Ways to the Center

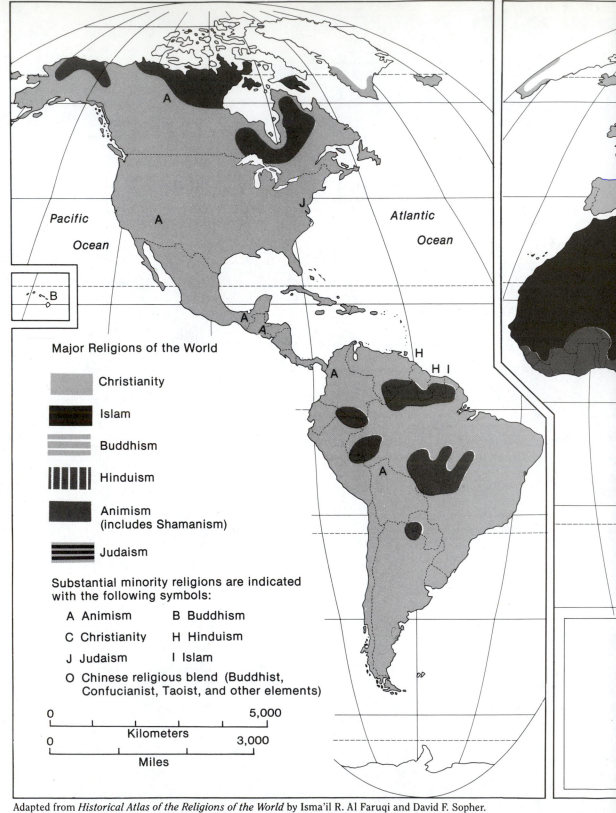

Major Religions of the World

Christianity

Islam

Buddhism

Hinduism

Animism
(includes Shamanism)

Judaism

Substantial minority religions are indicated
with the following symbols:

A Animism   B Buddhism

C Christianity   H Hinduism

J Judaism   I Islam

O Chinese religious blend (Buddhist,
Confucianist, Taoist, and other elements)

0   5,000
Kilometers
0   3,000
Miles

Pacific

Ocean

Atlantic

Ocean

Adapted from *Historical Atlas of the Religions of the World* by Isma'il R. Al Faruqi and David F. Sopher.
Copyright © 1974 by Macmillan Publishing Company, Inc. Reprinted by permission of Sakhr Faruqi.

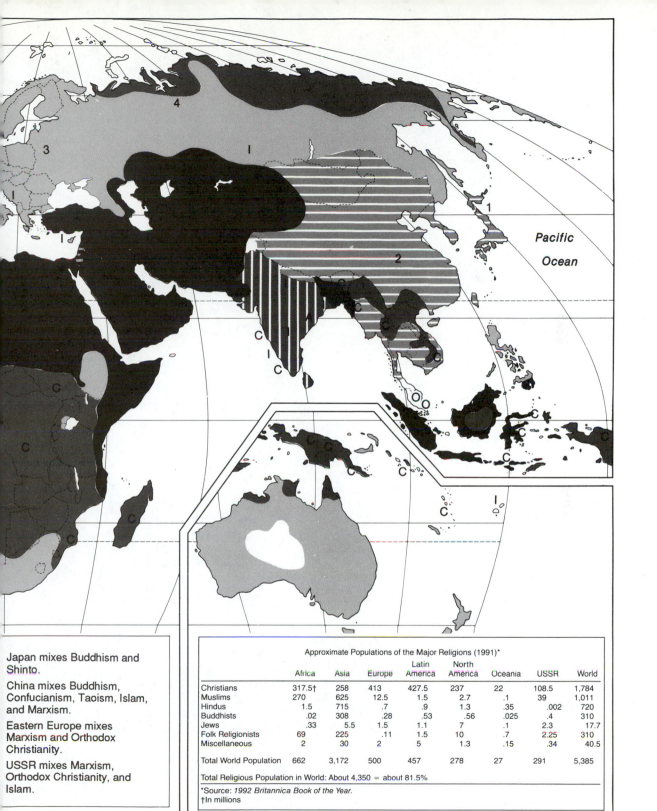

*Pacific
Ocean*

Japan mixes Buddhism and
Shinto.

China mixes Buddhism,
Confucianism, Taoism, Islam,
and Marxism.

Eastern Europe mixes
Marxism and Orthodox
Christianity.

USSR mixes Marxism,
Orthodox Christianity, and
Islam.

Approximate Populations of the Major Religions (1991)*

	Africa	Asia	Europe	Latin America	North America	Oceania	USSR	World
Christians	317.5†	258	413	427.5	237	22	108.5	1,784
Muslims	270	625	12.5	1.5	2.7	.1	39	1,011
Hindus	1.5	715	.7	.9	1.3	.35	.002	720
Buddhists	.02	308	.28	.53	.56	.025	.4	310
Jews	.33	5.5	1.5	1.1	7	.1	2.3	17.7
Folk Religionists	69	225	.11	1.5	10	.7	2.25	310
Miscellaneous	2	30	2	5	1.3	.15	.34	40.5
Total World Population	662	3,172	500	457	278	27	291	5,385

Total Religious Population in World: About 4,350 = about 81.5%

*Source: *1992 Britannica Book of the Year.*
†In millions

WAYS TO THE CENTER
An Introduction to World Religions

Fourth Edition

Denise Lardner Carmody
UNIVERSITY OF TULSA

John Tully Carmody
UNIVERSITY OF TULSA

Wadsworth Publishing Company
Belmont, California
A Division of Wadsworth, Inc.

Religion Editor: Peggy Adams
Editorial Assistant: Dorothy Zinky
Production Editor: The Book Company
Print Buyer: Diana Spence
Designer: Detta Penna
Cover: Michael Rogondino
Compositor: Weimer Incorporated
Printer: Malloy Lithographing

This book is printed on acid-free paper that meets Environmental Protection Agency standards for recycled paper.

1 2 3 4 5 6 7 8 9 10——97 96 95 94 93

Library of Congress Cataloging in Publication Data

Carmody, Denise Lardner, 1935–
 Ways to the center : an introduction to world religions / Denise
Lardner Carmody, John Tully Carmody. — 4th ed.
  p. cm.
 Includes bibliographical references and index.
 ISBN 0-534-19182-7
 1. Religions. I. Carmody, John, 1939– . II. Title.
BL80.2.C34 1993
291—dc20   92-24866
                                                    CIP

IN MEMORY OF

Catherine R. Carmody

Stephen J. Carmody

Denis Lardner

Martha Comen Lardner

CONTENTS

INTERLUDE

ASIAN RELIGIONS
70

INTERLUDE

NEAR EASTERN RELIGIONS
232

PREFACE TO FOURTH EDITION

This revision incorporates changes made for new editions of *Western Ways to the Center* (1991) and *Eastern Ways to the Center* (1992). Perhaps the most significant are more discussion of: (1) the sources on which analysis of the traditions must depend and; (2) how students may think critically about the claims the various religions make.

Otherwise, the text retains its destinctive two-fold format of both historical and systematic (philosophical) analyses. Also, it remains an effort to welcome students who know little about the world religions and leave them exposed to a wealth of information and challenging ideas.

Our thanks to all the scholarly readers who have advised us over the years, especially those involved in this fourth edition: John Crosley, University of Southern California, and Daniel R. Sheridan, Loyola University.

Ways to the Center

INTRODUCTION: ON THE STUDY OF WORLD RELIGIONS

A symbol of the concentricity of the natural, the social, the divine, and the personal that religious searches for the center reveal.

The religious life of humanity is a vast spectacle hard to keep in perspective. Therefore, we should make our goals and methods clear from the outset. Our primary goal is to make clear how the world's religious traditions have oriented billions of human lives. Our primary method is to place the study of religion in the context of the humanities and approach the traditions with a consistent format. Let us explain these notions in more detail.

THE NATURE OF RELIGION

Picture yourself in New Delhi. You are outside *Rajghat,* the memorial to Mahatma Gandhi, the politician and holy man who led India to freedom from British colonial rule. Before you, squatting on the broken sidewalk, are three small boys with wooden flutes. They are piping tunes toward round wicker baskets. When they lift the baskets' covers, three silver cobras slowly weave their way out. You watch for several minutes, fearful but entranced. Then the boys shove the cobras back into their baskets and approach you for their fee.

A few rupees seem fair enough—you don't want to upset those cobras.

Does this picture shine a light on the exotic East? Is it a minor revelation of Indian culture? Yes, but only if you know a little background. In India, as in many other countries with ancient cultures, serpents have been potent symbols (think of the story in the third chapter of Genesis). Perhaps because they appear menacing or phallic (penislike), they have stood for something very basic, something very close to the life force. For centuries, groups of Indians have specialized in snake handling, and the skills have been passed along from father to son. Their profession has combined show business and a bit of crude religion. It has been both entertainment and an occasion to shiver about the implications of death and life.

Now picture yourself in medieval England. In 627 C.E. ("common era" = A.D.) the monk Paulinus came to King Edwin in northern England and urged him to convert his people to Christianity. After some debate, one of Edwin's counselors stood up and said: "Your majesty, on a winter night like this, it sometimes happens that a little bird flies in that far window, to enjoy the warmth and light of our fire. After a short while it passes out again, returning to the dark and the cold. As I see it, our human life is much the same. We have but a brief time between two great darknesses. If this

Religious Wisdom: Twenty-five Key Dates	
ca. 1500 B.C.E.	Vedas
ca. 1360	*Hymns of Akhenaton*
1000–500	*Redactions of* Pentateuch
800–400	Upanishads
750–550	*Hebrew Prophets*
550	*Oldest Parts of Zoroastrian* Avesta
500	*Oldest Parts of* Analects
400–250	Job; Ecclesiastes; Bhagavad Gita
ca. 350	*Plato's* Laws; Tao Te Ching
ca. 330	*Aristotle's* Metaphysics
ca. 160	*Buddhist* Prajna-Paramita
ca. 80	Lotus Sutra, *Key Buddhist Text*
ca. 50	*Buddhist* Dhammapada
ca. 50–90 C.E.	New Testament *Writings*
413–426	*Augustine's* City of God
425	*Buddhist* Visuddhimagga
ca. 500	*Babylonian* Talmud
ca. 650	*Canonization of the* Qur'an
712–720	*Shinto* Chronicles
ca. 1100	*Al-Ghazali's* Revivification of the Sciences
1175	*Chu Hsi's Neo-Confucian Synthesis*
1190	*Maimonides'* Guide for the Perplexed
1270	*Aquinas's* Summa Theologica
1536	*Calvin's* Institutes
1581	*Compilation of* Adi Granth, *Sikh Scripture*

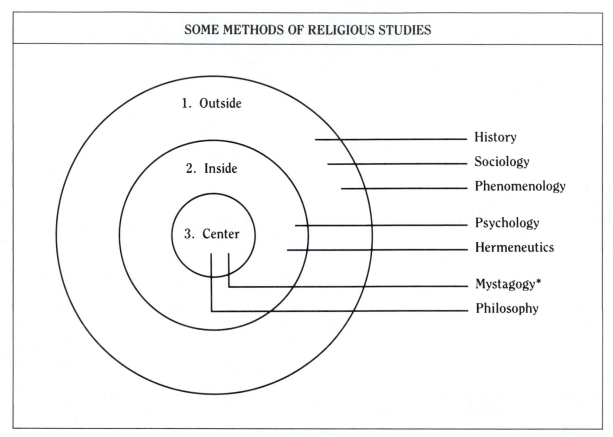

SOME METHODS OF RELIGIOUS STUDIES

1. Outside

2. Inside

3. Center

— History
— Sociology
— Phenomenology
— Psychology
— Hermeneutics
— Mystagogy*
— Philosophy

*Appreciating the religion's approach to ultimate mystery.

monk can show us warmth and light, we should follow him."[1]

For most of medieval Europe, the warmth and light that made life seem good radiated from Jesus Christ. At the core of Europe's complex and in many ways crude culture at that time was a faith that a personal father God so loved the world he had given his son to heal and enlighten it. When they shared that faith, European monks, kings, and kings' counselors largely agreed on their conception of life. Monks, for instance, were willing to give up family life in order to bear witness to God's love. Kings tried to show that their rule derived from what God had done through Jesus, and counselors tried to show commoners how the rule of kings mediated God's will. Often, of course, monks and kings and counselors did things that we find hard to square with Jesus, pursuing wealth and power by means of guile. But their culture forced them all to confront Christian warmth and light, as

Indian culture forced Indians to confront sex, death, and life.

Our two pictures are not quite compatible. The modern Indian scene stressed rather primitive sexual or vital energies, while the medieval English scene stressed lofty love and vision. Westerners have tended to view Indian and European life in that way, as the writings of early Christian missionaries to India suggest. However, the past century of scholarship in religious studies has shown the deficiencies of such an attitude, so we must add a few comments on the two scenes.

First, drawing a picture of medieval Europe that is raw and primitive would not be hard. In Ingmar Bergman's movies about the medieval period, such as *The Seventh Seal* and *The Virgin Spring*, death and sex and life are jammed together like serpents in a basket. Because of the Black Death, the plague that killed about three-quarters of the late medieval Euro-

Figure 1 *Corpus Christi, Spanish, second half of
the thirteenth century. Wood with polychrome, 72
in. high. The crucifixion was a central focus of
medieval Christian piety. The Nelson–Atkins Museum
of Art, Kansas City, Missouri.*

pean population, monks and commoners marched in
processions beating themselves, scourging their flesh
with whips to do penance for their sins and keep death
away. The harshness of medieval life also led to brutal
wars and brutal rapes. The knight and the squire of
The Seventh Seal, who watch the procession of peni-
tents, have kept company with death since they went
to war as Crusaders. The rape and murder of the young
girl in *The Virgin Spring* sums up medieval primitive-
ness. Sex and death pour out in her blood, and only
after her father has slain the rapists do we see hope for
new life trickle forth in a fresh spring. Medieval Europe, Bergman suggests, was as raw as India has ever
been.

Second, were we to go inside the memorial to
Gandhi and look at the scene at his commemorative

stone, the sublimity of Indian culture and its visions
of warmth and light might rise up and parallel those
of Christian Europe. *Rajghat* blends green grass, elegant black marble, and fresh flower petals of orange
and pink. They symbolize the beautiful spirit of the
Mahatma, the little man of great soul. Gandhi was a
politician who moved people by *satyagraha*—the force
of truth. Without military arms, much money, or even
much respect from British leaders, he forced the whole
world to take notice. When he vowed to take no food
until India's just claims were met, the world held its
breath. When he led groups of nonviolent *satyagrahis*
into the midst of club-swinging soldiers, he upset the
conscience of the world. By the simple rightness, the
sheer justice, of his cause, Gandhi showed how his
Hindu conception of God could be very powerful. His

God was "Truth," and it finally shamed the British into withdrawal.

Snakes and scourges, love and truth—they have shot through India, Europe, and most other parts of the world. In contemporary America, they or their offspring live with us yet. For instance, our nuclear missiles are for many citizens and analysts eerie phallic symbols. Like cobras we are trying to get back in their baskets, the missiles give us shivers. Many people see the missiles' thrust, their destructive power, and the claims that they give us security or economic life as brutalizing and raping our culture. From Hiroshima to Three Mile Island, nuclear power muddles our wellsprings and hope.

So too with the ways that we whip ourselves for guilt, the ways that we still crave love, the ways that we search after light. Our guilt keeps psychiatrists in business. Our searches for light fill churches and schools. Clearly we are sisters and brothers to religious Indians and medieval Europeans. Clearly their snakes and saviors relate to our own.

Religion is the issue of ultimate meaning that this discussion of cobras and monks spotlights. It is the part of culture—Eastern, Western, or contemporary American—that we study when we ask about a people's deepest convictions. For instance, Hinduism is the animating spirit, the soul, the way of looking at the world, that has tied snake handling and *satyagraha* together for most Indians. Christianity is the way of looking at the world that has joined scourging to Jesus for most medieval Europeans. Religion, then, is what you get when you investigate striking human phenomena to find the ultimate vision or set of convictions that gives them their sense. It is the cast of mind and the gravity of heart by which a people endures or enjoys its time between the two great darknesses of prebirth and death.

STUDYING RELIGION

Certain attitudes should be cultivated in all study, but the study of religion demands more self-awareness and personal engagement with its materials than most other disciplines do. For instance, although reducing physical science to "objective" observing and testing is simplistic, since all knowledge is ultimately personal,[2] physical science does not make great demands on a student's inner experiences of suffering or love. The humanities (those disciplines that study our efforts at self-expression and self-understanding) involve more of such inner experiences, because suffering and love shape so much of history and literature, yet even the humanities seldom deal with direct claims about ultimate meaning. Only in philosophy and religion does one directly encounter systems about God, evil, and humanity's origin and end. Philosophy deals with such concepts principally in their rational forms, while religious studies meet them more concretely in the myths, rituals, mysticisms, behavior patterns, and institutions through which most human beings have been both drawn to ultimate meaning and terrified of it.

More than in any other discipline, the student in a religious studies course is confronted with imperative claims. The religions are not normally warehouses where you pay your money and take your choice. Rather, they are impassioned heralds of ways of life. More than most people initially like, the religions speak of death, ignorance, and human viciousness. However, they also speak of peace and joy, forgiveness and harmony. Whatever they discuss, though, they are *mystagogic,* which etymologically means "mystery working." The religions work mystery. Their preoccupations, when they are healthy, are nature's wonder, life's strange play of physical death and spiritual resurrection, and the possibility of order in the midst of chaos. The religions say that the kingdom of God is in your midst, because you are a being who can pray, "Abba, Father." They say that the *Tao* ("the Way") that can be named is not the real *Tao.* Above all, they say that the person who lives divorced from the mysteries of rosy-fingered dawn and wintery death is less than fully human. So Sioux Indians revered the East, because dawn symbolizes the light of conscience. So Jewish scripture speaks of love as strong as death. So, finally, Islam speaks for all religions when it says that Allah—Muslim divinity—is as near as the pulse at our throats. Clearly, then, we cannot study the religions well if we are afraid of mystery or are in flight from death and life.

We also cannot study the religions well if we insist on forcing them into the categories of our own faith. We must first take them on their own terms, giving their experiences and problems a sympathetic hearing. After we have listened to the wisdom of a scripture such as the Hindu *Bhagavad Gita,* we may and should compare it with the wisdom of our Western faiths. Even then, though, unless we can say with the Christians' Saint Peter, "I see now how true it is that God has no favorites, but that in every nation the person who is God-fearing and does what is right is acceptable" (Acts 10:34), we risk acting with prejudice and condescension.

A second reason for remembering life's mystery, then, is that it helps us clear away prejudice. Talk of the New Testament superseding the Old or of revealed religion besting paganism—without strong qualifications—is self-serving and naive. Used as a word of God, Jewish scriptures open onto a divinity ever new, ever fresh, and ever free. Taken in its experiential vividness, a Zen Buddhist's enlightenment *(satori)* tears the veil of ignorance and comes as revelation and grace.[3] As Thomas Aquinas insisted, we do not know what God is. As John Calvin knew, the mind without mystery is a factory of idols. The most authoritative Western theologians have fought against prejudice.

Third, it is worth pointing out that the religious studies course offered here is not theology, at least not the theology of a church. Church theology tends to be a search for an understanding of one's own faith that is directed by the particular creed or commitment of an individual or group. Spontaneously the search spreads to a probing of all life's dimensions in terms of such a commitment. So there develops a theology of art, a theology of history, and even a theology of the world religions.[4] In these theologies, however, the main goal is to square data with one's own faith or religious group. Moreover, a church theology's ultimate goal is to promote its own faith. It studies art, history, or the world religions to beautify, advance, or defend its own vision of things, whether the "church" be Muslim, Buddhist, Jewish, or Christian. The understanding that theology seeks in such study is not necessarily distorted, but it is in the service of preaching, ministering, and counseling. When it is not in such service, church theology becomes divorced from the life of its community.[5]

In a university, however, neither students nor teachers are expected to confess their faith (or nonfaith). We, the authors, have argued elsewhere[6] that it is proper and healthy to make clear one's position on the *implications,* for thought and action alike, to which a course's studies lead. In other words, there is nothing wrong and much right with teachers and students becoming personal—dealing with concrete, practical implications. There is much wrong, however, in university courses that place their own values on other people's art, history, or religion and thereby distort them. One must listen with an open mind before judging and deciding.

So we urge you to get inside the religions' experiences and values and to compare them with your own. In fact, we very much hope that your study will enrich your appreciation of nature, will increase your wonder about life's meaning, and will increase your resources for resisting evil. But we do not set these hopes in the framework of any one faith. We are not, in other words, doing church theology. You may be Christian, Jewish, Buddhist, agnostic, atheistic, or anything else. To us such labels do not matter. What matters is that you be human: a man or woman trying to hear the Delphic oracle's "Know thyself," a person humble with the Confucian virtue of sympathy or "fellow feeling" *(jen).*

Fourth, what benefits will this effort to study humanistically bring you? At least two spring to mind. First, you will have the chance to grapple with some of the most influential, wisest personalities of the past. Second, you will better understand the world of the present, in which all peoples on the globe are much closer than they have ever been before.

To illustrate the first benefit, let us call on the Chinese sage Confucius. In his time (551–479 B.C.E.) some people were advancing the proposition that it is better to pay court to the stove (to practicalities) than to heaven (to ideals) (see *Analects* 3:3). Confucius batted their proposition back. If you do not pay court to heaven, he said, you will have no recourse when practicalities fail to bring you good life. In other words, the mystery of life is more than food and drink, more than shelter and pleasure. Important as those things are, they do not make the truly good life. Only moving in the Way *(Tao)* of heaven makes us human beings what we ought to be, what we most deeply want to be. If we settle for the stove, we halve our human potential.

To illustrate the second benefit of the humanistic study of religion, we must comment briefly on current history. Today it is a commonplace observation that the world is becoming one. That does not mean that all peoples are agreeing on a common government, economy, or philosophy. It does mean that communications, transportation, economics, and other forces are tying all nations together. Thus, commentators speak of a "global village" or a "planetary culture." They remind us of the novelty of the twentieth century, the only time when it could have happened that when Gandhi fasted, the world held its breath; that when Mao died, his funeral reached every capital. Furthermore, in our nuclear age all curtains can be raised. In our age of escalating population and hunger, all the silos of Kansas cast shadows on East Africa. In our age of ecological pollution, the wastes of one country foul the air, water, and land of others.

The implications of this current state of affairs are too numerous to detail. We may be on the verge of a new phase of evolution; the human sciences may just be approaching their maturity. The outer complexity of human affairs may just be developing a self-consciousness among human beings so that we will be able to cope with these affairs. Or we may devastate the entire planet through nuclear war or ecological disaster. In either case, religion acquires an added significance, because we cannot learn much about the evolution or self-consciousness of the global village unless we listen to its members' deepest perceptions and convictions. We cannot understand human motivation unless we study what people have considered the highest good. Religion shows a people's deepest perceptions and convictions. Hinduism, Buddhism, Christianity, and Islam form the souls of a majority of the world's population today. To live together in the future, we human beings will have to understand the world religions very well.

SCHOLARLY METHODS

In pursuing such understanding, it is well to take note of the different methods that scholars of religion have developed. W. Richard Comstock, the author of a useful introduction to religion, once offered a list of five basic methods.[7]

First, there is the *psychological* perspective. Since the time of Freud (1856–1939), who was quite interested in religion's parallels with neurosis, Western scholars have been sensitive to the inner drives that set people to work, parenting, religion, and the many other aspects of human culture. For example, sexual satisfaction, acceptance by our peers, and a sense of control all play a part in our development of human culture. C. G. Jung (1875–1961) broke with Freud over the interpretation of sexual and religious drives. For Jung the second half of life tends to be a pursuit of meaning (giving one's time and experience coherence). Often the symbols people use in pursuing meaning are religious, so even today psychoanalysts

probing patients' dreams can come upon archetypal symbols reminiscent of ancient religious mythologies.

If we generalize the sensitivity that recent psychological studies sharpen, the main point seems to be that we must stay alert to the complexity of human motivation. For example, in studying a holy man from the Hindu tradition, such as Mahatma Gandhi, we should realize that his asceticism had a basis in his adolescent sexual traumas and that his political ambitions were forged by his experiences of racial discrimination in young adulthood. At these formative times in his life cycle, Gandhi was tested to an unusual degree. He found himself unready for the erotic aspects of marriage, and his experience as a "colored" person in South Africa told him he had to champion India's oppressed.[8]

On the one hand, if we so focus on psychological issues such as these that we neglect the history, sociology, economics, politics, and other aspects of Gandhi's life and times, we become reductionists, trying to squeeze all of reality onto the psychoanalyst's couch. On the other hand, if we neglect such inner demons and angels, we divorce ourselves from a powerful tool of understanding (perhaps because we do not want to face the similar demons and angels warring in our own souls). As usual, a balanced use is the ideal.

Just as scientific psychology is a fairly recent development, not available to scholars of religion a century ago, so is *sociology*. And just as the pioneer psychologists were quite interested in religion, so were pioneer sociologists such as Max Weber (1864–1920) and Emile Durkheim (1858–1917). In both cases, their interest was religion's role in making a group cohesive. The religious ideas of a tribe, or even a large culture, are always in part a projection of the tribe's or the culture's sense of its own identity. For example, Hindus have been people stratified by traditional wisdom into four main social classes. Chinese have been people living at the center of the world in accordance with the *Tao* they thought moved both nature and the wise ancients. Americans have been high-minded refugees come to make a place of justice and freedom in a new world. Thus neither Hindu caste nor Chinese misogyny nor American racism could be the patent inhumanity an outside observer might think it. Sacralizing the way they talked about themselves, all three peoples claimed heaven had approved their customs.

Recently, cultural anthropologists such as Clifford Geertz and Victor Turner have tuned the interests of the classical sociologists more finely. Living in the midst of the societies they wanted to interpret, they have sought the deep structures and threshold moments through which a people reveals how it constructs its world view. Geertz's study of the Balinese cockfight,[9] for example, is a marvel of sophisticated participant observation. Sensitive to the drama of what he calls "deep play," Geertz makes the cockfight a microcosm of the Balinese thought-world.

A third methodological orientation popular in recent religious studies is the *historical*. One of the drawbacks of the psychological and sociological approaches is that they can seem to bracket time past (and time future), as though their analyses were moved by an Archimedean lever standing outside the flowing stories of either their subjects or themselves. But such ahistoricism obviously is fallacious. The self always enacts a story, a unique version of the common life cycle, and a society is always being pushed by its past and lured by its future. Since the modern discovery of evolution, and the rise of modern retrieval techniques such as archeology, the study of religion has become more historical, and so more faithful to the traditions' ongoing changes. Even the most conservative tradition alters in at least small ways, generation by generation. Though they perform the same rituals and tell the same myths, a people of any era understands itself somewhat differently than its forebears did or its children will.

The good historian's goal is telling the story of these changes. Representing the past as it most likely was, good historians bring their readers from point alpha to point omega. Thus a Buddhist historian might muse: In the beginning, at the earliest point we can reconstruct, Buddhists understood Gautama in such and such a way. A thousand years later, when controversies inside the community had caused much debate, there were the three following major interpretations. Today, in Japanese Buddhism, the third of these interpretations prevails, due to such and such factors.

One thinks, then, of a continuum or a map. In the image of the continuum, the historian grants all centuries a certain equality, showing how Buddhism changed century by century. In the image of a map, the historian plots the journey from the Buddha's India to modern Japan, showing the geographic and cultural routes the Teaching (Dharma) traveled. The result should be a sense of perspective and interrelationship. Alpha led on to beta, because of factor alpha prime, just as today omega seems to be

leading on to omega-plus-one, because of factor omega prime.

Comstock's fourth methodological perspective is *phenomenological*. Referring to the work of scholars such as Geradus van der Leeuw (1890–1950), who have concentrated on the different *forms* that many religious traditions seem to share, one can emphasize the concern many phenomenologists have to find *typical* patterns that show up repeatedly across the full range of religious data. So, for example, sacred people appear in most traditions. East and West, monks or ascetics or yogis have won great veneration. One can distinguish among these three categories of holy people, but they share an orientation away from worldly affairs, toward contemplation and self-discipline. The typical Hindu holy man fits the pattern of withdrawal, as does the typical Buddhist monk. In China and Japan, both Buddhism and Taoism prized withdrawal from worldly affairs, seclusion in order to grow better attuned to the Dharma or the *Tao*.

Phenomenological studies tend to stress the sameness of certain structural features, providing a basis for discussing how Hindu yogis differ from Buddhist monks in cultural details, or how Eastern ascetics differ from Western ascetics. By grouping functionaries together in general terms, we are stimulated to ask how they differ in particulars. The results of such generalizations can seldom be ironclad, since there are usually exceptions to general trends, but phenomenological inquiries can be very stimulating.

Comstock's fifth methodological perspective is *hermeneutical*. If anything, this perspective has increased in importance since the time he made his survey. Hermeneutics is the study of interpretation. It concerns processes such as that by which a teacher from Maryland tries to explain to a student from Oklahoma what it was like to live in medieval China or India. In one sense, hermeneutics applies to all parts of this communication. Even the gap between Maryland and Oklahoma can be significant, but the gap between twentieth-century America and medieval China or Japan is enormous. Thus, hermeneutics tends to be most concerned with how we can tease from texts or artifacts reliable interpretations of past or foreign cultures. The cultural anthropologists we mentioned have come to the forefront of the hermeneutical debates, but historians, psychologists, sociologists, and philosophers of language have also been prominent. These debates tend to get very technical, generating schools such as structuralism and subdisciplines such as semiotics and deconstructionism.

Thus, the scholarly end of the hermeneutical "turn" is not yet in sight and its overall significance is still emerging.

For undergraduates, though, the gist of the hermeneutical perspective is clear enough: Try to be quite sensitive to the sources and ranges of the meanings you are studying. Above all, realize that in studying a text, or any other cultural artifact, you are involved in a two-way conversation. A text is not a brute object whose meanings are obvious to any beholder. Physically, a text is simply some marks on a piece of paper or some impressions in clay. To convey meaning, these marks have to "speak" from the mind of the person who set them down to the minds of people like you who are trying to pick them up. Thus, the languages and assumptions of both minds come into play, your own as much as the author's. You can assume that you and the author share a great deal, since you are both human, but you must be careful about how you use this assumption. The death of a child in ancient China was both very like the death of a child in contemporary America, and very different. Boiled down, hermeneutics is walking the tightrope between the sameness we have as members of one species and the differences we have as individuals, people of different cultures, and people of different historical eras.

One might suggest how these five different methods complement one another by trying to apply them to a single religious phenomenon. Suppose, for example, that one were studying the place of Torah, Divine Instruction, in Judaism. Psychological methods could help one probe what Torah has meant to the millions of men and women formed in traditional Judaism—how it consoled them in hard times, why they clung to it with might and main, why trying to enter into the thought-world of an ancient text proved fascinating, how Torah barred the door against meaninglessness. Sociologically, one might probe the status accorded those who became expert in Torah, moving on to study why bright little boys traditionally were encouraged to become masters of the text and why little girls were not encouraged. One might also analyze how the community divided when modernity called much of traditional Judaism's docility to Torah (regarding diet, keeping the Sabbath, resisting assimilation into the gentile culture, and the like) into question.

Historical studies could teach us about the original conception of the Torah in biblical times, how this conception changed when Jews were cast out of Jerusalem in the first century C.E., what Torah had come to mean by the time the Babylonian Talmud had been collected and edited (about 500 C.E.). We might study the connection between Torah and the Jewish philosophy of a great medieval thinker such as Moses Maimonides, between Torah and the devotional fervor of the Baal Shem-Tov (who founded Hasidism in eighteenth-century Eastern Europe), and between Torah and Zionism, the twentieth-century movement to return to Israel. In each case, we would be rounding out the notion of "Torah" by tying it to specific coordinates on the map of space and time.

Phenomenological studies of Torah could lead us to compare it with other instances of Divine Instruction, such as the Hindu Vedas, the Buddhist Tripitaka, the writings of the Confucian Canon, the Christian Scriptures and Creeds, and such Muslim analogues as the Qur'an and the Shariah (Law). Or, within Judaism itself, we might study how Divine Instruction was both the same and different for the prophets and wisdom writers of biblical times, for the early rabbis and the later Hasidim, for Reformed Jews and Jews who in reaction to Reform became "Orthodox." Phenomenology could help us see both what emerges as common to all these instances and what proves variable, maybe even contradictory, among the different instances.

Last, hermeneutical studies would engage us directly in the task of interpreting the Torah, of trying to bridge the centuries between the Five Books of Moses, or the early rabbinic codes known as the Mishnah, and the twentieth century. We would have to try to get inside the "system" of the Torah, to see how it comprises an integral, consistent world view. We would also have to criticize the assumptions behind that world view, so that we came to appreciate how the choices the biblical authors and rabbis made were free and full of consequences—things they might have taken in a different direction.[10]

Three further issues pertaining to the scholarly methods now favored for studying religious phenomena beg consideration. The first is the matter of the source-critical basis for studies of ancient texts, personalities, movements, and the like. The second is the matter of such descriptions as "Western" and "Eastern" used in this text and many other places. The third is the matter of the philosophical foundations for studies that compare different religious traditions, even to the modest extent that we do in this text.

Concerning the question of the source-critical basis for studies of ancient texts, personalities, movements, and the like, the frank answer is that although scholars have made significant advances in editing primary written sources, much remains less exact than what present-day ideals of reliability require. Judaism, Christianity, and Islam all stem from periods when oral tradition was more significant than written tradition. What one finds in the Bible and the Qur'an, for example, is more mythic, poetic, indebted to memories handed down for generations, and less "scientific" than what present-day critical history requires. The same judgment holds for nonscriptural materials from these three traditions, as well as for sources bearing on the origins of Greek, Iranian, Mesopotamian, Egyptian, Native American, Eskimo, and African traditions. The modern development of critical study postulated a detached point of view, according to which one could sift competing claims and assemble an account of a given action, belief, or career that could stand up to outside, skeptical scrutiny. Much of the spirit behind modern critical scholarship likened it to legal proceedings in court. Evidence and cross-examination were highly prized. The text or traditional memory was subjected to scrutiny from the viewpoint of those trying to prove its innocence (reliability) and from the viewpoint of those trying to prove its guilt (unreliability). Indeed, the presumption developed by source-critical studies has tended to be in favor of unreliability rather than reliability, lest the credulity so powerful in religion infect humanistic scholarship.

The result of this modern mentality has been both to sharpen judgments about the historical reliability that a given piece of evidence carries and to make it plain that some of the most crucial sources of evidence are simply never going to yield testimony able to stand up to the demands of critical history. In other words, there is no way that the Bible or the Qur'an can be turned into a witness acceptable in a contemporary courtroom, because neither the Bible nor the Qur'an ever wanted to be a detached observer, a disinterested party. In addition to all the lapses in memory and corruptions in copying that specialists can sniff out in the scriptural texts, there remains the more fundamental problem that the materials always assumed and required faith. By definition, the religious studies scholar cannot give such faith, so the religious studies scholar, trying to establish the humanistic credibility or sense of key texts, is always going to come up short. The problem is not that the Bible or the Qur'an or the other, analogous sources on which the historical representation of Western religious experience depends have been mendacious, deliberately trying to conceal or mislead. The problem is that the sense of reality, of

what actually happened and what that happening meant, operative in the most important sources bearing on Western religion has been shaped by convictions of faith that God was doing such and such. Therefore, careful scholarship in religious studies always has to put many qualifications on the conclusions it draws about actual, historical happenings when its primary sources have been documents or other artifacts forged in faith.

Second, concerning the use of "Western" religions, one has to confess that it is at best a useful convenience, at worst a significant distortion. Christianity now has a presence in all 254 of the countries represented in the *1989 Britannica Book of the Year*'s statistical chart on the populations of the world's religions.[11] Does the fact that the majority of the Christian population still resides in the West, along with the fact that Christianity has had more impact on the historical development of the West than the East, continue to justify describing Christianity as a "Western" religion? Perhaps so, but only with the qualification that the 82 million Christians in East Asia and the 132 million Christians in South Asia are not insignificant populations. Even more significant are the 282 million Christians resident in Africa. These populations are changing the traditionally Western or European visage of Christianity, as befits a global culture in which West and East increasingly interpenetrate and so dilute many of their differences.

One could argue that Christianity, and even more Judaism and Islam, are better described as "Near Eastern" religions, in view of their places of origin, than they are as "Western" religions. All of them arose in what we now call the Near, or Middle, East. Christians and Jews continue to have sizable fractions of their populations there, even though they have spread to many other geographic areas. About 84 percent of present-day Jews are Ashkenazim (people of German/European cultural background), so "Western" continues to be defensible in the Jewish case.

It is harder to defend the use of "Western" in the case of Islam, because the vast majority of Muslims live in Africa (253 million) and South Asia (560 million). The Indian subcontinent and Indonesia house hundreds of millions of Muslims. On the other hand, there are two good reasons for considering Islam along with Judaism and Christianity and so casting the mantle of the term "Western" over it. One reason is the family relationship among the three traditions, all of which consider Abraham their father. Christianity confessedly derives from Judaism, while the Qur'an clearly is concerned to position Islam in relation to Judaism and Christianity. Muslims speak of Jews and Christians as "people of the book," and Islam thinks that the prophecy given to Muhammad perfected the prophecies that structure Judaism and Christianity. Inasmuch as Judaism and Christianity fall into the category "Western," Islam may be placed there too, as a topographical convenience.

The second reason is more pragmatic. In dividing the world's major religious traditions, it makes some sense to consider their place of origin as the first demarcator. It follows, then, that Buddhism, Hinduism, Confucianism, Taoism, and other Asian religions end up in the "Eastern" half of a simple division, while Judaism, Christianity, and Islam are left for the other part of the division, which inevitably gets labeled "Western." For our purposes, the main lesson to draw is that the term "Western" is quite loose and debatable, and that we are using it more for reasons of convenience than for strong theoretical reasons.

Third, concerning the philosophical foundations for the comparative study of the world's religions, suffice it to say that we follow a philosophical anthropology (an understanding of human nature) indebted to thinkers such as Eric Voegelin and Bernard Lonergan, according to which religion expresses drives of human consciousness found in all people. Because all people press forward to know the structures of their world and find something worthy of their wholehearted love, all people exhibit some similarities in their religious traditions (which tend to be the parts of their culture where ultimate concerns most clearly focus). From the side of the human agent, then, one can postulate a likeness sufficient to permit the side-by-side comparison of Confucians and Jews, Muslims and Hindus. Granted the assumption (itself based on empirical observation) that all human beings desire to know and love ultimately, the religious traditions may be studied, and compared, in terms of the myths, rituals, artifacts, social structures, and the like that their desires have generated. Alternatively, they may be studied in terms of the fourfold delineation of reality that analyses of human consciousness such as Lonergan's and Voegelin's have disclosed: nature, society, the self, and divinity.

So, the basic assumption behind our comparative efforts is the transcendental (ever ongoing) character of the human spirit, while the basic diagram of the objective correlative of the human spirit (the world with which it is always involved) considers reality to have four irreducible dimensions: divinity (ultimate reality), human society, the physical world, and the human self. These are the main philosophical pillars undergirding our comparative work, and they position us as "critical realists." That is, we believe that one can gain some purchase on reality (what is so objectively) if one strives to be attentive, intelligent, judicious, and responsible. By disciplining one's senses, imagination, judgment, and will, one can gain reasonable confidence that what one finds making sense of one's data in fact obtains in reality.

OUTSIDE, INSIDE, AND CENTER

Difference and sameness apply to all our interactions with other human beings, so the study of Asian people's religions is not radically different from the study of the child-raising practices of the people next door. Still, one can lean more heavily on difference or sameness, make the people one is studying stranger or more familiar, depending on one's point of view. Generally speaking, sociological, historical, and phenomenological approaches tend to stress differences. Concerned with other people's customs, stories, and distinguishing features, they tend to detail things peculiar to Japanese, or Nigerians, or Italians. Psychological and hermeneutical studies perhaps lay greater stress on sameness. Because motivation plays an important role in psychological studies, and because the meaning of a people's customs or the assumptions behind their rituals loom large in hermeneutical studies, the common humanity that observer and observed share is emphasized. This is not to say that sociologists, historians, and phenomenologists neglect motivation and meaning. It is not to say that psychologists or hermeneuticists neglect external behavior or detail. It is simply to suggest that studying other people involves an outside and an inside, a blend of alien details and perhaps more familiar motivations, and that different methods may stress either the alien or the familiar.

In this book we shall try to give both the outside and the inside their due. Recognizing that what a scholar chooses to stress is usually in part a function of that scholar's personality, let us confess from the outset that our own interest tends more to the inside than to the outside. It is their meanings, motivations, assumptions about the world that make a people interesting to us. Of course, we are also interested in how they build their houses, how they raise their children, and what festivals they have created to pace themselves through the calendar year. But we find an unrelieved concentration on such matters somewhat tedious, a focus of diminishing return. Subjects of study become interesting to us in the measure that they show themselves profound, or brave, or innovative at handling the problems that rivet all human beings to mystery. "What does this people make of birth?" we will ask. "How do they reconcile themselves to death?" "What is this people's symbol for the best of human times?" "How do they picture the darker sides of human experience, the evils one must most try to avoid?"

Suppose, for instance, that you were an anthropologist, living in the midst of an Indian tribe in the Amazon jungle. If you witnessed a ritual boxing match, in which each man clouted the other as hard as he could, winding up to deliver a mighty blow to the opponent's chest, you might at first think this a strange way to while away an evening. Then, when you learned that the purpose of this ritual was to test the power of each man's spirits, the vitality of the *hekura* lodging in his chest, you probably would find it making a little more sense. Nonetheless, it likely would remain a quite foreign, if not bizarre, custom until you got a handle on the concern of this (rather typically shamanic) tribe to build up vitality, the power to resist disease and other enemies, by drawing on the forces of its surroundings, the spirits of the plants and animals that shared its habitat. At that point, you might sense a parallel to the psychosomatic concerns of modern Western medicine, the efforts of your own people to feel sturdy and confident.

In any study of the religion of other people, we do well to move back and forth between their differences from us and their likenesses to us. If we respect the ways that they conceive of the world, give their own reports a fair hearing, we can move on to try to assimilate their reports to our own experiences and convictions. Then a process of dialogue can develop that may grow richer and richer, showing the people we are studying to be both stranger and more familiar than probably we found them at our first meeting.

In an ideal study, however, one finally verges upon the center of the other people's experiences and finds that it can virtually coincide with one's own. Florinda Donner, an anthropologist who went to the Amazon, observed the strange boxing matches, and learned about the *hekura*, was fortunate enough one

day to grasp the beauty of her subjects' world and so come to understand their tendency to live almost completely in the present: "An overwhelming sense of awe brought me to my feet as the sky in the east glowed red and purple along the horizon. The clouds, obedient to the wind, opened to let the rising disk through. Pink mist rolled over the treetops, touching up shadows with deep blue, spreading green and yellow all over the sky until it changed into a transparent blue. . . . Like the Iticoteri [the tribe she was studying] I had learned to live in the present. Time was outside of me. It was something to be used only at the moment. Once used, it sank back into itself and became a perceptible part of my inner being."[12]

THE STRUCTURE OF THIS BOOK

In this book we shall try to build our descriptions of other people's outside features and inside convictions into a climactic presentation of the sort of peak experience, vivid and peaceful, that gives their world a center. Thus, we shall try to present the world religions as various "Ways to the Center."

Where the data allow, we begin our chapters with a sketch of the history of the tradition in question. Behind this historical section lies the conviction that one gains valuable insights into a people's sense of reality by learning the story of where they have come from, how they were formed into a people, what crucial experiences forged their deeper senses of who they are and what they believe. Such historical sections afford us the opportunity to mention many of the people's external characteristics. Sketching where they have come from and where they now seem to think they are going, we can try to move them from "once upon a time" to today.

Following on the historical section will be a "structural analysis" of the tradition's view of reality. Assuming that each religion has a certain consistency, a drive to make sense out of reality as a whole, we shall indicate some of the major pillars of the adherents' world view. The schema that we have found most adequate for this work has four headings: nature, society, self, and ultimate reality. Both the external data of the world religions and an internal analysis of human experience East and West seem to justify using this schema as a loose working format.

For example, all peoples must contend with nature. The physical world affords all of us our food. The skies and the seas and the plains provide all of us our environment, spiritual as well as physical. Indeed, it is characteristic of most ancient peoples to strive for a close harmony with physical nature. As though they instinctively knew many of the lessons that scientific studies in ecology have been teaching our contemporary world, ancient peoples typically sought kinship with the plants and animals of their area, knowledge of their area's weather and terrain. Nor is it hard to find connections with our own situation as twentieth-century individuals. If we find that we tend to perform differently on a high pressure day (when the skies are open and the sun is bright) than on a low pressure day (when the skies are low and gray), we have half the stimulus we need to become interested in the ecological sensitivity of other people, in how they pictured their weather and environment.

More easily than with ourselves, we find that most ancient peoples sacralized at least portions of nature: treated them with reverence or even worship. This tended to be a rallying point for the people, whether the people was at the stage of hunting and gathering or had unified itself under an impressive king. Through their rituals and ceremonies, most people have tried to move with nature's annual flow and ebb. Spring awakening and Fall harvest, Summer heat and Winter cold, have all cried out for recognition. In giving nature such recognition, people have helped define who they were: people of the forest, or people of the mountain. Depending on the way that it has pictured reality as a whole, a people usually has appointed headmen or shamans or priests to deal with these important matters. We shall see more of this in our first chapters, but it brings us to a point worth underscoring from the beginning. In most religions, the people's attitudes toward nature and their own social organization have fit together, have been complementary pieces of a single puzzle.

The same with a people's attitudes toward self and ultimate reality. When religious people the world over have asked "Who am I?", their answers have reached out to include situating themselves in the physical cosmos, placing themselves in the history and social structure of their tribe, and making at least fumbling attempts to connect themselves with the ultimate power or reality they have considered the origin, destiny, or most important feature of the whole, the universe, of what human beings can see and conceive. Nature, society, self, and ultimate reality are

Figure 2 *Buddha image, northwest India, Gupta period (300–620). Bronze, 14¾ in. high. This representation of the Buddha is typical in suggesting light, peace, and teaching authority. The Nelson–Atkins Museum of Art, Kansas City, Missouri (Nelson Fund).*

not artificial or isolated categories, fashioned simply for the convenience of teachers and textbook writers, who must try to give the mass of data about the world religions some shape. We are convinced they are interconnected dimensions of each human life that become more significant and fascinating as our exposure to human history expands and we continue our descent into the depths of our own consciousness.

So, for example, you can find in any bookstore writers telling you that: you are what you eat, your American nation is in peril, your self will flower only through physical love, and "God," a benevolent ultimate power, numbers every hair of your head. Behind each of these assertions is both knowledge and questioning. For centuries people have studied diet, national history, sex, and the mystery of the universe. Today these topics continue to imply vital questions, matters that any of us would be better for having probed. Moreover, we can use them to build bridges to other people, other eras, other faiths. That is how we plan to use them in our structural analyses: as useful ways of presenting some of the most important aspects of ancient, nonliterate, Hindu, Buddhist, Chinese, Japanese, Egyptian, Iranian, Greek, Jewish, Christian, and Muslim experience.

At the end of our structural analysis we conclude each chapter with a short summary essay on the heart of the tradition's convictions, the center of the tradition's world. Admittedly, such essays are always just our own interpretations, but we have felt we owed students the best parting word we could write. If you use our structural analyses and summary essays comparatively, noting how a given tradition both is like the others and differs from them, you should close this textbook with a fairly adequate sense of humanity's worldwide religious beliefs.

One does not get to the center of a religious tradition by methods (controlled ways of approach) strictly so called. One works more by intuition or a sense of where the different weights of a tradition come to rest. Among the approaches that hone such intuition, however, one can mention philosophy and mystagogy. Philosophy, in the Platonic sense of the love of wisdom, involves contemplating and trying to come into harmony with the highest good a tradition reveres. Mystagogy, as we have previously described, is sensitive to the mystery (fullness and perplexing character) of existence—to ultimate reality or God. By trying to reflect back upon the coherence of a tradition with philosophical and mystagogical attunement, one often finds one's own judgments about the tradition's center emerge rather clearly.

Discussion Questions

1. What is the difference between a humanistic and a theological approach to world religions?

2. Why does the interconnected character of today's international scene spotlight the significance of religion?

3. What are the main methods scholars recently have used to study religion?

4. How does "religion" relate to peoples' approaches to the mystery of human existence?

5. Why does an adequate view of a religious tradition require attending to its "outside," "inside," and "center"?

6. Briefly sketch the history, world view, and center of your own religious tradition.

7. How would you counsel your friends to increase their openness to people of other religious traditions?

Glossary

archaic: old; premodern and prescientific. When one speaks of archaic religious traditions, usually the term is not pejorative. Rather, one is stressing the antiquity of such traditions, their roots in prehistory and humanity's quite direct experience of the mysteries of nature, life, and death. Granted hundreds of thousands of years of truly human existence and so culture, the archaic stratum of human religiosity understandably underlay the religions not just of the hunters, gatherers, and early agriculturalists but also of the great civilizational religions, including Hinduism, Confucianism, Judaism, and Christianity. The more these religions interacted with rural peoples, the more significant the impact of the archaic strands.

contemplation: an attempt to focus the spirit on the whole of a scene or experience, or to commune with ultimate reality directly. Contemplation may be distinguished from meditation, as something more holistic, more affective, and less intellectual. As well, contemplation may be considered the early stages of mysticism, inasmuch as it schools the human spirit in letting go of particulars and reaching out to receive the divine whole directly and lovingly. Whereas traditional religions regularly developed contemplative regimes, modern rationalism has complicated the issue of how such a holistic outlook or state of soul should be correlated with an empirical bent or a rigoristically analytical outlook.

esoteric: concerning things that are thought secret, hidden, possessed only by a privileged few as the truth necessary for salvation. Esoteric groups divide society between insiders and outsiders. What they say and do among outsiders then has an exoteric character—is something less than the full truth. Only insiders deserve to know the inmost meanings of sayings or actions, because one ought not to cast pearls before swine. Esoteric teachings easily become gnostic and in general religious traditions have sought a balance between approving efforts to penetrate the deeper meaning of common teachings, ritual practices, mores, and the like and disapproving any prideful tendency to constitute elite groups thinking themselves possessed of saving wisdom not available to the general religious membership.

ethics: study or teaching concerned with morality—right and wrong in the realm of behavior. In traditional societies ethics and religion have little separation, as metaphysics and religion have little separation. Moreover, ethics tends to be very traditional—what "our kind" have done since time out of mind. Such ethics regularly are assumed to have been encoded in the cosmos by the divine powers when they gave the cosmos birth, so the political and social orders are not secular but wholly religious.

exoteric: concerning the outward, more readily apparent side of a religious existence, set of doctrinal truths, ritualistic activity, and the like. The exoteric aspects of religion tend to sponsor an empirical approach to understanding both people and institutions, while the esoteric aspects tend to invite an intuitive, contemplative, or mystic approach. Probably the two sides are best seen as necessary complements and one ought to worry only when one side tries to oust the other from all influence.

faith: belief; commitment or assent beyond factual surety or proof. All religion, if not indeed all of life, requires faith, for we are always having to go beyond what is empirically certain. The religions spotlight the demand for faith, because they deal with a mystery one cannot measure, asking that we trust prior trav-

elers on the way to gaining a healing relationship with such a mystery. The intellectual side of religions, their theologies and philosophies, do good work by offering faith a serviceable language and conceptual scheme, but faith itself always remains rounder, closer to the ineffable core of the personality and the mystery it encounters, than what any theology or philosophy can render.

folk religion: the beliefs and practices of the common people, in contrast to the views of the intelligentsia and religious officials. Folk religion virtually by definition is somewhat inarticulate and unreflective, but it may be no less rich or even sophisticated for that. It embraces the cult of the saints honored in a given religious tradition, the full round of paraliturgical devotions and religious practices, and the simple everyday acts of piety, prayers of petition, and other practices that get unlettered believers through the day. Some generations ago folk religion received rather short shrift from scholars, who depreciated it as untutored, but with the advent of anthropological investigations many students of religion have realized that peasant ways often house amazingly persistent and profound views of both the particular religious tradition in which they occur and the basic problematic of human existence that religious mythology regularly has kept lively, persuasive, and beguiling.

fundamentalism: the tendency, found in many religious traditions, to fixate on the literal level of scriptures or official doctrines (or rituals and moral teachings), under the conviction that fidelity to the letter is asked by God or is the safest way to guarantee one's religious fidelity. Fundamentalism can express an heroic effort to keep faith with the Buddha, Christ, Muhammad, or other aspects of a given religious pathway, but it can also express a neurotic fear of divine mystery and a debilitating refusal to accept the role that critical intelligence must play if one is to gain a mature, well-reasoned and well-tested faith. The crux perhaps comes in how people regard questioning: Can questioning express a movement of the religious spirit toward God, or must it represent a decline from pure, wholehearted faith?

God: the supreme being, holy and creative, that Western religions have considered fully personal and unique. Precisely what "God" names is a question that has long exercised both theologians and philosophers, both of whom have seen that the word intends something beyond the empirical or everyday order. In religious perspective, the word points toward the sense of transcendence and holiness many people feel, suggesting that these common stirrings of human beings are best explained by there being an objective correlative—a Being who corresponds to them as their potential fulfiller. God then becomes imagined and conceived as full of truth, beauty, justice, love, mercy, and the other qualities that human beings frequently long to meet in pure, unlimited, deathless form.

hermeneutics: the study of interpretation—how to extract the legitimate meanings of a text or artifact. The hermeneutical "turn" of recent religious studies has greatly enriched our awareness of the complexity and sophistication of the exchanges among writer, text, and readers. On the other hand, sometimes hermeneutical works get so complicated that they seem to call impossible what manifestly has happened in many times and places: effective communication of meaning from a writer or speaker to an audience. In the case of religious communication, the mysteriousness of many of the references only heightens the need for hermeneutical scholars to test their own range of experiences, feelings about religious symbols, and assumptions about the ultimate construction of both reality as a whole and religious consciousness in particular, asking that those who would preside over how meaning is established come clean about their own theoretical and personal prejudgments.

humanism: an appreciation of human virtues and needs that leads to focus on human concerns, sometimes to the neglect of divinity or ultimate reality. Humanism may go hand in hand with religion, or it may appear to be religion's enemy. The social programs of the religions, and their appreciation for the wonders of human nature, tend to make them humanistic. However, when humanism becomes delimiting—a way of saying that human beings are the measure or the limit—religion usually must protest. Religion lives from transcendence: going beyond any present attainment, reaching out to the infinite. Humanism can define itself so as to be compatible with such transcendence, but frequently it does not. Secular humanism expressly does not, taking its name from the this-worldly horizon that at best brackets divine transcendence.

mystery: something that has not been explained or cannot be explained. The religious philosophers tend to agree that the divine mystery is a fullness, a surplus, that no amount of human scholarship—indeed, no amount of divine revelation to humanity—will ever remove. So, for example, there is the Christian notion that the beatific vision of God in heaven can be endless (eternal), because the fullness of the divine intelligibility is endless—literally without limit. Theologians also speak of mysteries when in fact they might better speak of surdities: things that appear intrinsically irrational. Evil may be such a surdity or mystery. Why should people do what is to the hurt not only of others of their kind but also of themselves, since it closes them to the divine life for which they have most basically been made? Perhaps the most difficult mysteries are the natural disorders (earthquakes, cancers) that cannot be held to the account of free human beings and seem to bring God into the dock. On the testimony of Job, one can only confess one's nescience and let the problem remain with God, neither denying the ways that God seems guilty nor presuming to be certain that God can't still be bringing goodness out of what human perception can only call evil.

mysticism: experience of or direct communion with ultimate reality. Mystics come in different garbs and may be found across the religious traditions, monotheistic and polytheistic alike. Problems of definition abound, but most commentators stress an ineffable experience that brings the person into direct contact with ultimate reality or God. How important union with ultimate reality is, or how lasting the indubitable character of the experience must be, can be debated. What mystics commonly share is the conviction that the world open to the senses is only a fraction of total reality, as well as the conviction that direct communion with ultimate reality, through gracious divine love or human enlightenment, is the most precious experience any human being can have.

nature: physical reality in its totality; whatness or character. Nature in the sense of the physical world or cosmos virtually coincides with divinity in many religious traditions. Not everything in nature is divine, because divinity has depths or boundaries that escape the cosmos—transcend the natural matrix. On the other hand, nature tends to be perceived as having come from a divinity stronger and less perishable than itself. Nature therefore remains mysterious, something whose foundations, rhythms, purposes, and willfulness human beings cannot fathom. Nature in the sense of essence or whatness stems from rather refined philosophical analysis. When people distinguish between the fact that something is and the character of that thing (the way that it exists—as human or rabbit, tree or rock), they have begun to press beyond commonsensical naming and started to wonder about how things give up their whatness, how mind correlates with names and essences, and so forth. Philosophy, poetry, and natural science differentiate from a primordial wonder about this process, taking humanity in several different enriching directions and then asking to be correlated again.

primitive: original or underived; undeveloped. This word clearly can have at least two quite different connotations. As pointing to religious ways that are original, not derived from long-standing cultural traditions, primitive can suggest vitality, creativity, raw power, closeness to a nature or a divinity that has not been tamed by convention. Thus the primitive theology of the Yahwist gives the Pentateuch much of its religious power. However, as undeveloped, unsophisticated, unrefined, primitive religion is liable to confusion and shallowness. Its myths may be incredible fantasies rather than lovely poetry. Its rituals may be crude exhibitions or orgies, rather than artful expressions of how the world was born, how the deities move, what human beings need to hear, say, and do to be reconciled. Scholars generally have dropped the designation "primitive religion," because the nonliterate or small-scale cultural complexes with which it dealt proved too admirable to justify risking the condescending or negative possibilities in the term.

religion: communion with, service of, or concern for ultimate reality. The etymological origins of the term stress binding or tying, to the gods or holy forces. Religion traditionally has been little distinct from the mores of a people, naming most of what has animated its art, legal conventions, ethical expectations, role models, and senses of destiny. Religion inevitably traffics in mystery, contending with the Beginning and Beyond that the human mind cannot comprehend, but religious people come in various personality types, some inclining more to social service (as their expression of devotion to ultimate holiness) and others inclining more to solitary contemplation.

revelation: disclosure (of sacred truth). The core image is of tearing or removing a veil that previously has shrouded the truth. People can make self-disclosures that merit being called revelations, but for religions the primary revelations always come from the ultimate powers. The paradox hanging over the theology of revelation is that even when divinity unveils itself, as in the Incarnation of the Logos or the gifts of the Qur'an, it remains so mysterious that one has to continue to say that what human beings do not know about it outweighs what they do know. Philosophical theologians have gained some insights into the process of revelation by appropriating the views of thinkers such as Martin Heidegger, whose essential notion of truth (*a-letheia*) was the unveiling of bits of reality that comes when a word enters the mind as a fresh naming.

ritual: prescribed, formalized religious action or ceremony. With myth, ritual constitutes the typical and basic way traditional humanity spoke to itself about the world, who it was as a people, individual destiny, and the divine forces responsible for its world and fate. Rituals tend to dramatize existence, and their appeal is holistic: to the senses, memory, feelings of social solidarity, symbolic or artistic faculties that engage people's feelings and make their experiences vivid. Few people are thoroughly convinced of truths that have not been communicated ritualistically, and instinctively most peoples have employed music, dance, special costumes, and the like to make ritualistic occasions the more impressive. Rituals carry the danger of becoming overly aesthetic, ends in themselves, antagonistic to doctrinal clarity, and rubricized (legislated in all their details), but many commentators think that the repristination of myth and ritual is essential if present humanity is to reacquire the feelings necessary to have a beautiful and fully meaningful existence.

scripture: a writing thought to be especially holy and authoritative because closely connected with God, ultimate reality, or final wisdom. Literate religious traditions regularly produce scriptures, although the precision with which they define their scriptural canons varies greatly. The production and reception of a scripture involves members of the tradition in the complicated textual issues recently highlighted by literary studies: hermeneutics, reading passages against their apparent sense, altering the religious experience from something that originally generated a text to something the text now generates, and so forth. Those who revere a scripture and use it regularly tend to dwell within a world organized by the text, loving the images, cadences, and assurances which that textual world brings to mind. Scriptures need not create fundamentalist readers driven to take them literally, but they always carry that potential. They may also, however, stimulate symbolic or iconographical readings that find it richer to treat the scriptural master-images and texts as "material" presences of a holy spirituality that is bound to be dynamic, creative, alive, and so always shifting (without necessarily changing its basic identity).

sect: a party or smaller group within a larger whole, often distinguished by its dissent from doctrines or practices usual for the larger whole. This basic denotation of the term reflects the tendency of most religious groups to generate internal controversies and so divisions. Sectarian groups usually are sufficiently alienated from the parent or larger body to define themselves as much in opposition to it as positively, but in the larger context of a pluralistic world with many other religious or cultural traditions they retain much likeness to the parental body and so will tend to be seen by outsiders as simply idiosyncratic Jews, Muslims, Christians, Buddhists, or whatever. Clearly sectarianism is in part a function of the rigidity with which a parental body or long-standing tradition defines its boundaries. The less specific and dogmatic a tradition, the more easily it may accommodate diversity and avoid sectarian splits. In recent sociological usage the term has come to overlap with "cult," insofar as groups pivoted on a dominant personality and requiring total dedication usually bear some relationship to a longer-standing parental body and define themselves as a purification or new prophetic form of that body, which must live somewhat in opposition to it.

tradition: teaching and practice that have been handed down. Religions generally look to the past for their standards, models, and wisdom. Indeed, many religions are nostalgic for a golden age when relations with the gods supposedly were better than they have been recently. Tradition can imply a precious connection to this better past and the way a people stays in touch with the paradigms given by the gods at the creation of the world. In religions that look back to a historical revelation, tradition tends to make that revelation its starting point and golden age. Thus Moses, Jesus, and Muhammad all launched strong traditions. Philosophically, tradition depends on and expresses the historicity of religion and the rest of human culture. Faith and morals, as well as art and scientific lore, are always evolving. As well, every people has to contrive ways to pass its culture on to the next generation. So tradition intersects with a people's ways of educating its young. The religious problems raised by traditioning boil down to finding a balance between neglecting the past, and so being condemned to repeat its mistakes, and being immobilized in the past, afraid or unwilling to make the adaptations necessary if what was believed in the past is to continue to be vital in the future.

ultimate reality: the endpoint the mind reaches when it seeks the source of the being, intelligibility, and goodness it experiences. This term may also indicate divinity in an impersonal mode. Religious traditions that shy away from calling themselves theistic sometimes are comfortable speaking of ultimate reality. Generally the term does not depend on revelation and may represent a philosophical or mystical extrapolation from the sense that finite realities do not furnish their own reason to be. The so-called proofs for the existence of God frequently amount to explorations to ultimate reality. The cosmological proof argues from contingency to a necessary being. The teleological proof argues from efficient action to goals and purposefulness. The ontological argument argues from the inclusion of existence in the concept of a supreme or perfect being to the actual reality of such a First, Source, or Divinity. When religions confess an ultimate reality, they virtually confess the presence of that reality to all proximate beings and situations, whether ontologically or in the sense that one cannot fully estimate the significance of any proximate reality without taking the ultimate reality into account.

worship: adoration and veneration, usually offered directly to God or truly ultimate reality. Worship can provide for prayers of petition and sacrifices aiming to dispose the deity to grant favors, but most liturgists place the heart of worship in praise and thanksgiving. Religious traditions concerned about idolatry and polytheism usually insist that only the One God merits worship. Thus biblical Judaism, Protestant Christianity, and Islam have all had iconoclastic impulses designed to protect the purity of their worship. More sacramental religions have thought worship ought to engage the senses, employ material elements, and invite nonhuman creation to participate. Iconographic traditions usually have distinguished between the veneration accorded their saints and the worship rightly offered only to God. So, for example, Catholic and Orthodox Christian theologians have separated the *latria* suitable for God from the *dulia* one might offer the saints or the holy images.

CHAPTER 1

THE ANCIENT RELIGIOUS MIND

Egyptian sign for divine wisdom

We begin our study of the world religions by trying to understand the mentality of prehistoric human beings. **Prehistoric** implies having no literature or writing, because we moderns require writing for a critical, trustworthy account of what happened—a history. The ancient religious mind is the mentality that we hypothesize characterized humanity when it was without written records. It is the oldest human mentality, because the first human beings did not write. It is also the newest human mentality because it is the "beginner's mind" with which human beings meet the world most freshly.[1]

To feel sympathy for the earliest religionists, we must be convinced that they were as human as we are. In a way, the description that follows will argue this case, but it will also assume it. Right now, then, we need a quick and brilliant proof—a case that will banish all doubt. Consider the cripple of Shanidar.

From excavations at a Paleolithic cave ("Shanidar cave") in northern Iraq, archeologists have described the skeleton of a man whose arm had been severed in his youth. He must have been useless for hunting or self-defense. He could not have dragged fuel, extended a territory, stalked or stunned a foe. Life in his time was hand-to-mouth, and there was little extra food to go around. Surely, then, he was a liability. Like animals, his fellow cave dwellers should have let him die where the accident occurred. They did not. There must have been something about the cripple, something more than the ability to hunt and gather. Maybe he sang, bringing cheer to the dark night. Maybe he loved children—was patient, kind, quick to tell stories. Maybe he was a great wit, or a great lover, or a great reader of signs. Or maybe he was just a good man in pain—a man whose smile broke your heart. Whatever, his family kept him on, made sure he got food and clothing. He did not die by famine or by beast. He died in a cave-in, at home in his family circle.

The Ancient Religious Mind: Twenty-five Key Dates

4.6 billion years ago	*Formation of the Earth*
3.6 billion years ago	*Rise of Life*
4 million years ago	Australopithecus, *Advanced Hominid in Africa*
2 million years ago	Homo Habilis; *Stone Tools*

Key Dates Continued

1.5 million years ago	Homo Erectus; *More Sophisticated Tools*
500,000 years ago	*Use of Fire*
100,000 years ago	Homo Sapiens; *Ritual Burial*
75,000 years ago	*Mousterian Cave Dwellers; Clothing to Survive Northern Winters*
40,000 years ago	Homo Sapiens Sapiens, *"Modern Man," Full Hunting Culture*
35,000 years ago	*Clothing Adequate for Life in Siberia*
30,000 years ago	*Prehistoric Painting and Sculpture*
30,000–25,000 years ago	*Migrations across Bering Strait to New World*
20,000 years ago	*Colonization of Europe, Japan*
15,000 years ago	*Extensive Cereal Collecting*
10,500 years ago	*Humans throughout South America*
9,500–6,500 years ago	*Cereal Cultivation, Domestication of Animals*
8000 B.C.E.	*Full Withdrawal of Glaciers*
8350–7350 B.C.E.	*Jericho, First Walled Town (10 acres)*
6250–5400	*Catal Huyuk (Turkey), Large City (32 acres)*
ca. 6000	*Rice Cultivation in Thailand; Pottery and Woolen Textiles in Catal Huyuk*
ca. 5000	*Irrigation of Mesopotamian Alluvial Plains*
ca. 4000	*Bronze Casting in Middle East*
ca. 3500	*Megaliths in Brittany, Iberian Peninsula, British Isles; Invention of Wheel*
ca. 3100	*Pictographic Writing in Sumer*
ca. 3000	*Spread of Copper Working*

Such a valuing of humanity for itself, with little concern for pragmatic benefits, indicates that prehistoric people were more than our peers. Sometimes they were our betters.[2]

In this chapter we deal with four places where one can observe important stages of humanity's first period of religious evolution: earliest religion, hunting and progress toward agriculture, the period after agriculture, and the period when many people built great stone constructions (called megaliths) on the order of Stonehenge in England.

EARLIEST RELIGION

What we are calling earliest religion begins with the oldest remains of human culture. Since humanoid beings have been walking the earth for perhaps 3,500,000 years, and since true humans *(Homo sapiens)* surely existed 100,000 years ago,[3] this is an enormous time span. On the basis of archeological evidence, scholars are persuaded that religion is virtually as old as humanity itself.[4] The earliest forms of religion are quite vague, but since the time of what we might call "developed" human beings (beings capable of abstraction and calculation), which began at least with the Aurignacian era 32,000 years ago,[5] there probably has been a reflective religion that we ourselves could recognize.

Indeed, as we shall show, we moderns continue to manifest many facets and interests of ancient religion, and psychoanalytic theory suggests that strata of early evolutionary experiences live on in our unconscious.[6] Because we have become aware of this, and because anthropological studies have shown that contemporary nonliterate tribes probably have as much native intelligence as we, contemporary attitudes toward ancient religion are very different from attitudes during the formative years of academic religious studies, when the so-called classical approaches emerged.[7] Then a scholar such as K. T. Preuss, who flourished at the turn of the century, could locate the beginnings of religion in what he called "primitive stupidity" *(Urdummheit)*. Bedeviled by the evolutionary perspective that had burst on the scene with Darwin's *On the Origin of Species* (1859), many of the classicists considered nonliterate peoples to be savages, more bestial than rational.

SOME CORRELATIONS AMONG PHENOMENA OF PREHISTORIC RELIGION	
Earliest existence	Burial rites
	Interest in soul
Hunting	Kinship with animals
	Life taking life
	Study of game
	Importance of men
	Eventual domestication of animals
Gathering	Kinship with plants
	Appreciation of nature's cycles
	Importance of women
Agriculture	Control of crops
	Basis for settled life
	Emphasis on mother earth
	Source of wealth and leisure
	Stimulus to new technology
Megaliths	Permanence of stone
	Honoring of dead
	Bones of mother earth
	Ritual centers

But rational they were, and such remains as cave paintings and rock incisions lead us to conclude that they were thoroughly absorbed in making religious sense of their condition. It is perilous to generalize about a regular or typical prehistoric religious mentality (in North America alone, before the coming of whites, there were up to 2,000 separate cultures, many of them based on mutually unintelligible languages),[8]

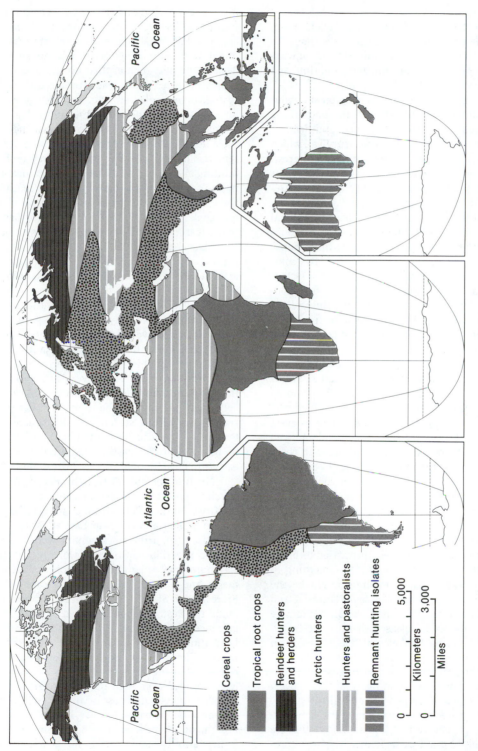

Figure 3 *Original economies of the world. Adapted from* The Times Atlas of World History, *edited by Geoffrey Barraclough, 1979.* © Hammond, Inc., Maplewood, New Jersey. Reprinted by permission of The London Times, New York, New York.

Cereal crops

Tropical root crops

Reindeer hunters and herders

Arctic hunters

Hunters and pastoralists

Remnant hunting isolates

Kilometers

Miles

0   3,000

0   5,000

Pacific Ocean

Atlantic Ocean

Pacific Ocean

but Native Americans, Africans, Australians, and others do seem to have shared some basic beliefs. From these beliefs we can tender a few hypotheses about the earliest human cultures, which similarly had no writing, usually depended on hunting and gathering, and sought intimacy with nature.[9]

What do scholars of prehistoric religion say about the earliest human mentality? That its most absorbing issues were probably birth, subsistence, and death.[10] The first human concern probably was survival, which meant food and children. The first religious interest, consequently, probably was how to get the mysterious surrounding powers to provide food and children. Developing this thesis, the British scholar John Bowker has proposed that early religion clarifies the general biological or evolutionary situation, in which a species must sufficiently crack its "compound of limitations" to gain another generation's worth of life.[11] By "compound of limitations" Bowker means the set of factors that threaten a species' existence. This includes needing food, being liable to disease, being vulnerable to natural disaster, and the like. For human beings it also includes spiritual vulnerabilities: madness, loss of hope, and noncooperation.

At first Bowker's theory, which owes much to computer science, seems very sophisticated, but it soon works out to be rather basic: The first human beings strove mightily to survive. They hunted and gathered for food; they did what they could to avert sickness and cure disease; they begot children and tried to protect them. Part of their recourse in these efforts, though, went beyond what we might call practical means. Part of it was religious in the sense of reaching out to the unseen. There is evidence, for instance, that more than 500,000 years ago, in the Dragon Bone Hill caves of China near Beijing, people buried bodies in the hope of an afterlife.

Some of the earliest peoples, then, tried to break death's stranglehold by imagining that something in them survived death. That something might be the part that traveled in dreams, that could fantasize and construct realities other than the physical. It might be like the smoke that wood releases when it is destroyed by fire, or like the part of plants that makes them flower again after winter. Whatever, these prehistoric peoples used their imagination and at least rudimentary reflection to project meanings that could overcome their biological weakness and mortality.

At this stage of human existence, the hard distinctions between nature and human beings that we have been taught did not exist. Rather, the art of prehistoric caves suggests that animals and plants were intimate fellow creatures, close links to humans in the chain of life. What happened to plants in the spring might well illumine what would happen to human dead in the next turn of their cycle. So as the earliest people mourned their dead, treasured their frail offspring, or marveled at sexuality, they probably drew on a sense of the life chain, the continuum of plants, animals, and themselves. We know that they anointed their dead with substances like red ochre, which resembles life-giving blood. As well, they probably saw hunting and gathering as sacred affairs, dealings with nature's awesome powers of life and death. Nature, then, was the great interest and educator of the earliest people. Much more than we moderns, they felt part of the seasonal cycles, dominated by sun and cold.

This concern with nature seems to have made certain objects related to fecundity, hunting magic, and the cult of the dead potent symbols. Whether ancient peoples thought in terms of a single, overarching power (a "god") that would organize these symbols is still debated. More likely, their most general conception was of a universal bounty—a source of life that kept replenishing the animals and plants. Two apparent locations of this life-power were the sky and the earth. The sky, vaulted over everything, was in a position to observe and perhaps control everything, and it contained the sun and the rain; thus, it regularly attracted the mind's search for an ultimate principle. From the experience of human birthing, people seem to have given the earth a maternal modality very early—to have thought of it as a **Great Mother**.

Much of the **cult** of early humanity, much of its worship, probably focused on generative powers and the Great Mother. Relics from a swath of land extending from Siberia to the Near East attest to the prehistoric use of figurines of pregnant women and to the likely conception of God as a woman.[12] In the same way, numerous relics attest to a concern with hunting magic and animal fertility. In the cave called Trois Frères, near St. Girons in Ariège, France, explorers found the head of a lion engraved on a stalactite. The presence of numerous arrows suggests that the lion head functioned as a target in a ritual of hunting magic. The famous "sorcerer" painting discovered elsewhere in the same cave depicts a figure who may have presided over such hunting magic. His legs are human, his eyes are those of an owl, and he has reindeer antlers, the paws of a bear, the tail of a horse, and prominent genitals. Some scholars suggest that he is a "master of the animals,"[13] who led a dance or ritual in which his people expressed their needs and hopes for the hunt.

So prehistoric peoples probably understood their world largely in terms of quite concrete, emotion-laden interactions with the life powers. From nonliterate peoples living today, we can hypothesize that the earliest peoples probably developed stories about the origin of the world and of themselves based on their observations of human and animal birth. Moreover, because they could create by making things, and so sensed their special powers of consciousness, prehistoric peoples may frequently have claimed to have a special soul—a source of psychic or spiritual life. Such a soul may have been thought to linger after death, giving ancestors a semiphysical presence, making them more than just their children's memories. Because of this conception of a soul, they may have thought of death as a passageway, a threshold to a new level of existence. As one passed thresholds at birth and puberty, so one might pass a last threshold at death. In death one might even curve to a new phase in a circle that led the soul back to earthly life—one's life force might animate another breathing creature, even another human body.

In this way, the fascination and dread experienced by early human beings in their encounters with death could have generated a rudimentary philosophy. As a result, they may have tried to explain both the interconnectedness of living things, which often take life from one another, and the apparent end signified by an individual's death. Because they felt so dependent on the sky and the earth, early human beings probably petitioned their aid, asking the sky and earth to carry the dying across to a new life. Thus, the interplay of life and death probably formed the center of prehistoric religion.

HUNTING AND PROGRESS TOWARD AGRICULTURE

For the more prosaic, and more certain, aspects of the history of religion before the rise of civilization, a useful guide is the first volume of Mircea Eliade's history of religious ideas.[14] In it, Eliade, a very influential historian of religion, summarizes the major religious advances from prehistory to the time of the city-state.

At the beginning, more than two million years ago, our ancestors often pondered life's mysteriousness in terms of the implications of hunting. Living off animal flesh, they both established a mystical bond with the animal world and made a significant change in their own evolution: "Hunting determined the division of labor in accordance with sex, thus reinforcing 'hominization'; for among the carnivora, and in the entire animal world, no such difference exists."[15] Thus, well before 500,000 B.C.E. (the date of the first documented use of fire), human beings had moved into a world of new meanings by specializing in hunting.

The earliest remains believed to have been used for religious purposes are bones, and those from the Mousterian period (70,000–50,000 B.C.E.) suggest the practice of burial with hopes for an afterlife. The problem in interpreting ancient artifacts (many of them much older than the Mousterian), though, is that they are "opaque": Their meanings are uncertain. Without written texts or at least semididactic ("teaching") art, we can only imagine how the earliest people used such artifacts—what they thought when they laid the dead in the ground, why they sang and danced, and so on. The situation is somewhat better in the Paleolithic period (30,000–9000 B.C.E.), since many cave paintings reflect the theme of animal life. They make it clear that Paleolithic peoples were bonded to animals out of need, reverence, and fear.

Some of the motifs in the cave paintings correspond to what we know from shamanist hunting peoples of modern times. For instance, many paintings combine animal and human forms (the **shaman** often identifies with a bird or wolf), and certain "x-ray" paintings manifest an interest in skeletal structures (many shamans meditate on skulls and bones, which they consider the crucial animal elements). Other motifs emerge in remains from the Mesolithic period, after the last glacial period (about 9000 B.C.E.). For example, there is a new concern with women and human fertility, as evidenced by many statues of females who either are pregnant or have exaggerated sexual features. Along with excavations of a village in Siberia, in which men and women lived in different quarters, this motif suggests an increased interest in human procreation and sexual complementarity. Such complementarity no doubt had more than human significance. Probably it meshed with the hunters' views of animal life, calculations of astronomical cycles, dances, mythic-ritualistic accounts of creation, and so on.

If the apparent similarities between certain early remains and the arts of hunting peoples living today are valid, we can infer that Mesolithic tribes had a complex world of signs and symbols—a cosmos (ordered whole) with many sacred layers. We know that shamanist ecstasy goes back to prehistoric times. We can guess that wonder about human language lent great imaginative power to such ecstasy, as it did to ritual and myth. From at least Mesolithic times, then, human beings probably have tried to coordinate sex, sacrifice, death, animals, the moon, the stars—all the striking, impressive phenomena of their lives.

Moreover, the end of the Ice Age seems to have marked a division among prehistoric peoples. From Mesolithic times there is mention of a golden era, a paradise when human relations with heaven and the animals were more harmonious. Probably this idea represents the culmination of hunting peoples' myths and reflection—an early form of mythic speculation on the ways things ought to be. In any case, when the glaciers melted, the flood brought the world's strangeness into sharper focus. Also, questions arose of moral responsibility and guilt: What caused the flood? How did we lose paradise? Ancestors, believed to linger on as ghosts or spiritual presences, also stimulated such questions: What is our relationship to our predecessors who knew better times? To increase their chances of living in a good age, ancient hunters probably developed a code of behavior and a cluster of taboos that they attributed to their ancestors: "Live this way and you will prosper."

Just as hunting trained people to pay close attention to the characteristics of the game—where they fed, when they migrated south or north—so gathering trained people to pay close attention to the characteristics of plants. Gatherers, the majority of whom probably were women, had to know where to find the roots, nuts, berries, fruits, and other plant products that furnished the staple portion of the earliest peoples' diet (meat from hunting was unreliable). Moreover, gatherers experimented to learn the different properties of the plants in their area—which ones yielded savory spices, which ones had healing or hallucinogenic properties, which ones could be boiled or dried to produce dyes, decorative hangings, or good fuel for the fire.

All of this attention to the cycles and characteristics of plants paved the way to agriculture: the control of plant production. With agriculture human beings made a great leap in their mastery of their environment. Like the domestication of animals, agriculture meant people no longer were at the whim of natural cycles they did not understand. They could stabilize their food supply, lay in better stores for winter, and free some members of their group for artistic work, for developing religious lore, or for planning how to dominate neighboring peoples. The very successes of hunters and gatherers therefore moved these earliest people toward a significantly different way of life (and so toward significantly different religious interests and concepts).

AFTER AGRICULTURE

The great practical advances of the Mesolithic period were the settled communities made possible by the domestication of plants and animals. In the Near East, especially in Palestine, these advances created a period of strong cultural activity, as people strove to understand and express the far-reaching changes in their life-styles. The remains of the Natufian culture at Wadi en-Natuf, for instance, show a people who built a village of circular huts, harvested wild cereals with stone sickles, and ground seeds with mortar and pestle. (There is evidence that cereals were a dietary staple in the valley of the upper Nile as early as 13,000 B.C.E.) By 6500 B.C.E. different Near Eastern communities had domesticated sheep, goats, and pigs. The Mesolithic period also produced numerous important inventions, among them the bow, cords, nets, hooks, and boats.

In Eliade's view, such inventions have more than just practical or economic effects. When people work with different materials imaginatively and creatively, they develop a sophisticated sense of the many possibilities in matter—the many analogies between tools and artifacts, between human work and natural processes. Then they easily create rich symbolisms or mystiques. Thus ancient peoples often gave mining, harvesting, or weaving a densely symbolic value. A fairly direct line runs from their prehistoric world to that of the medieval alchemist and even that of the modern engineer, in that all have been absorbed with the changes one could work on matter and through matter on social life.

Before the Mesolithic turn to agriculture and a more settled life, nomadic cultures depended on hunting, blood sacrifices, and a close identification with animals. In later times, these Paleolithic themes continued to play in the background. Through military groups, myths of the days of nomadic life, hunting for sport, and occasional orgies (with frenzied tearing of animals and eating of raw flesh), agricultural peoples kept contact with their past. Nonetheless, along with village life came "vegeculture" (the civilization of roots, tubers, and rhizomes), and then agriculture (the cultivation of cereals and grasses). The religious impact of these cultivations was revolutionary.

For instance, to be steady producers of food, human beings had to calculate the seasons much more accurately. This led to astronomical calculations, astrology, and the worship of planets and stars. Furthermore, agriculture led to a more intimate knowledge of the natural cycle of death and rebirth. In the myth of Hainuwele, from New Guinea, we can see the ancient struggle to comprehend this new set of mysteries.[16] By her murder and dismemberment, the semidivine Hainuwele allowed tuberous plants to spring forth. In other words, vegeculture was thought to have depended on a primordial murder. More deliberately than hunters, who found available animals, cultivators buried life to secure their food. Summarizing the psychic impact of this new situation, Eliade says, "All responsible activities (puberty ceremonies, animal or human sacrifices, cannibalism, funerary ceremonies, etc.) properly speaking constitute a recalling, a 'remembrance,' of the primordial murder. It is significant that the cultivator associates with a murder the essentially peaceful labor that insures his existence, whereas in societies of hunters the responsibility for slaughter is attributed to *another*, to a 'stranger.' "[17] Thus, as people reflected on their new relations with nature, they had to confront their own responsibilities in the cycle of nature's fertility.

Succeeding the mystical solidarity between hunters and animals, then, is a mystical solidarity between cultivators and plants. Whereas in earliest times blood and bone were the essential, most sacred elements of life, in agricultural times the generative elements—masculine sperm and feminine blood—became the most sacred. Above all, women dominated agricultural life, and "mother earth" was the prime focus. Through the millennia before the biology of reproduction became clear, the earth was believed to give birth independently, without need of any male. Because women developed agriculture and controlled it, and because women issued all human life, Mesolithic culture connected women to mother earth. Thus, from this period came the best known great goddesses. Sexuality became a sacred drive and process, because all nature—the whole cosmos—moved through a religious cycle of conception, gestation, birth, nurturance, growth, decline, and then death (which could be a new conception).

Houses, villages, shrines, and burial vaults all reflected the womb architecturally. The earth itself seemed uterine: From it we come, to it we return. Accordingly, very old myths of human creation speak of first ancestors crawling forth from mines or caves, and funerary rituals consign the dead offspring back to the Great Mother. Finally, during this initial period of agriculture, there was an increased stress on polarities—earth and sky, dirt and rain, yin and yang (the Chinese dual elements).

This focus on the earth in the Mesolithic era continued into Neolithic times, when village life developed into city life, agriculture became more extensive and secure, and arts and crafts such as pottery, weaving, and tool manufacturing were established. Also, in the Neolithic period, cults of fertility and death assumed even greater prominence. From sanctuaries excavated in Anatolia (modern Turkey), we know that around 7000 B.C.E. worship involved skulls and various gifts, such as jewels, weapons, and textiles. The principal divinity was a goddess, who was manifested in three forms: a young woman, a mother, and a crone (old woman). Figurines represent her giving birth, breasts adorn her cave sites, and drawings portray her among animals, especially bulls and leopards. In many caves the double ax, symbol of the storm god, underscores the fertility theme (stormy rain fecundates mother earth).

Representations of bees and butterflies relate this fertility theme to the burial skulls and gifts, since both bees and butterflies pass through distinct stages in their life cycles. Worshipers likely tried to fit death into such a scheme—to see it as another transformation of the life force, another stage. Subordinate to the goddess was a male god, a boy or youth, who seems to be her child and lover and who has some correlations with the bull.

With the discovery of bronze about 3500 B.C.E. in the Middle East, new weapons and tools came into use. Also, more specialized work developed, such as mining, smelting, and casting metal. In turn, this work created more efficient farming implements, which led to the production of surplus food. Surplus food allowed a new class of religious specialists (who were agriculturally unproductive) to arise, while the metals "industry" stimulated the exploration and colonization of new territories for raw materials.

From 1900 to 1400 B.C.E., following the Hittite invention of tempering, iron came into widespread use, and the production of bronze and iron further stimulated the human imagination and increased the symbolic content of mother earth. Whereas the earliest iron was a gift from the sky (coming in the form of meteorites), mined iron came from the womb of the earth. Indeed, miners developed regimes of fasting, meditation, and purification, since they had to go into sacred depths and extract a new form of life. Their mythology spoke of elves, fairies, genies, and spirits who inhabited the underground, assisting or witnessing the slow gestation of mother earth's strangest children, the ores. Metallurgists, like blacksmiths and potters, had to be "masters of fire," which associated them with the shamans, who were masters of inner, magical heat. Also, metallurgists took on some of the paradoxical nature of metal itself. Coming from mother earth and being a boon to humanity, metal was sacred. However, being invulnerable and easily made into an instrument of death, metal was too close to evil for humans to handle comfortably. Thus, the smith entered the mythology of the gods, fashioning weapons for their heavenly battles and tools for their heavenly enterprises. In India, Tvastr made Indra's weapons for the fight against Vrtra; in Greece, Hephaestus forged the thunderbolt that enabled Zeus to triumph over Typhon.

MEGALITHS

The Bronze and Iron ages begot the first great Near Eastern civilizations, which we discuss in Chapter 7. Here, however, we survey one last prehistoric phenomenon, the megaliths. **Megalith** means "great stone," and it brings to mind the prehistoric European cultures that left remains such as the famous cromlech (circle of huge stones) at Stonehenge in England. Actually, prehistorians speak of a megalithic cultural complex, centered at Los Millares in southeastern Spain and covering Portugal, half of France, western England, and parts of Ireland, Denmark, and Sweden. In some cases, prehistoric peoples in these areas arranged either cromlechs or *dolmens* ("immense capstone[s] supported by several upright stones arranged to form a sort of enclosure or chamber")[18] from slabs weighing as much as 300 tons.

What was the point of all this labor? Apparently the megalith was the major symbol for a cult of the dead. For Neolithic peasants of the fifth and fourth millennia B.C.E., stone was the symbol of permanence—of resistance to change, decay, or death. Unlike peoples in central Europe and the Near East, who strictly separated themselves from the dead, the megalithic tribes of western Europe sought close communion with the deceased, probably because they regarded death as a state of security and strength. To these people, ancestors could be powerful helpers and great allies. With the discovery of agriculture, human life perhaps seemed even more frail than it had before. Like that of the plant, it was ephemeral, bound to a cycle of birth, life, and death. By associating with "ancestral" stones—the bones of mother earth—humans might overcome their frailty and impermanence.

The megaliths represent burial vaults or ritual areas where this faith was practiced. At Stonehenge, for instance, the cromlech was in the middle of a field of funeral mounds. (Stonehenge was also a sophisticated instrument that could be used for making astronomical calculations.) At Carnac in Brittany, there was an avenue large enough for thousands to parade. Both sites likely were ceremonial centers or unenclosed temples—areas of sacred space for communing with ancestral stones.

Practically the whole island of Neolithic Malta was a megalithic sanctuary system. There a great goddess presided as the guardian divinity over a cult of the dead. One necropolis, now called the Hypogeum, has yielded bones of more than 7,000 people. Previously, scholars thought that this cultural complex, like the European ones, derived from a cultural basin around the Aegean Sea. However, radiocarbon datings show that the megaliths are older than the remains from the prehistoric Aegean, so western Europeans apparently developed their megalithic death cult independently.

Moreover, megaliths later cropped up in a vast geographic area extending from Algeria to Korea and North America. Thus, huge stones probably prompted in many different peoples similar ideas about death, ancestors, permanence, and escape from time and decay. If most prehistoric peoples were moved to ponder their mortality more deeply because of agriculture, perhaps they tended to use stone to assist them in this contemplation. Indeed, studies of megalithic societies that continued into the twentieth century C.E. confirm this hypothesis. In Indonesia and Melanesia, stone monuments defended the soul during its journey to the beyond, ensured an eternal existence after death,

Figure 4 *Prehistoric "Standing Stones" on the Isle of Lewis, Scotland at Callanish. Photo by J. T. Carmody.*

linked the living and the dead, and fertilized the crops and animals through their sacred durability. Certain customs of European peasants in megalithic areas further confirm this hypothesis. As late as the early twentieth century, peasant women in parts of France slid along stones or rubbed themselves against stones to stimulate conception. For them as for women who lived in their locales 5,000 years earlier, stone was powerful and fertilizing.

SUMMARY: THE CENTER OF THE ANCIENT RELIGIOUS MIND

We said earlier that the cyclical conflict between life and death probably formed the center of prehistoric religion. With a life expectancy less than half our own,

the earliest human beings knew death as an intimate partner. So they probably struggled to make friends with the forces that seemed to oppose death: the sun, the rain, the personages they pictured as controlling the animals. They probably prayed to these forces, offered these forces things good to eat or beautiful to behold, and tried to purify themselves of evil or abusive thoughts that might alienate the powers of life. When they themselves had to kill, to secure food or ward off enemies, they probably did so with some uneasiness, feeling a need afterward to purify themselves. Indeed, the killing power of warriors probably seemed to conflict with the nurturing power of mothers, so prehistoric people perhaps kept these two powers apart, insisting that both mothers and active warriors seclude themselves from the community at large.

One can interpret the various religious rites that the remains in prehistoric caves suggest as ways to try to make contact with the powers of life that controlled the world of prehistoric peoples. In their stories and dances, the earliest peoples probably identified themselves with different natural forces and animals that impressed or appealed to them. The link between human beings and other living things would have been strong—human beings, for instance, feeling that they held as many things in common with animals as they held apart. Thus to dance in the gait of a bear, to prowl in the step of a tiger, could be to associate oneself with the bear's strength, to take on some of the tiger's deadly grace. Similarly, to draw these animals, or other life-associated forces, could be to project oneself into the world of their vitality, as could chanting, dancing, or making drug-induced voyages of the spirit.

Björn Kurtén, a scholar of prehistory, has written a fine novel about life 35,000 years ago, when the European glaciers thawed. Using his scientific knowledge to give his literary imagination a solid footing, Kurtén has brought to life a very full mental, social, and ecological existence that the earliest members of our species may well have led. In his portrait, one glimpses the identification with animal power that the artistic remains of the European caves seem to suggest. A man named Tiger has watched two tigers slowly and masterfully isolate a mammoth calf from its mother and then kill it for food. Thinking about his own name, and the need he feels to avenge his father against an enemy who had killed him, Tiger decides to put his artistic talent to good use.

Then one morning the tigers were gone. Their tracks showed that they were heading north. Tiger was tempted to follow them, but he kept his head. He knew that he had things to do, and now he thought he knew how to do them. He would appear gentle and innocent, but behind that mask he would be as swift and deadly as the tigress. There was one thing he had to do before he went on. Not far away, he found what he was looking for: a great granite hogback with a smooth, ice-polished surface, where the wind had swept away much of the snow and the sun had melted the rest. Tiger built a great fire and, armed with charcoal and mammoth fat, went to work.

He sketched out a great picture of the scene he had witnessed. The immense black mammoths took shape under his hand. Then came the tigers. He worked in ecstasy to reproduce in sensitive lines the flow of power, the clownish insolence,

the mastery of the male tiger; to catch the urgency and precision of the female, her single, high-rising attack, the one unerring stroke of violence in the whole combat. . . . Then he drew a different image, which came from another secret place in his mind. There were only two figures here: one, a majestic shelk [the name and symbol of his murderous enemy]; the other, a black tiger moving in to attack. The shelk, for all its glory, was touched by the premonition of death, while every line in the tiger was alive with implacable anger.

After days of toil, all was finished. Exhausted, yet with a consciousness of purpose and resolution that was new to him, Tiger contemplated his work. "That is the way it will be done," he said. The pictures sealed his compact with the great Guardian.[19]

This is an imaginative reconstruction, of course, taking considerable literary license. Nonetheless, it has the great advantage of making Tiger, one of the earliest members of our line *(Homo sapiens sapiens),* seem as intelligent and sensitive as we are. The differences between Tiger and ourselves, which quite likely represent the actual historical differences between ourselves and people of Tiger's prehistoric era, pivot on his greater immersion in the forces of nature. Not having literacy to mediate between him and nature, he more closely identifies himself with the interactions of the other members of his natural environment than we do. For him the changing of the seasons, the migrations of the herds, the flights of the birds were both economically and aesthetically more absorbing. Consequently, they were more significant religiously. Thus the mysterious sources of life seemed to be directing the interactions of human beings and tigers to some inscrutable purpose. Feeling intensely alive, Tiger referred his whole natural ecology to a guardian power. Feeling alive, or lonely, or bewildered, many of us living tens of thousands years later reach into the darkness with spiritual efforts not so very different. Quite like Tiger, we continue to dance around life and death.

Discussion Questions

1. What do the grave sites of very ancient peoples suggest about the earliest religious interests?

2. How does literacy serve as a shield between human beings and nature?

3. Why have the sky and the earth always been religiously significant?

4. How did religion shift with the rise of agriculture?

5. What did early peoples probably make of the killing power of the hunter and warrior?

6. How did women and mother earth function in symbolisms of the cycles of life, death, and rebirth?

7. What were the main functions of the megaliths?

8. What was Tiger doing in making his great drawing?

Glossary

animism: the tendency to attribute a spiritual center or force to all realities. Animists usually believe that all happenings are due to the agencies of spirits, whether benevolent or malign, and that everything has a living principle, endowed with power if not will. Consequently, much of their energy usually goes into trying to pacify potentially harmful spirits and enlist potentially beneficial spirits on their side.

anthropomorphism: personification—the tendency to treat something nonhuman as though it were human. Many religions have anthropomorphic deities or ultimate powers: for example, Zeus or the Wisdom-That-Has-Gone-Beyond that resembles a gracious lady. Many religions also anthropomorphize animals and plants in their mythological accounts of creation, the origin of death, and the like, speaking of snakes that steal the plant that would have given human beings mortality, or of a turtle that dived to the bottom of the earth to bring up the beginning of the world, as though they had been free, willful agents.

archetype: a first form that serves as a model for later members of the same class. In most religious mythologies primal figures and events, such as Adam and Eve and the Fall, serve as archetypes through which later members of the tradition interpret their own experiences. Archetypes therefore have something paradigmatic about them, offering themselves as basic patterns that will always prove illuminating about human weakness, possibility, mortality, and the like.

cosmological myth: the notion that the whole of reality is an ordered and living unity composed of a single primal matter or essential being. Many archaic peoples have stories of the birth of the world and the differentiation of the different species that express such a conviction (about the consubstantiality of all living things) in poetic form. The religious philosophies that speak of a single ultimate reality providing the being of all the things that exist as numerous and diverse on the phenomenal level have taken a step away from the mythic form of this thesis about consubstantiality without fully breaking with its thrust. Only the religions that develop a doctrine of creation from nothingness (and perhaps their impersonal, Eastern equivalents, if such may be defended) have decisively broken with the cosmological myth and separated the physical world from the spiritual reality of divinity or primary being.

cult: this word can mean worship, usually in the sense of the formal thanksgiving, praise, and petition that a religious group offers its deity on a regular basis. The word also can mean an idiosyncratic group that in effect offers its founder or leader so intense an obedience that the life of the group verges on idolatry and seems a worship of the will of its leader. Cult in the first sense has been at the foundations of culture, implying the leisure (both physical and psychological) in which to create and appreciate works worthy of God.

god: written with a small *g*, the word implies a partial possessor of ultimate holiness, power, and the like, and so something considerably less than the fullness of divinity intended by the monotheistic religions. Whether polytheism—profession of many divinities—is best considered a defective religious option opposed to monotheism or an alternate outlook intent on stressing the many manifestations of what might be the single source or font of holiness and creative power is a difficult question. Much depends on one's definitions of terms, especially on what one wants "monotheism" to denote and how one is going to express the presence of divinity in all creatures, each of whom may well only exist because of the direct grant of being God makes to it.

Great Mother: the female divinity found in many ancient cultural areas who seems to stand for ultimate reality in the mode of a fertile, nourishing, and perhaps kindly personification. Archeological excavations in central Europe and Asia have yielded many artifacts suggesting veneration of a Great Mother in Mesolithic and Neolithic times, if not before. Scholars usually associate such veneration with the great interest prehistoric peoples had to have in fertility of all sorts—human, animal, and vegetative. As the manifest sources of human life, human females would have suggested a Great Mother as the source of all the life in the cosmological whole—or at least as the One people did well to imagine interested in their problems of life and death and so properly honored with sacrifices, prayers, and faith.

heaven: the realm of the gods or the force that oversees human affairs. It seems an almost universal human tendency to associate the sky and its forces (light, from the sun and moon; rain, from the clouds) with the ultimate powers shaping creation, observing human activity (and so able to pass judgment upon it), and calling the human spirit to ascend toward greater vision and purity. Heaven, therefore, stands in tension with earth, sometimes as a pure zone judging a corrupt zone, but other times as symbolic of a reality needing union with earthly (maternal) powers of fertility if it is to co-create a fully vital and truly human (or truly saving) religion.

holy: set apart and dedicated to the worship or service of the divine. Modern religious thought has tended to associate holiness with moral perfection or saintliness, but the older connotations correlate it more with "most real, most truly existent." The divine was supremely holy, but such holiness might express itself as a raw power that could terrify. One took off one's shoes when entering on holy ground because not to come humbly, well aware of one's creatureliness and sins, could get one destroyed. Human beings could not see the divine and live, because the divine itself was a vortex of fire, a burning purity of energy, power, and creative will.

magic: the word probably comes from the Magi (Persian priests), and in the most positive usages it denotes efforts to gain spiritual effects through rituals, special knowledge (such as astrology), and attunement to spiritual forces running throughout the universe. As used by anthropologists and many scholars of religion, it refers to spiritual efforts to try to control natural processes for human ends. Black magic would be control that sought to harm other people, whereas white magic would be control that sought helpful results. As used by some theologians, magic is opposed to genuine religion because it seeks to manipulate di-

vinity rather than submitting to divinity (as true religion always does). Virtually always, therefore, the word demands further precision if it is to signify anything exact.

megalith: a prehistoric monument constructed of huge stones. Scholars debate the origin and intent of most aspects of the megalithic remains scattered over a large range in western Europe (but found as far east as Indonesia). The major conjectures include their use as ceremonial sites, places for burying the dead, and astronomical laboratories for making solar and stellar calculations. Clearly, they depended on sizable outlays of labor, and possibly they had social ties to promoting the significance of a chieftan class, somewhat the way the Egyptian pyramids dovetailed with the status of the pharaohs. Stone may have appealed as seeming the most immortal of substances, or as representing the bones of mother earth. Either way, it could symbolize a transhuman sort of "life" that represented something sufficiently other or transcendent to focus numinous powers.

Neolithic: relating to the latest period of the Stone Age, beginning in southwestern Asia around 8000 B.C.E. in many locales. The Neolithic period was when agriculture came firmly into human control, along with animal husbandry and village life. Writing tended to occur at the end of the Neolithic or the beginning of the Bronze Age. Nonetheless, social and ritual patterns derived from older hunter days continued to be influential, as did various mother goddesses.

oral peoples: those whose cultures had or have no writing. Obviously all cultures have been oral in the sense that living speech has been the first mode of communication. But peoples that develop writing change their cultures significantly. Writing starts to mediate a great many relationships—official, personal, religious, economic—and education may become more reflective. And while oral peoples often have prodigious memories, they do not develop the archives on which history in the modern academic sense depends. Thus they tend to be somewhat ahistorical, all the more so when they remain entranced by mythic accounts of creation, the rise of their culture, and where their time will end.

patriarchy: a social system in which authority is vested in the male elders or "fathers." Patriarchy seems virtually the universal rule in the historical cultures, almost everywhere men having been in control of the sources of official power: military, political, economic, religious. Women could in fact exert significant, even controlling, power by indirect means, but the lack of women's official equality to men tended to make feminine influence subtle or even manipulative. Patriarchy generally has worked to women's detriment, if equal opportunity and self-confidence be one's criteria, and feminist students of religion tend to account the patriarchal religious traditions some of the worst offenders in the historical record of women's oppression.

prehistoric: before written history. In one sense, there are no prehistoric beings, in that all true human beings have had memory and language and so have defined themselves through stories of their origin and destiny. In another sense, writing clearly leads to a different sort of history, based on archival records and the possibility of much later reconstructing a synoptic view of events from many different sources. But we should not exaggerate the difference between these two sorts of histories and so sorts of existence, because even well-documented events always remain elusive—never can be reconstructed in their full impact nor set in a larger narrative framework that is free of assumptions and prejudices.

sacrifice: an offering that "makes holy" the thing offered or the people doing the offering; an oblation of something of value (such as an animal) to God or the sacred powers. Sacrifices provide human beings with a way of expressing their desire to honor the deity, or make amends for their failures, or try to influence the deity to favor their petitions. Frequently the background assumption is that the deity provides all life and value and so has a right to either first fruits or regular recompense. In developed religious views of sacrifice, the outward actions are supposed to represent inner dispositions of dedication and service. Like all rituals, sacrifices run the danger of becoming merely formal performances that lack inner dedication. Judaism, Christianity, and Islam have all employed sacrifices of various sorts, while the religions of most nonliterate peoples have stressed sacrifices of both crops and animals. Early Hinduism was pivoted on physical sacrifice, but the notion has had mainly spiritual implications in Buddhism. Confucianism approved sacrifice as part of the public cult, but philosophical Taoism gave it little place. Religious Taoism and Shinto, however, both kept the folk traditions of sacrifice.

shaman: a specialist in ancient techniques of ecstasy. The shaman normally is a functionary for a nonliterate community, serving as its healer, intermediary with the gods, guide of the souls of the dead to their rest, and custodian of traditional tribal lore. The typical shaman comes to this role through either heredity or having manifested idiosyncratic traits (epilepsy, sexual ambiguity, poetic sensitivity, dramatic dreams). Psychologically, shamans depend on an ability to function in two worlds, the ordinary reality of daily life and the extraordinary reality they encounter through their ecstatic journeys. As well, they serve their tribe as a defense of meaning, by incarnating a contact with the powers thought to hold the tribe's destiny.

shelk: Björn Kurtén's term for a magnificent prehistoric deer. Kurtén's novel develops the scientific views that paleontologists have of the entire life of prehistoric Europeans, from the plants and animals of their environment to their hunting, gathering, art, and religion. His shelk is both an actor on the physical scene and a totem—an animal that symbolizes powers a given human tribe or individual reveres.

supernatural: beyond ordinary capacities, sometimes with the connotation of occult or weird. God and the divine life often have been considered beyond the capacity of either physical or human nature to understand or receive. In that sense Christianity has spoken of grace as creating a supernatural order—something that exists only by God's special institution. The use of the term *supernatural* to point to the occult or weird carries overtones of common sense: what doesn't occur in most times and places, what is paranormal. The term has raised many problems on both counts, sometimes inclining orthodox groups to make religion otherworldly and sometimes inclining occultist groups to suggest that religion or spirituality should be more concerned with the bizarre than with the (marvels of the) ordinary.

theocracy: a political regime in which religious and secular authorities are fused and lie in the hands of a single set of leaders, who claim to hold their authority from God. The majority of premodern regimes have been theocracies, in that the majority of premodern cultures have not sharply distinguished the sacred and secular realms. The medieval European tensions between popes and emperors show the theocratic impulse working both ways, kings claiming divine sanction and popes claiming authority over temporal as well as spiritual affairs. Traditional Jewish law, Muslim law, and Hindu law was theocratic in that the one power expressed was religious, thought to be derived from God. Theocracies now supposedly are few—the rule of the Ayatollah Khomeini is often given as the best recent example—but one may find the theocratic impulse in totalitarian regimes that, paradoxically enough, deny religious and civil liberties. In these lat- ter cases, the ideology (for example, Marxist) in control claims an exhaustive sovereignty like that previously claimed by theology, or the will-to-power of the rulers' (for example, the rightist juntas) claims that "national security" must determine all questions of justice and rights.

CHAPTER 2

RELIGIONS OF RECENT NONLITERATE PEOPLES

Australian aboriginal hunting symbol

COMMON THEMES

Let us begin by describing some of the basic characteristics of the religious lives of recent nonliterate peoples, focusing on three topics: the sacred, myth and ritual, and the shaman.

The Sacred

As we saw, life and death dominated prehistoric religion, as they dominate much religion today, but the broadest notion in the prehistoric mind perhaps was what we call the sacred or the holy. The Oxford English Dictionary defines sacred as "set apart for or dedicated to some religious purpose." For recent nonliterate people it has meant the realm of the truly real, the realm of the gods or venerable powers.

This idea of the sacred probably was vital among the first human beings. We believe this because recent nonliterate peoples have sensed that one can live in passionate connection with what is most real and valuable or in dissociation from it. They have sensed that they ought to be in harmony with the power that courses through sky and earth and sea and that often they were not. Furthermore, they, and no doubt the first human beings, have seen the destruction that disharmony can bring—natural disasters, disease,

100,000 years ago	Homo Sapiens *in Africa*
70,000–50,000 years ago	Homo Sapiens *in Australia*
30,000–25,000 years ago	*Mongoloid Peoples Cross Bering Strait*
8500 B.C.E.	*Mongoloid Peoples throughout South America*
5000	*Agriculture and Domesticated Cattle in Nile Delta*
4000	*Intense Hunting, Gathering, Fishing in Boreal Regions*
3000	*Farming in Central Africa*
2000	*Metalworking in Peru*
1500	*Maize Farming in Central America*
1100	*Lapita Civilization in Polynesia*
1000	*Colonization of Arctic*
900	*Foundation of Nubian Kingdom of Kush*
500	*Iron Making in Sub-Sahara; First Hieroglyphic Writing in Mexico*
300	*Rise of Hopewell Chiefdoms in Illinois and Ohio*
300 C.E.	*Rise of Mayan Civilization*
700	*Islamic Domination of North Africa; Rise of Empire of Ghana*
800	*Polynesians Reach Easter Island and New Zealand*
900–1500	*Emergence of African States*
1000	*Reindeer Hunting in Boreal Regions*
1200–1300	*Eskimos Appear in Greenland*
1325–1470	*Aztec and Inca Civilizations*
1526–1870	*Ten Million Slaves Shipped from Africa*
1645	*Tasman Circumnavigates Australia*
1741	*Russian Traders Cross Siberia to Alaska*
1880–1913	*Western Powers Partition Africa*

slaughter, and death. So the realm of ultimacy, the realm of power and the truly real, has been both concrete and mysterious. Either way, it has been the massive given with which ancient peoples have had to contend. They may not have abstracted the powers of the sacred into a "realm" or personified it as an expression of a primordial will, but they have completely turned their spirits toward its puzzles and sway.[1]

The experience of the sacred, in Rudolf Otto's celebrated description, involves the sense of a mystery that is both fearsome and fascinating.[2] It has been most vivid in nature's manifestations of power, but it might also occur in initiation rites, ceremonial ecstasy, or other intense experiences. With modifications, we can glimpse the experience of the sacred in accounts of enlightenment and peak experiences from religious and psychological literature. The visions of Isaiah (6:1–13), Ezekiel (1:1–29), and Revelation (1:1–29) show some of the biblical expressions of the sacred. In all these cases, we can see human imagination dazzled by the pure power that makes everything that is. Perhaps this power, Van der Leeuw has argued, is religion's central object.[3]

As many scholars have shown, the sacred can touch any aspect of creation or life. Van der Leeuw himself deals with stones, trees, water, fire, sky, mother, father, demon, angel, king, life, death,

LEADING NONLITERATE RELIGIOUS FUNCTIONARIES		
American Indians*	Shamanic Healers	
Eskimos	Shamanic Healers	Guides for dead Intercessors with deities Keepers of tribal lore
Australians	Medicine Men	Healing Guidance in ceremonies Guidance into the dreamtime Keeping tribal lore
Africans	Diviners	Foretell future Determine cause of troubles Keep tribal lore
	Witch Doctors	Healing
	Priests	Sacrifice
	Kings	Sacrifice Keep fertility of people
	Prophets	Express divine voice Guide social change

*Most North American Indians sought shamanlike visions and intimacy with animal spirits. South American Indians tended to accept them but not seek them.

KEY ASPECTS OF NONLITERATE RELIGION		
Sacred	Order of Being	Main social goal: Harmony with what was considered most real, most holy
Myth	Order of Thought	Group defining its identity by telling stories about how the gods made the world and human beings
Ritual	Order of Action	Ceremonies to enact the myths, bring people into contact with the original order of creation, dramatize progress in the life cycle, unite the tribe
Shamans	Order of Salvation	People with access to the sacred who could heal and mediate restoration to right order

preacher, priest, community, family, church, nation, soul, and more. The sacred may even focus on human hair and fingernails.[4] Clearly, ancient humanity felt the power of creation, the awesome force of life and being, everywhere. During a storm, the power could be manifested as thunder and lightning. More tranquilly, it could play on the waters.[5] Regularly it would rush in at birth and death. Hunting, planting, weaving, metalworking—all occupations felt the touch of sacred power. Thus, ancient peoples lived with a fact that the early Greek scientist Thales only glimpsed in a vision: "The world is full of gods." For them nothing that one saw or did was without its heavenly archetype.[6]

This omnipresence of sacred power is perhaps our best thread through the labyrinth of the nonliterate religions. To dramatize such omnipresence, let us draw on some examples of sacredness that Mircea Eliade has assembled in his thematic sourcebook *From Primitives to Zen*.[7] The Dyak of Borneo, for instance, thought of themselves as a sacred people. Their land was sacred, too, because it had been given to them by the divinity, which made it from the remains of the sun and the moon. For the Delaware Indians of North America, the four directions of the compass were sacred and merited prayers of thanksgiving. They thanked the east for the morning, when the light is bright and everyone feels good. They thanked the west for the end of day, when the sun goes down and everyone can again feel good. To the north they owed thanks for the wind, whose cold coming reminds us that we have lived to see the leaves fall again. To the south they owed thanks for the warm winds that make the grass turn green.

Thus, the land and its directions were regularly thought of as manifestations of creation's holy power. So, too, were the phases of life. The Ngaju Dayak of South Borneo saw marriage as a sacred stage in life's unfolding. Therefore, the two marital partners were made to die symbolically so that they could be reborn by sticking the stem of the Tree of Life, represented by a spear, in a human head taken in a raid or from a slave. Thus, the couple was made vividly aware that their new state dealt with awesome powers. (Recently the head has been replaced by a coconut.)

For the Naskapi Indians of Labrador, hunting was especially sacred, since it was their most important occupation. The Naskapi believed that the animals they hunted had emotions and purposes like their own, and that in the beginning animals could talk like humans. So the Naskapi would sing and drum to them

as to friends. Similarly, they would take great care not to mutilate certain bones of the elk or beaver believed to enclose an inner soul, a spirit like the hunter's own. Indeed, they thought that at death the animals gathered in their animal realm, just as human spirits gathered in the human realm. Both realms were conceived as stages in a cycle of reincarnation (rebirth in a new form), and so both sets of spirits were bound together. If the hunters did not know the behavioral principles governing their sacred connections with the animals, all sorts of misfortune could ensue. The hunt would be fruitless, the people would be without food, sickness or even death might descend.

As hunting peoples have considered their pursuit of game sacred, so agricultural peoples have considered farming sacred. The Native Americans who raised corn (maize) reverenced it as the gift of the Corn Maiden and harvested it ceremonially.[8] Other Native Americans insisted on treating the earth especially gently in the spring, for then it was like a woman pregnant with new life. To plow it, even to walk or run on it without care, would have been to mistreat a full womb.

In a word, just about every aspect of human experience has at some time been held sacred. Thought and sex, trees and waters, stones and ancestors—all have been considered manifestations of power or holiness. We can say, therefore, that the sacred is the ultimate or deepest significance that any thing, place, or person can manifest if seen at the right angle. For instance, the beggar can seem to wear a coat of holiness. On the other end of the social scale, chieftains and kings have regularly been reverenced as sacred. In fact, the king has been not only a ruler by divine right but also frequently a sacrificial figure, killed for the sake of his people.[9]

More understandably, perhaps, the shamans, yogis, and medicine men who have been prominent in nonliterate societies' dealings with the sacred have taken on the aura of holiness. Because they have been mediums for encountering the venerable powers, they themselves have been venerated and feared. Normally nonliterate peoples have felt that the sacred itself was a good or at least an indifferent force. If one was not in harmony with it, however, it could be destructive. Therefore, one had to approach sacred functionaries with some caution.

A story by the contemporary Native American storyteller Durango Mendoza captures this feeling of caution.[10] Two children make fun of an old man. He has a reputation for witchcraft—the ability to turn special powers against his enemies. When one of the children later becomes sick, the story suggests an almost palpable presence of evil: The old man is taking revenge. As studies of Navaho witchcraft have shown, this evil (power turned malevolent) is often a strong component of the American Indian world view.[11] In dealing with the holy, human beings risk being consumed in burning flames. If humans are not protected, the holy can destroy them.

Many ancient aversions and **taboos** (irrational or magical forbiddings of contact with items thought to be dangerous) can be explained by the belief that the sacred demands purity. Contact with the dead, for instance, is often a source of **pollution**. Because many ancient peoples considered contact with a menstruating woman to be polluting, ancient woman was a powerful figure.[12] In neither case is the pollution something moral—it is not a matter of bad will, bad choice, or sin. Rather, it is a matter of being out of phase with the sacred and so endangered.

It is difficult for us in modern technological societies to appreciate this ancient sense of the sacred. However, our own interests in the occult, astrology, demonology, and parapsychology indicate that we still sense part of its world. Indeed, the ancient world portrayed so effectively by Carlos Castaneda forces us to realize how much our own reality is the product of social consensus and the inner dialogue that we constantly carry on.[13] If we lived in the midst of people who were awestruck by the sun, we, too, would likely reverence its rays.

Today, what science tells us about simple vegetative forces is capable of humbling us. For instance, Annie Dillard reports that a single plant of winter rye grass can send forth 378 miles of roots with 14 billion root hairs. One cubic inch of its soil can contain 6,000 miles of root hairs.[14] The power coursing through the natural world is staggering, and when we are staggered, we are open to the sacred.

Myth and Ritual

Nonliterate peoples have usually described the sacred through myth and ritual. A **myth** is a story, an explanation of what has happened. History began in the tendency of peoples to tell myths explaining how they came to be where and what they were. Of course, our present-day critical history distances itself from myth by rigorously controlling sources and arguments.

Nonetheless, critical history could not have developed without the capacity of human beings to remember what had happened to them and what it meant.

Ritual refers to the conduct of ceremonies. In the nonliterate context, it consists of the dances and dramatic presentations by which tribes have displayed their mythic histories and realities. Together, myth and ritual constitute the characteristic means by which nonliterate peoples have explained the world, interacted with the sacred, solidified their community, and baffled many scientific observers. If one takes ancient cultures seriously, without presuming that they are inferior or subhuman, one has to search for the meaning of their myths and rituals.[15] Let us see what that might entail.

Until the French anthropologist Marcel Griaule was tutored by a blind tribal elder, he could only deal superficially with the culture of the Dogon, an ancient tribe living near the Upper Volta region of northwestern Africa.[16] But when Ogotemmeli, the elder, led him through thirty-three days of indoctrination, Griaule came to realize that this "primitive" people had an amazingly complex traditional lore through which they explained all the important facets of their life. Essentially, their explanations were stories of how each thing or practice had come to be.

Weaving and smithery, for instance, were considered activities of heavenly origin. The weaver's ginning iron and the smith's hammer both reflected the celestial granary, which symbolized the whole world system. Because the granary contained seeds, and the heavenly smith had brought these seeds to human beings on his hammer, and because the ginning iron both resembled the smith's hammer and dealt with seeds (cotton), the smiths (men) and the weavers (women) could both be confident that their work had come from heaven and was supremely significant. In the same way, the weaver's carding stick was like the rod by which the archetypal smith had sprinkled water on his fire, while the skin on which a woman spun was like the sun, because the first leather had belonged to the bellows of the smithy, and the smithy had contained the solar fire.

Clearly, the mythic mentality of the Dogon gave them a reality that is very different from what modern imagination gives us. The logic governing the Dogon world, like most mythic worlds, was a logic of correspondences. Blacksmithing and weaving corresponded because their tools were similarly shaped and their materials were used in similar ways. Furthermore, they both fit into more comprehensive patterns used by the heavenly forces who had formed the world by design. As a result, things were more "alive" than they are in a scientific culture. A scientific culture tends to fix relationships to universal patterns rooted in the sensible world. Unless items correlate according to these patterns, they are not considered real but merely imaginary or fabulous. Like the centaur, the phoenix, or the unicorn, they can be represented but are not truly real.

Ogotemmeli did not follow such patterns. His ancestors had explained the world to him in terms of what the Nummo, the heavenly forces, had done in creating and ordering it, and this explanation had served him well. It had given smithery, weaving, harvesting, and his people's other occupations dignity and coherence. What could be more dignified than a work designed by the gods? What could be more coherent than a culture in which all occupations related, in which all occupations were strands in a single tapestry? Ogotemmeli's world was not simply a cartoon that was colorfully imagined. His mythic mentality knew as well as the scientific mentality that human relations and farming are objective and demand common sense. But often his mentality brought a different, indeed a more creative, mythic sensitivity to such common sense.

For example, the Dogon viewed speech as a means of organization, and as such thought it essentially good. Nonetheless, from the start of the world, speech had loosed disorder. This was because the jackal, God's deluded and deceitful son, desiring speech, had laid hands on the skirt (where speech was hidden) of his mother the earth and so had begun an incestuous relationship that set the world careening. As a result, there were many bad words whose utterance had quite physical effects. To Ogotemmeli they actually smelled, and their smell traveled from the nose to the throat and liver, and then to the sexual organs, where it affected potency and procreation. Was this not a vivid way of symbolizing our human psychosomatic constitution? Might it not make us rethink the effect that bad words of lust or hate have on children, both in the womb and outside?

Creation Myths.   The myths of other nonliterate peoples prompt similar thoughts. For example, though American Indian creation myths are no scientific competition to current astronomy, they offer considerable insight into our condition as creatures. The Winne-

bago, for instance, pictured creation as a process of pure divine thought. When the Father, the Earth-maker, came to consciousness, he cried because he did not know what to do. Noticing that his tears, which had fallen from heaven, had become the waters, he realized that by wishing he could make other things become. So he wished light and earth, which became. Then he made a likeness of himself from earth, and when it did not answer him he made for it a mind and soul and breathed into it so that it could reply. Thus, in one myth, the Winnebago taught that the world was made by design and that humans were made in God's image to converse with him.

Creation is the subject of the most basic myth, which ritual frequently uses to integrate a people with the sacred. Scholars have lavished much attention on this type of myth and have found explanations of creation involving thought, sacrifice, masturbation, a cosmic egg, diving into the primeval waters, and many other motifs. Indeed, the Boshongo, a Bantu tribe of central Africa, said that the creator Bumba produced the world because he had a stomachache. In pain, he vomited up the sun, the moon, living creatures, and finally humans. Thus, again and again, in tales both funny and sobering, nonliterate people have oriented themselves in the world and suggested why things are as they are.

Rites of Passage.   As a final mythoritualistic motif common to many peoples, we mention what scholars call "rites of passage." **Rites of passage** are ceremonies of the life cycle, religious dramas for birth, puberty, marriage, and death. For nonliterate peoples, each of these times has been the threshold to a new stage of development, a new stage of intimacy with the sacred. As the gods did at the beginning, so human beings have given birth, passed over to adulthood, married, and buried their dead. Most impressive have been the rites for puberty. Rites for young men regularly have stressed enduring suffering. Those for young women have stressed preparing for feminine tasks, as the particular society conceived of them. For both sexes, puberty has been a time to learn about sexuality, the tribal gods, and the discipline that adulthood demands.

In Black Elk's account of the seven rites of the Oglala Sioux,[17] the pattern for the female puberty rite was set by a vision of a buffalo calf being cleansed by its mother. Out of this grew the traditional ways that young women were cleansed (as the Sioux thought necessary for their fertility power) so that they could bear children and raise them in a sacred manner, and so that their fertility power would not conflict with the killing power of Sioux males (who were hunters and warriors).

For the BaMbuti, the forest pygmies of the northeastern Congo, female puberty rites have been less solemn. These rites, called the *elima,* have consisted of dancing and singing in praise of life.[18] Since the BaMbuti have had a quite positive view of the life that their forest gave them, the *elima* has been but one of a number of occasions on which they sang with their *molimo* (a long tubal instrument that produced hauntingly beautiful sounds and was thought to represent the forest animals' collective voice). What has emerged in the *elima* is the equality of men and women among the BaMbuti. This was reflected in the economic cooperation among the pygmies, but during the *elima* it emerged as something more basic—an instance of androgyny, of the ancient conviction that both sexes are needed for a complete, fully human life that will mirror divinity.[19]

The Shaman

The central figure of nonliterate religion, found in many areas, is the **shaman**, who offers the most striking example of what happens when one meets the sacred with a mythoritualistic consciousness. According to Mircea Eliade,[20] the shaman is a specialist in archaic techniques of ecstasy. Specifically, tribes of Siberia and central Asia (which some scholars consider the most purely shamanistic) often select their shamans for psychological features and capacities that render them apt for ecstasy—for going outside themselves. The typical candidate is sensitive, introverted, inclined to solitude, and perhaps sickly (perhaps epileptic or given to fainting). By adolescence he (males predominate in Siberian shamanism) is thought to be different—peculiar, brooding, religious. If he has an emotional crisis or something strange happens to him (such as getting very sick or being struck by lightning), elders will consider him appropriate for initiation into shamanism. That will entail learning tribal lore and ecstatic techniques and then passing an initiatory ordeal.

In Siberia the initiatory ordeal amounts to a ritualized experience of suffering, death, and resurrection. The candidate's body is dismembered; he dies and is transported to the realm of the gods. There his organs are replaced or renewed, sometimes with special

stones or other tokens of his visit added. Depending on the beliefs of his tribe, he may fly to heaven as a bird, climb a sacred pole or tree (the *axis mundi* connecting earth to heaven), or travel up the rainbow. Which organ is replaced seems to depend on what his tribe thinks is the organ that ultimately quickens human beings. Bone and blood are popular choices. The constant feature of the ordeal is bodily sundering and death. As noted, the death usually takes place in the realm of the gods, after a flight or ascent, and a benefactor god or ally typically reconstitutes the candidate's body (replaces the removed organ) and returns him to life.

This experience takes place while the candidate is in ecstasy, outside his normal consciousness. If the initiation is public, the community gets a running narration of how it is going, with descriptions of the ascent, the celestial realm, the dismembering, and sample voices of the gods. A modern Westerner would probably call the proceedings imaginary, but nonliterate peoples tend to equate the real with the vividly experienced, so they consider it quite real.[21] Furthermore, studies show shamans to be the healthiest members of their tribes psychologically, not the most schizoid, hysterical, or neurotic. Performing his duties makes the shaman feel good and heals him of his ills, so whenever he is out of sorts, the shaman will sing or drum and go out of himself to the gods.

When the candidate has passed his initiatory ordeal, he is usually accepted by his community and can start functioning as a shaman. His principal functions are healing, guiding the dead to the afterworld, and acting as a medium between the living and the dead. These functions show much of what a shaman's tribe believes, which is essentially that the universe and the human being are both dualistic. The universe is dualistic because it includes the human realm, where the shaman's body remains, and the spiritual realm, to which his spirit travels. The human being is dualistic because he or she has both a bodily and a spiritual part. The spirit's "travel" is the shaman's colorful experience of ecstasy.

Ordinarily, a shaman goes into ecstasy to gain knowledge or power. He must find out from the gods what is ailing a patient or what the right medicine is. (For nonliterate peoples, illness is as much a spiritual matter as a physical one.) Similarly, to find where the game has gone, the shaman must be able to go to the gods who keep the game. For example, to the coastal Eskimos, this meant the shaman's swimming to the depths of the sea, where the goddess Sedna, who ruled

Figure 5   Eskimo mask, Alaska, nineteenth century. Wood, feathers, paint; 15 in. high. This seal mask, with bubbles extending upward, depicts what a shaman saw in a vision. The Nelson–Atkins Museum of Art, Kansas City, Missouri.

the seals and the fish, had fenced them in. To guide the souls of the departed, the shaman must also be able to travel to the land of rest. If a tribal member suffers soul loss (which causes sickness), the shaman must be able to trace the soul and retrieve it.

Wherever he goes, the shaman reports on his progress. His functioning therefore re-creates the community in two senses: (1) He helps his people reassert their view of the world, and (2) he gives them an entertaining account of his plunge to the bottom of the sea, his fight to get past Sedna's vicious watchdog, and so forth. When he returns from a mission, he often requires the community to renew itself. Sedna may be withholding the fish because someone has broken a taboo—a hunter may have mistreated a seal, two brothers may have had a violent fight, or spouses may have aborted a fetus. Such a violation of the tribe's ethic must be atoned, for it has ruptured their harmony with nature. Thus, the skillful shaman creates a forum in which his people can confess their guilts and express their regrets and fears. He tries to reconcile

enemies and convince the whole tribe to reaffirm its ethical ideals.

How do shamans gain their tribe's confidence to do this? Some develop paranormal powers, including clairvoyance and clairaudience (seeing and hearing beyond the normal range). Others possess an impressive knowledge of herbs, drugs, tribal traditions, or special vocabulary. Probably the shamans' greatest success, though, comes from their mastery of techniques of suggestion, which are especially effective with peoples of vivid imagination.

Eliade's description of shamanism stresses ecstasy and the shaman's ability to go into a trance and travel to the realm of the sacred powers. Other scholars interpret shamanism more loosely, stressing its social dynamics. Overall, though, it is clear that the shaman has been a very important figure in many nonliterate tribes.

In contrast to the Siberian shaman, some functionaries in nonliterate societies give guidance by taking in a spirit. In other words, rather than going out to the gods, the gods come into them. That is the case for much of the spiritualism or shamanism in China and Japan. Typically shamans there sing songs and go into a trance as a way of being taken over, being temporarily inhabited or possessed. Significantly, such shamanism has been practiced more by women than by men. In China, the female shaman's song to her guiding spirit often has had a romantic tone, as though a beloved were pining for her lover.[22] In Japan, the *kami,* or spirits, who come can be erotically intimate. In both places, the possessed shaman performs divination, discerning what the spirits want or what the future will require. Additionally, the Japanese shamans used to band together and walk a regular beat through the local villages, offering personal advice and medical healing. In performing this work they developed teaching techniques that contributed to Japanese theater and dance.[23]

I. M. Lewis's anthropological study of spirit possession and shamanism[24] reveals important sociological aspects. Lewis finds that many of the spirit-possessed live on the margins of society. This contrasts with Eliade's theory, in which the shaman is a key social figure. Part of the contrast may lie in the fact that Lewis deals more with modern societies, whose power structures are more differentiated and complex. Another part may lie in Lewis's concentration on the "enthusiasm" of "little people" (marginals) in highly developed religious traditions (including Islam and Christianity).

Etymologically, *enthusiasm* means "being filled with the god." In Lewis's study it tends to mean emotional exaltation, as we can observe in rural American religion, where the devout may swoon, sing ecstatically, or dance. Interestingly, societies that grant women little status tend to have a substantial number of female enthusiasts. Most likely, such women use their religious experience to gain a little respect and influence. So, too, with the powerless people prominent among other groups of ecstatics. Their religion may be genuine, but the attention they receive can be very welcome.

If shamanism is to be considered in general terms, the phenomena of visions and tutelary spirits must be included. Among Native Americans the vision quest is a regular feature of an adolescent's passage to maturity. This quest is especially clear for men (it is less clear for women), and some of its most famous examples occur in *Black Elk Speaks*.[25] There we read that even before adolescence and without a quest, Black Elk was taken into the air on a cloud, saw groups of prancing horses, was told by "grandfathers" about his people's sad future, and finally was taught the sacredness of his nation's hoop—the circle representing all the Sioux.

This vision stayed with Black Elk throughout his life, dominating his interpretation of all that he observed and experienced. After he had grown old and witnessed many sadnesses, he climbed Harney Peak (for the Oglala Sioux the center of the world), prayed to the grandfatherly spirits, and confronted for the last time the broken hoop, the withering of the tribal tree. As if in answer to the tearful conclusion of his life, a raincloud appeared in the clear sky—a dramatic expression of the Great Spirit. Perhaps a majority of Native Americans were shamans like Black Elk (though not necessarily in such dramatic fashion), for many of them lived by a personal vision and spirit.

Not all shamanist figures have been exalted personalities or seers. Some have been charlatans who performed for applause or money, and some "black" shamans, who solicited the powers of evil to inflict harm. In fact, shamans have run the full gamut: from holy persons, expert in venerable lore, stooped from bearing the tribe's burdens, to quacks and half-mad mutterers. (Films show Nepalese shamans performing the crudest of cures, with filthy fetishes—objects believed to have protective power—and the blood of cocks. No doubt they offer some psychological comfort to their people, but they must be hygienic disasters. Similarly, films of Yanomamo shamans, who practice among the fierce people living at the border of Venezuela and northern Brazil, indicate that their visions come from ingesting hallucinogenic snuff. The snuff induces visions of *hekura*, tiny humanoid figures who may be used for healing friends or making enemies sick. The Yanomamo shaman's vocation demands some dedication—periods of celibacy, for instance—but most Yanomamo shamans practice in order to ingest snuff and fight.[26])

Shamanism is so widespread that it cannot be explained by cultural diffusion from a single original center. Eliade's study treats central and northern Asia, North and South America, Southeast Asia and Oceania, central Europe, Tibet, China, and East Asia. Edmans's volume *Studies in Shamanism* studies Eskimos, North Americans, Nepalese, people of Kalash-Kaffir, Israelites (on the basis of biblical evidence), Hungarians, and Swedes.[27] Other studies have dealt with Greek and Malay cases. If the definition of shamanism is extended to include divination by trance, we could cite many African instances, including some influenced by devotional Islam (Sufism).

What does this worldwide phenomenon suggest? That shamanist ecstasy accomplishes something that most peoples have desired. To go out of oneself to deal with supernatural powers is a way of extending one's world. Many peoples have found it a way to encounter the sacred, a way to experiences both tremendous and fascinating. Surely that is why so many different tribes have employed shamanism.

We have seen something of the prehistoric religious mind. In the rest of this chapter, we examine four nonliterate peoples from different parts of the world: American Indians, Eskimos, Africans, and Australians. Each area has many cultural subgroups, so what we can say about each group as a whole is limited. Nonetheless, this chapter should give us a better understanding of how several aspects of the prehistoric religious mind have endured to the present.

AMERICAN INDIANS

Because of their contact with white culture, which has altered their reality markedly, few American Indians now live as their great-grandparents did. However, on the western reservations enough of the old traditions and native mentality remains to distinguish Indian children from those of other ethnic groups. At least,

Figure 6   Traditional tepee. Harvard, Massachusetts. Photo by J. T. Carmody.

that is what child psychiatrist Robert Coles concluded after extensive contacts with Pueblo and Hopi children of New Mexico.[28] They showed an instinctive reverence for the land, a living relationship with their departed ancestors, and a revelatory dream life that he had not found in black, white, or Chicano children. All these characteristics indicate ancient beliefs, but the most significant is the orientation to the land. As Coles himself puts it:

> There is a seemingly impersonal quality to the words and gestures a Pueblo or Hopi parent uses when pointing at some element in the surrounding landscape. There is a pantheistic side to Indian life—an emphasis by parents upon the sacral quality of *both* the living and the inanimate world. And, too, there is a subdued but persistent eroticism that is expressed in the contemplative wonder and awe that Indian children learn to feel when they stare at the sky, the horizon, the land both near and far. A thunderstorm, a windstorm,

or simply a bright, clear day—and the Pueblo or Hopi child is happy, is ready (if it were possible) to reach out and touch with great satisfaction the sun, the dark clouds, the air rushing by so noisily.[29]

Consider what the life of a Pueblo Indian even fifty years ago might have been like. For years, he or she would have been living "on the roof of the world," at a high elevation, absorbed by the sun, the sky, and the mountains. In youth, there would have been leisurely, wonderful ceremonies that drew the young person into the meanings and mysteries of the sun, the sky, and the mountains. In adulthood, much of life was arranged so one could contemplate these elements—think on them from the heart. Increasingly the elements came to dominate one's life. The sun, was it not a great god? Were not all human beings children of its light and warmth? The mountains—did they not give us water and make us the streams necessary for life?

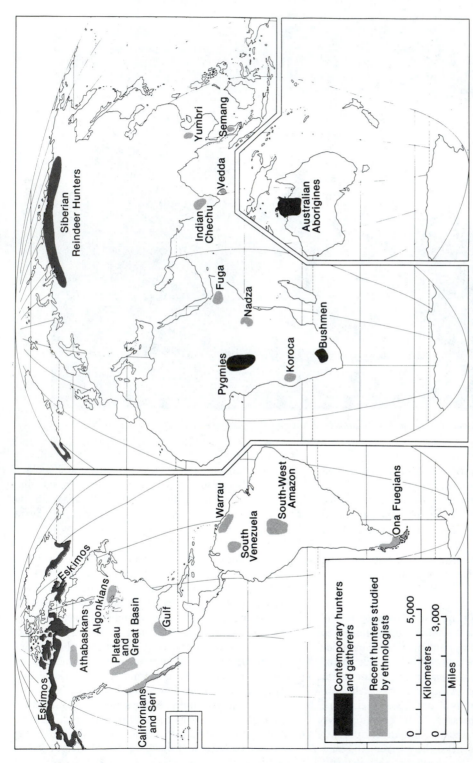

Figure 7 *Modern hunters. Adapted from* The Times Atlas of World History, *edited by Geoffrey Barraclough, 1979. © Hammond, Inc., Maplewood, New Jersey. Reprinted by permission of* The London Times, *New York, New York.*

All that such an Indian cared for came together in such ceremonies and contemplation. Dancing and gazing, the Indians did their part of the holy work. Ultimately, the Pueblos believed the world itself would cease to function if they did not practice their religion: The sun would not travel the sky, the mountains would not stand tall. In the utterly clear air, this belief was absolutely certain. Without thanks from human beings and exchanges with human beings, the forces of the world would not abide human beings, would not function. Indians and sun, then, kept a holy compact. All that gave Indians life came from the sun, the sky, and the mountains. Yet Indians had great dignity, for Indians kept nature going, kept furnishing it a reason to be.[30]

For our purposes, these attitudes link recent American Indians with their most ancient forebears, who probably began to come from Siberia across a land bridge at the Bering Strait as much as 30,000 years ago. Upon contact with Europeans in the fifteenth century, native North Americans comprised several distinct geographic groups.[31] In the East were woodland tribes, who both hunted and planted. Southeastern tribes cultivated the land extensively, midwestern Plains tribes were primarily buffalo hunters, and southwestern tribes lived in pueblos or were nomads. Along the Pacific Northwest coast, fishers predominated. In each case, the tribal economy determined the life-style. Depending on the buffalo meant a life quite different from that which depended on salmon or corn. Nonetheless, scholars think that some basic attitudes were held by all North Americans.[32]

At the core of these attitudes lay belief in a primary holy force. For the Sioux it was *wakan;* for the Algonquin, *orenda.* Other tribes gave it other names. But shamans throughout the continent agreed that a holy force held all things together. North American Indian life largely revolved around this force. It made nature alluring and intimidating, a source of benevolent influences that on occasion turned severe. Perhaps the key goal of most American Indians was to keep harmony with such holy natural power, to move with its cosmic pulse. Harmony was the way to fertility of both tribe and field, to success in both hunting and war, to a full life. By contrast, disharmony led to disaster: ruined crops, sickly children, defeat in war. As a deliberate exercise in disharmony, witchcraft caused a perceptible shudder. It strove against the natural rhythm, willfully tempting power to run amok. Death was too good for a witch.

Figure 8   Indian boy by George Catlin (1796–1872). Oil on canvas, 49⅛ in. × 39½ in. Seminole prince Nikkanochee is shown as a young warrior. The Nelson–Atkins Museum of Art, Kansas City, Missouri (Nelson Fund).

As noted, these ideas probably had originated many millennia previously in the past. In fact, many of the myths, rituals, and beliefs of the native North Americans resemble those of Siberian tribes, and the two groups share numerous physical characteristics. The North Americans' original myths, rituals, and beliefs likely developed in a culture centered on hunting, warfare, and shamanistic activities, which North Americans pursued until recent times.[33] Even today Navaho ritual attempts cures by singing, and Zuñi ritual shows traces of hunting ceremonies (though the Zuñi have been settled agriculturalists for some time).

Divinity

For the most part, native North Americans have not worshiped a supreme "God." For them, the categories "nature" and "divinity" have been largely indistinguishable. Some of the agricultural tribes thought of a supreme power associated with the sky or the sun, but most peoples have worshiped several powers. For instance, scholars studying Indian myths find a variety of creator spirits. Earth Diver (an animal or bird who brings the earth up out of the water) is a common one, but the Zuñi tell of numerous workers who disappeared once the world was organized. According to the creation myth of the Maidu of California, a turtle collaborated with a heavenly spirit called "Earth Initiate" to pull the land up out of the waters. The turtle wanted a place to rest from his ceaseless swimming, so he volunteered to dive down for some earth. Earth Initiate held a rope tied to the turtle's left arm. The turtle went down, stayed six years, and returned covered with green slime. Under his fingernails was some sand, which Earth Initiate rolled into a ball that swelled up and became the earth.[34] In the slightly different version of the Yauelmani Yokuts of California, a duck and an eagle replace the turtle and Earth Initiate.

Less revered than creative deities are the culture heroes celebrated in myths, whose function was to socialize the tribe. Often they are twins to whom the people trace their arts and crafts. Another superhuman figure in many tribal mythologies is the spirit who owns the animals. Unless the people reverence this spirit, they will not have good hunting or fishing. A third power in North American mythology is the antihero called **Trickster**. He is both a cunning person and a dupe, a principle of both order and disorder, the founder of convention and yet its chief defier. Typically, he has enlarged intestines, an insatiable appetite, and an extended, uncontrolled penis that goes off on adventures of its own. Trickster will not control his bowels or bladder, and he makes practical jokes and humbles the haughty. In short, he is human impulsiveness, the psychoanalytic id, set free to be an entertainer.[35]

By contrasting *wakan* with lesser figures such as Trickster or culture heroes, we can focus on the more comprehensive North American notions of divinity. These include the Dakota Wakan Tanka, the Lenape Mani, and the Pawnee Tirawa. Wakan Tanka is the oneness of all holy *(wakan)* beings. Mani, on the other hand, is the chief among many gods who function as his agents. Most Lenape prayers address these agents, but the greatest ceremonies address Mani himself. Tirawa seems more like Wakan Tanka than like Mani. Though "Father Above" is one of its titles, Tirawa is usually impersonal. Perhaps we can best conceive of it as the power in all creation that sustains all things.

These native divinities, of course, were not principally ideas. If we imply that they were philosophical conclusions or abstract inferences, we misrepresent them. Rather, they have been the stuff of storytelling, song, and dance. North Americans have lived with them, spoken to them from the heart, and sought access to their sacredness through traditional ceremonies. Perhaps such ceremonies are the best introduction to American Indians' sense of both society and self.

Ceremonies

Some ceremonies, which we might call negative, have emphasized the dangers of falling out of harmony with sacred power. For instance, warriors and homicides have had to be purified, lest they infect the tribe; relatives of dead persons have had to be protected against ghosts. Even scalping ceremonies were negative, insofar as they were efforts to tame and tap the male spirit power, which resided in the head. Death, then, was a time of crisis demanding ritual protection to restore the harmony it had upset.

Much other Native American ritual, however, was positive, aiming at intimacy with a benevolent supernatural power. A good example of this is the vision quest. Many North American Indians strenuously sought a vision of a guiding spirit. (South Americans accepted visions that came but tended not to pursue them.) The vision quest became a rite of passage, a threshold to maturity. Without a vision as a guiding experience, one could not walk with direction or live with full purpose. If a young man's vision quest failed, he might become a tribal marginal, forced to dress in women's clothing and barred from male roles.

Along the Great Lakes and Mississippi Valley, the vision quest was largely used to train boys. In the Plains, men used it throughout life, whenever they felt the need. On the Pacific coast, it often took the form of spirit possession.[36] When the vision quest was used as training, children as young as seven years learned to fast. Boys heard that they would amount to nothing if they did not see a spirit and obtain its guidance. Girls could quest until puberty, when a different kind of power came, the power of motherhood.

As Charles Eastman, a Santee Sioux, tells it, a young man would begin the vision quest with a steam bath, putting off all worldly thoughts. Then he would ascend the most commanding summit, strip to his moccasins and breechcloth, and stand erect and motionless for several days.[37] To prove his sincerity, he might cut off his little finger or offer strips of flesh from his arm. When his vision came, it usually included a promise for his tribe, a glimpse of a tutelary animal (often a wolf or eagle), and a token (perhaps a feather or hair) that became his most prized possession. Finally, the youth would also receive his song—the particular chant that he alone could sing on important occasions. If he had other visions in the future, he could accumulate a "medicine bundle" of tokens. Often shamans who were great healers relied on such tokens to work cures.

An important variation on this vision theme was the Hopi representation of spirits through ceremonial masks. In that tribe, children up to eight or nine believed the *kachinas,* or masked dancers, were real spirits in their midst. The crisis of the Hopi passage to adulthood occurred when the dancers dropped their masks, for then the young person had to accept that the reality of the *kachinas* was not physical but completely spiritual. In a painting by Louis Aiken,[38] the *kachina* has horns, a marionette face, a block nose, speakerlike ears, and a collar of fur. Emory Sekaquaptewa has described how Hopi adults assumed the characters of the masks they wore by projecting themselves into the spirit world and becoming what they were representing.[39]

Other tribes achieved such projection through the use of narcotics. Peyote is the best known, but at the time of Columbus, American Indians used perhaps a hundred different substances.[40] Far fewer were available in the Old World, which may explain why the vision quest was much less common there.

Largely through their visions, Native American shamans functioned as healers, prophets, and diviners. As healers, they tended to suck from victims' bodies objects thought to be the tools of witches or ghosts. Shamans from the Navaho and other tribes of the Southwest stressed healing by ritual singing, while holy people of planting tribes specialized in spells for crop fertility. The Pueblos of New Mexico were agriculturalists who shifted from shamanist, rather individualistic, ceremonies to more formalized, priestly rituals. However, even their lengthy chants for healing and fertility retained ecstatic elements from a preagricultural, nomadic, and shamanist past.

Constantly, then, American Indian peoples interacted with spirits, divinities, and animals, since their principal goal was to be in balance with them. Tribal rituals served this end, for they kept human beings on the right path. No North Americans seem to have thought in terms of original sin or a fall, but all tribes recognized a need for discipline and renewal. A religious ceremony such as the punishing Sun Dance of the Sioux combined such social and personal functions, renewing the tribe's good standing with sacred nature and giving warriors stoic courage.

The Self and Destiny

Among hunting tribes, the concept of the self or soul was not well defined. Human beings were thought to have several souls, one or more of which might live on after death. In fact, the Sioux were exceptional in not fearing the dead. Other tribes would have a child "adopt" a deceased relative to tame the relative's loosed soul. Reincarnation was a common belief, and the Hopi buried dead infants in the hope that their souls would return in future children. The Pueblos had a singularly clear and happy conception of the afterlife. For them the dead would either join the *kachinas* or become rain clouds. More typical was the Hopis' muted hope—they buried women in their wedding dresses, anticipating the women's passage to the next world.

Despite the importance of these notions, most Native Americans were less concerned with salvation in a future heaven than with a good life in the present. Happiness or success was to enjoy the beautiful land, to have many children, and to know the spirits intimately. Our modern notions of getting ahead would have meant little to a traditional Native American. Far more important than possessions was the power to see.

Recent Movements

In the nineteenth century, a pantribal movement called the Ghost Dance responded to Indians' depression and being subjugated by whites and temporarily lifted their spirits. The Ghost Dance was a cult based on trance and a spiritual message promising that if the Indians renewed their old ways and danced the new dance, they would defeat the whites and witness the return of the buffalo. In 1886 a Paiute named Wowoka rallied hundreds of Paiutes, Kiowas, and Cheyenne in Nevada. By 1890 the Sioux, who had lost nine million acres of their best land, turned to the Ghost

Dance as a last resort. Across the country, Indians sang of the message brought by a spotted eagle: The dead are returning; the nation is coming; the Father will return the elk, the deer, and the buffalo. But the whites killed Sitting Bull, and the movement ended in the tragedy of Wounded Knee.[41]

Today one of the most interesting Native American religious movements is the Peyote religion. It was introduced in the late nineteenth century by Apaches, who traded for peyote across the Mexican border. Slowly a body of rituals developed, many of them from the Plains Indians, until there was a complete ceremonial of confession, singing, drumming, and praying. The movement incorporated some Christian elements, reached many tribes of the Plains and the Southeast, and filled some of the void left by the Ghost Dance. Today, incorporated as the Native American Church, the Peyote religion offers Indians the legal right to take peyote as their ritual sacrament.

In these and other ways, some of the tribes are preserving their traditions. Pueblos, Navahos, and Hopis have returned to some of their rituals, while in the Plains the Sun Dance ceremony of dedication and endurance is being revived. On the reservations, though, the main heritage seems to be the intimacy with nature that Coles witnessed and the concern for living at the center of nature that has so impressed some Christian observers.[42] With the Native American understanding of suffering,[43] this heritage makes for a powerful, underappreciated religious resource. However, American scholars still have a hard time appreciating the holistic, more than rational character of American Indian religion.[44] Perhaps for that reason, foreign scholars have worked more vigorously to show the importance of American Indian religion.[45] But a desire for greater intimacy with earth powers has brought feminist writers such as Margaret Atwood close to an American Indian psychology,[46] and ecological concerns may bring more of us to it in the future.[47]

ESKIMOS

Far north of the American Indians, but having some contact with them and sharing a common Siberian past, have lived the Eskimos, our next ancient religious group. The Eskimo groups differ significantly among themselves, especially the coastal and inland groups. However, most of the 50,000 or so who called themselves "Inuit" understand one another. From Greenland, across Canada and Alaska, and to the Bering Strait, their life has traditionally revolved around fishing and hunting. Naturally, their culture has been most shaped by their environment. Because sheer survival is a formidable feat, Eskimo children learn to disregard egocentric or self-indulgent impulses. From their earliest years, they are part of a group dominated, regulated, and challenged by the wind, the river, the tundra, and, above all, the snow and ice.

What sort of a personality does a child brought up in such a world have? Were you to ask Eskimo children about the world, you might be discomfited by the answer. They might quietly summarize the ruin that whites have brought Eskimo culture (especially Alaskan Eskimo culture), and they might describe a confrontation with death that the elements seldom force on those living in warmer climates.

If the children draw you pictures, the pictures will probably strike you as abstract: no people, a few uncontrolled lines, and a few bleak colors. Such a picture may well represent a storm that no one survived or the last moments of a village, or the child's own final day. Frequently, it will show only a little blue fighting an immensity of white. The white is winning—the snow, the ice, the cold.

In a strange way, this clear acknowledgment of icy death may liberate Eskimo children. They see the harshness of life so clearly that the behavior demanded by their parents makes sense. Furthermore, the opportunities to express kindness and friendliness are all the more precious. Wary yet full of grace, Eskimo children can grow up to carve wonderful seals or spirits in ivory or stone. Or they can grow up to try to drown their pain in alcohol.[48]

The Supernatural

The full history of the Eskimos' habitation in the far north is beyond recovery. Their location, physical characteristics, and culture argue for a North Asian origin. Like that of traditional, shamanist Siberian tribes, traditional Eskimo life was dominated by the supernatural. Spirits and powers were as real as ice and snow. Eskimo notions of creation, however, were rather vague. For example, north Alaskans held that when Great Raven was sitting in darkness, he came to consciousness and was moved to create trees and humans.[49]

Figure 9   Alaskan house post: Haida; Sukkwan Island, about 1850. Wood, paint; 11 ft., 11½ in. high. The post is designed to placate friendly spirits and to ward off the unfriendly. The Nelson–Atkins Museum of Art, Kansas City, Missouri (Nelson Fund).

Eskimos of northern Canada had a myth of Sedna, goddess of the sea and source of the sea animals. Originally, Sedna was a handsome girl who proudly spurned prospective suitors. One spring a fulmar flew in from across the ice and wooed her; his song described the soft bearskins she would rest on and the good food she would never lack were she to become his wife. However, the fulmar never fulfilled his promise, and the new bride found herself in the most wretched conditions, bitterly lamenting her rejection of previous human suitors. To avenge her, Sedna's father killed the fulmar; but he and Sedna then became objects of the other fulmars' wrath. While Sedna and her father were fleeing from their attack, a heavy storm arose, and the father decided to surrender Sedna to the birds by throwing her overboard. She clung to the side of the boat, but he cut off her fingers. The first joints became whales, the second joints became seals, and the stumps became ground animals. The storm subsided and Sedna returned to the boat with a fierce hatred for her father. While he was sleeping, she had her dogs gnaw off his feet and hands. He cursed her, the dogs, and himself, whereupon the earth opened and swallowed them all. Ever since, they have lived in the nether world, where Sedna is mistress of sea life.[50]

In a Greenland version of this myth, Arnaquagsaq, the old woman living in the ocean depths, sits in her dwelling in front of a lamp and sends out the animals that Eskimos hunt. Sometimes, however, parasites settle on her head, and in her anger she keeps back the game. Then the *angakoq* (shaman) must brave the way to her and remove the parasites. To do this, he must cross a turning wheel of ice, negotiate a kettle of boiling water, skirt terrible guardian animals, and finally navigate a bridge as narrow as a knife's edge.[51] He narrates this journey to the community, who follow the tale breathlessly in their mind's eye.

On the traditional Eskimo earth lived the goblin people—dwarfs, giants, trolls, shadows, and the like—who could either help travelers or carry them off to torture. Below the earth was an underworld—a warm, comfortable place where the dead could enjoy what they liked in life. The sky was usually considered a good place, too, although western Greenlanders pictured it as being cold and deserted. When the northern lights appeared in the sky, the dead were believed to be playing football with a walrus head.[52]

Eskimos traditionally regarded rocks, animals, food, and even sleep as alive. Their whole world was alive, though only humans and animals had true souls. The basic image for those souls was either a shadow or a breath. The souls were miniatures of what they animated; thus, they were pictured as tiny humans, tiny caribou, and so on. A child was named for a dead person in the belief that he or she inherited that person's soul and qualities. For that reason, the Caribou Eskimo called a child who had inherited an ancestor's name "grandmother" or "grandfather." Many Eskimos also believed in animal reincarnation. For instance, the fish soul was thought to dwell in the intestines, so they threw fish intestines back into the water to replenish the schools.

The most general Eskimo religious conception, however, was "Sila." Najagneq, a shaman whom the explorer Knud Rasmussen met in Nome, described Sila as "a great spirit, supporting the world and the weather and all life on earth, a spirit so mighty that his utterance to mankind is not through common words, but by storm and snow and rain and the fury of the sea; all the forces of nature that men fear."[53] On the other hand, Sila could also express himself gently, by sunlight or calm of the sea. Frequently, he spoke to small children. Since many of his messages warned of danger, children were directed to alert the shaman. When all was well, Sila dwelt in endless nothingness, apart from everything. He was a mystery, whether he was close or far away. Thus, Najagneq concluded, "No one has ever seen Sila; his place of being is a mystery."[54]

The Eskimo Shaman

Normally, the shaman mediated between Sedna or Sila and the tribe. Another of Rasmussen's informants, Igjugarjuk, said this about shamanist power: "All true wisdom is only to be learned far from the dwellings of men, out in the great solitudes; and is only to be attained through suffering. Privation and suffering are the only things that can open the mind of man to those things which are hidden from others."[55] The hidden powers themselves chose the people who were to deal with them, often through revelations in dreams.

Igjugarjuk, for instance, became a shaman because of strange visions he had at night, which marked him as a potential *angakoq*. He was therefore given an instructor. In the dead of winter, his instructor placed him in a tiny snow hut and left him without food or drink. His only provision was an exhortation to think of the Great Spirit. Five days later the instructor returned and gave him some lukewarm water. Again he

exhorted him to think of the Great Spirit and left. Fifteen days later, the instructor gave Igjugarjuk another drink of water and a small piece of meat. After ten more days—a total of thirty days of nearly complete solitude and fasting—Igjugarjuk saw a helping spirit in the form of a woman. For five months after this he was kept on a strict diet and forbidden sexual intercourse, to consolidate his new power. Throughout his later career, he fasted whenever he wanted to see his spirit and gain her help.

Other Eskimo shamans have reported initiations involving being shot through the heart or drowned. One who was drowned described being tied to a pole and carried out onto a frozen lake. His instructor cut a hole in the ice and thrust him into it, so that he stood on the bottom with his head under water. He claimed to have been left in this position for five days, and when he was hauled up, his clothes were not wet. He had overcome death and become a great wizard.[56]

In these accounts, we can see that the Eskimo shaman's way to power is through an initiatory ordeal that often has had a death-resurrection motif. Eliade's materials on Eskimo shamans detail other initiatory techniques.[57] For instance, a neophyte might have to rub stones over and over until helping spirits came, or an older shaman might extract the neophyte's soul from his eyes, brain, or intestines, so that the spirits could determine what was best in him. Through this process, the neophyte learned how to draw out the soul himself, so as to travel on mystical journeys. Still another initiatory motif focuses on sudden illumination. In the shaman's brain flashed a sort of searchlight or luminous fire that enabled him to see in the dark, perceive coming events, or read others' secret thoughts. Finally, Iglulik Eskimos spoke of the shaman's ability to see himself as a skeleton, all of whose parts he could name in a special language. The skeleton represented elemental human stuff, that which could best resist sun, wind, weather, and even death. By going in spirit to his skeleton, the shaman stripped himself of perishable flesh and blood and readied himself to deal with the holy.

Worldview

In traditional Eskimo religion, then, divinity, nature, and self were all related. Although Sila was a force moving through the universe, it could be personified as a woman who was especially concerned that humans treat the animals kindly. The mythic Eskimo mentality sensed Sila or divinity in a wide variety of places, and it did not nail down the status of spirits, ghosts, or Sedna. More important was the typical ancient conviction that nature was alive, willful, holy, and dangerous. Because the shaman came into contact with this dimension of life most directly, the shaman best exemplifies the Eskimo self. "Animistic," "impressionable," and even "hallucinatory" are tags that commentators have used, but these terms are probably more confusing than explanatory. Quite simply, these very practical people, who often expressed themselves in exceptionally skillful hunting, sewing, and art, were, like American Indians, extraordinarily aware of the elements' impact on their psyches.[58]

Traditional Eskimo society focused on survival: gaining shelter against the cold and obtaining the seal, fish, or deer that furnished food and clothing. The basic social unit was the married couple, and the male hunted and the female sewed. Both the hunting and the sewing took place in the midst of complex taboos. As interpreted by the shaman, these taboos formed a system for dealing with the spirits. Shamanist ecstasy, then, served social as well as individual ends. The shaman fasted, danced, or ingested tobacco to gain for the tribe access to the control center of the natural world.

This culture may go back beyond the Bronze Age.[59] Since that time, Eskimos have been hunters, and the elaborate taboo system that they developed seems to have been designed to conciliate the game who had to suffer so that the Eskimos could live. As one Iglulik shaman put it, "Life's greatest danger lies in the fact that man's food consists entirely of souls."[60] Therefore, great precautions were taken to placate the spirits of the game and avoid their anger. For instance, Eskimos poured water on the snout of the ringed seal when they killed it, because it lived in salt water and was thirsty. The harpoon had to stand by the blubber lamp the first night after the kill so that the soul still in the harpoon head might stay warm. If one killed a bearded seal or bear, no one could work for three days; also, such a prize deserved presents— for example, sole skin for the bear, because bears walk so much. The Bering Sea Eskimos spent a month preparing for their festival of the bearded seal, during which they returned to the sea the bladders of all seals caught in the preceding year.[61] In honor of the whale, they held masked dances and gave gifts.

The Eskimos of central Canada had taboos to separate land animals from sea animals. For instance, eating walrus and caribou meat on the same day was forbidden. Before seal hunting on ice could begin, the hunters had to smoke their weapons over fires of seaweed to remove the smell of the land. Similarly, all sewing of caribou skins had to cease on a particular day.

Such a taboo system depends on a network of relations among the different forms of life. Because of those relations, many Eskimos carried amulets or fetishes—bits of bone, feathers, or the like. An amulet represented a power bond between the wearer and the animal of origin. One might give a baby some owl claws so that the baby would have strong fists. A man would wear a piece of caribou ear to gain sharp hearing. Even soot was given to impart strength, since it is strong enough to extinguish fire.

Many analyses of Eskimo culture linger somewhat pruriently over marriage.[62] According to Freuchen, Eskimo marriage traditionally began by the man's "capturing" the woman (carrying her off more or less against her will). It was not sexually exclusive, for a man might offer his wife to a visiting friend, regularly arrange to share her with other men, take another man's wife on a hunt with him if his own were pregnant, and so on. Some groups practiced polygamy, and the general attitude was that sexual desire is just another appetite like hunger.

In part, these marital arrangements usually reflected a shortage of women. Fathers prized male children, and many female infants were killed by strangling or exposure because raising them and providing a dowry loomed as too great a burden. In daily life, however, women were indispensable. They cooked the food and made all the clothing, often chewing for hours on an animal skin to soften it for sewing. Women went on dogsled trips, and some could handle the dogs better than men. Eskimo men feared menstrual blood, so women were forbidden contact with game. For the same reason, men isolated women who were in labor. In fact, both birth and death were awesome events involving dangerous forces. A new mother was restricted in what she could eat, whom she could see, what clothing she could wear, and more. Only certain persons could touch the dead, and, if possible, a person died outdoors. If death occurred indoors, everything in the house had to be destroyed.[63]

The "spirit songs" recorded by Rasmussen offer our final glimpse into the Eskimo mind.[64] They breathe both loneliness and sensitivity. Fighting their vast, barren land, Eskimos remind us about how many trials ancient peoples endured. Their lives were short, their labors heavy. Eskimo children often died in birth, and Eskimo hunters were frequently lost at sea or frozen in storms. Nonetheless, the Eskimo human spirit devised implements for building igloos at breakneck speed and for hunting, fishing, and traveling by sled. It also produced a somber yet poetic thought world. Although that world was poorer mythologically than those of the American Indian or African, it was equally impressive in imagining life's elemental forces. Sitting on their ice floes and working animal skins, Eskimo men and women did what had to be done to survive. Their wisdom about Sila was no cheap grace. Sila was in both storm and quiet. It moved the bear as well as the child. Knowing Sila, one could call life good. Knowing Sila, one could be glad to be an Inuit.

AFRICANS

As American Indians and Eskimos have been shaped by their environments, so traditional Africans have been shaped by their land. They have been forest people, such as the BaMbuti, or mountain people, such as the Ik. In fact, the habitat of Africans has even determined their sense perception, how they see and hear the world. Anthropologists have found Africans from the forest who could not see things in perspective at far distances. For instance, one anthropologist took a BaMbuti friend from the forests of Zaire on a trip to the Ruwenzori Mountains of Uganda. At home in his forest, the Pygmy was a skillful hunter, able to pick his way through the dense growth with ease. He knew dozens of plants at a glance, and very little escaped his gaze. The trip was a great adventure for the Pygmy, who was shrewd, alert, and interested in every detail.

In the mountains, however, for the first time no trees blocked the Pygmy's view. The anthropologist only realized how significant this was when they stood looking down over miles of grassland. Several miles away, yet clearly in view, was a herd of grazing buffalo. "What are those insects?" the Pygmy asked. The anthropologist thought he was joking until he realized that the Pygmy had never had to make much allowance for distance when he judged something's size. The same thing happened later when they were viewing a distant lake; the Pygmy refused to believe that a large boat was in the middle, insisting that it was just a floating piece of wood.[65]

Figure 10   *Head of an* oba *(king), Benin, Nigeria, seventeenth century. Bronze, 11 in. high. Heads such as this were placed on the king's altar to propitiate his ancestors' spirits while he was away. The Nelson–Atkins Museum of Art, Kansas City, Missouri.*

The Africa most germane to our study in this chapter is south of the Sahara.[66] In the north, Islam is now the major influence, while in the south, ancient religion mingles with Christianity. A 1980 census estimated that 200 million Africans were Christians, 190 million were Muslims, and 65 million adhered to traditional ancient ways.[67] However, those figures are deceptive. Ancient notions persist so strongly that African Islam and Christianity differ markedly from their counterparts elsewhere.[68]

Because traditional Africans were not literate, no written materials are available for a history of the cultural development. Still, some analysts of African mythology find indications of very ancient thought patterns, as well as of extensive cross-cultural influences. For instance, one analyst sees in Dogon thought evidence of a time of hunting and gathering, a time of early land cultivation, a time of grain cultivation, and a time of contact with Hellenistic culture.[69] Another analyst, in a famous study of Near Eastern kingship, draws extensive parallels between Egyptian notions more than 4,000 years old and twentieth-century African views.[70] A third, like scholars of ancient peoples generally, underscores the conservatism and tenacity of oral traditions. Some African tribes have kept a ritual language that is different from contemporary speech and that goes back countless generations, just as liturgical Latin or Old Slavonic does.[71]

Worldview

In analyzing traditional African religion, one first notes that most tribes have had a supreme being. In East Africa, its most common name has been Mulungu, which connotes an impersonal spirit that is far away.[72] Mulungu is creative, omnipotent, and omnipresent. It may be heard in thunder and seen in lightning. Originally Mulungu was intimate with the world, but in later days it withdrew. When personified, Mulungu is envisioned as having a wife and family. He molds human bodies and gives all life its breath.

Under Mulungu are subordinate powers.[73] Africans have reverenced both these powers and their own departed ancestors. The most important of the subor-

*Figure 11   Sacred Ashanti stool, Ghana, about 1860. Wood and silver, 15 in. high ×
23½ in. wide. According to tradition, the power and well-being of the Ashanti state
were vested in a king's stool thrown down from the heavens. The Nelson–Atkins
Museum of Art, Kansas City, Missouri (Nelson Fund).*

dinate natural powers are the spirits of the storm, but earth spirits, water spirits, and spirits associated with crafts (such as blacksmithing and weaving) exert considerable influence, as do gods associated with divination.

Traditional West Africans have families of gods and build temples. They tend to pray every day, using simple, personal words, and frequently they pray at one of the many shrines that dot the countryside. Usually their prayers are quite practical—petitions for health, security, good farming, or safe travel. They commonly sacrifice something to a god, usually offering a liquid or cereal. The first-fruits offering at harvest time is especially important. Special occasions may prompt an animal sacrifice, and in ancient days humans apparently were sacrificed, largely to provide companions for deceased kings.[74] (Kings were crucial mediators of cosmic harmony, and so somewhat divine.)

The ox sacrifice of the Nuer shows African religious ceremony in high style. It only takes place on such important occasions as weddings or feud settlements. Once the ox has been brought in, the ceremony unfolds in four phases: presentation, consecration, invocation, and immolation (killing). The animal is tethered to a stake; officiants rub ashes on it to consecrate it; a priest raises his spear and invokes the spirit; he then spears the animal, and all members of the community eat from it.[75] (Africans in general show great regard for cattle, and the main idea in cattle sacrifice seems to be to revere and tap the powers of procreation that bulls and cows represent.)

Traditionally Africans also emphasize rites of passage, investing birth, adolescence, marriage, and death with religious significance and giving the self a sense of development. Usually these rites are performed at home under the guidance of a family elder. At a birth, the family will make offerings to the ancestors. They will also divine to which deity the child should be dedicated. Adolescent ceremonies stress endurance. They are ordeals designed to toughen children into adults and to impart adult sacred lore. Frequently they take the form of circumcision or clitoridectomy.

Many tribes are polygynous, and so African women often are co-wives. As the operation of a women's society such as the Sande of Sierra Leone shows, one of the purposes of clitoridectomy is to develop deep sisterly ties, lest husbands play women off against one another. Thus, the painful excision of the initiate's clitoris is performed amid strong group support; other women console the initiate with food, songs, and dances, promising her that her present suffering will ensure her future fertility and be a sign to her husband of her moral and religious maturity. It is also likely that clitoridectomy is thought to remove any maleness (since the clitoris is perceived as a penislike organ), allowing the woman to fit into her female social status more easily.[76] Understandably, feminist scholars have suspected a patriarchal desire to control women's sexuality. Anthropologists also furnish interesting accounts of African circumcision.[77]

Almost all Africans consider marriage a sacred duty and children a great blessing. For that reason, the menarche (first menstruation) can be a time of tribal rejoicing and for such celebrations as the Pygmies' *elima* feast for young women. Indeed, female fertility is linked directly to tribal prosperity. With no social security system, African parents see many children as their hedge against old age. Thus, polygyny and large families are frequent. Westerners trying to lower the birthrate sometimes find themselves upsetting an old economic system.[78]

Funeral rites are intended to separate the dead from the living without offense. One must perform them most carefully, for they can influence the dead person's peace in the spirit world. Funerals keep the living in view, too, stirring up consoling memories and reminding the bereaved that all life is fleeting. Africans have tended to place great stock in dreams, often because there they could meet their departed ancestors.

Representative Myths

African religions are especially rich mythologically, so studying the tribes' tales has become a preferred way of understanding the African social outlook. In a Yoruba creation myth, the supreme God sends to a marsh an artisan who is carrying a bag that lay between the great God's thighs. From this bag the artisan shakes out soil and then a cock and pigeon, which scratch the soil until the marsh is covered. Thus, the land is holy, given from above. The Dogon say that God created the sun and moon like pots with copper rings. To make the stars he flung pellets of clay into space, and he also made the earth of clay. The Fon think that a great snake gathered the earth together after God made it and that the earth still rests on this snake's coils. For the Kikuyu of Kenya, God is the divider of the universe. He made Mount Kenya, the "Mountain of Brightness," as evidence of his wonders and as a divine resting place. The Luyia say that God first made the moon brighter and bigger than the sun. The sun became jealous, and the two fought. The moon was thrown into the dirt, resulting in its muddy face.[79]

Through many images, then, traditional Africans made their world sacred. It was a living whole, not modern science's objective collection of matter. Perhaps relatedly, African art tends to avoid representing the supreme God. Indeed, there are numerous myths of his withdrawal to the distant heaven. The Mende of Sierra Leone say that God moved away because humans were always bothering him. Ghanans and Nigerians say that humans became too familiar with God. Originally God's heaven was just above their heads, but children came to wipe their hands on it, women hit it when pounding grain, and finally a woman with a long pole hit heaven in the eye. God then moved away. The Burundi of central Africa say that God went off because a crippled baby was born, and some humans wanted to kill God, whom they held responsible. In African mythology, God often leaves by climbing a spider's thread. If there were a great emergency, humans might be able to find the thread and obtain God's help again.

Though these stories stress God's distance and so reflect an African sense of a fall from heavenly grace, African prayers show that divinity is still thought to be present and operative, in ordinary times through intermediary gods and in times of crisis through the high God. Thus, a prayer to Imana, creator God of the Ruanda-Urundi, begs, "Give me offspring, give me as you give to others! Imana, what shall I do, where shall I go? I am in distress, where is there room for me? O Merciful, O Imana of mercy, help this once."[80]

A hymn to Mwari, God of the Mashona of southern Zimbabwe, recites his attributes and accomplishments (he piled the rocks into mountains and sewed the heavens like cloth), then asks a hearing and mercy. A South African bushman asks his God Gauwa for help in hunting, complains that Gauwa is cheating him, but concludes on a note of hope: "Gauwa will bring something for us to kill next day, after he himself hunts and has eaten meat, when he is full and feeling well."[81]

The African God, then, is both far and near, both inscrutable and able to be petitioned. In general, he is considered kind and good, a father or friend. He creates and sustains all things, but no one has ever seen him. In a number of myths, he creates humans out of the ground. The Zulu of South Africa and the Thonga of Mozambique both have a tradition that the first man

and woman came out of an exploded reed bed. A Pygmy story says that the chameleon heard a strange, whispering noise in a tree. When it cut the tree open, out came a flood of water, which spread over the earth, and the first humans, who were light skinned. The Ashanti of Ghana revere Mondays and Tuesdays, because the leopard, who is sacred to some clans, emerged on those days. Also, the first human leader consoled his followers, who were frightened on coming out from under the earth. Because that leader was killed on Wednesday, Wednesday is a feared day.[82]

Overall, Africans seem to experience nature as being bountiful and good, unlike the Eskimos. Perhaps as a result, Africans show little tendency toward asceticism. God's heavenly world is but a larger and happier version of their present good life. Many tribes hope that after death there will be a rebirth from the world of ghosts into another part of the sunlit earth.

Because nature is bountiful, natural processes, including sex, are accepted without great question. The Ashanti of Ghana say that sexual knowledge came when the python sent man and woman to lie together. Consequently, many Ashanti thank the python for their children. If they find a dead python, they sprinkle it with white clay and give it a ritual burial. Africans tend to fear abnormal births, however, and disfigured people become outcasts. Twins are regarded differently by different tribes. Some tribes expose them to die, but others welcome and honor them. Like Eskimos, Africans think that souls are numerous, that the world is alive, and that a new child may inherit a soul from an ancestor.

Several of the most poignant African myths deal with life's troubles. A Zambian story tells of an old woman who wanted to follow her dead relatives because she had been left all alone. First she cut down tall trees and piled them on top of one another, trying to reach the sky. When this failed, she went looking for the road to heaven, which appears to touch the earth at the horizon. She could not find it, but in her travels she met many tribes. They assured her that suffering is normal. A myth of the Chaga of Kenya tells of a man determined to shoot God because his sons had died. When he found God, however, there were his sons, more glorious than they had been on earth.

From these and other sources, it follows that many Africans have attributed death to a mistake. The Kono of Sierra Leone, for instance, explain death as the failure of a messenger dog. God gave the dog new skins for human beings, but the dog put them down in order to join a feast and a snake stole them. Since then the snake has been immortal, changing skins, while human beings have died—and tried to destroy snakes.

Divination

The African religious functionary who merits most attention is probably the diviner. One scholar has suggested that there are several levels of African divination, and that the diviner at the deeper levels is equivalent to a profound shaman.[83] The two polar categories this scholar uses are "possession" and "wisdom." In possession, the diviner is filled by a spirit that reads omens, interprets movements of sacred animals, and so on. In wisdom, the spirits, gods, and the diviner's own personality are subordinate to the cosmic order. Thus, wisdom is a protoscience or protocosmology—an effort to set the facts of nature and experience into some overarching scheme. Often through wisdom the diviner arrives at the notion of a Supreme Being who intelligently controls all cosmic flux. In other words, the diviner of wisdom is an intellectual, not an ecstatic or spirit-possessed functionary. His or her religious talent is to conceive a comprehensive view of how all events fit into a sacred scheme.

However, possession and wisdom are not clearly differentiated. Intermediate forms lie between them. The Mwari cultists of the Matopo Hills of Zimbabwe, for instance, believe that God speaks through mediums whom he possesses deep in certain caves, and that these messages give a comprehensive view of his operations in the world.

Also, there are numerous African intuitive diviners, famed for their ability to find lost articles, identify thieves, recognize witches, and so on. Whether they are inspired by a spirit or instinctively sense particular events is unclear. Perhaps neither explanation is adequate. These diviners show high intelligence, can pick up oblique clues from their clients' stories, and give evidence of extrasensory perception.

Evan Zuesse suggests that the typical Dogon sage is a wisdom diviner, insofar as the mythoscientific scheme that he reveals functions, with its archetypes and creation accounts, as the Dogon's most profound way of situating themselves in the world. The myths of the scheme's first level, which are made known to noninitiates, have themes such as the loss of paradise and the withdrawal of God, which are common to hunters and gatherers. A second level deals with the marriage of heaven and earth, which is a theme typical of early cultivators. The third-level myths of the cosmic egg have been found among grain cultivators, while the highest esoteric knowledge, concerning the "Word," suggests the *logos* (Word) of Hellenistic culture. Therefore, through the centuries Dogon sages probably assimilated the deepest insights of each new culture with which they came into contact, weaving them into their own philosophy.[84]

Another evidence that African world views reflect centuries of cultural exchange is the common divinatory systems that stretch from Zaire to South Africa. In one system, for example, a basket containing 205 pieces of bone or wood represents all reality. To answer a question, the diviner shakes the basket and analyzes the pattern into which the pieces fall. The possible combinations are enormous, so students travel long distances to study with famous teachers. In effect, the basket and its pieces are a microcosm of the African world's social institutions and forces. The diviner can feed into this system the problem at hand and then read out an answer. As with the shaman's report from the gods, the diviner's answer often becomes a means to healing or reconciliation.

Like the African witch doctor, who is a sort of physician, the diviner supports the forces of good, just as **witches** (to be distinguished from witch doctors) and **sorcerers** are agents of evil. Most tribes think that witches work at night, are usually women, and inherit or buy from demons a power to inflict harm.[85] The sorcerer taps the power that witch doctors use, but turns it to harm. He or she may make potions, cast spells, or put pins in an image of the victim. Needless to say, sorcerers and witches are greatly feared and hated.[86]

African religion, therefore, is a good example of the "undifferentiated" consciousness we meet throughout nonliterate cultures. On the whole, it presents a compact sense of reality in which material, imaginative, and spiritual components more run together than they are clearly distinguished. The positive effect of such compactness or lack of differentiation is that the African reality has been rich and weighty. Africans have lived close to the earth, at ease with their bodies, in the midst of spiritual forces that could touch their bodies by touching their minds. The African psychology has been holistic and full of feeling, little sundered by wars between body and spirit.

The negative potential in all compact consciousness, African included, has been a vulnerability to irrationality—such fear of witches and spirits that people could die, such immersion in dreams and sensation that neither technology nor theology could make clear, consistent progress. Thus we have seen the African tendency to solve the problem of making God both transcendent of the world and immanent to the world by postulating a high God aloof from the world and lesser gods immersed in daily activity. Most other nonliterate religious cultures have worked out similar solutions, not agreeing with the monotheisms that accept the otherness of full divinity, its lack of the limitations we find in all nondivine realities, that makes it the realest, closest of beings. On the other hand, most other nonliterate cultures have shared with African cultures a solid love of the world in which they have found themselves and so an enviable realism and mental health.

AUSTRALIANS

Australians lived far from the influence of the madding European crowd until the end of the eighteenth century. Of the settlement that followed Cook's exploratory voyage of 1770 it has recently been said: "The spread of settlement proved a disaster to the delicate ecology of aboriginal civilisation, which perished from all but the centre and far north almost before it was noticed, let alone understood."[87] Consequently, the reconstruction of how native Australian religious culture must have first appeared takes considerable imagination.[88]

The prime impression that the natives made on observers was of living in a different sort of time. Australian natives were not just sensitive to the seasons—they seemed to have a different set of aspirations. Their apparent listlessness seemed to grow more intense with age. A young man or woman who was manifestly alert and able to solve practical problems steadily became more dreamlike.

The first European observers did not know that this psychological makeup had a firm rationale. Were the native informants clearly to have spoken, they might have said something like the following: "In our religious ceremonies, we are initiated ever more deeply into the dream time of the eternal ancestors. That is the world's own time, by which creation moves. Around us, at the places in the landscape that we memorialize, the ancestors exert the pull of this

dream time. Slowly, they return us all to our origins, to where we were before this life. How strange that you whites rush and bustle. You must not know the dream time, must not want to return. Too bad. Life is for returning. We are as the ancestors have dreamed us."

Historically, the Australian aborigines probably migrated from Southeast Asia (southern India and Sri Lanka) about 50,000 years ago. They spread throughout the continent and were isolated from outside influences until the arrival of Europeans in the eighteenth century. From the time of Cook's voyage interest grew, and in 1778 the British settled a penal colony in the area that is now Sydney. At the time of European contact, the aborigines probably numbered about 350,000. Some aspects of their culture suggest that they had had contact with peoples of Melanesia and New Guinea. Presently they number about 120,000, and about 45,000 are of pure stock. In the semidesert northern region, they maintain much of their original culture, which is based on hunting and gathering and which was fairly uniform across the numerous tribes.

Worldview

The secrecy and foreignness of much Australian lore have made it hard for Western investigators to penetrate its history or philosophic structure. Nevertheless, E. A. Worms has suggested a list of the original religion's essential features, which include the belief in a personal sky being, belief in helpful spirit beings, belief in holy, powerful objects left by the sky being, ritual drama to renew divine creativity, initiation rites for both sexes, sacrifice and prayer, and a medicine man leader.[89]

T. G. H. Strehlow has complemented this list by sketching the beliefs that were held over the entire continent.[90] According to Strehlow, most tribes believed in eternal supernatural beings, whom they linked with totemic animals, plants, or natural phenomena. In fact, the concept of totem came into religious studies largely as a result of research in Australia.[91] As Webster defines it, a totem is "an animal, plant, or other object serving as the emblem of a family or clan." The eternal supernatural beings were therefore ancestors and clan founders.

In the beginning, many tribes say, these supernatural beings slept under the earth's crust. Time began when they were "born out of their eternity" and burst to the surface. According to the Unambal of northwestern Australia, in the beginning Ungud lived

Figure 12 *Garden in Sydney representing aboriginal motifs. Photo by J. T. Carmody.*

in the earth as a snake, while in the sky was Wallanganda, the Milky Way. During the night they created everything through a creative dream. Ungud transformed himself into the beings that he dreamed; Wallanganda threw out a spiritual force, shaped it into images, and projected them onto the rocks of the present landscape.[92] Next, spirits arose, shaped as either animals or humans and based on Wallanganda's images. In turn, they shaped the rest of the earth—mountains, sand hills, plains, and so on. The ancestors were also responsible for the aborigines' sacred songs and rituals, which were preserved with great care.

The ancestors were restrained only by a vague superior force that could punish any crimes, although they were also subject to age, sickness, and decay. Eventually they sank back into their first state of sleep, having produced the sun, moon, stars, death, labor, and pain. In the Northern Territory, scholars have found cults and art honoring the ancestors' fertility. In other regions, natives venerate rocks, trees,

and *tjurunga* (distinctive slabs of wood) as sites where ancestors left supernatural powers.

Thus, Australians parceled divinity out among several supernatural figures. Central Australians believed that human beings came into existence as semi-embryonic masses that were joined together by the hundreds. The totemic ancestors then sliced these masses into individual infants. The traces of these masses left in the landscape became a principle of human life, for pregnant women would receive them and pass them on to the unborn. In other words, a soul could enter the fetus from a certain point in the landscape. It would be an immortal gift from one of the ancestors, the ancestor's own reincarnation. The newborn was thus a being of high dignity. Also, the newborn had strong links to a particular rock or tree, since from it had come the ancestor's spirit.

If humans were linked with eternal ancestors, why did they die? According to the Wotjubaluk of southeastern Australia, originally the moon raised the dead. Then an old man said, "Let them remain dead."

So now only the moon itself returns to life. An Aranda myth says that the dead used to emerge from the grave for a second round of life, but a magpie who witnessed this became angry, grasped a heavy spear, thrust it into the neck of a dead man, and shoved the man back into the grave, saying, "Remain rooted down for all time."[93]

Now mortal, humans pass through a temporal circuit. Life begins when one's parent perceives the coming of the ancestor's spirit to the womb. This most often occurs in a dream but may be prompted by morning sickness or even birth pangs. During initiation into maturity, one partially reenters the dreamtime—the time when he or she originated out of eternity. Adult life means returning deeper and deeper into this time through religious ceremonies. At death one crosses the final threshold and again becomes a sacred spirit in the sky.[94]

Ritual

Puberty rites were a crucial occasion. Scholars first thought that they existed only for men, but more recent scholarship suggests that menstruation and childbirth were ritualized as religious experiences.[95] Puberty rites took place in considerable secrecy on sacred ground. Often this sacred ground represented the world as it was in the beginning, for in the puberty ceremonies the participants relived the time of creation. The puberty rites of the Kamilaroi, for instance, reenacted the time when their god Baiame was on earth and founded their ceremonies; in this way the tribe reactualized his presence and regenerated the world.

Accordingly, the Kamilaroi prepared the sacred ceremonial ground in terms of a cosmic symbolism. The dominant features were two circular enclosures. The large enclosure, about twenty-three meters in diameter, had a pole about three meters high with emu feathers on top. In the smaller circle were two young trees with their roots in the air. The Kamilaroi drew figures on the ground or modeled them in clay. The largest was a five-meter representation of Baiame. Then they pantomimed the sacred history of Baiame's creative acts. For the adolescent initiates, this was their first exposure to the tribal lore about how things were in the beginning. For the adults who directed the ceremony, it was a renewal of faith.

One tribe, the Kurnai, separated adolescent boys from their mothers matter of factly, but most tribes even today begin the ceremonies with much weeping and lamentation. Initiates may vary in age from six to fourteen, and they undergo various bodily operations. Most ceremonies follow a regular pattern of segregation of the initiates, instruction, bodily operations, revelation of some sacred objects and ceremonies, washing, and returning to ordinary life.[96] The dominant symbolism of the entire ceremony is death and resurrection. The novice dies to the child's world of irresponsible ignorance and is reborn as a mature, spiritual being. Supposedly the mothers take the death motif literally. Thinking hostile supernatural beings have killed their sons, they mourn as at a funeral. When the boys return, the women treat them as new beings, quite different from what they were as children.

During the ceremony, the boys are covered with branches or rugs. They may not use words, only sounds and signs. In the ritual operations deadly supernatural beings act upon them. When the bullroarer (a slat of wood tied to the end of a thong that roars when whirled) is sounded, the supernatural beings may knock out a tooth, pull out hair, or scar the body. Circumcision is the key act, however, because it is a direct slash at a life source.

Six months to three years after circumcision, many tribes perform a second operation called subincision. Students of Australian religion debate its significance. Subincision involves slitting the underside of the penis and permanently opening the urethra. Some tribes give it overtones of bisexuality, likening the wound to a vulva. In that case, it may represent males' efforts to arrogate powers of mothering. Supporting this is the sociological fact that the boys pass from female to male control at this time. Other evidence indicates that subincision is a way to gather blood, which is needed for other ceremonials. From this perspective the act approximates menstruation. Eliade explains this ritual as follows: "Just as the women get rid of 'bad blood' through menstruation, the initiate can expel his mother's blood by laceration of the subincision wound."[97] The deeper goal of all these initiation ceremonies, however, is to instruct the young men in the sacred lore necessary for an adult male life.

Girls' initiations are tailored more for the individual, since they are triggered by the onset of menstruation. In seclusion older women teach the girl songs and myths relating to female dignity and duties. After this instruction, they lead the young woman to a lagoon for a ritual bath and then display her to the community as an adult. In some tribes, a girl's initiation includes defloration with a sort of dildo, followed by ritual intercourse with a group of men. No doubt this act has more than a sadistic or carnal motive, but its exact religious significance is unclear. Certainly nonliterate peoples sometimes treat sexuality as an impersonal dimension of tribal life, so perhaps this aspect of the ceremony is a way of tying the potential mother to the gods' and tribe's forces.

The female puberty rite is only the first rite in an Australian woman's life. Marriage, childbearing, menopause, and old age occasion further instruction in the nature of the sacred. As the revelations become more profound, the ceremonies become more secret. Westerners have found a pattern in the women's rituals similar to that in the men's—the reenactment of mythical events from the time of creation.

In early times, women apparently played important parts in the men's rituals. Myths speak of female ancestors who were more powerful than male ancestors and of men stealing songs, powers, and artifacts that had belonged to the women. The bullroarer is one of the artifacts that the men supposedly stole. Women may have originally functioned in the male circumcision rites, for among some tribes today the initiate gives his foreskin to his sister, "who then dries it, anoints it with ochre, and suspends it from her neck."[98] No myth speaks of women stealing important religious items or doctrines from men. Most likely, then, in earlier times religious collaboration between the sexes was greater than it has been recently. In modern times, women have not been privy to male lore. For that reason, men say that women do not progressively reenter the sacred dream time—that female ceremonies are not a steady return to spiritual existence in the sky.

The Medicine Man

The principal figure in traditional Australian ritual life has been the medicine man, who derives his healing powers from visionary contacts with supernatural beings. Usually he possesses magical items that symbolize these powers: quartz crystals, pearl shells, stones, bones, or the like. Mircea Eliade has described the ecstatic, highly imaginary making of a medicine man among the Wiradjuri of southeastern Australia.[99] First his father places two large quartz crystals against the boy's breast. They disappear into his body, making

him clever and "able to bring things up." These crystals felt warm, but other ones that the boy drinks look like ice and taste sweet. From this time on, the boy can see ghosts.

During the boy's puberty rites, after a tooth has been knocked out, he learns to go down into the ground and bring up quartz crystals. The initiators take him to a grave, where a dead man rubs him to make him clever. The dead man also gives him a personal totem, a tiger snake. By following the snake, the boy and his father find the living places of various gods. At the initiation's climax, they climb a thread to Baiame's place in the sky. Baiame looks like an old man with a long beard, and from his shoulders extend two great quartz crystals.

Evidently, the medicine man is a sort of shaman whose healing powers derive from his ability to "travel to heaven." They are represented by his quartz crystals, which are part of divinity itself, and his animal spirit, the tiger snake, helps him in his tasks. An Unmatjera medicine man from central Australia reported that an old doctor threw crystals at him during his initiation and then cut out his insides. He was dead until the old man put more crystals in his body, covered it with leaves, and sang over him. The singing caused him to swell up. Then the old man gave him new internal organs and brought him back to life. From that time the medicine man was able to produce quartz crystals within himself at will, and they gave him the power to heal.

Thus, the Australian ancient religion over which the medicine men ruled bound people to the land and to one another through imaginative myths and rituals that brought them into contact with ancestral totemic spirits or divinities. Its basic goal was to keep harmony with these powers. By integrating themselves with them through ritual, participants supported nature as well as personal and tribal life. Death broke one's ties with the supernatural beings, so funeral rites had two functions—consoling the bereaved and helping the deceased to find his or her new station. The Aranda believed that finding one's new station entailed the immortal soul's going back to the place where it first passed into the fetus. The dead person's second, mortal soul turned into a ghost and was capable of malicious acts. Consequently, the mourning ceremonies tried to mute any anger that the deceased might have borne against relatives and friends. After a stated time, the ghost was incapable of mischief, because it departed for other haunts or faded away.

Figure 13   Ritual mask, Sepik River, New Guinea, twentieth century. Basketry, clay, bamboo, feathers, paint; 42 in. high. This mask was used in men's ceremonies, hanging high on the gable of the man's house to represent a helpful spirit. The Nelson–Atkins Museum of Art, Kansas City, Missouri (Nelson Fund).

THE PERSISTENCE OF ANCIENT THEMES

When we observe our contemporaries interested in the occult, astrology, and witchcraft, we should get an inkling that the world of our prehistoric and nonliterate ancestors is not so far away as we tend to think. When we find ourselves longing for a pace that would be more humane, a medicine that would treat the mind and the body as fully integral to our holistic self, a technology that would try to go with nature rather than thinking it had to assault nature, we may realize that in any dialogue between such ancestors and our contemporaries the ancients would have things to teach as well as things to learn. But perhaps the clearest indication of how ancient themes continue in current Western culture emerges when we consider the three topics with which we began this chapter: the sacred, myth and ritual, and the shaman.

The sacred peeks through whenever people turn toward the mysteries of being and goodness. For example, when people respond to a philosopher such as Martin Heidegger, whose ruminations about being continue to command respect, they find their minds quieted and pointed toward something both basic and potentially holy: the mystery that anything at all should exist, that creatures should continue to step out of the void of nonbeing.[100] When people follow the wry yet troubling narratives of a novelist such as Walker Percy, they find themselves confronting very old questions about good and evil, about God and the demonic, about what true holiness, and so true humanity, entail.[101]

Clearly, therefore, many of our writers still work under the allure of the old questions that set the agenda of our early ancestors' discussions around the campfire.

The question of being plays less philosophically but no less actually in Florida sunsets, in otters sporting off Point Lobos, in a lover's eyes. Indeed, there is no place we can fly, the Psalmist says, where the divine source of being does not hover. The very structure of our minds, some religious analysts say, implies the question of God.[102] Certainly the structure of our hearts, their constant search for what is truly worth loving, what is stable in goodness, keeps open the question of the sacred, of that which might be wholly good, untouched by the evil that compromises our worldly experiences. So our own senses, minds, and hearts continue to present us with mysteries quite like those that dominated ancient human cultures.

As a consequence, we also retain a sense of the **profane**, the nonsacred. It comes from losing oneself in cooking, clerking, welding, or tennis—from gaining bread or freeing sweat. Our surfeit of busy-ness and pragmatism is a major form of profanity. Perhaps because of it, we have few awesome shrines, our woods are not full of helper spirits. We still intuitively distinguish the sacred from the profane, however, for we still sense that some things are truly real and others are but passing.

We also still make myths and ritualize the life cycle,[103] though few commentators find our myths effective or our rituals profound. For decades, we Americans lived a civil myth now called "manifest destiny." It began with the Pilgrims' errand in the wilderness, moved west to establish a New Israel, and finally led us to think we were guardians of the free world, able to destroy villages in order to save them. The shattering of this myth was close to a national trauma, suggesting how powerful ancient peoples' self-definition through stories must have been. Whether we shall fashion a new myth or a ritual cycle to make our children brave remains to be seen. We could do better than the current New Year's Day, Memorial Day, Fourth of July, and Thanksgiving or the current American way of wedding and dying. We might learn from feminist religionists' revolt from tradition and return to the goddess.[104] We could tell stories from E. F. Schumacher's *Small Is Beautiful*.[105]

Last, what about shamanism today? Are there still ecstatic people able to communicate with the sacred? The poet T. S. Eliot was rather doubtful. In *The Cocktail Party*, he made the psychiatrist our priest. One could do worse, though, than a Robert Coles or an Erik Erikson. They know a great deal about the spirit's quests. Similarly, Michael Polanyi and Eric Voegelin suggest the religious import of creative scholarship; Doris Lessing, Lawrence Durrell, Walker Percy, Patrick White, Isaac Singer, Saul Bellow, and many others show the art and mystery of modern love. Shamanism is not dead. Its essence lives in such tribal comforters.

To be sure, these people offer no panacea, no unguent for every bruise. With Aeschylus, they know that wisdom comes through suffering. But they keep heaven open, so they are deeply encouraging. Beating their drums, spinning their tales, they climb the cosmic pillar. Had we eyes to see, we might follow them to an ancient beauty, a wonder viable yet.

SUMMARY: THE CENTER OF NONLITERATE RELIGIONS

In an interesting book, whose title alone reveals a great deal about the progress of scholarship in dealing with nonliterate peoples, Sam Gill has tried to summarize the salient findings of recent researches. Gill's book is entitled *Beyond the Primitive*, and near its conclusion he reflects:

> The most general concern of this book has been to demonstrate: (1) the immense variety of religions which may be found among nonliterate cultures and (2) the complexity and sophistication of the religious beliefs and expressions. We have shown that these religious systems are comparable in many ways to those of literate peoples and to the great religious traditions which have a worldwide influence. And we have found that the religions of nonliterate peoples are not different in kind, nor in any single distinguishing feature, from the rest of the religions of humankind. However, this is not to say that there are not distinctions to be made nor that all religions are the same. Indeed, we have seen that there is a whole set of religious categories in which certain tendencies may often be associated with nonliterate peoples. Furthermore, we have shown that at least one way to address and understand these tendencies is to focus on the fact of nonliteracy, the lack of a written counterpart to the spoken language. Yet we fully acknowledge that this tie is perhaps only one of many ways these tendencies may be meaningfully associated and understood.
>
> Nonliteracy is linked with limits on the potential size of a culture, its forms of economy and political system, its modes of thought, and its forms of expression. Nonliteracy also shapes conceptions of time and space, fundamental to the process of religious conception and expression. We can see this fact clearly when we consider the various forms which are so ingeniously used to express complex ideas—art, artifacts, architecture, colors, odors, verbal arts, and symbolic movements. We can see how belief is both shaped by and expressed through the most commonplace aspects of sustenance activities. Nonliteracy shapes relationships and orientations within time. It encourages the face-to-face, person-to-person transmission of culture in forms especially appropriate to the needs of such processes—stories, songs, prayers, and other aspects of oral tradition.[106]

In other words, the center of nonliterate peoples' religions is much the same as the center of prehistoric and literate peoples' religions (life and death, the sacred, enlightenment, or God), but nonliterate peoples tend to color this center distinctively, because of their very nonliteracy. Not having the means to fix their histories, traditions, myths, rituals, and beliefs in unchanging form, they tend to have quite flexible histories, traditions, myths, rituals, and beliefs. They may have marvelous memories, capable of retaining orally matters that go back hundreds of years; but the sharp accent of their cultural life, and so of the faiths that inform them, is on the present, the immediate, the interpersonal.

Where literate peoples always run the risk of becoming bookish, abstract, cut loose from the living immediacy of the sacred, nonliterate peoples run the risk of quite opposite dangers. For them the problem is gaining sufficient critical distance or control over their ceremonies and beliefs to *differentiate* the various aspects of the complex reality in which their dreams, hunts, memories, and economic needs all whirl together. The shaman may well touch psychic depths that technical, literate modern cultures have neglected. The way of the shaman may well have a lot to teach modern Western medicine.[107] But the nonliterate shaman has only a slippery hold on the distinction between imagination and reason, knows only a little bit, and that intuitively, about the distinctions that might separate the sacred, the psychic, the aesthetic, and the therapeutic.

Beyond the nonliterate lies the objectifying mentality that can make these distinctions, for both weal and woe. For weal, the distinctions lead to modern science, modern political theory, modern economic arrangements. For woe, they lead to alienation, bureaucracy, systemic injustices, institutionalized neuroses. The center of nonliterate religions is a vividly sacral world, an impressively mysterious nature, that might teach aberrant modernity a great many lessons in what is necessary to regain a healthy, peaceful human nature. It would be sheer romance to make the nonliterate life of the American Indian or central African the measure of human achievement, but that sort of life often had satisfactions, healths, that literate peoples came to lose. How many modern Westerners, for example, have a vividly sacral world? What percentage of Europeans and North Americans find nature alluring, welcoming, hospitable, daunting, pacifying, as most nonliterate peoples have?

For most nonliterate peoples, nature has not been cut off from the divine or ultimate reality. It has not been raw material to be exploited, developed, subdued as human beings saw fit. It has rather been a milieu, an environment to be reverenced and enjoyed, re-

spected and celebrated. The spirits of the trees and the animals have made nature round rather than flat, alive rather than inert, impressive rather than factitious. The beauty of the forests, the jungles, the rivers, and the skies has made nature most centrally a benevolent mystery. The world's core force or greatest divinity has been awesome, worthy of great thanksgiving and applause. Because they could not write their emotions down and be done with them, nonliterate peoples have told stories and composed dances to express their thanksgiving, petition, and applause. Because they could not separate out the part pertaining to the brain from the parts pertaining to the body, they have had to make a religious return that was whole. As we struggle to gain a postmodern wholeness, we would do well to keep nonliterate peoples' wholeness toward the front of our minds.

Discussion Questions

1. Describe your reaction to Figure 8, "Indian Boy," by George Catlin.

2. What was the significance of the Eskimo concept "Sila"?

3. Why would traditional Africans consider marriage a *sacred* duty?

4. Explain the significance of the Australian medicine man's crystals.

5. Explain the sentence "The power coursing through the natural world is staggering, and when we are staggered, we are open to the sacred."

6. What are the assets and liabilities in Ogotemmeli's myth about speech?

7. What is the function of the shaman's ecstasy?

8. How does profanity, the lack of sacredness, influence contemporary Western culture?

9. Why does nonliteracy encourage a stress on the here and now?

10. What does a romantic view of nonliterate cultures tend to forget?

11. How does sacredness relate to wholeness?

12. Compose a religious myth about the Fourth of July.

13. Create a religious ritual for Thanksgiving.

Glossary

angakoq: an Inuit term used to denote the major religious figure, a shamanic healer, keeper of tribal lore, intermediary with the deities, guide of the souls of the dead, and general protector of the tribe's psychological peace against the forces of nature, the spiritual world, and the gods and goddesses that might threaten chaos.

divination: the art of discerning future events, the cause of sickness, the will of a god, and the like, practiced by the majority of archaic peoples. Diviners—specialists in this art—have used innumerable methods in their work: studying the entrails of special animals, determining the flight of birds, reading the cracks in tortoise shells, shaking out yarrow stalks or chits in a basket, and much more. Regularly the "system" developed has been a miniature of the social structure, if not the whole world view, of the tribe involved and has served the diviner as a framework for intuiting many psychological and social aspects of personal, familial, and tribal tensions.

exorcism: the process of trying to cast out evil spirits thought to have possessed a person. Exorcism depends on the belief that malign forces can take over at least portions of the body and psyche, and that representatives of holy counterforces can intercede to cast the malign forces out. The whole phenomenon trades in interactions among psychic and somatic forces that make it hard to determine precisely what the undeniable phenomena of possession—swellings, cursings, supernormal strength, apparent hatred of everything holy, bestial whoops—represent, and one cannot say definitively whether it proves the objective, independent existence of either devils or God.

fetish: an object believed to have protective powers. Fetishes, like geomancy, flourish in an animistic world, where one needs protection from powers that may be either malign in themselves or sent on malign errands by one's enemies. By giving the frightened personality something specific upon which to fix its hopes for defense, the fetish provides a measure of psychological comfort. Although the technologies of the sophisticated religious traditions certainly can bring forward other rationales, the beads of pious Muslims, mezuzah of pious Jews, and icons of pious Christians all draw much of their impact from the same need and psychodynamics that earlier peoples fixed on fetishes and amulets.

kachina: a masked dancer prominent in Hopi Indian ceremonies such as that for coming of age. The dancer usually stands for an ancestral spirit, and part of the revelation made to those in the process of becoming adults (full human beings) was that the *kachinas* were "actually" human beings. On the other hand, when wearing their masks the dancers themselves felt they had entered upon a different identity, so the revelation about their humanity was not just a debunking. Rather, it probably served to free the borders between "spirits" and "human beings," opening to the newly minted young adult the possibility, the wonder, that traffic crossed both ways. As in other societies that used masks in their rituals, the Hopi aimed at an ecstasy that would both expand their sense of "reality" and renew the wonder of the entire created world.

medium: a go-between, usually in the sense of the person who goes into trance to transmit messages from the dead or from intelligent spirits. Mediums flourish in shamanic milieus, for their practice depends on accrediting their ability to work in a nonordinary mode of consciousness. Most mediums appear to be passive instruments taken over by the deceased or the spirits in question. They may employ ouija boards, divination baskets, tarot cards, and similar methods, in which case they become mediums between the present and the future (or the fate that exists outside of time). One might say that premodern consciousness regularly was more fluid than what we usually see in the West nowadays, and so that "travel" or "possession" was less remarkable.

myth: a storied form of explanation, usually traditional, that may discard the limits of ordinary experience and portray divine or ultimate realities acting beyond the constraints of space and time. Scholars distinguish myths into different kinds. Usually a people's most important myth concerns the cosmogony—how the world was born. This sets the pattern for all the things in creation, tends to be renewed at the turning of each new year (often through rites of dissolution [orgy] and reformation), and may be invoked at any other new start, such as erecting a house, passing from childhood to adulthood, marrying, or passing from the living to the dead. Etiological myths explain the origin of particular aspects of the natural or cultural world; teleological or eschatological myths deal with the goal of history and the end of time. Myths of judgment describe what will happen after death to reward the good and punish the wicked. Myths often are sung, danced, and ritualized. Overall, they make people's basic notions vivid, memorable, capable of empowering human beings to live with direction and conviction.

oral peoples: those whose cultures had or have no writing. Obviously all cultures have been oral in the sense that living speech has been the first mode of communication. But peoples that develop writing change their cultures significantly. Writing starts to mediate a great many relationships—official, personal, religious, economic—and education may become more reflective. And while oral peoples often have prodigious memories, they do not develop the archives on which history in the modern academic sense depends. Thus they tend to be somewhat ahistorical, all the more so when they remain entranced by mythic accounts of creation, the rise of their culture, and where their time will end.

pollution: being sullied or rendered unfit for participation in sacral activities, because of some action (for example, murder) or some state (for example, menstruation) thought incompatible with proximity to the divine or ultimate reality. Pollution frequently is not a moral matter but rather a matter of what a people "feels," psychosomatically, is not compatible with divine power. The concept is of energies or vitalities whose collusion would bring disaster. However, one also can be polluted through sin, which also frequently is pictured as being out of kilter, disharmonious, with both one's better self and the legal or sacral order ordained by the divinity (either through positive precept or through the natural laws it has encoded in the human tribe or conscience).

priest: a religious functionary usually primarily concerned with performing sacrifices, rituals, and at least semiofficial interpretations of doctrine and morals. Priests tended to arise alongside writing and to become the custodians of the religious lore that multiplied after writing, but one can find ritualists in oral societies who fit most of the rest of the priest's profile. Priests may be innovators, prophets, or mystics, but as priests they tend to have debts to tradition and the current religious establishment that make them conservators rather than innovators. Frequently, priests become specialists in law and other verbal occupations—preaching, teaching—and sometimes this leads them to overstress the mental, conceptual, or semantic sides of religion. As concerned with sacrifice, priests mediate between heaven and earth, trying to placate the deity and sympathetically represent human needs before the heavenly throne.

profane: the opposite of sacred; that which exists outside the shrine or realm of the holy; ordinary reality when taken without reference to its ultimate source or goal. Scholars debate the usefulness and applicability of the twin terms *sacred* and *profane,* usually agreeing that many traditions themselves have equivalent notions but disagreeing about how precise or ultimate the notions are. For on the one hand virtually all peoples have separated off certain times and places as special—holy, given over to divinity, deserving of respect or even awe—whereas on the other hand they have thought that the divine could invade any realm and so have put brackets around mental or physical efforts to make airtight distinctions between the holy and the ordinary or even the depraved. Modern Western consciousness has increased humanity's general sense of profanity by removing many portions of reality from the divine influence. Thus the processes of nature, and many of the processes of the human mind and social consensus, now tend to be viewed as implying nothing sacred—nothing showing the direct imprint of the transcendent, other, holy reality traditionally called God. How much here is perception and how much ontology remains unclear. What presently is very clear is the difference, if not antagonism, between secular outlooks in terms of which virtually everything is profane and religious outlooks that suspect that everything positive is a gift of God and that with a properly contemplative or mystical spirit normal people could appreciate them as such.

rite of passage: a ceremony in which one moves from one state to another, for example, from puberty to adulthood, or from life to death. The great stages regularly ritualized as passages through the life cycle have been birth, puberty, marriage, and death. Many peoples have conceived of human time as an ongoing initiation, and the rituals of traditional peoples have carried the motif of further disclosures of tribal wisdom. The rites themselves tend to create a free zone, different from ordinary existence, in which people may bond in fresh and deeper ways and their ordinary identities are laid aside. One finds analogies to rites of passage, therefore, in such other ritual occasions as the Islamic Hajj and the Western Mardi Gras.

ritual: ceremonial action designed to express a people's beliefs, fears, and hopes. Rituals allow people to participate in their myths and dramatize their beliefs, so that they make a full, psychosomatic impact.

sacred: holy, more real and significant than ordinary reality, purer and deserving purer handling. The sacred stands in contrast to the profane, which is experienced as nonultimate, secular, business-as-usual, perhaps even sullied. Sacredness often elicits piety, as people experience the goodness of what is most ultimate and perhaps has been merciful to them. Awe, fear, and intoxication also may result from dealings with the sacred, as the exalted spirit either appreciates the blinding holiness and power of the sacred or loses its footing in the world. Cultures differ as to how they conceive of the sacred, but virtually all premodern cultures agreed that sacredness was the crux of meaning. In modern times secularity has risen to challenge and purify sacredness, but also to tempt humanity to try to do without sacredness—a move most religious people think disastrous.

sorcery: the use of power gained from evil spirits. Sorcery is like black magic or negative witchcraft in seeking to use its powers for harm. It usually depends on a world view in which impersonal powers can be brought to one's side or spiritual forces may be divided into those serving evil spirits and those serving good. Thus in some situations sorcery has meant diabolism—the attempt to gain and serve satanic powers.

taboo: a Polynesian word used to designate something one should avoid because of its sacral or dangerous character. Scholars tend to associate taboos with nonliterate or tribal religious traditions, but one easily finds analogies in literate and civilizational traditions. Thus, while it is clearly a taboo when Eskimos avoid contact with the seals in certain periods, or when any tribal group segregates menstruating women, it is arguably something quite the same when Jews establish kosher laws and Muslims, Buddhists, and some Christians proscribe alcohol. The common denominator in most taboos, when they are viewed psychologically, is that one is to avoid particular items not because it can be shown they are simply evil or opposed to sacredness but because cultural factors have linked these items with the human spirit's general needs to defend itself against violations of nature's strange (never fully knowable) laws, or to keep its tribe distinctive, or to preserve a sense of cleanliness that it tends to equate with godliness.

totem: an animal, plant, or other object that serves as a clan emblem. The totem suggests the symbiosis between human and animal life. A clan usually thinks of its totem as a helper, as well as a symbol of its special qualities. Thus an eagle could be a messenger from heaven, as well as a symbol of freedom and speed. A bear could be a source of wisdom about the ways of the forest, as well as an emblem of strength. It would be natural to speak to the clan totem, venerate it in regular rites, and let it summarize the whole animal economy on which one's people depended for food and clothing.

Trickster: a figure found in many nonliterate societies who usually plays a part in founding the tribe's culture and shows a deceitful, clownlike, yet powerful character. Trickster has struck some psychoanalytically inclined observers as a projection of the id—the faculty or source of irrational human impulses. Often the myths about Trickster deal with inordinate appetites—for food, sex, rascality. Trickster tends to perform gross, scatalogical pranks, and overall may often have been a safety valve—a way for a people to project their animal appetites, mock law and order, and tame with humor the destructive potential in their instinctual makeup. The pranks played by Susanoo, the wind, on the Shinto sun queen Amaterasu are a good example of tricksterish behavior.

witch: one who performs sorcery or magic with evil intent; or simply a wise woman rooted in the pre-Christian traditions of European religion. Witches could be advocates of naturalistic methods of healing, childbearing, and worship. They could be people stigmatized as social deviants. Some were men (warlocks), but most have been women. When engaged in sorcery, witches tried to tap powers of animals or malign spirits. In societies that both accredited witchcraft and feared it as a source of black magic, people proven to be witches could be marked for death.

INTERLUDE

ASIAN RELIGIONS

Building on Chapters 1 and 2, we may introduce the Asian religions by noting how they manifest ancient, nonliterate aspects of religious thought and activity. In India, for example, ancient religious interests have long remained vital. The veneration of life forces, sex, and natural phenomena has long been popular. Similarly, a keen sense of the sacred and a rich body of rituals and mythology link Hinduism and Buddhism to oral traditions. Neither of these great Indian religions took a predominantly shamanist turn, but through the early literature of both shines the magic of the spoken word. Thus, both employ oral elements in a new synthesis rather than casting them away or leaving them behind.

From the Vedas (the Hindu scriptures) and the Tripitaka (the Buddhist scriptures), though, we can sense that Indian religion early distinguished itself from the traditions of shamanist peoples by developing a strong tradition of yoga. *Yoga* means "discipline," especially the interior discipline of meditation. Since prehistoric times, Indian yogis have given their culture an appreciation of spirituality and a profound hunger for peace by going deep into their own consciousnesses. Though some Indian meditators and philosophers studied psychology and epistemology (the structures of human awareness and knowledge), most pursued a wisdom lying beneath the rational mind. Sitting in a stable position, such as the lotus, most yogis tried to bring their consciousness to "one-pointedness"; that is, they focused on mental awareness itself rather than on its images, thoughts, or feelings. Heightening their sense of psychosomatic unity through regular breathing and other techniques, they strove for what Mircea Eliade has called *enstasis*—self-possession.

Etymologically, enstasis is the opposite of ecstasis. Where ecstasis goes out, enstasis goes in. Thus, the shaman and the yogi present a dramatic contrast. The former specializes in techniques that take the spirit out to travel, the latter in techniques that settle the spirit down at home. The religion of civilized India seems to have stepped away from the ancient shamanic mind through a disciplined search for spiritual autonomy or self-possession. Instead of wild singing and hair-raising flights of imagination, it emptied the mind of imagination to achieve tranquillity and trance. Probably from these states Indians got their intui-

tions of Hindu **moksha** or Buddhist **nirvana**—of release from the burdensome human condition.

We will strive to justify this hypothesis throughout two fairly long chapters, thereby assuring that our contrast between ancient and contemporary Indian religion not be simpleminded. In its bhakti or devotional religion, for instance, India was quite ecstatic. In its mythology of the gods and heroes, it was quite imaginative. Still, you might begin your move from nonliterate to Indian religion by paying special attention to the yogic strain. For after all due qualification, yoga remains a distinctively Indian concept, a characteristic feature of the Hindu-Buddhist religious mind.

The chapters on Chinese and Japanese religion present an analogous situation. From prehistoric times, shamanism and a concern for the sacred prevailed in both lands. Both the Chinese and Japanese were ritualist, and both generated full mythologies. In Confucianism and Taoism, though, China discarded the ancient religious mind somewhat. By stressing ethics and nature's "Way" (Tao), respectively, these two Chinese traditions forged the foundation of a vast civilized religion. (Buddhism's arrival in China strengthened this foundation.) The result was a culture that was quite formal, socially stratified, and yet aesthetic. Moreover, China developed a culture of apparent permanence, surviving numerous social upheavals through its blend of religious and ethnic spirit.

The case is somewhat different with Japan, because the native Japanese religion, Shinto, has a quite ancient point of view. In it nature bulks large, and shamanist elements are strong. However, Japan, like China, adopted Confucian, Taoist, and Buddhist influences. Together with an articulate, self-conscious Shintoism, Japan like China developed a civilized religion that has been both formal and aesthetic. Thus, formalism and aesthetics distinguish the East Asian religions from ancient shamanism.

The East Asian sage is a quite elegant figure. If the shaman is an impressive ecstatic and the Indian yogi an impressive enstatic, the East Asian sage is a sober, worldly, yet graceful dancer to the Tao—to nature's song. That, too, is impressive.

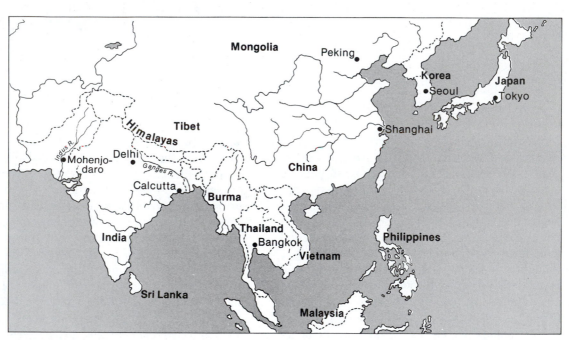

Figure 12 *Asia.*

CHAPTER 3

HINDUISM

(Hindu) Om: Mantra expressing the unity of reality

HISTORY

Our sketch of the historical evolution of Hinduism unfolds in six chronological phases: the pre-Vedic phase; the Vedic phase; the phase of native challenges to Vedic orthodoxy; the phase when Hindus responded to such challenges by reforming, renovating, and elaborating the Vedic tradition; the phase when outside, modern Western ideas challenged reformed Hinduism, and the present phase—what we might call recent or contemporary Hinduism. Naturally, these phases overlap, since ideas and practices from early periods often have continued to exert great influence. Indeed, there is a sense in which all of the last five phases in our schema are "Vedic," since virtually all Hindus have accepted to some degree the proposition that the Vedas enshrine what we might call the constitutional beginnings of their culture (much as virtually all Christians could consider all twenty centuries of Christian history biblical, because all were informed by the New Testament).

Moreover, for an idea or practice to be challenged did not necessarily mean that it ceased or immediately was reformed. Overall, however, we find this six-phased description of how Hinduism has unfolded faithful to the historical data. The organic character

Hinduism: Twenty-five Key Dates	
ca. 2750 B.C.E.	Growth of Civilization in Indus Valley
ca. 1500	Aryan Invasions; Vedic Literature
800–400	Upanishads
600–500	Challenges of Mahavira and Buddha
ca. 500	Aryans as Far South as Sri Lanka
500–200	Epic Poetry: Mahabharata (Bhagavad Gita), Ramayana
322	Chandragupta Founds Mauryan Empire
100 B.C.E.–100 C.E.	Rise of Bhakti Literature
480 C.E.	Fall of Gupta Empire
680	Flourishing of Tamil Bhakti Movement
788–820	Shankara, Leading Philosopher
800–900	Rise of Hindu Orthodoxy
1017–1137	Ramanuja, Leading Philosopher
1175	First Muslim Empire in India
1485–1533	Chaitanya, Leader of Krishna-Bhakti
1498	Vasco da Gama Visits India
1526	Beginning of Mogul Dynasty
1653	Completion of Taj Mahal
1690	British Found Calcutta
1707	Decline of Mogul Power
1818	Beginning of British Rule
1869–1948	Mahatma Gandhi
1885	Founding of Indian National Congress
1947	Indian Independence; Partition of Pakistan
1971	Founding of Bangladesh

of Hindu culture, which has stemmed from Indians' tendency not to discard previous ideas and practices so much as to place new ones alongside them, means that one can seldom be precise about what was waxing when and what was waning. But one can suggest the "additive" logic of the Hindu religious story by noting the new ideas and movements that slowly enlarged Hinduism into the rich and varied entity one finds today.

Pre-Vedic India

Before the first invasions of Aryans from the northwest around 2000 B.C.E., an impressive Indian culture already existed. Its beginnings stretch back to the second interglacial period (400,000–200,000 B.C.E.), and its earliest religion, if we conjecture on the basis of ancient peoples living in India today, was shamanist, focusing on the worship of nature—especially on the life force. In 1924, excavations at two sites along the Indus River, called Harrapa and Mohenjo-daro, furnished the first extensive evidence of a high ancient Indian culture. This culture, called the Harrapan, stretched over about 500,000 square miles[1] and was distributed in small towns between the two "capitals" of Harrapa and Mohenjo-daro. Other excavations in what is now Pakistan have disclosed cultures predating the Harrapan, but this Indus Valley culture is the larg-est source of information about pre-Aryan Indian ways. Carbon dating suggests that the Harrapan cul-ture flourished about 2150–1750 B.C.E., and some evi-dence suggests that the culture was remarkably stable throughout that period.

Harrapa and Mohenjo-daro seem to have had pop-ulations of 30,000 to 40,000. Both were about one mile square. That few weapons have been found suggests that their people were not very warlike. Outside each city was a citadel, which was probably used for worship rather than for military defense. There were large granaries in the cities, two-room apartments nearby for the granary workers, and high city walls. Most building was done with kiln-dried bricks, which were standardized at 3 by 10 by 20 inches. Through the city ran an excellent sewage disposal system, with terra-cotta pipes and manholes through which workmen could enter to clean the pipes. The houses were mul-tistoried dwellings with thick walls and flat roofs. Out-side stairways to the roofs suggest that people slept there on hot nights.

The entire city plan suggests orderliness: Streets were wide and rectilinear, houses had chutes for slid-ing trash down into collection bins, and apartments had bathrooms and toilets. Larger buildings included a bathhouse 108 by 180 feet, with a tank 20 feet wide by 39 feet long by 8 feet deep. If this tank was used like similar ones outside Hindu temples today, proba-bly its purpose was ritual bathing.

Some of the most significant remains from the Harrapan culture are small sandstone seals, engraved with a pictorial script and apparently used to mark property. They are decorated with various animals, both real and imaginary, and indicate a modest eco-nomic and artistic life. Other interesting finds include a small bronze statue of a dancing girl, lithe and graceful, and a red sandstone sculpture of the torso of a young man, also artistically impressive. Some schol-ars hypothesize that these finds indicate creative po-tential that was stifled by conservative forces, but others logically suggest that these artifacts are the only remains we have of a rather vigorous art whose other products perished. The first scholars, in their interpretations of pre-Aryan culture, believed that the artistry of the Harrapans was static and even monoto-nous, and that it changed little over 400 years. The uniformity in the bricks and buildings suggests a strong deterrent to innovation, and the people were likely ruled by autocratic priests, who insisted on con-formity to a theopolitical tradition based on worship at the religious citadels and lavatory tanks. Since the mid-1960s, however, this interpretation has been dis-puted because of scholars' both finding new artifacts and learning of comparably stable groups that did not have autocratic priests. Though much of what we know of the Harrapan culture does suggest stability, it probably had its ups and downs, like most other cultures.

By about 1500 B.C.E., the Harrapan culture was destroyed, after perhaps a millennium and a half of existence. (Most scholars postulate a long growth pe-riod before the 400 years of prosperity.) The destruc-tive Aryan conquerers were a pastoral and nomadic people who loved fighting, racing, drinking, and other aspects of the warrior life. They probably came from the north, where the cooler climate favored such vigor, and they thought of themselves as the salt of the earth—their name means "from the earth" or "no-ble." (This name survives in *Iran* and *Eire;* in addition, all European languages save Finnish, Hungarian, and Basque are related to the Aryans' language.)

The Aryans had fair skin and pointed noses, a fact perhaps responsible for their hostile reaction to the dark, snub-nosed Harrapans. They moved by horse, ate meat, and hunted with bow and arrow. There is no evidence that they ever learned to navigate or sail, and they produced no striking art, although they did know about iron and fashioned good weapons. Like many other warrior, nomadic peoples (for example, the Celts), they loved storytelling and singing. Indeed, their culture and religion were highly verbal. Their society was male dominated, with a primarily patriar-chal family structure, priesthood, and cast of gods.[2] Above all, they were mobile, pushing through Greece, Italy, Iran, and India. After 2000 B.C.E., they were strong enough to dominate the native Indians, but they may have started trickling into India from the northwest as much as 2,000 years previously.

Troy Wilson Organ suggests that the Aryans' fa-vorite god, Indra, whom we shall study when we turn to the *Rig-Veda,* was a projection or personification of their own sense of character.[3] He was exuberant and warlike—a boaster, a thunderbolt thrower, a big drinker, a slayer of dragons. He ruled by seizure rather than inheritance, loved action rather than stability. Thus, according to Aryan myth, Indra aggressively seized the waters of heaven, released them, and fash-ioned the earth. Some have suggested that Indra was first a culture hero and only later a leading god, but from their earliest time in India, the Aryans undoubt-edly looked to him as the source and model of their prowess in war. Even in his fondness for drinking Indra was a great model, for what hardy people has not sanctioned its love of drink?

Two peoples thus contributed to the beginnings of Hindu culture. If the Harrapan culture was representative, the people who came before the Aryans in the Indus Valley were stable, even conservative, city dwellers who perhaps developed (or took from earlier peoples) important fertility rites. The Aryans were a rough, fighting people who had a much simpler technology than the Harrapans but whose poetry and religion perhaps were imaginative. These Aryans became the dominant force militarily and politically, imposing their will and their gods (*devas*) on the subjugated Harrapan (or Dravidian) natives. Inasmuch as the Aryans produced the Vedas, their culture always had more official status.

However, Indian culture never lost its Dravidian features, especially in the less Aryanized south. At most they were dormant for a while. After the demise of Vedic culture, Dravidian interests in fertility re-emerged (the Aryans had their own fertility interests). The complex devotionalism of later Hinduism is best explained in terms of many non-Aryan factors.

Vedic India

By Vedism most scholars mean the culture resulting from the mixture of Aryans, Harrapans, and other peoples of the Indus and Ganges valleys. This culture expressed itself in the earliest Indian writings, which are a collection of religious songs, hymns, spells, rituals, and speculations called the Vedas. It is convenient to consider them as representing the first stages of Hinduism, for although later India abandoned many of the Vedic gods and practices, the Vedas retained scriptural status throughout the later centuries, weaving themselves deeply into India's fabric.

The word *veda* means "wisdom" (cognates are the English *wit* and the German *wissen*). The Vedic pieces were originally oral. In fact, the proto-Hindus considered human speech divine, so singing and praying to the gods became sacred actions. Scholars have found that the Aryans composed some of the hymns found in the oldest Vedic literature before they entered India. The hymns honoring the sky and the dawn, for instance, are remarkably like the religious literature of other Indo-Europeans, indicating that they go back to the time before the Aryans split into their Iranian and Indian branches.

Consider, for example, the following lovely verses in praise of Varuna, the *deva* of moral order:

> He has put intelligence in hearts, fire in the waters, the sun in the sky, and the *soma* plant on the hills. . . . I will speak of the mysterious deed [*maya*] of Varuna renowned, the Lord immortal, who, standing in the firmament, has measured out the earth, as it were, with a yardstick. (*Rig-Veda* 5:85:2,5)

To the traditional Hindu, the Vedic literature represents the highest intuitive knowledge that the *rishis* (holy persons or seers) had attained.[4] The technical term denoting such a state of wisdom is **shruti,** which translators often render as "revelation." *Shruti* does not connote that divinities outside the human realm broke through the veil separating heaven and earth in order to impart light from above; as we shall see, Hinduism does not have such a remote view of the divine. Rather, *shruti* implies that the eminent holy person has heard certain things in peak experiences (often induced by the ritual drink soma). Therefore, Vedic literature, representing what the *rishis* had heard, was considered the best and holiest presentation of knowledge.

The Vedas consist of four separate collections of materials. Together, these four collections are known as the *Samhitas*. *Samhitas* therefore can be a synonym for Vedas. The individual collections are called the *Rig-Veda, Sama-Veda, Yajur-Veda,* and *Atharva-Veda.* The *Rig-Veda* is the oldest, largest, and most important. It contains more than a thousand *suktas,* or individual units, which are hymns to the *devas,* magical poems, riddles, legends, and the like. They show considerable learning and poetic skill, which argue against their being the spontaneous poetry of freewheeling warriors or rude peasants. More likely, they represent the work of priestly leaders—the careful creation of an educated class concerned with regulating contact with the gods and maintaining its own social status.

Most of the *Rig-Veda*'s hymns have two purposes. First, they praise the god being addressed; second, they ask the god for favors or benefits. For instance, the *Rig-Veda* praises Agni for deeds that show the splendor of his status as the god of fire. (These deeds appear to be not so much mythical allusions to feats that the god performed in the beginning as similes drawn from human experience. For example, Agni's flame is like the warrior's battle rush: As the warrior blazes upon the enemy, so the god of fire blazes through the brush or woods.) Then, having admired the god, the hymn singer makes his petition. In *Rig-Veda* 6:6 he asks for wealth: "wealth giving splendor, . . . wealth bright and vast with many heroes."

Though this ritual exchange is the most usual focus, the *Rig-Veda* has other interests. For instance, it includes petitions for forgiveness of sins (such as having wronged a brother, cheated at games, or abused a stranger) which indicate a developed moral sense. Although the *Rig-Veda* may not separate itself completely from an ancient worldview, where being out of phase with the cosmic processes is almost physically dangerous, it provides solid evidence of a religion centering on free, responsible choices made for good or evil. As well, some of the hymns of the *Rig-Veda* are speculative, wondering about the source of the many phenomena of the world. A famous speculative text is 10:129, where the poet muses about the creation of the world. At the beginning there was no being and no nonbeing, no air and no sky beyond. It was, in fact, a time before either death or immortal life had begun. Then only the One existed, drawn into being by heat that interacted with the primal waters and the void. However, from desire the One started to think and emit fertile power. Thus, impulse from above and energy from below began to make the beings of the world. But, the hymn asks in conclusion, who knows whether this speculation is valid? Even the gods were born after the world's beginning, so who can say what happened? Only one who surveys everything from the greatest high heaven knows, if indeed even that being knows.

The Vedic Gods. A study of the Vedic gods suggests what the earliest Hindus thought about the deepest forces in their world. The gods are many and complex (tradition said there were 330 million), but of course a few stand out as the most important. Indeed, for many later sages, all the gods were manifestations of a single underlying divinity: "They call it Indra, Mitra, Varuna, Agni, or again the celestial bird Garutman; the one reality the sages call by various names . . ." (*Rig-Veda* 1, 164.46). They are all *devas* (good divinities), as distinguished from *asuras* (evil divinities). (In Iran the terminology is just the reverse, suggesting that the Iranian-Indian split may have been theological.[5]) The Vedas cast most *devas* in human or animal form. Since the main feature of the *devas* was power, we may consider them functional forces: the warmth of

the sun, the energy of the storm, and so on. To express these larger-than-life qualities, later Indian artists often gave the *devas* supernumerary bodily parts. An extra pair of arms, for instance, would indicate prowess in battle; an extra eye would indicate ability to discern events at a distance. Typically, a *deva* was a male deity associated with a female consort, who represented his energetic force (*shakti*). (In developed Hindu speculation, the male principle was passive, or cool.) Later, Tantrist Hinduism focused on *shakti*, sometimes through the practice of ritual sex.

By textual analysis, scholars have uncovered different generations of the Vedic gods. The oldest group consists of the gods of the sky and the earth that the Vedas share with other Indo-European religious texts. For instance, the Vedic Father Sky (Dyaus Pitar) is related to the Greek Zeus and the Roman Jupiter. Like them, he is the overarching power that fertilizes the receptive earth with rain and rays of sun. The Vedic earth is the Great Mother, the fertile female.[6] These deities are not the most prominent Vedic gods, but they echo in the background as the oldest.

The second oldest group, whose age is confirmed by Iranian parallels, includes Indra, Mithra, Varuna, Agni, and Soma. As noted, Indra was the warrior god of the storm much beloved by the Aryan conquerors. Mithra was the god of the sun. Varuna was the god of cosmic and moral order, and Soma was the god of the exhilarating cultic drink. Known in Iran as *haoma*, soma gave visions so dazzling that it became integral to the sacramental cult (scholars dispute whether the drink was hallucinogenic). Agni, finally, was the god of fire, whose importance increased as the sacrifice focused more and more on fire. It is worth noting that most of the deities in this second generation represent earthly and especially heavenly forces. Perhaps the storm, the sun, and the sky were all originally joined in Dyaus Pitar, but later they became separate objects of devotion.

The third generation of gods includes Brahma, Vishnu, and Shiva. They arose after the Aryans arrived in India and so perhaps indicate Dravidian influences. We shall consider them more fully below.

Finally, the fourth generation, which comes to the fore in the philosophical texts called the Upanishads, comprises abstract deities such as One God, That One, Who, and the Father of Creation (Eka Deva, Tad Ekam, Ka, and Prajapati).[7] Upanishadic seers had become dissatisfied with the concrete, world-affirming outlook at the core of the *Rig-Veda* and searched for simpler, more spiritual notions.

Overall, then, we find a development within the Vedic literature from an acceptance of many divinities, to a desire for unity, and then to a focus on knowledge that culminated in the Upanishads. On the way to the Upanishads, however, Indians went through a period when rituals were all-important.

Brahmanism. In the early Vedic period, the sacrifice was quite simple. It required no elaborate rituals, no temples, no images—only a field of cut grass, some ghee (clarified butter) for the fire, and soma (some poured onto the ground for the gods and some drunk by the participants). Later the sacrifice became more elaborate, involving the chanting of magical sounds, reenacting the world's creation, and slaying a variety of animals.[8] Since this elaboration went hand in hand with the increasing importance of the priest (brahmin, or brahman), commentators often refer to sacrificial Vedic religion as Brahmanism. Always, however, the sacrifice intended to make human beings holy by giving them an operational way to please the gods.

Brahmanism reached its greatest elaboration with the horse sacrifice, a ceremony that lasted more than a year. In the first step of this complicated ritual, attendants bathed a young white horse, fed it wheat cakes for three days, consecrated it by fire, and then released it and let it wander for a year. Princes and soldiers followed the horse, conquering all territory through which it traveled. After one year, servants brought the horse back to the palace. During the next new moon, the king shaved his head and beard. After an all-night vigil at the sacred fire, the queens went to the horse at dawn, anointed it, and decorated it with pearls. A sacrifice of 609 selected animals, ranging from the elephant to the bee (and sometimes a human), followed.

The sacrifice reached its climax after attendants slaughtered the horse itself and placed a blanket over it. The most important queen then slipped under the blanket to have (simulated?) sexual intercourse with the horse, while the other queens and the priests shouted obscene encouragements. After this, participants ate the horse in a ritual meal. The entire ceremony fits the pattern of ancient celebrations of the new year, which often involved sacrifices and orgies designed to renew the world's fertility. Most of the symbolism centers on the virility of the king, in whose person the people hope to find strength like that of a lusty stallion.

Caste. When one considers the distinctive organization of traditional Indian society that goes back to the Vedic roots, the word **caste** comes to mind. In fact, it is a Western word, covering two distinct though related native Indian concepts and phenomena. The first native concept has been conveyed through the word *varna,* the original meaning of which is uncertain but perhaps had connections with "color." Varna mainly has referred to the division of social ranks and tasks developed by the Aryans and established by them as regulative for the India that they came to dominate. Although this social structure became more pronounced and influential in India than in the other areas (Iran, northern Europe) where Aryan ancestral stock (the proto-Indo-Europeans) prevailed, one finds that ancient Persians, Celts, Greeks, and others shared its general delineation of the main social classes. This delineation was into the three groups of priests, nobles or warriors, and commoners/farmers/merchants.

As has been true in other ancient cultures, India did not think of its social structure as designed, worked out, by human beings who might well have fashioned things quite differently. It did not think varna had arisen the way one might divide a present-day business organization into executives, managers, and secretaries, or the way one might divide an army into generals, majors, and privates. No, India thought of varna as part of the divinely ordered cosmos—part of the heavenly scheme of things. Thus the *Rig-Veda* (10:90) speaks of a primal sacrifice of a protohuman being that gave society its four varnas (India added servants). Later, the most influential law code, that attributed to Manu, repeated such Vedic justification, tying the ways Indians had come to think of their principal social classes to the divinely given order of things.

The second native Indian word usually covered by the English "caste" is *jati,* which refers to the many particular, familial, clanlike groups that have made Indian society a complex quilt of separable yet tangent entities. As one recent study of varna and jati puts it: "There are thousands of *jatis* scattered throughout the subcontinent, and they vary widely in their attributes and characteristics. Each is characterized by a set of rules governing acceptable occupations, foods, associations (that is, with members of other *jatis*), marriage rules (concerning widow remarriage, for example), and much else. European observers have long been particularly interested in three areas of *jati* regulation: the rule of endogamy [the necessity of marrying within one's own jati], the presence of a characteristic (or at least traditional) *jati* occupation, and the rules whereby *jatis* in proximity rank themselves and each other."[9]

In practice, this has all meant that most Indians have not grown up free to pursue what work they wished, marry as they and any with whom they established a mutual attraction might have wished, and interact with other Indians mainly on nonclannish, democratic grounds.

The simplest correlation between varna and jati, which many Hindus themselves have used, is to consider jatis subdivisions of varnas. Thus, while there might be thousands of different brahmanic jatis separating the priestly caste into various subgroups who could have only limited contact with one another, all such jatis held something in common and were more closely connected to one another than to such members of the third social echelon (the farmers/merchants) as barbers, potters, and leatherworkers. The latter three groups, although constituting different jatis that kept them apart in many significant areas of daily life, shared membership in the third social echelon and so were closer than they could be to priests, warriors, or the lower-class workers of the fourth echelon.

Most Indians have considered both varna and jati related to, indeed, derived from, their karma (a concept we discuss shortly). In other words, both aspects of social status have come under the general Indian assumption that one's movement (toward release from the painful human condition or away from such release) was a constant byplay between individual choices and outward circumstances (such as one's work, extended family, and geographic area).

The Upanishads.   Before the end of the Vedic period, Brahmanism declined for at least two reasons. First, common sense dictated that society had more to do than listen to priests chant all day. The texts imply that even during the times of the *Rig-Veda*, people were unhappy with the priests' constant prating. A satire in 7:103, for instance, likens them to frogs croaking over the waters. Second, intellectuals desired something more satisfying than an understanding of sacrifice that tended to remain on the surface. The

Upanishads reveal the intellectuals' turn to interiority, which resulted in sacrifice becoming less a matter of slaughter, ritual, and words and more a matter of soul cleansing and dedication to the divine powers.

The word *Upanishad* connotes the secret teaching that one receives at the feet of a guru. Out of hundreds of treatises (over the period from 800 to 300 B.C.E.), a few Upanishads came to the fore.[10] They show that the intellectuals embraced a variety of styles and ideas and that their movement was poetic as much as philosophical. Whether poetic or philosophical, though, the movement's goal was quite religious: intuitive knowledge of ultimate truths, of the unity behind the many particulars of reality.

The Upanishads themselves do not agree on whether the unity behind everything is personal, impersonal, or a mixture of the two. However, they do tend to use two words in discussing it, both of which are more impersonal than personal. The first word is **Brahman**, which generally means the first principle, cause, or stuff of the objective world. Brahman, in other words, is the final answer for the Upanishadic thinkers who wondered about how things are founded—especially things in the material world.

The second word, **atman**, means the vital principle or deepest identity of the subject—the soul or self. Probing this reality by thought and meditation, the Upanishadic seers moved away from Vedic materiality to spirituality. The internal world, the world of atman and thought, was a world of *spirit*.

Combining these new concepts of Brahman and atman, some of the Upanishadic seers found a coincidence—the basic reality within and without, of self and the world, was the same. Atman is Brahman. So in the Chandogya Upanishad 6:1:3, the father Uddalaka teaches his son Shvetaketu that Shvetaketu himself *is*, most fundamentally, Brahmanic ultimate reality: *Tat tvam asi* ("That thou art"). The soul and the stuff of the world are but two sides of the same single "be-ing" or "is-ness" that constitutes all existing things.

In the Brihad-aranyaka Upanishad, one of the most important, an interesting discussion occurs between the thoughtful woman Gargi and the sage Yajnavalkya about the ultimate "warp" of reality (the relevant definition of "warp" is "the basic foundation or material of a structure or entity"). Gargi has pressed the sage to tell her about the weave of reality: "That, O Yajnavalkya, which is above the sky, that which is beneath the earth, that which is between these two, sky and earth, that which people call the past and the present and the future—across what is that woven, warp and woof?" The sage answers that she is asking about space. Sensing that she still has not gained the final goal of her inquiry, Gargi presses one further question: "Across what then, pray, is space woven, warp and woof?" This is the capital question, eliciting from the sage the capital answer: the Imperishable.

To describe the Imperishable, Yajnavalkya launches into a long list of negatives: "It is not coarse, not fine, not short, not long, not glowing, not adhesive, without shadow and without darkness, without air and without space, without stickiness, odorless, tasteless, without eye, without ear, without voice, without wind, without energy, without breath, without mouth . . . without measure, without inside and without outside." Only by denying the limitations implied in each of these attributes can the sage suggest the unique, transcendent character of ultimate reality.

The Imperishable does not consume anything and no one consumes it. It is the commander of the sun and the moon, the earth and the sky, and all other things. Without the knowledge of the imperishable, other religious attainments are of little worth: "Verily, O Gargi, if one performs sacrifices and worship and undergoes austerity in this world for many thousands of years, but without knowing that Imperishable, limited indeed is that [work] of his." For the Imperishable is the unseen Seer, the unthought Thinker, the only One that understands. "Across this Imperishable, O Gargi, is space woven, warp and woof."

The Imperishable, then, is the Upanishadic sage's ultimate wisdom. When pressed for the material cause of things, the "that from which" everything is made, Yajnavalkya can only say "Something that is of itself, something that does not perish." This is a characteristic answer, one that many sages, West as well as East, have fashioned. Pushing off from the perishable nature of the things of sensory experience, they have conceived of the ultimate foundation of reality as other than sensible things, other indeed than anything within the range of human experience. The best we can say of the origin of the universe, the final reason for everything that exists, is that it *is* independently, in a mode that does not perish, pass away, or suffer change. To uphold the world it must be different from the world. Either in the midst of worldly flux, or apart, it must surpass the "world," the mental construct of the material and spiritual whole that we limited humans fashion.

On the other hand, the ultimate material cause of things must be enough like us, discernible by us,

to warrant our giving it negative names and seeking to know it. Were it absolutely other, completely apart from our human realm, we could not even discuss it negatively. It was by pondering this equally primordial fact that the Upanishadic seers came to focus on the human spirit or soul as the best analogue or presence of the Ultimate. This spirit or soul (atman) seemed the best candidate for the presence of the Ultimate that makes human beings exist. While they live, human beings are imperishable: something keeps them from total change and decay. Thus while they have a given identity they draw upon the Imperishable, depend upon It, and express It. Between It and them must obtain a connection, maybe even an identity. Certainly the most real part of them is the presence of the Imperishable, without which they would actually perish. So perhaps the best way to regard them (ourselves), or anything, is as a form of the Imperishable, one of its myriad extrusions or expressions. If so, one can say that, in the last analysis, only the Imperishable is real or actual or existent. Everything else at best receives a passing reality from the temporary presence to it, presence in it, of the Imperishable. For that reason, Yajnavalkya can rightly call it "that across which even space is woven, warp and woof."

For the Upanishadic thinkers, this realization was liberating because it avoided the multiplicity, externalism, and materialism that had often corroded Brahmanism. Though sacrifice and the gods continued to have a place in Upanishadic religion, they were quite subordinate to monism.

In addition, the Upanishadic thinkers felt an urgent need for liberation (*moksha*), unlike the Vedists. Perhaps echoing Buddhist beliefs, the writers of the Upanishads worked with experiences they found more dismal, depressing, and afflicting than the first Aryans had. Whereas those vigorous warriors had fought and drunk, living for the moment, these later meditative sages examined the human condition and found it sad. To express their beliefs, they fashioned the doctrines of samsara and karma, which did not appear in the early Vedas.

Samsara (the doctrine of rebirths or reincarnation) implies that the given world, the world of common sense and ordinary experience, is only provisional. It is not the ultimate existence. To take it as ultimate or fully real, therefore, is to delude oneself and thus to trap oneself in a cycle of rebirths. Only when one penetrates Brahman, the truly real, can one escape this cycle. Otherwise, one must constantly travel the scale of animal life (up or down, depending on one's advances or backslidings in wisdom).

Karma is the law that governs advancement or regression in the samsaric life of deaths and rebirths. Essentially, it is the reality that all acts have unavoidable consequences. In an almost physical way, they determine one's personality. Karma also explains one's status: A person's present life is shaped by that person's past lives. The only way to escape the round of rebirths, the pain of samsara, is to advance by meritorious deeds and be saved or freed. (Hinduism chooses to live with the illogic of a law both necessary and capable of being undercut by freedom.[11])

Case Study: The Isa Upanishad.   The Isa Upanishad, one of the shortest, offers a good specimen of the Upanishadic style. Robert Hume, a respected translator of the Upanishads into English, divides the Isa into eighteen stanzas.

The strong emotions the stanzas of the Isa display remind us that the Upanishadic seers were *religious* philosophers—people pursuing a vision that would bring them *moksha*. The Isa's passionate quest for a single principle to explain the diversity of the world's many phenomena also reinforces the impression that many of the Upanishadic seers had grown soul-sick from the complexity of Brahmanic religion.

The first stanza of the Isa announces the monistic theme: Unless we see that the Lord (Isa) envelops all that exists, we misunderstand reality. There must be a stable principle giving rest to all the moving things. Religious people renounce all these moving things and so come to enjoy human life. Such renunciation takes them away from coveting the wealth or possessions of other people, which so frequently is a cause of sadness.

Stanza two develops this basis of freedom. It is possible to live in the world, performing the duties of one's station, without being attached to one's deeds. In that case, the deed (*karman*) does not adhere to the personality or weight it down. Detachment therefore is the antidote to karma. If one is free from concern about the effects of one's actions, one can work for *moksha*.

But, as stanza three emphasizes, those who do not detach themselves receive a stern punishment after death. If they have slain the Self (the presence of Brahman within) by desirous, badly motivated deeds, they will go to dark worlds ruled by devils.

Stanza four shifts back to a positive viewpoint. The One that does not move, that stands free of the changing things of the world, is swifter than the human mind and senses. Wisdom is placing one's action in this One, reposing one's self in what is so swift it is stable.

Human life therefore faces a paradox, as stanza five shows. The principle underlying everything that exists seems both to move and not to move. Insofar as it is the inmost reality of whatever exists, it moves in all things' movement. Insofar as it gives all these things their basis, it is free of their movement, self-possessed rather then dependent on another. So, too, the One can be both far and near, both outside and within any being of the samsaric world.

Stanza six suggests a focus to bring this blur into clarity. By looking on all beings as though they reposed in the Self (the world's soul), and looking at the Self as though it were present in all things, the wise person stays close to the Brahman that is the world's ultimate significance.

According to stanza seven, the profit in this focus is the freedom from delusion and sorrow it brings. The person who perceives the unity of reality, seeing the single Self everywhere, achieves a knowledge and joy that the ignorant, mired in the world's multiplicity, never know.

This leads, in stanza eight, to an imaginative flourish. Picturing the world ruler, the human being who has realized full human potential, the Isa unfurls a flag of glowing attributes: wise, intelligent, comprehensive, self-sufficient. By dealing with what is bright, bodiless, pure, and unaffected by evil (by dealing with the Self), this person has reached the summit, come to stand close to eternity.

Stanzas nine and ten are quite mystical, probing the nature of religious enlightenment. If those who worship ignorance (who neglect the Self) go into a blind darkness, those who delight in true knowledge go into a greater darkness or mystery, a state beyond the dichotomy between knowledge and nonknowledge. The wise people who have handed down Vedic wisdom confirm this: Enlightenment and *moksha* are mysterious.

Stanza eleven adds another dimension: The wise person, holding knowledge and nonknowledge together, passes over death and gains immortality.

ĪŚĀ UPANISHAD[1] [12]

Recognition of the unity underlying the diversity of the world

1. By the Lord (*īśā*) enveloped must this all be—
   Whatever moving thing there is in the moving world.
   With this renounced, thou mayest enjoy.
   Covet not the wealth of anyone at all.

Non-attachment of deeds on the person of a renouncer

2. Even while doing deeds here,
   One may desire to live a hundred years.
   Thus on thee—not otherwise than this is it—
   The deed (*karman*) adheres not on the man.

The forbidding future for slayers of the Self

3. Devilish (*asurya*[2]) are those worlds called,[3]
   With blind darkness (*tamas*) covered o'er!
   Unto them, on deceasing, go
   Whatever folk are slayers[4] of the Self.[5]

The all-surpassing, paradoxical world-being

4. Unmoving, the One (*ekam*) is swifter than the mind.
   The sense-powers (*deva*) reached not It, speeding on before.
   Past others running, This goes standing.
   In It Mātariśvan places action.[6]

5. It moves.   It moves not.
   It is far, and It is near.
   It is within all this,
   And It is outside of all this.[1]

6. Now, he who on all beings
   Looks as just (*eva*) in the Self (*Ātman*),
   And on the Self as in all beings—[2]
   He does not shrink away from Him.[3]

7. In whom all beings
   Have become just (*eva*) the Self of the discerner—
   Then what delusion (*moha*), what sorrow (*śoka*) is there
   Of him who perceives the unity!

Characteristics of the world-ruler

8. He has environed. The bright, the bodiless, the scatheless,
   The sinewless, the pure (*śuddha*), unpierced by evil (*a-pāpa-viddha*)!
   Wise (*kavi*), intelligent (*manīsin*), encompassing (*paribhū*), self-existent (*svayamblū*),
   Appropriately he distributed objects (*artha*) through the eternal years.

Transcending, while involving, the antithesis of knowing

9. Into blind darkness enter they
   That worship ignorance;
   Into darkness greater than that, as it were, they
   That delight in knowledge.[4]

10. Other, indeed, they say, than knowledge!
    Other, they say, than non-knowledge![5]
    —Thus we have heard from the wise (*dhīra*)
    Who to us have explained It.[6]

---

[1]So called from its first word; or sometimes 'Īāsāvāsyam' from its first two words; or sometimes the 'Vājasaneyi-Samhitā Upanishad' from the name of the recension of the White Yajur-Veda of which this Upanishad forms the final, the fortieth, chapter.

[2]Compare the persons called 'devilish,' *āsura*, at Chānd. 8. 8. 5. A variant reading here (accordant with a literalism interpreted in the following line) is *a-sūrya*, 'sunless.'

[3]The word *nāma* here might mean 'certainly' instead of 'called.'

[4]This idea is in apparent contrast with the doctrine of Katha 2. 19 d (and BhG. 2. 19), where it is stated that 'he [i.e., the Self] slays not, is not slain.' The word *ātma-han* here, of course, is metaphorical, like 'smother,' 'stifle,' 'completely supress.'

[5]The whole stanza is a variation of Brih. 4. 4. 11.

[6]So Com. But *apas* may refer, cosmogonically, to 'the [primeval] waters.'

---

[1]The very same ideas as in this stanza, though not all the same words, recur at BhG. 13. 15 a, b, d.

[2]This universal presence is claimed by Krishna for himself at BhG. 6. 30 a, b.

[3]The indefinite word *tatas* may mean 'from these beings,' or 'from this Self,' or 'from this time on,' or pregnantly all these. The whole line recurs at Brih. 4. 4. 15 d; Katha 4. 5d; 4. 12 d.

[4]This stanza is identical with Brih. 4. 4. 10.

[5]The point here made is that both knowledge and lack of knowledge are inadequate for apprehending the Ultimate.

[6]A somewhat more concrete, and perhaps earlier, form of this stanza occurs as Kena 3 e–h.

11. Knowledge and non-knowledge—
    He who this pair conjointly (*saha*) knows,
    With non-knowledge passing over death,
    With knowledge wins the immortal.[1]

The inadequacy of any antithesis of being

12. Into blind darkness enter they
    Who worship non-being (*a-sambhūti*);
    Into darkness greater than that, as it were,
        they
    Who delight in becoming (*sambhūti*).

13. Other, indeed—they say—than origin
        (*sambhava*)!
    Other—they say—than non-origin
        (*a-sambhava*)!
    —Thus have we heard from the wise
    Who to us have explained It.

Becoming and destruction a fundamental duality

14. Becoming (*sambhūti*) and destruction
        (*vināśa*)—
    He who this pair conjointly (*saha*) knows,
    With destruction passing over death,
    With becoming wins the immortal.

A dying person's prayer

15. With a golden vessel[2]
    The Real's face is covered o'er.
    That do thou, O Pūshan, uncover
    For one whose law is the Real[3] to see.[4]

16. O Nourisher (*pūsan*), the sole Seer (*ekarsi*),
        O Controller (*yama*), O Sun (*sūrya*, off-
        spring of Prajāpati, spread forth thy rays!
        Gather thy brilliance (*tejas*)![5] What is thy
        fairest form—that of thee I see. He who is
        yonder, yonder Person (*purusa*)—I myself
        am he!

17. [My] breath (*vāyu*) to the immortal wind (*an-
        ila*)![1] This body then ends in ashes! *Om!*
        O Purpose (*kratu*[2]), remember! The deed
        (*krta*) remember!
        O Purpose, remember! The deed remember!

General prayer of petition and adoration

18. O Agni, by a goodly path to prosperity (*rai*)
        lead us,
    Thou god who knowest all the ways!
    Keep far from us crooked-going sin (*enas*)![3]
    Most ample expression of adoration to thee
        would we render![4]

---

[1]This formula recurs at Brih. 5.15. The idea that at death the several parts of microcosmic man revert to the corresponding elements of the macrocosm is expressed several times in Sanskrit literature. With the specific mention here, compare 'his spirit (*ātman*) to the wind (*vāta*)' in the Cremation Hymn, RV. 10.16.3a; 'with his breath (*prāna*) to wind (*vāyu*),' Śat. Br. 10.3.3.8; 'his breath (*prāna*) to wind (*vāta*),' Brih. 3.2.13; and even of the sacrificial animal, 'its breath (*prāna*) to wind (*vāta*),' Ait. Br. 2.6.
[2]Compare the statement in Chānd. 3.14.1, 'Now, verily, a person consists of purpose (*kratu-maya*).'
[3]Other prayers for freedom from sin (*enas*, compare also *āgas*) are at RV. 1.24.9d; 3.7.10d; 7.86.3 a, 4d; 7.88.6 c; 7.89.5 c, d; 7.93.7 c, d; 8.67 (56). 17; 10.35. 3 a, c; 10.37. 12; AV. 6.97. 2 d; 6.115. 1,2,3; 6.116. 2,3; 6.117; 6.118; 6.119; 6.120.
[4]This stanza is identical with RV. 1.189.1, and the second line also with AV. 4.39.10b.

---

[1]This stanza occurs again in Maitri 7. 9.
[2]The sun.
[3]For the petitioner (who calls himself '*satya-dharma*') to see through; or 'For Him whose law is Truth (or, true) to be seen,' [as, e.g., for Savitri in RV. 10.34. 8; 10.139.3; or the Unknown Creator, RV. 10.121.9; VS.10.103; or Agni, RV. 1.12.7]; or, 'For that [neuter] which has the Real as its nature [or, essence; or, law] to be seen.'
[4]These lines occur with slight variations at Maitri 6.35 and Brih. 5.15.1.

[5]According to this translation the idea is entirely honorific of the effulgence of the sun. Or, with a different grouping of words, the meaning might possibly be the petition: 'Spread apart thy rays [that I may enter through the sun (as well as see through—according to the previous petition) into the Real; then] gather [thy rays together again, as normal]. The brilliance which is thy fairest form, . . .' At best the passage is of obscure mystical significance.

The "beyond" or transcendent character of true enlightenment appears even more clearly in stanzas twelve and thirteen. Both nonbecoming (changelessness) and becoming (change) can be illusory. The ultimate truth of Brahman transcends such oppositions. So too it transcends the opposition between origin (being the source of everything) and nonorigin (not being the source). The saving intuition that brings *moksha* takes the perceiver to another realm, where the dichotomies and antagonisms thrown up by ordinary human intelligence do not pertain.

According to stanza fourteen, this saving intuition also conjoins becoming and destruction. If one understands their relation, he can ride destruction across the chasm of death, ride becoming to the far shore of immortality.

The Isa concludes prayerfully, in stanza fifteen praising the sun as a cover of reality and asking divinity to uncover its face, that we might fulfill our primary human obligation, which is to grasp reality. (Note that this prayer is answered in the *Bhagavad Gita*.) Stanza sixteen calls divinity the nourisher, the sole seer, the controller of fortunes, the one who is yonder yet the inmost reality of the personality. Stanza seventeen prays that while our body ends in ashes, our breath may take us to the immortal wind. This will happen if we remember our purpose, grasp the import of our deeds. The Isa's last prayers, in stanza eighteen, are addressed to Agni: Lead us to prosperity by a godly path, you who know all the ways. Keep us from the crooked ways of sin, for we want to offer you ample adoration.

The Period of Native Challenge

From about 600 B.C.E. to 300 C.E. the Vedic religion, including its Upanishadic refinements, was seriously challenged by some Indians. We have already seen that the Upanishads represent a critical reaction to sacrificial Brahmanism.[13] However, even the Upanishads themselves, the final fruits of the Vedic tradition, were eventually contested by materialist, Jain, Buddhist, devotionalist, and other religious views. Not that "Vedism" or "Brahmanism" had ever been either a monolith or a system clearly considered official and in control. Always there had been resistance among the warrior and merchant classes, along with teachers of meditation and new philosophical views. As well, the entire Vedic tradition of revelation kept growing through commentaries and instructions. Hindus refer to these materials collectively as *smriti* (memory or tradition). Still, while some Hindus remained loyal to early Vedic gods and sacrifices, the strong challenges decisively changed the religion of the majority.

Materialistic, Jain, and Buddhist challenges to Vedism first arose in northeastern India, where warrior tribes were more than ready to contest the priests' pretensions to cultural control. By this time (600 B.C.E.), the Aryans had settled in villages, and India was a checkerboard of small kingdoms, each of which controlled a group of such villages. Some intellectuals, radically opposed to the Vedas, strongly attacked the Vedic belief that there is a reality other than the sensible or material. It is hard to know precisely what these materialists taught, because few of their writings have survived, but Buddhist literature reports that Ajita, a prominent materialist thinker, said that earth, air, fire, and water are the only elements—the sources of everything in the universe. According to Ajita, the differences among things just reflect different proportions of these elements. Human beings are no exception, and at death they simply dissolve back into these four elements. There is no afterlife, no reincarnation, no soul, and no Brahman. During the brief span of their lives, people should live "realistically," enduring pain and pursuing pleasure. Nothing beyond the testimony of the senses is valid knowledge, and what the senses reveal is what is real.

Jainism was a very different challenge that grew from the struggles for enlightenment of Vardhamana, called the Jina (conqueror) or Mahavira (great man). He was born to wealth but found it unfulfilling, so he launched a life of asceticism. After gaining enlightenment by this self-denial, he successfully preached his method to others. The Jina opposed both the ritualism and the intellectualism of the Vedic tradition. The only significant sacrifice, he said, is that which conquers the self. Similarly, the only worthy knowledge is that which enables the personality to gain full freedom.[14]

The Jina's followers became opponents of all forms of violence and pain. Consequently, they opposed the Vedic sacrifice of animals, calling it an assault on life that opposed true religion. Also, Jains became critical of matter. Their "karma" was a semisolid entity that attached itself to the spirit through acts involving material objects.[15] In memory of the Jina, whom they considered to be a great *tirthankara* ("crosser of the stream of sorry life"), Jains eschewed eating meat, harming anything believed to have a soul, and physical activity. Since total avoidance of these activities was practically impossible, Jains tried to balance any injury that they inflicted or bad karma that they generated by acts of self-denial or benevolence.

The popularity of Jainism and of Buddhism, which arose only slightly later, testifies to the vulnerability of Vedism that many Indians experienced during the sixth century B.C.E. At the time of the Mahavira's death (due to voluntary starvation), his followers have been estimated at more than half a million. There were more women than men, and many more laypeople than monks and nuns. For laypeople and monks alike, however, Jainism developed guiding vows, similar to commandments, which have been a principal reason for the persistence of Jainism in India to the present.

The lay vows include commitments not to injure living beings, not to lie or steal, not to be unchaste, not to accumulate large sums of money, not to travel widely or possess more than what one needs, not to think evil of others, and not to pursue evil forms of livelihood. There were also positive vows to meditate and to support the community of ascetic monks.

Today there are about two million Jains in India. Prominent centers include Gujarat in the west and Karnatuku in the south. There is also a significant Jain population in Calcutta. In Jain temples one can see pictures of nude, ascetic saints who represent an ideal of complete detachment, and the Jain doctrine of **ahimsa** (noninjury) has made a permanent impression on Indian culture.[16]

Since we discuss Buddhism at length in the next chapter, we note here only that from a Hindu perspective, Buddhism arose, much like Jainism, as an anti-Vedic protest in the sixth century B.C.E. It was another stimulus to Hindu reform, another flowering of Vedic interest in improving people's ability to cope with an often painful world, another attack on both the Vedic sacrifices and their Brahmanistic rationale. If by "Hinduism" we mean the full-bodied tradition that evolved in response to the challenges of Jains and Buddhists, then those challenges were crucial to what Hindus later believed and did.

Bhagavata. Especially in western India, movements arose that, unlike materialism, Jainism, and Buddhism, brought changes from less radical critics. A collective word for these movements is *Bhagavata* (devotionalism), which connotes an emotional attachment to personal gods such as Krishna and Shiva. Devotees *(bhaktas)* continue to claim that such devotion is a way of salvation or self-realization superior to sacrifice or intellectual meditation.[17]

In the central Indian city of Mathura, devotion was focused on the god Krishna. There has been much debate about the background of this god (his name means dark blue or black and was a common one). Some have claimed that Krishna originally was a solar god, others that he was a vegetative god, and still others that he was a mythical hero. Organ suggests that the Krishna cult may have appropriated five minor religions that flourished in the Mathura area.[18] All these religions related to a solar deity, whom the local people worshiped as a personal god and petitioned for gifts.

Whatever its origins, the Krishna cult became very popular, and it developed a wealth of legends about Krishna's birth and adventures that ultimately made Krishna the most beloved of the Indian deities.

In one legend, demons tried to kill the baby Krishna, but he was stronger than they. When the demoness Putana, who had taken the form of a nurse, tried to offer him a breast covered with poison, Krishna took it and sucked out all her milk and blood. When another demon approached him, Krishna kicked the demon so hard that the demon died. Another cluster of legends describes the child Krishna's pranks (he was always stealing his mother's butter, for which he had a great appetite)[19] and the young man Krishna's affairs with young girls. Consequently, Krishna became the object of love—the love for an infant and the romantic and sexual love for a handsome young lord.[20]

The premier work of the Bhagavata tradition is the *Bhagavad Gita,* in which Krishna is the featured god. (The contrast between the warrior Krishna of the *Gita* and the pranksters of the Bahagavata tradition reminds us that we are dealing with a complex, mythological character.) The *Gita* offers ways of salvation to all types of people, but **bhakti** (devotional love) appears to be its highest teaching.[21] This is especially so if one reads the *Gita* as the progressive instruction of a pupil (Arjuna) by his guru god (Krishna). The *Gita* is set in the context of a great battle (the subject of the epic poem the *Mahabharata*), and it deals successively with (1) the ethical problem of war (one must do one's caste duty; there is no killing of the soul), (2) the valid ways to wisdom and realization (sacrifice, meditation, and action without attachment to its results), and (3) the divinity's unveiled countenance (the dazzling vision that is recounted in chap. 11). Then, in what seems to be the work's climax, Krishna tells Arjuna that the best "way" *(marga)* is love of Krishna and that he, Krishna, loves his devotee in return. In other words, there is a divine love for humanity as well as a human love for divinity (chap. 18). This final teaching, probably even more than the *Gita*'s catholic offering of many religious ways, has made it Hinduism's most influential text.

In later Hindu theology, Krishna became an avatar, or manifestation, of Vishnu, whom we discuss shortly. However, to complete our discussion of Bhagavata, we should first describe the beginnings of a devotional cult to Shiva. This cult, too, was in part a reaction against Vedism, and one of its fascinating texts is the Svetashvatara Upanishad. For the devotees of Shiva, this text serves much as the *Bhagavad Gita* serves Krishnaites—as a gospel of the personal god's love. It is unique among the Upanishads for its theism (focus on a personal god), yet it shares with the monistic Upanishads an effort to think logically.

The author begins by asking momentous questions: What is Brahman? What causes us to be born? Then the author rejects impersonal wisdom, materialism, and pure devotion as inadequate answers. His own answer is to interpret Brahman (the ultimate reality) as a kind of god who may become manifest if one meditates upon him. In the Svetashvatara Upanishad, the preferred designation for Brahman is Rudra-Shiva. Rudra probably was the Dravidian form of Indra and Shiva a god of fertility.[22] In the post-Dravidian combination of these gods, the accent was on slaying and healing, destroying and creating—Shiva as the lord of the two rhythms of life.

According to this Upanishad, Shiva is in everything. He has five faces and three eyes, which show his control of all directions and all times (past, present, and future). The devotee of Shiva therefore deals with a divinity as ultimate and powerful as Krishna but whose destructive capacities are more accentuated.

Devotion to Krishna (Vishnu) or Shiva, then, satisfies the person who wants religious feeling and a personal god with whom to interact. Probably this sort of person predominated in Hindu history. From the legends about the gods and from the epics (especially the *Mahabharata* and the *Ramayana*), the *bhaktas* found models for religious love and for faithful living as a good child, husband, wife, and so on.

Smriti. During this period of challenge to Vedic authority, one other development merits attention because it was responsible for a great deal of Hindu religious literature. This movement was commentary on the Vedic literature that was intended to make it more comprehensible, practicable, and contemporary. The authority of this commentary movement is described by the word *smriti* (tradition). *Smriti* provided such diverse literatures as the *Dharma Shastras*, or law codes (of which the Laws of Manu are the most famous); the writings of the six orthodox schools of philosophy; legendary works such as the *Mahabharata* and the *Ramayana;* the *Puranas* (more legendary materials, often from folk or aboriginal sources); commentaries appended to the Vedas (for example, the *Ayur-Veda*—the "Life-Veda," devoted to systematic medicine—which tradition added to the *Athavara*); tantric writings on occult and erotic matters; writings ("Agamas") peculiar to sects such as the Vaishnavites and the Shaivites; and writings on logical or ritualistic forms of thought.

The basic form of the *smriti* was the sutra, an aphorism or short sentence designed to expose the pith of a position.[23] By the end of the third century C.E., the *smriti* tradition had developed some very important and common ways of understanding the Vedic heritage that greatly shaped Hindu social life.

The great social development of the *smriti* period was the caste system. The Vedas, as noted, had spoken of the creation of humanity in terms of the four ranks: priests, warriors, merchants, and workers. In the original sacrifice, Purusha, the primal man, gave his mouth, arms, thighs, and feet to make those four ranks. However, law codes such as Manu's were required to justify casteism.[24] Apparently, casteism precedes the Aryan subjugation of the native Indians, being something common to proto-Indo-Europeans, but whether it was first based on color, occupation, tribe, or religious beliefs is unclear.[25] Modern India has tried to deemphasize both varna and jati, but they remain influential. Modern India has also tried to improve the lot of the untouchables, who lie outside the caste system, but they still exist. Thus, even now, only certain groups of people carry garbage, clean homes, work in banks, and so on.

Personal Life. From the *smriti* elaboration of Vedic tradition came another influential doctrine, that of the four legitimate life goals. These were pleasure *(kama),* wealth *(artha),* duty *(dharma),* and liberation *(moksha).* Kama was the lowest goal, but it was quite legitimate. *Kama* meant sexual pleasure but also the pleasure of eating, poetry, sport, and so on. *Artha* was also a legitimate goal, and around it developed learned discussions of ethics, statecraft, manners, and the like.[26] Because the person of substance propped society, wealth had a social importance and was thus more significant than pleasure.

Dharma, or duty, was higher than pleasure or wealth. It meant principle, restraint, obligation, law, and truth—the responsible acceptance of one's social station and its implications. So in the *Bhagavad Gita,* Krishna appeals to Arjuna's dharma as a warrior: It is his duty to fight, and better one's own duty done poorly than another's done well. *Moksha* meant liberation, freedom, and escape. It was the highest goal of life, because it represented the term of one's existence: self-realization in freedom from karma (the influences of past actions) and ignorance. The concept of *moksha* meant that life is samsaric—precarious and illusory. It also meant that pleasure, wealth, and even duty all could be snares.

As a complement to its exposition of life goals, *smriti* also analyzed the stages in the ideal unfolding of a life.[27] For the upper classes (excluding the workers), the four stages, or *ashramas,* were student, householder, hermit, and wandering mendicant. In a one-hundred-year life, each would last about twenty-five years. In studenthood, the young male would apprentice himself to a guru to learn the Vedic tradition and develop his character. Depending on his caste, this would last eight to twelve years and dominate the first quarter of his life. Then he would marry, raise children, and carry out social responsibilities. Hindu society honored marriage, and the economic, political, and social responsibilities of the householder gave him considerable esteem. Indeed, Buddhist asceticism caused some Hindu thinkers to reemphasize the dignity of this phase of the life cycle.

When the householder saw his children's children, however, *smriti* urged him to retire from active life and start tending his soul. He could still give advice and be helpful in secular affairs, but he should increasingly detach himself from the world. Finally, free of worldly concern, seeking only *moksha,* the ideal Hindu would end his life as a poor, wandering ascetic. Thereby, he would be an object lesson in the true purpose of human life, a teacher of what mattered most.

In effect, this scheme meant an ideal development (not often realized but still influential) of learning one's tradition, gaining worldly experience, appropriating both tradition and experience by solitary reflection, and finally consummating one's time by uniting with ultimate reality. From conception to burial, numerous ceremonies have paced the Hindu through this cycle. The most important have been adornment with the sacred thread (signaling sufficient maturity to begin studying the Vedas), marriage, and funerary rites. Women have fallen outside this scheme. During most of Hindu history, their schooling, such as it was, took place at home, and they were not eligible for *moksha.*[28]

Case Study: Stories from the Mahabharata. Two stories from the *Mahabharata* illustrate the ambivalent status to which the brahmins had fallen by the time native Indian developments were challenging and expanding the religious outlook one finds in the Vedas.

The first story might be called "The Curse of a Brahmin."[29] It shows the power attributed to brahmins and also the colorful world of supernatural forces that has long delighted Hindus.

Once the great King Parikshit went hunting. Wounding a deer, he chased it deep into an unfamiliar forest. There he came upon a hermitage with an old ascetic priest sitting near some cows. The king approached the brahmin, told him who he was, and asked him whether he had seen the wounded deer. But the brahmin gave the king no answer, for the brahmin had taken a vow of silence. The king repeated his question, and when he again received no reply, he got very angry. Gazing around, he spied a dead snake, lifted it with the end of his bow, and hung it around the priest's neck to shame him. The brahmin still did not utter a sound, so the king gave up and returned home empty-handed.

The old brahmin had a son, and when the son's friends heard of the incident, they teased the boy about his father's disgrace. The son asked his friends how his father had come to have a dead snake hung round his neck, and the friends told him the story of King Parikshit's visit. The son reacted angrily, cursing the king: "May Takshaka, the king of the serpents, kill this wretch who placed a dead snake upon the shoulders of my frail, old father."

When he returned home, the son told his father how he had cursed the king. The old brahmin was not pleased. Ascetics, he said, should not behave so impetuously. The son had forgotten that they lived under the protection of King Parikshit, who defended all the

MAJOR VEDAS	
Rig-Veda	Hymns manifesting mythology and prayers
Atharva-Veda	Materials concerning magic of special interest to Brahmins
Sama-Veda	Mantras to be chanted at various sacrifices of soma (ritual liquor)
Yajur-Veda	Priestly textbook on the Vedic ritual as a whole

MARGAS (PATHS)	
Meditation *(Dhyana)*	Experience one's unity with the ALL. Gain self-possession. Go below sensations, feelings, images, ideas, volitions to essential spirit (experience *samadhi*).
Study *(Jnana)*	Gain an intuitive understanding of religious truths. Grasp the wisdom expressed in the scriptures and tradition, through mystical insight.
Work (Karma)	Purify one's action through detachment from its fruits. Carry out one's social responsibilities blamelessly.
Love (Bhakti)	Devote oneself to a god or goddess. Make service and emotional attachment to a divinity the core of one's life and hope.

priests of his realm. The king had not known of the father's vow, so he should be forgiven much of his anger and bad behavior.

To try to repair the damage of his son's action, the brahmin promised to send a messenger to warn the king. Both the father and the son knew, though, that the curse of a brahmin could never be thwarted.

When the old brahmin's messenger told the king of the curse, Parikshit was saddened by how he had abused the priest. He was also worried about his life, so he took counsel with his ministers about how to protect himself. They advised him to build a high platform, standing on tall posts, so that no one could approach him unobserved, and to remain there for seven days. The king followed this advice and moved his living quarters to the platform.

Toward the end of the seven-day period, the serpent king Takshaka sent several of his servants to King Parikshit disguised as ascetics. Not sensing any danger, King Parikshit allowed the ascetics to mount his platform and accepted their gifts of water, nuts, and fruit. When the ascetics had departed, King Parikshit invited his counselors to enjoy the gifts with him. But just as he was about to bite into a piece of fruit, an ugly black and copper-colored insect crawled out. The king looked at the setting sun, which was ending the seventh day, gathered his courage, and dared Takshaka to assume his true form and fulfill the brahmin's curse. No sooner had he said this than the insect turned into a huge serpent and coiled itself around the king's neck. Bellowing a tremendous roar, Takshaka killed the king with a single mighty bite.

The story has several morals. First, it teaches the exalted status of priests. Dealing with holy things and marshaling great spiritual power by their ascetic practices, priests can perform marvels that ordinary humans can barely conceive. Therefore ordinary humans, including kings, ought to deal respectfully with priests.

Second, however, a brahmin's very power imposes on him the responsibility to stay above petty emotions that might lead him to abuse this power. Thus the old father was deeply disturbed by his son's intemperate curse. A brahmin's power ought to serve the people around him, improving their lives. The many Hindu stories in which priests do not act as ideally as they should suggest that the common people often found their priests wanting.

Third, the story piquantly illustrates the intimacy with nature that popular Hinduism has retained. Even though the Upanishads were pressing toward a purely spiritual conception of reality, in which a single Brahman would relativize the reality of both human beings and snakes, the popular religion that came out of the period of native challenge stayed deeply immersed in the cosmological myth. (The cosmological myth is the assumption that all things that exist live within physical nature, the span from heaven to earth. With this assumption, gods and human beings, serpents and kings, become more alike than unlike one another.) This made for a very lively and imaginative "reality," in which curses such as the brahmin's were plausible enough to teach both priests and commoners a religious lesson.

The second story from the *Mahabharata* might be called "The Well of Life."[30] It offers a dramatic picture of the dangers of samsaric existence.

Once there was a brahmin who wandered into a dark forest filled with wild animals. Indeed, so ferocious were the lions, elephants, and other great beasts of this forest that even Yama, the god of death, would only enter it when absolutely necessary. The brahmin only came to sense the wicked nature of the dark forest gradually, but then he grew more and more fearful. Panicking, he found himself running in circles, becoming more and more confused.

Finally the brahmin looked about on every side and saw that the forest was caught in a huge net held by a giant woman with outstretched arms. There were five-headed serpents everywhere, so tall that their heads nearly reached the heavens. Then the brahmin came to a clearing, with a deep well covered by vines and underbrush. Running frantically from a wild elephant that was pursuing him, he stumbled into the well, fell through the brush, and lodged halfway to the bottom, held upside down by a few vines.

At the bottom of the well was a huge snake. Above him waited the great elephant, which had six faces and twelve feet. To the side, in the vines that held him, were many bees that had built hives and filled them with honey. When the honey dripped toward him, the brahmin reached out to catch it in his mouth. The more honey he ate, the more he could not satisfy his thirst for it. Meanwhile, black and white rats gnawed at the vines holding him. Though the elephant stood guard above, the serpent stood guard below, the bees buzzed on all sides, and the rats gnawed at his lifeline, the brahmin continued to grope for more honey.

As many Hindu commentators have made clear, the story is an allegory for the human condition. The forest is the limited sphere of our life, dark and filled with dangers. The woman holding a net over the forest is the process of aging, which allows no human life to escape. The beasts of the forest are the diseases and other forces that can destroy us, while the serpent at the bottom of the well is time, which eventually receives all living things. The six-faced elephant with twelve feet is the year, with its twelve months, while the black and white rats are night and day, the devourers of our life spans. Finally, the honey is the pleasures of life, for which our thirst seems unslakable.

The allegory, then, paints human life as tragic. Despite danger on all sides, we persist in pursuing transient pleasures. This is illusion with a vengeance. It is attachment making us oblivious to the great questions of what direction we should be taking and how we ought to be battling death. If we are ever to escape the painful circle of rebirths, which ensures that life after life we will suffer fear and pain, we must realize our self-imposed bondage. Plunging heedlessly into a dangerous life, we are soon fleeing in panic. We have gotten in over our heads, and before long we are upside down in an inescapable pit. Above and below, the many forms of time wait like jailers, ensuring that we stay in terrible danger. Meanwhile, day and night nibble our life span away.

Clearly, the story wants to impress upon its hearers the fearsome nature of unreflective living. If we simply live instinctively, pursuing the pleasures of the senses and fleeing the pains, we will end up in the most trying of circumstances. Only by estimating correctly the lay of the land and refusing to get trapped in life's forests or fall into time's snares can we escape a tragic ending. Only by avoiding the whole battlefield of time can we enter into true freedom.

The Hindu keys to true freedom, therefore, are attention and detachment. We must watch where we are going, and we must stay free of worldly desires. The brahmin of the story is pathetic because his calling or station especially should have educated him in these virtues. Were he noble in substance rather than just noble in name, he would not have wandered into the forest aimlessly. Similarly, he would not have abandoned himself to the sweet honey, forgetting his mortal peril. By meditation, sacrifice, austerities within and austerities without, he would have had hold of his time and been powerful in spirit. Then the beasts would have held no terrors, the well would have gaped to no avail. But, the story implies, few priests or few people of any station are true brahmins, strong in spirit, so most people find aging a fearsome process.

The Period of Reform and Elaboration

From about 300 to 1200 c.e., the various movements that criticized or amplified the Vedic heritage resulted in a full reform and elaboration of Hinduism. Of course, it is difficult to distinguish additions, such as those of the *smriti* writings, from revisions, but we can see in the growth of the six orthodox philosophies (described below) and the rise of the major Hindu sects developments that effectively revamped Hinduism.

A convenient distinction in the discussion that follows is that between those who reject the Vedas (for example, materialists, Jains, and Buddhists), called *nastikas* ("those who say no"), and those who accept the Vedas, called *astikas* ("those who say yes"). The orthodox philosophies, or *darshanas*, originated with *astikas*. In other words, the orthodox philosophies were conceived as explanations of *shruti* (revelation). There are six such philosophies or schools: Mimamsa, Samkhya, Yoga, Nyaya, Vaisheshika, and Vedanta.[31] We can content ourselves with explaining **Vedanta**, the most celebrated *darshana*.

Vedanta. Shankara, the greatest of the Vedanta thinkers, was a Malabar brahmin of the ninth century who tried to systematize the Upanishads in terms of "unqualified nondualism" (*advaita*). In other words, he tried to explain the basic Upanishadic concepts of

Brahman and atman with consistency and rigor. To do this, Shankara first established that there are two kinds of knowledge, higher and lower. Lower knowledge is under the limitations of the intellect, while higher knowledge is free of such limitations.

The limitations of the intellect include its reasoning character, its dependence on the senses, and its dependence on the body to act. These limitations are all subjective, since they are limitations of the knower, or subject. The objective limitations to knowledge, due to aspects of the known thing, are space, time, change, and cause-effect relationships. Because of objective limitations, we tend not to see or grasp reality in itself.

Higher knowledge comes by a direct perception that is free of either subjective or objective limitations. In practice it is the direct vision that the seers who produced the Vedas enjoyed—*shruti*. Quite likely, therefore, Shankara assumed that the Vedanta philosopher practices a yoga like that of the ancient sages. If so, he assumed that the Vedanta philosopher experiences a removal of the veil between the self and Brahman (with which the self is actually identified).

Shankara then applied this theory of higher and lower knowledge to *hermeneutics,* the study of textual interpretation. According to Shankara, all passages of the Upanishads that treat Brahman as *one* derive from higher knowledge; all references to Brahman as *many* or dual derive from lower knowledge. We can paraphrase this by saying that Brahman in itself is one and beyond all limitations, while Brahman for us (as we perceive it through sensation and reasoning) appears to be multiple—to be both in the world and beyond it, both material cause and prime mover.

With the subtlety of a great philosopher, Shankara wove the two edges of Brahman-in-itself and Brahman-for-us into a seamless whole. With the religious hunger of a mystic, he sought to correlate the within and the without. Shankara's core affirmation in his philosophical construction was that reality within is identical with reality without: Atman is Brahman. In other words, when one realizes through revelation, or higher knowledge, that there is no change, no space-time limitations, no cause-effect qualifications to the real, one then discovers that there is no self. Rather, there is only the Self, the Brahmanic reality that one directly perceives to be the ground of both internal and external being.

From the perspective of lower knowledge, there is, of course, a personal, separate, changing self. In absolute terms, though, there is one indivisible reality that is both subjectivity and objectivity, that is atman-Brahman. Since we rarely perceive directly, we often live and move in maya (illusion). The world of maya is not unreal in the sense that there are no elephants in it to break your foot if you get in the way of a circus parade. The elephants in the world of maya are substantial, their dung is mighty, and their step will crush your foot. But this viewpoint has limited validity. From a higher viewpoint, all that goes on in maya has no independent existence. The elephants' movement is a "play" of the only reality that exists independently—that is uncaused, unconnected, sovereign, and fully real.[32]

Vaishnavism. In the period of reformation, then, keen speculative minds tried to rehabilitate the Vedic heritage by showing the reasonableness of *shruti*. It is doubtful that they directly converted more than a few intellectuals, but they did impressively demonstrate that orthodox Hinduism, through Vedic revelation, could enable one to make powerful interpretations of reality. The more popular reformations of Vedism were theistic movements that brought the energies of Bhagavata (devotionalism) back into the Vedic fold. Two principal such movements centered on Vishnu and Shiva. Although both these movements were targeted at the common person's allegiance and presented quite different versions of divinity, they both advanced Vedic tradition and made a religion that combined some intellectual clout with much emotional enthusiasm. The main determinant of why one clung to one's particular god was a combination of social factors (the religion of one's family, jati, geographic area) and personal temperament.

The theistic religion centered on Vishnu (Vaishnavism) got its impetus from the patronage of the Gupta kings in the fourth century C.E. Perhaps the most winning aspect of Vaishnavite doctrine was its notion that the god is concerned about human beings, fights with them against demon enemies, and sends incarnations of himself (avatars) to assist humans in troubled times. In one traditional list there are ten avatars, the most important being Rama (the hero of the epic *Ramayana*), Krishna, Buddha(!), and Kalki (who is yet to come).

Vishnu himself is associated with water. According to tradition, the Ganges flows from under his feet while he rests on the coils of a great serpent. He is gracious to human beings, sending them many avatars of himself to help them when they are in need. Often

he rides the great bird Garuda and is pictured as blue. Like an ancient monarch, he carries a conch shell, a battle discus, a club, and a lotus. Frequently he has four arms, to signify his great power to fight evil, and his consort is the much-beloved Lakshmi.

Vaishnavism promoted itself in several ways. Two of the most effective tied Vishnu to the bhakti cult. Between the sixth and the sixteenth centuries, the *Puranas* (legendary accounts of the exploits of gods and heroes) pushed Vishnu to the fore. The *Bhagavata Purana*, perhaps the most influential, was especially successful in popularizing the avatar Krishna. In fact, the tenth book of the *Bhagavata Purana*, which celebrates Krishna's affairs with the girls who tended cows *(gopis)*, mixes erotic entertainment with symbolism of the divine-human relationship. As the cow-girls were rapt before Krishna, so could the devotee's spirit swoon before god. When one adds the stories of Krishna's extramarital affairs with Radha, his favorite *gopi,* the religious eros becomes quite intense. The *Puranas* were thus the first vehicle to elevate Vishnu and his prime avatar to the status of bhakti (devotional) gods.

Vaishnavite bhakti was promoted in southern India during the seventh and eighth centuries.[33] There Tamil-speaking troubadours called *alvars* ("persons deep in wisdom") spread devotion to Vishnu by composing religious songs. However, their wisdom was simply a deep love of Vishnu, a love that broke the bonds of caste and worldly station. The constant theme of the songs was Vishnu's own love and compassion for human beings, which moved him to send his avatars. The *alvars* were so successful that they practically ousted Buddhism from India, and they were the main reason that Vishnu-Krishna became the most attractive and influential Hindu god.

Vaishnavism also had the good fortune of attracting the religious philosopher Ramanuja,[34] who is now second only to Shankara in prestige. Ramanuja lived in the eleventh century, and his main accomplishment was elaborating the Upanishadic doctrine in a way that made divinity compatible with human love. This way goes by the name *vishishtadvaita*—"nondualism qualified by difference." It opposed the unqualified nondualism of Shankara, whom Ramanuja regarded as his philosophical enemy. For Ramanuja, Brahman consisted of three realities: the unconscious universe of matter, the conscious community of finite selves, and the transcendent lord Ishvara.

Furthermore, Ramanuja held that the Upanishadic formula "This thou art" meant not absolute identity between atman and Brahman but a relationship: the psychological oneness that love produces. The highest way to liberation was therefore loving devotion to the highest lord who represented Brahman. Knowledge and pure action were good paths, but love was better. By substituting Vishnu or Krishna for Brahman or Ishvara, the Vaishnavites made Ramanuja a philosophical defender of their bhakti. For those who wanted to reformulate revealed doctrine through love, Ramanuja was the man.

Shaivism. An alternative to Vaishnavism was Shaivism—devotion to Shiva. Shankara had been a Shaivite, but his intellectualism hardly satisfied the common person's desires for an emotional relationship with divinity. Shiva was the Lord of the Dance of Life and the Destroyer who terminated each era of cosmic time. From the earliest available evidence, Shaivism was a response to this wild god. It was frequently a source of emotional excesses, and its tone always mixed love with more fear and awe than Vaishnavism did.[35]

For an extreme example, one of the earliest Shaivite sects, which the *Mahabharata* calls Pashupati, taught that to end human misery and transcend the material world, one had to engage in such rituals as smearing the body with cremation ashes; eating excrement, carrion, or human flesh; drinking from human skulls; simulating sexual intercourse; and frenzied dancing. Through such bizarre behavior, it wanted to symbolize the reversal of worldly, samsaric values that true religious devotion implied. Less defensibly, members of other sects, such as the eleventh-century Kalamukha (named for the black mark they wore on their foreheads), became notorious as drug addicts, drunkards, and even murderers.[36] Even when Shaivites were thoroughly respectable, their religion was more fiery and zealous in its asceticism than that of the love-struck but more refined Vaishnavites. Shaivite priests came from all social classes, and Shaivite followers often regarded the *lingam* as Shiva's main emblem. The *lingam* symbolized the phallus and sexual creativity in general, as well as the dedication and intensification of this power through asceticism. Parallel to the Vaishnavite *alvars* were the Shaivite *adiyars,* whose poetry and hymns were a principal factor in Shiva's rise to prominence, especially in southern India.

The Shaivite movement also received royal patronage in southern India from the fifth to the tenth centuries. During those centuries the Shaivites waged war against both the Buddhists and the Jains. After winning that fight they turned on the Vaishnavites, singing of Shiva's superiority to Vishnu. In their theology they stressed not only the Lord of the Cosmic Dance and the god of fertility and destruction but also the hidden god. (Shiva also had such forms as the householder and the ascetic, representing several stages in the life cycle.) Even the worship of the phallus was enshrouded in mystery by placing it behind a veil. In addition, Shaivites often substituted representations of Nandi, Shiva's bull, or one of his *shaktis* (consorts) for the god himself. Finally, to stress Shiva's ability to transcend all opposites, his followers often depicted him as androgynous. Since the Shaivite often became identified with the god, Shaivism was more like yoga than was Vaishnavism, in which the worshiper and deity remained two.

The worshiper of Shiva grew conscious that he or she was a sinner through mysterious rituals and Shiva's own symbols of fire and a skull. As a result, there was less equality, less of the lover-beloved relationship, between the devotee and Shiva than what one found in Vaishnavism. The Shaivite might deprecatingly refer to himself or herself as a dog. That the god would come to such a person was pure grace. Worship, then, was essentially gratitude that the tempestuous god chose to forgive rather than destroy.

Shaktism. A last reformation of the Hindu tradition came through movements that scholars group as Shaktism or Tantrism.[37] This sort of Hinduism focused on secret lore whose prime objective was to liberate the energies of imagination, sex, and the unconscious. Insofar as Shiva's *shaktis* represented the energy of female divinity, they exemplified Tantrist powers. The general name of the ancient female divinity is Maha-Devi, whom we discuss below in her form of Kali.

It is hard to know exactly what *shakti* sects believed and practiced, because most of their rites were secret, but one of their main beliefs was that the union of coitus is the best analogy for the relationship between the cosmos and its energy flow. This belief seems to have spawned a theory of parallels or dualisms, in which male-female, right-left, and positive-negative pairings all had highly symbolic aspects. Like some of Shaivism, **Tantra** downplayed class distinction and violated social conventions to symbolize the reversal of ordinary cultural values implied in religious conversion and realization (of union with divine reality).

One of the many Tantrist rituals for gaining *moksha* was called *chakrapuja* (circle worship). In it men and women (Tantrist groups tended to admit members without regard for sex or caste) used a series of elements (all having Sanskrit names beginning with the letter *m*) that might facilitate union with Shakti: wine, meat, fish, parched rice, and copulation. In right-hand Tantrism these elements were symbols. Left-hand Tantrism used the actual elements [not hedonistically but with ritual discipline, to participate in maya (reality's play)]. Other Tantrist practices involved meditation to arouse the *kundalini*—the snake of energy lying dormant at the base of the spine.[38]

Overall, the reformation and elaboration of the Vedic tradition meant expanded roles for some Vedic gods and a shift of popular religion from sacrifice to devotional, theistic worship. The renovators tried to defend and extend their ancient heritage, allowing people to respond to any part of it that they found attractive. In this way they created an eclectic religion tolerant of diversity in religious doctrine and practice.

The Period of Foreign Challenge

From about 1200 c.e. on, Hinduism increasingly contended with foreign cultures, rulers, and religions. Islam and Christianity both made serious impacts on Indian life, and their presence is felt to this day. Islam, a factor in India from the eighth century on, first affected Indians of the Sind and Punjab regions in the northwestern part of ancient India, where Muslims traded and made military conquests. Invasions in the eleventh century put much of the Indus Valley region under Muslim control, and by 1206 Islam had conquered most of northern India. By 1335, Muslims controlled the south as well, and their final dynasty, the Mogul, did not end until 1858.

The policies of Muslim leaders toward Hinduism varied. Many were tolerant and allowed the Indians freedom to practice their traditional ways. Others, such as the Mogul zealot Aurangzeb (ruled 1658–1707), attempted to establish a thoroughly Muslim state and so tried to stop drinking, gambling, prostitution, the use of narcotics, and other practices that were prohibited by Islamic doctrine. Aurangzeb destroyed more than 200 Hindu temples in 1679 alone, and he discriminated against Hindus in the collection of taxes, custom duties, and various other ways.

The permanent changes that Islam made in Hinduism and that Hinduism made in Indian Islam are hard to determine because the two faiths are intertwined. Islamic architecture and learning influenced Hinduism deeply, while Hindu casteism affected Indian Muslims as well. Muslim fundamentalism, based on the belief that the Qur'an is God's final word, probably upgraded the status of the Hindu Vedas, and many Hindus found Sufism, the devotional branch of Islam, quite compatible with their native bhakti practices.

On the other hand, Muslim tendencies to regard many Hindu devotional practices (for example, reverencing cows and praying to many deities) idolatrous complicated relations between the religions. Indeed, in modern times tensions have led not only to the partition of India but to much bloodshed.

One definite result of Islam's presence in India was a new religion, Sikhism. Traces of it were found among Hindus who considered aspects of Islam very attractive, but it actually began as a result of the revelations of the prophet Nanak, a Punjabi born in 1469. Nanak's visions prompted him to sing the praise of a divinity that blended elements of the Muslim Allah and the Hindu trinity of Brahma, Vishnu, and Shiva. This God he called the True Name. The religious prescriptions for serving the True Name that he set for his followers were rather severe and anticeremonial, steering away from Hindu pilgrimages and devotions and favoring compassion and neighborly good deeds. The Sikhs developed into a small but hardy religious band, and on numerous occasions they proved to be excellent warriors. They number about six million in India today, and their great shrine remains in Amritsar in the northwest. Many of the other holy Sikh sites, however, are now in Pakistan because of the 1947 partition.[39]

Christianity has been present in India since the first century c.e., according to stories about the apostle Thomas's adventures there. It is more certain that a bishop of Alexandria sent a delegation to India in 189 and that an Indian representative attended the Council of Nicaea (325). Only in the sixteenth century, however, did the Christian missionary presence become strong, in the wake of Portuguese (and later Dutch and English) traders. The British East India Company, founded in 1600, increasingly controlled the Indian economy and trade, and after the Sepoy Mutiny in 1857 the company, which had become a sort of government, gave way to direct colonial rule. When India became independent in 1947, after almost a century of British colonial rule, it had some experience with the political ideas and social institutions of the modern West. Christianity therefore usually has had a colonial character.

The Christian impact, as distinguished from the Western impact, has not been impressive statistically.

According to 1990 census figures, only 2.43 percent of all Indians considered themselves Christians. Nevertheless, Christians opened hundreds of charitable institutions, especially schools, and were responsible for the first leprosaria. They also promoted hospital care for the tuberculous and the insane. In fact, Christianity's greatest impact was probably the rousing of the Hindu social conscience. The tradition of dharma as social responsibility had not resulted in the establishment of institutions for the poor and sickly. While Western culture opened India to modern science, technology, and democratic political theory, Western religion drove home the ideal of social concern. Mother Teresa of Calcutta continues that tradition today. On the other hand, a colonial Christianity often seemed racist and blind to native Indian genius and needs.

Modern Bhakti. The native Hindu movements during the past seven centuries have not been particularly social.[40] Perhaps in reaction to foreign rulers, the masses tended to focus on somewhat privatized, devotional religion. After the elaboration of the ancient tradition, Hinduism directed itself toward the further development of bhakti. Islamic Sufism stimulated this tendency, as we suggested above. In the religious poetry of Kabir (1440–1518), a forerunner of the Sikh founder Nanak, the love of God became the heart of a religion that ignored distinctions between Muslims and Hindus, priests and workers.[41] For Kabir this love correlated with a pure heart only.

For Ramananda, who was both the teacher of Kabir and a follower of the philosopher Ramanuja, the important thing was to adore God, whom Ramananda called Rama, with fervent devotion. Rama considered all persons equal. In southern India, especially among the people who spoke Tamil, the Lord Vishnu increasingly appeared as a god of pure grace. Self-concern is useless and distracting, the Tamils told their northern Vaishnavite brethren. Not works but love is redeeming.

In west-central India, from the thirteenth to the seventeenth centuries, a poetic movement called the Maratha renaissance carried the message of bhakti. Tukaram (1607–1649), the greatest poet of this movement, stressed God's otherness and the sinfulness of human beings. His god was not the Brahman who was identical with one's innermost self but a free agent and lover whose goodness in saving sinners was the more impressive because of their distance from him.

In these and other movements, modern Hinduism increasingly focused on bhakti, moving away from Vedic orthodoxy. The singers of bhakti cared little whether their doctrines squared with the Upanishads or the great commentators. The notions of *shruti* or *smriti,* in fact, meant little to them. They thought that the love they had found undercut traditional views of social classes, sex, and even religions. The god of love was no creator of castes, no despiser of women, no pawn of Hindus against Muslims. With little concern for intellectual or social implications, the singers and seers who dominated modern bhakti gave themselves over to ecstatic love.

Perhaps the greatest representative of bhakti was Chaitanya, a sixteenth-century Bengali saint whom his followers worship as an avatar of Krishna.[42] Chaitanya, originally a brahmin, converted to Vaishnavism and spent his days worshiping Lord Krishna in the great Bengali temple of Puri. Increasingly his devotions became emotional, involving singing, weeping, dancing, and epileptic fits. He died in delirium in the surf off Puri, where he was bathing. Somewhat typically for modern bhakti, Chaitanya repudiated the Vedas and nondualistic Vedanta philosophy as opposing a gracious god. All were welcome in his sect, regardless of caste, and he even sanctioned worship of a black stone, thinking it might help some followers' devotion. He stressed the followers' assimilation with Radha, Krishna's lover, arguing that the soul's relation to God is always female to male.

Yet Chaitanya also stressed the necessity to toil at religious love and opposed those who argued that grace was attained without effort. His followers deified him, seeing his unbounded religious ecstasy as the ideal communion of divinity and humanity. He was the major figure in the devotional surge toward Lord Krishna that produced some remarkable Bengali love poetry during the sixteenth and seventeenth centuries.[43] His movement has continued in the United States through the work of Swami Prabhupada, founder of the International Society for Krishna Consciousness and of the Bhaktivedanta Book Trust. The swami's monks in saffron robes on street corners, and his numerous publications,[44] have made "Hare Krishna" part of our religious vocabulary.

Partly in opposition to the excesses of bhakti and partly because of the influence of Western culture, a group of Bengali intellectuals in the early nineteenth century began to "purify" Hinduism by bringing it up to the standards that they saw in Christianity. The first such effort was the founding of the group Brahmo Samaj by Rammohan Roy in 1828. Roy was a well-educated brahmin whose contacts with Islam and

Christianity led him to think that there should be only one God for all persons, who should inspire social concern and criticism of any abuses, Hindu or Christian.

God should, for example, oppose such barbarism as suttee *(sati),* the relatively rare Hindu practice in which a widow climbed on her husband's funeral pyre and burned with him.[45] In 1811 Roy had witnessed the suttee of his sister-in-law, whom relatives kept on the pyre even though she was screaming and struggling to escape. He knew that in Calcutta alone there were more than 1,500 such immolations between 1815 and 1818. Roy pressured the British to outlaw the practice, and in 1829 a declaration was issued that forbade it (though it did not completely stamp it out). Members of the Brahmo Samaj thought this sort of social concern was essential to pure religion.[46]

Another movement to modernize Hinduism that originated in Bengal in the nineteenth century was the Ramakrishna Mission. Its founder, Ramakrishna, was an uneducated brahmin who became a mystic devotee of the goddess Kali, whom he worshiped as a divine Mother. After visions of Kali and then of Rama, the epic hero, Ramakrishna progressed through the Tantrist, Vaishnavite, and Vedanta disciplines, having the ecstatic experiences associated with the traditions of each. He even lived as a Muslim and as a Christian, learning the mystic teachings of those traditions. From such eclectic experience he developed the joyous doctrine that we can find God everywhere: Divinity beats in each human heart. Ramakrishna's teachings achieved wordwide publicity through his disciple Vivekananda, who stressed the theme of worshiping God by serving human beings. The Ramakrishna Mission has sponsored hospitals, schools, and cultural centers, and it keeps an American presence through the Vedanta Society, which has chapters in many American cities.[47]

Tagore and Gandhi.   In the twentieth century, these currents of domestic and foreign stimuli to religious and social reform inevitably affected the controversies over Indian nationalism and independence. The controversies themselves largely turned on the assets and liabilities of the British and Indian cultures. Not all Indians opposed the British, largely because they did not have a single national tradition themselves. Rather, Indians tended to think of themselves as Bengalis or Gujaratis or Punjabis—natives of their own districts, with their own respective languages and traditions. What the Indian tradition meant, therefore, was far from clear. This fact emerges in the lives of

two of the most intriguing modern-day personalities, Tagore and Gandhi.

Rabindranath Tagore (1861–1941), modern India's most illustrious writer, won the Nobel Prize for literature in 1913. His life's work was a search for artistic and educational forms that would instill Indians with a broad humanism. For this reason, he was leery of nationalism, fearing that it would crush individual creativity and blind Indians to values outside their own country. In the West, Tagore found a salutary energy, a concern for the material world, which seemed to him precisely the cure for India's deep cultural ills. However, he despised the Western industrial nations' stress on machinery, power politics, and democracy. In Tagore's renewed Hinduism, India would give and receive—give resources for individual creativity and receive Western energies for using that creativity to improve society.

Mohandas Gandhi (1869–1948) was a political genius who made some of Tagore's vision practical. He trained as a lawyer in England and found his vocation as an advocate of the masses in South Africa, where he represented "colored" minorities. In India Gandhi drew in part on a Western idealism that he culled from such diverse sources as the New Testament, Tolstoy's writings on Christian socialism, Ruskin's writings on the dignity of work, and Thoreau's writings on civil disobedience. He joined this Western idealism with a shrewd political pragmatism of his own and Indian religious notions, including the *Bhagavad Gita*'s doctrine of karma-yoga (work as a spiritual discipline) and the Jain-Hindu notion of *ahimsa* (non-injury). Gandhi's synthesis of these ideas resulted in what he called **satyagraha** (truth force). To oppose the might of Britain he used the shaming power of a simple truth: Indians, like all human beings, deserve the right to control their own destinies.

Mahatma Gandhi's autobiography, *The Story of My Experiments with Truth,* shows how his personal strivings for purity of spirit intertwined with his leadership of a political movement rooted in nonviolence. Gandhi fasted, followed a vegetarian diet, and practiced celibacy in order to free his spirit from bodily constraints, to prepare a vessel fit for the inspiration of God. He studied nonviolence in the intuitive conviction that this part of the Indian religious tradition held the key to humanity's future survival. Among his many reflections on *ahimsa* the following is typical:

> *Ahimsa* is a comprehensive principle. We are helpless mortals caught in the conflagration of *himsa*

Figure 15 *Rajghat, memorial to M. K. Gandhi in Delhi. Photo by J. T. Carmody.*

[violence]. The saying that life lives on life has a deep meaning in it. Man cannot for a moment live without consciously or unconsciously committing outward *himsa*. The very fact of his living—eating, drinking, and moving about—necessarily involves some *himsa*, destruction of life, be it ever so minute. A votary of *ahimsa* therefore remains true to his faith if the spring of all his actions is compassion, if he shuns to the best of his ability the destruction of the tiniest creature, tries to save it, and thus incessantly strives to be free from the deadly coil of *himsa*. He will be constantly growing in self-restraint and compassion, but he can never become entirely free from outward *himsa*.

Then again, because underlying *ahimsa* is the unity of all life, the error of one cannot but affect all, and hence man cannot be wholly free from *himsa*. So long as he continues to be a social being, he cannot but participate in the *himsa* that the very existence of society involves. When two nations are fighting, the duty of a votary of

ahimsa is to stop the war. He who is not equal to that duty, he who has no power of resisting war, he who is not qualified to resist war, may take part in war, and yet wholeheartedly try to free himself, his nation and the world from war.[48]

Violence, Gandhi admits, is part of the evolutionary and political build of reality. Insofar as species live off one another, violence is a law of life that we cannot avoid. Nonetheless, we can strive to minimize our violence and destructiveness, not injuring any fellow creature needlessly. By a vegetarian diet, we can minimize our injury to fellow animals. By such traditions as the protection of the cow, India has long tried to focus nonviolence on a highly visible symbol of animal vitality. Such practices foster self-restraint and compassion, virtues especially needed in modern social affairs. The phenomenon of war, which for Gandhi probably reached its most tragic expression in the bloody conflicts between Indian Hindus and Muslims that followed upon independence from Britain, depends upon our lack of restraint and compassion.

Surely a sagacious society, one that listened to the wisdom of its elders and traditions, would be able to muster the minimal spiritual power needed to keep itself from civil war. That India could not muster such minimal virtue sickened Gandhi's spirit. As a final irony, he ended his life the victim of a Hindu assassin, a fellow-religionist so unwise he thought killing a champion of peace would advance the Hindu cause.

Erik Erikson, whose psychoanalytic study of Gandhi won great praise a generation ago, has described the Mahatma as a "religious actualist":

> If, for the sake of the game, I should give his unique presence a name that would suit my views, I would call him a *religious actualist.* In my clinical ruminations I have found it necessary to split what we mean by "real" into that which can be known because it is demonstrably correct (factual reality) and that which feels effectively true in action (actuality). Gandhi absorbed from Indian culture a conception of truth *(sat)* which he attempted to make actual in all compartments of human life and along all the stages which make up its course . . . while he learned to utilize craftily what was his first professional identity, namely, that of a barrister English style, and while he then became a powerful politician Indian style, he also strove to grasp the "business" of religious men, namely, to keep his eyes trained upon the all-embracing circumstance that each of us exists with a unique consciousness and a responsibility of his own which makes him at the same time zero and everything, a center of absolute silence, and the vortex of apocalyptic participation. A man who looks through the historical parade of cultures and civilizations, styles, and isms which provide most of us with a glorious and yet miserably fragile sense of immortal identity, defined status, and collective grandeur faces the central truth of our nothingness—and, mirabile dictu [marvelous to say], gains power from it.[49]

Gandhi was a genius at symbolizing truth force. In Joan Bondurant's study,[50] one can see how he worked out *satyagraha* campaigns of civil disobedience, striking, marshaling public support, and so on. In Erik Erikson's study of Gandhi at middle age, one can see the psychological roots of *satyagraha* and something of its promise as an instrument for sociopolitical change in the nuclear age. In Gandhi himself one can see the conflicts, confusion, and

riches of the Hindu tradition in the mid-twentieth century, for he called himself just a seeker of *moksha,* just a servant of the one god found whenever we harken to truth.

Contemporary Hinduism: Popular Religion

As we have already stressed, Hinduism is an umbrella for a great variety of different religious ideas and practices. Of necessity, we have concentrated on the ideas and practices that stand out when one attempts a historical overview. The outstanding ideas, however, tend to be the possession of intellectuals, at least in their reflective form. For the common people, it tends to be the many rituals of the Hindu religious year that mediate the sense of unity with the world that religion seeks to inculcate. To conclude our historical survey, we concentrate on a few of the rituals that fill popular Hinduism today. Let us begin with an anthropologist's description of how a village of central India celebrated *Naumi,* a high point of a festival devoted to nine goddesses.[51]

Naumi occurs in the fall, in either September or October. It is the ninth day of the festival of the nine goddesses—a sort of arithmetic highpoint. In the afternoon of Naumi, the main activity is a procession of men possessed by gods. Throughout the entire festival of the nine goddesses mediums are constantly making contact with the supernatural world, so the procession of possessed men is a kind of climax to their work.

In this village, the two principal mediums were a weaver and a carpenter. The weaver claimed that his tutelary spirit was the mother goddess *(Mata),* while the carpenter claimed that he was directed by the spirit of a local incarnation of Vishnu. The weaver's behavior was the more elaborate of the two. For the entire nine days of the festival, he fasted, living in a small hut adorned only with a picture of Mata, five baskets of sprouting wheat, and a few ritual objects. People visited him during these days, asking for help with their personal problems. For example, a woman asked the weaver what she should do for pains in her back. He gave her some grains of sorghum to eat and told her to offer a gift to the goddess.

The carpenter claimed that he could not afford to spend the whole nine days away from his work, so he held only limited sessions for clients. However, the carpenter's sessions had the strong support of the local headman (and so drew the wealthier people), because the headman had once consulted him about obtaining a son and had his request granted by the carpenter's guiding spirit.

On the afternoon of Naumi, at the climax of the feast, both mediums held rites in their houses. The followers of the carpenter sacrificed rice and ghee to his god, while the followers of the weaver sacrificed a goat. Both mediums then led their followers to the center of the town, where they processed to the pounding of drums. On this occasion some magicians enlivened the proceedings. Indeed, one magician continually excited the weaver, who was in trance, by sleight-of-hand tricks with limes. The magician would make the limes appear and then disappear. Since limes are thought to accompany the mother goddess, each time the limes appeared the weaver would become beside himself with expectation, thinking his special god had drawn near. The procession also had a fertility aspect, for some of the men carried seedlings which they finally sunk in a well outside the village, to "cool" them for the best growth.

In the evening the people sacrificed a goat at each of the three principal shrines, trying to assure the town's good fortune in the coming year. They also purified themselves with fire, walking between two flames and passing through the flames their tools, butter churns, swords, and the like. The anthropologist reporting these customs was advised to pass across his ever-present pen and camera.

Although the afternoon procession was the most popular part of Naumi (in large measure because it drew magicians and other showmen), the evening sacrifices, performed for the welfare of the whole village, were no less important. In fact, in the evening some people visited all forty-four of the village's shrines, praying for all the gods' help during the coming year. (Since there were only about 900 people in the village, there was one shrine for about every twenty people.) The order of visitation shows how the village ranked these shrines: mother goddess, smallpox goddess, Vaishnavite Temple, another mother goddess, lord of the south village gates, Shaivite Temple, local small god, god of the nath caste, temple where a treaty was signed with some marauders, local mother goddess, temple of the brahmin caste, another Vaishnavite Temple, and more.

The anthropologist reporting this bevy of temples did not always know precisely what function a given god was thought to perform, and his mention of so many castes shows the splintered character of Indian village society even in recent times. The temples concerned with smallpox, cholera, and leprosy are a sad commentary on rural Indian health, while the several temples dedicated to the mother goddess show that recent folk Hinduism has continued India's millennial adoration of the Great Mother, the primal source of life and comfort.

The rituals of folk Hinduism vary from geographic area to geographic area, depending on local gods and customs. Among Hindus of the Himalayas, a strong shamanistic influence remains. Many of these people's religious ceremonies involve a shaman's possession (much like the possession of central Indian mediums such as the weaver and carpenter). More often than not, a family calls upon a shaman because of some misfortune: "Most supernatural beings make their presence felt by imposing difficulties or troubles upon people—usually disease or death to people or animals, and sometimes other troubles such as hysteria, faithless spouses, sterility, poor crops, financial loss, or mysterious disappearance of belongings."[52] When such things happen, people usually ask a shaman to hold a seance. Thus, a goodly number of ad hoc ceremonies supplement the annual cycle of ceremonies similar to Naumi.

The shaman may be from any caste, and he tends to make his living by acting as the medium of a particular god. Usually he opens a consultation by singing prayers in honor of his god, to the steady beat of a drum. As he enters into trance, often he becomes impervious to pain, as he demonstrates by touching red-hot metal. When the god has taken full possession of the shaman, the god usually uses the shaman's voice to tell the client what is troubling him and what should be done to cure it. The god may also identify thieves or harmful articles that have brought the misfortune. If the clients do not like the god's diagnosis or advice, they simply go to a different shaman.

More often than not, the treatment the god suggests is performing a *puja* (short ceremony) in honor of the being that is causing the trouble. (In the case of a ghost, the *puja* amounts to an exorcism.) Other popular treatments are making pilgrimages or removing harmful objects causing disease. If the case is impossible to cure (for example, a person deranged beyond healing), the god may prescribe an impossible treatment (for example, the sacrifice of a cow; since the cow is sacred to Hindus, sacrificing a cow is unthinkable).

If the suggested cure is performing a *puja*, other religious specialists generally enter the scene. Their job is arranging and executing a ceremony in which the god can enter a human body, ideally that of the victim, dance in it, and make known any further demands. These *puja* specialists usually come from the lower castes, and their basic method of inducing the god's possession of the victim is playing percussion instruments.

The ceremony tends to unfold in three parts: the dance, the *puja* or prayer proper, and the offering. Usually the ceremony takes place in the shrine of the god who is concerned. The shrine itself is very simple, generally consisting of one to four iron tridents about 8 inches high. The people place these in a niche in the wall, if the shrine is indoors, or at the base of a large stone, if it is outside, in effect marking off a sacred space. During the ceremonies the shrine is lighted by a small oil lamp, and often a container of rice and small coins hangs near it, as an offering to the god.

The dance, which begins the ceremony, is intended to attract the god (or any other spirit or ancestor who likes to dance in the bodies of humans). The gods are thought to like dancing because it gives them a chance to air their complaints and needs. Dancing most often occurs in the evening, but sometimes it is repeated the following day. As the drummers increase the intensity of the beat and the room fills with onlookers, smoke, and heat, the rhythms become more compelling, until someone, either the victim or an onlooker, starts to jerk, shout, and dance, first slowly but then more wildly. The possessed person is honored with incense and religious gestures, and fed boiled rice, because for the moment he or she is the god.

After the god has danced his fill, he usually speaks through the possessed person, telling the cause of his anger (the source of the misfortune) and detailing what it will take to appease him. The victimized person and his or her family then make a short prayer to the god, expressing reverently their desire to comply with his requests, after which they make the offering the god has demanded.

The most frequent offering is a young male goat. The people place the goat before the shrine and throw rice on its back, while the ritual specialist chants mantras. When the goat shakes itself, the onlookers believe the god has accepted their offering. An attendant (usually from a low caste; higher caste people tend to consider this defiling) takes the goat outside and beheads it. The attendant then places a foot and the head of the animal before the shrine, as an offering to the god, along with such delicacies as bread and sweet rice. The ritual specialist eventually gathers these up,

as part of his fee, and the family and guests share the rest of the goat.

The anthropologist describing this kind of ceremony found that the villagers strongly believed in its efficacy. Thus one teenage boy attributed his father's recovery from pneumonia to a possession ceremony, while another informant opined that the gods are like lawyers: The more you give them, the more they will do on your behalf. Clearly, therefore, the villagers of the Himalayas, as much as the villagers of central India, have continued to supplement the more official festivals of the Vedic gods with many local folk practices.

A third sort of ritual common in contemporary Indian religion deals with a stage of the life cycle, helping a person cope with puberty, marriage, parenthood, or widowhood. The *habisha* ritual performed by middle-aged women in the eastern province of Orissa illustrates this sort. To begin, the anthropologist making the report notes that the *habisha* ritual is a *brata* or vowed observance: "Historically, vows have been an important part of Hindu ritual life for centuries. People make vows mainly to secure something in this world, such as progeny, wealth, good fortune, health, fame, or long life; sometimes people make vows to secure something in the next world; and occasionally, as in the *habisha* rites, people make vows to gain something both in this world and in the next."[53] The vows may last as short a time as a day, or as long as the rest of one's life, but whatever their time, they are serious business. As the stories of the *Puranas* emphasize, failure to fulfill a vow can lead to dire consequences.

Consequently, the person who makes a vow usually prepares assiduously to fulfill it, by fasting, worshiping gods, taking frequent purificatory baths, abstaining from sexual relations, refraining from drinking water or chewing betel nuts, and not sleeping during daylight hours. From this asceticism, as well as the fulfillment of the vow itself, the vower gains spiritual power. In the case of the *habisha* ritual, the spiritual power focuses on preventing the death of the woman's husband. Most *habisha* participants, in fact, are menopausal women trying to protect their husbands from death (and trying therefore to protect themselves from the sad fate of the Hindu widow).

For the women whom our source studied, participating in the *habisha* ritual, and especially going on pilgrimage to the holy town of Puri, had been the high point of their lives. Typically, the women dedicated a thirty-five-day period in October–November to purificatory rituals and fasts in honor of Jagannatha, a local version of the young god Krishna. The imaginative context of these devotions was the legendary scene of the young Krishna among his female devotees (*gopis*). Krishna was the cow herdsman and the *gopis* were the milkmaids. The *habisha* women drew scenes from this legend in rice powder, churned milk in imitation of the *gopis*, offered coconuts and cowrie shells to a replica of Krishna, and danced ecstatically to express their great love of the god. If possible, they concluded their season of devotions with a 40-mile trip to the temple of Lord Jagannatha in Puri.

The elaborate preparations of one informant show the seriousness with which Indian women can enter upon rituals like *habisha*. This informant, a fifty-five-year-old married woman named Tila, was a member of the confectioner caste. Six days before the beginning of *habisha* in 1971, she had a barber trim her fingernails and toenails. Then she took a ritual bath and summoned the brahmin who usually performed ceremonies for her family. He further purified Tila by sprinkling cow-dung water on her head. Ideally, he said, people would purify themselves for *habisha* by drinking *panchagavia,* as in the old days, but nowadays few people were so thorough. *Panchagavia,* it turned out, was the five holy substances of the cow: milk, curds, clarified butter, urine, and dung. Tila apparently forewent this treat, promising, however, that she would be the brahmin's disciple for the full month, that she would listen to his daily recitation from a sacred book, and that she would fulfill her vows of fasting, purification, and sexual abstinence.

The typical day of the votive period began with a chilly predawn bath at the village pond. Facing in each of the four directions, the women involved prayed to the gods, to their ancestors, and to other sources of help, dipping into the water and purifying themselves. Then they made mud-pictures of the god Vishnu as a child, offered prayers to the rising sun, and took burning wicks to the village temple, where they chanted and prayed. These ceremonies, as well as their common dedication, bonded the women together, so that for the *habisha* month they put aside their rivalries, jealousies, and gossip. From the village temple they retired to their individual homes, where they cooked the one meal they were allowed to eat each day at sundown. Tila was allowed to eat only rice, lentils, green plantain, taro, cucumber, ginger, and custard apple—foods considered pure. She could have no spices, but each of her meals had to contain clarified butter, a holy substance from the cow.

During the *habisha* days, Tila was especially careful to avoid such defiling contacts as stepping on animal feces or touching a person from a low caste. She would join the other women for ritual baths, prayers, drawings, and above all, dances reenacting the legends of Krishna. The psychosocial explanation for these ceremonies is the upper caste Hindu woman's fear of an early widowhood. The younger the widow, the worse her fate, because widowhood means marginal status as a financial dependent, a potential source of sexual disturbance, and a being polluted by contact with death. The religious explanation is the devotional satisfaction that immersion in the theistic cult of Krishna, loving communion with Krishna, sponsors. Insofar as Krishna becomes the center of the women's emotional lives, the chance *habisha* offers them to concentrate on Krishna intensely for a whole month is a religious delight.

Two hundred fifty miles directly south of Delhi, in the town of Bharatpur, is a famous temple, the Balaji, to which many Indians come for the cure of psychosomatic illnesses. The main assumption behind the healing rituals of the temple is that most petitioners are possessed by a destructive spirit. Usually the destructive spirit has suggested its presence through symptoms such as stomach pains, headaches, or fits of uncontrollable rage. To relieve the patient of such afflictions, the priests of the temple have developed formalized processes focused on a warfare between the offending spirit and one of the protector deities resident in the temple. The ordinary start of the formalized process or ritual is the patient's overt possession by the demon, the clearest evidence of which is a rhythmic swaying of the upper half of the body and violent sideways shaking of the head. The demon may also manifest its presence by making patients beat the floor with their hands, hit their backs against the wall, or lie down on the floor with heavy stones piled on their backs. The patients enter a trancelike state (what a psychoanalyst might call a *dissociation*). They are able to carry on a conversation but generally will not remember what went on during the ritual.

The center of the process usually is a struggle between the demon and the protector god who has been invoked. The demon shouts, curses, and makes accusations or complaints through the mouth of the patient, while the onlooking crowd (the family of the patient or other pilgrims) berates the offending spirit. Generally the demon finally agrees to leave the patient, after greater or lesser struggle, and the temple priests arrange for the continuing protection of the helpful deity by giving the patient talismans to signify the protection of a good spirit. The good spirit usually will manifest itself through a shorter and calmer trance, during which the patient will offer prayers and prostrations to the protector deity. A psychoanalyst might see most of the patient's pains as symptoms of the sexual inhibition or repressed anger that Indian ideals of self-control and family peace can cause, but the framework in which the patients and priests view the sicknesses is the folk Hindu conviction that the world is populated with many spirits, both good and evil.[54]

To balance the stress on popular religion we have made in dealing with contemporary Hinduism, we should point out that the centuries-long concern for transcendence and *moksha* certainly has continued. If the rituals we have described mainly are pragmatic, concerned with helping people in everyday life, the yogic practices, study, and asceticism practiced by the religious virtuosi have kept alive the realization that religion entails more than the pragmatic and everyday. Certainly rituals such as those we have described go back to Vedic times. Certainly in all periods Hindus would have offered anthropological observers rich materials such as those mined by observers nowadays. But throughout the ages the thirst for *moksha,* leading to withdrawal from everyday affairs, celibacy, meditation, and austerity, also has been a strong component of Hindu culture. So we are wise to think of the overall tradition as a balance— a diet that offered much to both those concerned with earthly problems and those seeking heavenly release.

Critique.   In the mid-1970s, Indira Gandhi, head of the Indian government, imposed an "Emergency" to try to get her country's political and social problems under control. V. S. Naipaul, a journalist of Indian ancestry, has ruminated on the underlying causes of such problems as follows:

> In a speech before the Emergency, Jaya Prakash Narayan, the most respected opposition leader, said: "It is not the existence of disputes and quarrels that so much endangers the integrity of the nation as the manner in which we conduct them. We often behave like animals. Be it a village feud, a students' organization, a labor dispute, a religious procession, a boundary disagreement, or a major political question, we are more likely than not to become aggressive, wild, and violent. We

kill and burn and loot and sometimes commit even worse crimes."

> The violence of the riot could burn itself out; it could be controlled, as it now was, by the provisions of the Emergency. But there was an older, deeper Indian violence. This violence had survived untouched by foreign rule and had survived [Mahatma] Gandhi. It had become part of the Hindu social order, and there was a stage at which it became invisible, disappearing in the general distress. But now, with the Emergency, the emphasis was on reform, and on the "weaker sections" of society; and the stories the censored newspapers played up seemed at times to come from another age. A boy seized by a village moneylender for an unpaid debt of 150 rupees, fifteen dollars, and used as a slave for four years; in September, in Vellore in the south, untouchables forced to leave their village after their huts had been fenced in by caste Hindus and their well polluted; in October, in a village in Gujarat in the west, a campaign of terror against untouchables rebelling against forced labor and the plundering of their crops; the custom, among the untouchable men of a northern district, of selling their wives to Delhi brothels to pay off small debts to their caste landlords.

> To the ancient Aryans the untouchables were "walking carrion." Gandhi—like other reformers before him—sought to make them part of the holy Hindu system. He called them *Harijans,* children of God. A remarkable linguistic coincidence: they have remained God's chillun. Even at the Satyagraha Ashram [community] on the riverbank at Ahmedabad, which Gandhi himself founded after his return from South Africa, and from where in 1930 he started on the great Salt March. *Son et Lumière* at night these days in the ashram, sponsored by the tourism Development Corporation; and in the mornings, in one of the buildings, a school for Harijan girls. "Backward class, backward class," the old brahmin, suddenly my guide, explained piously, converting the girls into distant objects of awe. The antique violence remained: rural untouchability as serfdom, maintained by terror and sometimes by deliberate starvation. None of this was new; but suddenly in India it was news.[55]

There are some qualifiers one should place on Naipaul's observations. First, although born in Trinidad (of Indian parents) and educated at Oxford, Naipaul brings to India the sort of special sensitivity that an American of Irish extraction might bring to "the troubles" of Northern Ireland. Because the country he is observing has shaped his own genes, he sees its failures with a special acuteness. Second, one could document the failures of other religiocultural systems as graphically as Naipaul has documented the Hindu failures. His own later work, *Among the Believers,* is a scathing indictment of the foibles and horrors of the fundamentalist Islams of Pakistan, Iran, Malaysia, and Indonesia. Nazi, Soviet, Latin American, Cambodian, Chinese, African, and other failures, atrocities, and inhumanities blot the social records of the religions that have held sway in those areas. The treatment of Amerindian tribes and black slaves in the United States raises similar hackles and cautions.

Still, it remains that Hindu caste has been a powerful ingredient in what to the outsider looks like the nearly unrelieved misery of millions of Indian poor. Simply by the accident of their birth, the majority of Indians have been assigned to the bottom levels of the social pyramid. Of course, to the traditional Hindu, birth was nothing accidental. One was born into a priestly caste, or into a caste of workers, in virtue of one's karma from previous lives. While this might provide some consolation—"my fate is what the gods have meted out to me, or what I have earned from previous existences"—it meant that Indian society as a whole could become static. If many people thought that their poverty, or their wealth, was fated, they were less likely to work hard. Certainly, talent and industry could make a difference in any individual life. On the whole, however, the tendency to think of themselves as fenced in by their caste or particular trade sapped the vitality of many Indians. In the worst cases, it also supported discrimination and outright cruelty. The upper castes had every right to think themselves superior to the lower castes, and they felt few pressures to treat lower caste people kindly. The more religious people were, the more the "impurity" of the lowest castes could vex them, leading at times to violence, even murder. So Naipaul's critique is telling. Unless one accepts a traditional worldview in which most things are dictated by birth (as the expression of divine or cosmic forces), caste seems to be a formula bound to produce pervasive injustice.

Among all classes, but especially the poor, Indian women have suffered the worst burdens. The poverty, slavery, and general abuse into which untouchable women often have fallen, simply because they had been born into a certain social stratum, call into question all the religions' tendency to justify the status quo as a matter of divine ordinance. One need not employ Marxist analyses of ideology and class conflict to clarify the self-advantage that the upper classes have pursued through the Hindu caste system. Simple common sense will do.

A good critique is aware of its own biases and tries to balance negative data with positive. For Westerners, a regular bias has been the assumption that Western technology, democracy, and higher culture have been simon-pure boons to the people colonized, missionized, or taken into trading relationships with Western powers. While often this has been true, and many Indians have taken to heart Western objections to such Indian traditions as caste, it remains equally true that technology, religious proselytizing, and trade, to say nothing of political rule by Western powers, often have upset traditional Indian culture and generated many sufferings. In addition to the humiliation and resentment caused by being forced to submit to others' rule and culture, Indians and other colonized people have had to suffer attacks on their native ways and misunderstandings that sometimes have threatened to undermine their confidence in who they were.

On the matter of positive data, scholars of Hinduism often note that bonding between women, affection between spouses, and respect for wives, mothers, and daughters regularly have softened the negative potential latent in the traditional sexual roles. Similarly, the castes and jatis often have coexisted amicably, keeping their distinctions without making them cause for disrespect, animosity, or violence. Insofar as most Hindus through the ages have accepted the caste system as simply the way things were, they have shrugged off many of the criticisms or feelings of outrage an outsider might expect. None of these positive, countervailing data ought to place Hinduism beyond criticism, but any of them can help restore balanced perspective.

WORLDVIEW

For Hinduism, as all other religious traditions, the relationship between history and worldview is dialectical—that is to say, each influences the other. What Hindus have believed about the structures of reality (worldview) has developed in the course of their history. Conversely, their worldview has directed many of the choices that have determined the patterns of their existence over time (history).

Perhaps the most significant feature to emerge from Hindu history has been pluralism. Hindus have developed such a wealth of rituals, doctrines, devotions, artworks, social conventions, and other ways of dealing with ultimate reality, one another, and nature that they could not be uniform. More than such religious traditions as the Jewish, the Christian, the Muslim, and the Buddhist, whose basic convictions have been relatively uncontested, Hindus have admitted variety and debate into the core of their religious culture. One sees this when examining the impact of such a Hindu notion as that of the four legitimate goals of life. To say that pleasure, wealth, duty, and liberation (salvation) are all legitimate ends for human beings to pursue, and then to allow numerous ways of interpreting each of these ends, has been to ensure that Hinduism would allow a vast range of options in prayer, family life, economic activity, and dealings with the natural environment.

Thus the interaction of history and worldview in Hinduism has been especially creative. The vaunted color of Hindu life, the teeming variety of sights, smells, tastes, and sounds, stems from this creativity. The tradition has encouraged people to find their own pathway, to develop the special genius of their own little group, and people have responded creatively. Even when caste or poverty seemed to limit their potential, many Hindu men and women have found a devotion that gave them hope, a god or goddess who made them feel significant, a way of finding beauty in nature or human affairs that made them smile now and then.

Nature

For the most part, Hinduism considers nature (the physical cosmos) to be real, knowable, and orderly. The cosmos is a continuum of lives; consequently, human life is seen as an ongoing interaction with the lives of creatures above and below it. Furthermore, most Hindus consider divinity to be more than physical nature and think human self-realization *(moksha)* entails release from the laws of karma. Let us develop these ideas.

The statement that the physical cosmos is real requires some qualification. Through history, the average Hindu, concerned with making a living and caring for a family, has had little doubt that the fields, flocks, and other physical phenomena are real. Also, the hymns of the Vedas that revere the sun and the storm express a vivid appreciation of nature. Even many of the philosophers spoke of the world as *sat*—having being or reality. Only the idealistic thought of the Upanishads, as the Vedanta developed and somewhat organized it, called the reality of the physical world into question.

Furthermore, because of the Vedic notion of *rita* (order, duty, or ritual) and the later notion of karma, Hinduism found the natural world quite orderly. *Rita* presided over such phenomena as sunrise, sunset, and the seasons. Karma expressed the Hindu belief that all acts in the cosmos result from previous causes or choices and produce inevitable effects. To be sure, there are various religious paths *(margas)* for escaping karmic inevitability, and we discuss those paths below. Nonetheless, *rita* and karma suggest that the world is patterned, regular, and dependable. This does not mean that flood, famine, earthquake, sickness, or war cannot occur, but it does mean that none of these calamities makes the world absurd.

Karma is connected with the notion of transmigration and rebirth. *Rita* is involved with the vast space-time dimensions in which Hindu cosmology delights. Together these concepts give nature a gigantic expanse that is replete with connections. The connections that most interested the average Hindu linked the myriad living things. Astrology and astronomy brought some people in contact with planetary forces, but the average Indian was more interested in other people and animals. Shaivites expressed this interest by venerating the powers of fertility. Ancient rites honoring the Great Mother and other rites stressing Shaktism reveal other Hindu responses to the wonders of life. The symbolism surrounding Shiva and his consorts (such as Kali) explicitly links life with death. At a level above ancient concerns with the vegetative cycle of death and rebirth and the taking of life by life, Hinduism placed the connection between death and life in the context of the universal cycles of creation and destruction: the Brahma Day and Brahma Night by which the universe pulsated, Shiva's dance of life and death, and the sportive play of illusion (maya).

The Jain notion of *ahimsa,* which many Hindus adopted to varying degrees, implied the connectedness of all lives through its practice of not harming animals. Many Indians refused to eat meat out of the desire not to harm animals. Nonviolence toward the cow, which one might not kill even to help the starving (but which might itself starve), epitomized for many Hindus a necessary reverence for life. Taking karma and **transmigration** (the passing of the life force from one entity to another) seriously, Hindus thought that life, including their own, was constantly recasting itself into new vegetative and animal forms. Such life was not an evolutionary accident or something that ended at the grave. The inmost life principle continued on, making nature a container of life forces.

Frequently, maya and samsara carry negative overtones. In fact, the whole thrust toward *moksha* suggests that the natural sphere is of limited value. For more than a few Indians, the natural sphere has been a prison or place of suffering. Yogis of different schools, for instance, have tried to withdraw from materiality to cultivate enstasis. Other Hindu mystics have sensed that there was something more ultimate than the ritual sacrifice, the play of natural processes, and even the emotions of the devout worshiper of the bhakti god. In this sense samsara opposed the freedom suggested by *moksha,* and *moksha* meant exit from what one had known as natural conditions.

However, it is misleading to label Hinduism as world denying or life denying, since India's culture has produced many warriors, merchants, artists, and scientists—a full citizenry who took secular life seriously.[56] Nonetheless, Hindu culture was seldom secular or materialistic in our modern senses, usually stabilizing society by referring to a god or Brahman transcending human space and time. (We may say the same of traditional premodern societies generally.) In addition, Hinduism's reference to metaphysical concepts probably held back its concern with health care, education, and economic prosperity for the masses. (Again, we could say this of many other traditional cultures.) When he argued for a secular state and a turn to science rather than religion, Premier Nehru spoke for many modern, educated Indians. Even today, the religion of the villages, which is often quite primitive, hinders the improvement of agriculture, family planning, housing, and health care.

Thus, Hinduism's Aryan beginnings, which were so bursting with love of physical life, and its Dravidian beginnings, which were tantamount to nature and fertility worship, were negated in some periods of history. The most serious blows came from intellectual Hinduism and bhakti, which found life good by spiritual exercises and thus were not concerned with social justice or transforming nature for human benefit.

In Eric Voegelin's terms, neither the early Hinduism that began close to nature nor that which withdrew from nature to focus on human spirit escaped the cosmological myth. In Israel, Greece, and European Christian culture, such a withdrawal made nature less than divine. Unlike the religions of these Western cultures and the prophetic theology of Islam, Hinduism tended to keep gods and humans within the cosmic milieu and to think of nature as a stable entity that one could little affect or change. *Moksha* is an exception, but *moksha* was seldom articulated clearly. It primarily proposed that human self-realization comes by escaping the given world.

One confirmation of the view that Hinduism did not differentiate the realms of nature, divinity, and society is that the concept of creation from nothingness never became a dominant Hindu belief. In Hindu cosmology the universe goes its rhythmic way of Brahma Days and Brahma Nights; it has always existed and always will. Insofar as the concept of *moksha* suggests that we may transcend this cosmic rhythm, it carries seeds of a doctrine of creation from nothingness. However, the usual Hindu explanation of creation involves gods molding the world from preexisting stuff.[57] Thus Hinduism differs from Western religion by considering the world divine. It always remained somewhat under the cosmological myth and so it has lessons to teach Westerners who have lost reverence for nature. The Western notion of creation from nothingness is equally mythical, but its myth was different in stressing the freedom of a single personal deity.

Society

As we have seen, Hinduism structured society by caste and numerous occupational subclasses. In addition, families traced themselves back through their departed ancestors.[58] Outside the four castes were the untouchables, and there were also instances of slavery. The basic structure of the four castes received religious sanction in the *Rig-Veda* 10:90, where the priests, warriors, merchants, and workers emerged from the Great Man's body after he was sacrificed.

The Laws of Manu, expanding the doctrine of casteism, specified the castes' social duties. The brahmin, for instance, had six required acts: teaching, studying, sacrificing for himself, sacrificing for others, making gifts, and receiving gifts. Brahmins also were to avoid working at agriculture and selling certain foods (such as flesh and salt). Were they to do these things, they would assume the character of people of other castes. In a similar way, Manu set duties and prohibitions for the warriors, merchants, farmers, and workers, giving the entire society a comprehensive dharma. As a result, Hindus considered their dharma to be something given rather than a matter of debate or free choice. Indeed, such caste obligations were the basic cement of Hindu society.[59]

Nonetheless, various religious inspirations and movements introduced some flexibility. Many of the bhakti cults rejected caste distinctions, contending that all people were equal in the god's sight. The possibility of stepping outside the ordinary organization of things to become a full-time ascetic or seeker of liberation loosened the stranglehold of both dharma and caste. Throughout history, the patchwork organization of the Indian nation also added to social flexibility. Since most of the people lived in villages, and most of the administrative units were local rather than national, local customs were very strong.

Thus, Hindu society was remarkably diverse and tolerant despite its official rigidity. The complexity of social stations and religious allegiances meant that there were many legitimate ways through life. In the family, which was usually quite large, or extended, the chief figure was the father. Family organization was usually patriarchal, as was property administration. Women had some property rights, according to some legal schools, but their position was generally inferior. In fact, the place of the female, 50 percent of Hindu society, illustrates well the overall Hindu social and religious outlooks.

Women's Status.   We know little about the earliest Indian women's social status. There is evidence of fertility rites among the pre-Aryans, as we have seen, suggesting a cult of a mother goddess or a matriarchal social structure. In Vedic times women clearly were subordinate to men, but in earlier times they may have held important cultic offices, created canonical hymns, and been scholars, poets, and teachers.[60] In the Brihad-Aranyaka Upanishad, the woman Gargi questions the sage Yajnavalkya, indicating that wisdom was not exclusively a male concern.[61] It therefore seems likely that in early India at least some girls of the upper castes received religious training like the boys'.

However, between the first Vedas (1500 B.C.E.) and the first codes of law (100 C.E.), women's religious roles steadily declined. A major reason for this was the lowering of the marriage age from fifteen or sixteen years

to ten or even five. This both removed the possibility of education (and consequently religious office) and fixed women's roles to being wife and mother. In fact, in later Hinduism being a wife was so important that a widow supposedly was prohibited from mentioning any man's name but that of her deceased husband. Even if she had been a child bride or had never consummated her marriage, the widow was not to violate her duty to her deceased husband and remarry. If she did, it was thought she would bring disgrace on herself in the present life and enter the womb of a jackal for her next rebirth.

Thus, the widow was the most forlorn of Hindu women. Without a husband, she was a financial liability to those who supported her. If menstruating, she could be a source of ritual pollution. If barren, she was useless to a society that considered women essentially as child producers. In such a social position, many widows must have felt that they had little to lose by throwing themselves on their husband's funeral pyre.[62] (Even suttee, though, was not simple. If the widow did not burn herself out of pure conjugal love, her act was without merit.)

Women were sometimes admitted as equals into the bhakti and Tantrist sects. However, two circumstances in Tantrism minimized the social liberation that the open admission might have effected. First, the Tantrist sects tended to be esoteric, or secret, which made their public impact minor. Second, the Tantrist interest in tapping *shakti* energies often led to the exploitation of women by men. Thus, the males sometimes tried to gain powers of liberation *(moksha)* by symbolic or actual sexual intercourse, with the result that the females became instruments rather than equal partners. Nevertheless, the Tantrist image of perfection as being androgynous tended to boost the value of femaleness. How much this ideal actually benefited Indian women is difficult to say, but it probably helped some. Nonetheless, women were not generally eligible for *moksha;* the best that a woman could hope for was to be reborn as a man. There is little evidence that Tantrism eliminated this belief, though the *Bhagavad Gita,* 9:32, seems to contradict it.

In fact, the overall status of women in Hinduism was that of wards. They were subject, successively, to fathers, husbands, and elder sons. As soon as they approached puberty, their fathers hastened to marry them off, and during their wedded lives they were to honor their husbands without reservation. According to the *Padmapurana,* an influential text, this obligation held true even if their husbands were deformed, aged, debauched, lived openly with other women, or showed them no affection. To ritualize this attitude of devotion, orthodox Hindu authors counseled wives to adore the big toe of their husband's right foot, bathing it as they would an idol, and offering incense before it as they would to a great god.[63]

Worse than ward status, however, was the strain of misogyny (hatred of women) running through Hindu culture. The birth of a girl was not an occasion for joy. Hindus attributed it to bad karma in a previous life and frequently announced the event by saying, "Nothing was born." A girl was a financial burden, for unless her parents arranged a dowry there was small chance that she would marry, and the Vedic notion that women were necessary if men were to be complete (which the gods' consorts evidence) lost out to Manu's view that women were as impure as falsehood itself. In fact, Manu counseled "the wise" never to sit with a woman in a lonely place, even if that woman were one's mother, sister, or daughter.[64]

Consequently, Hindu religious texts sometimes imagine a woman as a snake, hell's entrance, death, a prostitute, or an adulteress. In Manu's code, slaying a woman was one of the minor offenses. In the Hindu family, the basic unit of society, woman therefore carried a somewhat negative image, although, of course, some women entered happy households. The high status of the householder did not extend to his wife or female children. India mainly honored women for giving birth and serving their husbands. (In a study of the emotional attitudes that this pattern has inculcated in modern India, Aileen Ross found the following intensity ratings for the listed relationships [the higher the number, the more intense the relationship]: mother-son, 115; brother-sister, 90; brother-brother, 75; father-son, 74; husband-wife, 16; sister-sister, 5. She gives no rating for the mother-daughter relationship.[65])

Ma Jnanananda.   To show the sort of exception that relativizes general statements such as those that we have been making about Hindu women, let us briefly consider a contemporary female guru, Ma Jnanananda of Madras.

Ma is a familiar form of *mother.* Jnanananda is a spiritual mother to numerous followers in present-day Madras. She is both a *guru* and a *sannyasi.* A guru is a religious teacher. A sannyasi is "one who has taken a formal vow renouncing all worldly life, including family ties and possessions. Such a vow, in effect, means death to one's former life. This renunciation allows

full-time pursuit of spiritual goals and fosters spiritual development. Such vows have been common in India from ancient times to the present."[66]

Ma gained her lofty position as a guru because one of the leading Advaita Vedanta figures of contemporary India, Shankaracharya of Kanchipuram, recognized that she had penetrated the deepest truths of Hinduism, through mystical absorption with Brahman. Jnanananda had done this while living in the world, married and raising five children. That probably accounts for her great ability to relate the teachings of Vedanta to her disciples' daily problems at work or in family life.

Photographs of Ma taken before she became a guru show a lovely woman, well dressed and well groomed. The beauty still lingers, but now it seems a reflection of her inner peace. She has traded her fine clothes for a simple sari of ochre cloth, cut her hair short, and painted on her forehead and arms horizontal stripes of a thick paste made from ashes, to symbolize her death to vanity and worldly desires.

Ma's teaching is rooted in her profound experiences of *samadhi. Samadhi* is a state of deep trance, an experience of the basic consciousness that has no form yet relates the person to all other things. Here is Ma's description of her earliest experiences. "In that state I used to ask myself, 'Where am I?' Then I would try to think of myself at some point, but I immediately felt myself to be at the opposite point."[67] The result of such *samadhi* is a profound conviction that all things are one, that the world at bottom is a simple unity.

To help her disciples gain this perception, from which flows great peace and integration, Ma Jnanananda stresses four principles or virtues, all of which have venerable roots in traditional Hinduism. First, she insists on absolute truth, on trying always to stand in the light of conscience and the light of objective reality. One who would seriously pursue the Advaita Vedanta path toward enlightenment has to employ truthful means. Second, she urges purity. This means clearing the inner waters, letting all immoral thoughts and desires sink toward the bottom, like useless silt. Third, the disciple must develop his or her dharma, the righteousness that comes from fulfilling the duties of one's state in life. Last, Ma stresses *ahimsa* or nonviolence, the attitude of trying to do no injury to any fellow creature.

Together, these four virtues compose a spiritual program that Ma calls "action without desire." It is at least as old as the *Bhagavad Gita,* yet completely practical in the contemporary world. Essentially, it means self-surrender, so that one's life more and more stands free of either worries about the past or troubling anticipations of the future.

The end result of such a self-surrender should be a complete focus on God (ultimate reality). In the regime Ma would have a disciple follow, the day begins with some prayer or meditation to the deity of the disciple's choice. After this, the disciple turns to the work of the day, trying to perform duties in such a way that they do not distract the mind from God. The ideal is always to surrender completely to God. When distracting thoughts enter the mind, one should return to God by substituting a prayer or *mantra* (sacred sound). The goal always is "realization" of God, experiential awareness of the divinity in everything.

As this realization increases, worldly things lose their allure. Bit by bit one is skirting the dark forest of fear and desire, moving away from the powers of samsara and time. We can never control all the events of our lives, but we can control our attitude toward them. If we regard what happens to us as intended for our detachment from samsaric things, intended for our attachment to God, all things will become profitable. Such is Ma's teaching.

The final state of realization brings a great love of God. As one's union with divinity increases, one's fulfillment overflows. In this conviction, Ma Jnanananda is a sister to the great mystics of other religious traditions. East and West, they agree that union with God or ultimate reality is the greatest success a human being can attain. Ma Jnanananda therefore shows that Shankara's stress on the sole reality of Brahman is neither eccentric nor ethereal. As it works in her own life, and the lives of many of her disciples, it is a source of great fulfillment and love. She also shows that Indian women of talent can escape the limits of the image Hinduism has given them.

Conclusion. The social rewards of Hindu religion were in the hands of a relative few. By excluding most women, untouchables, and workers, intellectualist Hinduism told well more than half the population that their best hope was rebirth in a better station sometime in the future. (For the most part, only a member of a high caste could reach *moksha*.) However, in the family and the different trades, dharma gave all castes some legitimacy. Nonetheless, if the fundamental belief of Hinduism is considered to be the struggle for self-realization, these honors were rather tainted. For instance, in the ideal life cycle men of the upper three

castes were to leave their families in middle age and retire from social life. A husband might take his wife into retirement with him, but he had no obligation to do so. If anything, tradition probably encouraged him to go off alone. What a person intent on self-realization did for children, servants, or the lower classes in his city was secondary to what he did for his own atman. Thus, in the Brihad-Aranyaka Upanishad 2.4.5, Yajnavalkya praised his wife Maitreyi for wanting his help in gaining immortality rather than in gaining wealth. This made her dear to him, not because he loved her earthly self but because he loved her atman.

The smaller units of Hindu society were less honored religiously than they were in other cultures. For instance, although Hindu marriage involved a sacramental rite, it was not regarded as highly as in Judaism, where it is one of life's three great blessings (the Torah, good deeds, and marriage). The larger social organizations in India never approached the unity of a nation or empire, so one does not find the analogies between earth and heaven that one finds in Mesopotamia or Egypt, where the king was the mediator of divine substance, or *maat*—the mediator between the above of the gods and the below of the human realm. Indians may have sometimes pictured the realm of the many gods as a sort of government with superiors and subordinates, but this imagery was not so strong as it was in Greece or China. Indian society was simply too diverse and too fragmented to be considered a mirror of the macrocosm.

Thus, Hindu society is very complex. Dharma has meant that religion supported a responsible attitude toward society, and the law treatises specified these responsibilities. On the other hand, *moksha* and bhakti militated against taking worldly life too seriously. For those absorbed in religious liberation or religious love, political, economic, and even family structures could seem of negligible importance.

Understandably, many of the great religious figures of Indian history left the social scheme. The Mahavira and the Buddha both left high-caste homes (the Buddha, in fact, left a wife and small child). Shankara urged celibacy and skipping the two middle stages of the life cycle so that one could pursue liberation wholeheartedly. The wandering minstrels of bhakti clearly did little for their families' or towns' social stability. Since pleasure and wealth meant less than duty and liberation, they were less effective ties to worldly responsibilities than they have been in other cultures. Thus, Hindu society has been notably "unhistorical"—not simply in the sense that it has kept

Figure 16   Narasimha, Madras, India, eleventh century. Bronze, 19⅜ in. high. Narasimha is an avatar of Vishnu, in which he appears as half-man and half-lion. His four arms suggest his powers to help his devotees, and his semiyogic posture suggests a masterful repose. The Nelson–Atkins Museum of Art, Kansas City, Missouri (Nelson Fund).

relatively few records of temporal affairs but in the deeper sense that it has defined itself by a striving for something that lay outside space and time.

Self

Obviously, the average Hindu did not think about the self in isolation from nature and society. The social caste system and the cosmic samsara-transmigration

system were the framework of any studious self-examination. Within this framework, however, an individual might set about the task of trying to attain *atmasiddhi,* the perfecting of human nature. This was another way, more concrete perhaps, of posing what *moksha* or the *mahatma* (the "great soul") meant.

In the *Rig-Veda, atmasiddhi* was the pious man who faithfully recited the hymns and made sacrifices to the gods.[68] The ritualistic texts called the *Brahmanas* changed the ideal to the priest who could faultlessly conduct the expanded ritual. The Upanishads shifted perfection toward the acquisition of secret knowledge about reality. The *smriti* literature such as the Laws of Manu valued more worldly achievement. There the most excellent man was he who could rule public affairs and lead in community matters. The *Bhagavad Gita* spoke of love as the highest attainment, but it described the realized human personality as being stable in wisdom and having overcome the desires of both the flesh and ambition. Recently Indian saints such as Ramakrishna and Gandhi have stressed, respectively, the mystic loss of self in God and the service of Truth. Clearly, therefore, Hindu tradition allows the self many ideals. Generally speaking, though, full success has implied emotional, intellectual, and spiritual maturity and has honored the social side of human being as well as the solitary.

The Upanishads jostled the classical life cycle for many. As we have seen, the Upanishadic self was the atman identified with Brahman. For this revered part of the Hindu tradition, then, the most important aspect of the self was the spiritual core. More than the body, this spiritual core was the key to escaping rebirth. If one was serious about escaping rebirth, why wait for the final stages of the life cycle? Why not cultivate the atman full time? Some such reasoning surely prompted those who became wanderers long before old age. Whether through study or meditation, they pursued a way that implied that the self's needs or aspirations could outweigh social responsibilities.

In the past thousand years or so, the individual Hindu has therefore had a variety of ways of viewing his or her life journey. The four stages of the life cycle, the Upanishadic or bhakti wandering, the household devotions—any of these concepts could give people's lives meaning. Hinduism explicitly recognized that people's needs differed by speaking of four *margas* (paths) that could lead to fulfillment and liberation. Among intellectuals, the way of knowledge was prestigious. In this *marga* one studied the classical texts, the Vedic revelation and commentators' tradition, pursuing an intuitive insight into reality. Shankara's higher knowledge is one version of this ideal. If one could gain the viewpoint where Brahman was the reality of everything, one had gained the wisdom that would release one from suffering.

But philosophy patently did not attract everyone, and many whom it did attract could not spare the time to study. Therefore, the way of karma (here understood as meaning works or action) better served many people. The *Bhagavad Gita* more than sanctioned this way, which amounted to a discipline of detachment. If one did one's daily affairs peacefully and with equanimity of spirit, then one would not be tied to the world of samsara. Doing just the work, without concern for its "fruits" (success or failure), one avoided bad karma (here meaning the law of cause and effect). Gandhi, who was much taken with this teaching of the *Gita*, used spinning as an example of *karma-marga* or *karma-yoga* (work discipline). One just let the wheel turn, trying to join one's spirit to its revolutions and paying the quantity of production little heed. When *karma-yoga* was joined to the notion that one's work was a matter of caste obligation, or dharma, it became another powerful message that the status quo was holy and meaningful.

A third *marga* was **meditation** *(dhyana),* which meant some variant of the practices that Patanjali's *Yoga Sutras* sketch.[69] (This is the most popular meaning of **yoga.**) Contrasted with the way of knowledge, the way of meditation did not directly imply study and did not directly pursue intuitive vision. Rather, it was usually based on the conviction that one can reach the real self by quieting the senses and mental activity to descend without thinking to the personality's depths. In this progression, one approached a state of deep sleep and then went beyond it to nondualism. "Seedless *samadhi*" (pure consciousness) was the highest of the eight branches of yogic progress, but to enter *moksha* one had to leave even it behind. Along the way to *samadhi* one might acquire various paranormal powers (such as clairvoyance or telepathy), but these were of little account. Below even the subconscious one wished to rest without desire on the bottom of pure spirit. For the many who meditated, the way of *dhyana* usually meant peace, a great sensitivity to body-spirit relationships (through, for example, posture and breath control), and a deepening sense of the oneness of all reality.

Finally, bhakti had the status of a *marga,* and, according to the *Bhagavad Gita,* it could be a very high way. Of course, *bhaktas* ran the gamut from emotional hysteria to lofty mysticism. The *Gita* qualified the self-assertiveness that could arise in bhakti, however, by making its final revelation not human love of divinity but Krishna's love for humans. On the basis of such revelation, the *bhakta* was responding to divinity as divinity had shown itself to be. In other words, the *bhakta* was realizing human fulfillment by imitating God. (That was true of the yogi as well, which suggests that in India, as in other religious cultures, the self was finally an image of divinity.)

Case Study: The Hindu Child. We can get further glimpses into the Hindu sense of the self by considering how Hindus tended to regard their children.

The Hindu child was subjected to religious ceremonies well before birth. For devout Hindus, there were rituals to ensure conception, to procure a male child, and to safeguard the child's time in the womb. Birth itself involved an important ceremony, which ideally took place before the cutting of the umbilical cord, and that included whispering sacred spells in the baby's ear, placing a mixture of ghee and honey in its mouth, and giving it a name that its parents were to keep secret until its initiation. Birth made both parents ritually impure for ten days, which meant they were not to take part in the community's ordinary religious rites. Ten days after birth the child was given a public (as contrasted with the secret) name. Some households also solemnized both an early ear-piercing and the first time the parents took the child out of the house and showed it the sun.

A. L. Basham, from whose book *The Wonder That Was India* we are taking this description of Hindu childhood, lists some of the other rituals that devout parents included in a child's first years:

> More important [than the first vision of the sun] was the first feeding *(annaprasana).* In the child's sixth month he was given a mouthful of meat, fish, or rice (in later times usually the latter) mixed with curds, honey, and ghee, to the accompaniment of Vedic verses and oblations of ghee poured on the fire. The tonsure *(cudakarma)* took place in the third year, and was confined to boys; with various rites the child's scalp was shaved, leaving only a topknot, which, in the case of a pious brahmin, would never be cut throughout his life. Another ceremony, not looked on as of the first importance, was carried out when the child first began to learn the alphabet.[70]

There was a pressing motive for parents to have sons, in that at least one son was thought necessary to perform the parents' funeral rites, without which they could not be sure of a safe transit to the other world. Adopted sons were better than nothing, but they were nowhere near so good as natural sons. Girls were of no use whatsoever, because girls could not help their parents in the next world, and at marriage girls passed into the families of their husbands. Although Indian history shows some evidence of female infanticide, this practice seems to have been relatively rare. Despite their lesser desirability, many girls were cared for and petted like sons.

Indeed, Indian literature shows few instances of such maxims as "Spare the rod and spoil the child," and one gathers that most Hindus had relatively happy, indulged childhoods. In Indian poetry, for example, children are often shown laughing, babbling, and being welcomed onto their parents' laps, even when it was likely they would leave those laps quite soiled. On the other hand, poor children were set to work soon after they were able to walk, and wealthier children started their studies as young as four or five. Thus boys usually were set to studying the alphabet by their fifth year. Richer families engaged tutors for their children, and through the Indian Middle Ages (before the Muslim invasions) many village temples had schools attached. The education of girls was considered much less pressing than that of boys, but most upper class women became literate. Before his initiation, when he was invested with the sacred thread and set to studying the Vedas, an upper-class boy usually concentrated on reading and arithmetic.

The initiation of brahmin boys usually occurred when they were eight. For warriors the ideal age was eleven, and for merchants twelve. The key element in this initiation was hanging a cord of three threads over the boy's right shoulder. The cord was made of nine twisted strands (cotton for brahmins, hemp for warriors, and wool for merchants). To remove this thread anytime during his subsequent life, or to defile it, involved the initiate in great humiliation and ritual impurity.

Another important element in the initiation was whispering the *Gayatri,* the most sacred verse of the *Rig-Veda* (3:62:10), in the ear of the initiate. Whereas previously he had been a child, not really a member of the Aryan people, this access to the Vedas began his spiritual, fully human life. The *Gayatri* is addressed to the old solar god Savitr, and it functions in Hindu ceremonies much as the Lord's Prayer functions in Christian ceremonies, as a basic and privileged expression of devotion. In Basham's translation it runs: "Let us think on the lovely splendour of the god Savitr, that he may inspire our minds."

In later times initiation and investment with the sacred thread became limited mainly to brahmins, but in Vedic times the other upper classes initiated their children, often including their girls. The initiation made the child an Aryan, a member of a noble people, opening the door to his first serious task, that of mastering the sacred Aryan lore. Accordingly, soon after initiation the child was apprenticed to a brahmin in order to learn the Vedas. During this period he was to be celibate, to live a simple life, and to obey his teacher assiduously. There were no sexual overtones to the initiation rite, and other ceremonies took care of the passage to physical maturity.

What was the Hindu child being taught through rituals such as these? That he or she was a being who, in addition to social responsibilities, had the potential to cope with desire and karma, thereby becoming free enough to recognize that the grounds of selfhood were divine and that full freedom lay in discovering this divinity.

Ultimate Reality

Our final consideration is how Hindus experienced and conceptualized ultimate reality. This is no less complex than the dimensions of nature, society, and the self. In the early Vedic literature, the gods are principally natural phenomena. It is the wondrous qualities of the storm or fire that elevate Indra and Agni to prominence. By the time that the Brahmanic emphasis on sacrificial ritual dominated, the gods had come under human control. The final stage of Brahmanism was the view that the ritual, if properly performed, inevitably attains its goals—it compels the gods to obey. When we couple this subordinating view of the gods with the notion of samsara, the gods become less venerable than human beings. Human beings have the potential to break with samsara and to transcend the transmigratory realm through *moksha.* The gods, despite their heavenly estate, are still within the transmigratory realm and cannot escape into *moksha.*

The Upanishads, as we saw, moved away from the plurality of gods toward monism. One can debate whether this view is atheistic or religious, but the debate turns on semantics. However, both the Upanishads and the Vedanta philosophers stated that the knowledge of Brahman or atman is redemptive. Such knowledge, in other words, is not simply factual or scientific but has the power to transform one's life—it is light freeing one from existential darkness. Therefore, from the side of the one who experiences Brahman's dominance, we can surely speak of "religious" (ultimately concerned) overtones.

As well, the place that Brahman has in the world view of the Upanishads and the Vedanta correlates with the place that God has in monotheism. Brahman is the basis of everything, if not the creator. It is the supreme value, because nothing is worth more than the ultimate being, which, once seen, sets everything else in light and order.

Attending to Brahman, Hinduism's major concept for ultimate reality, we can note finally that the two aspects of Brahman approximate what monotheistic religions have made of their God. Being beyond the human realm *(nirguna),* Brahman recedes into mystery. This parallels the Christian God's quality of always being ineffable and inconceivable. But being within the human realm *(saguna),* Brahman is the basis of nature and culture. In this way it approximates the Christian conception of the Logos, in whom all creation holds together.

Brahman, of course, is impersonal, whereas most monotheistic religions conceive their deities on the model of the human personality. Still, it is the functional equivalent of the most comprehensive realities of other religions. Like the Chinese *Dao* it cannot be named, yet it mothers the ten thousand things. Like the Buddhist suchness or buddha-nature, it must be described in both absolute and relative terms.

The bhakti cults have revered still another form of Hindu divinity. Vaishnavites do not strictly deny the reality of Shiva or Brahma, nor do followers of these other gods deny the reality of Vishnu or Krishna. The mere fact that bhakti sects devoted to different gods contend among themselves shows that they take the other gods seriously. But the emotional ardor of the devoted *bhaktas* suggests that they grant their gods the ultimate value of a monotheistic god. The same holds for devotees of goddesses, who may actually outnumber devotees of the male gods. The Devimahatmya writings, for instance, have fashioned a warrior queen who is the equal of Vishnu.[71]

In Krishna's manifestation to Arjuna in the *Bhagavad Gita,* we can see how this monotheistic value took symbolic form. Krishna becomes the explosive energy of all reality. In the *Gita,* his theophany (manifestation of divinity) is the ultimate revelation of how divinity assumes many masks in space and time. Whatever reality is, Krishna is its dynamic source. Much like the Upanishadic Brahman, he is the one source capable of manifesting itself in many forms. But whereas the atmosphere of Brahman is serene and cool, the bhakti-prone Krishna is turbulent and hot. When J. Robert Oppenheimer, one of the developers of the American atom bomb, saw the first nuclear explosion, Krishna's dazzling self-revelation came to his mind: "If the light of a thousand suns should effulge all at once, it would resemble the radiance of that god of overpowering reality" (*Bhagavad Gita,* 11:12). Thus, the Hindu divinity, like the Hebrew divinity of the chariot or the Zoroastrian divinity of the sacrifice, could be a refining fire.

This refining fire makes the world rise from and fall back into formlessness. The Hindu trinity of Brahma, Vishnu, and Shiva stands for creation, preservation, and destruction. Shiva himself, however, presides over life and death as the Lord of the Dance of Creation. The Shaivites, in this belief, indicate more clearly than the Vaishnavites how many Hindus retain a quite ancient notion of divinity.[72] Shiva is a complex reality, to be sure, but his ascetic and destructive aspects reflect quite ancient encounters with spiritual forces.

The Problem of Evil.   The problem of evil is that so much in human experience seems to be dark and disordered. For many Western observers, Indian philosophy has seemed strangely silent about evil. (Their greater interest was the problem of ignorance—why human beings fail to see things as they truly are, realize that only ultimate reality is fully real.) In these observers' eyes, the Hindu doctrine of rebirth shifted the problem of evil away from the Western orientation, in which individuals (like Job in the Bible) can accuse God of having dealt with them unjustly, having caused them to suffer through no fault of their own. Rebirth, coupled with the notion of karma, meant that one existed through long cycles of time whose overall justice was beyond human calculation, and that one's fate in a given lifetime was the result of one's actions in a previous existence. Thus there was no unmerited punishment and consequently no "problem" of evil. The gods did not have to justify themselves before innocent sufferers and evil was not an absurd, irrational force corroding human sanity.

Wendy Doniger O'Flaherty has challenged the simplicity of these Western assumptions:

Philosophers and theologians may set up their logical criteria, but a logical answer to an emotional question is difficult both to construct and to accept. The usual example of extraordinary evil given in Indian texts is the death of a young child. If one says to the parents of this child, "You are not real, nor is your son: therefore you cannot really be suffering," one is not likely to be of much comfort. Nor will the pain be dulled by such remarks as "God can't help it" or "God doesn't know about it." It is only the ethical hypothesis that is *emotionally* dispensable: God is not good, or God does not wish man to be without evil (two very different arguments). And this is the line most actively developed by Hindu mythological theodicy.[73]

By "Hindu mythological theodicy" O'Flaherty means the effort one can find in the Hindu epics and devotional literature to justify God's ways, or the way things occur in the world. One of the early reasons why Hinduism developed an articulate response to the problem of evil was the attacks of the Buddhists, who found evil a soft spot in Hinduism's armor. Thus Buddhist texts satirically ask why the Hindu gods do not set the world straight. If Brahman, for instance, is lord of all things born, why are things so confused and out of joint? Why is there such unhappiness and deception? If we are honest, it seems as though Brahman ordained not dharma (a good working order) but adharma (chaos).

Hindu thinkers struggled to meet this challenge. In trying to understand evil, they tended to regard natural disasters, such as earthquakes, and moral wrongs, such as murder, as but two aspects of a single comprehensive phenomenon. Thus the Sanskrit term *papa* (evil) embraced both natural and moral evil. In the *Rig-Veda,* probably the moral sense prevails: People are evil-minded, committing adultery or theft. Still, the *Rig-Veda* does not necessarily see such evil as freely chosen. Moral evil or sin may occur without the sinner willing it. Therefore, one finds few prayers of personal repentance in the *Rig-Veda,* though numerous prayers for deliverance from the bad things other people can do. The *Atharva-Veda* also tends to blend natural and moral evils, and to see moral evil as an intellectual mistake rather than a culpable flaw in character. There are exceptions to these tendencies, such as the *Rig-Vedic* hymn of repentance to Varuna (5:85), but the overall inclination of the Vedic texts is

to regard evil not as something we humans do but as what we do not wish to have done to us.

Although Hinduism tried out many different responses to the problem of evil, in O'Flaherty's opinion it favored myths that blamed God for evil (in contrast to the West's favorite myths, which blamed human beings). This gives Indian mythology a rather tragic tone. When it moves from the drama of creation to the pathos of creation's defects, the Indian imagination is inclined to picture reality as intrinsically misbuilt. The result is a worldview in which evil is an integral factor. In the comprehensive system of this world, as enlightened minds perceive it, there is both the purity of healthy-minded people and the dirt of sick-minded people.

We can turn to the Vedas as a source of optimism, stressing healthy-mindedness, or to the Upanishads as a source of pessimism, stressing sick-mindedness. The Vedas emphasize benevolent gods whom one can invoke as aids in attaining heaven, while the Upanishads emphasize inadequate or even malevolent gods who are a central cause of our human problems.

In the subsequent tradition, through the epics and *Puranas,* one finds an integration of both emphases, a sort of dualism or unity of opposites: "Evil is recognized as horrible, death terrifying, heresy wicked, but these are accepted and integrated with the healthy goals of the Vedic life-view."[74]

In our opinion, this traditional tendency would have enhanced the attraction of proposals to undercut the entire dualistic realm. *Moksha* would then have become an escape from a world in which tragedy was inevitable because evil was as aboriginal as good. The sages could say very little about the sort of life that *moksha* would bring, because all expressible experience was mottled by suffering. They intuited, however, that *moksha* was full of being, bliss, and awareness—was an existence beyond evil's reach.

Kali. One female deity whom scholars have studied thoroughly is Kali, the mistress of death, an important expression of Maha-devi, the ancient great goddess. In her, many of the popular ambivalences about ultimate reality come into focus. Part of the fascination Kali has evoked stems from her dreadful appearance. Usually she is portrayed in black, like a great storm cloud. Her tongue lolls, reminding the viewer that she has a great thirst for blood, and she shows fearsome teeth. Her eyes are sunken, but she smiles, as though enjoying a terrible secret. Round her neck is a garland of

Figure 17   The god Ganesha dancing, northwest India, tenth century. Light gray sandstone, 39 in. high. Ganesha, the elephant-headed son of Shiva, is very popular because he bestows wealth and success. The Nelson–Atkins Museum of Art, Kansas City, Missouri (Nelson Fund).

just fine. (It is interesting that the cult of Kali flourished in areas most profoundly influenced by British colonial rule, as though to express a sense that life had turned horribly oppressive.)

Moreover, certain historic associations have besmirched Kali's name, linking her with some of the most loathsome, degenerate streams in Hindu culture. For example, she has been linked with blood sacrifices, including those of human beings, and she has served as the patron goddess of the Thugs, a vicious band of criminals that flourished from ancient times until the late nineteenth century and devoted themselves to strangling carefully selected victims as a way of honoring the goddess of death. (It is from this group that our English word *thug* has come.) Nonetheless, a careful study of Kali's full history as a major Hindu deity suggests that she has functioned as more than simply a lodestone for the soul's blacker passions.

First, Kali does not appear in the earliest Hindu texts, but comes on the scene fairly late. Second, throughout her history it is largely peripheral people, marginal groups, that populate her cults. In this her cult reminds one of Shavaism and Tantrism. Third, the geographic areas most devoted to Kali have been Bengal and the Vindhya Mountain region of south-central India. Fourth, when Kali became associated with the tantric cults her appearance changed, for a potential benevolence more clearly emerged.

Tantrism's concern with tapping libidinal energies led to the rise of many female deities from the seventh century C.E. on, and by the sixteenth century Kali was intimately connected with the more adventurous "left-hand" tantric sects. For some important left-hand tantric sects, religion became a dramatic effort to conquer the fractured world and gain *moksha.* An indispensable ally in this effort was the *shakti* power of female divinity.

> In his attempt to realize the nature of the world as completely and throughly pervaded by the one Sakti, the *sadhaka* (here called the hero, *vira*) undertakes the ritual known as *panca-tattva,* the ritual of the five ("forbidden") things (or truths). In a ritual context and under the supervision of his *guru,* the *sadhaka* partakes of wine, meat, fish, parched grain, and sexual intercourse. In this way he overcomes the distinction (or duality) of clean and unclean, sacred and profane, and breaks his bondage to a world artificially fragmented.[75]

snakes, a half-moon rests on her forehead, her hair is matted, and often she licks a corpse. In her hand is apt to be a necklace of skulls. She has a swollen belly, girdled with snakes, and for earrings she has corpses. Her face projects a calm contentment, as if the savage realities of life, its evil and deathly aspects, suit her

Kali is a personification of the most forbidden or truthful thing, death. Therefore, the tantric hero presses on to confront Kali, trying to transform her (death) into a vehicle of salvation. Consequently, the hero is apt to go to Kali's favorite dwelling place, the cremation grounds, meditate on each terrible aspect of her appearance, and try by penetrating her fearsomeness to pass beyond it. Translating the hero's rationale we might hear him say: "By embracing death with my every pore and synapse, I will make Kali rid me of all fear of death, all alienation from this death-infiltrated world."

It is doubtful that the average Hindu worshiper of Kali has had such an adventurous, or highly conscious, rationale as that of our tantric hero, but the devotionalism of many followers, especially those from the Bengal area, shows a similar effort to make worship of the goddess a way to come to grips with life's worst features. Thus the poetry of Ramprasad (1718–1775), one of the most influential Bengali singers of Kali's praises, speaks of a mother who makes those attached to her as mad as she is. Ramprasad begs Kali to deal with him as a mother and help him accept her wild, incomprehensible behavior. As the *Bhagavad Gita* swells the figure of Krishna, so that he becomes coextensive with the whole of mysterious creation, so Ramprasad swells the figure of Kali, so that she becomes coextensive with the whole of mysterious creation. By remaining devoted to her, despite her forbidding appearance, the poet expresses a blind faith that somehow, sometime, life will show itself to have been worth living.

Ramakrishna (1834–1886), another very influential Bengali devotee of Kali, taught much the same message, but in more ecstatic and joyful terms. Going out of himself in adoration of the goddess, Ramakrishna pointed to a realm beyond good and evil, beyond all the dichotomies we make in everyday life. This is a realm where the deepest forces of death and life intermingle, moving the world to a rhythm only divinity can comprehend.

The ordinary Hindu, man or woman, who was not a saint like Ramakrishna, tended to interact with a favorite god or goddess without understanding that this deity was merely the face of a universal divinity or ultimacy. Throughout history, most Hindus have not been literate, so their sense of the gods and goddesses has come from the oral tradition. It was the great cycle of stories about Krishna and Devi, about Rama and Sita, that filled the imagination of the ordinary person and so shaped what he or she said at prayer, thought during the religious festivals, feared in the depths of night or at the bed of a sickly child. This is not to say that the average Hindu had no sense of the unity among the different deities. In all probability, even the humblest peasant believed that the many different deities were reconciled in the realm of the gods. But for the present age, the trials of this round of the samsaric cycle, it was more helpful to focus on a particular deity than to speculate about a divine unity beyond or underneath all of the divine diversity.

A second feature of popular Hindu religion, the culture of the masses, has been a certain passivity. Sometimes Muslim ideas about the sovereignty of God (Allah) encouraged this feeling, but the Hindu notion of karma made a greater impact. Ideally, karma moved people to live on the border between acceptance and resignation. Acceptance is something positive: thinking that one's life is in God's hands, thinking that Providence must in the final analysis be benevolent. Resignation is something negative: we can't do much about our situation, in the long run, so we had best detach ourselves from foolish hopes and let happen what will.

In their prayers and rituals, Hindus tried to draw from their favorite deities a blend of acceptance and resignation fitting and powerful enough to keep them going. Popular religion certainly had its ecstatic moments, when love of a dazzling deity might move people to transports of delight, but on a daily basis Hindu piety or spirituality tended to be sober. The problems were great and the chances of solving them satisfactorily were small. The suffering was omnipresent and could easily become oppressive. Much popular piety therefore was an exercise in gaining reasons to keep going, in working out strategies for coping. The impressive thing is that it succeeded so often.

Conclusion. Indian ultimate reality thus has had many levels and many facets. In our opinion, the dimensions of nature, society, and the self are subordinate to the dimension of divinity, since the last determines the places of the first three. In other words, we suspect Hindus have arranged nature, society, and the self in view of the Agni, Brahman or Krishna who centered their lives in divine mystery. If Brahman is the ultimate reality, then nature, society, and the self are all versions of maya, are all illusion and play. If Agni, the god to whom one directs the fire sacrifice, is the ultimate reality, then nature stands by divine heat, society stands by priestly sacrificers, and the self strives after *tapas* (ascetic heat) or lives by ritual mantras (verbal formulas for controlling the divine forces). Finally, if Shiva is the ultimate reality, then ultimate reality destroys castes, is the arbiter of life and death, and reduces the self to a beggar for grace.

Nevertheless, one could begin with the view of nature, society, or the self and develop what ultimate reality and the other two subordinate dimensions meant. In other words, cosmology, sociology, and psychology all have their legitimate places in religious analysis.

However, historians of religion believe that no system of interpretation can truly substitute for the system that the religion itself implicitly uses. In other words, we cannot reduce the religions to their cosmological, sociological, or psychological factors. They must remain essentially what they claim to be: ways emanating from and leading to the divine. For this reason, the concept of ultimate reality in a religion will always be the most crucial concept. God or ultimate reality is by definition the ultimate shaper of a worldview, because divinity determines the placement of the other dimensions and thus the worldview as a whole. Having had many forms of divinity, Hinduism has had many worldviews.

SUMMARY: THE HINDU CENTER

How, overall, does Hinduism seem to configure reality for its adherents? What is the center, or summarizing pattern, that the Hindu "ways" appear to depict? It seems to us that the Hindu center is an alluring sense of unity. From the time of the Vedas, reflective personalities in India sought to put together the many disparate facets and forces of reality. Thus *Rig-Veda* hymns, Upanishads, and the later theistic cults all proposed a mystery, or ultimate reality, or god that stood behind things, promising the believer, the devout adherent, or the self-disciplined yogi, a satisfying peace. The peace would come from the order that union with Brahman or Krishna would produce. Thus the individual was not to cling to the passing multiplicity of social, natural, or even personal life. Samsara was an enemy trying to keep the individual in a state of disunion, and so of suffering. Illusion was samsara's main ally. If one broke with illusion, appropriated the wisdom of the ancient seers who had fought through to, or been blessed by a vision of, the ultimate unity of all things, one could find being, bliss, and awareness.

Moksha probably is the watchword best symbolizing this typically Hindu cast of mind, yet *moksha* could have several different weightings. For the passionate, those either suffering with special pains or burning for being, bliss, and awareness with a special ardor, *moksha* could be an imperative. There being nothing more important than coming to right order, finding the ultimate truth and meaning of life, the passionate Hindu could pursue *moksha* wholeheartedly, opting out of India's highly structured caste and family life. For personalities either less pressured by suffering or less drawn by the prospects of fulfillment, *moksha* could carry a somewhat comforting and palliative set of overtones. If not in this life, in some future life one could hope to attain *moksha*. With such a good future prospect, the turmoils and troubles of the present life could somewhat slacken.

Theistic Hindus, bhaktas devoted to Krishna, Shiva, or one of the goddesses, tended to picture the center in terms of their beloved God. Thus the theophany or revelation that Krisha gives Arjuna in the *Gita* shows Krishna to be the center of all reality, a sort of Brahman, but more personalized, dazzling, and energetic. As the force of life and death, Shiva could have a similarly universal power to organize reality, a similarly profound religious clout. Love for such a god could give the devotee's life great meaning. Sacrifices to the god, celebrations of the god's festivals, visits to the god's temples, prayers for the god's help in time of sickness or distress—this sort of intense, personalized religion probably pictured *moksha* as an unbroken enjoyment of the god. If the god was one's lover, the Krishna who could espouse the devotee's soul, then the enjoyment beckoned as quite erotic. If the god was a mother, a goddess of comfort or even frightening command (recall Kali), then the release of *moksha* might carry overtones of a child returning to its first home or a servant hoping for the rewards of a job well done, a life of devotion well lived.

Throughout these and the other forms of Hindu religion, something beckoned Hindus to hold present times lightly, treat the things they encountered respectfully but ungraspingly. Of course, a great many Hindus disregarded this beckoning. The violence and

Figure 18   Birla Temple, a modern Hindu temple in New Delhi, replete with statues of gods and animals. Photo by J. T. Carmody.

cruelty of the subcontinent, the poverty of its so many millions, remind us that karma could be a grinding enslavement, *moksha* could be an escapist strategem of last resort. Thus V. S. Naipaul, the brilliant novelist and journalist, on returning to the land of his ancestors, found India to be a "wounded civilization," weighted down with a sense of the past that mottled its present and future.[76] In Naipaul's impression, karma had helped millions, both intellectuals and illiterate peasants, to accept the wretched injustices of caste, the manifold bondages of the vast majority to poverty, ignorance, and a dearth of worldly prospects.

Be that as it may (and it may be more accurate about the recent India than about the India of the pre-Muslim era), the impression remains that the Hindu center has been as ambivalent in its social effects as most other religious centers have been. By the standards of a radical contemplative wisdom that would

penetrate to the core of reality's mystery and a radical social justice that would treat all human beings as equals who deserve fair dealing, the Hindu worldview emerges as more wise than just. So, of course, do most other worldviews, if only because it is usually easier to contemplate the grand source of order, the fair center of a mystery revealing itself as beautiful and healing, than it is to promote other human beings' equal access to the good life that such a mystery suggests.

The world over, religious people rightly have their proposed wisdoms challenged because their concrete social and cultural lives show continuing malignancies, ongoing patches, large or small, where they treat one another worse than wolves. Thus the critics of religion usually have plenty of ammunition, many rocks with labels such as "hypocrisy," "escapism," and "neurosis" ready to hand. That would be true for any who might want to criticize Hinduism. On the other hand, the Hindu religionist, like the adherent of most other religions, has had a simple and effective response: Where is your more beautiful, profound, or hope-inducing *moksha?* Where is your society free of caste, cruelty, and injustice?

So it goes, the dialogue or battle between religion and irreligion, anti-Hinduism and Hinduism. In our view, Hinduism's mantra of *om*, its central symbol of unity and peace, still sits on the table, awaiting from its opponents a response equally comprehensive and deep.

Discussion Questions

1. Why did Vedic religion come to stress sacrifice?

2. How could Upanishadic knowledge bring salvation?

3. Translate *moksha* into terms that your contemporaries would find attractive.

4. In what sense did bhakti personalize Hindu divinity?

5. What does the status of Indian women through the ages say about Hinduism?

6. How could we adapt the classical Hindu life cycle to the needs of Americans today?

7. Does Indian religion show that ultimate reality is as much impersonal as personal? How?

8. Explain the significance of Kali.

9. Why would you like or not like to be a disciple of Ma Jnanananda?

10. How satisfactory is the Hindu view that evil is an intrinsic part of this world? Why?

11. Explain the emotional aspects of devotion to Krishna.

12. Describe the fusion of religion and politics for Mahatma Gandhi.

13. Write a brief essay on the relations among *ahimsa,* fertility, and the cow.

14. What were your impressions when reading the accounts of possession by a god or force that required being placated?

15. What could be the positive aspects of a belief in transmigration?

Key Terms

ahimsa: an Indian term for nonviolence or noninjury. Both Hindus and Buddhists have made *ahimsa* part of their religious ideal. The liberated personality would feel no desire to hurt, abuse, manipulate, or otherwise disorder other finite beings and so would be a source of peace in nature as well as society.

asceticism: discipline; abstinence from self-indulgence. Most religious traditions have ascetical moments or streams, suggesting that when people strive to gain enlightenment or union with a holy divinity they tend to think they must discipline their desires, sensual appetites, spontaneous chatter, and the like. Asceticism should be ruled by the goal the tradition makes paramount, and so kept in the order of means to an end, but frequently it becomes a powerful if not all-absorbing interest in its own right, as people who fast, separate themselves from sexual activity, keep silence, live in solitude, and the like find they have more intense spiritual (visionary, ecstatic) experiences.

atman: Indian term for self or substantial reality. Where the Buddhists denied there was a self, many Hindu philosophers, influenced by the Upanishads, considered the atman the inmost presence of divinity. In other words, the true nature of the self could not be separated from that which made everything else exist and be what it was: Brahman.

bhakti: an Indian term for devotional religion centered on love. Bhaktas, devotees of a Hindu deity, usually conceive of their relationship with the deity in question on the model of a love affair, or at least an intense friendship. Thus women have tended to associate themselves with the cow-herding girls featured in legends about the young god Krishna, or they have associated themselves with one of the wives of a god celebrated in the epic literature. Men devoted to a god such as Shiva have tended to picture themselves as servants, even slaves, of the god, while both men and women devoted to one of the forms of the mother goddess have generally approached her on the model of a child seeking maternal help or comfort.

Brahman: Hindu term for ultimate reality. Brahman carried overtones of being the ultimate basis of nature and the cosmos, somewhat in contrast to the psychological overtones of atman. Both effable and ineffable, Brahman existed within human experience as the ground of what people felt and knew, but it also transcended this realm and stood for the basis of all that existed beyond human perception.

brahmin: a member of the highest, priestly Hindu caste. Brahmins traditionally have had responsibility for ritual, sacrifice, and religious knowledge. Some interpretations of caste made being a brahmin a prerequisite for *moksha,* and even when this interpretation did not hold, brahmins tended to enjoy great social prestige. They could expect being protected by warriors, having available the goods of traders, and being able to call on workers to care for their mundane needs.

caste: the Hindu social system that grouped people into four main ritualistic classes (priests, warriors, merchants, and workers) and innumerable occupational groups (jatis). Scholars debate the origins of caste, many now being less confident than past generations that color was the dominant motivation. Caste received cosmic sanctions in the Hindu accounts of the birth of human society from the sacrifice of a gigantic original human being and so came to be thought encoded in the way the universe had been born. Modern, secular India legally abolished caste, but it continues to exert a considerable cultural influence. Those who have fallen outside the caste system and become known as untouchables—people ritually impure—have suffered great alienation and been forced to support themselves by carrying out the most abhorred tasks (sewage disposal, garbage collection, animal slaughtering, and the like).

dharma: an Indian term for teaching and duty. Buddhists have stressed the idea of teaching, speaking of the dharma of the Buddha as one of their three great treasures (Buddha, dharma, community). Hindus have more vaguely spoken of dharma as a Truth rooted in their tradition (most notably in the Vedas). The word has had a more precise set of Hindu connotations when used in a social context, pointing to the responsibilities attendant on one's caste and the teachings of the famous law codes (such as that of Manu) that regularized social relationships.

karma: an Indian term for the relations among past deeds, present character, and future fate. Indian thought was intrigued by the problem of why people are what they are and do what they do. It related this problem to the basic problematic summed up in sam-

sara: Why are people immersed in webs of relationships that bring them suffering, death, and rebirth? The doctrine of karma postulated that each choice or action shaped one's character, and that what one's character had become at death shaped what one's next existence would be like. Most Indian thinkers wanted to leave individuals the freedom to choose their acts, and so their characters, and so their future fates, but the overall weight of taking karma seriously was to make one's fortune seem predetermined. Still, Indians felt urged to live virtuously by the general consensus that one would only gain release from samsara by having gained a good karmic condition, which in turn could only be gained by virtuous living.

maya: a Hindu term for reality taken to be so marvelous that it proves incomprehensible and thus unreliable. Human beings tend to be seduced by maya and so live unrealistically, in illusion. Maya can be understood to be a divinity, wooing the mind away from what is really so, playing with human beings for the sport of seducing them. To combat maya, one must attend to the scriptures and root out one's desires, on which maya trades. Insofar as maya predominates in most situations, it becomes a synonym for unenlightened living and so quite cognate to samsara and the wheel of rebirths.

meditation: mental exercises aimed at clarifying one's sense of the truth, advancing one toward enlightenment, and actualizing one's best spiritual potential. The term varies in connotation from context to context, in the East having yogic overtones while in the West suggesting either simple rumination or the first stages of mental prayer. Yogic meditation can be quite contemplative, trying to undercut the discursive mind and exercise the holistic powers of the basic spirit or heart. All meditation carries the danger of overmentalizing reality and religion alike, so many meditational regimes self-consciously require complementary manual labor or devotional prayer that engages the senses. A further question is the relation between meditation and social life, or even ecology, which some traditions solve by requiring common meditation halls, or communal prayers in a more devotional (liturgical) style, or walks and works calculated to make one's purifying mind penetrate the spiritual significance of nature and society.

moksha: the Hindu term for release, liberation, salvation from the bondage of samsara. *Moksha* necessarily must be approached "negatively," by way of denying the limitations afflicting daily human experience. So it implies what is not limited, mortal, bound to the cycle of births and deaths, afflicted with desire, deluded, and the rest. Positively, Hindu thinkers have spoken of being, awareness, and bliss. *Moksha* is lasting, self-sufficient, truly real, in contrast to the fragility, passingness, and dubious reality of ordinary existence. It is full of the light of knowing and the joy of loving. As such, it can symbolize a good sufficient to justify the asceticism and toil necessary to escape samsara.

puja: a Hindu term for ceremonial prayer or worship, especially that which occurs in the home or local temple. The many small offerings, prayers of praise, prayers of petition, sacrifices, vows, and festival celebrations that punctuate the traditional Hindu year suggest that *puja* carried the Hindu spirit along from day to day. What the grand myths and ceremonies did on a great scale, the humble species of *puja* did in the home, for the small group, or for the individual concerned with personal problems. Women were prominent in *puja,* their many devotions to local goddesses, prayers for the health of their families, reverences to Lord Krishna, and the like being a prominent strand in the Hindu tapestry.

reincarnation: the notion that the vital force survives after death and returns to animate a new body, usually in a nearly endless, cyclical way. Theories of reincarnation flourish within the orbit of the cosmological myth, which justifies thinking of the many different creatures in the cosmos as democratic sharers in a single basic stuff. Then the movement of the vital aspect of such stuff from one temporary housing to another poses little imaginative difficulty. Some advocates of reincarnation point to psychic experiences (for example, that of déjà vu) as evidence for reincarnation, and philosophers as diverse as Plato and the Buddha have promoted it. A corollary question usually is how one merits incarnation up or down the scale of creatures and how one ought to treat other creatures, in view of their probably being reincarnations of other forms of being.

samadhi: an Indian term for the highest state of meditation or yoga. *Samadhi* usually is described as an imageless trance, an experience of pure human spirituality. Mircea Eliade has explained *samadhi* in terms of a yogic goal of defeating time and space. The yogi who realizes *samadhi* has such control over the body and spirit that the usual constraints of space and time

seem broken. Insofar as yoga is trying to defeat samsara and lead the person (or the atman) to an unconditioned state (*moksha*), *samadhi* is a sort of down payment on *moksha,* much as mystical experience serves many theistic traditions as a down payment on heavenly communion with the deity. The philosophical question *samadhi* sharpens is whether humanity can be perfected by withdrawing from ordinary dependencies on the body. Incarnational religious systems tend to dispute the claim that it can, although any adequate comparison of traditions' views on this matter would involve many further questions and distinctions.

satyagraha: an Indian term meaning "the force of truth." Mahatma Gandhi employed the term and made it famous as the rationale for his various strikes, demonstrations, and efforts to arbitrate grievances between the British and Indian communities. Coupled with Gandhi's dedication to nonviolence and his conviction that God was the ultimate foundation of all truth, *satyagraha* undergirded the remarkable discipline of Gandhi's followers. *Satyagrahis* frequently were brutally clubbed, if not exposed to rifle fire, but Gandhi consoled them that the truth of their cause one day would bring them justice. So *satyagraha* stands in the modern world as a challenging proposition: If one nonviolently demonstrates the truth of one's situation, the justice of one's cause, one will preserve one's own integrity and will shame or encourage one's adversaries into hearing their own better voices of conscience.

shakti: the generative energy of divinity or ultimate reality, often represented as the wife or consort of a Hindu god. In Hindu typology, the male gods were accounted cerebral, passive, and detached. The female consorts were the bodily, active, involved, creative side of the divine dimorphism. The *shaktis* needed the control of their male counterparts if they were not to run amok. Many folktales depict the awesome power of a mother goddess or wife of a powerful god on the verge of annihilation. The notion of *shakti* undergirded tantric attempts to tap into ultimate creativity, and it helped make the Hindu female an ambivalent figure. No doubt *shakti* has roots in ancient Indian awe about female fertility, as well as in philosophical speculation about the relationship of spiritual and sexual energies.

shruti: a Hindu term for revelation or scriptural truth, the highest sort of wisdom, found in the Vedas. *Shruti* came from ancient seers (*rishis*) who saw ultimate realities in deepest trance or spiritual transport. Hinduism has maintained a flexible sense of revelation, tending to be inclusive rather than exclusive. Nonetheless, it reserved the highest official respect for the Vedic scriptures, which have included the principal Upanishads one finds at the end of the Vedas. On the testimony of the Upanishads, the ultimate reality grasped by the *rishis* was a simple unity of being, bliss, and awareness—a Brahman with the features one attains by escaping samsara and achieving *moksha*.

smriti: a Hindu term for traditional truth, such as that found in commentaries on the Vedas or traditional law codes like Manu. *Smriti* therefore has less dignity than *shruti* and is considered less revelatory, more the product of human reasoning. Where the *rishis* intuited in mystical vision, the makers of tradition studied and reasoned. On the other hand, *smriti* had great influence in Hindu culture, because any elaboration of the social responsibilities of the different castes (their dharmas) involved such traditioning. Hinduism was sufficiently this-worldly, patient with space and time, to honor the station of the householder, which in turn meant thinking about family life, business, law, the arts, military matters, and political science. All of this fell to the conservers and developers of tradition.

tantra: a Hindu and Buddhist term for a ritual manual; by extension, the term has come to mean the effort to gain liberation that uses rituals, the imagination, and libidinal energies. The tantras—texts and adepts alike—were holistic, sensing that only by getting mind, body, and psyche to pull together could they generate the maximal force and enlist it in the service of enlightenment. Tantric Buddhism predominated in Tibet, where it sponsored a tradition of one-to-one instruction from a guru. The guru would supervise one's practice, and many of the most famous gurus developed dramatic, even hyperbolic, personas. Tantric Hinduism sometimes has flouted convention, to make disciples realize that convention alone can be a dead letter. Thus it has played with sexual and dietary taboos, even urging the eating of meat or the drinking of alcohol, to stimulate the insight that the ultimate reality itself undercuts all such distinctions as those between the socially approved and the socially forbidden.

transmigration: the passing of the life force from one entity to another. Transmigration assumes a distinction between soul (life force) and body, such that the soul does not perish along with the body. It further assumes an interaction among the various forces of the natural world, such that the soul can come to animate another body, whether that of another human being or that of a nonhuman animal. Some defenders of transmigration point to experiences of reminiscence and déjà vu, which they think suggest previous lives. Others speak of a collective unconscious, a sort of racial memory encoded in the genes, that carries the sum of human experience. The Indian systems of karma and samsara imply something like transmigration, though the Buddhists deny there is any soul to migrate.

Vedanta: one of the six orthodox Hindu philosophical schools. Vedanta is associated with the sage Shankara (about 788–820), who taught a strict monism. To his mind, reality is nondual and all variety and change should be attributed to illusion. Vedanta may be said to have systematized and deepened the teachings of the monistic Upanishads, taking their equation of Brahman and atman to its logical consequence. Vedanta has had considerable influence in the West, and often (wrongly) has been considered the sum or best representative of Hindu spirituality. In fact, Indian history has furnished numerous other respectable schools, such as Shamkya, which have allowed for duality (matter and spirit, for example). The philosopher Ramanuja (eleventh century C.E.) attacked Shankara's system, arguing for a qualified nonduality that would permit love between the deity and the disciple.

yoga: an Indian term for discipline. Both Hinduism and Buddhism fostered several different yogas, most of which ideally were in the service of liberation from samsara. Yogas focused on the body aimed at achieving better tone, relaxation, digestion, suppleness, and the like. A discipline focused on the breath might try to unify the matter-spirit composite. The most prestigious yoga was the *jnana* discipline aimed at gaining an intuitive understanding of reality and so liberation. The yoga of trance and meditation sought to gain *samadhi*, or at least much better mental concentration. *Karma-yoga* was geared to purifying action, by bringing people to work and strive without desire. *Bhakti-yoga* was a discipline for emotion and love, by which one might unify one's heart and focus it entirely on one's favorite deity. Overall, yoga testified to India's conviction that to escape pain and gain enlightenment one had to marshal one's energies and put oneself under discipline.

CHAPTER 4

BUDDHISM

Wheel: Buddhist symbol for the dharma or teaching

HISTORY

Overview

The term *Buddhism* derives from Western scholarly efforts to organize the movements, ideas, and practices that appear to have been spawned by the Buddha (ca. 563–476 B.C.E.). As well, it covers the diverse things done and thought by followers of the Buddha, who in the early centuries of the Common Era spread from India throughout Asia and recently have established roots on other continents.

Buddhism began as an Indian sectarian religion— a way of seeking release from life's problems that clashed at some points with the prevailing Indian (Hindu) patterns. Gautama, the Buddha, drew followers because of his remarkable insight and compassion, which he claimed were based on an experience of enlightenment that others minimally could find helpful for improving their own lives and in some cases could replicate. It appears that the Buddha's authority over those who came to follow his way and comprise his community at times was contested by more ascetic disciples, such as his cousin Devadatta. After the death of the Buddha, his disciples began to collate his teachings, but they also began to go separate ways, depend-

Buddhism: Twenty-five Key Dates	
563–476 B.C.E.	*Buddha*
519	*Gautama's Enlightenment*
473	*First Buddhist Congress*
363	*Second Buddhist Congress*
273–236	*Reign of Buddhist Emperor Asoka*
236	*Rise of Mahayana Tradition*
160	Prajna-paramita *Literature*
80	Lotus Sutra
ca. 200 C.E.	*Nagarjuna, Leading Philosopher*
220–552	*Missions to Vietnam, China, Korea, Burma, Java, Sumatra, Japan*
430	*Buddhaghosa, Leading Philosopher*
594	*Buddhism Proclaimed Japanese State Religion*
749	*First Buddhist Monastery in Tibet*
805–806	*Foundation of Japanese Tendai and Shingon Sects*
845	*Persecution of Chinese Buddhists*
1065	*Hindu Invasions in Sri Lanka*
1175	*Honen; Japanese Pure Land*
1193–1227	*Rise of Japanese Zen Sects*
1260–1368	*Tibetan Buddhism Influential in China*
1360	*Buddhism Becomes State Religion in Thailand*
1543–88	*Final Conversion of Mongols*
1603	*Tokugawa Government Begins Domination of Japanese Buddhism*
1646–94	*Basho, Great Japanese Buddhist Poet*
1868–71	*Meiji Persecution of Buddhism in Japan*
1954–56	*Sixth Buddhist Council in Rangoon, Burma*

ing on their interpretations of what he had taught. Thus the meetings (councils) that took place in the fourth century B.C.E. failed to keep the community completely intact. Indeed, the split between Hinayana (small vehicle) and Mahayana (great vehicle) Buddhists that had become perceptible by the beginning of the Common Era had its beginnings in the aftermath of the early councils.

During the reign of Asoka (ca. 270–232 B.C.E.) Buddhism received imperial favor. Asoka wanted to reject the violence that prevailed in his early years of conquest and establish a regime consonant with Buddhist nonviolence. Within fifty years of his death, however, the Mauryan dynasty to which he had belonged collapsed and was replaced by one more sympathetic to Hinduism.

From the second century B.C.E. to the first century C.E., Buddhism was a powerful force throughout the whole Indian subcontinent, from the northwestern areas influenced by Greek ideas to Sri Lanka in the south. Buddhist influence also spread into Central Asia. Scholars sometimes speak of the transition during this period from an imperial to a civilizational impact—that is, Buddhism no longer depended on the favor of a king but had become a widespread influence throughout Indian culture (even when its power at the royal court had declined).

	THERAVADA	MAHAYANA
Monks	Makes the *sangha* the center	Considers compassion for others the best way to nirvana; monks especially compassionate
Buddha	Stresses the historical figure Gautama	Develops a wealth of devotional and metaphysical buddhas
Saint	One detached and highly ethical (*arhat*)	One noted for great compassion toward all living things (*bodhisattva*)
Geography	Sri Lanka, Burma, Thailand	East Asia
Philosophy	Rather scholastic and tied to meditation and ethics	Boldly speculative and tied to Zen and devotional schools

The 700 years from the second to the ninth century C.E. were a time when Buddhism enjoyed great cultural vitality, flourishing in Sri Lanka, India, and Central Asia. As well, it became firmly established in both north and south China, and also in Southeast Asia. After 500 C.E., it had taken root in both Tibet and Japan. Between 400 and 700 C.E., there was great traffic between China and India, much of it due to Chinese Buddhist monks seeking contact with the origins of their faith. By 500 C.E., a new branch of tradition, called the Vajrayana (thunderbolt vehicle) and stressing esoteric techniques, had developed out of Indian Mahayana insights and come to have great allure. During the eighth and ninth centuries C.E., it spread to Tibet and Japan.

After 900 C.E., the rise of Islam was disastrous for Buddhist interests in both India and Central Asia. As well, the intensification of Hindu bhakti movements gave it problems. Thus, by the end of the first millennium C.E., the influence of Buddhism had waned in both India and Central Asia. Although it continued to be significant in Sri Lanka, the future lay with such lands as Burma, Thailand, China, Japan, Korea, and Tibet. During the second millennium C.E., those have been the great Buddhist cultures, although usually there have been notable adversaries (Confucianism and Shinto, for instance) that have kept the Buddhists from gaining complete control. The wealth, vigor, and influence of the Buddhist monasteries have waxed and waned, new schools and reinvigorations steadily appearing but slack periods of laxity and stultification also occurring rather regularly. In the twentieth century Buddhism has suffered greatly from the spread of Communism in East Asia, but it has somewhat been compensated by a significant penetration of North America. Our historical treatment will assume this chronological skeleton and concentrate on the complex of ideas and ritualistic practices that gradually created the rich Buddhist system.

The Buddha

The Buddha was born about 536 B.C.E. outside the town of Kapilavastu in what is now a part of Nepal just below the Himalayan foothills. His people were a warrior tribe called Sakyas and his clan name was Gautama. The religious climate in which he grew up was quite heated. Some objectors were challenging the dominance of the priestly brahmin class. As we saw in

KEY SUMMARIES OF BUDDHIST BELIEF	
Three Jewels	The Buddha, dharma, *sangha*
Three Pillars or Main Concerns	Wisdom, morality, meditation
Three Characteristics (Marks) of All Reality	Painful, fleeting, selfless
Four Noble Truths	All life is suffering. The cause of suffering is desire. Removing desire removes suffering. The way to remove desire is to follow the noble Eightfold Path.
Five Ethical Precepts	Not to kill, lie, steal, be unchaste, take intoxicants
Eightfold Path	Right views, intention, speech, action, livelihood, effort, mindfulness, concentration

Chapter 3 the writers of the early Upanishads reveal the dissatisfaction with sacrifice that was burning among intellectuals, while the accounts of the Mahavira are evidence of the ascetic movement that also challenged the priestly religion of sacrifice. In secular culture, the sixth century B.C.E. saw a movement from tribal rule toward small-scale monarchy, a growth in urban populations, the beginnings of money-based economies, the beginnings of government bureaucracies, and the rise of a wealthy merchant class.[1] Thus, the Buddha grew up in a time of rapid change, when people were in turmoil over religion and open to new teachings.

Religious faith heavily embellishes the accounts of the Buddha's birth and early life, so it is difficult to describe this period accurately. Legend has it that his father, Suddhodana, was a king, and received a revelation that his son would be a world ruler if the child stayed at home but a spiritual savior if the child left home. According to other legends, the Buddha passed from his mother's side without causing her any pain, stood up, strode seven paces, and announced, "No more births for me!"[2] In other words, the child would be a spiritual conqueror—an Enlightened One.

As the Buddha grew, his father surrounded him with pleasures and distractions, to keep him in the palace and away from the sights of ordinary life. When the Buddha came of age, the father married him to a lovely woman named Yasodhara. So Sakyamuni ("sage of the Sakyas") lived in relative contentment until his late twenties. By the time of his own son's birth, however, the Buddha was restless. (He named the child Rahula [fetter].)

What really precipitated Sakyamuni's religious crisis, though, were experiences he had outside the palace. On several outings he met age, disease, and death. They shocked him severely, and he became anxiety ridden. How could anyone take life lightly if these were its constant dangers? Meditating on age, disease, and death, the young prince decided to cast away his round of pleasures and solve the riddle of life's meaning by becoming a wandering beggar concerned only to gain enlightenment. Renouncing his wife, child, father, and goods, he set off to answer his soul's yearning. (Indian tradition allowed renouncing the world after one had begotten a son.)

The teachers to whom the Buddha first apprenticed himself when he started wandering in pursuit of enlightenment specialized in meditation and asceti- cism. Their meditation, it appears, was a yogic pursuit of enlightenment through *samadhi* (trance). From them the Buddha learned much about the levels of consciousness but was not fully satisfied. The teachers could not bring him to dispassion, tranquillity, en- lightenment, or nirvana (a state of liberation beyond samsara). In other words, the Buddha wanted a direct perception of how things are and a complete break with the realm of space, time, and rebirth. He sensed that to defeat age, disease, and death he had to go beyond ordinary humanity and tap the power of some- thing greater.

To try to attain his goal, Sakyamuni turned to asceticism—so much so that he almost starved him- self. The texts claim that when he touched his navel, he could feel his backbone. In any event, asceticism did not bring what Sakyamuni sought either. (Because of this, he and his followers have always urged mod- eration in fasting and bodily disciplines. Theirs, they like to say, is a Middle Way between indulgence and severity that strives to keep the body healthy, as a valuable ally should be, and to keep the personality from excessive self-concern.) The Buddha was learn- ing key lessons for the conquest of self—key strata- gems for getting the body, mind, and spirit to agree to seek liberation wholeheartedly.

Perhaps what liberated the Buddha was recall- ing moments of peace and joy from his childhood, when he had sat in calm but perceptive contemplation. According to the traditional accounts, Mara, the per- sonification of evil or death, tried to tempt Buddha (who sat meditating under a fig tree) away from his pursuit.[3] First, he sent a host of demons, but the Bud- dha's merit and love protected him. Then, with in- creased fear that this man sitting so determinedly might escape his realm, the evil one invoked his own power. However, when Mara called on his retinue of demons to witness to his power, the Buddha, who was alone, called on mother earth, which quaked in ac- knowledgment. As a last ploy, Mara commissioned his three daughters (Discontent, Delight, and Desire) to seduce the sage. But they, too, failed, and so Mara withdrew. (Psychological interpretation can illuminate the details of this legend, considering them as symbols of dramatic changes in the person- ality — the challenges, fears, resistance, and final breakthrough one experiences when pursuing liber- ation. Then Mara would stand for the dread the per-

sonality feels at having to be converted to a radically new path.)

Enlightenment. The enlightenment (realization of the truth) itself occurred on a night of the full moon. According to tradition, Buddha ascended the four stages of trance. In later times these four stages were considered as a progressive clarification of conscious- ness: (1) detachment from sense objects and calm- ing the passions; (2) nonreasoning and "simple" concentration; (3) dispassionate mindfulness and consciousness with bodily bliss; and (4) pure awareness and peace without pain, elation, or depression.[4]

According to tradition, then, the Buddha pro- gressed in his contemplative sitting by moving from confusion and sense knowledge to pure, unemotional awareness. The assumption was that this progress fa- cilitated his direct perception of reality—seeing things as they really are. Enlightenment might bring in its train magical powers (the ability to walk on water, to know others' minds, or to remember one's previous lives, for instance), but its most important result was to eliminate desire, wrong views, and ignorance, the bonds that were tying Gautama to samsara. To break these bonds was to free his consciousness for nirvana.

Another traditional way of describing the Bud- dha's enlightenment is to trace his progress through the night. During the first watch (evening), he ac- quired knowledge of his previous lives. This is a power that some shamans claim, so it is not Buddha's distin- guishing achievement. During the second watch (mid- night), he acquired the "divine eye" with which he surveyed the karmic state of all beings—the cycle of dying and rebirth that is their destiny. With this vision he realized that good deeds beget good karma and move one toward freedom from samsara, while bad deeds beget bad karma and a deeper entrenchment in samsara. This second achievement made Buddha a moralistic philosopher, one who saw the condition of all beings as a function of their ethical or unethical behavior.

During the third watch (late night), the Buddha reached the peak of perception, attaining "the extinc- tion of the outflows" (the stopping of desire for sam- saric existence) and grasping the essence of what became the **Four Noble Truths**: (1) All life is suffering; (2) the cause of suffering is desire; (3) stopping desire

Figure 19   Head of Buddha, Afghanistan, third century C.E. *Polychrome stucco, 7 in. high. The half-closed eyes suggest the Buddha's repose, while his trace of a smile suggests his cool joy. The Nelson–Atkins Museum of Art, Kansas City, Missouri (Nelson Fund).*

connections that link all beings. Beings not only depend on one another in what might be called a field of relations, they also arise (come into being) together—thus the "co" in coarising.

Enlightenment seems to have been the dramatic experience of vividly perceiving—seeing, understanding, feeling—that life, which Sakyamuni had found to consist of suffering, had a solution. One could escape the terror of aging, sickness, and death by withdrawing one's concerns for or anxieties about them—by no longer desiring youth, health, or even life itself. By withdrawing in this manner, one could lessen the bad effects of karma, since desire was the means by which karma kept the personality on the wheel of dying and rebirth. Removing desire therefore took away karma's poison. To destroy desire for karmic existence, though, one had to penetrate and remove the illusion of its goodness. That is, one had to remove the ignorance that makes sensual pleasures, financial success, prestige, and so on, seem good. Buddha designed the Eightfold Path and the doctrine of Dependent Coarising to remove such ignorance and rout desire.

The picture of the Buddha sitting in repose after having gained enlightenment has always been a great consolation to his followers. With the pictures and stories about his kindness as a teacher, his affection for his disciples, his wisdom in instructing kings, and the like, it has given the Buddha the human qualities most followers of a religious leader seem to need if they are to follow the path with enthusiasm. The general rule seems to be that followers must love the leader if they are to love the path. Admiring the clarity of the leader's teaching and experiencing the benefits of the path are not enough. The leader inevitably becomes the model, the prime evidence, the proof that the teaching indeed is wholly wise, that the path in fact is fully efficacious. So Muhammad became the prime Muslim, beloved of all who confessed Allah, while Jesus became not only the way, the truth, and the light but the personal face of a God who was love to the core. The teaching of Krishna that we found in the *Bhagavad Gita,* where he finally revealed that bhakti was the great way and he himself loved those who loved him devotedly, applies in many other religious contexts. The Buddha was an effective teacher because his students loved him. They did not find his detachment something cold and forbidding. They found it just the far side of the compassion, the kindness, the charm that made him seem to reach into their very beings

will stop suffering; and (4) the Eightfold Path (explained below) is the best way to stop desire.

The **Eightfold Path** outlines the life-style that Buddha developed for people who accepted his teaching and wanted to pursue nirvana. As such, it is more detailed than a description of what he had directly experienced in enlightenment—something that he probably elaborated later on. The explanation of reality that Buddha developed out of his experience of enlightenment, which became known as the doctrine of **Dependent Co-arising,** also came later. It explains the

and loosen the bonds in which ignorance and fear had kept them tied.

The Dharma (Buddhist Doctrine)

Buddhists have seen in Sakyamuni's enlightenment the great act centering their religion. The Buddha is worthy of following because in enlightenment he became shining with knowledge *(bodhi)*. What he saw under the bodhi tree in the third watch was nothing less than the formula for measuring life and curing its mortal illness. The Four Noble Truths and Dependent Coarising are two favorite ways of presenting the essential truths of Buddha's knowledge.

Dependent Coarising and the Eightfold Path. Often Buddhists picture the doctrine of Dependent Coarising, which provides their basic picture of reality, as a wheel with twelve sections or a chain with twelve links (the first and the last are joined to make a circuit).[5] These twelve links explain the round of samsaric existence. They are not an abstract teaching for the edification of the philosophical mind, but an extension of the essentially therapeutic analysis that the Buddha thought could cure people of their basic illness.

The wheel of Dependent Coarising turns in this way: (1) Aging and dying depend on rebirth; (2) rebirth depends on becoming; (3) becoming depends on the appropriation of certain necessary materials; (4) appropriation depends on desire for such materials; (5) desire depends on feeling; (6) feeling depends on contact with material reality; (7) contact depends on the senses; (8) the senses depend on "name" (the mind) and "form" (the body); (9) name and form depend on consciousness (the spark of sentient life); (10) consciousness shapes itself by samsara; (11) the samsara causing rebirth depends on ignorance of the Four Noble Truths; and (12) therefore, the basic cause of samsara is ignorance.

One can run this series forward and back, but the important concept is that ignorance (of the Four Noble Truths) is the cause of painful human existence, and aging and dying are both its final overwhelming effects and the most vivid aspects of samsara. Thus, the chain of Dependent Coarising is a sort of practical analysis of human existence. It mingles concepts of physical phenomena (for example, aging and dying depend on rebirth) and concepts of psychological phenomena (for example, appropriation depends on desire). The result is called Dependent Coarising (or origination) because it is a doctrine of coordinated

influences—of how the basic factors shaping reality impact on one another. The links of the chain are both sequential and simultaneous.

In the Buddha's enlightenment, as he and his followers elaborated it, there is no single cause of the way things are. Rather, all things are continually rotating in this twelve-stage wheel of existence. Each stage of the wheel passes the power of movement along to the next. The only way to step off the wheel, to break the chain, is to gain enlightenment and so detach the stage of ignorance. If we do detach ignorance, we stand free of karma, karmic consciousness, and so on, all the way to aging and rebirth.

The result of enlightenment, then, is no rebirth, which is the implication of nirvana. Nirvana is the state in which the chain of existence does not obtain—in which desire is "blown out" and one escapes karma and samsara. Thus, nirvana begins with enlightenment and becomes definitive with death. By his enlightenment, for instance, the Buddha had broken the chain of Dependent Coarising; at his death his nirvana freed him from rebirths.

The Eightfold Path (which is the Fourth Noble Truth) details how we may dispel ignorance and gain nirvana by describing a middle way between sensuality and extreme asceticism that consists of (1) right views, (2) right intention, (3) right speech, (4) right action, (5) right livelihood, (6) right effort, (7) right mindfulness, and (8) right concentration.[6] "Right views" means knowledge of the Four Noble Truths. "Right intention" means dispassion, benevolence, and refusal to injure others. "Right speech" means no lying, slander, abuse, or idle talk. "Right action" means not taking life, stealing, or being sexually disordered. "Right livelihood" is an occupation that does not harm living things; thus, butchers, hunters, fishers, and sellers of weapons or liquor are proscribed. "Right effort" avoids the arising of evil thoughts. In "right mindfulness," awareness is disciplined so that it focuses on an object or idea to know its essential reality. "Right concentration" focuses on a worthy object of meditation.

The first two aspects of the Eightfold Path, right views and right intention, comprise the wisdom portion of of the Buddhist program. If we know the Four Noble Truths and orient ourselves toward them with the right spiritual disposition, we are wise and come to religious peace. Tradition groups aspects three, four, and five under morality.[7] To speak, to act, and to make one's living in wise ways amount to an ethics for nirvana, a morality that will liberate one from suffering. Finally, aspects six, seven, and eight entail meditation. By setting consciousness correctly through right effort, mindfulness, and concentration, one can perceive the structures of reality and thus personally validate the Buddha's enlightened understanding.[8]

The three divisions of the Eightfold Path compose a single entity, a program in which each of the three parts reinforces the other two. Wisdom sets up the game plan, the basic theory of what the human condition is and how one is to cope with it. Morality applies wisdom to daily life by specifying how one should speak, act, and support oneself. Regular meditation focuses one on the primary truths and the reality to which they apply. In meditation the Buddhist personally appropriates the official wisdom, personally examines the ethical life. As a result, meditation builds up the Buddhist's spiritual force, encouraging the peaceful disposition necessary for a person to be nonviolent and kindly.[9]

The Buddha's Preaching. Buddha himself apparently debated what to do after achieving enlightenment. On the one hand, he had this dazzling light, this potent medicine, to dispense. On the other hand, there was dreary evidence that humanity, mired in its attachments, would find his teaching hard to comprehend and accept.[10] Legend says that the god Brahman appeared to the Buddha and pleaded that the Enlightened One teach what he had seen for the sake of wayward humanity. Out of compassion (which became the premier Buddhist virtue), the Enlightened One finally agreed to Brahman's request.

According to tradition, his first sermon occurred in Deer Park near Benares, about five days' walk from where enlightenment took place. He preached first to some former ascetic companions who had rejected him when he turned away from their harsh mortification, and his calm bearing won them over. What Buddha first preached was the Four Noble Truths, but he apparently prefaced his preaching with a solemn declaration of his authority as an immortal enlightened one. From this preface Buddhists have concluded that one must offer the authority behind the **dharma** (the teaching) if the dharma is to have its intended effect.

Opening ourselves to the Buddha's authority, let us imagine that we are listening to his famous Fire Sermon, preached after the sermon in Deer Park. He was following his customary pattern, dwelling in one place as long as seemed profitable and then moving on

to the next. So, having finished a stint in Uruvela, he set out for the town of Gaya Head. With him went a great band of monks. When they got to Gaya Head, the Blessed One addressed the monks as follows:

O priests, [monks], all things are on fire. The eye is on fire, as are the forms the eye receives, the consciousness the eye raises, the impressions the eye transmits, the sensations—pleasant, unpleasant, or indifferent—that the eye's impressions produce. All that has to do with our seeing is on fire.

And in what does this fire consist? It consists in the flame of passion, the burning of hate, the heat of infatuation. Birth, old age, death, sorrow, lamentation, misery, grief, and despair are all expressions of the fire that comes into us through our eyes.

In the same way, the ear is on fire with burning sounds. The nose is on fire with burning odors. The tongue is on fire with flaming tastes. The whole body is on fire with flaming touches. Even worse, the mind is on fire; hot ideas, burning awareness, searing impressions, smoldering sensations. Again I say, the fire of passion, birth, old age, death, sorrow, lamentation, misery, grief, and despair is burning you up.

What, then, should you do? If you are wise, O priests, you will conceive an aversion for the eye and the eye's forms, the eye's consciousness, the eye's impressions, and the eye's sensations, be they pleasant, unpleasant, or indifferent. If you are wise, you will conceive an aversion for the ear and its sounds, the nose and its odors, the tongue and its tastes, the body and the things it touches, the mind and all that passes through it.

If you conceive this aversion, you will divest yourselves of passion. Divesting yourselves of passion, you will become free. Being free, you will become aware of your liberation and know that you have exhausted rebirth. This will prove that you have lived the holy life, fulfilled what it behooved you to do, and made yourselves subject to this world no longer.

When the Buddha finished his sermon, many of the monks' minds became free from attachment and they were delivered of their depravities.[11] This set them on a path toward the heights of meditation where they might defeat the problem of suffering by understanding the illusions on which it feeds.

What, though, about ourselves, twentieth-century hearers of the Buddha? Can the Fire Sermon carry across 2,500 years? Many Buddhists think it can. After all, we are still possessed of eyes, ears, nose, tongue, and hands eager to touch. We are still the strange animals possessed of minds flowing with ideas, reflex awareness, sensations to drive our days and bedevil our nights. As with the Buddha's contemporaries, unless we have these faculties under control, we are burning with useless passions. If our senses lead us, instead of our leading them, we are bound hand and mind. Thus when Buddhists addressed lay people they urged them to moderate their behavior (though not as a project asserting the force of the ego or self).

Look around you. See how many of your contemporaries rush like lemmings to the sea. Some rush after money. Others rush after pleasure. A third group hustles to gain power. From dawn to midnight, their brains teem with schemes, images of success, numbers adding up to bigger and bigger bank accounts. Do they not seem feverish? Is there not within them a fire wisdom would have to douse?

And how could wisdom go about dousing this fire? Could it not scoop up the old Buddhist verities, the millennial lessons in detachment? "If you want peace," Buddhist wisdom continues to say, "you must gain control over your senses and your mind. To gain control over your senses and your mind, you must detach yourself from their blandishments. Not every image that floats before your mind is profitable. Not every lissome limb or attractive scheme brings you good. Indeed, few images, limbs, or schemes conduce to your peace and freedom. Unless you have conquered your passions, most visitors to your soul will do you harm."

How pressing is this teaching? That depends on how seriously you take death, aging, sickness, and the other limitations and sufferings that make human existence deeply problematic. If you think your basic task before death is gaining enlightenment, wisdom to free you from death's hold, you will find the Buddha's teaching pressing. If you do not think your basic task is gaining enlightenment, you will let the Buddha's teaching pass by. The Buddha's own criterion for evaluating your state likely would focus on your degree of inner pain. If you find your current circumstances depressing, and you long deeply to change who you are, you are apt to be open to the dharma. The Enlightened One gained his wisdom through struggles with sadness and discontent; so can you. His wisdom means

little to those content with their lot, happy to eat, drink, and be merry. For them the wheel must turn again. They need a deeper experience of life's burning.

The Buddha's preaching won him innumerable converts, men and women alike, many of whom decided to dedicate their lives to following him and his way. A great number entered the *sangha,* or monastic order, assuming a life of celibacy, poverty, and submission to rules of discipline.[12] Other followers decided to practice the dharma while remaining in their lay state, and they frequently gave the Buddha and the Buddhist community land and money.[13] In both cases people became Buddhists by taking "refuge" in the **three jewels** of the Enlightened One's religion: the Buddha himself, the teaching (dharma), and the community (*sangha* can mean either the monastic community or the entire community of Buddhists, lay and monastic, past and present).[14]

By uttering three times the vow of taking refuge, one became a follower in a strict, official sense. (This act reflects the special, almost mystical effect that words had in ancient India. When the Buddha preached, just as when the Vedic priests uttered sacrificial formulas, an active force was believed to be released. When one took refuge, the words effected a binding to the Buddha, the teaching, and the community.)

Buddhist Catechetics.   In time a catechism developed to explain the Buddha's teaching. One of the catechism's most important notions was the "three marks" of reality. Together with the Four Noble Truths and Dependent Coarising, the **three marks** have helped countless Buddhists hold the dharma clearly in mind. According to this conception, all reality is painful, fleeting, and selfless (*dukkha, anicca, anatta*). This formula adds something to the insights of the Four Noble Truths. That all life or reality is painful is the first truth: the reality of suffering. By this Buddhists do not mean that one never experiences pleasant things or that one has no joy. Rather, they mean that no matter how pleasant or joyous one's life, it is bound to include disappointment, sickness, misunderstanding, and finally death. Since the joyous things do not last, even they have an aspect of painfulness.

Second, all life is fleeting, or passing. Everything changes—nothing stays the same. Therefore, realistically there is nothing to which we can cling, nothing that we can rely on absolutely. In fact, even our own realities (our "selves") change. On one level, we move through the life cycle from youth to old age. On a more subtle level, our thoughts, our convictions, and our emotions change.

Third, there is no self. For Buddhists, the fleetingness of our own consciousness proves that there is no atman—no solid soul or self. In this the Buddhists directly opposed Hinduism as well as common belief. All people, it seems, naturally think that they have personal identities. Buddhists claim that personalities consist of nothing solid or permanent. We are but packages of physical and mental stuff that is temporarily bound together in our present proportions.

The tradition calls the component parts of all things *skandhas* (heaps), which number five: body, feeling, conception, karmic disposition, and consciousness. Together the *skandhas* make the world and the person of appearances, and they also constitute the basis for clinging to existence and rebirth. To cut through the illusion of a (solid) self—Buddhists do not deny that we have (changing) identities—is therefore the most important blow that one can strike against ignorance. This is done by being open to the flowing character of all life and decisively pursuing nirvana.

The early teachers described the realms of rebirth to which humans were subject and in so doing developed a Buddhist version of the Indian cosmic powers and zones of the afterlife. Essentially, the Buddhist wheel of rebirth focuses on six realms or destinies. Three are lower realms, which are karmic punishment for bad deeds. The other three are higher realms in which good deeds are rewarded. The lowest realm is for punishing the wicked by means befitting their particular crimes. However, these punishments are not eternal; after individuals have paid their karmic debt, they can reenter the human realm by rebirth. Above the lowest realm is the station of the "hungry ghosts," who wander the earth's surface begging for food. The third and least severe realm of the wicked is that of animals. If one is reborn in that realm, one suffers the abuses endured by dumb beasts.

The fortunate destinies reward good karma. The human realm is the first, and in it one can perform meritorious deeds. Only in the human realm can one become a buddha. The two final realms are those of the demigods (Titans) and the gods proper. Both include a variety of beings, all of whom are subject to rebirth. Since even the Buddhist gods are subject to rebirth, their happiness is not at all comparable to the final nirvana. Better to be a human being advancing toward enlightenment than a divinity liable to the pains of another transmigratory cycle. Perhaps

for that reason, the Buddhist spirits and divinities, as well as the Buddhist ghosts and demons, seem inferior to the human being. Apparently Buddhism adopted wicked and good spirits from Indian culture without much thought. In subjecting these spirits to the powers of an *arhat* (one who achieves nirvana), however, Buddhists minimized their fearsomeness.

Despite its sometimes lurid description of the six realms, the dharma basically stated that each individual is responsible for his or her own destiny. The future is neither accidental, fated, nor determined by the gods. If one has a strong will to achieve salvation, a day of final triumph will surely come. As a result, karma is less an enslavement than an encouragement. If one strives to do good deeds (to live by the dharma in wisdom-morality-meditation), one cannot fail to progress toward freedom. At the least, one will come to life again in more favorable circumstances. Thus, Buddhism ousts the gods and the fates from control over human destiny. This is interesting sociologically, because Buddhism has been most appealing to people who have wanted control over their own lives, such as warriors and merchants.

The simpler folk, who might have had to spur themselves to such a sober and confident state of mind, drew encouragement from Buddhist art, which illustrates the delights of heaven and the torments of hell. Many renditions of the wheel of life, for instance, show Mara (Death) devouring the material world and those who cling to it. In the center of the wheel are such symbolic animals as the cock (desire), the snake (hatred), and the pig (delusion), who work to keep the wheel turning.[15] "Break with these," the art shouts. "Rise up. You have nothing to lose but your chains."

The dharma, therefore, began as a proclamation of diagnosis and cure. Likening himself to a doctor, the Buddha told his followers not to lose themselves in extraneous questions about where karma or ignorance comes from. Furthermore, he told them not to concentrate on whether the world is eternal or how to conceive of nirvana. To ponder such issues, said the Buddha, would be like a man severely wounded with an arrow who refuses treatment until he knows the caste and character of the man who shot him. The point is to get the arrow out. Similarly, the point to human existence is to break the wheel of rebirth, to slay the monstrous round of suffering, fleetingness, and emptiness.

For about forty-five years after his enlightenment, the Buddha preached variants on his basic themes: the Four Noble Truths, Dependent Coarising, and the three marks. His *sangha* grew, as monks, nuns, and laypeople responded to his simple, clear message. He had to suffer painful threats to the unity of his group, but on the whole he did his work in peace. At his death he had laid the essential foundation of Buddhism —its basic doctrine and way of life. Thus, his death (*parinirvana*) came in the peace of trance. The physical cause of his death was poisoning by either pork or mushrooms (depending on which commentator one reads), but in the Buddhist view the more profound cause was the Buddha's sense of completeness. When he asked his followers for the last time whether they had any questions, all stood silent. So he passed into trance and out of this painful realm. According to legend, the earth quaked and the sky thundered in final tribute.

Early Buddhism

After the Buddha's death his followers gathered to organize the dharma (which for some centuries remained largely oral) in part because he had said it should be their leader after him. According to tradition, they held a council at Rajagraha during the first monsoon season after the *parinirvana* to settle both the dharma and the **Vinaya** (the monastic rules). The canon of Buddhist scriptures that we now possess supposedly is the fruit of this council. Today the **Pali canon** (the authoritative collection of materials in the Indian vernacular that the Theravadins use) consists of five *nikayas,* which are collections of discourses (**sutras**) that the Buddha supposedly preached. Just one of these collections, the middle-length *Majjhima Nikaya,* runs to 1,100 pages in modern printing.

In addition to these sutras and the monastic rules, early Buddhists added to the canon the *Abhidhamma* treatises of the early philosophers, who tried to analyze reality by correlating the Buddha's teaching with the experiences of meditation. Therefore, the Buddhist tendency in forming a canon (etymologically, a ruler) by which to measure faith and doctrine was to be as comprehensive as possible.

However, within 100 years of the Buddha's death, dissensions split the *sangha.*[16] These were the precursors of the major division of Buddhism into the **Theravada** and **Mahayana** schools, which we consider below. The apparent forerunners of the Mahayana

schools were the Mahasanghikas, who seem to have considered the Vinaya adaptable, while the Sthaviras (Elders), the precursors of the Theravadins, stressed the importance of the letter of the monastic code. About 200 years after the Buddha's death the Pudgalavadins branched off from the Sthaviras. They taught that there is a person or self (neither identical with the *skandhas* nor separate from them) that is the basis of knowledge, transmigration, and entrance into nirvana.

These first schisms prefigured later Buddhist history. New schools have constantly arisen as new insights or problems made old views unacceptable. As a result, the *sangha* has not been a centralized authority and Buddhism has not kept a full unity. Nonetheless, the *sangha* has given all Buddhists certain essential teachings (almost all sects would agree to what we have expounded of dharma so far). Also, it has fostered a very influential monastic life. The monastic order, which has always been the heart of Buddhism (monks have tended to take precedence over laity as an almost unquestioned law of nature), has been a source of stability in Buddhism. Let us therefore turn to the lives of Buddhist monks and nuns.

Monasticism. A major influence on the Buddhist monastic routine has been Buddha's own life. According to Buddhaghosa, a Ceylonese commentator in the fifth century C.E., the Buddha used to rise at daybreak, wash, and then sit in meditation until it was time to go begging for food. He stayed close enough to a village (wandering from one to another) to obtain food, but far enough away to obtain quiet. Usually devout laity would invite him in, and after eating lightly he would teach them the dharma. Then he would return to his residence, wash, and rest. After this he would preach to the monks and respond to their requests for individual guidance. After another rest he would preach to the laity and then take a cool bath. His evening would consist of more individual conferences, after which, Buddhaghosa claims, he would receive any deities that came for instruction.[17]

The Vinaya established rules that would promote such a steady life of meditation, begging, preaching, and counsel. Originally the monks always wandered except during the rainy season, but later they assumed a more stable setting with quiet lands and a few simple buildings. From the Vinaya's list of capital offenses, though, we can see that a monk's robe did not necessarily make him a saint.

The four misdeeds that merited expulsion from the order were fornication, theft, killing, and "falsely claiming spiritual attainments." Committing any of thirteen lesser misdeeds led to a group meeting of the *sangha* and probation. They included sexual offenses (touching a woman, speaking suggestively to a woman, urging a woman to gain merit by submitting to a "man of religion," and serving as a procurer), violating the rules that limited the size and specified the site of a monk's dwelling, falsely accusing other monks of grievous violations of the rule, fomenting discord among the monks, or causing a schism. With appropriate changes, similar rules have governed the nuns' lives.

There are hundreds of other things that monks and nuns cannot do, and all of them suggest something about the ideals of the *sangha*. Prohibitions against lying, slander, stealing another's sleeping space, and "sporting in the water" testify to an ideal of honest and direct speech, mutual consideration, and grave decorum. Similarly, prohibitions against digging in the ground and practicing agriculture reflect the ideals of not taking other creatures' lives and of begging one's food. Rules for good posture and table manners indicate that an ideal monk has stood erect, kept his eyes downcast, refrained from loud laughter, and not smacked his lips, talked with his mouth full, or thrown food into his mouth. The refined *bhiksu* (monk) also cannot excrete while standing up or excrete onto growing grass or into the water. Finally, he is not supposed to preach the dharma to monks or laypeople who carry parasols, staffs, swords, or other weapons, or wear slippers, sandals, turbans, or other head coverings.

The *sangha* accepted recruits from all social classes, and many of them were youths. From this circumstance one can understand the concern for the rights of the growing grass and the water. In addition, historians regularly note that the Vinaya is remarkably free from taboos (irrational proscriptions of contact with certain items labeled dangerous, such as menstrual blood, corpses, hair, or fingernails), although Buddhism has developed its share of irrationalities. Monks often carried their two principal fears (of taking life or being sexually incontinent) to extremes. Especially regarding matters of sex, the monastic legislation was quite strict.

The Laity. From earliest times, Buddhism encouraged its laity to pursue an arduous religious life.

Though his or her white robe never merited the honor that a monk's colored robe received, a layperson who had taken refuge in the three jewels and contributed to the *sangha*'s support was an honorable follower. From early times Buddhism has specified morality (*sila*) for the laity in five precepts. The first of these is to refrain from killing living beings. (Unintentional killing is not an offense, and agriculturalists have only to minimize their damage to life.) The second is to refrain from stealing. The third precept deals with sexual matters. It forbids intercourse with another person's wife, a nun, or a woman betrothed to another man. It also urges restraint with a wife who is pregnant, nursing, or under a religious vow of sexual abstinence. Apparently relations with courtesans were licit. The commentators' explanation of this precept assumes that it is the male's duty to provide control in sexual matters (because females are by nature wanton). The fourth precept imposes restraint from lying, and the fifth precept forbids drinking alcoholic beverages.

This ethical code has been the layperson's chief focus. Occasionally he or she received instruction in meditation or the doctrine of wisdom, and later Mahayana sects considered the laity fully capable of reaching nirvana. (In the beginning only monks were so considered; nuns never had the status of monks, in part because of legends that the Buddha established nunneries only reluctantly.) The principal lay virtues were to be generous in supporting monks and to witness to Buddhist values in the world. The financial support, obviously enough, was a two-edged sword. Monks who put on spiritual airs would annoy the laity who were sweating to support them. On the other hand, monks constantly faced a temptation to tailor their doctrine to please the laity and so boost financial contributions. The best defenses against such abuses were monasteries in which the monks lived very simple, poor lives.

Other practices that devout laity might take up have included regular fasting, days of retreat for reading the scriptures, praying, hearing sermons, giving up luxurious furniture and housing, abstaining from singing, dancing, and theater, and decreasing their sexual activity. Clearly, such practices have further advanced the pious layperson toward a monastic sort of regime and have sometimes smacked of puritanism.

Scholars suggest that early Buddhism did not develop many new ceremonies or rites of passage; in-

Figure 20 *Temples of the Imperial Compound, Bangkok. Photo by J. T. Carmody.*

stead it integrated local celebrations and customs into its practices. To this day, birth and wedding ceremonies do not involve Buddhist priests very much, but funeral services do. In early times, the Indian Buddhists likely celebrated the New Year and a day of offering to the ancestors, both of which were probably adopted from Hinduism. In addition, Indian Buddhists commemorated the Buddha's birthday and the day of his enlightenment. Robinson and Johnson suggest that cults of trees, tree spirits, serpents, fertility goddesses, and funeral mounds all came from preexisting Indian religious customs.[18] However, the bodhi tree under which the Buddha came to enlightenment prompted many Buddhists to revere trees. Such trees, along with **stupas** (burial mounds) of holy persons, were popular places of devotion.

The worship of statues of the Buddha grew popular only under the influence of Mahayana thought after 100 C.E., but earlier veneration of certain symbols of the Buddha (an empty throne, a pair of footprints, a wheel or lotus, or a bodhi tree) paved the way. These symbols signified such things as the Buddha's presence in the world, his royal renunciation, and the dharma he preached. The lotus became an especially popular symbol, since it stood for the growth of pure enlightenment from the mud of worldly life.

Meditation. A central aspect of early Buddhist life was meditation, which has remained a primary way to realize the wisdom and inspire the practice that lead to nirvana. Meditation (*dhyana*) designated mental discipline. For instance, one could meditate by practicing certain devotional exercises that focused attention on one of the three jewels—the Buddha, the dharma, or the sangha. These would be recalled as the refuges under which one had taken shelter, and the meditator's sense of wonder and gratitude for protection would increase his or her emotional attachment. Thus, such meditative exercises were a sort of bhakti, though without sexual overtones.

Indeed, both the saints (*bodhisattvas*) and the Buddha could become objects of loving concentration. However, such devotion was not meditation proper, for *dhyana* was a discipline of consciousness similar to yoga. As is clear from the story of his own life, Buddha's enlightenment came after he had experienced various methods of "mindfulness" and trance. It is proper, then, to consider Buddhist meditation a species of yoga.[19]

From early times the mindfulness of Buddhists has usually been a control of the senses and imagination geared to bringing "one-pointed mental consciousness" to bear on the truths of the dharma. For instance, one fixed on mental processes to become aware of their stream and the *skandhas,* and to focus on the belief that all is fleeting, painful, and selfless. In addition, meditation masters sometimes encouraged monks to bolster their flight from the world by contemplating the contemptibleness of the body and its pleasures.

Buddhaghosa, for example, proposed lengthy exercises concerning the repulsiveness of food. To help monks control eating, he suggested that they consider (1) that they have to go get food and thus leave their solitude; (2) that they have to search it out through muddy streets and often suffer abuse from villagers; (3) that chewing food crushes it to a state of repulsiveness, "like a dog's vomit in a dog's trough"; (4) that the four effluvia (bile, phlegm, blood, and pus) go to work on the ingested food; (5) that the food goes into the stomach, which "resembles a cesspool that has not been washed for a long time"; (6) that the food has to pass through this cesspool and its malodorous regions, which are traversed by the stomach's winds; (7) that digested food is not like gold or silver but gives off foam and bubbles, becoming excrement and filling the abdomen like yellow loam in a tube; (8) that digested food brings forth various "putridities," such as hair and nails, and that poorly digested food produces ringworm, itching, leprosy, eczema, and dysentery; (9) that excreted food is offensive and a cause of sadness; and (10) that eating and excreting soil the body.[20]

This master has similar proposals for meditations on corpses and even beautiful women. A beautiful woman, for instance, is really a bag of bones and foul odors. In a few years she will be a corpse, and like all dead corpses she will be full of worms and maggots. Only a fool would risk nirvana for illusory pleasure with her.

However, wisdom was more than just attacks on hindrances to freedom and nirvana. In careful meditations, Buddhist adepts tried to replicate the Enlightened One's experience during the night of vision, cultivating first his one-pointedness of mind and then his dispassionate heightening of awareness. Adepts also composed meditations focusing on doctrinal points such as the Four Noble Truths or the three marks in order to see their reality directly. This was similar to the insight practices or the way of knowledge (*jnana-marga*) that Hinduism offered, though of course Buddhist beliefs often differed from Hindu.

Case Study. The Theravada tradition, which claims ties with pristine early Buddhism, has stressed the importance of meditation for gaining freedom from the illusions of the self, and this teaching has experienced a vigorous renaissance in contemporary Burma. By and large, most of the recent Burmese meditation masters have emphasized attaining insight into the true nature of reality, in contrast to meditation masters in other eras or lands who have emphasized attaining a formless yogic trance. Since they claim that insight was the original Buddhist emphasis, while trance was the Hindu emphasis, the recent Burmese masters have rather self-consciously striven to give preference to the Buddhist, rather than the Hindu Brahmanistic, influences that Indian history bequeathed them.

For most contemporary Burmese practitioners of meditation, the goal is improving one's karmic state and so gaining a fortunate rebirth. In contrast to the Hindu yogic tradition, which pays close attention to body-mind control, the Buddhist insight tradition pays close attention to *observing* the body-mind unity in its actions, thoughts, and feelings. Control is secondary and less important.

The preferred Burmese focus for observing the human unity is the breath or the body's tonus (feeling). By cultivating a regular breathing that integrates the body-mind components and stressing feeling, the Burmese masters have shifted away from the visual emphasis of the yogic tradition. They urge that one try to grow more sensitive to the touch of the breath at the nostrils or the rise and fall of the abdomen. Then, with practice, one can expand this tactile awareness to other dimensions of experience, for example the pleasures or pains one is experiencing. The result should be a heightened attention to what seems most real—stimulating, pleasing, or irritating—to the body-mind unity at a given moment. Behind the efforts to gain this heightened attention lie the conviction that the three marks, if vividly experienced, will bring one great progress.

The descriptions of a European Buddhist who learned Burmese meditation may concretize some of these theoretical remarks. The man was in Rangoon on a business trip in December of 1952. He had been a practicing Buddhist for eighteen years, had grown interested in meditation while spending a year in monasteries in Mongolia and Tibet, and therefore contacted Guru Sithu U Ba Khin, a prominent Burmese meditation master. Guru Sithu put him on a regime of insight-meditation (vipassana), beginning with two half-hour introductory sessions. These were all the man required to see clearly within himself a remarkable light. He took this light to be the powerful and bright illumination the mind gives off when we free it from disturbances and let it be pure and serene. The basic method the man used to come to this illumination was concentrating on his breath, which allowed him to still and focus his consciousness to "one-pointedness."

The man continued meditating, shifting his concentration to his bodily sensations. The first sensation that preoccupied him was his body's burning or suffering. As he focused on his bodily temperature, a burning within him grew to the point that he felt like steam on the surface of boiling water. As he stayed with this sensation, it expanded to the point that it seemed to envelop the core of his being. The suffering he felt was almost unbearable, since all of him seemed on fire.

> At the last moment, when I felt myself about dying, it was as if my heart was pulled out of my body and at the same moment—wanting eagerly to be freed from Dukka [suffering]—with a sudden but a small flash of light, I was out of it and felt a refreshing coolness and delight, which words cannot describe. It is an escape and a refuge from all daily trouble, too great to be understood, when not experienced. And the great bliss is that every one can achieve this state; provided he has a pure mind at least for the time of concen-

tration, has the right intentions, attentiveness and concentration, and anyhow tries to live as pure as possible.[21]

Guru Sithu glossed this account of the man's meditational experiences with the following remarks: (1) He and the European Buddhist had agreed that morality, meditation, and wisdom were the three indispensable steps to Buddhist development. (2) He had found the man morally sound and already well advanced in meditation, as the man's quick access to the light of the mind revealed. (3) The man understood theoretically the Buddhist (and contemporary scientific) notion that everything in the universe is in flux. By developing his insight-meditation, he would soon be able to realize the true nature of the forms and names under which ever-changing reality appears. (4) The man's experience of heat was a breakthrough on the way to realizing the fluctuating and painful character of all reality. (5) He assured the man that experiencing suffering is one of the best ways to extinguish suffering. (6) The coolness the man experienced was a sort of rebirth, showing that he had burned up a significant portion of the impurities that cause our human suffering.

So, we find in this Burmese example the traditional truths of suffering and transiency. Drawing on centuries of meditators' experience, many contemporary Buddhists are hard at work trying to change their body-mind condition, so that one day, one lifetime, they may experience no-self and be ready for nirvana.

Mahayana

In the development of Buddhist sects, which reached its most important point in the years 100 B.C.E. to 100 C.E. with the rise of Mahayana Buddhism, wisdom, meditation, and mortality were important to all parties. However, the saintly ideal and the place of the laity differed among Theravadins and Mahayanists. Even more, the notion of the Buddha and the range of metaphysics varied considerably. The rise of Mahayana was the first major change in Buddhism.[22] Before its emergence, early Buddhism was fairly uniform in its understanding of Buddha-dharma-sangha and wisdom-morality-meditation. (Theravada has essentially kept early Buddhist beliefs, so the description of Buddhism thus far characterizes Theravada.)

Of course, Mahayana was not without forerunners. We have indicated the liberalizing orientation of the Mahasanghikas, and also the split among the Sthaviras that occurred when the Pudgalavadins advocated the reality of the person. However, the hallmark of Mahayana was its literature, which placed in the mouth of the Buddha sutras describing a new ideal and a new version of wisdom. *Mahayana* means "great vehicle," symbolizing a large raft able to carry multitudes across the stream of samsara to nirvana. *Hinayana* is the term of reproach that Mahayanists used to characterize those who rejected their literature and views. It means "lesser vehicle," symbolizing a small raft able to carry only a few persons across the samsaric stream. Theravadins, pointing with pride to the antiquity of their traditions and claiming to have preserved the original spirit of Buddhism better than the innovating Mahayanists, do not refer to themselves as Hinayanists.

Why did Mahayana conceive the need for a greater vehicle? The answer seems to be twofold: the sense that the career of the Buddha showed him to be so full of compassion that one could not limit Buddhist doctrine or practice in any way that confined the outreach of the Enlightened One's mercy, and the sense that people everywhere, indeed all living creatures, needed such compassion—were burning with desire and could only be saved by the wisdom of Gautama. Thus the Mahayanists came to think that the ideal follower of the Buddha, the saint they call a *bodhisattva* (one who had the knowledge and being of a Buddha, who essentially was an Enlightened One), would so extend compassion that any notion of self-concern would fall away. Somewhat in contrast to the *arhat,* the holy person whose concentration on self-perfection had brought deep wisdom, goodness, and peace, the *bodhisattva* would vow to postpone entrance into nirvana (postpone gaining the fruits of his or her perfection) and stay in the samsaric world to labor for the salvation of all living human beings.

In Mahayana, therefore, the self-giving symbolized by Gautama's decision to return to the world and preach the dharma empowered a considerable outreach. Emotionally, horizons expanded to include all beings in need. In terms of missionary impulse, the Mahayanists felt impelled to preach to people everywhere. Culturally, Mahayanists sensed that all aspects of life ideally would be colored and enriched by the Buddha's compassion. As well, they realized that lay-

people had to be better appreciated and shown how any state of life, married life and work in the world as much as monastic living, could be a means to enlightenment and a place where one could do good. Finally, the Mahayanists put great effort into developing Buddhist wisdom so that it could accommodate the large-heartedness they found in the Buddha's career. Thus their metaphysics came to look for traces of *bodhi,* liberating wisdom, everywhere, and they soon came to question any facile distinction between nirvana and samsara.

Historically, Theravada spread to southern India and Southeast Asia, while Mahayana became the "northern" tradition, spreading to Central Asia, China, Korea, and Japan. Today Theravada Buddhism dominates Sri Lanka, Thailand, Burma, and Laos. Other Asian countries are dominated by Mahayana Buddhism. Tibet has been dominated by Vajrayana, as we shall see.

In focusing on Mahayana doctrine, let us deal first with two innovative teachings of the Mahayana schools, emptiness and mind-only, and then consider the Mahayana views of the Buddha himself.

Emptiness. Emptiness *(sunyata)* is a hallmark of Mahayana teaching. In fact, the Mahayana sutras known as the *Prajna-paramita* ("wisdom-that-has-gone-beyond") center on this dynamic notion. By the end of the Mahayana development, emptiness had in effect become a fourth mark of all reality. Besides being painful, fleeting, and selfless, all reality was empty. Thus, further rumination on the three marks had led Mahayana philosophers to consider a fourth mark, emptiness, as the most significant feature of all beings. No reality was a substance, having an "own-being." Obviously, therefore, none could be an atman, be constant, or be fully satisfying.

The Heart Sutra, a short specimen of the *Prajna-paramita,* exemplifies the dialectical reasoning with which Mahayana worked on emptiness. In this sutra, we can also perceive the paradoxical result of such reasoning: Nirvana and samsara are not two. The sutra begins with an act of reverence (which reminds us that this is religious wisdom, not arid speculation): "Homage to the Perfection of Wisdom, the Lovely, the Holy."[23] "The Lovely" (*Bhagavati*) is feminine, indicating that Buddhism conceives of wisdom as a goddess or maternal figure, out of whom issues the light of knowledge.[24] Next the sutra speaks of the *bodhisattva*

Avalokitesvara (who in East Asia became known as Kuan-yin) moving in the course of the wisdom that has gone beyond (that has reached the shore of nirvana) and looking down compassionately on our world. He beheld but five heaps (the *skandhas*), and he saw that they were in their own-being (their substance) empty (*sunya*).

The word *sunya* conveys the idea that something that looks like much is really nothing. Etymologically it relates to the word *swelled*. As a swelled head is much ado about nothing, so things that are *sunya* appear to be full, solid, or substantial but actually are not. The spiritual implication of emptiness (*sunyata*) is that the world around us should not put us in bondage, for it has nothing of substance with which to tie us. Philosophically the word implies *anatman* (noself): nothing is independent of other existents. For the Mahayana, all dharmas (here meaning items of existence) are correlated, and any one dharma is void of classifying marks—characteristics that would give it a distinctive independent being.

Dialectics.   Having recalled these staples of Mahayana tradition, the Heart Sutra then employs dialectics (the act of playing both sides of an issue) in analyzing the five *skandhas:* Form is emptiness, and this very emptiness is form. Feeling, perception, impulse, and consciousness are all emptiness, and emptiness is feeling, perception, impulse, and consciousness. This identification, the sutra emphasizes, can be seen by anyone "here"—from the viewpoint of the wisdom that has gone beyond. Therefore, reminiscent of Shankara's two levels of knowing Brahman, the *Prajna-paramita* says that there are several ways of looking at ordinary reality. From the lower point of view, feeling, perception, impulse, consciousness, and form are all "something." From the higher viewpoint of enlightenment or perfect wisdom, however, these terms all designate something that is empty, that has no solid core or own-being. A third, middle viewpoint, is that both of these truths are true.

To deal with any dharma as though it were full, therefore, would be to deal with it at least erroneously and possibly desirously—thus, karmically. If, however, we see that *nothing* is pleasant, stable, or full, then we will deal with all things in detachment, moving through them toward nirvana. So, according to the sutra, a *bodhisattva* sees things without "thought coverings," does not tremble at the emptiness that this attitude reveals, and thereby attains nirvana. That is

what all buddhas (Gautama is not the only one) have done, and it shows that the *Prajna-paramita* is a great spell of knowledge (the sutra concludes with a mantra, a chanting of a wisdom spell: "Gone, gone, gone beyond, gone altogether beyond, O what an awakening, all-hail—this completes the Heart of perfect wisdom").[25]

Case Study: The Diamond Sutra.   Another good example of the *Prajna-paramita* literature that Mahayana Buddhism developed is the Diamond Sutra, which probably originated in India in the fourth century C.E.[26] This sutra begins by setting the stage for a dramatic discourse. Once when the Buddha was dwelling in the garden of a person named Anathapindika, with a group of 1,250 monks, he rose, went on his round of begging, returned, washed his feet, and sat down to meditate. Many monks approached him, bowed at his feet, and seated themselves to await his teaching. One of them, a monk named Subhuti, ventured to ask the Enlightened One how a son or daughter of good family, having set out on the path toward enlightenment, should stand, progress, and control his or her thoughts. The Buddha graciously replied that such a person ought to entertain the thought that although the Enlightened One has led many beings to nirvana, in reality he has led no being to nirvana. How can this be? Because, as any true *bodhisattva* or enlightened person understands, the notion of "being" or "self" or "soul" or "person" is actually an illusion.

With various subtleties, examples, and further inferences, this is the sutra's main teaching. Thus somewhat later the Buddha repeats the message: *Bodhisattvas* are those who do not perceive a self, a being, a soul, or a person. They do not perceive a dharma (individual item of reality), or even a nodharma. They neither perceive nor nonperceive. Why? Because they have reached a realm beyond the dichotomies that perception usually entails, beyond our ordinary tendency to organize things in terms of beings, persons, or selves. Such a tendency seizes on individuals and turns aside from the whole. By concentrating on beings it neglects nirvana. Nirvana is not a thing, nor an entity. Those who think in terms of things or entities cannot enter nirvana. Only those who have gone beyond, to the higher knowledge that is unified, intuitive, and comprehensive, can enter nirvana.

To try to jar the hearer from ordinary consciousness, the sutra even moves to outright paradox: "The Tathagata [Buddha] has taught that the dharmas special to the Buddhas are not just a Buddha's special dharmas. That is why they are called 'the dharmas special to the Buddhas.' " If we try to make sense of this, we find ourselves straining at the edge of logical reason. The dharmas — realities or teachings—applying to buddhas (fully enlightened beings) and making them buddhas are not just peculiar to buddhas. They are what enlightenment finds intrinsic to all reality, the way things are. For that very reason, however, grasping them makes one a buddha. In other words, buddhahood consists in grasping what is so for everyone, for all beings. The special, distinguishing feature of buddhas is that they *realize* what the rest of us only experience or are. The rest of us, in the final analysis, deal with the same (empty) reality as the buddhas do. The rest of us are potentially enlightened, potentially *bodhi-* (knowledge) beings. But only the buddhas realize or actualize this knowledge. Only the buddhas become what they are, illumine their full selves (which are no-selves) with the light of nirvana or emptiness. One can see how this viewpoint could encourage all people, laity as well as monks, to find their true, *bodhi*-being, and how it could inspire the development of Mahayana schools such as **Zen**, where meditation aims at triggering insight into the enlightened being one already is.

Because he understood this line of discourse, Subhuti could reply to the Buddha in kind.

I am, O Lord, an arhat [saint] free from greed. And yet, O Lord, it does not occur to me, "an Arhat am I and free from greed." If, O Lord, it could occur to me that I have attained Arhatship, then the Tathagata would not have declared of me that "Subhuti, this son of good family, who is the foremost of those who dwell in Peace, does not dwell anywhere; that is why he is called a dweller in Peace."

Once again, the key to understanding is to take the text as a paradox, the uneven sort of speech that comes when we have one part of our mind on the level of superior knowledge and the other part on the level of ordinary, worldly knowledge. In terms of ordinary knowledge and discourse, Subhuti is an *arhat* free of greed. That is how the man in the street rightly would describe him. In terms of ultimate knowledge and discourse, however, this view of the man in the street is seriously flawed, because it assumes that "Subhuti,"

"arhat," "greed," and the like are solid things. Ordinary discourse tends to reify what it deals with, to invest it with the solidity of a "thing." Forgetting that everything is painful, fleeting, and possessed of no-self, ordinary speech withdraws from the interrelational field of mutual influence, the wheel of Conditioned Coarising, that, on deeper analysis, shows everything to be without an "own-self."

As one who has passed beyond ordinary speech, Subhuti does not allow himself reifications. Not for him such expressions as "an *Arhat* am I and free from greed." He would not be dwelling in the peace of enlightenment, the fulfilling realm of nirvana, were he still pervaded by such substantial and dichotomizing thinking. Indeed, for him truly to be an *arhat* is for him to appreciate the omnipresence of emptiness. *Arhat* and emptiness therefore coincide. Emptiness defines the outlook of an *arhat,* and the outlook of an *arhat* discloses everything to be empty. How very important, then, are the exercises of meditation that cut below the ordinary mind, the exercises of morality that root out normal egocentricity. Without them, we will never reach the state of wisdom, never will become an *arhat* (that is, a no-*arhat*). Even less would we become *bodhisattvas,* determined to help all beings realize their (empty) buddha-nature.

Mind-only.   Emptiness was the special concern of the **Madhyamika** Mahayana school.[27] The second major Mahayana school, the **Yogacara,** which became influential from about 300 C.E. on, proposed another influential teaching on ultimate reality, mind-only.[28] Like the teaching on emptiness, it went beyond early Buddhist teaching, and the Theravadins rejected the sutras that attributed this teaching to the Buddha. The teaching of mind-only held that all realities finally are mental. There were antecedents to this viewpoint in the morality literature that Mahayana shared with the Theravadins, such as the *Dhammapada,* and the proponents of emptiness implied it in their belief that all phenomena are illusory, because we do not grasp them in their ultimately empty reality. The *Dhammapada*'s interest, however, was practical, not speculative: "What we are today comes from our thoughts of yesterday, and our present thoughts build our life of tomorrow: our life is the creation of our mind."[29] The Yogacarins wanted a fuller explanation of mental reality, probably because their intuitions grew out of meditational or yogic practices (whence their name).

One of the principal Yogacarin sutras, the *Lank-avatara,*[30] described a tier of consciousness in the individual culminating in a "storehouse" consciousness (*alayavijnana*) that is the base of the individual's deepest awareness, the individual's tie to the cosmic. The storehouse consciousness is itself unconscious and inactive, but it is the repository of the "seeds" that ripen into human deeds and awareness. Furthermore, Yogacarins sometimes called the storehouse consciousness the Buddha's womb. Thereby, they made the Buddha, or Tathagata (Enlightened Being), a metaphysical principle—a foundation of all reality.

From the womb of the Buddha issued the purified thoughts and beings of enlightenment. The symbolism is complex (and interestingly feminine, suggesting a Buddhist version of androgyny or primal wholeness). Its main point, though, is clear: The womb of the Buddha (*Tathagata-garbha*) is present in all living beings, irradiating them with enlightenment. Like the feminine *Prajna-paramita,* then, the ultimate reality of the Yogacarins "mothers" the many individual things (that are themselves empty). It is the great mental storehouse from which they issue, the matrix that holds them all in being. It stimulates their dancing flux.

Mahayana Devotion.   Both major Mahayana schools developed sophisticated theories to correlate the many beings of experience with the simple finality of nirvana. It was not philosophy that brought Mahayana popular influence, though, but its openness to the laity's spiritual needs, its devotional thought. Early Buddhism held monks in great regard, considering them the only true followers of Buddha. They were the teachers, the determiners of doctrine, and the guardians of morality. They were the stewards of tradition who made the *sangha* a jewel alongside the Buddha and the dharma. Consequently, the laity considered themselves to be working out a better karma, so that in their next lives they might be monks (or, if they were women, so that they might be men). The central lay virtue, as we have seen, was giving financial support to the monasteries, and the *sangha* seldom admitted laity to the higher occupations of philosophy or meditation.

Mahayana changed this view of the laity. As we have seen, by stressing the Buddha's compassion and his resourcefulness in saving all living creatures, it gradually qualified the Theravadin ideal of the *arhat* (saint) and fashioned a new, more socially oriented ideal, the *bodhisattva*. Mahayana thereby prepared the way for later schools that were in effect Buddhist devotional sects, such as the Pure Land sect. Such sects believed that through graceful compassion, a buddha or *bodhisattva* only required that one devoutly repeat his name and place full trust in him for salvation. In this "degenerate age," the difficult paths of wisdom and meditation were open only to the few. Therefore, the Enlightened One had opened a broader path of devotion, so that laity as well as monks might reach paradise and nirvana.

Mahayana did not destroy monastic dignity. Rather, it stressed the social side of the ideal. The Mahayanists saw the Hinayana *arhat* as too individualistic. To pursue one's own enlightenment and salvation apart from those of other living beings seemed selfish. Out of great compassion (*mahakaruna*), the full saint would remain in the samsaric world, for eons if need be, content to put off final bliss if that would help save other living beings.

Mahayanists stress six great "perfections" (*paramitas*) in becoming a *bodhisattva,* and these effectively summarize Mahayana religious living. First is the perfection of giving: giving material things to those in need, but also giving spiritual instructions, one's own body and life, or even one's own karmic merit. In a life of compassionate generosity, everything could be given over to others. Mahayanists understand the five other perfections of morality, patience, vigor, meditation, and wisdom in a similarly broad fashion. Thus, they have applied the traditional triad of wisdom-morality-meditation in more social ways. Giving, patience, and vigor have meant that one became selfless in more than a metaphysical way. For the love of others, for the grand vision of a totally perfected world, the saint may cheerfully donate his goods and talents, suffer abuses, and labor ceaselessly.

Finally, Mahayanists began to contemplate the Buddha's preexistence and the status he had gained as a knowledge being. In this contemplation, his earthly life receded in importance, so much that some Mahayanists began to say that he had only apparently assumed a human body. Then, linking this stress on the Buddha's metaphysical essence with the Indian doctrine of endless kalpas of cosmic time and endless stretches of cosmic space, Mahayanists emphasized the many buddhas who had existed before Sakyamuni and the buddhas who presided in other cosmic realms. All became potential objects of adoration and petitionary prayer.

In this way the notion of buddhahood greatly expanded. First it was the quality shared by many cosmic beings of wisdom and realization. Later, in East Asian Mahayana, buddhahood became the metaphysical notion that *all* beings are in essence enlightenment beings. As we have seen in the *Prajna-paramita* sutra, enlightenment implies grasping how all beings are empty of individual solidity. Enlightenment, therefore, is just realizing one's buddha-nature, the knowledge and light that dawn when the grasp of emptiness allows true human nature to show itself. It is the beginning of nirvana, the break with samsara, and the achievement of perfect wisdom all in one.

Buddhahood thus became complex and many-sided. The Buddha came to have three bodies: The dharma body, in which he was the unmanifest aspect of Buddhahood or Enlightenment-being; the human body, in which he appeared on earth; and the glorification body, in which he was manifest to the heavenly beings, with all his marks and signs. Moreover, the distinction between buddhas and great *bodhisattvas* blurred and largely dissolved in the popular mind, giving Buddhist "divinity" a full spectrum of holy beings. Citing the Mahayana understanding of divinity, therefore, is a sure way to refute claims that Buddhism is not a religion. By the fifth or sixth century after the Buddha's death, Mahayana Buddhists were venerating a variety of divine figures. This was especially true in East Asia, where Mahayana devotionalism built on pre-Buddhist traditions (for example, many Japanese kami became *bodhisattvas).*

Tantrism

We have seen the Hindu mixture of occult and erotic practices called Tantrism or Shaktism. Indian Buddhism helped create this trend and incorporated many of its notions. Buddhist Tantrism in India seems to have originated around the sixth century C.E., flourishing first in the northwest. From the eighth century on it prospered around Bengal, combining with *Prajna-paramita* philosophy and native symbolic practices. It later reached Sri Lanka, Burma, and Indonesia.[31] Often it merged with Shaivism, but in Tibet it combined with native Bon (shamanist) practices and became the dominant Buddhist faith.[32]

Tantrism had antecedents in both Buddha's teaching and in the surrounding Hindu Brahmanism. Buddha appears to have allowed spells, and the canon contains reputed cures for snakebite and other dangers. *Prajna-paramita* sutras such as the Heart often ended with spells, transferring certain key ideas and words from strictly intellectual notions to mantras. In Brahmanic sacrifices, as we noted, the prayers were understood so literally that they became mantras; if a priest recited a prayer properly, it was sure to accomplish its end.

Buddhist Tantrists took over such sacred sounds as *om,* as well as esoteric yogic systems, such as *kundalini,* which associated sacred syllables with force centers (*chakras*) in the body. They also used mandalas (magic figures, such as circles and squares) and even stupas (shrines). The Buddhist Tantrists were thus hardly bizarre or innovative, mainly developing ancient Hindu esoteric practices in a new setting.

What novelty the Tantrists did introduce into Buddhism came from their creative use of rites that acted out mandalas and esoteric doctrines about bodily forces. Perhaps under the influence of Yogacara meditation, which induced states of trance, the Tantrists developed rituals in which participants identified with particular deities. If it is true that many meditation schools, such as the Yogacara, employed mandalas for the early states of trance in order to focus consciousness, then the Tantrists probably built on well-established practices. In their theoretical elaboration, however, they retrieved certain ancient cosmological notions.

For instance, they came to see the stupas as replicas of the cosmos. The railings that separated the stupa precinct from secular ground divided the sacred from the profane. The edge of the moving mandala that the Tantrist troupe would dance or act out had a function similar to that of the railings. Often Tantrism strove to symbolize the entire cosmic plan. Indeed, the Tantrists tried to draw heavenly worlds (*bodhisattva* realms) and gods into their meditations and rituals.

A principal metaphysical support of Tantrism was the Madhyamika doctrine of emptiness, which the Tantrists interpreted to mean that all beings are intrinsically pure. Consequently, they used odd elements in their rituals to drive home the truths of emptiness, purity, and freedom. For the most part, these ways did not become public, since the Tantrists went to considerable pains to keep their rites and teachings secret. In fact, they developed a cryptic language that they called "twilight speech," in which sexual references were abundant.[33] For instance, they called the male and female organs "thunderbolt" and "lotus," respectively. As with Hindu Tantrism, it is not always possible to tell whether such speech is symbolic or literal. Some defenders of Tantrism claim that it tamed sexual

energy in the Indian tradition by subjecting it to symbolization, meditative discipline, and moral restraints.
Other critics, however, view Buddhist Tantrism as a
corruption of a tradition originally quite intolerant of
libidinal practices. For them the Tantrist explanation
that, since everything is mind-only, the practice of
erotic rites means little is simply a rationalization.

In a typical Tantrist meditation, the meditators
would begin with traditional preliminaries such as
seeking refuge in the three jewels, cleansing themselves of sins (by confession or bathing), praying to
past masters, or drawing a mandala to define the sacred space of the extraordinary reality that their rite
was going to involve. Then the meditators would take
on the identity of a deity and disperse all appearances
of the world into emptiness. Next, using their imaginations, they would picture themselves as the divinities whose identities they were projecting.

So pictured, a man and his consort would sit on
the central throne of the mandala space and engage in
sexual union. Then they would imagine various buddhas parading into the sacred space of the mandala
and assimilate them into their bodies and senses. In
that assimilation, their speech would become divine,
they could receive offerings as gods, and they could
perform any of the deities' functions. So charged with
divinity, they would then return to the ordinary world,
bringing back to it the great power of a buddha's divine understanding.[34]

The relation of the master (guru) and the disciple
was central in Tantrism, because the master represented the tradition. (Zen has maintained this stress
on the master. The Tantric guru was the authority
needed to help the striver receive the original enlightenment disclosed by the Buddha. Texts were too pale
and ambiguous.) The Tantrist gurus occasionally
forced their pupils to engage in quite bizarre and painful practices, to teach them to examine the mirror of
their minds, to learn the illusory character of all phenomena, and to stop the cravings and jealousies that
clouded their mirror.[35] Pronouncing the death of old
judgments and the birth of new ones of enlightenment, the guru might confuse pupils, punish them
and push them to break with convention and ordinary
vision. When Buddhism had become vegetarian, some
Tantrist masters urged eating flesh. When Buddhism
advocated teetotalism, some urged intoxicating spirits. In such ways, Tantrist wisdom could become paradoxical and eccentric.[36]

Tibet.   Perhaps the best place to examine the Tantric
tradition full-blown is Tibet. Tantrism was welcomed
in Tibet and came to dominate in the region between
India and China. Our first historical records date from
only the seventh century C.E., when Chinese historians
started mentioning it. Under King Srongsten Gampo
in 632, Tibet borrowed both writing and Buddhism
from Kashmir. Toward the end of the eighth century,
two notable Indian figures came to Tibet, Santaraskita
and Padmasambhava, who founded a lasting Tibetan
sangha. Tradition credits Padmasambhava with inau-
gurating the influential Nying-ma-pa Tantrist sect,
while Santaraskita apparently was responsible for the
triumph of Indian traditions over challenges from
Chinese schools (especially Chan). Since that triumph,
Tibet has owed more to Indian scholarship and philosophy than to Chinese.

Indian academic structures greatly influenced Tibetan Buddhism.[37] During the Indian Gupta dynasty
(320–540 C.E.), great monastic universities became the
pillars of Buddhism. The "curricular Buddhism" of
these schools encompassed all the arts and sciences.
Furthermore, meditation integrated with scholasticism, assuring that the academic efforts to correlate
Buddhist beliefs with existing knowledge never divorced themselves from practical religion. The Tibetan
adoption of an Indian rather than a Chinese religious
style correlated with this union of study and meditation, for the Indian schools favored a gradual penetration of enlightenment, in which study could play an
important role.

One characteristic of Tibetan Buddhism has
therefore been its line of scholars based in monastic
universities. They have produced voluminous translations and commentaries for the canonical scriptures,
as well as a tradition that learning should inform ritualist life. Learning and ritual, in fact, became the
primary foci of the Tibetan monastic life. The king and
the common people looked to the monastery for protection through ritual against evil powers, while individual monks utilized both meditation and ritual in
their pursuit of enlightenment.

The typical day of a traditional Tibetan monk began with a private ritual contemplation (Tantrist) before dawn for an hour and a half. During the morning,
the monk regularly participated in the community's
prayers for two hours and then worked in the monastic
library. He devoted the afternoon to more work and
public ceremony and again meditated in the evening.

Many monks spent a lifetime in this regime, coming to the monastery at the age of nine or ten and receiving a thorough training in the scriptures, meditation techniques, and ceremonial details. As suggested above, the king supported this life-style, because ritual could prop his authority. (Pre-Buddhist Tibetan culture thought of the king in ancient sacred terms, as the tie between heaven and earth. Something of this ancient view continued when monks prayed and conducted rituals for the king's good health.) The common people, whose shamanist heritage emphasized many malevolent spirits of sickness and death, saw in the ritual spells and ceremonies a powerful defense. As a result, the monasteries were quite practical institutions for them, too.

By emphasizing ritual in both public ceremonies and private meditations, Tibetan Buddhism created its own version of the Tantrist belief that the imagination, senses, and psychological and bodily powers are all potential sources of energy for enlightenment and wisdom. When we discussed Indian Tantrism, we considered how the adept tried to identify with divine forces and gain control over a *cosmion*—a "little world" that represented universal space and time. The Tibetan Tantrist cult acted out many such identifications, so that the common people could indwell something comfortingly universal. The worship of the goddess Tara, for instance, which monasteries and popular festivals promoted, gave the world a motherly and protecting aspect. Monks and laity both prayed personally to Tara for help, while many of Tibet's musical and dancing arts developed through festivals devoted to her.

The success that Buddhism enjoyed in Tibet may also be linked to its ability to capitalize on native shamanist themes and political institutions. The ancient Tibetan Bon ("he who invokes the gods") was a shaman very like the archetypal Siberian shaman. Beating his drum, whirling in dance, weaving his spells, he fought against the demons of sickness and death.[38] In addition to developing its own Tantrist rituals to cover these interests of the older religion, Tibetan Buddhism also produced a type of wandering, "crazy" saint who drew much of the awe and respect that the older shamans had.

The prototype of this ascetic, visionary holy man in Tibet was the much beloved Milarepa (1040–1123).[39] After a harsh initiation by family suffering and a cruel guru, he took to the mountain slopes and gained a reputation for working wonders. In his songs he poetically expressed profound insights into both the nature of dharmic reality and the psychology of the ascetic life. Other famous saints, such as Tilopa and Naropa, were similarly poetic. They show that for personal religious life, Tantrism could cast all conventional values and assumptions in doubt in order relentlessly to pursue enlightenment.

Buddhism capitalized on the demise of kingship in Tibet in the ninth century to establish a theocratic regime with the monastery at its heart. Despite early persecutions during a period of kings' intrigues and assassinations, by the eleventh century the monasteries were strong. Until the Communist takeover, in fact, the monasteries and the Dalai Lamas (religious leaders) dominated Tibetan politics (often with much intrigue and sectarian strife).[40] The Mongol emperor Kublai Khan granted the abbot 'Phags-pa (1235–80) temporal power over all Tibet, firmly establishing a theocratic rule. By the fourteenth century, however, Tibet was a cauldron of various Buddhist sects vying for power. The Nying-ma-pa sect that Padmasambhava had founded claimed a certain primacy because of its antiquity, and it also kept close ties with the ancient shamanist loyalties.

Of the sects that developed after the demise of the Chinese Tang dynasty in the ninth century, the most important was the Ge-lug, which shrewdly employed the idea of reincarnation. Consequently, the Mongols both recognized the Dalai Lama as a spiritual leader and considered him a grandson of the Mongol chief. From the sixteenth century onwards, the Ge-lug wielded great political clout. The Dalai Lamas, for the most part, have been men of considerable spiritual and political acumen, and their rule has meant a vigorous *sangha*. The fourteenth, and current, Dalai Lama (b. 1935) was exiled by the Chinese Communists, but he is still the spiritual leader of tens of thousands of Tibetan Buddhists, working for the day when Tibetans will again govern their own lives and be free to practice their religion.

Tibetan Buddhism thus stands out for two things: its Tantrist bent and its especially knotted political history. Few cultures have so absorbed one version of Buddhism as Tibet has absorbed the "thunderbolt vehicle" (Vajrayana or Tantrism). Perhaps the most famous Tibetan religious text to reach the West is the Tibetan *Book of the Dead*,[41] which purportedly describes the experiences of the deceased during the forty-nine days between physical death and entry into a new karmic state. By employing vivid imagery and specifying rituals designed to help the deceased to achieve nirvana, the *Book of the Dead* exemplifies the Tantrist mentality well. It is a journey through the imagination and unconscious that severely challenges most notions of reality, since it maintains that the period right after death is the most opportune time for liberation.

Recent Trends. Much of the Tibetan tradition continued a vigorous life well into the twentieth century, as one learns from travelers such as Alexandra David-Neel, whose *Magic and Mystery in Tibet*,[42] originally published (in French) in 1929, makes fascinating reading. Neel was not long into her travels through Tibet when she had the opportunity to meet the Dalai Lama. Watching him bless a large crowd (one by one), she was struck by the people's manifest belief that physical contact with the Dalai Lama would put them in touch with a magical beneficent power. Indeed, great throngs gathered in Kalimpong, where the Dalai Lama was staying, seeking to benefit from his power.

However, not all the onlookers shared the general faith, and Neel's contact with one skeptic opened a door to Tibet's Tantrist past. She noticed that a man wearing dirty, much torn monk's robes seemed to be watching the crowd cynically. His matted hair wound around his head like a turban, and he had the small traveling bag of a wandering ascetic. In fact, Neel's interpreter described him as a *naljorpa,* an ascetic possessing magical powers. Upon inquiry, the interpreter found that the man was a wandering monk from Bhutan, who usually lived here and there—in caves, empty houses, or under the trees. He just happened to be passing through Kalimpong when the crowds gathered for the Dalai Lama's blessing.

Reflecting on the monk's strange behavior, Neel decided to seek him out at the local monastery, where he had said he was headed. She and her interpreter found him finishing his meal in a room containing the holy images before which the monks prayed. When Neel and her interpreter tried to begin a conversation, the monk only grunted through a mouthful of rice. Then he began to laugh and mutter. "What is he saying?" Neel asked. The interpreter was embarrassed, explaining that he did not know whether he should translate the monk's rough speech. Neel urged him to translate accurately, since she was in Tibet precisely to capture the local color. So licensed, the translator said

that the monk had asked him, "What is this idiot here for?" To Neel this was the sort of insult Indian yogis frequently threw out, so as to put off or test those who approached them. She told the interpreter to tell the ascetic she wanted to know why he had mocked the crowd that had come to seek the blessing of the Dalai Lama.

The *naljorpa* muttered, "They are insects fluttering in dung, puffed up with their own importance." Once again, this seemed the sort of iconoclasm Neel had witnessed in India. "Are you yourself free of all taint?" she asked. The monk laughed noisily and then launched into a speech worthy of Milarepa, Naropa, or one of the other ancient Tantrist saints. "The person who tries to get out of the dung only sinks in deeper. Therefore I roll in it like a pig. I swallow it, trying to turn it into golden dust, into a brook of clear water. That is the great work: to turn dog dung into stars." He said this with great delight, evidently enjoying himself.

Neel decided to press him. "What was wrong with the people approaching the Dalai Lama? They are simple folk, unable to study the high doctrines. Why should they not take what blessing they can?" The ascetic broke through her little objection. "The only efficacious blessing is that given by a person who truly possesses the power he professes. If the Dalai Lama were genuine, he would not need soldiers to fight the Chinese or his other enemies. He would be able to drive all his enemies out of his country, surrounding Tibet with an invisible barrier no enemy could penetrate. Padmasambhava had such power, and his blessing still reaches those who worship him twelve centuries later, though he now lives in the heavenly land of the sages." The ascetic then suggested that he himself had experienced Padmasambhava's genuine blessing.

Neel tried to extricate herself from the situation gracefully, feeling that the ascetic was perhaps a little crazed, but she made the mistake of having her interpreter offer the ascetic some money. Insulted, he refused the money, and when the interpreter tried to insist, the interpreter was hurled backwards and doubled over in pain, as though he had received a terrible blow in the stomach. He was convinced the monk had loosed a spiritual force against him, and none of Neel's Western, commonsense efforts to explain the incident would appease him.

Throughout her journey, Neel found Tibetan Buddhism undergirt with a great respect for the occult. Ordinary people thought meteorological phenomena were the doings of demons or magicians. A hailstorm, for instance, was one of the demons' favorite ways of preventing pilgrims from journeying to the holy places. It was also the way magicians kept intruders from their hermitages and tested would-be disciples. Many mediums found steady employment communicating with the dead or transmitting messages of the gods. In the Himalayas, the centuries-old tradition that sages and ascetics have to battle powerful forces of darkness was alive and well.

The Demise of Indian Buddhism

Buddhism declined in India after the seventh century, only in part because of Tantrist emphases. Invaders such as the White Huns and the Muslims wrecked many Buddhist strongholds, while the revival of Hinduism, especially of Hindu bhakti sects of Vishnu and Shiva, undermined Buddhism. Mahayana fought theistic Hinduism quite fiercely, not at all seeing it as equivalent to the Buddhist theology of *bodhisattvas* and buddhas, but Hinduism ultimately prevailed because of its great ability to incorporate other movements. Indeed, Buddha became one of the Vaishnavite avatars.

By the seventh century the Indian *sangha* had grown wealthy and held much land—facts that contributed to a decline in religious fervor and to antipathy among the laity. From the time of its first patronage under Asoka (around 260 B.C.E.), Buddhism had enjoyed occasional support from princes and kings, and its ability to preach the dharma, to enjoy favor at court, and to influence culture depended on this support. The Kusana dynasty (ca. 78–320 C.E.), for instance, was a good time for Buddhists, while the Gupta age (320–540 C.E.) revived Hinduism. When the Muslims finally established control in India, Buddhism suffered accordingly. Early missionary activity had exported it to the south and east, however, and Buddhism proved to be hardy on foreign soil. So Hinduism, which has largely been confined to India, became the native tradition that opposed the Muslims, while Buddhism became an internationalized brand of Indian culture.[43] We deal with the East Asian version of Buddhism in the next two chapters.

Contemporary Buddhist Rituals

The austere meditational focus of Zen and the continuing challenge of lofty Buddhist philosophy have captivated most Western observers of Buddhism, perhaps preventing them from properly appreciating Buddhist ritual. To fill out our historical account, let us focus on how contemporary Buddhist piety actually functions in such disparate locales as Burma and California, remembering that a similar ritualism has been important throughout all of Buddhist history.

Melford Spiro's informative anthropological study, *Buddhism and Society*,[44] includes a chapter on the ceremonial cycle of Burmese Buddhism that he witnessed. Of special interest are the devotions that paced the individual through the day. Although participation in these devotions was voluntary, and those who did not participate neither sinned nor lost merit, most Burmese took part (children being observers until they reached their teens).

The pious Burmese Buddhists whom Spiro met in the late 1950s and early 1960s began and ended the day with devotions performed in front of a small household shrine. This shrine usually consisted of a shelf for a vase of fresh flowers and a picture of the Buddha. It was always located on the eastern side of the house (the most auspicious side) and placed above head level (to place the Buddha below head level would be insulting). During the time of devotions, householders would light candles and place food offerings before the Buddha.

Coming before this shrine, the householders would begin by saying: "I beg leave! I beg leave! I beg leave! By act, by word, and by thought, I raise my hands in reverence to the forehead and worship, honor, look at, and humbly pay homage to the three gems—the Buddha, the Law, and the Order—one time, two times, three times, O Lord." Then they would petition to be freed from the four woes (rebirth in hell, as an animal, as a demon, or as a ghost), from the three scourges (war, epidemic, and famine), from the eight kinds of unfortunate birth, from the five kinds of enemy, from the four deficiencies (tyrannical kings, wrong views of life after death, physical deformity, and dull-wittedness), and from the five misfortunes, that they might quickly gain release from their pains. They would end the morning prayer by reciting the five precepts, renewing their commitment to abstain from taking life, from stealing, from drinking intoxicants, from lying, and from sexual immorality.

Clearly, therefore, the Burmese Buddhists sought to orient each day by honoring the Buddha, begging his protection against misfortune, and rededicating themselves to the Buddhist ethical code. In the evening many Burmese, especially the elderly, would conclude a similar session of homage, petition, and rededication by praying a rosary. The Buddhist rosary consisted of 108 beads, one for each of the 108 marks on the feet of the Buddha (which, in turn, represented his 108 reincarnations). While fingering a bead the devotee usually would say either "painful, selfless, fleeting" or "Buddha, dharma, *sangha*" three times.

In addition to these devotions held in the home, the villagers whom Spiro studied held a public ceremony every evening after sunset in the village chapel. This was located in the center of the village and consisted of a shed open on three sides. The fourth side enclosed an ark containing a statue of the Buddha. Attendance usually was sparse, except in special periods such as the Buddhist Lent, and more sophisticated believers, who thought meditation was the central expression of a mature Buddhist faith, spoke disparagingly of the chapel services as magical or superstitious.

Nonetheless, the village service was interesting because it was led by laypeople, rather than monks, and because it used the Burmese vernacular, rather than Pali, the formal liturgical language. Thus, it was a place where common folk and Burmese youth could experience their religion in a form easy to understand.

The ceremony usually began with an invocation of the gods, and then an invocation of the Buddha, before whose image fresh cut flowers had been placed. The worshipers asked permission to reverence the Buddha and prayed that their worship might bring them to nirvana or the higher abodes (the states near to nirvana). Other prayers followed, asking the Buddha to grant the petitioners strength to fulfill the five precepts and understand the three marks.

The central portion of the village ceremony began with an offering of flowers, candles, and water— symbols of beauty, reverence, and purification. Following this, the faithful expressed their veneration of the Buddha, the teaching, the order, their parents, and their teachers. Next came recitations of parts of the scriptures, a profession of love for all creatures, a recitation of the doctrine of Dependent Coarising, a recitation of the Buddha's last words, a recitation of the five "heaps" (*skandhas*) of which human individuality is composed, a prayer to the eight planets, and a confession of faith.

The ceremony concluded with a water libation that called the merit of the worshipers to the attention of an ancient earth goddess, the release of the gods who had been called into attendance, and an enthusiastic "sharing of merit" (of the benefit the participants had gained from the service) with the participants' parents and all other beings. Overall, the ceremony reinforced the main points of Buddhist teaching, reminding the participants how to orient their lives and encouraging them to express both their reverence for the Buddha and the main concerns for which they wanted the Buddha's aid.

Since 1970 there has been a successful Buddhist monastery near Mount Shasta in northern California. It has seventeen buildings (a Zendo or meditation hall, a founder's shrine, a shrine to the *bodhisattva* Kannon, a sewing room, a laundry, a tool shed, a store room, a library, eight residences, and a common room). The monastery was founded by an Englishwoman named Peggy Kennett (Jiyu Kennett-Roshi), who is a guru in the Soto Zen tradition. (Soto and Rinzai are schools that began in China but underwent a further development in Japan.) While maintaining traditional Soto teachings, the Shasta monastery has tried to adapt to American cultural forms. Thus members eat their meals American style at a table rather than Japanese style sitting on the floor, they chant in Gregorian tones rather than Japanese tones, they usually wear Western clerical garb rather than Japanese robes, and they serve English rather than Japanese tea.

The central occupation of the monastery is *zazen*, or sitting in meditation. Most members of the monastery spend two to three hours in meditation each day. Charles Prebish has described the daily schedule of all the monastic duties as follows:

5:45 A.M.	Rising Bell
6:15	Zazen
7:00	Morning Service
7:45	Community Tea
8:15	Breakfast
8:45	Community Clean-up
9:15	Trainees' Class
11:00	Community Tea
11:30	Junior Trainees' and Laypeople's Class
1:00 P.M.	Lunch
1:30	Rest
2:00	Priests' Class (Work Period for Others)
3:00	Community Tea
3:30	Work Period
5:00	Zazen
6:00	Dinner
6:30	Choir Practice
7:30	Evening Service

7:45	Zazen
8:30	Tea
9:00	Return to Residences[45]

During the morning service, the trainees make three bows and offer incense to the celebrant, Kennett-Roshi. The community then intones and recites portions of the Buddhist scriptures. There are three more bows, and then the community processes to the founder's shrine, where they recite more scriptures. During the evening ceremony, in addition to the scripture recitations, there is a reading of the rules for *zazen*. At meals someone recites portions of the scriptures while the food is passed, to help community members increase their sense of gratitude for what they are about to receive. Since the meditation hall is closed on any day of the month having a four or a nine (for reasons Prebish does not disclose), six times in most months there is a "closing ceremony." Vespers finish the evening service, and through the day monks say prayers before such activities as shaving their heads and putting on their robes.

If this schedule inculcates the same dispositions that the similar schedules of strict Christian monasteries do, the result is a great focusing of attention. The day passes largely in silence, for speech is allowed only at stated times, and most community members expend much effort in meditation. At Mount Shasta there are regular periods throughout the year when the monks concentrate on meditation almost full-time, making a strong effort to come closer to enlightenment. Yet the Soto conviction that buddha-nature should emerge peacefully tempers such effort.

The recitation of the Buddhist scriptures potentially has the effect of creating mantras, for when sounds enter consciousnesses that have been purified by discipline and made alert by meditation, they can develop almost mesmerizing cadences. The ritual bows, use of incense, use of flowers, and the like help to engage all the senses and focus all the spiritual faculties, so that the prayer or meditation to be performed can be wholehearted.

A major difference between the monastic ritualism of Mount Shasta and the lay ritualism of the Burmese Buddhism we described is the stress the lay ritualism placed on petitioning the Buddha for protection against misfortune and help with worldly needs. Part of this difference stems from the greater stress that Theravada lay doctrine places on gaining merit. Whereas the monastic doctrine of Soto Zen stresses the enlightenment nature of all reality, the Burmese

Figure 21 *Standing Buddha, Kashmir, tenth–eleventh century. Bronze; 10⅜ in. high. This statue blends the styles of north-central India with Hellenistic influences. The upraised right hand is a gesture of protection. The Nelson–Atkins Museum of Art, Kansas City, Missouri (Nelson Fund).*

Buddhists live in a thought-world filled with ghosts and gods that constantly make them aware of a need to improve their karmic state. Consequently, Burmese ritual seems more anxious. While the Burmese stress the merit one must attain for a better future, the Soto ritual stresses the grace, harmony, and peace that enlightenment brings. (Of course, Soto ritual is also an effort to inculcate the dispositions that conduce to enlightenment, such as inner silence, gratitude, and a sense of harmony with all of creation.)

As we saw, Burmese ritual also tends to be a constant reminder of staple Buddhist doctrine. It has an important place for honoring the Buddha, and for expressing the worshipers' needs, but a great deal of its energy goes into reviewing, or trying to deepen the worshipers' hold on, the five precepts, the three jewels, and so on. Mount Shasta appears to take care of doctrine in the classroom.

In both cases, however, Buddhist rituals encourage believers to worship, the central religious act, as other religions' rituals bring adherents to worship. At worship, members of quite different religious traditions appear to draw much closer to one another. Despite massive doctrinal differences (which, of course, shape what the worshipers understand themselves to be doing), the members of the different traditions all seem to be trying to collect themselves, praise what they take to be ultimate reality, and gain the spiritual aid they need. Not surprisingly, therefore, some of the most fruitful comparative study of religion occurs when scholars try to enter the inner dispositions of the worship and sense what the different rituals are trying to bring about.

WORLDVIEW

We have stressed the intellectual aspects of Buddhist history, the development of key notions and important philosophical schools, because Buddhism is a tradition that has stressed enlightenment: grasping experientially the structures of reality. Often, this "grasp" has involved a lot of un-knowing—realizing ways in which spontaneous, commonsensical views of reality are erroneous. Such views are not innocuous, because they keep people chained in samsara. The Buddha's personal experience was that he broke the chains of samsara only when he had the insight that gave rise to the Four Noble Truths. Ever since, attaining a personal understanding of the Four Noble Truths—replicating something of the Buddha's genetic insight—has been very important. The Buddhist *sangha* has existed to facilitate gaining such an understanding. The monastic life has been geared to putting aside desire and preparing the spirit for nirvana. Laity have venerated monks and nuns because these spiritual athletes have striven for experiential wisdom.

Naturally enough, Buddhism has made accommodations for the laity, since they were bound to be the majority of the members of the community. The Japanese holy man Shinran (1173–1262) made explicit what many other Buddhist leaders have done implicitly, adapting the dharma to the needs of married people, unlettered people, people who have to work in the world. Shinran went farther than most others, stressing faith in the Buddha more than a grasp of the dharma, but whenever it allowed rituals and devotions to multiply, the *sangha* accommodated the Buddha's Way to the needs of ordinary people.

Thus, the worldview that we now study has usually come to ordinary laypeople through ceremonies, festivals, traditional stories, and Buddhist culture at large. Music, poetry, views of sickness, views of good fortune—all aspects of a popular religious culture carry parts of the core religious message. If the core religious message has always been the Four Noble Truths, young people have heard it differently from old people, women have heard it differently from men, the wealthy are bound to stress one side of the message and the poor bound to stress another. That is how popular culture works. It is never straightforward, completely clear, univocal. It is always complex, many-layered and many-voiced.

Thus, you have to imagine the intellectualism that we have stressed working its way out in terms of images and feelings—thoughts and hopes that the average Buddhist seldom brought to clarity or full articulation. For example, you have to imagine the typical devout Buddhist family centering its religious life on the little altar in its home. When family members decorated the altar with flowers and fruit and incense, they expressed concretely their love of the Buddha, their trust that Buddhist tradition would make their lives meaningful, their inclination to go to the Buddha and tradition in time of trial. We should not despise religious traditions for being most powerful in time of trial. We ought to accept the fact that, the world over, most human beings only think completely seriously when suffering, death, injustice, evil, and other trials or hardships force them to. Paradoxically, and mercifully, that is how the bad things that happen to good people sometimes turn out to have brought a blessing. The blessing does not remove the badness, but it can become a solid consolation.

In the same way, we have to accept the fact that the majority of Easterners, like the majority of Westerners, have gone beyond what a restrained orthodoxy might have preferred and sought human faces in which they might concretize the ultimate reality that they needed to worship. For example, a great many

Buddhists have worshiped Gautama, even though some schools of Buddhism have taught that he was only a man who embodied a universal wisdom. The distinction between venerating a holy man and worshiping a truly ultimate, divine reality escapes many laypeople in many different traditions. The popular treatment of the Virgin Mary in Christianity and of Muhammad in Islam are cases in point. Rather than debate about the propriety of the cultus that grew up around Gautama, as around central figures in other religious traditions, we do better to appreciate the human needs that the cultus expresses.

In the case of the Buddha, the people who have bowed, offered gifts, chanted verses from the scriptures, and in various other ways given flesh to their vow to place their trust in the Buddha (as in the dharma and the *sangha*) have expressed their need for a center—a holy place of refuge. The Buddha has functioned for most Buddhists as such a place, just as Christ has functioned that way for Christians. The Buddha has meant that reality is not chaotic, life is not meaningless, suffering and defeat are not the final word. More positively, the Buddha has meant that, in the ultimate analysis, human existence is blessedly good and carries a wonderful potential. That is what human beings most need to hear. That is the sort of "place" the human heart most needs to be able to go, if it is not to feel like a motherless child—an orphan in an uncaring, hostile world.

So, as you consider the Buddhist worldview, think of how it probably played itself out in a Buddhist of your own age, sex, and socieconomic situation. Think of what the Buddha might have meant to a person in the equivalent of our modern business, or art, or science, or family life. If one studies the world religions with a sympathetic eye, it is easy to find an equivalence among their different symbolisms. All have been faced with the same basic problems: survival, justice, hope for a meaning that goes beyond the grave. All have tried to bless love and creativity, stand against untruth and cruelty. And so all have invited people to do the same things: reflect, reform their lives, detach themselves from destructive private and social behavior, commit themselves to what brings light and peace. That has been the reason-to-be of the Buddhist worldview and so the key to Buddhist history.

Nature

Stepping back from the historical view of Buddhism, we find that Buddhist attitudes toward nature do not fit together neatly. From its Indian origins, Buddhism assumed much of Hinduism's cosmological complexity. That meant taking up not only a world that stretched for vast distances and existed for immense eons (kalpas) but also the Aryan materialism and yogic spiritualism that lay behind such a cosmology. However, Buddhism came to contribute its own world views. Its numerous "buddha-fields," for instance, are realms with which our earthly space-time system shares the boundless universe.

Buddhism has had few equivalents to Vedic materialism, but Buddhism used the doctrine of samsara early in its history to justify acceptance of one's worldly situation and working only to improve it (rather than to escape it for nirvana). On the other hand, the ancient Indian yogic practices impressed the Buddha and his followers deeply. Since Gautama had in fact become enlightened through meditation, and since this enlightenment expressed itself in terms of the antimaterial Four Noble Truths, Buddhism could never settle comfortably in the given world of the senses and pleasure.

Initially, therefore, Buddhism looked on nature or physical reality as much less than the most real or valuable portion of existence. Only consciousness could claim that title. Certainly the belief that all life is suffering reflects a rather negative attitude toward nature, and it indicates that what the eyes see and the ears hear is not the realm of true reality or true fulfillment. Also, to analyze physical reality in terms of three negative marks (pain, fleetingness, and selflessness) further devalues nature. At the least, one is not to desire sensory contacts with the world, because such desire binds one to illusory reality and produces only pain. Thus, Indian Buddhists separated themselves from nature (and society and self).

Philosophy and Popular Buddhism. Because the great interest of early Buddhist philosophy was an analysis of dharmas (elements of reality) based on probings of consciousness sharpened by intense meditation, the material aspects of the natural realm fell by the way. At best they were background realities and values. The scholastic Abhidharmists did not deny nature, for they were acutely aware of the senses, but they did deflect religious consciousness away from it.[46] Far more impressive than natural phenomena were the states of consciousness that seemed to go below the gross phenomena to more subtle phenomena. They were the places where the Indian Buddhists preferred to linger.

In considering the Buddhist view of nature, we must distinguish between the inclinations of the meditators and scholars, who were interested in nonphysical states of consciousness, and the inclinations of the laity, who saw the world more concretely and less analytically. As we might expect, the laity were more worldly than the monks. When they heard that all life was suffering, they probably thought of their family burdens, their vulnerability to sickness, and the many ways in which nature seemed out of their control. The comforts they received from Buddhist preaching, therefore, lay in the promise that right living would take them a step closer to the kind of existence where their pain would be less and their enjoyment greater.[47]

Thus, it is no surprise that the most popular Buddhist movements were built on the Indian traditions of devotion. Just as popular Hinduism fixed on Vishnu, Krishna, and Shiva, popular Buddhism fixed on **Amitabha, Avalokitesvara,** and **Vairocana.** These celestial buddhas or *bodhisattvas* drew the popular religious imagination away from the historical Buddha and the commonplace world of the here and now to the realm of future fulfillment. In that way, popular Buddhism lay in between the deemphasis of the physical realm that the monks and scholars practiced and the simple acceptance of physical life that a worldly or naturalist outlook (such as that of the early Vedas) produced. Emotional Buddhism influenced the sense perceptions of the laity so that this world became just the preliminary to the Western Paradise.[48]

Samsara and Nirvana.   We have seen that as the intellectuals and contemplatives worked further with immaterial consciousness and its philosophical consequences, they changed the relationships between samsara and nirvana. In the beginning, Buddhism thought of samsara as the imperfect, illusory realm of given, sense-bound existence. Nature, therefore, was part of the realm of bondage. The Buddha himself exemplified this view when he urged his followers to escape the world that was "burning" to achieve nirvana. His original message regularly said that spontaneous experience makes one ill, and that health lies in rejecting attachments to spontaneous experience. With time, however, the philosophers, especially the Mahayanists, came to consider the relations between nirvana and samsara more complex. From analyzing the implications of these concepts, the philosophers determined that nirvana is not a thing or a place. The Buddha realized this, for he consistently refused to

describe nirvana in detail. But while the Buddha's refusal was practical (such a description would not help solve the existential problems of being in pain), the refusal of the later philosophers, such as Nagarjuna, was largely epistemological and metaphysical. That is, they thought that we cannot think of such a concept as nirvana without reifying it (making it a thing), and that the reality of nirvana must completely transcend the realm of things. Therefore, nirvana could be the deepest reality of nature.

To follow this line of thought is no easy task, so only the elite grasped the philosophy of the *Prajnaparamita,* with its concepts of emptiness and transcendence. That philosophy influenced the devotional life of Mahayana and the ritual life of Tantrism, however, because even the simple people could grasp its positive implications as presented by the preachers. These positive implications, which blossomed most fully in the East Asian cultures, amounted to seeing that all reality is related. The other side of saying all dharmas are empty is to say that the buddha-nature (or nirvana, or the other ways of expressing the ultimate totality) is present everywhere. Even if one had not entered into Nirvana fully, so that no mark of karma remained, one could sense the presence of nirvanic ultimacy as the foundation of nature. This belief gave religion a very positive tone. For instance, if all things contain the buddha-nature, then the natural and social worlds can become glowingly fresh and beautiful, as one realizes their potential.

Tantrist Buddhism, finally, shared the belief in the nonduality of samsara and nirvana that Indian Mahayana developed but differed in its expression of this belief through ritualistic imagination. Tibetan practices, for example, played with the world, both loving nature and kicking it away, through sights (mandalas), sounds (mantras), and ceremonies (symbolic intercourse) that engaged the participant both psychologically and physically. All of this, of course, implied using nature as a somewhat sacramental way to gain liberation. Insofar as physical nature reaches into the human being through the subconscious and unconscious, Tantrism has both honored and provided for nature's "depth psychology."

Society

The Indian society of the Buddha was divided into castes, which were religiously sanctioned as a way of maintaining social order. Moreover, casteism was part of Vedic India's cosmological myth, since according to legend human society's order resulted from the sacrifice of Purusha, the primal human being. In Brahmanism, the priests merited their primary status because they derived from Purusha's mouth.

Buddha, himself a member of the warrior class, brought a message that clashed with this hierarchy. His dharma taught that beings are to free themselves from painful worldly life. Since this invitation was from human nature, from what we are, it was more compelling than the call to accept the caste tradition. At least, Buddhists could strongly refute the cosmological myth that legitimated casteism. Many warriors and merchants no doubt also found Buddhism a convenient weapon in their struggles with the brahmins for power. So they and others who wanted to change the status quo gave Buddhism a close hearing.

There was great liberation potential in the Buddha's message. Indeed, there was considerable social radicalism. Buddha did not concern himself very much with politics as such, but his stress on enlightenment, nirvana, and the human calling to conquer karma and samsara challenged the politics of his day, as did the decision to admit people of all castes into the *sangha* and to include women. This decision was a logical application of the belief that all humans were in misery and might gain enlightenment.

In application, though, Buddhism never fully realized these ideals of liberation and radical equality. Caste was too much a part of Indian society to be exorcised without great difficulty. For instance, the *Dhammapada* (vv. 383–423) uses the brahmin as a figure of perfection. The "true Brahmin," it is at pains to show, is not he who is born into a priestly bloodline but he who gains a noble character through morality, meditation, and wisdom. Nonetheless, the *Dhammapada* does not choose to reinterpret the sudra (lowest class worker). It is the brahmin who continues to denote nobility.

Women's Status. Buddhism offered Indian females considerably more than had been available to them previously.[49] Women were capable of enlightenment and could join the monastic community as nuns. This was in stark contrast to the classical Hindu view, which held that women had to be reborn as men to be eligible for *moksha*. By opening religious life to Indian women, Buddhists gave them an option besides marriage and motherhood—a sort of career and chance for independence. No longer did a girl and her family have to concentrate single-mindedly on gathering a dowry and arranging a wedding. Indeed, Buddhists

viewed Hindu child marriage darkly, and they thought it more than fitting that women should travel to hear the Buddha preach. In later times, women could preach themselves, but from the beginning they could give time and money to the new cause.

Moreover, by offering an alternative to marriage, Buddhism inevitably gave women more voice in their marriage decisions and then in their conjugal lives. In fact, Buddhism viewed spouses as near equals. The husband was to give the wife respect, courtesy, faithfulness, and authority, while the wife was to give the husband duties well done, hospitality to their parents, faithfulness, watchfulness over his earnings, skill, and industry. One concrete way in which a Buddhist wife shared authority was in choosing their children's careers. For instance, to enter a monastery, a child needed both parents' consent. Married women could inherit and manage property without interference. Buddhism did not require or even expect that widows be recluses, and suttee was abhorrent to a religion that condemned animal sacrifice, murder, and suicide. Finally, Buddhist widows could enter the *sangha*, where they might find religious companionship, or they could stay in the world, remarry, inherit, and manage their own affairs.

Still, Buddhism never treated women as full equals of men. Though the logic of equal existential pain and equal possession of the buddha-nature could have run to equal political and educational opportunities, it seldom did. Nuns had varying degrees of freedom to run their own affairs in the monasteries, but they were regularly subject to monks. Women never gained regular access to power over males, either in Buddhism's conception of the religious community or in its conception of marriage. Insofar as celibacy became part of the Buddhist ideal, marriage could become a second-class vocation and women could become a religious danger.[50]

Politics. In its relations with secular political powers, Buddhism had varying fortunes. The Buddha seems to have concerned himself little with pleasing public authorities or worrying how his spiritual realm related to the temporal. No doubt his assumption was that if people became enlightened they would relativize social problems and solve them fairly easily. At the time of Asoka, however, the importance of royal patronage became clear. Much of Buddhism's influence outside India began when Asoka dispatched missionaries to foreign lands, and his efforts to instill Buddhist norms of ethics and nonviolence in his government became a model for later ages. As Christianity rethought Jesus' dictum about rendering unto Caesar the things that are Caesar's when it found a potentially Christian Caesar in Constantine, so after Asoka Buddhism longed for a union of dharma and kingly authority, thinking that such a union would beget a religious society.

Historically Buddhists tried to gain favor at court.[51] In Sri Lanka, Burma, Thailand, and the rest of Southeast Asia, this effort often succeeded, and temporal rulers played a large role in Theravada's victory over Mahayana and Hinduism. In China, Buddhism's fortunes depended on whether it fared better or worse than Confucianism in getting the emperor's ear. During the worst periods, it became the object of imperial persecution. The same was true in Japan, where such persecution had much the same rationale: Buddhism was not the native tradition. Overall, however, Buddhism fared well in East Asia. It had to coexist with Confucian and Daoist cultural forces, but it regularly dominated philosophy, funeral rites, and art. Tibet realized the theocratic ideals that Asoka had sparked: Throughout most of its history religious leaders doubled as temporal powers. However, the intrigue, murder, and moral laxity that this binding of the two powers produced during certain periods of Tibetan history suggested rethinking the relation between the religious and the secular powers.

As with Christianity, there is a built-in tension between the Buddhist religious community and any temporal state. The *sangha* and the church both make claims upon their followers that can bring them into conflict with secular powers. Since these claims are made in the name of dharma or God, they carry an aura of sacredness or of coming from a higher authority. To be sure, Buddhism took pains to establish an ethics that urged peaceful citizenship.[52] But the proviso always lurking behind these sincere efforts was that secular rulers not order things unjust, evil, or irreligious. The things that rightly are Caesar's are limited. So long as there is a Christ or a Buddha, a God or a nirvana, Caesar cannot claim everything.

One ploy that Caesar can develop, however, is to claim that he, rather than the priests or monks, is the representative of God or dharma. In other words, employing the aspect of the cosmological myth by which the human ruler is the link between heaven and earth, the king can claim a sacredness of his own. Many Christian successors to Constantine claimed this, and in effect many Buddhist rulers after Asoka did also. Eric Voegelin has sketched the preparation for this sort of claim that a society such as the Mongol had. According to his hypothesis, Kublai Khan gave the Buddhists authority over Tibet as an administrative extension of his own sacred power.[53]

Despite its focus on otherworldly matters, then, Buddhism remained knotted in secular-religious controversies. Since it did not clearly establish an authority outside the cosmos (for instance, by coming to a doctrine of creation from nothingness), it was always liable to attack from kingly Buddhists who wanted to make doctrinal dharma serve the state.

The Sangha. The *sangha* alternately raised and dashed hopes that most human beings might live together in harmony and peace. Energetic monasteries, run by learned and holy monks or nuns, were models of what human society could be. Living simply, obeying a common rule and a common authority, such Buddhist professionals acted out a vision of equality and cooperation. When a monastery was in good spiritual fettle, one survived there only if one's motivation was religious. Meditation, hard work, austerity in diet and clothing, long periods of silence, celibacy—these staples of Buddhist monastic life offered little to the worldling. However, monasteries of the devotional sects could be quite different. Often people entered them rather grudgingly and briefly, to learn the minimal ritual and doctrine necessary to function at the inherited family temple. Meditation-centered monasteries also differed from the pampered, court-favored centers of learning, art, and intrigue frequently spawned by East Asian Buddhism. Still, as long as the genuine articles existed, Buddhism was alive and well.

The life of Buddhist laity has always reflected the state of the monastic *sangha*. When the monasteries were spiritually active, the laity tended to support them generously. In return, the monks usually served the laity spiritually. During these periods, the notion that the layperson's vocational obligation was primarily to support the monks evoked no cynicism. The monastery was embodying the social ideal and so encouraging the whole *sangha* to think that dharma could be an effective social philosophy. On the other hand, when the monks were lax, the reaction of the laity was ambivalent. The laity enjoyed seeing clay feet under yellow robes, but they missed the examples and teachings that might have dissolved some of their own clay. Ideally, then, the monks and nuns and the laity have provided mutual support.[54] A lively interaction between monks and laity could grow from the notion that by giving generously to the monks lay people could draw on the "field of merit" created by monastic holiness. Mahayana and Tantra have acted on this ideal by relating nirvana and samsara in such a way that vocational differences between the laity and the clergy are lessened. Even for these schools, however, the monasteries have symbolized idealistic places of retreat, meditation, study, and ritual devotion.

Buddhist Ahimsa. In an appendix to his study of Theravada ethics,[55] Winston King has some interesting remarks about recent Buddhist attitudes toward killing. Perhaps they will somewhat bridge the way from the Indian tradition of *ahimsa* to our present age, with its pressures from nuclear weapons, ecological disorders, and dietary researches, to rethink our modern aggression. If so, it may suggest the perennial power of Buddhist social thought.

Traditionally, Buddhism laid great stress on the precept of nonkilling, not only because this precept inculcates a respect for all living things, but also because carefully observing it leads to great self-control and promotes peace. For example, if one is to stay away from killing or injuring other creatures, one must control anger, greed, hatred, and the other vices that usually spur our injurious actions and inhibit social justice.

Nonetheless, in countries such as Burma, where many political figures profess to be faithful Buddhists, the question of how to apply the precept of nonkilling in public policy has grown quite vexing. Thus, one candidate in the 1959–60 elections pointed out the difficulty of adhering to strict interpretations of nonkilling while trying to suppress rebel insurgents or run such important government industries as fishing and mutton production. This dilemma differs little from that of the Christian pacifist, but nonviolence probably has been closer to the core of Buddhist tradition than to the core of Christian tradition. Leading Buddhist politicians, such as U Thant, who became head of the United Nations, therefore have had to make some distinctions. Generally they have tried to moderate public policies in the direction of nonkilling but have conceded that a thorough application of *ahimsa* (for example, prohibiting all military action) is not always practical.

Capital punishment is another problem that the precept of nonkilling heightens. Ideally, most Buddhists probably would oppose a law of capital punishment, urging sentences of life imprisonment for capital crimes. Not only would this honor *ahimsa,* it would also offer the criminal an opportunity to repent

and be converted to Buddhist convictions. Still, through history to modern times most Buddhist countries have practiced capital punishment. This has caused some analysts to speak of a conflict between the mundane morality of the state and the ideal morality of the Buddhist religion. In their view, the state needs capital punishment to maintain order, so one must reluctantly kill the worst social offenders. This might seem to relegate Buddhist ideals to complete impracticality, but further reflection has led some ethicians to a more dialectical notion of nonkilling.

For these dialecticians, there are circumstances in which *not* slaying heinous offenders would be a great violence. Those charged with protecting the common good would seriously fail their charge were they to allow murderers to continue operating without fear of capital punishment. So the dialecticians come to the conclusion that committing the lesser evil is doing a species of good. In other words, they justify capital punishment as a necessary evil, a means public officials must employ if they are to honor the precept of noninjury in more general, far-reaching terms. To prevent great injury to the public at large, one must injure some criminal offenders. Once again, it would not be hard to draw parallels to Western debates over capital punishment.

Still another implication of the precept of noninjury is that one must avoid contributing to the *conditions* that lessen or warp the span of living things, especially human beings. This is parallel to the Latin American theoreticians' discussions of *violencia blanca. Violencia blanca* is the white or invisible violence that an unjust system perpetrates through its inequitable distribution of wealth and power. Thus, when they are accused of corrupting their revolutionary cause by resorting to military violence or violence against the property of the rich, some Latin Americans argue that the prevailing *violencia blanca* in the slums, poverty, shortened life spans, bloated stomachs of little children, illiteracy, and the like, is a greater evil, though of course one to which most people have grown accustomed.

The Buddhist parallel quoted by King is quite exact. In it a contemporary Burmese ethician urges his fellow countrymen to apply the precept of nonkilling to "crowded and ill-ventilated buildings, workshops and factories; slum conditions in big cities and towns; the overworking of children as well as adults; careless driving of steam boats, rail engines, planes, motor and other vehicles and engines; sale of spurious and other adulterated foodstuffs; unskilled use of syringes with or without license; treatment of sick people by quacks; sale of foodstuffs not fit for human consumption," and so forth. Anything that violates human health or dignity can be subsumed under the precept of nonkilling.

Self

The practical accent of Buddha's original preaching made the issues related to self paramount. Yet, paradoxically, a capital thesis in that preaching was that self is an illusion, "the most pernicious of errors, the most deceitful of illusions."[56] Consequently, Buddhist religious experience and doctrine concerning the self have been complex. On the one hand, Buddhism has directly addressed individuals, insisting that only the individual can change his or her life. On the other hand, Buddhism has counseled that to escape samsara and achieve nirvana, we have to rid ourselves of the notion that we have or are an atman, a soul, or self. This belief has prompted some of Buddhism's central meditational practices and philosophical doctrines.

Historically, the teaching of *anatman* most distinguished the Buddha's way from that of his Hindu predecessors. As we have seen, a staple of Upanishadic wisdom was that the self is part of the great Atman (the interior aspect of Brahman). In yogic meditation, the Hindu tried to realize this ultimate identity, to experience the oneness of everything in Atman. When Buddha turned away from this teaching, calling human identity just a bundle of elements (*skandhas*) temporarily fused, he laid down a philosophical challenge that Hindu and Buddhist philosophers seldom neglected in later centuries. What motivated this new conception of the human being?

The principal motive, it appears, was Buddha's conviction that the key to human problems is desire. If pain expresses the problem ("All life is painful"), then desire expresses its cause ("The cause of suffering is desire"). These, we have seen, are the first two Noble Truths. The Third Noble Truth ("The removal of desire leads to the removal of suffering") extends the first two, and when Buddhists pondered its meaning and implications, they came to the doctrine of no-self (*anatman*).

The Third Noble Truth itself is psychological. For instance, we may analyze the suffering in human relations in terms of desire. Parents desire their children's success and love. When the children choose paths other than what the parents have dreamed, or when the children demand distance in order to grow

into their own separate identities, the parents suffer pain. They feel disappointed or rejected, or that their toil and anxiety have gone for naught. Buddhists would tell such parents that their relations with their children have been unwise or impure. Because they have desired success and love, instead of remaining calm and free, they have set karmic bonds that were sure to cause pain.

But to cut the karmic bonds, the Third Noble Truth implies, one must get to the root of the desire. At this point one must turn psychology into metaphysics—one must realize that the self from which desires emanate is neither stable, fixed, permanent, nor, ultimately, real. In our distraction and illusion, we gladly accept the fiction that we have stable selves. Under the prod of analysis and meditation, however, we start to see what Alfred North Whitehead (the Western philosopher currently touted as the most "Buddhist" of our metaphysicians)[57] called the "fallacy of misplaced concreteness."

In simple terms, the prime reality in our interior lives is flux. At each moment we are different "selves." True, some continuity exists in that we remember past events and project future ones. But this continuity hardly justifies clinging to or relying upon a permanent self.

What Buddhists stressed, therefore, was the change and coordination of the "self's" components, just as they stressed the interconnectedness and flux of the entire world (through Dependent Coarising). They developed a view of both the interior realm of consciousness and the exterior realm of nature that became quite relational. Their metaphysics focused on nature's coordinated interdependencies, its continual movement. The self could not be the exception to such a worldview. Humans were too clearly a part of the total natural process to violate the process's fundamental laws. And just as analysis showed all the natural elements to be empty, so, too, analysis showed the self to be empty.

Therefore, Buddhists directly denied what Western philosophers such as Aristotle called a "substance." To live religiously, in accordance with the facts of consciousness, one had to cast off the naive assumption that the human person is a solid something—one had to slide into the flux. In so doing, one could both remove the basis for desire and open up the possibility for union with the rest of coordinated reality.

This movement toward coordination with the rest of reality became the positive counterweight to the

Buddhist negative view of the self. That is, as people advanced in their meditation and understanding, they started to glimpse what Mahayana saw in enlightenment: the realization that all buddha-nature is nondual. According to the *Prajna-paramita,* ultimately only buddha-nature existed. All multiplicity or discreteness resulted from a less than ultimate viewpoint. Yogacara texts such as the Chinese *Awakening of Faith*[58] explicitly correlated this view of ultimate wisdom with meditation. Stressing the centrality of mind, the *Awakening of Faith* tried to lead the reader toward the realization that his or her own consciousness reflected the ultimate connectedness. Such a realization, of course, meant the death of the illusion that one was an independent atman.

We have belabored this teaching of *anatman* (noself) because it seems most important to the Buddhist attitude toward the individual. It is also the key to the Buddhist view that nature flows together and that society should strive for ultimate reality by means of enlightenment. Because of no-self, the individual could move toward greater intimacy with nature. There were no barriers of separate identity, no walls making him or her isolated. For those who attained enlightenment through the dharma, this nonseparation of self, nature, and society was a personal experience. As a contemporary account of enlightenment puts it, "The big clock chimes—not the clock but Mind chimes. The universe itself chimes. There is neither Mind nor universe. Dong, dong, dong! I've totally disappeared. Buddha is!"[59]

Buddhism regularly counseled the individual to regard the body, the family, society, and even a spouse or a child with detachment. One was to revere and discipline the body according to the Middle Way. Clearly, though, the body was only a temporary station on the way to nirvana or one's next incarnation. Wealth and pleasure were not, as they were for Hinduism, worthy life goals. The family was a necessary unit, biologically and socially, but frequently it was also an impediment to spiritual advancement, as the Buddha's own life showed. Society would ideally be a context for mutual support in realizing enlightenment. Personal bonds, therefore, could not be passionate and karmic, and even a spouse or a child came under this law.

The love proper to a Buddhist was "great compassion"—desire for the other's good in nirvana. This became no-desire in worldly terms. So alcohol, sex, clothing, and other items affecting the body were governed by the ethical rule of detachment (and came

under the "Buddhist economics" that E. F. Schumacher made a cornerstone of his book *Small Is Beautiful*).[60] So business, politics, and art ideally sprang from a free spirit. East Asian painting, poetry, and calligraphy, for instance, ideally occurred in a state of no-mind.[61] Contrary to the regular Western view of the artist, in which the person agonizes through his or her work to produce a vision (and a self), the East Asian artist was to let art flow out of a meditative experience. Its hallmark was to be spontaneity, and the major stumbling block to spontaneity was self-concern.

Tantrism seems to qualify the Buddhist view of the self, since it allowed a more intense connection with food, alcohol, sex, and material ritual items. However, according to its own masters, the watchword in Tantrist rituals was still discipline and detachment. To use alcohol or sex licentiously was just a quick way to attachment and bad karma. The point to Tantrist ritual was to master these items and retain the energies that would have flowed out to them.

Even if not carried out, the doctrine of *anatman* (no-self) shaped Buddhist culture. Wherever Buddhist religion was vigorous, the doctrine of *anatman* was influential. In fact, we often can sense its effects in the peace and humor of Buddhist texts. Many texts, of course, are complicated and complex. However, some raise serenity, irony, paradox, and wit to a high religious art. For instance, in one story two monks meet a fetching damsel by a rushing river. One charitably hoists her and carries her across. Later the second monk chastises the first for such sensual contact. The first monk replies, "I let the girl down when we crossed the river. Why are you still carrying her?" The Buddhist ideal was to carry nothing, to have a self utterly free.[62]

Case Study: Nagarjuna. Nagarjuna gained such a lofty reputation in later Buddhism, especially that of Tibet, that he deserves special consideration as an example of the wise Buddhist personality, the ideal Buddhist "self." He probably lived between 150 and 250 C.E., most likely in south India, and his style of argumentation, as well as his analyses of his opponents' positions, suggests that he was trained as a Hindu brahmin before he converted to the budding movement of Mahayana Buddhism.

Although Nagarjuna is known as the most acute of the Mahayana dialecticians, Tibetan tradition also reveres him as a guru who offered his disciples sound ethical advice. Some verses from the "The Staff of Wis-

Figure 22   Head of a Buddha image, northwest India, first–second century. Stone; 19¼ in. high. The topknot, long ears, mark of knowledge on the forehead, and half-closed eyes are marks of authority, vision, and peace. The Nelson–Atkins Museum of Art, Kansas City, Missouri (Nelson Fund).

words never come to the core. This insistence expresses the conviction of all Buddhist gurus that words can be deceptive. If we allow words a life of their own, detached from the experiences they are trying to describe, words can distract us from reality. To grasp the dharma or the treatises of wisdom, we must both meditate on the realities to which they point and practice the virtues they extol. The same with the holy mantras that the tradition urges us to pray. Unless we experience the states from which they flow, the realities to which the saints have spontaneously directed them, the mantras will be but nonsense sounds.

Nagarjuna then reflects on the sort of knowledge that is truly valuable. We only know what this knowledge is in time of need, when we are hard-pressed. Then it is clear that the knowledge contained in books is of little use. Unless we have made an insight our own, it will give us little light or peace. In this, knowledge is parallel to wealth. Time of need shows us that wealth we have borrowed from others is no real wealth. It is nothing on which we can depend, for it can be taken from us at a stroke. Whether it be a matter of knowledge or of wealth, need, pressure, or suffering shows us the stark contrast between what we truly own and what we have merely borrowed. Thus hard times can have a silver lining. If they strengthen our resolve to gain our own wisdom, possess our own (incorruptible) wealth, they can advance us toward fulfillment.

We should consider our work in the same vein. The accomplishments of a teacher of ants, as Nagarjuna describes a person concerned with trivial affairs, are but ways of earning a living. Even the master baker, carpenter, or clerk deserves only the praise we can accord worldly skills. But suppose we meet a person studying liberation. Helping us terminate our earthly incarnation, such a person deals with heavenly affairs, the only things truly necessary. Were we wise, we would turn our admiration from masters of trivial affairs to those few masters who teach the only things truly necessary. Thereby, we would clarify our own essential task, making the study of how to terminate our earthly incarnation *the* great accomplishment to which we aspired.

Even master-teachers wander off the track at times, and Nagarjuna's next verse seems a tangent to his main line. If you have a chosen truth, a pearl of special wisdom, he says, be careful to whom you give it. Make sure that you scrutinize the character of any

dom," a work attributed to Nagarjuna, suggest his ethical style.[63]

First, Nagarjuna insists that the only way to gain the real meaning of the dharma, the Buddhist sciences, and the holy mantras is directly to experience them. Those who merely analyze the meaning of

person to whom you would impart the dharma. Unscrupulous people can turn the best of teachings to injurious use. Remember the legend of the man who took compassion on a monkey and gave him a small place to live. Before long the monkey had taken over the whole house and the man was out in the street. The same can happen with careless teachers. Unscrupulous disciples can turn the dharma against their teachers, making an act of charity into a shambles.

Bending back to the main stream of his thought, Nagarjuna turns to two kinds of teaching. Some people teach with words; others instruct silently. This is reminiscent of the reed-flower, which has no fruit, in contrast to the walnut, which has both fruit and flower. It is also reminiscent of the kataka tree, the fruit of which clears mud from the water. If you only mention the name of the kataka tree, you will not remove the mud. You must make your teaching bear fruit, make it deal with more than words. You must extend it to the realm of action, instructing by silent deeds as well as wordy lectures. Indeed, if you do not apply your knowledge, you are like a blind man with a lamp. Though you have in hand a source of great illumination, you do not shed it on the road, do not light the way for others to travel.

Stanza after stanza, Nagarjuna tosses out aphorisms like these. Line after line, his advice is poetic, symbolic, image-laden. From deep meditation and reflection, he finds emptiness a font of great illumination. For one who sees, the spiritual life is paradoxical and parabolic. As we come close to enlightenment, the main structures of the holy life stand clear, but these structures (meditation, wisdom, and morality) are capable of endless application. The key is having the experience, grasping the center, knowing emptiness directly. When we realize that reality is a seamless cloth, we can enjoy all its various designs. At that point, Buddhist selfhood will be properly achieved (and empty).

Ultimate Reality

Debate has raged over the question of whether Buddhism is a theistic religion. For instance, the late Chogyam Trungpa, a Tibetan master living in the United States, complained, "It is especially unfortunate that Buddhism has been presented as a theistic religion, whereas in fact it is a nontheistic spiritual philosophy, psychology, and way of life."[64] On the other hand, there is a good reason why scholars have frequently presented Buddhism as a theistic religion: It has frequently seemed to be such.[65] Devotional Buddhism has venerated a variety of buddhas and *bodhisattvas,* treating them as other religions treat gods and saints. Also, the Buddhist concepts of nirvana, buddha-nature, and emptiness have on occasion evinced the sacred aura of divinity, generating language that can only be called, by its difference from ordinary language, religious. In its perceptions of nirvana, Buddhism has made ultimate reality the touchstone of all wisdom. While this reality has been judged ineffable, all the meditation-masters imply that it is wholly positive. One cannot speak about it because it is too full, whole, basic, and brilliant for human language to describe. It is impersonal and reached by meditation more than by words. Therefore, Buddhism frequently has seemed to be both theistic or religious and matter-of-factly nontheistic.

To be sure, the Buddha himself does not appear to have claimed divinity. For example, he cast no speeches in the "I am" form that the Jesus of John's Gospel assumed. Rather, Gautama seems to have been a human being who thought that he had found the key to living well. The key was enlightenment, whose expression was the Four Noble Truths. In the enlightenment experience, Gautama encountered ultimate reality. The overtones to this encounter gleaned from the texts are not those of meeting a personal God. Whether that differentiates Gautama's ultimate reality from the God of Western religion is another question, the answer to which depends on careful analysis of peak experiences and conceptions of ultimate reality. The personal character of the Western God is not so simple as many Westerners assume, and the impersonal quality of Gautama's encounter with nirvana is less absolute than many assume.

Images of the Buddha. We may suggest the status of the Buddha by drawing on some of the images in which the sutras have delighted. A first image, of the Buddha's dharma as a raincloud, comes from the Lotus Sutra, a scripture very influential in such Mahayana sects as the Chinese Tien-t'ai and the Japanese Nichiren.

The sutra puts the image of a raincloud in the Buddha's own mouth: "The King of Dharma I am, who arose in the world to crush becoming; Dharma I teach to beings, after I have discerned their dispositions.

. . . It is like a great cloud which arises above the earth, which covers up everything and overshadows the firmament. And this great cloud, filled with water, wreathed with lightning, resounds with thunder, and refreshes all the creatures."[66]

A few verses later, the Buddha says that he has arisen in this world like a raincloud. And when he has arisen, "the World's Savior" speaks, to show all living beings the true course they ought to travel. For this he is honored by the whole world, with all its gods. He is the Tathagata, the one who has gone over to enlightenment, a conqueror who has arisen in the world like a raincloud. He refreshes all living beings, whose bodies are withering away because they cling to the lower worlds. The Buddha will ease the pains that are withering them. He will give them pleasures and the final rest of nirvana.

Moreover, he preaches the dharma to all beings, always making enlightenment the foundation of his teaching. This teaching is the same for all hearers. There is no partiality in the Buddha's message, no alteration of voice, for he is beyond hatred and love. Once again, this makes him like a raincloud, which releases its rain evenly on all. Enlightenment applies equally to the noble and the mean. It is the message the Blessed One offers the immoral as well as the moral. The depraved are no different in their need for enlightenment than those whose conduct is good. In all cases, final fulfillment depends on grasping, realizing, the dharma. Thus people who hold false views and people who hold right views, people who hold unsound views and people whose views are pure all stand in need of the Buddha. Prescinding from their merit or demerit, enlightenment presses on all of them as a fierce imperative. Without enlightenment, they are equally needy, equally bereft of the truth that saves. The Buddha is the one doctor dispensing the medicine needed by all the world's sickly souls.

For that reason, the Buddha spends himself, preaching dharma to beings of inferior intellect and beings of superior intellect, to beings whose faculties are weak and beings whose faculties are strong. Setting aside his own fatigue, he rains down dharma on them all. Feeling this rain, the world is well refreshed. Each being who comes under the shower of truth benefits, according to its own capacity. Each finds the well-preached teaching to its taste. In this the dharma is again like the rain, which falls on shrubs and grasses, bushes and smaller plants, trees and great wooded tracts, doing good to each. Throughout all the realms, earthly and celestial, the Buddha's teaching makes beings glow with refreshment and satisfaction.

Thus, the sutra concludes, it is the nature of dharma always to exist for the good of the world, offering a continual refreshment. From this refreshment the world should, like a well-watered plant, burst forth in blossoms of insight, purity, good behavior, and compassion.

If we step back to analyze this imagery, it is clear that the sutra pictures the Buddha and his teaching as the heavenly dew that makes the world green. Without the Buddha's dharma, the world would be a desert, arid and joyless. In the empty wastes of suffering, there would be no cause for hope. But the words of the Blessed One are so powerful and creative they make what was barren burgeon with sturdy growth. Cool, detached, above all the world's tribulations, the Buddha serenely makes the rain of truth fall on just and unjust alike. Only the sun moving in its heavenly circuit, or the clouds drifting high above, can symbolize the Buddha's equanimity and evenhandedness. To him all creatures are in need of the truth, so all have a claim on his enlightened compassion. Whatever their station or disposition, his message is apt and helpful.

The sutra depends on the conjunction of natural imagery with a conviction of Buddha's "skillfulness in means." In this phrase the tradition epitomized its belief that the Enlightened One could find a way into any heart, no matter what that heart's condition. Possessing the light of salvation in all its effulgence, the Buddha knows how to make the light shine into every corner of the world. So deeply does his wisdom go, it is always relevant, always able to clarify the hearer's condition. Just as all creatures need the rain of the skies, so all rational creatures need the heavenly truth. The Buddha was so closely associated with heaven, the supervising powers that rule the world, that the Lotus Sutra instinctively expressed his compassionate aid in terms of heavenly phenomena. Taking up the awe and gratitude human beings have always directed toward the heavens, the sutra focused them on the teaching, the Buddha's way out of this vale of tears.

Consequently, in a comparative perspective he was the great Buddhist divinity. Although at times *bodhisattvas* such as Kuan-yin drew more attention, often because they projected a maternal mercy, the core tenets of Buddhism ran toward placing Gautama, man and primary manifestation of enlightenment, at the center of the bull's-eye. As human, he modeled the pious life. As the primary manifestation of enlightenment, he brought nirvana into the midst of samsara. So his dharma became *the dharma,* the teaching that ran the world. So all enlightened people grew in his lineaments (though Zen masters and others fought any tendency to a literalist aping; for them the essential following of the Buddha was doing what he did, realizing one's own enlightenment-nature). For the common people, reverencing the Buddha was a main way to a better life, in which they might win release from suffering and gain the bliss of nirvana.

If Gautama has represented the personal aspect of Buddhist ultimate reality, putting into human form the truth that might free the human mind, heart, soul, and strength from the sufferings of samsara, it remains to be said that both Gautama himself and many subsequent Buddhists have considered nirvana, or the state of liberation, to be impersonal, a kind of no-thingness that both psychologically and ontologically (that is, in both the shifts in consciousness it denoted and what it suggested about being or the build of reality itself) did not fully square with either theistic or religious terminology.

Buddhist masters often explained that nirvana was something positive, as we have mentioned. Yet both etymologically and in terms of some of the classical descriptions of it, nirvana implied the denial of the limitations humanity presently suffered. So it would be like the state of the flame when the candle of desire had blown out. It would be an unconditioned—unfettered, unbound—way of being. When ignorance, pain, mortality, and disease (both physical and moral) had passed away, or had been escaped, one could speak of nirvana. When the last residue of karma, the final traces of debt to dying and being reborn, had been erased, one would be at the nirvanic far shore. Sometimes Mahayana thinkers translated this sort of thought into terms that seemed to equate it with a shift in consciousness: Think in nondesirous terms, live free of karmic impurity, and you could experience the substance of nirvana. Often such translations used the calm, the peace, the compassion of Gautama as emotional and behavioral anchors: That is what nirvana looked like in the life of the Enlightened One.

Moreover, such a focus tended to make light of, if not ignore, the question of whether there was a nirvanic realm of being—a place or state to which one went, or into which one entered, when one died as an enlightened being. The result was a peculiarly Buddhist form of secularism: a stress on the here and now that urged a nongrasping, fluid, sort of harmony. One was not to exploit the beauty, or even to flee the outward pain, of life in the here and now. Neither was one to take the here and now as an icon of eternity or God's otherworldly grace. Rather, one was to accept and join the flux of all beings, enjoying their being, light, and change. This was the way things were, and from the supreme realism of agreeing to the way things were one would both gain ultimate wisdom and enact it. Certainly one was to be compassionate toward the sufferings woven through most unenlightened people's perceptions of the way things were, but this compassion need not rouse one to anger at natural disaster or social injustice, need not shake one's deep-seated peace with agonies over evil, worries that reality itself had cancerous lesions.

The ontological correlative of this psychologically impersonal appreciation of ultimate reality largely traded in negation and silence. One could not define or describe nirvana as a state, a thing, a realm without falsifying it. Nirvana was in the midst of samsara. It was true being in contrast to mottled, desire-ridden, mortal being. Yet it was so whole, so basic, so pure that the human mind, intrinsically given to dichotomies and partialities, was bound to distort it. So the best approach was simply to let nirvana be, treating it as the wonderful, even the gracious partner to the wholeness, freedom, and delight one had entered upon with enlightenment. It was primary and human awareness of it was secondary. It was true or real, while most metaphysical schemes, like most human lives, were illusory—because they did not stem from the center of a healed, enlightened personality. One might use the Buddha to exemplify this appreciation of nirvanic ultimate reality; one might even sanction devotions such as reading the sutras or praying at the shrines of the *bodhisattvas.* But these were instrumental things, limited to the order of means. If they helped people, especially the common people, to sense the grandeur of what the Buddha had discovered and nirvanic reality always offered, fine. In itself, however, nirvana simply was, grounding all of samsaric existence and offering a perennial basis for hope, yet never yielding itself up to human control, never becoming less mysterious or less paradoxically both the treasure that might fulfill human longing and something so transhuman it could never be tamed, it would always remain somewhat alien.

SUMMARY: THE BUDDHIST CENTER

The Buddhist center seems to us to lie in enlightenment. This is the experience that gives the religion its name; this is the experience from which the Middle Way proceeds, to which it conduces. At various times we have spoken about enlightenment. In these last lines we would speak about it summarily, epitomizingly, in a final effort to cut to the heart of the Buddhist matter and find therein a lotus of peace.

Historically speaking, enlightenment made Gautama the Buddha. He became the person who knew the way to happiness, the secret of good living, by bringing his meditations under the bodhi tree to fruition. Flooded with light, realizing how things were and always had been, the Buddha solved the problem of suffering, broke the chains of samsara, gained a light and peace that made him compassionate, able and willing to succor all beings in need. Come to rest and insight himself, he could give order to the flux of human existence, see the implications of the light that he had found this flux to bear. So he became the great promulgator of the Teaching, the Noble Middle Way. He became the guide who was sufficiently skillful in means to mediate the Truth to any who would hear. As one of the devotional texts that we saw put it, his teaching "is like a great cloud which arises above the heart, which covers up everything and overshadows the firmament. And this great cloud, filled with water, wreathed with lightning, resounds with thunder, and refreshes all creatures."[67]

A center, however, should be perspicuous to most beholders. However much a full appreciation of it depends on a deep immersion in its presuppositions and implications, a center of a living, well-tested faith should have some allure for outsiders, should sparkle with the possibility of becoming their center, reorienting their lives for the better. Can we gain a sufficient appreciation of Buddhist enlightenment for this to

happen to us? Can we see ourselves, in our mind's eye, becoming flooded with light like the Buddha's and so gaining the Buddhist sense of reality, the Buddhist feel for the world? Let us try.

For many Buddhists, what Gautama experienced or discovered was neither new nor unique. Other enlightened beings had preceded him, and enlightenment is a possibility for all human beings. Why? Because reality itself is lightsome, knowing and knowable. To exist is to be mind-oriented, making sense, taking one's place in a scheme of things. Thus Yogacara Buddhists could come to the position that only Mind exists. Becoming greatly impressed with the mental or knowing aspect of all reality, they could put brackets around any nonknowing remainders, push them to the side of reality's essential definition. Zen Buddhist masters often speak in similar tones. For them reality itself is intrinsically perfect, complete and undefiled. It is only our ignorance or illusion that prevents us from seeing reality's perfection. As we grow more accustomed to right views and the rest of the Eightfold Path, through study, meditation, and good living, reality will grow brighter and brighter for us. At the lightsome center of the mind that has meditated well, the reality that has been well studied, there is only a stunning emptiness, a brilliant freedom from fixity, stolidity, desire.

When the Buddha realized this, he broke free of suffering. There was nothing to desire, and so nothing to suffer from. He and the rest of reality were not two or many. They were not one, in the Hindu sense of atman and Brahman. Their relation was ineffable, impossible to fix in clumsy human language. Only one who had come to understand this relation, to enjoy the light of being itself, could fully sense, feel, and profit from it. The best advertisements for enlightenment were the wisdom, freedom, and compassion that it generated. The serenity of nonattachment was like a breeze that blew out samsara, a dawn that unveiled nirvana. Were human beings to relate to nature, one another, and themselves in the light of such freedom, all things might go well. With humor and humility, intense presence to the given moment and great common sense, human beings might make their own organization a place of refuge. Then the *sangha* would indeed be a jewel, a worthy object of trust.

The humility and joy of enlightenment make it a very attractive center. Perhaps for that reason, William Johnston, one of the best translators of Buddhist spirituality to the West, has reminded his readers of a famous koan (a puzzling Zen saying meant to break down commonplace approaches to understanding). "A monk asked Ummon, 'What is the Buddha?' Ummon replied, 'A dried shit-stick.' A shit-stick was used in China instead of toilet paper. And Ummon, asked about the wonderful buddha-nature that is the true self, makes this shocking and iconoclastic answer. What does he mean? He means that however noble our aspirations, we must remember that we are (in the words of one commentator) 'a bag of manure.' Nor is it sufficient to give an intellectual assent to this proposition. One who would solve the koan must live it, realize it, act it out with his or her body, demonstrate to the master that one has identified with this ugly shit-stick . . . [yet] the Buddhist realization that the one is a dried shit-stick is also accompanied with great joy. There is no gnawing guilt in this koan but a great emancipation from anxiety together with the overflowing joy that always accompanies the recognition of the truth."[68] At the Buddhist center, we may find the liberating truth of our nothingness. Not all traditions would express this truth so graphically, but all would agree that humility makes one free, emptiness is fulfilling.

Discussion Questions

1. What was the essence of Gautama's enlightenment?

2. Is wisdom-morality-meditation a comprehensive, fully adequate religious regime? Why? Why not?

3. In what sense was Mahayana both more popular and more speculative than Theravada?

4. How did Tantrist Buddhism utilize the imagination?

5. Does Buddhism merge nature and divinity?

6. How would you try to persuade your best friend that he or she has no self?

7. Explain the Buddhist symbol of the lotus.

8. What do the various images of the Buddha seem to be saying?

9. What would you expect from a session with guru Nagarjuna?

10. How attractive do you find the daily routine of Mount Shasta Monastery?

11. What sense do you make of nirvana?

12. How can Buddhism be both religious and non-religious?

13. What is the significance of Buddhist compassion?

14. What would be the main thesis of a Buddhist social ethics?

15. How has Buddhism regarded sexuality?

16. What did the Buddha's acceptance of women into the *sangha* say about his views of contemporary Indian culture?

Key Terms

Amitabha: the Buddha of light, who presides over the Pure Land. Known in Japan as Amida, this buddha has been a prime object of veneration among such devotional groups as the followers of Shinran, who preached that faith in the mercy of Amida would suffice for salvation, due to the religious difficulties of his time.

anatman: the Buddhist doctrine that there is no substantial self and so nothing to which desire actually can cling. Buddhist philosophers have analyzed all the realities human beings experience as empty of either duration or permanent significance, trying to enlist disciples' minds in the pursuit of a complete detachment from the karmic allure of anything finite or conditioned.

arhat: a Buddhist term for one who has reached nirvana. In contrast to the *bodhisattva*, the *arhat* usually is considered to have been a rather solitary pursuer of enlightenment and full release, not much interested in the social side of liberation, where one would take up the burdens of other people, indeed of all living things, who also suffer from ignorance and desire.

Avalokitesvara: one of the greatest of the *bodhisattvas* reverenced by Mahayana Buddhism. Avalokitesvara is noted for his great compassion, and one finds in the *Prajna-paramita* sutras an indication that he presides over the philosophical way to enlightenment, being associated with Lady Wisdom herself in the effort to get believers to realize the emptiness of all dharmas and the coincidence of nirvana and samsara.

bodhisattva: a Mahayana Buddhist term for the enlightened one or saint who is a buddha-to-be. Typically, the *bodhisattva* postpones entrance into nirvana to labor for the salvation of other living beings, and generally the *bodhisattva* becomes a figure of help and mercy. Thus Kuan-yin, the *bodhisattva* most influential in the popular Buddhist religion of East Asia, has functioned as a kindly maternal figure, ever-available to help people with their worries about sickness, having a child, business problems, and the like.

buddha: one who comes to enlightenment and so becomes a knowledge-being, full of light and compassion. Gautama therefore has been only one of the many buddhas, but his making clear in earthly, historical terms the requirements for enlightenment has kept him central in Buddhist faith. Some Buddhist schools urged freeing oneself from overdependence on Gautama, under the conviction that each person was a potential buddha and had to develop this potential by self-reliance.

Dependent Coarising: the Buddhist doctrine about the structure of reality as a chain of mutually connecting influences. This chain straddles what we might call the physical and the moral realms, linking desire with death and rebirth but also specifying how desire works through the senses and intellect. One result of the doctrine of Dependent Coarising was to distance Buddhists from Hindus who thought in terms of a Brahman behind the phenomenal world and responsible for its patterns. Dependent Coarising meshed with the Buddhist view that all reality is empty and processive—moving along like a dance or even a flux.

dharma: an Indian term for teaching and duty. Buddhists have stressed the idea of teaching, speaking of the dharma of the Buddha as one of their three great treasures (Buddha, dharma, *sangha*). Hindus have more vaguely spoken of dharma as a Truth rooted in their tradition (most notably in the Vedas). The word has had a more precise set of Hindu connotations when used in a social context, pointing to the responsibilities attendant on one's caste and the teachings of the famous law codes (such as that of Manu) that regularized social relationships.

Eightfold Path: the Buddhist program of right views, right resolve, right speech, right action, right livelihood, right effort, right mindfulness, and right concentration. This is the fourth of the Buddha's Four Noble Truths, and traditionally Buddhists have understood it as undergirding wisdom, morality, and meditation, the three principal foci of their religious enterprise. Of course one could only learn what was

"right" in each of these areas from the Buddha, the dharma, and the *sangha,* but the Eightfold Path laid out the principal things on which one was to concentrate when thinking about the outlook, ethics, and reflective life necessary for enlightened living.

emptiness: an important concept in Mahayana Buddhist philosophy, stressing that no reality is substantial and that reifying language is misleading. Emptiness does much of the work in a Buddhist scheme accomplished by "contingency" in some of the Western religious schemes. By pressing hard on the limitations of the things we experience, on the mortality of human beings, on the ignorance of all living beings, and the like, Buddhist philosophers could show that none of these beings grounded or explained itself and so that all were "empty" of both fixed reality and ultimate significance. Practically, this meant good reasons for not clinging to any such entities in desire and so not being ensnared in samsara through their influence.

enlightenment: In Buddhist circles enlightenment names the experience that made Gautama the Buddha and that could take any human being out of the vicious circle of death and rebirth, onto the path toward nirvana. Enlightenment usually came with a flash of understanding, mainly that most of the dualisms we propose are illusory and most of the desires we have are misguided. In addition to light, enlightenment therefore also suggested liberation from bondages that had taken away one's peace and joy.

Four Noble Truths: the epitome of the Buddha Gautama's preaching and teaching, which says that all life is suffering, that the cause of suffering is desire, that by removing desire one can remove suffering, and that the way to remove desire and travel freely through human time is to follow the Noble Eightfold Path. The Four Noble Truths, therefore, have served Buddhists as an easy reminder of the heart of their religion's matter, although when one starts to investigate any one of the four one finds things considerably more complicated than they first appeared to be.

Hinayana: a somewhat pejorative term (meaning "the smaller vehicle") used by Mahayana Buddhists for the groups that opposed their liberalizing policies. "Theravada" (referring to the traditions of the elders) is the term these groups themselves prefer. The Mahayanists claimed to be providing a greater vehicle or raft, which would carry more living beings across the stream of samsaric existence to the far shore of nirvana. The Hinayanists objected to the liberties taken with the image of the Buddha, to the proliferation of sutras professing to be authoritative, to making laity more equal with monks, and to other such tendencies. They also resisted a certain supernaturalizing of Buddhist faith and practice, preferring a more sober, humanistic focus on Gautama's basic teachings about the need to root out desire and come to a clear understanding of reality.

Kuan-yin: the female form of the *bodhisattva* Avalokitesvara, who became the great savior figure in much of East Asia. Kuan-yin is the Chinese name, which in Japan became Kannon. In both countries an East Asian desire for a motherly divinity seems to have been responsible for the change of sex. Kuan-yin was the special refuge of women seeking children, a healthy birth, or help for family problems. She became a great favorite in East Asian art, often personifying the compassion and serenity of Buddhahood (enlightenment). Like the *Prajna-paramita,* the Wisdom-That-Had-Gone-Beyond, she softened the potential harshness of Buddhist discipline and probably linked up with the Daoist sense that the ultimate Way runs by a motherly love.

Lotus Sutra: a Mahayana scripture that pictures the Buddha Amitabha and the Western Paradise over which he presides. This sutra became one of the texts most influential in devotional Buddhism, especially that of Japan. Thus, the Jodo and Nichiren schools have made the Lotus Sutra central to their faith and practice, the latter chanting homage to the Lotus Sutra, which it has seen as an epitome of all Buddhist teaching. The Lotus Sutra is seen as a condescension to the moral weakness of modern times, when people can hardly be expected to accomplish more than to believe in the mercy of the Buddha and throw themselves upon it in faith. Thus reverence of the Lotus has gone hand in hand with a lay orientation and a stress on faith (a sort of Buddhist bhakti) rather than intellectual or meditational attainments.

Madhyamika: a moderate school of Mahayana Buddhist philosophy, founded by the famous dialectician Nagarjuna in the second century C.E.. The Madhyamika stressed the teachings of the *Prajna-paramita* sutras on emptiness, and through its dialectical analysis of the relations between nirvana and samsara justified a this-worldly focus. That in turn supported later Mahayana developments such as Zen, which assumed one could find nirvana in the midst of samsara and sought to give emptiness full impact in meditation, aesthetics, the martial arts, and other aspects of Japanese life. The Madhyamikas contrasted with the Yogacarins as moderate realists to idealists, because they did not subscribe to the Yogacara position that all reality is mind-only. Rather, they stressed that the ultimate is inexpressible, must be present to give any existent thing its existence, and appears differently depending upon whether one speaks of it as an enlightened person does or as one still immersed in samsara.

Mahayana: a branch of Buddhism that arose in controversies during the second century after the Buddha's death. Mahayana became opposed to Hinayana or Theravada, as the "great vehicle" to the "lesser vehicle." It paid more attention to the spiritual needs of the laity, broadened the saintly ideal from that of the individualistic *arhat* to that of the *bodhisattva* filled with great compassion for all enslaved creatures, and developed many metaphysical systems, some of which involved an extensive Buddhology that greatly advanced the simple appreciation of the man Gautama. Mahayana came to predominate in East Asia, whereas Theravada came to predominate in Sri Lanka, Burma, Thailand, and other countries between India and China.

nirvana: the Buddhist term for the goal of liberation or fulfillment. Nirvana has been likened to the state of the flame when the fire has gone out. In that figure, the implication is that nirvana is what one gets when desire, and so the cycle of birth, death, and rebirth has been fully extinguished. Other similes stress unconditionedness: what one gets when the various lets, hindrances, barriers, limitations that afflict everything of present experience have fallen away, when one has existence pure and simple, without qualifications or dependencies. Insofar as enlightenment opens the door to nirvana, and enlightenment is fully positive, one can think of nirvana as like the Hindu *moksha:* full of being, awareness, and bliss. The Buddha was leery of philosophizing about nirvana, thinking that talking about the ineffable soon was profitless and that it was more important to cure the disease than to speculate on the qualities of the postdisease state.

Pali canon: the collection of the scriptures (Tipitaka) judged authoritative by the Theravada Buddhists and written in Pali, one of the Prakrit languages associated with Sanskrit. The three baskets of the Pali canon contain discourses associated with the Buddha, as well as other early, foundational writings. Some of them were only recorded generations after their first utterance, having been preserved in the community's memory. The early Buddhist conciliar meetings that discussed right doctrine and monastic practice perhaps inevitably also discussed canonical texts and so were a stimulus toward making official collections.

Prajna-paramita: a group of Mahayana sutras concerned with the perfection of wisdom. Some of these sutras are very long, but others (such as the Diamond and the Heart) are able to put the perfection of wisdom quite concisely. Usually it boils down to grasping the emptiness of all dharmas. From the standpoint of enlightenment, nothing has an own-being. The *Prajna-paramita* has built on such staple Buddhist notions as that of the three marks (painful, fleeting, selfless) of all realities and Nagarjuna's dialectics of emptiness. One should remember that the point of this literature is not an academic analysis of ontology, much as ontology may be involved. It is, rather, to clarify the nature of reality and so develop the right thinking necessary for enlightenment.

Pure Land: the world of bliss (Sukhavati) pictured by the Lotus Sutra as the place in the West where Amitabha Buddha dwells and the devout will be reborn. The Pure Land became the focus of much East Asian devotional Buddhism, which frequently taught that the mercy of Amitabha was sufficient to bring his devotees thence with more regard to their faith than their merits. On the other hand, those Buddhists absorbed with karmic merit could think that they were building a dossier capable one day of winning them entrance to the Pure Land. The colorful descriptions of the Pure Land in the Lotus Sutra and other devotional texts greatly influenced popular Buddhist imagination, providing much of the sense of "heaven" that kept the common people hoping one day to enjoy a better world.

sangha: the Buddhist community. The term may refer to either the entire community or just the monastic part, in reflection of the paramount role monks played in the formation of the Buddha's community. Tradition records Gautama gathering disciples through his preaching and offering them spiritual direction. Laity were enrolled as supporters of the monastic ventures and from quite early times women were admitted into the monastic life. The *sangha* is placed alongside the Buddha and the dharma when the faithful enumerate the jewels of their faith. One formally becoming a Buddhist takes refuge in these three, which implies that the *sangha* will provide not just a haven from the samsaric world but also help with coming to know the Buddha and the dharma. As well, it should provide companionship along the Eightfold Path and instruc-

tion. The *sangha* has not been so unified or institutionalized as has the Christian church. Like the Jewish and Muslim communities, local variations have been tolerated, without giving up the sense that all the faithful are members of one overarching or organic community.

sila: a Buddhist term for morality—the ethical precepts incumbent on all members of the *sangha*. In briefest compass, these have been five: not to kill, not to lie, not to steal, not to behave unchastely, and not to take intoxicants. More broadly, *sila* has added further precepts proportioned to the lives of monks and nuns, to the lives of laity, and drawn from such key doctrines as *ahimsa*. Along with wisdom and meditation, Buddhist morality has been a basic component of the Middle Way, so *sila* has been as significant as meditation and philosophical study—perhaps more so in most lay lives. Characteristically, Buddhist ethics has focused much more on the individual's actions than on social questions, in part due to Buddhist convictions that the key to proper social behavior is enlightened individual consciousness.

skandhas: a Buddhist term for the "heaps" thought temporarily to comprise the human "person." The *skandhas* give the human being what integrity or identity it has as it passes through time. Traditionally they have been enumerated as five: form (or bodily shape), sensation (or feeling), perception, the aggregates of consciousness, and consciousness (or the faculty of consciousness). None of these should be pictured as static, independent, or substantial. Each is in flux and is empty. But Buddhist psychologists realized that if they wanted to analyze consciousness they had to make distinctions and namings such as these five, so the *skandhas* figure in most discussions of how to purify consciousness or gain a wise view of what happens in consciousness. Buddhists say the *skandhas* dissolve at death and are not carried over to the next existence; only karma links one life to another.

stupa: a mound of earth or stone that serves as a shrine to a Buddha or *bodhisattva* and so becomes a focus of Buddhist piety. The stupas, along with the devotional use of statues, flowers, incense, and other material objects, give Buddhism its sacramental side. They make it analogous to Islam, Catholic and Orthodox Christianity, and Hinduism in honoring saints and thinking the body, the material world, and the lives of fellow pilgrims all capable of being endowed with sacredness. Stupas become points of pilgrimage, giving Buddhists access to some of the religious effects pilgrimage regularly produces (entrance into a zone free of ordinary, profane, concerns, divisions, and sullied-ness). Like the shrines that have developed in East Asian Buddhism, they provoke observers to consider the geography of Buddhist faith: where the faithful tend to find their convictions refreshed and revivified.

sunyata: a Buddhist term for emptiness. This term appears most significantly in the Mahayana *Prajna-paramita* literature and was developed by the philosopher Nagarjuna into a keystone of his understanding of both nirvana and samsara. To the traditional three marks—painful, selfless, fleeting—emptiness added a metaphysical conclusion: insubstantial. *Sunyata* has had the ethical and devotional implication that one should not cling to anything one experiences, because there is no-thing really there to justify one's grasping. It can be developed into a profound appreciation of the mysteriousness of existence: a Buddhist variation on the basic Western problem of the one and the many, or a Buddhist version of the Western question about why there is something rather than nothing.

sutra: a Buddhist text or discourse, especially one attributed to the (or a) Buddha himself. The sutras arose shortly after the death of Gautama, first in oral traditions, then in written texts. They appear to have been a blend of memories of what Gautama himself actually taught and what devoted disciples imagined Gautama might or would have taught on other given occasions. The Mahayana Buddhist movement spotlighted Buddhas other than Gautama and sparked the creation of sutras, such as the Lotus, that purported to be discourses from heavenly places such as the Western Paradise (Pure Land). The Buddhist canon (Tipitaka) collects a great number of sutras. The Mahayana sutras include discourses by famous *bodhisattvas* such as Avalokitesvara and may be quite metaphysical. Different Buddhist sects have favored different sutras, sometimes (as in the case of Nichiren Buddhism's absorption with the Lotus Sutra) relegating most others to irrelevance.

Tathagata: a title of the Buddha, usually taken to mean "One who has fully realized thusness or such-ness," the state of ultimate, unconditioned perfection. The title suggests Buddhist realism: desire to be what one ultimately is, to see what ultimately is there just as an incontrovertible reality. Enlightenment, there-fore, is just dispelling illusion, letting unfold what always was true or so, was always waiting to be allowed to show itself. The Tathagata is close to the *dharma-kaya,* the body of the Buddha that makes reality be as

it is, although probably the accent of the former is more on the subject Gautama whose enlightenment made him objective. In using the title as a term of praise, Buddhists in effect praise the wisdom of the Buddha, his utter realism, implying that association with him may make them similarly realistic.

Theravada: the older, conservative school of Buddhism that contrasts with the Mahayana schools. Theravada sometimes is described as the sole present survivor of the several Hinayana schools in existence at the time of the divergence of what became the Mahayana. It predominates in the Asian lands closest to India—Sri Lanka, Burma, Thailand—and has tended to be less metaphysical and lay-oriented than the Mahayana. The Buddhist scriptures of the Tipitaka have been the textual authority in Theravada, and such beloved texts as the *Dhammapada* express that school's ethical cast. Yet Theravada has also sponsored a full cultural development—art, political theory—as well as distinctive contributions to Buddhist views of meditation and the monastic life.

three jewels: the mainstays of Buddhist faith—the Buddha himself, the dharma, and the *sangha*. By "taking refuge" in Gautama, his teaching, and his community, Buddhists could save themselves from the pains of samsara. They could follow the path to liberation. As "jewels," these three foci of trust seemed to adorn or beautify the Buddhist way of life. They called to mind, and comprised, most of what was attractive. Gautama had been a model of wisdom and liberation, as well as its prime spokesman. His teaching was the font of everything good that his followers had experienced. And his community provided the context, tradition, and further modeling that a living religion required.

three marks: the Buddhist view that all of reality is painful, selfless, and fleeting. The three marks may be considered elaborations of the First Noble Truth, carried out under the influence of the Buddha's insight into how to solve the human problem. By elaborating why one should not desire ordinary existence—why one should flee a life that is intrinsically painful—the three marks gave Buddhist students intellectual ammunition, for themselves even more than others. No rational person would cling to something so illusory as an item of ordinary life. Developing Buddhist detachment therefore became an eminently sane thing to do.

Vajrayana: a development of Mahayana Buddhism that came to stress tantric methods and to predominate in

Tibet. Known as the "thunderbolt" vehicle, Vajrayana combined the scholastic interests of Indian Buddhism with the East Asian desire to vest authority in lineages of gurus. Its own special contribution was an interest in the psychology of enlightenment that led to experiments with psychosomatic influences and symbols that might engage the whole personality. The psychosomatic influences included social conditioning, through inculcation of accepted mores, and sexual desire. By challenging convention and rousing the libido contained in both of these psychic areas, Vajrayana often was able to work dramatic changes in the personality of the disciple striving for enlightenment. The mandalas, mantras, *chakras* (ritual circles within which the gods could be encountered or impersonated) furthered the Vajrayana experiments in enlightenment, while such texts as the *Tibetan Book of the Dead* expressed the Vajrayana sense that the end of a given existence was an especially propitious time for escaping from the wheel of karma.

Vinaya: the code of Buddhist monastic discipline. The Vinaya developed in the first centuries after the death of the Buddha, as monks and nuns tried to work out the discipline under which they would live. While there have been points of dispute and minor variations between Theravadin and Mahayanin monks, on the whole the Vinaya has been a force unifying Buddhism. In addition to obeying the basic precepts of *sila*, monks and nuns have been expected to obey the detailed rules regarding their clothing, admission into the order, housing accommodations, diet, and interactions with other monastics. They have been guided by the Buddha's Middle Way between austerity and laxity toward a sparse but healthy diet, have been expected to obey the directions of the abbot or head of the monastery, frequently have begged their food, have offered counsel and good example to laypeople, have kept the festivals traditional in their area, have participated in the special periods of increased meditation,

and so forth, in all cases trying to eliminate desire and concentrate single-mindedly on following the Buddha's path.

Yogacara: a school of Mahayana Buddhist philosophy, founded by Asanga and Vasubandhu in the fourth century C.E., that taught that only consciousness is real. As the name suggests, Yogacara speculation had debts to the experience of yoga (meditation). In teaching that only consciousness was fully real, it amounted to being an idealism that doubted the reality of matter. The implications of Yogacara included the need to purify one's mind and the conviction that as one thought, so would one be or become. Yogacara speculation took up such topics as the functioning of consciousness and the debts of human consciousness to a matrix of cosmic consciousness. It influenced such practical schools as Zen and in general was a greater prop to meditation than to wisdom or morality, although it did not deprecate either.

Zen: the Japanese name for the school of Buddhism that has most stressed meditation. In China this school went by the name Chan and was attributed to Bodhidharma, a meditation-master come from India. Zen has considered meditation to epitomize the Enlightened One's teaching and methodology. Historically it had great influence in Japanese culture, shaping the ideals of the samurai and undergirding such practices as swordsmanship, floral arrangement, the tea ceremony, and gardening. Rinzai Zen has tended to seek sudden enlightenment, urging disciples to strive hard and keep up a firm discipline of work, silence, and obedience. Soto Zen has been more relaxed, thinking that enlightenment should come gradually, as the ripening of an overall maturation in Buddhist faith and practice. Soto has also lessened the distinction between meditation and the rest of life, thinking that as one's practice developed one would always be cultivating one's innate buddha-nature and helping it manifest itself.

CHAPTER 5

CHINESE RELIGION

Chinese character for Dao ("Way")

HISTORY

Preaxial Chinese Religion

The philosopher Karl Jaspers has spoken of an "axial period" of human civilization, during which the essential insights arose that spawned the great cultures.[1] In China the axial period was the sixth and fifth centuries B.C.E., and the two most important figures were Confucius and Laozi, whose Confucianism and Daoism, respectively, formed the basis for all subsequent Chinese culture. Before them, however, were centuries, perhaps even millennia, of nature- and ancestor-oriented responses to the sacred, when the prehistoric mind dominated the Chinese people. In China, for instance, divination mixed with the Confucian ethical code, so that the prime divinatory text, the *Yi Jing*, became one of the Confucian classics. As the popular Chinese folk novel *Monkey*[2] shows, other ancient attitudes were alive well into the sixteenth century C.E. So the preaxial worldview that we now sketch was a constant feature throughout Chinese religious history.

First, though, we must qualify the concept of Chinese religion. China, like most ancient cultures, did not develop religion as a separate realm of human concern. The rites, sacred mythology, ethics, and the like that bound the Chinese people were simply their culture. These cultural phenomena were not distinguished from the daily routine. So, what we underscore for our purposes is not necessarily what the Chinese underscored. Second, the Chinese attitude toward ultimate reality stressed nature—the physical world. Nature was the (sacred) essential context of human existence, and there was no clear Creator outside nature.

Of course, nature appeared to be both constant and changing. The cosmos was always there, but it had seasons and rhythms, as well as unexpected activities such as storms and earthquakes. To explain this tension between stability and change, the Chinese of the Han period (206 B.C.E.–220 C.E.) thought in terms of a union of complementary basic forces. **Yang** was the force of light, heat, and maleness. **Yin** was the balancing force of darkness, cold, and femaleness. The changes in the relations between yang and yin accounted for the seasons, the moon's phases, and the tides.

Another aspect of nature was the mixture or proportions of the five vital forces (water, fire, wood, metal, and earth) at any given time. They were the qualities that activated nature—that gave particular things and events their character. Together, the yin-

Chinese Religion: Twenty-five Key Dates

ca. 3500 B.C.E.	*Earliest Chinese City*
ca. 1600	*Shang Bronze Age Culture*
551 – 479	*Confucius*
520	*Traditional Date for Death of Laozi*
403 – 221	*Warring States Period*
206	*Han Dynasty Reunites China*
ca. 200	*Rise of Religious Daoism*
ca. 112	*Opening of "Silk Road" Links China with West*
ca. 150 C.E.	*Buddhism Known to Exist in China*
304 – 589	*Huns Fragment China*
607	*Beginning of Chinese Cultural Influence in Japan*
658	*Height of Chinese Power in Central Asia*
700	*Golden Age of Chinese Poetry*
ca. 730	*Invention of Printing in China*
845	*Great Persecution of Non-Chinese Religions*
1000	*Flourishing of Painting and Ceramics*
1130 – 1200	*Ju Xi, Leading Neo-Confucian Thinker*
1234	*Mongols Destroy Dynasty*
1275	*Marco Polo in China*
1585	*Matteo Ricci in China*
1644	*Manchu Dynasty; Confucian Orthodoxy*
1850	*Taiping Rebellion*
1893 – 1977	*Mao Zedong*
1900	*Boxer Uprising*
1949	*Communist Victory*

	CONFUCIANISM	DAOISM
Key Figures	Confucius (Kongzi) Mencius (Mengzi)	Laozi Zhuangzi
Key Texts	*Analects*	*Dao De Jing*
Key Ideas	1. Humaneness 2. Ritual 3. Subordination of younger to elder and women to men 4. Good ethical example the key to political prosperity	1. Active not-doing (*wu-wei*) 2. The Uncarved Block (presocialized human nature) 3. Following the way of nature (*Dao*) 4. Resisting convention and routine
Key Influences	Government, family life	Private life, arts, philosophy, meditation

yang theory and the theory of the five vital forces formed the first Chinese explanation of nature.[3]

Above the system, not as its Creator from nothingness but as its semipersonal overlord, was the heavenly ruler. His domain was human and natural behavior. The heavenly ruler probably was the first ancestor of the ruling dynasty. That is, the Chinese first conceived of him as the clan head of the ancient ruling house of Shang.[4] Later they modified this anthropomorphic conception to heaven, a largely impersonal force. Then the emperor became the "Son of Heaven," not in the sense that he was the descendant of the first ancestral leader of the ruling clan but in the sense that he represented the force that governed the world.[5]

Another name for the director of the natural system was *Dao*. Essentially, *Dao* means "way" or "path." The Confucians spoke of the *Dao* of the ancients—the customs or ethos that prevailed in the golden beginning times. Similarly, the Chinese Buddhists described their tradition as the "Way of the Buddha." However, the Daoists most directly appropriated the naturalistic overtones of *Dao* and focused on nature's

directing path. For them, the *Dao* was an ultimate reality, both within the system and beyond it.

We shall see how the *Dao* was characteristic of the different Chinese religious traditions. The point here is that they all assumed the ancient view that nature is sufficiently orderly to suggest an overseer and a path. Within the natural system, however, the prehistoric Chinese stressed harmony. That is, they tended to think that trees, rivers, clouds, animals, and humans compose something whole. As a result, natural phenomena could be portents, while human actions, whether good or evil, influenced both heaven and earth. As the Native Americans identified closely with their forests, so the oldest Chinese were citizens of nature, not a species standing outside and apart from it. Consequently, they did not consider human beings apart from the other creatures of the cosmos.

When the Daoist philosopher Zhuangzi spoke of reentering the Great Clod,[6] he spoke from this ancient conviction. To die and return to the material world, perhaps to be a tree or a fish in the next round, was natural and right. With some qualifications that we shall mention, the Chinese have favored long life

ers developed prescriptions for both social and individual life. In that way, ancient reflection helped form the rational framework of classical Chinese culture. More influential, though, was the nonrational heritage of the preaxial days. The vast majority of China's billions have been peasants, who, with relatively few changes, continued to stress animistic forces, amulets, and divination rites up to the beginning of the twentieth century (if not right up to the present).

Folk religion is always an effort to explain nature, but it employs a logic that is more symbolic than that of yin-yang, the five dynamic qualities, or *Dao*. Rather, it emphasizes similarities and differences, whether in shapes, sizes, or names. As close to dreaming as to science, folk religion easily allows the subconscious great influence. So, for instance, diviners thought they had a key to nature in the cracks of a baked tortoise shell, or the flight patterns of birds, or the broken and unbroken lines that the ancient text called the *Yi Jing* interpreted as ratios of yin and yang. It was but a small step to use these interpretational techniques to control nature—to use them as magic.

One functionary who has specialized in this symbolic magic is the practitioner of *feng-shui*.[7] *Feng-shui* is the study of winds and water, or geomancy. Essentially, it involves how to position a building most auspiciously. In a convoluted symbolism employing dragons and tigers, it has tried to make the living forces of nature yield good fortune by figuring out the spiritual lay of the land. What nature disposed, according to *feng-shui,* architecture could oppose or exploit. For instance, straight lines were believed to be evil influences, but trees or a fresh pond could ward them off. Consequently, the basic design of Chinese villages has included trees and ponds for protection. Similarly, a winding approach to a house has diverted evil forces. The *feng-shui* diviner would plot all the forces, good and evil, with a sort of compass that marked the different circles of power of these forces. *Feng-shui* has prevailed well into modern times, a fact attesting to its perceived importance.

Other important ancient functionaries were the mediums and the shamans. As Waley's translations suggest,[8] the shaman's song frequently called on a personal spirit to come down and enlighten him. Perhaps, then, the Chinese shaman (or shamaness) was more a subject of possession or a medium than a traveler to the gods.[9] More importantly, the existence of the shaman shows that ancient China believed in a realm of personified spirits.[10] These spirits could come

Figure 23 *Animal spiral, western Zhou dynasty, early ninth century* B.C.E. *Bronze; 13½ in. high. This spiral was made to be fitted to a pole, perhaps for protection or use in shamanistic rituals. The Nelson–Atkins Museum of Art, Kansas City, Missouri (Nelson Fund).*

rather than immortality, enlightenment that polishes worldly vision rather than enlightenment that draws one out of the world. Chan Buddhism's transformation of the Mahayana philosophy of nirvana owed much to Daoist philosophy and this ancient worldliness.

The Peasant Heritage. The preaxial views of nature, therefore, provided the axial thinkers with basic beliefs about nature's patterns, elements, and the consubstantiality (substantial sameness) of humans with other forms of life. From these beliefs, the axial think-to susceptible individuals with lights and messages or be the spirits of departed ancestors speaking through a medium who was in trance. If one did not revere them, speak well of them, and give them gifts of food, the ancestor spirits could turn nasty.

In later times, ordinary people thought that the ancestor spirits lived in a spiritual equivalent of the human world, where they needed such things as food, clothing, and money. Thus, pious children would burn paper money to send assistance to their departed parents.[11] In fact, one's primary obligation of a religious sort was just such acts of commemoration, reverence, and help. This **reverence for ancestors** so impressed Western missionaries that they fought bitterly among themselves about its meaning. Some missionaries found ancestor rites idolatrous, while others found them praiseworthy expressions of familial love.[12]

Exorcism.   Another feature of ancient Chinese religion was the personification and exorcism of evil. In historical times, the Daoist priesthood dominated exorcism, but the roots of exorcism go further back. Peter Goullart has given an eyewitness account of a modern Daoist exorcism,[13] complete with descriptions of weird phenomena like those enacted in the American film *The Exorcist*. The assumption behind exorcism, of course, is that evil forces invade and possess a person. In part, this assumption is just the logical conclusion of a thought-world in which shamanism is possible. If the Chinese shaman could be invaded by his helping spirits, and if evil spirits existed, then other people could be invaded by evil spirits. Along another line of interpretation, demon possession is just the development of ancient fears of evil, while exorcism is just the development of ancient ways of combating such fear.

Goullart's description of the "energumen" (demoniac), however, renders the evil most concrete. The possessing power curses, threatens, and pours out hate (in a terrifying distortion of the demoniac's own voice). It bloats the demoniac's body, pushing the bedspring on which he rests down to the floor. The demoniac howls like an animal, gives off horrid smells, and empties his bladder and bowels repeatedly. Onlookers are terrified, and the Daoist priest strains to the utmost in his spiritual struggles with the evil one. The reader senses something absolutely primitive: human shock before the possibility of naked evil. Exorcisms were not daily occurrences, but they open a window onto the recesses of the Chinese psyche.

In his summary of the religious beliefs of the Chinese Neolithic age,[14] Mircea Eliade sketches the general context for such shock, as well as for shamanism, divination, and other ancient features that we have discussed. There was from earliest times a connection between life, fertility, death, and afterlife that took the form of a regular cosmic cycle and gave rise to annual religious rites. Furthermore, the ancestors were a source of magical and religious power, and all natural forces had an aura of mystery—the mystery of the conjunction of opposites: of life and death, good and evil, rational and irrational. Possession and exorcism, then, are but vivid instances of a generally volatile mix. The ancient Chinese world was thoroughly alive, and one never knew precisely where its power would go.

Confucianism

Inasmuch as it furnished many Chinese with the ideas about order and ultimate reality that directed their lives, Confucianism fulfilled many of the functions of a religious tradition.

Confucius (551–479 B.C.E.) became the father of Chinese culture by transforming the ancient traditions into at least the beginnings of a code for directing social life. More than two centuries passed before his doctrine became the state orthodoxy (during the Han dynasty, 206 B.C.E.–220 C.E.), but from the outset it had a healing effect on Chinese society. Confucius lived during a warring period of Chinese history, an epoch of nearly constant social disorder. For Master Kong (the Chinese name of Confucius), the way from such disorder toward peace could be obtained from the ancients—the venerable ancestors who were closer to the beginning and wiser than the people of the present age. What the ancestors knew, what made them wise, were the decrees of heaven. As we have seen, heaven meant nature's overlord. Thus, Confucius accepted the ancient, preaxial notion that nature has some order. In his view, the way to a peaceful and prosperous society was to adapt to that order. People could adapt externally through sacrificial rites and hierarchical social relationships. Internally, one had to know the human mind, and the human mind had to be set in *ren* (fellow-feeling or love).[15]

For external order, the emperor was paramount. As the Son of Heaven, he conveyed heaven's will to earth. In other words, the China of Confucius' time held to the cosmological myth. With many other ancient societies, it shared the notion that the king was the sacred intermediary between the realm of heaven and the realm of earth modeled upon it. What the king did for human society, then, was both priestly and exemplary. By officiating at the most important rites, through which his people tried to achieve harmony with heaven, the king represented society before the ultimate judge of society's fate. By the example that he set at court and by the way that he directed imperial policy, the king not only served as a good or bad model for his followers, he also led the state in following or defying heaven's intent. The king achieved his power simply through his close connection to heaven.[16]

Confucius approved of the model leadership of the legendary kings, and he also approved of the notion that ritual makes what we might call a sacrament of the vital flow between heaven and earth. One focus of his teaching, then, was historical: He concentrated on how the ancients reportedly acted. Another focus was liturgical. He was himself a master of court ritual, and he thought that proper sacrifice and etiquette were very important. Probably Confucius' most profound impact on Chinese culture, though, was his clarification of human virtues, or spiritual qualities.

Having had little success in public affairs (he never obtained high office or found a ruler willing to hire his counsel), he turned to teaching young men about politics and the way to private virtue. In other words, he became the center of an academic circle, like that of Plato, which had ongoing dialogues about the good life, political science, private and public morality, and so on. Confucius consistently stressed practicality in his tutoring. The wisdom that he loved built up the good society, the commonweal. It was not a yogic or shamanic regime dedicated to a single individual's spiritual development.

The *Analects* are a collection of fragments from the Master. In them we can see why Confucius impressed his followers, who finally made him the model wise man. (After his death, Confucius gained semidivine status and became the center of a religious cult.)[17] Especially in the third through ninth books, the Confucians preserved sayings that seem to be original, although Confucius himself claimed no originality. In fact, he did not even claim divine inspiration. His Way was nothing novel; he only studied the past and then transmitted the ancients' customs.

"The Master said, At fifteen I set my heart upon learning. At thirty, I had planted my feet firm upon the ground. At forty, I no longer suffered from perplex-

ities. At fifty, I knew what were the biddings of Heaven. At sixty, I could hear them with docile ear. At seventy, I could follow the dictates of my own heart, for what I desired no longer overstepped the boundaries of right" (*Analects,* 2:4).

It is clear, then, that the mystical union with the Way that consummated the Master's life was the fruit of many years' labor. This example reminds us that wise or holy people tend to become identified with the models, texts, or rituals that they use to interpret ultimate reality. We become what we study, meditate upon, and establish as the treasures on which our hearts are set. Perhaps that is why Confucius was so insistent on hard study—constant effort during one's youth and maturity to master the wisdom of the past.

For Confucius, the Way manifests itself as a golden mean. It opens a path between punctiliousness and irregularity, between submissiveness and independence. Most situations are governed by a protocol that will produce graceful interactions if it is followed wholeheartedly. The task of the *junzi* (true gentleman or superior person) is to know that protocol, intuit how it applies in particular cases, and have the discipline to carry it out. The death of a parent, for instance, is a prime occasion for a *junzi* to express his love and respect for his parent. According to the rites of mourning, he should retire from public affairs, simplify his living arrangements, and devote himself to grieving (for as long as three years).

As that example suggests, filial piety was a cornerstone of Confucianism. If the relations at home were correct, other social relationships would likely fall into line. The Confucian classic *The Great Learning*[18] spells out this theory, linking the individual in the family to the order of both the state and the cosmos. Moreover, the family circle was the training ground for a *junzi*'s lifelong dedication to humanity (*ren*) and ritual propriety (*li*). When a man developed a sincere love for his parents and carried out his filial duties, he rooted himself firmly in both *ren* and *li*. (We consider the place of women below.) Confucius' own teaching, therefore, called for a balance between interior goodness and exterior grace. He thought that if people knew their inner minds (grasped at "inwit," in Ezra Pound's translation)[19] and manifested their knowledge through social decorum, society would have both the substance and the appearance of humanity.

Different followers developed different aspects of Confucius' teaching. Mencius, for instance, softened the Master's view of *ren*, drawing it down from the lofty status accorded it by Confucius and making it a possibility for everyman.[20] For Mencius, human nature was innately good. We are evil or disordered only because we forget our original nature. Like the deforested local hill (Mencius 6.A.8), the typical human mind is so despoiled by abuse that we cannot see its spontaneous tendency toward altruism and justice. If we would stop deforesting it with vice, we would realize that virtue is instinctive. Just as anyone who sees a child at the edge of a well rushes to save the child (Mencius 2.A.6), so anyone educated in gentlemanliness will rush to solve civic problems.

Thus, Mencius centered Confucius' teaching on the goodness of human nature. Living two centuries after the Master, Mencius tried to repeat Confucius' way of life. He searched for an ideal king who would take his counsel, but he had to be satisfied with having a circle of young students. Mencius, though, somewhat lacked Confucius' restraint in discussing heavenly things (Confucius considered the human realm more than enough to master). According to Lee Yearley,[21] Mencius practiced a disciplined religion to increase physical vigor by acting with purity of heart, and he was willing to die for certain things such as justice and goodness. So, just as one can consider some of Confucius' sayings quite religious (for example, "It is not better to pay court to the stove than to heaven"), one can view Mencius as having transcendent beliefs. Both Confucian thinkers, we believe, appealed to more than human prudence.

Mencius also proposed an ultimately religious theory that history moves in cycles, depending on how a given ruling family handles the *de* (the power to govern well) that heaven dispenses.[22] The sharpest implication of this theory (which clarified some traditional notions) was that an unjust ruler might lose the mandate of heaven—that a revolutionary might be justified in establishing a new regime. Furthermore, Mencius advanced the view that the king brought prosperity only when he convinced the people that the things of the state were their own. This view was in part shrewd psychology: A people who have access to the royal park will think it small even if it is 100 miles square; a people denied access to a royal park one mile square will complain that it is far too vast. As well, however, this view brought Confucius' stress on leadership by example and virtue up to date: Only if the king demonstrated virtue could he expect the people to be virtuous.

A legalistic wing among Confucius' later followers, led by Xunzi, opposed both Mencius' teaching that human nature is essentially good and the non-Confucian Mozi's doctrine of universal love.[23] Xunzi taught that only strong law can confine human nature to right action; for lack of strong law, a great many states flounder. Furthermore, Xunzi connected this belief with Confucius' own stress on ritual, arguing that law and etiquette have the pedagogical function of showing the inner spirit what goodness and justice really mean. Unfortunately, later apologists for the state took some of Xunzi's ideas as a warrant for government by compulsion. In themselves, however, his ideas perhaps complemented Mencius' program as much as they opposed it, since they clarified the place for external codes. Arthur Waley, at least, has tried to show that Xunzi mainly reacted against possible abuses of Mencius' views on human nature.[24]

In summary, then, the hallmarks of the original Confucians were a reliance on ancient models, a concern for the golden mean between externalism and internalism, a stress on filial piety, and a deep respect for the ruler's connection with heaven. These socially oriented thinkers emphasized breeding, grace, and public service. Their goal was harmony and balance through a hierarchical social order.[25] They gave little attention to the rights of peasants or women, but they did prize ethical integrity, compassion, and learning. Against the blood and violence of their times, they called for a rule through moral force. This was their permanent legacy: Humanity is fidelity to virtue.

Neo-Confucianism

During the Song dynasty (960–1279 C.E.), the seminal Confucian thought that lay in the teachings of Confucius, Mencius, and Xunzi grew into a full-fledged philosophy that included metaphysical interpretations of nature and humanity. That was largely in response to the impressive systems that Buddhism, with its Mahayana doctrines of emptiness and the Buddha's cosmic body *(dharmakaya)*, and to a lesser extent Daoism, had developed, and it produced a new synthesis known to scholars as neo-Confucianism. To Confucius' ethics the neo-Confucians added an explanation of all reality. They accepted the ancient worldview, granting an important place to sacrifices for the state and the family. As well, they accepted the moral supremacy of the sage, whose virtuous power might move society or even nature. But they went on and reasoned about the sort of reality that nature must be if the sacrifices or the sages were to be efficacious. This neo-Confucian development gave the Song rulers and their successors a doctrine that buttressed their practical preference for Confucian ethics.

The neo-Confucian philosophy of nature that gained the most adherents involved the interaction of two elements, principle and ether. Ether, or breath, was the basis of the material universe. All solid things condensed out of ether and eventually dissolved back into it.[26] In the dynamic phases of this cycle, ether was an ultimate form of yang. In the still phases, it was the ultimate form of yin. The neo-Confucian view of material nature therefore preserved the tension of bipolarities—of, for example, hot and cold, male and female, light and dark—that had always fascinated the Chinese. One reason for the acceptance of neo-Confucianism, in fact, was that it appeared to be just an updated version of the ancient patrimony. The second element in nature's dualism, principle, etymologically related to the veins in jade or the grain in wood. It was the *pattern* running through all material things, their direction and purpose. If you opposed principle (went against the grain), all things became difficult. In terms of cognitional theory, the neo-Confucians invoked principle to explain the mind's ability to move from the known to the unknown. They also used it to ground the mind's appreciation of the connectedness of things. Principle was considered to be innate in human beings—it was nature's inborn guidance. The main task of human maturation and education was to remove the impediments that kept people from perceiving their principle. This task implied a sort of asceticism or moral diligence, sometimes involving meditation and self-denial.

Finally, the neo-Confucians tried to assimilate the folk aspect of Confucianism by finding a place for the spirits. They preferred not to venerate the ancestors' ghosts, but they allowed that *shen* and *kuei* (the two traditional kinds of spirits) could be the stretching and contracting of ether. In that way, they could agree that the "spirits" worked the planets, the stars, the mountains, the rivers, and so on. Once again, neo-Confucianism was less personal than the earlier traditions, but its new, rather rationalistic system stayed in touch with the old roots.

Ju Xi (1130–1200 C.E.) was the master thinker who systematized these neo-Confucian ideas.[27] His predilection was sober analysis, a sort of scientific philosophy, and he concentrated on physical nature. Another more idealistic wing of the neo-Confucians took to the Chan Buddhist stress on mind and tended to place principle in the context of a meditative, as well as an analytic, cultivation of reason. Because Ju Xi's ideas became authoritative in such government-controlled areas as the civil service examinations, neo-Confucianism inculcated in the educated classes a realistic, affirmative view of material nature. As well, it accepted meditation enough to stay competitive with Buddhism,[28] and it tried to stay open to such artistic movements as the magnificent Song dynasty landscape painting.

Despite these metaphysical developments, neo-Confucianism retained a commitment to the traditional Confucian virtues associated with character building. The paramount virtue continued to be *ren*. The ideogram for *ren* represented a human being in relationship: *ren* is humaneness—what makes us human. We are not fully human simply by receiving life in a human form. Rather, our humanity depends upon community, human reciprocity.[29] *Ren* pointed in that direction. It connected with the Confucian golden rule of not doing to others what you would not want them to do to you. Against individualism, it implied that people have to live together helpfully, even lovingly. People have to cultivate their instinctive benevolence, their instinctive ability to put themselves in another's shoes. That cultivation was the primary education task set by Confucius and Mencius.

The neo-Confucians also kept the four other traditional virtues: *yi, li, zhi,* and *xin. Yi* meant duty or justice, and it signified what is right, what law and custom prescribe. Its context, therefore, was the Chinese culture's detailed specification of rights and obligations. Where *ren* undercut such formalities, giving justice its heart, *yi* took care of contractual exactitudes.

Li, which meant manners or propriety, was less exact than *yi.* To some extent it depended on learning, so Confucius tried to teach by word and example what a gentleman would do in various circumstances, but it also required instinct, breeding, or intuition. Handling authority over household servants, men in the fields, or subordinates in the civil service involved *li.* So, too, did deference to superiors, avoidance of ostentation, and a generally graceful style. *Li* therefore was the unguent that soothed all social friction. In a society that prohibited the display of hostile emotion, that insisted on a good "face," *li* was very important.

Zhi (wisdom) was not a deep penetration of ultimate reality like the Buddhist *Prajna-paramita;* it depended on neither enlightenment nor mystical union with *Dao*. Rather, it was the prudent sense of right and wrong, decent and indecent, profitable and unprofitable that one could hope to gain by revering the ancients and living attentively. *Xin* meant trustworthiness or good faith. It was related to *ren* insofar as what one trusts in another is his or her decency or humanity, but it pertained more to a person's reliability or dependability. A person of *xin* was not flighty or capricious.

Case Study: The Cult of Confucius.

Although the intelligentsia resisted efforts to deify Confucius, the Chinese people at large long reverenced the Master with rituals and cult. To communicate the flavor of this cult, let us briefly describe some of the ceremonies that regularly took place at Confucius' shrines in the southwestern part of Shandong Province. Before the Communist revolution, such ceremonies were an important part of the Chinese ritual year.

A Western visitor who witnessed the rites at Confucius' ancestral temple in Chufu in 1903 was first received by the Yeng-sheng Kung ("the Duke who propagates"), as the head of Confucius' clan officially was known. The duke took the visitor around the temple grounds, which covered about 35 acres well-wooded with old cypress, yew, and fir trees. Tradition said that one of the trees was planted by Confucius himself and that two others were planted during the Tang and Song dynasties. The temple proper was divided into six courts, the innermost of which was venerated as the area where Confucius had lived. In front of this innermost precinct were various tablets with inscriptions of praise by various Chinese emperors.

Inside the central area stood an altar, commemorating the spot where Confucius had received people who came for his instruction. Behind this altar lay a great hall containing a statue of the Master. The statue was 16 feet high and portrayed the Master seated on a throne. Near it were screens, embroidered with dragons, that could be arranged as a shield. Magnificent pillars of white and black marble supported the great hall, its floor was lined with black marble, its roof was covered with yellow tiles, and its ceiling consisted of 486 square panels gilded at the edges and ornamented with dragons.

Two of the principal festival days for worshiping at the Confucian temple were the Ting days of spring and autumn, when the stems and branches of the foliage were supposed to be flourishing. The minister of music would open the ceremonies, which featured music used in Confucius' own day (but composed even earlier, supposedly about 2000 B.C.E.). The entire ritual employed symbols and artifacts considered to come from the ancient days, when the model heroes whom Confucius had revered had led Chinese society wisely by faithfully following the dictates of heaven. The dominant cloth, for instance, was a pure white silk, which ancient chiefs used to give people they wished to take into their employ. Other symbols of the Ting ceremony included the head of an ox (chief of the domestic animals, who leaves broad, permanent footprints); a pig (an animal with a will of its own, as its bristles suggest); and a sheep (plump for food and useful for wool). The incense used suggested the fragrance of virtue, while the wine and food typified the abundance of a virtuous kingdom. The boys performing the ceremonial dance dressed in ancient costumes, bearing in one hand a flute and in the other a pheasant feather. The flute represented the refinement music produces, while the feather stood for the adornment of learning.

Obviously, this ceremony, like most of the others that took place in Confucius' temple throughout the year, was meant to convey elegantly the benefits of virtue and breeding. In tune with the cosmic rhythms, the dancers suggested how any diligent student of virtue might hope one day to live, how any well-ordered state might hope to flourish.

Some of the hymns sung during the sacrifices to Confucius suggest the respect, veneration, and religious need his cult expressed. In one hymn, the choir begins, "Great is Confucius!" Why is Confucius great? Because he perceives all things accurately, knowing them before they even arise. Because he stands in the realm of heaven and earth, the primal realities, and so can teach the ten thousand ages. Because his power brought lucky portents: The unicorn's horn gained a tuft of silk. Because he unveiled the sun and the moon, making heaven and earth fresh and joyful.

During the offering of the gifts to Confucius the choir members would sing: "I think of thy bright virtue." Never had there been a human being equal to the Master. His teaching was in all respects complete. The vessels people offer today are filled as vessels have been filled through thousands of years. From time immemorial, the Ting days have been sweet with the smell of sacrifice, adorned with clear wine.

Later in the ceremony, the choir referred to the traditional sounds of the drum and the bell. Echoing as the celebrant offered the ritual wine, the drum and bell expressed the reverence and harmony at the heart of the ceremony. The rites proceeded, the music cleansed the participants' hearts, and the liturgy reached a point of perfection—let all rejoice!

Then the choir would remember how people had performed these holy rites since antiquity. Even primitive people performed them, wearing rough skin hats. Though these ancient ancestors had only the fruit of the ground to offer, their music was orderly. Only heaven has ever guided any people well, and only a sage of Confucius' stature could have suited his instructions to the needs of any given hour. Following him, present-day people could carry out their moral duties properly, reverencing the emperor and their elders. Confucius taught his followers the link between sacrifice and happiness. Who would dare not be reverent in his hall? In their joy, all who prosper remember him as the source of their culture. Like the mountains of Fu and Yi, the rivers of Zhu and Si, Confucius' beautiful acts have spread his influence high above and all around. The sacrifice reminds all of his great virtue. He renovates thousands of the people. He fosters their schools and instruction halls.[30]

As elements of the cult to Confucius suggest, Confucianism built on Chinese customs that had long antedated the Master. Indeed, sacrifices such as the one we have described can be traced as far back as the Shang dynasty, which is the limit of current archeological research. Insofar as most emperors gravitated toward Confucianism rather than Buddhism or Daoism, because Confucianism offered social thought more likely to produce docile subjects, they found it useful to involve themselves in the Confucian sacrifices. Thus the emperor himself would officiate at the major ceremonies, as clan heads had since earliest times, while Confucian bureaucrats would officiate at lesser ceremonies in the capital and at state occasions in the provinces. This meant that there was no special caste of Confucian priests. In Confucianism, state official and religious priest merged, becoming but two faces of one public functionary.

Characteristically, the Confucian public functionary opposed innovation, both in the cult and at the government bureau. The party line was that the Confucian literati merely handed on the wisdom and customs of the venerable ancestors, as Confucius had definitively interpreted them. Thus Confucius was in effect the patron saint of the literati. As other clans had their divine protectors, so the literati had Confucius. The difference was that the literati headed the corps of civil servants. Their "clan" staffed the government offices, transmitted the imperial will. As teacher, cult figure, and model, Confucius gave civil servants the sanction of tradition and sober wisdom. Through him came the *Dao* of the ancestors, the basis of good order in his or any time.

By the seventeenth century C.E., the diverse elements of the Confucian tradition had been merged into a rather unwieldy official cult. According to an official list of those to whom imperial worship was due in the seventeenth century, there were three classes of worthies. First came the Empress Earth, the imperial ancestors, and the guardian spirits of the land and the harvest. Second came the sun, the moon, the emperors of the preceding dynasties, the patrons of agriculture and sericulture (raising silkworms), the spirits of the earth, the planet Jupiter, whose revolution around the sun regulated the Chinese calendar, and Confucius. (In 1907 Confucius was moved up to the first class.) Third came the patron saints of medicine, war, and literature, the North Star, the god of Beijing, the god of fire, the dragons of several pools in Beijing, the god of artillery, the god of the soil, the patron saint of the mechanical arts, the god of the furnace, the god of the granary, the gods of the doors, and many official patriots.

This list illustrates the amalgamating tendency of the Confucian tradition. On the list's map of reality are the imprints of ancestor veneration, veneration of the deities of the earth, veneration of the patron gods or saints of particular clans, and veneration of Confucius, the mortal whose interpretation of the past was most congenial to the crown. Some of the deities in this list are very ancient, going back to the Shang and Zhou dynasties, at the very beginnings of Chinese history.

During the Qing dynasty (1644–1911), the government instructed its officials in the particulars of worshiping the cult figures of the several ranks. The official was to bathe, fast, prostrate himself, and offer prayers. He was to make thanksgiving offerings of incense, lighted candles, gems, fruits, cooked foods, salted vegetables, wine, and other gifts. For special occasions sacrifices of whole oxen, sheep, pigs, deer, or other game were appropriate, as was a burnt sacrifice of a whole bullock. Music and dancing were to accompany these sacrifices. If the sacrifice was to a deity of the first rank, the official had to "fast" for three days before it. For sacrifices to deities of the second rank, two fast days sufficed. Fasting meant refraining from flesh, strong-smelling vegetables (such as leeks and onions), and wine.

Moreover, officials were to see to it that during important ceremonial seasons there were no criminal proceedings, no parties, no visits to the sick, and no mourning of the dead. They were especially to forbid entering the chamber of a dead woman, sacrificing to spirits, and sweeping a tomb. The government commissioned inspectors to check on the officials delegated responsibility for the Confucian cult, to make sure that they followed these prescriptions scrupulously. Behind this concern that the officiants be properly prepared lay the Confucian conviction that a province follow the moral character of its officials. If the officials were scrupulous in performing the rites, the people would be orderly. As Confucius was reputed to have said (*Analects,* 2:3): People led by laws and restrained by punishments will avoid laws and punishments without qualm. People led by moral example and restrained by social ritual will develop a sense of shame and become good.[31]

Daoism

The classical, axial-period Daoists responded to the troubled warring period quite differently from the Confucians. They agreed that the times were disordered and that the way to set them straight was by means of the ancients' *Dao.* But the great Daoist thinkers, such as Zhuangzi and Laozi, were more imaginative and mystical than the Confucians. In their broad speculation, they probed not only the natural functions of the Way and the interior exercises that could align one with it but also the revolt against conventional values that union with *Dao* seemed to imply. Of the two great Daoists, Zhuangzi is the more poetic and paradoxical. His stories stress the personal effects of living with *Dao.* Laozi's orientation is more political. For him, *Dao* gives a model for civil rule, lessons in what succeeds and what brings grief. Insofar as Zhuangzi is more theoretical and less concerned with political applications, he enjoys a certain logical

priority over Laozi.[32] Thus, even though he probably came after Laozi historically, we treat him first.

Zhuangzi. What impressed Zhuangzi most was the influence of one's viewpoint. The common person, for example, can make little of the ancients' communion with nature, their unconcern for human opinion, and freedom. Such things are like the great bird flying off where the sparrow has never been. Yet if one advances in the "fasting of the spirit" that the ancients practiced, their behavior starts to make sense. Apparently such "fasting of the spirit" was a meditative regime in which one laid aside distractions and let simple, deep powers of spiritual consciousness issue forth.

Zhuangzi pictured those powers rather dramatically: They can send the sage flying on the clouds or riding on the winds, for they free the soul so that it can be directed by *Dao* itself. *Dao* is the wind blowing on the ten thousand things, the music of the spheres. With little regard for petty humankind, it works nature's rhythms. The way to peace, spiritual ecstasy, and long life is to join nature's rhythms. But by joining nature's rhythms, one abandons social conventions. *Dao* throws off our human judgments of good and bad, right and wrong. Thus, the true Daoist becomes eccentric with respect to the rest of society, for he (or she, though women seldom predominated in Chinese society) prefers obscure peace to troubled power, leisurely contemplation to hectic productivity.

In rather technical terms, Zhuangzi attacked those who thought they could tie language directly to thought and so clarify all discourse. If *Dao* touches language and thought, he showed, they become highly symbolic. Moreover, Zhuangzi made his attack on conventional values and language into simple good sense. It is the worthless, cast-off, unpopular trees and people that survive. Those who would be prominent, who would shine in public, often end up without a limb (as punishment for crime or disfavor). When he was asked to join the government, Zhuangzi said he would rather drag his tail in the mud like a turtle. When his wife died, he sang and drummed instead of mourning. She was just following *Dao,* just taking another turn in the process by which matter keeps changing. Puncturing cant, deflating pomposity, excoriating our tendency to trade interior freedom for exterior position, Zhuangzi ridiculed the sober Confucians. They, like other prosaic realists, seemed too dull to be borne— too dull for a life of spiritual adventure, for a *Dao* as magnificent as the heavens and as close as the dung.

Laozi. Thomas Merton has published a delightful interpretation of Zhuangzi that relates him to the contemplative spirit of Western poets and monks.[33] No one has done quite the same thing for Laozi or the *Dao De Jing,* perhaps because Laozi's style is more impersonal. The *Dao De Jing (The Way and The Power),*[34] like the *Zhuangzi* (the book left by Zhuangzi and his school), is of undetermined origin. Indeed, its author's very existence is less certain than that of Confucius. But the book itself has become a world classic, in good measure because of its mystic depth (and vagueness). In it a very original mind meditates on *Dao*'s paradoxical qualities, gleaning lessons about human society. Interpreters vary in the weight they give to the mystical aspects of the *Dao De Jing,*[35] but in any interpretation it is clear Laozi thought that *Dao* held the secret to good life.

Consequently, a major concern of the *Dao De Jing* is to elucidate just how nature does operate and how society should imitate it. The text's basic conclusion, presented in a series of striking images, is that *Dao* moves nature through *wu-wei* (active not-doing). Three of the principal images are the valley, the female, and the uncarved block. Together, they indicate *Dao*'s distance from most human expectations. The valley symbolizes *Dao*'s inclination toward the lowly, the underlying, rather than the prominent or impressive. Laozi's female is a lesson in the power of passivity, of yielding and adaptability. She influences not by assault but by indirection, by nuance and suggestion. The uncarved block is human nature before society limits it. These images all show *wu-wei.*

Wu-wei is also shown in the power of the infant, whose helplessness can dominate an entire family. It is in the power of water, which patiently wears away rock. Wryly Laozi reminds us of the obvious: A valley resists storms better than a mountain, a female tends to outlive a male, an infant is freer than a king, and a house is valuable for the space inside it, not the furniture or the wall hangings. Such lessons underscore a reality that common sense tends to ignore because common sense tends to notice only what is prominent. In contrast, *Dao* moves nature by a subtle, elastic power. Were rulers to imitate *Dao,* moving others by *wu-wei* rather than *ba* (violent force), society might prosper.

Wu-wei, it follows, tries to short-circuit the law of the human jungle, the round after round of tit for tat.[36] But to gain *wu-wei,* human nature must become like an uncarved block, which is perhaps the most important of Laozi's symbols. (Holmes Welch, who argues that we can read the *Dao De Jing* on several levels, makes the uncarved block its key.[37]) It symbolizes the priority of natural simplicity over social adornment. A block of wood or jade, before it is carved, has infinite potential, but once we have made it into a table or a piece of jewelry, its use is fixed and limited.

Impressed by the limitless creativity of nature, Laozi wanted to recover human nature's originality. In his eyes, the Confucians tended to overspecialize human nature. A society with fewer "modern" advances, less technology, and more spontaneous interaction with nature and fellow humans would be much richer than the Confucians'.[38] The Daoists, who took their lead from Laozi and Zhuangzi, tried to show how less could be more, how neglect could be cultivation. If people would shut the doors of their senses and thus cut off distractions, how less can be more would be obvious. The good life was not to be found in having but in being. By being simple, whole, alert, and sensitive in feeling, one could find joy.

Throughout history, many commentators have criticized Laozi and his followers for both naivete and obscurantism. They have especially jumped on the Daoist precept that a good way to promote peace and simplicity is to keep the people ignorant. Daoists believed that by not knowing about a wide range of possibilities, and therefore not having many desires, a populace would be quite docile. Critics have maintained that it is but a short step from such docility to sheephood and being at the mercy of evil rulers. The commentators have a point: The ideas expressed in some of Laozi's sayings invite easy abuse. For instance:

> Heaven and Earth are ruthless;
> To them the ten thousand things are
> but as straw dogs.
> The sage too is ruthless;
> To him the people are but as straw
> dogs.[39]

However, a close reading of the *Dao De Jing* shows that *wu-wei* is quite different from mindless docility or even complete pacifism. Rather, it includes the regretful use of force to cut short greater evil. As well, *wu-wei* is not sentimental, which further distinguishes it from most Westerners' views of "the people." As easily as nature itself, *wu-wei* discards what is outworn, alternating life with death. Because of this objectivity, Daoism can seem inhumane. For a people close to nature, though, humaneness is a less anthropocentric virtue than it is for ourselves. It is less personal and more influenced by the belief that self-concern or forgetting how nature and death dwarf human existence leads to folly.

"*Dao* is empty, but it never exhausts itself through use. Fathomless, it seems to be the genesis of all things. It dulls its sharpness, unties its tangles, dims its luster, and mixes with the dust. Hidden as it is [it] exists. I do not know whose son it is. It seems to have existed before the emperor of heaven" (*Dao De Jing*, 4).

In this passage Laozi is working in his usual oracular fashion. Again and again, he makes the *Dao* the opposite of what human beings expect and honor. For example, *Dao*, the ultimate reality, is more like emptiness than fullness. The fertility that it lavishes upon the world comes from something unstructured, something rich in the mode of an infinite treasure house, too vast or simple for us human beings to grasp. Where our minds crave clarity, sharpness, it is dull. Where we love complexity and sophistication, it unravels itself to appear completely plain. It has no polish or vanity. It is so real, so elementary, that it mixes with the dust of ordinary creation. Yet, though it is hidden in all of these ways, it is the most real thing we could know. If we doubt its reality, we miss the point of our human condition. We cannot know the lineage of the *Dao*, because it is at the very beginning of any world that we could grasp. So we have to make do with unknowing.

Like many mystics, Laozi finds that his encounters with ultimate, primary reality leave him in the dark. He has to yield to the *Dao*. He cannot bend the *Dao* to his understanding or will. So the practical message of Daoism is both obvious and radical: Submit yourself to what is greater than you are. Organize your reality in terms of what is objectively so: an Other has all of the priority.

Religious Daoism and Aesthetics.   Two great consequences of the school in which Zhuangzi and Laozi predominated had considerable influence through subsequent Chinese history. One consequence was religious Daoism, which was considerably different from the philosophical Daoism of the founding fathers.[40] The other was a Daoist aesthetics.

Religious Daoism owed as much to Chinese folk beliefs and practices as it did to the reflective, mystical, ironic musings of Zhuangzi and Laozi. Scholars call this use of the *Dao* "religious" because it deals with myth, ritual, faith, and even superstition and magic—in contrast to the poetic but still rational accents of philosophical Daoism. In fact, religious Daoism owed a great deal to Laozi and Zhuangzi, but it tended to interpret their poetry literally, becoming preoccupied with their oblique remarks about extraordinary powers and immortality, so that it actively pursued such gifts through chemical experiments and yogic techniques. In addition, religious Daoism had a considerable influence on Chinese art, furnishing it many themes and sometimes suggesting that artistic work could occasion an experience of the *Dao* that would yield special power or even immortality.

The religious Daoists formed a "church," generated a massive literature complete with ritualistic and alchemical lore, and earned the wrath of modern educated Chinese, who considered religious Daoism a bastion of superstition. Also, religious Daoists sometimes became embroiled in politics and sponsored violent revolutionary groups.[41] Their rituals and revolutionary politics went together, because from their rituals they derived utopian visions of what human society ought to become.

The religious Daoists sought physical immortality by diverse routes.[42] Some sponsored voyages to the magical islands in the East, where the immortals were thought to dwell. Others pursued alchemy, not to turn base metal into gold but to find the elixir of immortality. A third Daoist interest was hygiene. The two favorite regimes were breathing air and practicing a quasi-Tantric sexual yoga. Along with dietary oddities, some religious Daoists counseled trying to breathe like an infant in the womb, so as to use up vital force as slowly as possible. Adepts would lie in bed all day, trying to hold their breath for at first a hundred and eventually a thousand counts. Perhaps some became euphoric through carbon dioxide intoxication. The yogis of sex practiced retention of the semen during intercourse, thinking that this vital substance could be rechanneled to the brain and thereby enhance one's powers and longevity. In these exercises, the proximate goal was prolonging physical life, and the ultimate goal was a full immortality.

Religious Daoism also developed regimes of meditation, which it coupled with a complicated roster of gods. The basic assumption behind this venture was that the human body is a microcosm—a miniature world.[43] Within it, certain gods preside over particular organs and functions. By visualizing one of these gods, Daoists thought, one could identify with its powers of immortality.[44]

Daoism had as strong an impact on Chinese aesthetics as it did on Chinese popular religion.[45] As a guide to creativity, it stressed spontaneity and flow. Largely because of Daoist inspiration, calligraphy, painting, poetry, and music ideally issued from a meditative communion with the nature of things. In what Chan Buddhism popularized as "no-mind," artists worked spontaneously, without calculation or design. Their products were the outflow of a fullness far more comprehensive than logic or method. In fact, the artists were supposed to render both the stream of nature and the way that particular items suddenly focus that stream. So a bird alighting on a tree, a rush of wind, the striking colors of persimmons at daybreak—these were typical themes of poetry and art. Daoist artists owed a great deal to the "retirement" that Daoism advocated as a respite and counterpoint to Confucian "office."[46] Mixed with Buddhist aesthetics, Daoism provided China most of its artistic depth. Nature, art, and the spirit so came together for the traditional Chinese that they considered their Way superior to the rest of the world.

Buddhism

Buddhism may have entered China as early as the beginning of the first century B.C.E. and almost certainly established itself by the middle of the second century C.E.[47] Buddhist missionaries traveled along the trade routes that linked northeastern India and China, probably entering at Dunhuang in the west. By 148 C.E., monks such as Anshigao had settled at Luoyang, considerably to the east, and begun translating Buddhist texts. The first interests of these translators and their audiences appear to have been meditation and philosophy, which suggests that the Chinese first considered Buddhism similar to Daoism. However, as the translating progressed through the Han dynasty (ended 220 C.E.), sutras on morality became popular, too.

From this beginning, Buddhism slowly adapted to Chinese ways. Most of the preachers and translators who worked from the third to the fifth centuries C.E. favored Daoist terminology. This was especially true in the south, where the intelligentsia had created a market for philosophy. In the less cultured north, Buddhism made progress by being presented as a powerful magic.[48] By the middle of the fifth century, China had its own sectarian schools, comparable to those that had developed in India. Thus, by that time most

of the major Buddhist philosophies and devotional practices had assumed a Chinese style, including the *Abhidhamma* (a system that employed erudite philosophy and psychology in interpreting the scriptures) and the Indian Madhyamika and Yogacara schools. In general, Mahayana attracted the Chinese more than Hinayana, so the native schools that prospered tended to develop Mahayana positions.

The Chinese brought to Buddhism an interest in bridging the gap between the present age and the age of the Buddha by constructing a line of masters along which the dharma had passed intact. The Master was more historical than timeless scriptural texts were, and the authority-minded Chinese were more concerned about history than the Indians had been.

Indeed, conflicts over the sutras were a sore problem for the Chinese, and in trying to reconcile seemingly contradictory positions, they frequently decided to make one scripture totally authoritative. A principal basis for the differences among the burgeoning Chinese Buddhist sects, therefore, lay in which scripture the sect's founder had chosen as most authoritative. (The notion of sects is distinctively Chinese, since it is based on the old concept of the clan. Chinese culture venerated its ancestors, and each Chinese Buddhist school accordingly had its dharma founder or patriarchal teacher.)

Buddhist Sects. The most popular sects were the Chan and Jingtu, which devoted themselves to meditation and the Pure Land, respectively. The Chinese took to meditation from the beginning of their encounter with Buddhism. There are evidences of yogic practices in the Daoist works attributed to Laozi and Zhuangzi, and certainly Daoist imagery of what the sage who knows the "inside" can accomplish had made many Chinese eager to tap interior powers. Chan capitalized on this interest, working out a simple regime and theory that focused on meditation.[49] (Chan is the transliteration of the Indian *dhyana;* the Japanese transliteration is Zen.) Its principal text was the *Lankavatara Sutra,* which the Yogacarins also much revered, because that text stressed the mentality of all reality.

According to legend, Bodhidharma, an Indian meditation-master devoted to the *Lankavatara,* founded Chan in the fifth century C.E. Paintings portray Bodhidharma as a fierce champion of single-mindedness, and he valued neither pious works nor recitations of the sutras. Only insight into one's own nature, which was identical with the dharma-nature of

all reality, was of significance; only enlightenment justified the Buddhist life. Tradition credits Bodhidharma
with developing the technique of "wall gazing," which
was a kind of peaceful meditation—what the Japanese
later called "just sitting" *(shikan-taza).*

Probably the most eminent of the Chan patriarchs
who succeeded Bodhidharma was the sixth patriarch,
Hui-neng. According to the *Platform Sutra,* which
purports to present his teachings, Hui-neng gained his
predecessor's mantle of authority by surpassing his
rival, Shenxiu, in a demonstration of dharma insight.
To express his understanding, Shenxiu had written:

> The body is the Bodhi Tree
> The mind is like a bright mirror and
> stand.
> At all times wipe it diligently,
> Don't let there be any dust.

Hui-neng responded:

> Bodhi really has no tree;
> The bright mirror also has no stand.
> Buddha-nature is forever pure;
> Where is there room for dust?[50]

This juxtaposition and evaluation of the two rivals' verse reflects the beliefs of the southern Chan
school, which looked to Hui-neng as the authoritative
spokesman for its position that enlightenment comes
suddenly. Because all buddha-nature is intrinsically
pure, one need only let it manifest itself. The northern
school held that enlightenment comes gradually and
thus counseled regular meditation. (Hui-neng himself
probably would have fought any sharp distinction between meditation and the rest of life. In wisdom all
things are one and pure.) The southern school finally
took precedence.[51]

Pure Land Buddhism (Jingtu) derived from Tanluan (476–542). He sought religious solace from a
grave illness, and after trying several systems, he
came to the doctrine of Amitabha Buddha and the
Pure Land. Amitabha is the Buddha of Light, devotion
to whom supposedly assures one a place in the Pure
Land or Western Paradise. Tanluan stressed faith in
Amitabha and the recitation of Amitabha's name as
ways to achieve such salvation. This, he and his successors reasoned, was a doctrine both possible and
appropriate in the difficult present age. The Pure Land
sect greatly appealed to the laity, and it developed
hymns and graphic representations of paradise to fo-

cus its imagination. In stressing love or emotional
attachment to Amitabha (called A-mi-to fo in China),
it amounted to a Chinese Buddhist devotionalism. By
chanting "na-mo a-mi-to-fo" ("greetings to A-mi-to fo
Buddha"), millions of Chinese found a simple way to
fulfill their religious needs and made A-mi-to fo the
most popular religious figure of Chinese history.[52]

Case Study: Medieval Buddhism.   "For the first two
hundred years of the T'ang, Buddhism flourished as
never before. Supported by the lavish donations of the
devout, guided by leaders of true piety and brilliance,
graced by the most gifted artists and architects of the
age, Buddhism was woven into the very texture of
Chinese life and thought. These centuries were the
golden age of an independent and creative Chinese
Buddhism."[53]

The Tang dynasty (618–907) followed on the Sui
(589–618), under which north and south China had
been reunited. Buddhism had made steady gains in
China even before this reunification, but after reunification it grew by leaps and bounds. A major reason for
this growth was the perception of both the Sui and the
Tang rulers that Buddhism could help them knit together the northern and southern cultures. Thus the
founder of the Sui dynasty presented himself as a universal monarch who was both a pious Buddhist believer and a generous patron of the *sangha.* He likened
his wars to campaigns to spread the ideals of Buddha,
calling his weapons of war incense and flowers offered
to the Enlightened One. It is hard to see how this
squared with Buddhist nonviolence, but the popularity
of Buddhism among the emperor's subjects led him to
associate himself with the dharma as much as he
could.

On the other hand, both the Sui and the Tang
rulers feared the power of the *sangha* and took steps
to limit its influence. Thus they insisted on regulating
the admission, education, and ordination of the
Buddhist clergy and on licensing the Buddhist temples. As well, the emperors put pressure on the *sangha*
to enforce the Vinaya strictly, for its rules governing
monastic life tended to restrict the clergy's economic
enterprises. Such imperial efforts to control Buddhism were only partly successful, for many medieval
empresses and wealthy merchants saw to it that
temple wealth grew. The merchants' support of Buddhism is an interesting example of fitting a religious
rationale to economic goals. For the merchants, the
Mahayana notion that money gifts should be put to
productive use became a justification for widespread

commercial enterprise. Since the prevailing economy was, by imperial design, focused on agriculture, the Mahayana notion in effect buttressed the merchants in their conflict with the state comptrollers.

The government did its best to limit the ways that Buddhist doctrines might become politically subversive, guarding against the revolutionary implications of Mahayana dharma. For example, potential rebels had available to them the Mahayana belief that Buddhism would pass through three ages. In the third age, religion would come close to extinction and no government would merit the full allegiance of the Buddhist faithful. A wealthy and powerful sect called the San-chieh chiao seized on this notion and tried to use it to undermine the imperial authority, but the Sui and Tang rulers reacted vigorously and had the sect suppressed. The Mahayana teaching about Maitreya, the future buddha, was similarly dangerous. Enough Buddhists believed that the advent of Maitreya was close at hand to present the government a sizable problem. The popular understanding was that when Maitreya came, a new heaven and a new earth would begin. Thus both the Sui and the Tang emperors had to battle rebels moving against them under banners of white (the color associated with Maitreya).

Still, the golden age that Buddhism enjoyed in these dynasties flowed from the positive support the emperors gave it. For all their care that Buddhist fervor not become subversive of their own rule, the Sui and Tang leaders made Buddhist ritual an important part of the state ceremony. Thus the accession of a new emperor, the birth of a prince, and the ceremonies in honor of the imperial ancestors all incorporated Buddhist sutras, spells, and prayers. When the emperor ritualized important occasions, the monasteries and temples received handsome donations, which of course increased their patriotic loyalty and pliability.

At the great capital of Changan, Buddhist art dominated a vibrant cultural life. The architecture of the pagodas and temples gracefully blended Indian and native Chinese elements, producing a distinctively Chinese Buddhist appearance. The images and paintings that adorned the temples drew on the full range of sources with which the great Chinese Empire came in contact. Thus there were not only native Chinese art forms but also Indian, Persian, Greco-Roman, and Central Asian. With sufficient freedom married to sufficient imperial support, Chinese Buddhist artists enjoyed a period of great prosperity and created a distinctive new style.

This sort of syncretism—a core of Chinese Buddhist inspiration in touch with many other sources of inspiration—extended to literary art. The Tang dynasty was a high point in the history of Chinese poetry, and the moving forces behind this poetry were the two congenial streams of Buddhist and Daoist philosophy. Thus the celebrated poet Bozhui was representative in filling his work with references to the Buddhist rituals and temple grounds that gave him and his contemporaries spiritual nourishment. In one poem he remembers visiting a great hall called the Jade Image, in which rows of white jade buddhas sat like serried trees. He and his fellow journeyers shook the dust from their clothes and bowed to worship the buddhas, whose faces were like frozen snow. The buddhas' white cassocks hung like folded hoarfrost, and their crowns glittered like a shower of hail. So perfect were these white images that the journeying poets scrutinized them in wonder, feeling that here was a work of heavenly spirits, a work more exalted than any earthly chisel could have managed.[54]

The following lines from the renowned Du Fu (712–770) show the moving humanism that Tang art could achieve. The poet is speaking of his absent wife:

Tonight, the moon over Fu-chou,
From her room she can only watch alone.
Far away, my poor little children
Don't know they should remember the capital.
Fragrant mist moistens her hair, dark as clouds.
Clear rays chill her arms, fair as jade.
When shall we lean against the empty curtain,
With the moon drying the tears of us both?[55]

Medieval Buddhism also permeated the life of the common people, including the village peasantry, for the government developed a network of official temples that linked the provinces to the capital. On official feast days, ceremonies held throughout the land reminded the people that they shared a uniform religious faith. The provinces also used the Buddhist temple grounds for their fairs, thereby making them the centers of the local social, economic, and artistic life. The great feast days were the Buddha's birthday and the Feast of All Souls, when large crowds would gather to honor the Buddhist deities, listen to the sutras, or hear an accomplished preacher expound the dharma.

When local organizations met for vegetarian dinners, clergy and laity had a fine chance to socialize. Fashioning close bonds of mutual interest, these dinners became a great source of fund raising for the monasteries and blessings for the mercantile and personal interests of the laity. The village clergy usually were not well educated, but they tended to know the laity intimately and to provide them considerable solace at such important times as weddings and funerals. Many of the village Buddhist clergy also functioned as healers and mediums, as well as storytellers and magicians.

The state and the *sangha* therefore had a symbiotic relationship throughout the Sui and the Tang dynasties. Whether pulling in the same direction or wanting to go opposite ways, they were mutually influential. One place where Buddhist views considerably modified traditional Chinese customs was the penal codes. The traditional customs were quite cruel, so the Buddhist ideals of compassion and respect for life served as a mitigating influence. Both the Sui and the Tang rulers granted imperial amnesties from time to time, and when the rulers remitted death sentences they often justified their actions in terms of Buddhist compassion or reverence for life. Specifically, both dynasties took up the custom of forbidding executions (indeed, the killing of any living thing) during the first, fifth, and ninth months of the year, which were times of Buddhist penance and abstinence.

The emperors also converted Buddhist notions of the soul to their own ends, using them for the psychological conditioning of the imperial armies. Whereas the traditional Chinese cult of filial piety had weakened martial fervor, teaching that a good son should return his body to the earth intact, out of gratitude to his parents, the Buddhist stress on the soul (or spiritual aspect of the "person") downplayed the importance of the body. The traditional cult had also taught that immortality depended on being buried in the family graveyard, where one's descendants could come to pay tribute. Thus a soldier buried far from home would have no continuing significance. The Sui and Tang dynasties made it a practice to build temples at the scene of foreign battles and endow these temples with perpetual services for the souls of those slain in military service. In this way, they lessened the conflict between a generous service in the army and a generous filial piety.

Medieval Buddhism also increased the charitable helps available in Chinese society. Monks were the first to open dispensaries, free hospitals (supported by the Tang government), and hostels for travelers. They built bridges, planted shade trees, and generally broadened China's ethical sensitivity. Whereas the na-

Figure 24 *Sakyamuni Buddha, northern Wei dynasty, 494 C.E. Gray stone; 21¼ in. high. This statue shows Gautama as the sage of his tribe (the Sakyas). The* mudra *or gesture of his right hand is a symbol of his protection. The nimbus behind him emphasizes the peace and power of buddhahood. The Nelson–Atkins Museum of Art, Kansas City, Missouri (Nelson Fund).*

tive ethic seldom took much charitable interest in affairs outside the clan, Buddhism encouraged an interest in the welfare of all living things. For example, it said that giving alms to poor people outside one's clan was a fine way to improve one's karma. This Buddhist universalism never displaced the formative influence of the Chinese clans, but it did move many Chinese to great magnanimity.

Finally, it was during the medieval flourishing that Buddhist philosophy became fully Chinese. A hallmark of this domestication was the rendering of the abstractions in which Indians delighted into the concrete images the Chinese preferred. For example, the Indian "perfection" became the Chinese "round," while the Indian "essence" became the Chinese "pupil of the eye." Chan, the school that most stressed meditation, carried the Chinese spirit to the heart of Buddhist spirituality, distrusting abstract words and stressing metaphors, paradoxes, gestures, or direct, person-to-person intuitions. Chan and the other native schools also stressed living close to nature, in the conviction that nature held many of the secrets of enlightenment. This had great appeal for medieval Chinese artists, poets, and philosophers, many of whom would refresh themselves in retreats at Buddhist monasteries.

The Traditional Synthesis

Confucianism was the most influential religious tradition for the public functions of the Chinese family and the state, and in that sense the most official. For private worship, philosophy, and art, however, Buddhism and Daoism were quite influential. Buddhism and Daoism contended for influence at court and sometimes gained dominance. After the fall of the Han dynasty (third century C.E.), for instance, Confucian influence waned, and Buddhism gained great influence that lasted well into the ninth century. Nonetheless, in most periods the state bureaucracy hewed to the Confucian line.

Buddhism's major impact in the public sphere was its control of burial rites. In time, China associated funerals with monks. Partly out of envy at such influence and partly out of its own searches for enlightenment, Daoism established monastic communities in the fourth century C.E. Along with the rituals of the Daoist priesthood and the Daoist political parties, these communities were strong sources of Daoist public influence.

However, in their struggles against Confucian dominance, Buddhism and Daoism primarily depended on their greater appeal to individualist and artistic sentiments. In comparison, the sober Confucians offered relatively little to nourish a private, meditative, philosophical, or aesthetic life, although they were not completely lacking resources for meditation, self-improvement, and aesthetics. The Master's love of music, for instance, though he set it in a traditional and public context, could have inspired personal creativity in the arts. However, such inspiration tended to fall to Buddhists and Daoists.

In addition, the Buddhist and Daoist texts seemed richer and more mysterious to middle-aged people seeking meaning in their existence. Few Chinese could live fifty years and not suffer some surfeit from rules, laws, ceremonies, or traditions. At such point, the lean paradoxes of Zhuangzi, Laozi, the *Prajnaparamita*, and Chan could be very attractive. So could the *Dao* that could not be named, the Buddhist emptiness that one had to attend to in silence.

Peasant Religion.   Only the educated upper classes, of course, had the opportunity to immerse themselves in any of the high three traditions. For the majority of the population, the influence of these traditions only vaguely affected a world dominated by family loyalties and naturalistic animism, largely because the Chinese population was always overwhelmingly composed of peasants. Close to nature, these people filtered Buddhist and Daoist ideas through a primal reverence and fear of nature's powers.

For instance, the Chinese peasants incorporated Buddhist demonology, Daoist demonology, and both traditions' concern with saints into their ancient world of ghosts and helpers, which was home to the ancestors. This world was real because it affected the peasants each day, as the family sacrificed or tried to avert bad luck. The world of the spirits was alive. Daily the phenomena of the sky and the fields expressed that world's mysteries, and the wind and the sea carried great swans and dragons. The cities and the imperial court had their influence on the hamlets, but real life there confronted nature with little polish or form. What we might call an instinctive Confucianism about family relations blended with an instinctive Daoism about nature and human destiny to produce a curious mixture of formality and fear.

Moreover, the peasants had not separated, either through study or through deep meditation, rationality from mythical or pragmatic hopes and fears. Getting enough food, sheltering one's family, warding off sickness, continuing the family line—those were the concerns of the villagers. To meet them, different gods were honored at festivals for the New Year and for the changing seasons. As well, the Buddhist Goddess of Mercy drew those seeking easy births and strong children, and the Daoist cult of the immortals attracted a few who wanted longevity or knowledge of the rulers of their bodily organs. Tradition sanctioned these quests for meaning, but it was a tradition with many cracks. Daily life was shadowed by a greater need to avoid the wrath of the ancestors or the evil spirits.

Mercantile Religion.   By the fourteenth century C.E., guilds of artisans and businessmen had developed, and folk religiosity in China had become more mercantile. The guild became a sort of family or clan and had its patron gods and rituals. People now invoked the spirits who were the patrons of good selling, and a folk mentality affected the examinations that were part of the way to civil office. For instance, masters of the Confucian classics who did well in the examinations and secured good jobs took on an aura of religious power. As well, numerous stories were told of scholars who had received miraculous help from a patron deity, and these scholars gave the Confucians their own measure of magic and mystery.[56]

The common people could go to a great variety of shrines and temples to find out their futures. In addition, students prayed for success in their examinations, travelers prayed for safe journeys, and young people prayed for good marriages. Popular Chinese religion thus became almost economic. Gods and powers were the foci of business—the business of getting along well with an unseen world of fate and fortune. Confucianism, Daoism, and Buddhism all were mixed into this economic popular religion, but its base was preaxial closeness to nature. Few Chinese were so far from nature or so safe from adverse fortune that "secularism" was a live option. The state somewhat controlled religion by keeping the Buddhist and Daoist clergy in check, but the religious life of the family and the individual ran all the traditions together in a form that was largely outside the government's control.

The Communist Era

For more than two millennia, the ideas and beliefs that we have described prevailed in China with amazing stability and consistency. (Indeed, Hans Steininger has said of Confucianism, "It is these ethics which even today we meet all over East Asia."[57]) Despite new dynasties, wars, changing artistic styles, and even dramatic new religions such as Buddhism and Christianity, the general culture perdured. In the family, the government bureaucracy, and the villages, the folk/Confucian tradition was especially solid.

However, that changed in the early twentieth century. From without, Western science and Western sociopolitical thought dealt it heavy blows; from within, the decay of the imperial government led to the birth of the republic in 1912. Belatedly, China entered the modern world. In the twentieth century, its ancient culture showed cracks and strains everywhere. As a result, Chinese religious traditions, especially Confucianism, came under strong attack. Identified with the old culture, they seemed out of place in the modern world. Since the "cultural renaissance" of 1917, China has tried to cast off its Confucian shackles; since the Communist takeover of 1949, it has espoused a program of ongoing socialism and modernization.[58]

The paramount figure in this program, of course, was Mao Zedong. Mao was born in 1893 in Hunan (a south-central province) of a "middle" peasant family (that is, not one of abject poverty). His father had little culture or education, and his mother was a devout Buddhist. Mao himself received a traditional primary school education, whose core was memorizing the Confucian classics. (As a result, he developed a profound distaste for Confucius.) He had to leave school when he was thirteen to work the land, but prompted by his desire for more education, he ran away and enrolled in a modern high school. There he first encountered Western authors who challenged traditional Chinese culture. (At that time many educated Chinese felt humiliated by their defeat by the British in the Opium War of 1839–42, their defeat by the Japanese in 1895, and the repression of their Boxer uprising in 1900 by a coalition of mainly Western powers. In the opinion of biographer Stuart Shram, Mao probably saw China's need to gain respect in the international community more clearly than he saw its internal needs.[59])

Slowly Mao adopted a more positive program as a result of increased engagement with the developing Chinese Communist party, increased knowledge of developments in Russia, and then years as a guerrilla soldier. Before long, Mao was a convert to Marxism-Leninism. He joined the Chinese Communist party in 1921, took part in the Communist collaboration with Jiang Kai-shek's Guomindang party until 1926, and then led Communist forces that opposed Jiang. By 1935 Mao was in charge of the Communist party and engaged in what became his legendary "Long March." Through World War II the Communists and the Guomindang collaborated uneasily against the Japanese; after the war the final conflict with Jiang led to the Communist takeover in 1949. Throughout this period

Mao pursued the twofold career of military general and political theoretician. While gaining power he collaborated with the Russians, but he eventually decided that China had to go its own way. The result was a massive experiment in agrarian reform, enfranchising the lower classes, and trying to control economics by Marxist-Leninist and Maoist dogma.

The reason for this brief biographical sketch of Mao is that he was the most important figure in China's break with tradition and plunge into modernity. Influenced by the Confucian classics and Buddhism, he nevertheless repudiated both. On the surface at least, Maoism took shape as a secular humanism—a system that referred to nothing more absolute than "the people." Some of its doctrines and programs dramatically changed the life of the people. The women's movement, for instance, and the related changes in the marriage law raised an entire segment of the population from subjection to near equality.[60] By stressing agricultural production, local health care, and "cellular" local government, Chinese Communism has become an even more grandiose socialist experiment than the Soviet.

As part of the program instituting these changes, Mao's party denounced religion. Instead of gods and sacrifices, it offered self-reliance, hard work, and the mystique that the people united are invincible. Temples became government property, religious professionals were persecuted, and religious literature was derided or proscribed. The party likewise attacked the Confucian classics, virtues, and traditions. Throughout, its goal was to destroy the old class society and make a new people with one will and one future.

However, as one might expect, religion and tradition died harder than the Communists had hoped. In the rural regions, peasant traditions continued to have great influence. Among the intellectuals, conforming to the party line resulted in rather wooden, if not second-class, philosophy, science, and art. According to R. J. Lifton,[61] Mao himself ruminated on immortality in his last years, for he saw the problem of keeping the revolution "green"—retrieving for a new generation the experiences of the Long March and the other peak events that had united the wills of the founding generation.

Something of that concern comes through in the last of Mao's poems.[62] "Two Birds," supposedly written in 1965, contrasts a sparrow, concerned only with beef-filled goulash, with a soaring roc that sees how the world is turning upside down. The options, Mao seems to say, are settling down in material comfort

and keeping the revolution green. Many commentators saw in Mao's sporadic activism (periods of stability followed by upheavals such as the Cultural Revolution) an effort to ward off stagnation.

Since the death of Mao Zedong, China has opened to the West. The "four modernizations" (in industry, science and technology, agriculture, and military affairs) urged by Mao's successors aimed at bringing China into the modern world. "To 'handle the problem of religion' correctly, the regime has recently convened 2 major study conferences: the China Atheistic Seminar (Nanking, December, 1978) calling for scholarly research on atheism, and the National Planning Conference on Religious Studies (Kunming, February, 1979) calling for scholarly research on religions from the Marxist standpoint. On 15 March 1979, the regime promulgated a new policy statement entitled 'Religion and Superstition,' re-establishing the pre-1966 religious policy as 'correct.' The Religious Affairs Bureau in Beijing formally resumed operation the next day. Open persecution of believers is now expected to decline, but authentic legal toleration remains unlikely."[63]

Before 1966, the policy, expressed in article 88 of the Constitution of 1954, had been that the people of the People's Republic enjoy freedom of religious belief. During the Cultural Revolution of 1966–69, the policy was to promote atheism. The Constitution of 1975 stipulated in article 28 that citizens have the freedom to practice a religion, and the freedom not to practice a religion and to propagate atheism. In mid-1980, the demographic results of these policies were estimated as follows: nonreligious Chinese, 527 million people, or 59 percent of the population; folk religionists, 179 million people, or 20 percent of the population; atheists, 107 million people, or 12 percent of the population; Buddhists, 53 million people, or 6 percent of the population; Muslims, 21 million people, or 2.4 percent of the population; Christians, 1.8 million people, or 0.2 percent of the population.[64]

The upheavals in China in the late 1980s called the future of all individual liberties seriously into question. By putting down the movement among students and intellectuals for democracy, the regime, headed by elderly successors of Mao, ensured that a Communist orthodoxy would continue to dominate official culture, at least for the short run. While some religious groups had made progress and seemed to be on the verge of gaining a considerable following, the suppression of free speech and criticism by the government caused all such groups, along with all other

Chinese coalitions seeking reforms and greater freedoms, to hold their breath. At the time of this writing
(May 1992), the future of religion in mainland China
remains very unclear.

WORLDVIEW

The history of religion in China is a story of the
interaction of many forces and traditions. The oldest
and deepest stratum, which reveals a folk religion
much concerned with fertility and various supernatural forces, always predominated for the great numbers of Chinese who were peasants. The "higher"
indigenous traditions, expressed in Confucian and
Daoist ideas and convictions, assumed this deepest
stratum and labored to clarify the stances that educated people, people of reflective awareness and refinement, ought to take toward it. The Confucians
dominated social attitudes, inasmuch as education
could shape them. Confucian convictions about how
the wise people of the fortunate past had lived and
thought established a preference for ritual, ceremony,
class consciousness, the rule of men over women, and
above all, reverence for one's elders and ancestors.

Certainly all of these features of Chinese culture
owed much to folk convictions, but the Confucians
gave them an anthropocentric focus. Inasmuch as
sages such as Confucius and Mencius experienced
themselves to be living repositories of tradition, existential awarenesses of the Way, they felt powerful
enough to oppose both the dysfunctional views of human arrangements that could develop in folk religion
and the disorders of people who held considerable political or military power but had been seduced by force,
greed, vanity, lust, or any of the other vices that were
bound to bring social disaster in the long run.

The Daoists agreed with the Confucians that wise
people, filled with the spirit of the golden past and
attuned to the Way not only revered in that past but
running the cosmos in the present, were the living
repositories of tradition. They differed from the Confucians in their distrust of the efficacy of ritual, mores
that would prop the distributions of power constituting the status quo, and convention. The Daoists found
more paradox in the ways of the Way, and they thought
that the sage had to be more individualistic. As well,
he or she (the Daoists were minor champions of wom-

en's wisdoms) had to be more attuned to the patterns
of nature, where the Way constantly gave instruction
on how to live well. We are speaking of the philosophical Daoists, of course. The religious Daoists kept less
distance from folk religion and more subordinated
such masters as Laozi and Zhuangzi to it than they
subordinated it to them.

The Buddhists never replaced the folk religionists,
Confucians, or Daoists, philosophical or religious.
Their tendency was, rather, to supplement, deepen,
and occasionally challenge the indigenous ways. That
is not to say that Buddhism did not make a deep impact on China. It did, especially in such areas as the
philosophy of nature, meditation, and both the understanding and the ritualization of death. But the
Chinese pattern was to extend a Confucian instinct
about social relations so that Buddhist instincts might
enrich it. Similarly, the tendency was to combine
Buddhist philosophy with philosophical Daoism, so
that Buddhism became simpler and more paradoxical,
as it did in Chan schools.

This interpretation of the religious history of
China suggests that, in studying the Chinese worldview, students do well to concentrate on the cooperation of the different major forces or strata. The way of
regarding nature, society, the self, and ultimate reality
that one finds in the typical Chinese man or woman
was almost always an amalgam of folk, Confucian,
Daoist, and Buddhist influences. These influences
were not uniform or equal. A given tradition might
play a stronger or weaker role in a given area (for
instance, social outlook) or with a given person (for
instance, the peasant woman Wang). But for the abstract that we can derive from the total mixture of
influences, we have to take into account the constant
contributions of all the major traditions in all of the
major areas. Pay attention, then, to the amalgamated,
syncretistic character of the Chinese worldview. Do not
consider the various Chinese traditions competitors
(though they were that on occasion) so much as complementary stimuli—pressures to make the typical
Chinese person aware of other options, sensitive to
further complexities.

Nature

All ancient societies lived deep in what we have called
the cosmological myth, and China was no exception.[65]
However, China did not have India's tendency to call
sensory experience into question. Throughout its axial
period, China's attitude was that nature is utterly

real—more primordial than human beings. After the axial period, when Buddhism had a deep effect, native Chinese thought and the dharma were joined in more than a marriage of convenience. For instance, the Chan and Huayen schools translated the Mahayana philosophy of emptiness into a Chinese version of the theory that nirvana and samsara are not two. Furthermore, although Buddhist devotional sects among the masses drew attention to the heavenly Pure Land, they also described the Pure Land as a present reality. Overall, then, nature bulked large and unquestioned. The vast majority of Chinese doubted neither its reality nor its ultimacy. If there had been a question of subordinating one of the four dimensions of reality (nature, society, self, and divinity), nature would have been the last to go.

Physical reality took form through *Dao*. *Dao* was the most basic force holding nature together. To be sure, the *Dao* most to the fore here is that which humans can name. The nameless *Dao* (which to Laozi was the more real) was too vast, too primordial, too womblike for humans to grasp. It was so unlimited as to be somewhat beyond the world, so full or complete as to be beyond our comprehension.

So, it was the worldly Way—the cause of the seasons, the peculiarities of history, the laws of gravity and the tides—that dominated most Chinese reflection on nature. Most Chinese reflection on nature concerned manifest entities, patterns and forces that affected human beings. The other latent *Dao* was only the intuition of an intellectual, indeed of a mystical, elite. Not only could that *Dao* not be named, it could not be brought under human control. Consequently, it was the best candidate in pre-Buddhist Chinese thought for the mystery whose uncontrollability is our primary indication that something more powerful and basic than what we see is at the origin of things.

Dao, it follows, was both Logos and mother. As Logos, it was the reasonable pattern, the intelligence running through nature. As mother, it was the womblike source of all things. Neither being nor nonbeing, the maternal *Dao* existed in a realm of its own. Yet this transcendent realm was also the basis for all the other realms of nature. The fish, waters, clouds, trees, mud, dung, and other elements of observable reality existed by *Dao*. Both the manner in which they existed and the fact that they existed implied this ultimate. So *Dao* functioned as the within and the without. Not many Chinese reasoned in this somewhat relentless way, but their more poetic and circular descriptions take us to such conclusions. Nature had a sense and a

mystery, and this sense finally was owed to its mystery. The pregnant word *Dao* signified both.

Throughout Chinese history, *Dao* retained this richness. Confucians and Buddhists used it to express their understanding of nature, as did Daoists themselves. Frequently *Dao* was associated with heaven *(Tian)*, which often gave it a sacred aspect. Originally heaven was the overseer (a notion that the Chinese shared with Indians and Near Easterners). There was nothing that heaven did not notice and record. Heaven itself, though, never took on personal features among the Chinese. No father with a white beard, no Apollo with a dashing chariot, became its emblem. Neither the sun nor the moon solicited reverence as the primary form of heaven. If anything, the sky itself, broad and indistinct, was the focus of Chinese devotion.

Opposite to the sky was the earth. Yet the earth seldom was viewed maternally, as it was by many ancient peoples. The Chinese acknowledged the mysteries of vegetation, seasonal changes, the fallow and the productive, and they touched their newborn to the earth in recognition of their origin. But the maternal aspect of nature's bounty they attributed more to *Dao* than to the earth. Perhaps they were more attuned to pattern and flow than to dirt-bound production. (Or perhaps we are speaking mainly about the beliefs of poets and intellectuals, whose writings shape our impressions overmuch.)

In any event, Laozi, Zhuangzi, and the Buddhists consistently invested nature with an aura of ultimacy and preferred to bow before *Dao*. For instance, Zhuangzi's Great Clod is more than mother earth. Returning to the Clod at death keeps one in a universal rhythm. The Great Clod is the material system, the massive lump, that *Dao* turns. Similarly, Buddhist landscapers and gardeners went beyond mother earth to Suchness, buddha-nature, or emptiness for their inspiration. Although the Japanese developed the aesthetic resulting from this inspiration more fully, it first came from China.

Folk Views. More mundane matters—such as yin and yang, the five dynamic qualities, and the ghosts and helping spirits—absorbed the masses. These concepts rendered Chinese nature lively.[66] Of course, virtually all ancient peoples thought of nature as alive. Although the Chinese stressed the cult of ancestor spirits more than comparable peoples, such veneration was yet present among other peoples as well. Indian Buddhists, for instance, thought that the dead would turn malevolent unless the living venerated them.

Chinese folk religion is also distinctive (although, again, not unique) in its concern for the compass directions. The geomancy of *feng-shui* is a clear expression of Chinese emphasis on nature's four directions. Of course, other peoples were concerned with directions; Native Americans made a great deal of the four geographic directions, while early civilized peoples such as the Egyptians built their temples with great concern for their orientation toward the sun. However, China carried this concern to a high art. Even for the average person, the angle of the wind or the shape of the terrain was magically influential.

Chinese divination expressed another set of naturalistic assumptions. The *Yi Jing,* for instance, elaborated on the belief that yin-yang components shape human participation in nature's course of events. Like the African diviner who studied the patterns of chits in a magical basket, the Chinese fortune-teller believed that numbers and designs expressed nature's coherence. In popular Chinese religion, then, there was a primal sense that nature coordinates with mind. That sense did not develop to the point of gaining a control over nature, as it would in modern Western science and technology, but for Chinese diviners, astrologers, and even fortune-tellers, that sense had great mythic power.

Such a mythic mentality may largely derive from a deep appreciation of what might be. Anything that is not contradictory might be. Therefore, anything non-contradictory can, under the pressure of imaginative suggestion, be accepted as something that is or that soon will be. From faddish "cures" for cancer to the stock market, we can see the same dynamics at work in late twentieth-century America.

In using the *Yi Jing*'s patterns of broken and unbroken lines, Chinese diviners were moved by the powerful human tendency to blur the distinction between what might be and what is, between the imaginable and the real. The interest motivating mathematicians, physicists, novelists, and theologians is little different from this tendency.[67]

Case History: Classical Chinese Aesthetics. The traditional Chinese notions of beauty were so intimately involved with nature that we can consider both classical poetry and classical painting in a naturalist context. To be sure, classical poetry did not neglect the supernatural world, for one finds poems concerned with God, nature deities, Daoist "immortals," and ancestors. In addition, there were numerous poems concerned with family ties, friendship, love, social jus-

tice, war, and other human themes. But nature tended to be the encompassing orbit (for example, "God" was *Tian,* heaven) and the great source of inspiration.

In the earliest poetry, from the *Book of Poetry* (about 1100–600 B.C.E.), nature often offers analogies to human life. Thus the first poem in this classical collection speaks of the cries of ospreys on an island in a river, which remind the poet of a man longing for the love of a virtuous maiden. As the poem unfolds, the river becomes a backdrop for the shifting emotions of human love.

Another early theme was just the opposite. In poetry from the early centuries C.E., we can read of nature's distance from human ways. Where human beings feel things intensely, hoping and sorrowing, nature goes its way in indifference. Where human affairs are always changing and the human life span is brief, nature goes its way with little alteration, confident in its endlessness. Unlike metal or stone, human beings cannot be expected to endure. The poet finds this contrast poignant, even bitter: Why should human life be so fragile and fleeting?

Still a third theme of classical Chinese poetry is the personification of nature, according it feelings like the poet's own. Thus some lyrics of Li Yu (937–978) describe flowers in the woods losing their red bloom, paling because of chilly rains or strong night winds. The flowers are like rouge-stained tears asking the poet to stay and share nature's sorrow. Other notable Chinese poets indulged in this "pathetic fallacy," as John Ruskin called it. Conventional imagery, for instance, attributed to rivers a great grief, as though their spring rising were the effect of voluminous tears, or their endless flow were a ceaseless lament for the harshness human beings must endure.

A fourth way the classical corpus treats nature is more subtle and sophisticated. Seeming to depict a natural scene objectively, the poet actually evokes almost stylized emotions, through the conventional associations his naturalistic images would stimulate. Thus a ninth-century C.E. poem of Wen Ting describes a tower backed by a river, a moon gazing down on the sea, and mists along a seacoast punctuated only by two lines of migrating geese. Adding images of frontier sparseness, the poet insinuates the melancholy of the homesick traveler, alone while his family and friends have gathered at night. The Western reader can catch the general mood, but the Chinese reader would have been affected by such details as willows waving along the dike, because traditionally one gave a willow branch to a friend departing on a journey.

Like artists everywhere, the classical Chinese poets turned their materials this way and that, searching for the best inspiration. They felt little need to be "logical" and treated nature sometimes directly and at other times indirectly. Thus an eighth-century poem of Wang Chang-ling portrays nature subjectively, as a stimulus of emotions. The poem, "A Woman's Complaint," tells of a young wife, hitherto carefree, who first experiences regret when she climbs to the top of a tower on a spring day and catches sight of some willows along the road. They remind her of the gift she gave her husband, when he acceded to her urgings and went off to seek his fortune. Led by the sight of the willows, the woman enters a new land, the domain of regret. For the first time, she wonders whether her impetuous urging was wise. The poet's lesson seems to be that nature can nudge us along the painful passage to wisdom. The timeless powers that move the world can open us to quiet reflection through flowers and sunsets.

Perhaps the most important motif in the classical poets' view of nature, however, was that peace comes from submerging the self in nature. Here the influence of Daoism and Buddhism seems strongest. For example, a work of the eighth-century poet Wang Wei speaks of birds returning home at evening, having traveled the vast void of the sky. At dusk the sky and earth invite the mind, too, to come home from its travels. If the mind would merge with the earth and sky, it would find rest. One feels through the poem the natural whole that birds or the setting sun can reflect. The human spirit finds its best place, the poet seems to say, when it lets birds and sunsets unite it emotionally with nature's mystery.[68]

Classical Chinese painting was equally preoccupied with nature. Before the rise of landscape painting, which is probably the most lauded Chinese development, there was a concern with depicting figures, such as impressive Buddhas, and after the heyday of landscape painting there was a concern with birds and animals, grasses and flowers. But landscape painting holds the central panel in the Chinese triptych, so we do well to concentrate on landscape painting.

There is no evidence of landscape painting before the Jin dynasty (265–419). The first specimen of natural scenery, attributed to Gu Kaizhi, a famous figure-painter of the fourth century C.E., shows a mountain inhabited by wild beasts. The animals are disproportionately large, as though they might gobble up the mountain, but for the first time we come upon a Chinese mind able to detach itself from human concerns and contemplate the wilderness. Zong Ping, who succeeded Gu as the leader of the new movement, wrote an essay entitled "Preface to Landscape Painting," in which he expressed what was to be the guiding philosophy of this school: "The complete form of the mountain cannot be seen when the eye is quite close to it, but from a distance the eye can take in its whole compass, since the size of the mountain diminishes as it recedes from sight."[69] From this bit of common sense, the landscape artists drew the conclusion that one best deals with naturalistic scenes by stepping back to see them whole.

During the Tang dynasty landscape painting flourished. Both of its essential components—the composition of the whole and the brushwork detailing the parts—grew more skillful. The northern school favored rugged brush strokes, leading to a more severe style, while the southern school favored more delicate strokes, leading to a more graceful style. Thus a snow scene by Wang Wei of the southern school is rather misty, with fine bits of snow falling on thin bare branches. A little bridge crosses a cloudy stream, its pilings and railings whitened by snow. A tiny human figure approaches the door of a house apparently lighted for the evening. The man likely is looking forward to the cheerful fire but regretting having to leave the peaceful winter scene. Such poetic, imaginative emphases were typical of the southern Tang school.

Landscape painting reached its greatest heights during the Song dynasty. The fashion of painting richly colored landscapes developed, although a majority of the masters finally favored simple shadings of black ink. Gradually brush strokes became the distinguishing feature of the great masters, and color faded to insignificance, but there are some early paintings with beautiful rich colorings. The southern Song school gained most renown for its fusion of poetry and painting. Not only would the artist usually run a text down the side of the scroll, he would also blend the scene with the poetry so that sight and sound married perfectly. A small snow scene by Liu Songnian, for example, perfectly pictures the literary contents of its poem: mountains, a little bridge, lonely pavilions, and a desolate willow tree. The total effect is "poetic" rather than objective, a tug at the heart rather than an analysis by the eye. "Winter is beautiful but bitter," it seems to say. "Much of life's loveliness is bleak and cold." The artist presents the natural forms in considerable detail, conveying a great respect for nature's intricacies.

Figure 25 *Fishermen (handscroll detail) by Xuning, about 970–1051. Ink on silk; 82 in. long, 19 in. high. The picture stresses the vastness and permanence of a nature that dwarfs human beings and wraps them in emptiness. The Nelson–Atkins Museum of Art, Kansas City, Missouri (Nelson Fund).*

Later southern Song landscapes moved away from this detail, preferring a mere hint of nature's intricacies. Thus their canvases grew sparse, with large areas of empty space. The artists would show only the topmost peaks of a mountain or a single spray of flowers. Since this southern Song development, *space* has dominated Chinese landscapes. Whether one considers this a triumph of Buddhist "emptiness," or a maturation of an inner artistic perception (an indirect way of suggesting nature's mystic whole while emphasizing its striking individual parts), it is singularly effective, pleasing the onlooker in both eye and soul. The eye is drawn to the perfectly executed flower or thin cloud, while the soul delights in leaving details,

busyness, behind so that it can simply contemplate. Communing with the *all* that runs behind, in, and through the details, the soul can aspire to "unknowing" facts and intuiting reality, as many mystics might have put it.

Thus a painting of Mi Feng entitled *Pine and Bower* has only several mountaintops, a tree, and a little hut. Half the picture is empty space, which might be clouds obscuring the bottom half of the mountains or a lake behind the little hut. There is no human presence except that suggested by the hut. The entire scene is tranquil: nature perfectly in balance, because left alone. Mi breaks the stereotype of southern delicacy, however, through a predilection for rugged natural features. This squares with a story told of him. Once he was walking along a forest path when he saw a large rock blocking his way. The rock was grizzled and oddly shaped, but his heart went out to it. So he knelt in the dust and embraced the rock, calling it "my elder brother." For this he got the nickname Mad Mi, but any good Buddhist or Daoist could understand his emotion. He developed a technique of "Mi dots" to help him express his love of strong particulars. Thus the mountains of *Pine and Bower* are wonderfully grainy, and the clouds have a thick consistency, as though unknowing were wrapping itself around the mind prior to enlightenment.

Nature in Buddhism.   Richard Mather has shown that the concept of nirvana only won acceptance in China after the Buddhists had modified it considerably.[70] At the outset, ultimate Buddhist reality seemed wholly contradictory to Chinese concreteness. Thus, Chinese Buddhists accomplished a rather thorough cross-cultural translation. They had predecessors in the Indian Mahayanists, who identified samsara with nirvana, but the Mahayanists were far more abstract than the Chinese. Indeed, Chan probably became the most successful of the sects rooted in Mahayana metaphysics because it most thoroughly domesticated nirvana. Little interested in words or speculations, Chan focused on meditation, by which one might experience nirvana. It also stressed physical work, art, and ritual that deemphasized dualistic thinking. This deemphasis is more familiar to Western readers in its Japanese (Zen) form, but it had a Chinese beginning.[71]

So the radical buddha-nature (whether as emptiness or as mind-only) found in Chan a natural form. It could be the essence of all physical things, so present that one need not flee the world nor even close one's eyes to experience it. Since meditation expresses this conviction through the bodily postures that one assumes, one has only to sit squarely in the midst of natural reality and focus on its is-ness. (Not incidentally, one does not close one's eyes. The proper focus is neither a direction within nor a withdrawal to fix on the passing mental stream. In Chan it is a gaze with eyes open toward the end of one's nose.) The objective is to see without reasoning the reality that is right here. Such seeing should not focus on particulars, or concern itself with colors and forms. Rather, it should appreciate reality's wholeness by not making distinctions. When such appreciation flowers, there is enlightenment: "I came to realize

clearly that Mind is no other than mountains and rivers and the great wide earth, the sun and the moon and the stars."[72]

Society

Historically, China used Confucianism as its binding social force, and Confucianism thoroughly subordinated individuals to the community. Consequently, the Chinese individual felt inserted not only into a nature more impressive than the self but also into a society greater than its parts. Furthermore, the great Confucian thinkers based their theory of ideal social relationships on legendary rulers of the past. Such rulers embodied the social *Dao.* Their way, then, was a paradigm that ordered society by exemplary morality. Somewhat magically, the virtue *(de)* that went out from the legendary kings and dukes brought those it touched into harmony, at least according to Confucianism.

The Confucian mythic history evidences the common ancient notion of sacred kingship. Because the ruler stands at the peak of the human pyramid, he can conduct heaven's governing power to earth. The Chinese king manifested this holy meditating role by offering sacrifices to the gods of heaven and earth. In pre-Confucian times, he sacrificed human beings.[73]

The imperial cult, consequently, was the keystone in the Chinese social edifice, and the Confucian notion of *li* (propriety) applied especially to the punctilious execution of its ceremonies. To know the music and ritual appropriate to different occasions was the mark of a high gentleman. In fact, from this cultic center radiated something religious that touched all social relationships. Since human activities related to heaven, they partook of cultic propriety. By maintaining a harmonious family, for instance, individuals contributed to the most important order, that between natural divinity and humanity.

The harmony that the Confucians encouraged, though it extended to all aspects of social life,[74] expressed itself most importantly in its rating of key human relationships. It rated men over women (and so pictured marriage not as a partnership but as the wife's servitude to the husband). It rated children (among whom the eldest son was the plum) distinctly inferior to the parents—so much so that obedience and service toward the parents (most importantly toward the father) dominated the lives of children.

Likewise, rulers were rated over subjects, masters over peasants, and, to a lesser extent, elder brothers over younger brothers.

In logical extension of their veneration of the past, the Chinese honored ancient ancestors more than more recent ones, and they rated children according to the order of their birth. Surely some parents loved a younger son more than an elder son or a gracious girl more than a mulish boy, but in determining the important matter of inheritance, age was the main standard. In these and many other ways, Chinese society looked backwards. The past was the age of paradigms; the elderly were the fonts of wisdom. The axial masters of Chinese political thought give little evidence of celebrating youth or brave new worlds.

Social space was similarly static. From the ruler's key connection to heaven, the social classes descended in clearly defined ranks with little egalitarian or democratic moderation. The Confucians especially felt that the rank of a person was important. One said quite different things to a fellow noble riding in a hunting carriage and the carriage driver. A person of breeding knew and respected such differences. If Confucius and Mencius themselves are representative, such a person was almost prickly about his social rights.

For example, the master would not visit just anyone, and for a pupil to come into town and not quickly pay a visit of homage was a serious slight. Somewhat like Plato, the Confucian master protected his dignity and honor. Perhaps surprisingly, the Confucians turned their insistence on moral worth into a partial break with the cosmological myth (and with sacred kingship). Implicit in their exaltation of virtue over external rank or status was a turn to the wisdom of the sage—a turn from cosmology to anthropology.[75]

Women's Status. Among the Confucians, a peasant or a woman, however virtuous, had a hard time gaining respect. In fact, of the three Chinese traditions, Confucianism was the most misogynistic. The woman's role in Confucianism was to obey and serve her parents, husband, and husband's parents. She was useless until she produced a male heir, and her premarital chastity and marital fidelity were more important than a man's. In some periods, obsession with female chastity became so great that society insisted on total sexual segregation.[76] No doubt some men genuinely loved their wives and treated them tenderly, but the Confucian view of marriage gave little place to romance.

Since a Chinese woman's destiny was early marriage, childbearing, and household duties, her education was minimal. She was not necessarily her husband's friend, confidante, or lover—males and courtesans could fulfill these roles. A Chinese woman was primarily her husband's source of sons. They were the reason for her marriage—indeed, for her sex. As a result, the ideal Chinese woman was retiring, silent, and fertile. Custom severely curtailed her freedoms, but never more cruelly than through foot binding. Mary Daly described this custom in graphic terms: "The Chinese ritual of footbinding was a thousand-year-old horror show in which women were grotesquely crippled from very early childhood. As Andrea Dworkin so vividly demonstrates, the hideous three-inch-long 'lotus' hooks—which in reality were odoriferous, useless stumps—were the means by which the Chinese patriarchs saw to it that their girls and women would never 'run around.' "[77] One should add that footbinding was not a universal practice, either historically or throughout all ranks of Chinese society. Wherever it occurred, though, it maimed a woman significantly. Nonetheless, there is anthropological evidence that many Chinese women overcame their submissive role by cleverly manipulating gossip so that abusive husbands or mothers-in-law would lose face.[78] Still, until the Communist takeover, women had no place in the official political system and did very well if they merely outwitted it.

The Daoists were kinder to women and to the socially downtrodden generally. They were responsible for curtailing the murder of female infants by exposure, and their more positive regard for female symbols as examples of how the *Dao* worked upgraded femininity.[79] This was not an unmixed blessing, since it involved the "strength" of the one who was submissive and the manipulative power of the one who got herself mounted. Still, by bestowing feminine or maternal attributes on the *Dao* itself, the Daoists made femininity intrinsic to ultimate reality.[80] Analogously, the Buddhist symbolism for ultimate reality and the admission of women to the *sangha* were boons.

Case Study: Women Warriors and Shamans. In Maxine Hong Kingston's *The Woman Warrior,*[81] one glimpses how the Chinese sense of women echoed in the twentieth century. As a child, Kingston heard from her mother innumerable stories about Fa Mu Lan, the woman warrior. Stretching the imagination that would later make her a fine writer, she pictured what it would be like to be Fa.

It would be like a little girl coming upon a little hut in a forest and having the door open. An old man and woman would come out carrying bowls of rice, soup, and a branch of peaches. They would offer the little girl a share of their meal, she would refuse out of politeness, but they would press her to honor them with her presence. After lunch the three would go for a walk, the little girl enjoying the lovely mountains and pines, the old couple walking so lightly their feet would not disturb so much as a pine needle. The old couple would invite the little girl to spend the night and she, fearing the ghosts of the forest, would thankfully agree. Being tucked into a little bed just her width, the little girl would hear the old woman say, "Breathe evenly, so that you do not fall out." The old couple would then raise the roof over the girl's bed, and she would fall asleep watching the moon and the stars.

The next day, the old couple would invite the girl to stay with them, so that they could train her as a warrior. "What about my family?" the girl would ask. Stirring the water in a drinking gourd, the old man would show the little girl her family discussing the honor of their daughter being invited to become a warrior. So she would agree and begin her strict training.

First, she would learn to be quiet. The couple would leave her by streams, that she might watch the animals that came to drink. If she were not absolutely quiet, she would scare them away. With time the squirrels would come and bury their hoardings near the hem of her skirt, taking her for part of the landscape.

Next would come years of strengthening. With time her body would be strong enough to run with the deer, to leap twenty feet into the air, to control even the dilation of the pupils of her eyes. Then she would be ready for her first test, surviving alone in the forest. Fasting, she would find out how much her body could endure, how sharp her senses could become, the energy that comes when the body grows pure. She would grow so intimate with the forest a rabbit would toss himself into her fire, making himself her meal. The trial in the forest would end with a vision of a man and woman made of gold dancing together, like the axis of the earth's turning. They would be lion dancers, all light. They would be angels with high white wings. They would become so bright they would make the girl's head swim, and she would faint. Later she would be able to see ordinary people as golden dancers, understanding all the meanings of their

movements. When she awoke from her dreams, the old couple would feed her hot soup and ask for an account of her adventures. They would be satisfied, and so set her onto the next phase of her training.

This would involve learning all about dragons. Tigers connote adolescent power, but dragons are the source of a mature wisdom. The mountains are but the heads of dragons. A person climbing a mountain is like a bug moving along the forehead of a great beast. The quarries in the mountain show the dragon's veins and muscles. The minerals are its teeth and bones. The soil is its flesh and the trees are its hairs. One can hear its voice in the thunder and feel its breath in the winds.

The girl's training would conclude with the martial arts, and then she would return home to her family, whose need of a champion would have grown desperate. Indeed, so strong would be their desire for revenge on their enemies, they would carve in the girl's back a whole series of oaths. When she recovered from this operation, she would get ready for battle. A white horse would come into the courtyard, as a magical sign the drama was to begin. Donning her armor and mounting the horse, the girl would begin gathering her army. When her troops met marauders and gangs of criminals, she would lead them forward, screaming a mighty scream and swinging two great swords over her head. From her mouth would come rousing songs urging her troops to victory. Wherever they went order would be restored.

Finally they would come to the capital in Beijing and prepare to face the wicked emperor who had caused all the hardship in the provinces, all the hunger and conscription of sons. So quickly that it would be anticlimactic, the woman warrior and her husband (she would have married during the campaign and brought forth a child) would behead the emperor, clean out the palace, and set on the throne a peasant who would preside over a new social order. Then they would journey along the Long Wall, chasing back the Mongols.

Still, the woman warrior would not yet have avenged her brother, whose conscription had caused her family's great sorrow. To gain this revenge she would have to slay the fat baron who had led her brother away. Finally she would confront the baron, tearing off her shirt and showing him the oaths inscribed in her back. While he stared at her breasts, shocked that the famous warrior was a woman, she would slash him across the face and cut off his head.

Then she would ride back to her family, and the whole village would celebrate a great festival.

Kingston's girlhood fantasies drew on a great treasury of Chinese folktales. The dragons, tigers, golden dancers, and warriors with which her brain seethed had delighted Chinese children for centuries. However, she wanted to draw closer to actual history, so she began to collect stories of her mother's life; but all her efforts seemed only to tie her more tightly to myth.

Her mother had trained as a doctor in China in the 1920s. Before the family's flight in 1939, her mother had been a person of prestige. The laundry the mother ran in San Francisco's Chinatown was a great comedown from her previous station. At night she would tell the children stories of her training to be a doctor, which involved much more than battles with textbooks. It involved battles with ghosts, for even in her time Chinese doctors kept one foot in the shaman-ist tradition. Though the medical schools were open-ing to Western science, they had not completely closed the door on ghosts.

Kingston's mother was older than the other med-ical students, having lied about her age. She therefore made fun of their reports that a ghost had occupied an abandoned dormitory room. When the other students challenged her for affecting unconcern, she offered to spend the night in the ghost's room. Her account of that night burned itself into her daughter's mind, and so was reconstructed years later, as a young Chinese-American author tried to fix herself and her mother to paper. The ghost of her mother's medical training came to stand for all the ghosts transplanted people must exorcise. To become American and modern, Kingston felt she had to conquer the incubi of her unconscious, which said that in Chinese scales no fe-male, no matter how glorious a warrior, could ever balance a male.

Her mother was reading in the ghost's lair, slowly making herself sleepy. Her eyes drooped and she turned out the lamp. The darkness was so black it shocked her awake. All her nerves grew taut, like the time she had been caught in a snowstorm on a moun-tain. A rushing came at her from under the bed. Fear seized the soles of her feet, as something alive climbed the foot of the bed, rolled over her, and sat on her chest. It pressed against her, sapping her breath. "It is a sitting ghost," her mother thought. The more she pushed against it, the heavier it became. She grabbed the ghost's thick hair, which was like an animal's coat. She pinched its skin and tried to gouge its flesh with

her fingernails. She searched for its eyes, to stab them, but it seemed to have no eyes. So she grew discour-aged. The more she fought, the more her strength oozed away.

If only she could reach the knife lying on the lampstand. The ghost sensed her thoughts and spread itself over her arms. Rallying her spirit—the spirit that her daughter later found so indomitable—she be-gan to hector the ghost:

> You will not win, greedy ghost. There is no pain I cannot endure. This school has big jars of alcohol. I will get some alcohol, put it in my bucket, spread it across the floor, set fire to it, and burn you out. You have made a big mistake, greedy ghost. I will track you all over the school and burn you out. What an ugly ghost you are. You must be one of the lower spirits. Now I am going to chant tomorrow's lessons. There are no such things as ghosts.

When she awoke in the morning, Kingston's mother told her classmates of her adventure. After class she gathered them all in the ghost's room and began the great burnout. In twos and threes, they ar-ranged their buckets and jars of alcohol. Down poured the alcohol, up flared the flames, across went the rows of fire. Back and forth, they burned the room free of its ghost. "I told you, stupid ghost. Your end has come. There is no place for you in this school of medicine. You have to go—back to your dark haunts, back to the old villages, back to the depths of our minds."

When the smoke cleared and the mops stood idle, the room rested in peace. Under the bed where King-ston's mother had slept was a piece of wool, dripping with blood. They burned it in a bucket, and the stench was like a corpse exhumed for its bones.

In her inner rites of passage, Kingston could not tell which ghosts to laugh at, which ghosts to accredit. Her mother was a fabulous woman, a creature from a different age. Storyteller and shaman, warrior and healer, her mother was the tip of a mythic iceberg. How could a child of the new world manage such a mother's psyche? What could women's liberation say to a dragon ironing sheets?

Kingston's novel reminds the reader that none of us is only the person our social group reflects back to us. Each of us is also the person our imagination con-jures up: the hero riding forth in dreams of the day, the ghost-slayer battling in dreams of the night. Daoists like Zhuangzi who rode the winds knew much about the spirit of fancy. Healers who tapped pulses and drove off devils imagined a better balance for bodies and souls. Writing her way through the labyrinth to her self, Kingston put Chinese characters on American paper. Her fingers typed an IBM Selectric, but her mind reproduced images of tattered scrolls. Our character and our images imprint one another. Much more than what we eat, we are what we imagine. Because we can imagine more than our society assumes, we are always somewhat free.

Buddhist Social Influence. Buddhism downplayed social differences in another way. By teaching that the buddha-nature is present in all reality, it said that equality is more basic than social differentiation. The monastic *sangha* institutionalized this equality. It would be naive to think that background or wealth played no part in monks' evaluations of one another, but the *sangha* was governed by a monastic code that underplayed wealth and severely limited monks' possessions.

Furthermore, during many periods in Chinese history, the *sangha* was genuinely spiritual. That is, its actual raison d'être was religious growth. In such times, the only "aristocracy" was determined by spiritual insight. For instance, though Hui-neng, who became the sixth Chan patriarch, was born poor (and, according to legend, brought up illiterate), his spiritual gifts mattered far more. Because he was religiously apt, a reading of the Diamond Sutra opened his mind to the Buddha's light. After enlightenment, his peasant origins became insignificant.

The Buddhist *sangha* also improved the lot of women. It offered an alternative to early marriage and the strict confinement of the woman's family role. In the *sangha* a woman did not have full control of her life, but she did often have more peer support and female friendship than she could have in the outside world. In fact, Confucian traditionalists hated Buddhist nuns for their influence on other women. By telling women there were alternatives to wifely subjection, the nuns supposedly sowed seeds of discontent.[82] Besides the jealousy of their Confucian and Daoist rivals, then, and the sometimes warranted outrage at their extensive landholdings, the Buddhists suffered persecution because they offered attractive alternatives to traditional Chinese family and social structures. The government frequently forced monks and nuns into lay life during a time of purge to force them back into traditional social patterns.

Thus, although persecution was not the norm, Buddhists and other effective religionists often felt the controlling hands of the state. Formally, there was little independent religious authority. In times of peace, Buddhists and Daoists were left to go their own ways. When they perceived any threat, however, the rulers clamped down and made it clear that religion was a function of an integrated Chinese culture, not something outside the culture that could set itself up as the critic of culture. As the Daoist revolutionary sects showed, the rulers had good grounds for their fears.

As a result, Chinese religion was what C. K. Yang has called "diffused."[83] Stronger by far than any institutional achievements was a pervasive sense of the supernatural. In good part because it propped the state against the potential rebellion that Daoism and Buddhism housed, Confucianism became the state orthodoxy. Daoism and Buddhism, by contrast, were always somewhat heterodox.[84]

Among the common people, an important function of religion was to shore up received culture and authority. Apart from advanced positions in Daoist and Buddhist thought, religion did not liberate the individual. In this sense, Chinese religion broke neither the cosmological myth nor what we might call the social myth (conceiving of the political community as being divine). Both nature and the state (or the local duchy during the many periods of fragmentation) existed before the individual and predominated over him or her.

Consequently, China had little sense that the human mind makes its own reality—little enlightenment, in the European sense. Thus it remained closer to nature and more socially unified than later Western religious society did. The Chinese defined themselves by their land and their group. Happy to be the center of the earth, the Chinese Empire regarded all outsiders as barbarians and less than fully human. Millennia of living within a shared myth of nature and society had wrought so strong a cultural identity that this attitude was almost invincible. That was both Confucianism's triumph and its limitation.

Self

By our stress on the primacy of nature and society, we have indirectly suggested the Chinese view of the self. Nevertheless, the Chinese experimented with various conceptions of the self, just as they experimented with gunpowder, acupuncture, and pottery. As Donald Munro has shown,[85] axial Chinese thought, both Confucian and Daoist, wrestled with the possibility that human beings are essentially equal (at least male human beings). The effect of this belief on the hierarchical structure of Confucianism is complex, but the Chinese concepts of *ren* and *li* (goodness and propriety) indicate that the Chinese sensed that all people have something to share as a basis for mutual respect.

In the structure of society, then, the self had some right to acknowledgment. Despite one's subordination to the whole (or, in many cases, one's near slavery), the common person found in such an author as Mencius a champion of the self's essential goodness. Mencius counseled princes to take their people's welfare to heart; his counsel was clearly more than a pragmatic bit of advice about how to avoid rebellions.

Furthermore, the Confucians exercised considerable care on the self's education, at least for the middle and upper classes. Their major motivation seems to have been societal needs (as opposed to the self's intrinsic dignity), but by stressing character formation, the Confucians had to probe what the self's substance and dignity were. They decided, with considerable prodding from Confucius himself, that the paramount human faculty was the inner mind. If one could act from this inner mind with clarity and dispassion, one could act humanely and civilly. The core of the Confucian view of the self, therefore, was a certain rationalism. Confucianism did not stress speculative reason (that which gives rise to abstract theory), since Confucianism was not concerned with the human capacity to illumine or be illumined by the Logos of nature, but it did stress practical reason or prudence. Laying aside passion and prejudice (which required self-control), the good Confucian could hope with experience to discern the appropriate and harmonizing course of action.

Either through reflection on history or further rumination on the mind, the Confucians eventually linked practical reason with the ancients' *Dao*. It was clear from the myths handed down that the foremost ancestors were people of composed, effective good sense, which enhanced their subjects' common good and even prosperity. Because they were not venal or petty, the ancestors were able to lead by example—by radiating the power of *ren*.

On further reflection the Confucians confirmed that the zenith of human achievement (which Confucius himself later came to epitomize) was such inner-directed action. In other words, the ideal human spirit feared no outer laws or sanctions. It was autonomous—it delighted in the good for its own sake. Though Confucius and Mencius both longed for public office, a major reason that neither ever achieved it was that neither would compromise his standards. This

uncompromising integrity became a lesson to disciples for centuries. When a devout Confucian observed an inhumane ruler, he felt more pity than envy.

The Daoist Self.   The Daoists, who paid greater attention to the relationship between human consciousness and the cosmic *Dao,* produced a more paradoxical view of the self. They went against the Confucian standards of sagehood. Their masters were either cryptic eccentrics such as Zhuangzi or magical "immortals" possessing paranormal powers. The eccentrics' suspicion of human reason developed into a strong attack on logic and Confucian prudence. Logically, the *Zhuangzi*'s chapter on seeing things as equal suggests that the philosophical Taoists found conventional language and morality both arbitrary and relative.[86] Standard terms in Confucian discourse such as *great* and *small, good* and *bad* (which were also used in the Chinese linguistic analysis contemporary with Zhuangzi) turned out to be wholly relative. In fact, the Daoists cast doubt on the entire realm of discursive reason, which plods along from premise to premise and often misses the whole. If one could argue either side of a proposition, as lawyers always have tended to do, one clearly was not in the realm of ultimate concern.

For the philosophical Daoists, the realm of ultimate concern pivoted on *Dao.* They attempted to reach that realm by meditation and *wu-wei.* Consequently, they individualized the self more than the Confucians did. The Confucians, of course, realized that the talents of people differ, including the talent to reach the still inner reason from which humane action emanates. But the Daoists went beyond reason itself, encouraging each person to write his or her own script. What was important was that one write to the tune of the *Dao.* What the specific story was, how one chose to enact *Dao*'s inspiration, was secondary.

One of Daoism's greatest influences on Buddhism shows in Chan's acceptance of this individualism. Placing little stock in doctrines or formulas, the Chan master determined enlightenment by the pupil's whole bearing. The flash of an eye, the slash of a sword—a single gesture could indicate an enlightened being. One could even "slay the Buddha"—throw off all traditional guidance—if one had drawn near to the goal. To the unenlightened majority, one's actions and life would be strange. Quite literally, one would be eccentric. But if the *Dao* or buddha-nature really became the self's treasure, such eccentricity was but the near side of freedom.

The religious Daoists saw the self as a mortal physical body. Therefore, by the several "hygienic" regimes mentioned, they tried to prolong physical life. As a result, religious Daoists experimented with yogic practices, many of them in the vein of Indian *kundalini* or Tibetan Tantrism, both of which viewed the body as a repository of energy centers.[87] Depending on the particular interest of a religious Daoist group, the self might focus on breath or semen or some other quintessence.

Furthermore, most Daoists regarded the body as a warehouse of tiny gods, each in charge of a particular bodily part. In yogic exercise the adept was to visualize the god in charge of the spleen or the heart, and so gain health or blessing there. By their quests for immortality (in the sense of continued physical existence), then, the religious Daoists simultaneously underscored mortality and suggested that humans can defeat death. They did not distinguish an immaterial part of the self as the best candidate for such survival, but they did probe the relations between contemplative ecstasy and nature's apparent immortality.[88]

Karma and Selflessness.   Through Buddhism, China received a heavy dose of belief in karma. That was most effective in the popular Buddhist sects, among which Pure Land headed the list, but it entered the general religious stream, influencing even those who rarely participated in Buddhist rites. Karma, of course, meant that the self was immersed in a system of rewards and punishments. All its actions, good or bad, had their inevitable effects. Past lives pressed upon the present, and the present was but a prelude to a future life. In popular Buddhism, this doctrine encouraged a sort of bookkeeping. Sometimes quite formally, with ledgers and numbers, Buddhists tried to calculate their karmic situation and plan out a better destiny. More generally, the concept of karma prompted the belief that the self's present existence was a trial that would be evaluated at death. How heavily this sense of trial pressed on the average person is hard to say. Combined with the rather lurid popular pictures of the several hells awaiting the wicked, karma probably sparked its share of nightmares.

The philosophical and meditative Chinese Buddhist sects accepted the traditional doctrine of *anatman*. So, the Chinese thinkers who followed Madhyamika or Yogacara speculation agreed that emptiness or mind-only implied an effort to rout the illusion of a permanent personal identity. To grasp buddha-nature and join the dance of reality, the individual had to annihilate samsaric misconceptions about the substantiality of the self. The Chinese appear to have been more concrete than the Indians in such efforts. That is, where the Indians often reasoned over the self very closely, trying by dialectics to understand the illusion of selfhood, the Chinese tried to get the self to see reality's totality. Such seems to be the intent of pictures that Tiantai and Hua-yen masters drew, as well as the intent of the more radical techniques of Chan. Bodhidharma's "just sitting" and "wall gazing," for example, were exercises designed to make clear that only buddha-nature is real.

Overall, these various Chinese religious views of the self made for considerable confusion and complexity. Despite Buddhist philosophical influence, the average person through Chinese history apparently did not doubt the reality of his or her self. The educational and governmental establishments in most periods were shaped by the Confucian ideal of a sober, restrained, altruistic personality. One aimed at discipline and grace, at becoming a source of wisdom. The force that shaped the Confucian self was political in the sense that living together with family members and fellow citizens rather than in isolation was the norm. Only the few artistic and religious professionals seem to have broken this pattern. For them Daoist or Buddhist contemplative solitude stressed the mystery of the self insofar as the self was where the *Dao* or buddha-nature most directly manifested itself. According to Laozi, one would find *Dao* by shutting the "doors" (the senses) and going within.

The conceptions of the self that were presented in the three high traditions blurred when they entered the common culture. Most of the people came to Confucianism, Buddhism, or Daoism from its folk side. So the Confucian scholar became a sort of wonder worker, the Buddhist *bodhisattva* glamorized holiness, and the Daoist "immortal" represented victory over death. From the ancient spirit world ancestors and ghosts said that being a conscious self meant participating in a cosmos that was alive, a system of heavens and hells that impinged on the present.

Ultimate Reality

China was only holistically, diffusely, aware of sacred powers and ultimate reality. At most, certain high points of Buddhist and Daoist speculation, and to a lesser extent of Confucian speculation, indicated a monism—a single, impersonal principle considered the inmost reality of all beings. As we have seen, the first stirrings of religious consciousness probably apotheosized (deified) the clan founder, making him the "face" of overwatching Heaven. As nature became better understood, however, heaven became less personal, more the general symbol of the vast sky. Earth, in association with a maternal *Dao,* took on overtones of a Great Mother, but with less of the humanity and intimacy that other cultures developed.

For most Chinese throughout history, nature has been the effective divinity. In other words, nature and divinity have run together. The physical world itself was something sacred and mysterious. This world intimated something beyond itself that was grasped by those who saw nature with mystic clarity, but the majority at best sensed this something beyond only vaguely. To sense clearly the *Dao* that cannot be named, one must reject the adequacy of all things nameable. Realizing that water, air, fire, wood, earth, yang, yin, and so on, do not explain the totality of heaven and earth, the mind senses that the ultimate is of a different order. It is without the limitations that characterize all the primal elements. As such, it must dwell in obscurity, too full or great or bright for mere human intelligence. Philosophical Daoism and Buddhism sometimes intimated that line of thought.

A muted reference to ultimacy probably plays in Confucius' laconic references to heaven. For the most part, the Master refrained from speculating about heavenly things. Like Alexander Pope, he believed that "the proper study of man is man." But Confucius' reverence toward the sacrifice to heaven suggests that, had such a modern Western notion been available to him, he would not have explained the sacrifice as a humanistic means of social bonding. Rather, he probably saw a link between the ancients' *Dao* and the way of sacred nature, and so viewed the sacrifice as humanity's chance to align itself with the power that most mattered, the power behind all life and all things.

Confucius made heaven the ultimate sanction for his ethical program. He believed that those who pay full court to the stove have no recourse when they fail. The true judge of success and failure must be more stable than a human creation. Against the Daoist belief that heaven treats all creatures as straw dogs, Confucius believed that heaven is the great champion of *yi* (justice). We go well beyond Confucius himself if we work this commitment to heaven into a theology or a theodicy (a vindication of God's justice). Clearly, however, the Confucians justified their calls to virtue by appealing to suprahuman standards. Indeed, the depth of Confucius' analysis of what is necessary for a

Figure 26 *Lohan* (arhat), *Liaojin dynasty, 900–1200* C.E. *Pottery with three-color glaze; 40 in. high. This figure, found in the hills south of Beijing, has his hands in the* dhyana mudra, *a posture signifying deep meditation. The individuality of the* arhat's *quest for personal salvation (in contrast to the* bodhisattva's *concern for all beings) leads to a quite distinct portrayal. The Nelson–Atkins Museum of Art, Kansas City, Missouri (Nelson Fund).*

full humanity makes his overall program an invitation to explore the sacredness of the mystery of human potential.

Buddhism, of course, addressed ultimacy more squarely. In the philosophical mainstream, nirvana, buddha-nature, Suchness, or emptiness held sway. This mainstream suggested that the ultimate is the interconnected whole. For the idealists, the accent was on the mentality of the ultimate. In their view, the many things that we perceive by sense are fraudulent because only spirit or mind finally makes something be. For the less idealistic schools, material things and ideas were equally fraudulent. To accept the apparent plurality of either physical nature or consciousness was the folly of an unenlightened mind. The idealists were less concerned with physical nature than the nonidealists. By calling all dharmas empty, the followers of Madhyamika went directly to the rather radical (and potentially worldly or incarnational) point of the wisdom-that-has-gone-beyond. By contrast, those who followed Yogacara idealism stayed apart from the physical world mentally.

In popular Buddhism, such as Pure Land, some divinities had quite precise features. In its popular religion, then, Chinese Buddhism offered an access to aspects of ultimate reality that Confucianism barely indicated. (Daoism is more complicated: The *Dao* was a mother, and religious sects made Laozi into a cosmic principle.) The cult of Confucius himself qualifies this judgment somewhat, but overall the Buddhists offered the most personal concepts of divinity.

The beliefs of philosophical and religious Daoists, of course, must be distinguished. As we have seen, the philosophical Daoists, following Zhuangzi and Laozi, fixed on the cosmic Way. Often they seem to have invested it with divine attributes. For the philosophers, *Dao* was the source, the ultimate power, the model, and the prime value of the world. Inspiration from it, communion with it, and direction by it were the ways to wisdom, wholeness, and fulfillment.

Nonetheless, despite intuitions in Laozi that *Dao* is beyond the physical world, Daoist philosophers tended to equate *Dao* with nature. The naturalistic symbolism they preferred suggests this, as does their unconcern with immortality or an afterlife. If *Dao* had been independent of nature, union with *Dao* should have generated thoughts about escaping the cycle of birth and death. In India, for instance, the *nirguna* (unmanifest) Brahman and the Buddhist ultimate led to doctrines of *moksha* and nirvana as human release. For Zhuangzi and Laozi, natural harmony in the present was all-important, and they paid little heed to future enjoyment of some otherworldly states. Consequently, the divinity of *Dao* was preeminently the undergirding and direction it gave cosmic nature.

Reaching back to prehistory, the religious Daoists conceived of a pantheon of divine forces, often giving them picturesque names and features. Furthermore, the goal of religious Daoist practices was to prolong life, and so religious Daoists ventured into alchemy and yoga, as well as voyages to the Lands of the Blessed (the Immortals). What they shared with their philosophical counterparts, however, was a characteristically Chinese concern with the body. Their ideal was not an extinction of suffering humanity in nirvana, not a release in *moksha*, but a consolidation of vital powers so as to resist death. Their divinities, consequently, were gods who could help this process, or "immortals" (who probably spanned the often narrow gap between saints and gods) who had successfully accomplished such a consolidation. In either case, they offered followers encouragement and models.

How did Chinese divinity appear in the popular amalgamation? Through ritualistic, emotional, and shamanic points of entry.[89] The prevailing popular mind, which was primarily interested in warding off evil fortune and attracting good, and the great importance of ancestor veneration, gave ultimate reality a rainbow of colors. Ceremonies at the family hearth reaffirmed the clan by acknowledging the reality of its ancestors. Ceremonies in the fields, for building a new dwelling or for curing someone seriously ill, brought people face to face with spooky forces of life, luck, and disease. Shamans and mediums were the key figures, contacting spirits and ancestral souls. Diviners gave advice and told fortunes. The average person gathered talismans and totems, but also Buddhist and Daoist saints. The educated people patronized Confucius, but even they were open to other sacred figures who offered help. To say the least, then, the Chinese religious mind was syncretistic, and the study of folk religion, as recent studies suggest,[90] has to be very comprehensive.

However, most characteristic of China is its commitment to physical nature. It shares this with Japan and with many ancient peoples, but China most directed its various intimations of divinity toward nature. The *Dao*, the Chinese buddha-nature, the field of spirits—these far outweighed personal qualities. The Chinese divinity was the arc of the sky, the pulse of the earth, the life force itself.

SUMMARY: THE CHINESE CENTER

The clan and the Way held life together for most Chinese. The clan was the defining social reality, the psychological milieu in which the individual found his or her identity. Somewhat parallel to the way that Indian caste positioned a person in Hindu society, the clan positioned a person in Chinese society. However, the Chinese clan had a more pronounced historical dimension. The ancestors that one venerated in the household rites formed a golden chain back to better times. For the people as a whole, the best of times were the ages when the fabled nobility that Confucius and Mencius venerated had walked the land and embodied virtue. The way that they had lived was the benchmark against which traditional China measured itself. Their grace and reverence in executing the liturgical rites, their sense of restraint and propriety, and their freedom from all venality defined what humaneness or full development could be.

The Way therefore was something objective. One only walked it confidently, unswervingly, if one embraced it from the heart, but its general import was as much natural and social as personal. It was the way of the cosmos as well as the way of the clan. It moved in the heavens and the depths as well as in the individual heart. And it was a way that produced balance, harmony, and prosperity. When the yang and the yin forces were both given their due, the Way shone forth splendidly. When the people followed the lead of a virtuous leader and themselves lived virtuously, the mandate of heaven manifestly was in good hands. In office, the Chinese tried to bureaucratize the Way. What stability persisted through their millennia of political upheavals was in good part due to the consistency of the Confucian civil service. Taking pride in their high culture, traditional Chinese accounted themselves the center of the world. The *Dao* that formed their ancient culture ruled everywhere, but theirs was the land that had been most blessed with eyes to see and ears to hear.

In people's retirement, Daoist and Buddhist insights gave both the clan and the Way their poetry and metaphysics. If one backed away from the bureaucratic mind, accepted the lure of Zhuangzi and Laozi, the Way took on sharper angles, more vivid hues. It remained remarkably realistic, determinedly focused upon the commonsensical order of things. But it showed intriguing wrinkles of humor, elusive bends of fillip and paradox. So Zhuangzi carries across the thousands of years, speaking playfully to any generation that has kept some wit.[91] So Laozi remains a quite relevant political study, challenging all our established views of power and virtue. How, in fact, does the suc-

cessful natural organism survive and prosper? What, in reality, are the evolutionary and ecological virtues? As a matter of experience, how lasting or thorough is the victory that does not conquer the enemy's heart? In the best of personal times, when one does hear the Way in the morning, what is the contentment for which one would willingly die?

These are the sorts of questions that make a culture profound, concerned with ultimate realities or religion. Without them, a people's rites and social arrangements lack any special distinction, are matters of instinct and pheromones as much as matters distinctively human. China was fortunate in having Buddhists and Daoists who kept these questions throbbing. Through their influence on art, philosophy, and social ethics, they made the Way properly empty. Emptying the Chinese mind of the excesses to which its Confucian practicality tended, Daoists and Buddhists gave this great people inner space. So Chinese landscape paintings can haunt the beholder as few other artworks. So a lonesome, allusive poetry let thousands of gentlemen give voice to their inmost feelings.

This lonely, allusive persona sits awkwardly atop the teeming world of Chinese politics and clan intrigues, yet it does seem to distinguish the Chinese center. Something stoic and clear-eyed keeps the Chinese world less tangled than the Indian, the Chinese atmosphere less steamy. Those pictures of snowy mountain fastnesses can exert undue influence, but most of Chinese wisdom seems astringent and disciplined. Thus the Chan clarity of gaze, control of the emotions, and focused wholeness seem of a piece with the scenes of mountain snow. Thus silence seems quintessentially Chinese, a direct "word" from the center.

There is much irony in this word, much well-tested humor. The Way that collects us, giving us our vision and our depth, turns out to be sportive and unpredictable. To the sober-sided it is quite regular, but the sober-sided are more mummified than enlightened. To the sage, each day is fresh, each particular fights generalization. The sage does not master life by formulas and bureaus. The sage does not master life at all. Mastery is really discipleship, docility and constant attention. When a docile, empty mind meets a fluid, allusive way, things fall apart. There is no center fixed or certain. There is only a center moving, always being re-created, ever arranging itself in new yet ancient patterns, like a kaleidoscope. The way that can be told is not the real way. The real way is compressed in a glance, hinted in a gesture, sounded in the pure tones of an emptied life.

Discussion Questions

1. Sketch the outline of axial Chinese religion in terms of *Dao*.

2. What are the positive aspects of Chinese ritual propriety *(li)*?

3. What are the negative aspects of *wu-wei*?

4. Why were the ancestors such a potent symbol in popular Chinese religion?

5. Explain some of the likely assumptions and dynamics of Chinese divination.

6. If you meditate on the practice of foot binding, how do you picture Chinese social arrangements?

7. Why did philosophical Daoism long exist alongside religious Daoism, and how can one reconcile their different views of immortality?

8. Describe some of the leading motifs of Chinese aesthetics.

9. What were some of the most important influences that Buddhism had on China?

10. Is the Confucian hierarchical view of reality viable in the modern era? Why?

11. What did Laozi learn from the valley and the female?

12. What sort of a divinity did Confucius become?

13. Why did Mao Zedong reject the Confucian classics?

14. Why was China so taken with geomancy?

15. How did the religion of Chinese merchants differ from the religion of Chinese peasants?

Key Terms

Confucian classics: Confucius himself drew on several sources that became classical expressions of the golden age that he used to ground and illustrate his teachings. These sources included the *Book of History (Shu Jing),* documents purporting to record the words and deeds of ancient leaders; the *Book of Songs (Shi Jing)* an anthology of lyrics from the early feudal states and the court of Zhou; the *Book of Changes (Yi Jing),* a manual for divination; the *Springs and Autumns (Chunqui),* the annals of the state of Lu; and the *Canons of Ritual and Protocol (Li Jing),* three works on *li* (protocol). In addition, the Confucians came to revere four works as canonical expressions of the wisdom that the Master himself had inspired: the *Analects (Lun Yu),* sayings and dialogues of Confucius; the *Great Learning (Da Xue),* a short study of how cultivating perfection can contribute to the ordering of society; the *Doctrine of the Mean (Zhung Yung),* a somewhat metaphysical treatment of how the moral person is at the center of the universe; and the *Book of Mencius (Meng Zi),* a collection of sayings and dialogues of the foremost exponent of Confucian thought. Both the *Great Learning* and *Doctrine of the Mean* are excerpts from part (the *Li Ji*) of the *Canons on Ritual and Protocol.* Collectively, these nine works constituted the literary corpus that the Confucian literati strove to master.

Dao ("dow"): a Chinese term for the cosmic or moral Way or Path. Daoism most directly focused on understanding the Way and gaining harmony with it, but Confucianism also was interested in the Way, meaning both the traditions of the wise men of yore and the patterns encoded in nature. The *Dao* is perhaps the closest equivalent in native Chinese religion to the Western notions of God, the Logos, and the Law of Nature. Laozi spoke of the Way that was known, but also of the *Dao* bound to be unknown. The movement of the *Dao* explained the movement of the ten thousand things making up creation, and the movement of the *Dao,* as the philosophical Daoists interpreted it, was a not-doing *(wu-wei).* The female, infant, and valley better exemplified the Way than the male, the adult, and the mountain. Water was a better exemplar than rock, the uncarved block better than the finished piece of sculpture.

feng-shui: Chinese geomancy; the art of locating favorable sites for buildings, graves, and other constructions. *Feng-shui* assumes a premodern worldview in which directions, astral influences, the winds, and the waters are considered to have (animistic) powers significant for human beings' well-being, both bodily and spiritual. In effect, it is a divination of the forces, auras, and spirits of the lay of a particular land, to assure people considering inhabiting that land the most favorable siting of themselves (their beings as well as their buildings) upon it.

folk religion: the beliefs and practices of the common people, in contrast to the views of the intelligentsia and religious officials. Folk religion, virtually by definition, is somewhat inarticulate and unreflective, but it may be no less rich or even sophisticated for that. It embraces the cult of the saints honored in a given religious tradition, the full round of paraliturgical devotions and religious practices, and the simple everyday acts of piety, prayers of petition, and other practices that get unlettered believers through the day. Some generations ago folk religion received rather short shrift from scholars, who deprecated it as untutored, but with the advent of anthropological investigations many students of religion have realized that peasant ways often house amazingly persistent and profound views of both the particular religious tradition in which they occur and the basic problematic of human existence that religious mythology regularly has kept lively, persuasive, and beguiling.

li: the Confucian term for propriety, ritual, protocol, etiquette. *Li* was the virtue that ideally presided over social interactions, the gentleman's participation in public life and external affairs. It required knowledge of the traditional ceremonies and mores, discipline, and grace. Probably the origins of *li* lay in ancient ideas about ritual, especially that surrounding the king. If such ritual were properly performed, it was thought bound, or at least very likely, to bring such good effects as bountiful harvests and social rest. *Li* tended to encourage politeness and social sensitivity, including a keen awareness of the different social ranks. It supported a somewhat formal persona, with considerable care given to preserving dignity, appearance, and face. At its best, when fully animated by *ren,* it suggested that all public living ought to be artful and sacramental.

ren: the primary Confucian virtue of humaneness. *Ren* signifies human nature as it ought to be, full of fellow-feeling or even love. It is what makes social life attractive, what long study and practice ought to develop. Confucians have seen ritual, filial piety, and the other important virtues (powers of the mature character) as expressions of *ren* or ways to build up *ren.* Insofar as *ren* has run low, Confucianism has been liable to legalism, formalism, pedantry. *Ren* therefore has been the spirit without which much of the Confucian teaching would have been empty letters. The Mas-

ter himself probably reached the ideal measure of *ren* when, at seventy, what the Way (the call to live humanely) required and what his own heart desired were one.

reverence for ancestors: The traditional Chinese did not worship their ancestors, but they did reverence them greatly. Just as young people were to reverence their elders (who had not only given the young people existence but had lived long enough to be wise), so the present generation was to reverence its forebears. The previous generations had accomplished the essential task of handing on life and keeping humanity in existence. Moreover, in many periods of Chinese history the past seemed a more ideal time than the present, so one's ancestors were assumed to have been more fully human. Something sacred attached to the ties between the present generation and the past. The obligation of the present generation to keep its ancestors in mind, to offer them material gifts in token of a spiritual gratitude and remembrance, was so strong that it was a major reason for having children. People who did not procreate failed to supply a crucial link in the chain of remembrance. Certainly, this Chinese attitude expresses close ties with nature and nature's mysteries of death and birth. Certainly, it also bespeaks a profound appreciation of how much the present depends upon the past—of how formative tradition has to be. But it also represents a deliberate choice, best articulated by the Confucians, to keep alive a sense of history. Those who ignored the past, in the specific form of their ancestors, would be bound to live truncated lives. They would not appreciate the mysterious depths out of which their own flesh, to say nothing of their culture, had arisen. It was not superstition but a profound humanism that moved the best Confucians to place veneration of elders and ancestors at the center of Chinese social life. They were convinced that those who contemplated the wonders of family history and lineage would be little inclined to deface their own lives—to shame their ancestors and call into question the worth of their having passed human existence along to subsequent generations.

wu-wei: Daoist not-doing or active-inaction. *Wu-wei* epitomizes how the philosophical Daoists thought the Way acted. It shone in the water that wore away rock, the cook who realized the best way to prepare fish was to stir them as little as possible. The infant who wrapped the adult household around its finger, the ruler who got others to do his will by silent example or subtle persuasion—both were good imitators of the *Dao*. Opposed to *wu-wei* was *ba* (force). *Ba* might win temporary victories, but in the long run it was bound to bring violent reactions and so do more harm than good. Laozi and Zhuangzi urged the Chinese to return to simpler days, when there were fewer laws, fewer criminals, less education, less sophistication, and more simple vigor.

yang: the Chinese principle of nature that is positive, light, dry, and male. Yin-yang theory was a dualism that conceived of natural processes as shaped by the relative proportions of male and female principles each contained. Yang usually was considered the positive force and yin the negative. These judgments should not be taken in a moral sense, but rather like the plus and minus poles of a battery. Each was equally necessary for life and the ongoing circuits of the cosmos.

yin: the Chinese principle of nature that is negative, dark, wet, and female. In diet, ritual paraphernalia, and the like, yin had to be coordinated with yang, if one were to get health and good fortune. Yin-yang theory correlated with astrology, geomancy, exorcism, and natural philosophy. It had ties with theories of divination and functioned as a protoscience. The Chinese search for harmony and to hold opposites in creative tension meant that neither yin nor yang ought ever achieve a definite triumph. Both were to be accepted and cultivated, although patriarchal China preferred the yang side.

CHAPTER 6

JAPANESE RELIGION

Torii: Gate to Shinto shrines

HISTORY

The Ancient-Formative Period

According to ethnologists, the people we now call the Japanese perhaps are a mixture of an indigenous people (the Ainu) and peoples from the Asian mainland and the southern islands. This mixture is one clue to the composite character of Japanese religion as well as to the general tolerance that has historically marked Japanese culture. The native religion goes back to the Japanese prehistoric period, which lasted until the early centuries of the Common Era. Clay figurines that archeologists have excavated from this earliest Jomon period indicate a special concern with fertility.[1] As the hunting and gathering culture of the earliest period gave way to agriculture and village settlement, religious practices came to focus on agricultural festivals, revering the dead, and honoring the leaders of the ruling clans. According to the primitive mythology, which existed long before the written versions that date from the eighth century, such leaders were descendants of the deities—once again a version of sacred kingship.

However, the mythology and cult surrounding the ruling family were but part of the earliest Japanese religion. Research suggests that in the villages outside the leading families' influence, people probably conceived of a world with three layers. The middle is the realm of humans, where we have a measure of control, but the realms above and below, which spirit beings control, are far larger. The kami dwell in the high plain of heaven and are the objects of cultic worship; the spirits of the dead live below, condemned to a filthy region called Yomi.[2] (In some versions, the dead go to a land beyond the sea.) Apparently Yomi was especially important for the aristocrats' cult, which suggests not only a connection between folk and imperial religion but also indicates why Shinto came to stress ritual purification, especially from polluting contacts with the dead.

The Kami. The kami represented the sacred power involved in the principal concerns of prehistoric Japanese religion (kingship, burial of the dead, and ritual purification).[3] They were rather shadowy figures or spiritual forces who were wiser and more powerful than humans. From time to time, kami would descend to earth, especially if a human called them down and helped them assume a shape (in their own world the kami were shapeless). They were called down by means of *yorishiro*—tall, thin objects that attracted the kami. Pine trees and elongated rocks were typical *yori-*

Japanese Religion: Twenty-five Key Dates

ca. 4500–250 B.C.E.	Jomon Period: Hunting and Gathering
ca. 660	Jimmu, Traditional First Emperor
ca. 250 B.C.E.–250 C.E.	Yayoi Period: Blending of Ethnic Groups
5 C.E.	Building of National Shrine at Ise
285	Confucianism Introduced
ca. 550	Buddhism Introduced
594	Buddhism Proclaimed State Religion
645	Taika Reform Remodels Japan on Chinese Lines
712–720	Completion of Shinto Chronicles
805–806	Introduction of Tendai and Shingon Buddhist Sects
ca. 890	Cultural Renaissance: Novels, Landscape Painting, Poetry
1175–1253	Pure Land, Zen, and Nichiren Buddhist Sects Arise
1333	Civil War
1549	Francis Xavier Arrives in Japan
1600–1867	Tokugawa Era: Confucianism Prospers, Buddhism Controlled by State, Japan Closed to Foreigners
1646–94	Basho, Leading Buddhist Poet
1650	Beginning of Popular Literary Culture
1730–1801	Motoori Norinaga, Leader of Shinto Renaissance
1850	New Religions Emerge
1854	Commodore Perry Forces Trade with West
1868–71	Meiji Persecution of Buddhism; Shinto Brought under State Control
1894–1905	Successful Wars with China and Russia
1899	Religion Forbidden in Public Schools
1939	Department of Education Controls All Religious Bodies
1945	Japan Surrenders in World War II; Shinto Disestablished

	SHINTO	BUDDHISM
Main Source	Indigenous Japanese culture	Chinese schools
Main Ideas	Holiness of nature Importance of purity and beauty Integrity of Japanese people (as a whole and in clans)	Emptiness Meditation Monasticism Significance of death
Influence	Nationalistic ideology National mythology Aesthetics Marriage ceremony Folk arts	Funerals Discipline Philosophy Meditation Devotional faith

shiro, and they suggest that the kami had phallic connotations. To a lesser extent, rocks of female shape also attracted the kami, and relics from the great tombs of the third and fourth centuries—a profusion of mirrors, swords, and curved jewels—suggest that these artifacts also drew the kami. (Such objects became part of the imperial regalia as well as the special objects of veneration in shrines.) There were also kami on earth, and revered ancestors who assumed a status like that of kami, so not all kami came from heaven.

Because the kami held key information about human destiny, it was important to call them down into human consciousness. That occurred through the kami's possession of shamans or mediums. Most of the early shamans *(miko)* were women, and they functioned in both the aristocratic and the popular cults. Ichiro Hori has shown that female shamans persisted throughout Japanese history.[4] The *miko* were quite important to society. They tended to band together and travel a circuit of villages, primarily to act as mediums for contact with the dead but also to serve as diviners and oracles. They also ministered to spiritual and physical ills, which popular culture largely attributed to malign spirits. As a result, the *miko* developed both a poetic and a pharmacological lore. In composing songs and dances to accompany their ministrations, they contributed a great deal to the formation of traditional Japanese dance, theater, balladry, and puppetry.

Essentially, the kami were the sacral forces of nature and impressive aspects of social life. They impressed the Japanese ancient mind, as they impressed the ancient mind elsewhere, by their striking power. Sensitive individuals could contact them, but the kami remained rather wild and unpredictable. Later, Shinto shrines stressed natural groves of tall trees and founders of religious cults were often possessed by spirits. As the early mythology shows, however, the kami remained in charge.

As the eighth-century chronicles, the *Kojiki* and *Nihon-shoki,* have preserved it, Japanese mythology adapted to Chinese influences early on. For example, redactors regularly changed the Japanese sacred number 8 to the Chinese sacred number 9,[5] and they were influenced by the Chinese cosmogonic myths. The result was a creation account in which the world began as a fusion of heaven and earth in an unformed, egg-shaped mass that contained all the forces of life. Gradually the purer parts separated and ascended to heaven, while the grosser portions descended and became the earth.

Shinto Mythology. Chinese influence disappears when the chronicles come to the myths of the kami's origin and to the related question of how the Japanese islands came to be. The first kami god was a lump that formed between heaven and earth; he established the first land. Six generations later, the divine creator couple, Izanagi and Izanami, arose by spontaneous generation. They married and by sexual union produced the many kami, including the Japanese islands.

For instance, heaven commanded Izanagi and Izanami to solidify the earth, which hitherto had been only a mass of brine. Standing on a bridge between heaven and the briny mass, they lowered a jeweled spear and churned the brine. When they lifted the spear, drops fell, solidified, and became the first island. The couple descended to this island, erected a heavenly pillar (the typical shamanistic connector to heaven), and proceeded to procreate. The account of their interaction is both amusing and revealing:

> Now the male deity turning by the left, and the female deity by the right, they went around the pillar of the land separately. When they met together on one side, the female deity spoke first and said: "How delightful! I have met with a lovely youth." The male deity was displeased, and said: "I am a man, and by right should have spoken first. How is it that on the contrary thou, a woman, should have been the first to speak? This was unlucky. Let us go round again." Upon this the two deities went back, and having met anew, this time the male deity spoke first, and said: "How delightful! I have met a lovely maiden."[6]

This account influences the Shinto wedding ceremony to this day, tabooing the bride from speaking first (under pain of perhaps having a deformed child).

In tortuous logic, the myth describes the fate of the first two. Izanami died giving birth to fire, and Izanagi followed her to the underworld. Izanagi then produced many deities in an effort to purify himself of the pollution of the underworld. By washing his left eye he produced the sun goddess **Amaterasu**, and by washing his right eye he produced the moon god. When he washed his nose he produced the wind god Susanoo. In this story of descent to the underworld and divine creation, scholars see an expression of the aboriginal Japanese rites of purification and fears of death. The sun goddess, who became the supreme being of the Yamato clan, a powerful Japanese family, and the focus of the clan's cultic center at Ise, presided over the land of fertility and life. Opposing her was the domain of darkness and death. Rituals were performed to keep darkness and death from afflicting sunny fertility—harvests, human procreation, and so on. As Izanagi purified himself of death by plunging into the sea, the Japanese throughout their history have used

salt as a prophylactic. People still scatter it around the house after a funeral, place it at the edge of a well, set a little cake of it by a door jamb, and even scatter it before the bulging sumo wrestler as he advances toward his opponent.[7]

In subsequent myths, Amaterasu and Susanoo have numerous adventures arising from the antagonism between the life-giving sun and the withering wind. These figures also demonstrate the Trickster and noble sides of the divinity found in nature. Susanoo, the Trickster, committed "heavenly offenses" that later became a focus of ritual purification: He broke the irrigation channels for the imperial rice field that Amaterasu had set up; he flayed a piebald colt and flung it into the imperial hall; and, worst of all, he excreted on the goddess's imperial throne. Unaware, she "went straight there and took her seat. Accordingly, the Sun Goddess drew herself up and was sickened."[8] These offenses reflect practical problems of an agricultural society (respecting others' fields), cultic problems (a sacrificial colt was probably supposed to be of a single color and not be flayed), and speculation on the tension between divine forces of nature.

From these and other materials in the earliest chronicles, it is clear that the ancient-formative period of Japanese history centered on natural forces, some of which were anthropomorphized. In the background were the kami, whom we may consider as foci of divine power. Anything striking or powerful could be a kami. To relate themselves to the natural world, the early Japanese told stories of their love for their beautiful islands (worthy of being the center of creation) and of the divine descent of their rulers. The fact that Amaterasu is a sun goddess suggests an early matriarchy, as does the fact that kingship on the Chinese model of a rule possessing the mandate of heaven (rather than by heredity) only came with the Taika reforms of 645 C.E. Shinto maintained the divinity of the emperor until the mid-twentieth century, when the victorious Western Allies forced the emperor to renounce his claims.

Buddhism

Buddhism infiltrated Japan by way of Korea during the second half of the sixth century C.E. It first appealed to members of the royal court as a possible source of blessing and good fortune. Also, it carried overtones of Chinese culture, which had great prestige. The Japanese rulers, in the midst of trying to solidify their country, thought of the new religion as a possible

means, along with Confucian ethics, for unifying social life. So, during the seventh century, emperors
built shrines and monasteries as part of the state apparatus. In the eighth century, when the capital was at
Nara, the Hua-yen school (called Kegon in Japan) established itself and began to exert great influence. The
government ideologues expediently equated the emperor with the Hua-yen Buddha Vairocana, and they
made the Hua-yen realm of "dharmas not impeding
one another"[9] a model for Japanese society. Kegon has
survived in Japan to the present day and now has about
500 clergy and 125 temples.

The Medieval-Elaborative Period

Most commentators consider the move of the capital
from Nara to Kyoto in 794 a pivotal event. Indeed, the
Heian era (794–1185), when Mount Hiei in Kyoto was
home to as many as 30,000 monks,[10] was a golden age
whose memorials may still be found in Kyoto. Politically, Japan passed from a centralized bureaucracy to
feudalism. While the imperial court still held nominal
power, in fact a few aristocrats, especially those from
the Fujiwara clan, were responsible for the main political initiatives. With the loosening of centralized authority, Buddhists were freer to innovate, although
they had to keep good relations with the leading clans.

The first decades of the Heian era saw the rise of
two new schools of Japanese Buddhism, Tendai and
Shingon. Dengyo Daishi (767–822), the founder of
Tendai, went to China to learn about the latest forms
of Buddhist doctrine and practice. Upon returning to
Japan, he established a new monastic foundation on
Mount Hiei. The school that Dengyo Daishi founded
derived from the Chinese Dien dai sect. Dien dai
taught a quite syncretistic outlook, laying special
importance on the Lotus Sutra. It was especially
interested in joining philosophical speculation to
meditation. Dengyo Daishi broadened the syncretistic
outlook by adding moral discipline and ritual to the
program he wanted his monks to follow. He also gave
Tendai a nationalistic aspect, believing that Buddhist
practice would help protect the Japanese nation. The
result was a well-rounded school in which just about
any traditional Buddhist interest could be pursued.
Dengyo Daishi struggled with the government to gain
recognition for his group, but after his death his followers got a full go-ahead and could ordain monks. It
is difficult to overemphasize the importance of the
establishment of Tendai on Mount Hiei, because from

its ranks in the Kamakura era (1185–1333) came the
leaders of the Pure Land, Zen, and Nichiren sects.

Shingon was founded by the monk Kobo Daishi
(774–835), who, like Dengyo Daishi, went to China to
find fresh inspiration. The term *Shingon* derived from
the Chinese term for *mantra,* and the school that Kobo
Daishi established in Japan amounted to a branch of
Buddhist tantra. Through elaborate rituals, Shingon
expressed deep metaphysical notions thought capable
of achieving through cult a great, magical power. Kobo
Daishi was a talented writer, so he was able to furnish
Japan a full manual on esoteric Buddhism. Through
his influence, mantras, mandalas, and *mudras* (ritual
gestures) became influential religious vehicles. As
well, they made a great impact on Japanese iconography and fine arts.

Both Tendai and Shingon were open to outside
influences, so during the Heian period Shinto and
Buddhism came into closer contact than previously
had been the rule. For instance, there arose numerous
jinguji (shrine-temples), where Buddhist rituals took
place within the precincts of a Shinto shrine. Relatedly, the idea arose that the kami were manifestations
of the Buddhist *bodhisattvas.* Until the beginning of
the Meiji era (1868), when there was an official reform
aimed at cleansing Shinto, Tendai and Shingon
fostered such a syncretism between Shinto and
Buddhism.

Last, we should note that during the Heian era
there arose the conviction that Buddhism was bound
to devolve through several ages (on the order of the
Indian kalpas), and that the present age was the lowest—a time when religious practice was especially difficult. This eventually laid the foundation for the rise
of various savior figures during the Kamakura era—
for example, Amida Buddha, the merciful figure who
presided in the Western Paradise so eagerly pursued by
the Pure Land sects.[11]

Kamakura Buddhism.[12]   In many scholars' opinion,
the rise of the Pure Land, Nichiren, and Zen Buddhist
sects during the Kamakura dynasty (1185–1333) produced one of Japan's most distinctive religious
achievements. Pure Land Buddhism, which focused on
Amida, the *bodhisattva* of light, became the most influential form of devotional Buddhism. It was popularized by evangelists such as Ippen (1239–1289), who
encouraged songs and dances in honor of Amida.
Ippen taught that devotion to Amida and the holy
realm where Amida presided was "the timely teaching"

Figure 27 *Amida Buddha, late Heian to Kamakura dynasty, twelfth–thirteenth century. Gilded wood; 9 ft., 2 in. high. Amida Buddha, who presides over the Western Paradise, is shown here in a posture of deep meditation. The Nelson–Atkins Museum of Art, Kansas City, Missouri (Nelson Fund).*

suitable for a degenerate age. By practicing the ***nembutsu*** or recitation of "homage to Amida Buddha," followers could gain great merit or even full salvation (entry to the Pure Land). This prescription was simple, practicable, and available to all. It did not require deep philosophy or meditation, simply faith. The laity found Ippen's message very appealing.

As one of Ippen's devotional works makes clear, he encouraged followers of Pure Land with a steady stream of moralistic advice. Verse after verse, the work tells devotees to adore the Buddha, not ignore the Buddha's virtue, revere the three jewels, not forget the power of faith, devoutly practice the *nembutsu,* forget other religious practices, trust the law of love, not denounce the creeds of other people, promote a sense of equality, and avoid discriminatory feelings. They

were to awaken a sense of compassion, be mindful of the sufferings of other people, cultivate amiability, not display an angry countenance, preserve a humble manner, and not arouse a spirit of arrogance. It is as though Ippen found all the traits of a good character to flow from faith in Amida. Were the faithful to yearn for the bliss of the Pure Land and not forget the tortures of hell, they would lead wonderfully meritorious lives.

Honen (1133–1212) was more insistent on the singularity of the *nembutsu,* in effect separating Pure Land Buddhism from other sects and making the *nembutsu* the be-all and end-all of the Middle Way. Honen personally suffered persecution for his position and for his success in winning converts. In a letter written to the wife of the ex-regent Tsukinowa, Honen described the essentials that a convert to Pure Land would have to embrace. The gist of his exposition was that the *nembutsu* was the best way to rebirth in the Pure Land, because it was the discipline described in Amida's own vow to become a *bodhisattva* and open salvation to all creatures. Indeed, the earthly Buddha Sakyamuni entrusted the *nembutsu* to his disciple Ananda, that Ananda might make it Sakyamuni's main bequest to posterity. Finally, all the buddhas of the six quarters of the world endorsed the *nembutsu.* So while other religious practices, such as meditations or ritual ceremonies, had considerable value, only the *nembutsu* had the highest stamp of authority. What did it matter that some critics claimed the *nembutsu* was too easy, fit only for simpletons? Amida and Sakyamuni had endorsed it; would one rather stand with earthly critics or heavenly masters?

Shinran (1173–1262), Honen's most successful disciple, came to feel that the successful propagation of the *nembutsu* depended on the clergy's closer identification with the laity. He therefore urged breaking with the tradition of clerical celibacy and with the permission of Honen he himself took a wife. So strong was his conviction that salvation depends purely on the grace of Amida that he rejected practices such as monastic vows and disciplines as possible impediments to genuine faith. Whereas some conservative Pure Land preachers urged a continuous recitation of the *nembutsu,* Shinran thought that a single invocation of Amida Buddha, if filled with loving faith, would suffice for salvation. Shinran's hymns ring with this loving faith: Amida endlessly sends forth his pure, joyous, wise, universal light. It is brighter than the sun and the moon, illumining numberless worlds.

Sakyamuni came into the world only to reveal Amida's vow to help human beings and the primacy of faith in Amida's grace. By faith even the worst of sinners will come to Amida's mercy, as surely as all mountain water finally comes to the ocean. Eventually, Amida's faith in the disciple will make things right.

Pure Land has the effect of providing Japan a very appealing form of Buddhist devotionalism. The mercy of Amida rang true to the Japanese tendency to seek an ultimate reality who shows signs of maternal kindness. Nichiren (1222–1282) agreed with the Pure Land Buddhists that simple devotional forms like the *nembutsu* were desirable, but he found their stress on Amida unwarranted. For Nichiren the be-all and end-all of Buddhist faith was the Lotus Sutra. He considered this scripture the final teaching of Sakyamuni, in which his three bodies (historical, doctrinal, and blissful) came together in a marvelous unity. Other schools had overlooked one or more of these three aspects, slighting either the historical life of the Buddha, his existence as the dharma giving all reality its true form, or his existence as the perfection of salvation (the center of the abode of the blessed). Devotion to the Lotus Sutra assured that a balance would be restored. Thus Nichiren urged the practice of chanting homage to the Lotus Sutra. In rather uncompassionate style, he called Amida Buddhism a hell and Zen a devil. Today there are many subsects of Nichiren Buddhism that together make this school second only to Pure Land in popularity.

Zen. Two of the great pioneers who launched Chan on its illustrious career in Kamakura Japan, were Eisai (1141–1215) and Dogen (1200–53). Eisai studied Chan in China and then established himself in Kamakura, the new center of Japanese political power. His teaching won special favor among the hardy warlords who were coming to dominate Japan, and from his time Zen and the samurai (warrior) code had close bonds. For Eisai, mind was greater even than heaven. Buddhism, which concentrated on the mind, had known great success in India and China. Among the different Buddhist schools, the one founded by Bodhidharma especially stressed mastering the mind. From Bodhidharma's missionary ventures in China, Zen had made its way to Korea and Japan. Now it was time for Japan to capitalize on Zen's great potential.

By studying **Zen**, one could find the key to all forms of Buddhism. By practicing Zen, one could bring one's life to fulfillment in enlightenment. To outer appearances, Zen favored discipline over doctrine. Inwardly, however, it brought the highest wisdom, that of enlightenment itself. Eisai was able to convince some of the Hojo regents and Kamakura shoguns of this message and make them patrons of Zen, so he planted Zen solidly in Japan.

If Eisai proved to be a good politician, able to adapt to the new Kamakura times and to benefit from them, Dogen proved to be the sort of rugged, uncompromising character Zen needed to deepen its Japanese roots and gain spiritual independence. After studying at various Japanese Buddhist centers without satisfaction, he met Eisai and resolved to follow in his footsteps and visit China. After some frustration in China, Dogen finally gained enlightenment when he heard a Zen master speak of "dropping both mind and spirit" (dropping dualism). Returning to Japan, he resisted the official pressures to mingle various forms of Buddhism and would only teach Zen. Nonetheless, within Zen circles Dogen was quite flexible, teaching, for example, that study of the Buddhist scriptures (scholarship) was not incompatible with a person-to-person transmission of the truth (the guru tradition).

Within Zen circles, Dogen also distinguished himself for his worries about the use of koans. The Rinzai school of Chan that Eisai had introduced to Japan stressed the use of these enigmatic sayings as a great help to sudden enlightenment. In Dogen's opinion, the Chinese Soto school was more balanced and less self-assertive. He therefore strove to establish Soto in Japan, teaching a Zen that did not concentrate wholly on the mind but rather on the total personality. This led him to a practice of simple meditation *(zazen)* that ideally proceeded without any thought of attaining enlightenment and without any specific problem in mind. Disciplining the body as well as the mind, Dogen aimed at a gradual, lifelong process of realization.

In some of his "conversations," Dogen movingly expressed his great faith in the power of Zen Buddhism. Quoting Eisai, he spoke of a monk's food and clothing as gifts from heaven. The teacher is but an intermediary between the pupil and heaven. Heaven gives each of us what we need for our allotted life span, and we should not make a fuss over these things. The student should direct his gratitude to heaven, much more than to his master, opening himself to all of heaven's gifts. The greatest of heaven's gifts is truth, and it is the good fortune of monks to be able to pursue truth full time. The difficulties monks or any of us face in securing life's practical necessities should not obscure this central point. Such difficulties should merely make us serious, willing to sacrifice for being able to pursue the truth. If monks lived utterly leisurely lives under full patronage, they likely would grow lazy and selfish. If, on the contrary, they live in poverty, begging for their food or working the land, they likely will grow hardy in spirit.

Dogen's compassion was equal to his faith, for he also liked to tell his disciples the story of Eisai's decision to give some copper to a destitute man who had come to the monastery begging help for his wife and children. The copper had been destined to make a halo for a statue of the Buddha. When some of Eisai's monks complained that he had forgotten this lofty designation for the copper, Eisai agreed that ideally the copper would have gone into a halo for the Buddha's statue. But the Buddha's own example of spending himself for the sake of needy human beings had urged Eisai to be generous, sacrificing some of the monastery's goods for the lives of fellow human beings.

Both Pure Land and Zen made their great impressions on Japanese culture largely in terms of the goodness they encouraged. From its deep faith in the goodness of Amida Buddha, Pure Land taught the Japanese people Shinran's concern for sinners, outcasts, men and women tending to doubt their own worth. From its deep experiences of self-realization, Zen matured a gratitude for all of creation that easily became a great compassion for all creatures suffering pain. Situating themselves within the common Buddhist tradition, the Kamakura schools suggested that faith and insight, devotion and practical charity, are not antagonistic but complementary. If one goes deeply enough into faith, one reaches a gratitude that is almost identical with the gratitude that rushes forth in enlightenment. If one goes deeply enough into meditational insight, one reaches a gratitude that is almost identical with the wholehearted faith that Amida Buddha is utterly trustworthy and good. The legacy of the Kamakura schools, finally, was their depth. Shinran and Dogen were such heroes of the spiritual life that all subsequent Japanese aspirants to sanctity or wisdom saw in them clear models of the way.

Francis Cook has summarized the overall innovations that these Japanese masters introduced into Buddhism.[13] First, the Japanese tended not to adhere to traditional codes of conduct, whether for laity *(sila)* or for monks (Vinaya). Eventually, priests were able to marry, eating meat and drinking alcoholic beverages were allowed, and monks could have more than a spare robe. Second, Japanese Buddhism tended to move re-ligious activity from the temple to the home. As a result, emphasis was shifted to the laity, and monks or priests were relegated to the care of temples and the performance of ceremonies (especially funerals). Caring for temples frequently came to be a family affair, as fathers passed a priesthood on to their sons.

Third, during the Kamakura period several sects promulgated the notion that one particular practice summarized Buddhism. In that they were to a degree reacting against the syncretism of the Shingon and Tendai sects. As we have seen, Honen made chanting Amida's name *(nembutsu)* the only way to be reborn in the Pure Land. Dogen thought that meditative sitting summarized everything essential. Nichiren, finally, insisted that chanting "homage to the Sutra of the Lotus of the True Law" was the way to identify with the Buddha.

Shinto. During the Kamakura period, Buddhism sometimes eclipsed Shinto, but the native tradition always lay ready to reassert itself. Whenever there was a stimulus to depreciate foreign influences and exalt native ones, Shinto quickly bounced back. Also, Shinto only defined itself in the seventh century, when Buddhism, Confucianism, and Daoism started to predominate. In defining itself, Shinto picked up something from Buddhist philosophy, Confucian ethics, and Daoist naturalism. The result was a nature-oriented worship with special emphasis on averting pollution. Furthermore, Shinto domesticated Buddhism as a religion of *kami-bodhisattvas,* and it modified Confucian social thought to include the emperor's divine right.

Earhart defines the medieval-elaborative period of Japanese history as the years 794 through 1600.[14] This stretches from the Heian era, when the court at Kyoto had a glorious culture, through the Kamakura and Muromachi eras, and ends with the fall of the Momoyama era. While Japan worked its changes on Buddhism, Shinto was liberally borrowing from the foreign traditions. Since it represented the oldest native traditions, the result was a great enrichment, or at least a great complication, of what constituted Shinto. From Buddhism, as noted, Shintoists developed the notion that the kami were traces of the original substances of particular buddhas and *bodhisattvas.* As a result, Buddhist deities were enshrined by Shintoists (and kami by Buddhists). So thoroughly did Buddhism and Shinto combine that Dengyo Daishi and Kobo Daishi, the founders of Tendai and Shingon, thought it natural to erect shrines to honor the kami of the mountains of their monastic retreats.

Figure 28 Torii *(sacred gateway) to National Shrine at Ise. The* torii *separates the sacred space of the shrine grounds from the profane space outside. Ise is the most venerable Shinto shrine, distinctive for the rough, unadorned character of its buildings. Photo by J. T. Carmody.*

From Shingon, Shintoists absorbed certain esoteric practices, such as using mandalas to represent the basic dualities of mind-matter, male-female, and dynamic-static.[15] Because of such dualism, people began to call Shinto "Ryobu," which means "two parts" or "dual." In one of its most dramatic actions, dualistic Shinto gave the Ise shrine an inner and an outer precinct to make two mandalas that would represent the two sides of Amaterasu. She was the sun goddess of the ancient traditions, but she was also Vairocana, the shining Buddha of Heaven.

Later in the medieval period, a number of Shinto scholars took issue with syncretism.[16] Some of them just wanted to upset the evenhandedness that had developed, so that the kami would predominate over the *bodhisattvas* or so that Amaterasu would predominate over Vairocana. Others wanted to rid Shinto of its accretions and return it to its original form. The most

important of these medieval Shinto reformers were Kitabatake and Yoshida, who worked in the fourteenth and fifteenth centuries. They drew from writings of Ise priests, who wanted to give Shinto a scripture comparable to that of the Buddhists. Another step in the consolidation of Shinto's position was the organizing of its shrines, which began in the tenth century and continued through to the twentieth. The resulting network provided every clan and village with a shrine to represent its ties with the kami.

Christianity. In the mid-sixteenth century Christianity came to Japan in the person of the charismatic Jesuit missionary Francis Xavier. It flourished for about a century, until the Tokugawa rulers first proscribed it and then bitterly persecuted it. The first Western missionaries made a great impact because Japan was used to religions of salvation. Pure Land

Buddhism, for instance, was then popular among the common people. By impressing the local warrior rulers (often by holding out prospects of trade with the West), the Christians gained the right to missionize much of Japan and made some lasting converts. Western artifacts fascinated the Japanese as well, and for a while things Western were the vogue.

However, before the missionaries could completely adapt Christianity to Japanese ways, the shoguns became suspicious that the missionaries had political and economic designs. The shogun Ieyasu (1542–1616) killed many who had converted to Christianity, and after his death Christianity's brief chapter in Japanese history came to a bloody close. Shusaku Endo's novel about the Christians' persecution, *Silence*,[17] caused a stir in the contemporary Japanese Christian community because of its vivid description of the trials (in faith as well as body) that the missionaries underwent.

Summary. At the end of the medieval period of elaboration (around 1600), then, five traditions were interacting. Buddhism brought Japan a profound philosophy and system of meditation that stressed the flux of human experience, the foundation of being, and death. In return, it was revamped to suit Japanese tastes and the interests of the diverse social classes: rulers for rituals, warriors for discipline, common people for devotional love and hope. Confucianism furnished a rationale for the state bureaucracy and for social relationships. It stressed formality and inner control, which especially suited merchants and government officials, and one can see its imprint in the Bushido Code, which prevailed during the Tokugawa period.[18] Daoism most influenced folk religion, while, as we have seen, Shinto developed a rationale for the kami and a strong shrine system. Christianity came to represent foreign intrusion, but since it converted perhaps 500,000 Japanese, it also satisfied a hunger for other ways to salvation. Probably the average person mixed elements from these traditions with folk beliefs to fashion a family-centered religion that would harmonize human beings with the forces—kami, *bodhisattvas,* and evil spirits—that presided over good fortune and bad.

The Modern-Reformative Period

During the Tokugawa shogunate (military dictatorship), which lasted from 1600 to 1867, Japan experienced peace and stability. The Tokugawa rulers expelled the Christian missionaries and severely limited contacts with the West. The biggest shift in the social structure was the rise of the merchant class, which went hand in hand with the growth of cities.

Regarding religion, the Tokugawa shoguns made sure that all traditions served the state's goals of stability. In the beginning of the seventeenth century those goals had popular support because the preceding dynasties had allowed great civil strife. Buddhists had to submit to being an arm of the state. Neo-Confucianism eclipsed Buddhism in state influence, perhaps because it was less likely to stir thoughts of independence or individualism. Shinto suffered some decline in popular influence but retained a base in folk religion. As well, Shinto generated a clearer rationale for separating from Buddhism.

Early during the Tokugawa period there arose a movement called *Kokugaku* ("National Learning"), designed to furnish Japan a more impressive native religious/cultural tradition. In terms of positive goals, the leaders of this movement wanted to improve historical learning about Japanese culture, thinking that scholarship about Shinto and other aspects of the native ways were in a deplorable state. Negatively, many of the leaders attacked the way that Japan had adopted Confucian and Buddhist ways. The tendency of the leaders of the Kokugaku movement was to schematize Japanese history into three phases. In the early period, a pristine native culture and spirit had flourished. During the middle period, foreign imports had contaminated Japanese culture. They hoped to make the modern period a time when the ancient native ways would be restored and their country would be purged of foreign contaminations.

In fact, the beginnings of this reform movement owed something to the Buddhist priest Keichu (1640–1701), who proposed aesthetic reforms that would return poetry to ancient forms, and who noted the differences between Shinto and both Buddhism and Confucianism. He showed special respect for the kami, claiming they were beyond human understanding, and generally provided some of the initial impetus to restore ancient Japanese traditions. A Shinto priest from Kyoto, Kada Azumamaro (1669–1736), contributed one of the first influential critiques of the synthesis between Confucianism and Shinto that had arisen, arguing that Shinto ideas were not well interpreted through such Confucian notions as yin and yang or the five basic elements constituting reality.

A second generation of Shinto reformists came with Kamo no Mabuchi (1697–1769) and Motoori

Norinaga (1730–1801), who sharpened the focus of Kokugaku to precisely religious matters. Mabuchi founded a school of "ancient learning" dedicated to reviving the Japanese spirit that had prevailed before the introduction of Buddhism and Confucianism. Norinaga edited the *Kojiki,* the chronicles that became regarded as the Shinto scriptures. His commentaries on the *Kojiki,* along with his other writings on such topics as the kami, and his poetry, gave the Shinto revival much more intellectual clout than it had had previously. Hirata Atsutane (1776–1843) represents a third generation of the Kokugaku movement. He was the most passionate advocate of Shinto religiosity, arguing that the way of the kami was superior to all other religious ways.

Despite their claim to be purifying Japanese religious traditions of the foreign accretions that had denatured them, the later reformers in fact drew on the Daoist philosophers Laozi and Zhuangzi. Atsutane even borrowed from Christianity, which the Tokugawa leaders had proscribed. The rationale for such borrowings seems to have been twofold. First, Shinto traditions themselves were proving too thin on theoretical matters to undergird the revival the reformers wanted. Second, Buddhism and Confucianism were the great rivals or enemies, so borrowing from such politically weaker traditions as Daoism and Christianity amounted to a minor evil.

In their attacks on Buddhism and Confucianism, the Shinto reformers argued that those traditions had arisen through human contrivance, while the way of the kami was natural—completely in accord with the dictates of heaven and earth. The Daoist notions of spontaneity and nonstriving *(wu-wei)* seemed to support the superiority of such naturalism and so were adapted to the argument on behalf of the superiority of Shinto. Norinaga used the further Daoist concept that things are self-explanatory (do not require a full chain of causes) to rebut Neo-Confucian ideas about the workings of nature that he felt had invaded the Shinto view of the world. He also explored medicine, his profession, with an eye to reviving ancient theories, which were quite empirical (concentrated on simple facts and cures), and to ousting the complex, more rarefied theories of the Neo-Confucians. The religious payoff Norinaga found in this contrast was a support for his view that one ought to give the kami complete obedience, respecting the mysteriousness of their ways and not poking into how they had arranged nature. Thus what he considered Shinto naturalism, bolstered by Daoist views (Chinese naturalism), seemed more

properly religious (worshipful) than what had infiltrated Shintoism through Neo-Confucianism.

Some later Shinto scholars have argued that Norinaga also was shaped by Christian views of the Creator, but the clearer Christian influence appears in the works of Atsutane, who apparently incorporated materials from translations of books on Christian doctrine brought by Western missionaries to China such as Matteo Ricci (1552–1610). The missionaries had been searching for ways to show the superiority of Christianity to Confucianism and some of their arguments seemed relevant to Shinto attacks on Confucianism. As well, Atsutane adapted Christian notions of the Trinity and the last judgment to a theology of the nature and works of the kami. A third feature of his theology was its special emphasis on Japanese ancestor veneration, which he found superior to Chinese ancestor veneration because it was broader in its range of devotion (Japanese ancestor worship was dedicated not only to members of one's own clan but also to the great kami associated with the imperial family). This latter point was extremely important in the nineteenth-century Meiji restoration of the power of the imperial family, for it provided a basis for discrediting the Tokugawa leaders (who were shoguns, not members of the imperial line) and bolstering the sacredness of the restored royal line. The subsequent "divinization" of the Japanese emperor, which went hand in hand with the extreme nationalism of late nineteenth-century and early twentieth-century Japan, owed much to the last phases of the Kokugaku movement, when the kami had come to reoccupy the royal ancestral line, much as Shintoists believed they had done during the earliest period, before Japan had been tainted by foreign religious ways.[19]

The New Religions. During the Tokugawa period the first "new religions" arose. They were eclectic packagings of the previous, medieval elements, and they gained their success by contrasting favorably with the highly formal, even static, culture that had prevailed in the early nineteenth century. The new religions usually sprang from a charismatic leader who furnished a connection with the kami—indeed, whom his or her followers took to be a kami. By personalizing religion and addressing individual faith, the new religions stood out from the dominant formalism and offered something attractively dynamic.

Since the government was pushing Shinto, the new religions tended to join the nationalistic trend. Tenrikyo and Soka Gakkai both owe as much to

Figure 29 *Moss Temple grounds, Kyoto. The sunlight filtering through the trees illumines and shades the rich vegetation into a wondrous variety of green colorings. The rocks and waters add a calming contrast, making for a sense of fertility and peace. Photo by J. T. Carmody.*

Buddhist as to Shinto inspiration, but other new religions found it useful to shelter under the nationalistic umbrella. Tenrikyo sprang from a revelation that its founder, Nakayama Miki, had in 1838.[20] She had been a devout Pure Land Buddhist, but while serving as a medium in a healing ceremony for her son, she felt a kami possess her—the "true, original kami Tenri O no Mikoto" ("God the Parent"). Thereafter, her religion had a distinctively shamanic character. Miki embarked on a mission to spread her good news, healing sick people and promulgating the recitation of "I put my faith in Tenri O no Mikoto." The Tokugawa authorities harassed her somewhat, but in time a large number of followers accepted her as a living kami. Her writings became the Tenrikyo scripture, her songs became its hymns, and her dances shaped its liturgy. Recalling the creation myth of Izanagi and Izanami, she built a shrine "at the center of the world," where she thought

the first parents had brought forth the land. The shrine had a square opening in its roof and a tall wooden column—ancient symbolism for the connection to heaven.

Miki's teachings stress joyous living. In the beginning God the Parent made human beings for happiness, but we became self-willed and gloomy. By returning to God the Parent and dropping self-concern, we can restore our original joy. The way to return is faith in God the Parent and participation in Tenrikyo worship. Earhart has suggested that Tenrikyo's success comes in part from its return to peasant values.[21] By stressing gratitude for (sacred) creation, social rather than individual good, hard manual work, and the like, this sect has generated great popular enthusiasm. By the end of the nineteenth century, Tenrikyo claimed more than two million members, testifying to the power of combining old, shamanistic elements with new organizational forms and liturgies. Tenrikyo even revived the ancient Shinto concern for purification by focusing on an interior cleansing of doubts and untoward desires.

Soka Gakkai derives from Makiguchi Tsunesaburo (1871–1944), who preached a new social ethic based on three virtues: beauty, gain, and goodness.[22] Makiguchi found Nichiren Buddhism attractive, so he worked out his ethics in terms of the Lotus Sutra: Beauty, gain, and goodness came from faith in the Lotus. During World War II the leaders of Soka Gakkai refused the government's request that all religionists support the military effort, arguing that compliance would compromise the truth of the Lotus Sutra (by associating Soka Gakkai with other Buddhist sects and with Shintoists). For this he went to prison. Makiguchi died in prison, but his movement revived after the war through the efforts of Toda Josei. By 1957, Toda had reached his goal of enrolling 750,000 families, largely through his fine organizational abilities, and his shrewd use of enthusiastic youths. As well, Soka Gakkai capitalized on the frustration of Buddhists committed to the Lotus Sutra but alienated by the bickering among the various Nichiren groups. In a time of national confusion, Soka Gakkai's absolutism (all other religious options were held to be false) carried great appeal. According to Soka Gakkai, commitment to the Lotus Sutra (and to itself) would dissolve all ambiguities.

Many observers have criticized Soka Gakkai for its vehement missionizing and its political involvement. It offers a "cellular" structure like that of Communists, a simple program for daily devotion, pilgrimages to the National Central Temple near Mount Fuji, and an extensive educational program. Under the name Nichiren Shoshu, it has exported itself to the West, and though Soka Gakkai has separated from its political arm (Komeito), the party continues to have considerable political effect.

The Bushido Code. The **Bushido Code** provides a good summary of the religious and ethical values that formed the Japanese character throughout the late medieval and early modern periods. Bushido was especially significant for gathering together the sense of honor most samurai warriors and their consorts held to be more precious than life itself. John Noss has said of Bushido:

Bushido did not consist of finally fixed rules. It was a convention; more accurately, it was a system

of propriety, preserved in unwritten law and expressing a spirit, an ideal of behavior. As such, it owed something to all the cultural and spiritual forces of the feudal era. Shinto supplied it the spirit of devotion to country and overlord, Confucianism provided its ethical substance, Zen Buddhism its method of private self-discipline, and the feudal habit of life contributed to it the spirit of unquestioning obedience to superiors and a sense of honor that was never to be compromised.[23]

Bushido was the "way of the warrior," whether he was a **samurai** (warrior) in fact or only in spirit. For Japanese women, the Bushido concern for honor focused on chastity. Manuals instructed young girls who had been compromised how to commit suicide (with the dagger each girl received when she came of age), including details of how, after plunging in the blade, she should tie her lower limbs together so as to secure modesty even in death. When a powerful lord would not stop his advances, the noble Lady Kesa promised to submit if he would kill her samurai husband first. The lord agreed, and she told him to come to her bedroom after midnight and kill the sleeper with wet hair. Then she got her husband drunk, so that he would sleep soundly, washed her hair, and crept under the covers to await her fate.[24] This was not typical, but it is instructive.

Recent History. From the close of the Tokugawa period in 1867 to World War II, Japan was in transit to modernity. It abolished the military dictatorship and restored the emperor. It also changed from a largely decentralized feudal society into a modern nation organized from Tokyo. Japan made astonishing strides in education and culture, assimilating Western science and again opening itself to the outside world (at first under duress, due to Commodore Perry and the U.S. gunboats during 1853 and 1854, then voluntarily). Success in two major wars with China and Russia between 1895 and 1905 gave the Japanese great confidence, and the first third of the twentieth century was a time of increasingly strident nationalism. One of the main foci of this nationalism was what became state Shinto. Because of its chauvinist potential, some Japanese thinkers and politicians stressed the divinity of the emperor and the unique dignity of the Japanese people.

During this period Buddhism lost its official status as a branch of the government, Shinto was established as the state religion, and Christianity was reintroduced. In addition, more new religions appeared, which, like Buddhism and Shinto, took on nationalistic overtones.

For our interests the modern period, beginning with the Meiji Restoration (of the emperor) in 1868, is most significant because of the revival of Shinto. This was largely a political operation, designed to glorify the imperial family and to unify the country around its oldest traditions. Edwin Reischauer has described the widespread changes in secular life that the Meiji leaders introduced.[25] Japanese cities were revamped, and Western ideas of individual rights and responsibilities that are part of a modern state were brought in. H. B. Earhart provides documents of the propaganda that Meiji leaders generated to link the nation with religion and reestablish Japan's sense of divine mission.[26] "The Imperial Rescript on Education" (1890),[27] for instance, explicitly linked the imperial throne ("coeval with heaven and earth") with filial piety to make nationalism the supreme personal virtue. To bring their tradition up to date and do what their revered ancestors had done, the modern Japanese had only to be utterly loyal to the emperor. In fact, Joseph Kitagawa has argued that the Japanese notion of national community (*kokutai*) "incorporates all the major thrusts of individual and corporate orientation of the Japanese people to a sacral order of reality."[28]

Japan's defeat in World War II produced great national trauma, prompting the success of hundreds of new religions. Culturally, defeat meant a shattering of national pride; religiously, it meant a body blow to state Shinto. The Western conquerors, led by Douglas MacArthur, force-fed the Japanese democracy and the concept of individual liberties. On its own, Japan rebuilt with incredible speed, soon becoming the economic giant of Asia. The new constitution disestablished Shinto and allowed complete individual religious freedom. The older traditions, which people identified with the national self-consciousness of prewar times, were shattered, and the new religions rushed in to fill the void. In the past two decades or so, the older traditions have regrouped, especially Buddhism, but secularism has been a strong trend. Caught up in its technological spurt, Japan has seemingly put aside nationalistic and religious issues, preferring to let the traumas of the war heal by benign neglect.

Today the Japanese religious picture is quite complicated. The culture is secularistic, at least outwardly, but in the byways Buddhism and Christianity struggle to revive themselves. Confucian and Daoist elements remain part of the Japanese psyche, but in rather muted voice. Strangely, perhaps, it is Shinto—the ancient version rather than the state—that is the strongest religious presence. Divinity in nature, which Japanese religion has always stressed, continues in the shrines that connect present times to the aboriginal kami. The place of the emperor remains a touchy issue.

WORLDVIEW

How ought we to regard the relation between history and worldview in Japan? Perhaps the most profitable way would be to imagine the historical influences interacting with a strong ethnocentrism. As Confucian, Daoist, and Buddhist influences penetrated Japan, the Japanese people worked steadily to make them their own. Shinto arose, as the articulation of the native traditions, and the strong social cohesiveness of the Japanese gradually shaped how the new ways would color the old.

As in China, the different religious traditions seldom competed on the Western, individualistic model. By and large, people did not feel forced to choose between a wholehearted allegiance to Shinto or a wholehearted allegiance to Buddhism. Confucianism proved useful in expressing Japanese convictions about social relations. Daoism provided help in articulating native feelings about nature, in aesthetics, and also in expressing aspects of Buddhist philosophy. But the typical Japanese person felt free to pick and choose from the wealth of ideas and rituals that the several traditions offered. Any showdown that occurred tended to be between Shinto and Buddhist loyalties, and Shinto always had the great advantage of being intimately bound up with the symbolism of the royal family and the birth of the Japanese islands. The Confucian influence was more indirect or internal than imposed from without. Many more people thought about family life and social relations in Confucian terms than studied the Confucian classics or considered themselves disciples of Master Kong.

From the relative homogeneity of its people, Japanese religion could rely on many tacit assumptions. People long schooled to living closely together and taking pride in their beautiful land did not need to be lectured on consensus or veneration of natural beauty. Certainly, modern technology has shown that Japanese respect for nature is vulnerable; ecological problems are serious. Similarly, modern Western political ideas have posed significant challenges. But Japan's genius for taking foreign ideas, technology, and other accomplishments into itself and refashioning them to fit its own sense of peoplehood and social values has continued strong into the contemporary era. What seldom cracks is the ability of the people to work cooperatively, for a common good. In the case of religion, that has meant creating a digest of foreign influences that mixed well with Shinto convictions about the significance of beauty and the primacy of the Japanese people.

It should prove useful to focus on the ways that Japanese religion has not only offered the usual ministrations (ways of coping with death and other deep questions, ways of hallowing everyday life) but has also helped to energize the Japanese people. This is perhaps clearest in the case of Zen Buddhism, but one can probe for an energizing influence in the acceptance of other Buddhist schools, of Confucian convictions, of Daoist aesthetic notions, and even of Christian ceremonies (for weddings, for Christmas). The Shinto sense of being the people privileged to live on a beautiful string of islands has moved the Japanese to draw from other traditions what might enhance such a life—give it more vitality, increase its pleasures and decrease its pains. So, for example, the discipline that Zen Buddhism developed made it seem useful for more than personal enlightenment. Samurai warriors found in Zen a spiritual training to ground their martial arts and clarify their complete dedication to the service of their lord. Some contemporary industrialists have looked to Zen for a similar service, thinking that it could sharpen the attention of their workers and so improve efficiency.

Thus Japanese religion has been an important part of an energetic, creative culture—one more stimulated by the challenges of foreign influences, including those of Western modernity, than intimidated. The worldview that has developed in Japan, with considerable religious support, has canonized hard work and loyalty to one's kind (clan, fellow workers). It has been a worldview clearer than many others about the high survival value of social cohesiveness—the way that social cohesiveness keeps life relatively simple and keeps all significant ranks closed to outsiders.

Nature

From its earliest beginnings, Japanese religion has been enraptured by nature. Y. T. Hosoi has detailed prehistoric Japan's focus on the sacred tree;[29] Manabu Waida has described the rich mythology that surrounded the moon;[30] and ancient mythology, as we have seen, featured the sun goddess Amaterasu and the wind god Susanoo. Furthermore, we best describe the kami as nature forces (though they could also possess human beings), and the Japanese Buddhists' love for nature, which poets such as Saigyo and Basho dramatize, developed from a pre-Buddhist base. A closeness to nature, a love of natural beauty, an **aesthetic** geared to flowers and trees, seasons and vistas— these have been Japanese characteristics.

Japanese folk religion, which exerted a hardy influence, viewed nature with a peasant's eye. Nature was fertile and fickle, nourishing and devastating. The early myths reflect this paradoxical quality. The sun goddess was benevolent—a source of warmth, light, and the power to make things grow. The wind god was unpredictable, often destructive. Susanoo's punishment for his misdeeds belies a peasant hope that nature's order and benevolence will prevail. However, Susanoo and his like might have destructive outbreaks at any time; Japan has been a land of earthquakes, volcanoes, floods, and typhoons. Japan is a very beautiful land, but rugged and not easily tamed, and controlling the effects of nature has been a herculean task. Perhaps that accounts for the Japanese delight in gardens and groves—places where they have brought peace to nature.

As we noted in describing the Japanese innovations in Buddhism, this sort of delight showed in the Japanese embellishment of religious ceremonies. Not only do most temples have some sort of grounds, often quite lovely, but their liturgies employ flowers, incense, candles, and other adornments. Along with the Japanese stress on order and cleanliness, which goes back to ancient concerns for purification, a desire has grown to make living graceful. Buddhism has benefited from this desire, as the breathtaking Moss Temple and the Rock Garden Temple grounds show. In Shinto shrines, such as Ise, Heian, and Meiji, gardens, pools, fields of flowers, and lofty trees also reflect this desire.

The mode in which the Japanese have received these nature lessons, we suggest, has been "religio-aesthetic." Japan is not very concerned with a philosophy of nature in the Western sense. It does not analyze "prime matter" or nuclear particles. Its religion appears to move more by a sense of harmony. If the folk interest is nature's agricultural energies (and the powers responsible for sickness), the higher class interest is nature's ability to soothe. Sensing that the groves and gardens represent something primal, the warrior, merchant, and bureaucrat have returned to it to escape the human concerns that threatened to swamp them. By communion with nature, the samurai warrior could collect his spirit for a single-minded attack. By slipping away from his accounting, the merchant could anticipate a "retirement," which, in Japan as well as China, allowed more poetic, Daoist preoccupations. The same applies to the bureaucrat. Even Emperor Hirohito, who after World War II was merely a figurehead, specialized in marine biology. Somewhat inept in social situations, he came alive in his pools and gardens.

This interest in nature is religious in the sense that nature has regularly represented to the Japanese something ultimate. Thus, concern for nature has often been an ultimate concern—a stance before the holy. This stance seldom involved violent beliefs. The major prophetic figures do not tell tales of burning bushes or theologize out of mysteriously parted seas. Rather, the predominant mood has been peaceful.[31] Japanese religion tries to gain access to the core of the personality, where the personality touches nature's flow. It tries, probably semiconsciously, to let the moss and rocks work their influence. These objects can summarize existence, giving messages from mind-only. Such Buddhist ideas suggest emptiness—the strangely satisfying "no-thingness" that the spirit disgusted with ideas, the spirit more holistically inclined, often finds in open space or the sea.

The religious veneration of nature, or even the religio-aesthetic use of nature for soothing the soul, implies an impersonal ultimacy. Furthermore, it implies that humanity, as well as divinity, is more at one with nature than over or against it. Religion based on nature, in fact, tends to collapse humans and gods into nature's forces or nature's flows. As a result, Japan has not seen the world as created by a transcendent force. Rather, Japan has let nature somewhat suppress knowledge and love of divinity, subordinating them to energy and flow. Human beings have been encouraged not to exploit nature (though recent technological changes qualify this statement). Through most of Japanese history, one would prune or rake nature rather than lay waste to it, at least in part because human

beings did not have a biblical writ to fill the earth and subdue it.[32] Rather, they had a call to live with nature. Today we might hear that as a call to be ecological, grateful, and thus graceful.

This emphasis on nature relegated intellectual concerns to second place. Many Japanese monks have lived in mountain fastnesses, while relatively few have been theoreticians of divinity's word. The reasoning of theoreticians tends to be sharp, attacking, and dialectical. The reasoning of contemplative monks tends to be poetic, symbolic, and expressive. Those who ponder the "feminine" intelligence of Eastern cultures come upon this contemplative mind. Generally, Japan has sought the whole rather than the part, the movement rather than the arrest, the beauty as well as the utility. These are feminine characteristics only if *masculine* refers to only one sort of logic (the shortest distance between two points). If a culture moves more circuitously, Western men will likely call it feminine. We are fortunate to live in a time that challenges such stereotypes.

Case Study: Japanese Aesthetics.[33]   Much of the Japanese effort to gain religious peace has expressed itself aesthetically, in artistic pursuits. Classical Japanese painting, for instance, tended to portray the physical world realistically, with great attention to details. It was not abstract or surrealistic. On the other hand, classical painting also was not photographically objective, but tended to use a flat, undistanced surface to express subjective perceptions of reality. A good example is a series of screens by Kano Naizen from the Momoyama period (1568–1600). The screens portray the arrival of Portuguese merchants and the conversion of some Japanese citizens by Christian missionaries. In one street scene the foreground presents the foreign priests and merchants mingling with the Japanese natives. In the background, a local shop and a pine grove are portrayed without depth, covered by golden mists. The effect is a standoff between time and eternity. The busy street scene with the newly arrived foreigners argues that times are always changing, novelty is nearly rampant. The golden mists, pine grove, and stylized shop argue that the more things change the more they stay the same. Novelty is but a small wrinkle on the surface of an ancient culture and a timeless nature.

Some of the oldest Japanese ceramics, the *haniwa* figurines from the fifth and sixth centuries C.E., display what became an almost standard Japanese love of simple, austere presentations. The *haniwa* figurines tend to have oval eyes and tiny mouths, as though they were timeless masks, suitable for the ceremonial dances that take us out of profane time. They are sober and archetypal, yet poised on the brink of motion (for the sacred dance is always occurring, always inviting us to join in). Some historians find Chinese influences in these early ceramics, but they express qualities that Japan soon made wholly its own. Buddhist influences brought an increased concentration on portrait sculpture in order to represent the Enlightened One. In the best of these representations, artists captured the Buddha's humanity, giving him the slightest trace of a smile, a bit of warmth and playfulness. Portrait sculpture of the Nara period (710–794) included monks among its subjects. Thus the sculpture of the famous blind monk Ganjin shows a holy man deep in meditation. The smile lines at the mouth and the corners of the eyes help to heighten his attractiveness. Though physically blind, he probably had great insight into human nature. Though concentrating on the timeless dharma, he probably had been molded to a timely humaneness, becoming a person we would like to know.

Zen masters of the Muromachi period (1392–1568) were instrumental in Japan's appropriation of the landscape techniques developed during the Chinese Song dynasty. This led to the *suiboku* style (ink on paper with splashed-ink wash). The conventions of the *suiboku* landscapes called for a vertical perspective, featuring craggy mountains or deep basins with lakes and canyons. Clouds or empty spaces tended to divide the pictures into three realms, reminiscent of the doctrine of the Buddha's three bodies. The lower level of the painting usually dealt with earthly and human concerns: a lake, a hermit's hut, several fishermen. The middle of the picture would have temples or pagodas suggesting paradise. At the top the picture would portray icy mountain peaks, to symbolize the perfection beyond all human imagining.

Working within this conventional form, a Zen master such as Sesshu (1420–1506) was able to introduce some striking originality. His *Winter Landscape*, for example, shows jagged mountaintops lost in clouds, a temple in the middle range, and near the base a traveler in a broad-brimmed hat. The traveler is lost in the immense landscape, quite vulnerable as he picks his way. Though this is all quite conventional, Sesshu has invested the painting with an electric energy. Using short, ragged lines, he has expressed the Zen sense that nature is tremendously alive. Thus the

impression is not of a soft, misty nature but of sharp angles, well-defined particulars. That this effect at the bottom is in tension with empty space at the top, which makes a white, heavenly vagueness, makes the picture an epitome of Zen philosophy. Emptiness accents particulars. Mystical absorption at the top should lead to vitality and decisiveness at the bottom.

Another interesting Japanese art form was the *ukiyo,* which means a picture of the "floating world." The hallmark of this style was the changeableness of things, the world's transiency. Yet whereas transiency had traditional Buddhist overtones of sadness, the *ukiyo* artists tended to be happy. The excitement of the latest gossip, the fun of seizing the day, ran through their work. One of their favorite subjects was Kabuki actors. In a celebrated series of portraits done by Toshusai Sharaku in 1794–95, the arresting feature is the actors' facial expressions. They show brilliant rage, triumph, coyness, defeat—all the emotions required on the Kabuki stage. The faces are heavily made up, and the total effect is to drive home the energy and pathos of the actor's life.

Japanese aesthetics also led to notable architecture, gardens, and rituals such as the tea ceremony. The traditional Japanese house was a model of simplicity, even austerity. It had straw-mat floors, sliding-screen walls, and very little furniture. The custom of removing one's shoes on entering the house suggested coming into a new, venerable space. The screen walls offered minimal protection against nature, but they were flexible enough to accommodate to quick changes of mood. In summer, the screens easily opened to the elements, eliminating the barriers between the family and nature.

During the Muromachi period Zen monastic influence made the style of the abbot's quarters attractive for laypeople's houses. The main room therefore came to center around a floor-level writing desk, and there would usually be an alcove for arranged flowers. A scroll usually would hang in the corner, the floors would be covered with *tatami* (straw mats), and the walls would be sliding paper doors and screens. Among the wealthy, who could afford large houses with many screens, there would be special arrangements for viewing the moon or the snow to best advantage. The Katsura imperial villa on the edge of Kyoto is a good model of such large houses designed for beautiful views.

For many Japanese, the most beautiful views have opened onto exquisite gardens. The Shinto roots of the gardening tradition stressed gnarled old trees and

Figure 30   *Teahouse of the Rock Garden Monastery. Photo by J. T. Carmody.*

large rocks in places set aside for the kami. When Chinese culture began to shape Japanese tastes, Daoist and Buddhist influences became important. Traditional Chinese gardens sought to reproduce the islands and grottoes of the Daoist immortals or the beauty of the Buddha's Pure Land. Chinese geomancy set many of the stylistic ideals, and harmony between yin and yang forces was a high requirement. Thus a large yang boulder would be counterbalanced by a low yin pool. Waterfalls represented life and bamboo represented strength.

Once again, Zen was the native Japanese development that most directly varied the Chinese model. In the case of gardening, Zen pushed the designs in a more abstract and asymmetrical direction. In the Zen scheme, gardens were not so much places for leisurely strolling as places for meditation. Translating many notions from Song landscape painting, the Zen gardeners stressed emptiness and the lack of human or emotional touches. So the Zen gardens tended to have no benches or wine cups. Instead of showy flowers they

stressed moss or rocks. The Ryoanji or Rock Garden Monastery of Kyoto, built around 1500, epitomizes this abstract style. There are no ponds or streams, only white gravel raked to resemble eddies—phenomenal reality playing on the surface of emptiness.

The tea ceremony was one of several rituals the Japanese developed to beautify each part of daily living. Often it would take place in the teahouse of a shrine garden (see Figure 17). Indeed, many Zen Buddhists came to consider the tea ceremony a sort of sacrament, symbolizing the grace, austerity, and concentration that good living requires. While the core of the ceremony was simply making and sipping whipped green tea, the teahouse, the utensils, and the manner of serving all played important parts. Ideally there would be lovely surroundings: a garden of great beauty, flowers, a *suiboku* painting or a scroll of elegant calligraphy. Aficionados paid special attention to the bowl in which the tea was served, and master potters often strove to produce simple, elegant tea vessels. Although the upper classes sometimes embellished the tea ceremony with ostentatious displays, the protocol developed by Sen no Rikyu, the greatest of the tea masters, stressed "poor tea": absolute simplicity and ordinariness.

Ideally the tea ceremony would take place in its own teahouse, usually a small structure apart from the main house. Failing that, it would occur in a special room within the main house. The goal in designing the teahouse was to achieve a simplicity both rustic and refined. At one end of the house usually was an alcove decorated with a hanging scroll and floral arrangements. Another usual feature was a small sunken fireplace for heating the tea kettle in winter. During summer months people would use a portable brazier. Bowing to enter the small, low door of the teahouse, guests would begin the ceremony in a spirit of humility.

The ceremony itself has usually consisted of the host bringing tea utensils into the room, offering the guests sweets, and then preparing and serving tea made of pulverized tea leaves stirred in hot water. Normally the tea one prepared was thin and frothy, but on occasion a heavier tea might be served. At times the ceremony would be preceded by a light meal, which made the tea the climax of a social and culinary occasion. After the consumption of the tea, guests often would inquire about the implements that had been used, for as noted these often were considered art objects.

The tea ceremony has long had special ties with Zen Buddhism. Zen monks of the Kamakura period drank tea to stay awake during their meditation periods. Later they made tea drinking part of their ceremony for honoring their founder Bodhidharma. By the fifteenth century the tea ceremony itself had become a much loved art form, if not a religio-aesthetic ritual, as well as a vehicle for friends to gather and discuss aesthetics in a congenial atmosphere.

At the beginning of the Tokugawa period, the ceremony was somewhat codified and simplicity became the approved note. The ideal was to achieve harmony between the guests and the implements being used; respect among the participants and for the implements; cleanliness (a Shinto note), which led to ritual washings before entering the teahouse; and tranquility, encouraged by a slow, careful use of each article in the ceremony. Thus the tea ceremony itself became something of a religious "way"—a distinctively Japanese blend of aesthetics and religion.

Flower arrangement (*ikebana*) brought aesthetic refinement home to many Japanese family circles. In a sense, the goal of flower arrangement was to make a miniature garden, and so a miniature, domestic paradise. Like the tea ceremony, flower arrangement became a "way": an avocation both refreshing and disciplining. In flower arrangement the great virtues were simplicity, asymmetry, and form (color was secondary). The preferred forms were understated rather than obvious, subtle rather than bold. The ideal was to hint at a mysterious meaning and suggest old, somewhat formal ways. During the Tokugawa period (1600–1868) a threefold style developed. A high and a low branch on one side would represent heaven and human beings. A middle branch on the opposite side would represent earth. One would gain variety by changing the flowers, grasses, leaves, sticks, and other elements placed in these three positions. The result was a timeless pattern varied by new materials.

Throughout all their arts, the Japanese have tried to express and develop their sense of emptiness, form, the changeableness of human beings, and the primacy of nature. Rarely did a Japanese art form flourish without close ties to religion. In the tea and flower ceremonies, for instance, one is hard pressed to say where art leaves off and religious contemplation begins. A certain blankness signals the touch of Buddhist emptiness. A certain austerity signals the touch of Shinto antiquity, when life was close to nature, unemotional and strong.

Society

Women's Status.   It is ironic that a culture that has had many stereotypically feminine refinements has been almost oppressively male dominated. Although there are traces of an early matriarchy and strong influences from female shamans and their successors in the new religions, women have regularly occupied a low position in Japanese society. Of course, women's influence in the traditional home and even the modern office is stronger than superficial sociology suggests.[34] Expert in the very refined Japanese tact, wives and mothers have found ways of influence despite their institutionalized powerlessness. As well, they have run the home and controlled the purse strings. Officially, however, Japan accepted Confucian notions of social relationships (no doubt because they fit traditional predilections), so the female was almost always designated as the underling.

The important religious roles played by females in Japanese history should be further discussed. Perhaps their phallic overtones made it fitting that the kami should possess females. Or perhaps shamanism offered the powerless a chance to gain attention and influence. Whatever the reasons, women were the prime contact with divinity in folk Shinto, despite strong menstrual taboos. As well, they were the prime contact with the spirits of the dead and so were central in maintaining the sense of the clan. The figurines from the prehistoric Jomon period suggest that women were originally considered awesome because of their power to give birth. The difficulty of the women's liberation movement in contemporary Japan suggests that the powers of women represented by these former roles have long been suppressed.

No doubt for a variety of reasons, the men dominating Japanese society have found it advantageous to place religion and femininity in opposition to warfare and business. As the recourse to nature (retirement) has been in contrast to things official, so the recourse to monasteries, female shamans, and even geishas has been in contrast to workaday life. In part, of course, this contrast links religion with recreation, art, and family life. (In modern Japan a man identifies as much with his job and company as with his family.) Thus, nature, religion, and women are considered surplus commodities and yet especially valuable ones: surplus in that they do not figure much in modern work, but valuable in that work alone does not constitute a complete existence.

Clan Emphasis. The modern stress on a man's work, identifying him with his corporation, is the result of the group structure of Japanese business. Consequently, the typical businessman takes much of his recreation with his fellow workers apart from his family. Considered in the context of Japanese religious history, this situation is somewhat anomalous. Earhart, for instance, has gathered documents that testify to the religious significance of family life,[35] showing the sense of clan that has predominated. (In fact, the modern corporation exploits this sense of clan loyalty.)

Moreover, a characteristic of the traditional family was concern with the dead. As in China, ancestor veneration was a significant portion of the average person's religious contacts with ultimate powers. Originally, the Japanese probably believed that the departed continued to hover around the places where they had lived. The Japanese tended to associate their ancestors with kami and *bodhisattvas* after these figures were introduced by Shinto and Buddhism. Therefore, in its

petitions and venerations, the clan reminded itself of its own identity (the function that some sociologists, such as Durkheim, have considered the main rationale for religion) and kept attuned to the natural forces of life and death.

Thus, the family tended to be the locus of daily worship, and the family shrine tended to predominate over the village or national shrine. Still, there was not a sharp division between the family clan and the national clan. The emperor was often considered the head not only of his own line but also of the entire Japanese people; the gods of Shinto mythology were the gods of the collective Japanese group; and national shrines such as Ise were the site of ceremonies performed on behalf of the entire nation.

Overall, Japan is not a place where A. N. Whitehead's definition of religion (what a person does with his or her solitude) is very helpful.[36] Although standing alone before a striking shrine such as the Golden Pavilion has shaped for many Japanese a sense of ultimacy,[37] group activities—at home, in war, or at work—have been crucial factors in developing such a sense.

The Confucian cast of much traditional Japanese social thought is evident from the first article of a constitution developed by Prince Shotoku in 604. The implication is that throughout the land, harmony—cooperation—ought to be the watchword:

> Harmony is to be valued, and an avoidance of wanton opposition is to be honored. All men are influenced by partisanship, and there are few who are intelligent. Hence there are some who disobey their lords and fathers, or who maintain feuds with the neighboring villages. But when those above are harmonious and those below are friendly, and there is concord in the discussion of business, right views of things spontaneously gain acceptance. Then what is there which cannot be accomplished?"[38]

Ethics. This historical sense of clan was accompanied by certain ethical assumptions that were immensely influential in shaping the Japanese conscience. The medieval samurai felt that his life belonged to his feudal lord. If he failed his lord, by being defeated or less than fully successful, he was expected to offer to commit ritual suicide—to petition his lord for this "favor," so that he might mend the honor he had violated. In contemporary Japan, the individual worker is supposed to promote the honor of his bosses above all. He is to assume any failures by his group and to attribute any successes to the group's leader. Thus, the boss (or at most the group as a whole) always gets credit for a bright idea or increased productivity. If the worker does not rock the boat, the corporation will take care of all his needs until he dies.

Buddhism offered an alternative to the Japanese group orientation. Though the Buddha's own thought was quite social, as manifested by the *sangha,* his original message stressed the uniqueness of each individual's situation. It is true that each being possessed the buddha-nature (at least according to Mahayana Buddhism, which introduced the Buddha to Japan), and that this belief, coupled with the doctrine of no-self, led to a conception of the relatedness of reality. Practically, however, the Buddha made the existential personality the religious battleground. Only the individual could remove the poison of karma and rebirth; only the individual could pronounce the Buddhist vows for himself or herself, let alone live them out. However, early Japanese attempts to appropriate Buddhism were sponsored by the state, because the state leaders thought they might enlist its magical or ritual power.

In Japan Buddhism both kept some of its individualism and suffered a socialization. As Zen perhaps best shows, the *sangha* could gear itself to making free spirits. Its discipline could be odd, even cranky. At least, the Zen masters brim with spontaneity, venerating their tradition but often in iconoclastic ways. Yet Japan acculturated Buddhism. Indeed, Buddhism became a government agency, propping warlords and nationalistic ideology. Ultimately, Japan decided that Shinto served nationalism better than Buddhism, but that was not for Buddhism's lack of trying.

Self

Theoretically in Buddhism there was no self and so no barrier (for the enlightened) to union with nature or the group. Shinto defined the self less clearly than it defined nature or the group. Thus, when Confucianism brought an elaborate social protocol, the sense of self in Japanese religious consciousness was bound to be deemphasized.

In fact, Japanese religion does not emerge as a champion of freethinking. Compared with religion elsewhere, Japanese religion does not support individual initiative or responsibility to a significant degree. Except for Zen, Japan has told the individual that ful-

fillment is a matter of harmonizing with nature and society. For instance, the traditional Japanese artist does not agonize in the creative process like Western artists do. Japanese art has not been primarily for working out a self. We may doubt, therefore, that many Japanese artists have thought of their lives or work in terms of Patrick White's "vivisection" (of experience).[39]

More prominent has been the Daoist notion that the artist goes to the center of nature, where the Way rules, and from union with the Way spontaneously expresses a fleeting glimpse of reality.[40] The fall of a cherry blossom, the pattern of a scarf, the rumble of a mountain—those are the subjects that seize a classical poet such as Basho or a modern novelist such as Kawabata. In the tea ceremony, the No play, archery, or swordsmanship, the ideal is selflessness. Such activities, in fact, are but active forms of what the meditator pursues in *zazen.* Cast off the dichotomizing mind, the culture has said. Distinguish no more between your self and the world. Distinguishing makes for multiplicity and illusion. Buddha-nature is one. Full attainment, in the Japanese aesthetic religion, is the unitive mind, the mind lost in Mind.

Perhaps as a consequence of selflessness, the individual Japanese may appear ethically underdeveloped to the Westerner. Such a description can provide confusion, as well as misperception and offense. Still, a Western student has to begin with existing Western categories, even if they prove inappropriate. In Western ethics, the individual person judges right and wrong, largely because Greek philosophy and Israelite religion, the bases for Western culture, made the individual an intellectual and moral subject of revelation—in the Greek case, revelation from a nature or personal experience structured by reason (Logos); in the Israelite case, revelation from a willful God. By the time of the Enlightenment (the eighteenth century), the West had developed this patrimony to the point that the individual could be autonomous and ethics a matter of individual reasoning. Even though recent thought has found this view to be inadequate, it remains influential and at least partially true.

For instance, Western scholars of Shinto such as Bownas[41] and Blacker[42] go out of their way to underscore that its persistent concern with pollution had little to do with morality. Pollution did not pertain to the intentions of the actor, and no distinctions were made between accidental and deliberate violations. Merely to shed blood or encounter death was polluting. Consequently, the polluted person did not have to assume responsibility, to repent, or to renew the self morally. Essentially, both the pollution and the purification were external to the violator and amoral. Polluting acts occurred in the context of rather physical forces, akin to electricity or the shark's response to blood. (Buddhist teaching veered away from an amoral pollution, stressing personal responsibility. People with both Shinto and Buddhist loyalties therefore suffered some ambiguity.)

In the medieval period, the warrior or serf let his master be his will. The master held the power of life and death over the servant; morality was more a matter of loyalty to conscience. This deemphasis on conscience in personal life has persisted even in the modern period. As the honor accorded ritual suicide suggests, the individual has been subject to the social code in nearly all matters.

From medieval times, as we suggested earlier, an individual's proper bearing toward the group was loosely codified in Bushido, the warrior's way. Robert Bellah's study of Tokugawa religion suggests that Bushido discipline is largely the basis for the vitality of the modern Japanese economy, serving a purpose similar to what Protestant worldliness did for Western capitalism.[43]

The watchwords for the individual in Japanese religious history, then, were discipline and self-effacement. Fulfillment would come from submission to nature and service to the group, not from self-development or personal contact with God. The religious traditions, consequently, tended to help satisfy society's need for good workers and compliant citizens. Although this is true of religious traditions in most places, it stands out in Japan. The happy life that a new religion such as Tenrikyo holds out to its faithful is the result of reviving ancient concepts, including the submersion of the individual in the group. Soka Gakkai and other politically active religions stress service to the group.

Just as radical and Marxist political groups in the West offer their faithful a cause in which to lose themselves, the Japanese new religions have capitalized on the security that an individual feels in being part of a large group. In the clan, the nation, or the religious group, the Japanese individual has felt secure—safe from meaninglessness and partner to something large and compelling. All the beauty in Japanese culture, all the intelligence in Japanese technology, ought to incline us to study such "belonging" carefully.

Ultimate Reality

Japanese divinity, though complex, is essentially an impersonal collectivity of natural and clan forces. Although devotion to a particular kami, Buddha, or Daoist god qualifies this assertion somewhat (the people who place offerings at the "baby shrine" of the Bodhisattva of Mercy in Tokyo no doubt pray to an individual figure), the sharply defined personage that we associate with the God of Western religion hardly appears in Japan. The gods of Shinto mythology, for instance, have a quite finite knowledge, love, and power; they have not separated from the cosmos to make particular demands. (Particular kami do take over individuals such as Miki, the foundress of Tenrikyo, so we must qualify that statement, too.)

In the course of Japanese history, there have been numerous personal claims to divinity such as Miki's. In the thirteenth century, Nichiren was confident enough of his success in propagating Buddhist dharma to proclaim himself "Bodhisattva of Superb Action,"[44] taking advantage of the common doctrine about the buddha-nature residing in all living things. For the common populace, though, divinity did not reflect individual humanity. Its best representations were nature or the clan. Yet insofar as people always conceive of divinity through their sense of perfection or power (and through their revelatory experiences), even impersonal Japanese divinity occasionally touched the human qualities of knowledge and love.

The Buddhists best showed deep knowledge to Japan—the ultimate reality that shone in enlightenment. Insofar as Japan deified the Buddha, it deified glorious understanding. From enlightenment, further, one could reason that the buddha-nature was the basis for the world's intelligibility. It was what makes things be and what gives things meaning. It was also an active source, issuing all things from its womb. The generation of all things from buddha-nature was not the same as the "logical" creation that Hellenized Western religion developed, but it did correlate Buddhist ultimate reality with mind and understanding.

Love was another matter. The *bodhisattva* vow, of course, was based on great compassion, and all East Asia best loved the *bodhisattva* Kannon, the *bodhisattva* of mercy, to whom it looked for motherly care. Amida Buddha, dispensing mercy from the Pure Land, was another divine figure both personal and encouraging warm emotion. In keeping with the injunction to stop craving, though, love or compassion was not

to stir desire, however noble. So one could work for
the salvation of all beings in good cheer, believing that
their present sufferings were no cause for raging
against divinity's or even society's injustices. So the
love of the *bodhisattva,* even when it entailed suffering, was of a different sort than the redemptive love
(*agape*) of Western religion.[45] For Japan evil has been
more an illusion than a disordered love or an idolatry.
In the eons of time, in the vastness of *ku* (emptiness),
present problems have been but fleeting. If one would
abandon thinking about them and loose one's attachment to them, one could relate to them properly. Then
death would lose its sting and suffering have no
fangs.[46]

The Buddhists were by far the most acute Japanese philosophers; the conceptions of divinity in the
other traditions were far less clear. For Japanese folk
religion, which touched all but the most intellectual,
divinity was quite piecemeal. Its representation was
the local shrine or the house altar; neither negated
the other, and neither denied the divinity of the
shrines in the neighboring villages or of the altars in
the next block. Folk religiosity therefore was quite tolerant—and quite confusing. It was relatively happy to
multiply divinities without seeming necessity. A
Shinto wedding, a Buddhist funeral, and a good many
charms in between were the common custom. The
gods of Shinto mythology, Daoist magic, and popular
Buddhism but varied a sacredness felt to be quite near.
For the few who hungered after simplicity, nature or
the Buddhist void sufficed. Either could anchor spirituality in the present. Either could rouse wonder and
make any time or space profound.

To the present, the times and spaces that are most
wonderful, though, are the folk festivals and the popular pilgrim shrines. As the diary of a pilgrim to Ise
puts it: "One does not feel like an ordinary person any
longer but as though reborn in another world."[47]
At special festivals or shrines, one passed a threshold
(*limen*) and went from the ordinary to the sacred
world. The diary of the Ise pilgrim describes this lim-
inal experience in the aesthetic manner noted above:
The pine groves have an unearthly shadow; the rare
flowers that survived the frost carry a delicate pathos;
most of the adornments in the shrine recall the ancient days, when religious life was honest, simple, and
rough. The pilgrim notes the spray over the hills, the
solitary woods that beckon to the meditative. He
washes in the sea to gain outer purity and strives for
a clean Shinto worship (with no Buddhist interfer-

ence) to gain inner purity. Throughout, the physical
beauty of Ise engrosses him.

Shinto Shrines.[48] To set off places where people
might venerate the kami, the Japanese have long fashioned wooden shrines with encompassing groves.
They have not designed the shrines for communal
worship, but rather as simple sites where people might
recite ritual prayers and make offerings to the kami.
Unlike the Buddhist temples, the Shinto shrines originally did not contain statues. The official focal point
of veneration usually was an old sword or mirror,
which was considered to be the kami's resting place or
"body." However, these ritual objects were seldom
seen, even by the Shinto priests, so the general impression most visitors received was of a simple wooden
pavilion where one might make a personal petition
or venerate the kami in the course of a village
celebration.

Usually the encompassing grove was almost as
important as the wooden pavilion. The grove typically
was of rectangular shape, and one entered it through
a sacred archway or *torii*. At the entrance stood a well,
where visitors were to take some water in a wooden
dipper and purify their hands. At the entrance to many
Shinto shrines two stone lions stood guard. Even today the tall trees create an atmosphere of quiet, which
the trees' association with the kami turns in the direction of religious respect. The general appearance of
both the grove and the shrine buildings is unadorned.
Thus the grove's vegetation burgeons almost wildly
and the shrine buildings usually are of rough wood.
Exceptions occur, as in the red-painted Heian shrine
of Kyoto, but even there the total effect is subdued, in
flight from anything fancy or garish. The roofs of the
large Heian buildings are shingled with natural materials, and the gardens behind the buildings are understated. As with the great shrine at Ise, the grove keeps
a fairly dense appearance, probably so that the natural
influences of the kami can seem to outweigh the cultural influences of human beings.

When visitors approach a main shrine, they usually clap their hands and ring a suspended bell to attract the gods' attention. They then bow, in reverence
or prayer, and deposit their offerings in a money chest.
Another building, at the innermost part of the shrine,
is a sort of holy-of-holies, where the deities actually
dwell. Laity have no access to this building, and the
popular attitude has been that to peek into it, and
observe the ritual objects that attract the kami, would

be to court blindness or death. Buddhist influences caused some Shinto shrines to erect pictures of human beings or images of gods, but generally the "bodies" of the kami have been impersonal objects. In addition to the old swords and mirrors, stones, sacred texts, ancient scrolls, jewels, and balls of crystal have predominated. All these objects have associations with natural forces (or, on occasion, heroic human figures) thought to embody the kami. When the influence of Buddhist *bodhisattvas* came to color the Shinto notion of the kami, and so led to deifying especially loyal subjects of the emperors, the headgear, batons, weapons, clothing, writing implements, and other possessions of such deified subjects also became "bodies" of the kami.

Before the disestablishment of Shinto after World War II, the government classified shrines on twelve levels. At the head of the list was the Great Imperial Shrine at Ise. Below Ise came the various large government or national shrines, such as the Heian Shrine in Kyoto and the Meiji Shrine in Tokyo, and then the smaller local shrines. Not even on the list were the tens of thousands of little village or domestic shrines, at which a great deal of Shinto worship actually occurred. Before World War II there were about 111,000 official shrines and about 15,500 Shinto priests.

Two major themes sound in most pilgrims' accounts. One is the holiness of nature, and nature's superiority to our cultural gewgaws. If not interfered with, nature offers us a lush growth and quiet that can reorient our souls. The second major theme is the antiquity of the Shinto shrines and their traditions. Japanese told themselves: Ancestors have come to shrines such as this, prayed prayers such as these, for hundreds of years. Shinto has been the native Japanese way, the tradition that has made us who we are. Coming close to nature, doing as our ancestors have always done, we approach the sacred center of reality, where things work as they should.

SUMMARY: THE JAPANESE CENTER

Characteristically, the Japanese have shown a remarkable talent for taking other peoples' works and giving them a distinctive polish or perfection. This has hap-

pened recently with Western technology, and historically it has happened with non-Japanese religion. Most of the religious influences that Japan appropriated and perfected came from China. To its native Shinto orientations, Japan welded Confucian, Daoist, and Buddhist components. The result was an energetic, disciplined, elegant religious ideal. Aesthetic as well as philosophic, solitary yet bounded by clan psychologies, the Japanese way could take nationalistic and militaristic turns without completely losing sight of a beautiful center.

At the midmost portion of the Japanese imagination, a cherry blossom stands threatened by an unseasonable frost. Cool, refined, melancholic, this image says that the center of reality is an emptiness that incises natural details. In both the lonely novels of a Nobel laureate such as Yasunari Kawabata and the serene lectures of a Zen roshi such as Shunryu Suzuki, the center keeps particulars lean and alert, makes tea utensils objects of art.

The Japanese center that provokes such responses is not personal. The nature that gives serenity and proportion is not warm. No divine face waits to break through the emptiness of the Rock Garden. In the reflecting pond of the Golden Pavilion one sees only trees, pavilion, and sky. Buddha upon Buddha, the rows of statues in the Kyoto temples depersonalize as well as multiply the possibilities of enlightenment. Like the many haiku depicting different moments of spiritual arrest or insight, the buddhas diversify as much as they unify. Thus they make the unity of the buddha-nature cumulative: Since any being can flash forth the light of being, a single force of light, a uniform no-thingness, might remove the barriers between us and the rest of the world. When such barriers are removed, the central light can shine. Then our problems reduce to delusion, rather than to the Hindu illusion. The world itself is completely real and lightsome. Only our ignorance keeps us in the dark.

At the Japanese center, reality is polite. Cleanliness and formality, mediated through Shinto concerns with purity and the vital forces of nature, obtain. The rituals of the traditional religious year express different aspects of this vitality. For harvests, marrying, the New Year, and burials, different measures of Shinto and Buddhist beliefs color life's mystery fertile, familial, regenerative, or transmigratory. It is a beautiful land that the Japanese people celebrate. It is a cohesive national identity.

At the Japanese center throbs an amazing energy, coupled with a redoubtable discipline. Yet the center itself remains elusive. The shrines and statues cannot sum it up. It is a whole pictured by preference in peace. It is a flux stopped just long enough to become art. The center sheds much light on death. Death to the body can be as near as failure to serve one's lord perfectly. Death to the self can be as familiar as a popular sutra. Nature dies and is reborn so regularly that the death and rebirth of the personality seem quite fitting. Shame and honor revolve so inexorably that detachment is but common sense.

Detached, the Japanese personality stands a good chance of following up its affinities for beauty, of tending its gardens, and throwing its pots. Detached, the personality finds life's inequities more bearable. Rich and poor, male and female, honored and downcast are the ways things are. Things can change, but they do not have to change for there to be meaning, order, and a reasonable tradition. Reality may seem to be diverse, but in fact Japanese culture shows those who penetrate to the center that it has a remarkable unity.

The polite center judges all brutality harshly, but brutality had many inglorious seasons in Japan. For peasants, women, and ordinary people, it has been easy to be in the wrong place at the wrong time. Then the ruling powers have crushed people thoughtlessly, like a cart rolling over a bug. The consolations of nature never shroud the fact that nature itself can be very cruel. In a land of volcanoes and fierce storms, beauty and violence have often commingled. In a land of warriors and artists, discipline has had several faces. The Japanese center more lets these disparities be than reconciles them in some thicker mystery. Atonement and redemption are not the Japanese way. True, Shinran came to a profound sense of self-abandonment, in which he let the ultimate do its own chanting in his heart. But Shinran seems emotionally extraordinary, the warm exception proving the generally cool rule.

Warm and cool, raw and cooked—both sides of our dichotomies apply in most lands. The best one can do is speak of tendencies, generalities, proclivities— quite fallible impressions that the reader should test warily. We keep coming back to moments in quiet Japanese gardens, when rain gently dimpled the waters. The message then was primitive, ungilded by human contrivance, preferring rough timber and clean thatch. The message was: "Be attentive! Focus your gaze; give the wind and rain good hearing." There wasn't more than the wind and rain at the Japanese center. Quiet and sun added nothing essential. Any time one perceived the force of nature, whether the kami were gentle or the kami were wild, one perceived ultimate, defining reality. This was cool and raw, strong and beautiful, astringent yet ineffably peaceful.

Discussion Questions

1. In what sense is Shinto a fertility religion?

2. What seem to have been the primary psychodynamics of the new religions?

3. Analyze the feminine and masculine components in native Japanese culture.

4. How does the Japanese sense of shame differ from the Western sense of sin?

5. Does Japan make any hard distinctions between aesthetics and religion? Explain.

6. Where would you locate Confucian influence on Japan?

7. Explain how the tea ceremony could become a religious pathway.

8. What were the main Buddhist developments of the Heian period?

9. What was the significance of the Kokugaku movement?

10. How did the kami figure in the average Japanese person's life throughout history?

Key Terms

aesthetic: concerning the beautiful or artistic. In many religions it is hard to separate aesthetic values from the people's sense of what is fitting or filled with divine splendor.

Amaterasu: the sun goddess who has been the chief deity among the Shinto kami. The myths about Amaterasu place her in tension with such other natural forces as the wind and make her the ancestor of the Japanese ruling clan.

Bushido: the ethical and disciplinary code of Japanese samurai (warriors). Bushido was more cultural than expressly religious, but it drew on Confucian notions of responsibility to one's superiors and Buddhist (especially Zen) notions of the disciplined spirit. Those formed by the Bushido Code considered dishonor worse than death and offered their superiors (the lords for whom they fought and served) complete loyalty. For women, the Bushido Code stressed loyalty, fidelity, and above all chastity, creating a feminine parallel to the warrior's commitment to honor.

kami: the Japanese (Shinto) term for the gods or spirits. Traditionally one numbered the kami at 800,000, a round figure probably intended to suggest their profusion. Although most of the kami apparently originally were natural forces (wind, storm, sun; spirits of various striking local phenomena—tall trees, distinctive rocks), heads of the clan and other heroes also could be kami. Indeed, when Buddhism had made a great impact in Japan, the line between kami and *bodhisattvas* often vanished, leading to Buddhist saints being accounted kami and kami being considered *bodhisattvas.* The kami prompt reflection on why it is that people around the world seem to personify or animate the striking things in their natural and social orbits. With the rise of modern critical consciousness this tendency has atrophied, but one can see remnants of it in poets' talk about their muses and naturalists' descriptions of their love or awe for particular desert, mountain, or seaside sites.

nembutsu: an invocation ("Homage to Amida Buddha") central to the practice of Pure Land ("Jodo") Buddhism. The *nembutsu* combines characteristics of a typical Eastern mantra with characteristics of Christian prayer. As mantric, it offers the disciple a familiar, repetitive sound that can calm and direct consciousness, freeing it to sense reality as Buddhist devotionalism has found most useful. As similar to Christian prayer, it offers a personified focus, a divine being one can imagine (because of traditional iconography) and love. "Homage" is an awkward translation of something that combines reverent acknowledgment with submission, respect, and praise.

new religions: a name applied to largely Shinto sects that arose in Japan from the nineteenth century on. As a general phenomenon, the new religions clearly expressed a need for religious ways more vital than what were available by the end of the Tokugawa shogunate. Most of the founders of the new religious groups were charismatic personalities who felt taken over by a kami or called to restore old religious ways rooted in traditional village life. The loose lines between Buddhism and Shinto meant that Buddhist elements were not excluded, while a desire for warm ties with the divinity sometimes led to making the chief deity a parental god. Some of the new religions ran afoul of the government, but others were apolitical and sought only a renewal of charismatic religious authority.

samurai: Japanese warriors of the feudal period who swore fealty to their lord under pain of death. The samurai became renowned for their courage, sense of honor, and discipline, as well as for their outbursts of cruelty and their share in the infighting of Japanese politics. Many samurai found Zen Buddhism congenial, since it seemed to offer a spiritual discipline to inform their life of dedication to their liege-lords. Despite the traditional Buddhist demand for noninjury *(ahimsa),* the samurai developed swordsmanship, archery, and hand-to-hand combat as holistic disciplines. For women, the Bushido virtues of chastity and honor offered a parallel field for spiritual discipline.

torii: the sacred gateway that stands at the entrance to Shinto shrines. Most interpreters see the *torii* as dividing the sacred realm of the shrine from the profane outside world. Usually there is a well nearby, for purification, and visitors become more serious after having passed through the *torii* (though Shinto shrines are not grim places). The shrine itself is thought of as a domicile of the kami, who not only reside at a special holy building but also are present in the trees, the streams, and the other aspects of the natural beauty. Some say the *torii,* which has the form of two posts with a double horizontal lintel, represents perches for the birds *(tori),* in thanks for the help they gave the gods.

Zen: the Japanese name for the school of Buddhism that has most stressed meditation. In China this school went by the name Chan and was attributed to Bodhidharma, a meditation-master come from India. Zen has considered meditation to epitomize the Enlightened One's teaching and methodology. Historically it has had great influence in Japanese culture, shaping the ideals of the samurai and undergirding such practices as swordsmanship, floral arrangement, the tea ceremony, and gardening. Rinzai Zen has tended to seek sudden enlightenment, urging disciples to strive hard, try to crack their koans, and keep up a firm discipline of work, silence, and obedience. Soto Zen has been more relaxed, thinking that enlightenment should come gradually, as the ripening of an overall maturation in Buddhist faith and practice. Soto has also lessened the distinction between meditation and the rest of life, thinking that as one's practice developed one would always be cultivating one's innate buddha-nature and helping it manifest itself.

INTERLUDE

NEAR EASTERN RELIGIONS

You now know a fair amount about how Asian religion has regarded nature, society, the self, and ultimate reality or divinity. The religions that arose in the Near East differ notably on these points.

First, Near Eastern religion is more realistic about the natural world than Asian religion is. By realistic we mean "undoubting": Judaism, Christianity, and Islam show little of the Hindu or Buddhist inclination to consider physical phenomena illusory (as evidenced in maya or samsara). As you know, India has doubted the physical world more than East Asia, but East Asian Buddhism brought samsara to China and Japan. In contrast, the major Near Eastern religions were tutored by the Bible and the Qur'an to consider nature as God's creation. That somewhat relativized nature—nature did not exist independently—but more important, it verified the reports of the senses and prevented any concept like samsara.

Second, the Near Eastern religions have generally been more cohesive (at least in their theory) and action oriented than Asian religions have been. Hinduism was part of Indian culture, which it considerably informed, but through most of its history

India was a rather loose collection of quite disparate kingdoms. Buddhism became a multiethnic religion, and perhaps for that reason its key social concept, the *sangha,* was more inclusive than anything comparable in Hinduism. (Indeed, the *sangha* is quite parallel to the Church or the Muslim *Ummah.*) However, neither China nor Japan developed a religious collectivity (apart from the *sangha*) that stood out from existing ethnic or cultural groupings.

Furthermore, none of the Asian religions strikes the Western reader as passionate for social justice, corporal works of mercy, or institutionalized charity. Hindu dharma, Buddhist morality, and Confucian ethics had many lofty social ideals, but they did not produce the drive toward democracy and equal sharing that their Western counterparts did. They did not, for instance, make as much of popular education, nursing, or almsgiving, though Buddhists were supposed to support mendicant [begging] monks. Similarly, their castes, peasantry, and poor seem more tolerated, more condoned or even sponsored, than Western slaves, peasantry, and poor have been. We do not make this observation judgmentally (the Asian religions have their own basis for judgment). We make it with all due qualification and certainly with no boosterism for the West.

Third, the Near Eastern religions differ from the Asian religions in several ways concerning the self. The Asian religions (more so in India than in East Asia) have been focused on the human spirit in such a way that the human body has been perceived as less unquestioned than has been true in the West. The mature self of wisdom or enlightenment in Asian religions differs from the West's prophet, as elaborated below. The Near Eastern scriptures clearly refuse to dichotomize the personality—to split body and spirit. For them the human person is a unity, and the reality of the body and the spirit is never doubted. Thus, Near Eastern religions show neither a great urge to leave the body nor a doctrine of no-self (*anatman*). (Greek, Iranian, and Gnostic thought accounts for the dualism that sometimes shows in Christianity; such dualism is hardly apparent in either Judaism or Islam.)

The wise person in India or the Far East is enlightened. As the word *Buddhism* (from *bodhi* meaning "knowledge") suggests, Asia seeks light

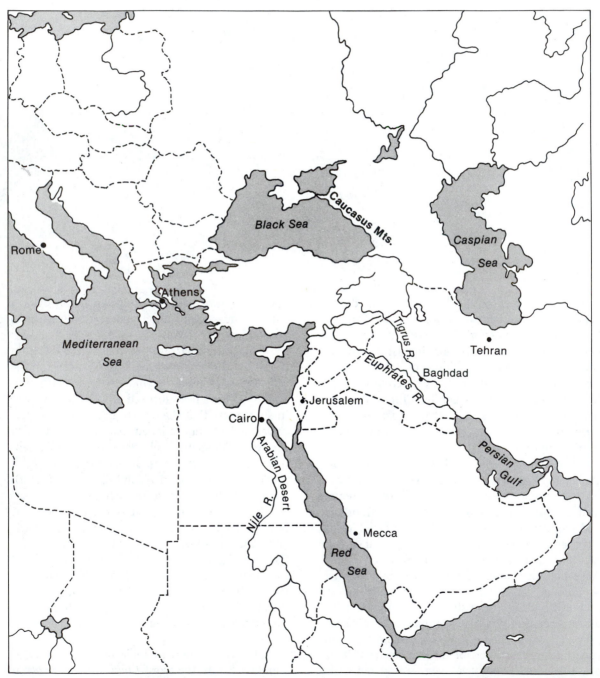

Figure 31 *Egypt, Iran, and Greece.*

for the mind and clarity for the spirit. The West does not dispute this quest, especially when it turns toward secular education (which narrows the meaning of *knowledge*). However, the West uses a different metaphor. While Eastern "light" or wisdom is associated with seeing, prophecy is associated with hearing. In part because many influential Near Eastern religious personalities came from the desert, where the eye has little food, aural imagery prevails in the Bible and the Qur'an. (Greek thought, however, was oriented toward seeing and light.) The word of God, spoken to the heart (of the faithful listener), is the foundation of the Near Eastern religious program. The prophet, then, is not so much enlightened as inspired— addressed and directed by a spirit that uses him or her as a mouthpiece.

Fourth, these models for the religious self clearly correlate with the different conceptions of ultimate reality or God. The Asian conception is of an impersonal entity or condition, while the Near Eastern conception is of a personal one. The Hindu *Brahman,* Buddhist *Nirvana,* and Chinese *Tao* were all more coextensive with nature than beyond it. Furthermore, none was a superperson prone to uttering a directive word. Thus, neither India nor the Far East broke with the cosmological myth by proposing a doctrine of creation from nothingness. In the following chapters, we will maintain that although the Near Eastern religions sense the dangers of anthropomorphism, the God of the Bible and the Qur'an knows and loves in such a way that Western religion becomes fundamentally interpersonal. To be sure, Asian divinities took on human features and solicited not just meditation but petitionary prayer. To be sure, no one has ever seen the biblical God's face, and the Qur'anic God is not a person with whom you casually chat. Nonetheless, India senses an impersonal foundation for the world and East Asia glides toward the *Tao* in ways that the Near Eastern religions do not.

If India is meditative and East Asia is aesthetic, then the Near East and West are ethical. India stresses rational spirit, East Asia stresses harmony, and the three Near Eastern religions, at their foundations, stress will. Greek thought does give the West, especially the Christian West, a charge of speculative intellectualism. Nevertheless, love (the primary act of the will) is the greatest Christian virtue, and both Jews and Muslims prize deeds over thoughts. "Ethical monotheism" is a phrase that scholars sometimes use to describe biblical religion; with some elaboration it will serve you well in what follows.

To be sure, these descriptions are all perilously brief. In each cultural area, folkways and the sameness of the human desire for wholeness have clouded any too-clear distinctions. As well, secularism—born in the modern West but now spread throughout the world—challenges the primacy we, and the traditional religions themselves, have accorded divinity. But that chapter is something of an epilogue, as you will see.

CHAPTER 7

RELIGIONS OF ANCIENT NEAR EASTERN CIVILIZATIONS

Zoroastrian fire symbol representing purity

We begin our study of traditions that began in the Near East with four great ancient cultures: Mesopotamia, Egypt, Iran, and Greece.

MESOPOTAMIA*

Ancient Near Eastern culture began in Sumer, which lay in the southern part of what is now Iraq, where the Tigris and Euphrates rivers come together and flow into the Persian Gulf. (The term *Mesopotamia* means "between the rivers.") The Sumerians arrived there as colonizers in prehistoric times and were not related either racially or linguistically to their neighbors to the north, the Akkadians. Sumer was a flat, marshy region, and the first settlements consisted of huts built on mud. Flood was a constant, potentially devastating threat. Silt made the land fertile, however, and the

*We are indebted in this section to Professor Eugene Webb of the University of Washington, who furnished us his materials on Mesopotamian religion. Any defects, however, are entirely our responsibility.

ca. 6500 B.C.E.	First Farming in Greece and Aegean Countries
ca. 5000	Agricultural Settlements in Egypt
ca. 3100	Unification of Egypt; Memphite Theology; Rise of Writing in Sumer
2700–2200	Old Kingdom in Egypt
2590	Great Pyramids at Giza
2050–1800	Middle Kingdom in Egypt
2000	Beginning of Minoan Civilization in Crete
1570–1165	New Kingdom in Egypt
ca. 1500	Iranian-Speaking Peoples Rise
1370	Akhenaton's "Monotheistic" Reform
1200	Collapse of Mycenaean Civilization in Greece
776	First Olympic Games
750	Homer's Iliad and the Poetry of Hesiod
ca. 588	Zoroaster Begins Prophetic Work
550	Cyrus II Founds Persian Empire; Zoroastrianism the Official Religion
525	Persian Conquest of Egypt
525–406	Aeschylus, Sophocles, Euripides
521	Persia Extends from Nile to Indus
469–332	Socrates, Plato, Aristotle
332–329	Alexander in Egypt, Persia, India
323–30	Ptolemaic Dynasty in Egypt
312	Start of Seleucid Era in Persia
247	Arsaces I Founds Parthian Empire
224 C.E.	Foundation of Sasanian Dynasty
637	Muslims Invade Persia

Sumerians were able over the millennia to transform the swamp into a garden. They were highly creative people, and by the time they developed cuneiform (wedge-shaped) writing—approximately two centuries before the Egyptians developed hieroglyphics—they had already built great terraced, multistoried temple towers (ziggurats) with bricks, and they were using sailboats, wheeled vehicles, animal-drawn plows, and potter's wheels. The country included a dozen small cities, each belonging in principle to its god and centered upon his temple. These cities included Eridu (traditionally considered the earliest, dating from about 4000 B.C.E.), Ur, Nippur, and Uruk or Erech. Sumerian kings served as representatives of the gods, enforcing their justice and promoting wealth to be used in their service. Cuneiform writing developed primarily as an instrument for recording contracts and accounts in the affairs of the temples, which controlled up to one-third of the land and owned great wealth.

It was also in Sumer, toward the middle of the twenty-fourth century B.C.E., that the idea of imperial rule was born, when a king named Lugalzaggesi (Zaggesi the Great) conquered a large part of the valley. An inscription that Lugalzaggesi placed on a monument in Nippur tells how Enlil, the supreme god and king of all countries, gave dominion to Lugalzaggesi, who

MAJOR CHALLENGES TO THE COSMOLOGICAL MYTH		
Egypt	Akhenaton Amon hymns	"Monotheism" Negative theology
Iran	Zoroaster	Interior, spiritual experience as source of divine attributes
Greece	Philosophy	Correlation of mind and reality; rationality as crux of reality

then prayed that his rule might be peaceful and prosperous forever.

Sumerian political power never extended northward into Akkad, but Sumer had enormous cultural influence there. Over the centuries the Akkadians learned writing from the Sumerians and adopted much of their mythology and technology. Despite Lugalzaggesi's prayer for perpetual dominion, he was later defeated in battle and taken captive by an Akkadian, Sargon I, who founded an empire of his own—and also claimed the authority of Enlil. Sargon's rule was short-lived, however, and the Sumerians regained their independence for a while. But by the time of Hammurabi in the eighteenth century B.C.E., the Sumerians were completely absorbed into the civilization that is now known as the Babylonian, after its principal city, Babylon (*Babilani* or "the gateway of the gods"), which grew to prominence after the demise of Ur.

Although we have some Sumerian fragments, most of the writings now available come from the Babylonian period, so we see Sumerian myths through Babylonian eyes and with Babylonian adaptations. One reason that the evidence is so fragmentary, in addition to its enormous antiquity, is the fact that the cuneiform tablets were not used primarily for the recording of myths, but for business accounts. In many cases the tablets with myths seem to have been the exercise books of schoolboys learning to write by copying out stories. Still, we have enough evidence to provide a fairly clear picture of the religious conceptions not only of the Babylonians, but also of the Sumerians.

Sumerian Creation Myths

The great legacy of Mesopotamia is its mythology. To begin with the beginning, let us consider one of the earliest Sumerian creation myths, the story of Enki and Ninhursag in the land of Dilmun.[1] Dilmun, the poem tells us, was pure, clean, and bright, free from death and disease, until the mother goddess, Ninhursag, was impregnated by Enki, variously interpreted as the god of earth or of water. These events took place in primordial time, the time of the ordering of the cosmos. In the myth, Ninhursag and Enki produce a daughter, with whom Enki also mates and who then gives birth to another daughter, with whom Enki also mates. This last birth brings Uttu, Enki's great granddaughter. Ninhursag warns the girl that Enki lurks in the marsh and lusts for her, and that she should not yield herself to him until he offers her the appropriate gifts for a bride. He does so, however, and she gives herself to him joyfully.

At this point it seems (the text is broken) that Ninhursag intervenes, takes Enki's semen, and uses it to bring forth eight plants. Enki, noticing the eight new plants, decides he must "know" them and decide their fate, and therefore he eats them. Ninhursag becomes furious at this usurpation. She curses him and says she will no longer look on him with the eye of life. Enki then languishes and the land becomes dry and dusty. Alarmed, the other gods, with Enlil as their spokesman, intercede through the help of a clever fox to get Ninhursag to restore Enki. She does so by placing her vulva next to the ailing parts of Enki's body and bringing forth eight goddesses, each of whom heals the part with which she is associated. The eight goddesses evidently replace the eight plants that Enki had misappropriated. The poem ends with the naming of the goddesses and the assignment of their destinies. It is not clear who speaks at that point, Enki or Ninhursag, but since the ending is one of reconciliation and restoration of life, it seems that the naming takes place with Ninhursag's approval. The last line of the surviving text praises Father Enki.

It is not easy to interpret a text that comes to us from a time so distant, in fragments, and possibly with many layers of revision along the way, but the main outline is not too difficult to discern. Clearly the myth depicts the beginning of the ordered world (or "cosmos") as we know it— a world in which nature brings forth living creatures. Before natural life with its cycles of birth, fertility, and death begins, there is no death or disease, but with life comes the problem of evil in its various forms. The form of evil that this story emphasizes is the evil of disorder. Exactly why Enki's claim to preeminence (that is what his eating of the plants seems to imply) is a source of disorder is not altogether clear. Many ancient myths take the preeminence of the father god for granted, but this one does not. Possibly, therefore, there was an earlier version with a matriarchal emphasis, that is, with the idea that the female principle is preeminent in generation. At any rate, what we see is a struggle between the male and female sources of life to define their relative dignity.

When Enki, the male principle, claims eminence that Ninhursag finds excessive, she demonstrates her own importance by withdrawing her life-giving power. The other gods subsequently realize her importance, as does Enki himself, who must ask her to heal each part of his body that is afflicted. At the end an appropriate balance seems to emerge. The masculine principle's usurpation of knowledge and power is represented as a sort of fall that must be purged through suffering and the reestablishment of proper order.

Thus we see a fairly typical mythic pattern in which disorder in creation is repaired by dissolution, and right order is established through a new act of creation (the healing of Enki and the birth of the goddesses who replace the plants). Since this sequence of creation, death, and rebirth is also the pattern of the annual cycle of vegetation, the myth seems to do double duty as both a story of creation and commentary on the cycles of nature.

Case Study: **Enuma Elish.** Another widespread motif is that of a battle between creative and destructive forces. In the Dilmun myth this motif takes the form of a personal conflict between mother and father deities. In the famous *Enuma Elish* myth, it becomes a regular military campaign. Both myths explain the seasonal renewal of nature and also the continuing

need for the creative forces in the cosmos actively to counter threats of disorder and returning chaos. (*Cosmos* and *chaos* are Greek terms that have come to be used generally to refer on the one hand to the ordered totality of things, including all the levels of being and even the gods, and on the other hand to a state of unformed, unordered being. The term *chaos* originally meant an abyss and comes from the verb "to yawn." *Cosmos* originally referred to the village as compared with its surrounding wilderness. Eventually it came to refer to whatever was harmonious, civilized, beautiful, and constituted an ordered whole.)

The *Enuma Elish* (the title means "When on high" and is from the first words of the Akkadian text) has come down to us mainly in its Babylonian form, but some fragments of a Sumerian original have also survived. In the Sumerian version everything begins with the union of sky and earth, represented by the first "thing," a cosmic mountain whose base is earth (female) and whose summit is the sky (male). The Babylonian version begins with the precosmic chaos: "When on high the heaven had not been named. Firm ground below had not been called by name. . . . No reed hut had been matted, no marsh land had appeared. . . ."[2] Neither gods nor humans had yet been created. There was only the primordial pair, Apsu (male, associated with fresh water) and Tiamat (female, the sea), "their waters commingling as a single body." Time and the world begin when they give birth to the first gods (perhaps representing the accumulation of silt where the river water meets the sea). These beget other gods and goddesses who mate in turn to produce the gods of earth (Ea) and sky (Anu) and so on. (Interestingly enough, earth and sky are here both represented by male gods, evidently because the Babylonians wanted to give honor to the earth god, Ea, progenitor of their own special god, Marduk. They seem to have been more emphatically patriarchal than the Sumerians.)

As the story proceeds, the younger gods annoy their original ancestors through their poor manners and overbearing character. Apsu complains that he can gain no rest by day or by night because of their incessant noise and he proposes to annihilate them. Tiamat, though she too is angry with them, urges restraint, but he ignores her. When the younger gods hear of his plans, they become virtually paralyzed with fear, except for Ea, who casts a spell of sleep on Apsu and then slays him. Afterward Ea builds his home on Apsu's body and begets Marduk. (The image suggests earth, perhaps mud from the river, building up above the level of the water so that habitations may be built and the Babylonians eventually generated.)

The poem proceeds with lavish praise of Marduk (the sun), who is said to be the tallest and strongest of the gods. Marduk himself creates the four winds and produces streams, both of which annoy Tiamat. She decides to put an end to all of this nuisance and to avenge Apsu. She takes a new consort, Kingu, and raises an army with which to make war on the younger gods. When they hear of this they are at a loss until they think of asking Marduk to lead them. Ea bids Marduk come to the assembly of the gods. Marduk promises to be their champion but asks in return that he become supreme among them and receive all their authority to "determine the fates." They willingly proclaim him king and confer on him throne, scepter, and royal vestments.

When Tiamat sees Marduk ride into battle against her, she goes wild, taking leave of her senses and shaking to her lowest parts—an image not only of a stormy sea, but of chaos itself. Slaying her, Marduk splits her in two like a shellfish and thrusts one-half upward to make the sky and the other downward to make the sea, setting guards to ensure that her waters will not escape and threaten the world again. He makes the dome of heaven correspond to earth as its heavenly counterpart. Then he executes Kingu and creates human beings from his blood so that the gods will have servants to maintain the earth when they have withdrawn to the heavens. As their final work of creation the gods build Babylon and at its center, as a temple to Marduk, the great ziggurat of Esagila, described as reaching as high as Apsu, as high as the primordial waters were deep.

Notice in this myth that the gods need human beings that they may rest from labor. The gods are not unlimited in power, but constitute only a part of the larger system of things that is the cosmos as a whole. They themselves must struggle to establish creation and keep it in proper order. Also, they do not create the world from nothing but make it from a preexisting reality. The world as we know it comes from the body of the subdued Tiamat, and human beings come from the blood of Kingu. One might say that the gods do not "create" the world in the same sense that the God of the Judeo-Christian-Islamic tradition creates. Rather they are the world, and we are of the same substance as they. Theogony (the birth of the gods) and comogony (the birth of the ordered whole) are here one and the same.

Order

The plot of the *Enuma Elish* describes both the creation of the cosmos as a whole and the evolution of the political order of Mesopotamia, as seen from the perspective of Babylonians in the second millennium. The authors are looking back to the origins of an order in which they have preeminence over their neighbors but are themselves under the authority of the gods and divine justice. The movement from a democratic assembly of gods to a centralized monarchic system under the rule of Marduk, god of Babylon, parallels the historical movement from independent city-states in Sumer and Akkad to the Babylonian Empire. That the Babylonian emperors interpreted their own authority as subordinate to and representative of an overarching divine order can be seen, for example, in the preamble to the Law Code of Hammurabi (approximately 1750 B.C.E.), which opens with a description of how Anu and Enlil, lords of heaven and earth, committed lordship ("the Enlil functions over all mankind") to Marduk and then called Hammurabi personally to enforce their justice in the land.

The underlying idea in this picture of historical development seems to have been that earthly kingship was conferred from a superhuman source and was an imitation of and participation in the ordering power of a divine original, the order established by the gods of the empire at the beginning of the world. This meant that royal rule was intended to be sacred rule in the service of true justice. It also meant that human life and its order were connected with the cosmic order and the life of the gods. If human farmers did not cultivate their crops, if reverent worshipers did not offer sacrifices, if justice among human beings was allowed to deteriorate, then the life of the gods would also suffer injury.

This interpretation of the relationship among human beings, the world, and the gods is a good example of cosmological symbolism: symbolism in which human life and society are interpreted by analogy with the cosmic order. That was the predominant pattern of symbolism in ancient Mesopotamia, and we will see it again in Egypt. It is not the only possible pattern of symbolic interpretation, but all over the world it seems to have been the first to develop.

Anthropomorphic symbolism, such as that which flourished in classical Greece, likens society and the cosmos to a human existence. Specifically, it depicts reality in terms of the inner order of a wise and virtuous person. Anthropomorphic symbolism usually develops after cosmologically symbolized societies have broken down and disappointed their members so deeply that the members feel the need for an entirely new way of discovering meaning and purpose. This sort of disappointment never seems to have afflicted the ancient Mesopotamians, at least not enough to have caused a radically new development in their culture. Most of the myths the Mesopotamians have left us suggest that they found the evil of the universe intelligible in terms of the basic model we have seen: a precarious balance of interdependent forces.

Case Study: Gilgamesh   Nonetheless, the Mesopotamians did finally wrestle with the problem of a suffering that is genuinely personal and calls the cosmological principle into question. The epic of Gilgamesh is their famous meditation on personal suffering. It concerns a famous early king of Uruk in Sumer and probably dates from the late third millennium B.C.E. The most complete surviving text is in Assyrian, but there are fragments of earlier versions in Sumerian and Akkadian.[3]

Gilgamesh, the poem tells us, was of mingled parentage, divine and human, but he was a mortal all the same, and his mortality is the poem's main theme. At the opening Gilgamesh is a vigorous and effective ruler, in fact too vigorous: His constant demands for labor and military service lead the people of Uruk to appeal to the gods for relief. The goddess Aruru responds by creating another energetic creature, Enkidu, to attract the interest of Gilgamesh. Enkidu is humanity in its most primitive state. He is naked, covered with hair, enormously strong, and lives among animals in the wilderness. Befriending the animals, Enkidu protects them from hunters, who, unable to fight him themselves, appeal to Gilgamesh. Gilgamesh sends a sacred prostitute, Shamhat, to civilize Enkidu. Shamhat goes to the wilderness to wait for Enkidu by a water hole. When he comes, she attracts his interest by uncovering her body. They enjoy a week of heroic lovemaking, at the end of which Enkidu tries to return to the company of his animals but finds them shying away from him. Shamhat tells him that he no longer belongs among animals but has become wise and godlike. She offers to take him to see the great walls of Uruk and mighty Gilgamesh. Enkidu decides to go with her and to challenge Gilgamesh. He arrives in Uruk at the moment of Gilgamesh's wedding procession and bars Gilgamesh's path to the bride. The two powerful figures hurl themselves at each other and fight like young bulls, shaking the walls of the bride's house. Gilgamesh turns out to be the stronger of the two, but his generous praise of Enkidu makes them fast friends. Looking for adventure together (Gilgamesh seems to have forgotten all about his bride), they set out to kill a monster named Huwawa. When they return victorious the goddess Ishtar falls in love with Gilgamesh and proposes to him. He turns her down. Furious, Ishtar appeals to her father, Anu, to unleash the bull of heaven. Anu warns her that this monster will be so destructive that there will be a famine for seven years, but she persuades him to unloose it anyway. However, Enkidu gets behind it and twists its tail while Gilgamesh plunges his sword into its neck. Enraged by Ishtar's curses, Enkidu tears off the bull's shank and throws it at the goddess.

This means trouble. The gods hold an assembly and sentence Enkidu to death. Enkidu is horrified and launches into a long lament in which he curses everything that has led to this end: his departure from the animals, his lovemaking with Shamhat, his migration to the city, and even his friendship with Gilgamesh. The sun god Shamash, however, intervenes and persuades him to withdraw his curses and bless his friend before dying. In a dream Enkidu has a vision of Irkalla, the land of the dead. It is a house of dust and darkness, devoid of real life, in which one is no more than a shadow. Far from representing a form of immortality, it is death depicted in the most graphic terms.

After his friend's death Gilgamesh falls into an extreme despondency, not simply due to the loss of his companion, but because death, which had always been a remote abstraction to him, has now become a vivid reality. He realizes that however long and glorious his life may be, death awaits. This thought becomes an obsession, undermining any joy in his own or his city's glory and any consolation from the balance of forces in the cosmos. The thought of his death haunts Gilgamesh day and night. Finally he decides to search for an escape from mortality. He has heard of an ancestor named Utnapishtim who once won eternal life as a gift from the gods and now dwells at the end of the earth. The sun god, Shamash, reproaches him for his lack of moderation, but Gilgamesh is not interested in reasonableness; his heart is set on only one thing: not to die. Eventually he arrives at the shore of the great sea that encircles the earth, where he finds a tavern run by a woman named Siduri. She offers the conventional wisdom, urging him to accept his mortality, enjoy food, drink, and merriment, wear beautiful clothing, bathe in fresh water, rejoice in his children, and give satisfaction to his wife. This, she says, is the task of human beings. Gilgamesh refuses to listen and persuades her to tell him how to find Utnapishtim. She directs him to the boatman, Urshanabi, who takes him to Utnapishtim's island.

The result, however, is bitterly disappointing. Utnapishtim tells Gilgamesh that he did not win immortality through deeds of valor. It happened at a time when the gods had decided to destroy humankind in a great flood. Ea, more foresighted than the other gods, realized that without human beings to maintain the earth the gods would languish for lack of sacrifices. Ea told Utnapishtim to build an ark and save his family and pairs of all animals. (The story is similar in many details to the biblical story of Noah, which, as far as written records indicate, it predates by perhaps a millennium.) After the flood the gods realized the fault of their hastiness and were so grateful to Utnapishtim that they conferred eternal life on him. Unfortunately that was something that could happen only once.

Utnapishtim suggests, evidently mockingly, that if Gilgamesh wishes to conquer death he might begin by trying to conquer sleep. No sooner does Gilgamesh take up the challenge than sleep overcomes him. Utnapishtim would happily let Gilgamesh sleep himself to death, but his wife takes pity on Gilgamesh and persuades Utnapishtim to wake him and let him go home. She also persuades him to tell Gilgamesh about a plant that will perpetually renew his youth. This thorny plant grows in the Apsu, the sweet waters deep under the earth. (In the Mesopotamian cosmology the earth is a great floating island.) Gilgamesh dives for it by tying stones to his feet and sinking to the bottom. When he gets the plant he is overjoyed, thinking his basic goal achieved. On the way home, however, feeling the heat of the day, he decides to take a swim in a cool pond. He leaves the plant with his clothes and while he is swimming a serpent comes out of its hole and eats the plant. Immediately the snake sloughs off its old skin and is renewed, shiny and young.

With that, Gilgamesh completely despairs. Following his despair, however, come resignation and composure. Essentially Gilgamesh accepts the wisdom of Shamash and Siduri that he had rejected earlier. At the end of the poem he takes the boatman around the great walls of Uruk, praising the grandeur of his royal domain.

Is the poem a lesson in moderation and the acceptance of human limitations, or is it a radical protest against those limitations? There is no easy answer. How far did the challenge to Mesopotamian cosmological assumptions proceed? Did anyone seriously doubt them to the point of considering another perspective? The ending of the poem seems designed to reassert the old beliefs. In the perspective of the conclusion, Gilgamesh's obsession becomes a temporary disorder that must be overcome if one is to live in proper harmony with the cosmos and the gods.[4]

EGYPT

Today Egypt is a powerful center of Arab and Muslim culture. Taxi drivers careen through Cairo with a Qur'an on the dashboard to protect them; common people lay rugs in the train station and kneel at the call to prayer. Yet the treasures of Tutankhamen, the Giza pyramids, and above all the Nile tie modern Cairo to the pre-Islamic Egypt of more than 5,000 years ago. Merely follow the Nile by train to Alexandria and you will see in its delta peasants drawing water with buffalo much as they did in the Old Kingdom.

The Nile itself is a principal player in Egyptian history. Its moods, both varying and constant, reflect the Egyptian soul. Historically, the Egyptian soul appears ageless. For the best part of 2,500 years Egyptian life remained the same. At the Great Pyramids near the Sphinx, the desert seems to have mimicked the Nile's behavior. The endless sand, like the river water, changes with the wind. Actually, though, little changes. Sky, sun, sand, and water—they all endure. Like stable props, they are set on every stage.

On the Egyptian stage, pharaohs and peasants enacted a mortality play. As the pyramids show, death kept adamant hold on this people's soul.

Beyond life under the sun, life in the flesh, lay deathlessness. The tomb then was an archway through which everybody passed. Sanity was preparing to pass well.

Standing before the Sphinx, an Egyptian might have offered a prayer such as this: "O god of the puzzle, well do you symbolize our situation. Strong as a lion, winged like thought, you beguile us like a woman. In this flesh, we mainly know contradiction. Body and thought, we go diverse ways. Clearly, though, all ways end in the underworld. Help us stand judgment there before Osiris. Help us enter Re's course through the sky. May our time in the sun go smoothly. May our afterlife be content. Help us solve our riddle."

History

Scholars debate the history of Egyptian religion, but the major events are clear. Unification of Upper (southern) and Lower (northern) Egypt occurred about 3100 B.C.E., and with it began the central Egyptian religious dogma—*divine kingship*.[5] In the prehistoric years before unification, Neolithic culture gradually developed small-town life, characterized by domestic animals, significant crafts (especially pottery), and probably the burial of the dead with hopes of an afterlife. From the beginnings of Egyptian history, local gods had great influence, and throughout the long dynasties they comprised a pantheon (assembly of divinities). It is well established that ancient Egypt was amazingly stable culturally. Divine kingship, concern with an afterlife, and a rather unorganized complex of gods exemplify that stability, for they characterized the entire 2,000 years of the native dynasties.

Egyptian splendor began vigorously in the period 3100–2200 B.C.E., which historians divide into the Early Dynasties (3100–2700 B.C.E.) and the Old Kingdom (2700–2200 B.C.E.). A famous product of Old Kingdom religion is the Memphite theology, developed to justify the new, unified kingdom centered at Memphis. Central to the justification is that the god of Memphis, Ptah, is the foremost creator god. Ptah originated Atum, the supreme god of the older cosmogony, and the other gods by an idea in his heart and a command on his tongue. Scholars are fascinated by this notion, because it suggests that 2,000 years before the Hebrews or Greeks came up with the notion of a first spiritual cause, an Egyptian had more than suspected it.[6]

From about 2200 to 2050 B.C.E., there was an intermediate period of disorder. The social order rooted in the permanence of nature and the gods gave way to chaos. We catch overtones of that upheaval in the famous "Dispute over Suicide," a remarkable text from the end of the third millennium. A man says to his soul, "To whom can I speak today? My fellows are evil, my friends do not love, . . . the land is left to those who do wrong." So, he considers suicide: "Death faces me today like the recovery of a sick man, like going out into the open after a confinement, . . . like the longing of a man to see his home again, after many

years in captivity."[7] Clearly the prehistoric Egyptian hope of a happy afterlife with the gods functioned for this desolate writer as a way to justice—a way to symbolize the friendship and social order that life must have if it is not to seem absurd.

The Middle Kingdom (2050–1800 B.C.E.) was centered at Thebes. It nurtured several trends that brought important changes, although they worked below the surface constancy of Egyptian life. The most important of these trends was a democratization of certain religious rights, as the distance between the pharaoh and the common people narrowed. Also, there was an effort to elevate the more important gods and an increasing inclination to worship gods who were in the form of animals,[8] two phenomena that we shall observe when we analyze the complex Egyptian sense of divinity. The most important religious rights that democratization brought the middle classes were privileges in the afterlife and a chance to participate in ceremonies that had been confined to the king and a few priests.

A second intermediate period (1800–1570 B.C.E.) dissolved the Middle Kingdom and included a century or so of rule by the Hyksos (Shepherd Kings), who were probably Syrians. The New Kingdom (1570–1165 B.C.E.) began with the famous XVIII dynasty, which made Egypt a true empire that stretched to the Euphrates. For our limited review of the high points in later Egyptian religious history, the New Kingdom's speculation on monotheism and a purer divinity is important. In the XIX dynasty under Akhenaton (1369–1353 B.C.E.), there was a move to make Aton, previously just the sun disk, the sole deity. Apparently Akhenaton himself bullied through this change (Egypt quickly reverted to polytheism after his death) because of his own spiritual perceptions (which many of his contemporaries considered fanatical and heretical).

Eric Voegelin calls Akhenaton "a new voice in history, the voice of a man intimately sympathetic with nature, sensitive to the splendor of light and its life-spending force, praising the god and his creature."[9] In a joyful climax, one of Akhenaton's hymns cries out: "The Aton is the creator-god: O sole god, like whom there is no other! Thou didst create the world according to thy desire, while thou wert alone."[10] Moreover, Aton was not the god of Egypt alone. Akhenaton saw that a true creator god must have established all peoples, whatever their country, speech, culture, or skin. This was truly a remarkable leap toward universalism, especially coming from the leader of a resolutely eth-

Figure 32 *Great Sphinx near Giza pyramids, outside Cairo, Egypt. Photo by J. T. Carmody.*

nocentric people, and it was the centerpiece in the so-called Armarna Revolution that gave the New Kingdom a great charge of cultural energy.

Another high point of New Kingdom theology consisted of the Amon hymns, which probably date from the reign of Ramses II (1290–1224 B.C.E.). They illustrate a return to Amon and the demise of Aton, as well as a deep sense that the first creator god must be mysterious. Amon is "far from heaven, he is absent from the underworld, so that no gods know his true form. His image is not displayed in writings. No one bears witness to him. . . . He is too mysterious that his majesty might be disclosed, he is too great that men should ask about him, too powerful that he might be known."[11] Along with the hymns of Akhenaton, these praises of Amon represent the greatest advance in Egyptian theology.

For the most part, the Egyptians were not intellectually rigorous. They easily tolerated many gods and relied almost unquestioningly on ethical maxims and proverbs. In the Amon hymns, however, we see traces of a negative theology—a rising of the mind to the true nature of divinity by denying that creatures can represent it adequately. Because negative theology is a paramount way of breaking the cosmological myth, the Amon hymns show how close Egypt came to the revolutions that Israel and Greece accomplished.

In the centuries after the New Kingdom, the capital moved to Tanis, Bubastis, and Saïs—a good indication of the political turmoil of that era. Persians ruled Egypt from 525 to 405 B.C.E., and the last native dynasties (405–332 B.C.E.) ended with the conquest of Alexander. In the period from Alexander to about 30 B.C.E., the Hellenistic Ptolemies ruled, and the city of Alexandria was the luminary of the eastern Mediterranean. Christian influence rose in the Roman and Byzantine periods (30 B.C.E.–641 C.E.), bequeathing

Egypt the Coptic church. Since 641, Egyptian culture has been largely Muslim, but its native orientations have never completely died.

Worldview

Ultimate Reality.   With regard to divinity, the proliferation of Egyptian gods and symbols is overwhelming. The basic hieroglyph for God is a pole with a flag—the emblem flying in front of major temples, which designated purity and the creative life force. Since the Egyptians sensed purity and creativity in many places, they split divinity into many gods. The gods most important in the old cosmogony were four male-female pairs. The males bore the head of a frog, and the females the head of a snake—symbols, apparently, of self-renewal (the frog begins as a tadpole, while the snake sheds its skin). The belief (before the Memphite theology established Ptah as the creator) was that an invisible wind moved over primal waters and used these four pairs of gods to make life.

Throughout Egyptian history, the most important gods were associated with the sun and death-resurrection. Their names and images varied from cultural center to cultural center, but the most common name for the sun god was Re, symbolized by either the sun's disk or the falcon. Another name was Khepri, represented by a scarab pushing the sun disk; a third name was Atum, whom people at Heliopolis worshiped and represented as the setting sun. In the mythology of Heliopolis, Atum generated himself on the primordial hill of creation (the Great Pyramids of the Old Kingdom represented this hill). He conquered chaos, took charge of the world, and established *maat,* the eternal cosmic order. The *Book of the Dead* (17:3–5), from the New Kingdom, says that Re became king of the gods in the earliest times by defeating all his opponents. Maat is his daughter but also his mother, because in his course through the sky, the sun god follows her cosmic order.

That course determined Egyptian reality. The west was the land of the dead, and the east was where the daily miracle of the sun's return from the dead occurred.[12] On the walls of royal tombs near Luxor, twelve sections divide the night realm, or underworld, through which the sun god's boat travels. Although the sun god is dead during this time, he still possesses the power of resurrection. Middle night is the realm of Sokaris, who appears in human form with the head of a falcon. His area is a desert through which Re's boat has to be dragged before the sun can reemerge into the light.

It was Osiris, however, around whom developed the funerary cult that made the underworld almost an Egyptian obsession. Nowhere is the myth of his descent to the underworld detailed, but it probably had the following plot. Osiris and Seth were brothers, and Isis was Osiris' sister and wife. Osiris ruled the world as a good regent, but Seth hated him and killed him by guile. He got Osiris into a coffin and sent it down the Nile. Isis recovered Osiris' corpse and uttered a soulful dirge (which inspired litanies used in Osiris' worship). This dirge had a magic power that revived Osiris. Once again Seth moved against Osiris, this time hacking Osiris' body into fourteen pieces and then scattering them. Isis recovered them all and buried each piece properly wherever she found it (this explained the many Osirian sanctuaries). Furthermore, Isis conceived a son Horus by the dead Osiris and brought Horus up in the marshes to hide him from Seth.

When Horus reached manhood, Isis arranged for a trial at which Seth was condemned for murdering Osiris and Horus was recognized as Osiris' heir. Osiris himself remained in the underworld, accepting the roles of lord of the nether realm and judge of the dead. Osiris seems to represent the growing power of vegetation, which roots in the earth, and he relates to all buildings that are set on the earth, to the moon, and to the dead. Isis represents the throne, the sacred seat of the king. As such, she "makes" the king and is his mother. For instance, on a relief in a temple at Abydos, the pharaoh sits on Isis' lap. Thus, Horus and the pharaoh are correlated. As Horus owed his throne to his mother Isis, so did the pharaoh.

Horus had many appearances, but most frequently he wore the head of a falcon. He was the model son but shows traces of an older sky god. In the Osiris myth, Horus fought Seth and lost an eye, while depriving Seth of his testicles. They reconciled, however, to suggest that life and death are paired. Thoth, originally a moon god, was the agent of their reconciliation. Usually Thoth was represented as a baboon or an ibis. He was also a god of the dead and is thought to have found Horus' lost eye and have returned it to him. This eye became a token of life returned from the dead.

The prime attribute of Egyptian divinity, then, was life. It shone in the sun, who daily accomplished the miracle of being resurrected from darkness, bestowing life-giving light and warmth. Life flowed in the Nile, whose annual flooding was necessary for crops to grow. Even the underworld became a realm of life. Osiris ruled there, judgment took place there, and vegetation rooted there.

Nature.   From this association of divinity with life, it follows that nature itself had a potent sacredness. Henri Frankfort, in fact, has analyzed Egyptian divinity in terms of the sun's power of creation, the power of procreation in cattle, and the power of resurrection in the earth.[13] We have seen a little of the sun and the Osirian earth. Apis, the bull god, was a focus of procreative power, as was Min, a mummy with a huge projecting phallus.

By the "cosmological myth," we mean the tendency to run these various sacred forces together so that nature and divinity are coextensive. Apart from the brief ventures behind the hymns to Aton and Amon, Egypt little doubted the cosmological myth. It could support so many gods because, like oral ancient peoples, Egyptians sensed sacredness everywhere. Unlike Jews, Christians, and Muslims, however, they did not fashion a popular, effective negative theology that said, "True divinity is actually in no one place—it is beyond all place, all time, all this-worldly containment." As a result, nature's cycles and changes all represented aspects of the basic Egyptian divinity, which was the world itself. This cosmos of rocks and trees, water and land, living things and dying things— this was the ultimate reality.

The Egyptian people participated in the sacred cosmos through their king, who to them was quite literally divine. The king represented Horus, Re, or Osiris. In the analytic terms of Western scholars, he mediated between nature's divine order and his people. Society and politics were part of one natural circuit; the *maat* (goddess of order) that gave the world its law or reason ran from heaven through the pharaoh to the people. Thus, the *pharaoh* was under *maat* and yet, for the common people, was the source of *maat*. Psychologically, this order was a major reason for the stability of the Egyptian culture. With divinity in their midst, what need the people fear?

Through many agricultural ceremonies and many regal rituals, these beliefs took dramatic form.[14] At first the common people had limited access to most kingly ceremonies, but in the later centuries their participation increased. The greatest threat to social stability, understandably, was the king's death. Consequently, the most influential mythic cycle was that of Osiris and Isis, which explained where the king (identified with Osiris) had gone at death. Relatedly, the most important ceremonies were the old king's burial and the new king's accession. For a hint of how effective this mythic-ritualistic faith was, consider the pyramids. The common people supplied the immense, brutal labor needed to build the pyramids, because they assured the king's happy afterlife and the state's continuance.

Society.   Ancient Egypt had a powerful caste of priests, and at times, despite the dogma of the king's divinity, this caste clashed with the crown. The conflict between Akhenaton and the priests of the old god Amon was a vivid instance of such friction, but conflict was almost always on the verge of breaking out. When Akhenaton moved the capital from Thebes to Amarna, he bruised theological, class, and local sensitivities all at once. The local priesthood, fighting for its own gods and people, consistently defended those sensitivities. As a result, the priesthood was a powerful sociological force.

Women were quite subordinate in Egyptian society, but were not without influence and religious importance. The goddesses Hathor, Nut, Neith, Maat, and Isis represented the feminine aspects of divinity, while the queen had vital roles in the political theology.[15] Hathor, Nut, and Neith were forms of the mother goddess—both sacred representations of fertility and figures of comfort. Maat ruled cosmic justice, while Isis was sister and wife of the god as king. On rare occasions a queen could rule (Hatshepsut, 1486–1468 B.C.E., is the most famous instance), and as the source of the divine king, the queen mother was much more than just another harem wife.

Egyptian proverbs encouraged husbands to treat their wives well so that their property would prosper, but they also pictured women as "frivolous, flirtatious, and unreliable, incapable of keeping a secret, untruthful and spiteful as well as naturally unfaithful. To the storytellers and moralists [women were] the epitome of all sin and an endless source of mischief."[16] Women of the New Kingdom served in the temples and as popular entertainers, but in both cases they risked reputations as prostitutes. In both formal and popular religion, Isis was a focal point for women's own religion, especially in Hellenistic times. Related to Osiris, she was the ideal wife (and a potent exemplar of grief); related to Horus, she was the ideal mother. Through Isis, then, women in ordinary roles participated in divinity.

Perhaps because of this divinity, legal documents from about 500 B.C.E. suggest that Egyptian women had the right to own property, buy or sell goods, and testify in court. They were taxpayers and could sue; they could inherit from parents or husbands.[17] On the other hand, husbands could dismiss wives at their pleasure (but not vice versa), and concubinage, adultery, and prostitution were widespread. Because many Egyptian women worked the fields or had other important economic roles, their lot was better than that of women in other ancient civilizations (Mesopotamia, for instance). Still, women were not equal to men, in part because of a prevailing male suspicion of woman: "She is a deep water whose twisting men know not."[18]

Self. The Egyptian religious conception of the self relates intimately to the Egyptian concern with death, burial, and the afterlife. That concern, John Wilson insists,[19] was a result not of gloom but of optimism. The ancient Egyptians loved life, despite its dependence on such uncertain phenomena as the Nile's proper rising, and they looked forward to another, better chapter after death. The remains of many burial sites, well preserved because of the desert sand and dry climate, show that the departed took with them favorite utensils and even favorite servants. The *ba* was that aspect of a person that continued after death, which contrasted with the *ka,* or vital force, the impersonal power animating the living. A third concept, the *akh,* was the shining, glorious aspect of the dead in heaven. With these three notions, the Egyptians had a sense of what moves the living and what continues on after death.

As indicated in our outline of his myth, Osiris judged the dead in the underworld. The pyramid texts of the Old Kingdom, coffin texts of the Middle Kingdom, and *Book of the Dead* from the New Kingdom show a constant concern with judgment, hence a certain awareness of personal responsibility. The *Book of the Dead* contains a famous "negative confession" that illustrates both the posthumous trial Egyptians imagined and some of their principal ethical concerns. The deceased claims before Osiris: "I have not committed evil against men. . . . I have not mistreated cattle. . . . I have not blasphemed a god. . . . I have not done violence to a poor man. . . . I have not made anyone weep. . . . I have not killed. . . . I have not defamed a slave to his superior. . . . I have not had sexual relations with a boy." In all, thirty-six declarations of innocence are made.[20] Then, to complete his show of religious virtuosity, he gives each of the forty-two divine jurors, by name, a specific assurance. For example, "O Embracer-of-Fire, who comes forth from Babylon, I have not stolen. O Eater-of-Entrails, who comes forth from the thirty [judges in the world of the living], I have not practiced usury. O Eater-of-Blood, who comes forth from the execution block, I have not slain the cattle of the god."[21]

In ancient Egypt, then, the gods were everywhere. Economics, politics, the arts, nature—all aspects of life were religious. In symbolically mythic ways, nobles and peasants alike looked to the king, tried to discern *maat,* and hoped for mercy before Osiris. The sun, the river, and the land all witnessed the interplay of death and resurrection and offered comfort. Each dawn, each annual flood, each spring sprouting was a pledge of hope. Therefore, one could live optimistically and even with good humor; on most days, ancient Egyptian life probably was good.

IRAN

Recently Iran has been a nation in the throes of choosing its identity and direction, as well as a nation wracked by a prolonged war with neighboring Iraq. On first view, the principal choices Iran has faced in determining its identity have been Western secularism (almost unavoidable because of Iran's massive petroleum industry) and a volatile form of traditional Islam. These forces alone are more than enough to bewilder analysts, but the snowcapped mountains rimming Tehran suggest there is much more—the long history of culture that crossed the Iranian plain. When one sees Iranian women draped in black, showing only a panel of dark eyes, something flickers that is more ancient than Islam.

That something is the spirit of Zoroaster, priest and prophet from 2,500 years ago. In the mind's eye, it burns toward Truth. Picture Zoroaster as being fiery, choleric, fierce of face. He is angry that some Iranians do not accept his Wise Lord. In their dimness, they stick to the old vital forces. Zoroaster, though, knows better—he knows the battle between Evil and Good.

Ask about Zoroaster on the streets of Tehran today, however, and you will likely be rebuked. "We are Muslims!" the typical residents will say. True enough, fewer than 30,000 Zoroastrians remain in Iran (perhaps 100,000 remain in India). Nonetheless, Zoroaster was the greatest religious influence in the epochal Persian Empire, the strongest molder of the Iranian spirit. As well, he was the first son of Asia adopted by the West.[22]

Zoroaster first intrigued the Greeks, whose explorers encountered his culture 400 years before Christ. Much later he impressed Western historians, philosophers, and artists as a cultural hero—a founder of civilization and conscience.

History

The historical context for estimating the significance of Zoroaster stretches from the tenth century C.E., when the Arab military conquest of the seventh century began to affect Iranian culture, back beyond 1500 B.C.E., when speakers of Indo-Iranian filtered through the Caucasus Mountains to the Iranian plateau. Before that date, "cave man," as Ghirshman calls him, lived around that plateau in holes dug into wooded mountainsides.[23] Indeed, archeological remains suggest that human beings have inhabited Iran since the beginning of a dry period, 12,000 to 17,000 years ago.

According to Ghirshman, in the primitive agricultural societies that developed on alluvial deposits, such as on the Iranian plateau, women had an economic, political, and religious superiority. Indo-European conquerors who settled in Iran probably adopted their matriarchal social structure from these first inhabitants of what is present-day Iran.

Those first inhabitants were great potters, and archeologists have found among their relics designs and figurines of a naked goddess, whose mate was likely a god who was her son. This belief would be the most direct explanation for the early Iranian customs of marriage between blood relations, descent through the female line, and, in certain tribes (for example, the Guti of Kurdistan), female army commanders. Later archeological remains, dating back to 2000 B.C.E., suggest a people both artistic and hopeful, for impressive pendants, earrings, bracelets, and the like found in gravesites imply a strong belief in an afterlife.

In the second millennium B.C.E., Indo-Europeans, pressured by population shifts in the neighboring geographic areas, left their homelands in the plains of southern Russia and migrated southeast across Iran. Some of them eventually ended up as far south as India.[24] In the west they established the Hittite Empire, sacked Babylon, and confronted the Egyptians. From the east, Indo-European tribes called the Mittani conquered northern Mesopotamia and allied themselves with Egypt in about 1450 B.C.E. Linguistic, religious, and social parallels suggest that pre-Zoroastrian Iranian culture, as well as the culture of the peoples who conquered the Indus Valley in India and produced the Vedic culture, derived from the Mittani, Hittite, and other Indo-European "Aryans" (from an Indo-European word meaning "noble"). In particular, the Iranian and Indian Aryans had similar gods and similar social structures. (French scholar Georges Dumezil has argued that the Aryan gods correlated with a three-part social structure—priests, warriors, and agriculturalists—in which each social class had both a legal and a symbolic aspect.[25])

The native Iranian religion that Zoroaster challenged was probably controlled by Median priests (the Medes were a later Aryan tribe) from western Iran called **Magi**. Apparently that religion was an animistic **polytheism** (devotion to many divine spirits) similar to that of early Aryan India. After Zoroaster's death, the Magi fused their ideas onto his new notions, making Zoroastrianism an amalgam of conflicting gods and practices.

Zoroaster is estimated to have lived from 628 to 551 B.C.E., but the only direct source for his message is a fragment of the sacred Zoroastrian liturgical text, the *Avesta.* That portion, called the *Gathas,* along with later Greek and Persian traditions, suggests that Zoroaster's enemies (Magi and men's societies of the old religion) forced him to flee from his native western Iran westward into ancient Chorasmia (the area today of Khurasan, western Afghanistan, and the Turkmen Republic of the Soviet Union). There, when about forty years old, he found a patron in King Vishtapa and his message began to have social effect.

R. C. Zaehner has suggested the following summary of Zoroaster's main doctrines:[26] (1) There is a supreme God, the Wise Lord (**Ahura Mazdah**), who has thought all things into existence by his Holy Spirit. The Wise Lord is holy, righteous, and generous, and he expresses himself through the Holy Spirit, Good Mind, and Truth—three entities inseparable from his essence. Wholeness, Immortality, and Right-Mindedness are his attributes. (2) The world is divided between Truth and the Lie. Ahura Mazdah made Truth, but Zoroaster does not say who made the Lie. (3) Creatures of the Wise Lord (spiritual beings and humans) are free to choose between Truth and the Lie. Angra Mainyu (the Destructive Spirit), twin brother of the Holy Spirit, chooses to do evil. "This he does of his own free will as do the *daevas,* the ancient gods whom, on account of the violence associated with their wor-

Figure 33 *Beaker with winged lions and bulls, Persian, about 1000 B.C.E. Gold; 6¾ in. high. The Nelson–Atkins Museum of Art, Kansas City, Missouri (Nelson Fund).*

radical discovery of reason and that suggests some parallels with such near-contemporaries as the Buddha and the Mahavira, Zoroaster generates his images of divinity and human destiny from the operations of his own spirit. He turns away almost completely from nature toward the inner light of human conscience. In so doing he steps at least halfway out of the cosmological myth.

Two verses from perhaps the most autobiographical of Zoroaster's hymns suggest the religious experience at the core of his preaching:

> As the holy one I recognized thee, O
> Wise Lord,
> When I saw thee at the beginning, at
> the birth of existence,
> Appoint a recompense for deed and
> word:
> Evil reward to the evil, good to the
> good,
> Through thy wisdom, at the last
> turning-point of creation [43:5].[27]

> As the holy one I recognized thee, O
> Wise Lord,
> When he came to me as Good Mind.
> To his question: "To whom wilt thou
> address thy worship?"
> I made reply: "To thy fire! While I
> offer up my veneration to it,
> I will think of the Right to the utmost
> of my power"[43:9].[28]

In Iran in the early sixth century B.C.E., only an exceptional personality could have cut through the welter of Aryan gods, spells, and semimagical practices and discerned a clear religious call to identify divinity with justice. Similarly, only an exceptional personality could have lingered over abstractions such as Good Mind and the Right and made these terms God's best names.

It is true, as most scholars remind us, that Zoroaster's revelations had a social background and significance;[29] for instance, he championed the farmer over the nomad. Nonetheless, the deeper explanation of Zoroaster's religious power is the interior, spiritual experiences indicated by the *Gathas*. Like Jesus and Muhammad, Zoroaster met a holy, compelling divinity or ultimate reality. His mission was simply to spread the truth of this divinity far and wide. The origins of Zoroastrian history, then, are the visions and the reli-

ship, Zarathustra [Zoroaster] considered to be evil powers." (4) Because human beings are free, they are responsible for their ultimate fates. By good deeds they win the eternal reward of possessing Wholeness and Immortality; by evil deeds they merit pain in hell. (5) The great outward symbol of Truth is fire, and the center of the Zoroastrian cult is the fire altar.

When we set these doctrines in the context of Zoroaster's times, they are striking for their interiority. Before this prophet, little in Indo-European, Mesopotamian, or Egyptian religion focused on the mental concepts of truth and lie, the spiritually intuitive concepts of immortality and right-mindedness. In a way that prefigures the Greek philosophers' more

gious insights of a founding genius. Through all its later changes, Zoroastrianism and the world religions that it influenced retained something of the dazzling vision of Zoroaster's Wise Lord.

After Zoroaster.   The great leaders of the Achaemenid Empire who followed Zoroaster were the Persians Cyrus II (599–530 B.C.E.), Cambyses II (530–522 B.C.E.), and Darius I (522–486 B.C.E.). They conquered eastern Iran, the prophet's initial sphere of influence, and we can read in inscriptions that they left something of Zoroastrianism's function as the religious rationale for a new, energetic empire.

Following Alexander's victory over Darius III in 331 B.C.E., the Achaemenid dynastic line begun with Cyrus II gave way to the Greek Seleucids. Under the Seleucids, for almost a century, Hellenistic cultural ideals blended with Persian. Zoroastrian influence probably declined, being overshadowed by a Greek-Iranian *syncretism* (combination of two forms of belief). While the practice of pure Zoroastrianism seems to have remained in Fars (the southern province called Persis), the old Iranian goddess Anahita, fused with the Mesopotamian goddess Nanai, complicated the religious picture in other provinces.

Also complicating the picture was the Greek hero Heracles, who joined with local gods. Heracles was the patron of the gymnasium, the place of physical exercise, an important feature of Hellenistic culture. Also, he was one of several "savior" gods (gods who made life whole) whose influence grew apace with the disintegration of the previously secure city-state religions. The *Avesta* was probably still evolving at this time, incorporating hymns to the god Mithra, who had existed before Zoroaster and later became an important savior god for the Romans. In the *Avesta,* Mithra's main functions are to preserve cattle, sanctify contracts, and render judgment on human actions.[30]

The Era of Many Religions.   The Greek Seleucids yielded to the Parthians, who entered Iran from the area southwest of the Caspian Sea. The Parthians dominated Iran, bit by bit, from the first conquest by Arsaces in about 238 B.C.E. until about 226 C.E. While sources are scanty, Zoroastrianism apparently made some gains against syncretism under the Parthians, achieving a privileged status. Richard Frye relates this to the influence of the Magi: "We may suspect that Magi, in various parts of Iran, upheld the worship of Ahura Mazdah and/or other old Aryan gods in varying forms and degrees of piety."[31] Nonetheless, in Parthian

times the cultures of the different geographic areas varied considerably. Coins, art, and other remains indicate different local preferences for a variety of gods. Ahura Mazdah and Mithra certainly were influential, but the cult of the goddess Anahita was probably the most important.[32] The northern Magis' custom of exposing the bodies of the dead on mountains (burial would pollute the earth) spread as far south as Susa, capital of the old Elamite kingdom. We also know that the Parthians were tolerant of religious minorities, so much so that Jews regarded them as great protectors.

The history of Zoroastrianism under the Parthians remains rather vague. Under the Sasanians (ca. 226–637 C.E.), it is more definite, as is the story of Persian culture generally. The early Sasanian king Papak probably was the director of the shrine to Anahita in Istakhr in Persis (south-central Iran), and his successor Shapur had quite liberal religious policies. That soon changed, however, largely because of the influence of Kartir, a zealous Zoroastrian priest. By the last third of the third century, he had made Zoroastrianism the established Persian "church." Kartir favored proselytizing, establishing fire temples for worship and instruction, purging Zoroastrian heretics, and attacking all non-Zoroastrian religions. Consequently, he persecuted Jews, Buddhists, Hindus, Christians, and Manichaeans, destroying their centers and proscribing their faiths. From his time marriage between blood relations became a common Zoroastrian practice, and the Zoroastrian clergy were a political power.

The Manicheans—followers of the native Iranian prophet Mani—were the chief heretics. Under Shapur I, Mani had been free to travel and preach, but soon after Shapur's death the Zoroastrians martyred him. Nonetheless, his ideas gained considerable acceptance, both in Iran and throughout the Roman Empire. They stressed a *dualism* of good and evil, equating good with the spirit and evil with matter. Consequently, Manicheans denigrated the body, sex, marriage, women, and food—anything perceived as carnal. As we shall see, Manicheanism had significant effect on Christians, influencing St. Augustine and spawning several medieval heresies. At the end of the fifth century C.E., Persian Manicheans led a socioeconomic movement called Mazdakism (after its leader Mazdak), which preached a sort of communism that included the division of wealth and the sharing of wives and concubines. Many poor people embraced this movement, but Prince Chosroes Anosharvan massacred the Mazdakite leaders about 528 C.E.[33]

In the last decades of Sasanian rule, the Zoroastrian church sanctioned a rigid caste system based, somewhat like that of India, on an ideal division of society into priests, warriors, scribes, and commoners. Ritual tended toward a sterile formalism, and a number of speculative or gnostic (relating to secret knowledge) tendencies emerged. At the beginning of the Sasanian period, Zurvanism had become the dominant Zoroastrian theology, in good part because of an increasing interest in the problem of evil. Zurvan was Infinite Time. Slowly, he displaced Ahura Mazdah (now called Ohrmazd) as the first principle. Ohrmazd then became identical with Holy Spirit, and Zurvan became his father, as well as the father of Holy Spirit's twin, Destructive Spirit. Thus, Zurvanism begot a dualism: Holy Spirit and Destructive Spirit. However, unlike Mani's dualism, Zurvanism did not make matter evil. For Zurvanite Zoroastrians, nature remained God's good creation.

Muslim Era.   After the Muslims conquered Persia in the seventh century, the Zoroastrian communities that survived continued to have significant influence. Zoroastrian priests were instrumental in creating a renaissance of religious literature in Pahlavi, the native Persian in its "middle" period. They kept alive the notion that the prior Sasanian Empire had been a fortunate time for the "good religion" that had preceded the Muslims, and also for such Zoroastrian doctrines as the coming of the future savior and the approach of an apocalyptic era when Judgment would occur. Zoroastrians also fought against the Arabs, Romans, and Turks in their midst, assuring the faithful that God would soon give them revenge against these interlopers.

However, the actual political revolts that the Zoroastrians attempted tended to be completely crushed. That was dramatically true of an uprising attempted in the city of Shiraz in 979, the result of which was a series of harsh repressions instituted by the Muslim rulers. As a consequence, around the end of the tenth century, Zoroastrians began to leave Iran and head toward India, where their small but successful community became known as Parsis. They left a reduced community in Iran, centered in the regions of Yazd and Kerman. Both these Iranian Zoroastrians and the Parsis have perpetuated the religion begun by Zoroaster, although what one finds practiced nowadays naturally has been deeply transformed by a further millennium of historical changes.

Until the sixteenth century, the Zoroastrian communities in Iran and India had little contact with one another. In the sixteenth century they began to exchange *rivayat,* texts providing answers to questions that had arisen about liturgical and doctrinal matters. The Iranian communities usually felt isolated in the midst of a hostile Muslim environment, but the Indian Parsis flourished and exerted considerable influence on their neighbors, all the more so when British rule gave them special privileges. Bombay has been the center of the Indian community.

In India, the Zoroastrians have had considerable contact with other religions: Hinduism, Islam, Christianity. They have also encountered modern spiritualism: astrology, theosophy (occult systems about divinity based on supposedly direct intuitions). The result of such contact has been pressure to rethink traditional views about monotheism (Ahura Mazdah) and dualism (Truth and Lie). Indian Zoroastrians (Parsis) have also struggled with internal questions of reforming liturgical rites and doctrine, to make them more attractive to modern members. Such matters as the cult of the dead, questions related to the liturgical calendar for religious celebrations, and interpretations of the scriptures (the *Avesta,* rediscovered in the eighteenth century and thereafter studied with modern philological tools) have all been occasions for debate and division.[34]

When British rule ended in India in 1947, a small group of Parsis (perhaps 5000) were isolated in Pakistan. There was also a small community in Sri Lanka. A census in 1976 estimated that there were about 130,000 Zoroastrians worldwide, about 80,000 of them in India, 25,000 in Iran, and most of the others in North America. They held an international symposium in Tehran in 1960 and subsequent, similar meetings in Bombay in 1964, 1978, and 1985. A 1986 estimate of the religious complexion of Iran's 46 million people listed less than 2 percent as non-Muslim, while in India Parsis were less than 0.4 percent of the estimated 777 million. In India Parsis have kept the fire sacrifice, exposed their dead in "towers of silence" where vultures might strip their flesh, and become one of India's best educated and most prosperous groups.

Worldview

Ultimate Reality.   Before Zoroaster, Iranian ultimate reality included a number of *ahuras*—good celestial spirits. The most prominent were lucidity (the brightness that glances off the waters or that leaps from fire); the sacred liquor *haoma,* used in the old Aryan cult; and plain water, symbol of purity and motherliness.

Zoroaster pushed to the fore one wise Ahura, whose special qualities, such as Wholeness and Good Mind, were expressions of divine being. In later Zoroastrianism, these qualities became angelic beings who served Ohrmazd and influenced humans.

Opposing the good angels were powerful, antidivine forces led by the evil one, Ahriman. According to speculation after Zoroaster, Ohrmazd realized that to destroy Ahriman he would have to lure him out of eternal time (Zurvan) into finite time. Zoroastrian theology thus became highly eschatological (interested in the last events of humanity) and developed imaginative doctrines of judgment, heaven, and hell. Ultimately Ohrmazd and goodness would triumph, and hell would cease after the wicked had been purged of their sins.[35]

If Ohrmazd and Zurvan represent the most refined aspects of Zoroastrian divinity, Mithra and Anahita express aspects no less influential. Both relate divinity to nature—Mithra to the sky and sun, Anahita to water. On the folk level, Anahita was very powerful, in effect giving Iran a great goddess. For instance, in one *Avestan* text (*Yasht* 5:17), Ahura Mazdah asks Anahita to make Zoroaster think, speak, and act according to good religion. Clearly, then, there was considerable confusion in developed Zoroastrian theology. Pressed by pre-Zoroastrian traditions and by outside cultural influences, Zoroastrianism tried to accommodate a variety of divinities within its monotheistic stress on Wise Lord. As a result, the goddess of plenty, the god of wind, the star Sirius, the Fravashis (the preexistent souls of good men and women), and more were objects of veneration.

Nature. Though Zoroaster's theology turned away from nature and toward mental processes, the physical elements continued to shape Iranian religion. Mental processes and physical elements conspired in practical living, since the basic ethical imperative was to maintain goodness and life by fighting against evil and death. As a result, Zoroastrianism has frowned on fasting, asceticism, and celibacy. Rather, humans have been counseled to foster the powers of generation in nature and humanity alike. One basis for this view was Zoroaster's own stress on the holiness of agriculture, which to him was a cooperation with Ahura Mazdah. The farmer who sows corn, he said, "feeds the religion" of the Wise Lord.

Society. Ancient Iranian society established a pronounced caste system, but most of its cultic practices cut across class distinctions. Some common people were quite interested in magic, but the orthodox leaders feared the occult, treating sorcerers and witches as criminals. Folk beliefs and totemic practices (for example, rubbing oneself with the wing of a falcon to ward off an evil spell) flourished, in part because of contact with Mesopotamia. Both divination and astrology were common, and other nations considered Persian Magis to be specialists in dream interpretation. Finally, occasionally there was trial by fire or molten lead (if the person survived, he or she was deemed innocent).

Zoroaster himself seems to have disapproved of blood sacrifices, going out of his way to try to protect cattle. Blood sacrifices survived in later Zoroastrianism, though, the most important being the bull sacrifice. Also important to later Zoroastrians was the preparation and offering of *haoma,* the sacred liquor, which until recently served as a sort of sacrament for the dying. The most important sacrifice and cultic focus, however, has been the fire sacrifice. The flame has to be "pure" (obtained by burning "pure" materials such as sandalwood), and it has to pass to another flame before its fuel becomes embers. The fire sacrifice has overtones of an ancient wonder at the source of light and heat, but its major emphasis has always been to symbolize the blazing purity and potential sensing of the Wise Lord.

Self. Through their several sacrifices, Zoroastrians have kept a sense of righteousness before Ahura Mazdah. For individuals, rites of passage at maturity, marriage, and death are important, as are various purifications. At maturity, both men and women have received a sacred thread and shirt. The thread is a compound symbol: Cosmically it stands for the Milky Way, the thread of the stars through the heavens; mythologically, it recalls Ahura Mazdah's gift of *haoma;* personally, it symbolizes taking up adult responsibilities. The shirt is white, to symbolize purity and the garment that the soul dons after death.

Death and bloodshed are prime occasions for purification, because they are prime pollutants. As noted, Zoroastrians have exposed the dead so as not to defile other persons, the earth, fire, or water. In some periods of Zoroastrianism, blood from a cut or from an extracted tooth, or even menstrual flow could render one ritually unclean. Emily Culpepper, who has surveyed Zoroastrian menstrual taboos, suggests a strong ancient element in this concern with purity.[36] (Complicated rites in which bodily impurities were passed through bull's urine, sand, and water also evidence this concern.[37]) In general, women have played only a small part in the Zoroastrian world. Their part in redemption has been to furnish males to fight against Ahriman. Most of the tradition has held that in the beginning women defected to the Destructive Spirit. Theologically, then, Zoroastrianism has viewed the female nature as unholy.

Zoroastrianism is important beyond its own confines. Because its eschatology attracted Jews, Christians, and Muslims, it has influenced perhaps half the world's believers. That is its historical prestige. In terms of philosophical prestige, where the issue is wisdom—the clarification of reality—Zoroaster is a prime religious figure because he made a strong contribution to the discovery of order, the proper perspective on reality that comes when we determine the relations among nature, society, self, and divinity.[38]

GREECE

Mesopotamia calls to mind a rich mythology. Egypt amazes the world historian by the stability of its civilization. Iran-Persia impresses the historian of religion by Zoroastrianism's contribution to the clarification of order and its influence on Judaism, Christianity, and Islam. Greece, the final land of ancient Near Eastern civilization that we study, dazzles both world historians and historians of religion with its cultural diversity and splendor. Like classical Egyptian and classical Iranian religious culture, classical Greek religious culture has passed from the scene. Its influence in modern Greece lies under the surface of Eastern Orthodox Christianity, much as classical Egyptian religion lies under present-day Egyptian Islam and classical Zoroastrianism lies under present-day Iranian Islam. It is dead, but not without its influence.

Moreover, the influence of classical Greek religion is active in a sense different from that of its Egyptian or Iranian counterparts. Through the philosophy, science, literature, politics, and art that it nurtured, classical Greece became tutor to the West. For example, it furnished Christianity and Islam with many of their intellectual categories. Insofar as those categories have been developed in modern science and technology, classical Greece has been absolutely instrumental in shaping the present global society.

History

In his world history, Arnold Toynbee locates the beginnings of Greek culture about the middle of the third millennium B.C.E., when Sumerian and Egyptian influences apparently stimulated civilization in Crete.[39] Sir Arthur Evans, the foremost archeologist of ancient Crete, called the Bronze Age culture that had developed by 2000 B.C.E "Minoan," after Minos, the legendary king of Crete. By about 1700 B.C.E. the Minoans had a linear script, and in the period 1580–1450 B.C.E. a splendid civilization flourished. The first true Greeks, called Minyans, were Aryan-speaking Indo-Europeans. They established relations with Minoan Crete, and between 1450 and 1400 B.C.E. (at which time they were known as Mycenaeans) the Greeks had settled at the Cretan capital city of Knossos. The Mycenaean period (1400–1150 B.C.E.) constituted Crete's last glory; a people known as the Dorians invaded from northern Greece and cast a "dark age" over the Aegean from 1100 to 650 B.C.E.

During that period, literacy largely passed from the Greek scene. Consequently, much of our knowledge of Minoan religious culture comes from archeological excavations. These reveal that caves were great cultural centers from Neolithic times, serving as dwellings, cemeteries, and churches all in one. (Insofar as they gave rise to the mythic labyrinth, Cretan caves influenced the religious psyche permanently.[40]) As the archeological excavations show quite clearly, the foremost deity of Cretan cave religion was a goddess, whose primary features were fertility and mastery of animals. This corresponds with remains found on Cretan mountains, where Minoans also celebrated fertility.

However, the goddess cult probably did more than simply venerate natural life. The many burial remains, symbols of butterflies and bees (change-of-state beings), and other artifacts suggest a complex religious interest in life, death, and rebirth. Probably participants underwent initiation into these mysteries, much as tribal Africans or Australians have long done. The remains or artistic representations of bull horns, double axes, trees, animals, cosmic pillars, and blood sacrifices testify to a particularly rich Neolithic agricultural goddess religion like that described on page 28.

In light of later Greek initiations—for example, those into the Eleusinian and Orphic mysteries—it is likely that the Minoan goddess cult aimed at ensuring a happy afterlife.[41] If so, it probably had conceptions of

Figure 34   Mycenaean tomb figurine, 1400–1200
B.C.E. *Painted terra cotta; 4½ in. high. The figurine*
may stand for protective spirits or for the departing
soul of the deceased. The Nelson–Atkins Museum of
Art, Kansas City, Missouri (Nelson Fund).

the *Laws,* Plato placed his characters on Crete, walking from Knossos into the hills to the temple cave of Zeus.

Case Study: Olympian Religion. The Cretan or Minoan strand of Greek religious history wove itself deep into the Hellenic fiber. The Mycenaean strand, however, was throughout more predominant. Linear B shows that the Minyan people who came to Crete were Indo-Europeans—the people that shaped both Iran and India. One of the outstanding characteristics of Indo-European religion was its interest in sky phenomena—storms, wind, lightning, the sun, and stars. Zeus, the prime Greek Olympian god, is a close relative of both Vedic and Iranian sky gods. (In proto-Indo-European religion, Mother Earth was polar to Father Sky but less powerful.) Furthermore, the Indo-Europeans were much concerned with the human word—in sacrifices, chanting, spells, and sagas. Their traditions were largely oral, and they opposed writing when they first encountered it among Near Eastern peoples. It is worth underscoring that they had a powerful, double sense of the sacred—the sacred was both charged with divine presence and forbidden to human touch. Throughout its later development, Greek religion never lost this sense of awe-filled untouchability. Last, as we noted in connection with Iran, Indo-Europeans divided their society and gods into three groups. As a result, Vedic India, Aryan Iran, and preclassical Greece all thought in terms of priests, warriors, and commoners (though in Greece the priestly class was underdeveloped), as did Celts and Romans.

If both Crete and mainland Greece maintained earlier traditions during the dark age,[42] we can assume that the emergence of Homeric, Olympian religion was quite slow. By the time of the great poet Homer, however, the Indo-European religion had a distinctively Greek flavor. For instance, Zeus had acquired a mythological lineage. According to a later work, Hesiod's *Theogony,* he was born in the third generation of gods, after the original period of Earth and Heaven and the second period of the Titans. When Zeus overthrew his father Kronos, the present world resulted. (Eliade sees in the rather violent mythology of the *Theogony* a Greek account of creation. Heaven and Earth separate: nature's forces assume their present order.[43])

Zeus came to preeminence slowly. Most likely, his many liaisons with local goddesses represent a reli-

immortality that continued through the dark age and served as a counterpoint to the later Zeus and the Olympian gods. In the Olympian scheme, the afterlife was only a shadowy, dismal existence. The mystery religions that offered a more hopeful view may well have derived from the Cretan earth goddess.

At any rate, as the script that archeologists have discovered and called Linear B shows, people spoke Greek on Crete from 1400 B.C.E. By that time, Minoan and Mycenaean cultural forces were interacting. One important effect was that later Greek religious culture appropriated Minoan Crete as its golden age. For instance, according to Olympian legend, Zeus was born on Crete, and Apollo, Heracles, and Demeter (and even the non-Olympian Dionysus) performed prodigies or had high adventures in Crete. Crete thus became the *omphalos,* the navel or birth center, of the classical Hellenic world. At the end of his life and literary career, when he composed his masterpiece

gious and political takeover, as a unified Greek culture emerged out of local traditions. These local traditions did not disappear, but instead entered the large complex of Greek religious notions, enriching both Greek mythology and religious practices. For instance, the local Cretan dances of armed youths during their initiation ceremonies became part of the colorful story of the infant Zeus' birth in Crete. The noise of the youth's clashing shields drowned out the infant's cries, and so saved him from Kronos, who wanted to devour him. Furthermore, the Cretan Zeus merged with the child and lover of the Cretan goddess, linking him to the island's Neolithic past.

In classical Greece, Zeus was first among the gods dwelling on Mount Olympus, as Homer portrayed him. He was the father of humans, the ruler of their destinies, and, despite his own moral waywardness, the ultimate upholder of justice. In addition to Zeus, the roster of the foremost Olympian gods included Hera, Zeus' wife; Poseidon, god of the sea; Hephaestus, the divine blacksmith; Apollo, god of law and order; Hermes, the divine messenger; Artemis, mistress of wild beasts; Athena, patroness of feminine and practical arts; and Aphrodite, goddess of love.

Of these gods and goddesses, Apollo deserves special mention, because he came to symbolize many virtues that seemed typically Greek, such as serenity, harmony, balance, and order.[44] Through his oracle at Delphi, Apollo gave counsel on matters of liturgical propriety and ritual purification. For example, Apollo had charge of purifying homicides, who had to cleanse themselves of their "pollution." One would take serious matters needing counsel to Apollo's pythia (priestess) at Delphi. In trance, she would exclaim the wisdom with which Apollo filled her. The origins of the pythia's exclamation may lie in shamanism, but by classical times Apollonian wisdom had distanced itself from the emotional and irrational, becoming primarily intellectual *theoria*—relatively serene religious contemplation. As epitomized in the Delphic oracle's command "Know thyself," Apollonian religion deified thought and spirit. For that reason, it encouraged science, art, philosophy, and music.

Somewhat the antithesis of Apollo was Dionysus, an eccentric among the gods of the Olympian period. A son of Zeus by a mortal woman, Dionysus apparently always remained an outsider. His cult was not native to central Greece, while psychologically its concern with the irrational and emotional made many fear it.

In his well-known study, *The Greeks and the Irrational,* E. R. Dodds associates Dionysus with "the blessings of madness."[45] Unlike the ecstasy of the Apollonian pythia, that of the followers of Dionysus (for example, of the women called maenads)[46] was wild, frenzied, and orgiastic. Such ecstasy represented the enthusiasm (being filled with divine force) that could come from dancing and wine drinking.

For Eliade, Dionysus conjures up "the totality of life, as is shown by his relations with water and germination, blood or sperm, and by the excess of vitality manifested in his animal epiphanies (bull, lion, goat)."[47] Finally, Dionysus was a god of vegetation who would disappear to the underworld and then spring back to life. The most influential literary source on the Dionysian cult, Euripides' play the *Bacchae,* portrays the god's followers as wildly joyous. If the play is accurate, their mountain revels culminated in tearing apart live animals and eating the flesh raw (so as to commune with the god of animal life).

Strangely enough, the Greeks recognized something essential in the non-Olympian Dionysus. Call it the need for madness, reverence for the life force, or the value of temporarily escaping one's moral bonds—they blessed it and called it good. As a result, Apollo vacated Delphi during the three winter months and allowed Dionysus to reign.

Earthly Religion. The sky-oriented, rational aspect of Olympian religion never was the whole story. From the Minoans and the psyche came an earthly religion to balance the sky. Certainly the Dionysian cult was a major manifestation. So, too, were the many mother goddesses. Hera, Artemis, and Aphrodite, for example, all relate to fertility and mother earth. In Hesiod's *Theogony,* Gaea (earth) actually precedes and produces heaven. In popular religion, Demeter and Persephone were very influential. In fact, Demeter's search for Persephone in the underworld was a major theme of the Eleusinian mysteries, which are described below.

The result of this earth-oriented counterweight to the somewhat overbearing Olympian gods who resided in heaven was a view that humans should aim to become, in Plato's phrase, "as much like God as possible." Through contact with the forces of life and fertility (in the Eleusinians' case) and with the forces of intellectual light (in the philosophers' case), the limits of mortality were challenged. "No," many Greeks said, "we are made for more than a few days in the sun. If we truly know ourselves, we can find undying life."

The Eleusinian mysteries were practiced in Athens from about 600 B.C.E. on, though they clearly originated much earlier. They evolved from the myth of Demeter's search for Persephone in the underworld,[48] which included a subplot about Demeter's unsuccessful (because of human folly) attempt to make Demophoon, the infant prince of Eleusis, an immortal. Thus, the mysteries consisted of rites and revelations that gave initiates precious knowledge in this life and bliss in the world to come.

We do not know the particulars of the mysteries, which were strictly secret, but the *mystery religions* probably grafted Neolithic agricultural ideas onto the Olympian theme that the gods are immortal. If so, the mysteries moved beyond the myths of the Polynesian Hainuwele type, in which agriculture entailed ritual murder and gods that died. The result was a new, powerful synthesis of sexuality and death (as reflected in Persephone being carried to the underworld by Pluto) and of agriculture and a happy existence beyond the grave (as in Demeter representing mother earth). This religious synthesis made Eleusis an important cultic center for almost 2,000 years. Adherents to the Eleusinian mysteries lived in all parts of the Greek world and came from all social classes. Anyone who spoke Greek and had "clean hands" (including women, children, and slaves) could take part. Poets of the stature of Pindar and Sophocles praised the mysteries, and they were a powerful force in Greek life.

The background of the somewhat similar Orphic rites was a mythology like that of Demeter and Persephone.[49] Orpheus was a prominent Thracian hero, the son of Calliope by Apollo. His great gift was for music—when he played the lyre wild beasts grew calm, trees danced, and rivers stood still. Orpheus married the nymph Eurydice, who died from snakebite while fleeing Aristaeus, another son of Apollo. Orpheus could have regained Eurydice from the underworld if he had been able to resist looking at her. But he could not, so he had to wander inconsolably until followers of Dionysus tore him apart (because of his devotion to Apollo). From this background Guthrie concludes: "The story throws light upon the Orphic religion because that is exactly what, in its main features, it stood for, a blend of the Thracian belief in immortality with Apolline ideas of *katharsis* [purification]. From the one it took *ekstasis,* enthusiasm, and a deep spiritual

hope; from the other a formalizing influence, an almost legal atmosphere of rules and regulations."[50]

For eternal blessedness, Orphics preached, one had to follow a strict moral code, abstain from the flesh of living creatures, and cultivate the Dionysian part of human nature. When fully pure, the soul would be reincarnated no more. No more would it drink of the spring of Lethe (forgetfulness), but, light as air, it would live in union with the divine mind. The Orphics appealed to persons of refinement, and Orphism certainly influenced Plato, the natural philosopher Empedocles, and the Roman epic poet Virgil.

Both the Eleusinian mysteries and the Orphic rites sought immortality, the one by a profound ritualization of the life force, the other by purifying the divine soul. Together, they were a strong counterforce to the pessimism fostered by the heaven-oriented Olympianism, which taught that once one passed from the sun everything became a shadowy darkness. Another counterforce to the sky were the *chthonioi,* the spirits who lived in the dark recesses of the earth.[51] Though they were hardly mentioned in Homer, in popular religion they tended to spell out the twofold function of mother earth: fertility and rule of the dead. For the most part, the *chthonioi* were local spirits, concerned with a particular town's crops or deceased. Sometimes their cult blended with the cult of a local hero. Other times sacrifices to the *chthonioi* had overtones of devotion to Gaea, Demeter, Pluto, or Trophonious—divinities of fertility or Hades. Whether the *chthonioi* were gods or shady figures imagined to populate the afterlife is not clear. Regardless, they elicited considerable fear, and the common people tried not to offend them.

Case Study: Philosophy. The common people did not build Athenian culture or make the breakthrough called philosophy (the "love of wisdom"). Rather, an aristocratic elite, working for several centuries, slowly distinguished the realms of myth and reason and in so doing wrote a pivotal chapter in the history of human consciousness. Before philosophy, the concept of reason was vague. We have seen the prehistoric suspicion that something can travel in dreams, rise in shamanist flight, and survive the grave. In Egypt, the Amon hymns exhibited a strong sense of transcendence—of the human mind passing beyond materiality to divine mystery itself. In Iran, Zoroaster's interior dualism (the battle between Truth and the Lie) revealed a striking grasp of the abstract spirit.

Nonetheless, only the culture of the Greek city-state identified reason and controlled it. Only the line of pre-Socratic thinkers—most prominently, Pythagoras, Xenophanes, Parmenides, and Heraclitus—so disciplined their dissatisfaction with Olympian culture that they saw the human mind (*nous*) itself as being divine and real. India approached this belief but never came away with Greece's counterbalancing faith in the reality of the material world.

The story of the pre-Socratics, which weaves into that of the dramatists and Sophists (teachers of shallow philosophy), is a fascinating chapter in religion.[52] Partly from interior experimentation and partly from an empirical study of nature, the early philosophers moved beyond what most previous peoples had meant by the word *god*. As we have seen, peoples believing in the cosmological myth considered the world to be a living whole. With the rise of civilized religion, Mesopotamians, Egyptians, Iranians, and others focused on the political aspect of the cosmos. In other words, divinity to them was in good part a symbolic representation of their own society. Even Ahura Mazdah had a strong political function. For Darius I, Ahura Mazdah sanctioned the building of an empire of Truth.

Out of its dark age, Greek creativity produced a pantheon—a roster of gods—that was neither natural nor political. The Olympians were anthropomorphic, evidencing human aspects. To be sure, Zeus was a sky god and Athena fought for Athens. But although nature and politics played important roles, they did not make the Olympians distinctive. What made the Olympians distinctive was the rich, anthropomorphic mythology surrounding them. In these divine characters or personalities, human passions were blown up to divine stature. Contemplating such divinity, ruminating on the Olympian mythology, the Greek philosophical geniuses clarified where and how *mythos* shatters on *logos*—where story must yield to analytic reason.

Of course, this realization was prompted by historical events. It did not spawn at a seaside resort. Looking around them, the Greek geniuses of the fifth and fourth centuries B.C.E. saw a succession of empires. The decline of Babylon, Egypt, and Persia evoked the question, "What is the meaning of history's process?" As a result, historians such as Herodotus and Thucydides wanted a break with myth, an explanation of the flux in political affairs.[53] As a result, Socrates, Plato, and Aristotle labored heroically to produce such a break.

When the Athenians sentenced his teacher Socrates to death for impiety, they shocked Plato to the depths of his soul. If Athens could reject the one wise person who might save it, what chance did truth have?[54] Eventually Plato correlated the Athenian city-state experience with the flux of empires that had bothered the historian and came to wonder about the very possibility for human beings finding or making order—stable meaning. The *Republic* and *Laws*, which constitute about 40 percent of Plato's writings, testify to how long and deeply problems of political order absorbed him. His great problem, in fact, was the disorder of most humanity—citizens, empire builders, the great and small alike. Grappling with this problem, Plato saw that all order—personal, sociopolitical, and historical—depends on a truth only luminous because given by an incorruptible divinity. Since Plato's great problem remains our own, we do well to attend to his insight.

From instinct, observation, and reflection, Plato decided that history must mean more than wars and power struggles. Restricted to that level, history is literally absurd—a cause for despair—and yields no truth that might give the soul peace and joy (except negatively, as an analysis of cultural destruction).

Rather, Plato thought that we must become aware of a reality not distorted by our lusts, that divine mystery must shine forth an ordering light. Where warmongers and powerbrokers close themselves, philosophers must be receptive and willing to change. Where politicians restrict reality to money and influence, philosophers must go to the center of things—to the soul's passion for justice and love. Like a new Prometheus bringing fire to humanity's soul, the Platonic lover of wisdom wanted to make justice and love humanity's great passion. The presence or absence of that passion made for either health or disease. Plato minced no words. One either admitted divine mystery or one faced disaster.

The fire and order of the Platonic soul clarified human reality. From Plato's time, some people have realized that the meaning of their existence is to move through experience toward the intellectual light of God. Thus, since Plato the process of human questioning—human searching for flashes of insight and then sustained visions—has been a primary task for those seriously religious. The Western development of science, philosophy, and the humanities was possible because of the Greek consecration of this task of seeking wisdom.

Figure 35 *The Parthenon, remains of a prime symbol of Athens' golden age. Photo by J. T. Carmody.*

Plato himself used myth and symbols to suggest the psychology, politics, and natural philosophy of the newly clarified human consciousness. His uses of them were deliberate, calculated attempts to keep in touch with the whole field of human awareness, to keep from getting lost in abstraction. Aristotle, more prosaic, commonsensical, and scientific than Plato, analyzed the new clarification of consciousness in drier, more technical terms.[55] As he saw it, a person first experiences ignorance about the meaning of human existence. This ignorance, however, is peculiar: It is knowing that one does not know—being aware that one is in the dark. Instinctively we seek release from the tension that this realization produces. Aware of our confusion, upset that we do not know how our lives make sense, we are moved to clarify things. If distractions, whether personal or social, do not interfere, we may pursue enlightenment, and our search may become inner directed. We may grope forward by an intuition or foreknowledge of what we seek, just as we work a math problem by a knowing ignor-ance that enables us to recognize when our answer is correct.

Likewise, in the profound problem of human understanding that Aristotle was working on, there is a sense of the answer or goal from the beginning. Looking for the reality that will order both ourselves and our world, questioning and following the thoughts of our mind, we slowly advance toward the divine light, the divine mind, the divine being. Indeed, divinity itself, Aristotle finally realized, had been attracting him from the beginning. From the first, his glimmerings of light, of intellectual understanding, had been sharings in God. Developing this Platonic and Aristotelian insight, the Christian theologians Augustine and Aquinas wrote a new treatise on the image of God, stating that our human intellectual light is a share in the activities of the Father, the Son, and the Holy Spirit.[56]

The Hellenistic Religions.   Following the cultural flowering of Greek religion in science, the arts, and philosophy, the Hellenistic religions dominated. This postclassical period resulted from Alexander the Great's conquests (*Hellenism* is the term for his vision of an ecumenical, transnational culture). The Hellenistic era extended from Alexander (who died in 323 B.C.E.) well into the Roman and Christian periods. According to historians who love classical Greek culture, it was not a time of glory. Gilbert Murray, for instance, speaks of a "failure of nerve," while E. R. Dodds speaks of a "fear of freedom."[57] From our standpoint, perhaps the most significant feature of Hellenistic religion was its syncretism. In an imperial area populated by numerous ethnic groups, many different gods, beliefs, and rituals swam together. We can conclude our historical survey of the main movements of Greek religion by describing the most important aspects of this syncretism.

Alexander himself was something of a visionary, for what lured him to empire building was the idea of a realm in which conquered peoples "were to be treated not as uncivilized and barbarous members of subject races but as equals with whom one must live in concord."[58] Before Alexander, the Greeks had some knowledge of foreign religions through travel and trade, but, in general, Oriental deities had made little impact on their own piety. (One exception might be Cybele, a mother goddess imported from Phrygia [central Turkey], who was identified with Rhea, the mother of Zeus.) However, from the time of the Diadochi, the rulers who succeeded Alexander, Oriental cults began to spread. By the beginning of the second century B.C.E., they were predominant. The most popular gods were Cybele, Isis, and Serapis. In the later Roman period, Mithra also flourished.

As noted, Cybele was a mother goddess (and mistress of the animals). Usually she was accompanied by her young lover, Attis. (We may hypothesize that to the Greeks Cybele and Attis echoed the Minoan cave goddess and her consort.) She was severe and vengeful, and accompanied by lions. When Attis was unfaithful, she drove him insane. Eventually Cybele became a maternal deity like Demeter, Hera, and Aphrodite—a patroness of life, protectress of particular cities, and defender of women.

In Cybele's ceremonies devotees reenacted Attis' insanity and consequent self-castration. They would take the pine tree (Attis' symbol), bury it, mourn for the dead god, and then observe his resurrection. Resurrected, Attis would rejoin Cybele, which was cause for great feasting. The cult seems to have promoted fertility, and its rituals have overtones of the vegetative cycle and sexuality. Celebrants went to emotional extremes, dancing, scourging themselves, and even on occasion imitating Attis' castration. We could say that the worship of Cybele attracted Dionysian energies.

In ancient Egypt, as we saw, Isis was the wife of Osiris and the mother of Horus. In the Hellenistic period she achieved a wider influence, often in the company of Serapis. Serapis was an artificial creation, the result of the Greeks' aversion to the Egyptian tendency to worship gods in animal form. Fusing Osiris with his symbol (Apis, the bull), the Greeks made a new god: Serapis. He was bearded and seated on a throne, like Zeus, Hades, and Asclepius, some of whose functions he shared (such as rule of the sky, rule of the underworld, and healing). Joined with Isis, Serapis was primarily a fertility god, bedecked with branches and fruit.

Isis rather overshadowed Serapis, for she became a full-fledged, several-sided deity. As the consort of Osiris-Serapis, she was the heavenly queen of the elements, the ruler of stars and planets. Because of such power, she could enter the underworld to help her devotees or to stimulate the crops. Indeed, as a vegetative goddess she blended with Demeter and also the moon goddess Selene. Perhaps her most important role, though, was to represent feminine virtues. In distress, she had sought the slain Osiris and brought him back to life. Sensitive and compassionate, she would do the same for her followers. As the mother of Horus (she was often represented suckling him), she would help women in childbirth and with child raising. Unlike Cybele, the Hellenistic Isis was soft and tender. Yet, as recent scholarship has shown,[59] her devotees assumed a code of high ethics and her cult was strikingly free of orgiastic tendencies.

Like those for Cybele and Attis, the ceremonies for Isis and Osiris-Serapis amounted to a cycle of mourning and rejoicing. Mourning, followers reenacted Isis' search for Osiris and her discovery of his dismembered parts. Rejoicing, they celebrated Osiris' resurrection and the return of Isis' joy. The initiate Apuleius' famous account gives some of the details of the rituals, which included bathings, ten days of abstinence from sex, "approaching the gates of death," and entering the presence of the gods.[60] Clearly, the ceremonies were elaborate and effective, much as the Eleusinian mysteries must have been. Through the cycle of Osiris' death and resurrection, followers would gain confidence that their own lives were in good hands. Through the dramatic symbolization of the afterlife, they could anticipate security and bliss.

Mithra, whom we know from Iran, never took strong hold among the Hellenistic Greeks, but he did become important among the Romans influenced by Hellenism, especially the Roman soldiers. Indeed, his transformation illustrates almost perfectly the religious amalgam that cross-cultural contact produced at this time. In Mithra's Romanization, Jupiter (Zeus) took on attributes of Ahura Mazdah and became a great champion of Truth. Mithra, in turn, became Jupiter—Ahura Mazdah's faithful helper in the battle against the Lie. In this later mythology, Mithra was born of a rock (symbol of the celestial vault), and from birth carried a bow, arrows, and dagger (much like a Persian noble). He shot the arrows into the heavens from time to time to produce a heavenly spring of pure rain water. Very important was his sacrifice of the bull, from whose blood sprouted the corn (symbol of vegetation).

Thus, Mithra was both a celestial deity (later associated particularly with the sun) and a fertility god. His followers would trace his circuit through the sky, reenact the mythology of his birth, and celebrate a bull sacrifice in his name. After the sacrifice they would feast together, believing that the bull's meat and blood contained the substance of eternity. As the Mithraic doctrine developed, it generated a complicated astrology, by which the progress of initiates' souls through the heavens was shown. At its peak, Mithraism ran underground "churches" and schools. Today excavations under Christian churches, including St. Clement's in Rome, reveal statuary, classrooms, and altars used by Mithraists.

In summary, the Hellenistic period was a time of profuse religious activity. Onto Greek and then Roman religious culture, a cosmopolitan era grafted elements from the Egyptians, Persians, Phrygians, and others. We have not even mentioned the Syrian cults of the mother goddess Adonis and of various baals (Canaanite and Phoenician local deities), which constituted another strand of Hellenistic fertility religion.[61] Beyond doubt, a certain cultural confusion underlay all this excitement. Thrown into close contact with foreigners, all people in the new empire had to face new divinities and beliefs. Partly as a result, many people felt great need for signs of salvation or assurances of a happy afterlife. The upshot was a frenzy of mysteries through which devotees could feel stirring emotions or see marvelous sights. With a rush of sorrow, sexual excitement, or hope for rebirth, an initiate would feel passionately alive. In a time of disarray and ceaseless warfare, when the city-state or clan no longer offered security or guidance, such a sense of vitality was more than welcome.

Worldview

Nature and Ultimate Reality.   Nature and divinity run together in pre-Christian Greek religion. Throughout its history, the Greek religious mind associated all major natural phenomena with particular gods. As noted, the sky, sea, and earth were powerful deities. The major stress was on fertility (which was the focus of most local festivals), perhaps due to the poor quality of the rocky Greek soil. The Homeric hymns, for instance, sing praise to mother earth, who feeds all creatures and blesses humans with good crops. Relatedly, they make the man with good crops a symbol of prosperity. The earth, mother of the gods and wife of the starry heavens, has blessed him—his children can play merrily.[62] As a result of its prehistoric roots, then, Greece saw much divinity in natural growth.

Society.   In *social* terms, Greek religious culture reflects the ethical ideas that bound first the early clanspeople and then the citizens of the city-state. The ethics of the early historical period evolved from the extended family. There was no money, and banditry was rife, so a man's great virtue was to provide food, shelter, and defense—whether by just means or otherwise. Consequently, most men (it was a patriarchal culture) petitioned the gods for material prosperity and success in arms. They called one of their number good (*agathos*) and praised him for excellence (*arete*) if he was a survivor. The more elevated notions of justice later developed by philosophers clashed with the less moral early tradition. Since early Greek religion did not associate godliness with justice, the philosophers called for its overthrow.

Another primitive concept that died hard was "pollution." This was the dangerous state of being unclean, or at odds with the natural powers because of some dread deed. Homicide was especially polluting, but incest, contact with a dead person, or even a bad dream or childbirth could also be polluting, each in varying degrees. Washing in a spring would cleanse away a bad dream; purification by fire and the offering of pig's blood cleansed a homicide. The concept of pollution seems to have been a way for the Greeks to deal with dreadful, amoral happenings that might bring destructive contact with the sacred, even though they were unintentional. Since polluted persons could contaminate others, they were often banished.

Greek cults used magical formulas, prayers, sacrifices, dances, and dramatic scenes—a wealth of creative expressions. Magical formulas probably were most prominent in agricultural festivals, where peasants mixed models of snakes and phalluses with decomposing, organic materials, such as pine branches and remains of pigs, to excite powers of fertility. Greek prayers would recall a god's favors and the sacrifices that the praying person had offered previously. This implied a sort of barter: We will honor you and offer a sacrifice if you give us success in crops (or war, or family life, or whatever). Occasionally texts indicate pure admiration for divine power or beauty, but the ordinary attitude was quite practical. Since the gods were not necessarily rational or holy, they had to be cajoled. Indeed, a Greek tended to pray and sacrifice rather parochially, addressing the family Apollo or Athena, who might remember fat sacrifices offered in the past. Each family or city-state had its own traditions, customs, myths, and gods, which served both to bind the members together and to keep the different tribes from uniting.

Sacrifice was a primary way to keep local religion in good health. By giving the local god good things, one could expect prosperity in return. (Significantly, this implied that the gods blessed those who were wealthy and had good things to sacrifice and that those who sacrificed and met bad luck had secret sins or wicked ancestors. Either way, human success and goodness were rather arbitrary.) In a sacrifice, usually parts of an animal were offered and the rest was consumed. According to a Homeric account, for instance, a pig was cut up, pieces of each limb were wrapped in fat and thrown on the fire, and barley grains were sprinkled on the fire. The meal that followed was a mode of communion with the deities.

Greek cults produced many priests, but their status and functions were limited. In principle, any person could pray and sacrifice to any god, so priests had no monopoly. They tended to be limited to particular temples and were seldom organized into bands or hierarchies. A large clan might have its own officiating priest, and the priest of a prosperous temple might make a good living from sacrifice fees. Otherwise, priesthood was not a road to status or wealth. Priests seldom gave instruction or performed divinations, though some priests in the mystery rites did both.

Many Greek religious authors were rather harsh on women. Hesiod, for instance, reported the myth of Pandora and the box of evils, which made woman the source of human woes. In other places he called woman "that beautiful evil," the "snare from which there is no escaping," and "that terrible plague."[63] Socrates, when asked about the advisability of marriage, balanced the boon of heirs against the woes of a wife: "One quarrel after another, her dower cast in your face, the haughty disdain of her family, the garrulous tongue of your mother-in-law, the lurking paramour."[64] In Plato's *Republic,* women were to be equal to men socially and sexually, having rights to education and rule. Nonetheless, Plato tended to consider women less independent than men, in good part because of their physique: "The womb is an animal that longs to generate children." Aristotle, however, was the most unequivocal misogynist. To him women were simply inferior, both intellectually and morally. In his matter-and-form theory, women supplied only the matter for human reproduction, men supplying everything effective and active.

Women did have legal rights in Athenian society, but their lives were largely circumscribed by male control. Their basic function was to bear children. The playwright Euripides summarized the impact of this socialization, putting into the mouths of the women of his *Andromache* such self-evaluations as: "There's a touch of jealousy in the female psyche"; "For nature tempers the souls of women so they may find a pleasure in voicing their afflictions as they come"; "A woman even when married to a cad, ought to be deferential, not a squabbler"; and "And just because we women are prone to evil, what's to be gained from perverting men to match?"

On the other hand, we have seen that Greek divinity frequently was powerfully feminine. In the Minoan-Mycenaean period, a great goddess was the prime deity. In the Olympian period, Demeter, Hera, Athena, Artemis, and Aphrodite all exerted great influence. In the Hellenistic religions, Cybele and Isis more than equaled Mithra. Psychologically, then, Greek culture never doubted the divinity of the feminine. More than Israelite, Christian, or Muslim culture, Greek divinity was androgynous. Furthermore, certain religious groups offered women escape from social oppression, for example, the Eleusinian and Dionysian sects. There, in a sort of utopian free zone, women could experience equality and dignity. Although these cults never compensated for women's lack of dignity or status in ordinary life, their egalitarianism was an implicit admission that ordinary life was quite imperfect.

Self.   The personal side of Greek religion is perhaps most manifest in myths dealing with human creation. In the most famous collection of myths, Hesiod's *Works and Days,* ancient Greeks read that they were the last and lowest in a series of human generations. During the first ages, races of gold, silver, and bronze had flourished, but they came to various bad ends. A flood intervened, followed by the age of the heroes. Finally the present iron people arose. In other words, Hesiod's myth put into Greek form the widespread belief in a golden age or a previous paradise, with the accompanying message that the present age was a low point, a period of decline.

Partly from this religious heritage, the prevailing mood of many Greek writers was pessimistic. As Sermonides, a writer of the seventh century B.C.E., put it, "There is no wit in man. Creatures of a day, we live like cattle, knowing nothing of how the god will bring each one to his end."[65] Others echoed Sermonides: Human beings have only a short time under the sun; their powers fade quickly, their fortunes are uncertain. By comparison, Delphic wisdom was more positive: Gain self-knowledge and moderation. Self-knowledge, above all, was accepting one's mortality. By moderation, one could avoid hubris (overweening pride) and tragedy. There were overtones of jealousy in this advice from Apollo, however, as though the god feared humans yearning for immortality or resented their craving a life of passion.

Indeed, passion was ever a danger, for the Greeks were competitive and lusty. In the end, they would not give up their dreams of immortality. So becoming godlike became a central theme of philosophy and mystery religion. The philosopher Empedocles, for instance, thought that his wisdom made him a god among mortals. Plato taught that the soul is divine and deathless. The common person would more likely find divinity in one of the mystery rites, through a union with Demeter or a knowledge from Isis, either of which could bring victory over death.

The personal implications of Greek religion were greatest in the philosophers' clarification of reason, universal humanity, and the participation of divinity in human thought. As we have noted, the poets, dramatists, and early philosophers slowly clarified the nature of human reason, separating it from myth. By focusing on mind (*nous*) and its relations with being (*ousia*), the pre-Socratics prepared the way for Plato

and Aristotle, who realized how mind and being coincide. Moreover, this work did not take the Greek intellectuals away from either religion or politics. Rather, it introduced them to an order that set all the fundamentals—nature, society, self, and divinity—in harmony. In other words, it took them to the heart of what it means to be human.

Finally, the philosophers' order meant a new perspective on death. In early times, death was shadowy. For Homer, the dead had only a vague existence around their graves or in the underworld. There was no judgment or punishment for injustice toward one's fellows. Only those who had directly affronted the gods had to suffer. The mystery cults said one could conquer death by union with an immortal divinity, and their great popularity indicates the hold that death had on Greece starting in the sixth century B.C.E. The philosophers spoke of judgment and punishment because they were acutely aware that justice rules few human situations. In quite deliberate myths, Plato symbolized the inherent need we have for a final accounting. Without it, he suggested, reason would lose balance.

In the eyes of many scholars, the Greeks were among the most religious of ancient peoples. From heaven to under the earth, from crude emotion to the most refined spirituality, their great culture put a religious shine on everything. Today, if we find the world "sacred" (deeply meaningful) through science or art, if we find the human being "sacred" (deeply valuable) through medicine or philosophy, if we find the political order alive with counsels to flee disorder and pursue justice—if we ever think in these ways, it is largely because of the Greeks. They made the "transcendental" qualities—unity, truth, goodness, and beauty—part of all subsequent Western religion.

SUMMARY: THE ANCIENT NEAR EASTERN CENTER

We have surveyed the rise of ancient Near Eastern civilized religion. We should now reflect at least briefly on the central patterns that our survey reveals.

First, civilization—culture and social organization at a scale larger than that of the tribal village—developed on the foundations of agriculture. The increase in population, the sedentary life, and the economic and cultural specialization that farming allowed made cities and their cultural advances possible. Not surprisingly, then, many agricultural or earth-related motifs continued on in the religions of the first great civilizations. For all their moments of spiritual achievement, Egypt, Iran, and Greece all remained immersed in peasant views.

Second, the discovery of writing was essential in the advances of civilized religion. Through writing— even the hieroglyphic writing of the Egyptians—came the records that the early civilizations themselves used and that we, their latter-day students, have used to retrieve what they thought and felt. Within the early peoples' own religious horizon, the sense of history that came with writing was a significant development. Of course, oral peoples have memory and tradition, but writing makes historical consciousness more formal.

Writing also raises the possibility of a new attitude toward the realities of the traditional world. For writing makes the realities of the traditional world *mediated,* as they previously were not. Spoken language has a holistic quality, conveying its message immediately, in a rather imperative or at least solicitous way. Written language is more detached and indirect. To the benefit of science, and perhaps the detriment of religion, it tends toward scholarship. For example, once the biblical legends were written down, scholars could dissect them at leisure. In the development of the early civilizations, we catch sizable traditions at their very revealing transition from oral to written religion.

Third, this chapter has mainly dealt with religious traditions that lasted for long stretches of time. Of course, Mesopotamia, Egypt, Iran, and Greece all changed significantly during the times that we studied. Nonetheless, Egypt had a quite coherent religious culture that lasted longer than Christianity has so far, and Iran and Greece both provide impressive instances of religious cultures that endured and evolved through many centuries. Because of their long duration, we can reconstruct and analyze the world views these cultures generated. Concerning nature, they all preserved close ties with a living cosmos. In rites, myths, and popular religion, for instance, they all kept strong agricultural influences. On the other hand, each separated itself from the cosmological myth somewhat. Akhenaton's reform was Egypt's most dramatic separation, but the Amon hymns and man's dispute with his soul about suicide provide additional evidence.

Zoroaster made Iran break with the cosmological myth more sharply than Egypt did, but later Zoroas-

trianism retreated on this point. Only Greece took the full step toward the realization of spirit. The philosophers discovered the mind; for Plato and Aristotle, what is and what can be thought coincided.

Still, none of the early civilizations broke the cosmological myth entirely. None conceived of a personal creator God wholly independent of the cosmos. All their divinities were world forces, and all their ultimate world views tended to follow nature's rhythms.

Socially, Egypt appears as the most hierarchical and rigid civilization; its culture is remarkably static. Iran appears as a welter of ethnic influences and a welter of religious trends. It was in great turmoil, but few personalities, other than military kings, stand out. Personalities stand out most dramatically in Greece, despite its large patches of social conservatism. Especially in the Athenian golden age, tradition seemed just flexible enough. Thus, Greece fostered geniuses. In art and philosophy, we study them still. If viewed as the culmination of the developments of ancient Near Eastern civilizational religions, they suggest that the center for which these developments were groping was the consubstantiality of mind and holy being, the mutual penetration. In the Greek discovery of reason, human beings glimpsed the possibility that divinity is eminently rational, that the sacred is a holy word. That glimpse changed the history of Western religion and now is rewriting the history of the entire world.

Discussion Questions

1. Why was the sun so prominent in Egyptian religion?

2. How does the myth of Osiris illumine the religious significance of the pyramids?

3. In what sense did Zoroaster differentiate Iranian religious consciousness?

4. What emerges when you compare Ahura Mazdah and the Egyptian Amon-Re?

5 How did the Greek love of wisdom definitively clarify the nature of human reason?

6. Do Dionysus and Apollo together compose a complete symbolization of divinity? Why?

7. Is it fair to summarize the Hellenistic religions as a return to a prephilosophical emphasis on fertility, or did their "salvation" entail considerably more?

8. What is the main lesson in the myth of Gilgamesh?

9. What were the main features of popular, local Greek religion?

10. What significance have the Zoroastrians given to fire?

11. What does Greek religion suggest about the religious significance of death?

12. What were the main feminine motifs in the ancient Near Eastern religions?

Glossary

Ahura Mazdah: the Wise Lord who has been the main Zoroastrian divinity. Ahura Mazdah represents Zoroaster's version of the extrapolation from the demands of a refined conscience to the existence of a good, intelligent first principle one finds in other reflective religious seers.

cosmos: the universe conceived as an orderly system. Opposed to the cosmos is the chaos of a nature that seems unordered and a human realm that defies rational analysis. Religious systems that have posited an intelligent power at the foundations of reality usually have imagined the universe as a cosmos. On the other hand, the irrationalities in creation and its nonhuman scale have kept the specter of chaos alive and influential. The more sophisticated theologies—for example, the Hindu—have sometimes incorporated both aspects into their divinity, and even the theologies (for example, those of the monotheistic Western religions) that have pictured the divinity as wise and loving have had pockets in which the raw power of the deity came close to being an irrationality (or a suprarationality) so strong that human beings could never comprehend it and had always to fear it.

divine kingship: the concept, common to many ancient societies, that the monarch so mediates between the people and ultimate reality that he should be considered a god. Usually the society involved has a rather fluid notion of divinity, applying it to any forceful or crucial entity that mediates relations with the ultimate powers. In the typical scheme, the assumption of the cosmological myth makes the leading ruler the connection between heaven and earth, where the power that keeps the one consubstantial realm in order passes from above to below. Thus the vitality of the king is extremely important, and the moment when the king dies and mediating functions pass to a new ruler is the most dramatic time in the people's existence.

dualism: bifurcating reality, usually so that it separates into forces of good competing with forces of evil. The experiential basis of most dualisms is the complexity of the moral realm, in which goodness and evil seem irreducible (one cannot be collapsed into the other and neither is able to defeat the other decisively). Manicheanism and Zoroastrianism are two dualistic religions that exemplify this tendency. The Christian St. Augustine thought he solved the problem of evil, and so in good conscience could quit Manicheanism, by seeing that evil, rather than being something positive or existent in its own right, is always a privation of the being, order, and goodness that health or virtue demands. Thus sickness is the disordered functioning of cells or bodily mechanisms, whereas sin is the lack of reason and love that rationality and faith demand. Every theism has to contend with the data sparking dualism, either by distancing evil from God or by postulating what in effect is evil at the very foundations of the world (in divinity itself). Hinduism sometimes seems to take this latter position.

Hellenism: the cultural ideals, usually credited to Alexander the Great for their genesis, that dominated eastern Europe and the Near East from the late fourth century B.C.E. through perhaps the first five centuries of the Common Era. Alexander sought an ecumenical empire in which perception of a common humanity would allow different ethnic groups to be citizens of a common political realm. The religious implications included a tolerance of many different gods and cultural traditions, which in turn frequently sponsored a syncretism in which gods from different traditions overlapped or ran together.

maat: an Egyptian term (and goddess) referring to cosmic order. *Maat* was something like the Law or *Logos* guiding creation. Personified, it had the obligation of constraining or persuading creatures to follow the laws natural to them. The pharaoh mediated *maat* to the common people, and the laws of the state sanctioned by the pharaoh spelled out what *maat* was to mean in many concrete circumstances. The pharaoh had responsibilities to *maat,* but he served as well as a metaphysical link between the order of heaven that *maat* expressed and the order of earth that needed ordering. *Maat* had many competitors in the Egyptian pantheon, probably standing psychologically for the rights of reason in competition with will, desire, fertility, and the other urges of both the conscious and the unconscious mind.

Magi: ancient Persian and Zoroastrian priests. If one finds the roots of the Magi in ancient Indo-Iranian culture, they may originally have been a hereditary class like the Brahmins. Their name has overtones of (spiritual) riches, and in later periods they presided over the Persian rituals, including the Zoroastrian rites. By the time of Christ, the Magi had a reputation throughout the Hellenistic world as astrologers and interpreters of dreams.

mystery religions: traditions of the Hellenistic period that focused on ways to gain immortality and used secret sacramental rites. The mystery religions stemmed from various sources—Greek, Egyptian, and Mesopotamian. They influenced Judaism and Christianity inasmuch as they were competitors in a battle for the allegiance of people interested in wisdom and salvation. Many of the recurrent themes dealt with fertility—the dying and rising of nature that might hold promise that human beings would enter a new cycle after death. Others enacted myths of the immortality of the human soul, recalling its divine origin and speculating about its happy afterlife.

pharaoh: the king or presiding figure of ancient Egypt who mediated heavenly power and *maat* to the people. Pharaohship took place within the Egyptian version of the cosmological myth, the pharaoh being less important as an individual than as a mediator between heaven and earth. The pyramids witness to the Egyptian desire to secure pharaohship against death, while the care taken for the transition from old pharaoh to new suggests how the office of the pharaoh served Egypt as a fence against chaos.

polytheism: having many gods, or allowing all the many places or ways in which ultimate reality expresses itself to be venerated. Sometimes polytheists unify the many expressions of the divine by speaking of a single divine substance or of a great divine overlord. Usually, however, they are not metaphysicians and do not trouble themselves greatly about the relationship between the many deities and the one divine power that makes them all kin. Egyptian and Mesopotamian religions are good examples of polytheism in a developed, in its own way quite sophisticated, mode that generally felt little pressure toward henotheism or monotheism.

syncretism: the tendency to run several gods, ceremonies, beliefs, or other aspects of two or more religious traditions together. The result usually has been an undigested mixture or rather infertile hybrid. Syncretism was influential during the Hellenistic period and so presented both Judaism and Christianity many serious questions. One should distinguish syncretism from the acculturation that a religious tradition undergoes when it is transplanted from one geographic locale to another, though in fact such acculturation does sometimes lead to syncretism. For example, the translation of Buddhism from India to China and Japan was not itself syncretistic, but when Japanese Buddhists and Shintoists agreed that *bodhisattvas* and kami could be two faces of the same reality, they were accomplishing something syncretistic.

CHAPTER 8

JUDAISM

Jewish menorah

Judaism is the oldest of the three major prophetic religions. The founding and development of Christianity and Islam could not have occurred without the preexistence of Judaism. (Zoroastrianism can claim some prophetic equality with Judaism, but its prophecies never became dominant in Near Eastern and Western beliefs. Zoroastrianism's major influence in the West was its eschatology—its ideas of death, judgment, resurrection, punishment, the warfare between good and evil, and so on.) Abraham, Moses, David, Elijah, Isaiah—they are the personalities that dominated the Western prophetic beginnings.

HISTORY

The Biblical Period

In dealing with the roots of Judaism in the biblical period, we encounter serious questions about the sources that any historical treatment must use. The Bible is not a simple, straightforward book, and thus the evidence it provides for the evolution of Israelite

Judaism: Twenty-five Key Dates	
ca. 1200 B.C.E.	*Exodus from Egypt*
ca. 1013–973	*David*
722	*Fall of Northern Kingdom to Assyria*
586	*Fall of Southern Kingdom to Babylon*
331	*Alexander Conquers Palestine*
168	*Maccabean Revolt*
63	*Romans Conquer Jerusalem*
70 C.E.	*Romans Destroy Jerusalem*
80–110	*Assembly of Hebrew Scriptures*
ca. 200	*Promulgation of Mishnah*
ca. 500	*Babylonian Talmud Complete in Rough Form*
640	*Muslim Conquest of Middle East*
1041	*Birth of Rashi, Bible and Talmud Commentator*
ca. 1135	*Birth of Maimonides*
1187	*Muslims Reconquer Jerusalem from Christians*
1290–1309	*Expulsion of Jews from England and France*
1492–1496	*Expulsion of Jews from Spain and Portugal*
1516	*Introduction of Ghetto in Venice*
1521	*Jewish Migrations to Palestine*
1648	*Massacre of Polish and Ukrainian Jews*
1654–1658	*Jewish Communities in New Amsterdam and Rhode Island*
1760	*Death of Baal Shem-Tov*
1897	*Founding of Zionist Movement*
1938	*Every Synagogue in Germany Burned*
1948	*Creation of State of Israel*

faith is not simple or straightforward. The current scholarly consensus is that the Jewish scriptures (Old Testament) come from many sources and represent many different points of view. Circles of priests, prophets, and people interested in wisdom (sapiential circles), for example, probably preserved memories of battles, of traditional laws, of the reigns of different kings, of prayers to be sung on special occasions, and much more. Each such circle had its own traditions, its own political goals, its own understanding of what Israelite history had been in the past and signified in the present. For perhaps a thousand years (from the time of the monarchy of David to the time when the rabbis reached a final rough consensus about what writings should be deemed regulative and so "scriptural"), Israelites (early Jews) worked over records and leavings. Northerners had traditions that differed from southerners. Poets put things one way and chroniclers put things another way. Indeed, in just the first five books of the Bible, traditionally attributed to Moses, scholars have discerned at least four major strands of tradition. Weaving their way through Genesis, Exodus, Leviticus, Numbers, and Deuteronomy, these strands sometimes offer us different perspectives on the same topic. For example, the account of creation that opens the Bible (Genesis 1) stresses the orderly arrangement of the physical world, while the

KEY JEWISH DOCTRINES	
Revelation	Divine will expressed in Torah Divine nature shown in history
Covenant	Special bond created between God and Israel Chosen people called to a special holiness
Redemption	Divine action to save the people Key experiences: Exodus, return from Exile, establishment of the state of Israel
Prophecy	Divine inspiration to announce God's will Call to right worship and social justice
Monotheism	Only the God of the ancestors is a true divinity Need for vigilance against idolatry
Ethics	Need to follow Jewish Law (Torah) Call above all to justice and mercy

account that we find in chapters 2 and 3 is more interested in how the first human beings arose and what happened to them.

Materials such as these different strands of the Pentateuch were edited, usually several times, into the order of the biblical "books" that we find today. Each book of the Bible therefore is a composite work, and sometimes one finds conflicts, both within a given book and between one book and another. So, for example, Exodus gives us one view of Moses and Deuteronomy gives us another. Moreover, although the first five books of the Bible have been accorded the most dignity and authority, the second section of the Bible, traditionally called "the Prophets," also has been revered, and this second section contains reinterpretations of the events (especially the establishment of the covenant between Israel and God) suited to later crises, such as the removal of many leaders of the Israelite community to Babylon in the sixth century B.C.E. Still a third section of the Bible, traditionally called "the Writings," collects later and disparate materials, and while as a group it has had less status than either the first five books (Pentateuch, Torah) or the Prophets, its works have still been considered authoritative interpretations of the meaning of Israelite existence. Together, these three sections of the Bible comprised the *TANAK*, an anagram comprised from the first letters for each in Hebrew.

Any sketch of the history of biblical Israel, therefore, both depends on questionable sources and tends to distort what the Bible itself was all about. The Bible itself is about "paradigmatic" history: key events and personages that could serve as three-dimensional lessons about the significance of Israel's experiences sojourning with its Lord though time. As we turn now to such a sketch of the biblical period, it is important to remember that the biblical writers on which we or the authorities we are using depend were themselves usually more interested in the significance a given event had for contemporary existence (the cultural challenges existing at the time of the writer or editor) than in what happened, in a literal sense, originally. In other words, we are always involved in interpreting interpretations—dealing with the meanings, symbolic and historical alike, that people using the Bible paradigmatically found most absorbing.

To begin our historical survey, we take up an "integrationist" point of view, assuming a continuity between biblical Israel and later Judaism. As one prominent Jewish scholar has put it: "From the point of view of the Jew, Judaism and the Religion of Israel are the same, and what is called the religion of [biblical] Israel is but one chapter of a long and variegated historical continuum."[1] We accept this point of view, avoiding the tendency to make a great disjunction between biblical Judaism and Judaism in the Common Era. While the Roman destruction of the Temple in Jerusalem in 70 C.E. changed Jewish religion, the rabbis continued to look to the Torah of Moses for their inspiration.

In the beginning, the Jews were most likely a loose collection of seminomadic tribes that wandered in what is today Israel, Jordan, Lebanon, and Syria. They may have cultivated some crops, but their self-designation was "wandering Aramaeans" (Deut. 26:5). Thus, when scouts returned from Canaan (present-day western Israel) with grapes, pomegranates, and figs (products of settled cultivators), they caused quite a stir.[2]

Members of an early Jewish extended family tended to worship their particular "god of the father," defining themselves largely in terms of their patriarch and his god. The cult therefore centered on clan remembrance of this god, who wandered with the tribe in its nomadic life. The common name for such a clan divinity was *el.* Before their settlement in Canaan, the people seem to have worshiped a variety of *els:* the god of the mountain, the god of seeing, the god of eternity, and so on. Usually they worshiped at altars constructed of unhewn stones, which they considered to be the god's house. In addition to the *els* were household deities and minor divinities and demons of the desert. In later orthodox Jewish interpretation, Abraham drew on whatever sense there was of a unity among these *els* or of a supreme *el* over the others to dedicate himself to a God who was beyond nature. That God, the creator of the world, Abraham called Yahweh (YHWH).[3] (The influence of Exodus 3:14 on the Genesis story of Abraham is clear.)

For later orthodoxy, Abraham became the "Father" of the Jews and his God YHWH ("I am who I am") became their God. In that sense, Judaism began with Abraham. Abraham probably lived around 1800 B.C.E. His descendants Isaac and Jacob, whose stories are recounted in the biblical book of Genesis, kept the Abrahamic faith in the unique name of YHWH, "the Lord." From about 1650 to 1280, the people of Abra-

ham, then known as Hebrews, were in Egypt, subjects of the Egyptian kingdom.[4] According to the Book of Genesis (39–50), the Hebrews' presence in Egypt was due to the success there of Jacob's son Joseph. Their leader at the end of their stay in Egypt was Moses. In later Jewish theology, Moses functioned as the founder of the Jewish people, because God revealed through Moses his will to make a covenant and fashion himself a people. In the incident at the burning bush (Exod. 3), Jewish faith said, Moses experienced God's self-revelation. God then commissioned Moses to lead the people out of Egypt, giving as his authoritative name only "I am who I am" (or "I am whatever I want to be").

Moses then led the Jewish people out of Egypt, an event that dominated the biblical authors' interpretation of everything that preceded and followed it. In the most significant episode in that *exodus,* Egyptian pursuers drowned in the sea. Free of them, the Israelites (the descendants of Jacob, Abraham's grandson) wandered in the desert until they entered the homeland that God had promised them. The deliverance from Egypt through the unexpected event at the Reed Sea (not the present-day Red Sea) marked all subsequent Jewish faith. Looking back to this event, later generations clung to the belief that their God ruled history and would continue to liberate them from oppression.

In the desert, Moses and the people tested the meaning of their exodus experience. They came to believe, through what the Bible pictures as God's miraculous speaking to them, that they were bound to God by a *covenant.* In this compact, based on the relation between a Near Eastern overlord and vassal, God pledged care and the people pledged fidelity. The commandments accompanying this covenant gave the binding relationship (which some later commentators saw as prefigured in Adam, Noah, and Abraham) an ethics. They became the basis of the Law (Torah) and the revelation that bound the people together.

This *Torah* has been the mainstay of Jewish life for over 3,000 years. In the beginning, it encompassed the oral revelation of God, believed to have been given to Moses as a sort of charter or constitution for the life of the covenanted or chosen people. When Jewish religious writings about the formative period (of the earliest ancestors and Moses) arose, they were attributed to Moses. Thus the first five books of the present Bible, now known as the Torah or the Pentateuch, were long considered to have come from Moses' hand (modern biblical scholarship disputes this). When subsequent writings eventually included in the Hebrew Bible (the two groups of writings known as the Prophets and the Writings) gained status as authentic revelation from God, they too partook of the dignity of Torah. Thus the Tanak (Torah-Prophets-Writings) or Hebrew Bible has all been considered Torah.

In the same way, later Judaism came to consider the rabbinic writings (such collections as the Mishnah, the Gemara, and the Talmud [the Mishnah plus the Gemara]) sufficiently authoritative to have the status of God's revelation or direction, so such rabbinic writings also came under Torah. Torah, then, is the expression of the divine will, given through human intermediaries, on which pious Jews have depended for their basic sense of what God is like, what God has done in their history, and how God wants them to live (in keeping with their call to be the special people of a holy deity). From laws about how to keep the Sabbath to traditions about how to sway while praying, Torah has encompassed all the traditions cherished as the basis of the people's identity and way to live worthy of their Lord.[5]

When the Israelites finally settled in Canaan (in the latter half of the thirteenth century B.C.E. under Moses' successor Joshua),[6] they changed from a nomadic to an agricultural people. They were still a group of confederated tribes, but in settlement their bonds tended to loosen, as each group kept to its own area and developed its own ways. Only in times of common danger would the groups weld together, but war was so constant a feature of the period from the Exodus to the sixth-century Exile in Babylon that the people had to cooperate. Settlement also meant religious changes, as local sanctuaries replaced the wandering ark of the covenant as the house of God. A somewhat professional priesthood apparently developed around these sanctuaries, and as the Israelites conquered Canaanite temples, they probably took over the scribal schools attached to the temples. These schools were probably the first sources of written Hebrew religious literature. In addition, the Canaanite religion itself was a great influence on the Israelites. Before long it produced a conflict between Israelites who favored the older God YHWH—the God of Abraham, Moses, and the covenant—and those who favored the agricultural gods (baals) of the Canaanites.

Kings and Prophets. From about 1200 to 1000 B.C.E., the Israelites had a government by "judges"—charismatic leaders, usually men but occasionally women, who took command in times of common danger. However, they eventually adopted monarchical rule, orga-

nizing a sturdy little kingdom under David at a new capital: Jerusalem. This kingdom unified the tribes of both north and south, and under Solomon, David's son, it had a brief but golden age of culture and empire. Some of the most striking narratives of the Hebrew Bible (Old Testament) derive from this period, including the brilliant memoir we find in 2 Samuel, chapters 13–20.[7]

In these narratives, David is portrayed as the ideal king and yet a man undeniably human—lustful for Bathsheba (willing to murder to get her), tragically at odds with his son Absalom. Much later, David's achievements in war and his fashioning a kingdom for peace made him the focus of messianic hopes—hopes for a king anointed by God who would usher in a new age of prosperity and peace. David, then, was the Jewish prototype for sacred kingship. Similarly, David's son Solomon became the prototype for wisdom. Just as many pious Jews attributed the Psalms to David, so they attributed much of the Bible's wisdom literature to Solomon.

Following Solomon's death, the northern and southern portions of the kingdom split apart. The north (Israel) lasted from 922 to 722 B.C.E., when it fell to Assyria. The south (Judah) lasted until 586, when it fell to Babylon. (Both Assyria and Babylon lay to the northeast.) These were centuries of great political strife and military conflict. They spawned a series of important religious *"prophets,"* who dominate the next phase of biblical history. Greatest of the early prophets was Elijah, who preached in the north against the corrupt kings Ahab and Ahaziah and the queen Jezebel. The legendary stories about Elijah portray him as a champion of YHWH and true prophecy against the false prophets of the Canaanite baals. What is clear from these stories is the influence at the time of charismatic personalities who felt that God inspired them to stand up for the old religious ways—even if doing so infuriated the royal establishment.

Around 750 B.C.E., Amos, an originally southern prophet working in the north and the first of the writing prophets, issued a clarion call for justice. Changing the notion that YHWH was simply Israel's protector, Amos made divine blessings dependent upon repentance from sin. His God was clearly in charge of nature, but the key access to divinity was social justice. In other words, YHWH was a God of people and history, especially concerned that human beings deal with one another fairly.

Hosea, another northern prophet, also spoke up for mercy and justice (and for nonidolatrous cult), but he expressed God's attitude as that of a spouse willing to suffer infidelity, unable to cast off his beloved (the people covenanted to him). In the south, the successors to these northern prophets were Isaiah, Jeremiah, and "Second Isaiah" (the source of Isaiah, chapters 40–55). They made the same demands, but with greater stress on punishment by foreign powers. Reading the signs of the times, they thought that God would subject his people to captivity because they had not relied on him in pure faith. However, both Jeremiah and Second Isaiah held out hope for a new beginning, assuring Judah that a remnant of the people would keep faith.

During the reign of the southern king Josiah (640—609 B.C.E.), there was a religious reform that many scripture scholars see as the source of the "Deuteronomic" recasting of the early Jewish tradition. It shaped not only the Book of Deuteronomy but other historical writings as well. Among the influential ideas were that YHWH had elected Israel to be his people; that observing the covenant laws was necessary for religious prosperity; that Jews ought to repudiate contacts with foreigners and foreign gods; that the cult should be consolidated in Jerusalem; and that Israel ought to rely only on YHWH, since he controlled history and oversaw nature.

Case Study: Jeremiah. It will be useful to consider the personality, career, and message of Jeremiah, for Jeremiah is a striking example of both the prophetic vocation and biblical spirituality. Born in the middle of the seventh century B.C.E. (in 645, according to some scholars), and coming from a priestly family, Jeremiah preached during the reigns of kings Josiah, Jehoiakim, and Zedekiah, until he was deported around 582 to Egypt, where he died. We know more about Jeremiah's personal life than that of the other prophets, and Jeremiah's personal life shows a man completely dominated by God's call. He did not marry, because he wanted to symbolize that most children would not survive the troubles coming because of Israel's infidelities (Jer. 16:1–4). He would not take part in mourning ceremonies or festivals, because soon there would be none left to mourn and nothing good to celebrate (16:5–8).

As one might expect, these dire forecasts made Jeremiah very unpopular. Enemies conspired against his life (11:18–23), he was confined in the stocks (19:14–20:6), and for announcing the coming destruction of the Jerusalem Temple he was tried for blasphemy. King Jehoiakim considered Jeremiah his deadly enemy and had him flogged. Jeremiah reciprocated Jehoiakim's enmity, flogging him verbally. Indeed, his indictment of King Jehoiakim reveals so much about Jeremiah's character that the verses are worth reproducing:

Woe to him who builds his house by
unrighteousness, and his upper rooms
by injustice;
who makes his neighbor serve him for
nothing, and does not give him his
wages;
Who says, "I will build myself a great
house with spacious upper rooms,"
and cuts out windows for it, paneling
it with cedar, and painting it with
vermilion.
Do you think you are a king because
you compete in cedar?
Did not your father eat and drink
and do justice and righteousness?
Then it was well with him.
He judged the cause of the poor and
needy; then it was well.
"Is this not to know me?" says the Lord.
"But you have eyes and heart only for
your dishonest gain,
for shedding innocent blood, and for
practicing oppression and violence."
Therefore thus says the Lord
concerning Jehoi'akim the son of
Josi'ah, king of Judah:
"They shall not lament for him,
saying,
'Ah my brother!' or 'Ah sister!'
They shall not lament for him, saying
'Ah lord!' or 'Ah his majesty!'
With the burial of an ass he shall be
buried,
dragged and cast forth beyond the
gates of Jerusalem." (22:13–19 RSV)

Whence came this lashing tongue, this need to accuse the mighty to their faces? Jeremiah felt his painful vocation had been laid upon him by God, who had chosen him to be a prophet from the moment of his conception (1:5–10). His mission would extend beyond Israel, bringing the Lord's message to all the nations.

Jeremiah apparently came to this understanding of his vocation while still a teenager, and the responsibility it imposed overwhelmed him. But the Lord would hear none of Jeremiah's protests, assuring him that if he spoke divine words he would receive divine support: "Behold I have put my words in your mouth" (1:9). "Be not afraid of them, for I am with you to deliver you" (1:8). So a prophet was formed, a man dominated by "the word of the Lord," the message his God impelled him to deliver.

Along with Jeremiah's calling came two visions (1:11–19). The first vision was of an almond tree. Punning on the similarity of the Hebrew words for *almond tree* and *to watch,* God told Jeremiah that his vision of the almond tree was accurate: The Lord would watch over his word to perform it. The second vision was of a boiling pot, facing away from the north. Just as boiling water spilled out of the pot and swept away twigs and pebbles, so foes would sweep out of the north and inflict evil on Jeremiah's countrymen. Jeremiah himself would face strong opposition for delivering these oracles, but his enemies would not prevail. The Lord would be with him, to deliver him.

From the outset, therefore, Jeremiah was a troubled man. He felt a charge to bring before his people the unpleasant news that hard times were coming, as the just desserts of their irreligion. From the outset Jeremiah was also a poetic man, brimming with powerful imagery. In a few lines he could sketch the whole career of a dishonest king, withering him by contrast with his righteous father. In a few phrases he could etch the king's coming demise, depicting the funeral that none would mourn. The word of the Lord pouring from the mouth of this troubled man riveted his people's imagination and lashed their soul. Jeremiah's passion for justice, his almost obsessive sense that the people had abandoned the very basis of their existence by falling away from the true God, gave him the courage to flay kings and leaders publicly. Thus he asked the people, in the name of God, "What wrong did your fathers find in me, that they went far from me, and went after worthlessness, and became worthless?" (2:5).

As Jeremiah read the political situation, God would punish this worthless people, using Babylon as his instrument. King Zedekiah consulted with Jeremiah about the political situation, but the king's advisers were bitterly opposed to the prophet, feeling that his predictions of woe were destroying the people's will to resist the Babylonians. Babylon did lay siege to Jerusalem, and when in 588 or 587 Jeremiah used a brief break in the siege to leave Jerusalem, his enemies arrested him for desertion. Zedekiah soon released him from the dungeon but had him kept in confinement. Undeterred, Jeremiah continued to proclaim that the Babylonians would defeat the Jews, and for this stubbornness his enemies threw him into a cistern, with the intention that he should starve there. When Jerusalem finally fell in 586, the victorious Babylonians treated Jeremiah well, offering him the choice of living either in Babylon or Judah. Jeremiah chose Judah, and he urged his countrymen left in Judah to try to live in peace.

Peace was not to be, however, for some discontented Jewish fugitives from the army killed Gedaliah, the governor appointed by the Babylonian ruler Nebuchadnezzar. Most of the Jewish community feared Babylonian vengeance for this murder, but when the community appealed to Jeremiah for a divine oracle on whether they should flee to Egypt or stay where they were, Jeremiah told them to stay in their own country. The people would not accept this oracle, however, so they took Jeremiah and his scribe Baruch with them to Egypt. In Egypt Jeremiah continued his unpopular ways, predicting that the Babylonians would defeat the Egyptians and castigating Jews who fell to worshiping a heavenly queen. The Jews in Egypt rejected this rebuke, and, according to later legend, stoned Jeremiah to death.

Overall, most of Jeremiah's warnings, visions, symbolic actions, and oracles were gloomy. Thinking that his people had enmeshed themselves in secular politics to the neglect of their religion, the prophet saw Judah becoming crushed by the much larger foreign powers surrounding it, and thought this fate a fitting punishment for Judah's defections. Still, not all Jeremiah's prophecies were gloomy. Like the other great prophets, his message balanced judgment with consolation. If God was judging the people harshly, because of their wanton irreligion, God was also assuring the people that the future would bring better times. Jeremiah's most consoling assurances occur in chapters 30–32, which are a high point of biblical poetry and theology.

Chapter 30 begins with the formulaic introductory phrase, "The word that came to Jeremiah from the Lord." This word was positive. The days were coming when God would restore his people's fortunes. He would bring them back to their land, lost when the northern kingdom fell in 722 to Assyria and threatened by Babylon. No matter how great the present pains grew, God would save the people from them. He would break the yoke of their foreign rulers, leading them back to serve him, the Lord their God, and a king like David.

With great poetic skill, the prophet plays variations on this theme. Behind the people's present sufferings is the hand of the Lord, punishing them for their transgressions. But that same hand will punish Israel's enemies: "Therefore all who devour you shall be devoured, and all your foes, every one of them, shall go into captivity, those who despoil you shall become a spoil, and all who prey on you I will make a prey" (30:16).

Similar poetry sings of what the restored people will enjoy: good fortune for the tents of Jacob, compassion on all Jacob's offspring's dwellings, songs of thanksgiving throughout the city and the palace, many voices making merry. "And you shall be my people, and I will be your God" (30:22). Hearkening back to the exodus from Egypt, the prophet has God say that the people who survived the sword and found grace in the wilderness would come to know God most intimately. Why? Because "I have loved you with an everlasting love; therefore I have continued my faithfulness to you" (31:3).

So in the future weeping would be for joy rather than sorrow, walking would be along lovely brooks of water and straight paths of virtue. God would gather his scattered people, like a shepherd gathering his flocks. Maidens would join in the dance, young and old alike would make merry. And the voice of Rachel, lamenting the exile of the northern kingdom, would cease. In the future, voices would not be for mourning, eyes would not be for tears. After the present time of painful chastening, the people would realize that God had never forgotten them, never stopped feeling merciful toward them.

In the good future, no longer would it be said, "The fathers have eaten sour grapes, and the children's teeth are set on edge." Rather, each person would be responsible for his own good or evil. Indeed, there would be an entirely new covenant, better than the covenant the people had entered upon after God led them out of Egypt. The people broke that covenant, though God was their husband. "But this is the covenant which I will make with the house of Israel after those days, says the Lord: I will put my law within them, and I will write it upon their hearts; and I will be their God, and they shall be my people. And no longer shall each man teach his neighbor and teach his brother, saying, 'Know the Lord,' for they shall all

know me, from the least of them to the greatest, says the Lord; for I will forgive their iniquity, and I will remember their sin no more" (31:33–34). In all the literature of the world religions, few passages express the divine love more beautifully.

Both the prophets and the Deuteronomic historian-theologians testified to the dangers to survival that Jews of their time felt. Political subjugation by the much larger neighboring powers was ever a possibility, but it was less ominous than cultural assimilation. To preserve their identity Jews would have to keep clear of their neighbors' fertility religion. Only an adherence to a quite different god—YHWH, the God of Moses and Abraham—could keep the people true to themselves.

Thus, the stress on nonidolatrous cult and detailed religious law that we find after the period of captivity to Babylon was most likely a reaction to the threat of adopting non-Hebrew influences. For instance, both adopting kingship and holding agricultural celebrations could be false steps, because they could take the Israelites away from YHWH. When the Israelites were dispersed into Babylon, Jews of the southern kingdom tested the prophets' theology. A few realized what they had lost by playing power politics and relying on new gods. When the Persians gained control of the region from the Babylonians, Cyrus allowed Jews to return to Jerusalem. The relatively small number who did return lived a reformed life under Nehemiah and Ezra, choosing to rebuild the Temple the Babylonians had wrecked and to reestablish themselves on the basis of a strict adherence to the covenant law. Marriage to foreigners was interdicted, and priests strictly controlled the new Temple.

Covenantal Theology. From their *Exile* to Babylon, Jews thought they had learned a capital lesson. They now viewed their history as one of wavering fidelity to the covenant, and this view suggested to them that infidelity to Torah led to national disaster. God had chosen them by covenanting with them in a special way, and unless they responded with signal fidelity, they would reap not blessing but judgment. Consequently, the returnees stressed their isolation and uniqueness. Still, historical experience also suggested, at least to some prophets and religious thinkers, that God himself was universal, Lord of all peoples. His dominion included the foreign nations, for they had obviously served as his instruments for chastening Israel. He had punished through the Assyrians and Babylonians and freed through the Persians.

As a result, conquest, exile, and return made Jews focus more and more on Jerusalem and its cult (centered in the Temple) as the source of their identity. At the same time, they clarified their ideas about God's worldwide outreach, finally realizing that God had to be the Creator of all things. Views of the covenant changed somewhat, but the predominant view was that God would punish Israel for infidelity and reward it for standing firm. However, God was not bound to be merciful. Mercy, rather, was an outflow of his unpredictable, unmeasurable goodness. Somehow, despite all human weaknesses, God would give a new future. Often the Jews envisioned this future as messianic—coming through a holy ruler anointed by God.

The stress on covenant by the Deuteronomic and postexilic leaders exalted Moses as the religious figure par excellence. However much David stood for kingly success, indeed for the very establishment of Jerusalem, Moses stood for the Torah—revelation, teaching, law. The Torah was a much more solid foundation than either kingship or Jerusalem. By the words of God's mouth, the heavens were made. By the words God spoke through Moses' mouth, the Jews were made a people. If the people kept to those words, they would choose life. If they forgot them or put them aside, they would choose death. Thus, Moses had said: "I call heaven and earth to witness against you this day, that I have set before you life and death, blessing and curse; therefore, choose life, that you and your descendants may live, loving the Lord your God, obeying his voice, and clinging to him" (Deut. 30:19–20). In the sober climate that followed the return from exile, the wise way for Jews seemed to be to keep to themselves and their own special laws.

Wisdom and Apocalypse. Two other movements marked the later Jewish biblical period. The first is found in the wisdom literature of the Hebrew Bible. As many commentators point out,[8] Ecclesiastes and Proverbs bear the marks of the prudential, reflective thought, expressed in maxims, that was available from Egypt. Somewhat incongruously, it grafted itself onto Jewish speculation about God's action, which suggests that postexilic Judaism found its times rather trying. At least, the wisdom literature is dour and sober compared with the historical and prophetic sections of the Bible. It retains a faith that God still has his hand on the tiller but it finds the seas gray and choppy. Suffer-

ing had tempered the fire in the Jewish soul for poetry and prophecy.

The Book of Job, however, is an exception. Job probes the problem of suffering, which surely is a wisdom concern, but it reaches poetic depths. Job reveals that the innocent do suffer mysteriously—that we cannot understand our fate, because all human life unfolds by the plan of a God whose mind we cannot know. This God set the boundaries of the seas, made the different species of all living things. He is not someone we can take to court, not someone who has to account to us. Rather, we can only cling to him in darkness and in trust. Because Job does not profess the older theology, in which punishment was in response to sin, instead proposing a mystery beyond legalistic logic, it brings the postexilic centuries some religious distinction.

By the end of the third century B.C.E., however, the constraints on Jewish national life brought about another reaction to the problems of suffering and providence. Job refers to Satan, an "adversary," and, perhaps due to Iranian influences, in the last years before the Common Era, a dualistic concern with good and evil came to the fore. God and his supporting angels fought against Satan and his minions. The world, in fact, was conceived of as a cosmic battlefield, with God and the forces of light against the forces of darkness. For the first time, Jewish religion started to focus on an afterlife. Pressed by the problem that the good do not necessarily meet with reward nor the evil with punishment, Jewish religion raised the notion that a divine judgment would mete out proper justice. Correspondingly, it started to imagine heavenly places for the good who pass judgment and infernal places for the wicked who fail.

The Book of Daniel expresses these concerns through what scholars call "apocalyptic" imagination.[9] This imagination purports to be a revelation *(apocalypsis)* from God about how the future will unfold. Psychologically, it is an effort to comfort people who are under stress with promises that they will find vindication. Theologically, it puts a sharp edge on the question of whether God controls history. The historical context of Daniel was the pressure of Antiochus Epiphanes, the pagan ruler, to profane Jewish worship. The revolt of the Jews led by the Maccabees stemmed from this pressure.

Daniel joins apocalyptic concern with the older prophetic concern with a messiah, casting the future vindication of the Jews in terms of a heavenly being (the "Son of man") who will come on the clouds. His coming is the dramatic climax in the eschatological scenario that Jews developed in postexilic times. Thus, the Son of man came to figure in many apocalyptic writings (most of them not included in the Bible), and among apocalyptic believers he was the preferred version of the messianic king. (Christians seized on this figure as a principal explanation of Jesus.)

Hellenism.   From the end of the fourth century B.C.E., the political fate of the Jews lay in the hands first of the Greeks and then of the Romans. Thus, Greek and Roman influences mixed with Israel's wisdom and apocalyptic concerns. The ideals that some Jews accepted from Alexander the Great are commonly labeled "Hellenistic." They included the notion that all people have a basis for community *(koinonia)* in human reason and so can share an inhabited world *(ecumene).*[10] Contact with Hellenism divided the Jewish community. Some priests and intellectuals took to the notion of a common humanity, as well as to Greek science, philosophy, and drama, but the majority of the people, sensing a threat to their identity, reacted adversely. By the time that Antiochus Epiphanes tried to enforce pagan Hellenism and destroy traditional Judaism, most Jews supported the (successful) revolt that the Maccabees led in 168 B.C.E.[11] Herod the Great, appointed king of the Jews by the Roman Senate in 40 B.C.E., helped to promote Hellenistic influences in Judea after the Roman conquest.

Overall, Hellenism influenced the Jewish conception of law, and it sparked the first strictly philosophical efforts to make the Torah appear reasonable to any clear-thinking person. Philo, a contemporary of Jesus, was a great expositor of this sort of philosophy. In the final decades of the biblical period, however, political and religious differences divided the Jewish communities. Some people, called the Zealots, urged political action, in the spirit of the Maccabean rebellion. These Zealots opposed those (such as the Essenes of the Qumran community around the Dead Sea) who urged a withdrawal from political life and a purification for the coming of the Messiah. The *Pharisees* and *Sadducees,* lay and priestly groups, adopted centrist positions, urging both a political accommodation and a reliance on the Torah.

Rabbinic Judaism

The forces who urged revolt against the Romans suffered a crushing defeat in 70 C.E., when Titus destroyed the Temple in Jerusalem and cast most of the Jews out into the *Diaspora* (in this context, *Diaspora* refers to the settlement of Jews outside Palestine). Despite the heroic resistance of many Zealots at Masada, a fortress of King Herod near the Dead Sea Valley, foreign (pagan) rule stamped down all the harder. The Pharisees and their successors picked up the pieces. The Pharisaic movement owed much of its concern for the punctilious observance of Torah to the lay scribes (lawyers) who arose in the postexilic Hellenistic period, but the Pharisees did not organize themselves as a distinct party until the second century B.C.E. Maccabean revolt.[12] The Pharisees stood for a close observance of the covenant law, applying it in all aspects of daily life, trying to adapt it as new times required. This belief had come to dominate the scribes who preceded the Pharisees, and it dominated the *rabbis* (teachers) who came after them. The Pharisees sponsored vigorous debate about the application of Torah, which became a feature of subsequent rabbinic Judaism.

In the Diaspora these rabbis became the center of communal life. The Temple had fallen and with it the cultic priesthood. So the alternative to cultic sacrifice—an alternative that had begun in the Babylonian exile, when Jerusalem and the Temple were far away—filled the religious void. This alternative was the *synagogue*—the gathering place where the community could pray and hear expositions of the Torah. The synagogue became the central institution of Judaism in exile, and the study necessary to expose the Torah well made Judaism an intellectual powerhouse.

What we call rabbinic Judaism focuses on the synagogue, exposition of the Torah, and study that increases the importance of the teacher (the rabbi). Increasingly, the teachers wanted to base their expositions on the teachings of their eminent predecessors, so they gathered a great collection of commentaries. Eventually, this collection became the *Talmud* ("the Learning"), a vast collection of the oral law that was composed of the *Mishnah* (itself a collection of interpretations of biblical legal materials) and the *Gemara* (commentaries on the Mishnah).[13] As noted, all of these rabbinic materials became part of Torah.

The Mishnah arose at the end of the first century B.C.E. from the new practice of settling legal disputes by a systematized appeal to recognized authorities. This practice prompted a conflict between the Sadducees and the Pharisees. The Mishnah represented a Pharisaic effort to outflank the Sadducees, who denied the binding character of the oral law and relied on the literal biblical text alone. After the Temple fell in 70

C.E. and times became tumultuous, a written record of all the great teachers' legal opinions became highly desirable. The recording took place in Jabneh, a town on the coast west of Jerusalem. Many teachers moved to Jabneh, among them the great Rabbi Akiba (50–135), who later set up his own influential academy at Bene-Berak to the north. They began the real systematization of the Mishnah (the word implies repetition). The Mishnah continued and even intensified the scrutiny of every scriptural jot and tittle, but it went hand in hand with more pastoral activities.

Under the Roman emperor Hadrian, the Jews felt so oppressed, especially by his decision to build a temple to Jupiter on the site of the great Jewish Temple in Jerusalem, that they mounted the short-lived revolt led by Bar Kokhba. The Romans crushed it in 135 C.E., and thenceforth Jews could enter Jerusalem only on the anniversary of the destruction of the Temple, when they might weep at the Western Wall (Figure 36).

In Babylon (present-day Iraq), to which many of the teachers fled, the talmudic work went on. When Hadrian died in 138, Palestinian Jews' fortunes rose, and a new intellectual center soon was established in Galilee in northern Israel. There, under Rabbi Judah, the Mishnah was elaborated to the point where, when written down (around 200 C.E.), it could be both a practical code and a digest of the oral law. It consisted of six parts, whose subject matter reveals a great deal about the rabbis' conception of religious life.[14] The first Order (part) deals with the biblical precepts concerning the rights of the poor, the rights of priests, the fruits of the harvest, and other agricultural matters. The second Order deals with the Sabbath, festivals, fasts, and the calendar. The third Order (entitled "Women") contains laws of marriage and divorce and other laws governing the relations between the sexes. The fourth Order, entitled "Damages," addresses civil and criminal law. The fifth Order deals with cultic matters and the slaughtering of animals, and the final Order concerns ritual cleanliness.

Law and Lore.   Perhaps the best-known portion of the Mishnah is the *Pirke Avot* ("Sayings of the Fathers"), the last tractate of the fourth Order.[15] It contains opinions of some of the oldest and most influential rabbis, but it is especially venerated for the spirit, the animating love, with which it infuses both the study of the Torah and the ethical life that the Torah should inspire. Often commentators on Judaism state that the Talmud represents a psychology of defense. It is a "fence" for Torah—a protective device to keep people from violating the Law on which their identity and survival depend.

But the religious spirit of the Fathers forces us to reconsider this interpretation. The Fathers built an ethics and religion that are, if not aggressive, at least positive and constructive. On first reading, the *Pirke Avot* suggests not defensiveness but the thought of sober, disciplined, studious minds—minds not unlike that of Ecclesiastes and the other wisdom writers. However, further study shows that the Fathers' sobriety encourages a study that reaches the heart and brings joy. This is explicit in Johanan ben Zacchai (2:13), but surely it is implicit in Hillel (1:12), Simeon the Just (1:2), and many others.

The rabbis called the legal portion of the Torah *halakah.* Through reason, analogies, and deep thought, halakah made the most minute applications of the Torah. For instance, it concerned itself with the dietary laws intended to keep the Jews' eating practices clean or fitting (*kosher*). It also went deeply into the laws for the observance of the *Sabbath.* For centuries such laws, in their biblical forms (for example, Leviticus and Numbers), had kept the Jews separate from their neighbors. As the scribes, Pharisees, and then the Diaspora rabbis concentrated their legal expertise, however, halakah became very complex. Certainly in the Roman Empire, non-Jews strongly associated the Jews with their laws. Thus, halakah partly contributed to anti-Semitism, insofar as it stressed the sense of "otherness" that often is used to justify bigotry.

Balancing the strictly legal teaching and lore, however, was the looser, more folkloric *aggadah.* This was a treasury of exegetical and homiletic (explanatory and preaching) stories that applied biblical passages to a congregation's present circumstances.[16] Where halakah reasoned closely, aggadah was apt to employ mythic devices, including paradigmatic figures and symbols. Aggadah drew much of its authority from the fact that Jewish theology had always held (at least in the ultimately dominant Pharisaic opinion) that an oral Torah accompanied the written Law of Moses and the other books of the Hebrew Bible. Aggadah often presented unscientific but pious reflection about traditional passages, especially those of scripture, that pictured God in his holy freedom—God at work creating this world in which we live.

Thus, the aggadic tradition tells of Rabbi Hanina bar Pappa's teaching on how God guides conception: "The name of the angel appointed over conception is Night. He takes the seed and lays it before the Holy One, blessed be he, and says to him: Master of the

Figure 36 *Jerusalem: the Western Wall. The Dome of the Rock lies behind. Photo by J. T. Carmody.*

universe, what is this seed to be—mighty or weak, wise or foolish, rich or poor? But he does not say 'wicked' or 'righteous.' So according to Rabbi Hanina. For Rabbi Hanina said: 'All is in the hands of heaven, except the fear of heaven.' " In other words, the aggadah tried to explain how a phenomenon (such as conception) was under God's control. It also urged certain attitudes (such as fear of heaven) to make faith consonant with such control. This method probably began with Ezra in the postexilic period, and it dominated what Jewish historians call the Soferic period, when the scribes came to dominate the reassembled community's spiritual life. Aggadah continued to develop side by side with halakah for at least a millennium, ministering to the needs that common folk had for a teaching that was vivid and exemplary.

In Babylon, under the rule of the Exilarch (as the head of the Diaspora community was known in the Common Era), scholars collected the fruits of discussions of Rabbi Judah's Mishnah conducted at various academies. In addition, they immersed themselves in the ideas and *responsa* (masters' answers to questions about the Law's application) that flowed back and forth between Babylon and Palestine. Both halakah and aggadah contributed to this broad collection of legal materials, and the final redaction of the Babylonian Talmud, probably accomplished early in the fifth century, amounted to an encyclopedia of scholarly opinion not only on the law but also on much of the other learning of the day, including biology, medicine, and astronomy, that formed the background for many of the discussions.

Talmudic Religion. In terms of theology proper, the Talmud (whether the Palestinian or the more influential Babylonian version) clung to scriptural faith.[17] Its central pillar was the *Shema* (Deut. 6:4): "Hear, O Israel: The Lord our God is One Lord." A second pillar was the biblical notion of election. The Talmudic view of the Shema was practical rather than speculative. That is, the rabbis did not spend much energy probing the unity of God, the confluence of the divine attributes, or the like. The oneness of God meant to them God's sole dominion over life. He was the Lord of all peoples, the world's only source and guide.[18] The most practical of God's attributes were his justice and his mercy, but how they correlated was not obvious. Clear enough, though, were the implications for ethics and piety: A person ought to reckon with God's justice by acting righteously and avoiding condemnation. A person also ought to rely on God's mercy, remembering that he is slow to anger and quick to forgive.

Through such righteous living, a person could look forward to God's kingdom, which would come through the *Messiah.* The Messiah would rejuvenate or transform this earthly realm, which was so often a source of suffering. Of the Messiah, Isadore Epstein says, "At the highest the Messiah is but a moral leader who will be instrumental in fully rehabilitating Israel in its ancient homeland, and through a restored Israel bring about the moral and spiritual regeneration of the whole of humanity, making all mankind fit citizens of the Kingdom."[19] This description rejects the Christian tendency to equate the Messiah with a divine son and also provides a foundation for the Zionistic fervor to return to the land. The concept of God's kingdom eventually included a supernatural dimension (heaven), but Judaism rather distinctively has emphasized that personal fulfillment comes through daily life.

The thrust of the Talmud, therefore, is not so much theological as ethical. The rabbis were more interested in what one did than in how one spoke or thought. So they balanced considerable theological leeway with detailed expectations of behavior. One could hold any opinion about the subtleties of God's nature, but how one observed the Sabbath was clearly specified.[20] A major effect of this ethical concern was the refinement of the already quite sensitive morality of the Hebrew Bible. For instance, the rabbis wanted to safeguard the body against even the threat of mortal injury, so they called wicked the mere raising of a hand against another person.

Similarly, since the right to life entailed the right to a livelihood, the rabbis concerned themselves with economic justice, proscribing once accepted business practices such as cornering a market, misrepresenting a product, and trading on a customer's ignorance. In the same spirit, they pondered a person's rights to honor and reputation. To slander another obviously was forbidden, but they reprehended even putting another to shame, likening the blush of the shamed to the red of bloodshed.

Despite the caricature that they were concerned only with legal niceties, their writings show that the rabbis were very sensitive to social interaction. Lying, hatred, infringement on others' liberty—all these were targets of their teachings. The rabbis held that the goods of the earth, which prompt so much human contentiousness, were to be for all people. Thus, after a harvest, the owner should leave his field open for the public to glean; the wealthy are obligated to help the poor; and no bread should ever go to waste. Moreover, the rabbis did not limit their lofty social ideals to the Jewish community. Glossing the injunction of Leviticus (19:34) to love the stranger "who sojourns with you . . . as yourself," the talmudists made little political or social distinction between Jew and non-Jew. Human rights applied to all.

The spirit of talmudic ethics, thus, is both precise and broad. The Talmud goes into extreme detail, but it applies to all humanity. According to the Talmud, the great vices are envy, greed, and pride, for they destroy the social fabric. Anger is also destructive, so the rabbis lay great stress on self-control. On the other hand, self-control should not become gloomy asceticism. Generally speaking, the Talmud views the goods of the earth as being for our enjoyment. We should fear neither the body nor the world.

In fact, God, who gives us both the body and the world, obliges us to keep them healthy and fruitful. To spurn bodily or material goods without great reason, then, would be to show ingratitude to God—to withdraw from the order God has chosen to create. Wealth and marriage, for instance, should be viewed as great blessings that one should accept with simple thankfulness. For the truest wealth, finally, is to be content with one's lot. In faith, the pious Jew tried to raise his sights beyond everyday worries to the Master of the universe, from whom so many good things flowed. The ultimate purpose of religious life was to sanctify this Master's name—to live in such love of God that his praise was always on one's lips.

Hallowing Time.   Through religious observances the talmudists designed the social program for inculcating their ethical ideals. In practice, every day was to be hallowed from its beginning. At rising the faithful Jew would thank God for the night's rest, affirm God's unity, and dedicate the coming hours to God's praise. He was supposed to pray at least three times each day: upon rising, in midafternoon, and in the evening (women were exempt, because of their family responsibilities). Ritual washings, as well as the kosher diet, reminded the faithful of the cleanliness that dedication to God required. Prayer garments such as the fringed prayer shawl; the phylacteries, or *tefellin* (scriptural texts worn on the head and the arm); and the head covering reinforced this cleanliness. The mezuzah (container of scriptural texts urging wholehearted love of God) over the door was a reminder to the entire home to adopt this attitude. Home was to be a place of law-abiding love. When possible, Jews would say their daily prayers together in the synagogue.

The synagogue, of course, was also the site of congregational worship on the Sabbath and on the great feasts that punctuated the year. Primary among such feasts have been Passover, a spring festival that celebrates the Exodus of the Israelites from Egypt; Shavuot, a wheat harvest festival occurring seven weeks after Passover; Booths (Sukkoth), a fall harvest festival whose special feature is the erection of branch or straw booths that commemorate God's care of the Israelites while they were in the wilderness; the New Year; and the Day of Atonement (Yom Kippur).

The last is the most somber and solemn of the celebrations: the day on which one fasts and asks forgiveness of sins. It is a time when estranged members of the community should make efforts to reconcile their differences, and when all people should rededicate themselves to the holiness that God's covenant demands. There are other holidays through the year, most of them joyous—like Hanukkah, a feast celebrating liberation by the Maccabees—and collectively they serve the several purposes of a theistic cult: recalling God's great favors (anamnesis), binding the community in common faith, and expiating offenses and restoring hopes.

In the home, celebration of the Sabbath did for the week what the annual feasts did for the year. It gave time a cycle with a peak that had special meaning. From midweek all looked forward to the Sabbath joy, preparing the house and the food for the day that came like God's bride. When the mother lit the candles and the Sabbath drew near, even the poorest Jew could feel that life was good. Special hospitality was the Sabbath rule; rest and spiritual regeneration were the Sabbath order. Regretful as all were to see the Sabbath end, a glow lingered that strengthened them so they could return to the workaday world.[21]

The principal rites of passage through the life cycle were circumcision, through which males entered the covenant community on their eighth day; bar mitzvah, to celebrate the coming of age; marriage; and burial. Through communal celebration, these rites reinforced the faith that life is good, the Torah is life's crown, marriage is a human being's natural estate, and death is not the final word.

The Medieval Period

From the seventh century on, this talmudic religious program structured the lives of Jews who were mainly under Muslim rule.[22] As a subjugated people, the Jews tended to look inward for their fulfillment. Muhammad himself took rather kindly to Judaism, because he thought that his own revelation agreed with biblical thought: "Hence his uncompromising monotheistic doctrine, his insistence on formal prayers, fasting and almsgiving, his adoption of the Day of Atonement, his introduction of dietary laws (such as the prohibition of swine's flesh), and his [initial] requirement that his followers turn toward Jerusalem in prayer."[23] However, things grew more complicated when the Jews refused to convert to Islam, and under both Muhammad and his successors the Jews had to endure not a little trouble. Nonetheless, Muslims frequently found Jews useful as translators or businessmen, and Muslim countries were generally tolerant. As long as non-Muslim religious groups posed no threat to security or orthodoxy, they could have a decent, if second-rate, civil status.[24]

During the first centuries of Muslim power, the Jewish community's prestigious center of learning was at the heart of its Diaspora in Baghdad (in Babylonia). According to talmudic tradition, the leaders of the Baghdad schools gave *responsa* to points of law and held sway over community religion. They also fixed the pattern of communal worship, which hitherto had been a source of confusion and controversy. During the ninth and tenth centuries, the scholars of the Babylonian schools also standardized the pronunciation for the Hebrew Bible. These scholars (Masoretes) supplied the vowel points, accents, and other signs necessary to make readable a text that had consisted only of consonants. (Pronunciation, consequently, had been a matter of oral tradition.) The same work went on in Palestine, and eventually the version of a Palestinian author named Ben Asher won acceptance as the canonical Masoretic text.

At the end of the first millennium of the Common Era, talmudic scholars emigrated to Europe, North Africa, and Egypt, taking with them the scholarship of the talmudic school to which they felt the closest ties. The Babylonian traditions were more popular, but in countries such as Italy, which had close ties with Palestine, Palestinian influence was great. In Europe, of course, the Jews were largely under Christian rule, although southern Spain and southern France were under Muslim rule.

The two great Jewish traditions, the *Sephardic* (Iberian) and the *Ashkenazic* (East European), can be characterized by their subjugation under either Muslim or Christian rule, respectively. The two traditions shared more than they held separately because of the talmudists, and their different styles in intellectual matters and in piety largely derived from the different cultures in which they evolved. In the tenth and eleventh centuries, the Sephardim in Spain developed a golden culture, with philosophy, exegesis, poetry, and scientific learning at their peak. Toledo and Cordoba were great centers of learning, but so were Avila and Lisbon.

The major internal problem during this period was the rigorist Karaite heresy, which began under the leadership of Anan ben David in the eighth century. This movement rejected the Talmud and based its beliefs on a literal reading of the scriptures. For instance, Karaite Sabbath law forbade washing, leaving the house, carrying anything from one room to another, wearing anything except a shirt, making a bed, or any other activity construed as work. Karaites interpreted the injunction of Exodus 35:3, to kindle no fires on the Sabbath, to mean that one had to spend Friday night and Saturday in darkness and cold. They were so scrupulous about incest laws that finding an acceptable marriage partner was difficult.

Because *Karaism* appealed to individual conscience and had some master propagandists, it mustered considerable support. Anan withdrew from Babylonia to Jerusalem, where he set up a community, and he pushed for a complete break with talmudic Jews (called Rabbanites). In the ninth and tenth centuries Karaism spread to Persia, Egypt, Spain, and parts of Asia and seemed to be on the verge of replacing Judaism. When we add to its appeal the confusion that the Muslim recovery of Greek learning was producing in scholarly circles, we can understand the complexity of the Jewish religious situation and why it came close to crisis. With literalist Karaites on their right and rationalistic Hellenists on their left, the talmudists felt besieged.

The talmudists responded to the Karaites with an intensive campaign of biblical study, which included exegesis, Hebrew grammar, philology, and the other learning necessary to defend their own interpretations

of the sacred text. Against the rationalists they took up the tools of philosophy, logic, and physical science in an effort to show the compatibility of reason and faith. The great champion in this talmudic or Rabbanite counterattack was Saadya ben Joseph (892–942), who lived in Upper Egypt. He combined Hebrew and Arabic learning, biblical scholarship, and philosophical erudition. In addition, he wrote halakic *responsa,* codified rules of talmudic logic, resolved problems with the calendar, and composed an order for public worship.[25] The counterattack that he spearheaded was successful, and when the Jews fled from Babylonia at the breakup of the Muslim Empire into the eastern and western caliphates, they took with them at least the beginnings of a renewed talmudic tradition. The golden age in Spain was in no small measure possible because of this renewal.

Philosophy.   The early medieval period thus saw a ferment in talmudic learning. As well, a Jewish philosophical theology arose.[26] While Philo, in the first century of the Common Era, worked at what could be called philosophical theology, trying to reconcile Hellenistic thought with biblical thought, the medieval thinkers, especially Maimonides, brought philosophy into the Jewish mainstream.

Philo, whose strong point had been what he called *allegoresis* (a reading of scripture on several levels, so as to remove the problems that the philosophical mind might have with anthropomorphism), never exerted a decisive influence on his contemporaries. Maimonides did. He was the response that made Judaism competitive in the new arena opened by the Muslim retrieval of Aristotelian logic and science. As such, his work was apologetic, making Judaism a strong contender in the debates that were being conducted by the Western religions on the supposedly common ground of rational analysis. However, Maimonides' work was also constructive, setting talmudic and traditional learning in the context of a philosophical system. Finally, the philosophical services of thinkers such as Maimonides were very useful in internal fights with literalists such as the Karaites, who (despite their fundamentalism about points of biblical law) mocked both biblical anthropomorphism and much of aggadah (because it was poetic and symbolic).

The great questions of this period of philosophical debate were the criteria of biblical *exegesis,* the relation of faith to reason, the nature of the human personality and its relation to God, God's existence and attributes, the creation of the world, and providence and theodicy (God's justice). In debating these questions, the philosophers based their work on the Greek view that contemplation *(theoria)* is the most noble human work. Thus, the Jewish philosophers made rationality the source of human imaging of God. From that they derived an obligation (they would have called it a religious obligation) to develop one's reason—to explore God and his world.

Whereas for the talmudist, study of the Torah was the highest activity, many of the medieval philosophers considered the contemplation of God's eternal forms (through which he had created the world) the highest human activity. Maimonides became the prince of Jewish philosophers largely because he was also learned in the talmudic tradition and so could reconcile the old with the new. For him philosophical contemplation did not take one away from the Torah, because the proper object of philosophical contemplation was the one Law we find in both scripture and nature.

A key teaching in Maimonides' system was divine incorporeality. God had to be one, which he could not be if he occupied a body, since matter is a principle of multiplicity. To rationalize the anthropomorphic biblical descriptions of God, where he has bodily emotions if not form, Maimonides allegorized as Philo had done. The dynamic to his system, however, was the conviction that philosophical reason can provide the key to scripture. As his own *Guide for the Perplexed* puts it, "This book will then be a key admitting to places the gates of which would otherwise be closed. When the gates are opened and men enter, their souls will enjoy repose, their eyes will be gratified, and even their bodies, after all toil and labor, will be refreshed."[27]

Maimonides has probably been most influential through the thirteen articles in which he summarized Jewish faith, and which even today are listed in the standard prayer book: (1) the existence of God, (2) God's unity, (3) God's incorporeality, (4) God's eternity, (5) the obligation to worship God alone, (6) prophecy, (7) the superiority of the prophecy of Moses, (8) the Torah as God's revelation to Moses, (9) the Torah's immutability, (10) God's omniscience, (11) reward and punishment, (12) the coming of the Messiah, and (13) the resurrection of the dead.[28] In this summary a philosopher gave the key headings under which reason and biblical revelation could be reconciled.

However, Jewish philosophy before Maimonides expressed a somewhat contrary position. The lyrical writer Judah Halevi (ca. 1086–1145), for instance, insisted that the God of Aristotle is not the God of Abraham and the biblical Fathers. (Halevi's position is reminiscent of the later Christian philosopher Blaise Pascal, and it draws on the same sort of religious experience that made Pascal visualize God as a consuming fire—no Aristotelian "prime mover" but a vortex of personal love.) Halevi did not despise reason, but he insisted that it is less than full religious experience, faith, or love. Moreover, he was concerned that Judaism remember where it had found God in the past. Concrete historical acts had furnished the Jews their election and destiny as God's covenanted people, not eternal forms or timeless philosophical truths ever available for human contemplation.

Mysticism. The devotional current in influential medieval philosophers shows that the appropriation of Greek rationality did not extinguish Jewish mystical life, any more than it extinguished talmudic preoccupation with law. Law, in the sense of guidance for a daily practice of faith and ethics, certainly predominated over philosophy in the popular religious mind, but both philosophy and mysticism colored legal interpretation. Gershom Scholem has treated the major trends in Jewish mysticism admirably,[29] tracing them back to biblical origins. The major influence, discernible even in Maimonides' doctrine of God, was Ezekiel's vision (Ezek. 1) of the divine chariot *(merkabah)*. Philosophers and mystics alike agreed that under this symbolism lay the most profound mysteries of the divine nature. The talmudists tended to stay away from the subject, lest they fall into impious speculation, but the mystics, even though they cautioned about dangers, repeatedly went back to it.

In medieval Germany a movement arose among people called the Hasidim, who upheld a relatively new spiritual ideal. Biblical religion had spoken of the poor of God *(anawim),* and from biblical times a *hasid* was one poor in spirit who piously devoted himself to God. The medieval expression of this piety, in which intellectualism was subordinate to devotion, contested rabbinic learning. What characterized the truly pious person, this movement argued, was serenity of mind, altruism, and renunciation of worldly things. The renunciation, implying asceticism, especially ran counter to traditional Judaism, for it seemed to entail turning away from the world. Indeed, Hasidic speech relates to the experience that has always drawn mystics and caused them to neglect the world—the experience of glimpsing the divine being itself, of tasting the biblical "goodness of the Lord." Then the divine love exalts the soul and seems far more precious than anything the world can offer.

Hasidism in its medieval, Germanic form is not the direct ancestor of the modern East European Jewish pietism that goes by this name. Intervening between Hasidism's two phases was a most influential Jewish mysticism, that of the *cabala*. *Cabala* means "tradition," and the cabalists sought to legitimize their movement by tracing it back to secret teachings of the patriarchs and Moses.

Such secret or esoteric overtones stamp cabalism as a sort of Jewish gnosticism (secret knowledge); indeed, several cabalistic doctrines smack of the Gnostic concerns with the divine *pleroma* (fullness), the emanations of different divine aspects, and secret doctrines explaining how divinity intends to redeem the wicked fallen world.[30] Thus, R. J. Zwi Werblowsky characterizes cabalism as a "theosophical" (concerning wisdom about God) movement especially concerned with the *pleroma*.[31] This fullness, which the prophets glimpsed in their ecstatic visions, ordinary human beings can only conceive symbolically. Hence, cabalists engaged in their own brand of allegorical exegesis of scripture, trying to decode secret symbols about divinity that the Hebrew Bible couched in deceptively simple language.

For cabalistic thought, the divine and the human spheres are interdependent. The fallen state of the world (most acutely manifested in the suffering of the Jews, God's chosen people) signals a disruption within the divine essence itself. Human sinfulness, it follows, reflects this divine wounding. On the other hand, human holiness contributes to God's repair, and so every human act takes on cosmic significance. In fact, human life can become a sort of mystery play or theurgy (divine work), in which the significant aspect of people's actions is their wounding or repairing of the divine life.

When the Spaniards expelled the Jews from the Iberian Peninsula at the end of the fifteenth century, the cabalists had the perfect crisis on which to focus their somewhat fevered imaginations. Isaac Luria, who taught in Jerusalem in the sixteenth century, and Sabbatai Zevi, the "false messiah" of the seventeenth century, interpreted the expulsion as an effect of a cosmic disaster that actually occurred before Adam's fall. They had great popular impact.

The paramount book of the cabalistic movement, and the most representative of its symbolism, was the *Zohar*—the "Book of Splendor." From 1500 to 1800, the *Zohar* exerted an influence equal to that of the Bible and the Talmud. Analysis of the work suggests that it was written in Spain at the end of the thirteenth century, most likely by Moses de León.[32] The *Zohar* is similar to aggadic materials in that it interprets scriptural texts symbolically and in pietistic fashion rather than in the legal manner of halakah. What distinguishes the *Zohar* from traditional aggadah is its suffusion with the Gnostic ideas mentioned above. For instance, its commentary on the first verse of the Hebrew Bible (Gen. 1:1) goes immediately to what the divine nature was really like "in the beginning." Within the most hidden recess of the infinite *eyn sof,* the divine essence, a dark flame went forth, issuing in the *sefiroth*. The *sefiroth* were what the philosophers called the realm of divine attributes, but the mystics saw them as the emanations of God's own being. Such a view makes the world alive with divinity. It gives history and human experience eternal implications, because the emanations move through our time, our flesh, our blood.

The *Zohar* turns over each word of Genesis, searching for hidden clues to the divine plan. It concerns itself with the numerical value of the words' letters (for example, a = 1) and correlates clues in Genesis with clues from other visionary parts of the Hebrew Bible, such as Ezekiel, chapter 1, and Isaiah, chapter 6. To align its interpretation with respectable past commentary, it cites traditional rabbis, but the *Zohar*'s immediate concern is not the rabbis' interest in ethics but an imaginative contemplation of divinity and the divine plan.

In other words, the *Zohar* draws people by the splendor of its vision, its graphic display of divinity. With its beauty, the *Zohar* can move the spirit to ecstatic joy. No doubt the cabalists devoutly hoped that such an imaginative and contemplative experience would build up faith and inspire good works. However, they differed from the talmudists (some of whom had secret sympathy for cabalism) in their predilection for visionary appreciation of the Law's source rather than a sober perusal of the Law's applications.

The Modern Period

If the mark of modernity is a turn from rather mythical religious authority to human authority and self-reliance, modernity did not begin for Judaism until the end of the eighteenth century—although some intellectuals realized early on the challenge that the Enlightenment raised to traditional Jewish Law. In fact, thorough exposure to a secularized, technological culture did not come to most of the rural population of the Eastern European *shtetls* (villages), where much of the Jewish population lived, until close to World War II. Until that time enlightenment and reform made little impact, for talmudic and Hasidic orthodoxy kept the tradition basically unchanged.[33]

Cecil Roth[34] and Leon Poliakov[35] have described the constant repression and persecution that Jews endured in medieval and early modern times. What Roth calls "the crowning tragedy" was the Jews' expulsion from the Iberian Peninsula in 1492, since that devastated what had been Jewry's greatest cultural achievement. In its aftermath, the Eastern European ghetto became home to most Jews, and the false messiah Sabbatai Zevi, who finally apostatized to Islam, shows the intensity that Jewish messianic yearning reached by the mid-seventeenth century. Part of the success of Israel Baal Shem-Tov (1700–1760), the father of modern Hasidism, resulted from the effects of Sabbatai Zevi. In his wake lay a void into which apostasy, nihilism, and antinomianism (lawlessness) threatened to rush.

The Baal Shem-Tov (Besht) and his followers taught a religious inwardness, a joyous communion with God.[36] They sought to restore the traditional faith, which they saw as endangered by false messianism, arid intellectualism, and talmudic legalism. Hasidism did not attack the Law and traditional practice itself. Rather, it shifted Jewish religious focus from the "scientific" rabbinic leader to the gifted Hasid or holy person, who manifested divine wisdom and joy. The movement quickly caught fire in Eastern Europe, and thousands rushed to the Hasidic "courts" where charismatic masters presided. In their vivid portrait of *shtetl* life, Zborowski and Herzog[37] have shown the attraction that the Hasidim exerted in the typical village. Many of the villagers (usually men) yearned to go off to the courts for spiritual refreshment, and many would leave their families for substantial periods of time.

Case Study: Hasidic Tales. The Hasidic masters made a deep impression on the Jewish imagination, and some of the tales about them are wonderfully entertaining, as well as deeply instructive. For example, there is the story of the burning of the Torah, which deals with "the terrific struggle between the Baal Shem-Tov and the Enemy, who by foul trickery sought to have the Torah taken away from the Jews."[38]

Satan was tormented by the good he saw the Baal Shem-Tov doing on earth, so he schemed to overcome the Master. Calling all his servants of darkness together, he disclosed to them a wicked plan. He would station devils on all the roads that led to heaven. Whenever a prayer rose upward, toward heaven's gates, the devils would be able to throttle it, and so keep it from getting through. Thus no prayers would come before God's throne. After some days without prayers getting through, Satan would be able to go to God and say, "Look, your people have deserted you. They no longer send you prayers. Even your favorite puppet, Rabbi Israel Baal Shem-Tov, has ceased to pray. Take back his wisdom, then. Take away his people's Torah."

The soldiers of the Evil One listened attentively, and then slunk out to execute the foul scheme. Leaving no bypath unguarded, they lurked silently in wait for any prayer. When a prayer came, they leaped upon it, pummeling and kicking it. They could not kill the prayers, but they flung them sideways into chaos. Thus all of space became filled with wounded prayers, whimpering and moaning, lost from their way. On Sabbaths the flux of prayers was so great that many got through to heaven's gate, but there a great army of devils saw to it that the prayers were rebuffed. Three weeks passed in this fashion, and Satan thought it time to confront God.

Going before the divine throne, Satan said: "Take away the Torah from the Jews." But God said, "Give them until the Day of Atonement." Satan struck a hard bargain: "Give the command today, but hold back on its execution until the Day of Atonement." So God gave the terrible edict, and the Jews were to lose the Torah. On earth, the archbishop issued a proclamation. In ten days, the bishops were to have all the Hebrew books of learning confiscated. Men were to be sent into the synagogues to seize the Torah, and into all the Jews' homes. Then they were to heap all the Hebrew books into a great pile and set fire to them. The bishop of Kamenitz-Podolsky in Russia was the most zealous in obeying, sending his servants into all the Jews' homes. On the Day of Atonement, a great fire would destroy all the books of God's Law.

When the Baal Shem-Tov saw these things happening, he knew Satan was mounting a terrible attack. Yet he did not know how Satan was accomplishing this great evil, nor how to counteract it. Each day the horror mounted, as Jews were stripped of the Torah. In home after home cries of anguish rent the night. Fasting and sleepless, the Baal Shem-Tov struggled on behalf of his people, sending mighty prayers toward heaven day and night. They rose on colossal wings at incredible speed, but the Enemy himself caught them outside heaven's gate and cast them aside. So the heart of Baal Shem-Tov emptied, becoming a great cave of grief.

At last the Day of Atonement dawned. Rabbi Israel went into the synagogue to hold the service, and the people saw the fever of his struggle on his face. Hope rose in their hearts. "He will save us today," they said. When the time came to sing the *Kol Nidre* ("All Vows"), Rabbi Israel's voice poured out the pain of his heart, freezing all who listened.

It was the custom for Rabbi Yacob to read each verse of the lamentations aloud and then for Rabbi Israel to repeat it. But when Rabbi Yacob read out the verse, "Open the Portals of Heaven!" Rabbi Israel did not utter a word. The people first were confused, and then waited in growing fear. Once again Rabbi Yacob repeated, "Open the Portals of Heaven!" but still Rabbi Israel did not utter a word.

Then, like a trumpet blast into the monumental silence, Rabbi Israel threw himself upon the ground, beat his head, and roared like a dying lion. For two hours he remained doubled over, his body shaking with the force of his struggle. Those watching in the synagogue dared not approach him. They could only worry and wait.

At last, the Baal Shem-Tov raised himself from the ground, his face shining with wonders. "The Portals of Heaven are open," he said, and then he ended the service.

Years afterward, it became known how Rabbi Israel had passed those terrible two hours. He had gone to the Palace of the Eternal, traveling by the road that goes directly to the throne. There he had found hundreds and hundreds of prayers huddled before the gate. Some were wounded, some lay gasping as though they had just ended a terrible struggle, some were emaciated and old, and some were blind from having wandered so long in darkness. "Why are you waiting here?" the Baal Shem-Tov asked them. "Why don't you go in and approach the throne?"

The prayers told Rabbi Israel that only his approach had scattered the dark angels. Before he came, no prayer could pass through the gate. "I will take you in," the Baal Shem-Tov told them.

But just as he started to pass the gate, the Baal Shem-Tov saw the army of evil spirits rush forth to close it. Then Satan himself came forward and hung a great lock, as big as a city, upon the heavenly gate. The Baal Shem-Tov walked all around the lock, looking for a crack through which to enter. It was made of solid iron, however, so there seemed no way he could pass through. Still, Rabbi Israel did not despair.

Now, for each of us living on earth, there is an exact duplicate living in heaven. So, Rabbi Israel called across the gate to his heavenly counterpart. "What shall I do," he asked, "to bring the prayers before the Name?" Rabbi Israel of heaven told him, "Let us go to the Palace of the Messiah."

They went to the palace, where the Messiah sat waiting for the day when he might go down to earth. As soon as they entered, the Messiah told them, "Be joyous! I will help you," and he gave the Baal Shem-Tov a token. The Baal Shem-Tov took the token back to the heavenly gate. When he brandished the token, the heavenly portals swung open, as wide as the earth is large. So all the prayers entered, going straight to the Throne of the Name. Heaven fell to ecstatic rejoicing, and all the angels sang hymns of praise. But the dark angels fled back to their hellish dungeons, routed and fearful again.

On earth, the bishop of Kamenitz-Podolsky was lighting a great fire. Beside him was a mountain of Hebrew books, which his minions had readied for the flames. He took a tractate of the Talmud and hurled it into the fire. He hurled another and another, until the flames leaped high as the clouds. But then his hand began shaking, and he fell down in an epileptic fit. The crowd was seized with terror, and ran out of the central square. The fire soon died down, and most of the books were saved. When the news of this happening spread to other towns, they abandoned their plans to burn the Torahs. Fearing they too would be struck by seizures, the other bishops gave back all the stolen books. That was how the Baal Shem-Tov saved the Torah for the Jews, on the Day of Atonement.

When we reflect on this little story, it reveals volumes about premodern Jewish belief. The Baal Shem-Tov is the central hero, but there are many other actors in the drama. The evil genius threatening Jewish life is Satan, the angel of power and light who had turned bad. Hating God and everything good, Satan is constantly plotting against God's people. If the Jews had not had saints like Rabbi Israel, there was no telling how their misfortunes might have grown. Bad as life was in the midst of unsympathetic Christians, it would have been much worse without the sainted rabbis.

As the story shows, the central treasure of premodern Jewish life was the Torah. Enclosed in the holy pages of the treasured books lay the only wisdom worth pursuing. Without the Torah, the Jews would not have been God's people. Without the Bible and the Talmud, there would have been no faith, no joy, no hope. For the common people, the volumes of Torah were both pledges and holy presences. To destroy a book of Torah therefore was to slash at the central artery, to snuff out the breath of life.

The theater for the drama of Satan against the Torah was not limited to earthly cities. For the popular Jewish mind, heaven was a central factor in the play. Before the throne of God, all parts of Jewish life passed review. God's ways were terribly inscrutable, but no pious Jew doubted the efficacy of prayer. If the people would pour out their hearts to the Master of the Universe, he would find them a way to survive. The Torah spoke of many past acts of salvation and of the coming of the Messiah, the one who would bring lasting peace. Prayer and strict observance therefore became the people's armor. Often helpless in earthly terms, the Jews looked to their learned rabbis as to spiritual generals. By the holy power they generated, the rabbis might storm heaven's gates and keep Satan's dark forces at bay.

Of course, it is hard to say how literally the average person took imagery like that of our story. Whether heaven had a big gate, whether there were roads to heaven, whether prayers could be kicked and wounded—all that is hard to tell. Most likely, all that was quite secondary. Lost in a good, gripping story, most Jews probably indulged their imaginations. To picture prayers like little people, or like swift birds winging up to God, made the act of praying more dramatic. Most people knew they could never picture God accurately. They knew heaven was beyond any tongue's ability to describe. So they let their imaginations paint whatever settings most helped them in their prayers and inner struggles. There had to be close connections between this world and heaven, for otherwise God would not be involved in what his people were doing. But it was the essence of the theology of the covenant that God was always deeply involved in what his people were doing, were suffering, and were hoping. So the

life of the Jewish home and the services of the Jewish synagogue encouraged many vivid pictures of heaven. Indeed, the worse earthly life became, the more heaven gleamed in contrast.

Village Life. Hasidism ran the danger of irrationalism and an intolerance of anything modern, but for discerning contemporary Jews such as Martin Buber[39] and Abraham Heschel,[40] it became a valuable resource. Although large portions of the educated, who were desirous of a Jewish enlightenment and emancipation from Christian discrimination, strongly opposed Hasidic piety, it remained vigorous in the villages well into the twentieth century. There it tended to commingle with talmudic faith, blending legal observance with emotional fervor. Indeed, Jewish village life hinged on the Sabbath (in the time-organizing way described above) and on three blessings: the Torah, marriage, and good deeds.

The Torah meant God's revelation and Law. In practice, it meant the exaltation of learning. *Shtetl* parents hoped that they would have learned sons, well versed in the Law, who would bring glory to the family. Thus, the ideal son was thin and pale, a martyr to his books. From age five or so he marched off to a long day of study, beginning his education by memorizing a Hebrew that he did not understand and then progressing to subtle talmudic commentaries. The Torah shaped the economic and family lives of *shtetl* Jews, because men tried to free themselves for study, placing the financial burdens on women. The poor scholar, revered in the *shul* (synagogue school) but master of a threadbare family, exemplified the choices and values that the Torah inspired.

Many men did work in trades (the state usually prevented Jews from owning land and farming), but even they would try to gain dignity by devoting their spare time to learning. Glory for women came from caring for the home, the children, and often a little shop. So much were those responsibilities part of religion for women that no commandments prescribed for them exact times for prayer, fasting, synagogue attendance, charitable works, or the like. Women's three principal *mitzvoth* (duties) out of the traditional 613 were to remove a portion of the Sabbath bread, to light the Sabbath candles, and to visit the ritual bath *(mikvah)* after menstruation.

In the *shtetl,* marriage was the natural human situation and children were its crown. Father and mother were obligated to create a home steeped in Torah and good deeds (fulfillment of the *mitzvoth* and acts of charity). In semiserious popular humor, nothing was worse than an old maid, while an unmarried man was pitied as being incomplete. Of course, kosher rules and keen legal observance marked the devout home, which was but a cell of the organic community. That community supported needy individual members with material goods, sympathy in times of trouble, and unanimity in religious ideals. One had to share one's wealth, whether wealth of money or wealth of mind, and the seats of honor in the synagogue went to the learned and the community's financial benefactors.

Tribulations.   The community exacted quite a toll through the pressure it exerted to conform to its ideals and through the gossip and judgment that ever circulated. Nevertheless, most Jews gladly accepted being bound by the common laws and custom, and few Jews could avoid being bound by the equally overt and common suffering. The urban populations in the Russian and Polish ghettos shared an almost paranoid life, with pogroms (persecutions) a constant specter, while the rural populations of the rest of Eastern Europe never knew when some new discrimination or purge would break out. In both situations, Jews' mainstay was their solidarity in faith. Consequently, we can understand how threatening movements to change the faith, such as the reform or enlightenment (described below), must have been. The old ways had been the foundation of Jewish sanity. New conditions, as in Germany and the United States, seemed much less solid than long familiar suffering and endurance.

The bulk of the Jewish population in the late 1700s was in Eastern Europe: the pale of the Russian Empire, Austria, and Prussia. Their life was rather precarious, and attacks by Russians and Ukrainians produced a stream of emigrants to the New World. Yet European Jews contributed to the formation of the notion of the modern, secular state, probably because they hoped that it would offer them greater religious freedom. Thus, the Jewish philosopher Spinoza (1632–1672) suggested such a political arrangement, and Moses Mendelssohn (1729–1786), a German man of letters, plumped for a secular state before the French Revolution. Generally, Jews' civil status seemed to prosper in countries or under regimes that were open to the new, liberal ideas of equality. However, when nationalism prevailed, Jews tended to experience more anti-Semitism, since non-Jews then considered them all the more outsiders.

Jacob A. Agus has noted three principal Jewish reactions to modern nationalism.[41] First, many Jews identified themselves with the people among whom they lived. For instance, German Jews became great supporters of German culture, which was enjoying a golden age in music and philosophy. Second, some of the Jewish intelligentsia embraced the new universalist philosophies that downplayed race or ethnicity and stressed the common humanity all people share through their reason. Third, some Jews incorporated nationalistic feelings into their own group consciousness by thinking of the cohesiveness of the "nation" of Israel. Agus sees these reactions working, respectively, in the time of Emancipation in France (see below), the socialist movements in Europe and Russia [which led to the formation of the Jewish *Bund* (party), influential in Poland during the two world wars, and also to the Reform movements in Germany and the Anglo-American world], and the Zionist movement, which he conceives of as a Jewish nationalistic renaissance.

Dissolution of Traditional Judaism.   Jacob Neusner attributes the breakup of traditional Judaism in the modern period to two factors, the enlightenment and Hasidism.[42] The enlightenment, whose main feature according to Kant was the realization that humanity should be guided by its own reason and not by institutional authorities, in effect attacked the legal and philosophical underpinnings of traditional Judaism. By extending political rights to Jews ("Emancipation"), the gentile thinkers of the enlightenment in principle took away the basis of the Jewish community—it was no longer a ghetto or a world set apart from the national mainstream, because all citizens were to be equal.

By its philosophical turn to individual reason, the enlightenment attacked the talmudic assumption that traditional law and its interpretation by the Fathers were the best guides for life. Thus, intellectual Jews who accepted the ideals of the enlightenment tended to abandon talmudic scholarship (or at least deny that it was the most important learning) and devote themselves to secular learning. This movement spawned the distinguished line of modern Jewish scientists, social thinkers, and humanists, but it meant that the Jewish community lost some of its best talent to secular concerns. It also often meant intellectual warfare between the advocates of the new learning and the defenders of the old.

The relation of Hasidism to traditional, talmudic Judaism is more complex. On the one hand, as we have seen, Hasidism accepted traditional assumptions about the Law, the specialness of the people, the coming of the Messiah, and the reality of God's reign over the world. On the other hand, Hasidism set the charismatic holy man rather than the learned rabbi at the center of the community.[43] This new figure, the *tzaddik* (righteous one), Hasidim revered for his intimacy with God, his ability to pray evocatively, and his gifts as a storyteller. (As a storyteller he was an updated version of the ancient aggadist.) But the simple faithful held the *tzaddik* to be a wonder worker.

Thus, as illustrated, the Hasidim abounded with stories of God's coming to the aid of his oppressed people through the special interventions of the *tzaddik*.[44] The story with which the contemporary Jewish writer Elie Wiesel (who explicitly situates himself in the Hasidic tradition) prefaces his novel *The Gates of the Forest* epitomizes the impact of Hasidic faith in the masters' powers:

> When the great Rabbi Israel Baal Shem-Tov saw misfortune threatening the Jews it was his custom to go into a certain part of the forest to meditate. There he would light a fire, say a special prayer, and the miracle would be accomplished and the misfortune averted. Later, when his disciple, the celebrated Magid of Mezritch, had occasion, for the same reason, to intercede with heaven, he would go to the same place in the forest and say: "Master of the Universe, listen! I do not know how to light the fire, but I am still able to say the prayer" and again the miracle would be accomplished. . . . Then it fell to Rabbi Israel of Rizhyn to overcome misfortune. Sitting in his armchair, his head in his hands, he spoke to God: "I am unable to light the fire and I do not know the prayer; I cannot even find the place in the forest. All I can do is to tell the story, and this must be sufficient." And it was sufficient. God made man because he loves stories.[45]

Reform. Thus, the traditional legal authority at the heart of rabbinic Judaism crumbled because of both the new secular learning and the greater attractiveness of the charismatic *tzaddik*. From within, Judaism succumbed to a desire for more intellectually and spiritually satisfying evidence of God's helpfulness. In response to this crisis of the tradition came a "Reform" of orthodox conceptions. On a popular level (though we are still speaking of the relatively educated), Reform meant an effort to accept modern culture and

still remain a Jew. In other words, it meant searching for new definitions of Jewishness that would not necessitate alienation from the intellectual and political life of gentile fellow nationalists.

Among the "virtuosi," as Neusner calls the important personalities of the Reform movement, the effort was not just accommodation but rethinking the tradition to bring it up to date with integrity. A good part of the virtuosi's effort emphasized the Jewish philosophical and ethical beliefs that seemed eminently rational (and so applicable to all people). In effect, emphasis shifted from what was distinctive in Judaism, what gave Jews their unique status as God's chosen ones, to what Judaism could offer to all humanity.

The stress of Reform was ethical. Reform Jews saw their tradition as offering all peoples a moral sensitivity, a concern for the rights of conscience and social justice, that derived from the prophets and the great rabbis but could serve the dawning future age of equality, political freedom, and mutual respect. In part, this ethical stress was the result of wishful thinking. Reform Jews tended to be talented people who were either formally or informally excluded from national and university life. As a result, their visions of a new day led them to stress what in their own religious past might abet equal opportunity.

A response to Reform within Judaism was self-conscious *Orthodoxy*. It tended to recruit those who shared many of the Reformers' perceptions but who disagreed with their reinterpretation of the tradition. Instead, Orthodoxy insisted that the Torah be the judge of modernity and not vice versa. Positively, however, the Orthodox conceded the possibility that living with gentiles might be a good, God-intended arrangement. No doubt, the breakup of Christian control over culture that marked the Western shift from medieval to modern times played a strong role in this reevaluation. That is, the Orthodox saw the wisdom in the Reform argument that, despite its evident dangers to faith, living among modern gentiles might free Jews of the prejudice endemic in medieval Christian faith by letting Christians see that Jews could be amiable fellow citizens (in its most virulent form, that prejudice branded all Jews as "Christ killers").

In their contests with the Reformers, the Orthodox could draw on factors that tradition had driven deep into the Jewish psyche. First, there was the conservatism that was almost intrinsic to a faith built on teaching "Fathers" and the father-figure of the family. Such conservatism made it difficult for the younger

Figure 37   Infamous gate at Dachau concentration camp, outside Munich, Germany, reading "Work frees." Photo by J. T. Carmody.

generation to convince the older. Second, the Orthodox could claim, much more plausibly than the Reform, that they represented the wisdom and experience of the past by which the people had survived. Third, the Orthodox could seem more genuinely religious than the Reform; although the virtuosi wanted to develop faith, the majority of the Reformers were secularly minded, drawn by goods outside the traditional culture. Last, the combination of these factors gave Orthodoxy the advantage of appearing safer and surer than Reform.[46]

Conservative Judaism represented an effort to find a centrist position between Reform and Orthodoxy. Its founder was Rabbi Zecharias Frankel (1801–1875), chief rabbi of Dresden and later head of the Breslau Theological Seminary in Germany. Frankel's position was that Judaism should change slowly, remaining true to its traditional character and only allowing slight modifications of traditional practice. In

the United States, Solomon Schechter of the Jewish Theological Seminary of America was the central promoter of Conservative Judaism.

Presently Conservative Judaism is the largest of the three main groups of American Jews. Its intellectual center is the Jewish Theological Seminary in New York, its rabbinical assembly numbers more than one thousand members, and its league of synagogues (the United Synagogue) numbers more than one thousand congregations. Building on Reform initiatives, the Conservative worship service has introduced family pews, developed a modernized liturgy in the vernacular, and allowed women a fuller role in the congregation's ritual life.

Reconstructionism, a U.S. Jewish movement founded by Mordecai Kaplan (1881–1983), has taught that past Jewish concern with otherworldly salvation is no longer credible, and that consequently Jews should translate their traditional concern for salvation into this-worldly terms: human betterment in health, political rights, education, and the like. Other reconstructionists have kept the same this-worldly emphasis but focused more on Jewish culture than "salvation."

Zionism. The movement most responsible for the establishment of the modern state of Israel is *Zionism.* Most of the medieval piety movements anticipated Zionism insofar as their messianism regularly involved the notion of returning to the ancestral land (and to the holiest of cities, Jerusalem). Thus, the Karaites of eighth-century Iraq (Babylonia) emigrated to Israel, and some of the cabalists took up residence in Galilee. In the eighteenth and nineteenth centuries, Hasidim in Poland sent many people to the holy land, with the result that there were circles of devout Jews in Jerusalem, Tiberius, and Safed.[47] The upsurge of nationalism in modern Europe tended to make Jews consider their own national roots, while new movements of social thought, including those led by Marx and Tolstoy, caused many Jews to dream about a new society based on the *kibbutz* (collective).

The greatest impetus to Zionism, however, was the persecutions that convinced European Jews they were in peril on the Continent: pogroms in Russia from 1880 to 1905, Ukrainian massacres from 1917 to 1922, persecutions in Poland between 1922 and 1939, and, above all, the Nazi persecution that began in 1933 and climaxed in the Holocaust of perhaps six million Jews in Nazi death camps. By 1948 about 650,000 Jews lived within the British Mandate of Palestine, and at the birth of modern Israel many hundreds of thousands more emigrated from Europe and from Arab lands (where, after the 1948 war, conditions were difficult). The main ideologist for the modern Zionist movement was a Viennese named Theodor Herzl. His witness of anti-Semitism during the Dreyfus affair in France at the end of the nineteenth century had convinced him and many other Jews that only by having their own nation could Jews be free of constant persecution.

Today Judaism is most vital in Israel and the United States, and in both places the battles over what it means to be a Jew in the modern world continue unabated. Israel has become the spiritual center of Judaism, and what faith can mean after Auschwitz and the Holocaust has become the prime topic of theological discussion.[48] Because of its vigorous intellectual tradition, Judaism disproportionately contributes to the debates about the value of modernity, and its voice is now influencing many Christian thinkers.[49]

WORLDVIEW

Nature

Generally speaking, nature has not been so important in Judaism as peoplehood. For example, Maimonides did not refer to it in his thirteen articles of faith, and scholars dealing with the biblical period,[50] a historical perspective,[51] or even Jewish values[52] do not focus on nature. That does not mean, of course, that Jews had no consciousness of their land or that the physical world played no part in their religion. Indeed, the promise of a land of their own kept the people going during their wanderings in the desert under Moses and encouraged all Jews during the centuries of the Diaspora.

In the biblical period nature was quite important, because the earliest "Jews" were shepherds or farmers. The earliest theology appears to have been a veneration of different *els* (gods) related to natural powers, and the constant lament of the prophets and other biblical theologians that the gods of the neighboring peoples (the Canaanites especially) were seducing the people away from true religion is testimony that the cosmological myth held considerable attraction.

Still, contesting the cosmological myth (in which divinity is immanent to the world and natural processes are divinity's most intimate operations) were the "great acts" of YHWH in his people's time. Eric Voegelin has argued that "history" itself (our human conception of time) is substantially the product of Israelite theology.[53] For Voegelin, history gets periodicity from the revelations of a God outside the world, and it is those revelations that decisively shaped the Jewish people. So YHWH, the most transcendent of Gods, was also the most interactive. He was the God of the Fathers, Abraham, Isaac, and Jacob. He was the one who had led the ancestors out of Egypt, struck the covenant on Sinai, and ushered the people into the promised land.

From the beginning, the Jewish conception of God, coupled with the Jewish ethnic memory and sense of identification through religious history, combined to deemphasize nature as a religious focus. As the Psalms show, YHWH was the lord of nature as well as of time. He was the creator of the physical world, the benefactor of good harvests, a God who could appear with clouds and lightning. What made him special in Jewish eyes, though, was his redemptive activity and covenanting—actions in which he stepped out of natural phenomena and acted on a personal basis.

For instance, the liturgical feasts, though they began as nature festivals, ran through the agricultural year, and were expressions of gratitude for harvests, reached their peak at Passover and Yom Kippur—celebrations of historical events and of a moral requirement based on the covenant. Furthermore, the sacrificial aspect of early Jewish worship was replaced by the sermonizing and Bible reading of the synagogue. In fact, as the Torah grew in influence, the human qualities of law, reason, study, and ethics came to the fore. Celebrations still involved food, drink, and dance, but they were probably due more to a social sense, from a desire to affirm a common identity, than from a close connection with mother earth or father sky. (Interestingly, though, in their elaboration of the Torah, the rabbis were remarkably sensitive to animals' welfare. They glossed the biblical injunction not to muzzle the grinding ox, and they demanded that ritual slaughtering be as painless as possible.)

Urban Values.   Many of the countries in which Jews lived, as a distinct and often inhibited minority, forbade them ownership of land, while their tradition of study tended to lead them into intellectual occupations and business. The tensions between *shtetl* Jews and *goyim* (gentiles) in Eastern Europe, for instance, were due as much to different occupations as to different theologies. The gentile peasants worked the land and valued rather brutish strength. The *shtetl* Jews did not farm very much, tending, rather, to engage in small businesses and study.

As a result, the qualities valued by the Jews were not the goyish qualities of strength and violence. Jews were not to fight, engage in hard labor, drink, or carouse. They were to be disciplined, cultured, and family and community oriented. Because few Jews lived on farms, they had to concentrate on living in densely populated areas. The gentile peasants needed customers for their goods, middlemen for their trades, craftsmen, and doctors, and Jews tended to fill these roles. Thus, they clearly stood at some remove from nature.

Zionism.   With Zionism and the return to the holy land, Judaism has brought back to center stage a theme that was prominent in premodern times—the predilection for Israel and Jerusalem as the most religious places, favoring the prosperity of Jewish faith. In the centuries of Diaspora, the typical Jew felt something of what the first biblical exiles lamented—the inability to sing and rejoice in a foreign land. No doubt that feeling did not afflict the descendants of the actual exiles as intensely, for few of them returned from Babylon when they had the opportunity, but it mixed a certain nature orientation with Jews' desire to have a place of their own. Consequently, Israel became not just a venerable place but also a beautiful, fruitful, arable, desirable land. Thus, the biblical theme of a promised land joined with messianic hopes to link the new age that the Messiah would usher in and the people's return to a place flowing with milk and honey. Zionism drew on these traditional themes, joining them to socialistic (if not utopian) theories of working the land and living together in close cooperation.

Though few American Jews farm or do their religious thinking along cosmological lines, quite a few Israelis live on kibbutzim and work the land (and quite a few American Jewish youths join them for a summer or a year). The land, if not nature, is most important to kibbutzniks. Because of Israel's ancient history and Jews' present need to have their own place in the sun, the Israelis now are more agrarian than their recent predecessors were. How that affects their religious consciousness is hard to determine. Many do not consider themselves religious, and they often view their life on the land, even though it brings them close to nature, in sociological rather than naturalistic terms. Frequently, then, they resemble other idealistic groups who form communes and farm in order to augment their freedom (and often to "purify" their lives). On the other hand, those who do form kibbutzim out of religious motivations are often fundamentalists trying to regain their biblical heritage. Still, that heritage is not so much harvesting God's earth as living where God made the Jews his special people.

Thus, Judaism has tended to view nature rather prosaically. To be sure, some Jews have farmed, and some non-farming Jews have found religious significance in seasons, sunsets, flowers, and stocks of grain.

However, the Hebrew Bible, the Talmud, and other products of the mind have been more central to the tradition.

Society

Few religions are as community minded as Judaism. Even when we consider that modern individualism is a historical novelty, the fact remains that the Jews were the chosen *people*—chosen as a group or line rather than as individuals. From tribal beginnings, through kingdom, Diaspora, and ethnic diversification, Jewish religion has always been a group affair. Of course, the Torah is inseparable from this phenomenon, for it is a special law designed expressly for the chosen, covenanted people. It sprang from a group sense that life must flow to "our" God, who led us out of captivity to be his own people. The Torah also specified the theological direction of Jews by giving election and covenant the forms by which they shaped social life.

Thus, the synagogue has been a popular gathering place, uniting the action of the people. The Christian *ecclesia* ("church") has a similar etymological meaning ("gathering," "being called out"), but the building it names has been almost as much a place for private prayer as for public. Perhaps the relative smallness of the Jewish population has helped it to gain a more worldwide sense of community than Christians have had. Perhaps, as well, the relative mildness of its sectarian divisions has helped to keep Judaism a family affair. In any event, Muslims, despite their democratic worship and pilgrimage, have been less united than Jews have been, and Christians, despite their lofty theology of the Church, have been more individual oriented and divided. Finally, nothing in Hinduism or Buddhism prompts a different judgment: Judaism is unified and social to a remarkable degree.

Women's Status. Jews, then, have focused more on culture than on nature.[54] Anthropologists sometimes use these two concepts as opposing points on a spectrum to determine a people's attitudes toward itself and cosmological processes. For instance, anthropologists have used this spectrum to study sex roles.[55] Women have generally been associated with nature, because of menstruation, childbirth, nursing, and—to male eyes—more instinctive, less cerebral behavior. Men have been associated with culture: craft, art, literature, and politics. It does not take a great deal of research to dispute this construct, but many societies have used it, more or less consciously, to characterize sex roles. Therefore, the construct is useful in analyzing how societies view the play of physical nature in human societies.

This sexual stereotype is somewhat applicable among Jews. As we noted, during many periods of Jewish history women worked or ran the home while the men studied. The biblical portrait of women,[56] and the portrait of women in the Talmud[57] and in the *responsa*,[58] reflect a traditional view that placed women away from law and the mind and toward nature and the body. Separating the patriarchal structure of Middle Eastern society, the Jewish religious conception of God (usually as a husband or father, seldom as a wife or mother), and the Jewish perception of nature is almost impossible. The facts, however, are that women and nature went together and that they were subordinate to men and culture.

For instance, women did not read the Torah in the synagogue (usually they could not read Hebrew), did not have many legal obligations (only three *mitzvoth* pertain only to them), could not be priests or rabbis, were tabooed during menstruation, and were both indulged and criticized for their "flightiness." Under biblical law, Jewish women were partially considered as property—akin to animals and goods. For instance, the laws concerning adultery and rape were principally intended to protect the rights of the male—the injured husband or father. The principal value of women throughout Jewish history was motherhood—a quite "natural" function. They seldom could have careers and usually had difficulty obtaining the education that would have enabled them to be their husbands' best friends. They were the source of the family line and of emotional support, not leaders. In good measure because he enjoyed being the cultural center, the male Jew traditionally prayed thanks to God for not having created him a woman.[59]

Case Study: Jewish Rituals. Traditionally, Jewish social life has involved many rituals. To begin with, there was circumcision, the ritual through which males entered the covenant community. Herman Wouk, the celebrated novelist, has tried to explain circumcision and other Jewish rituals to sympathetic gentiles.[60] He begins by noting the scorn that often has been directed at circumcision and similar Jewish customs. Thus the

French Enlightenment writer Voltaire mocked a God who could care whether people cut off their sons' fore-skins. On the other hand, Spinoza, the rationalistic Jewish philosopher, thought that circumcision alone was sufficient to keep the Jews a separate people. How-ever, whether mocked or made a subject of philosophy, circumcision can be a key to Jewish faith.

In the perspective of Jewish faith, circumcision is not a matter of hygiene. It is a sign of the pledge made between Abraham and God, a sign in the very organ of life. For the rest of his life, the man signed this way stands out from the rest of unsigned humanity. Naked, the Jewish man is clearly a Jew. In Wouk's in-terpretation, the swing of modern medicine to cir-cumcision was but a ratification of the sound policy Jews have always expected God's law to entail. With or without such a ratification, however, Jews would continue to circumcise their males on the eighth day after birth, the time when Abraham circumcised Isaac.

The circumcision ritual is called a *bris*, the He-brew word for covenant. When most children were born at home, the bris meant a family feast, with crowds of relatives and friends, learned speeches, and general merrymaking. Each step of the ceremony was something to be stored in the memory for later medi-tation. Contemporary ceremonies retain what they can of this tradition, gathering relatives and friends to cel-ebrate the new birth. The bris intensifies the ordinary joy parents feel at the gift of a child, by emphasizing that the covenant community is being extended an-other generation.

So the father of the child pronounces a joyous blessing: "Blessed are you, Lord our God, Master of the Universe, who have made us holy with your com-mands, and have commanded us to bring this boy into the covenant of Abraham our father." Ideally the father would do the circumcision himself, as Abraham did, but the accepted practice has become to employ a *mohel* or ritual circumciser to perform it. The mohel may or may not be a medical doctor, but he has been well trained in medical safeguards and antisepsis. In Wouk's view the mohel is preferable to an ordinary doctor, both because the mohel likely has fuller tech-nical training and because he understands the full meaning of the ritual. Thus, he can stand in for the father more adequately.

Following circumcision, the next rite of passage for the Jewish child is the *bar mitzvah* or ceremonial accession to adulthood. Recently, American Jewish feelings about this ceremony have become quite sen-

sitive, and Wouk reports having received many bitter, even violent complaints about his somewhat humor-ous depiction of a bar mitzvah in his novel *Marjorie Morningstar*. Where he thought he had portrayed the bar mitzvah accurately and affectionately, many of his fellow Jews thought he had been satirical, even disre-spectful. His reply is that when people lose their sense of humor, becoming unable to see the foibles of their tribe, it is time they take themselves to the mirror.

Sticking to his humorous guns, Wouk likens the American bar mitzvah to a Christmas feast orches-trated by Charles Dickens. The lengthy preparations, the incredible eating, the enormous wassailing, and the swirl of family emotions seem parallel in both cases. In both cases, a great deal of purely human gusto dances on top of a religious rationale. In the case of American Jews, the bar mitzvah seems to have become an occasion to celebrate a relative freedom from discrimination. While Wouk applauds this free-dom, he wonders whether American Jews aren't in danger of losing the religious significance of the bar mitzvah, much as American Christians are in danger of losing the religious significance of Christmas, through all their buying and partying.

The religious tradition behind the bar mitzvah assumes that a child does not develop the capacity to grasp the concepts of Judaism, nor to fulfill Judaism's disciplines, until the age of thirteen. Before that time, the father is responsible for the child. The bar mitzvah marks the child's transition to personal responsibility. Donning the phylacteries that an adult wears when he prays, the boy bar mitzvahed can now receive an *aliya*, a call to speak the blessing over a part of the weekly reading of the Torah.

The most honorific aliya is the last one, the call concerning the weekly piece from the prophets. In Eu-ropean Jewish communities the custom arose of giv-ing this special aliya (called the *maftir*) to a boy on his bar mitzvah Sabbath, and this custom has been re-tained in the United States. Often, however, the solid preparation in Hebrew that the European tradition as-sumed has been lacking. Thus, in Wouk's view, the American bar mitzvah frequently became a time of crisis, the young person feeling that his blitz of prep-arations was a sham. In a number of communities, this has led to a renewal of Hebrew studies, so that the ceremony can express a genuine mastery of Judaism's foundations.

With the rise of a Jewish feminist consciousness have come rituals for bringing girls into the covenant and adulthood. Thus Judith Plaskow, a prominent Jewish feminist and theologian, has written a bris ceremonial for a girl. It begins with the song Hannah sang on the occasion of the birth of her son Samuel (I Sam. 2:2–8), including the words: "The bows of the mighty are broken, but the feeble gird on strength. Those who were full have hired themselves out for bread, but those who were hungry have ceased to hunger. The barren has borne seven, but she who has many children is forlorn. God creates and destroys; She brings down to Sheol and raises up."[61] With similar adaptations of other scriptural passages, Plaskow weaves together a celebration of a baby girl's entrance into the community's life parallel to that for a baby boy.

Concerning a girl's coming of age, Wouk indicates some of the reasons for the absence of a special ceremony in the past, and why present times have led to coming-of-age ceremonies for girls. Traditionally, women were exempted from most Jewish rituals, that they might be free for family tasks. When the bar mitzvah was a rather minor ceremony, for which boys began intensive studies at the age of five, "a girl would have been out of her head to agitate for the burdens of scholarship." But when the preparation for the bar mitzvah dwindled, and the event came to occasion a great party, there were good reasons for girls to want an equal celebration. Thus, there has arisen the *bas* (or *bat*) *mitzvah* ceremony for girls, an improvised way to ritualize girls' graduation from religious-school training and to recognize their new status as adults. (Wouk seems insensitive to the traditional correlation between learning and religious status in Judaism, as well as to the deeper hopes of feminists for full sexual equality.)

In most religions' ritualization of the life cycle, the third recurring ceremony has been marriage. Judaism has been no exception, giving marriage a great deal of ritual attention. *The Jewish Catalogue*, a high-spirited collection of lore and advice that tries to make Judaism attractive to contemporary Americans, begins its section on marriage with a story from the talmudic traditions.[62] Once a Roman matron asked Rabbi Jose bar Halafta how long it took God to create the world. The rabbi replied it took six days. The woman then asked, "What has God been doing from then until now?" The rabbi answered, "The Holy One, blessed be He, is occupied in making marriages." The matron scoffed at this, saying that marriage should only take a short time. Indeed, she went home and in one night married off a thousand of her male slaves to a thousand of her female slaves. The next day the slaves came before her, broken, wounded, and bruised. Each slave

said, "I do not want the one you gave me." So the woman went back to the rabbi and apologized. "I see now that your Torah is beautiful—praiseworthy and true." The rabbi replied, "Yes. God considers making a suitable match as difficult as dividing the Red Sea."

Difficult or not, Jews, like all other peoples, have persisted in marrying, generation after generation, for better or worse, for richer or poorer. Traditionally, their marriages have taken place under a canopy *(huppah)* supported by four poles, the original purpose of which was to provide the ceremony a sacred space. The day itself usually entailed a fast, and other similarities to the Day of Atonement, in the belief that on their wedding day God forgives a couple all their past sins, so that they may begin their life together afresh. Another custom was for the bride and groom to wear white as a symbol of purity.

Jewish betrothal occurred by writing a legal document binding on both parties. The rabbi asked the groom if he was prepared to fulfill his obligations as stated in the contract *(ketubbah),* and the groom answered affirmatively by taking hold of a handkerchief or some other object given him by the rabbi. After the groom signed the contract, the men present surrounded the groom and danced with him over to the bride, who sat regally on a throne. The groom lifted the veil from the bride's face, while the rabbi recited the phrase, "O sister! May you become the mother of thousands of myriads" (Gen. 24:60). The bride and groom then processed to the huppah, the bride circled the groom seven times (entering all seven spheres of her beloved's soul), there were psalms, hymns, a blessing of wine, and then the essential act occurred.

The essential act was the groom putting a ring on the index finger of the bride's right hand and saying, "Behold you are consecrated to me with this ring according to the Law of Moses and Israel." After this the marriage contract was read, seven blessings were recited, and the groom smashed a glass by stamping on it, to conclude the ceremony. Traditionally, the bride and groom then retired to consummate the marriage. Nowadays they retire to break their fast. When they emerge, their families and friends greet them with music, dancing, and celebration.

Funeral rites, the last stage on life's way, have involved Jews in a final confession of faith. Ideally the dying person said, "Understand, O Israel, the Lord our God is One. I acknowledge before Thee, my God, God of my fathers, that my recovery and death are in your hand. May it be your will to heal me completely, but if I should die, may my death be an atonement for all

Figure 38 Judith with the Head of Holofernes,
*by Simon Vouet (1590–1649). The Nelson–Atkins
Museum of Art, Kansas City, Missouri (Nelson
Fund).*

sins that I have committed." After death there was a
ritual washing of the body, a funeral dominated by the
recitation of psalms, a ritualized burial, a meal for the
mourners, and then the *shivah,* a seven-day period of
mourning, during which friends were expected to visit
and a *minyan* (quorum of ten) was to gather each day.
The mourning period concluded with visiting the synagogue the first Sabbath after the shivah.

A Jew has usually prayed in the plural, for the
sake of the many. When a student or scholar devoted
himself to Torah, it was usually in common. In the
shtetl, one clearly lived very much with people—at
times oppressively so. As we noted, wealth was for the
common good and study had teaching as its goal. Unlike Christian society, Jewish society had no monastic
alternative (neither solitary nor communitarian) to
marriage and family life.[63] (The Essene community at
Qumran, if it was an exception to this rule, was short-
lived.) Generally, then, Jewish existence has been distinctly social or communal.

Relatedly, the rabbinic mind uncompromisingly
intended that all the people live socially. The scholar
pondered a law incumbent on all; the working person

normally was in business rather than in the solitude
of the fields or the forests; in the home, which was
largely the woman's province, feelings were gotten
"out," almost compulsively expressed. In fact, silence
was considered antisocial and even cruel behavior. The
two things that a child could do to punish its mother
were not to eat and not to speak. Finally, community
conversation buzzed with a detailed analysis of each
member's learning, wealth, and family lineage. Small
wonder, then, that being called forth to read the Torah
before the community was an honor, placing one
among the *sheyneh yidn,* the "beautiful Jews."

As we have seen, this communitarian consciousness is rooted in patriarchal times. Jews first identified
themselves by their tribal origins, which they tied together under the concept of "the twelve tribes." They
attributed their sense of commonness to fatherly figures: Abraham, Moses, and David. Abraham was the
source of the seed. To him had been the promise of a
progeny as numerous as the stars in the heavens or
the grains of sand along the sea. Moses was the founding father, in the sense of being the lawgiver. David
was the sacred king, the mediator between heaven and
earth, the top of the human pyramid. From his line
would spring the Messiah. In a special way, the capital
city of Jerusalem was the city of David.

Jerusalem. When the Jews gained a new homeland
in 1948, fulfilling decades of Zionist longings, Jerusalem again became the real center of Jewish geography.
All the biblical overtones of the city of David lie inside
the old walls. Outside the old walls is much evidence
of the surrounding and hostile Arab population. Historically, Jerusalem summons images of kingship,
prosperity, a golden age, a pawn of Christians and Muslims. Sociologically, Jerusalem gives the Jewish people
a realized dream, a place of their own to which, next
year, the Messiah just might come and all the blessed
might journey.

Psychologically, contemporary Jews are apt to
overflow with feelings about Jerusalem, some of them
quite conflicting. On the one hand, there is a desire to
support the powers in the new capital that are trying
to promote Israel's survival and prosperity. On the
other hand, there is the knowledge that the majority
of Jews still live outside Israel, often more prosper-
ously than if they lived inside Israel, and that not all
the things done in the Knesset (parliament) merit full
support. Some policies emanating from the Knesset
have made barren land spring back to life. Yet on the
West Bank the ecological policies have become so

mixed with religious aims that they often seem to be a military weapon aimed against the troublesome Palestinians. It is hard for sensitive Jews to know where to direct their support.

Historically, Jerusalem has suffered from the conflicting aims of its leaders. The classical prophets often found themselves spiritual spokesmen, pitted against kings and opposing worldly powers. They feared that worldly reliances, above all military recourses, would keep the Jewish people from pure religion, and weaken Israel's firm faith in God. The kings often rejected the prophets' perspective, preferring to play power politics. The resulting split of the kingdom, as well as the fall of the southern portion to Babylon, stands in biblical history as a great vindication of the prophets. Through the many centuries when Jews had no power over their ancestral land, and the many more centuries when they lived mainly outside it in the Diaspora, the priests and rabbis could deal with questions of power politics rather distantly, regarding them as theoretical rather than practical issues. Today, however, conflicts between the religious and secular sides of Jewish faith have once again come to swords' point in Jerusalem, as in the 1982 Israeli slaying of hundreds of Palestinian refugees in Lebanese camps.

The Special Commission of Inquiry that reported on the Israeli slaying based their findings, in part, on a Jewish law and tradition with roots extending back to the Bible. They combined modern jurisprudence with the talmudic heritage, and the result was an arresting confluence of democratic self-criticism and religious sensitivity. While the proximate blame for the massacre fell squarely on non-Jewish shoulders (those responsible for the slayings were right-wing Christians), the Commission found leading Jewish military and political officials guilty of indifference and imprudence. Because the highly developed traditional moral code held that one who is able to avert an evil and does not do so is somewhat responsible for such evil, leading generals, the defense minister, and even the prime minister drew the Commission's blame. These findings were deeply disturbing to many Jews. But the form of the findings, their deep and honest self-criticism, was an act of healing, a step of therapy and hope. As many commentators the world over pointed out, there are only a handful of other nations in the world where such a public self-criticism would be conceivable, and few if any of them are in the Middle East.

The prophetic emphases on justice, conversion to God, and walking in the ways of truth continue to shape daily life in Jerusalem. Down the streets hurry bearded Hasidic Jews and visiting Americans, devout religionists and Jews nearly completely secularized. The land and the ethnic solidarity have become lodestones to chosen people all over the globe. The Jews of European origin (Ashkenazim) who have been the main reference point of our story increasingly find that they must accommodate the Jews of Spanish origin (Sephardim) and Oriental Jews. Within a small country, an amazing variety obtains. Fundamentalists seeking to establish new settlements believe they are fulfilling a biblical mandate. Twenty miles away in the Hebrew University, professors teach that such fundamentalism is foolish. Meanwhile, the specter of the Nazi death camps hovers outside Jerusalem at Yad Vashem, the memorial set in the nearby hills. This specter has led many to vow "Never again!"

Prophecy and the Chosen People. Of the three key biblical figures, Moses predominated, because the Law that came through him has been the backbone of Jewish religious life. As different cultures were assimilated by Judaism, Abraham's lineage became less important than his exemplary faith. Similarly, as political sovereignty became a dim memory, David's kingship became rather metaphorical, propping future hopes more than guiding present living. Moses, however, stayed wholly relevant: He was thought to have authored the code that kept Jews united; he was the mediator of the covenant into which the community circumcised each male. When prophecy had become central to Jewish religion, Moses became the prophet par excellence.

Prophecy, which often distinguishes Western religion from Eastern wisdom religion, is not so much the predictions that appear in today's tabloids as a discernment of what the divine spirit is saying to the people of God. The great biblical prophets analyzed the contemporary state of faith and, from that analysis, shrewdly estimated political or military fortunes. A goodly portion of such recorded prophecy was, of course, written after the fact. No portion of respectable prophecy, though, pried into the divine mystery. God remained God; the prophet had only the word that God deigned to speak. The establishment of Moses as the supreme prophet testifies to the social utility that Jews have expected communication with God to bear. They expected such communication to result in communal renovation, strengthening, and redirection. Prophecy was not a display of individual virtuosity or a matter involving crystal balls.

As prophecy intimates, the ultimate bonding agent of Jewish society has been God; only the atypical, modern secular Jew would dispute this. Through history the master of the universe, the Adonai ("My Lord," substituting for Yahweh, which was considered too holy to utter) that all prayers bless, has bound Jews together as his people. Physically and legally one is a Jew if one is born of a Jewish mother; spiritually one is a Jew if one identifies with the people fashioned at Sinai, framed by the Torah, and covenanted to God. To be sure, many problems attend election as God's people, and Jews have not been unmindful of them. Indeed, the relation between the chosen people and the gentile nations has been a constant topic for Jewish meditation. In good times, such meditation has turned over history's mysteries gratefully: Why were we chosen when we show no special merit? What are our obligations to the nations?

Indubitably, the gentile nations were under God's direction, too. It could not be that God had no fulfillment in store for them. So Jewish thinkers worked out the notion of the Noachian covenant: God made a pact with the gentile nations modeled after the promise he made to Noah, in which he stressed the need for human beings to respect life, especially by avoiding bloodshed. The Bible sees the rainbow as a symbol of God's fidelity to this pact: He will never destroy humanity, never again allow it to suffer as it did in the flood. Yet God could well have more in store for the nations than this Noachian covenant, and Israel's vocation was to be a light unto the nations—to provide them with a greater knowledge of God. In that way, being the chosen people became less a matter of honor than a matter of responsibility.

In bad times, however, reflection on being chosen by God had to probe darker mysteries. For instance, the prophets almost fixated on the horror that many Israelites refused their election. Most people wanted kings like the nations had, cults like those to Baal, fertility from the land rather than from the covenant. With some deliberateness, many Jews turned their backs on God because they could not endure living in faith; God's self-naming to Moses, "I am whatever I want to be," was too much for them. For the prophets, this flight from God was the deepest sickness of the soul, the most debilitating sin, as well as a rejection of Israel's better self. The worst of biblical times, then, occurred when people left the covenantal faith.

At such times, the prophets brought the whole question of what the Jewish people at core were into paradox. They then spoke of a remnant, of an Israel within Israel that was composed of the few who did keep faith. A major Jewish-Christian controversy has hung on this point, for Christians have claimed to succeed Israel by accepting God's later revelation (specifically, his revelation in Jesus the Christ). Within the Jewish community itself, prophetic religious leaders have always worried about the correlation between bad faith and loss of membership.

The Law. For rabbinic Judaism, the Law helped to ease the problem of bad faith. Without abandoning their ideal of the perfect faith outlined in Maimonides' thirteen articles, the rabbis generally have focused more on performance than on motivation or thought. What one believed about God, within broad limits, has been less important than keeping the Sabbath and fulfilling one's communal obligations. This attitude encouraged considerable intellectual freedom, including lively debate, tolerance, and theological ambiguity. As well, it prevented the establishment of a clear-cut religious authority and dogma, such as that encountered by Roman Catholics in the magisterium of their councils and popes. The Law, which seemed so specific, had dozens of interpreters. On and on the Talmud grew, because most interpreters had insights worth preserving.

The result was a subtle but significant shift in the notion of the faith requisite for community membership. Faith was expressed in action, not in speculation or confession. How one used one's body, money, and time was more important than how one used one's mind or tongue. Such a practical view of faith meant that the community could bind itself through rituals, ethics, and laws without excessive concern about their meaning (although the rabbis did not ignore their meaning or the proper motivation behind ritual actions).

This emphasis on action relates to the Jewish refusal to separate mind and body and to the Jewish commitment to hallowing life. Traditionally, one obeyed the Law to express and learn that God, who is holy, wants holy people. Through the quite overt keeping of the Law, Jews reminded themselves that they were the people called to sanctify God's name. A Jew knew that his neighbor accepted this identity because he could see that his neighbor obeyed the Law. Not accidentally, withdrawal from the Law and from the traditional God whom the Law hallowed have gone hand in hand in modern times.

The Holocaust. Last, contemporary Jewish identity has been annealed as a result of the Holocaust. While exodus and entry into the promised land characterized Jews in biblical times, suffering and persecution have characterized Jews since the expulsion from Jerusalem in 70 C.E. Jewish commentators have no consensus on what recent history and the Holocaust mean. For Richard Rubenstein, they mean the death of the traditional God.[64] For Emil Fackenheim, they mean a call to hold together both evil and divine providence.[65] For Hannah Arendt, they show that history can make evil utterly commonplace or banal.[66] Such commentators do agree that we must not ignore, deny, or explain away the evil of the Holocaust. As Elie Wiesel has said, it is better to keep silent than to depreciate the suffering of so many innocent victims with "explanations."[67] Thus, Jewish identity, the theme of so many American novels, has yet to be fully resolved.

Self

An intense community life, such as that of traditional Judaism, can heighten individualism. One can prize the individual because the richer the individual, the richer the group. Judaism appears to have appreciated this proposition.

For example, after the prophets (such as Ezekiel and Jeremiah), individual responsibility separated from collective responsibility. No longer could one hold, rather magically, that the fathers had eaten sour grapes and so set the children's teeth on edge. Furthermore, both Hellenization and internal legal development set apart individual reason. For instance, Jewish thinkers in Alexandria reflected Platonic, Aristotelian, Epicurean, and Stoic interests in mind and reason. Philo, the luminary of these thinkers, tried to correlate Mosaic teaching with a cosmic law. In the medieval period, Maimonides, Halevi, and others tried to square the Torah with rational demands for a less mythic, more analytic explanation of faith. Since the individual soul is the site of reason, such concerns inevitably clarified the personality's partial independence of group thought. That is, it underscored that any particular person might grasp or miss the divine Law.

Moreover, the Torah and the Talmud themselves inculcated something of this sensitivity. As a scriptural religion, Judaism demanded literacy and encouraged learning. But, literature and learning are obviously cultural developments deriving from a common human nature that tend to distinguish people according to their talent. Thus, the bright little boy may distinguish himself by the age of ten. Through his unique gifts he may stand out from the crowd, and even increase regard for his family. If he develops into a sage, he will join the line of masters whose commentaries on the Law are the classics. So, by stressing personal insight, legal study encouraged individuation.

To a lesser degree, Jewish mysticism and Jewish attitudes toward wealth also encouraged individuation. Mysticism, like study, is a personal inward phenomenon. Despite its debt to tradition and its occurrence within a community of faith, mysticism is a solitary pursuit involving an "I-Thou" relation. When mysticism flowered in Judaism, it produced revered personalities, such as the Baal Shem-Tov and the Magid of Mezritch. To their disciples, these *tzaddikim* were stunning demonstrations of the ardor that divinity could inspire. Their personalities were special, set apart, distinguished. Despite the threats that mysticism posed for the traditional rabbinic authority, the mystics were precious for strengthening the common people's faith. Thus, one could aspire to Hasidic distinction, as one could aspire to rabbinic distinction. Because mystical prowess edified the community, it was a worthy ambition.

Analogously, one could aspire to the (lesser) distinction that came with wealth. Judaism is not, comparatively speaking, an ascetic religion. As much as Hinduism, it views wealth or prosperity as a legitimate life goal. For his good fortune and financial talent, as well as for his philanthropy, a successful Jew could win recognition. True, with success he was sure to gain a host of petitioners, but their attestation to his generosity somewhat offset the burden they imposed.

This description of the self must be qualified in discussing women. Since their vocation was marriage and practicality, their distinction was basically reflected—that of being a rich man's wife or a scholar's mother. Nevertheless, women had rights to self-expression, at least regarding nonscriptural matters. The *shtetl* tradition that a woman had no soul did not mean that she had no say. In matters of the home or the shop, she probably had the dominant say. In matters of affection or emotion, she surely did. Thus, few distinguished Jews were not first signalized by women, and most *shtetl* neighborhoods recognized certain girls as being especially nubile and certain mothers as being especially benevolent.

Mind-Body Unity.   Judaism has stressed the unity of mind and body, eschewing a body-soul or matter-spirit duality. Scholars usually contrast biblical Jewish notions of personhood and the then-contemporary Greek notions. This contrast can illumine the tendency of Judaism toward an existential concreteness that most of Western culture has been struggling for centuries to recapture.

For instance, Descartes, the father of modern European philosophy, worked hard to reconcile the opposition within the human being between its *res cogitans* (thinking part) and its *res extensa* (material part). In contrast, the "soul" *(nepesh)* of Hebrew biblical thought was a unity of mind and body that could not be divided into thinking and material parts. So the heart rather than the head stood for the center of thought and emotion. Out of the fullness of the heart the mouth would speak. This conviction fought against the Hellenization of Jewish theology, which would have made the mouth speak what reason dictated. It fought against the legalism possible in rabbinic theology, keeping space for aggadic tales whose appeal was more than mental. The earthiness that one finds in Hebrew literature, from biblical times to the present,[68] reflects these convictions about the heart and body.

Furthermore, through his or her body, the Jewish personality maintained contact with the natural world. In the beginning, God had formed human beings from the earth, breathing into them a living spirit. Various biblical figures, such as Job, acknowledge this connection with the earth when they humble themselves before God and say, "We are but dust and ashes." The connection with the earth is more intense in the command to be fruitful and multiply, for the command implies that living things have an inbuilt drive to survive and grow. Biblical notions of stewardship over the earth found an evolutionary aspect in the command to be fruitful and multiply. (They also subordinated nature to human need.)

The command to be fruitful and multiply also influenced Jewish attitudes toward marriage. The fulfillment of the spouses certainly was much valued, at least in talmudic times, but a strong focus also remained on procreation. As many commentators point out, the late development of the notion of personal immortality in Judaism is due not only to the lack of a clear sense of a spiritual (immaterial) soul, but also to the tendency to think that one continued to exist through one's offspring. In other words, the family line was a sort of concrete immortality. To some extent, this limited the significance of the individual.

On the other hand, marriage was a treasure of Jewish faith in part because it prevented the individual from being totally lost in the abyss of death. From this and other benefits attributed to marriage, sexual activity derived a certain dignity, even a certain obligation. It is true that in rabbinic Judaism prudery could offset the high evaluation of sexual love. For instance, rabbis counseled against raising one's eyes to a woman's face, and some desired that the sexes be segregated as much as possible. Most laid on women the same heavy burden of the temptress that one can see in other religions. Indeed, in Judaism, unchastity was not only sinful but deplorable, because it drew the mind down from the heights of the Torah and prayer.

In most traditional homes (which for the poor often had only one or two rooms), husband and wife did not sleep in the same bed. Tradition encouraged them to have relations except during the menstrual flow but to keep the sexual appetite in check. One of the customs of the Sabbath, however, was that in its leisure spouses should make love. As the cabalists stressed, the Sabbath was the bride of God. Consequently, they found in the coexistence of man and woman a supplement to the notion that human reason is an image of God. Humanity also images God through sexual love, acting in accordance with the Genesis line "male and female created he them."

The Human Spirit.   In prophecy Jewish religion found understandings of God's relationship to the human spirit new to human history. That is, the ecstatic experience of the prophets, who seem to have begun as wandering bands of exultants *(nebi'im),* evolved into something other than ordinary shamanism (which we may take as the typical model of ancient ecstasy). For where shamanism usually kept the world divine and usually confused the relations between imagination and reason in the ecstatic experience (though some shamans were well aware of the divine incomprehensibility), the prophets had experiences that burned below imagination to the base of the spirit. The burning bush, for instance, occasioned the realization that we only know of God what the divine mystery shows in time. Elijah's small, still voice suggested that God comes more through spiritual recollection than through natural storms. Jeremiah, finally, went to the core of the matter: Divine creativity best expresses itself by writing its law upon the human heart.

That did not mean that the prophetic, or later the mystical, Jews did not mix myth, symbol, and imagination. The *merkabah* (chariot) imagery, as we mentioned, dominated even the philosophers' ruminations about God, while the cabalists' bliss was to imagine the divine emanations. Still, the union of the entire numinous experience (the entire experience of divinity) with ethical demands refined what it meant to be religious by stressing communion with a transcendent God. Implicit in the prophetic and talmudic program was the proposition that true religion is doing justice and worshiping purely. Implicit was the twofold commandment of loving God (who is one) and loving one's neighbor (who is another self). This outlook developed a powerful concept of individual conscience: God alone is the mystery that should dominate and constitute the human person in its being or its morality. When Jewish theologians clarified such a *monotheism,* they dealt a deathblow to all *idolatry.* History continues to unfold the implications of this ethical monotheism. From biblical times, then, Jews have cast the self, as well as the people, in partnership with a single God.

Ultimate Reality

The question of the place of ultimate reality in Judaism is difficult for Westerners, because the Jewish God is inseparable from Western culture. We can no more filter out Israelite ethical monotheism from the Western world view than we can filter out Greek reason. It requires considerable imaginative energy, therefore, to grasp the origins of Jewish divinity and trace how those beginnings developed into theological conceptualizations.

The biblical beginnings were extremely novel, constituting a "leap in being" rivaled only by the Greek clarification of reason. The biblical beginnings were deep spiritual experiences: irruptions of divinity that seized and formed the soul (more than they clarified reason). The God who was revealed was lively, personal, and free.

Perhaps because the genius of Israelite religion was not reason but spirit, the biblical Jews expressed this God's character as the world's origin and destiny in myths. That is, they expressed the truth of order, of humanity's proper place in and with nature and God, symbolically, from the "dead spot," the bottom of the

soul, which revelation seizes. Moreover, having expressed its order mythologically, the Israelite religious genius hardly criticized its symbols, making little effort to interpret them in clearer, if less complete, conceptual terms. In other words, it did not attack the problems of inner coherence that today's analytic philosophy associates with meaning.[69] So the God of Moses "is" only what time shows him to be; the God of Genesis makes the world "in the beginning" from primal chaos, the status of which is quite unclear; and the God of Isaiah is placed beyond the world by a dazzling cluster of symbols.

In the midst of a splendid reflection on the Book of Ruth, the contemporary Jewish novelist Cynthia Ozick probes the significance of the monotheism to which Ruth committed herself when, unlike her sister-in-law Orpah, she threw in her lot with their mother-in-law Naomi and committed herself to Naomi's God:

Who will demand of Orpah—think of the hugeness of the demand!—that she admit monotheism to the concentration and trials of her mind? Offer monotheism to almost anyone—offer it as something to take seriously—and ninety-nine times out of a hundred it will be declined, even by professing "monotheists." A Lord of History whose intent is felt, whose Commandments stand with immediacy, whose Covenant summons perpetual self-scrutiny and a continual Turning toward moral renewal, and yet *cannot, may not, be physically imagined*? A Creator neither remote and abstract like the God of the philosophers, nor palpable like the "normal" divinities, both ancient and contemporary, of both East and West? Give us (cries the nature of our race) our gods and goddesses; give us the little fertility icons with their welcoming breasts and elongated beckoning laps; give us the resplendent Virgin with her suffering brow and her arms outstretched in blessing; give us the Man on the Cross through whom to learn pity and love, and sometimes brutal exclusivity! Only give us what our eyes can see and our understanding understand: who can imagine the unimaginable? That may be for the philosophers; *they* can do it; but then they lack the imagination of the Covenant. The philosophers leave the world naked and blind and deaf and mute and relentlessly indifferent, and the village folk—who refuse a lonely cosmos without consolation—fill it and fill it and fill it with stone and wood and birds and mammals and miraculous potions and holy babes and animate carcasses and magically divine women and magically divine men: images, sights, and swallowings comprehensible to the hand, to the eye, to plain experience. For the nature of our race, God is one of the visual arts.[70]

The fight of the best Jewish theologians has been to preserve the instinct, traceable to Moses and the prophets, that God is not one of the visual arts and that the nature of our race cannot be the measure of God. God has to be beyond our measures—visual, emotional, even intellectual. God has to be allowed to be as God presents the divine nature: sovereignly free, though deeply committed to the welfare of human beings. Human beings have to suffer the fact that God is always going to be strictly mysterious: a fullness that human beings can never comprehend, let alone control. One can debate whether Torah became an infringement on this passionate Jewish instinct, a loss in the fight to preserve strict monotheism, but probably not to any good conclusion. For the weight of Jewish theological tradition has been that Torah offers guidance for how to live with the God who cannot be visualized, who must always be allowed the divine mysteriousness—guidance that divinity itself had offered as a gracious gift and kindly command. The core of some of the most significant Jewish theology lies in the intimate connection between Torah and the divine mystery—in guidance to honor above all the unimaginable Guide of Jewish existence.

Case Study: The God of Jewish Prayer.[71] Through more than 2,500 years of liturgical experience, Jews have developed the biblical notion of God. Probably the prime characteristic of the Jewish God that has emerged is his unity. As a summary of Jewish belief and prayer, the Shema has said it all: "Hear, O Israel: The Lord our God is One Lord." Thus the daily prayers of the individual Jew, as well as the communal prayers of the synagogue, have always lauded the divine unity. Nonetheless, the divine unity is not the only word in Jewish theology. The God of the Fathers has not only been One, he has also been the Creator, the revealer, and the redeemer. In his actions toward the world and his people, he has made new things, disclosed his will, again and again saved the people from dead ends.

All these motifs are manifest in the prayers that we shall describe. One should picture the community assembled in the synagogue as abuzz with these pray-

ers, since the basic form of the Orthodox liturgy has been for each person present to say such prayers aloud. That is what the basic Jewish word for prayer *(daven)* has meant: to say the liturgy aloud yet quietly and privately.

In the Jewish Prayer Book one finds praise for the One God who is King of the Universe: "Praised are you, O Lord our God, King of the Universe." This prayer then itemizes the great things the King of the Universe does. He fixes the cycles of light and darkness. He ordains the order of all creation. He is the source of the light that shines over all the earth. His mercy radiates over all the earth's inhabitants. Because he is so good, he recreates the world day by day. His manifold works reveal his great bounty. Their beauty and order reveal his great wisdom.

And what does the devout Jew ask of the King of the Universe? That he continue to love his people. He, the only One exalted from of old, the One praised and glorified since the world began, has been all Jews' shield and protection: He has been the Lord of our strength, the rock of our defense. In his infinite mercy, may he continue to love us. His goodness is for all time, so we may hope for this mercy. Daily he renews the work of creation, so daily he may be our reliance. The Psalmist knew this and sang, "Give thanks to Him who made the great lights, for His loving-kindness is everlasting." O God, make a new light to shine on Zion. Make us worthy to behold its radiance. All praise to you, O Lord, maker of the stars.

The One God is also the revealer of the Torah. The Prayer Book expresses this conviction in connection with God's compassion: Out of tender regard for his people's needs, the Lord has taught our Fathers the laws of life. For their sakes, may he continue to teach us. May we, too, learn the divine Laws, trust more and more in the divine guidance. May we observe all the precepts of the divine Law, fulfill all its teachings. If we are to do this, God must enlighten our eyes and open our hearts. He must gather together our scattered thoughts, uniting our whole beings in reverence and love. This reverence and love will keep us from shame, and help us to feel God's aid. If we trust in God's holiness, we will come safely from the corners of the earth to the dignity of our own holy land. It is you, God, who are our deliverance, you who have chosen us from all peoples and tongues. We praise and thank you for having drawn us close to you. "We praise You and thank You in truth. With love do we thankfully proclaim Your unity, and praise You who chose Your people Israel in love."

When the Prayer Book reproduces the Shema, it includes much of the Shema's original biblical gloss. Thus after expressing the call to love God with whole mind, soul, and strength, the Prayer Book reminds the people that the words of the Shema should ever be in their hearts. They should teach these words diligently to their children. They should talk about the Shema at home and abroad, day and night. The words of the Shema ought to be a sign upon the hand, or as frontlets (browbands) between the eyes. They should be inscribed on the doorposts of the home and on every gate. If the people fulfill these injunctions, they will find God favoring. He will give them rain in the autumn and rain in the spring, that their harvests may flourish. He will provide them grain, wine, and oil. Their grass will grow thick in the field for their cattle. They will have food enough to eat in contentment.

The way away from God is the way to disaster, so the people must take care not to wander after false gods. If they forsake the true God, they will find the heavens closed, unwilling to provide them rain. They will find the earth barren, unable to provide them food. Before long, there will be no good land for the people to enjoy. The good land will disappear, and with it the once good people. So all Jews should stay mindful of God's words of the Shema, keeping them in their hearts and souls. The words should sign the hand, to guide all that the hand works. They should be stamped between the eyes, to guide all that the eye sees, all that the mind conceives.

In speaking of God as redeemer, Jewish prayer spotlights his intervention on his people's behalf. God has been the king of each generation, the people's only sovereign guide. He has been the redeemer of each generation, the One to whom all Jews must go in time of need. Creator, he has been a victorious stronghold, a fort no enemy could overrun. Through his redemptive interventions, he has shown that there is no God but he.

Though God dwells in the heights of heaven, his decrees reach all of creation. The very ends of the earth stand or fall by God's Laws. Happy is the person who takes these Laws to heart, obeying the commands of God's Torah. Such a person experiences what it really means to have a Lord, a defender and mighty king. The true God is the first and the last. The true people have no king or redeemer but him.

Addressing God directly, the weekly Prayer Book prays: "You, O Lord our God, rescued us from Egypt; You redeemed us from the house of bondage." As though retreating to a favorite haunt of memory, Jewish prayer again and again goes back to the Exodus. God slew the firstborn of the Egyptians, and saved his people's firstborn. He split the waters of the Red Sea, rescuing his faithful and drowning the wicked. When the waters engulfed the enemies of Israel, not one of the arrogant remained.

God the redeemer is therefore God the powerful, God the One not to be trifled with. In the Exodus episode, Israel received its greatest lesson in redemption. Ever since, Jews have sung great hymns of thanksgiving to God. Ever since, they have extolled God with psalms of praise. For ever since they have known that the Lord their God is a mighty king, overseeing everything from his high heaven. Great and awesome, he is the source of all blessing, the ever-living divinity exalted in majesty.

As the Exodus episode revealed, the God of Israel humbles the proud and raises the lowly. He frees the captive and redeems the meek. Helping the needy and answering the people's call, he shows himself no respecter of earthly persons, a respecter only of what is right. So let all voices ring out with praise for the supreme God: Ever praised be he! As Moses and the children of Israel sang, "Who is like You, O Lord, among the mighty?" Who is like God in holiness, wonderful deeds, worthiness of praise? There is none like God, because there is only One God. The people God saved in the Exodus sensed this stunning uniqueness. They sang a chorus of praises by the sea. The Lord will reign forever. Rock of Israel, may he ever rise to his people's defense. "Our Redeemer is the Holy One of Israel." Lord of Hosts is our God's name. May the Lord be praised, the Redeemer of Israel.

Such prayer combines a remembrance of God's past deeds with a meditation on God's constant nature. Its regular accent is thankful and praising. God has made everything that exists. He has revealed his will to Israel. And he has saved Israel from its enemies. For these and all his other splendors, he deserves his people's full worship and confidence. Though king, Lord, ruler of heaven, he has deigned to concern himself with his people's needs. Though holy and righteous, he has manifested mercy and steadfast love.

When a person or a group prays in this mood, its words and images fall into an easy rhythm. One image sparks another, one memory brings another memory to mind. Phrases tend to repeat themselves, for the point is not innovation. The point is moving one's soul back to the dispositions of one's forebears in faith, who forged the canonical expressions. In their time, God was manifest in nature and was a fellow-warrior, with them against their foes. In their time, good harvests and military victories derived directly from God's hand, while bad harvests and military defeats suggested the people had faltered in their religion.

What has predominated in the Jewish liturgy, however, is the memory of God's saving deeds. In times past God has shown himself the people's redeemer. Times present and times future will reveal God to have remained faithful and true. Reviving their faith by journeying back to the biblical experiences, generations of Jews have been able to open their spirits to the God who lay ahead of them, in the mystery of the future. God has given his people a way to walk into the future with confidence. Not only has he promised he would reveal himself to Israel through time, he has given his Torah, to detail what holy living with him requires.

So Jews prayed for God's help to fulfill God's Torah. They wanted to be good, to do what was right, and they sensed that for this they needed God's help. Unless God gave them light for their minds and purity for their hearts, they would miss the path of Torah. Unless they did justice to their neighbors and worshiped God day and night, they would lose their heavenly protector. One can see how modern experiences of persecution could put this faith in God's redemptive activity to a severe test. Nonetheless, the Prayer Book has continued to promote the biblical phrases, confident that Jews of today need to worship God wholeheartedly no less than Jews of the past.

SUMMARY: THE JEWISH CENTER

The center of traditional Judaism is the Torah. That there is a law or guidance, come from God and leading to God, has been Judaism's first conviction and main treasure. With such a guidance, life is meaningful, reasonably clear. When such a guidance loses its persuasiveness, as it did for large numbers of Jews in modern times, almost all aspects of life demand rethinking. Then the zeal with which the rabbis studied Torah may shift focus to such new concerns as physical science, social justice, or simply making money. Kept under high pressure for centuries, Jewish intelligence cannot just relax and take a leisurely stroll. In old

tracks or new, it has pressed forward to set things clear, gain new knowledge, redress old wrongs. So the summons to Torah has continued to echo in the modern Jewish psyche. When a Jew marshaled intellectual or moral energy, the old summons suggested that things might subserve a higher plan, society ought to succor its widows and orphans.

To summarize the biblical portions of Torah, one speaks of the Law, the Prophets, and the Writings. The Law is historical as much as juridical, a story as much as a blueprint, and its gives Jewish faith a certain at-home-ness in the world. If God comes through time, and is the master of time's universe, then time is not samsara. True, history falls short of God's eternity, human understanding is inadequate to the divine counsels; but time itself is deeply humane. Though the sufferings that human beings inflict on one another call God's guidance of time into question, the Book of Job remains a powerful denial that human confusion or despair should be indulged. Thus Job suggests that much of the difficult trick of *feeling* time to be humane is to accept one's ignorance of time's final patterns. Then the very minutiae of the biblical and rabbinal codes can be ironic lessons in human finitude. If the greatest masters of Torah reach the grave ignorant of the total picture, the humblest lover of God may be closest to the final truth.

The prophets, biblical and later, pressed for Torah's social consequences. In their eyes, the guidance that came with the covenant asked Jews to weave bonds of justice and care. If righteousness stamped all the doings of the prophetic God, then fair measure and kind-heartedness ought to identify the devout Jewish believer. This conviction, too, was colored by traditional Jewish assumptions about time. Since the Creator's world was basically congenial, marred more by human malice than by any cracks at its core, it ought to be possible to make the human portion of creation humane and enjoyable. Were all Jews to keep the Law, remember their ancient traditions, and help their kin, things would surely go well. Did not the Sabbath give most weeks a patch of human perfection? Was not the Day of Atonement proof that new beginnings could occur? The hatred of outsiders would remain a heavy burden, but the community life itself could keep a strong halo of hope. Indeed, one righteous man might carry this hope so high that the Messiah would come to end all suffering. When the Baal Shem-Tov strode the land, the signs and portents were strong.

The Writings, both biblical and subsequent, added judicious perspectives. Turning over their wisdom literature, Jews learned that it was possible to accept the Law, admire the Prophets, and still feel weary from human vanity. Equally, it was possible to ride time like a poet, singing psalms of praise, psalms of grief, even songs of erotic love. This variety of mood, diversity of outlook, rounded out the Lord's guidance of time. What one felt for a lover, or on a day of defeat, or in vivid memory of the people's redemption from Pharaoh could take wing to the Holy One, advance yet more grounds for blessing his name. If one ascended to the highest heavens, the Holy One was a God of lights. If one fell to the lowest pit, the Holy One was an unshakable recourse. Torah therefore went beyond the borders of reason. One could believe and act far beyond what one understood.

And so the central Jewish instinct has been ethical, performative. Tongues might wag, minds work furiously, but doing has ruled the day. Words—what are they but phantoms and trial balloons? Thoughts—who can be sure they are accurate or will last? The surer coin is deeds, the more reliable religion. Do what Torah prescribes and one day you may understand your tradition. Sever yourself from the common way and surely you will find disaster. Through times of persecution without, schism within, Torah kept inviting and commanding performance. Those who went to the prayer hall, studied the texts, recited the prayers, kept the holidays, and supported the common projects were Jews in deed, members who could be relied on. The others? Well, times were hard, the flesh was weak, wisdom always was rare.

Discussion Questions

1. Why was David's kingship an ambiguous symbol?
2. What is the main theme of the history that the Hebrew Bible writes?
3. In what ways does rabbinic or talmudic religion differ from biblical religion?
4. How would you summarize the religious mentality expressed in Maimonides' thirteen articles of faith?
5. In what ways has Judaism focused more on culture than on nature?
6. Discuss the significance of celebrating a Sabbath each week.
7. Define exactly the senses in which the Jewish God is *creator* and *redeemer*.
8. Describe the faith of the prophet Jeremiah.
9. What is your impression of Jewish rituals?
10. How has the circumcision ceremony concretized Jewish faith?
11. What are the main religious questions raised by the Holocaust?
12. What has been the significance of the traditional exclusion of women from the Rabbinate and talmudic study?
13. What are the main advantages of a religion's having a clear Torah (divine guidance)?
14. What gives the story of the Baal Shem-Tov's storming heaven its charm?
15. What have been the main sources of anti-Semitism?

Glossary

aggadah: Jewish stories and teaching lore. The aggadah somewhat complements the drier, more precisely legal halakah. In the aggadah Jewish writers gave themselves imaginative license to personalize the biblical stories and draw out pious or moralistic lessons for faith in their days. Aggadah suggests the entertainment value that folk religion usually blends into its teachings, and by its vividness and storied character it made a great impact on the common people, for whom the legal treatises could seem rather abstract and remote.

Ashkenazim: Jews of German origin, who have predominated in Eastern European Jewish culture and contributed most of the founding figures of the modern state of Israel. Although many of the Ashkenazim lived in small villages and close to nature, many others entered fully into the Enlightenment streams of modern European culture as well as into commercial life. This family of Jewry suffered some cultural crisis with the rise of Nazism, because Nazism suggested that cultural sophistication was no guarantee that violent racism and anti-Semitism would not flourish.

cabala: a Jewish mystical movement that flourished during the Middle Ages. The cabalists usually considered themselves faithful followers of the Torah who were developing an esoteric wisdom to complement the esoteric wisdom of the halakic law. In their mystical writings and exercises, the cabalists emphasized the emanations of the divinity into the created world and the marriage of the divinity with the Torah, which gave religious living a nuptial or erotic aspect. Many of the rabbis worried about the gnostic possibilities latent within cabalism, but perhaps equally as many rabbis dipped into the cabalistic lore, often secretly studying such influential texts as the *Zohar.*

covenant: the semicontractual bond between Israel and YHWH, such that Israel would be his people and he would be their God. The Mosaic covenant was influenced by legal treatises of the ancient Near East by which a vassal pledged fealty to an overlord and in turn received protection. The various other biblical covenants—between God and Noah, God and David, God and Adam, and God and Christ (or the Church)—amounted to variations on this theme. Whether God was bound to the covenant regardless of human fidelity was a major question in the Hebrew Bible, while Christian faith has taken the position that the covenant, renewed and reset by the death and resurrection of Christ, is eschatological: accomplished once and for all, by God's grace.

Diaspora: a Jewish term for dispersion or exile from the homeland in Judah. Jews often lived in exile from their holy land following the Babylonian captivity or Exile of the sixth century B.C.E. After 70 C.E., however, when the Romans destroyed the Temple in Jerusalem and ousted the elite, Diaspora life became the norm. Rabbinic Judaism developed the Mishnah, the Gemara, and the Talmud in the Diaspora, the Babylonian Talmud tending to prevail over the Talmud of the land of Palestine. Zionism may be seen as the countermovement through which Judaism tried to overcome the alienations of being dispersed throughout foreign lands, and since the establishment of the modern state of Israel in 1948 the term Diaspora has had less weight, since even those Jews who lived outside Israel (in the free world) easily could visit the homeland.

exegesis: the process of elaborating the meaning of texts. Usually the term refers to biblical texts, but in principle it is applicable to the scriptures of all religions—indeed, to the elucidation of any text. As modern critical method has come to inform both historical and literary analyses of texts, exegesis has moved from rather commonsensical, mystical, and allegorical tendencies toward hermeneutics: trying to determine the meanings intended by the original authors and latent in the text as a somewhat transhistorical entity. Exegetes usually stress knowing the original language in which the text was written, informing oneself about the original historical context, and studying the symbols through which the text seems to be trying to express its assumptions, messages, hopes, and the like.

Exile: the term usually applied to the deportation of many Judeans into Babylon when Judah fell to Babylon in 586 B.C.E. This was a major divide in biblical history, everything before it qualifying as preexilic and everything after (or everything after within the pre-Common Era) qualifying as postexilic. The Exile highlighted the paradoxes of trying to give theological interpretations of history (say what were God's purposes in the Babylonian captivity, as well as the significance of autonomous rule in one's own land for the full flowering of biblical faith). Some of the most profound prophetic poetry of the Bible came from the cauldron of the Exile—parts of the present books of Isaiah, Jeremiah, and Ezekiel.

Exodus: the movement of the Hebrews out from Egypt under the leadership of Moses. This escape from the oppressive rule of the pharaoh was attributed to the intervention of YHWH and later served as the primary evidence for believing in God's will to make Israel his own special people. The Exodus so countered worldly expectations and likelihoods that it seemed a miracle. All of our accounts of it are filtered through later religious experience, so the historical core of the event is unclear, but every year Jews have celebrated the Passover as the memorial of this liberation that launched their peoplehood and the main reason they should continue to believe God would guide their lives. Christians typologized the Exodus, making it a symbol of the general liberation from sin that was accomplished through the death and resurrection of Jesus.

Gemara: comments on and discussion of the Mishnah. Gemara represents a second stage in the evolution of rabbinic Judaism, as the rabbis who gained more and more control during the Diaspora of the early centuries of the Common Era elaborated their views of the oral Law (which they thought had long accompanied the Tanak) and moved from collecting the teachings of the revered early sages (accomplished in the Mishnah) to collecting reflections, additions, and commentaries upon this first stratum of collected oral tradition.

halakah: Jewish legal tradition. The regulations, interpretations, juridical decisions, and the like that have been the backbone of rabbinic religion. Seen as continuing the priestly legislation one finds in such biblical books as Leviticus and Deuteronomy, the halakic works called for a keen memory and developed a particular sort of (religiously) legal mind. Halakah testifies to the priority that behavior or praxis has had in traditional Judaism, where people have been more interested in keeping the customary law than in developing doctrinal innovations. In modern times halakic lawyers have had to face major questions of how to adapt their tradition to a much changed culture and to face the implications of the widespread secularization of the Western cultures in which most Jews have lived.

idolatry: the worship of something less than God as ultimate reality. "Worship" implies giving one's complete loyalty and love. It implies adoration. For the monotheistic religions, the One God alone merits worship and worshiping anything other than the One God is terribly wrong. How purely monotheists in fact have lived and thought is a complicated question. In principle, however, one can see that when people have experienced God as a reality uniquely unlimited, good, and holy they are bound to feel that they can worship no other. Idolatry misleads the human spirit, and so human culture, by fixing it on things unworthy of it— money, pleasure, crude symbols of ultimacy—that are bound to distort it.

Karaism: a movement among Middle Eastern Jews of the eighth to twelfth centuries who rejected oral Torah. The movement was conservative if not puritanical, and it tried to establish the written Torah, above all the five books of Moses, as the sole authority in Jewish life. This directly attacked the power the rabbis had been accumulating, which was based on the legitimacy of claiming that an oral tradition had always accompanied the written Torah. As keepers (interpreters, developers) of this oral tradition, the rabbis claimed the power to legislate how the community ought to eat and drink, marry, and do business. The Karaites wanted greater freedom from this rabbinic authority, but mainly so as to impose their own more literalist sense that God's will was more concisely and clearly laid out in the written Torah.

kibbutz: a collective, often agricultural, settlement in Israel. The kibbutz movement usually partook of both an attachment to the land (Zionism as nostalgia for the promised land) and socialist convictions about how people would best prosper (spiritually, if not materially) by living in cooperatives, sharing child rearing and manual labor, and creating a community life that treasured learning, the arts, and other aspects of higher culture. Some of the kibbutzim were religious, but many were not. On the religious kibbutzim, ortho-

dox or even fundamentalist views tended to prevail, one of the customary ideas being that when the Torah was fully observed in the ancestral land Jews would have the best possible chance to realize the potential of their chosenness.

kosher: fit, proper, suitable according to Jewish law. Kosher especially applied to dietary matters, but more broadly regarded actions, ideas, and moral habits that were considered consonant with the Torah. The dietary laws appear to have developed from a combination of ancient ideas about what was hygienic (apt to promote health and discourage disease) and what was fitting or normal in nature itself—for example, separating dairy and meat foods. Kosher observance became a badge of Jewishness in many periods, serving to demarcate Jews from gentiles and helping to preserve the purity of the chosen people. Probably more Jews kept the laws for this reason than out of any strong sense that certain foods were intrinsically unclean or that God from all eternity had wanted housewives to need two sets of dishes.

Messiah: the anointed king that Jews have awaited as their deliverer since the late biblical era. The present scholarly consensus is that the prophetic allusions to the Messiah had in mind an earthly leader on the model of David and did not foresee Jesus Christ, but any such judgment entails theological preconceptions about the nature of the Bible. For Christians many of the messianic passages seemed fulfilled in the life, death, and resurrection of Jesus, especially the songs of Second Isaiah about the suffering servant of YHWH. Jews probably thought of this figure as a corporate personality, standing for Israel as a whole, but Christians understandably found the passages anticipatory of what happened to Jesus. Thus, in their polemics with Jews, the early Christians argued typologically, trying to show that what had been prophesied about the Messiah had been fulfilled. The Gospels are strongly colored by this way of thinking, especially the Gospel of Matthew.

mikvah: the Jewish ritual bath. Visiting the *mikvah* became one of several Jewish rites of cleansing and purification, complementary to the kosher laws and the laws for observing the Sabbath. Women had the obligation to visit the *mikvah* at the end of their menstrual period, to help divide the times when sexual intercourse was illicit and licit. Men tended to visit the *mikvah* at times of the religious calendar when purification was encouraged. Although Judaism did not develop so strong a notion of human sinfulness as what developed in some branches of Christianity, it retained from its biblical lawyers the sense that one was to approach God with clean hands and a clean heart. The ritual bath, then, was more symbolic than physical (although in ancient and medieval times the physical washing could be culturally distinctive), the main idea being a spiritual renewal.

minyan: the quorum of ten needed for Jewish worship. Traditionally the ten had to be men, but recently some branches of Judaism have allowed women to be counted. The ten would be sought both for daily worship or study in the synagogue and for such memorial prayer sessions as sitting shivah for a person recently deceased. The minyan had the effect of specifying the social character of Jewish study and prayer, since official worship had a minimal number and a few scattered individuals would not suffice.

Mishnah: the collection of Jewish learning formalized by rabbis in the Diaspora around 200 C.E. The Mishnah was the first compilation of the oral tradition that had been building since the Second Temple period, and it became the core of the Talmud. The Gemara, which collected commentaries on the Mishnah, plus the Mishnah itself, yielded the Talmud. The interest of the mishnaic teachers was relatively practical, as they divided Jewish reality into different tractates and discoursed on how relationships ideally would be. For example, in the tractate on women they discussed especially the transitions that ought to occur when a woman passed from her father to her husband at marriage or when she passed from marriage to widowhood.

mitzvah: a Jewish commandment; a scriptural or rabbinic injunction. A mitzvah also could take on the connotation of a good deed—something commanded or required because it would bring good. In the Jewish community one struggled to become full of good deeds, not only by obeying the 613 commandments (for men) but also by helping the poor, feeding the hungry, teaching the ignorant, and the like.

monotheism: holding for only one God, who becomes the ultimate source, goal, and treasure of creation. Pure monotheisms are hard to find, but certain strands of biblical religion seem motivated by a genuine insight into the Oneness of a truly transcendent God, as does much of the Qur'an. The experience underlying monotheism is bound to be ineffable, and most monotheisms suffer when cast into doctrinal form, because the doctrines tend to ossify and suggest

that one can map the sole deity comprehensively. Thus the mystical dimensions of the monotheisms have the constant task of calling adherents back to the wellsprings, while the metaphysical dimensions have the constant task of reminding people that the being of a truly monotheistic deity has to be of another order than anything people can grasp—indeed, that it has to be the creator of everything else from nothingness. Judaism, Christianity, and Islam all claim to be monotheistic, and in their high traditions no doubt have been. But in their little traditions, where saints and sprites have frolicked, they have been closer to the supposedly polytheistic traditions (Hinduism, Shinto) than many of their theologians have admitted.

Pharisees: Jews of the late Second Temple period who defended the oral Torah and tried to update it. The Pharisaic party triumphed after the Diaspora of the first century C.E., making them a fairly direct link to the rabbinic religion that generated the Talmud and dominated Judaism in the common era. The Pharisees usually are described as a lay group, much concerned for fidelity to the precepts of the Torah, and somewhat distant from the Temple that was the center of priestly, ritualistic Judaism. The portrait of the Pharisees in the New Testament is colored by Jewish-Christian polemics and cannot be considered objective in its charges of hypocrisy.

prophet: a spokesperson for God or a divinity. The prophet is one who delivers the divine message, sometimes quite unwillingly. For the classical biblical prophets, the divine message (Word) came as an inrush of understanding and will they could not avoid, much though they might have wished to. Prophets in other contexts deliver oracles at local shrines or speak to the people about the fate they feel is soon to arrive. Muhammad, for instance, preached a coming judgment, as had Zoroaster, John the Baptist, Isaiah, and Jesus. Popularly, prophets have been pictured as able to foretell the future, but usually the sharper import of their message has been a judgment on present times as being out of kilter with divine ethical standards.

rabbi: a Jewish title for teacher or master, most often applied to those who focused on the oral Law. The rabbinic movement shows ties to the priestly circles that were involved in the formulation of biblical law, and during the Second Temple period, after the return from Exile, the focus of much Jewish piety seems to have shifted from ritual to Law and wisdom. Torah exfoliated as the precepts whose following allowed one to keep the covenant well, and the rabbis became revered as the teachers of what would keep the chosen people worthy of their special election. They became the arbiters of how to interpret the Law, adjusting it to varying cases, and from their decisions, obiter dicta, and stories came the talmudic literature that has been the backbone of Judaism in the common era.

sabbath: a day set aside for worship; the Jewish day of worship. The origins of the tradition of making a sabbath are obscure, but biblical Judaism correlated its sabbatical traditions with the account of creation in Genesis, encoding the notion of a seventh day of rest in the foundations of the cosmos. Keeping a sabbath means maintaining a fence against this-worldly preoccupations, and so it may be seen as a line of sacrality delimiting secularity. By insisting that work is not all, and that worship, play, and recreation have their rights, traditional peoples have kept supple the imagination, feelings, and muscles necessary to fit human beings to the rhythms of nature and defend them against both overwork and a loss of wonder.

Sadducees: an ancient Jewish party of priests and upper-class members who were associated with the Jerusalem Temple and stressed the written Torah. Their main opponents for influence during the Second Temple period were the Pharisees, who were mainly laity and approved the oral Torah that explicated the scriptures. The Sadducees disappeared after the fall of the Jerusalem Temple in 70 C.E. They are presented in the New Testament as denying the notion of a resurrection and agreeing with the Roman establishment that Jesus was a threat to security in Judea.

Sephardim: Jews of Hispanic or Iberian cultural background. The Sephardim established a glorious civilization in medieval Iberia, and the expulsion of the Jews from Spain in 1492 was a trauma so great it led many cabalists to expect the coming of the Messiah. The Sephardim suffered greatly from the Inquisition, and after their expulsion from Spain many went into the Turkish Empire, which they hoped would be more benign than the Christian. Sephardim often are contrasted with Ashkenazim, who adapted Jewish culture to a Germanic and Eastern European subsoil. The two families shared most articles of faith, holidays, and law codes, but their different cultural complexes colored everything somewhat differently.

Shema: the Jewish proclamation of God's unity based on Deuteronomy 6:4–9. The Shema has served as an epitome of Jewish faith, reminding believers that they are covenanted to the unique deity responsible for the creation of the world and the guidance of history. Their relation to this God ought to be one of wholehearted love, and they have the obligation to make this God the focus of the education they give their children, the culture they develop, and all the distinctive features of their community life. The Shema could stand in contrast to the many laws of the rabbis' Torah, but usually it was considered their digest and pulse. The call to "hear" implied listening, to the divine or prophetic or rabbinic word. It also implied obedience and loyalty, as well as a regular effort to remember the great things God had done for his chosen people, especially the victory of the Exodus and the gift of the promised land.

synagogue: a Jewish house of assembly, study, and prayer. The term, like the Christian term *church,* implies both a building and a congregation. The historical origins of the synagogue are not fully known, but it seems likely that after the destruction of the Temple of Solomon and the deportation of many Jews to Babylon in the sixth century B.C.E., the custom of gathering for common study and prayer gained momentum. The synagogue rather naturally gave rise to the rabbinic movement, in that it emphasized study of the tradition, focused in the Torah, more than ritualistic sacrifice. Following the Diaspora of 70 C.E., the synagogue became the major Jewish institution, although archaeological remains suggest that synagogues varied considerably in their architecture and their degree of involvement in the movement that led to the Mishnah, the Talmud, and the rabbinic hegemony over Judaism.

Talmud: the primary source of Jewish law and focus of rabbinic learning, composed of the Mishnah and the Gemara. The Talmud was probably virtually complete around 500 C.E. and existed in at least two important versions, that from Babylon and that from Palestine. It collected teachings, opinions, and decisions of rabbis concerned with continuing the tradition of the oral law—the ongoing interpretation of the Mosaic Torah. As talmudic scholarship grew throughout the Middle Ages, the talmudic texts became an encyclopedia of Jewish learning—science, linguistics, and theology, in addition to halakic theory. A traditional Jewish education was based on the Talmud, and it inculcated a good memory, a concern for legal precedent, a willingness to weigh authorities against one another, and a realization that interpretation was intrinsic to the Jewish experiences of both scripture and God. Modernist Jews challenged talmudic authority, but to the present day the Talmud continues to be a conduit of ongoing Jewish religious development. Partly because of the variety of opinions enfolded in the Talmud, Judaism has tended to sponsor considerable doctrinal freedom and to consider behavior a more crucial index of faith than theology.

Torah: Jewish Guidance, Revelation, or Law. The Torah came from God, most inaugurally to Moses. It was developed by successors of Moses, reaching the literary form of Tanak: Torah (Pentateuch), Prophets, and Writings. The rabbis insisted that an oral Torah had always accompanied the written Torah—tradition to interpret the scriptures. The Talmud codified many of the rabbinic opinions, and after the Talmud further rabbinic writings amplified the teachings of the Talmud. Thus Torah is a fluid concept, having stricter and broader denotations. Some rabbinic speculation thought of the Torah as eternal, having existed alongside God when he created and being something God himself loved to contemplate. Thus the study of Torah became the centerpiece of rabbinic Judaism, sometimes even more important than prayer.

Zionism: the Jewish movement to establish a homeland in Palestine. Zionism has biblical roots, from the time that Israel gained a land of its own centered on Mount Zion in Jerusalem. During the Exile Jews longed to be back in their promised land, where they alone could sing their native songs joyously. The Dia-spora that occurred in the first century C.E. made nostalgia for Zion and the Western Wall that symbolized the Temple ingredient in all Jewish culture. During the nineteenth century Jews led by Theodor Herzl (1860–1904) began practical movements to resettle Palestine, which came to climax in the establishment of the modern state of Israel in 1948. The aftermath of the Second World War, and the sufferings that Jews had endured in the Holocaust (as the climax of centuries of anti-Semitism in Europe) had made conditions ripe. Recently bitter discussions have arisen about Zionist ideology, while the ties between Zionism and such doctrines as chosenness and the gift of the promised land continue to beg clarification.

Zohar: a prime text of Jewish cabalism. The *Zohar* probably was written by Moses de León in thirteenth-century Spain. Known as the "Book of Splendor," it consists of imaginative contemplations of the emanations of the divinity through the different layers of creation. The *Zohar* stimulated many mystics, Hasidim, and even orthodox rabbis to view creation as shot through with sparks of the divine seeking to return to God in redemption. It supported the notion that God is metaphysically married to the Torah and that the splendor of God *(Shekina)* is a nuptial entity that sets sexual complementarity and love at the center of the heavenly realities.

CHAPTER 9

CHRISTIANITY

Cross of Christ

If we gather all its parts, Christianity is the largest religion in the world. What began as a Jewish sect has carried its version of the Torah and prophecy around the globe.[1] We begin our study of Christianity by describing its history.

HISTORY

Jesus

Christianity developed from the life and work of Jesus of Nazareth,[2] as Buddhism developed from the life and work of Gautama. Jesus (whose historical reality is attested to by such non-Christian authors as Josephus, Tacitus, Suetonius, and Pliny the Younger) was born about 4 B.C.E. (by current calendars) in Palestine. It is likely that "Jehsus," a Greek form, derives from the Hebrew "Yeshua," which means "savior." We know little about his youth except through Gospel stories, such as those of his circumcision and his dialogues with religious teachers. (The stories of his birth are probably legendary, in the service of the various New Testament authors' theologies.[3]) One may assume that

ca. 30 C.E.	*Death of Jesus of Nazareth*
ca. 65	*Death of Apostle Paul*
ca. 95	*Last of New Testament Writings*
ca. 100–165	*Justin Martyr, Leading Apologist*
ca. 185–254	*Origen, Leading Theologian*
313	*Christians Freed of Legal Persecution*
325	*First Council of Nicaea*
354–430	*Augustine, Leading Theologian*
451	*Council of Chalcedon*
ca. 480–550	*Benedict, Founder of Western Monasticism*
ca. 540–604	*Pope Gregory I, Founder of Medieval Papacy*
787	*Second Council of Nicaea (Last One That the Orthodox Church Considers Ecumenical)*
869–870	*Rome Declares Photius in Schism*
1054	*Mutual Anathemas between Rome and Constantinople*
1096–1099	*First Crusade*
1225–1274	*Thomas Aquinas, Leading Theologian*
1369–1415	*John Hus, Bohemian Reformer*
1517	*Luther's Ninety-five Theses*
1509–1564	*John Calvin, Leading Theologian*
1545–1563	*Council of Trent*
1620	*Mayflower Compact of the Pilgrims*
1703–1791	*John Wesley, Founder of Methodism*
1869–1870	*First Vatican Council*
1910	*Beginning of Protestant Ecumenical Movement*
1962–1965	*Second Vatican Council*

he grew up as a Jewish youth of his times. About the year 27 C.E. he started from his native Galilee on a career as an itinerant preacher. Geza Vermes has described the contemporary political and religious context, suggesting that Jesus was a preacher and healer on the model of the Jewish *hasid* (pious one) familiar to his time and locale.[4]

While Jesus' message has been interpreted in very different ways, certain essentials seem quite clear. Joachim Jeremias's careful study argues that Jesus' own voice echoes in the New Testament parables, riddles, discussions of the reign of God, the peculiar use of *amen,* and the peculiar use of *Abba* (Father) for God.[5] On etymological and historical grounds, these are the safest leads to how Jesus himself preached (with concrete, lively language) and to what he had to say (that a new time was dawning and that God is intimately parental). In their admirable digest of Christian theology, Rahner and Vorgrimler state that Jesus' main theme was an announcement that the reign of God was at hand in his (Jesus') own person.[6] That reign or kingdom was a new beginning, a time of justice and holiness.

According to the New Testament writers, this theme meant that Jesus had fulfilled Jewish religion and superseded it, making a new covenant with God. Jesus himself solicited a radical commitment to the

KEY CHRISTIAN DOCTRINES	
Trinity	God as a community of knowing and loving Father (unbegotten), Son (begotten), Spirit (breath of divine love)
Christology	Jesus one integral being, fully human and fully divine
Grace	Communication of divine life Strength to overcome sin Divine favor and forgiveness
Sin	Freely chosen evil Absence of divine life
Church	Body of Christ Community of disciples
Eschatology	Divine judgment Heaven and hell
Scripture	Word of God Norm for Church

new opportunities that God's reign offered, which included intimacy with God and friendship with other people. The morality that Jesus anticipated in the kingdom[7] is most graphic in his Sermon on the Mount. There the evangelists have him bless those who are poor, gentle, mourning, hungry, and thirsty for what is right, merciful, pure in heart, peacemaking, and suffering for the cause of justice. They are the citizens of the kingdom; dispositions or circumstances like theirs render human beings open to divine love. The gist of Jesus' own life, according to the New Testament, was just such love.

Information on Jesus' public life and ministry remains imprecise (because of the limited sources). Apparently he linked his work with that of John the Baptist, his message raised opposition from the religious establishment, he worked out only some of the particulars for living in the kingdom, and he predicted woe to those who rejected his program. Furthermore, he planted at least the seeds of the Christian Church by gathering disciples and co-workers, and he gained a reputation as a healer. His death

came by order of the Roman procurator Pontius Pilate on the dubious grounds that he threatened the peace.

Interpretations. Beyond this bare outline, historical and theological interpretations diverge. Indeed, all of the Gospels are theological interpretations of Jesus, developed in the light of at least a generation's worth of the Christian community's experience of faith, of controversies with Jews who did not accept Jesus as the Messiah, and of efforts to explain the significance of Jesus to gentiles. According to the New Testament and the orthodox faith of later centuries, the old reign of Satan and sin died with Jesus. Furthermore, after death Jesus was raised (**resurrected**) and was disclosed to be "Lord" or ruler of humanity. More tersely, Jesus was the divine Son whose dying and rising brought the world *salvation.* The traditional interpretation thus stresses a twofold quality in Jesus: He was both human and divine. The church councils that specifically discussed and defined Jesus' being found this interpretation to be the intent of the Gospel and Epistle writers, who in turn considered themselves interpreters of the Hebrew Bible.

Another interpretation of Jesus found in the New Testament is that he was the Messiah—the anointed king of the age of grace which Judaism had long been anticipating, where *grace* came to mean not just peace and material plenty but intimacy with God and sharing in divine life. From the titles that the New Testament gives to Jesus, his own reported claims, and the miracles (healings, raisings from the dead, and so on) that the New Testament attributes to Jesus, we can conclude that the New Testament writers found him most remarkable—so remarkable that he had to be more than human. For them he was the bringer of salvation, God's Word incarnate, the Christ (Messiah), and the divine Son.

The New Testament was shaped considerably by the traumatic break of the Jews who accepted Jesus as the Messiah with the synagogue that rejected him. All the gospels are at pains to show Jesus fulfilling Messianic expectations and justifying Christians' commitments to him; those who reject Jesus are deemed people of bad faith. This judgment of the New Testament writers has colored Jewish-Christian relations for more than 1900 years.[8]

In the earliest portions of the New Testament, the Pauline Epistles, Jesus is a living spiritual reality. The assumption behind Paul's directions for Church life, for instance, is that "the Lord" lives in Christians' midst. After Jesus' death, his followers apparently thought that his movement was finished, but the events of the resurrection convinced them that he had assumed a new form of existence. They stayed together in Jerusalem; at Pentecost (fifty days after Passover, when Jesus had died), they experienced what they called the Holy Spirit, whom they thought Jesus and the Father had sent. The Spirit charged them to go out and preach about Jesus. Thus, the early Christians proclaimed that Jesus' life and death were the definitive act of salvation. The disciples also preached that Jesus was the Messiah. As such he was in accordance with Jewish tradition and yet responsible for its transformation. From a historical perspective, then, the first Christians appear as sectarian Jews—Jews with a new interpretation of messianism. The early Christians thought of themselves as the new Israel because they thought that Jesus had brought, and the old Israel had rejected, the kingdom of God sought by Jewish messianic expectation.

It took some time for the first interpretations of Jesus to sift out and clarify, and a principal catalyst in that process was Paul. From the accounts in Acts and his own writings, Paul was a Pharisaic Jew whose conversion on the road to Damascus (Acts 9:3–9) was quite dramatic. After his conversion he tried to show his fellow Jews that Jesus was their Messiah, but their opposition to his preaching, plus his own further reflection on Jesus' life and death, led Paul to think that in Jesus God had opened the covenant to all people—gentiles as well as Jews.

Consequently, Paul made the *gospel* (good news) about Jesus a transformation of the Torah. Because God had fulfilled in Jesus the intent of the Law, the Law's many detailed prescriptions were passé. Adherence to an external code could not make one righteous (acceptable to God). Only by opening to God's love and healing could one stand before him acceptably. Paul called that opening "faith." For him, Jesus was the agent of a shift from the Torah to the gospel, from works to faith. The way to become right with God was to commit oneself to Jesus. Thus, for Paul, Jesus himself represented the kingdom, embodied God's grace. As Paul's vision spread, he saw Jesus' transition from death to life as the climax of salvation history. Jesus the Christ was a new Adam, a new beginning for the human race. All who clung to him, who used him to interpret their lives, became members of his "body." Christ and the Church formed a living entity.

Paul's interpretation of Jesus was the key to early Christianity's developing into a universal religion. By dropping the requirements of the Jewish Law and extending membership to all who would base their lives on Jesus, the early Church broke with Judaism irreparably. In the beginning some followers of Jesus ("Judaizers") had urged keeping the precepts of the Jewish Torah, but they lost out. The Torah had been the cornerstone of covenantal life. Most Jews, understandably, were not willing to throw the Torah over or enter a new covenant. Some who had seen Jesus heal or heard him preach joined his cause; the apostles who began the church after Jesus' death, for instance, were Jews who journeyed from the Torah to the gospel. However, most Jews had not heard or seen Jesus, and for historical, psychological, political, and religious reasons they could not accept the claims about him.

The gentiles who warmed to the gospel lived in a Hellenistic milieu that was ripe for salvation.[9] Just as Judaism was in turmoil, with Zealots, Pharisees, Sadducees, and Essenes all urging different reactions to Roman rule, so, too, were the belief systems of the gentiles. Through the mystery religions, Gnosticism, and philosophy, a large number of gentiles were pursuing salvation avidly. Jesus as a savior figure fit many of their needs. In a short while, Christianity established itself as a new wisdom, or *gnosis* (secret knowledge), too. It offered fulfillment in this life, immortality in a world to come.

A New World View.   As a result of the gospel and Paul's theology, within a generation of Jesus' death Jewish and Greek thought had combined into a powerful new world view.[10] From Judaism came the concepts of prophet and messiah. From Hellenism came the notions of savior and god. In the Church's hands, they all were considerably developed. Jesus was the successor to Moses, the giver of a new Law, Daniel's Son of man come to inaugurate the messianic age, the conqueror of death and disorder, and the *Logos* (Word) of eternal divinity come into time. He was alpha and omega—the beginning and the end. All past history, from the first parent Adam, had been but a preparation for his coming. All of the future would unfold his implications, climaxing in a final judgment and a fulfillment in heaven.

At first the Christians expected the future to be short. Jesus would soon return in power and glory to consummate his work. As the years went by, the beliefs shifted. Jesus had accomplished the essentials of salvation through his death and resurrection. However long it took in God's dispensation for Jesus' salvation to work itself out, there was no doubt of the final success. The faithful would just have to endure. Living in faith and hope, they were to preach the good news to all whom they could reach.

Case Study: Jesus' Parables.   One of the main reasons Jesus has remained fresh for each generation of his followers is that the New Testament authors set down some of Jesus' lively teaching stories, his parables. Puzzling, enigmatic, and vivid, these parables have drawn the attention of preachers and audiences through all the Christian centuries. Today the parables have become a favorite topic of scholarly discussion. We can only hint at the main lines of this discussion, but studying one of Jesus' parables, that of the Great Supper (Matt. 22:1–10; Luke 14:16–24), will take us a few steps into what New Testament scholars are currently conjecturing about Jesus' own outlook.

As a background to our consideration of the parable of the Great Supper, let us first note the tendency of current New Testament scholars to emphasize the parables' underlying conviction of God's oneness. Believing in their bones that God was an absolute mys-

tery, the sole power responsible for all of creation, the authors of the parables (Jesus and the writers who set them in their New Testament form) instinctively used a paradoxical speech, through which they might hint at God's transcendence—God's overspilling of all human conceptual containers. The parables imply that God cannot be captured in any single set of images. The best way to indicate the divine nature is to juxtapose stories that flash forth now one, now another aspect of what God seems to be like.

Moreover, some of Jesus' parables opposed the assumption of some of his contemporaries that the only way righteous people could experience the rule of God would be through a dramatic, even cosmic, overturning of the prevailing political patterns, so that the sinners presently in charge would be thrown out. Not so, Jesus' preaching suggested. God does not need earthquakes or revolutions. The reign of God is subtler, and more powerful, than any prevailing political or religious conditions. No matter how bad the times, one could always find something of God in them.

For Jesus, God was always active, always reaching out to people in need. It required no more than common human experience to find the arena of God's actions. There was no need for aggression or technical training. "Even Jesus' way of speaking is nonaggressive and avoids setting up barriers between people. But this way of speaking has a powerful edge; the forgiveness and reconciliation imaged is demanded for everyone's life. The holiness appropriate to the rule of God belongs to all."[11]

Applied to Jesus' liking for parables, this attitude meant a calm "take it or leave it." A parable was an invitation to enter the world of Jesus' Father, to open oneself to Jesus' sense of what God was doing. It was not an oppressive command. The parable of the Great Supper suggests that one could meet Jesus and not even realize that this was the most important encounter of one's life. Jesus would not beat his hearers over the head. God would not flash forth lightning or bellow thunder. The Kingdom of God was in people's midst. To find it they had only to turn around and open themselves to Jesus' good news.

The parable itself tells of a man (or a king) who once gave a great banquet. Deciding to throw this feast, he sent his servants to announce it to those he wanted to invite. The servants told the invitees, "Come, for all is now ready." But the invitees began to make excuses. Not sensing the significance of the invitation, they told the servants such lame tales as "I have bought a field and I must go take a look at it," or "I have bought five yoke of oxen, and I must go examine them," or "I have just gotten married, so I cannot come." (However, Deuteronomy 20:5–7 and 24:5 suggest that these may traditionally have been considered legitimate excuses.) In each case, they asked to be excused.

The man hosting the banquet got very angry. In Matthew's version, the invitees had treated the man's servants shamefully, even killing them, so the man (who was a king) sent his troops to destroy the murderers and burn their city. In Luke's milder account, the host simply told his servants to go out into the streets and lanes of the city and bring in the most wretched people they could find: the poor, the maimed, the blind, and the lame. When the servants came back to report that they had done this and that there still was room in the banquet hall, the host told them to go out again, this time into the highways and hedges, and make people come in, until the banquet hall was completely full. Those whom he had first invited had shown themselves unworthy of the banquet, but one way or another he would have his house filled.

For Matthew, the story is an occasion to indulge in a bit of allegory. By playing up the theme of the king's punishment of the invitees' bad treatment of the servants, he can allude to the Roman destruction of Jerusalem in 70 C.E., which perhaps he saw as a retribution for the slaying of Jesus. Luke, on the other hand, presents a simpler plot line, and he is more interested in the redoubling of the host's invitation than in any rejection and punishment. Where Matthew makes an irreparable break between the king and the original guests, Luke passes over this relation, allowing the possibility that it might mend. Accenting the good fortune of the new invitees, he stresses that they are an unlikely group, outcasts and strangers. For Luke, the drama lies in the host's seizing the occasion of the original invitees' (the Jews') refusal or inability to come and making it a chance to be generous to another class of people. Thus, when most Jews rejected Jesus' message, God offered the gospel to the gentiles. In the background of the New Testament's use of the parable is the bitterness between Jews who had accepted Jesus (become Christians) and those who had rejected him.

Although they tend to stress the literary structure of the evangelists' different accounts, today's scholars do not neglect the historical or theological dimensions of the parables. For example, they point out that Jewish lore contemporary with Jesus had a story that praised a tax collector for doing one good deed during his (otherwise hateful) life: inviting some poor people to a banquet when the original guests did not come. Similarly, research into the social customs of Jesus' day has revealed a tendency in sophisticated Jewish circles to invite people twice. Important people, at least, did not take seriously a single invitation but had to have their egos stroked a second time. One of the rabbis used a person dressed and ready to go by the time of a second invitation as an example of wisdom, while a person not ready to go by the time of a second invitation, and so excluded from the good time, became an example of foolishness.

Moreover, by choosing the figure of a banquet, both Jesus and the gospel writers inevitably conjured up the messianic time. In the messianic time, when Israel's deliverer had come, Jewish tradition said the people would eat and drink joyously, banqueting together. It may be stretching the original intent of the parable to make it a full symbol of the messianic or heavenly time, as later Christian preachers often have, but the figure itself was bound to suggest inclusion in the occasion of celebrating God's victory or exclusion from it. If one stresses the confrontational side of the invitation and rejection, as Matthew does, one develops a rather harsh, judgmental view of Jesus' messiahship and the invitation to join the Christian community. The understated version of Luke simply hints at what a human situation—a generous host's disappointment that the people he first invited could not come—can reveal about God's ingenuity and goodness. Undaunted, the host finds new outlets for his largess.

Behind Matthew's harsher version probably lie the bitter experiences of the early Christian missionaries, who were confused and hurt that their proclamation of Jesus' good news brought them persecution rather than gratitude. However, this harsh attitude seems to contradict Jesus' own tendencies, which were to keep contact with people, avoid unnecessary ruptures, and find creative alternatives to strategies that had run into dead ends. Behind Jesus' own mission there seems to have lain a rather constant goodwill. If the members of the establishment were not interested in his message, there were always the crowds on society's margins. If the Jews proved intractable, there were always the Samaritans and the gentiles. Jesus may not have worked all this out into an explicit theology of his mission, but it seems latent in his regular style. For all that he seems to have been disappointed by the stupidity and hardness of heart he encountered, he kept speaking provocatively of the Kingdom of God, always hoping he would come upon a few people whom God's Spirit had prepared to accept his words.

In Luke's version of the parable, the social implications of the gospel also are important. It is no accident that the outcasts come into the banquet hall. Luke sees the good news of the Kingdom as especially intended for those people who have little other good news in their lives: the poor, the sick, the despised. At the least, his parable implies, those who have received much from God should share it generously with people less fortunate. The host who insists that his banquet not go to waste should be a role model for Christians.

In recent years, excavations at Nag-Hammadi in Egypt have made available to New Testament scholars gnostic versions of the gospel (see below) that they can compare with the canonical four *Gospels*. The Gospel of Thomas, for example, has a version of the parable of the Great Supper that is quite spare, more like Luke's than Matthew's account. Interestingly, however, the Gospel of Thomas makes several of the original invitees excuse themselves for monetary reasons. Thus one man has some merchants coming the evening of the banquet to pay him money they owe, while another man has bought some property and must go to collect the rent. When the host hears these excuses, he tells his servants to go into the streets and bring back whomever they find. The conclusion of the story is ominous: "The buyers and the merchants shall not come into the places of my Father." Not only does this conclusion make Jesus pass stern judgment on those who reject the invitation, it also castigates business (and by implication all this-worldly affairs) as incompatible with the Kingdom of Heaven.

Overall, the parables remain an absorbing topic for study. Because they stand so close to Jesus' own way of thinking and preaching, they offer some of the best keys to Jesus' intriguing personality. But the parables seldom admit of a clear-cut interpretation, any more than Jesus' other teachings or actions do. They contain so many different levels, possible allusions, and strata of metaphors that one is finally forced to leave off analyzing them and let them make a more synthetic, holistic impact. When one does this, it seems clear that Jesus, like many Eastern gurus, was a man filled with lively speech, because he was a man filled with God's presence, pregnant with God's love.

The Word of God had burned so deeply into his soul that all his human words sizzled and warmed.

The Early Centuries

The gospel writers—Mark, Matthew, Luke, and John—all interpreted the life of Jesus.[12] Even in the most journalistic portions of the New Testament, they have cast Jesus' sayings and doings in terms of their own theologies. Matthew, for instance, works largely with Jewish notions, trying to show that Jesus is the successor to Moses, the gospel is the successor to the Torah, and so on. The other Gospels, as well as the Epistle to the Hebrews and the Book of Revelation, are similarly theological. John arranges Jesus' public life around a series of signs giving him a sacramental glow and making him a thaumaturgist (wonder worker). The second half of John's Gospel concentrates on Jesus' "glory": his intimacy with the heavenly Father and his victorious death and resurrection. Hebrews tries to show that Jesus fulfilled Jewish types of sacrifice, while Revelation is a Christian *apocalypse* (disclosure) designed to shore up faith against Roman persecution.

By the end of the first century, then, the Church had a variety of theologies. The majority were extensions of Jewish religion in the light of Jesus as the Messiah. The "apostolic age" is the period that elaborated what Jesus meant and how the Church was to organize itself. It embraces roughly the period from the death of Jesus (ca. 30 C.E.) to the last decades of the first century. A central concern in both those years and the next centuries was authority. For the early Church, an *apostolos* was a person to whom God had delegated Church authority. The term depended on the Jewish notion of *saliah*—a Hebrew legal term that meant "the authoritative representation of an individual or group in juridical or legal matters."[13]

During Jesus' ministry, his twelve intimates were the *apostles* par excellence, since they had received their commission from Jesus himself. Clearly the Twelve formed a collegial group with Peter as their head,[14] and the Church accepted their authority. However, balancing this apostolic, "official" authority was a looser, *charismatic* leadership expressed through prophecy, teaching, speaking in tongues, and so on.

The earliest Church preaching was intended to show that Jesus fulfilled the promises of Jewish scripture. In their teaching, the first apostles relied on oral tradition about Jesus' person and words. The first great problem in the apostolic age, as we saw, was the Pauline (pertaining to Paul) problem of opening the Church to the gentiles.

During the second century the leadership of the Church passed from those who had seen Jesus themselves to those who had received the gospel from eyewitnesses but had not themselves known the Lord. The "Fathers" who led the second-century Church are therefore apostolic in the sense that they had direct contact with the Twelve. One of the apostolic fathers was Clement of Rome, whom tradition calls the successor to Peter as leader of the Christian community in Rome. Clement wrote an epistle in the style of Paul that called for Church unity. Another early Father, Hermas, wrote a pastoral piece that called for tight moral discipline. Ignatius of Antioch wrote several letters about keeping faith in the face of martyrdom. These three apostolic writers and other writers from the early second century[15] reveal something of the young Church's internal and external problems. Internally, keeping discipline was obviously a major difficulty. As Christ's return was delayed, human weaknesses and individualism asserted themselves. Externally, from the time of Nero (54–68) the Church was ever liable to persecution by the Roman authorities.

A celebrated non-Christian source describing the situation early in the second century is a letter written by the Roman Pliny the Younger, governor of Bithynia south of the Black Sea, to the emperor Trajan about 112. Romans had executed some Christians (their faith seemed incompatible with the pledge of loyalty to Caesar that Rome required), and Pliny described the Christians' religious activities, to give the emperor the information necessary to ascertain what sort of a threat they really were. According to the letter, the Christians would gather before dawn one day a week, sing hymns to a certain "Chrestus" whom they treated as a god, and take an oath to abstain from crime. Then they would end their meeting with a common meal. Trajan answered that if other Christians would recant and "worship our gods," Pliny might pardon them. Clearly the Roman authorities of the time worried about secret societies that might sow seeds of revolution. Since the Romans looked on religion as the bond of their realm, they were especially sensitive to groups who did not worship the traditional Roman deities.

Christians expanded throughout the Roman Empire during the second and third centuries. By 300 they probably constituted the majority population in Asia Minor and Carthage, and they were at least a noticeable fraction of the population along the northern shore of the Mediterranean. Their major political problem, gaining sufferance from the Roman authorities, was not solved until Constantine came to power early in the fourth century.

Gnosticism. More potentially destructive than Rome were the gnostic heresies. Their teachings varied considerably, but their common element was heterodox Judaism under the influence of Hellenistic and Iranian thought. In essence most *Gnosticism* involved a dualistic mythology. Matter, the negative principle, came from a Demiurge—a subordinate divinity whom the Father God begot as Wisdom but who fell from grace. Divinity itself was a *pleroma* (fullness) of times and levels. Gnosticism offered a revelation to certain "elect" persons: If they would hate this lower world of material creation (which was under the fallen Demiurge) and believe in a higher spiritual and divine realm, they might return to glory with God.

To explain their revelation, the Gnostics taught that each of the elect had a hidden spark from God's eternal world. The sparks fell into matter because of a heavenly war between darkness and light (or, in other versions, because of an accident during the production of the divine emanations). The jealous, inferior god who clumsily fashioned the material realm, which is subject to time and fate, was born in the same accidental process. He was the author of carnal humanity, in which the divine spark was a prisoner. Higher beings would one day dissolve this fallen world, but in the meantime they called to people's hidden sparks by means of saviors, revelations, and rites of baptism.[16]

Gnosticism blended the Hellenistic notion of divine emanation, mystery religion notions about salvation through sacramental rites, and Jewish notions of *sin* and *redemption*. It stressed the division between this world and heaven, the evil of matter and the flesh, and the need for asceticism (celibacy and bodily discipline) to gain freedom from matter. Valentinus is the most celebrated gnostic teacher, but we know his system largely through the apostolic father Irenaeus, whose influential *Against Heresies* attacked it harshly.

Other Challenges. Other threats to Christianity during the early period included the prophecies of Marcion, Montanus, and Mani, as well as Ebionism (an effort to restrict the understanding of Jesus to Jewish categories).[17] Marcion was a Christian excommunicate who maintained that the Christian gospel is wholly a matter of love rather than a matter of law. On that account, he completely rejected the Old Testament (Jewish scripture), finding the God of Genesis incompatible with the God of Jesus. Montanus led a heretical apocalyptic movement based on the primacy of the Holy Spirit. His followers expected the outpouring of the Holy Spirit on the Church. In its own prophets, Montanism saw the beginnings of the bestowal of the Spirit. Montanism developed an impressive asceticism, and it captured the estimable African thinker Tertullian, who found it more spiritual than Christianity under the discipline of Rome.

Mani lived from about 215 to 275 in Persia and India (to which he fled from Zoroastrian persecution). His system supposed a primeval conflict between light and darkness, and it, too, stressed asceticism. The object of Manicheanism was to release the particles of light that Satan had stolen and placed in the human brain. Buddha, the Israelite prophets, Jesus, and Mani himself were the messengers whom God had sent to teach human beings the way to salvation. Manicheanism spread to Egypt, Africa, and even Rome. During the early years of his adult life, the great Christian thinker Augustine was a Manichean.

The first Christian centuries, then, were a time of missionary expansion, the development of Christian doctrine (largely through opposition to gnostic rivals), and persecution. The Roman emperors Decius (249–251) and Diocletian (284–305) made enough martyrs to make professing Christian faith a serious matter. Christians had to meet secretly in catacombs (caves) or private homes, and their organization had to be informal. Their leaders (bishops and elders) were indistinguishable from ordinary people, and their teaching had a *disciplina arcani*–a strict code of secrecy. Those who died giving testimony to their faith (martyrs, etymologically meaning "witnesses") were great heroes, whom heaven would greet with open arms. One of the greatest early controversies, in fact, concerned the status of those who had recanted their faith to avoid martyrdom and then, in a period of calm, asked readmission to the Christian community. Donatus led a party of rigorists who insisted that traitors had no place in the Church and that any *sacraments* (holy rites) that they administered would be invalid. Augustine successfully opposed Donatus, arguing for greater clemency and for Christ's decisive role in the inner effect of the sacraments.

Only a thin line separates the apostolic fathers from the conciliar fathers and the great theologians of the "patristic" age (age of the Fathers), for the three centuries after the deaths of the Twelve were characterized by a continuity of theological themes. First, there was the task of defending Church discipline and morality against both laxness and rigorism. Second, Church leaders had to walk a middle way between inspiration through charismata and institutional authority. Against Gnostics, the Church had to affirm the goodness of material creation. Against those who denied Jesus' humanity (the Docetists), it had to maintain that he was fully human and had really suffered and died. The Christian Church had little power in the secular world until the conversion of the emperor Constantine (312), so even when it was not suffering active persecution, it was not very influential. From the time of the Edict of Milan (313), however, Christianity was free to proselytize within the Roman Empire. Church leaders continued to reflect on the relation between Jesus and Judaism, as well as on conceptions of Jesus and God that would make most sense to educated Hellenists.

The apostolic Church developed a rule by local bishops. They became the primary teachers of doctrine, the primary defenders of *orthodox* (straight) belief. The bishops led the common worship, settled community disputes, and, to the extent that their talents allowed, fought heresies through sermons and writings. They were the main line of Fathers around whom the early Church arranged itself. The great heroes, as we mentioned, were the martyrs, and the life of the community took its liturgical pattern from the *eucharist* (weekly communal meal) and *baptism* (rite of entry into the Church). Forgiving sins raised questions of moral theology, for after baptism all were supposed to keep their faith pure, but gradually the Church allowed sinners to return to the community rituals after they had done penance. In the first three centuries, then, the Church established elements of the character that it has borne ever since.

The Conciliar Age

During the fourth and fifth centuries, a number of meetings (councils) of Church leaders were held that formally established the discipline and official doctrine (*dogma*) that any group in union with the apostolic Church had to adopt.[18] From those meetings came the name for the next period of Christian history. Above all, the meetings, many of which were called by emperors concerned about the unity of the empire, dealt with the central issues of the Christian creed, hammering out the dogmas about God, Jesus, salvation, and the like that became the backbone of Christian *theology*. Various controversies made Church leaders realize that it was imperative to determine which apostolic sources were genuine expressions of faith and which were not. That imperative resulted in the establishment of a Christian scriptural canon (list of official books).

Three main factors determined the final *canon:* whether the writing in question came from an apostle or a close associate of an apostle, whether it was accepted by the Church at large, and whether its contents were edifying for faith.[19] As early as 170, leaders in Rome had determined a canon of authoritative books in response to the canon drawn up by the heretic Marcion. Yet for many decades no list was agreed upon by the entire Church because local traditions varied.

For instance, the East long hesitated to accept Revelation, while the West was chary about Hebrews. In the early decades of the fourth century, Bishop Eusebius of Caesarea (perhaps the first significant Church historian) divided candidate books into three categories: acknowledged, disputed, and spurious. The acknowledged and the disputed books constitute the twenty-seven books of today's New Testament. In 367, Athanasius of Alexandria published a "Festal Letter" that listed these twenty-seven books and earned the approval of Fathers such as Jerome and Augustine and the endorsements of synods (councils) at Hippo (393) and Carthage (397 and 419).

The first great dogmatic (official doctrinal) council occurred at Nicaea in Bithynia (south of the Black Sea) in 325. It produced a consensus that was especially important for clarifying Jesus' divine status as Logos or Son. The Council of Nicaea was called by the emperor Constantine, and without imperial support the Nicene party would not have triumphed. Before Nicaea, most churches had been content to repeat what scripture (Jewish and Christian both) said about God and Jesus. However, Church theologians did not know how to respond to questions that scripture did not address. One such question came from Arius, a priest of Alexandria, in Egypt, who proposed that Jesus, as the Logos of God (the divine Son), was subordinate to the Father. In short, Arius' proposition was that if one drew a line between created beings and the uncreated divine substance, the Logos would fall on the side of created beings, because "there was a then

when he was not." Arius' principal opponent was Athanasius.

Athanasius represented the theologians of Alexandria in Egypt, who descended from Clement of Alexandria (ca. 150–215), one of the first Christian theologians to cast faith as a philosophy that might persuade educated Hellenists, and Origen (ca. 185–254), the first great Christian speculator. (Working with Platonic philosophy, Origen had written immensely influential commentaries on scripture and expositions of Christian doctrine.)

Athanasius, drawing on this Alexandrian tradition, assaulted Arius' argument. Speaking for what he held to be orthodoxy, he said that the Logos was of the same substance as the Father, possessing the single divine nature. Nicaea agreed with Athanasius, making his position dogma. There were many political machinations, as different political factions chose different theological sides, and Arianism thrived among Germanic tribes well into the sixth century. However, the Nicene Creed, which codified the position against Arius, came into common use, with the result that the divinity of the Logos became common faith.

Trinitarian Doctrine. Athanasius also perceived that the canonical literature gave the Holy Spirit divinity equal to that of the Father and the Son. Therefore, he extended the meaning of his word *homoousios* (of one substance) to include the Holy Spirit and so set the lines of what would become, at the Council of Constantinople in 381, the doctrine of the Spirit's divinity. That completed the doctrine of the *Trinity:* one God who was three equal "persons," each of whom fully possessed the single divine nature.

Augustine, bishop of Hippo, in Africa, expressed this doctrine in terms of a psychological analogy that shaped Western Christian speculation. He proposed that as memory, understanding, and love are all mind, so (but without human imperfections) are Father, Son, and Holy Spirit all divinity. The Father is like an inexhaustible memory (from which all creation comes), the Logos is like the Father's self-awareness, and the Spirit is like their boundless love.

In the Trinitarian controversy (and perhaps even more in the subsequent Christological controversies [controversies about Jesus Christ]), the terminology that eventually became fixed was still quite fluid.[20] Bernard Lonergan has argued that the Church's decision to respond to Arius and so coin new language for new problems (problems not resolved by scripture) was a decisive advance in its self-understanding.[21] It would

have been obscurantism, or anti-intellectualism, to refuse to grapple with questions as serious and legitimate as Arius'. By responding to Arius' challenge, the
Church affirmed its ability to determine the meaning
of scripture and to develop doctrine as new situations
required.

Politics. The conciliar definitions gave Christian
faith considerably more precision and at least tacitly
encouraged theologians to study and speculate further
on the doctrinal tracts that they had laid out. The
conciliar age was also fraught with the intrusions of
secular leaders into Church affairs, for after Constantine and his successors made Christianity the favored
imperial religion, the emperors assumed that they had
the right, even the pious duty, to intervene in Church
affairs. Thus, the tension between Church and state,
as we now call it, started its long and tangled history
in the conciliar age. Whether this led to the Caesaro-
papism (domination of the Church by the emperor)
that many historians think afflicted the Eastern portions of Christianity before the schism of 1054 (when
East and West split) is a matter for learned specialists
to decide. We need only point out here that, because of
Christianity's favored status in the empire, the councils became a matter of imperial interest.

In fact, the councils were the spearhead of the
advances that the Church and state made into one
another's affairs.[22] No longer were Christians under
the constant threat of persecution and martyrdom.
They could enter worldly occupations, including government service—a situation that both weakened their
faith and made it more realistic. As a result, the original feeling of urgency gave way to the realization that
the Lord's return might be far down the road. Thus,
Christianity decided it had to become a faith that was
viable in the world.

Monasticism. Such worldliness stimulated new religious movements within the Church that opposed the
laxness or "accommodation" that worldly success easily begot. The most important reforms generated interest in monasticism and virginity (which overlapped,
insofar as monks took vows of celibacy). Both males
and females found a monastic life of dedication to
prayer and charitable works a way of maintaining their
martyrlike intensity of faith. Theirs was a "white"
martyrdom, not the red one of blood, and many found
that it led them to the desert for solitude and asceticism. The great hero of the day, in fact, was the desert father Antony, who made a great impression on

Athanasius. Thomas Merton has gathered a good
selection of the desert fathers' sayings.[23] In it one
sees both a bare faith and considerable shrewdness
about what happens to people when they set out to
meet God.

Partly because of the dangers of desert solitude,
many monks soon formed communities, and before
long these communities admitted women (nuns). In
the East, communal (cenobitic) monasticism took form
under the guidance of Basil, bishop of Caesarea. His
rule (which owed much to Pachomius, the founder of
communal monasticism) became the common law. In
the West the rule of Benedict predominated. So the
dedication that had previously been an informal option
(largely in terms of virginity or widowhood) took institutional form. Thenceforth monasteries were pow-
erhouses of Christian faith that laity and *clerics* alike
viewed as centers of holiness. That, too, was an innovation added to New Testament religion, which had no
monastic life. The Church's decision that monastic life
was truly in keeping with New Testament religion was
analogous to the decision to coin new doctrinal concepts. Quite consistently, the Protestant reformers of
the sixteenth century opposed the development of monasticism (as being unbiblical), just as they opposed
the development of the Catholic notion of authority.

Christology. The councils not only set the pattern of
Trinitarian faith that dominated the following centuries but also dealt with a host of problems that arose
when people started to think about Jesus as the divine
Word. Nestorius from Antioch and Cyril from Alexandria squared off in Christological controversy, and Alexandria won. Nestorius stressed the unity of the
Christian God, though he affirmed Christ's two natures (human and divine). Cyril thought that Nestorius' affirmation was not strong enough to safeguard
the single personhood of Jesus Christ the God-man, so
he pressed for a "hypostatic" (personal) union of the
two natures. The Councils of Ephesus (431) and Chalcedon (451) affirmed Cyril's doctrine of one "person"
and two "natures." Later Christological development
clarified that Jesus had a rational soul, two wills, and
two sets of operations, human and divine. This orthodox Christology resulted from trying to systematize
the scriptural teaching about God and Jesus. It
stressed that only the union of the divine with the
human in Jesus could save human beings from sin and
give them divine life. Orthodoxy cast many groups in
the shade, branding their positions as heretical, but it
also developed Christ's meaning considerably.

Orthodoxy

Orthodoxy has two principal meanings. It may refer to the Eastern churches that separated from Rome in 1054 or to the "right belief" established by scripture, tradition, and the councils. In this section we address the first concept, describing the growth of Eastern Christianity after the conciliar age (most of the great councils took place in the East). The term *Orthodox* was adopted for two reasons: The Orthodox church thought of itself as keeping the traditional faith, especially regarding the episcopal (pertaining to bishops) focus of Church authority; *orthodoxy* has also meant, especially in the East, "right praise." As "right praise" the term links the Orthodox conception of faith to the glorious Orthodox liturgy (which primarily is a praise of God).

Western theologians, many of whom were monks dedicated to a rich communal worship, coined the expression *"Lex orandi, lex credendi"*—the law of prayer is the law of faith. Similarly, Eastern theologians felt that the Church expressed itself most fully in the *liturgy*. During the apostolic age this communal worship (*liturgy* means "the work of the people") had developed a sacramental system in which baptism and the Eucharist ("the Lord's Supper") were especially important. In the early medieval period, when Orthodoxy took form, the liturgy flowered. The result was a full calendar of holy days and a full ritual that involved music, art, incense, iconography, and more. Thus, communal worship became the dramatic center of Eastern church life.

As we have noted, the councils of the fourth century occasioned theological division as well as theological clarification. In the fifth century, during the Christological controversies, more deviant versions of faith arose—Nestorian, Monophysite (one nature in Christ), and others—because as the councils established accepted beliefs, they excluded other options. Often the deviant minority party continued a church life, with the result that there were large numbers of heterodox Christians in the East. As Arianism remained robust even after its rejection by the Council of Nicaea, so the Christologically heterodox groups did not simply recant or go back into the woodwork. Thus, the major split between East and West that occurred in 1054 was not without Eastern forerunners.[24]

From the ninth to the fifteenth century, a complicated, still quite obscure process of alienation between Byzantine (Eastern) Christianity and Roman Christianity resulted in their separation. Each group finally rejected the other, charging it with having broken the traditional faith. Some of the factors in the separation were the fall of the Eastern Roman Empire, the failure of the Crusades, the growing antagonism of Islam, the growth of the papacy, the stirrings of what developed into the sixteenth-century Protestant reactions against the papacy, and the rivalry between Russia and Western Europe.[25] These factors take us to the beginning of modernity in Eastern Christendom, explaining why East and West have remained divided to the present.

Religious Issues. Thus, the break between Eastern and Western Christianity owed a great deal to political and cultural conflicts. Although separating these conflicts from theological differences is virtually impossible, we can delineate some of the more clearly religious issues. For instance, the patriarch Photius, who presided at the Eastern capital of Constantinople from 858 to 886, drew up a list of what Byzantines considered to be Latin (Western) errors in faith. This list reveals how the two portions of Christendom had developed different understandings of orthodoxy. In this list Photius cited irregularities in the observance of *Lent* (the period of penance before the great feast of Easter when the resurrection of Christ was celebrated), compulsory celibacy for the clergy, denying priests the power to administer confirmation (the Christian sacrament of adulthood), and false teaching about the Holy Spirit. Clearly, the list concentrates on points of Church discipline and administration. Such points have serious theological implications (for instance, for the structure of the Church and its authority), but they do not affect the cardinal doctrines of the Christian faith: Trinity, grace (God's favor and life), and Incarnation, except for Photius' last point on false teaching about the Holy Spirit.

The most acute point of theological difference between the East and the West was this last point, which came to be known as the *filioque*. According to the Nicene Creed, within the life of the Trinity the Holy Spirit proceeds from the Father. The Western Council of Toledo (589) made an addition to the Nicene Creed: The Holy Spirit proceeds not just from the Father but also from the Son (*filioque* means "and from the Son"). East and West each became attached to its Trinitarian formula, so the filioque became a sharp bone of contention. The East claimed that it was heretical; the West claimed it merely articulated a tacit understanding of traditional faith that Nicaea had assumed. The practical significance of the difference is not clear, but it probably shows the East's tendency to appreciate

Figure 39 *Byzantine book cover, Syria, sixth to seventh century. Gold, rock crystal, and ruby; 8⅞ × 6⅜ in. The handsome cross suggests that the cover was meant for a Bible. The Nelson–Atkins Museum of Art, Kansas City, Missouri (Nelson Fund).*

the Father's primal mystery—the Father's status as a fathomless source from which *everything* issues.

In response to Photius, Western theologians composed their own list of complaints about Eastern usage. In their view the Eastern discipline that allowed clerics to marry, that baptized by immersion, that celebrated the Eucharist with leavened bread, and that had different rules for fasting deviated from tradition. The debate even descended to such details as whether bishops should wear rings, whether clergy should wear beards, and whether instrumental music was valid at the liturgy. However, the main theological issue continued to be the filioque, while the main political issue emerged as the difference in the churches' understanding of authority. The Eastern church's tradition was a loose federation of bishops, all of whom were considered successors of the apostles. The Eastern church also stressed the rights of individual churches and ethnic groups. The Western tradition was a "monarchical" leadership by the bishop of Rome. As successor to Peter, he claimed primacy over the other churches.

When the Byzantine Empire was about to fall to the Turks, the Eastern and Western factions met for the last time at the Council of Florence (1439). That was long after the mutual anathemas of 1054 (described below), but the East hoped to secure both Church unification and Western help against Islam. On the agenda were only four points (the other disagreements having fallen away as trivial). They were the prerogatives of the bishop of Rome, the filioque clause, the doctrine of purgatory (the teaching that there is an intermediate state between heaven and hell, which the Orthodox condemned as unbiblical), and whether to use leavened or unleavened bread in the Eucharist. In retrospect, theologians have judged the last two items as relatively inconsequential. The first two were interrelated, because the Council of Florence came to focus on the question of whether the pope had the right to alter an ecumenical creed (that is, add filioque to the Nicene Creed). Because of their political problems (the menace of the Turks), the majority of the Greeks (Easterners) accepted the filioque and agreed to certain papal prerogatives. The union was confined to paper, though, because back at home Orthodox synods refused to ratify the agreements signed by their delegates.

Separation. The pivotal moment in the East-West division was the mutual excommunications of 1054, which were due more to politics (or to snappish personalities) than to theology. Pope Leo IX had sent a Western delegation to Constantinople headed by one Cardinal Humbert. The Normans were menacing Leo and also the emperor Constantine Monomachus, so a major goal was to unite the churches to oppose a common foe. Humbert seems to have been a narrow, contentious type, as was his Eastern counterpart, the patriarch Michael Cerularius. When Pope Leo died in 1054, Cerularius held that Humbert's credentials were void. Humbert responded by laying on the altar of Saint Sophia in Constantinople a letter that excommunicated the patriarch and all his associates. The patriarch then assembled his own council, which excommunicated Humbert in return. The emperor dispatched the cardinal back to Rome with presents, hoping that the next pope would appoint a new legate who could heal the breach. But the Normans prevented the popes from resuming negotiations, so the mutual excommunications stood until after the Second Vatican Council in the early 1960s.

In the opinion of many contemporary theologians and historians the division between the Eastern and Western branches of the Church was a tragic accident. (Historians now say much the same of the sixteenth-century Reformation split in Europe.) Political circumstances, differences in traditional ways of celebrating faith, and, above all, differences in temperament and cultural backgrounds were more decisive than hard theological differences. What Orthodox and Catholics (and Protestants and Catholics) held in common was far more significant than what they held apart. It took centuries for Christians to realize that millions of people (for example, Asians) knew little about their God, let alone their Christ—centuries for them to realize their own solidarity and so begin an "ecumenical (worldwide) movement" for Church unification. The sticking point through those centuries was a main factor in the East-West division—papal authority. Recently some ecumenical theologians have suggested ways that Protestant and Orthodox churches might acknowledge certain papal powers, but full accord remains quite distant.

Thus, the Orthodox church represents an understanding of Christianity somewhat different than that of Western Christianity.[26] It numbers perhaps one hundred sixty million people, depending on the estimates used for the Soviet Union, and within the family of Christian churches it stresses the conciliar tradition, the federation of local churches in geographic families, and a lofty theology of the Trinity, Christology, and grace. As we noted, the liturgy is its center, and it has a rich sacramental life.[27]

At the Orthodox liturgy, one feels a Christian "pneumaticism": The Holy Spirit is dramatically present to effect the sacraments. In the invocation made over the Eucharistic gifts (the *epiclesis*), Orthodoxy stresses the Holy Spirit's role in transforming the bread and wine into Christ's substance. In its baptism and confession of sins, Orthodoxy's accent is sharing God's life—beginning divine life in baptism or repairing it in penance. Overall, Orthodoxy places the mystery of the Christian God to the fore. For the East, God is less a lawgiver or a judge than a spiritual power operating through creation. Creation ought to respond to God's power and beauty, so the Divine Liturgy becomes a song of praise, a hymn to the goodness and love that pour forth from the Father of Lights. Orthodoxy especially venerates Mary, the Mother of God, for her share in the "economy" of salvation—her share in the design of grace that raises human beings to participate in the divine immortality. Bernhard Schultze has offered a full sketch of Orthodox doctrines and a full listing of its different family members.[28] He shows that, through many political troubles, Orthodoxy has kept faith with Jesus and the Christian beginnings.

Case Study: Orthodox Spiritual Wisdom. Both major branches of Eastern Orthodoxy, the Greek and the Russian, have fostered a strong monastic life, and from this strong monastic life has come a steady stream of holy people wise in the ways of the religious spirit. For a fascinating glimpse of such holy people, one need only pick up *In Search of True Wisdom: Visits to Eastern Spiritual Fathers,*[29] a work that beautifully conveys the Eastern Orthodox sense of prayer and asceticism.

This sense of prayer is a major focus in one of the authors' visit with a Russian recluse of Usui Valamao, a monastery in Finland to which some Russian expatriates retired after the Soviet rise to power. The visit took place in 1954, and the account of it transmits the spiritual advice of one Father Michael, a noted holy man of Valamo. Sergius Bolshakoff, the interviewer, was himself an expatriate Russian, who had decided to dedicate his life to the reunion of the Eastern and Western churches, by concentrating on the common monastic life that still kept the two churches quite close in their lives of prayer.

Bolshakoff was sitting with Father Michael at the end of the day in the holy man's little cell. Twilight filled the room, and a little oil lamp flickered in the corner before the holy icons. All was quiet and peaceful. Bolshakoff asked Father Michael to tell him about the tears of grace, one of the signs of advanced prayer. Father Michael replied that the tears of grace express a perfect prayer and the forgiveness of sins, referring to the authority of St. Isaac the Syrian, who had written on this subject. Opening a tome of St. Isaac's writings, he had Bolshakoff read certain passages he had marked off. The passages tell much about the Orthodox tradition of mysticism.

St. Isaac said that when a person is starting to leave obscure prayer, in which things are still confused, the person's heart will begin to burn like fire, and this will grow stronger day by day. No longer will worldly things hold any attraction, not even food or drink. Far more delicious will be the sweet, new, fiery thoughts in the person's soul. Then suddenly tears will begin to flow. They will run like a stream while the person reads, prays, eats, drinks, or works. Such tears signal a crucial period, during which a person can make great spiritual advances. Before them, the person has not climbed the mountain of God. When they come, the person has arrived, but he or she must redouble the efforts, so as not to lose a great opportunity.

The tears mean that a person has begun to smell the perfume of a wonderful new air. They announce that the birth of a spiritual child is near. "Our common mother, Grace, wishes to produce in us in her own mysterious way the divine image so that we may see the light of the age to come." After the flow of tears, which must last two years or more, there comes perfect serenity of mind. In this peace of mind, one can begin to contemplate the divine mysteries. The Holy Spirit opens the heavens, and God comes to dwell in the person, to resurrect in him or her the fruit of the Spirit.

Father Michael admitted that he himself had wept a great deal in his life. When Bolshakoff confessed that a certain book he used to read in the British Museum always moved him deeply, because it spoke so beautifully of a boy growing up in a pious Moscow family before the Communists' seizure of power, the monk nodded in understanding. That is not surprising, he said. Our time of unbelief and carnal living has made piety a lovely nostalgia. We think that tears manifest pitiful weakness or something else to be despised. We relegate them to old women. Stony indifference, hardness of heart, and coolness of spirit have become our marks of virility. The truth is, however, that an absence of tenderheartedness is merely a sign of spiritual death. As a Byzantine mystic said long ago, those who attend the Holy Liturgy without tears and a tender heart eat and drink the body and blood of the Lord unworthily. We must cultivate tears and tenderness of heart, because only through them can we purify our thoughts.

The interview passed on to other topics, most of them connected with prayer. At one point, Bolshakoff asked Father Michael to explain to him a puzzling passage from the writings of St. Seraphim. In the passage St. Seraphim says that when the Holy Spirit overshadows us, we must cease to pray. Bolshakoff wasn't sure he understood why. Father Michael said that all mystics have taught as St. Seraphim does, understanding "prayer" to be something we do by our human efforts. In contrast, when the Holy Spirit overshadows us, our efforts cease and there is no "prayer." Rather there is only a sentiment or heartfelt impulse of love that reaches out toward God without words or images. But Father Michael bade Bolshakoff to continue reading, for St. Seraphim also makes it clear that there are different gifts from the divine grace. Some people have the gift of mystical, unceasing prayer. Others are moved to watch their thoughts and pray in the sense of making human efforts. Still other people have the gift to fast, or to gather alms, or to live a virginal life. The point is to find one's own gift, one's own congenial path to God, and use it.

The next passage they discussed was also from St. Seraphim, and it concerned the lightning that one of Seraphim's disciples saw streaming from the saint's eyes, so bright it made the disciple's eyes ache. Seraphim told the disciple that the disciple himself was equally shining, because of God's life in him. The disciple then saw Seraphim's face become like the middle of the sun at its noonday brightest, a blinding light radiating in every direction. This filled the disciple with an inexpressible peace of soul. St. Seraphim explained that this peace is what Jesus meant when he told his disciples, "Peace I leave with you; my peace I give to you; not as the world gives" (John 14:27). It proved that the disciple truly had left the world.

When Father Michael commented on this and other writings of the holy fathers about light, he interpreted them as referring to a light like that which the apostles saw emanating from Jesus when they went with him to Mount Tabor and he was transfigured before them (Matt. 17:2). Still, such light did not keep the apostles from denying and abandoning Jesus at the time of his arrest, and it did not keep the saints, such as Simeon the New Theologian, from returning to a worldly life for a time. So we should think of it as a temporary strengthening for those who need shoring up, rather than a permanent acquisition or something essential to the state of grace. One can be in the fullest grace and not perceive or externally radiate such light.

The conversation then passed from light to warmth, as though Father Michael and Bolshakoff were exploring all the spiritual dimensions of the inner senses. In this case, however, Father Michael emphasized the supernatural warmth that Seraphim had asked his disciple to describe. "What kind of warmth do you feel, lover of God?" Seraphim asked. The disciple replied that, despite the snow all around them, he felt warmth like that which arises in a Russian bath, when one pours water on the heated stones and steam rises in a column. But the smell was completely different, like no perfume one can find on earth. St. Seraphim smiled in agreement. The consolations of the Holy Spirit are like no perfume on earth. What will the consolations of heaven be like? And, contrary to the warmth of a Russian steam bath, the warmth the disciple was feeling melted none of the snow surrounding the saint's hut. That showed it was warmth of a completely spiritual order, like the warmth the liturgy asks the Holy Spirit to give. For centuries, Seraphim pointed out, hermits who trekked into the deepest Russian forests did not fear the snows and the cold, because they relied on the inner warmth of the Holy Spirit. The grace of God, God's inner life, filled their hearts and heated their bones.

Again and again Father Michael and the classical authors he was explaining to Bolshakoff returned to the theme of grace, which has always been central in Orthodox theology. As Seraphim put it: "The Lord said, 'The Kingdom of God is within you.' By this Kingdom of God the Lord means the grace of the Holy Spirit. Well, this same Kingdom of God is now within us while the grace of the Holy Spirit shines and warms us, filling the air around us with various perfumes, and sweetens our organs of sensation with heavenly pleasure and our hearts with indescribable joy."

The Orthodox mystical tradition continues, alive and well, in places like Mount Athos in Greece, where monks meditate in the old ways and read the old classics. The center of their lives is something spiritual, something the eye cannot see nor the ear hear nor can it enter the hearts of human beings to conceive. Like Hasidim lost in the world of Torah, the Orthodox holy men and women are lost in the world of the gospel. For them the gospel words are shining jewels, the gospel scenes are blazing icons. Contemplating those icons, the Orthodox saints have enjoyed wonderful visions of the life of God that fills the holy soul, the mercy of God that courses through the world. Their meditations have made the scriptural scenes contemporary, much the way Jewish prayer has made the Exodus contemporary.

It is shocking to enter the thought-world of the Orthodox seers, and perhaps equally shocking to realize that a similar thought-world predominated in the Christian West less than 500 years ago. Less than 500 years ago, even theologians studied the Bible more for its religious feeling than for its literary structure. Even theologians were more interested in feeling compunction than in knowing its definition. Similarly, the terms of reference in Father Michael's world are not the historical or literary aspects of the Bible, but the spiritual experiences and verities the monastic tradition tells him the Bible can promote. What the Holy Spirit did for the apostles, and for the later saints like Seraphim, the Holy Spirit is poised to do today. After all, Jesus, the eternal Son of God, came from God precisely to give us human beings God's life, which the Holy Spirit wants to nurture in us. For Father

Michael, as for most of the saints, the great puzzle is why so many people seem uninterested in God's life.

God's life, the East always has emphasized, is the perfect community of the Father, Son, and Holy Spirit. It is the Trinity not as the subject of conciliar controversies, or the subject of theologians' dry reflections, but as the spiritual atmosphere in which human beings can live, move, and have their being, if they would open their souls in faith. What the Eastern liturgy has always sung, the Eastern holy people have always stressed: the substantial love of God poured out for the salvation of human beings; humanity's potential elevation to a new, heavenly mode of life.

One will not understand traditional Christianity without an imaginative effort to grasp spiritual convictions like Father Michael's. For the generations who gave their lives to praying over the gospel scenes, the Spirit offered a light, a warmth, a perfume surpassing anything the world had to offer. With the peace and joy of the Spirit, a person was infinitely blessed. Without the peace and joy of the Spirit, a person was greatly to be pitied.

The Medieval Period

In discussing the medieval period of Christianity, we shift focus from the East, where Orthodox faith took shape, to the European West, where a new historical epoch more clearly dawned. Evangelization (missionizing) of Europe progressed steadily from the time of the early councils, most of it presuming somewhat vaguely that the bishop of Rome was preeminent among the Church's episcopal leaders. During the fifth and sixth centuries, Christian missionaries made considerable inroads among the Germanic tribes. Frequently they would convert tribal leaders from paganism or Arianism, and then the entire tribe would convert. From 800 one could speak of the Holy Roman Empire—a tense mixture of political and religious drives for unity. However, Western state leaders tended to think that the Church was something for them to control. That tendency, plus problems of Church discipline, made the Western situation confusing. From the tenth century, however, there were efforts to reform the Church and increase its spiritual vitality. In the eleventh and twelfth centuries, such efforts—especially those that originated at the Abbey of Cluny in Burgundy—were fairly successful.

As well, individual Church leaders found that they could increase their freedom from local secular rulers by increasing their allegiance to the bishop of Rome.

The friction between Church and state therefore shifted to the interaction between the pope and the Germanic emperor. A key issue was who should appoint local bishops. The investiture controversy, as it is called, was solved by a compromise in the Concordat of Worms (1122). Secular rulers had to recognize the independence of the local bishop by virtue of his loyalty to the pope, and the pope had to consult the emperor and appoint bishops acceptable to him.[30]

During the twelfth century the Crusades to the holy sites in Palestine riveted the Christian imagination, but they tended to increase the alienation between Eastern and Western Christendom. When the Fourth Crusade (1204) conquered Constantinople, set up a Western prince, and tried to Latinize the Eastern church, relations deteriorated to their lowest point. By 1453, after the Councils of Lyon and Florence had done little to heal the wounds of division, and after Easterners had suffered centuries of Western domination, a popular slogan circulated to the effect that Turks would be better rulers than Western Christians.

During the twelfth century, Europe developed strong cities, with a concomitant shift of economic and political power. This development slowly transformed the feudal system of which the Church had been an intimate part. As a result, considerable resistance to the established Church power and faith arose among some groups, such as the Waldenses, who urged a return to apostolic simplicity and poverty. Groups that owed a debt to the Manicheans, such as the French Albigensians, pushed dualistic views in their war on the flesh and their contempt for the material world.

To meet the challenge of such reformers, the Roman church developed new orders of priests and monks, the most important of which were the Dominicans and the Franciscans. Dominic (1170–1221) organized his group to preach against the heretics, and one of the devotions it added was the rosary—a string of beads for counting prayers to the Virgin Mary. The Franciscans stemmed from the charismatic *poverello* (pauper) Francis of Assisi (1181–1226), who dedicated himself to simple living. His angelic love of nature and of the infant Jesus made a deep impression on subsequent generations of Christians. Both Dominicans and Franciscans were innovations on the established (largely Benedictine) model of Western monasticism. Principally, they had more freedom than Benedictines to move out of the cloister and its settled, agricultural rhythms. They were mobile, and therefore quite effective in responding to different religious trouble spots.

Scholasticism. The thirteenth century was the high point of medieval intellectual life, and the movement known as *Scholasticism* reached its peak then. The Scholastics systematized the conciliar and patristic (the Fathers') theological doctrines.[31] Augustine was their great master, but where Augustine worked with neo-Platonic thought categories (worked out by thinkers such as Plotinus, who developed Plato's ideas), Thomas Aquinas (1225–1274), the greatest of the medievals, worked with Aristotelian categories. Between Augustine and Aquinas lived Anselm (1033–1109), who developed the notion that theology is "faith seeking understanding." That is, on the basis of a firm Christian commitment (rooted in scriptural, conciliar, and patristic doctrines), the theologian ought to learn as much as the divine mysteries allowed.

Anselm's definition was a writ of intellectual emancipation. Though they accepted the disciplines of tradition and the Church's teaching office, the medieval theologians seized the right to develop reason and use it to illumine the realities of faith. Consequently, teachers such as Peter Lombard and Peter Abelard prepared lists of patristic opinions on different theological topics and started to reason them through dialectically. Franciscan theologians, such as Alexander of Hales and Bonaventure, and Dominican theologians, such as Albert the Great and Thomas Aquinas, developed the dialectics, writing voluminously on philosophical and theological topics.

After a great struggle, the position of Aquinas, who most carefully related reason and faith, gained the greatest following. Just as conciliar theology had moved beyond scriptural ideas (in order to illumine scripture), so Aquinas' scholastic theology moved beyond conciliar theology in order to illumine it through Greek philosophy. For Aquinas, philosophy was the wisdom available to reason. It was a universal basis for discussion, regardless of religious allegiance. Jews, Muslims, Christians, and pagans all had reason, and so all could philosophize. Theology, which rested on divine revelation, perfected philosophy, taking it into realms that it could not penetrate on its own (for instance, without revelation philosophy would not know of the Trinity or the Incarnation [the divine Word made flesh]). Aquinas developed a powerful system of philosophical theology, but he was by no means the only impressive medieval thinker. His school, Thomism, trusted in reason, had a hopeful view of the world, thoroughly analyzed the Trinity, Christology, and grace, made a careful analysis of human virtues and vices, and viewed the world as a hierarchy of levels of being, with matter on the bottom, humans in the middle, and God at the top.[32]

Hierarchy. Aquinas' hierarchy had counterparts in the medieval Church structure. The clergy had separated themselves from the laity, and within the clerical order there were numerous ranks: monks, priests, canons, bishops, abbots, archbishops, cardinals, and more. The papacy had a considerable bureaucracy and wielded great secular power. Because the general culture held a Christian world view, heaven and hell had a vivid reality. Thus, the papal power to bar people from Church membership and so from heaven made people fear the pope greatly. Considerable worldliness entered into the papal use of excommunication, interdict, and the like, because by medieval times the Church had largely laid aside the *parousia* (second coming of Christ) and was concentrating on shaping daily life.

The unsurpassed literary rendition of medieval Christianity is Dante's *Divine Comedy*. It shows the medievals' hierarchical thinking, their concern with heaven, hell, and purgatory, the venality of many medieval clergy, the infusion of pagan learning into medieval culture, and the sophistication of medieval moral theology, which catalogued virtues and vices quite precisely. Another wonderful source of insight into medieval Christianity is Chaucer's *Canterbury Tales,* which describes the daily habits of representative social types and the unconscious ways in which faith wove through medieval culture. From Dante and Chaucer one gathers that intellectuals of the late medieval period, especially nonclerical intellectuals, found many defects in the hierarchical Church yet basically accepted the terms of Christian faith. Their criticism focused on the discrepancy between the values that the Church professed and the all-too-human way in which many Church leaders conducted themselves.

The medieval cathedrals also exhibited hierarchy through their stretching from earth toward heaven. They instruct us about medieval faith, for towns built them to be a means of indoctrination. One can see this today in the gothic masterpieces of Notre Dame de Chartres and Notre Dame de Paris. The basic architectural thrust is toward heaven, as all commentators point out, yet within the cathedrals are windows and statues that bring God down into daily life. Most cathedrals were built over centuries, and sometimes the townspeople contributed free labor, as if they wanted the cathedral to praise God doubly. Significantly,

Chartres and Notre Dame de Paris both bear Mary's name. As the Virgin Mother of God, Queen of Heaven and recourse of weak human beings, Mary was a mainstay of medieval faith.

In their battles with the Arians during the fifth and sixth centuries, Church leaders had necessarily stressed Jesus' divinity, which the Arians denied. Consequently, the Roman liturgy had come to place Christ and the action of the Mass (eucharistic celebration) apart from the people (as befit Christ-God). The size of the cathedrals, the inability of many people to see the ceremonies, the inability of many people to understand the Latin in which the ceremonies were conducted—all these factors prompted devotion to Mary and the infant Jesus, which brought God closer and made faith more human. Divinity was not fearsome if one could shelter behind a young mother's kindness, a baby's vulnerability. So such devotions balanced the rather stern official cult.

Around the cathedral walls, in wonderful stained glass, were biblical scenes, pictures of saints, and the like that told even the illiterate what faith meant. With the statues of the Virgin and Jesus, they gave comfort to the person who slipped into the cathedral's darkness to pray. In its majestic space, one gained a proper perspective on one's problems. At a time when hard work, early death, and many sufferings were the rule, the cathedrals were for many a great support.

Monastic life progressed during the Middle Ages, though new orders such as the Franciscans and Dominicans neither completely replaced the more stable Benedictines nor completely abandoned their regimes. The great work of the monastic community was to celebrate the divine "office": liturgical prayers throughout the day and a communal Mass. By the thirteenth century, the Eucharist involved a rather complex ceremony, with choral music, gorgeous vestments, and precious vessels for the bread and wine. Gregorian chants best represent the music, which was lively and alert, giving many psalms a joyous lilt. For solemn moments, such as the celebration of Christ's Passion, chant could express deep sorrow, prefiguring, for instance, the music of Johann Sebastian Bach.

As it developed, the Mass increasingly tended to represent Christ's sacrificial death. That did not deny the motif of a common meal, but it shifted emphasis to the consecration of the elements (bread and wine), because in the theologians' interpretation, the separation of the bread and wine stood for the sundering of Jesus' body on the cross. As a prayer (the "sequence") for the feast of Corpus Christi (attributed to Thomas Aquinas) shows, the consecrated host (bread transformed into Jesus' body) came to epitomize God's presence and redemptive action. The consecration was a miracle that the liturgy enacted each day. Paradoxically, the host defied the senses and nourished the soul. Because Jesus' body remained in church, the church was indeed God's house. Indeed, in the host, Jesus made himself available for reverence and prayer. Along with the cult of the Virgin (see Figure 40) and the cults of the many medieval saints, the cult of the Eucharist gave people at the bottom of the Church pyramid another source of comfort.

Thus, the average person went through a harsh medieval life in fear and trembling but with many sources of hope that such a life would lead to heaven. The worldliness of much Church life was balanced by the sacramental ceremonies that stressed the primacy of heaven. Rather clearly, the faithful knew that they stood between heaven and earth. They were citizens of two worlds, and the best medieval theology and religious art counseled them to live their dual citizenship gracefully. For instance, the cathedral and monastic schools joined piety to learning. The mystery plays and even the *danse macabre* (dance of death) brought home to the common people that death leveled pope and pauper to strict equality. In fact, *"momento mori"* ("Remember death") was a pietistic watchword. Since death was a gateway to eternal life, *"momento mori"* had positive as well as negative overtones.

Case Study: Christian Art. As an interlude between the medieval and Reformation periods, let us consider the religious art of two great German painters of the early sixteenth century, Albrecht Dürer (1471–1528) and Matthias Grünewald (ca. 1470–1528). They show an interplay of the humanistic themes that grew out of the Renaissance (but had some forebears in medieval thought) and the emphases on human sinfulness that the Protestant Reformation spotlighted. We may note, however, that both poles of this interplay depended on faith in the Incarnation. Without a strong conviction that the Word of God had entered human history, had even assumed a body in order to suffer human sin, painters such as Dürer and Grünewald would never have seen the world as they did.

Dürer was born in Nuremberg, the son of a goldsmith. He showed great artistic ability even as a child, so his father apprenticed him to a wood engraver. In 1494–1495 he visited Italy and learned about a new technique, called "linear perspective," that made all parallel lines converge at a single vanishing point. He

Figure 40 Madonna and Child, *France, about 1475. Stone; 35¼ in. high. The Nelson–Atkins Museum of Art, Kansas City, Missouri (Nelson Fund).*

sance artists were reconceiving the artist as a human genius inspired to create his own personal world.

This new conception of the artist is evident in Dürer's *Self-Portrait,* painted in 1500. The painting suggests "a Christlike figure rather than a prosperous German painter of the turn of the century. The effect is intentional. The lofty gaze of the eyes underlines the solemn, almost religious nature of the artist's vision, while the prominent hand draws attention to his use of the pen and brush to communicate it to us."[33] The long, flowing hair is reminiscent of traditional portraits of Jesus, while the sadness of the eyes indicates the burdens the artistic seer has to carry, his heavy vision of human suffering.

In 1498 Dürer published a famous series of woodcuts illustrating scenes from the Book of Revelation. One of them, *Saint Michael Fighting the Dragon,* shows a warfare proceeding in heaven, while earth is represented by a peaceful German plain with a small town complete with a church steeple. Michael and the other angels look quite human, having long hair like Dürer's own. The demons, however, are gruesome creatures from the swamps of the unconscious, with long snouts and scaly tails. The general impression the woodcut conveys is of a cosmic battle between good and evil, the issue of which is still in doubt. The peace seeming to prevail on the human plain is misleading, since what is going on in heaven cannot fail to affect the human order. Apparently Dürer's sense of foreboding captured the popular imagination, for the fifteen woodcuts of his *Apocalypse* series sold well. The discontents of the period, which were to erupt only twenty years later in Luther's reform, made apocalyptic visions popular.

Dürer also produced many line engravings, incising his drawings on copper plates, and in this medium he achieved amazingly rich effects. His engraving entitled *The Fall of Man,* produced in 1504, shows an idealized Adam and Eve surrounded by animals representing the sins and diseases that have resulted from the Fall. Whereas Adam and Eve retain some of the splendor of their original creation, the animals emphasize the perverse effects of human beings' having eaten the fruit of the tree of the knowledge of good and evil.

A second trip to Italy in 1505–1507 brought Dürer in contact with the Venice school, which was then producing lavishly colored paintings. Thus his *Adoration of the Trinity,* finished in 1511, shows richly robed cardinals and kings adoring the Trinity. The heavenly host of martyrs and prophets are similarly clothed,

also absorbed the growing Italian interest in human anatomy. Still, perhaps the most important aspect of Dürer's trip to Italy was his exposure to a new conception of the artist's vocation. Whereas the traditional medieval artist had thought of himself as an artisan called to reproduce God's creation, the Italian Renais-

while the sublimity of the vision lifts the earthly worshipers right off their feet. In the right-hand corner Dürer himself stands in full-length portrait, as though wanting to stress that this glorious scene was his personal creation.

Colorful painting apparently could not hold Dürer's permanent interest, for he went back to engraving. His greatest engravings, produced between 1513 and 1515, included the famous *Knight, Death, and the Devil*. The knight, who may have been inspired by the Dutch humanist Erasmus' *Handbook of the Christian Knight*, published in 1502, represents vigilant Christian faith. He sits astride a magnificent horse, undaunted by either death, who brandishes an hourglass, or the devil, who looks like a mythical beast, complete with long snout and high horn. Beside the knight trots his faithful dog, whom some interpreters see as the tireless devotion that must accompany vigilant faith. The picture projects the great religious demands of the time, the inner warfare that Church corruption and the new humanistic ideals could provoke.

So, on the foundation of the medieval and fourteenth-century preoccupations with death, Dürer erected a new religious vision, equally serious but more appreciative of humanity's inner powers. Human beings were not sure to prevail against such powerful foes as death and sin, but Dürer's human figures said that men and women could fight great fights of faith, aided by the saints, angels, and Jesus, who were always ready to enter the picture.

Grünewald, whose given name was Matthias Gothart Neithart, worked for a while at the court of the cardinal archbishop of Mainz. In the Peasants' War of 1525 he took the side of the peasants against the ruling classes, and his enthusiasm for Luther's ideas lost him the cardinal's favor. Unlike Dürer, Grünewald's paintings show little influence from the new humanistic developments in Italy. Thus, there is little of the Italian Renaissance interest in an idealized human body and little effort to retrieve the humanistic subjects of classical Greek art. Instead, Grünewald turned to the traditional religious themes of medieval German art, suggesting the ferment of his own times through the intensity with which he painted familiar topics.

Two of Grünewald's best-known paintings are the *Crucifixion* and the *Resurrection* from the Isenheim Altarpiece, both completed in 1515. The *Crucifixion* depicts the intensity of Christ's anguish through straining hands, thorns stuck in a festering body, and a huge iron spike through the feet. The overall tortured effect is very different from the idealized humanity of Christ one finds in Italian Renaissance art. The figure of Christ so predominates over the other figures in the picture that ordinary humanity is made to seem of little account. At the foot of the cross Mary Magdalene kneels in grief, while to the left John the Apostle comforts Mary the Mother of Jesus. To the right stands a shaggy John the Baptist with an open Bible. He points to Jesus and above his hand are the words, "He must increase, but I must decrease." At John's feet is a small lamb (a traditional symbol of Christ) with a shepherd's crook. The lamb is shedding blood into a liturgical chalice. The power of the death scene comes from the force of the huge cross and strong corpus. This is not a man who died easily. The dark background suggests the brooding melancholy of Good Friday, when the sun was blackened for three hours, and the barren plain takes the picture away from Jerusalem, or any other earthly site, as if to say that history's deepest moment was a unity unto itself.

By contrast, the *Resurrection* shows a Christ of dazzling light. As powerful as the corpus of the *Crucifixion*, the central figure of the *Resurrection* floats in midair, as though he has just burst forth from the tomb. The soldiers who were guarding the tomb lie scattered like tenpins. A circular aura of light surrounds the Resurrected One, and his wounds stand out like jewels. The absence of any natural setting and the confused perspective give the painting an unearthly quality. If the *Crucifixion* seems abstracted from history, all the more so does the *Resurrection*. Yet the soldiers and the other physical details make it plain that this unearthly moment is the climax of Jesus' life. Where the great body on the cross droops with heavy defeat, the resurrected body is too light to be kept on earth.

When one realizes that the Isenheim Altarpiece was commissioned for the church of a hospital, the juxtaposition of the *Crucifixion* and the *Resurrection* gains further power. The sick people contemplating it could see that none of their sufferings would ever equal the pain of Christ crucified, but also that all their sufferings would be outweighed by Christ's resurrection, to which faith gave them access.

Thus, traditional Western Christian art took Jesus' humanity deeply to heart. By the eve of the Reformation, the scenes of the Bible had come to illumine the humanity of ordinary people. That Jesus was the Son of God did not mean that he was far from the rest of humanity. It meant that his death and resurrection held the key to all human beings' lives.

Thus Albrecht Altdorfer, a contemporary of Dürer and Grünewald, was unusual in painting landscapes that held no human figures. The Dutch painter Hieronymous Bosch, another contemporary of Dürer and Grünewald, was more typical in being fascinated by human concerns, even human depravities. Bosch's *Garden of Earthly Delight,* finished around 1510, crowds into its central panel hundreds of nude human figures engaged in erotic pursuits. The left panel of the tryptich portrays the Garden of Eden (with a naked Adam suspiciously interested in a naked Eve), and the right panel portrays an almost hallucinatory vision of hell, where the excessive pursuit of pleasure has finally received its just desserts. The middle panel, which presumably represents daily human life, is largely hell in anticipation. The final frustration and futility of hell are mainly but human pathos fully revealed.

By the early sixteenth century, Western Christian culture had become so disordered that the German and Dutch artists found little to cheer. Anticipating the pessimistic theologies of the Protestant reformers, the artists stressed the madness and sordidness that the fourteenth and fifteenth centuries had bequeathed to Europe. After the Black Death and Hundred Years' War in which millions had perished, even daily peasant life seemed twisted. Whereas the Italian humanists strove to create more optimistic images, the masters in the homeland of the Reformation brooded on folly. However, a generation later the best of them, Pieter Bruegel the Elder (1525–1569), painted human scenes with great compassion. For example, his *Peasant Wedding Feast* (1566–1567) takes a kindly view of a small child enjoying some tidbits and a poor, vacant-faced bagpiper waiting to perform. "Let them enjoy a brief time of happiness," the artist seems to say. "Their daily lives are hard enough."

The Period of Reform

In the piety that dominated the period between the high Middle Ages and the sixteenth-century Protestant Reformation, the most influential work was the *Imitation of Christ* by Thomas à Kempis (1380–1471).[34] The book evidences a sober awareness of death and a general view that life is a vale of tears. Both reflect a medieval heritage. Some church historians have called the *Imitation* the second most influential book in Christian history, second only to the New Testament. It breathes a certain air of discontent—the mood of the Netherlands, where it arose. It also breathes a de-

sire to experience religious consolation—the same desire that figured prominently in Martin Luther's spiritual biography.[35] However, the *Imitation* represents only one aspect of the period before the Reformation. Political factors certainly were a dominant influence, as was the fourteenth-century plague, which killed perhaps three-fourths of the population of Europe and Asia,[36] excited a great fear of devils and witches,[37] and made clear humanity's impotence and mortality.

During the late fourteenth and the fifteenth centuries, the papacy was in great disarray. At one point there were two claimants to the chair of Peter, one in Rome and one in Avignon. In the East the Muslims held Asia Minor and Greece, their most dramatic victory being at Constantinople in 1453. Well into the fifteenth century, southern Spain was under Muslim control, while in Italy the spirit of the Renaissance seemed stronger than conciliar attempts to reform the papacy. In addition, there were frictions among local rulers within the Italian, French, and German realms; the middle classes emerged as a result of city life and economic changes; and the pre-Lutheran attacks on Church corruption by the Lollards (followers of John Wycliffe in England) and the Hussites (followers of John Hus in Bohemia) took place.

The spark that set the Reformation blazing was Martin Luther (1483–1546), an Augustinian monk whose study and spiritual searches had convinced him that the heart of the gospel was the Pauline justification by faith (the belief that only faith makes one right with God). Only by reviving this Pauline theme could Christianity regain its pure beginnings. As John Kent has shown, there is a link between this central Lutheran idea and the themes of religious freedom and religious certainty that preoccupied later Protestants.[38] Justification by faith meant the fall of a whole system of "works" that the Catholic church had developed by late medieval times—the Mass, the sacraments, the rosary, and so forth.

Luther was precipitated into action by the prevailing practice of *indulgences* (papal remissions of purgatorial punishment due for sins), which one could obtain for various good deeds, including almsgiving. Behind this practice lay some simple economics. The popes had spent lavishly in their Renaissance enthusiasm for art and culture. Leo X, for instance, was perhaps 125,000 ducats in debt at the time that he endorsed the preaching mission of Johann Tetzel, Luther's first adversary,[39] which mission included granting an indulgence for a contribution to the building of St. Peter's in Rome. To Luther the whole system—the pope's extravagance, his pretension to control a treasury of merits generated by the saints, out of which he might draw "credits" to cover sinners' debts, and his focusing his economics on the Mass—was blasphemous. On October 31, 1517, tradition says, Luther nailed his Ninety-five Theses to the door of the castle church at Wittenberg, which amounted to a formal challenge to the system.

Many Germans who for political or religious reasons had grievances against Rome supported Luther. As his thought expanded, he made scripture the sole arbiter of Christian faith, declared the primacy of individual conscience, upgraded the status of the layperson, and urged the use of the vernacular rather than Latin. Luther also stressed the uniqueness of Christ's death on the cross and so taught that the Eucharist principally commemorates the Last Supper, rather than representing Christ's sacrificial death. On the basis of scripture, he judged the doctrine of purgatory unfounded and the practice of monastic life an aberration. Because Luther was a fine preacher, he made these ideas matters for discussion in the marketplace. By translating the Bible into marvelous German, he put the central basis for his reform within reach of all literate people (and just about standardized High German in the process). Finally, Luther's departure from monastic life and subsequent marriage led thousands more to leave their monasteries and convents.

The Spread of Reformation.   Luther's reform in Germany quickly generated uprisings elsewhere. Not only were many people eager for religious reform, separating themselves from Rome furthered their nationalistic sentiments. In Switzerland, Ulrich Zwingli (among the German speaking) and John Calvin (among the French speaking) led movements with similar themes. In England, Henry VIII and Thomas Cranmer separated their church from Rome. Generally, these reformers' writings show the influence of humanistic movements, from the Renaissance on, that had undermined the scholastic framework.[40] As well, they show a link to the spiritualist movements that were in search of a more emotionally satisfying faith. As the Reformation worked out, Lutheranism took root in countries with a primarily agrarian economy, such as Germany and Scandinavia, while Calvinism took root in countries with a commercial economy, such as French Switzerland, France, Flanders, and the Netherlands.[41]

Calvin had the greatest influence, however, on America, since France and Flanders largely returned to Catholicism, while Dutch Calvinism mixed with both the older piety espoused by the *Imitation of Christ* and the humanism of Desiderius Erasmus. In America, the Puritans from England were inspired by Calvin's desire to honor God by consecrating all of life to his kingship. Consequently, they tried to develop a theocratic state. Calvin's notions of God's sovereignty guided Jonathan Edwards, the first major American theologian,[42] and through Edwards much of the "Great Awakening" (the revivalist movement that Edwards sparked in New England from 1740 to 1743) and subsequent American religious life bore a Calvinist imprint. Through the preaching of John Knox, Scotland also became a home to Calvinism, and when they came to America Scottish immigrants brought their Calvinist tradition (Presbyterianism) to bear on business as well as Church life. Calvin's main work, *Institutes of the Christian Religion*, became the leading text of Reformed faith, while his efforts to establish a Reformed commonwealth in Geneva provided a model for other communities seeking to live by the gospel.

From the middle of the sixteenth to the middle of the seventeenth century, religious wars ravaged much of Europe. In France they subserved civil frictions. The Edict of Nantes (1598) preserved the status quo: Protestant areas would remain Protestant, Catholic areas (the majority) would remain Catholic. In the Netherlands the wars had the character of a rebellion against Spain. The northern Netherlands became largely Protestant, while the southern Netherlands remained under Spanish power and so Catholic. Germany was the most furious battlefield. Until the Peace of Münster (1648) there was constant carnage. The upshot in Germany was the famous dictum *"Cujus regio, ejus religio"*: Each area would follow the religion of its prince.

In England, Henry VIII found the Reformation currents useful in his struggle with the papacy to have his marriage to Catherine of Aragon annulled. Henry declared the king supreme in all matters that touched the Church in England, and he eagerly took monastic lands and income to finance his war against France. From 1553 to 1558 Mary Tudor made England papist again, but in 1571, under Henry's daughter Elizabeth I, the English bishops published their Thirty-nine Articles of Faith, which formalized their special blend of Protestantism and Catholicism.

Catholic Reform.   The Catholic response to the Protestant Reformation took place at the Council of Trent

(1545–1563). Trent affirmed the reliance of the Church on both scripture and tradition, the effective power of the sacraments, the need for human beings to cooperate in the work of justification (that is, no justification by faith alone), and the possibility of sin after justification (denied by some reformers). It also provided for reforms in clerical education and a general housecleaning to remove the laxness and venality that had made the reformers' charges more than credible. Probably the most powerful single agent of the Catholic Reformation was the Society of Jesus (the Jesuits), which Pope Paul III approved in 1540. Its founder was Ignatius of Loyola, a Basque.

Ignatius' companions quickly proved themselves the best combination of learning and zealous faith around. Therefore, they were assigned many of the tasks of teaching and missionizing that were central to Catholic renewal. Peter Canisius in Germany, Robert Bellarmine in Italy, and Francisco Suárez in Spain were intellectuals and educators (the first two also became prelates) who had a great deal to do with revitalizing Catholicism in their countries. Jesuit missionaries to Asia such as Francis Xavier, Matteo Ricci, and Roberto di Nobili, also had great success. Xavier was a charismatic figure of the first order, able to stir crowds without even knowing their language. Ricci and di Nobili took on the customs of the people with whom they worked (Chinese and Indians) and confronted the vast task of forming native versions of Christianity. Jesuits also ministered underground to Catholics in England (several lost their lives in the effort), and they went to the New World to missionize Canada, the American Southwest, and Latin America.[43]

Further Developments. A century after Luther's Ninety-five Theses, Europe washed in waves of Reformation and Counter Reformation (the Catholic Reformation). In Britain, the alternation of Catholic and Protestant monarchs led to a series of repressive measures, while the Calvinism first of the Scot John Knox and then of the rigorists called Puritans made great gains. The Spanish and Portuguese were exporting Catholicism through their great trading ventures, while the Dutch and English were exporting Protestantism. Consequently, Christian division became a worldwide affair.

Seventeenth-century America became a refuge for Protestants who opposed what they considered oppressive practices in their native lands and who stressed individual rights of conscience. The Church of England was strong in Virginia, Georgia, and the Carolinas. The Dutch Reformed Church dominated New York and New Jersey. Germans and Dutch flocked to Pennsylvania, while Congregationalists dominated New England. Catholics were an important group in Maryland. As the Reformation principle of individual conscience worked its influence, more and more groups splintered off to search out places where they could live their convictions in peace. According to Sidney Mead, the unique character of American religion has been that it formed a national culture and law on the basis of its pluralism.[44]

In its Reformation, Catholicism set new standards for its popes and clergy. It also obtained a new spirituality (largely Jesuit) that tried to adapt traditional piety to the new age of individual conscience. Commentators have nominated Loyola's *Spiritual Exercises* as the third most influential Christian book. If we substitute "Catholic" for "Christian," they are likely correct. The work is in the form of meditations on different gospel scenes, but Ignatius designed them to bring about a "discernment of spirits" and a choice of a way of life. Some commentators point out that the mysticism of the *Exercises* is a shift to the interior in keeping with the shift of the great contemporary Spanish mystics Teresa of Avila and John of the Cross, and that the *Exercises* bring the medieval mystical tradition up to date by tailoring it to a more active life. Other commentators have shown Ignatius' anticipation of a modern "mystagogy" (exercise in the experience of God) and mystical dialectics.[45] From the *Spiritual Exercises* and other works of the Catholic Reformation, the Roman church learned how people might work in the world with the hope of finding God in all things. That made it easier for Rome to bless new active orders of priests, brothers, and nuns.

As Robert McAfee Brown has shown,[46] the spirit of Protestantism that has come down from the sixteenth century stresses, first, the notion of reform itself—of always having to renew one's faith because of one's distance from God's holy will. Second, it stresses God's sovereignty, the authority of scripture, the priesthood of all believers, and the vocation of the laity to exercise their faith in the midst of the secular world. Ever since Luther and Calvin, the Bible has been the great text for both Protestant worship and Protestant theology, while, as historical sociologists such as Max Weber have suggested,[47] Protestant discipline has been a main ingredient in the rise of capitalistic culture. As capitalistic economies developed in Europe and the

United States, efficiency and wealth often became considered religious virtues—even signs of salvation.

The Reformation left Protestants and Catholics at odds, and the conflict has abated only in recent years. Today most seem to agree (despite such throwbacks as Northern Ireland) that the reformers had legitimate grievances and that the reformers' return to scripture renewed faith. On the other hand, Protestant and Catholic scholars also agree that many of the defects in modern Christianity result from its lacking the sense of a catholic tradition and common authority. The ecumenical task for the future, they would say, is for Christians to put their humpty-dumpty together again.

Modernity

In this section we concentrate on the eighteenth and nineteenth centuries, though aspects of modernity clearly are found in the seventeenth century and still persist today. From the myriad events and thinkers who shaped the eighteenth and nineteenth centuries we must select the most crucial. Clearly, the Enlightenment was crucial, as were the political revolutions in France and America, which were related to it. As well, the Industrial Revolution and the European colonization of large parts of Africa and Asia play in the background. Of the thinkers, the line from Descartes to Marx that passes through Hume, Kant, and Hegel is perhaps the most significant.

The religious life of the West changed dramatically in the modern period. It had to contend with new political, philosophical, and scientific thought. More profoundly, for the first time it met a passionate counterfaith, for as a movement or cause modernity opposed to reliance on God a deep commitment to humanity's own powers. (This was not true of Islam until the twentieth century.)

Heribert Raab has written, "The Enlightenment denotes the most revolutionary of all movements which the Occident has undergone in the course of history,"[48] making reference to Protestant historian Ernst Troeltsch's view that the Enlightenment marks the beginning of the modern period of European culture, ending the previous theological or ecclesiastical culture.

The Enlightenment began in the Netherlands and England in the mid-seventeenth century, but its most outstanding expressions arose in France and Germany. French rationalistic and materialistic philosophy (such as that of Voltaire, Helvétius, and Comte) and French revolutionary political action both derived from the Enlightenment. In Germany, Leibniz, Lessing, and Kant were its first philosophical offspring, while the "enlightened despotism" of Frederick the Great and Joseph II was a political result.

The Enlightenment thinkers saw themselves as part of a movement for progress, the watchword of which was criticism. They took as their enemy ignorance, intolerance, and repression, vowing to attack all such manifestations in national culture. To power this critical warfare they drew on the model of the new physical science (especially that of Newton). That meant setting goals of clarity, precision, and rational order. Thus, the Enlightenment was a tremendous affirmation of humanity's rational capacities. Furthermore, it assumed that both creation and human nature were essentially good, thus producing an expectation of great progress. Things would improve and freedom would increase as trustworthy critical reason expressed trustworthy human nature situated in a quite trustworthy natural order.

Quite obviously, the Enlightenment view of human nature clashed with that of traditional Christianity. Although reason held an important place in the medieval scholastic synthesis, the medieval mind never doubted that human nature is only perfectible through divine grace. In Reformation thought, Protestant and Catholic alike, both human reason and human love suffer the grievous effects of sin, with the result that only God can give the fulfillment they seek. The Enlightenment contested the beliefs of both periods.

In fact, Alexander Pope (1688–1744) epitomized his era when he said that the proper concern of man is man. Drawing on Renaissance humanism as well as on Reformation individualism, the Enlightenment thinkers concluded that things outside the province of human experience are of marginal concern. How we define human experience, of course, is a capital question. Enlightenment leaders tended to distrust both mystical experience and systematic reason (Hegel was an exception), preferring empiricism instead. Thus, Hume made a deep impression by limiting valid human thought to what sensation can verify. In the political sphere, the new thinkers sought to establish empirical laws of human nature that might help provide liberty, fraternity, and equality. Even when such philosophy or political science grew quite abstract (as in the case of the French revolutionary philosophies), there was agreement that theology and revelation were irrelevant.

For Kant and Hegel, the great innovators in the modern philosophy of consciousness, the reason that was to secure "the system" would not be subordinate to traditional faith. Thus, biblical, conciliar, and even Reformation notions of how things are in the world were rejected during the Enlightenment. By a turn to the thinking subject, reality became the domain that we now call the secular world. The transcendent domain, the holy world that past ages had called the most objective, had no place in the new world view. Only as a manifestation of human self-expression, individual or social, did religion merit attention.

A great many factors were at work in this subjective turn, of course, and not all of them sprang from human pride. A general disgust with religion—well deserved after a century of religious wars—certainly made a new humanistic beginning attractive. The overbearing weight of ecclesiastical institutions, which regularly stomped on individual rights and opposed free scientific inquiry, make anticlericalism rather healthy. (The Spanish Inquisition and Oliver Cromwell's massacre of the Irish are heinous instances of religion used to desecrate human beings.)

In the sciences, the excitement of empirical discoveries and the slow differentiation of canons of critical judgment were forces that seemed to oppose faith. Under the banner of religion huddled so much superstition and anti-intellectualism that simple integrity drove many educated people away from the Church. The best and the brightest frequently found themselves forced to choose between their love of human culture (the intelligence, sober judgment, and compassionate love that represent humanity at its best) and religion, Christianity, or even God.

However, applying Enlightenment beliefs to philosophy and politics did not prove to be an unqualified boon. Unfettered reason and humanism produced horrors that quite challenged those of the religious witch hunts and inquisitions. For instance, the bloodbaths of the French Revolution differed little from those of the religious wars, showing that not all fanaticism trumpeted about God. The American Constitution, despite its debt to Enlightenment humanism and its expression of democratic freedoms, was the framework of a culture that often treated nonwhites and women as less than human.[49] The Marxist-Leninist-Maoist brand of political religion, which is largely indebted to Hegel, produced inhuman totalitarian regimes. Small wonder, then, that Eric Voegelin found the path from Enlightenment to revolution a way of self-deification—a vicious way of placing selected human beings on the throne of divine mystery that they might crush all opposition.[50]

Those who defended the pre-Enlightenment order argued that the fallacies in the new order were both subtle and patent. On the subtle side, a thoroughly critical analysis of experience showed that there is more to reality than what Enlightenment philosophy acknowledged. For instance, mystical, mythical, poetic, romantic, and even creatively scientific thought all are poorly accounted for by Enlightenment epistemology (theory of knowledge). On the patent side, observation of human behavior showed that reason seldom guides public affairs. Putting these objections to the Enlightenment together, Christian apologists argued that an experience of God can take one beyond empirical reason and that an irrationality exists that is well labeled "sin." A major legacy of modernity is the continuing Western debate over the assets and liabilities of critical reason.

In our sketch of the historical development of Christianity, we have stressed the internal dynamics: how the original commitment to Jesus Christ as both the fulfillment of Jewish prophecy and the definitive Word of God offering human beings eschatological salvation developed into the great cultural force of the Western world. We have stressed this aspect because our main interest is Christian *religion*. For those more interested in Christian culture, or the interaction between ideas ultimately owed to Christian faith and such significant political developments as the rise of the Holy Roman Empire in medieval times or the rise of nation-states in modern times, greater stress on the struggles between kings and nobles, or between the upper and lower classes, or between capitalists and workers would be in order. We completely accept the principle that Christianity did not develop in a vacuum but was involved in a dialectical relationship with other cultural forces—political, economic, artistic, military. On Christianity's own terms, which lay rooted in the incarnation of divinity in space and time, everything human was relevant to religious faith, and religious faith was relevant to everything human. Thus one should picture the unfolding of religious ideas, theology, church life, and all the Christian rest as the result of an intense, ongoing, never-failing interaction between faith and worldly culture. Just as one cannot understand the significance of Jesus or the New Testament without appreciating how they were a response to the Jewish and Hellenistic cultures of their times, so one cannot understand later periods without realizing that Christianity was constantly molding and being molded by external forces. Religious ideas and practices never develop in a vacuum. Always the sociological pressures of a given time help to shape how people think about God, themselves, sin and grace, the sacraments of the Church, and so forth. If we have emphasized religious ideas more than secular currents, that is because religion is our main focus and obligation in this book. But students should never forget that throughout most of its history Christianity has been a highly complex phenomenon evolving in the cauldron of whatever was shaping its people.

The Contemporary Situation

The principles of Reformation and modernity have worked for more than four and a half centuries since Martin Luther. The reforming spirit continued both within and without Lutheranism and Calvinism, often simplifying Christianity to yield a stark biblical faith and worship. Thus, Puritanism, parts of Methodism, and Baptist religion moved Protestantism farther from Catholic dogmatic and sacramental theology. In reacting to this trend, Anglo-Catholicism tried to mediate between the ancient Catholic tradition and the Protestant instinct about the new religious needs of post-Renaissance society. However, the tide of the Protestant sectarians brought waves of individual, enthusiastic experience, which in turn promoted emotional preaching, revivalism, and biblical literalism. Meanwhile, traditional Catholic authority fought modernity tooth and nail, only accepting modern scholarship and modern conceptions of human rights in the twentieth century.

During the nineteenth century, the Enlightenment meant liberalism in religious matters. Christianity was adapted to the needs of the day, which liberals thought were primarily humanistic in character. Adolf Harnack's slogan that the Christian essence is "the fatherhood of God and the brotherhood of man" encapsules much of the liberal spirit.

On occasion, both liberals and *evangelicals* (people rooted in the gospel) pressed for social change. The Industrial Revolution produced some abysmal working conditions, and Christian exponents of the "social gospel" agreed with Karl Marx that such conditions destroyed human dignity. In the "liberation theology" of recent years, this kinship with aspects of Marxism has become explicit, for many liberation theologians are combining Marxist economic analyses with Christian beliefs. The most eloquent are Latin Americans,[51] but thought like theirs has penetrated the counsels of both Protestant Geneva and Catholic Rome. Recently Latinos, blacks, Asians, and feminists in North America who want to promote social change through radical Christian faith have all rallied around liberation theology.[52]

In American religious history, a central theme has been what Martin Marty calls "righteous empire."[53] With this phrase Marty tries to summarize the Protestant experience in the New World. It entailed divine errands in the wilderness, the sacred tasks of making God's new Israel, and a manifest destiny to show the world a truly Christian society. There was some breakup of the empire due to the divisions among the many American Christian churches, and so there was a rather reluctant settling for a civic code that granted *all* citizens religious liberty, freedom of conscience, and separation of church and state.

The effort of Enlightenment figures such as Jefferson and Franklin to make a state that was both humanistic and hospitable to the Christian majority has been a striking experiment. However, American civil religion has been neither fully Christian nor fully human if measured by either Christian dogma or post-Enlightenment criticism.[54]

Puritanism, liberalism, and Marxism may all be analyzed as forms of Gnosticism. Although these three viewpoints relate to the Enlightenment (and contribute to U.S. history) in quite different ways, they all depart from the classical political theory that developed from Greek reason and Jewish-Christian revelation. In other words, the majority movements in modern politics have not been concerned with maintaining a balance between divinity and humanity, faith and reason, transcendent reality and the world at hand. For the most part, they have concentrated on the second terms in these pairings or even tried to convert the first terms into the second.

The result has been an apotheosis (divinization) of humanity, a hearty optimism and faith in human reason, and a nearly mystical commitment to political action—with little feel for the irony involved. In the domain of scholarship, the historian has wielded more power than the theologian. In the domain of popular Christian religion, there has been considerable defense of the secular. Only after Vietnam, Watergate, and a proliferation of crises (ecological, nuclear, and economic), whose interrelationships challenge our cultural values, did Americans begin to suspect that modern Gnosticism had led them far astray. Within Christianity, these crises have become a common challenge. Only people who ignore reality do not feel their impact. They require a thorough rethinking of the faith handed down as well as a thorough critique of the gospel as lived by Wall Street.

Furthermore, Christians have had to rethink their assumptions about revelation, salvation, the centrality of Christ, and the position of "pagans" as they have learned about other religions. Because of both secular and religious developments, then, the current Christian situation is complex and demanding. Science, technology, politics, and history (in other cultures as well as those that derive from Christianity) all demand reconciliation with traditional faith.

Those concerns of current Western theologians press in upon even an introductory text in world religions. First, we cannot separate them from the assumptions with which scholarship approaches any religious tradition today. That is, we cannot cite religious phenomena, separate central ones from peripheral ones, and compose historical or comparative analyses without understanding just what religious phenomena are and why some are central. Even a student or scholar with no express theory about such things has a tacit theory about them.

For instance, some people think of religion in terms of social ceremonies. For them a person who does not attend church or synagogue regularly is not religious. Other people define religion as the urge to know and love that opens onto mystery. For them the irreligious person blocks off contemplative love. We favor the second interpretation.

Second, the concerns that modernity generated often spark a quarrel between scholarship and faith. Persons committed to religious traditions may feel that detached, critical, scientific treatment of their beliefs and worship distorts them. American Indians, for instance, have said that anthropologists' comments on their sacred dances are usually trivial. Without the experience of being lost in communion with the Great Spirit, the anthropologist can only ruminate about group contagion or the therapies of rhythm. There are analogies in every religion. At the heart of the effort to describe the reality of religious experience lie the unavoidable issues of critical reason and experiential faith.

As a result of the Enlightenment, contemporary scholars test every observation, every statement, every memory—they accept nothing uncritically. From traditional faith comes the axiom that one must believe in order to understand, love in order to see. That axiom finally implies that faith is an act greater and more comprehensive than reason.

Third, these interpretational issues are especially acute in contemporary Western culture because they arose due to the effects of Christianity. Indeed, the Christian blend of Israelite revelation and Greek reason may have carried their seeds from the beginning. By the happenstance (or providence) that Christianity became the dominant European world view, and the happenstance that European culture developed science, history, and philosophy into the massive critical apparatus that we possess today, these issues are fundamental to both contemporary Western culture and contemporary Christian faith. The result is a constant, if frequently subtle, interplay.

For instance, religion does not go away just because critical reason argues it off the property. Usually, it simply takes another form—the scientist or historian whose life turns on research becomes "religious" about his or her work. Indeed, the more creative such a historian or scientist is, the more passionate, even lyric and reverent, he or she will be about the commitment to truth and objectivity that the work demands. Similarly, the devoted social activist, whether Marxist or not, tends to survive through a largely unprovable faith that history has a meaningful direction or that giving one's life to improve other people's lot makes sense. Even the typical citizen who goes along without much reflection or passion hears a few whispers of God.

Case Study: Conversion. Against this background, Emilie Griffin's book *Turning: The Experience of Conversion*[55] sharpens many of the themes of recent Christian religious experience. Seeking the meaning of her own life, Griffin came to the critical point of personal choice: conversion from the secular values of the prevailing culture to an ardent Christian faith. In describing the motives and processes of her conversion, Griffin suggests that the Christian gospel still has the power to connect some lives to a deep, mysterious source of satisfaction. As we consider her case study of Christian faith, we can note where it challenges the mores of current Western culture and also where the modern critiques of Christian consciousness show faith vulnerable to self-deception.

For Griffin, the conversion process began with a great longing, an ache in her heart for something she had never experienced and could not even describe. This is reminiscent of the paradoxical remark of Blaise Pascal (1623–1662) that we would not seek God had we not already found God. Be it world weariness, or the passing of childhood satisfactions, or the strange inability of even great success to satisfy them for long, a disenchantment prompts many converts to consider a new way of life.

When she began to study the lives of converts, Griffin found that many reported having had intense experiences of nature in their youth, times when the universe stood as a fresh and dazzling immensity. A hunger for such experiences surfaced later in their lives, when they found a horizon of "everydayness" cramped and unsatisfying. For example, Thomas Merton, the Roman Catholic convert who became a famous Trappist monk, remembered being five years old and hearing all the birds in the trees start singing when some church bells began to chime. He asked his father why the two of them were not also in church, but his father only said that they would go to church some other Sunday. Similarly, C. S. Lewis, the well-known British convert, reported harkening back to an experience he had when he was six. He could see the Castlereagh Hills from his window, and they filled him with a great longing to touch their beauty.

In Griffin's early life both literature and nature had furnished her great joy. When she left her adolescent world of books and trees, however, and went to New York in search of a career, the joy seemed to drain away from her spirit. This made her brief trips to places like Central Park, or her times free for poetry reading, all the more precious, yet also all the more unable to satisfy her growing hunger. Almost accidentally she bought a leather-bound volume of the Anglican Book of Common Prayer, which surprised her by the force its words carried, as though something that had informed her distant ancestors was now speaking directly to her own soul.

Before long she became a frequenter of churches. Even when their bad art repelled her, Christian churches hinted at a wisdom about life and death, suffering and joy—the great human experiences she was trying to fathom. While the Christian teaching about immortality seemed to her illogical, she admired the concise statements of faith that rang forth in such venerable Christian formulas as the Apostles' Creed. Her upbringing in Christian Science made the question of the relation between flesh and spirit especially engrossing. Slowly she came to suspect that the attraction of Christian churches lay in their materialization of spiritual truths. In their glass and stone, they made faith, hope, and love visible, tangible.

From this suspicion it was but a short step to considering the center of Christian faith, the *Incarnation*. That Jesus had healed the man born blind (John 9:1–40) by spitting on the ground, mixing the spittle with dirt, and applying it to the blind man's eyes seemed utterly human—so human that it must have been orchestrated by God. Similarly, Jesus had turned water into wine, multiplied loaves and fishes, eaten broiled fish and honeycomb after his resurrection. Again and again, Griffin ran into this fusion of matter and spirit, this axis of incarnationalism or sacramentality. The Christian way, she came increasingly to see, was to place divinity in the world, to enflesh the Word of God in human form.

These discoveries only sharpened Griffin's longing to find a spiritual home. When she began to study traditional Christianity more deeply, her study did not spring from an academic interest in Christian religion. It was deeply personal and passionate. Perhaps this life-way held the truth of happiness, the sources of deep satisfaction. Perhaps it could slake the burning thirst of her soul. Reason and dispassion had their place, since she wanted a life-way that was realistic, not a bundle of convenient illusions. But her reasoning now was in the service of a heartfelt need for a whole, very human truth. In fact, the closer she came to seeing that she really hungered for God, for reality of a more-than-worldly order, the more she feared that affirming God would be an irrational leap spurred by her own needs. Perhaps "God" was only a projection of her great longings.

Yet this familiar argument against God seemed to have an obverse side. Would people long so for God if "God" had no reality? Could nature have made us so vainly, so certain to be frustrated? Back and forth the argument waged within her. Was her desire an unusual neurosis, or an unusual call to health? Before long, though, she decided that her desire for faith was too important to ignore. Better to risk disillusionment than never to test faith's truth. Better to pursue the desire for God to a frustrating conclusion than to hang back and remain divided. So Griffin determined to see the issue through, both intellectually and emotionally.

If we now generalize from Griffin's biography to the question of contemporary Christian faith at large, we find that the intellectual portion of the project of Christian conversion includes accepting the great propositions of the Christian tradition about sin, grace, the Incarnation, and the Trinity. Even if one gets through the door marked "God" and becomes able to affirm the existence of a Creator, Christian faith demands that one accept these further specifications of the Creator's nature and the Creator's actions on human beings' behalf. Finally, on the other side of the room to which the door marked "God" gives access, there are the Christian doctrines about the Church, the scriptures, and the sacraments. If one buys the Christian claims about God and Jesus, these other articles of faith also line up for adoption. Only if they form a coherent system can a responsible person like Griffin judge them an attractive, acceptable package.

Curiously, though, the more Griffin pursued the question of God, the more the entire package became plausible. Having once seriously entertained the possibility that God exists, Griffin found the biblical descriptions of God rather credible. Once again the Incarnation was to be crucial. That God should appear in human form, suffering and rising "for us human beings and our salvation," as the traditional creed put it, was certainly strange, but somehow in keeping with a God as good as the Bible proclaimed God to be.

It was not so strange that the world should have an intelligible source. It was more strange that this source should be as good as the father of the prodigal son described in Luke 15, as willing to sacrifice his eternal Son as Paul insisted in Romans 8. None of this was necessary, automatically entailed in the concept of "God." But all of it somehow was fitting. If God were to choose to make creatures with the spiritual capacities of reason and love, he might well choose to express himself in a human form and solicit their free love by a life of exceptional goodness. At least, this is the way that many converts like Griffin have found themselves starting to reason.

Moreover, this response to the intellectual challenges of accepting Christian faith tends to supply answers to most of the emotional challenges. Once the option of joining the Christian Church became intellectually respectable, Griffin found the emotional obstacles greatly diminished. The possible ridicule from supposedly sophisticated secular friends paled in comparison to the new meaning that conversion seemed to hold out. And her great longing for coherence, beauty, and a cause worth dedicating herself to seemed on the verge of finding fulfillment. So a certain at-homeness began to overtake Griffin's emotions. More and more the instruction classes she attended, the Church services she took part in, and the circle of new friends she met rang true, outlined a life-style that seemed to fit.

She realized quite well that the Church had many foibles, that her new friends were quite imperfect, and that much of the attractiveness of Christianity de-

pended on her making a prior commitment of faith. The sacraments were pregnant with lovely meaning only if she believed them to be life-giving actions of God's Spirit. Also, Griffin never forgot that her coming to the threshold of Christian faith and then stepping across into the Christian Church had been powered by her inner needs. She was like a sick person who had come in search of a cure, a puzzled person who had come in search of clarifications. Still, once she decided that this motivation need not discredit the help that Christian faith seemed to provide her, she could convert to Christianity in good conscience.

Griffin's sketch of the conversion process challenges the secular assumption that faith is unreasonable, in the very process of challenging the secular assumption that God is impossible. For Emilie Griffin, both Christian faith and the Christian God became more reasonable than the secular life of many of her friends. Indeed, increasingly she found secular living cramped and unsatisfying. If there was no more to life than good food, interesting work, and clever conversation, life was a cruel hoax. The issue boiled down to whether Christian faith or secularism laid out the richer world view, and for Griffin it finally was no contest. Jesus had words of eternal life and the world mainly spun its wheels.

It does not impugn this honest report on the dynamics of Christian conversion to point out that Christian faith ought to be judged more by its fruits than by its self-justification. That was Jesus' own criterion (Matt. 7:16), and it validates a certain healthy pragmatism. If Griffin's or any other convert's assumption of a religious world view produces a greater ability to love and to work (Freud's standard for psychic health), an honest observer will account that conversion a good thing. If, on the other hand, a religious world view injures or frustrates love and work, an honest observer will account that world view (or at least the particular convert's version of it) suspect.

What do these standards of "love" and "work" entail? No doubt some subjectivity enters in, but we would have "love" entail an increasing appreciation of the mystery of life, of our fellow human beings, and of ourselves. We would have "work" entail the ability to create, serve, and so make one's time advance the beautification, clarification, and betterment of one's time and space.

Admittedly, these are not precise criteria, but the ground-level question of human or religious authenticity can never be precise. Modern studies of human consciousness show that we are all very complex creatures, with many different motivations and needs. If, overall, we become creatures who are honest and loving, productive and helpful, the world view that forms us to such health deserves high praise. As well, it deserves thoughtful consideration by others, for it might just be the better way that they, too, have been seeking.

WORLDVIEW

Nature

Theologians who treat the meaning of nature in Christianity often show that nature has usually signified the human essence.[56] That does not mean that Christianity has denied the reality of the physical world. On the contrary, its Greek and Israelite sources both gave Christianity a realistic orientation toward the world. Moreover, the body of Jesus, insofar as Christian faith made him the Logos incarnate, was an anchor to realism. Against the Gnostics, who were their foremost adversaries, the early Christian writers insisted on the reality and goodness of matter. If God himself had made the world, and God's own Son had assumed flesh, both the world and human flesh had to be good.

Nonetheless, because of the early controversies about the being of God and Christ, the word *physis* (nature) connoted divine and human "whatness" more than it connoted external reality. During the early controversies about free will and sin, Christian speculation finally concluded that the redemption and salvation that Christ had worked were beyond that to which human beings had any right. Thus, they were supernatural gifts that came only by grace. Grace, it followed, was a generosity that God does not owe us. Furthermore, redemption and salvation so transformed human nature that it could share in God's own divine nature (2 Pet. 1:4). By itself, apart from grace, nature was unredeemed, unsaved, something far from the glory of divinity. These beliefs dominated classical Christian theology (Catholic, Orthodox, and Protestant alike).

In discussing creation we find more extensive Christian considerations of the physical world.[57] God stands to the world as its independent, uncaused source, who made it from nothing by his simple free choice. The first mark of the natural world for the traditional Christian, then, has been its subordination to divine creativity. Considerable time passed before the full conceptualization of creation as a Divine making of the world from nothingness developed (from a combination of biblical and philosophical sources), but from the beginning the God of the burning bush was sovereignly free.

In most periods of Christian history, nature was considered mysterious and overpowering, but the Genesis story that God gave human beings dominion over nature shaped a belief that the physical world existed for humanity's sake. Thus Christianity has taught its faithful to husband the physical world and use it. Little in the Christian message proposed that human beings should ravage the world, but equally little proposed integrating human life with nature's ecology or preserving nature's gifts through frugality and reverence. In most periods Christians found nature abundant and generous, so conservation was not a major concern.

Furthermore, the biblical fear of nature gods contributed to a semiconscious Christian effort to make nature undivine. In rural places (among European peasants, for instance), this effort succeeded only partially. Overall, though, it was quite central to the Christian theology of creation. Coming from God, the world was good. But since it came from God by his free choice, springing from nothingness, the world was definitely not divine. Thus, the Christian interest in transforming human nature combined with a continuance of the biblical prophets' objection to the nature gods; thus, the physical world was made a subordinate, even a somewhat ambivalent, concept. Inasmuch as nature and the human body could seem antagonistic to the spiritual destiny of human beings, nature could seem something that human beings had to restrain and control.

Science. The relative profanity (nonsacredness) that Christians attributed to nature played a rather complex role in the rise of Western science. When the Greek protoscientists, or early natural philosophers, developed a rude demythologizing of nature, they established the principle that the physical world is open to rational investigation. Thus, it was not blasphemous to pry into nature's secrets, and it could be profitable: Nature yields valuable information to those who pry well.

In Christian hands this demythologizing went several steps further. Pre-Renaissance scholars (many of them monks) worked at what we would call physics or biology, although such work was subordinated to theology. In other words, the basically religious culture preceding the Renaissance determined that theology would be the queen of the sciences. Thus, before the Renaissance, the Catholic church kept physical science on a rather short leash. The controversy that the new theories of Galileo Galilei (1564–1642) raised shows the Church attitude that still prevailed in the seventeenth century: Faith had to predominate over the evidence of the senses. Shoring up theological notions (that the earth was the center of the universe was a theological axiom) was more important than allowing intelligence the freedom to investigate nature as it would.

Enlightenment thinkers were reacting to that sort of dogmatism and theological control when they attacked Christian faith as irrational or anti-intellectual. Almost in the name of a higher religion (fidelity to conscience), they attacked theology as dishonest. Since the scientific method, as we now call it, that was disengaging itself from theology (despite the Church's protests) brought tangibly positive results, it drove the ecclesiastical authorities deeper and deeper into their indefensible corner. Still, the passion of their faith made the authorities fly their flag decades after it had turned to tatters. Long after the Galileo disgrace, when even the Roman Holy Office allowed the sun to be the center of the universe, the Church opposed new scientific theories on theological grounds. Thus, many Christian leaders denounced Darwin and Freud, because evolution and psychoanalysis seemed to refute the image of human nature that religious tradition had developed. The creature who was little less than an angel, the creature for whom Christ had shed his blood, the creature who was the very image of God could not have descended from an ape or have unconscious lust for its parents.

Regarding the investigation of nature, therefore, the Christian legacy has been mixed. At first Christianity supported reason, the reality and goodness of the world, and the value of scientific contemplation. However, when investigation seemed to threaten faith, Christian orthodoxy tried to check the scientific mind. In elite circles today things are much better, for theologians now analyze the implications of scientific findings for ethics and faith. For instance, they discuss genetic engineering, nuclear research, the medical definition of death, and the like from a belief in the Christian concept of human dignity. Some confusion still remains about the line between religion and science, but history has chastened theologians

considerably, and they are now slow to condemn scientific research.

On the other side, a significant number of scientists doubt that the scientific method alone is a comprehensive way of life. Not only does scientific research tend to ignore ethical questions about the social applications of its findings (for example, its findings about nuclear energy), it also finds itself more and more appreciative of nature's complexity—indeed, of nature's mystery. Every scientific discovery raises many more questions, whether in the realm of atomic particles, the realm of life, or the realm of the stars. Nature itself, we are finding, is a collection of mysteries.[58] Thus, nature commands a respect, even awe, that is quite different from the arrogance with which earlier, mechanistic scientists attacked it. In fact, for some philosophers of science, such as Alfred North Whitehead,[59] nature is the concrete form of divinity.

Sacramentalism and Mysticism. Christian sacramentalism has somewhat closed the gap (between the place of nature in Christian religion in contrast to pagan religion) that was opened by the Western separation of reason from myth. As well, Christian mystics such as St. Francis who have sensed a divine presence in woods and birds have been rather naturalist in their style. In its worship and sacramental theology, Christian religion often has pressed the belief that God called creation good. Often, it has applied a mythic and poetic intelligence that made the world mysterious, awesome, and alive. Baptismal water, eucharistic bread and wine, wax, incense, flowers, salt, oil—they have all enriched the liturgy. On the most solemn feast of Easter, the liturgy spoke as though all of creation got into the act, joining in the *Exultet*—the song of great rejoicing. In the liturgy of Good Friday, which commemorates Christ's death, the tree of the cross (the holy rood) became a new *axis mundi*—a new cosmic pillar linking heaven and earth. Taking over Psalm 150, Christians praised God in his firmament. Taking over other psalms, they made the mountains and the beasts co-conspirators to God's praise. All creation, then, was to resound to the music of the spheres. All creation ought to sing as it labored for redemption. Nature was part of a divine drama, part of a cosmic play of sin and grace.

Partly from such liturgical encouragement, Christian mystics have often shown a delight in nature like that of their East Asian counterparts. The accents have been different, since the Christian God is not the impersonal Buddha-nature, but they have not been contradictory. For instance, Francis of Assisi felt free to praise God as manifested in nature, and he composed famous canticles to brother sun and sister moon. Indeed the legends about his intimacy with animals are a sort of Christian prefiguring of the messianic age of fulfillment, recalling Isaiah's figures of the child playing at the asp's hole and the lion lying down with the lamb. In the messianic age men and women would once more be intimate with nature, as they were when God made them "in the beginning."

For the early desert fathers, the wilderness was a place to become sanctified. For many Puritans and early Americans, the wilderness brought to mind Israel's wanderings in the desert—the place where its religion was pure. Thus, a romantic strain of Christian thought has kept nature close to God. Sometimes it has made the city less desirable for religious life than the country. Often it has made solitude close to the elements a privileged place for prayer. As a result, the Christian God has been strong as the seas, everlasting as the hills, lovely as the lilies of the field.

Society

Central to the Christian notion of how people ought to join together has been the Church. It could oppose the state, standing as the religious collectivity against the secular. It has also been the place where Christian life was supposed to show itself as something mysteriously organic—as the "body" of Christ. In the earliest periods of Church history, before Theodosius established Christianity as the official Roman faith, Church leaders led quite unpretentious lives. Meetings of the community tended to be small gatherings in members' homes, and the bishop who led the liturgy might earn his bread as a cobbler or a craftsman. New Testament models suggested that carpentry (the occupation of Jesus) and tentmaking (the occupation of Paul) were more than honorable occupations. To those who waited idly for the *parousia,* the Church said, "Work—or no community support." In fact, most Christians in the beginning were nondescript working people. Thus, the *Epistle to Diognetius,*[60] an early Christian work, portrays a Christian existence in the world whereby faith would make one a solid citizen.

Nonetheless, from early times Christians also felt that preaching the gospel was an especially honorable work and that some community leaders ought to be free to labor at it full time. The decision to have deacons care for temporal affairs (Acts 6:1–6) suggests that Christians quickly established a hierarchy of tasks

parallel to the hierarchy of Christian authorities. The work that preoccupied Church leaders and that later theology regarded as the Church's basic duty was a ministry or service in terms of "Word and Sacrament."[61] "Word" was, in the first instance, the scriptures. From the outset, they guided worship, theology, and private reflection. Ministry of the Word included commenting on scripture to edify the assembly and preaching to the outside world (missionizing).

The Word itself was the gospel, but also the divine Logos. Thus, it implied reciting the dramatic story of what God, out of his love, had chosen to do for humanity. The decisive episode in that story was Jesus' death and resurrection. And Jesus—the Christ, the Logos—became present in a special way through the preaching of the Gospel. Faith in Jesus was the "entry" to the gospel view or "economy" of salvation, and faith demanded "hearing."

Developing biblical categories, recent theologians have shown that Jesus himself has been the Church's primal sacrament;[62] his flesh has been the greatest sign of God's nature and God's love. The Johannine writings contain the richest New Testament sacramental theology, but all the early literature makes clear that sacramental life has been a life of union with Jesus. Sacramental life continued the incarnation of divinity; through its cyclical recall of the mysteries of Jesus' life, it purported to lead Church members ever deeper into God's love.

Polity. Christian society has centered on worship through Word and Sacrament. Still, its structural organization was rather fluid at first and varied from place to place. In those early arrangements we can discern elements of all three of the later Church polities: the episcopal, presbyterial (of the elders), and congregational forms of Church government. With time, though, came the monarchical structure of Roman Catholicism, the collegial model of Orthodoxy, and the government by elders that has characterized much of Protestantism.

In the West before the Reformation, the structure of the Catholic church was pyramidal. At the top was the pope, along the bottom were the laity. In between, in descending order, were cardinals, bishops, and priests. The "religious" (those who had taken vows of poverty, chastity, and obedience, usually in the context of a communal life) were in the middle, though technically most religious groups had both clerical and lay members. Status, naturally and unbiblically enough, was accorded those at the top. Thus, the Council of Trent, reacting against Reformation notions that all Christians are "saints," denounced any diminution of virginity in favor of marriage. As a result, for many Roman Catholics the Church long meant the clergy. That was less true for Protestants and Orthodox, because their theologies stressed, respectively, the priesthood of all believers, and the mystical union of all believers with Christ their head. As well, the Protestant churches tended to have a strong theory, if not always a strong practice, that ministry was honorable in the measure it was a service.

Women's Status. In principle, the Christian Church was democratic in that all people, regardless of sex, race, or background, were welcome. Each Church member had her or his own gift from God, and each was a unique reflection of God. Thus, there was the Pauline dictum (Gal. 3:28) that in Christ there is neither Jew nor Greek, male nor female, slave nor free. In practice, however, women have been second-rate citizens in all branches of Christianity. Neither the Catholic nor the Orthodox churches would ordain women (that remains true today), nor would many Protestant churches. By associating women with Eve, the cause of Adam's fall (1 Tim. 2:14), the Church often suggested that they were responsible for human misery and sin. Thus, the fulminations of ascetics (usually celibate males) against women's wiles were a staple of the literature on how to avoid sin.

From the New Testament, men could buttress their supremacy by citing Pauline texts (Eph. 5:22–23; 1 Tim. 2:11–12) stating that wives were subordinate to their husbands and ought to keep silent in church. From the patristic age they could draw on what we can only call the misogyny of Jerome, Chrysostom, Tertullian, and others who portrayed woman as the gateway to hell. Augustine, perhaps from his personal experience of concubinage, made sexual congress the channel of original sin. Medieval theologians, such as the Dominican authors of the *Malleus Maleficarum (Hammer of Witches)* cited witches as being the cause of much psychological imbalance. In the name of preserving true faith, Church authorities tortured and killed thousands of witches.[63] Moreover, the Reformation did not relieve women's plight. Luther thought that woman's vocation was to "bear herself out" with children, while John Knox trumpeted against "petticoat" power in the Church. Reformation biblicism, then, meant merely a return to the patriarchy of the scriptures.

With a patriarchal God and an ambivalent role model in Mary the Virgin Mother, Christian women for the most part heard and obeyed, keeping any dissent to themselves. They had some measure of religious self-expression in their convents, and some of them gained leadership roles in the Protestant sects, but from the standpoint of today's egalitarian sentiments, their fate through most periods of Christian history was quite dismal.[64]

Church and State. The Christian view of society outside the Church varied over time. According to the New Testament Book of Revelation, Roman society was a beast that the coming Messiah had to slay if the earth were to become worthy of God. During the Roman persecutions, which some recent scholarship has downplayed, this view was influential. As a result, earthly life was held cheap compared to heavenly life. When the Church gained security with Constantine, it changed its tune. Eusebius, for instance, practically ranked Constantine with the twelve apostles. In reaction against this secularization, as we noted, the monastic movement restored the tension between time and eternity. The Western father Tertullian, for instance, cast doubt on the worth of secular culture, asking what Athens had to do with Jerusalem. However, other patristic figures, such as Clement of Alexandria and Augustine, recognized that Christianity needed an intellectual respectability if it were to prosper, so they started to give their theology an infrastructure of Greek philosophy.

By the medieval period, a certain harmony was achieved, as most of the culture was formed in accordance with Christian ideals (if not practice). There was a balance between reason and revelation, between emperor and pope. In practice, however, the competition between the emperor and the pope was fierce, for each tended to claim ascendancy over the other. Consequently, Church leaders such as Ambrose and Hildebrand, who stood up to kings or even brought them to heel, were accounted great heroes. In the Christian East, however, the emperor had more clearly God-given rights.

The Reformation depended in good measure on the political power plays of its day. Through application of the principle that a region would follow the religion of its ruler, a great deal of religious power returned to the local prince. Theologically, Luther tended toward a dualism of powers, religious and secular, while Calvin promoted a theocratic state in which citizens would live under Christian law. Thus, the

Reformation did not initially encourage the modern pluralistic state. In America the religious communities of the colonial period had to legalize pluralism if the colonies were to be united. With great reluctance on the part of many, the united colonies disestablished religion, and their act had enormous implications.

Since about the time of Voltaire (1694–1778), American pluralism has become something of a model for world government. Other nations have not formalized that model, with the slight exception of the United Nations, but its spirit has been at least a small counterweight to their nationalism. The model says that to live together well, human beings must find nondogmatic principles that can be common to all and that will generate the basic cooperation necessary for peace.

Through most of Christian history, though, the ideal society has been one that at worst allowed Christians freedom to exercise their religious convictions and at best institutionalized a Christian regimen. For instance, only recently has Roman Catholicism backed away from its teaching that it ought to be the established religion in any country with a Catholic majority. By its decree on religious liberty, the Second Vatican Council made an unprecedented acknowledgment of the rights of other religious communities. Orthodoxy has had difficulty with secular rulers through most of its history,[65] in part because of its organization as a cluster of national churches. To this day Russian Orthodoxy, the largest group, is shackled by its country's secular rulers. Protestantism has been more lay-oriented than Catholicism or Orthodoxy, so its ideas on the relations between church and state usually have been the most advanced.

What the Church ought to do for secular society, in contrast to what is has asked of secular society, has also varied historically. Generally, the Church has thought it should be a city on the hilltop—a witness to the commonweal that comes from mutual support and love. In other words the Church has thought it ought to be the place where society could see human community in action—could see love, cooperation, and mutual support. All human groups seek such community, and they have greater difficulty when they are large or their members have different values. The Church has thought it ought to manifest this community. In what Roman Catholic theologian Karl Rahner has called today's diaspora situation,[66] in which

Western churches are losing members, it becomes crucial that this concept of witness replace the ambition to rule over secular society that dominated most periods of the Christian past. Many contemporary theologians therefore want the Church to be with the poor, the oppressed, the people whom Jesus named in the beatitudes, for that would be where its witness would be most vivid.

Self

The conceptions of nature and society that we have sketched above suggest the Christian view of the self. The biblical teaching that God placed human beings over nature has meant to Christians that the human person is of much greater value than the plants and animals.

Furthermore, as Christian social theory interacted with the secular elaboration of human nature through Western history, the individual acquired greater stature than in Asia. In Asia, as in ancient societies generally, the group predominated over the individual. One was most importantly a member of a tribe and only secondarily a unique person. As an image of God, the individual was more significant under Christianity. Of course, at times both secular and religious authorities crushed individuals ruthlessly. Nonetheless, because they bore the life of Christ, individuals commanded respect. In matters of ethics, for instance, the notion of individual conscience counterbalanced the finespun codes of the canon lawyers and the moral theologians. The sacrament of penance epitomized this, for penance was essentially a self-accusation in which the individual, helped by the Church's representative, passed judgment on his or her standing before God.

By standing out from nature and having personal rights, the Christian individual was conscious of being a unique self. Historically, the Church did not lay great emphasis on fulfilling one's unique self by communing with nature, but it did lay great emphasis on fitting into the social body of Christ. In fact, the charity of the community united was to be the primary sign of God's presence. Beyond social fulfillment, however, Christian theology encouraged the self to commune with divinity itself—with the Father, Son, and Holy Spirit. During the biblical period that meant putting on the "mind of Christ." During the patristic age it meant that grace was considered a share in divine nature and that religion was a process of divinization. Since the Hellenistic divinity was above all immortal, religion was also a process of immortalization.

In medieval speculation, the self's fulfillment was the "beatific vision." By directly perceiving God's essence, our human drives to know and love (Augustine's famous "restless heart") would find a restful bliss. For the Thomists, participation in the divine nature through grace meant sharing in the "missions" of the Son and Holy Spirit. Thus, one's contemplation, knowing, and loving flowed into and out from the dynamic relations that characterized God's own inner life. The Reformation returned to biblical emphases, sending people to study the Word and to work in the world. For Orthodoxy the Divine Liturgy, with special accents on the Holy Spirit and the Mother of God, nourished one throughout life.[67]

In many periods, Christians never quite found the balance between life in the world and life that looked to heaven as its true home. Before the Reformation, Christians probably gave greater emphasis to the latter. Since the Reformation and the Enlightenment, they have emphasized social and political commitments in the world.

Religious Development. Stressing communion with God, traditional Christian spiritual masters developed certain models of what happens in the life of the serious religious person. One of the most influential traditions involved the "three ways" that the self would travel. First, one had to walk the "purgative" way, which meant purging oneself of sin and developing virtuous habits. Then one would enter the long way of "illumination," by which the Christian truths of Word and Sacrament would slowly become one's own. No longer would they be external concepts—in time they would become inner principles of judgment and action. Finally, consummating the spiritual life was the "unitive" way, by which the self would unite with God as in a deep friendship or even a marriage. Occasionally such union would produce experiences of rapture, and then one could speak of mysticism strictly so called ("infused contemplation"). Clearly, then, the paradigm of the three ways depended on the notion that final fulfillment was communion with God.

The saints who modeled Christian selfhood tended to be wholeheartedly given to communion with God. They also had to manifest charity for their fellows, but the spotlight was on their love of God. Because solitude or monastic withdrawal seemed to foster love of God, by allowing the freedom of deep, leisurely prayer, most saints went outside of family or civic life to lose themselves in devotion. That was the pattern up to the Reformation, and it took Christian selfhood some distance from the New Testament's view that prayer is important but not dominant.[68] Still, as the world became more important, the concept of saintliness expanded to include the service of other human beings. The Church had always honored certain holy married people, certain holy civic leaders, but by late medieval times it had to contend with a more dynamic society.

Consequently, the Protestant emphasis on holy worldliness found a ready audience among many post-medievals. This emphasis did not remove the notion that one was a pilgrim trying to make progress through time toward a more lasting city. However, it did upgrade the status of family life, business, and government. Indeed, by the nineteenth century, tracts appeared with the theme that Jesus was the greatest salesman of all time. As well, one could hear Andrew Carnegie defend capitalistic wealth as God's way of keeping the poor from squandering his gifts.

Sin. Related to the capital question of what the self should most value is the complicated Christian teaching about **original sin** (most developed in Western Christianity—Eastern Christianity has not stressed original sin to the same degree). At its crudest, the teaching said that all people not baptized were in thrall to Satan and on the road to hell. Hell was essentially the deprivation of God (the loss of the beatific vision), but because of a gruesome imagery of fire and brimstone, it was popularly conceived of as a place of physical suffering. The ceremony for infant baptism, then, contained an exorcism of Satan—to save the little one from evil and make it pure for God. (Unbaptized babies who died before reaching the age of responsibility, and so before the possibility of personal sin, went to "Limbo," a state of "natural" happiness without beatific vision. Although Limbo was never a matter of fully official Church teaching, it exerted considerable influence.)

A key moment in the development of the doctrine of original sin was Augustine's reading of the Fall as a social act. Adam's sin had alienated all human beings from God, for Adam was the head of the entire race.

Augustine took the seeds of this view from Paul (for instance, Rom 5:12–14). It suggested that Christ is the head of a new holy race, but that those not baptized into Christ belong to an old human nature destined for punishment.

The classical Protestant thinkers owed a great deal to Augustine; thus, their reform of theology emphasized original sin. Like Augustine, they interpreted Genesis and Paul rather literally, thinking in terms of corporate sinners and saints. The famous double *predestination* of Calvinism was an attempt to explain human beings' different fates (going to hell or heaven), as members of Adam or members of Christ, without removing the mystery of God's creative vision and providence. Whom God has destined for heaven will surely end up there. Likewise, whom God has set for hell will fall into the flame.

In a fateful development of Calvinistic predestination, the signs of election to heaven became outward decorum and even material prosperity. That meant the double burden of being both poor and damned and the double blessing of being both rich and saved. Eventually more careful Bible readers recognized that this correspondence contradicted the Sermon on the Mount, but a lot of Calvinists thoroughly enjoyed storing up plenty in their barns and letting their souls wax fat.

How inherently wicked or good the self is was an important question in the Reformation debates between Protestants and Catholics. Protestants, following Luther's stress on justification by faith and Calvin's stress on God's sovereignty, tended to emphasize the corruption of human nature through sin. Catholics, partly in reaction to that Protestant position and partly from their own emphasis on the sacraments and the Incarnation, saw an essential goodness in human nature (though they spoke of sin as darkening the mind and weakening the will). Clearly, though, Christianity made the West suspicious of human instincts. Many Christians were indoctrinated with the belief that they were virtually bound to be wicked sinners. Often that led them to oscillate between self-punishment and, in compensation, self-indulgence. However, most were taught that through penance one could experience God's mercy—the almost delicious sense of being loved gratuitously. Then the Johannine promise (1 John 3:20) that even when our hearts condemn us God is greater than our hearts could break out into joyous effect.

The Pauline discussion of sin and grace in terms of "flesh" and "spirit" focused Christian understanding of the self as embodied. That Paul's original language did not intend a matter-spirit dualism was almost forgotten after Christianity took up Greek thought. As a result, extremists tended to deprecate the body, marriage, and the world of human affairs as fleshly pursuits. In response to the Manichean and Albigensian heresies, the Church affirmed the goodness of the body, but the Church's general orientation toward heaven, its introduction of celibacy for holders of high Church offices, and its preference for ascetic saints tended to make the average person regret his or her flesh. For women this caused considerable suffering, because the male Church teachers often projected their sexual problems onto women. In that case, women became by nature wanton, seductive, and dangerous.

On the other hand, a certain realism about worldly life, in which imperfection if not sin was inevitable, tended to soften this rigorism. Christian moral theologians have usually taught that sins of the flesh are less grievous than sins of the spirit (such as pride, anger, or hatred). And, although at one point Roman Catholic moralists classified all sexual offenses as serious ("mortal" as opposed to "venial" sins), there were usually effective if unauthorized counterforces in the bawdiness of Chaucer and Boccaccio and the frequent concubinage of members of the clergy.

Case Study: Christian Rituals.   By means of its sacramental system, the Christian Church has ritualized its members' passage through the life cycle. The system has begun with baptism, the sacrament designed to celebrate a person's birth into divine life and Church membership. If the person was an adult, it was usual to require a profession of faith. The questions in the traditional inquiry into the candidate's faith show the transition that the sacrament of baptism was ritualizing.

First, the minister of the sacrament asked candidates whether they renounced Satan and the spiritual forces of evil that rebel against God. Assuming the answer was yes, the interrogation continued, soliciting affirmative answers to such questions as whether the candidates renounced the evil powers of this world that corrupt and destroy the creatures of God; whether they renounced all sinful desires that drew them away from God's love; whether they turned to Jesus Christ and accepted him as their savior; whether they put their whole trust in Christ's grace and love; and whether they promised to follow and obey Christ as their Lord. Along with a profession of the traditional creed, this profession of faith set the main lines of what the sacrament of baptism was enacting: a passover from a life of bondage to Satan and the world to a life of freedom in the grace of Jesus Christ.

The celebrant would then pray over the baptismal water, consecrate the oil with which the candidate was to be anointed, and finally baptize (pour water on the forehead of) the candidate in the name of the Father, and of the Son, and of the Holy Spirit. The concluding prayer summarized the effects the action was believed to have: "Heavenly Father, we thank you that by water and the Holy Spirit you have bestowed upon these your servants the forgiveness of sin, and have raised them to the new life of grace. Sustain them, O Lord, in your Holy Spirit. Give them an inquiring and discerning heart, the courage to will and to persevere, a spirit to know and to love you, and the gift of joy and wonder in all your works. Amen."[69]

The second sacramental rite in the normal Western life cycle was confirmation, the Christian celebration of coming-of-age. (The Eastern Christians celebrated along with baptism a rite called "chrismation" that bestowed the gift of the Holy Spirit.) The main motif in this celebration was asking God to give the candidates further strength from the Holy Spirit, in view of the services that adult life would require them to perform.

The Holy Eucharist has been the principal sacrament in the majority of the Christian traditions, and the ritual for the Eucharist has begun with a Liturgy of the Divine Word. After opening prayers, members of the congregation read several "lessons" from scripture, usually from both the Old and the New Testaments. There followed a sermon, to explain the scripture readings and apply them to daily life, and then a recitation of the Nicene Creed. Next came prayers for various needs, and then the eucharistic liturgy proper began.

This first offered thanks to God and praise of God's holiness. Then came the main action, a remembrance of the Last Supper that Jesus celebrated with his apostles before his death. The key words of this remembrance have been, "For in the night in which he was betrayed, he took bread; and when he had given thanks, he brake it, and gave it to his disciples, saying, 'Take, eat, this is my Body, which is given for you. Do this in remembrance of me.' Likewise, after supper, he took the cup; and when he had given thanks, he gave it to them, saying 'Drink ye all of this; for this is my Blood of the New Testament, which is shed for you,

and for many, for the remission of sins. Do this, as oft as you shall drink it, in remembrance of me.' "

After these prayers of consecration, there was a recitation of the Lord's Prayer ("Our Father"), more short prayers, and a Communion service, in which worshipers received the consecrated bread and wine. The prayers said when administering the bread and wine summarized the participants' sense of what they were receiving: "The Body of Our Lord Jesus Christ, which was given for thee, preserve thy body and soul unto everlasting life. Take and eat this in remembrance that Christ died for thee, and feed on him in thy heart by faith, with thanksgiving. The Blood of our Lord Jesus Christ, which was shed for thee, preserve thy body and soul unto everlasting life. Drink this in remembrance that Christ's Blood was shed for thee, and be thankful."

Overall, the Church celebrated the Eucharist as both a memorial of Jesus' death and a memorial of his last meal, when he gave himself to his friends under the signs of bread and wine. Since Jesus' death and resurrection were the central events in the Christian reading of history, each eucharistic memorial laid before the Christian faithful an epitome of their sense of reality. In Jesus' death and resurrection stood revealed the meaning and destiny of each human life.

Moreover, by receiving Jesus' body and blood, the believer was believed to be nourished in the divine life that Jesus' death and resurrection had made available. The Eucharist therefore was like the messianic banquet that Jews of Jesus' time had believed would accompany God's definitive victory. Celebrating the good news of Jesus' victory together, Christians renewed their spiritual strength by feeding on Jesus' substance. There was nothing cannibalistic in this. The eating and drinking were simply ways of expressing and strengthening the deep intimacy between Christ and Christians, who, according to Saint Paul (1 Cor. 12:12), were members of one body, or, according to Saint John (John 15:5), were united like a vine and its branches.

The people who found baptism, confirmation, and the Holy Eucharist insufficient to keep them from sin could have recourse to sacramental rites of penance, which were designed to reconcile sinners with God and the rest of the community. Normally the minister of this sacrament offered a prayer over the penitent, and then the penitent confessed his sins: "I confess to Almighty God, to his Church, and to you, that I have sinned by my own fault in thought, word, and deed, in things done and left undone, especially by [here the penitent would mention the specific sins most troubling him]. For these and all other sins which I cannot now remember, I am truly sorry. I pray God to have mercy on me. I firmly intend amendment of life, and I humbly beg forgiveness of God and his Church, and ask you for counsel, direction, and absolution." After whatever counsel and direction he thought appropriate, the minister would absolve the sinner of his or her sins, in the name of the Father, and of the Son, and of the Holy Spirit.

When the time came to marry, Christians have been expected to celebrate their union through a marriage ritual. The Christian theology of marriage has likened the conjunction of man and woman in matrimony to the union between Christ and the Church, and it has found in the Genesis creation account, in which God gave Eve to Adam, a prototype of the nuptial union. A Christian marriage was meant for both the mutual comfort of the spouses and the procreation of children. It had to be entered into freely by both parties, and usually the minister called upon the assembled community not only to witness the parties' vows but also to support them in their marital venture. The actual marriage took place when the betrothed said to one another, "I take you to be my wife [husband] to have and to hold, from this day forward, for better or worse, for richer or poorer, in sickness and in health, to love and to cherish, until we are parted by death." Then the couple would give one another wedding rings, as a sign of their union.

A sixth sacramental ritual deals with the ordination of the Church's ministers. In churches with several ranks of ministers, the bishop has usually presided at the ordination. After satisfying himself that the candidates were qualified, he solicited the approval and support of the community, prayed over the ordinand and then laid hands on the ordinand's head and prayed, "Therefore, Father, through Jesus Christ your Son, give your Holy Spirit to_____; fill him [or her, in churches that ordained women] with grace and power, and make him [or her] a priest in your Church."

Many churches also celebrated sacramental rituals for the healing and consolation of the sick and the dying. After prayers and scriptural readings, the sick person usually went through the penance ritual, and then the minister would lay hands upon the sick person and anoint her or him with holy oil. The prayers accompanying this anointing asked God for an inward anointing of the Holy Spirit, to forgive the sick person's sins, release the person from suffering, and re-

store wholeness and strength. Often the person then would receive Holy Communion.

The last stage on the Christian's way was the burial rite, which usually focused on the Holy Eucharist for the occasion of death and burial. The Liturgy of the Word featured psalms and scriptural passages concerned with death and the Christian hopes for resurrection, and the person would be buried in consecrated ground with prayers for forgiveness and the life of the blessed in heaven.

The Christian sacramental system is the basic framework of the traditional Christian's church life. While many churches of the Protestant Reformed tradition came to downplay the sacraments that Catholics and Eastern Orthodox celebrated, Protestants still assembled for baptism, a liturgy of the scriptural Word, and to solemnize such occasions as marriage, ordination, and Christian burial. Whatever reservations they had about the Catholic and Eastern Orthodox development of almost sumptuous rituals, Protestants retained the Christian conviction that God uses material things (if only words and music) to draw human beings in spirit and truth. The churches of the Catholic and Orthodox traditions extended this principle to bread and wine, oil and wax, and various "sacramentals" (signs, such as holy water and ashes, meant to solemnize smaller occasions). The result was a counterbalance to any Christian overemphasis on sin or unbridled condemnation of the world. If God's own Word had taken flesh, the body and the world had to be basically good. All of life, therefore, had "sacramental" possibilities. As the Holy Eucharist showed the deepest potentialities of an ordinary meal, so the union of Christ with the Church showed the deepest potentialities of ordinary sexual intercourse. Not every generation of Christians has preached this sacramentalism boldly, but it always has lain ready to hand in the mainstream tradition.

The sacramental system epitomizes the Christian sense of God's ways with human beings. Where God could have stood apart, in splendid isolation, God freely chose to make covenants, strike bonds, call his people not servants but friends. By enfleshing the eternal Word of his heart, God placed divinity in the very midst of human history. The death and resurrection of Jesus, which was celebrated each Sunday, said that God goes down with human beings in their deepest grief and raises human beings up beyond their wildest hopes. At its most gracious, Christian faith has become a dance that partnered time to eternity. God and humanity are joined sacramentally; through the things of matter, space, and time, the timeless Spirit of God has touched human beings and quickened them.

Ultimate Reality

The first Christian conception of God was Jewish. Jesus himself accepted the God of the Fathers—Abraham, Isaac, and Jacob. This God, as we have seen, interacted with human beings and was personal. His guidance of humanity peaked in his liberation of Israel from Egypt and his covenanting with Israel on Mount Sinai. As numerous theologians have pointed out, it was difficult for Jesus to designate himself as divine, because to do so would have confused his identity with that of his "Father." In other words, the God of Jewish faith was Jesus' Father, his source.

In dealing with the revealed God's inner nature, the concept of the Trinity became paramount. Orthodox catholic (universal) faith held that Father–Son–Holy Spirit was attested by the scriptures and defined by the councils. As we indicated, the psychological analogy that Augustine and Aquinas developed gained great respect, the West considering it the "purest" (the least material) analogy. Thus, the God of Christian speculation was a fullness of intelligence and love. He was perfection, in need of nothing outside himself. He was the Creator and Redeemer, moved only by his own goodness. The Incarnation was the main instance of his outpouring, but glimpses of God abounded everywhere. Subhuman creatures were his "vestiges" (footprints); human beings were his images. Christians were images of his great Image, for they reflected the eternal icon, the Logos-Son.

Regarding the Trinity, Christians stood in the Son's position, receiving their likeness to God from the Father and expressing it through Spirit-carried love. The similitude broke down, however, because the divine persons were only relationally distinct (that is, Son and Father differed only as begotten and begetter), while humans remained creatures distinct from God. Still, the consummation of faith, whether occurring in worldly mystical experience or in the beatific vision,[70] meant knowing with something of divinity's own knowledge, loving with something of divinity's own love.

Biblical Renewal. When Reformation thought returned to biblical conceptions, because it found the medieval synthesis too abstract and unhistorical, it revived the notion that faith is a living interpersonal relation to God. This contrasted somewhat with the position of most Scholasticism, which stressed the propositional knowledge (the information) that faith provides. As well, the reformers revived the twin notions of God's judgment and his merciful love. By faith, God became one's "rock and salvation"—the one on whom to rely. Between the time of Luther and the nineteenth-century Danish theologian Søren Kierkegaard, such faith became paradoxical—a leap. In the face of the "impossibility" of the Incarnation, Kierkegaard jumped into the intellectual abyss, proposing that what reason could not fathom divinity could yet do, because it moved by reasons the mind knew not, by reasons of the heart.

The Hebrew notion of *hesed* (steadfast, merciful love), which kept God to his freely chosen covenant, encouraged believers to trust that no situation in their lives was hopeless. If Ezekiel's God could raise dry bones back to fleshly life, Jesus' God could use even suffering and evil to his own inscrutable ends. Was not God's chosen way of salvation, the death of his only begotten Son, the surest sign that no one had ever understood him? As the heavens are above the earth, so were God's ways above the ways of human beings. For that reason, the Reformers wanted only a Pauline faith: God's power and wisdom are Christ crucified.

Did this finally mean a justification of God by surrender? For the deeper theologians, who had frequently wrestled with unbelief personally, the answer was yes. With Job and Paul, they said that the pot cannot tell the potter how to fashion. For the sake of their sanity, they had to affirm that God is wise and just (and even loving) in all his doings. How this worked out, however, they often could not say. Surrender was finally a matter of trust, a matter of unexpectedly feeling God's love. As the mistranslation of Job put it, "Though he slay me, yet will I trust him." The farthest reach of the Christian conception of God was an intimate marriage of lives and fortunes. What the prophet Hosea had written of God's constancy, even God's vulnerability, the new biblical theologians found in New Testament *agape* (love).

The Johannine epistles say God is this *agape*. The Pauline epistles say *agape* is the greatest of God's gifts. The biblical theologians translated *agape* as self-sacrificing love. Beyond *eros* (self-fulfilling love) or *philia* (the love of friendship), it worked through God's use of the cross. Thus, it was an attack on evil, on lovelessness. Thus, it broke the circle of tit for tat, of

Figure 41   Dead Christ with Angels, *by Edouard Manet (1832–1883). Etching and aquatint; 13 × 11 1/8 in. The Nelson–Atkins Museum of Art, Kansas City, Missouri (Gift of Mr. and Mrs. Milton McGreevy through the Westport Fund).*

At its better moments, Christianity was grateful to Judaism, since it had adopted most of Judaism's doctrine of God. As well, it was mindful of the continuing election of Israel that Paul had proclaimed (Romans 9–11). At its worst, Christianity condemned Jews as Christ killers and spoke of their responsibility for Christ's blood. Islam confronted Christianity with claims of a later, perfected revelation and prophecy, and with an adamant insistence on God's unity. For Islam, and for Judaism, the Christian doctrine of the Trinity violated monotheism. Christian claims that God is both one and three seemed to Muslims and Jews incoherent, while Christian allegiance to Jesus clashed with Muslim allegiance to the Qur'an and Jewish allegiance to the Torah. Those clashes remain with us yet.

As the center of the Christian world view, God in Christ dominated Christian conceptions of nature, society, and self. Nature was but God's cloak. It was a lovely gift, but it sprang from nothingness and was wholly under God's control. With each extension of space and time by science, the awe of sophisticated believers increased: A more complex nature only magnified their God all the more.

Similarly, God was the norm and goal of Christian society, because his law was the source of all natural law and because eternal life with God in heaven was the goal of all people. God wanted human beings to form a community. Christ showed them the love that could bring that about. Thus, the vocation of the self was to obey the great twofold command: to love God with whole mind, heart, soul, and strength and to love neighbor as itself.

sin and retribution. God the judge finally yielded to God the lover. In Jesus he suffered evil to undo evil, thereby making a new creation. The lamb who was slain for this new creation was worthy of all glory and honor, because his sacrifice showed a divinity greater than one could ever imagine. Only the nursing mother who could never abandon her child, the father of the prodigal son (Luke 15:11–32), or the lover to whom the beloved is more than another self could glimpse this *mysterion*—this plan of God's love, hidden from all ages.

In contrast to other religions' versions of divinity, Christian theology has stressed the personal, loving character of God that Jesus' flesh disclosed. Jesus was God in human terms. (He was also humanity fulfilled by union with divinity.) As a result, Christianity did not appreciate the impersonal divinity of nature so dear to East Asian and Indian thought. This divinity was implicit in Christian theology, but the personalistic emphasis placed it in the shade.

SUMMARY: THE CHRISTIAN CENTER

The Christian center is Jesus, for the God worshiped in the Christian liturgy, served in the Christian ministries, and crucial for the Christian Church is the Father known through the revelations of Jesus. In the New Testament (John 14:6) Jesus is the way, the truth, and the life. For the Christian monk, martyr, or layperson, Jesus has been the strong soldier in combat with Satan, the sacrificial victim dying for human beings' sins, or the good shepherd ever seeking his lost sheep. In the East, Jesus has been the *pantokrator,* the Lord of the World shining with heavenly glory. In the West, Jesus has been the great moral teacher, the supreme exemplar of selfless love. So it goes, in all times and places. At the center of the religion that bears his titular name, Jesus the Christ holds all things together, as Colossians (1:17) put it long ago: "He is before all things, and in him all things hold together."

The centrality of Jesus the Christ has meant that Christianity is supremely incarnational. Its theology, if not always its Church practice, has pivoted around the enfleshment of divinity. Orthodox and Roman Catholic Christians have developed this theology into rich sacramental rites. Protestant Christians have developed it into a profound reverence for holy scripture. With interesting but ultimately secondary differences, the main Christian families have agreed that God made Jesus the Christ his prime self-manifestation. Bluntly put, Jesus has been God in human terms—as much of ultimate reality as a single human being could convey. Often the startling result of this conviction has been that humanity itself has become profoundly sacramental or iconic. Not only has no one ever seen God; no one has ever seen the depth, or the height, or the breadth of the human potential to image forth God.

Thus one finds each Christian generation tending to picture Jesus, the central icon of God, according to its own interests and tastes. To a peasant age, Jesus could be a simple tradesman or a king in beggar's garb. When court ceremonial deeply impressed itself, Jesus could be clothed in elegant vestments: silk, fur, brocade. A Renaissance soldier might picture Jesus as the commander of his regiment, evoking the utmost loyalty and bravery. A passionate contemplative might picture Jesus as her spiritual spouse, the lover burning her deepest soul. Thus did the Incarnation vary, age upon age, temperament upon temperament. Jesus' preaching, healing, teaching, friendship, communing with the Father, battling with Satan, and other facets have offered artists and common folk limitless food for imagination. The New Testament portrait has been full enough to show that Jesus was completely human, an incarnation that took divinity into all of humanity's basic concerns. Yet the New Testament also has been empty enough, laconic enough, to allow readers to develop a Jesus after their own hearts.

Still, life and death have centered Christianity, as they have centered all religion, so the nub of the Christian center has been Jesus' death and resurrection.[71] That the Son of God died for human beings showed the lavishness of the Father's love. As well, it convinced millions that Jesus was indeed like them in all things save sin, did indeed know their utmost dreads. To outsiders the crucifix might be a stumbling block, or a sign of foolishness, but to believing Christians it has been a sign of God's peculiar power and wisdom. Because he completely embraced their death, Jesus made God burningly relevant to all people, a deity of blood and bone. As the Christian liturgy put it, "Dying he destroyed our death."

Rising, Jesus is believed by Christians to have restored the life for which human beings ever have longed. To be immortal, at one with the holy ultimate reality, filled with the creative love that moves the stars, has always been the human dream, the hope too good to be realistic. If Christmas has been the most popular Christian feast, because it celebrates God's nearness and humility, officially Easter has been the most profound Christian feast, because it celebrates a God so lavish he takes one's breath away.

Without Jesus' resurrection, Christian faith would only be a profound probing of life's tragic nobilities. To live for love, and so suffer injustice and misunderstanding, perhaps even cruel death, would be a very noble human way, but it would leave both God and human nature shrouded in uncertainty. If all things end in the grave, then the agony of the cross, the nobility of living for love, is pure but almost unbearably ambiguous. On the other hand, if all things end in the mystery of Jesus' resurrection, certainty beckons round the corner.

Very peculiar, this central Christian symbol of why life is worth living. The resurrection of Jesus, taken as a pledge of one's own resurrection, escapes the laws of ordinary human calculus, stands to the side in a clearing all its own. Its witnesses tell a very puzzling story. Its many abusers make the prudent very skeptical. Yet the mysterious thing itself keeps haunting the back alleys of one's soul, like a pencil of light one can neither escape nor trace down.

Discussion Questions

1. Why might Jesus have said that it is easier for a camel to pass through the eye of a needle than for a rich person to enter the Kingdom of God?

2. What is the significance of Jesus' parable of the Great Supper?

3. Elaborate on the following extract: "From Judaism came the concepts of prophet and messiah. From Hellenism came the notions of saviour and god."

4. Why were the Councils of Nicaea and Chalcedon important?

5. How did the Mass summarize medieval Christian symbolism?

6. Describe the main tenets of sixteenth-century Protestantism.

7. How does the eighteenth-century Enlightenment contrast with faith, mysticism, and symbolism?

8. How has Christianity both spawned physical science and frustrated it?

9. Compose a brief rite for Christian baptism, stressing the Orthodox reliance on the Holy Spirit.

10. Indicate the main issues a contemporary person should consider in converting to Christianity.

11. Why would you like, or not like, to have an interview with the Russian holy man Father Michael?

12. Give a brief digest of the overall Christian gospel.

13. Why has the understanding of Jesus changed from age to age?

14. What have been the main influences of the Christian doctrine of original sin?

15. What do the three ways of the Christian spiritual life—purgative, illuminative, unitive—suggest about religious maturation?

16. What has the Virgin Mary offered Christian women for a role model?

17. What have been the distinguishing features of Protestant, Orthodox, and Roman Catholic Christianity?

Glossary

apocalypse: biblical or extrabiblical literature that claims to be a revelation from God about the events that are soon to occur as the consummation of history. In the Bible the Books of Daniel and Revelation illustrate the literary genre of apocalyptic. Present-day scholars tend to emphasize the tradition—store of symbols, chain of historical influences—that one can discover the apocalyptic writers using, as well as the psychosocial roots of apocalyptic literature in anxie-

ties or resentments about worldly times, which might be bringing either persecution or marginalization from the centers of cultural influence.

apostle: one sent forth to proclaim an authoritative message. The early Christian leaders considered themselves authoritative emissaries of Jesus Christ, the most authoritative among them being the Twelve who had been the eyewitness companions and confidants of Jesus during his ministry. New Testament literature was associated with various leading apostles—Peter, John, Paul—and drew much of its authority from the such supposed sources. Apostolicity later became one of the four marks of the genuine Church, which was supposed to be one, holy, catholic, and apostolic.

baptism: the Christian sacrament of initiation, which proceeds by lustration—washing with water. The basic symbolism is of a cleansing from sin, but in baptism by full immersion in water the early Christians also developed the (Pauline) motif of going down into death with Christ and rising to new, divine life. Baptism has served as the rite of entrance into the Christian community, as well as the passover from sin to grace. Different churches have held different positions about the advisability of baptizing infants, which often was not done in the early centuries (yet can claim a fair antiquity). Insofar as parents and the community, as well as Christ and the Holy Spirit, have been granted primary places in the ritual action, defenders of infant baptism have claimed that such baptism is both moral and fitting.

canon: a list or body of writings considered scriptural, authoritative, or officially approved. The establishment of a canon of scriptural writings is always a momentous step in the development of a religious tradition, but usually it is not a neat, once-and-for-all process. Thus the canonization processes of both the Tanak (Hebrew Bible) and the New Testament remain somewhat obscure. Canonization implies an authority powerful enough to declare what writings authentically represent faith, and it has the effect of both narrowing the range of data that the orthodox will subsequently consider and widening the scope for creative interpretation of the group's religious traditions.

charism: a gift or talent thought to have been bestowed by God. Many religions have been reinvigorated by charismatic reformers, prophets, and mystics, whose gifts drew followers and seemed to reclarify the religious pathway. Charismatic authority usually stands somewhat in tension with official, institutional authority, and even so sophisticated a religious tradition as the Christian has never fully resolved the relation between the two types of authority. One can say that office and institutional leadership (or service) themselves are charismata, but on the whole the groups that have given special weight to charismata (eloquence, speaking in tongues, healings) have had weak institutional structures and easily splintered into smaller groups.

cleric: an official religious functionary. The word has ties to the ability of people destined for religious service to read and write, and usually it designates the group within a church or non-Christian religious body that constitutes its professional class—its full-time religious functionaries. The typical cleric is a priest, minister, or prayer-leader, and while much of the stability of religious organizations clearly has come from their clerical classes, the clergy have also been the usual target for charges of conservatism, stultification, legalism, and even corruption. So on the whole "cleric" usually stands somewhat in tension with "charismatic," and "clericalism" is not a term of praise.

dogma: official doctrine, set forth by a religious group's duly constituted authorities, that is considered binding on all who are members in good standing and so constitutes orthodoxy. In itself, dogma is a morally neutral term, having the advantage of clearly specifying what the given group believes and requires. As an adjective, however, "dogmatic" also connotes an authoritarian mind-set that is too quick to equate its own decrees with the (relatively few) truths the deity has revealed as necessary for salvation.

eucharist: a Christian term essentially meaning "thanksgiving" but regularly applied to the sacramental sacrifice and meal Christians have celebrated in memory of the Last Supper, death, and resurrection of Jesus. This meal owes debts to Jewish notions about the messianic banquet to be celebrated when God's anointed would bring deliverance and the consummation of history, as well as to the Jewish celebration of the Sabbath and Passover. It has ties with Christian views about the Incarnation of God's Word, the sacramental structure of faith, and the sense that grace has abounded over sin, making good news and thanksgiving Christian watchwords.

evangelical: referring to Christians who take an especially strong stand on the Christian scriptures, as the outward form of the "good news" (*euangellion*) of Christ. Evangelicals draw upon several principles of the Protestant Reformation, including the primacy of scripture over Church authority and the rights of the individual to interpret scripture as the Spirit inspires. Evangelicals run a considerable gamut in their degree of literalness about scripture, submission to Christian tradition and Church authority, and the like. In broadest connotation, any Christian who greatly prized the scriptures could claim to be an evangelical, while in narrow connotation neither Roman Catholics, nor Eastern Orthodox, nor (for many evangelicals) fundamentalists would qualify, because none would nourish the proper mystique about the presence of the divine power in the scriptural Word.

filioque: the Western Christian teaching that, within the Trinity, the Holy Spirit proceeds not just from the Father but also from the Son. Historically, this represented an addition to the explicit formulas of the earliest ecumenical councils. It became a bone of contention when Eastern and Western Christianity felt themselves estranged. How significant it is in itself depends on one's theology of the Trinity. Some Western Christian theologians think that giving the Son a role in the procession (the "active spiration") of the Spirit helps to prepare an understanding of the Spirit's actions in the order of salvation and this-worldly influence, while some Eastern Christian theologians insist that the filioque represents a move away from a previously more profound appreciation of the "Father," the originating source of the Godhead, as awesomely full and prior in everything relating to the Godhead.

Gnosticism: in general, the tendency to claim a privileged, secret, esoteric teaching about the true state of the world and the true path to salvation; in particular, the movement that challenged Christianity in the early centuries of the Common Era by proposing secret interpretations of either the teachings of Jesus or the divine plan for salvation. These interpretations stressed the fall of human beings from a previous intimacy with God, the need to purify oneself of material desires and let the continuing presence of sparks of one's old divine grandeur assert themselves, and joining with other Gnostics in rites and studies that would lead one back through the heavens to restoration with God.

gospel: the Christian term for the glad tidings announced by Jesus, and then by the Church, and then in the written form of the four evangelical writings that gained canonical status. In the ministry of Jesus the gospel centered on the announcement of the reign of God—the time and state when God would directly reorder all things so that justice and love would prevail. In the ministry of the Church, the gospel became the main content of preaching and liturgical celebration, often focusing on the victory of Christ and the new life brought by Christ's Spirit. In the New Testament the Gospels are seen as so many variants (there were many other "Gospels" that did not gain official approval) of the single proclamation about the time of grace that came with Jesus and continued in Jesus' community.

Gospels: the early Christian accounts of the life, death, and resurrection of Jesus that preserved originally oral memories of what Jesus did and taught. All four of the canonical Gospels are more than mere collections of different local churches' memories, however, because each offers a distinctive interpretation of who and what Jesus was (a distinctive Christology). The Gospels are our best indications of both the historical Jesus and the Christ believed in by the early Church, but on both counts none of them offers simply historical data because each of them is a construct by believers and for believers that begins by assuming the unique holiness of Jesus and his Lordship over the Church.

grace: divine favor, help, or life. Grace can refer to the special help believers believe God gives them to deal with ordinary life and also crises. It can also refer to the gratuity of God's having offered human beings salvation, through the whole mechanism of the salvation history laid out in the Bible and, for Christians, consummated in Christ. Third, it can denote the divine life poured forth in believers' hearts by the Spirit of Christ, a life of knowing and loving that stretches forward toward an eternal consummation ("heaven"). Last, grace can also indicate the presence of God to all people, everywhere, through acts of love and support that draw people toward integrity of conscience, courage in the face of death, and faith that honesty and love are more important than any temporary gains one may make by violating them.

Incarnation: the Christian doctrine that the divine Word (Logos) was made flesh in Jesus of Nazareth. This doctrine specifies the essential mystery of Jesus. For orthodox Christian faith, he is both fully human and fully divine: one "person" possessed of two different "natures." Christian incarnationalism flows from this doctrine, viewing matter as good because worthy of being taken into union with divinity. Christian sacramentalism and iconography look to the Incarnation

for their ultimate theological sanction: If God could use matter to make a primary sacrament (the flesh of Christ), then symbolizing the workings of grace and reverencing pictures of Jesus, Mary, and the saints must be legitimate, even required.

indulgence: the (largely Roman Catholic) notion of a pledge that some of the punishment due to one's sins will be remitted because of good deeds. The theology of indulgences depends on an organic notion of the Church (as the "communion of saints") in which the merits of one may be shared with others. Thinking itself the custodian of these merits, the Catholic hierarchy felt justified in dispensing the merits. At the time of the Protestant Reformation such dispensation had become rather commercial, appearing to Luther and others as a good symbol of the corruption that had degraded biblical faith. To restore the gratuity of salvation and the primacy of the merits of Jesus, they attacked the system of indulgences as unbiblical and scandalous.

Lent: the Christian penitential period (forty days) before Easter. The forty days no doubt derived from the biblical imagery of Jesus' time in the desert (which, in turn, reflected the forty years Israel wandered in the desert before entering upon the Promised Land). When the Christian liturgical cycle centered on the celebration of Easter (the Christian Passover, when Jesus moved from death to resurrection), it no doubt seemed fitting to prepare for this holiest season by doing penance. The regular discipline focused on food, all the faithful who were in good health being supposed to fast between meals and cut down on their overall intake of food. In some periods alcohol was frowned upon, as were sexual relations. Sundays were exempt from Lent, so many Christians relaxed or even partied on Sundays. Prior to Ash Wednesday, the beginning of Lent (when Catholics would receive ashes on their foreheads as a reminder of "ashes to ashes and dust to dust"), Mardi Gras ("Fat Tuesday") often was celebrated as a last, even bacchanalian fling.

liturgy: public, official, ritualized worship. The word comes from the Greek terms for "people" and "work." Thus, the work of the Christian people (and then, by scholarly extension, the worship of other peoples such as Jews and Muslims) was in the first place to praise God. The eucharist was the center of the traditional Christian liturgy, for there people most clearly remembered the grace to which they had been called, the love that had saved them from their sins. When monasticism arose in the Church, the monastic office—

singing psalms and praying prayers throughout the day—came to partake of liturgical dignity. The sacraments, as official acts of the Church, also had strictly liturgical status. But in practice even so-called paraliturgical forms of prayer, such as rosaries and novenas (nine-day sessions of prayer and renewal), carried a liturgical patina. As common prayer, done with ecclesial faith—a desire to benefit the entire community—all public worship more or less conformed itself to the pattern most clearly laid out in the eucharistic liturgy.

Logos: the divine Word that Christians identified with Jesus. The Christian doctrine of the Logos had predecessors in both Jewish and Hellenistic thought. The Word that came to the Hebrew prophets at times seemed an entity existing somewhat independently or alongside of God, much like the Wisdom celebrated in the Book of Proverbs. The Logos that interested pre-Socratic philosophers and by the end of the classical period had become part and parcel of the confluence of being and intelligibility served the Hellenistic philosophers (for example, the Stoics) in their speculations about the build of the physical and moral worlds (natural law). In Christianity, the Gospel of John was especially significant, identifying as it did the Word that was with God before the foundations of the world with the divinity that became incarnate in Jesus Christ. The overtones to the Logos included the idea of its being the Wisdom of God (a quality also associated with the Holy Spirit), its being that in which creation hung together (Col. 1:15–20), and its being the revelatory self-expression of the Godhead.

original sin: the Christian notion that the fall of Adam and Eve caused or represents a basic condition afflicting all human beings—a tilt that makes all human actions and thoughts somewhat unjust or impure. This notion owes much to Paul's Epistle to the Romans, especially chapter 5, and gained greater impact through the speculations of Augustine. It has a mirror image in Christian notions about the solidarity of believers in Christ, who like a new Adam gives the whole human race a fresh start. Paul and Augustine both taught that where sin abounded grace had abounded the more, but Western Christianity sometimes forgot this positive tilt. Eastern Christianity did better, stressing the divinization God offered and the pneumatic character of a creation filled by the Spirit of the resurrected Christ.

orthodox: straight, correct, or approved in belief or worship. Doxa can refer to either opinion or praise.

Thus, orthodoxy can refer to straightness, correctness, in either doctrine or liturgy. Eastern Christianity has sensed the correlation of the two, insisting on a worship that is primarily praise of the deity and that can only be shared by those who agree in creedal faith. Western Christianity has somewhat agreed, insofar as it has accepted the notion that worship expresses faith—gives the tipoff about what believers actually confess before God. In the context of other religious traditions, the word tends to be used by accommodation to this Greco-Christian etymology, signifying what has come to be accounted acceptable, nondeviant or nonheterodox, in a given area (doctrine, ethics, political policy).

predestination: the notion that God has determined one's fate (especially one's place in heaven or hell) as part of an eternal divine plan. All religions that speak of a deity omnipotent and omniscient have to contend with the problem of predestination, which in turn implies the problem of human freedom. Christian scripture is typical in asserting both that God guides all events and that human beings have a say in their own salvation or damnation. No speculative schema has definitively resolved the relationship between God's action and that of human beings, if only because human beings can never understand God's action (or any of the other infinite divine characteristics). However, some schemata have mitigated problems by underscoring that the divine knowledge and action do not occur in time and consequently do not occur "before" or "after" human choices. For God to know something (for example, the existence of a specific person in heaven or in hell) as existing coincides with the actual existence of that something. It does not precede it and so need not cause it (although it might have to concur in the existential operations that bring that something about).

redemption: retrieval ("buying back"); deliverance from sin. Part of the imagery is that of ransoming a slave from captivity. By paying the debt the slave had incurred, the redeemer satisfies the slaveholder and sets the indentured person free. The analogy to people's religious situations is simple enough. Insofar as sin or ignorance is viewed as bondage, who or what delivers people from sin or ignorance is a redeemer. One need not develop the analogy legalistically, as such theories of redemption as that of the medieval Christian theologian Anselm of Bec threatened to do, to make "payment" a significant image. However, the people redeemed ought to appreciate that effort, even cost, was expended on their behalf. Thereby, they will not think their redemption a cheap grace but rather will appreciate it as a great mercy of their liberator.

resurrection: the Christian notion of being raised from death and transported into the divine presence. Resurrection was a notion current at the time of Jesus, so it made cultural sense to depict his passover from death to Lordship at the "right hand" of the Father as an action of the Father raising him definitively into the heavenly sphere. Theologians sometimes contrast resurrection with immortality of the soul, describing the former as not positing a dualism of matter and spirit. Resurrection bears similarities to notions of rebirth found in many ancient peoples' rites of initiation, but in the Christian understanding it seems to carry a literal core that entails thinking of the risen Jesus as possessing a physical body and being in a "place" where the raised (and transformed) physical bodies of those he saves can join him.

sacrament: a sacred, empowering action, such as the Christian baptism and Eucharist or the Hindu investiture with the sacred thread. The term has flourished in Christian circles, but clearly it may be applied to many religious rituals. Sacraments typically employ symbolic materials—water, oil, bread, wine—that are believed to be filled with a pneumatic power that impresses a spiritual meaning on the person's soul. The sacramental mentality moves by analogy, seeing many correspondences between the literal import of the material used and deeper or higher religious possibilities. Thus, the physical bread and wine of the Christian Eucharist symbolize the spiritual nurture faith requires, and the two lines of thought join in the Christian conviction that in the Eucharist the bread and wine are transformed into the body and blood of Christ.

salvation: saving from sin; making whole and healthy. Insofar as religious cultures generally depict human existence as flawed, they present a situation in which people need salvation. The imagery may be of sickness or ignorance, but regularly it implies that the ordinary human condition requires healing, enlightenment, perhaps even transformation, if it is to measure up to the best aspirations people have. Salvation may focus upon the human personality, or human society, or people's relations with God. Occasionally it even extends to dealings with nature. The saved person claims to have become a unified personality. The saved community speaks of peace and brotherly/sisterly love.

Those saved by divine grace speak of being restored to friendship and good relations with the deity. Those for whom healing or enlightenment extends to people's dealings with nature speak of hurting the earth no more and experiencing both flora and fauna as friends. Salvation takes aim at the problem of evil and so is always a central religious concern. If one knows what a given tradition finds to be saving, one knows much of its potential appeal.

Scholasticism: the medieval Christian movement to develop a rational elaboration of faith. Scholasticism had its roots in Greek philosophy, which had disciplined reason and made it systematically analytical. During the patristic era, Christian theologians began the process of elaborating a Christian world view, trying to coordinate the various insights of the scriptures. Augustine combined a powerful speculative mind with great rhetorical skill, but the Scholastics sought something more detached and scientific. Peter Lombard (ca. 1100–1160) collected the opinions of authoritative Church thinkers on key points of faith, arranging them under the four headings of the Trinity, Creation and Sin, the Incarnation and the Virtues, and the Sacraments and the Last Things. Peter Abelard (1079–1142) introduced sharp dialectical skills, reasoning carefully about the reasons for and against many propositions about faith. Thomas Aquinas (ca. 1225–1274) brought the scholastic movement to a climax, producing the most esteemed of the *summas* that attempted to survey and coordinate all the major topics of faith. Overall, the Scholastics were responsible for placing much greater rigor into Christian theology, though sometimes at the expense of losing its symbolic and mystagogic character.

sin: an offense against God or the sacred moral order. Sin is moral evil—what should not be in the realm of free choice. Though some traditions use the word sin for indeliberate offenses or transgressions of tribal laws, the word has fuller resonance when it names the mysterious twistedness of the human mind and heart. Most theistic traditions are willing to say that all human beings are sinners, but what this means differs from group to group. Christians have emphasized sin more than Jews and Muslims, while Buddhists and Hindus have spoken more of ignorance. From Christian usage, as a secular aftermath, has come the modern Western inclination to speak of all human nature as dangerously pivoted on self-interest. Thus much modern political theory has tried to contrive checks and balances meant to keep a self-serving human nature at bay. This largely translates convictions of the classical Protestant reformers about the corruption of human nature and the necessity for divine grace. But it tends to leave out the possibility of divine grace and so to shift the focus from sin, strictly so called, which is an abuse of freedom that the love of God can overcome, to a humanity so flawed by evolutionary development (laws of the jungle) that nothing can heal it or make peace and justice more attractive to it than power and profit.

theology: study or teaching about God or the gods. In traditional cultures theology tended to be inseparable from general culture, since the basic traditional myths, rituals, and mores all bore on the people's sense of divinity and supposedly expressed the divine will. As knowledge differentiated into separate, specialized areas, theology became associated with ultimate questions, or with the corpus of tradition (scripture, liturgy, speculation about the divine) considered established by revelation. One traditional Western view is that theology is "faith seeking understanding," which puts well the priority belief often has had over vision or argumentative conclusions. Insofar as it purports to bear on the genuine God who exists transcendent to human ways, theology is intrinsically shaped by mystery—the inexhaustible nature of the divinity. What therefore sometimes is called mystical or negative theology is close to the essence, although equally necessary is an affirmative theology that does its best to find language in which to say the few essentials about divinity that human beings can and must say.

Trinity: the Christian God as Father–Son–Spirit. Christians have found the Trinity implied, though not clearly articulated, in the New Testament writings and recorded speeches of Jesus, who prayed to God as to his Father and spoke of the Spirit he would send. In orthodox Christian theology, the three "persons" do not make three gods. Each possesses divinity in its entirety. Each is equally and fully divine, though their relations indicate that the divine life is a system of knowing and loving with a certain structure. The Father is the unbegotten fullness, that beyond which one cannot go in primodiality. The Son is the expression of the Father's self-knowledge, while the Spirit is the result of the love that this self-knowledge issues. Creation is conceived as a work of all three persons, as are other works (salvation, divinization) "outside" the Godhead. Yet the missions of the Son and Spirit make it fitting to associate the divine contributions to the historical processes of creation and divinization (respectively) with them. Jews and Muslims generally have not accepted Christian arguments and have felt that the doctrine of the Trinity compromised strict monotheism. Christians have agreed that none of their arguments or symbols is adequate to explain the Trinity, which they have considered a strictly supernatural mystery, but they have felt the Trinity to be an essential part of biblical revelation.

CHAPTER 10

ISLAM

Crescent and Star: Ancient Byzantine symbols taken over by victorious Islam

The prophetic religion that began with Israel and took a new turn in Christianity gained a further career in Islam. Islam, which is the world's fastest-growing religion today, arose from the visions of the prophet Muhammad. At its height, Islam stretched from India to western Spain.[1] Today it is a great force in Africa, a middling presence in China, a strong presence in the Soviet Union, a shareholder in the petropolitics of the Middle East, a huge presence in Indonesia, and the religion of more than six million North Americans. To study the religion behind the crescent flag, we begin by describing its history.

HISTORY

Muhammad

Islam stems directly from the two precepts contained in the profession of faith: "There is no God but God, and Muhammad is his Prophet." *Allah* (the Arabic term for God) is the ultimate agent of Islamic revelation and religion, but he chose to work through Muhammad. Thus, Muhammad was the spokesman,

Islam: Twenty-five Key Dates	
570 C.E.	*Birth of Muhammad*
609–610	*First Qur'anic Revelations*
622	*Hejira (Flight to Medina)*
630	*Conquest of Mecca*
632	*Death of Muhammad*
636–640	*Conquest of Damascus, Jerusalem, Egypt, Persia*
ca. 650	*Establishment of the Canon of the Qur'an*
661–750	*Umayyad Caliphate*
680	*Murder of Husain, Shiite Saint*
711	*Muslim Entry into Spain*
713	*Muslim Entry into Indus Valley*
750–1258	*Abbasid Caliphate*
762	*Foundation of Baghdad*
909	*Rise of Fatimids in North Africa*
956	*Conversion of Seljuk Turks*
966	*Foundation of Cairo*
1099	*Christian Crusaders Capture Jerusalem*
1111	*Death of al-Ghazali, Leading Thinker*
1258	*Sack of Baghdad by Mongols*
1453	*Ottoman Turks Capture Constantinople*
1492	*End of Muslim Spain*
1707	*Decline of Mogul India*
1803–1804	*Wahabism Victorious in Mecca and Medina*
1924	*Secularization of Turkey*
1947–1948	*Creation of Pakistan and Israel*

the medium, of a definitive message and book (the Qur'an). Through it God expressed once and for all the divine mercy and judgment.

Muhammad was born in 570 C.E., in Mecca, which is in present-day Saudi Arabia. Around 610, he began to receive revelations. At that time, the religious milieu of the Arabian Peninsula was "a rather primitive *polydemonism* and worship of stones, stars, caves and trees."[2] Most of the people identified with one of the nomadic tribes that lived in the area. Mecca was a religious and commercial center, where people came to venerate the Black Stone, set in the shrine known as the Kaaba. Today scholars surmise that the stone was a meteorite. Whatever its origin, it served as a rallying point for local soothsayers and poets, who dominated the Arab religion that Muhammad witnessed as a youth. The likeliest forerunners of Muhammad's strict monotheism were the *hanifs,* a group who took offense at the polytheism and sought a purer faith, although to what extent they inspired Muhammad is not known.

W. Montgomery Watt has stressed the commercial strife that divided the people of Mecca during Muhammad's early years.[3] The conflict of the Byzantine and Persian empires affected Mecca, because traders from those realms passed through it. Among the Arabs in the Meccan area, a difficult social transition was under

MAJOR MUSLIM BELIEFS	
Oneness of God	Opposition to idolatry
Prophecy of Muhammad	Consummation of revelation Muhammad the model Muslim
Divinity of the Qur'an	Qur'an the "incarnation" of God's mind and will
Judgment Day	Separation of believers and unbelievers Consignment to Garden or Fire
Creation	God the Lord of all Worlds Humanity the vicegerent of God
Ummah	All believers form a brotherhood Pilgrimages to Mecca an experience of unity

way from a nomadic society, in which loyalty was to one's clan, to a mercantile society, in which loyalty was to one's business partners (or simply to profit). The result was considerable upheaval. Before that time people such as orphans and widows, who fell outside of nuclear families and trading groups, could find support in their larger clans, but the social change destroyed this support. Muhammad grew up as an orphan, so he must have felt some of the suffering experienced by children not raised by their own parents. Indeed, much of the social reform in his early message was to provide a religious basis for a unity extending beyond the clan and prompting concern for all orphans, widows, and the poor. At issue also were the tribal ethics that included the notions of honor and vendetta: feeling obliged to kill any outsider who had sullied the reputation of one's tribe, especially by bloodshed.

Muhammad grew up in a branch of the ruling Kuraish family under the care of his uncle, and he probably entered his family's caravan trade as a youth. In adulthood he married a wealthy widow, Khadija, who was some years older than he and who had been his employer. They had six children, of whom four daughters survived. Whether from personal troubles, challenges in the social situation, or a positive desire to understand the world more deeply, Muhammad de-

veloped the habit of going off to the hills near Mecca. There, in a cave, he enjoyed meditative solitude and began to have visions. His first visions, according to the Qur'an (53:1–18, 81:15–25) were of someone "terrible in power, very strong."[4] That person hovered near him on the horizon and imparted a revelation. It and subsequent revelations finally convinced Muhammad that God was choosing him to be a messenger.

At first, however, he wondered if he were going crazy. Nonetheless, Khadija encouraged him to believe in the revelations, and as his thought clarified, he attributed them to the angel Gabriel. Muhammad continued to receive revelations for the rest of his life (over twenty years), and those messages, which either he or early disciples wrote down on "pieces of paper, stones, palm-leaves, shoulder blades, ribs and bits of leather,"[5] formed the basis of the Qur'an.

From what scholars conjecture to be the early revelations, given to Muhammad before he moved to Medina, five major themes emerge: God's goodness and power, the need to return to God for judgment, gratitude and worship in response to God's goodness and pending judgment, generosity toward one's fellow human beings, and Muhammad's own vocation to proclaim the message of goodness and judgment.

At first, Muhammad's proclamation met with considerable resistance, principally because it threatened some powerful vested interests. For example, the absoluteness of God threatened the traditional polytheism. However, his message was much more than just a challenge to custom and traditional religion—it was a mortal challenge to the commerce that had grown up around the Kaaba. The livelihoods of the merchants who sold amulets, the soothsayers who sold fortunes, and the semiecstatic poets who lyricized the old gods were all imperiled.[6] Second, Muhammad's call for social justice implied a revolution—if not in contemporary financial arrangements, at least in contemporary attitudes. Third, the message of God's pending judgment was hardly welcome, for no age likes to find itself set before divine justice, hell fire, or the sword of retribution. Last, many Meccans ridiculed Muhammad's notion of the resurrection of the body.

Rise to Power. Initially rejected, Muhammad drew consolation from the fate of prophets who had preceded him. Increasingly, it appears, he learned about Judaism and Christianity from believers of those traditions who either lived in the area or traveled it for trade. The first converts to Muhammad's revelations came from within his own family. When he started to preach publicly, around 613, the leaders of the most powerful clans opposed him vigorously. He thus tended to be most successful among the low-ranking clans and those with young leaders ripe for a new order. Also, those who were considered "weak" (without strong clan protection) found the new prophecy attractive. Muhammad was proposing a religious association based on faith in Allah that transcended clan allegiances and so might make the weak stronger.

In 619 Muhammad suffered a personal crisis. His wife and uncle, who had been his foremost supporters, both died. *Muslims* ("submitters" to his God) were slowly increasing in number, but the future was very uncertain. In 622 he left Mecca and went to Yathrib, to the north, to arbitrate a long-standing dispute between two leading tribes. He settled there, and the town became Medina, the town of the Prophet. Muslims call Muhammad's departure or flight from Mecca the *Hejira,* and they view it as the turning point in the history of early Islam. Annemarie Schimmel interprets the Hejira as the complete breakup of Muhammad's relations with his own tribe—a definitive split from the old order,[7] which was a virtually unheard-of act in the clan-based society of the time.

Isma'il al Faruqi emphasizes the positive work that went on in Medina: the "promulgation of a constitution and the launching of the Islamic policy on its universal mission."[8] Muhammad proved to be a good politician, able to organize the immigrants who followed him from Mecca and the Medina clans into a single group.

One problem for Muhammad in Medina was the local Jewish community, which refused to accept him as a genuine prophet and ridiculed his interpretation of Jewish scripture. Apparently Muhammad either drove such Jews out of Medina or had them killed or sold into slavery.[9] After consolidating his power base and building support among the neighboring Bedouin tribes, Muhammad started to challenge his old foes at Mecca. He disrupted their trade in an effort to overturn the city's commercial base, and in 624 his vastly outnumbered troops won a surprising victory at Badr. Finally, after several further skirmishes, Muhammad won a decisive victory at the Battle of the Ditch.

Muhammad's greatest triumphs came through diplomacy among the tribes, however. Mecca finally fell in 630 without the stroke of a single sword. In control, Muhammad cleansed the Kaaba of pagan idols. He then consolidated his victory by a final military triumph over resistant Meccans at Hunayn. This settled the matter for most onlookers, and thenceforth the surrounding tribes were in Muhammad's hands.

In the two remaining years of his life, Muhammad further developed the educational program that he had set up in Medina. "The centre of all his preoccupations was the training, educating, and disciplining of his community. They were to be the leaven to leaven the whole lump—for he had no illusions about the Arab character and realized that any genuine conversion of the majority could only be the end of a long process extending far beyond his own lifetime."[10] Muhammad soon became the focus of Arab solidarity, and just before his death, he apparently contemplated action against the Byzantine powers in the north, perhaps because Muslim nationalism meant a growing hostility toward the Greeks and their Christian Arab allies. The quick military victories of his successors make most sense on the assumption that they simply executed plans that Muhammad himself had formulated.

Personality and Religious Impact. Although critics have decried Muhammad's violence toward his enemies, he certainly demonstrated an abundant humanity. In addition to his religious sensitivity and his political and military skills, the Prophet apparently manifested a notable sympathy for the weak, a gentleness, a slowness to anger, some shyness in social relations, and a sense of humor.[11] According to the *hadith* (traditions about Muhammad), for instance, one day the Prophet's second in command, Abu Bakr, started to beat a pilgrim for letting a camel stray. Muhammad began to smile and then indicated to Abu Bakr the irony that a pilgrim like Abu Bakr (a pilgrim through life) should beat a pilgrim to Mecca.

In glimpses obtained from the Qur'an and the earliest levels of the tradition, Muhammad seems to have been an ordinary man whom God singled out to receive revelations. Muhammad's virtue was to accept his commission and keep faith with it until death. The emphasis in the Prophet's own preaching on the sovereignty of God and the divine authority for the Qur'anic message led him to stress his own ordinariness, his liability to error, and the like. For example, at one point he thought that Muslims could compromise with Satan (the "Satanic Verses"), but then he realized that only God could receive Muslim devotion. He made no claim to miraculous power. The central miracle was the Qur'an itself—a message of such sublimity and eloquence that it testified beyond doubt to a divine source. In keeping with Muhammad's own humility, orthodox Islam has condemned any move to exalt Muhammad above ordinary humanity or to worship him as divine.

Nonetheless, popular Muslim religion sometimes seized on hints in the Qur'an and made Muhammad superhuman. The most famous of its images is Muhammad's "night journey" (miraculous flight) to Jerusalem, after which he ascended to Paradise, talked with the prophets who had preceded him, and experienced an ineffable vision of God. This story became so popular that it finally entered orthodox faith. Later religious faith also elaborated on Muhammad's preaching of the coming Last Judgment and tended to think of the Prophet as its shield and intercessor on the Last Day.

Sufis later elaborated a view of Muhammad as the supreme saint and mystic, while some Muslims given to cosmological speculation gave Muhammad an eternal existence prior to creation, which related to the eternal preexistence of the Qur'an as God's own Word. This belief gave Muhammad a role in creation as the intermediary between Allah and humanity. The mystic al-Hallaj, whom Islamic authorities killed because he claimed oneness with the deity, saw Muhammad as the first of the prophets—as the Light that was the source of all their lights: "He was before all, his name the first in the Book of Fate; he was known before all things

and all being, and will endure after the end of all."[12] In such understandings, the Prophet became the supreme exemplar, the mediator, something close to the Word of creation.

Qur'anic Religion

After Muhammad's death, his followers collected the texts of his revelations and established the orthodox version of the Qur'an during the rule of Othman (644–656). "To this day this version remains as the authoritative word of God. But, owing to the fact that the kufic script in which the Koran was originally written contained no indication of vowels or diacritical points, variant readings are recognized by Muslims as of equal authority."[13]

The present version of the collection of revelations follows the editorial principle that the chapters (suras) should be ordered in decreasing length. The result is that the present text tells the reader nothing about the chronology of the revelations. While scholars have attempted to distinguish the Meccan utterances from the ones given at Medina, their work is often so refined (distinguishing separate verses within a sura) that no one theory of the chronology of the revelations has won universal acceptance. Therefore, it is more expeditious simply to accept the fact that Muhammad's revelations were written down and collected unsystematically and that he used them as the basis of the program that he urged on his listeners. Among the earliest themes of his preaching, as noted, were the sovereignty of God, the imminence of judgment, and the need for fraternal charity.

Kenneth Cragg and other commentators insist on the importance of the Arabic used in the Qur'an.[14] Muslims consider the Qur'an to be written in the purest Arabic. The style of the Qur'an, as well as its message, proves to them that it must have come directly from God. Scholars such as Jeffrey and al Faruqi have both given thematic presentations of the Qur'an's religious materials.[15] They organize the Qur'an's seemingly repetitious or circular presentations, and by following their analyses we may get a sense of how Islamic revelation developed.

An early Meccan passage (96:1–5) emphasizes that Muhammad experienced his call as a command to *recite,* although what he was to recite only became clear as time passed. Sura 53, lines 1–18, richly symbolizes how Muhammad experienced his call. Because of Muhammad's vision of the angel Gabriel, the Muslim theology of revelation granted Gabriel an important role as the mediator in transmitting the Qur'an. In Sura 81, lines 15–29, are suggestions that Muhammad's early preaching met with disbelief and even contempt. Indeed, the Prophet seems to have had to defend himself against the charge of *jinn* (demon) possession.

Suras 73 and 74 buttress the tradition that Muhammad regularly used to go off to a cave to pray. Wrapped in a mantle against the night cold, he would seek God's comfort. This image has been a model for countless Sufis and ascetics as they have sought an experiential knowledge of God. Other Qur'anic passages that are considered reflections of Muhammad's early experiences boom forth a praise of God, a sense of God's overwhelming majesty, that suggests Rudolf Otto's classic definition of the holy: the mystery that is both alluring and threatening.

The later passages of the Qur'an, those that likely were written in Medina, concern more practical matters. As the head of an established political and religious community, Muhammad had to deal with questions of law and order. Thus, we can find the seeds of later Islamic law on inheritance, women, divorce, warfare, and the like. These seeds, plus the *hadith*, which contain what oral tradition said the Prophet himself taught and judged,[16] are the primary sources of Islamic law. Generally, Muhammad's law and social teaching were advances on the mores of his day. They improved the lot of the downtrodden and humanized both business and war. For instance, Muhammad made widows and orphans the prime beneficiaries of the *zakat* (almsgiving) required of all the faithful. Two points on which outsiders frequently have faulted Muhammad and the Qur'an are the doctrines of holy war *(jihad)* and polygamy. Nevertheless, in both cases Muhammad's views were improvements on the pre-Muslim practices and benefited both women and prisoners of war.

The Five Pillars. On the basis of the Qur'an's prescriptions for a true Islam, a true religion of submission to the will of God, Muslims have elaborated five cardinal duties known as the "pillars" of true faith. They are witnessing to faith (proclaiming the creed), ritual prayer, fasting during the lunar month of Ramadan, almsgiving, and pilgrimage to Mecca. The witness to faith epitomizes the Muslim's orientation in the universe. There is no God but God, and Muhammad is his Prophet. God is the only fit object of wor-

ship, and Muhammad is the last of the prophets—the "seal."

What a comparativist might call the rigorous monotheism of Islam has both negative and positive aspects. Negatively, in what amounts to an attack on false religion, Islam makes idolatry (associating anything with God) the capital sin. At the onset, then, Muhammad's revelation implied an attack on the prevailing Arab religion. Later it led to a polemic against Christian Trinitarianism and a check on any worldly pride or mammon that might diminish God's sovereignty. Positively, Islamic monotheism generated great praise for the "Lord of the Worlds"[17]—the Creator who guided all things, who was the beauty and power by which the world moved. For the Muslim mystics, the words of the creed swelled with hidden meaning. Like the Jewish cabalists, some Muslim mystics assigned each letter a numerical value and then composed numerological accounts of how the world hung together. Some Muslim mystics pushed the concept of divine sovereignty so far that they denied the existence of anything apart from God. Not only was there no God beside him, there was no being apart from his Being. While the orthodox Muslims found such pantheism blasphemous, the mystics tended to stress the oneness of the Lord's domain.[18] Last, rigorous monotheism implied that Muhammad himself was not divine. His high status was to be the *rasul*—the prophetic mouthpiece. (In later devotion, as we have seen, there was a tendency to exalt Muhammad, while later theology often viewed the Qur'an as coeternal with God, much as rabbinic theology saw the Torah as coeternal with God.)

The second pillar of faith is prayer, which has worked out as an obligation to pray five times daily. Authoritative authors such as al-Ghazali went to great lengths to specify the postures, words, number of bows, and proper places and times for prayer,[19] but the primary effect of the second pillar on the common people was to pace them through the day in the great Muslim practice of remembrance *(dhikr)*. At each call from the minaret (prayer tower), they were to remember the one God whom they served—remember his compassion, his mercy, and his justice. Ideally, by praying fervently at the appointed hours, one might forge a chain that linked together more and more moments of remembrance, so that God progressively came to dominate all one's thought, action, and emotion. And, in fact, witnessing Muslim prayer is a moving experience. The slow chant of the Qur'anic words becomes haunting, stirring even the non-Arabist. The voice (usually recorded today) is passionate—a lover's near sob, a tremulous witness to God's grandeur.

Third, what the prayer times are to the day, the holy month of Ramadan is to the year. *Ramadan* is the month of fasting and (interestingly enough) of celebration that helps give the year its rhythmic turning around God. Through all the daylight hours of Ramadan (from the time that one can distinguish a black thread from a white), no food or drink is to pass the lips. Thereby, the Muslim learns discipline, sacrifice, and the price that divine treasures cost.[20] In contrast to a secular succession of months, in which no time is finally more significant than any other, the religionist erects special times like Ramadan. These times oppose the flux, fencing off a portion of time as sacred.

Fourth, Islam has developed a similar paradigm for space by praying toward Mecca and by the obligation to make a pilgrimage to Mecca at least once in one's lifetime. For Muslims, Mecca is the center, the *omphalos* (navel) where the world was born. It is the holy city where Qur'anic revelation was disclosed to the world. Thus, the psychodynamics of the pilgrimage run deep. Without doubt, devout pilgrims feel that they are going to the holiest spot in creation.

On pilgrimage, Muslims dress alike, go through the same traditional actions tying their religion to the faith of Abraham, their spiritual father, and often experience an exhilarating sense of community. By going through ritual actions associated with Abraham, they dramatize their belief that Islam is not an innovation but the religion that preceded Judaism.

The fifth pillar, almsgiving, focuses this sense of community in a practical, economic way. By insisting that all contribute to the support of the poor (often one-fortieth of one's wealth annually), Qur'anic religion gives its community *(Ummah)*[21] food and clothing. The Muslim alms, then, is more than a tiny dole or act of charity—it is an act of social, corporate responsibility. Furthermore, it reminds the advantaged that they are one family with the disadvantaged and that the stern Judge will demand a strict account of what they have done with his gifts.

Case Study: Mary. Sura 19, entitled "Mary," shows some of the connections between the Qur'an and both Judaism and Christianity. The sura begins with an interpretation of the story of the birth of John the Baptist (Luke 1:5–80). Zacharias, the father of John the Baptist, approached God and prayed for an heir. He received the answer that he would have a son, to be called John, despite the fact that he and his wife were advanced in years. "It shall be no difficult task for Me, for I brought you into being when you were nothing before."[22] God instructed John to observe the scriptures with a firm resolve, bestowing on him wisdom, grace, and purity. John grew up to be a righteous man who honored his father and mother and was neither arrogant nor rebellious. So the Qur'an blesses the day John was born, and blesses the day of his death: "May peace be on him when he is raised to life."

Then Muhammad receives a command to recount the story of Mary, who left her people and betook herself to a solitary place to the east. God tells Muhammad that he sent to Mary the divine spirit in the semblance of a grown man. Mary saw the spirit and was seized with fear. But the spirit explained that he was a messenger of Mary's Lord, come to give her a holy son. When she asked how this could be, since she was a virgin, the spirit said that nothing was difficult to God and that this miracle was God's will. The son "shall be a sign to mankind," says the Lord, "and a blessing from Ourself. That is Our decree." Thereupon Mary conceived. When her time of delivery came, she lay down by a palm tree, wishing that she had died and passed into oblivion. But a voice from below her cried out that she should not despair. God had provided her a brook to run at her feet, and if she would shake the trunk of the palm tree it would drop ripe dates in her lap.

Mary took her child to her people, who abused her as a harlot. So she pointed to the baby in the cradle, who spoke up and said: "I am the servant of Allah. He has given me the gospel and ordained me a prophet." The child explained that God had commanded him to be steadfast in prayer, to give alms to the poor, to honor his mother, and to be free of vanity and wickedness. God had blessed the day of his birth and would bless the day of his death.

The sura then makes a polemical point: This is the whole truth about Jesus, the son of Mary, which "they" (probably the Christians) are unwilling to accept. "God forbid that He himself should beget a son!" In other words, though Jesus had a marvelous birth, he was in no way the divine Son of God. Only God is Muhammad's Lord, and the Lord of Muslims. Therefore only God is to be served. That is the right path. Any other path is erroneous. The unbelievers who cling to a different view of Jesus will experience woe on the day they appear before God, since they are in the grossest error (idolatry).

Next the sura takes up the story of Abraham. Abraham was a prophet and a saintly man. He asked his father, "How can you serve a worthless idol, a thing that can neither see nor hear?" Furthermore, he told his father that the truth had been revealed to him (Abraham), so that if the father followed Abraham he would follow the even path, away from the worship of Satan, who had rebelled against the Lord of Mercy. But Abraham's father only became angry, banishing him from the house and threatening him with stoning. Abraham prayed that the true Lord would forgive his father, but he departed, since he could not worship idols. God rewarded Abraham with sons called Isaac and Jacob, prophets of high renown.

The next story in the sura on Mary concerns Moses, who was a prophet, an apostle, and a chosen man. God called out to Moses from the right side of a mountain. When Moses came, Allah communed with him in secret and gave him his brother Aaron, also a prophet. Then there was Ishmael, also an apostle, a seer, and a man of his word. Ishmael enjoined prayer and almsgiving on his people, and thereby he pleased the Lord. Last there was Idris (Enoch), another saint and prophet, whom the Lord honored and exalted.

To all these men, God has been gracious. They are the line of prophets, from the descendants of Adam and the people God carried in the ark with Noah. They include Abraham and Israel (Jacob), and they stand out as the line God has guided and chosen. When they received divine revelations, these prophets humbled themselves, falling down on their knees in tears and adoration. In contrast, the generations that succeeded the prophets neglected prayer and succumbed to temptation. Assuredly they shall be lost.

However, those that repent, embrace the faith that Muhammad is preaching, and do what is right will be admitted to Paradise. They shall not be wronged, but shall enter the Garden of Eden, which the Merciful has promised to his servants as their reward for faith. What God has promised, God shall fulfill. In Paradise the just will hear no idle talk, only the voice of peace. Morning and evening they shall receive their sustenance. That is the bliss which the righteous shall inherit.

The sura then interposes a strange transition: "We do not descend from Heaven save at the bidding of your Lord." Muslim commentators tend to interpret this as the voice of the angel Gabriel, answering Muhammad's complaint that the revelations he was receiving sometimes stopped, making for long intervals of silence. Gabriel reminds Muhammad that revelation like this is solely God's affair. To God alone belongs what is before us and what is behind us, and all that lies between.

Gabriel goes on to comfort Muhammad. His Lord does not forget his servants. God is the ruler of the heavens and the earth and all that is between them. Muhammad's task is simple: Worship him and be loyal in his service. After all, what god compares with God? To whom else can a sane or devout person go?

But all human flesh is weak, so it finds faith hard to sustain. Thus human beings regularly ask, "When I am once dead, shall I be raised to life again?" God's answer is a call to remembrance. Why do human beings forget that God once had to create them from the void? Unless they put their lives in order, God will call them to account, placing them in the company of the devils, setting them on their knees around the fire of hell. Each sect of dissidents will have its stoutest rebels cast down into hellfire. God alone knows who most deserves to burn.

Sternly, the Lord issues a dire warning: Not one of the unbelievers shall not pass through the confines of hell. This is his absolute decree. God will deliver those who fear him, but wrongdoers will go to their knees to endure the torments of the fire. For the conduct of the unbelievers is wanton. When God's clear revelations are laid out before them, they say to God's faithful, "Will that way add to your glory or place you in better company than ours?" Such questioning and haggling will bring them speedy destruction. God has destroyed many generations of unbelievers before this present one. Faithless people far richer and more splendid than they have been sent on their way to destruction.

Yet Muhammad is to tell the unbelievers that God is merciful. He will bear with the unbelievers until they witness the fulfillment of his threats, be that a worldly scourge or the hour of doom, when all are called to judgment. At such times of reckoning, the unbelievers will realize the comparative worth of their way and the true way of God. Their worse plight and smaller following will make it clear they have chosen unto their woe.

On the other hand, God will more and more guide those who have chosen the right path. Their deeds will bring them lasting merit, a rich reward in God's sight, and an auspicious end. The unbeliever, in contrast, has only empty boasts. He expects wealth and children, as though he had had the future disclosed to him, or the merciful Lord, who alone knows what lies

Figure 42 *Dome of the Rock, Jerusalem, one of Islam's most splendid shrines, built in the seventh century. Photo by J. T. Carmody.*

ahead, had made him a solemn promise. The truth is far different. God will record every word of such vain boasts and determine punishments long and terrible. When the unbeliever is brought to judgment, he shall come alone, his expected wealth and children having proven only vain imaginings. The unbelievers have chosen other gods to help them. In the end, these useless gods will reject the unbelievers' worship and turn against them. So the unbelievers will be sent down to the devils that incite their irreligion. True believers like Muhammad should be patient. The days of the unbelievers are numbered.

On the day of reckoning, God will gather the righteous and bring them before him. But the sinful he will drive in great hordes into the fire of hell. Then no one will be able to intercede for the wicked, save the one (Muhammad?) who has received the sanction of the Merciful.

Again the sura lashes out at those who teach that God has begotten a son. That is such a monstrous falsehood that the heavens should crack, the earth should break asunder, the mountains should crumble to dust. Those who ascribe to God a son know nothing of the nature of the Merciful. It does not become him to beget a son. His sovereignty is beyond any such thing. For there is none in the heavens or the earth who shall not return to the Lord in utter submission. God keeps strict count of all his creatures. One by one, they shall all approach him on the Resurrection Day. Those he shall cherish are they who have accepted the true faith Muhammad is preaching and shown charity to their fellows.

Concluding, the sura has God remind Muhammad that he has revealed the Qur'an in Muhammad's own tongue so that Muhammad can proclaim good tidings to the upright and warnings to a contentious nation.

How many generations has the Lord not destroyed before this one? Is one of those past generations still alive? Does any still speak so much as a whisper?

From reading this remarkable bit of the Qur'an, one senses the overwhelming sovereignty of Muhammad's God. Not to believe him, not to accept the way he lays out, is tantamount to blindness or utter corruption of heart. Muhammad finds this way prefigured in the prior prophets of Judaism and Christianity, who deserve high esteem. Jesus, the miraculous child of Mary, the great heroine of faith, was a worthy precursor.[23] But the Christian notion that Jesus was God's son is sheer blasphemy, an effort to diminish the absolute uniqueness and sovereignty of God. The Creator is solely responsible for all that happens in the world. Those who confess this will merit good things in the Garden of Eden. Those who reject it will go to hell, the place of punishing fire and devils. So the choice is very simple: Believe and prosper, or reject belief and perish. The Lord is merciful, so belief is offered to all. The Lord is also just, so unbelief cannot evade due punishment. Those with any wit will open their hearts to God's last Prophet and believe.

The Age of Conquest

At Muhammad's death in 632 most of Arabia had accepted Islam, though often the allegiance was superficial. Some tribes took the occasion of the Prophet's death to attempt a revolt. General Khalid al-Walid, who served the first caliph (leader), Abu Bakr, crushed them within a year. Thus, when Abu Bakr died in 634, Arabia was united and poised for adventure. The obvious foes were Byzantium and Persia, which threatened Arabian prosperity and were ripe for religious and military conquest. The Muslim armies were amazingly effective. By the end of 636 they controlled both Damascus and Jerusalem. As important in this lightning conquest as their military skill, though, was the unrest of the peoples they conquered. Those peoples "welcomed the Muslims as kin-liberators from Byzantine politics, economic exploitation, Church persecution, and social tyranny."[24] On the eastern frontier, Muslim armies spread into Persian territory, and by 649 all of Persia was in Arab hands.

The quick conquest of Syria released men for further expeditions in the west; by 640 there were conquests in Egypt. Alexandria soon fell, and despite resistance from the Roman emperor Constans, the Arabs established themselves as a marine power

operating from the southeastern Mediterranean. By 648 they had conquered Cyprus; by 655 they were in charge of the waters around Greece and Sicily. On land in North Africa, the Muslims conquered the Berber region of Tripoli in 643 and then proceeded to Carthage and to the Nubian regions along the Nile, conquering the Nubian capital city of Dongola. When the Umayyad caliphate established itself in 661, the ventures became even more far-reaching. Soon Muslims were as far away as China, India, and western Europe. By 699 Islam occupied Afghanistan, while various campaigns south of the Caspian and Aral Seas brought Armenia, Iraq, Iran, and eastern India into the Muslim fold by 800.

At the beginning of the ninth century, Arab rule along the southern Mediterranean stretched from Palestine to the Atlantic. Muslims controlled three-quarters of the Iberian Peninsula, and most Mediterranean traffic had to reckon with Muslim sallies. European campaigns had brought Arab soldiers as far north as Orleans, and they strongly influenced the southern portions of the Frankish kingdom. In 732 Muslims had taken Toulouse and then the whole of Aquitaine, moving into Bordeaux and Tours. Charles Martel stopped them at Poitiers, but in 734 they crossed the Rhone and captured Arles, Saint-Remy, and Avignon. Then they fortified Languedoc and recaptured Lyons and Burgundy. In the ninth century, from their positions in southeastern France, they pushed northeast as far as Switzerland. By daring naval raids, they harassed such ports as Marseilles and even Oye on the coast of Brittany.

Toward the end of the ninth century, Islam controlled most of western Switzerland and ruled many of the Alpine passes. In the mid-tenth century Muslims were at Lake Geneva, taking Neuchâtel and Saint Gall. Only the attacks of the Huns and the Hungarians from the north and northeast and the deterioration of the Spain-based Umayyad caliphate kept them from ruling all of southern Europe. However, Muslim expansion ended after 1050, for the Normans pushed Islam out of southern France, southern Italy, Corsica, Sardinia, and Sicily.

By 1250, Islam's European presence had weakened considerably. Only southernmost Spain and eastern Anatolia (Turkey) held secure. However, Islam had spread through all of Persia, crossed northern India, and reached the western Chinese border. In East Asia, it had a discernible presence in Sumatra, Borneo, and Java. All of North Africa was securely Muslim, while

Figure 43   Mosque in New Delhi. Photo by J. T. Carmody.

down the East African coast as far as Madagascar it exerted a strong influence. In many of these regions, of course, substantial portions of the populations remained non-Muslim. For instance, in Egypt many Monophysite and Coptic Christians remained loyal to their own traditions, as did many Christians in Anatolia and Syria. Nestorian Christians in Iraq north of Baghdad held out, while portions of southern Persia remained Zoroastrian strongholds. In India the majority remained Hindu, especially in the central and southern regions.

Motivations.   Through this age of conquest and expansion, the basic Muslim strategy revolved around the use of the desert.[25] Just as modern empires, such as the British, made great use of naval power, so the Arabs exploited their experience with the desert, using it for communication, transferring supplies, and retreating safely in time of emergency. In their spread through North Africa, they established main towns at the edge of the desert. In Syria they employed such conquered cities as Damascus to the extent that they lay close to the desert. Through the Umayyad period (to 750), these garrison towns at the edge of the desert were the centers of Arab government. By dominating them and by introducing Arabic as the language of government, the conquerors exerted a disproportionate influence (they usually remained a minority of the total population). The towns served as the chief markets for the agricultural produce of the neighboring areas, and around their markets clusters of artisan quarters developed. By imposing discriminatory taxes on the outlying populations, the Arabs encouraged the citizenry to congregate in the cities, making their control easier.

Historians debate the motivation for all this expansion, and we can safely say that it was complex. The Arabs were likely suffering from population pressures on the Arabian Peninsula, which incited many of them to search for more land. Precedents for such an outflow occurred in the fifth and sixth centuries, before Islam, and apparently from even earlier times the land to the northeast, especially the Fertile Crescent, served as a safety valve for overpopulation. Bernard Lewis has suggested that older historians overestimated the role of religion in the Islamic conquests and that more recent historians have underestimated it. In his own view, "its [religion's] importance lies in the temporary psychological change which it wrought in a people who were naturally excitable and temperamental, unaccustomed to any sort of discipline, willing to be persuaded, but never to be commanded. It made them for a time more self-confident and more amenable to control."[26]

Symbolically, religion served as a rallying point for the Arab cause. It stressed common bondage to a single Lord, and it dignified the Arab movement with a sort of manifest destiny. Certainly the generals who dominated the era of conquest were as accomplished in worldly affairs as they were in religion. For Khalid and Amr, two of the most outstanding, the utilitarian values of religion seem to have been clear.

The Islamic administration of the conquered territories was also quite pragmatic. Rather understandably, the interests served were not those of the conquered subjects but those of the aristocracy that conquest created—the interests of the Arab rulers. Thus, the temper of the Arab military commanders and then of the quasi-military Arab governors most determined how Islam treated its new peoples. At the beginning of the conquest in Byzantium and Persia, Muslims kept the old administrative structures. In the 640s, though, they shifted to a new format, through which the caliphs could impress their will more directly.

However, at first there was no unified imperial law. The conquerors struck different bargains with different peoples, and some stipulated that local customs or laws remain in force. The Arabs tended to take only the property of the state (and that of the new regime's enemies); other landowners who were willing to recognize the new regime could keep their holdings provided they paid a sizable tax. Nevertheless, there were opportunities for Muslim "speculators," as we might call them, to gain lands outside the garrison center on which they would have to pay only light levies.

At first, the conquered peoples were allowed to retain most of their traditional civil and religious rights. The Muslims grouped most of the conquered non-Muslims together as *Dhimmis*—members of religions that Arab law tolerated. As "peoples of the book," Jews and Christians were *Dhimmis*, with title to special respect. There were nevertheless frictions, especially if Jews or Christians were blatantly derogatory of the Prophet and his Book, but usually people were not compelled to convert to Islam. Because Arab rule regularly promised to be more just than Byzantine rule, many Jews and Christians are on record as having welcomed the change. For example, in Palestine the Samaritans actively assisted the invaders. The Arabs were not always sure how to handle such complicity, especially when it developed into a desire to convert to Islam. Islam and Arabism were so synonymous that the first converts had to become *Mawali*—clients of one of the Arab tribes. In fact, converts seldom gained status equal to born Muslims, especially regarding such material benefits as the booty that warriors received after a conquest.

Internal Strife. Despite its enormous outward success in the age of conquest, the Islamic community suffered notable internal divisions. With the exception of Abu Bakr, the first caliphs, known as the *Rashidun* (rightly guided), all left office by murder. (Despite that fact, modern Islam has considered their time the golden age.[27]) Ali, the fourth caliph, was the center of a fierce struggle for control. His main opponent was Muawiya, the head of a unified stronghold in Syria. Muawiya maneuvered to have the legitimacy of Ali's caliphate called into question. As a result, Ali lost support in his own group, and dissidents called Kharijites appeared who had a hand in many later conflicts. A Kharijite killed Ali in 661, and the caliphate passed to the Umayyad dynasty—the followers of Muawiya.

However, Ali's influence did not end with his assassination. In fact, his assassination became part of Islam's deepest division, the one between the *Shia* (party), who were loyal to Ali, and the *Sunni* (traditionalists). The "party" supporting Ali believed that the successors to Muhammad ought to come from Muhammad's family—in other words, that Islamic leadership should be hereditary. (As the cousin and son-in-law of Muhammad, Ali was his closest male relative and so his heir.) This conviction was supported by certain verses of the Qur'an, in which the Prophet supposedly indicated that Ali would be his successor. The Shia therefore consider the first three caliphs, who preceded Ali, as having been usurpers. After Ali's death, they took up the cause of his sons, Hasan and Husain.

The word that the Shia gave to the power that descended through Muhammad's family line was *imamah* (leadership). Through its history, the Shia has made it a cardinal doctrine that Muhammad's bloodline has an exclusive right to *imamah*. The slaughter of Husain in Iraq in 680 was an especially tragic event, and the Shiites (who have been strongest in Iran) have come to commemorate it as the greatest of their annual festivals. It gives their Islam a strong emphasis on sorrow, suffering, and emotion that quite distinguish it from Sunni piety.[28]

Of course, our brief summary has presented only a slice of the dense military, political, and religious history that shaped the first unfolding of Qur'anic faith. Externally, Islam's quick successes testified as much to the political vacuum within which the conquered peoples lived and to their oppression as it did to Arab military genius. Internally, Islam's great energy made for considerable strife. However, during the following centuries, religion and culture caught up with the military wildfire of the initial expansion, consolidating the empire and making it much more than just a far-flung string of garrisons.

The Golden Civilization

In his history of science, Stephen Mason states that Muslim scientific culture began in the era of the Umayyads.[29] The Umayyads had been auxiliaries of the Romans in Syria, so when they established the caliphate in Damascus in 661, they brought an enthusiasm for Hellenistic culture. In particular, they became patrons of the sciences. For example, in 700 they founded an astronomical observatory at Damascus. However, the Umayyads fell to the Abbasids in 749, Umayyid rule continuing only in Spain. The Abbasids set their caliphate in Baghdad and turned to Persian rather than Hellenistic culture, supporting the Persian specialties of medicine and astronomy. Al-Mansur, the second Abbasid caliph, was also devoted to learning, bringing Indian astronomers and doctors to Baghdad and having many Indian scientific treatises translated. Under his successors, translation continued to be a major project, any nation's heritage being fair game. As a result, many Greek treatises (for example, those of Galen and Ptolemy) became available to Muslims. Partly because of Babylonian and Zoroastrian influences, the Baghdad caliphs deemed astronomy especially important. They imported Indian mathematicians to help in astronomical calculations and made Baghdad a center of astronomical learning.

Al-Razi (865–925) collected voluminous lore on medicine from Greek, Indian, and Middle Eastern sources. Indeed, he may even have drawn on Chinese sources, for there is a story that he entertained a Chinese scholar who learned to speak Arabic, and his successors' works include what seems to be the Chinese doctrine of what one could learn from the body's pulses. A Muslim alchemy arose in the ninth century with Jabir ibn-Hayyan, but in Islam alchemy remained somewhat suspect because the authorities linked it with mystical religion. Some radical Sufis became deeply involved in alchemy, but orthodox Sunni had the works of at least one such group, the "Brethren of Purity," declared heretical and burned. Principally, the orthodox favored the rational geometry and deductive science of the Greeks.

From 970, the Spanish branch of the Muslim Empire had a distinguished scientific center in Cordoba. Similarly, the religious authorities patronized science, especially medicine and astronomy, at Toledo from the early eleventh century. The Spanish Muslims tended to be critical of Ptolemy and to favor Aristotelian doctrines. Averroës (1126–1198) was a great Aristotelian synthesizer who composed a full philosophical corpus.

By conquering the territory between the Muslim East and the kingdom of Sung China, the Mongols expedited trade and the flow of learned information between East and West. Marco Polo (1254–1324) was able to travel to the East because of Mongol rule, which also enabled the Chinese Mar Jaballaha (1244–1317) to come West and become the Nestorian Christian patriarch. When the Mongols conquered China they left its bureaucratic structure intact. They set up an observatory in Peking and staffed it with Muslims. In the West they conquered the Abbasid capital of Baghdad in 1258, where they continued to support astronomical studies.

Albert Moore has shown the effects of Islam's monotheism in the field of art, arguing that it led to a classical concentration on the architecture and ornamentation of the mosque.[30] This art reached its peak in the sixteenth and seventeenth centuries, leaving impressive monuments in Ottoman Turkey, Safavid Persia, and Mughal India. Schuyler Cammann[31] has shown exceptions to the generally nonrepresentational character of Islamic art in Persian works, and Moore indicates that paintings of hunting and of love scenes were permitted in private Muslim homes. Nonetheless, the preponderance of Muslim art during the golden age was nonpictorial, including rugs, vases, lamps, and mosques.

A distinctively Islamic calligraphy developed from the trend to decorate pages from the Qur'an. The Qur'an itself praises the art of writing (96:4), and speaks of being written on a heavenly tablet (84:21–22). The favorite script was Kufic, which originated in the new Islamic town of Kufa near Babylon, and it was the standard scriptural model from about the seventh to eleventh centuries. It is vertical, massive, and angular, while its prime alternate, the Naskhi script, is horizontal, flowing, and rounded. A favorite subject of embellishment has been the *Bismallah,* the prefix to the Qur'anic suras ("In the name of God"). Through an extension of calligraphic swirls and loops, Muslims developed an ingenious ability to suggest flowers, birds, lions, and so on. The Sufi interest in numerology also encouraged artistic work.

Case Study: Architecture and Poetry. As we suggested, Islam also influenced architecture. The mosque was a sort of theology in the concrete. Muslim architects tried to embody the faith and conviction that all of life stands subject to God and so that no great distinction should be made between sacred dwellings and profane. The guiding idea in the construction of a mosque was simply to house a space for prayer and prostration. The *hadith* reported that the Prophet led his first companions outside the city, so that they could pray together in an open space. At Medina, the usual place for prayer was the open courtyard of Muhammad's own house. For convenience, the architects tried to construct a churchlike building that had the character of an open space where many faithful might go through the same rhythmic motions of bowing, kneeling, prostrating, and praying together.

Mosque architecture tended not to differ radically from that of Muslim palaces. Most of the renowned Muslim palaces have crumbled, but the Alhambra, in Granada, Spain, still stands, a glorious tribute to the Muslim golden age. The Alhambra was built between 1230 and 1354 and served as a great citadel for the Moorish kings. It was mutilated after the expulsion of the Muslims in 1492, but extensively restored from 1828 on. Its beauty suggests the Muslim notion of how religion and secular life ought to interpenetrate.

Physically, the Alhambra is located on a hill overlooking the city of Granada. Although it is surrounded by walls and has the look of a fort, only the lowest parts of the enclosure were actually used for military purposes. According to early Islamic tradition, palaces were supposed to be placed as the Alhambra is: close to the city, yet a little bit apart. Thus the Alhambra strikes us as a country villa, yet also like an urban citadel. One gets the same impression from similar palaces in Aleppo (northwest Syria) and Cairo. There, too, the effort was to retain the amenities of a royal palace while fortifying the ruler's residence against possible incursions. Such military considerations led to architectural innovations in the vaulting, gateways, and towers of the *qal'a* or urban citadel.

The Alhambra goes beyond a simple fusion of the villa and citadel traditions, however, by breaking its sizable area into a series of separate units. Some of these units are lovely gardens, in the Muslim paradisic tradition. For example, both Iranian and Indian Muslim palaces frequently sought to prefigure Paradise by developing lovely royal gardens. Of the other units of the Alhambra, the most celebrated is the Court of the Lions. The Court of the Lions has an impressive portico running along several sides, with slim, delicate pillars supporting strong arches. The open space in the center is handsomely tiled, and a small fountain with flowers at the base adds splashes of color. Off the court run complexes of square and rectangular rooms, as though the architect wanted to suggest sumptuousness. This is what one commentator calls the "additive" principle: adding room after room, to imply that the royal resources were limitless. The delicate, filigreed work on some of the wall panelings gives an impression of exquisite lace.

"The most important point is that very few of the halls and courts of the Alhambra had an architecturally definable purpose. A curious dissociation seems to have occurred between building and function, as though individual forms which are definable in architectural terms as courts, porticoes, square or oblong halls, and so forth, were merely generalized forms in which a variety of purposes, from traditional audiences to various pastimes, could be performed."[32] This dissociation, or apparent lack of precise function, was a feature of many other Muslim buildings. The masses of kiosks or pavilions in the palaces of Cairo or Istanbul, for example, were similarly "formal" constructions and did not suggest precisely what activities would take place in them. One could relate this Muslim style to recent Western tendencies toward "multipurpose rooms," which are capable of being turned into lecture halls, dining areas, or gymnasiums with little effort.

A third feature of the Alhambra, beyond its fortified and multipurpose aspects, is its extraordinary attention to decoration. When one is inside the

Alhambra, the most gripping feature is the careful ornamentation of the pillars, walls, ceilings, and floors. Once again, commentators generalize from the Alhambra to Muslim buildings of Iran, Central Asia, or Turkey. In all these places, the themes and techniques of internal palace decoration were spectacular.

If one asks why Muslims lavished such care on the internal aesthetics of their palaces, the Alhambra provides an important clue to the answer. The impressive stalactite domes, and the thin pillars of the Fountain of the Lions, apparently derived from the medieval Muslim understanding of Solomon, the famed biblical king. In the medieval mythology surrounding Solomon, the jinns made wonderful scenes of beauty for him and his queens. Thus medieval Muslim rulers had a certain stimulus to create scenes of an otherworldly, separate Paradise. Wanting to produce by natural means beauty such as that which Solomon achieved by supernatural power, they came to stress gardens, delicate decorations, and almost tours de force of engineering (thin pillars holding stupendous domes, for instance).

Less spectacularly, the motivations behind architecture like that of the Alhambra led to the "monumentalization" of many ordinary Muslim buildings. Thus in many urban areas, schools, shops, hostels, hospitals, baths, and even warehouses were built with great facades and intricate decorations. The caravanserais (motels, we might say) of thirteenth-century Anatolia, for example, employed the latest and most sophisticated techniques of construction. A religion that had a large place for "works"—business, pragmatic affairs, military matters—placed great stress on housing its social activities and secular affairs well. Also, in the medieval period Muslims tended to invest in land or buildings rather than trade or industry. The result was an architecture that little distinguished between the mosque and the secular building. Facades, for instance, seldom gave external viewers a basis for determining what sort of building they were entering. It was the internal decorations of the buildings, or the activity that occurred within them, that gave them their distinction.

In the history of architecture, the Muslim achievements stand out as the most significant development in the period from Roman times to the Middle Ages. Indeed, the Muslim development of monumental buildings for secular purposes was rivaled only by Roman lavishness. For the most part, this sort of construction seems to have gone forward haphazardly, out of an instinct that daily life ought to be housed well.

Exceptions to this general rule stand out: for instance, the organized city planning of Samarkand, Isfahan, and Istanbul.

Curiously, even the specifically religious architecture of Islam was influenced by Islamic secular monumentalism. From the tenth century on, the growth of domes, minarets, and mausoleums was mainly due to a desire to honor and publicize the people who were building the religious constructions, rather than to a desire better to serve the religious activities the constructions would house. Thus Islamic architecture differs from European medieval architecture as consciously more secular.

From the time of the building of the famous Jerusalem Dome of the Rock in 691, the decoration we stressed in the case of the Alhambra preoccupied Muslim builders. Indeed, increasing the decorative beauty of their buildings seems to have been a prime motivation in the Muslims' development of stucco, in their laying bricks to make bold designs, and in their creation of colored tiles. This concern with ornamentation leads to the question of how Muslim construction and decoration relate, a question historians of Islamic architecture debate with some vigor.

A good case to study is the mosque of Cordoba. In the *mihrab* (niche to designate the direction of Mecca) of the Cordoba mosque the domes contain such unusual features as ribs that appear to support the cupola yet form a static mass with the cupola. The squinches (a characteristic support of domes) that accompany the ribs do not really support anything. In other words, the ribs and squinches are present for decorative, rather than constructive, reasons. The north dome of the great mosque in Isfahan, Persia, built a century after the *mihrab* of the mosque in Cordoba, has an unusual articulation of supports that also seem more decorative than constructive. The supports correspond to every part of the superstructure and give the impression of being a grid or net filled with decorative masonry. Third, the Muslim use of *muqarnas*, three-dimensional shapes used in many different combinations, seems clearly intended for decorative, rather than constructive, purposes. The *muqarnas* draw attention to some principal parts of a building, but they usually have little significance in terms of engineering.

The debate among scholars of Muslim architecture seems to turn on what value one ought to give these decorative features. Perhaps the best resolution of the debate, for our lay purposes, is the one that stresses that Muslim architects apparently strove,

Figure 44 *Courtyard of Cairo Mosque, with purification fountain. Photo by J. T. Carmody.*

through their engineering and ornamentation alike, to produce a distinctive overall effect. In their great masterpieces, the whole is greater than the sum of its parts. Engineering and ornamentation have so blended that one gets an effect that is more than either brilliant constructive design or artful decoration. The *muqarnas* domes, for example, often give the effect of the revolving heavens. As the source of external light moves around the base of the dome, the complex surface that the *muqarnas* produce on the cupola gives an illumination that is always changing. Like the heavens, the top of the mosque never looks the same yet seems quite motionless.

Due to the secular impact of Muslim faith, then, Islamic architecture developed such characteristic features as a preponderance of activity (use) over form, a tendency to monumentalize buildings that served quite ordinary functions, and a tendency to fuse construction and decoration into one harmonious entity. However, Islam seldom created its architectural forms entirely from Muslim inspiration. Ordinarily it adapted non-Muslim forms influential in an area it had conquered. Thus in Iran Islamic architects made use of the pre-Islamic *aywan,* a large vaulted hall opening directly onto an open space. This became an axial feature of Iranian mosques, and of Iranian Muslim secular buildings as well. Similarly, in Ottoman Turkey the superb mosques of Istanbul adapted features of the famous Christian cathedral of Hagia Sophia (Holy Wisdom).

Since it conquered so many different areas, Islam had the opportunity, and the need, to graft Muslim ideas onto a variety of different architectural traditions. In India, for example, it tended to experiment with several different Near Eastern Muslim models, trying to adapt them to the local Indian traditions and materials. The result often was a fairly hybrid style, brilliant in such well-planned constructions as the Taj Mahal (Figure 47 on page 420), but often undistinguished in more commonplace undertakings.

Summarily, then, Muslim architecture suggests that (1) Islam tended to prize buildings as much for their versatility in being able to serve several functions as for their formal beauty, and (2) it tended to show more originality and brilliance in secular than in strictly religious constructions. Both these characteristics expressed the Muslim conviction that religion ought to breathe through all dimensions and activities of life. If one Lord ruled all of creation, overseeing each and every human activity, the distinction between sacred functions and profane was quite small.

The basic ornamental motif in much other Islamic art is repetition, seemingly endless patterns, whether representational (roses and leaves), semiabstract (vine tendrils and rosettes), or completely abstract (geometric patterns). This motif is known as the infinite pattern, and some suggest that it has theological significance. It does not want to rival God by creating anything fixed or permanent. Popular art often violated this pattern, suggesting that it most applied to mosques and official constructions. For instance, a Persian manuscript painting of the sixteenth century portrays Muhammad's ascent to Paradise, complete with winged angels, dishes of fruit, showers of pearls, and rubies.

Poetry. A. J. Arberry has translated a representative collection of Islamic writings,[33] and it suggests a great breadth and lyricism. Poetry had always held a place of honor among Arabs, for eloquence had always been considered a trait of a great man, even before the advent of Islam. Much as the Greeks valued military prowess and the ability to persuade others, so the Arabs honored both warfare and eloquence.

The ancient poetry was born in the desert, so it was replete with desert images and themes. With expansion and conquest, however, Islam became largely an urban culture,[34] so there was need to reshape its poetry. Meter, rhyme, and new imagery became the chief tools. The result was a very complex style: "We have called this poetry arabesque, and indeed it is fully as exquisitely and delicately ornamented as the finest Saracenic architecture."[35] The thirteenth-century poet Ibn al-Khabbaza fashioned an elegy that epitomized Arab eloquence: "Your life was of the order true of Arab eloquence; the tale was brief, the words were few, the meaning was immense."[36]

The themes that dominate Arberry's poetic selections are not especially religious: the beauty of a beloved, trees, battle, and, for humor, the flanks and shanks of an ant. Still, some of the religious mystics, such as Junaid, Rumi, and the woman Rabia, gained fame for their poetic skills. Most were Sufis—devotees of religious emotion and feeling. Among the religious poets of Islam, the Persians were most eminent. Their themes and images centered on the Sufi goal of self-effacement in the divine immensity. For instance, Rumi often portrayed the soul's sense of abandonment in moments of trial when it could not feel the divine embrace: "Hearken to this Reed forlorn, Breathing ever since 'twas torn from its rushy bed, a strain of impassioned love and pain."[37] In this way, the talented Sufi writers won considerable respect from cultured people. To be able to express their religious vision with eloquence made them seem less eccentric, more representative of traditional Arab cultural ideals.

Law and Theology. Within the inner precincts of Islam, neither science nor art constituted the main cultural development. Rather, the most important flowering of Qur'anic faith was the law (*Sharia*).[38] As the opening verses of the Qur'an suggest, a fundamental concern in Islam is guidance, and Islam went to lawyers, not to scientists, poets, or even mystics, for its most trustworthy guidance. In fact, Islam obtained little guidance from philosophical theology, which began a most promising career but foundered on the shoals of sectarian controversy and debates about the relation of reason to faith. Although numerous schools of law developed, the differences among them were relatively slight, and they usually subordinated speculative reason to faith and tradition. Thus, the authorities accounted them more trustworthy than philosophical theology—better cement for Muslim society.

Traditional Islamic law has thought of itself as derived from God's plan for the proper ordering of human life. Its province has extended to whatever impinged on human beings' passage to Paradise. A term equivalent to *Sharia, fiqh* ("understanding" or "knowledge"), implied that the laws developed by the lawyers expressed what was understood to be behavior that would keep believers on the straight path.

The classical *fiqh* treatises follow a similar format. First, they usually discuss people's obligations to God. For example, there are detailed rules for how to carry out daily prayers, the pilgrimage to Mecca, fasting during the month of Ramadan, and almsgiving. As well, one's obligations to God have included identifying sources of ritual pollution, carrying out ablutions to achieve ritual purity, the proper preparation of a corpse for burial, and the selection of a prayer leader for the community.

A second interest of the *fiqh* rules usually bears on what we might call horizontal relationships (in contrast to the vertical relationship between the believer and God): marriage, divorce, freeing slaves, oaths, criminal penalties, relations with nonbelievers, partnerships, contracts, the slaughter of animals, use of the land, fines, wills, sports, prohibited drinks, and much more. Some of these topics traditionally got more attention and development than others, in part because the religious courts were more able to detail and enforce laws concerning them: inheritance law, family law, and law concerning pious endowments for good works (schools, hospitals, etc.), for example.

On the whole, Islamic law has most concentrated on what sometimes is called "personal law": marriage, divorce, and inheritance. These areas continued to receive great attention and stay under the influence of religious lawyers even in the twentieth century, somewhat in contrast to the secularization of such other areas as taxation, criminal law, and constitutional law. Interestingly, however, with the rise of fundamentalist influences in many Muslim countries during the 1970s and 1980s has come a trend to rethink even these latter, secularized legal areas in terms of older traditions that assumed there was no unreligious, secular dimension in a good Muslim's life.

The early theological discussions dealt with the nature of faith. Idolatry and unbelief were the major evils for the Qur'an, so it was important to understand them well. The types of sins were also an important early theological focus. Later debates focused on the unity of God (in the context of discussing the divine attributes) and on the relation of the divine sovereignty to human freedom. While there was a full spectrum of opinions, in Sunni quarters the more moderate positions tended to win favor. Before long, however, Islam effectively curtailed speculation, favoring instead careful efforts to ascertain what legal precedents any *practical* problem had in the Qur'an, the *Hadith* of the Prophet, community consensus, or analogous situations. (These were the four main sources of religious authority).

To be sure, Muslims did not view religious law or theology as a human creation. Rather, it was divine guidance, the expression of God's own will. The goal of the teachers was to offer comprehensive guidance for all of life—much as the rabbis' goal was to apply the Torah to all of life. The lawyers classified theology among the obligations one owed to God, for theology was the science of right belief, and right belief was primary among the things that human beings owed to God. As they refined their science, the teachers also distinguished all human actions according to five headings: obligatory, recommended, permitted, disapproved, and forbidden. Thus, one had to confess the unity of God and the Prophethood of Muhammad, one was counseled to avoid divorce, and one was forbidden to eat pork. Since Muslim society was a theocracy, *Sharia* was the code of the land. While that made for a certain unity and order, it also prepared the way for the Sufi emphasis on personal devotion as a counterweight to legalism.

The Period of Division

A minor source of division within the Muslim community was the differences in law developed by the various schools. The Hanafite school came to dominate Muslim countries north and east of the Arabian Peninsula. Within Arabia itself the dominant school was founded by ibn-Hanbal. Northeast Africa was under Shafite and Hanafite lawyers, while Malikite opinions were the most prestigious in northwestern Africa. In Persia the Shia sect had its own law. On the whole, that distribution still holds today.

Given the four recognized legal codes of Sunni, the large Shia minority, and the division of the Islamic Empire into eastern and western parts centered at Baghdad and Cordoba, respectively, one can see that religious and political unity was less than perfect. Still, Muslims holding to the Five Pillars and the Qur'an had much more in common with one another than they had with any non-Muslim peoples. Thus, legal or creedal differences did not divide Muslim religion severely. In contrast, different devotional styles, such as *Sufism,* caused considerable hubbub.

Sufism. Opinions about the merits of Sufism differ. Fazlur Rahman, commenting especially on the work of al-Ghazali (1058–1111), speaks of the "fresh vitality" that al-Ghazali's devotionalism infused into the Muslim community.[39] Isma'il al Faruqi, on the contrary, cites Sufism as the first step in Islam's decline from its golden civilization.[40] It is true that al-Ghazali was not a typical Sufi (he had great learning as well as great piety), and that al Faruqi's sympathies lie with the reforming Wahabis (see below), for whom Sufism was an abomination. Still, a survey of studies shows quite mixed reactions to Sufism. Most commentators agree that its initial centuries (the ninth through thirteenth) were more creative and positive than its later ones.

At the outset, Sufism (the name likely comes from the Arabic word for wool, which Sufis wore as a gesture of simplicity)[41] stood for reform and personal piety. In a time when political and military success tempted Islam to worldliness, and the rise of the law brought the dangers of legalism, the Sufis looked to the model of Muhammad at prayer, communing with God. For them the heart of Islam was personal submission to God, personal guidance along the straight path. In later centuries, through its brotherhoods and saints, Sufism set a great deal of the emotional, antiintellectual, and antiprogressive tone of an Islam that had lost its status as a world power.

Several cultural streams ran together to form the Sufi movement. First was the ascetic current from traditional desert life, which was basic and simple—a daily call for endurance. Out of a keen sense of the religious values in such a harsh life, Abu Dharr al-Ghifari, a companion of the Prophet, chastised the early leaders who wanted to lead a sumptuous court life after their conquests. Second, many of the Sufi ecstatics, as we mentioned, drew on the Arab love of poetry. Their lyric depictions of the love of God, coupled with the Qur'an's eloquence, drew sensitive people to the side of a living, personal faith that might realize the beauties of Islam.

Third, the more speculative Sufis drew on gnostic ideas that floated in from Egypt and the Fertile Crescent. By the ninth century, Sufi contemplatives (especially the Persian Illuminationists) were utilizing those ideas to analyze the relations between divinity and the world. (The Sufis seem to have found most attractive the emanational ideas—the theories of how the world flowed out of the divine essence—rather than the dualistic theories of good and evil.) This kind of understanding, along with the alchemical interests noted previously, was the beginning of the esoteric and sometimes magical lore for which the orthodox theologians and lawyers held the Sufis suspect. Last, Indian (especially Buddhist) thought apparently influenced the eastern portions of the Muslim realm, and it perhaps was a source of the tendencies toward self-annihilation (loss of personal identity in God) that became important in Sufi mystical doctrine.

Taken at their own word, the Sufis desired to be faithful followers of Muhammad and the Qur'an. The more honored among them never intended any schismatic or heretical movements. Rather, they resembled spiritual writers of other traditions, such as the Christian Thomas à Kempis, in that they wanted to "feel compunction rather than know its definition." The most famous statement of this desire occurs in al-Ghazali's description of his withdrawal from his prestigious teaching post in Baghdad to settle the conflicts in his soul: "I was continuously tossed about between the attractions of worldly desire and the impulses towards eternal life."[42] Upon retiring into solitude to purify his soul, he found the peace he had sought. From being a learned philosopher, theologian, and lawyer, he became a follower of the mystical way, which the Sufis represented: "I learnt with certainty that it is above all the mystics who walk on the road of God; their life is the best life, their method the soundest method, their character the purest character; indeed, were the intellect of the intellectuals and the learning of the learned and the scholarship of the scholars, who are versed in the profundities of revealed truth, brought together in the attempt to improve the life and character of the mystics, they would find no way of doing so."[43]

In Idries Shah's collection of Sufi sayings,[44] one catches overtones of the pedagogical genius that the spiritual masters developed. Much like the Jewish Hasidim, they fashioned stories to carry their messages about the paradoxes of the spiritual life, the need for being focused and wholehearted, the way that God comes in the midst of everyday life. In these stories, the poor man turns out to be rich; the fool turns out to be truly wise. Like their counterparts in other traditions, the Sufis left no doubt that riches and prestige tend to be obstacles to spirituality. As well, they questioned the rational, "right-handed" portions of the personality, arguing that the more intuitive, "left-handed" portions must have their due if one is to achieve balance and fullness.

Predictably, this challenge to the expectations of society, of the religious authorities, and of the literally minded won the Sufis no love. Perhaps to intensify their opposition, some Sufis became even more provocative, challenging the establishment and suggesting that its religion was little more than dead convention. For instance, when Hasan of Basra was asked what Islam was and who were Muslims, he replied, "Islam is in the books and Muslims are in the tomb."[45] This oracular reply could mean that the Qur'an holds the secrets to true submission and that the earth holds the bodies of the great exemplars of the past. However, it could also mean that what people take to be Islam (the official version) is actually a dead letter, something buried and forgotten, because no one lives it anymore. Along similar lines is a story of a dervish who meets the devil. The devil is just sitting patiently, so the dervish asks him why he is not out making mischief. The devil replies, "Since the theoreticians and would-be teachers of the Path have appeared in such numbers, there is nothing left for me to do."[46]

Decline. By the beginning of the fourteenth century, the age of some of the greatest Sufi figures was over; Sufism started to decline, and with it much of Islam's religious vitality. The orders continued to multiply, and many princes and sultans continued to patronize them, but abuse, scandal, and superstition became more and more common. In Arberry's view, "It was inevitable, as soon as legends of miracles became attached to the names of the great mystics, that the credulous masses should applaud imposture more than true devotion; the cult of the saints, against which orthodox Islam ineffectually protested, promoted ignorance and superstition, and confounded charlatanry with lofty speculation. To live scandalously, to act impudently, to speak unintelligibly—this was the easy high road to fame, wealth, and power."[47]

Still, the Sufis played a considerable role in the expansion of Islam, largely by serving as models of piety for the common people and giving them hopes of wonder working. For instance, Sufi folk literature played an important role in the expansion of Indian Islam during the fifteenth through seventeenth centuries,[48] while genuine Sufi spirituality aroused strong devotion in North Africa well into the twentieth century.[49] The organizations carrying Sufi influence were the Sufi orders, or brotherhoods. The first seems to have dated from the twelfth century. Abd al-Qadir, who began his religious career in Baghdad as a student of Hanbalite law, converted to Sufism and became a preacher of the holy life. The many converts and followers that he gathered came to call themselves Qadiris, and historians often regard their association as the first brotherhood. It has been especially influential in India, where it has a presence even today. Al-Qadir was a traditionalist who called for strict adherence to the Qur'an and condemned any antinomian (lawless) tendencies. No doubt this helped his group become acceptable.

A second great order, also influential in India, derived from al-Suhrawardi (1144–1234), a moderate.

Other orders of significant number and influence were the Shadhiliya, who were especially successful in Egypt, North Africa, Arabia, and Syria, and the Turkish order of the Mevleviya, which derived from the renowned Persian poet Rumi.

Typically, at the order's local lodge, a small number of professionals resided to teach and lead worship. Most members have been lay adherents who came for instruction when they could and who supported the lodge by contributing money, manual labor, and so on. Each order tended to have its own distinctive ritual, whose purpose was usually to attain ecstatic experience. The ritual was the group's interpretation of the general virtue of **dhikr** (remembrance) that all Muslims seek. For instance, whirling dances characterized many of the Mevlevi dervish meetings, while Saadeeyeh Sufis developed a ceremony in which the head of the order rode on horseback over prone devotees.

The writings of the contemporary theosophist Gurdjieff have introduced a number of Sufi ideas into recent American consciousness. Overall, however, Islam has been making its greatest strides among Africans who have found that it suits their traditional tribal structure and their nationalistic mood better than Christianity.[50] The divisions and declines that sundered Islam before this modern resurgence were largely due to a combination of Sufi piety and orthodox rigidity, which undermined the fusion of piety and order that any vital religion has to have.

Islam also suffered from a counterattack by the countries that it had conquered. For instance, the European countries who supported the Crusades sharply contracted the empire that Islam had forged in its golden age. Historians date the point of decline differently. Bernard Lewis, however, holds that by the eleventh century Islam was in "manifest decay."[51] In addition to what they suffered at the hands of the Crusaders in the Holy Land and from the Europeans' counterattack in southern Europe, the Arabs found themselves superseded in the East by the Turks, who became Muslims, and by the Mongols, who at first showed no interest in Islam. The latter conquered both Persia and Iraq, causing a breakdown of Muslim power.

The Turkish Mamluks established themselves in Cairo by the mid-thirteenth century, ruling Egypt and Syria until 1517. When Vasco da Gama circumnavigated Africa in 1498, much of the Muslim economic and political power, which derived from Muslim control of the trade with India, quickly faded. The Ottoman Turks replaced the Mamluks in the early sixteenth century and ruled Middle Eastern Islam for almost 400 years.[52] Only in southern Arabia (Yemen) did speakers of Arabic remain largely free of foreign domination.

Late Empire and Modernity

During the period of empire (the Mamluks of Turkey and the Middle East, Persia,[53] and the Mogul dynasty in India[54]), at least three general changes occurred in Arabic-speaking society. The first was the transformation of the Islamic Near East from a commercial economy based on money to a feudal economy based on subsistence farming. The second was the replacement in positions of authority of Arabic-speaking peoples by Turks. The Arab tribes retained their independence in the desert regions, where they held out quite well against Turkish rule. In the cities and cultivated valleys (the plains of Iraq, Syria, and Egypt), however, the Arabs became completely subjected, and the glorious language that had been the pride of Islam became the argot of an enslaved population. Psychologically, the Turks grew accustomed to taking the initiative and commanding, and the Arabs grew accustomed to passivity and subjection. The third change was the transfer of the seat of Islam from Iraq to Egypt. Iraq was too remote from Turkey and the Mediterranean to be the base for the eastern wing of Islam, so Egypt—which was on the other principal trade route and which was the most unified area geographically—became the new center.[55]

As a result of this shift, Turkish and to a lesser degree Persian became the leading languages of Islam. At first many of the subject peoples welcomed the Ottoman takeover from the Mamluks as a return to political order. By the eighteenth century, however, the Ottoman Empire was in decay—corrupt, anarchic, and stagnant. The principal religious form of revolt during this period was Sufism. At first Sufism was mainly an escape for oppressed individuals, but with the organization of more brotherhoods, it became a social movement that was especially powerful among the artisan class. The long centuries of stagnation finally ended, however, with increased contact with the West. From the beginning of the sixteenth century, European expansion brought some of the new learning of the Renaissance and the Reformation. The French in particular had considerable influence in the Middle East, and Napoleon's easy conquest of the Ottoman Turks at the end of the eighteenth century was the final blow to Islamic military glory.

The Wahabis. Also during the time of Napoleon arose an Islamic reform that was designed to check the infection of Sufism.[56] One of the first leaders in this reform was a stern traditionalist named Muhammad ibn Abd al-Wahab, whose followers came to be known as Wahabis. They called for a return to the doctrines and practices of the early generations, of the ancestors whom they venerated.

In law, the Wahabis favored the rigorous interpretations of the Hanbalite school, and they abhorred the veneration of saints, which they considered superstitious. Thus, they inveighed against supposed holy personages, living or dead, and went out of their way to destroy the shrines that had become places of popular piety or pilgrimage. They further objected that the worship of saints presumed that they were "partners" of God and so was idolatrous. The punishment due such idolatry was death. Some of the more rabid Wahabis went so far as to classify the more lenient lawyers and schools as being guilty of idolatry (and so punishable by death). The Wahabis were based in Arabia, whence they waged war on their dissenting neighbors. They went down to military defeat in their 1818 Turco-Egyptian campaign, but their puritanical reform had much ideological success and spread to other parts of the Islamic world.

An immediate effect of the Wahabi movement was great hostility toward the Sufi brotherhoods. In fact, Muslims interested in renovating orthodoxy singled out the Sufis as their great enemies, although they also attacked the Scholasticism of such theological centers as al-Azhar in Cairo. One of the leaders of the nineteenth-century reform was the apostle of Pan-Islam, Jamal al-Din al-Afghani, who proposed the political unification of all Muslim countries under the caliphate of the Ottoman sultans. While Pan-Islam has never been realized, it stimulated the widespread search for an effective Muslim response to modernity. In India and Egypt, conservative groups arose that gravitated toward the Wahabi position. Many of the Sufi organizations lost their strength, and those that survived tended to back away from gnosis and return to a more traditional theology.

Even before this conservative threat, however, the Sufis had reformed on their own, sponsoring a number of missions in Africa, India, and Indonesia. For the most part these were peaceful, but occasionally they involved military ventures. In fact, some groups quite consciously took up the Qur'anic tradition of holy war, including the "Indian Wahabis" and the Mahdists in the Sudan. However, even in decline the Sufi brotherhoods kept dear to Islam the notion of bonding together for mutual support in faith.

The organizations that have grown up in recent times, such as the Association for Muslim Youth and the Muslim Brotherhood, seem in good measure an effort to fill the void created by the demise of the Sufi brotherhoods. The new groups differ by operating primarily in pluralistic cultures, where Muslims live in the midst of non-Muslims, while the Sufi orders drew on the ardor of a homogeneous culture that was secure in its unchallenged faith.

Western Influence. A characteristic of Islamic modernity was the invasion of Western secular ideas. These ideas came on the heels of modern Western takeovers in the Middle East, at first through the administrations of the Europeans who governed the newly acquired territories and then through the educational systems, which were Westernized. The new classes of native professionals—doctors, lawyers, and journalists—frequently trained abroad or in native schools run by Westerners. One political effect of such training was to raise Muslim feelings of nationalism and to provoke cries for Westernized systems of government. The new ideas challenged the *madrasas,* or religious schools, too, for it was not immediately apparent that these new ideas could be taught along with traditional theories of revelation and Qur'anic inspiration.

From the nineteenth century on, the economics, politics, education, social habits, and even religion of Muslims were increasingly affected by the upheaval that resulted from the European Renaissance and Enlightenment. Some countries remained largely insulated from Western notions, but they tended to be backward portions of the old empire with little political impact. As we might expect, the cities bore the brunt of the challenge. In theology the outward Muslim reaction was to close ranks. Still, even in the most fiercely traditionalist schools, modern notions—such as the freedom of human beings to shape their own destinies—softened the old propositions about providence and predestination.

Indeed, when it was convenient, theologians incorporated modern science into their argumentation. For instance, some Muslim theologians justified the doctrine that God creates the world continuously by citing atomic theory. The less theologically inclined among the modern educated classes contented themselves by asserting that Islam, as submission to the Master of Truth, in principle cannot conflict with modern science or with any empirically verified truths.

Controversy over societal matters has been more heated than that over theology because the guidance provided by the traditional legal schools diverged more sharply from Western mores than Muslim theology diverged from Western theology. Slowly Islamic countries have developed civil codes and separated civil courts from religious courts. In the mid-nineteenth century, the Turkish Republic breached the wall of tradition when it abolished the authority of the *Sharia* in civil matters. In other countries the *Sharia* has remained the outer form, but new legislative codes direct the interpretations. The tactic has been to invoke the Qur'an, the *hadith,* and the traditions of the schools but to leave the legislators and judges free to choose the authority that is most appropriate. Specifically, the legal reforms have applied primarily to marriage contracts (protecting girls against child marriage), divorce proceedings, and polygamy—central factors in the traditional family structure.

What new theology will emerge from the dynamics of these changes remains to be seen. H. A. R. Gibb has pointed out that by granting jurists freedom to interpret the traditional opinions and by departing from the old norm that there had to be a uniformity of interpretation throughout the Islamic community, the reformers have introduced a "Protestant principle" into the previously "Catholic" social consciousness.[57] Indeed, through its fairly rigid law, Islam had reified (made objective) its community more thoroughly than most other religions had.[58] Whether the demise of the former practice will result in a Protestant splintering of Islam is difficult to predict. On the one hand, it is hard to recall the critical or independent spirit once it has broken loose. On the other hand, there has arisen a growing Islamic fundamentalism similar to the fundamentalism by which some Protestant Christians are battling the spirit of Enlightenment criticism.

Relatedly, even some liberal Muslim reformers attracted to Marxist thought seem to bypass the Marxist call for a new order and to desire, rather nostalgically, the old social solidarity. On the other hand, traditionalists such as the Saudis find Marxism completely repulsive because of its atheism. Whether Saudi Arabia can progress satisfactorily by means of a capitalistic economy and technology, though, is far from certain. Critical-mindedness in the laboratory and simple faith in religion are not impossible, but few people in any faith manage them without a kind of schizophrenia.

Publications of the American Academic Association for Peace in the Middle East suggest that the history of such countries ("confrontation states") as Syria and Jordan explains much of the turmoil in the Middle East.[59] These countries have been trying to adapt their economics, their politics, and their religion to the modern world. On the one hand, their models for this transition have been the Western nations, who produced modernity. On the other hand, Western nationalism has taught them to insist on their right to a nationalistic expression of their ethnicity, their history, and their religious cohesiveness. The catalysts for this process have included the creation of contemporary Israel and Muslim oil resources.

In considering recent Muslim fundamentalism, one must realize that Islamic secularism never got so advanced as Western secularism. True, fundamentalism attracts a noteworthy number of Christians and Jews, but Christianity and Judaism more clearly differentiate the civic realm, the realm shared with citizens of other religious convictions (or of none), than Islamic culture has done. Conversely, Islam has kept the sacred and the secular more tightly conjoined than Christianity or Judaism has, professing that there is no secular realm—that everything lives by the will and touch of Allah, who is as near as the pulse at one's throat.

Case Study: Lessons from Recent Iran.   The rest of the Islamic world followed the Iranian upheavals of 1979 with great interest, to say the least, and many interesting commentaries on the meaning of Islam for the late twentieth century arose because of the Iranian events. One such commentary appeared in Cairo, at the instigation of the Islamic Student Association of Cairo University. Studying the reflections of this commentary may open a window on the likely future of Islam's blend of religion and politics.

The commentary begins with a quotation from the Qur'an (3:26) to the effect that God, the possessor of all sovereignty, gives earthly sovereignty to whomever he wishes. Just as freely, God takes earthly sovereignty away. Only God is powerful over all things. If God wishes to raise someone up, he does. If God wishes to debase someone, he does.

From this theological foundation the commentary moves to the Khomeini revolution in Iran, which was then riveting the whole world. This revolution, says the article, the violence and restraint of which

surpassed the calculations and wildest imaginings of most observers, deserves deep study. Muslims must ponder such marvelous happenings, if they are ever to fulfill their Qur'anic destiny (see 3:110) and "assume the reins of world leadership of mankind once again and place the world under the protection of the esteemed Islamic civilization."[60]

Beginning such study, the first lesson the commentary would underscore is the influence of the creed on the Islamic people. The Iranian people, who had appeared completely submissive to death and tyranny, exploded like a volcano, tossing their fears aside. Their spiritual conquest of the steely forces that opposed them recalls the heroes of earliest Muslim times, and it should remind everyone that faith might muster similar power in many situations. Islam is the religion with the power to redress the injustices of all peoples everywhere.

Second, the Iranian revolution reminds us that Islam is a comprehensive religion, legislating for both this world and the next. It provides alike for religion and state affairs, education and morals, worship and holy war. In fact, the Iranian revolution clarifies the errors in modern secularism, which would separate religion from state affairs. Clearly, it shows that secularism is the recourse of idolaters, who want to keep religion out of politics, so that they can plunder the wealth of the common people. The only adequate laws and constitutions are those that derive from the *Sharia* of Islam. When laws and constitutions are man-made, their status is no greater than the idols of the pre-Muslim Arabs. If the pre-Muslim Arabs got hungry, they would eat the Goddess of Pastry. In contrast, the *Sharia* of Islam, which comes from God, is permanent, just, wise, and perfect.

Third, Iranian affairs show that the true leaders of the Muslim people are the sincere, learned men of religion. These men (the *ulama*) have been the guiding lights of all the best modern Muslim liberation movements. The touchstone is justice. For forty years the tyrant shah betrayed his community and brought down on it the most repulsive forms of injustice. God takes his time with the wrongdoer, but when he takes him there is no escaping.

Fourth, shrewd observers will note how the false Iranian leaders had the courage of lions when dealing with their own people but were puppets in the hands of the rulers of the East and the West. Yet the West quickly disowned the shah, abandoning him like a worn-out shoe. To the lesson implied in this one should add the patent effort of Islam's enemies to exploit the sectarian differences between Shiites and Sunnis and tear the Muslim community apart. As well, the enemies of Islam tried to use the Iranian revolution to instigate local governments to strike out at Islamic movements.

Therefore, rulers in other Islamic locales must realize that their true strength lies in the strength of their people, and that the true strength of their people lies in Islam. Wise leaders are those that place their allegiance in God, his apostle Muhammad, and Muslim believers. As the Qur'an (5:49) teaches, only those who rule by what God has revealed can expect to be strengthened. Thus, to those who would instigate strife against Islamic movements, one should reply: God suffices for us. The Qur'an has said the last word in these matters: "God promised those of you who believe and perform good works that he would make you viceroys on earth as he did with those before and will make it possible for you to follow the religion which pleases you and will change your fear into safety. You will worship me, associating nothing else with me" (24:55).

Several concerns of the Cairo Students' Association merit special comment, because they have been present in the recent resurgence of a passionate Islam in other countries, such as Iran itself and Pakistan. First, some students obviously long for a return to traditional Muslim law. Chafing under what they think is their recent rulers' secularism, the students believe that returning to the principles of the Qur'an and traditional Muslim law will speedily redress all current wrongs. In its early stages, the revolution in Iran seemed a great vindication of this viewpoint. Even fervent Muslims were amazed that faith was able to bring down so powerful an enemy as the shah. Today, at a greater distance from the events of 1979, and with more experience of what the Ayatollah Khomeini understood the revolution to imply, even zealous students might take pause. The bloody chaos that afflicted the Muslim ranks in Iran after the revolution argues that the *Sharia* is open to markedly diverse and violent interpretations. The war between Iran and Iraq was a festering sore in the Muslim community.

Second, the chauvinism latent in the Islamic students' position paper is not likely to prove the most effective translation of the *Sharia* for the decades ahead. A great deal of the world does not want to be placed under the protection of Islamic civilization, even when one grants Islamic civilization its great due. Pluralism is a more powerful force than the students seem to realize, and any peaceful assumption of the reins of world leadership will have to handle pluralism quite sympathetically. Any forceful assumption of the reins of world leadership is almost unthinkable, both because Islam is hardly in the position to challenge the West or the East militarily and because military means to power inevitably raise the specter of nuclear war. No nations would profit from a contemporary translation of Islamic "holy war" that led to nuclear confrontations.

Third, students of religion might most profitably focus on the somewhat tacit pleas that run through the Egyptian students' commentary. For example, there is the tacit plea that the rest of the world take seriously and duly honor a proud religious tradition. Islam came on hard times when the West took charge of modernity. Its pride was wounded, and one can trace much of its strong rhetoric, even its hyperbole, to this wounded pride. Now that Islam is on the march again, more than competitive with the Western religions in Africa and other parts of the Third World, it is trying to recoup some of its emotional losses.

Another tacit plea is for an integral culture, in which religion and daily affairs might fit like hand and glove. Not only is this integration a part of Islam's traditional ideal, as we have seen, it is also a common human desire. Indeed, even the Western cultures play strains of this song. Christian and Jewish fundamentalists, for example, express a passionate desire to bring all of life under the domain of their God. Despite the cultural or religious imperialism to which this desire can lead, it is worth studying sympathetically. The rise of secular cultures in many nations of the world *has* made it more difficult to find transcendent meaning. There *are* many contemporary citizens, East and West, who feel fragmented or schizophrenic.

Probably the most viable solution to this problem is a synthesis at a higher level that avoids a fundamentalist reduction to blind faith, but such a synthesis is very demanding. One of the unfortunate features of our late twentieth-century times is the speed that evolution has reached. Whereas in the past people facing demands analogous to today's demand for a resolution of the conflict between a pluralistic secularism and a unified religious faith might have had thousands of years at their disposal, today we cannot be sure we have more than a generation. This should incline us to get on with the task, but also to comfort ourselves with a proper estimate of the task's magnitude. Nothing less than a truly ecumenic, universal humanity will solve our worldwide religiopolitical problems, and achieving a truly ecumenic, universal humanity is almost more than we can imagine.

Still another plea running through the students' manifesto is for simple justice. This plea is not at all tacit; it is quite express and eloquent. Iranians had been suffering injustice. Enough of them had been tortured and abused by the shah to make his regime hated. The popular support for the Khomeini revolution was only explainable on the basis of this hatred. Had the shah's innovations, his programs for modernization and economic development, not been perceived as brutally unjust, as well as destructive of the people's cherished religious heritage, the shah probably would not have become the Iranian Satan. Even when one allows for a considerable emotional excess in the rhetoric of the shah's opponents, and their considerable manipulation by religious leaders quite ambitious for power, the political facts seem clear. The clarion call of the religious revolutionaries was for a restoration of justice. A major attraction in the prospect of restoring a Qur'anic government was the possibility of achieving a much greater justice.

As statements by the Ayatollah Khomeini himself have suggested, the revolutionaries' ideal was a religious government free of the human caprice that so easily leads to injustice: "The venerable prophet, may God's peace and prayers be upon him, was appointed ruler on earth by God so that he may rule justly and not follow whims." However, things become ominous when Khomeini goes on to say, "The *Shari'a* and reason require us not to let governments have a free hand. The proof of this is evident. The persistence of these governments in their transgressions means obstructing the system and laws of Islam whereas there are numerous provisions that describe every non-Islamic system as a form of idolatry or a ruler or an authority in such a system as a false god."[61] For many Western observers, Khomeini's authoritarianism soon became precisely a demand for idolatrous obedience, precisely the arbitrary rule of a false god.

WORLDVIEW

Nature

The key to the Muslim notion of nature is Islam's concept of creation. As much as the biblical religion on

which it built, Islam sees God as the maker of all that is. Several Qur'anic passages establish this doctrine. For instance, Sura 10 describes the Lord as "God, who created the heavens and the earth in six days, then sat Himself upon the Throne directing the affair." This is the biblical imagery of creation: Genesis spreading God's work over six days. Moreover, the Qur'an finds significance in this creation in that through creation God has given God-fearing people signs of his dominion. By making the sun a radiance and the moon a light, by giving them "stations" so that astronomers can calculate time, and by alternating night and day, God has set over humankind a heaven full of signs. Just as the modern German philosopher Immanuel Kant spoke of the starry heavens above as a wonder that can incite a true grasp of the human condition, so Muhammad unself-consciously expressed the sovereignty of his God by referring to the divine guidance of the stars, the heavenly circuits by which the Creator periodizes our time.

Sura 13 repeats this theme, adding earthly phenomena: It is he who stretched out the earth, set firm mountains and rivers, and placed two kinds of every fruit. The abundance of nature testifies to the abundance of nature's source and ought to remind human beings of God's power and provision. Thus, the Creator is not only strong but also admirable in his design of the world and praiseworthy in his concern for human welfare as evidenced by his bounty. In this way the best features of nature become analogies for God in the Qur'an. The "Light-Verse" of Sura 24 gives one of the most famous of these analogies: God is the light of the heavens and the earth. His light is as a niche where there is a lamp. The lamp is in a glass, the glass is like a glittering star. The lamp is kindled from a Blessed Tree, an olive neither of the East nor of the West, whose oil would shine even if no fire touched it. Light upon light, God guides to the light whom he will.

Religiously, then, nature is replete with signs in which wise people discern God's creative presence. However, nature is not itself a divinity or a form of God's presence. Unlike East Asian thought, Islamic thought does not mix divinity with the cosmos. Islam separated from the ancient cosmological myth, in that God transcends the world. One may say that the biblical prophets' critique of nature gods combined with Muhammad's negative reaction to the polytheism of his times to correlate transcendence and anti-idolatry. So the signs that nature gives to the God-fearing are not themselves sacraments. They point beyond themselves; the divinity does not come in them. Water, oil, bread, wine—they are not miniature incarnations of divinity. The God of Islam has no incarnation, no personal or material forms by which he becomes present.

Isma'il al Faruqi tries to establish that Islam is rationalistic, meaning that Islam's highest religious certainty *(iman)* is not merely an act of believing, an "act of faith," but "a state in which religious knowledge produces an intuition of its certainty as a result of the consideration and weighing of all possible alternatives."[62] Then, in treating what he considers Islam's second essential quality (that it is "transcendentalist"), al Faruqi argues that Islam rejects all forms of immanentism for the divine. In other words, Creator is Creator, creature is creature, and never the twain shall meet. This transcendentalism provides the context for al Faruqi's discussion of the Muslim view of nature, the lead sentence of which is "Nature is not transcendent and constitutes an autonomous realm."[63] From this it follows that nature contains no divinity in its materials or its forces. It is totally real, wholly created. It is actual and objective, and "it contains no mystery."[64]

Thus, for al Faruqi, Islamic nature is utterly profane, in no way sacred (since nothing is sacred without mystery). That interpretation seems considerably more rationalistic than what most Muslims themselves have thought, for, as we suggested above, most Muslims have not followed Western Enlightenment by separating the sacred from the secular. When al Faruqi says that nature must be unmysterious to be autonomous, regular, and knowable, we are tempted to say that he protests overmuch. The mechanistic scientist of the nineteenth century could write such a description of nature, but few contemporary scientists and few traditional Muslims would do so.

Some Muslim thinkers might have lost contact with nature's mystery, but they were not in the majority, for that would have made Islam a comparative anomaly. For example, Jews and Christians, despite sharing with Islam the notion of a transcendent Creator, used psalms that glorified God's provision of food in due season. With Job, they found that the world and its train of strange animals were marvelous indeed. The Hasidim looked to the world for divine sparks, and the Christian poets drew on the sacraments and on the model of saints such as Francis of Assisi to consider the world pregnant with God's power. Both of Islam's sister faiths did develop veneration of nature less than the Eastern religions did, and both did fear the forces of fertility, the polytheism, that afflicted the lands of

their origin. But in the actual exercise of their faiths, nature was alive with the mystery of God and was neither profane nor autonomous.

Still, al Faruqi is right in implying that nature never dominated Islam or Arab culture. For instance, the earliest poetry deals more with war and nomadic life than with father sky and mother earth. Pre-Muslim Arabia worshiped natural and agricultural forces, but Qur'anic monotheism attacked them harshly. In religious art, as we have seen, the prohibition on images was not absolute, although religious art tended to avoid representations of natural scenes, let alone representations of God.

Still, the prime material for worship, the Qur'an itself, contained natural figures and not merely in the context of creation. Thus, it embellished its theme of judgment and recompense with naturalistic imagery. For instance, if one denied God's bounties—did not live the truth that God ever labors creatively for human benefit—then "against you shall be loosed a flame of fire, and molten brass" (55:35). Judgment is a day when "heaven is split asunder and turns crimson like red leather" (55:37), when sinners will go to Gehenna and hot boiling water. However, those who fear God will enter Paradise. The main image for Paradise is the Garden. There the virtuous will find two fountains running with water, fruits of all kinds, virgin maidens lovely as rubies and coral. Paradise has green pastures, gushing water, fruits, palm trees, pomegranates, and cool pavilions (55:50–70).

Thus, the Qur'an considered nature a factor in the mysteries of judgment, punishment, and reward as the images of Fire and Garden clearly show. Moreover, mythological elaboration of these themes in popular religion was quite unrestrained. "Hell, sometimes imagined as a terrible monster, is described as filled with fire and stinking water, and awful trees with poisonous fruits grow there."[65] In the popular conception, angels presided over hell, meting out punishments, while heaven became a place for enjoying fruit, wine, and the charming black-eyed virgins.

Like other religions, Islam maintained that justice would be served in the afterlife through reward for the pious faithful and punishment for the unbelievers. Sex was high on the list of pleasures, so Paradise was rich with sex. Islam depicted sex from the male point of view, with details of "maidens restraining their glances, untouched before them by any man or jinn" (55:55). As we shall see below, Islam did not declare the goodness of sex so loudly and clearly for women. In fact, there has often been ambiguity, puritanism, and a double standard concerning sex in Muslim society. Still, the basic fact that Islam does not paint heaven as an ethereal, wholly spiritual realm shows that it blesses human nature.

In summary, nature for Islam is one locus of God's signs to humanity. Nature is less prominent than in East Asian or ancient religion. Rather, Islam configures itself socially and theologically, focusing on the community and the sovereign Lord.

Muslim spirituality manifests something of this emphasis, in that one of its interests is to keep nature under control. By fasting, a Muslim tames the nature closest to the self. By confessing that there is no God but God, a Muslim clears the world of competitors to the Creator and Judge. That means that many devout Muslims' ideal is a bare vista. The Sufis manifested this ideal most fully, for many of them saw life as a pilgrimage to union with a God much more valuable than anything worldly. In less deliberate but still consoling ways, the poor merchant or soldier learned from misfortune how precarious a worldly vista was. Although the physical world was definitely real and on occasion quite good, the human being's role was to observe it closely enough so that it served as a guidepost to heaven. A Muslim can be comfortable in the natural world, then, but only as a visitor. Life in the natural world soon passes, and Judgment depends on higher things, such as one's faith, one's prayer, and one's generosity in giving alms. The tradition does not teach people that the Judge will ask them how they treated the environment or whether they tore the bosom of mother earth. Those issues are far less important than whether they remembered God and his Prophet.

Society

The Muslim social ideal has never distinguished between secular and sacred aspects of community life. Thus Islamic countries have been ambivalent about modernity, which usually sought to develop secular (nonreligious) codes of law and other cultural entities. Estimates of the social innovations that Islam introduced into prior Arab society and the degree of social perfection that it achieved vary considerably.

The proponent of Islam, Isma'il al Faruqi, begins with the thesis that Muslim society existed so that human beings might realize that "divine pattern." Elemental in that pattern was the family. Marriage was a civil contract, not a sacrament, and a man could marry more than one wife so long as he provided justice, equity, and loving care. Private property and the pursuit of wealth were inviolate rights, but wealth brought the obligation to care for the deprived. Concerning the right to life: "The life of one's fellowman is inviolate, except by due process of law. Nothing may henceforth be decided by force or violence. Such recourse is legitimate only in self-defense and in the safe-guarding of the security of missionaries. For the Muslim is duty-bound to bring his faith to the knowledge of mankind with sound preaching and wise counsel, to convey with warning and command of his Lord."[66]

The Muslim political unit has been the *Ummah,* which is as comprehensive a notion as the broadest notions of church or synagogue. Tradition says that the Qur'an teaches that the Prophet and his successors bore a theocratic power. That is, they had authority in both the religious and the secular spheres, because Islam does not much distinguish the two. Due to the concept of the *Ummah,* Muslims had to fight for brethren in other places who suffered tyranny (Qur'an 4:75). For Muslim leaders, the consensus of the community was an important goal, for they wanted a single divine rope to bind the *Ummah* together. Strong faith was to create an equality among all believers, and God would reward every man and woman who was faithful through difficulties and trials. Muslims were to bring their disputes to the Prophet or his successors, and they all had a common duty to worship God, to obey God's commands, and to do good and avoid evil.

Members were to be to one another as brothers and mutual guardians (9:71), respecting life and enjoying its good things. Woman came from the soul of man (4:1). Both men and women had the right to what they had earned, and both could enter Paradise, although "men have priority over women, by virtue of what God has endowed to them and by what they spend on women of their wealth" (4:34). Men were to provide their women tenderness and affluence if they could. Marriage was the usual state, and Islam did not support celibacy. Almsgiving was a primary obligation, and one was to go beyond justice to charity and forgiveness. From the call that God gave the Prophet, ideally all human beings would come to reason and felicity. Since God clearly did not compel non-Muslims to believe, Muslims themselves had no right to force others to believe (10:99, 108). However, the Qur'an regards balefully non-Muslims who contract with Islam and renege: "Lesser than the beasts in the eye of God are the unbelievers for they have cove-

nanted with you and violated their covenant shame-
lessly in every case. If you lay hold of them in war,
make of them a lesson to the others" (8:55).

The covenant of Medina that Muhammad composed gave Jews explicit rights: "To the Jews who follow us belong assistance and equal treatment from us
without either injustice or discrimination."[67] The
basic status of non-Muslims within the state that Muhammad envisioned was what might be called "col-
leagueship"—peaceful cooperation. The democratic
principles applying to Muslim citizenship were individual responsibility, equality, the leaders' responsibility to run the government, and the mutual security of
all citizens. In its law the state was to regard itself as
a replica of the cosmic state that God runs by strict
and unalterable laws. In effect, this meant buttressing
Islamic convictions with a sure faith in divine justice
on Judgment Day. The imam, or leader, led the community in upholding the law. This was the basis for his
quasi-contractual relationship with the *Ummah*.

The Islamic state made a threefold division of humanity: Muslims, covenanters, and enemies. The Muslim peoples who constituted the *Dar al-Islam* (House
of Islam) could not legitimately resort to war against
one another. Covenanters were non-Muslims who had
made compacts of peace, and their rights and duties
were the same as those of Muslims. Al Faruqi does not
specify the fate of enemies, although he notes the
Qur'anic teaching that Muslims are to preach to them
but not force them to convert. Presumably, holy war
only resulted when enemies rejected both conversion
and covenant. If an enemy responded with hostility,
Muslim security necessitated war. What happened
when the enemy simply wanted to be left alone or
considered a Muslim takeover of its area unacceptable
is not clear. However, clearly it was not blameworthy
for Islam "to combat with the sword the sword which
stands between it and man, preventing Islam from
conveying its call and man from listening to or receiving it."[68]

Ethics.   Annemarie Schimmel has sketched Muslim
ethics, which presumably directed Muslim actions.[69]
The guiding principle was to serve God as though you
saw him in front of you. In other words, belief in God,
Judgment, and the necessity of right deeds were the
bases of Islamic ethics. Religious bonds rather than
blood bonds, pure faith rather than idolatry, and sexual restraint rather than indecency—these were notable advances made by the Qur'an over Arab paganism.
In addition to the exhortations to justice and charity

found in the Meccan suras and the detailed legislation
of the Medinan suras, those who survived Muhammad
looked back on the Prophet's own life as the key to how
a Muslim ought to live.

The early disputes about the fate of a sinner and
the place of good works, which divided the theological
and legal schools, suggest that human beings were
considered free and responsible. As we noted, the
law distinguishes five kinds of action, from the
commanded to the forbidden. The Qur'an deals with
adultery, murder, and theft, prescribing stern
punishments for them. Women had the right to refuse
a proposed marriage, but men had greater rights than
women in divorce. The wife had to obey her husband,
who could punish her, and she always had to be at his
disposal. "If a husband kills his wife and her lover *in
flagrante delicto* [in the act of adultery itself] he is not
punishable. Sodomy is likewise forbidden (though
often practiced in a society that excluded women
largely from daily life. The object of Persian and Turkish love poetry is generally masculine)."[70]

The Qur'an takes slavery for granted, but it commends humane treatment and commends freeing
slaves. Only non-Muslim prisoners of war could legally
become slaves. Discrimination because of color and
race was unlawful, though some racial prejudice mars
Islamic history. When the law reached its final stage
of development around 1000, its detailed specifications
tended to become mechanical. The mystics therefore
tried to make ethics spring from a deeper relationship
with God. The first virtue they taught was *wara*—
abstention from everything unlawful or dubious. In
other words, one was not to nitpick but to act from the
heart and turn away from anything that might dis-
please God. Masters such as al-Ghazali developed a
shrewd psychology of virtue and vice, which they de-
ployed to bring about the highest perfection. That perfection was living every moment in the presence of
God. Finally, the general effect of Muslim ethics was
to heighten awareness of one's distance from the divine purity and so lead one to beg Allah's mercy and
forgiveness.

Women's Status.   The status of women in Islam says
a great deal about Muslim society.[71] In the Qur'an
there is some basis for sexual equality: Reward and
punishment in the afterlife depend on deeds, not gen-
der; marriage and conjugal life are precious; women
have dowry rights in some divorces, inheritance
rights, rights to remarry, and rights to protection in
time of pregnancy and nursing. However, women's

rights are not equal to those that the Qur'an gives males in either divorce or inheritance. Moreover, the Qur'an does not even consider the possibility that women might assume leadership roles in the community, receive an education equal to that of males, teach law or theology, or engage in polygamy (as males could).

Furthermore, the misogyny latent in most patriarchal religions had dark effects in Muslim society. As late as 1970, an Arab sheik offered the opinion that "educated or not a woman is a woman and the Prophet—God's prayers and peace on him—had said that women are lacking in mind and religion."[72] The tradition placed more women in the Fire than in the Garden, and the prime determinant of their destiny was their treatment of their husbands. In legend Muhammad virtually despised female nature as stupid and irreligious. Its specific defects were menstruation, which interfered with prayer and fasting, and unreliability, which made a woman's witness worth only half a man's in court. Obedience to her husband was the woman's first duty; failure to obey can still get her killed today.[73]

The Muslim woman regularly was considered erotic and empty-headed. Thus she was subject to purdah (seclusion and veiling), polygyny, concubinage, and the harem. Women were not to be taught to read and write ("a great calamity"), and they were morally "bent" because they came from Adam's bent rib. Thus, in many men's eyes, they had a dismal existence: "It were best for a girl not to come into existence, but being born she had better be married or buried."[74] Recent Muslims, especially Africans, have defended clitoridectomy and kindred operations, frequently with the following sort of rationale: "Circumcision of women releases them from their bondage to sex, and enables them to fulfill their real destiny as mother."[75] As she has done in the cases of Indian suttee, Chinese foot binding, and Christian witch burning, Mary Daly has vividly described African genital mutilation, writing more vividly than most scholars find comfortable.[76]

Another revealing view of women in Islamic society comes from the imagery of the Garden.[77] For many men, the best part of the heavenly Garden was the *hur*: dark-eyed, buxom virgins. In addition to his earthly wife, each male in heaven could expect to have seventy *hur*. They would never be sick, menstruating, pregnant (unless he wished), bad-tempered, or jealous. He would be able to deflower a thousand each month and find them all intact when he returned to them. In

descriptions of the Judgment scene, one sees the reverse of this fantasy: Women are in charge of men, which is a sure sign of disorder.

In fairness, Islam improved the lot of Arab women considerably, and certain parts of the community allowed women a function in the *Hadith*,[78] in scholarship, and in saintliness.[79] Some Muslim cultural areas had traditions more benign toward women than Arab culture was, and many modern Muslims deplore the injustices that women have suffered in the past. As well, they interpret Qur'anic religion in a way that gives women great dignity, and they bitterly oppose the drive of fundamentalists to return to such traditions as marrying girls off when they reach thirteen.

The recent resurgence of Muslim traditionalism in both Sunni and Shiite centers of learning (Cairo, Tehran) has brought more restrictions into many women's lives.

Variety.   The different Islamic cultures have all been bonded by the Qur'an despite their geographic, linguistic, ethnic, and even theological differences. The principal theological division, as we noted, has been between the Shiites and the Sunnis. However, as W. Montgomery Watt has shown, the formative period of Islamic thought saw a variety of controversies and then "heterodoxies."[80]

In India, as noted, Islamic elements fused with Hindu elements to create Sikhism, and Islam was also the inspiration behind Baha'i. Baha'i is a universalist religion that stresses the unity of all traditions and the basic oneness of the human race. It arose in nineteenth-century Persia when a Shiite Muslim, Sayyid Ali Muhammad, declared that he was the twelfth imam—the last, messianic leader whom the Shia awaits. Sayyid took the designation *Bab* ("gate"), and his follower Baha Ullah produced writings that became classic works of Baha'i faith. Today Baha'i has about five million adherents. Its world center is on Mount Carmel in Haifa, Israel, where there is a lovely garden and shrine to the Bab (Figure 45).[81]

Case Study: Islamic Rituals.[82]   Yoruba Muslims of West Africa have ritualized their religion for the life cycle, the religious year, and the ordinary week. By studying these rituals, we may glimpse not only how Muslims have expressed their faith over the centuries, but also how Islam has adapted itself to such new geographic areas as West Africa.

The life cycle of Yoruba Muslims begins on the day they become members of the worshiping commu-

Figure 45 *Shrine to the Bab, Haifa. Photo by J. T. Carmody.*

nity. This may be the day when, as adults, they formally convert to Islam, or the eighth day after their birth, when they receive their name. The major action in the adult conversion ceremony is an ablution, to symbolize the pure life the convert is entering upon. The candidates take off their clothes and don loin cloths. The presiding cleric washes each one's right hand three times, the left hand three times, the right leg three times, and the left leg three times. Then three times he washes the elbows, blows each one's nose, and washes the ears. Concluding, he pours water on the head and chest of each candidate, who, having been washed and become clean, is a true Muslim.

For the naming ceremony of a newborn child, the presiding cleric receives money in a covered dish. The cleric prays for the child, preaches a solemn sermon (often in Arabic), and then gives the child its name. Some West African Muslims also sacrifice a sheep or cut the infant's hair. (The Yoruba practice circumcision, as well as the drawing of tribal marks on the face or body. Apparently Islam did not introduce these cus-

toms but rather gave them a new interpretation.)

The second major stage on the Yoruba Muslim's way is marriage. The presiding cleric must divine that the proposed match is a good one and pray for the marital partners. Before the wedding, the groom has to pay the bride's family several monies and gifts. In modernized West African Muslim rituals, the presiding cleric asks the groom: "Do you take Miss _____ as your wedded wife? Will you love her, honor her, feed her, clothe her, and lodge her in proper lodging?" Then he quotes the Qur'an (4:34), to the effect that one of the signs God has given human beings is creating mates for them, that they may find quiet of mind. Putting love and compassion between these mates, God gives reflective people a sign of his goodness and care. The presiding cleric also asks the bride similar questions, including whether she will love, honor, and obey her husband. He repeats most of the quotation from the Qur'an, and reminds the bride that "the good women are therefore obedient, guarding the unseen as Allah has guarded." The ceremony concludes with prayers to Allah that he bless this wedding. (Most of the West African Muslim community supports the traditional polygyny.)

Funeral rites complete Islam's ritual impact on the Yoruba life cycle. When a person has died the neighbors come together and dig a grave. They then wash the corpse, repeating the ablutions of the conversion ceremony. They dress the corpse in a white cap, loin cloth, and sewn sheet, and then put it into the grave and cover it with earth. The presiding cleric prays for the deceased person, that God may forgive its sins. The dead person's family is expected to pay the cleric handsomely, with food as well as money. Some modernized sects hold a second ceremony, on the eighth day after the burial, with readings from the Qur'an, a sermon, and a eulogy of the deceased.

In addition to these three major ceremonies for the life cycle, Yoruba Islam has an annual cycle of feasting and fasting. The cycle begins with the Muslim New Year, which is a day for hearty eating in most sects and for orgiastic nude bathing and mock battles in a few. The New Year festival recalls Noah, who disembarked from the ark very hungry.

The next festivals in the annual cycle are two celebrations of Muhammad, his birthday and the night of his heavenly journey to Jerusalem and Paradise. The more conservative Yoruba Muslims have made much of the Prophet's birthday, using it as an occasion to display their learning. In their circles children act out scenes from the Prophet's life, and those who teach the Qur'an receive special stipends. The Yoruba do not understand the Prophet's heavenly journey well, so they tend to make little of it.

The month of Ramadan is the great time of fasting, but many of the Yoruba elderly fast during the month of Rajab as well. The last Friday of Ramadan is especially important, because then one may ask forgiveness for one's laxities in worship during the past year. Among the modernizing Yoruba Muslims the Ramadan ceremonies include the prayer, "O Allah! whom our obedience does not benefit and our disobedience does not harm, please accept from us what does not benefit you, and forgive us what does not harm you."

The two greatest feasts in the Yoruba Muslim calendar are the Feast of the Breaking of the Fast and the Feast of the Immolation. Each entails two days of public holidays in Nigeria. For the Feast of the Breaking of the Fast, worshipers dress elaborately and bring expensive prayer rugs. The ceremony includes an almsgiving, to solemnize gratitude for a successful conclusion to Ramadan, a visit to the ruler of the Yoruba, and a visit to the graves of the first two imams (religious leaders) of the community. The Feast of the Immolation reminds the Yoruba that their fellow Muslims in Arabia are performing this sacrifice in Mecca, as part of their pilgrimage. The immolation itself usually is the sacrifice of a small goat. After the communal ceremony many individuals also sacrifice goats or rams at the entrances to their own houses.

The last feast of the annual cycle is the *hajj,* the pilgrimage to Mecca. Since Nigerian independence, the government has supported the pilgrimage, making the *hajj* available to the prosperous farmer, shopkeeper, or local leader. If the individual can make an initial outlay of money, he or she usually will receive supplementary gifts from friends. Once the pilgrims return to their local communities, they enjoy great status, since they have been to the center of the Muslim world. Usually the experience of Islam as a worldwide fellowship greatly broadens the Yoruba pilgrim's horizons. Not all Yoruba Muslims have the opportunity to travel to Mecca, but each year at the time of the *hajj* all turn their imaginations to the holy city and picture what is taking place there.

In the weekly religious cycle of Yoruba Muslims, Friday is the crowning day, but Wednesday and Thursday also have special significance. The last Wednesday of each lunar month is esteemed as a day of special blessings. All are encouraged to increase their prayers, that they may protect themselves from the evil every month contains. The darkness of the moon at the end of the month is probably the spark for this attitude. A prayer of Muslim reformers expresses the last Wednesday mood: "In the name of God, the Merciful, the Compassionate: O God, O Terrible in power, O Terrible in cunning, O Strong One, O Thou Who guidest by Thy might everything in Thy Creation, shield me from the evil of everything Thou has created."

In folk Islam, Wednesday is considered replete with blessings, as is Thursday. Most Yoruba groups have adopted this folk attitude. Thus, most marriages, celebrations of a student's completion of the Qur'an, and groundbreakings occur on Wednesdays or Thursdays. One of the many functions of the Yoruba *alfa* (presiding cleric) is to divine an auspicious date for these celebrations. Conservative Muslims, who tend to be better educated, downplay such divinations, and do not attribute any special significance to particular days of the week.

However, Thursday evening has a special significance, because it is the threshold to Friday, the Muslim

Sabbath. Indeed, most Yoruba Muslims offer prayers for the dead on Thursday night. A popular tradition says that on Thursday evening God allows the dead to come back to the world and see what is going on. This ties into a Yoruba tradition of leaving gifts for the deceased. If a dead person does not have gifts left for him, he loses prestige among his peers.

A certain conflict between traditional, pre-Muslim notions about the dead and Muslim ideas confuses many Yoruba Muslims. The traditional pictures show the dead existing in a shadowy heaven *(orun)*, where they need the care of those they have left behind. The Muslim beliefs in judgment and resurrection do not square with these pictures, so the status of the dead is rather murky. Some Yoruba Muslims translate resurrection so that it becomes a state much like *orun*, but others accept the more orthodox Muslim notion that resurrection is a wondrous event that will occur in the future.

Friday is the center of the weekly cycle, when all good Muslims are supposed to gather at noon in the main mosque for communal worship. In the large towns the mosques are crowded with male worshipers. (A smaller number of women is allowed to worship, segregated from the males, at the back of the mosque.) The service begins with the call to prayer and then has a sermon in the vernacular. Often this "sermon" turns out to be more like a group session of petitionary prayer. People come up to the prayer leaders and whisper their intentions, which "megaphonists" then repeat in a loud voice, so that God and the community at large can hear them. The sermon sometimes amounts to no more than a few moral exhortations tossed in as editorial comments on the prayers people have offered. The people also contribute money.

After the sermon comes the heart of the Friday service, the communal *salat* or ritual prayer. Together the group go through the actions of the fivefold daily prayer—bowing, kneeling, and touching their foreheads to the ground. Muslim prayer is essentially this doing, this performative act. So "a mosque in the last resort is not a building: It is a place of prostration and any patch of ground in ritual purity suffices where a human frame may stretch itself—a fact about Islam which accounts in large measure for the naturalness of its occasions and the contagion in its expansion. A faith that does not need to house its worshipers has no walls to hide its creed."[83]

Through the life cycle, the annual cycle, and the weekly cycle, the great lesson the Yoruba or any other Muslims are learning is the lesson of prostration. Bow-

ing before God, the Almighty, the Muslim deepens her or his sense that only one power is in charge of the world. To be at peace with God is life's greatest accomplishment; to be at war with God is life's greatest tragedy.

Self

The strong control of the Muslim community by religious law has had two primary effects on the individual or self. First, the common code that governed external behavior shaped and constrained the majority. In other words, most Muslims accepted the ethics sketched above. Second, the Sufis and mystics drew a substantial minority to a more internal doctrine of the self shaped by personal devotion. Such devotion sought to unite the individual with God experientially. Thus, the first lesson that it taught was that the human person has a spiritual substance or capacity that can unite with God.

These two effects on selfhood produced a balance in Muslim religion: The self learned that membership in the House of Islam depended on observing the common law, which led to merit and the Garden, and that it could anticipate the Garden and taste God's joy in the present life.

The orthodox conception of the self began with the notion of creation. In Sura 96 the self is described essentially as a small thing that God made from a blood clot or a drop of sperm. The essence of Islam and of being a Muslim was to recognize the creator-creature relation: a sovereign God who is completely the Lord of a very insignificant vassal. The basic scriptural message of Islamic anthropology is submission, even a certain holy slavery.

This attitude was no false humility. Rather, it was the bare truth of the human condition. Human beings came from God, and their destiny depended on living out the pattern that God had in making them. Thus, they had no basis for self-glorification. Thus, the exclamations of an al-Hallaj, who claimed identification with God (through mystical union), could only sound blasphemous to the majority, who were immersed in the literal text. Between the divine Lord and the human vassal stretched an impassable gulf. However much genuine love might have drawn the spirit up to God, however much God's intimate mercy might have descended toward human flesh, the essential difference in their states remained.

From other Qur'anic accounts of creation one can gather the impression that, despite their lowliness,

human beings have a special status among all creatures. Al Faruqi calls this status being God's "vicegerent" on earth.[84] The word *lakum* ("for you") appears
in the stories of how God made the earth to produce
herbs, crops, and animals and of how God made the
sea to carry ships and the camels and sheep to bring
forth their offspring.[85] In the stories of Adam's creation (for instance, 2:28, 15:29, 32:8), the angels object
to God's making human beings, but God forms this
first man from clay and water, gives him a most beautiful form, and breathes his spirit into him. Then he
makes the angels bow before Adam, for Adam is to be
the *khalifa* (vicegerent) on earth, having in this capacity the right and duty to carry out God's orders. Echoing Genesis, Sura 2:31 speaks of God's teaching Adam
the names of all things, which means giving him
power over all things, since to control a being's name
was to have power over it. The end God had in mind
for such a creature, the recompense that He expected,
was adoration: "We have created men and jinn only for
adoration" (51:51).

We can see, therefore, the basis for the Islamic
view that God made the earth subject to human control. Along with the doctrine of God's transcendence,
this anthropocentricity in creation helped to deemphasize nature. As we argued above, naming and ruling the world did not remove nature's mystery. Even
with nature's mystery, however, the Muslim felt that
the earth had been given into his (and to a lesser
extent her) control. Nonetheless, Muslim teachings
about human nature honored its ties with the earth,
its creation from clay and water.

Anthropology. In traditional Muslim anthropology
(view of human nature) the spiritual faculties had several names. The *nafs* was essentially the animal soul,
the source of concupiscence (desire). It had the connotation of belonging to the lower part of the personality—to the flesh that incites evil. (Sometimes,
though, it just means "self.") The *ruh* was the spirit,
come from God, that animates the human body. Muslims often pictured it as a subtle matter that permeates
the human body. Reason *(aql)* was the spiritual faculty
by which human beings discern right and wrong. Finally, the mystics spoke of the *qalb*—the heart that is
the faculty by which one obtains direct knowledge of
God.

For some of the Sufis, the doctrine of creation in
God's image was crucial. On occasion, neo-Platonic or
gnostic notions colored this doctrine to mean that the
soul wanders in exile. It can return to its home,

Figure 46 *The Meeting of the Theologians, by 'Abd
Allah Musawwir, Persia, mid-sixteenth century. Colors on paper; 11³⁄₈ × 7¹⁄₂ in. The Nelson–Atkins Museum of Art, Kansas City, Missouri (Nelson Fund).*

though, if it appropriates secret teaching or learns certain meditative techniques. From the notion of creation in God's image, the Sufis also developed their
concept of the *insan kamil*, the perfect man. Usually
they applied it to Muhammad, who contained all the
divine attributes and served as a microcosm of
divinity.

The destiny of the human being, as we have seen,
was either the Fire or the Garden. Islam did not consider man and woman to be laboring under a "fallen"
human nature, for Muslims did not regard the sin of
Adam and Eve as being contagious or passed on to
their offspring. Thus, Islam did not speak of redemption. The prophet was a revealer or a medium of revelation; he was not a ransom, a victim, or a suffering
servant. Instead of sin (in the deep sense of alienation
from God by irrational actions), Islam tended to stress
human forgetfulness (of God's goodness). Human nature was weak—prone to a kind of religious amnesia.

In the Prophet's own conception of human destiny, men and women have a common responsibility to remember God's goodness and to respond by fulfilling his will. Originally, both men and women were to offer prayer and alms; however, in later times women's status deteriorated, and they did not have this obligation.

The self that was faithful to the identity set by the community could expect to gain Paradise. God would forgive sins (violations of religious law), so they did not mean a loss of community membership. (However, the dissident Kharijites said that every Muslim who committed a grave sin was an unbeliever.) What separated one from the *Ummah* in the orthodox view was to deny that the injunctions of the Qur'an came from God and thus were eternally binding. Among the Shia, who have predominated in Iran, faith also has included acknowledging the mystical imam of the time—the hidden successor to Ali whom the Shiites expect to come as the Messiah. By uniting with this hidden imam, one partook of salvation.

Historically, the major theoretical question concerning the self was the relation of human freedom to divine will. At least in the Meccan sections, the Qur'an takes human freedom for granted. Muhammad's call and his preaching make no sense without a capacity to respond. Similarly, the scenes of Judgment Day assume that human beings have been responsible for their actions—that they could have done otherwise than they did. However, later Qur'anic passages emphasize God's omnipotence. As a result, the question arises: Does God lead some people astray—or at least leave them in error?

In the Umayyad period a group of strict predestinarians (the Jabriya) stressed God's complete control. Opposing them were the Qasriya, who defended human responsibility. A third group, the Mutazilites, defended both human freedom and God's perfect justice. Still another position, that of al-Ashari, satisfied many people with the following formula: "God creates in man the will to act and the act, and man acquires the act by performing it." To say the least, the issue vexed Islam. In later times the common people frequently felt that life was fated—that it was out of their hands. Among the few monistic mystics, human freedom was lost in the divine nature.

In summary, Islam has given the self rather complex directives. The core message is that membership in the Prophet's community and submission to God fulfill the human duties. The way to realize oneself is to follow the community law. In the present, such self-realization means spiritual security; in the future, it will mean Paradise. While waiting for Paradise, one can work the earth, trade, fight, or enjoy the pleasures of the senses, so long as the chosen activity does not divert one from the ultimate reality of God. If one is submissive to God, most things are licit. More things are licit for men than for women, as we have seen, but many commentators think the Qur'an did improve the Arab woman's lot considerably.

Still, the popular image of Muhammad as a man who could satisfy nine wives and still receive revelations greater than those of Jesus inculcated a certain bravado in all but the most ascetic males. Since Islamic education deals primarily with religious lore, it does not necessarily demythologize Muhammad's popular image. As well, historically most Muslim women have been denied education. Therefore, tradition has tended to describe sexuality mainly from a male point of view. That point of view, in turn, has tended to meld with the patterns set forth in the eternal Qur'an. Following these patterns, one would let God more and more dominate the entire self.

Case Study: Muslim Saints.[86] When we considered the life cycle rituals, the annual rituals, and the weekly rituals of Yoruba Muslims, we glimpsed Islam's accommodation to the West African religious traditions that predated it. We get another glimpse of such cross-cultural accommodation by studying the different ways the different Muslim ethnic groups have conceived sainthood, the peak achievement of Muslim selfhood. For example, the Indonesian Muslims, who have been greatly influenced by Indian culture, have focused their religious imagination on saints whose style is markedly quieter than the style of the saints Moroccan Muslims have venerated. Since "Islam" starts to come into focus only when one begins to find the unity underlying such differences, let us attempt a comparative study of the Indonesian and Moroccan Muslim saints.

In Indonesian Muslim lore, Sunan Kalidjaga is the most important of the group of nine "apostles" considered to be the founders of Indonesian Islam. Legend has it that he was born the son of a high royal official of Madjapahit, one of the greatest and last of the Indonesian Hindu-Buddhist kingdoms, which dominated most of Eastern Java during the fourteenth and fifteenth centuries. In the sixteenth century Madjapahit declined, caught between the old Hindu-Buddhist order and the new Muslim order that was emerging. Pressured by this change, Kalidjaga moved to the new harbor state of Djapara, where he met another of the early apostles, Sunan Bonang, and was converted to Islam. Later Kalidjaga so greatly influenced Javanese politics that he is credited with Java's having become solidly Muslim. Symbolically, therefore, Kalidjaga serves as a bridge between the old Indic world of god-kings, ritual priests, and Indian shrines and the new Islamic world of pious sultans, Qur'anic scholars, and austere mosques. Indonesians love to contemplate the story of his conversion, for it recapitulates their good fortune in having gained access to the world of God, and it drives home the conviction that Islam is the best flower of the new phase of their history.

When Kalidjaga arrived in Djapara, he was a ne'er-do-well, accomplished in stealing, drinking, whoring, and gambling. So deep were his vices, he stole all his own mother's money, and when he had dissipated this he set out to steal from the public at large. Eventually he became a highwayman of such renown that people were afraid to go to the Djapara market lest they encounter him and lose all their goods.

Into this scene strolled Sunan Bonang, a Muslim (probably an Arab) dressed in gorgeous clothes and expensive jewels, and carrying a cane of solid gold. Naturally he attracted the attention of Kalidjaga, who put a knife to his throat and demanded all his finery. But, to Kalidjaga's amazement, Bonang laughed in his face. Calling Kalidjaga by his name (though he had never met Kalidjaga before), Bonang chided him as though he were a little boy: "Don't always be wanting this thing and that thing. Such material desires are pointless. We live but a moment. It is foolish to be attached to worldly goods. Look: there is a whole tree full of money."

Kalidjaga turned and saw a banyan tree transformed to gold and hung with jewels. At a stroke, he realized that material things were nothing compared with Bonang's power. What sort of a man must Bonang be, to be able to turn trees into gold and jewels and yet not care about gold and jewels at all? With this thought, Kalidjaga's life of vice repulsed him, and he begged Bonang to teach him spiritual power. Bonang agreed, but he warned Kalidjaga that such teaching was very difficult. Kalidjaga vowed he would persist until death, but Bonang merely told him, "Wait here, by the side of the river, until I return." Then he took his leave.

Kalidjaga waited by the side of the river for forty years, lost in thought. Great trees grew up around him, floods arose and receded, crowds jostled him back and forth, buildings went up and were torn down. Still he waited, lost in thought. Finally Bonang returned, and he saw that Kalidjaga had indeed been steadfast. So instead of teaching Kalidjaga the doctrines of Islam, Bonang simply told him that he had been a good pupil—indeed, that he had come to surpass Bonang himself. To prove this, Bonang asked Kalidjaga difficult questions about religious matters, and Kalidjaga answered them all correctly. Then Bonang told him to go forth and spread the truths of Islam, which Kalidjaga did with unsurpassed effectiveness.

What a remarkable story! The master apostle of Javanese Islam becomes a great saint without ever having seen the Qur'an, entered a mosque, or prayed a Muslim prayer. His conversion comes directly from a change of heart deepened by yoga-like meditation. It is not so much a change in belief (taking that word to refer mainly to matters of thought) as a change in will.

Because he had reformed his life, and penetrated the implications of his reform, Kalidjaga had become a Muslim. When he walked the meditative way that Indian culture had been impressing on Indonesia for centuries, he came out a Muslim—the new holy man forged in the fires of Indonesia's cultural transformation. So the message that was trumpeted whenever the legend of Java's greatest saint was told was that Islam is the obvious expression of the reformed, converted, highly developed religious personality. If one finds the depths of human authenticity, one eventually realizes that the Qur'an, the mosques, and the Muslim scholars are human authenticity's best expressions.

The Moroccan saint Sidi Lahsen Lyusi is quite a contrast to Kalidjaga. Lyusi was born into an obscure tribe of shepherds in the Middle Atlas Mountains of Morocco in 1631. Although he probably was of Berber descent, he claimed to be a *sherif* or direct descendant of Muhammad. Lyusi died in 1691, so the sixty years of his life coincided with the rise of the Alawite dynasty (which still rules today in Rabat, the capital of Morocco) from the chaos of a preceding sectarian strife. Like Kalidjaga's, therefore, Lyusi's sainthood was intimately tied to a difficult time of transition, when people were looking for models of a new social order. However, where Kalidjaga functioned as a miniature of the new harmony that Indonesia sought, Lyusi directly opposed the power he saw rising in his times. Thus Clifford Geertz, whose description of these two saints we are following, characterizes Lyusi's approach as moralistic, in contrast to the aesthetic approach of Kalidjaga.

The chaos of Lyusi's lifetime is sometimes called the Maraboutic Crisis, and it arose after the collapse of the last of the Berber dynasties, the Merinid. A *marabout* is a holy man, and during the Maraboutic Crisis Morocco splintered into different political groups clustered around different holy men. Lyusi wandered from political group to political group, always restless and on the move. When he arrived in Tamgrut, a desert oasis, he encountered the famous Muslim saint Ahmed ben Nasir. Ben Nasir was sick with smallpox, and so he asked his disciples, one by one, to wash out his loathsome nightshirt. Each disciple refused, repelled by the disgusting garment and afraid for his health. Lyusi, who had just arrived and was not known to ben Nasir, approached the saint and volunteered for the job. He took the shirt to a spring, rinsed it, wrung it out, and then drank the foul water it produced. When he returned to the master his eyes were aflame, not with sickness but with what Moroccans call *baraka:* the supernatural power that makes a marabout.

The story summarizes the Moroccan notion of sainthood. The main forces at work in Lyusi's transformation into a man of *baraka* were his extraordinary physical courage, his absolute personal loyalty to his "teacher," his moral intensity, and an almost physical passage of sainthood from teacher to disciple. Thus the Moroccan notion of Muslim sainthood seems more energetic than the Indonesian. Whereas Kalidjaga was transformed by forty years of meditation near a river, Lyusi was transformed by a single act of heroic courage.

Thirty years after this event, Lyusi had a momentous confrontation with Sultan Mulay Ismail, the great consolidator of the Alawite dynasty. In 1668 the Alawites had put an end to the Maraboutic Crisis and gained power in Morocco. The confrontation took place in the Sultan's new capital of Meknes, and it reveals the delicate relation between strongman politics and Maraboutism that has dominated Moroccan history. The warrior and the saint have been the two basic forms of heroism in Morocco, and this epic confrontation pitted a great warrior against a greater saint.

When Lyusi arrived in Meknes, Mulay Ismail received him as an honored guest. Indeed, he brought Lyusi to the court and made him his spiritual adviser.

The sultan was building a large wall around the city and treating the men working on the wall cruelly. When one of the workmen fell from exhaustion and was sealed into the wall, some of the other workers came to Lyusi secretly to complain. Lyusi said nothing, but that night, when his supper was brought to his chamber, he broke all the dishes. He continued to do this, night after night, until all the dishes in the palace were broken.

Eventually the sultan learned what was happening and ordered Lyusi brought to him. When he asked the saint why he was acting so outrageously, the saint asked in return whether it was better to break pottery of clay or the pottery of God (human beings). Then he proceeded to upbraid the sultan for his cruelty to the workers. The sultan was not moved. Lyusi had abused his hospitality (a high crime in Moroccan culture), so he ordered Lyusi out of the city.

Lyusi left the palace and pitched his tent near the wall that was being built. When the sultan asked why the saint had not obeyed the royal order, Lyusi said that he had left the sultan's city and taken up residence in God's city. At this answer the sultan was so enraged that he charged out on horseback. Interrupting the saint's prayers (another high crime), he again asked why the royal order had been disobeyed. Again he received the answer that Lyusi was now in the city of God. Wild with fury, the sultan advanced to kill the saint. But the saint drew a line on the ground and when the sultan's horse crossed the line the horse's legs began to sink into the earth. Terrified, the sultan begged mercy and promised that he would reform. Lyusi said he only wanted a decree acknowledging that he was a *sherif,* entitled to the honors of a direct descendant of the Prophet. The sultan gave him this decree and Lyusi left Meknes (fearing for his life) to preach to the Berbers in the Middle Atlas forests. After his death a great cult developed at his tomb, and he has since been revered as a most powerful marabout. In Lyusi, Moroccan Islam has found an ideal embodiment of its moral passion, just as in Kalidjaga Indonesian Islam has found an ideal embodiment of its meditative passion.

Ultimate Reality

Islam is perhaps the most theocentric of the major religions.[87] In Muhammad's revelation, God emerged to become the sovereign Lord. Before Muhammad, some Arabs had spoken of a high god "Allah" who was above the numerous idols. The divine name itself seems to fuse two words: al-Ilah ("the God"). It was an attempt to designate an ultimate divinity, a God who was beyond all demigods. From his visionary experience, Muhammad recognized that God is the only divinity, and that his primary designations are "Creator" and "Judge." As such, God leaves no place for other deities to function in either the world's creation or in the destiny of humankind.

Islam polished its theocentricity through controversy with polytheistic Arabs and then with Christians committed to the Incarnation and the Trinity. Sura 112, which Schimmel calls the logical end of the Qur'an,[88] puts the matter succinctly: "Say: He is Allah, One; Allah, the Eternal; He brought not forth nor hath He been brought forth; Coequal with Him there hath never been anyone."

The Creator made the world in six days (or in a single moment, according to Sura 54:50). Muslims trust that he guides the world wisely and unfailingly. God's knowledge of all creatures is total, and his mercy extends to all who acknowledge him. It is God in whose name every work is being begun and upon whose will every future action depends. Thus, one has to add "insha Allah" ("if God wills") to every sentence that refers to a future act or a new direction of thought. To try to indicate God's fullness, the Qur'an encircles him with "most beautiful names." He is the First and the Last, the Inward and the Outward. Above all, he is Merciful and Compassionate. He is the All-Holy, the Peace, the Light of Heaven and Earth. Transcendent though he be, he is also as near as the jugular pulse. Wherever one turns, there is his Face (the Qur'anic expression for God's essence).

Many scholars find the negative portion of the creed ("no God but God") very important, since it unequivocally rejects other peoples' gods. As well, it determined that the greatest sin in the Muslim code would be *shirk*—idolatry or "association" (of other objects of worship with God). The mystics sometimes took this to mean that nothing but God exists—that God alone is real. Among modern Muslims, anti-idolatry on occasion has worked against ideologies such as Marxism, capitalism, and nationalism, which some orthodox Muslims find incompatible with pure monotheism. Insofar as such ideologies gain the ultimate concern of many human beings, they amount to new kinds of paganism.

However, the theology of the Qur'an itself is not without ambiguity. After Muhammad's death, debates arose about God's nature. At the beginning, the ortho-

dox clung to the letter and imagery of the received text. That meant accepting descriptions of God that gave him a face, hands, and the like. The Mutazilites, who had contact with Hellenistic rationalism, pointed out the dangers latent in such anthropomorphism: When we think of God in human terms, we think of him as finite.[89] Thus, the Mutazilites clung to the absolute unity of God, accepting as a consequence that God cannot be imagined. In other words, they prized God's difference—the gulf that lies between the Creator and everything created. In Western terms, that made them "negative" theologians. Indeed, to safeguard God's unity, the Mutazilites even questioned the doctrine of the divine attributes (that God has speech, sight, and so on). For that reason, the orthodox described the Mutazilites as "those who deny the attributes," a charge of heresy.

In these debates, Muslims shared with Jews and Christians the consequences of an exposure to Greek reason. They had to ask whether their descriptions of God could be reconciled with what they could infer from the divine transcendence. For instance, they could infer that a Creator would be independent of the world, unlimited, unimaginable in created terms. From that it followed that any picture of God would be at best a happy convenience—a more or less useful fiction that might help some people's faith. As a further extension of such rationalism, the Mutazilites denied that the Qur'an is God's uncreated word. To them that would have made it a coeternal attribute, something ever existent with God. However, calling the Qur'an "created" deeply offended the orthodox, for whom the Arabic text expressed a heavenly prototype. The human Qur'an was unalterable (which led the orthodox to resist all attempts to translate it from Arabic), because it derived from eternity. Thus, the Mutazilites and the orthodox clashed in their theologies of revelation.

Furthermore, the Mutazilites insisted that God has to be just and true. For the divine will to be arbitrary would violate God's own inner consistency. Consequently, God has to reward the just with heaven and punish the evil with hell. As well, God cannot be the author of sin, so human beings must have free will. To the less intellectual Muslim majority, this logic seemed rarefied, and they could not follow its deductive chain. "Limiting" God's freedom jarred with their sense of the divine sovereignty. Indeed, popular orthodoxy never fully accepted either human freedom or the notion that God had to obey rules for creation, even if they were his own. Popular orthodoxy preferred to leave all things in God's hands and saw little reason to puzzle over human freedom, God's noncontradiction, or the other problems that vexed the Mutazilites.

Al-Ashari, who had mediated the debate on the question of divine providence and human freedom, also mediated the question of the divine attributes. To the Mutazilites, he insisted that God has attributes (thereby saving the picture in the Qur'an). To the traditionalists, he insisted that we cannot say precisely how God has his attributes. In al-Ashari's eyes, both anthropomorphism and the denial of attributes were grave sins.

Among the Arab philosophers,[90] such as Avicenna, Greek doctrines stimulated the conception of God as a first cause whose being is pure existence. In contrast, the Sufis tended to forego philosophical speculation, favoring instead a personal experience of the divine. For them the profitable way was not reasoning but intuition. Furthermore, the Sufis opposed Qur'anic fundamentalists by proposing that we should obey God out of love. To the fundamentalists, such a personal relationship seemed novel, for they admitted only a relationship of obedience: The Creator commanded and the creature obeyed. Because the Sufis were more ecstatic than either the fundamentalists or the philosophers, they are a richer source for ascertaining the beauty of the Islamic God—the allure of God's mystery and its fearsomeness. The Shiites also have been quite ecstatic, praying in remembrance of their martyred saints and for the coming of the seventh Imam, their Messiah.

The basic Islamic program for worshiping God has always been the Five Pillars. In the daily prayer *(salat)*, one expressed one's submission to God and so one's faith in God's Lordship. Historically, men attended the Friday common worship in the mosque, while women prayed at home. Sufi circles developed unstructured prayer, which frequently involved a repetition of God's holy names. On the folk level, magical practices mixed with worship. The Qur'an gave such practices some foundation by saying that the (bad) angels Harut and Marut taught the Babylonians magic (2:96). Ordinarily, the magician knew formulas that could conjure up the jinns or the angels. This has led to an expansion of the ways in which one can imagine the spirits and call them to one's aid. Amulets, reproductions of verses from the Qur'an, reproductions of God's names, and so on, are popular expressions of Muslim interest in attaining good luck. Similarly, Muslims continue to dread the "evil eye." To ward off its malignant influence, people constantly intersperse

their conversation with "as God wills." As well, they wear amulets or give their children ugly names to keep the evil ones away.

Popular religion also retains a considerable interest in astrology, prophecy, and fortune-telling. A favorite technique for divining the future is to open the Qur'an at random and take the first verse that one's eye falls on as a cipher for what is to come. Other popular methods are reading palms or coffee grounds.

Sacrifice also has a place in Muslim worship of God. Those who can afford it immolate a sheep on the Day of Slaughtering during the annual pilgrimage to Mecca. This sacrifice is in memory of Abraham, who was willing to sacrifice his son Ishmael. People also make votive offerings—cocks, sheep, and so on—at holy places such as the tombs of saints. The animal should be slaughtered ritually, by cutting its jugular vein and its trachea in one stroke; tradition recommends giving it to the poor. Finally, sacrifice is appropriate on almost any important occasion, such as starting construction of a house, celebrating a child's birthday, or expiating an offense.

Although Islam places no mediators between God and human beings, it has made both Muhammad and many saints quite important objects of devotion. The members of Muhammad's family have enjoyed special privileges, and Ali, his cousin and son-in-law, became a cult figure to those who considered him to be Muhammad's legitimate heir. The Shia expanded the creed to include the words "Ali is the Friend of God." The Shia also venerated the line of imams, with special emphasis upon the currently hidden imam. He is the ruler of the age, and he will return at the end of the world to fill the world with justice. In Iran this imam's name accompanies the promulgation of laws, and he is for pious Shiites an object of intense personal devotion.[91] Ali's son Husain also plays an important role, for the celebration of his assassination is a day of deep mourning.[92] Among the Sufis, the leaders of the orders were venerated, as were holy people who gained a reputation for miracles. The latter often received special tombs to which the faithful would go for cures and favors.[93]

Angels are also essential objects of Muslim faith. According to tradition, God created them from light. The Qur'an stresses that they are neither children of God nor female beings. They are intelligent and can become visible. From the Qur'an, Muslims know Gabriel as the angel of revelation. Israfil will blow the trumpet at Doomsday, and Azrael is the angel of death. Iblis is the fallen angel. Like Harut and Marut, he is a source of evil. Harut and Marut taught humankind witchcraft, but a beautiful woman seduced them and then imprisoned them in a well in Babylonia.[94] Thus, the sacred space between the creature and the Creator has been abuzz with personages of interest.

The Islamic divinity is similar to that of the other theistic religions. Though official Islamic doctrine insists on God's uniqueness, the comparativist finds that its popular practice also greatly honors Muhammad, angels, and saints. Muslims perhaps have read the Qur'an more literally than other religionists have read their respective scriptures, since Islamic orthodoxy reified it into God's eternal Word, but there are analogies in Judaism, Christianity, and Hinduism. Clearly, though, Muslim faith regularly has aspired to make things simple; a black-and-white doctrine of God, Muhammad, and Judgment; a program of genius (the Five Pillars) for reducing this faith to practice; a single community of believers dedicated to filling the earth with true religion—with submission to the Grand Lord of the Worlds.

SUMMARY: THE MUSLIM CENTER

God is certainly the Muslim center, and because the Qur'an is the definite expression of God, the Qur'an is the central place where the invisible Muslim God has become visible. How, then, does the Qur'an portray the Lord of the Worlds, the most ultimate and holy Muslim reality? It portrays him majestically, as a sovereign beyond compare, a power nothing earthly can approach. When God commands, the heavens thunder and the earth quakes. When God consoles, the winds quiet and the soul feels bliss. Were God not compassionate, merciful, life would be utterly terrifying. He is a severe judge, and none can abide the day of his coming. Yet he has sent prophets to warn humanity of his coming, has reset the strict boundaries of his laws. Muhammad is the seal of these prophets, in whom their work has come to complete fulfillment. As there is no God but God, so there is no final prophet but Muhammad. The eternal Qur'an that has been at God's side from the foundations of the world has taken definitive voice in Muhammad's recitals. All the *hadith,* ponderings of the lawyers, visions of the saints, and

virtuous living of the pious depend on this one everflowing font. Apart from the Qur'an, there would be no house of Islam.

For Qur'anic religion, the world is bare of idols. If we rightly perceive the Lord of the Worlds, nothing stands between divinity and creation. Whatever exists in space and time depends utterly on God. To God belongs all praise and worship; any worship of creatures is a wicked blasphemy. This does not mean that one should be an ascetic. The austerities of some of the Sufis are understandable, but they have never been the Muslim mainstream. The Muslim mainstream has rather been a sober, almost fated acceptance of whatever life brings. Thus wealth, power, or even plunder need not take a Muslim from healthy religion. Similarly, poverty and illness need not interfere with a solid holiness, since they too can be accepted "as God wills." The will of God dominates the Muslim psyche. What so splendid a Lord chooses to dispense obviously is one's true fate.

The best dispensation of God, his sovereign Word, has been the pious Muslim's fated solace. Thus small children memorizing the Qur'an, often without knowing its language, have slowly been formed to a passionate love of Islam's Arabic cadences. The rhythms of the Qur'an have become the rhythms of their souls. Muslim piety is poetic, rhapsodic, both burning and disciplined. When one bows and lets the verses sing through one's whole being, becoming like the Reed of whom the Sufis wrote, one's piety is almost instrumental. The poetry of God uses devout submission as its musical instruments—strings and drums of flesh and blood.

As a result, the Muslim mystics seem almost intoxicated with the Qur'anic God. His poetic voice fills their spirits like heady wine. In the stark clearing of Islam's powerful monotheism, the Muslim soul can see and feel divinity everywhere. The mystics who claimed strict union with God, utter identification, went beyond what orthodoxy would allow, but they built on an experience that mainstream Muslim piety fostered. A God as near as the pulse at one's throat, utterly in control of one's world, easily could invade one's spirit, break down the barriers between mine and thine. That usually he did not is a strong tribute to the effectiveness of the Qur'anic stress on his sovereign transcendence. Though he controlled all events, none captured more than a fraction of his power or being.

As a result, no event or creature could stand for God sacramentally, as the rites or icons of other the-isms could stand for their people's God. Muhammad could not be an incarnate divinity, as Jesus could be for Christians. (This is most true of Sunnis. Sufis have a more charismatic Muhammad, and Shiites make the seventh Imam close to divine.) No baptism or Eucharist could mediate the divine life, just as no meditation could actuate the divine enlightenment. The light of God was indeed a shining lamp. The path of God was indeed the Way that was straight. But the life of God, the being of God, dwelt beyond all this-worldly metaphors, ceremonies, or other means of conveyance. They even dwelt beyond all this-worldly experiences: The most intense mystical raptures did not allow one to claim possession of the divine nature. There is no God but God. There is no connection to God, no understanding of God, no commission from God that clouds the clear Muslim heaven. God is like the sun at its apex, blazing down on a beautiful desert stripped of all competitors to him.

Psychologically, then, the Muslim center is the submission in which one expresses one's creaturehood. God is great and the submitter is small. In the world of fellow human beings the submitter may be weak or strong, wealthy or poor, a simple soul or a complex tyrant. Under the aspect of God's eternity, the submitter remains but a creature of a day, a grain of sand along an endless shore. The best fruits of this psychology are the freedom and objective humility it has fostered. If one really lives under the aspect of eternity, few earthly tyrannies are impressive.

Discussion Questions

1. Contrast Muhammad with Jesus.

2. In what sense is Islam the preeminent religion of the Book?

3. Why do the Five Pillars make a comprehensive, fully adequate religious program?

4. Explain briefly how Qur'anic religion could inspire the golden age of Arabic civilization.

5. What does Sufism contribute to the family of Islam?

6. Compare the position of women in Islam, Judaism, and Christianity.

7. How well does submission describe the relation between the Muslim and God?

8. Contrast the sainthood of Lyusi and Kalidjaga.

9. Why is Islam so fervently opposed to God's having a son?

10. What are the assets and liabilities in the Muslim idea of a theocracy with no separation between religion and politics?

11. What are the main implications of believing God to be as near as the pulse at one's throat?

12. What are the main implications of believing that Judgment Day is soon to arrive?

13. What are the main psychodynamics you would expect to see at work during the pilgrimage to Mecca?

14. Why has Islam had no official sacraments?

15. How can God be all-powerful and human beings have free will?

16. How does Islam deal with the problem of evil?

17. What model of sanctity has Muhammad encouraged?

Glossary

Allah: God, singular for the degree to which Muhammad and Muslims have insisted he is the sole possessor of divinity, the Lord of the Worlds beside whom everything else pales into insignificance.

dhikr ("zicker"): a Muslim term for remembrance or recollection. This virtue became all-important when one linked it with the Muslim conviction that forgetfulness (rather than sin) was the main reason people disregarded God, fell into idolatry, violated the *Sharia*, and so forth. Thus the Qur'an called for constantly remembering the goodness of God, the promises and favors God had vouchsafed, the teachings of the Prophet, and the like. The call to pray five times a day externalized the importance of *dhikr*, and in general much Islamic spirituality sought to keep the disciple in the presence of the Qur'anic word or attentive to the presence of God to both human beings and the signs of physical nature.

hadith: Muslim traditions about Muhammad. The *hadith* function in Islam as one of the principal sources of authoritative teaching, standing with the Qur'an, community consensus, and analogical reasoning. They imply the paradigmatic faith of the Prophet, whose life believers have taken as the model or template for Muslim existence. Complicated rules govern how sayings became authenticated and entered the collections of *hadith*. Muslims tend to be confident that what is housed in the several authoritative collections accurately reports what the Prophet said and did, but scholars using the detached techniques of textual criticism find much that seems folkloric and mythic.

hajj: the Muslim pilgrimage to Mecca. One of the Five Pillars that summarize the practice of Islamic faith, the *hajj* has the special objective of binding believers to the birthplace of Islam and convincing them that all believers form a universal brother- and sisterhood. Pilgrims repeat ritual gestures more than a thousand years old, wear common, nondistinctive garb that levels their wealth and signs of worldly station, and regularly experience what the anthropologist Victor Turner has called "communitas": the sense of being a unified people that only can flourish in special circumstances, when one feels called out of the workaday world and has one's human relationships reset by direct experience of the divine holiness.

Hejira: Muhammad's flight or departure from Mecca to Medina in 622. The Hejira may be considered Muhammad's definitive realization that he would never get through to his fellow Meccans and so his striking out on a new chapter in his mission to spread Qur'anic revelation. In Medina he was given control of a community and so could develop a blueprint for a Muslim state. Having consolidated both his own thought and considerably more power, Muhammad then returned to Mecca and conquered his prior enemies, making the Hejira the prelude to the wholesale victory that established Islam as what would become a great religious empire and culture.

imam: a spiritual guide in Shiite Islam. Imams may be human teachers, offering the faithful instruction in Qur'anic religion. Or they may be mystical teachers ruling over given ages. The last of these mystical imams, ruling the final age in secret, is an object of great yearning in Shiite Islam. When he comes, Shiites will be justified in having followed Muhammad's bloodline for their successors and they will be recompensed for the sufferings of their great saints.

Islam: the faith, obedience, and practice of Muslims. The word has overtones of "submission," implying that the Muslim is in the first instance the one who submits to God. In practice this means submitting to the revelation of God (the Qur'an), to the Prophet of God (Muhammad), and to the community God had

Muhammad form through the Qur'an (the *Ummah*). Islamic piety carries through this notion of submission by having worshipers bow low at daily prayer and think of their relation to God as compassionate and merciful. God may be loved and may be experienced as love. But probably the stronger overtones in Islam are that God is the Lord and human beings are the servants, those who should hear and obey.

jihad: a Muslim term meaning holy struggle, warfare in defense, or pursuit, of a good cause. Muslims frequently make the point that jihad is broader than simply "holy war." It can connote the whole range of effort necessary to promote the faith in both personal and social life. Moreover, even when it refers to military matters, it need not primarily be offensive. The more ordinary reason for going to war, in the Muslim view of past history, was opposition that would have denied Muslims the chance to practice or spread their faith. Seeing such a denial as opposition to God, the Qur'an, and the Prophet, Muslims have felt obliged to fight, as they could feel obliged to fight on behalf of brother and sister Muslims who came under attack. The unity of the Muslim community justified such a sense of social solidarity, believers having ties among themselves that relegated their relations with unbelievers or outsiders to a lower level.

jinn: an Arabic term for a demon or spirit. Arab religion before Muhammad's time generally was polytheistic and animistic, believing in many spirits, both good and evil. The evil spirits or demons had to be warded off with prayers, sacrifices, amulets, and spells. Muhammad tried to cleanse the Arab psyche of its polytheistic impulses but he himself accepted the existence of angelic spirits and jinn. The jinn and angels certainly were not on the same level as God, but they had influence in human life and had to be dealt with. Popular Islamic religion frequently remained quite involved with fighting the jinn, retaining long-standing beliefs in the influence of the evil eye and the need to protect oneself against bad spirits by prayers and regular submission of one's fate to the will of God.

Muslim: a submitter to God; a follower of Islam and the Prophet Muhammad. Muslims accept the prophecies of Abraham and Jesus, but the Qur'an is their great charter. They think of Muhammad as the seal of prophecy—the definitive revealer. Islam correlates the submission of the believer bowing low in prayer with submission of the nonidolatrous mind. Just as the body bends and prostrates itself, so the mind should accept the sole Lordship of God and submit to the divine will manifested in the Qur'an.

polydemonism: the reverence or fear of many demons, spirits, or jinn. Polydemonism is simply a further specification of the animistic tendency to populate the world with frightful spirits. Witchcraft and black magic tend to abound in a polydemonistic world view, and usually the psychology of the people in question is troubled, even paranoid. In such cases, missionaries of either a single transcendent God or of a simplifying message such as the Buddhist call to enlightenment can seem liberators, offering people a way to escape thrall to irrational principalities and powers.

Ramadan: the Muslim lunar month during which the faithful are expected to fast from sunup to sundown. Keeping the fast of Ramadan is one of the Five Pillars basic to the superstructure of Islamic faith. Yet the fast is as much joyous as penitential, for in many Muslim countries those fasting celebrate each evening. Because lunar months move through the solar year, Ramadan may occur when the days are either short and cold or when they are long and hot, which means the severity of the exercise can vary considerably. The fast is supposed to discipline both body and mind, reminding all Muslims that their first obligation is to the will of God, and that to fulfill the will of God they need to be masters of their own personal beings.

rasul: Muhammad as the prophet or messenger par excellence. Islam admits that other prophets—Abraham, Jesus—preceded Muhammad, and it sees Muhammad as completing the prophecy of such predecessors. But with Muhammad has come the Qur'an, the Recital that "seals" prophecy. In other words, Qur'anic revelation is definitive. It completes what was begun but remained imperfect prior to Muhammad, and it itself will never be superseded. As the *rasul,* Muhammad is also the great exemplar of what God wants human beings to become. He is the compleat Muslim, modeling both proper piety and human maturation. Although Islam insists Muhammad was not divine, it has accorded him great honor and taken much offense whenever outsiders denigrated him.

Sharia: the path, teaching, canon law, and guidance of Islam. As law, *Sharia* is analogous to Jewish Torah. As a compendium of religious teaching, it is analogous to Buddhist dharma and Christian doctrine. Historically it rose from reflections on the Qur'an and the *hadith* that passed on the example and teachings of the Prophet. Generally it tends to connote the ortho-dox law codes Islam developed, which codified the consensus of the community and the conclusions the Muslim teachers had reached by reasoning from precedents. Traditional Muslims have looked to *Sharia* for guidance on the path to salvation, although they have admitted notable debate among their teachers over fine points of interpretation. *Sharia* has been the backbone of traditional Muslim culture, developing the revelations of the Qur'an and the example of the Prophet so that they could inspire a full body of architectural, scientific, political, and ritualistic expressions.

Shia: sectarian Islam that has opposed Sunni orthodoxy. The Shia arose from early disputes about succession to Muhammad in leadership of the Muslim community. It was the group championing Ali and the rights of blood relatives of the Prophet. It has usually been the Islamic minority and from its minority status, as well as specific historic sufferings such as the murder of the sons of Ali, has developed a religious consciousness dominated by suffering, persecution, and martyrdom. The Shia has predominated in Iran, which in some historical periods has been the cultural luminary of the Muslim world. Recently its relations with Sunni Islam have been tense, even combative. Shiites and Sunnis share more doctrines and practices than they hold separately, although the Shiites do have certain distinctive doctrines, such as the expectation of the return of the hidden imam to consummate history, and certain distinctive festivals, such as the commemoration of the martyrdom of the sons of Ali.

Sufism: devotional, ascetic, or mystical Muslim traditions whose adherents often are members of a lodge or brotherhood. Sufism appears to have arisen shortly after the Muslim military expansions and political successes, in good part as a protest movement. Fearing that worldly success would taint adherence to God, the Qur'an, and the Prophet, the Sufis turned their backs on worldly concerns to devote themselves to prayer and spiritual purification. Yet they did not advocate celibacy, and they usually did profess to be keeping faith with *Sharia.* Their critics have considered their support of saints and their sometimes eccentric, even credulous, religious practices a source of Muslim decline, comparing them disadvantageously with the sober demands of *Sharia.* The Sufis somewhat parallel the Jewish Hasidim, both groups seeking religious fervor and rejecting official legalism. Sufi mysticism added to the staple Muslim submission to God new notes of love, most notably in such writers as Rabia and Rumi. Sufi teachers, like Zen roshis, sometimes have spoken paradoxically, used pointed or parabolic stories, and employed theatrical gestures to prod their students.

Sunni: the majority denomination in Islam. The Sunnis have considered themselves both more traditional and more moderate than either the Shia or the Sufis. They have tended to think the *Sharia* the backbone of Muslim culture and to favor religious life that balanced between profession of the uniqueness of God and conviction that God had made the material world good for human beings to develop. Sunnis have predominated in most cultural areas other than Iran. Historically, they supported the view that the successors to Muhammad in leadership of the Muslim community need not be members of the Prophet's bloodline—a position with some foundations in pre-Islamic Arab political custom. Sunnis certainly are not monolithic, but the similarity of the several official Sunni law codes and the common rejection of doctrines peculiar to the Shia tend to harmonize them.

Ummah: the Muslim community. Islam thinks of all believers as comprising a brother- and sisterhood. The Prophet was the head of the entire community in his day, but after his death the question of headship of the community became entangled in political and cultural battles. Historically, the community has been led by different dynasties and has been divided geographically. In addition, the differences between Shiites and Sunnis have complicated estimates of how the *Ummah* actually subsists in time. But such occasions as the annual pilgrimage to Mecca have allowed Muslims to affirm their solidarity, while the common hold that the Prophet, the Qur'an, the *Sharia,* the Five Pillars, and other Muslim staples have kept on all the faithful has meant the community has been a solid reality, not just an unrealized ideal.

zakat: the Muslim alms. The *zakat* is one of the Five Pillars of Islam, not a charitable gift but a matter of obligation. How much it should be has varied with local custom, but everywhere it has symbolized the community all Muslims share and the obligations they carry to care for one another. In Muhammad's day clan society had broken down, with considerable suffering for widows, orphans, and others who had no immediate family. The alms in the first place was aimed at helping such unfortunates, but it can also take the form of endowing hospitals, schools, and mosques.

CHAPTER 11

ALTERNATIVES TO RELIGION—SECULARISM AND HUMANISM

A modern symbol suggesting human control

HISTORY

Traditional Sources of Secularization

In this chapter we look directly at the challenge the world religions have received—largely, but not exclusively, in modern times—from thinkers and social trends that have deprecated the significance of divine mystery and cut back the influence of religious professionals, institutions, doctrines, and behavioral patterns.[1] These influences have affected all the religious traditions, moving from the west to the east. While secularism and humanism now shape many religious people from within, as strong forces in their cultures, it is useful to examine both forces as alternatives to religion, because their internal logic makes them arguments for a world in which meaning is man-made.

Perhaps the first thing we should note is that the religious traditions themselves have always housed forces with a potential to decrease their hold on the common people and lessen the public perception that religion was the most important factor in anyone's life. For example, when Akhenaton promoted a "monotheistic" reform of Egyptian religion, he ran into opposition from the Egyptian priesthoods, because he threatened the existence (and so influence) of their particular

and fire the emotions, stories, dances, rites of passage, and the like have made ultimate questions things people could feel very deeply. Deep, intense feeling helps people enjoy being alive. Certainly it can be terrifying, when it focuses on all that is unknown, destructive, or threatening. On the other hand, it can be exhilarating, when it focuses on experiences, ideas, or spiritual powers that suggest ways of finding life to be beautiful, meaningful, something one can preserve from death and tragedy. So nowadays mythology usually commands considerable respect.[2]

Several generations ago, mythology commanded less respect because observers tended to focus on its irrational, unscientific, magical aspects. Often mythology seemed the enemy of an intellectual understanding of nature, rational attempts to improve health care and economics, and emancipation from taboos, superstitions, and crippling fears. We have mentioned the negative estimates of Sufism that many Muslim modernizers held—how they considered Sufism a bastion of backwardness. Much the same has applied to modernizers of other traditions: reforming Jews or rationalistic rabbis confronting the mythology indulged by Hasidim, Christian progressives confronting fundamentalist snake-handlers or pilgrims flocking to shrines in hopes of cures, Communist Chinese trying to rid rural villagers of their faith in demons, river sprites, and folk medicine.

Again and again, such attitudes, whether promoted by religious or antireligious people, have combined demythologizing with rationalization. Demythologizing is the effort to replace a storied, rather imaginative or magical view of reality with something more critical, more insistent on hard facts and rigorous logic. Rationalization, as social scientists such as Max Weber have used the term, is the effort to organize social institutions and culture generally in more reasoned—detached, disciplined, objective—ways. For example, when groups move from somewhat hit-or-miss family (clan) sources of help for the poor to government agencies operating according to clear laws or public policies, one can speak of welfare efforts being rationalized. Insofar as such rationalization can mean that the welfare efforts become more efficient, that they reach more people and distribute a group's resources more fairly, one can praise rationalization. Insofar as aid becomes depersonalized, cold, hampered by bureaucratic details, one can long for the less rationalistic, more spontaneous old days.

Relatedly, increasing the quotient of reason in a people's world view and religious existence can bring

gods. Somewhat similarly, when the Buddha preached the Four Noble Truths, he implied that the Indian gods were much less significant than popular Indian religion then held. People of the ancient Near East who heard about the Israelite God YHWH sensed that that God threatened their many naturalistic deities. European tribes who received Christian missionaries learned that if they embraced Christ their fields and streams would have less powerful natural spirits.

In none of these cases did popular religion change so radically that the world lost its mysteriousness and divine power ceased to be significant. Also, each of these reforms or innovations proposed a new object of worship or intense concentration that the innovators hoped would intensify people's efforts to find wholeness by communing with the most significant, sacred powers. Yet, in the maturation of every religious tradition, one can find seeds that only needed certain technological and social developments to manifest their potential for challenging the mythological outlook of the culture at large.

Nowadays scholars tend to be more appreciative of myth than they were a few generations ago, realizing that the stories people have told themselves about their origin, destiny, and identity have been mainstays of their cultures and sanity. By their very concreteness and holism, their very power to grip the imagination

INGREDIENTS OF MODERN ALTERNATIVES TO TRADITIONAL RELIGION	
Natural science and technology	New power over nature Need for independence from Church authority
Political liberalism	Focus on individual rights Sense that modern people had come of age Rejection of Church authority
Historical criticism	Realization that all texts and institutions are historically conditioned
Global exploration	Sense that European theism is only one of many different cultural options
Evolutionary theory	Human beings merely a part of nature Modernity far advanced over ages of faith
Humanism	Primary concern for human affairs
Secularism	Primary interest in "this world" Evil seen as proof there is no God
Marxism	Religion a source of alienation and oppression Concentration on economics and politics

both benefits and losses. Reason can clear up a lot of untidiness that irritated the thoughtful in the group. It can bring the focus back on important things—love of God, love of neighbor—and away from devotion to the saints or concern with cures that had taken center stage. Moreover, it can aid the reform of religious institutions and the lives of religious professionals, lessening the impact of unthinking custom, longtime systems of patronage, longtime assumptions of autocratic powers. Once again, however, people subjected to too sweeping or sudden a demythologizing or reform can feel that they have lost precious old friends. If they were used to praying to the saints or reverencing the clergy as presences of supernatural power, they may find the reformed religion thin beer.

To be sure, it is a far distance from religious reforms to secularism. Most of those who seek to make religious traditions more rational, less mythological in the pejorative sense, have no desire to oust divinity

and make the world (saeculum) seem the be-all and end-all. But whenever one focuses the powers of reason, starts to ask the old myths to make logical sense, wonders whether new ways being tried outside the tribe wouldn't be worth testing, one begins to tinker with the machinery that up to that point had kept the people relatively content and secure. Certainly that should not make people refuse to initiate any innovations, but it suggests why older people tend to become conservative. With experience, they have realized that change often is more radical in its implications than those proposing it realize.

Nonetheless, change is inevitable, as the historical record everywhere shows. Certainly change is not inevitably a move from mythology to rationalization, from a religious immersion in nature's mysteries to a secularist rejection of such mysteries. The lines can go forward or back, up or down, and applying values ("better," "worse") to "forward" and "back" is a perilous venture indeed. So we are not proposing that secularization is necessarily progress (or regress). But we are proposing that lines of change there will be, and as we see in the next sections, the changes associated with the modern period of Western history generally brought demythologizing, rationalization, and a lessening of the influence of traditional religious authority. More and more, this-worldly matters attracted people's energies, while otherworldly matters receded from center stage. More and more countries secularized their law codes and considered public affairs—business, entertainment, even education—something better kept out of the hands of religious professionals. If not considered dead, then, God seemed to be taking more vacations.

Modern Science

One can document the introduction of disciplined, critical, "scientific" reason in the history of several religions. For example, the Buddhist *Abhidhamma* literature, which pored over the experiences of meditation, shows that early Buddhists soon developed a scholastic mind—one passionate about precise definitions, catalogues, and close reasoning. By the time of the fourth-century Christian councils, technical terms had entered the discussion of Christ's nature, and Greek philosophy had become the infrastructure of Christian theological speculation. The rabbis who developed the Mishnah, Gemara, and Talmud show the final results of Second Temple Jewish efforts to establish the religious law as the center of Jewish life.[3] The Neo-Confucians who attempted a philosophy of nature to make their tradition competitive with Buddhist philosophy brought a rationalizing, demythologizing mind to their task. So did the Muslim lawyers and philosophers who tried to make *Sharia* something precise and tried to give Islam a world view clarified by Greek reasoning.

Nonetheless, the only place where what we mean by modern science developed was in the Christian West. Historians of science debate the whys and wherefores of this phenomenon, but it seems clear that neither Greece, India, nor China was fully hospitable to the blend of *empirical* observation and rigorous analysis that developed in the medieval West and flowered with such early moderns as Francis Bacon and Isaac Newton. Greece and India seem to have been inhibited by their sense that the cosmos went through endless cycles, repeating over and over again the same constant trends. True enough, the investigations of nature

one finds in the pre-Socratics and the naturalistic works of Aristotle display many of the intellectual characteristics one associates with modern science. But in fact Greece apparently did not generate sufficient faith in the intelligibility of empirical nature to launch the audacious enterprise begun in the later medieval to early modern West. Similarly, while India and Islam came to house considerable mathematical talent, as well as interesting technologies, their science never became the systematic investigation of nature intrinsic to the institutions of modern science. China certainly developed great technological ingenuity, but again one finds that the world view apparently could not undergird the modern patterns of detailed observation, bold hypotheses, and rigorous verifications.[4] Modern science may in fact have come in recent years into a postmodern phase, in which it requires a more nuanced and less mechanistic philosophy of nature than that which empowered it in the seventeenth, eighteenth, nineteenth, and early twentieth centuries. But it gained its present shape in significant part because its cultural underpinnings included a belief that nature was the creative work of an omniscient deity and human beings were images of that deity through their powerful faculties of reason and will.

The above is certainly a simple-minded sketch of the origins of modern science, and no doubt historians could dispute it at many points. But the exposition of this view that one finds in such distinguished works as Stanley Jaki's Gifford Lectures makes it a reputable hypothesis.[5] What is less questionable and more germane for our purposes is the character and the effects of modern science. Whereas originally the investigation of nature had been a branch of religious philosophy or theology, by the time modernity had become well launched in the *Enlightenment,* science was well on its way to becoming an independent, autonomous enterprise. To be sure, various other branches of knowledge gradually differentiated themselves from the compact medieval world view in which theology was the queen of the sciences and philosophy (which comprised much of what we would now distinguish as physical science, social science, logic, ethics, and political science) was the handmaid. Still, the most dramatic differentiation came through the emancipation of first the philosophy and then the empirical science that studied physical nature.

The dynamics of this differentiation of physical science reveal many of the roots of modern Western secularization. If at first late medieval scientists (some of them monks and clerics) went to nature thinking it a warehouse of of God's works (St. Augustine had said that nature everywhere showed the vestiges of God), gradually the divine origin of nature or the presence of divine power in nature receded into the background. In the foreground, commanding more and more of the interest, were the data and patterns of the natural phenomena themselves. As telescopes and microscopes improved, the range of the data broadened. As speculative naturalists saw the need for more powerful theoretical tools for handling the data and explicating the patterns, mathematics made leaps into such areas as calculus. True, the early modern scientific giants—Newton, Pascal, Leibniz—were philosophers as much as what we would call natural scientists. But large portions of their work and thought treated nature as a somewhat autonomous realm possessing laws that human reason (relatively or completely unaided by special divine graces) could master.

Such mastery had a twofold significance. On the one hand, there was the pure desire to know how nature was constituted—to understand how the planets moved, how peas changed genetically, how the blood circulated through the human body. On the other hand, there was the desire to bring nature more fully under human control. Francis Bacon, especially, proposed the thesis that scientific knowledge amounted to power. Modern technology owes much of its origin to this thesis, since everything from modern medicine to modern engineering could be promoted as research and application geared to increasing humanity's power to bend nature to its service.

In the controversy between the astronomer Galileo and the authorities of the Catholic church early in the seventeenth century, the old theological ways clashed with the new scientific ways quite dramatically. Galileo has been vindicated and made a champion by later modernity, but it is important to realize that in his own day his proposals were bound to seem impious. God then was thought much more immediately involved in the running of the natural world, and the priority of divine revelation (necessary for salvation from sin) was considered much more important than any understanding or practical benefits the investigation of nature might bring. Certainly most present-day theologians would say the Catholic authorities were unwise to connect a geocentric view of the solar system with Christian orthodoxy, but historians of ideas know that everywhere traditional peoples have tied their sense of how the cosmos came into being and was structured with their doctrinal and eth-

ical systems.[6] Certainly the vindication of Galileo was a victory for intellectual honesty, and certainly intellectual honesty should be high among the virtues religion defends. But in historical perspective it is not surprising that redefining faith so that it proved compatible with an intellectual honesty on the model of the autonomous investigations and speculations of modern science turned out to be a painful, traumatic business.

At any rate, their immersion in the data of physical nature, their sometimes intoxicating experience of the speculative powers of the human mind, and their witness of the practical changes to which scientific discoveries could lead when transmuted into modern technology all increased the scientists' conviction that they were the wave of the future. So science steadily developed its own canons of procedure, indeed its own orthodoxies.[7] The success of this development, combined with the greater wealth and health people came to enjoy from the labors of scientists and engineers, made the reservations of religious professionals seem either sour grapes or sheer timidity. Not until recent decades, when nuclear power burst on the scene with terrifying prospects of annihilation, chemistry and biology revealed horrible possibilities for polluting the earth, and military weaponry became unimaginably lethal, did confidence in modern science and technology take a significant body blow. Even now, huge portions of Western culture continue to cope with these and vast other problems (hunger, homelessness, drugs, economic dysfunctions, widespread criminality) as though physical science, technology, and behavioral science were the best sources for remedies. Religious believers, many of them fundamentalists, certainly oppose such an assumption, but it remains to be seen whether antiscientific religion proves any more effective than antireligous scientism and secularity. Religion that affirms the independence and value of science, and science that honors the mystery at the core of religion, could be good neighbors.

Liberalism

If modern science was the great arena in which independence of traditional religious authorities seemed to prove fruitful, modern political thought was the great arena in which the rights of human beings began to be defined apart from humanity's debts to the grace of God. There are many words and movements one could use to describe this political turn away from traditional, supposedly divine norms to rights defined by human beings themselves, but "liberalism" can stand duty for a goodly number of them. Probably the most influential liberal thinker was the Englishman John Locke (1632–1704), but other thinkers in England, France, Germany, and the United States both drew upon his thought and advanced it in new directions. Locke studied the classics, lectured on moral philosophy, and then took training as a physician. He became a political confidant of Lord Ashley, Earl of Shaftesbury, who led the parliamentary opposition to the Stuart kings. In 1675 Locke made a prolonged visit to France, where he deepened his understanding of the ideas of the French philosopher René Descartes, and in 1683 he was forced to follow Shaftesbury into political exile in Holland.

Locke's political philosophy ran to a constitutional monarchy, a parliamentary government, and an enumeration of human rights. Life, liberty, and property summarized much of his platform, which had great influence in the eighteenth-century revolutions in both the United States and France. While Locke wrote treatises in defense of the reasonableness of Christianity, his understanding of human nature in fact was considerably more empiricist (considerably less mythological) than that of traditional Christianity. Although raised as a Puritan, he tended to treat of theological themes (the existence of God, revelation) in a rather restrained way, separating faith from what one can determine by empirical reason. This helped him undergird an instinct that true religion is tolerant of others' religious opinions. Relatedly, Locke was skeptical of the claims of any one church or religious group to know with certainty the way to salvation. In the trade-off between institutional authority and the rights of individual conscience, he came down for individual conscience.[8]

One can see, then, that while Locke kept ties to prior views of religion and the priority of the divine, he paved the way for the later liberal stress on humanism. As science seemed to place more and more of the natural world under the influence of human beings, and as religious institutions showed themselves conservatively opposed to progress in either physical science or political efforts to emancipate people from the destructive control of kings or aristocratic classes, Lockean principles justified emphasizing the truth human beings could discover on their own and the political freedoms that ought to flow from considering the individual conscience something precious, indeed, something sacred. Many liberals in fact assumed that social morality would continue to follow patterns indebted to Christian culture, but liberalism itself tended to erode the doctrinal bases of that morality.

Two centuries after Locke, John Stuart Mill advanced the liberal outlook, writing persuasively about individual liberties (which included the emancipation of women). In France, Jean Jacques Rousseau had brought forward romantic notions of the benefits that would accrue were human beings left free to have their unspoiled (relatively unsocialized) natures develop. In the economic sphere, Adam Smith, the Scottish economist (or moral philosopher), had advocated laissez-faire policies that would give maximum play to individual initiative, trusting that a free market would somehow manage the best possible development and distribution of wealth.

What these various "liberal" thinkers held in common was a stress (now more, now less, exclusive) on the freedom of individual human beings to run their own lives. Often they assumed social agreements and controls that their later successors did not assume, but in general they wanted to move away from strict controls by either Church or state that would inhibit people from choosing to become what they thought best. Theological traditionalists tended to criticize such liberalism by arguing that sin made human beings much less trustworthy than the liberals assumed, while political conservatives argued that power was well handled by only a few and liberalism opened the door to anarchy. On the whole, the religious and political establishments supported one another in offering cautions against liberal views.

Whether or not they explicitly cast aside traditional religious guidance and traditional religious views of God and human nature, liberals tended to put divinity in the shade. They were more interested in such this-worldly questions as political freedoms, educational reforms, and license to develop entrepreneurial projects. The Industrial Revolution was an ambiguous phenomenon, for on the one hand it brought this-worldly expertise and drive to bear on creating previously unknown disbursements of wealth, while on the other hand it severely limited the actual liberty of thousands of workers. Behind the liberal stress on individual conscience lay the stress of the Protestant reformers on the rights of individual conscience in religious matters, but the reformers and their heirs certainly had assumed the priority of divine revelation.

Insofar as liberalism meant being free of oppressive authorities, it ran in tandem with many themes of the eighteenth-century Enlightenment. Both movements were excited at the prospect of human beings coming of age sufficiently to think for themselves, depend on their own resources, and solve their main political, economic, and technological tasks with energy and confidence. For both, traditional religion often seemed a source of ignorance and repression, so both contrasted human autonomy with an older, religiously based heteronomy, arguing that it was more honest, profitable, and fitting that human beings look to themselves.

As one can easily imagine, such a call to self-reliance tended to produce both fits of enthusiasm and fits of depression. While people who had chafed under what they took to be repressive theological or political regimes found the humanistic message emancipating, people who found human ingenuity or human goodness unequal to the tasks of producing wealth in which all might share and developing a fully inclusive political system could despair of life apart from divine assurances and controls. The freedom to which the liberal thinkers called their fellow human beings held both terrors and joys. To those who felt strong enough to depend on themselves, it was good news, pressed down and overflowing. To those who longed for a tidy sense of reality, a map through time that would lay things out quite neatly, the liberal call could seem a siren song portending disaster.

Nonetheless, liberal thought gained sufficient influence in modern Europe and modern America to become a dominant political outlook. For example, the instinctive belief of the typical citizen of the United States that one has the right to run one's own life with little outside interference owes much to the liberal tradition. Through history, of course, many notions originally associated with the liberal thinkers have been transferred to latter-day "conservatives," this instinct for individual autonomy primary among them. Under whatever label, however, originally liberal ideas have challenged the traditional religious systems that made God's laws the major determinant of everyday behavior and gave religious institutions the main say in determining what was real or how people ought to live.

Marxism

In the nineteenth century, Karl Marx (1818–1883) was the main influence in shifting liberal ideas into the sphere of economics. For Marx, *atheism* was a necessary postulate of human freedom, while the principal subjugation human beings suffered came from the exploitation of the working classes by their capitalist bosses. Marx saw history as a dialectical interplay of such forces as evolutionary matter and class conflicts. Although he borrowed considerably from the German idealistic philosopher G. W. F. Hegel (1770–1831), Marx had little patience with Hegel's interests in the operations of the divine Spirit. To his mind, the worlds of politics and economics, which mutually determined one another, were the things upon which to concentrate.

All this might have been peaceful enough had Marx not added the further notion that philosophy itself ought to be changed. Whereas in the past philosophers had thought of their task as being to understand or interpret the world, in modern times it had become clear that the great task was to change the world. In other words, Marx gave a certain priority to action or praxis over thought. But where other thinkers of such a practical bent, including the American pragmatists (Dewey, Peirce, James), refrained from advocating violent or revolutionary programs, Marx, his associate Engels, and his most influential interpreters Lenin and Mao all wanted to embody Marxist principles in strikes, uprisings, and revolutions that would take power from the oppressive ruling classes and place it in the working classes (whom they themselves would direct).

Scholars debate the extent to which Marx would have opposed a religion that made justice toward the poor a primary goal, but there is little debating about the general impact of Marxist thought upon the religious attitudes of those who espoused it. Marxist groups became the leading representatives of a wider socialist movement that regularly targeted religious bodies as props of an oppressive status quo. In the name of human progress toward justice and prosperity, they regularly denounced old religious beliefs and practices. For some, God and Jesus were not great problems, because they could be interpreted as champions of the poor. But for others, anything religious, otherworldly, dealing with spirituality and the sacred was atavistic—a throwback to the days of superstition and degenerate myth. Now that human beings had come of age, as modern science and technology surely showed they had, such backwardness was immoral. Those who indulged in it were either hopeless fools or knowing manipulators of forces designed to keep the common people in thrall to the owners—factory workers, upper-class nabobs—who were so handsomely profiting from their sweat.

Although Marxist groups often have been better at rhetoric than hard analysis, and although often their own accession to power has brought worse repressions than those they had promised to end, much of the Marxist vision has entered into the liberal humanistic tradition, as a sort of further transfusion of energy and idealism. Whereas the original liberals were rather individualistic and did not criticize the socioeconomic construction of reality with great penetration, Marx and his followers studied labor and capitalism with considerable acumen. In line with many of the ideas of the biblical prophets, they denounced piety that did not pay off in justice, indeed did not produce mercy and helpfulness toward society's least well-off. In their critiques of religion, they tended to demonstrate how religion could be an ideology: a scaffolding of ideas that supported current economic and political arrangements and so went hand in glove with the interests of the wealthy classes.

This sense of "ideology," according to which every group puts forward ideas, even a systematic world view, that works to its own advantage, of course could be turned back on the Marxists themselves, but usually they exempted their own positions, calling them expositions of such supposedly unassailable truths as the laws of class conflict, the determinism of economic factors, and the necessity of atheism. Of course this made the Marxists as dogmatic as any religious or politically conservative group they were attacking, but somehow they regularly managed to keep themselves from confronting such countercharges. Where they might have availed themselves of the insights of Friedrich Nietzsche (1844–1900) that all philosophers tend to build thought-systems that defend themselves, and that European culture by the mid-nineteenth century in effect had killed the living God (the God who called for creativity and spiritual life) by its hypocrisy and mediocrity, the Marxists preferred to style themselves "scientific" and so shied away from such poetry.

Marxism of course has changed shape considerably in the twentieth century, but what has remained constant in its many incarnations as the inspiration of political revolutions has been its assurances that history is on the side of the lower, working classes, who have only to rise up and fight their oppressors to advance the day when there will be a classless, egalitarian society. The Soviet and Chinese Communist regimes have been the two outstanding examples of wholesale efforts to remake states by Marxist principles, and the successes and failures of both have proved highly illuminating. For on the one hand both have certainly improved the material lot of their common people, while on the other hand neither has scrupled to shed rivers of blood in putting down any individuals or groups they felt threatened their dogmatic programs.

In these two Marxist regimes, the twentieth century has had object lessons in the assets and liabilities of a humanism defined as a break with traditional recourse to divine laws about human behavior. The third great object lesson, the Nazi regime of the 1930s and 1940s, certainly stemmed from different philosophical (or mythical) foundations, but it furnished an equally powerful lesson. The wrath of the movement was particularly directed against the Jews, whom the Nazis blamed for all modern evils, but Christians soon realized that Nazism was equally antithetical to their own views, requiring them to choose between Christ and the Führer.

Marxism, Nazism, and other forms of this-worldly, secularistic thought (scientific humanism, for example) certainly require careful study as individual developments, but for our purposes in this chapter they mainly are significant as examples of the rapidity with which modernity raced away from traditional religion. By the middle of the twentieth century, only four hundred years or so from the beginnings of the modern scientific, political, and philosophical stirrings, the mainstreams of Western art, science, and general culture serenely ignored God and traditional religious doctrines. Darwinian biology, modern geology, Einsteinian physics, Freudian psychology, and the sociology indebted to Comte, Weber, and Durkheim all inclined moderns to think that nature, society, and the self were all there was. "God" was at best a projection of human ideals, while religious tradition was at best a hodgepodge of commonsensical observations about humanity's place in a mysterious world. The experience of war and political unrest in the first half of the twentieth century had been enough to convince many moderns that meaning was nowhere to be found. History, whether recent or ancient, showed mainly a record of barbarities, while the new powers that science and technology were unveiling gave more reason for fear than hope. The result was the great wasteland dramatized somewhat self-indulgently by the existentialist literature that flourished after World War II. Human beings, in the phrase of Jean-Paul Sartre, were nothing but useless passions. They had no definite essence, nothing by way of a nature fashioned by God (which might have given them guidance). Their burden was to be completely free, and so completely responsible for what they made of themselves.

In contrast, much psychology and sociology was deterministic, teaching that early family life or social conditioning left people little if any freedom. Religion therefore found itself disregarded on two sides. Existentialists said that human freedom was incompatible with the existence of God, while much social science said that freedom, and so choice about ultimate destiny, were largely illusory.

Industrialization, urbanization, and the increasing complexity of business and national life all served to reinforce the secularist tendency not to accept the stimulus from physical nature to contemplate the turning of the seasons. Relatedly, the rush and relative superficiality of urban and suburban life tended to deflect people from pondering the mysteries of human community and selfhood, perhaps for fear they would glimpse the void or feel human life to be like vapor over a volcano.

Paradoxically enough, therefore, by the end of the third quarter of the twentieth century humanistic, this-worldly intellectual currents themselves were inclining many people to take up religious questions again. Although often they did not realize it, when such people tried to find ways to assure human existence some ultimate meaning they rejoined the great stream of what some have called the perennial philosophy—the sense of the whole that had made wonder at the mystery of existence the primary foundation of culture.[9]

WORLDVIEW

Nature and Divinity in Humanistic Perspective

Humanism is a term we have left undefined to this point, because we wanted to set it alongside secularism and let them both pick up rough and ready connotations from history. However, at this point it would be well to focus more clearly on both terms. Since the Italian Renaissance, *humanism* has connoted a turn to the human figure in art, a return to the classical literature of Greece and Rome that celebrated human pathos, and an assertion that human experience is worthy of interest and concern (in contrast to theological tendencies to deprecate human experience as disfigured by sin and overshadowed by the death and judgment soon to terminate one's passage through this vale of tears). One can connect humanism with religious views, as Christian humanists especially have done, in which case it tends to mean celebrating the grandeur of what God has done in making men and women of flesh and spirit. So, for example, the Christian father Irenaeus sang that God's glory was human beings fully alive. In recent years, humanism has become the bugbear of religious fundamentalists, who have contrasted it with a faith-filled acceptance of the primacy of God. Where religion has said life ought to be God-centered, arrogant humanists have said that human beings ought to be the measure and interest of all our doings. Thus humanism (or "secular humanism") has been taken to be atheistic, in fact if not in outright profession.

Secularization is the process by which this-worldly things have become more important and heavenly things have faded into the background. Industrialization, urbanization, and the demythologizing effects of scientific and critical thinking usually are nominated as major reasons why secularization has occurred in the modern West (and, through the cultural exports of the modern West, in other parts of the globe). Secularization is ethically neutral—whether it has been good or bad depends on further premises and judgments. *Secularism* is the viewpoint, the philosophical position, that secularization has been good because otherworldliness was a distraction or a vitiation of human development. In other words, secularism assumes or argues that God, grace, salvation, sin, and the other staples of the religious world views that have urged people to look beyond the here and now for their ultimate meaning have all been misguided notions.

Once again, one can make some distinctions and point out that many religious traditions have sponsored a sort of this-worldliness and so a sort of secularism. Christians claiming that the incarnation of Christ and the sacramental system made space and time God's chosen theater of salvation have been religiously this-worldly. Buddhists urging people to concentrate on the here and now, to find nirvana in the midst of samsara, to realize there is no self or Brahman behind or beyond the network of dharmas, have also been religiously this-worldly. But both usually have denied that human beings are the ultimate norm and measure. Rather, both usually have argued that human beings only find their full, proper measure when they realize they are situated in something greater than themselves: the mystery of God or the grandeur of the cosmic buddha-nature.

Through these semantic forays, we have suggested much of what secular humanists tend to think about nature and divinity. For those who do make human beings and/or this world of space and time the be-all and end-all, physical nature tends to be given rather than created. It did not arise from the creative fiat of a supreme power transcending the world. It is a fascinating system of material forces, but where it is going or what brought it into being is beyond our reckoning. It has no moral implications, and how human beings interact with it should be determined by such factors as the value one places on its beauty, its being the matrix of all life and thought, its having preexisted human beings, and its potential services to human beings, both present and future. Some secular humanists do find nature dwarfing human concerns and restoring perspective. Others find contemplating nature ultimately depressing, because the icy wastes of space and the infinities of both subatomic and cellular beings reveal nothing that cares about humankind. Insofar as all of nature heads toward destruction (entropy) and death, the matrix of humanity can seem casual—without either purpose or care. On the other hand, the grandeur of sunrise and sunset, the immensities of space and time, the variety and staggering beauty of the myriad species, and even the wonders of the human body and mind can all cause secular humanists to break out in praise. How far such praise is from what religious people do in acclaiming the Lord of the Worlds is a nice question.

The divinity of secular humanism either is completely missing—nonexistent—or lodges in the implications of behavior (such as acclamation of physical nature) that in fact seems to hunger for a purpose for human existence. When God is missing from people's world views, emotions, and practical calculations, the other three basic dimensions of reality tend to collapse together. Either nature, society, or the self may predominate, pulling the others more fully into its orbit by an intellectual gravity, but all three have only implicit grounding. For "God" and its equivalents function in human mentality as the ground and context for all other thought. They indicate, however vaguely,

the horizon, the backdrop, the whence and whither that neither nature, nor society, nor the self provides. One may say that concern about such a whence and whither is illusory or profitless. One may readily confess that questions about them move one to a transempirical realm where the mind may well be making up its data. But the fact remains that limiting one's constructions of reality to what sense and reason can produce by focusing on the phenomenal aspects of nature, society, and the self doesn't match what past cultures have dealt with nor what any healthy mind can be shown to vector toward.

Hindu, Buddhist, Taoist, Jewish, Christian, and Muslim cultures (to cite only the most obvious) all have concerned themselves with questions, experiences, perhaps realities that transcended "nature," "society," and "self" understood in empirical (sense-experienced) terms. Any healthy mind can be brought to a quiet and wonder that realize they are on the frontier of what may be a different sort of reality by placing it before a dead person and asking what the person's life has meant, or where the spirit of the person has gone, or why someone who enjoyed life should have to die, or what the outreach of the human mind and heart toward an understanding and love greater than mortality signifies. One doesn't have to answer these questions to sense the realm of *transcendence* that has meant so much to traditional religious cultures. One has only to raise them—only experience one's spirit move out toward them or be enveloped by their mystery. To be sure, many nominal atheists, humanists, and secularists have felt their spirits move into such mysterious matters. The question, then, is whether in fact they have lived apart from divinity and whether in consequence their world views have adequately accounted for their own spiritual experiences.

Society and Self in Humanistic Perspective

Areligious humanism may exalt society as the proper focus of human interest and endeavor, or it may view society as the source of most human corruption. By and large, the modern totalitarianisms have taken the first option, making "the people" the justification for their policies, whether benign or murderous. What has tended to suffer in modern humanistic social thought is the notion that "community" itself is a mysterious creation, a whole much greater than the sum of its parts and so a wonder suggesting divine aid.[10] To be sure, people who share military, political, or cultural ventures usually experience bonding. The question remains, however, what makes such bonding sacred—valuable enough to warrant reverence and sacrifice. Much the same question attends human love, as we shall see when we come to humanistic perspectives on the self.

On their own terms, most humanists do not raise such further questions. A few reflective humanists do not raise them as a matter of principle, having judged or postulated that such questions bring no profit or deal with a transcendent realm about which we can at best be agnostic. The majority of secular humanists, however, simply don't have the spiritual interest, need, or drive to press their first views of community toward something foundational. In this they are like the majority of believers, whose faith is equally uncritical. Nonetheless, secular humanism certainly can be developed into an impressive view of human community, if only by a logic such as the following.

Assume that there is no God demanding to be set at the center of one's system. Then survey what remains of human experience for what seems most valuable. You may decide that nature is the most valuable portion of reality, and so dedicate yourself to understanding, conserving, or developing nature. You may decide that personal freedom, individual autonomy, is the most precious thing you know, and so hymn the life of the artist, or the entrepreneur, or any other species of self that relies mainly on its own resources and tries to create meaning through its work or its love. If you choose either of these two courses, you certainly will not be alone. But probably you will find yourself with more company if you decide that helping suffering fellow human beings, or trying to create peaceful and beautiful human communities, best expresses your sense of where a godless world seems most worth inhabiting.

So one finds dedicated but humanistic doctors, lawyers, teachers, social workers, politicians, and the like who give their lives to helping other people or trying to bring peace and justice to a given portion of global society. One finds internationalists, even diplomats and soldiers, who have made their own the cause of trying to stay the forces of evil that ruin life for so many. Certainly it is rare to find someone both completely dedicated and fully convinced that all such social effort in no way reaches beyond the grave, but it is not unknown, perhaps not even extraordinary.

In a brave sort of *agnosticism,* many good people place brackets around ultimate questions and content themselves with doing here and now something they can be sure will make a positive difference. So they set broken bones, try to repair broken marriages, arbitrate grievances between owners and workers, try to smooth relations between alienated or warring nations. Realizing that most societies are much less just and enjoyable than they might be, such humanists decide they will spend themselves playing midwife to the birth of a somewhat better world. However slight their success, it will justify their time spent as police, firefighters, nurses, ministers of a gospel they believe centers on brother- and sisterhood.

The self emerges in humanistic perspective no less mysteriously than it does in religious perspective, because any probing of the self—psychological, artistic, medical—runs into reams of unknown factors. We have learned a great deal about the physical and psychological mechanisms that go into a human identity, yet we are so far from understanding the whole that what we have learned clearly is but a fraction of all there is to know. How our brains work, how our hormones interact with our brains, whether we have souls, how our nerves quicken our bodies, what causes some people to have brilliant memories, or imaginations, or computational skills, what causes other people to suffer severe depression, or schizophrenia, or to be idiot savants—these and hundreds of other aspects of selfhood await full understanding. We don't know why some people are shy and other people extroverted. We don't understand how children acquire language so easily, so naturally. Biological clocks, bodily intelligence, intuition, orgasm, mystical experience, loss of confidence, the acquisition of a social persona, the processes of aging—these research topics only skim the surface.

But perhaps the greatest of the self's mysteries continues to be the encounters with other selves that bring the healing and fulfillment associated with "love." Love is so common a phenomenon, and yet so precious a flower, that we understandably find it bruited about everywhere, advertised in the cheapest of bookstores, collapsed into sex to sell automobiles. Romantic love, the love of friendship, parental love, love of nature, love of God, love of creative work, the love that arises when two or three gather in the name of a common cause, suffering love, self-love—on and on the varieties go. Love is the foremost energy of the self, not to be divorced from the self's eros for knowledge but more central and profound. Children who are not loved do not thrive. Adults who are not loved and do not love in return do not thrive. Love naturally overflows into teaching, guiding, caring for, trying to heal, trying to help make amends. It takes form as forgiveness, reconciliation, peacemaking. And all of these forms of love, all of these facets of the self's adventure in search of love, of course intrigue humanists as much as religious people—sometimes more.

The humanistic self may be in special danger of turning narcissistic, but the religious self is in special danger of alienation—prematurely surrendering the self to "God" and so never maturing, becoming responsible, developing a healthy self-esteem. The humanistic self may be in special danger of despairing, since its philosophy offers it no ultimate reason for its brief time in the sun. On the other hand, the religious self can be repulsively full of answers, a know-it-all confusing the mystery of God with the doctrines of its little church, synagogue, mosque, or sect. On its own terms, the humanistic self has to consider the religious self liable to the same anxieties it is and so a fit object for compassion. On its own terms, the religious self has to say that the divine mystery plays in all people's lives, wooing them at the center where they occasionally go still and wonder about the whole. Neither humanistic wholeness nor religious grace can rightly be considered the exclusive preserve of a favored few.

Everywhere, people who enter into themselves, center down, and face both their terrors and their joys find an ambiguous darkness. Is it the blank nothingness of nature's muteness, the near side of a cosmic and personal meaninglessness? Or is it the cloud of unknowing about which the mystics speak, the presence of a God who can never be understood and always must be accepted in trust? Positioned this way, the two selves, humanistic and religious, seem more alike than different. The honest humanist who does not know about ultimacy and fears that professing faith would be hypocritical seems little different from the honest believer who confesses that God or the buddha-nature can never be mastered, will always force human hearts to abide in mute hope.

SUMMARY: THE HUMANISTIC CENTER

Although there are many varieties of humanists (people who do not configure reality in terms of God or a transcendent ultimate reality), they all qualify as humanists because they make humankind the main treasure or focus of their lives. A few think that the natural world onto which human intelligence opens is the most important consequence of there being a species that can understand and reflect, but more are preoccupied with social and personal questions. Indeed, probably the most typical center in a humanistic world view is the border between society and the self, where the group and the individual interact to construct "reality." Let us muse about this interaction.

Among the unreflective, who one is and for what one should strive tend to come from informal public opinion. "Image" is a great interest and influence, shaping young women to aspire toward beauty and power on the model of what they see in glamour magazines, studies of women's impact in the business world, or more traditional projections of what it might mean to be a wife and mother. Young men are manipulated by images of success in the work world, on the athletic field, with foxy ladies who admire their looks, muscles, brains, or tenderness. These many variations on the theme of the images laid out by one's society determine much of what plays in people's heads as they work at the main task of late adolescence and early adulthood: fashioning a self, a personal identity and sense of the world.

In traditional, premodern societies, most people gained their personal identity and sense of the world through dramatic rites of passage. At puberty and marriage they appropriated their people's sense of how reality was configured, of what the ultimate powers expected of a man or a woman. With the demise of the great, guiding myths typical of premodern societies, the social shaping of personal identities has become more diffuse and confused. Indeed, at times it seems that young people are the main targets in a war for influence over the future generation. Certainly parents, teachers, coaches, and friends continue to exert major influences, but the lack of heroic role models means that many young people will have only middling confidence that they know what they would like to become.

What is it that the typical secular humanist wants to become? Our estimate is someone self-reliant, realistic, and free. There being no privileged revelation in the humanistic world view, one has to make do with the best wisdom one can glean from either past humanistic traditions or personal experience. The best educated of humanists working with these tools soon find that little has changed in their project since the time that Plato or the Buddha ventured forth. Drop the few trappings of myth and divinity one finds in the Platonic dialogues or the sutras of the Buddha and you have two interesting models of the effort to find meaning without recourse to religious institutions. In fact, both Plato and the Buddha ended with visions of transcendent reality, but their methods seem quite amenable to adaptation by modern humanists.

In creating the literary identity of Socrates, Plato described a man bent on wringing wisdom from his experience, deflating the pompous fools who trumpeted unthinkingly about tradition, and listening to the inner voice of conscience, which he called his *daimon*. Socrates became the wisest man in Athens because he learned how much he didn't know—most of his wisdom was negative. For Plato the death of Socrates was a telling judgment on Athenian society. If the polis could not see the worth of the one man who might have saved its culture, it was blind unto spiritual death. The Platonic notion that one would only have a decent polis if one gained a philosopher-king extrapolated from the death of Socrates: the chance that a truly wise person would come to secular power was slim indeed.

The Buddha was humanistic in not relying on past Indian tradition but basing his teaching on his personal experience. Certainly he was formed by Indian meditation techniques and philosophical assumptions, but the crucial aspects of his medicinal program drew their authority from his own enlightenment experience. Above all, the proposition that the way to escape suffering is to eliminate desire went to the heart of every person's existence, presenting itself as something anyone might test at home.

In latter days, humanists have been most true to their own principles when they have followed Socrates and the Buddha in focusing on personal experience. In arguing that religious tradition was folly, they were most persuasive when they challenged religious institutions to show how religious doctrines formed people who were happy, productive, and left the world better for their having passed through it. In the light of such a challenge, the religions that had been responsible for slaughter in warfare, repression in sexual life, poverty in subjugation to wealthy upper classes, and crippling fear of divine wrath stood revealed as inhumane, perhaps even antihuman. On the other hand, the religions that could point to mystics rapt in love of a good God, to men and women spending themselves in caring for the poor, the sick, and the uneducated, and to thinkers who took away some of the sting of death and injustice, stood up to the humanists' challenge. Usually they had already accepted a pragmatism such as that of Jesus and agreed that one could know any group or intellectual position by the fruits it grew.

The perennial value of humanistic approaches to life resides in such pragmatism. By focusing intensely on what happens to human beings, how they are hurt or helped by the thought-systems they indwell, humanists have reminded all with ears to hear that what people promise is less significant than what people do. For a philosophical theologian, the implication of this reminder is that positions, theories about nature, society, self, and divinity, are best developed from what people who operate successfully in those areas must assume.

For example, no less a master in the realm of nature than Albert Einstein advised that one pay more attention to what successful scientists do than to what they say (about either the nature of science or the construction of nature). Applied in the political realm, this advice would imply that one should construct theories of human community from the instances of success—the times and places when people in fact have lived together peacefully, justly, making a profound culture in which buying and selling were in the service of art, science, and social service. Applied to the realm of the self, it would imply that one pay more attention to the dynamics at work in creative artists, creative scientists, signally successful parents, and people signally whole than to psychoanalytic, behavioristic, or other theories about human selfhood. Last, one would best explore the significance of divinity by examining the lives of the saints, the mystics who have communed with God, and the reformers who have spent themselves redeeming people from sin.

In all such experientially focused studies, one of course would run smack into evil, destruction, the dark side of human existence. The pessimistic humanisms pay such heed to this admittedly gigantic side that they come away with little hope that peace or justice will ever prevail. Perhaps the best question then becomes why light has continued to shine in the midst of such darkness, why the darkness has failed to snuff it out. For the metaphysician, the thrust of this question is toward the roots of existence, where one must wonder why there is something rather than nothing. For the anthropologist, the question becomes why creativity, goodness, and even holiness continue to emerge, generation after generation.

Are the light we have, the being that keeps nothingness at bay, the positive aspects of human nature sufficient to make life worth living? Humanists, no less than religious believers, all have to answer that question for themselves. No doctrinaire answer, humanistic or religious, cuts the mustard. At the heart of the human being, in the inalienable voice of conscience, all of us find our lives spelling out and boiling down to a radical choice. Will we say—are we saying—yes or no to the hands we have been dealt, the world in which we have been placed, the self we have received and made, the mystery into which all intimations of ultimacy usher us? Because this is the question we authors find at the center of the humanistic perspective, we think (with some amusement) that the center of the humanistic perspective is another window onto transcendence and ultimate mystery.

Discussion Questions

1. How has the tendency toward rationalization within the world religions contributed to demythologizing and secularization?

2. What are the advantages and disadvantages in bringing reason to bear on divine mystery?

3. Why did the empirical turn of modern science tend to dilute the premodern awe about nature?

4. How might empiricism coexist with a myth-making mind?

5. From what have most of the modern political liberals wanted to be free?

6. For what have most of the modern political liberals wanted to be free?

7. Why was classical Marxism dogmatically atheistic?

8. How has Marxism joined its analyses of work, ideology, and class conflict?

9. What are the main characteristics of a scientific humanism that makes nature and scientific method the kingpins of its world view?

10. What do the humanistic philosophies tend to put in the place of divinity when they try to configure the major dimensions of reality?

11. What should be the consequences of a humanistic philosophy that is pessimistic about the effects of socialization (formation by the common mores of one's group)?

12. Is there a core to the self that ties it to something or someone transcending its biology and culture formation? Why?

13. What should one conclude from the capacity and inclination of the human being to keep raising further questions?

14. How different would a balanced religious humanism be from a balanced secular humanism, and what would "balanced" mean in each case?

Glossary

agnosticism: the position that one does not know the ultimate structure of things. While there have always been some agnostics, Western modernity was the first historical period to associate agnosticism with a mainstream secularistic humanism. Within religions, agnosticism can suggest a mature theological or philosophical appreciation of the mysteriousness bound to attend God or ultimate reality.

atheism: the position that there is no God (or that none of the theologies or religions renders what would be worthy of a true God). While atheism has always had a small presence in developed religious cultures, because skeptics have always had intellectual or social reasons for thinking that no worthy deity could have sponsored the popular religion of the time, only in modern Western culture did a significant portion of the intelligentsia make atheism the prevailing assumption. Modern science and technology seemed to remove the need for a transcendent divinity, while the ambiguity of modern religious groups (their warfare, opposition to progress, and occasional venality or philistinism) made it easy to mock religion's claims to be representing the Creator or Savior of the world.

empiricism: the philosophical outlook that stresses sense experience and limits speculation. While one may point to instances in which empiricism has been religiously motivated, for instance, as an effort to live out a Christian incarnationalist view of reality, or a Hindu sacramental view, or a Buddhist conviction that nirvana is best found in the midst of the particulars of samsara, generally empiricism is a foe of religion, insofar as it finds little basis for the transcendental speculations that probe the nature of ultimate reality or God and finds equally little basis for the contemplative activities that try to deal with a formless, nonparticular, or specific whole.

Enlightenment: the eighteenth-century European movement that stressed the untrammeled use of human reason. Spurred by discoveries in natural science, many Enlightenment philosophers (Voltaire, Kant) urged human beings to take charge of their own lives, throwing off the constraints of Church authorities and traditional dogmas and becoming more autonomous. Through this Enlightenment modern critical history, social science, and other humanistic disciplines came to assume that their independent researches could produce valuable, perhaps definitive insights into the human condition and the build of reality itself.

humanism: an appreciation of human virtues and needs that leads on to focus on human concerns, sometimes to the neglect of divinity or ultimate reality. Humanism may go hand in hand with religion, or it may appear to be religion's enemy. The social programs of the religions, and their appreciation for the wonders of human nature, tend to make them humanistic. However, when humanism becomes delimiting—a way of saying that human beings are the measure or the limit—religion usually must protest. Religion lives from transcendence: going beyond any present attainment, reaching out to the infinite. Humanism can define itself so as to be compatible with such transcendence, but frequently it does not. Secular humanism expressly does not, taking its name from the this-worldly horizon that at best brackets divine transcendence.

Marxism: the politicoreligious system of philosophical thought and socioeconomic practice that has devolved from the work of Karl Marx. What Marx himself set out in germ regarding labor, capital, ideology, religion, class conflict, and the like has served as the basis for Marxist developments, but present-day Marxists often use terms and work with theories unknown in Marx's day. V. I. Lenin and Mao Zedong have probably been the most influential Marxist thinkers, each taking the thought of Marx (and Engels) in new directions. "Marxism" is now a quite protean notion, almost as much in need of further specification as "Christianity." It always denotes some debt to the thought of Karl Marx, and usually it connotes a dialectical materialism and commitment to achieving a classless society. Beyond that, convictions sometimes seem as numerous as there are Marxist writers.

secularism: the worldly view of existence that tends to deprecate transcendence and so be at odds with traditional religion. Secularism can have a healthy connotation, in which it is close to sacramentality in insisting on the worth and significance of this-worldliness: the human body, social justice, the production of culture. So doing, it rightly combats an otherworldliness that would deprecate the body, sexuality, social justice, beauty, and the other entailments of an incarnational religion. However, secularism regularly runs aground on the questions of death and evil, for which its this-worldliness provides no explanation or healing. The religious response that does claim to provide an explanation of sorts and healing would insert divine, more than worldly powers into space and time. Calling such an insertion grace or enlightenment, it would argue that the human being, human culture, and even the whole physical world cannot be themselves—realize their potential—on their own. What they postulate for fulfillment and beg for healing must come to them from an otherness, outside or within, that is free of the limits (physical, intellectual, moral) one finds in all creation.

transcendence: going beyond the usual limits, often out to the divine. One source of the human tendency to associate transcendence with divinity is the drive of the human spirit to know more and love more. A certain limitlessness in the human makeup suggests that the goal of human intentionality has to be a limitless intelligibility and love. Relatedly, human images of growth and maturation suggest that people ought always to be making progress, spiritually if not physically. The barriers human beings run into—death, ignorance, moral weakness—raise the question whether there is anything on the other side. Thus Buddhists have longed for the wisdom that has gone beyond the stream of human suffering. Other traditions, such as Judaism, Christianity, and Islam, have made divinity transcendent of the world and have spoken of a Judgment that would mediate human beings' way to living with the divinity definitively. Transcendence would seem to be polar to immanence (the inward presence of divinity), but most theologians find no contradiction in predicating both of God. God could go beyond even the barriers raised by human identity, being, as Augustine said, more intimate to us than we are to ourselves.

CONCLUSION: SUMMARY REFLECTIONS

A symbol of the concentricity of the natural, the social, the divine, and the personal that religious searches for the center reveal.

At the outset, we postulated that the religious life of humanity is a vast and diversified spectacle. Perhaps you now find that postulate only too well verified. The ancient religious mind, the wisdom religions of the East, and the prophetic religions of the West all combine to make a tapestry of unmanageable proportions. We have tried to discern some of this tapestry's principal patterns. We have tried to present the information and the themes that might make such terms as "Hinduism" or "Islam" intelligible. Our final task is to review the whole and suggest its implications.

UNITY AND DIVERSITY

The unity of the phenomena we have studied is religion—the common quest for a way to the center. The diversity of the phenomena makes the religions—the distinctive traditional ways in which sizable numbers of people have worked at this quest together. Specifically, we have studied the ancient, the Indian, the East Asian, and the originally Near Eastern traditional ways.

     The quests are all deeply humanistic, in that they all focus intensely on human welfare. For instance, according to C. G. Jung,[1] the American Indian or African who greets the sun as a daily miracle performs deep psychic work. The Hindu who makes *puja* (worship) or whom *bhakti* (devotionalism) carries to Krishna constructs a world that makes sense and provides emotional comfort. The same is true of Buddhists who ponder koans, Taoists who try to confect the elixir of immortality, and Hasidic Jews who learn diamond cutting to preserve what they can of the old *shtetl* life. In most times and places, the religions have supported or developed meaning unpretentiously, unobtrusively. For most people the traditions have worked subtly as sets of largely unquestioned assumptions.

Still, the traditions have varied in their subtleness. People who ate bean curd sensed the world differently from people who ate roasted lamb. The Prophet who recited, "There is no God but God," oriented Arabs away from the world that the Greek philosopher Thales saw when he exclaimed, "The world is full of gods." The recent introduction of social scientific and critical historical methods has made religious studies more empirically minded and so more sensitive to such variety. Thus, the differences among the religions have been in the spotlight.

Quite properly, we have seen that Hinduism and Islam are vast concepts. Indeed, they are quite abstract, for Hindus and Muslims have lived out their dharma and Qur'an very differently depending on time, place, and station. Therefore, to talk about Hinduism or Islam requires finding common qualities among great diversity, such as a regard for the Vedas or the Prophet, for karma or the Garden. Increasingly scholars debate whether there is a common quality among all the traditions, a common religion at the traditions' cores.

We believe that there is such a common quality or unity, and at various points we have described it as a common attraction toward mystery. Relatedly, we believe that the empiricism that misses such unity and mystery is at least an unwitting reductionism—an insistence that humanity is no more than as it behaves. Usually, that insistence indicates an impoverished imagination and interiority—an inability to intuit how two different behaviors (for example, shamanic ecstasis and yogic enstasis) might be directed toward the same goal: sacredness, the really real.[2]

The tricky thing about meaning, which extroverted observers tend to miss, is that ultimacy or mystery is always but a step away. Still, distraction and lack of reflection on the part of either the people under scrutiny or the scholars who are scrutinizing them are defenses that mystery easily breaks down. As Wakan Tanka, Brahman, nirvana, Tao, the Torah, God, and Allah, ultimacy broke down the defenses against deep meaning in the peoples we have studied. Whether they wanted it or not (and usually they did), sacred mystery defined their world.

If one can see the sacred, it breaks through the Iron, Bamboo, and other curtains that have divided our modern world. Perhaps the only traces of the sacred we can see are the anxieties on which the tranquilizer industry trades. Or perhaps we are able to appreciate it in the Nobel Prize–winning efforts of outstanding scientists and writers. Either way, with or without overt theology, ultimacy is always at hand. We may choose not to embrace it, not to call mystery our

Figure 47   *Taj Mahal: Islam on Hindu soil. Photo by J. T. Carmody.*

inmost vocation. However, as surely as we suffer and die, it will embrace us. All people by nature desire to know, Aristotle declared. Our mortal condition makes Aristotle's dogma existential: All people by nature desire to know the mystery from which they come and to which they go. All people are by nature set for religion.

Religion

The world *religion* refers to the inmost human vocation. By empirical fact as well as theoretical interpretation, *religion* pertains to all life that is reflective, that heads into mystery. Largely for that reason, the word *religion* was seldom uttered by the great teachers.[3] They rather spoke of meaning, the way to "walk," the traditional wisdom, the balance called justice, and the fire called love. Because they were embodied spirits speaking to other embodied spirits, they used familiar figures: mountains, rivers, widows giving alms. Furthermore, their speech led to common action: rhythmic prostrations, gutsy resistance to the emperor, dancing with the Torah, helping a friend. All these actions, though, were religious.

People organized communities around the great teachers' speech and actions. The communities expressed their religion (their venture after meaning into mystery) in ways that Joachim Wach has labeled theoretical, social, and active.[4] That is, they made theologies, brotherhoods and sisterhoods, and liturgies and laws. Regularly, the communities lost the spirit of their founders, as succeeding generations repeatedly prized order more than charisma, control more than inspiration, and orthodoxy more than creativity. Just as regularly, reformers tried to find their way back to the original vision. In China it was "Back to the ancients." In the Christian West it was "Back to the Word."

The various traditions have shaped their peoples in endless ways. Some have spoken rather simply—Judaism and Islam, for instance. Others have made strange bedfellows and cultures more complex, such as the religions of China and Japan. Still, all traditions have used the past to decipher the present and to prepare for the future. All have received and handed on.

That handing on is what we mean by *tradition*.[5] None of us fashions meaning free of external influences. All of us receive a cultural inheritance, meager or rich, to which we add. We do this willy-nilly—by having children, teaching students, working with colleagues, supporting friends. Original sin is the dark side of such a sense of tradition. According to this concept, we all take our first breath in air that is polluted, in a game that is tilted against us. How polluted or tilted the world is has been a matter of vigorous debate. The only consensus seems to be that evil is a sad fact and that there is sufficient good to justify hope. The handing on therefore leads all the religions to revile evil and buttress hope—a process that can be called a concern for salvation.

For instance, ancient peoples banded together for evolutionary salvation—against the evil of extinction and in hope that the race would go on. Close to the earth, they thought in concrete terms, undifferentiatedly, telling stories of life and death. Life came from the fatherly sky and the motherly earth. Life was as possible, as renewable, as heavenly water and productive dirt. Death was breathtakingly near, but perhaps the dead were as seed falling in the ground. Perhaps they were but a link in the chain of generations. Or maybe they passed to a new form of life. As smoke passes from burning wood, so perhaps the subtle part of a person, the part that thinks and travels in dreams, could pass to a new state. In those ways, perhaps, ancient peoples fought for hope, tried to block out absurdity.

To suffer, lose, rejoice, or trust—such acts know no religious, ethnic, or national bounds. We all walk a way (if only a way to death) that we cannot name. We all seek (if only covertly) a path that is straight, a path that mystery blesses. If some of our predecessors have been Nordic berserks, who heated up to feel mystery boil, others have been Eastern yogis, who so slowed themselves that they could be buried alive. If some of our predecessors have been erotics, convinced that the force of the way is sexual *shakti,* others have been lonely ascetics, convinced that meat clouds the spirit. There are few roads that no one has taken, few options that no one has tried. Though the options make all the difference for the individual, we can see from others where we might have gone. Indeed, that is a major reason why we study the humanities. There would be no basis for studying the humanities were there no unity called human nature. Likewise, there would be no religious studies were there no unity called religion.

Contending with nature, society, the self, and whatever ultimacy they have known, all human beings have mused about their sunrise and sunset. For all of them, the cosmos and the group have had effects, the self and ultimacy have beguiled. Without and within each person, the world has taken shape, changed, occasionally threatened to slip away. Since we are "synthetic" beings, whose incarnate spirits include the lowest matter and the heights of thought, we cannot escape religion's full span. Madness comes when the span tilts and the synthesis comes unglued. Boredom comes when we lose the span's tension, when imagination goes stale. In health, we find nature, society, and the self fascinating. In health, science, politics, and art are all essential, all deeply humanistic. If they become so specialized, so arcane, that their essential humanity is not apparent, we must speak of disease—of dysfunction, pathology, alienation.

Though disease has terrible power in our time, as nuclear arms and the prison systems show, it has always written arguments for despair. Parents who wept over dead children heard despair at Stonehenge, Gettysburg, and My Lai. Every woman raped, every man tortured, has heard voices within counseling her or him to abandon hope. Amazingly, though, human beings will not live by despair alone. Their very sense that the times are out of joint is a cry that there ought to be health.

Until we give up completely, we label health as normal. Disease, we say, is the lack of health. Evil, we say, is the lack of good—of proper order, right being, justice, and love. Indeed, so deep is our drive toward health that we cannot think of nonbeing and evil directly. They are irrational, absurd, and void. In their hope, then, the religions uncover more religion. In their hope, Marxists and religious believers can dialogue.

Meaning and Idiosyncrasy

The themes above are some of the constants that all the traditions carry. If they are general, it is because they pertain to all of humanity. In religious perspective, our human characteristics comprise a common condemnation (or consecration) to meaning. Thus, the differences among traditions are simply *how* their peoples have sought, conceived, and enacted meaning. That affirms, of course, that differences do differentiate.[6] It affirms that a Buddhist is not a Hindu and a Christian is not a Jew.

Because he or she is always dealing both with religion as a whole and with the individual religions, the student of religion must develop a peculiar balance. If she or he is blind to the unity behind all religions, the student will miss the deep humanity that the traditions can offer us. On the other hand, if the student sweeps all the information together, making

all Buddhists anonymous Christians or all Christians renegade Jews, he or she will miss the grainy texture that religion always has in people's lives. As is often the case, the ideal involves a duality: *both* cutting to the heart of the matter, where all human beings are siblings, *and* respecting the idiosyncrasies that differentiate people as nations, tribes, sexes, individuals, and traditional religionists.

The idiosyncrasies are mysterious. Why should the Buddha have proposed no-self? A first answer might be because no-self answered the question of suffering that the Buddha's personal life and the life of his Indian culture posed. Fine, but this is hardly an end to the matter. Why should death, disease, and putrefaction have troubled this particular prince so deeply? Presumably many other princes saw corpses without deciding to leave their palaces, wives, and children to adopt a life of asceticism; similarly, many other cultures experienced suffering. Why, then, did the Indians penetrate the psychology of suffering so profoundly? Why not the Babylonians, Chinese, Aztecs, or Mayans?

As those questions show, there is a limit to historical analysis. It can explain some of the differences among individuals or cultures, but their real origin lies beyond it. For the real origin of differences is the incomprehensible world order[7]—St. Paul's *mysterion*. We did not set the cosmic dust spinning. We don't know why it wove the combinations it did. Therefore, when we respect differences, we respect the totality of history and its mystery. We respect the ultimacy behind the facts, the often very brutal facts, that just this universal drama has played and no other.

Let us again try to be concrete. The Australian dream world, as scholars imperfectly reconstruct it from artifacts and interviews, reflects the peculiar landscape of the Australian continent. The aboriginal myths are similar to those of other areas that explain how the ancestors or demiurges fashioned the world, yet the aboriginal world is unique. The Australian use of the *tjurunga*, the sacred wooden boards, for instance, is distinctive. Other ancient peoples painted and carved, but none (that we know) with just the Australian concern for totemic ancestors. Or consider African peoples' use of masks. That, too, has analogies—with the American Indian use of *kachinas* and even the Greek use of theater masks. Yet in Africa masks relate to thought, such as Ogotemmeli's Dogon thought,[8] that speaks of man and woman, fox and ant hill, smithy and granary as the people of no other continent do. Again, the Chinese divination practice of *feng-shui* (geomancy) is like the complex basket divination of the Africans, yet they differ greatly. The two types of divination have the same purpose (to determine what will happen in nature and time), but they express it differently. *Feng-shui* would not seem appropriate in the Congo.

Differences also appear among religions about which we have more historical information. For instance, Judaism memorialized the Exodus (flight from Egypt) in a Passover ritual. Something happened to get the people out of Egypt, and Jewish religious memory attributed it to God and Moses. In time the happening became a paradigm for interpreting Jewish history. Because of what had happened in the past, faithful Jews endured their trials with hope. God would deliver them again somehow. That sort of historical memory, that "anamnesis," gave Jews an identity different from that of the Canaanites, Egyptians, Romans, or Germans. Indeed, without their religious memory, Jews today would have little identity crisis. It is the Exodus that makes the Holocaust so shattering. It is the Exodus and the Holocaust together that make the current state of Israel so taut.

For Christians, the Exodus was a prefigurement of the liberation that Jesus' death and resurrection worked. In their eyes, Jesus' "passover" made a new creation, Jesus' Spirit formed a new Israel, Jesus' teaching established a new covenant. The lamb of the old Passover was a figure of Jesus the victim and conqueror. In the heavenly Jerusalem, Jesus the lamb received all power, glory, and honor. In fact, the lamb had married the heavenly Jerusalem. Moreover, the heavenly Jerusalem had no temple, because "the Lord God Almighty and the Lamb were themselves the temple, and the city did not need the sun or the moon for light, since it was lit by the radiant glory of God and the Lamb was a lighted torch for it" (Rev. 21:22–23). This imagery—this radical reinterpretation of Exodus and Passover—developed within a century of Jesus' death. By then Christians and Jews had irrevocably separated. For nineteen centuries, they have thought of themselves as mutually opposed.

For Muslims, Muhammad makes a reality different from the reality that Moses makes for Jews or Jesus makes for Christians. The difference is rooted in pre-Islamic Arab culture and took form in Muhammad's own psyche, where he received visions not of a burning bush or a dove descending from heaven but of the angel Gabriel. This difference flowered in Islamic conquest, which made the Prophet's people imperial in ways that Jews and Christians never were. Muslims

swept across the Mediterranean world as Jews never thought to do, and they rejected priests, monks, and sacraments. Even their version of the religions' general abuse of women was distinctive: a peculiar blend of polygyny, purdah, the harem, clitoridectomy, and the *hur.*

A mosque, a synagogue, and a church all show likenesses to a Hindu or a Buddhist temple. All five enclose sacred space. But the first three have a family likeness that separates them from the latter two. Principally, their space reverberates with the Word of a Creator God. Still, one is not likely to confuse a mosque with a church or a synagogue. The Word takes different forms in St. Peter's, Rome, a synagogue in Skokie, Illinois, and a mosque in Cairo, Egypt.

Differences, then, are real. We could develop that theme for Hinduism contrasted with Jainism or Buddhism, for Catholics contrasted with Orthodox or Protestants. How great differences are, how divergent they make their adherents' realities, is difficult to determine. Often it seems as much a matter of the analyst's temperament as of the adherents' realities. In the terms of a recent debate,[9] the analyst who has an "esoteric" (inner-directed) personality tends to stress the unity in the traditions, while the "exoteric" (outer-directed) personality tends to stress the diversity.

Esoteric types respond to innermost notions and innermost realities. For them, a common mystery is as real as distinctive facts, even more real. Therefore, esoteric types tend to the negative way—the Hindu *"neti, neti"* ("not this, not that"). They may downplay or even disparage the diverse ways that people have chosen to pursue the supreme value. In contrast, exoteric types respond to outer phenomena—to the actual births, hungers, murders, orgasms, and deaths that make people's lives colorful, intense, palpably real. They fear that moving away from such realities ignores the way things are.

Besides exoteric blood, sweat, and tears, God does seem esoteric, pale and abstract. Looking closely, though, we find that esoterica have given religions most of their life. For instance, what would American Indian ceremonies—the Sun Dance, the vision quest, the potlatch (gift-giving feast)—have been without Wakan Tanka, the Great Spirit? What would the Egyptian pyramids have been without Osiris and Re? Those pale gods gave the ceremonies and massive stones their meaning. Apart from such meaning, exoterica are mute. The same applies in other traditions. Hindu *bhakti* festivals make no sense without a Krishna to play the flute, a Kali to wield the sword. Buddhist meditation depends on karma and nirvana. In the West, circumcision, the Eucharist, and the Muslim *hajj* (pilgrimage to Mecca) depend on the covenant, redemption, and the eternal Word. In the lives of religious people, the exoteric is a body for the esoteric. We think it should be the same in the writings of religion scholars.

COMPARING THE EASTERN TRADITIONS

When we discussed some of the methodological perspectives scholars are using to study religion today, we tacitly assumed the diversity and complexity of the world religions. In principle, most contemporary methods are supposed to be "value-free," assuming that all traditions are equally human. In our view, this does not mean that a scholar must refrain from all value judgments. We see no need to pass by Hindu caste, Chinese footbinding, or American racism with nary a discouraging word. We do need to explain how the traditions in which they occur see such phenomena and to make no assumptions that Indians or Chinese or Americans are more or less virtuous than other human tribes.

In this spirit, we shall attempt a summary comparison of the four Asian traditions we have studied, assuming that they are equally human, equally complex, but trying to distill the unique character, advantages, and liabilities of each. This distillation is bound to reflect biases we do not fully appreciate, but so would any other comparison, as well as the decision not to make a comparison at all.

Placed side by side, Hinduism, Buddhism, Chinese religion, and Japanese religion are four asymmetrical traditions. Although each is dizzyingly complex, and arguably is complete unto itself, their dependencies on one another are unequal. Hinduism generated a great deal of Buddhism, and continues to share a great deal with it, because of their common Indian roots. It shares much less with Chinese and Japanese religions. Buddhism shares much more with Chinese and Japanese religions, because of being transplanted to China and Japan. In the case of China, Buddhism set its seal very deeply, but in turn it was influenced deeply by Taoism, and to a lesser extent by Confucianism. In Japan, Buddhism interacted with

Shinto, receiving a further stimulus to focus on nature, and giving the Japanese love of nature a more profound philosophical underpinning. China and Japan themselves interacted, China having more cultural influence on Japan than Japan on China. Neither China nor Japan had a great cultural influence on India, but the lands between India and China often melded characteristics of the two. Thus Tibet, Burma, and Thailand sometimes seem to be midcountries, whose scripts, architectures, and religions have creatively blended Chinese and Indian elements.

Generally, India has been the great land of interiority and speculation. China has been the great land of exteriority and practicality. That does not mean India did not farm, fight, and organize political units. It does not mean China did not meditate, worship, and philosophize. It just means that when one searches for that elusive thing called a country's peculiar "genius," one does not point to India's political organization, nor to China's metaphysics. Despite all its wars and internal divisions, China has been the land of order and bureaucracy. Despite all its trade and kingdoms, India has been the land of karma and transmigration. Where China fingered the world like a piece of fine cloth, something to be delicately appreciated, India thought about the world like a mathematical problem or a dramatic plot, something to be grasped mentally. "Planting our feet solidly," the Chinese said, "let us make here a family structure, a cuisine, an aesthetic, a technology that allow us to live harmoniously with nature and one another." "Since the world of the senses is doubtful," the Indians said, "let us plant our feet lightly, and keep our spirits free. Pleasure and wealth are legitimate life-goals, but duty and salvation are higher."

Of course, these are simplistic comparisons—almost caricatures. In venturing to make them, we do not deny they can be terribly abused. Indeed, we are reminded of the Western "negative" tradition, which taught that God is more unlike than like even our true statements about him (or her, or it). There is a cultural analogue: If one could get down to specific villages and individuals, our comparisons might prove more untrue than true. From the vantage of a mental Goodyear blimp, however, the cultural contrasts we have made seem valid. India has been the more esoteric cultural basin, China the more exoteric.

The religious poles in this comparison would be philosophical Hinduism and Buddhism, on the esoteric side, and Confucianism, on the exoteric side. Devotional Hinduism and Buddhism, Taoism, and Shinto would occupy the intermediate ground. The cutting edge of Indian philosophy has been idealism—the priority of mind over matter. The cutting edge of Confucianism has been social realism—the priority of public affairs over private thoughts. In between, devotional Hinduism and Buddhism have worked the emotions and the imagination that mediate between human mentality and materiality. Taoism and Shinto have worked the mature spirits and human aesthetics that mediate between nature-centered humanity and political humanity. This does not mean that Indian philosophers did not have to consider economics and statecraft. It does not deny that Confucians made a place for meditation. It simply paints with the broad brush that "summary reflections" suggests, responding to those students who come to "summary reflections" hoping their teachers finally will risk a few generalizations.

Of the Asian traditions, to which should you go for a penetrating theory of nature? You should go to Hinduism or Buddhism for an analysis of how "nature" comes to us through the senses, and to Chinese or Japanese religion for directives on how best to enjoy natural beauty. For the foundations of natural science, you should go outside the Asian orbit, to Greek philosophy and Western revelation, since they were the main sources of the confidence in nature's intelligibility necessary for what we have come to call "natural science."[10]

To which Asian tradition should you go to for a penetrating theory of society? You should go to Confucianism and Taoism. Confucianism taught that only moral virtue will make any political unit healthy. The great Confucian key was the quality of a village's or a country's rulers. If such rulers were learned and good the village or country would prosper. To be learned, they had to know the ways of the ancients, the giants who first saw the lay of the political land. To be good, they had to attune themselves to the *Tao* of reality, disciplining selfishness, vanity, greed, and the other vices that kept people from walking the Way. The Way to social prosperity was "there," objectively available. If people had eyes to see and ears to hear, they could find it. But self-interest or seeking material profit so regularly blinded people's eyes or deafened their ears that most social units wobbled along or fell into the ditch. Until inner goodness (*jen*) joined with gracious protocol (*li*) social relations would continue to go badly.

Taoism agreed with much of this deeper Confucianism, but Taoism was appalled by the Confucian tendency to make stuffed shirts. When lesser spirits trumpeted the Confucian tunes about inner goodness and outer protocol, legalism and bureaucracy multiplied like cancers. For the Taoists, imagination was the crucial difference. Unless people stayed creative, their societies would bumble into dead ends or become impossibly boring. Only free spirits could keep the bureaucrats from driving everyone to drink. Only wit, irony, satire, and creative musing could keep politicians free to see the point. The point was justice, fair-dealing, and the way to justice was *wu-wei*: indirection, not-doing, the wink that's as good as a nod. Heavy-handedness, aggression, the lawyers' obsession with jots and tittles were the sure and rocky road to political disaster. People had to be lured, seduced, beguiled into cooperation. Unless you won their hearts and minds, you lost the long-range game. Because most would not grasp these rather obvious truths, China got generation after generation of wars and fatuous politicians.

To which Asian tradition should you go for a penetrating theory of the self? You should go to Hinduism or Buddhism. Their common font of wisdom is the centrality of detachment. If the human self is to become free, it must detach itself from layer after layer of illusion. Although Hinduism and Buddhism disagree about the final layer, Hinduism tending to retain a "self" and Buddhism tending to deny it, they agree that the individual is wrongly situated until he or she connects with the All. Whether the All is Brahman or nirvana, it is the only adequate context for human self-understanding. If we do not understand the mysterious envelope in which we are sealed, we do not understand our most basic characteristic.

In Western terms, the analogue that comes to mind is the Danish philosopher Søren Kierkegaard's view that the self is a relation relating itself to the Absolute. As a relation, my "I" is both a subject and an object: I can think about, reflect on, move myself. As a relation relating itself to the Absolute, my "I" moves its complex self toward God, whether it realizes this or not. For Kierkegaard, the great prod to grasping the human situation is sin, which shows itself in depression and despair. For Hinduism and Buddhism, the great prod is death, which shows itself in suffering and disease. Either way, the only solution is to realize, actualize, achieve what one is. Christian, Hindu, and Buddhist salvation all come from uniting the self with the All that lets the self be.

The Chinese and Japanese theories of the self have been more social and less profound. Behind that judgment, of course, is our conviction that social relations are less profound than the ontological (being) relation of the self to the Absolute. Many contemporary scholars would dispute this thesis, either speculatively or practically (either in their theories or the ways they choose to do their work). For them "the social construction of reality" makes all our selves intrinsically dependent on the cultures in which we live, move, and have our being. We have no language without our culture, no economics or politics. Language, economics, and politics more shape religion or metaphysics than they derive from religion or metaphysics.

There is a lot to be said for this thesis, but we do not think it finally wins the day. For all the massive influence of our cultures, we remain people who can move from language to language, religion to religion, economic system to economic system. Contrariwise, we can never move away from our relation to Brahman, nirvana, or God, because this relation is constitutive, built into the depths of reflective intelligence (selfhood).

To which Asian tradition should you go for a penetrating theory of ultimate reality? To devotional Hinduism or Zen. Devotional Hinduism, focused on Krishna or Shiva, spotlights the centrality of love. Binding the devotee to divinity with reasons of the heart, it makes religion a consuming passion. Zen Buddhism pivots on realizing one's pact with nirvana, one's intrinsic knowledge-nature. In silence, Zen sacramentalizes our ultimate enlightenment. The result can be a wonderfully gracious living, cool, serene, and artistic. Such living says that ultimate reality dances, paints, speaks itself forth in poetry. It says that ultimate reality is art, science, and ineffable light.

The Sage as Eastern Archetype

If asked to paint a picture of the ideal product the Asian traditions were trying to develop, we would entitle it *The Sage*. Whereas the nonliterate traditions have tended to pivot on the shaman and the Western traditions have originated from prophets, the Asian traditions have tended to pivot on the sage. To be sure, there have been shamans and prophets in India and East Asia, just as there have been sages in the West. But Buddha, Confucius, and Lao-tzu—the three most influential Asian personalities—have all been more sagacious than prophetic. It will be useful, therefore, to reflect on the differences in the Asian traditions' understandings of sagehood and then on the message the

Eastern sages offer students of the world religions today.

The Indian sage, Buddhist or Hindu, has tended to be a yogi. The *rishis* whose visions lay behind the Vedas, the Mahavira, and the Buddha all disciplined the flesh and the mind to win enlightenment and liberation. The Indian archetypal figure won his great wisdom by penetrating the veil of maya or samsara, by intuiting the reality of Brahman or Suchness. The popular tradition might embellish this victory with miracles and myths, but its core was yogic meditation. Meditation was the method, wisdom was the substance, and morality was the fruit. Archetypally, intuition *(jnana)* or trance *(dhyana)* were the principal yogas. *Karma yoga* (acting without attachment) and *bhakti yoga* (devotion) were accommodations, perfectly valid and effective for salvation, but spun off from the quieter core.

In East Asia, the sage had a more social inclination. For both Confucius and Lao-tzu, union with the *Tao* was a font of political order. One might say, therefore, that the East Asian sage was more prudent or ethical, the Indian sage more ontological. For example, there is little evidence that the Buddha aspired to political office. The world was burning; it would have been folly to plunge into worldly affairs. By contrast, Confucius greatly aspired to political office, or at least political counselorship. Like Plato, Confucius thought that good social order was the prime requisite and that good social order would come only when kings had sages for brains. From the demands of good social order, Confucius worked his way back to gentlemanliness, and then to *jen,* the heart of human nobility. By the time he was seventy, he could move nobly in all situations, letting his *jen* be the embodiment of the Way. Thus a certain mysticism shines through Confucius' last relations with the Way. He could hear the Way in the morning and in the evening die content because the Way had become his meat and drink, the other half of his heart and soul.

Lao-tzu is initially more mystical than Confucius, but eventually just as political. For Lao-tzu, all power *(te)* comes from union with the Way, for the Way runs nature and society alike. Therefore, the sage shuts the doors of the senses and places his spirit in the Way. Therefore, the sage advocates *wu-wei,* reveres the uncarved block. Backing away from social conventions and hackneyed speech, the sage is alert, poetic, and paradoxical. To the ordinary run of people, he is an eccentric, always trying to see the world afresh. Chuang-tzu pushed this eccentricity further than

Lao-tzu, delighting in affronting the sobersided Confucians. Soaring with the great birds, he was not surprised that the little birds found him very odd.

The deeper Confucians and Taoists joined with the East Asian Buddhist philosophers to make the sage's wisdom worldly. In the final frames of the Zen teaching pictures called *Herding an Ox,* the enlightened person comes back into the marketplace, able to enjoy enlightenment in the midst of buying and selling, eating and drinking. Empty and gone beyond, the *Prajna-paramita* is as near as a blooming cherry blossom, as full as the rugged rocks. Wisdom swirls in the master's whipped green tea, whistles in the flight of the archer's arrow. The enlightened life is graceful, integrated, at home in the world. By the time the dharma reached the Pacific, the world was no longer burning. It had cooled in the mountains of the Sung landscapes, lost its fever in the Shinto pools. So pacified, it looked outward as much as inward, found rest on the keen edge of body-mind. It grew to love subtlety and indirection, tactfulness and play. "There is no good and evil," the Zen disciple heard. "All jobs are worth doing well." What is is what is in front of us. After enlightenment, mountains are mountains and trees are trees.

It is hard to imagine Indian Buddhists and Hindus comfortable with this East Asian worldliness. In Delhi, Bombay, and Calcutta, life remains very steamy, burning with misery. The grass around Hindu shrines is seldom immaculate. The water buffaloes behind the Taj Mahal intrude an instructive dung and mud. Along with the blazing summer sun, they mock the sultan who thought the Taj would immortalize his lovely queen. The Taj will have crumbled long before the queen's soul has found rest.

Does the Eastern sage have a distinctive message for students of the world religions today? Perhaps so. If the students come from the West, they likely have been touched by the West's loss of confidence in wisdom. Western people who speak authoritatively about enlightenment, who persuasively incarnate the *Tao,* are few and far between. So, an increasingly influential argument has arisen. "Since so few wise people appear in our midst," the argument runs, "wisdom must be an endangered species, going the way of the dodo. Evolution must be in the hands of the technicians, the marines shouting 'can do!'" Swiftly and surely, the Eastern sages rebut this argument. Let Lao-tzu occupy your mind a half-hour and the marines will lie high and dry. "What can you do?" Lao-tzu politely asks. "What is the end of all your technique? If your graphs do not bring you beauty, your tanks do not win you peace, why all your plotting and piloting?"

The Eastern sages are sufficiently concerned with technique—in meditation, painting, ritual, and many other things—to make it clear that they are not opposed to engineering. They are merely opposed to calling a spade a pearl. A spade should be called a spade: an instrument for digging. With a spade, you may dig in the earth and come up with a goodly treasure. If you want a pearl, especially one of great price, you will have to dive into the sea, go down deep to rebirth. It is his deep intelligence, his midmost mind, that gives Confucius his clout. Were he to work the surface only, merely to push and pull his facts, we could read Confucius like a newspaper. Similarly, it is *samadhi,* the deepest consciousness, that gives the yogi his freedom.

Figure 48 *Landscape attributed to Kano Motonobu (1476–1559). Ink and light color on paper; 20 × 13½ in. This picture shows the Japanese appropriation of the Chinese aestheticoreligious notion of emptiness. The Nelson–Atkins Museum of Art, Kansas City, Missouri. (Gift of Mrs. George H. Bunting, Jr.)*

Were he merely to sense or reason, we could watch him like daytime TV.

For the Indian and East Asian sages, the way up remains the way down. If you want to glimpse the heavenly *Tao* or consort with the glorified Buddha, you will have to return to yourself, find who you are, see your face before your parents were born. It is your inner space, your emptiness, that will make your house useful. To focus attention on your walls or roof is to miss your house's meaning. Similarly, it is its spiritual drama that makes your community significant. To focus on your community's moving and shaking is to miss what your people might be.

You do not like these quirky phrases? Paradoxes put you off? Ah well, no Eastern sage ever promised you a garden of platitudes. If you want a good guru, an abbot who knows his business, you will have to knock and knock and knock again. Easy admittance means superficial discipline. Superficial discipline means shallow learning. Shallow learning means specious enlightenment, and so the sickening of the dharma. It is not cruelty that makes good gurus demanding. It is unusual kindness. In the spiritual life, you become what you do. In the spiritual life, outer persona and inner self must come closer and closer together.

"Consider yonder Bald Mountain," the sage Mencius said. "You know, once it was thick with trees. The mind of human beings is much the same. If they would nurture it, it would grow lush and very useful. But they neglect it, or abuse it, or hack it away without care, so it becomes barren and ugly, useless and an eyesore."

The *Dhammapada* begins: "Yesterday's thoughts make the self of today, and today's thoughts make the self of tomorrow. Our life is the creation of our mind." Is the *Dhammapada* passé? Have we found shortcuts to beautiful selfhood on our way to the mushroom cloud?

No. Many people in many nations now lament the lack of vision, the venality, the small-souledness in which they drown. But few Western people know that therapy is as near as the *Mencius,* as simple as the *Dhammapada.* You cannot have political vision if you never open your mind. You are bound to be venal and pusillanimous if you never feed your soul.

What doth it profit people if they can assemble any stereo and never hear the music of the spheres? What doth it profit people to place all their energies in the stock market? Stereos and the stock market have their place—all the Eastern sages allow them. What the Eastern sages do not allow them is primacy of place. If the *Tao* is in urine and dung, the *Tao* is in stereos and the stockmarket. But to hear the *Tao* in the morning and in the evening die content, one must vacate assembling and selling. The business of life is not business. The business of life is being. If we want to prosper significantly, we must be open, collected, and disciplined—"one-pointed" in soul and mind. It does not matter that many of our schools know nothing of such Eastern wisdom. The college catalogue is seldom a great book. Real learning occurs in dark nights and painful passages. Wisdom to live by goes far below figures and facts.

"Leave off, Buddha and Chuang-tzu," you may be saying. "Confucius, give us a break." "So sorry," the sages respectfully answer. "We thought you were asking Asia to try to gladden your heart."

If our hearts are ever to gladden, we must give them something to love. If we listen to the Eastern sages, we will give them natural beauty, social order, and personal depth. Day by day, one day at a time, we will try to make time graceful, to empty space for landscapes of peace. In emptiness we may possess our souls. In graceful time, the *Tao* may sing. If today you would possess your soul, you must empty it of what is tawdry. If today you would hear the *Tao,* you must attune your inner ear.

COMPARING THE WESTERN TRADITIONS

This attuning offers a first handle for comparing the Western traditions. American Indians, Egyptians, Iranians, Greeks, Jews, Christians, and Muslims have all had priests, shamans, or sages who have listened for the meaning of their peoples' lives.

For the nonliterate traditions of the West, the main meaning of the peoples' lives was to live harmoniously with nature. Nature was virtually coextensive with reality, and what was sacred, worthy of supreme veneration, was more nature's depth than something standing apart from the cosmos, from the world of space and time. To be sure, the Great Spirit was something that fleshly thoughts could never fathom. But the tribal peoples' many efforts to reach the Great Spirit almost always came to fruition as a vision or sense of communion that brought harmony with the natural world.

The Egyptian concern with life and death some-what extended this tribal sense of reality. Although the Egyptians enjoyed the pleasures of their life in the sun and their good fortune to live by the Nile, they pondered the afterlife so intensely that they left the pyramids as massive memos. As the pyramid texts suggest, the Egyptians sensed that the afterlife would be fortunate only if one could pass the test of a strict judgment on one's days of earthly life. Unless the soul were light and clean, it would gain no good immortality. The brief Egyptian flirtation with "monotheism" proved less powerful than an instinct that all the forces of nature, all the vectors of life and death, had to be represented, written large as divinities, if the people were to understand the tensions of earthly life and reach the depth their spirits sought.

Iranians who flocked to Zoroaster heard a different message about the spirit's wishes. To their great seer, the primal forces were Truth and the Lie—the human spirit as open to the light or the human spirit as closed. Thus Zoroaster seems to have meditated with his "topmost" mind, while his naturalistic predecessors in Egypt and among the Western tribes burrowed down toward the roots of the unconscious. Zoroaster's concerns with light, ideas, and images of heavenly forces all suggest a person aware of the human spirit's "transcendent" inclinations, its drive to rise higher and higher, go farther and farther beyond what it had conceived in the past.

The Greeks are remarkable for the fullness of their religious life, which spanned from the deepest roots of the unconscious to the most transcendent inclinations of the topmost mind. The riches of Greek mythology are a remarkable treasury, full of experiences of nature, family relations, and the struggles of the unconscious mind. The great Greek tragedians used this treasury most artfully, leaving the West unsurpassed renditions of humanity's most basic conflicts. The Greek philosophers seem to have taken the dazzling physical light of the Greek islands as a challenge to find dazzling mental counterparts. Building on the work of the early philosophers of nature, Socrates, Plato, and Aristotle finally accomplished the monumental feat of differentiating human reason. Following the light of the mind, the logos that made human beings a unique species, they saw that this light is the inreach of divinity, whose Light is coincident with any creature's reason-to-be. Although Hellenistic religion largely lost the classical philosopher's great achievement, enough of their differentiation remained to turn Western culture in a distinctively rational direction.

Along with Greek reason, biblical revelation also pushed Western culture to find its reason-to-be in God. However, where the Greek accent was the Divine Light, the biblical accent was the Divine Love. Thus Judaism formed a people around the free overtures of a God who wanted to make a people uniquely covenanted to himself. As biblical Jews understood this relationship, it was not the product of any special merit on their part. It was completely the product of God's own love. From his own goodness God decided to reveal himself over time, walking with the Jews as a fellow traveler. The Exodus was the warrant for Jewish faith that God could make the walk a liberation, while the covenant was the codification of the traveling relationship. Through the permutations of biblical history, biblical prophecy, biblical wisdom literature, rabbinic reflection, Cabalistic lore, and Hasidic piety, Judaism retained this sense of being bonded to a loving God. The Master of the Universe had shown the people a personal face. He had pledged them his mercy and steadfast love. This revelation and pledge held the deepest mystery of time.

Christianity accepted Judaism's stress on God's love, but by the fourth century it had added more of Greece's stress on God's Light. Jesus himself had preached and taught as a Jew, quite aware of the biblical traditions. For him the deepest mystery of time was on the verge of a definitive self-expression. The Kingdom of God, in which God's love and mercy would become dominant in many people's hearts, was as near as his intimate heavenly Father. When Christians reflected on Jesus' life and death, they moved the Kingdom into his person. This singular man, they said, himself embodied what God's love and mercy could do. Indeed, his resurrection was the pledge and first fruits of the Kingdom's cosmic import. Whoever clung to Jesus as Jesus had clung to the Father could hope to rise with Jesus to the Father's right hand. There Father, Son, and Spirit, the fullness of the Christian God, would give one a full understanding of time's mysteries, a full experience of love's beatitude.

The Jewish and Christian experiences of God's revelation somewhat shaped Islam, but the visions of Muhammad really determined the Muslims' world view. For Muhammad, Allah was Light and Love, but more powerfully Allah was the sole Creator, the omnipotent Lord of the Worlds. Thus Islam has accented human beings' need to submit completely to Allah. When Allah speaks, every creature ought to bow low, as in the daily prayer. When any creature considers the world, she or he ought to revere the many signs the world gives of Allah's great wisdom and power. Allah is a stern judge, demanding a full recognition of these truths. People who will not listen to Muhammad's recital are surely marked for the Fire. So for Islam the great disaster is unbelief. Sin and error play their woeful parts, but the core ruin to which human beings are prey is unbelief, which usually shows itself as idolatry. In all aspects of life, from Friday worship in the mosque to daily business in the street, the One God has set the standards. The devout Muslim prays each day to stay on the sole path that is straight, the path of Allah's guidance.

There are other strands in the history of Western religion, of course, but these traditions certainly account for most of the Western configurations. In modernity they ran up against a powerful atheistic revolt, so we "postmodern" Westerners tend to experience these religious traditions as somewhat strange. For example, the changes in Western consciousness that the Enlightenment and Marxist philosophies have worked suggest to many of our contemporaries that traditional religion is at best a curio, at worse an impediment to human growth. For the Enlightenment philosophers, the crux was our human capacity to make "reality." They saw that much that we think is "out there" comes from "in here," our own minds. For the Marxist philosophers, such speculative matters have been less important than the practical business of overthrowing current injustices. Understanding an imperfect reality, they have said, is only half the job. The full job includes building a new, better reality.

The traditional Western religions could agree with one part of the Enlightenment/Marxist program, but they would have to disagree with another part. Accepting the Greek understanding of humanity's vocation to follow the light of reason, the Western religious traditions could listen to the modern antireligionists quite sympathetically, marveling at how the moderns' rejection of traditional faith has helped them to make many splendid discoveries in physical science, epistemology, psychology, biological science, and sociology. These are all further disclosures of the inreaching Divine Light, so what is true and noble in them deserves religious veneration.

Accepting the biblical understanding of humanity's vocation to follow the love of covenantal sharing, the Western traditions could also listen quite sympathetically to the modern pragmatists. There is a biblical imperative to do justice and make a world fit for human beings to live in. There is a Qur'anic call to fellowship that transcends all boundaries of nations and races. Therefore, much in the modern Enlightenment/Marxist program preaches in terms almost identical with the Western religious traditions' own sacred scriptures.

On the other hand, the Western religious traditions could not agree with the modern antireligionists' hatred of God, nor with their murky view of human nature. For the religious traditions, only God gives human beings prosperity. Islam has driven this home like a stake into the heart: Idolatry is utter ruin. Unless the Creative Love and Power that makes the world afresh every day dominates human consciousness, human consciousness errs grievously and strews cruel wreckage left and right. Thus a clear view of human nature balances on a thin edge. It is neither optimistic nor pessimistic. It is hopeful, because open to God. Human beings have a limited capacity to follow the Light and understand. They have a limited capacity to give and receive love and so build peaceful communities. When they open themselves to God's help, human beings can do justice, make beauty, prosper in truth. When they close themselves to God, they truncate and warp their limited powers, and so produce trash, injustice, and great suffering. As the religious forms of arrogant closure to God have given the West many dreadful "holy" wars, so the irreligious forms of arrogant closure to God have given the West Gulag Archipelagos, Nazi concentration camps, Latin American butchery, and North American greed. To be human, our species needs the Light that Plato saw, the Love that Jeremiah hoped would make a new covenant. Without these, we treat one another worse than wolves. Without these, it does not matter whether we call ourselves religious or irreligious, for our true names are simply "Ruined."

When confronted by godless modernity, the Western traditions tend to pull together. For Judaism, Christianity, and Islam, the Creator is the creature's inmost definer. For the other Western traditions we have studied, the case is a little more complicated, but the upshot is much the same: Human beings are not the measure of reality.

In the eighteenth and nineteenth centuries, the Western religious traditions were thrown on the defensive, forced to grow beyond their insular, and in many ways self-serving, understandings of revelation. In the second half of the twentieth century, the irreligious humanisms have been thrown on the defensive, shown by their totalitarian tyrannies and nuclear horrors to be precipitous paths to hell. The question for the twenty-first century will be whether these two strains of current Western humanity can grow or purify themselves enough to cooperate and make the full circle of checks and balances that survival surely will demand.

The Prophet as Western Archetype

For the Asian traditions, it is relatively clear that the dominant personality, the religious ideal, has been the sage. Buddha, Confucius, Lao-tzu, and the various Hindu holy men have all been philosophic contemplatives, concerned with ordering or saving human life by penetrating the structures of the cosmos. For the Western religious traditions, the case is not so clear. The prophet seems to be the strongest personality, but often the sage and the mystic run a close second and third.

Among the nonliterate Western tribes, the dominant personality has been the shaman. Specializing in ecstatic techniques, the shaman has gone out of himself (less frequently, herself), to make contact with the sacred forces running the world. Thus the Eskimo shaman might go into trance to travel to Sedna, the goddess of the undersea who had fenced in the seals.

For Egypt, the priest, officiating at religious ceremonies, and the king, mediating divine order (*maat*), were highly visible personalities. Egypt also produced an interesting wisdom literature, most of it rather stoical. The message of Egyptian wisdom usually was that human experience teaches the value of prudence. The person who wants to prosper should keep the mouth shut and the eyes open.

For Iran, the Zoroastrian prophecies placed a high premium on the inner spirit of light. As the fire burned in the Zoroastrian rituals, so the truth should blaze in the human heart. The magi who later spoke for Zoroastrian wisdom earned a handsome reputation in the Middle East, much of it for their astrological learning. True to the continued immersion of their tradition in the cosmological myth, they set human affairs under the influence of the stars.

In Greece the philosopher, the lover of wisdom, ruled the psychological stage. Shamanist types and priests played strong roles in the days of Olympian religion, but after historians, natural scientists, political thinkers, and dramatists had come to the fore, the philosophers' search for the unseen measure prepared to take the place of honor. When Socrates, Plato, and Aristotle assumed this place, philosophy became a way of life, not an academic discipline. Speaking of their illuminations in religious terms, they would have dis-

missed any strong distinction between philosophy and revelation. In their experience, when the soul took wing and rose toward the idea of the good, God was the prime mover and drawer.

In both Judaism and Islam, prophets dominated the first stages of the tradition. Moses struck the covenant because he had received the Word of the Lord, while Muhammad was simply the *rasul,* the messenger commanded to recite God's Qur'an. In later periods both religions developed a less prophetic, more jurisprudential understanding of God's guiding Word (Torah or *Sharia*). Then the rabbis and lawyers dealt with an ethics both more complex and less explosive than the original prophetic Word. As well, both the Jewish rabbis and the Muslim lawyers assumed something of the philosopher's mantle, and both their cultures opened to Greek rationalism, though seldom to the point where prophetic revelation was endangered. For when rabbinical theology or Muslim law seemed in danger of running dry, the Hasidim, Cabalists, and Sufis rose up to water it with devotion. Thus Sufi teaching lore enlivened the Muslim lawyers' codes, while haggadah enlivened the Talmudists' halakah.

Overall, the biblical prophets and Muhammad *the* Prophet kept the notion of the Divine Word central. If both Judaism and Islam strike the comparativist as more ethical than metaphysical, it is because both thought of the Divine Word as more an imperative than an indicative. Revelation of God commanded that the people be holy, since they were to consort with the Holy One. In both traditions' understanding of this holiness, what one thought was less important than what one did. Such "doing" included worship as well as morality, but it had a distinct priority over speculative or purely contemplative theology. Speculation and contemplative theology had their places, but their potential for division was large. For the community to hold together, the people had first to keep the same Sabbath and kosher laws, to depend on the same Five Pillars.

In the case of Christianity, Jesus, also, seems more a prophet than a sage, despite the fact that the New Testament significantly casts Jesus in the lines of Old Testament wisdom. Jesus teaches the crowds, but what he teaches is mainly a view of God leading to a new mode of living. The centrality of love in Jesus' preaching somewhat distinguishes his prophecy from that of the Hebrew prophets, and even more from that of Muhammad, but we should not exaggerate this distinction. The love of God and love of neighbor that epitomize Jesus' program have strong analogues in both Judaism and Islam.

Where Christianity departs from the prophetic typology of Judaism and Islam is in divinizing its main prophet. Neither Moses nor Muhammad became Sons of God, sharers in the divine creative nature. Moreover, an infusion of Greek philosophy made Christianity quite ontological about Jesus and the Trinity. True, the conciliar controversies of the fourth and fifth centuries were passionate, rather than detached, bouts of speculation, but they determined that the Logos related intimately with the world's reason-to-be. The Christian God expressed his being in both an ongoing act of creation and the Incarnation of the Logos. Picking up hints from Pauline and Johannine literature (Col. 1:15–20, John 1:1–14), the Christian theologians came to think that creation occurred in the Divine Word, whom God had planned to incarnate from eternity.

The Incarnation made Christianity a prophetic religion instinctively sacramental. Where Judaism and Islam prohibited the representation of God, Christianity was fundamentally iconographic. Since God had made an icon of himself, uttering his Word into human flesh, all material things were open to the inspiration of God's Spirit. When the Spirit moved over the waters, the waters became baptismal. When the Spirit moved over the bread and wine, the bread and wine became the body and blood of the Lord. Above all, human affairs became the primary arena of God's action. Accepting the Jewish notion of covenant, Christianity said that Jesus and his people were bonded like a groom and bride. The story of the Church therefore was like the saga of an extended family, relating the increases and diminishments the original marriage had produced. To be sure, the marital compact would come to full fruition only in heaven, where the glory of the lamb (Rev. 5:12) would blaze forth, but even the days of earthly time could bring touches of conjugal union.

Although they rejected Christian incarnationalism and sacramentality, Judaism and Islam developed their own equivalents. Both became this-worldly religions, Judaism in large part by adding marriage and good deeds to Torah to make a trinity of holy blessings. As a result, Jews have influenced Western culture, literary and scientific alike, out of proportion to their small numbers. Since the Lord had made history his chosen field of interest, temporal things ranked high on the Jewish agenda. Islam largely agreed, sponsoring a splendid, full-bodied culture during its golden

age. The Islamic stress on Judgment and afterlife probably made it more eschatological than Judaism, more preoccupied with heaven and hell, but the Muslim theocratic ideal assured that politics, business, and war would all seem inseparable from religious practice.

Furthermore, neither Judaism nor Islam approved of celibacy, so neither had a corps of monks testifying to the rights of eternity. While the rabbis and Sufis hardly were robust in their encouragement of sexuality, they felt that God's command to increase and multiply, as well as ordinary human psychology, made marriage the healthiest estate. So, unlike their counterparts in much of Christianity, the prophetic and legal masters of Judaism and Islam felt a constant pressure to provide for wives and children. While this did not promote women to equal status with men, it did assure that family life received a thorough consideration. Thus the rabbis saw that the Genesis account of creation made humanity male-female, and that it suggested the Fall was in part a sexual awakening. Thus the Cabalists spoke of redemption in sexual terms, hoping that one day the fragmented world would return to God's full embrace.

Figure 49 Three Apostles, *Spanish (1140–1170). Limestone; 31 in. high. The apostles are Paul, Andrew, and John, part of a group of twelve. The Nelson–Atkins Museum of Art, Kansas City, Missouri.*

In hindsight, neither Judaism, Christianity, nor Islam gave physical nature the appreciation it deserved. Although the trail from the beginnings of these religions to today's ecological crises is tangled, there is little doubt that the biblical and Qur'anic subordination of nature to human beings helped the prophetic religious cultures to ravish the earth. Neither the Bible nor the Qur'an said to ravish the earth, but both so feared fertility religion and idolatry that they downplayed nature's sacredness. They knew the Creator had to be present to rocks and trees, if rocks and trees were to exist at all, but the prophetic religions shied away from the implications of creation, not wanting to say that whatever exists is inviolable.

So only at their most confident times did the prophetic religions make sacraments and humanisms that welcomed nature kindly. No doubt rural peoples of these traditions always sensed God's coming through the seasons, but the main word of the prophets stressed God's transcendence of the world, implying that God cared little for the seasons. (Therefore, high on the agenda of East-West religious dialogue should be discussing the East's greater appreciation of nature, and its greater appreciation of the impersonal side of God with which nature is allied.) The Western prophetic religions all experienced God as fiercely personal, a Word and Will impressing themselves mightily. Although the mystics in these traditions (especially the Christian mystics who were influenced by Greek spirituality) went beyond words and feelings to the naked divine immensity, the mainstreams in these traditions (especially the Christian mainstream) pictured God as a human person.

Today the most important legacy of the prophetic religions probably is their cry for justice. The Word of God the West has trumpeted is a shout for honesty and love. Through the Israelite prophets, Jesus, and Muhammad, God demanded that human beings treat one another well. Even though Judaism, Christianity, and Islam often have narrowed this demand, becoming ethnocentric and insular like other tribes, the demand itself is virtually their constitution. "If you would worship the true God," they all have heard, "you must do justice to your neighbors." So all the prophetic religions stand against the exploitation or oppression—capitalist, Marxist, or other—that denies the sanctity of human beings. So the racism, sexism, and religious bigotry that have spawned in the prophetic religions denounce them before their God. In evolutionary terms, this may be the prophetic religions' great significance. Imperfect though all their peoples have

been, the prophetic religions have still nursed an ideal of just, genuine living.

ON BEING AN AMERICAN CITIZEN OF THE RELIGIOUS WORLD

We have not paid special attention to America in this book, because in the history of religion, America has occupied only a small fraction. In general handbooks such as *The Historical Atlas of the Religions of the World, Historia Religionum, The Concise Encyclopedia of Living Faiths* and *The Encyclopedia of Religion*, American religion does not receive 2 percent of the space. The first lesson that the world religions offer Americans, then, is that America is not as important as Americans tend to think. Our 400 years of religious experience are not much beside India's 5,000. If our 6 percent of the world's population and almost 40 percent of the consumption of the world's raw materials are disproportionate, we need all the help we can get to become less important.

We are not advocating the suppressing of patriotism. Few existing cultures are very old. Europeans or Asians who sniff because their cultures go back more centuries than ours are hardly less ridiculous than we. All nations need a perspective on world history. All nations need to see things "under the aspect of eternity."

For most Americans, religion has been Christianity, and Christianity has often pivoted on Jesus and the founder of their own church. In some cases the dark ages between those two personages stretch 1,800 years. For such people, Catholics are not considered Christians, and Orthodox are beyond the pale. True, Americans have modified this intolerance by coexisting with their neighbors. Almost all Americans, though, are quite provincial and need a deep breath of cosmopolitan air.

The root of provincialism is what Erik Erikson calls "pseudospeciation"—pretending that we are the only true human beings. In the past, that "we" has been Chinese, Japanese, and Eskimos. It has been Boston Brahmins and Oklahoma dirt farmers. It has been Catholics who would never darken a Protestant church door, Orthodox who would never visit a synagogue.

Figure 50 *Prayer Tower, Oral Roberts University, Tulsa, Oklahoma. Photo by J. T. Carmody.*

Fortunately, we now know enough about the psychodynamics of pseudospeciation, largely through analyses of prejudice, to show that it has little to do with genuine religion. In fact, we now know that genuine religion directly opposes pseudospeciation.

In most cases, pseudospeciation stems from a combination of fear and self-interest. We fear the universal humanity, the radical equality, that a pluralistic world implies. It would force us to shed our shells; it would snatch away our platform for boasting. Similarly, we fail to grasp notions such as the Christian Church because it is to our advantage that "in Christ" there be male and female (Gal. 3:28). We fail to enact the notion of a union of all nations, because it is to our advantage to dictate prices to the world. Few of us are magnanimous willingly, textbook writers included.

If we Americans are to gain stature in religion's golden eye, we will have to become more realistic about time and space than we have tended to be. Throughout all time, most people have not been Americans, Christians, or whites, and any true God has blessed more lands than just ours. By today's standards, the colonial Puritans' "errand in the wilderness" was terribly naive. Those who launched it simply did not have our facts about human prehistory and human diversity. It was largely ignorance, then, that led them to locate salvation in New England. The same is true of those who proposed that America be God's new Israel. Sober students of American history wonder to what extent such notions were used to justify ravaging the Indians. Historians of religion stumble over the obvious fact that God's old Israel was perfectly well.[11]

If we deflate our egos, we may see things in better perspective. From the vantage point of an astronaut or the sun-god Re, Americans have never been *the* holy people. Long before the whites, reds revered every striking American locale. Shortly after the whites, blacks became America's suffering servants. Unbeknownst to our pioneers, peoples in Asia were living lives of grace under pressure.

The only holy people, in religious perspective, are of the single race, the single species. All divisions make but partial stories. There is a dictum in religious studies that he or she who knows just one religion knows no religion. By that dictum Americans urgently need to study world religions; if only to determine our own identity, we need to know what others have been, what alternatives there were.

In addition, the world religions can suggest what in American religious experience has been distinctive. This topic is immense, so we can only offer a few leads. First, the Reformation and Enlightenment had a marked effect on American religion. Together, they led to a peculiar blend of pietism and rationalism. Of course, pietism and rationalism have been present in other cultures. For instance, India embraced both bhakti and Vedanta; Islam embraced both Sufism and Law. In America, the mixture tended to set the Bible against the brain. Evolution and the Scopes trial of 1925 dramatized this tension. In colonial times, Calvinists made syntheses of biblical faith and intellectualism that pleased at least themselves. During the drafting of the Constitution, it appears that reason ousted piety—unless we should call the founding fathers pietistic.

One way of looking at American pietism and rationalism is aesthetic. William Clebsch has recently elaborated that point of view.[12] In his opinion, such representatively American thinkers as Jonathan Edwards, Ralph Waldo Emerson, and William James were most moved by the world's beauty. Another way of approaching American religion is to emphasize religious liberty. Sidney Mead has argued that the American experiment in religious pluralism proved as momentous as the establishment of Christianity in imperial Rome.[13]

Both these views owe much to the Enlightenment's advances on the Reformation. The Reformation established the principles of individual conscience and individual interpretation of scripture. The Enlightenment proposed that reason—nondogmatic thought common to all—should be the judge when individual interpretations shattered civic peace. In this new land, where individual opportunity was rich, reason sat in the official driver's seat.

In the matter of religious liberty through law, Americans made quantum leaps over their European forebears. There was much less than full political equality, as generations of blacks and women have underscored, but something novel was present that we have come to call pluralism. In religious terms, it was an attempt to live together as equals despite differences in creed. In secular terms, it was a search for a common sense to ensure economic and political cooperation. In theological terms, it conjured up natural theology—speculation about God apart from scripture or dogma. For Roman Catholics, the implications of American pluralism hit Europe only in the "Decree on Religious Liberty" of the Second Vatican Council, where the American model was accepted for the whole Church.

Despite its faults, America has done much that is commendable. In a world where the majority still seek basic human rights, including the right to religious liberty, America looks quite good. Even in the perspective of the world religions, our civic tolerance is remarkable.

At its most tepid, American religion has tolerated civic piety—mouthings on Memorial Day and the Fourth of July. However, it has also sponsored ecumenical debate, academic freedom, and political and religious dissent. The question now is whether pluralism is so inseparable from secularism that it condemns us to religious superficiality.[14]

Has our agreement to disagree about fundamentals relegated them to the private sphere? If religion is absent from the public places where we forge our national culture, our center may not hold. On the other hand, if religion is pursued only by the pious, genuine traditionalists will not want it to hold. Eric Voegelin has said that a crucial test of a culture is whether it enlists the best of its youth or alienates them. For both United States government and United States religion, that can be a hard saying.

We have become used to speeches telling us that our government has only to be as good as its citizens for America to prosper. In too many political assemblies, churches, and synagogues, that is a palliative, a placebo. It brings no health or distinction to the speaker or the audience. To a religious guru, it shows that the speaker ignores the human condition—the beginner's mind, the nature of enlightenment. Unreflective, unmeditative, the speaker cannot be terse, poetic, evocative; he or she can only pour forth the old, stale, placating language. Ignorant of ignorance and sin, the speaker sees no tragedy. Lacking rigor, stupid in the reasons of the heart, the speaker thinks hope is the same as good cheer.

Much the same is true of the audience, of ourselves. Not having gone down in spiritual death, we do not fly to the gods. Not set for spiritual combat, we do not resent that the seats are plush, the rhetoric easy. In part, that is because our culture tells us that only eggheads knit their brows and ponder. In part, it is because we are too lazy to live. In many cases it is a major accomplishment for us to endure ten minutes of silence.

From a religious perspective, the economic facts of American popular culture—the money we pay entertainers, athletes, and business executives—are absurd. Compared to what we pay the people who shape our nation's soul—the artists, scientists, nurses, teachers, and mothers—they are spiritual madness, what Aeschylus called *nosos*. Compared to how we treat the world's starving, they are beyond belief. Two thousand years ago, the *Book of Mencius* began by condemning profit. Wise people would have taken that lesson and banked it. We, however, have built a culture on profit. It is what makes our Ronny and Sally run. When will we see that they are usually running in circles?

People who say things that others do not want to hear, no matter how true such things may be, will suffer for their indiscretion. Socrates stands as the paradigm of their fate, and Socrates shows that in the political realm, prophets and sages are one. He also shows that prophets and sages cannot live for audience applause. They must do what they have to do, say what they have to say, because it is their truth, their good, their charge. Shamans, for further instance, must sing—because it relieves their sadness, because it makes them whole. Plato's "Seventh Letter" says that the philosophical soul must live by a love of the Good, that it can deny the Good only by denying its self. Religious people, creative people, humanity's benefactors have all found something more precious than human praise. Better, they have all been found by something more precious.

That something is the sacred, the numinous, the holy, the really real. It is Wakan Tanka, the Tao, Buddha-nature, God. Commonly, it is the essence of any conviction significant in the ultimate order, in the world as it finally is. The world as it finally is is the one place where you get what you are. It is where someone may finally tell you, "If you do not believe in mystery, God, or the Tao, be honest about it." By being honest you will reap two benefits. First, you will not bring ultimate realities into further disrepute. Second, you will take the first step in the pilgrimage toward wisdom, which is acknowledging the truth.

A second step is no less simple or heroic. It is to love the truth that you acknowledge. That may be the truth that mystery is beautiful or the truth that the religions often cant. It may move you to sound the ram's horn or to void at the flag. The point is not so much the content as the act. The dynamic of human consciousness, on which any genuine wisdom takes its stand, is a movement from one's present light to wherever that light leads. "Lead kindly light," Cardinal Newman and others have prayed. Go to your light's source, Augustine and others have counseled. Your light shines in the darkness, and the darkness cannot overcome it—as long as you want to be human, as long as samsara is not your all.

Whatever is noble, whatever is good, whatever is honest—think on it, St. Paul said. Whatever is your current belief about American religion, face it and start to love it. If it is a solid truth, your personality will ripen, your social circle will take fire. If it is a rotten pseudo-truth, you will hear a call to turn and change your heart. In the spiritual life, the only disaster is avoidance. Because they will not face their own beliefs, whether solid or rotten, many stay half-asleep.

Awakened, human consciousness reveals its intrinsic religiousness by pursuing the light to where it

Figure 51   The Sleep of Reason Produces Monsters, *by Francisco Goya, Spanish (1746–1828). Etching and aquatint; 7³/₁₆ × 4³/₄ in. The Nelson–Atkins Museum of Art, Kansas City, Missouri.*

is love. Worthy religious traditions and patriotism have nothing to fear from this pursuit. The pursuer does have some things to fear, but they pale in comparison with what there is to gain. In Eastern terms, the pursuer learns about ignorance: how much is samsaric in his or her starting "truth." In Western terms, the pursuer learns about sin: how difficult it is to follow only the light. Why we do not know the good we should know, why we do not do the good we should do—they are among our deepest mysteries. Only when you ponder them can you call yourself mature, let alone wise. Still, understanding these mysteries is the major therapy that any self needs. Understanding them is the heart of traditional political science.

However, the religions' dharma and prophecy illumine much more than ignorance and sin. Ultimately they lead to enlightenment and grace. Enlightenment happens: It is an empirical fact. Light floods some people, bringing them inexpressible joy. Similarly, grace happens: There are marvelous saints. They love God with whole mind, heart, soul, and strength. They serve sisters and brothers more than themselves.

In a dark and troubled time (that is, in any historical time), saints and enlightened people save our beleaguered hope. Just one of them is stronger than all the rubbish, all the valid ground for cynicism. For a single really holy, really religious, really humane person says that what we want and need is possible. We want and need light and love. Light and love are possible. By definition, light and love are buddha-nature and God. By saintly testimony, they are our center.

Discussion Questions

1. To what extent do the religions share a common attraction toward mystery?

2. Explain the following: "The final utility of religion is that it can teach us how to die and how to live."

3. What have been the principal strengths and weaknesses of American religion?

4. Write a brief definition of *religion* that takes into account the traditions' unity and the traditions' diversity.

5. What is the permanent lesson in the Eastern traditions' elevation of the sage?

6. What is the permanent lesson in the Western traditions' elevation of the prophet?

7. On what grounds might one defend "profit"?

8. How have the religions fostered or defended pseudospeciation?

9. Why does the experience of enlightenment or grace tend to lessen greed?

10. How valid is it to study a religion without personally confronting its call for conversion?

11. What have been the benefits of civil religions?

12. What is the mystical dimension in every human life?

Glossary

pseudospeciation: a term employed by the psychologist Erik Erikson to denote the tendency of people to deny the humanity of groups outside their own cultural circle. Erikson's point was the gap between psychology and biology at this point, as people who manifestly belong to the same biological species (who could, for instance, mate and reproduce) contrive to deny that the "others"—foreigners, aliens—are as human as their own kind. The extreme form of pseudospeciation is xenophobia—fear of foreigners to the point of hatred. Pseudospeciation thrived when peoples were isolated and so somewhat plausibly could keep their myths to the effect that creation had occurred in their neighborhood and they were the center of the earth. With the development of a planetary culture in recent decades, pseudospeciation stands revealed as more pathological than was first appreciated, and the religious contributions to pseudospeciation (bigotry, crusades, holy wars) stand revealed as dubious expressions of an estimable divinity.

NOTES

Introduction

1. This story is adapted from the Dutch Catholic bishops' work, *A New Catechism* (New York: Herder and Herder, 1967), p. 3.
2. See Michael Polanyi, *Personal Knowledge* (New York: Harper Torchbooks, 1964); Stephen Toulmin, *Human Understanding* (Princeton, N.J.: Princeton University Press, 1977). For a discussion of Western religion and the distinctive rise of Western science, see Stanley L. Jaki, *The Road of Science and the Ways to God* (Chicago: University of Chicago Press, 1978).
3. Philip Kapleau, *The Three Pillars of Zen* (Boston: Beacon Press, 1967), pp. 189–291.
4. For example, Heinz Robert Schlette, *Toward a Theology of Religions* (New York: Herder and Herder, 1966).
5. Another view of theology, geared to its easier practice in the university, is Shubert Ogden's "Theology and Religious Studies: Their Difference and the Difference It Makes," *Journal of The American Academy of Religion,* 1978, *46*(1):3–17.
6. John Carmody, "Faith in Religious Studies," *Communio,* 1976, *3*(1):39–49.
7. W. Richard Comstock, *The Study of Religion and Primitive Religions* (New York: Harper & Row, 1971), pp. 13–17.
8. See Erik Erikson's *Gandhi's Truth* (New York: Norton, 1969).
9. See Clifford Geertz, *The Interpretation of Cultures* (New York: Basic Books, 1973), pp. 412–453.
10. For a several-methoded approach to Judaism, see *Take Judaism, for Example: Studies toward the Comparison of Religions,* ed. Jacob Neusner (Chicago: University of Chicago Press, 1983). The methods are not precisely the five we have sketched, but the book's four stages (Analysis, Description, Interpretation, and Comparison) cover much the same ground. For a good introduction to the several different extensions of Torah, see *Back to the Sources,* ed. Barry W. Holtz (New York: Summit Books, 1984). As a way into the methodology most influential in recent studies of world religions, see Ugo Bianchi, "History of Religions," *The Encyclopedia of Religion,* vol. 6, ed. Mircea Eliade (New York: Macmillan, 1987), 399–408. (Hereafter cited as *ER*). Other stimulating sources include *The World's Religious Traditions,* ed. Frank Whaling (New York: Crossroad, 1986); and Jonathan Z. Smith, *Imagining Religion* (Chicago: University of Chicago Press, 1982). What these methodological studies most suggest is the crying need for a theory of consciousness that could map their different questions and coordinate them. We favor the views of Bernard Lonergan and Eric Voegelin. See Lonergan's *Insight* (New York: Philosophical Library, 1958) and *Method in Theology* (New York: Herder and Herder, 1972). See Voegelin's *Anamnesis* (Notre Dame, Ind.: University of Notre Dame Press, 1978) and *In Search of Order: Order and History,* vol. 5 (Baton Rouge: Louisiana State University Press, 1987).
11. See 1989 Britannica Book of the Year (Chicago: Encyclopedia Britannica, Inc., 1989), p. 299.
12. Florinda Donner, *Shabono* (New York: Delacorte, 1982), pp. 163–164.

Chapter 1:
The Ancient Religious Mind

1. Shunryu Suzuki, *Zen Mind, Beginner's Mind* (New York: John Weatherhill, 1970), p. xxx.
2. See John Bowker, *The Sense of God* (Oxford: Clarendon Press, 1973), pp. 57–58, 228. On prehistoric religion generally, see Mary Edwardsen, James Waller, et al., "Prehistoric Religions," *ER,* 1987, *11,* 505–522.
3. Sherwood Washburn, "The Evolution of Man," *Scientific American,* 1978, *239*(3):196–197.
4. E. O. James, "Prehistoric Religion," in *Historia Religionum, I,* ed. C. J. Bleeker and G. Widengren (Leiden: E. J. Brill, 1969), p. 23.
5. Mircea Eliade, "On Prehistoric Religions," *History of Religions,* 1974, *14*(2):141. (Hereafter cited as *HR*).
6. Eric Neumann, *The Origins and History of Consciousness* (Princeton, N.J.: Princeton University Press, 1971), pp. 5–101.
7. Jacques Waardenburg, ed., *Classical Approaches to the Study of Religion* (The Hague: Mouton, 1973), pp. 3–78.
8. Barre Toelken, "Seeing with a Native Eye: How Many Sheep Will It Hold?", in *Seeing with a Native Eye,* ed. Walter H. Capps (New York: Harper & Row, 1976), p. 9.
9. E. G. Parrinder, "Religions of Illiterate Peoples," in *Historia Religionum, II,* ed. C. J. Bleeker and G. Widengren (Leiden: E. J. Brill, 1971), p. 550.
10. James, "Prehistoric Religion," p. 23.
11. Bowker, *Sense of God,* pp. 44–65.
12. Merlin Stone, *When God Was a Woman* (New York: Dial Press, 1976), pp. 1–18. Behind this conception may well lie a more central role for women in biological evolution than they have hitherto been accorded. Recent

studies suggest that women were the primary socializers of developing humanity, as well as the source of from 50 to 90 percent of its food. See Nancy Tanner and Adrienne Zihlman, "Women in Evolution, Part I: Innovation and Selection in Human Origins," *Signs,* 1976, *1*(3):585–608; Adrienne I. Zihlman, "Women and Evolution, Part II: Subsistence and Social Organization among Early Hominids," *Signs,* 1978, *4*(1):4–20. On the rise of feminine deities, see James J. Preston et al., "Goddess Worship," *ER,* 1987 *6,* 35–59. For perspectives on why goddess worship did not necessarily improve the social lot of women, see Gerda Lerner, *The Creation of Patriarchy* (New York: Oxford University Press, 1986).

13.   Adolf E. Jensen, *Myth and Cult among Primitive Peoples* (Chicago: University of Chicago Press, 1963), pp. 135–146.

14.   Mircea Eliade, *A History of Religious Ideas,* vol. 1, *From the Stone Age to the Eleusinian Mysteries* (Chicago: University of Chicago Press, 1978).

15.   Ibid., p. 4.

16.   See Joseph Campbell, *The Masks of God: Primitive Mythology* (New York: Viking, 1970), pp. 173–176; Jensen, *Myth and Cult,* pp. 107–112.

17.   Eliade, *History of Religious Ideas,* vol. 1, pp. 38–39.

18.   Ibid., p. 115. For megalithic religion in general, see Marija Gimbutas and J. Stephen Lansing, "Megalithic Religion," *ER,* 1987, *9,* 336–346. On Stonehenge in particular, see Benjamin C. Ray, "Stonehenge: A New Theory," *HR,* February 1974, *26*(3):225–278.

19.   Björn Kurtén, *Dance of the Tiger* (New York: Berkeley Books, 1981), pp. 198–199.

Chapter 2:
Religions of Recent Nonliterate Peoples

1.   Mircea Eliade, *Cosmos and History* (New York: Harper & Row, 1959), pp. 8–16.

2.   Rudolf Otto, *The Idea of the Holy* (New York: Oxford University Press, 1958), pp. 12–40; see also Carsten Colpe, "Sacred and Profane, The," *ER, 12,* 511–526; Joel L. Brereton, "Sacred Space," ibid., 526–535; Barbara C. Sproul, "Sacred Time," ibid., 535–544.

3.   G. Van der Leeuw, *Religion in Essence and Manifestation, I* (New York: Harper & Row, 1963), p. 23.

4.   Bruce Lincoln, "Treatment of Hair and Fingernails among the Indo-Europeans," *HR,* 1977, *16*(4): 351–362.

5.   Manabu Waida, "Symbolisms of the Moon and the Waters of Immortality," *HR,* 1977, *16*(4):407–423.

6.   Theodore M. Ludwig, "Gods and Goddesses," *ER, 6,* 59–66.

7.   Mircea Eliade, *From Primitives to Zen* (New York: Harper & Row, 1967).

8.   Hartley Burr Alexander, *The World's Rim* (Lincoln: University of Nebraska Press, 1953), pp. 63–99.

9.   Joseph Campbell, *The Masks of God, I: Primitive Mythology* (New York: Viking, 1970), p. 151.

10.   Durango Mendoza, "Summer Water and Shirley," in *American Indian Authors,* ed. Natachee Scott Momaday (Boston: Houghton Mifflin, 1972), pp. 96–105.

11.   Clyde Kluckhohn, *Navaho Witchcraft* (Boston: Beacon Press, 1967), pp. 13–61.

12.   Ruth M. Underhill, *Red Man's Religion* (Chicago: University of Chicago Press, 1965), p. 51.

13.   Carlos Castaneda, *Tales of Power* (New York: Simon & Schuster, 1974), pp. 118–162.

14.   Annie Dillard, *Pilgrim at Tinker Creek* (New York: Harper's Magazine Press, 1974), pp. 163–164.

15.   Adolph E. Jensen, *Myth and Cult among Primitive Peoples* (Chicago: University of Chicago Press, 1963), pp. 1–79. W. Richard Comstock, *The Study of Religion and Primitive Religions* (New York: Harper & Row, 1971), 28–72; John J. Collins, *Primitive Religion* (Totowa, N.J.: Littlefield, Adams, 1978), pp. 55–158; Kees W. Bolle et al., "Myth," *ER, 10,* 261–285; Evan M. Zuesse, "Ritual," *ER, 12,* 405–422.

16.   Marcel Griaule, *Conversations with Ogotemmeli* (London: Oxford University Press, 1965), pp. xi–3.

17.   Joseph Epes Brown, ed., *The Sacred Pipe* (Baltimore: Penguin, 1971), pp. 116–126. Black Elk's exposure to Christianity makes it difficult to consider him a pure representative.

18.   Colin Turnbull, *The Forest People* (New York: Simon & Schuster, 1962), pp. 184–200.

19.   Mircea Eliade, *Myths, Dreams, and Mysteries* (New York: Harper & Row, 1960), pp. 174–175.

20.   Mircea Eliade, *Shamanism* (Princeton, N.J.: Princeton University Press, 1964), pp. 3–13.

21.   Odd Nordland, "Shamanism as an Experiencing of the 'Unreal,'" in *Studies in Shamanism,* ed. Carl-Martin Edmans (Stockholm: Almquist and Wiksell, 1967), pp. 166–185.

22.   Arthur Waley, *The Nine Songs* (London: Allen & Unwin, 1955).

23.   Ichiro Hori, *Folk Religion in Japan* (Chicago: University of Chicago Press, 1968), p. 181.

24.   I. M. Lewis, *Ecstatic Religion* (Middlesex, England: Penguin, 1971).

25.   John Neihardt, *Black Elk Speaks* (Lincoln: University of Nebraska Press, 1961), p. 20.

26.   Napoleon Chagnon, *Yanomamo: The Fierce People* (New York: Holt, Rinehart and Winston, 1968), p. 52.

27.   Carl-Martin Edmans, ed., *Studies in Shamanism* (Stockholm: Almquist and Wiksell, 1967; see also Mircea Eliade et al., "Shamanism," *ER, 13,* 201–222.

28.   Robert Coles, *Children of Crisis,* vol. 4, *Eskimos, Chicanos, Indians* (Boston: Little, Brown, 1977).

29.   Ibid., p. 522; see also Werner Müller, "North American Indians," *ER, 10,* 469–525; Catherine L. Albanese, "Exploring Regional Religion: A Case Study of the Eastern Cherokee," *HR,* May 1984, *23*(4):344–371.

30.   See C. G. Jung, *Memories, Dreams, Reflections* (New York: Vintage, 1963), pp. 246–253.

31.   Weston La Barre, "Amerindian Religions," in *Historical Atlas of the Religions of the World,* ed. I. al Faruqi and D. Sopher (New York: Macmillan, 1974), pp. 51–57.

32.   J. R. Fox, "Religions of Illiterate People: North America," in *Historia Religionum, II,* ed. C. J. Bleeker and G. Widengren (Leiden: E. J. Brill, 1971), pp. 593–608.

33.   A. Clos, "Religions of Illiterate People: Asia," in *Historia Religionum, II,* ed. C. J. Bleeker and G. Widengren (Leiden: E. J. Brill, 1971), pp. 573–592.

34.   Eliade, *From Primitives to Zen,* p. 88.

35.   Paul Radin, *The Trickster: A Study in American Indian Mythology* (New York: Philosophical Library, 1956); see also Klaus-Peter Koepping, "Absurdity and Hidden Truth: Cunning Intelligence and Grotesque Body Images as Manifestations of the Trickster," *HR,* February 1985, *24*(3):191–214.

36.   Underhill, *Red Man's Religion,* p. 104.

37.   Charles A. Eastman, *The Soul of the Indian* (Boston: Houghton Mifflin, 1911), pp. 6–8.

38.   See La Barre, "Amerindian Religions," p. 52.

39.   Emory Sekaquaptewa, "Hopi Indian Ceremonies," in *Seeing with a Native Eye,* ed. Walter H. Capps (New York: Harper & Row, 1976), p. 39.

40.   La Barre, "Amerindian Religions," p. 53.

41.   Dee Brown, *Bury My Heart at Wounded Knee* (New York: Holt, Rinehart and Winston, 1971).

42.   Carl F. Starkloff, *The People of the Center: American Indian Religion and Christianity* (New York: Seabury, 1974).

43.   Ake Hultzkrantz, "The Contribution of the Study of North American Indian Religions to the History of Religions," in *Seeing with a Native Eye,* ed. Walter H. Capps (New York: Harper & Row, 1976), pp. 86–106.

44.   Sam D. Gill, "Native American Religions," *Council on the Study of Religion Bulletin,* 1978, *9*(5):125–128.

45.   Ake Hultzkrantz, "North American Indian Religion in the History of Research: A General Survey," *HR,* 1966, *6*(2):91–107; 1967, *6*(3):183–207; 1967, *7*(1):13–34; 1967, *7*(2):112–148.

46.   Margaret Atwood, *Surfacing* (New York: Popular Library, 1976).

47.   N. Scott Momaday, "Native American Attitudes to the Environment," in *Seeing with a Native Eye,* ed. Walter H. Capps (New York: Harper & Row, 1976), pp. 79–85.

48.   See Coles, *Children of Crisis,* vol. 4, pp. 216–217; see also Inge Kleivan, "Inuit Religion," *ER, 7,* 270–273; and Daniel Merkur, "Eagle, the Hunter's Helper: The Cultural Significance of Inuit Mythological Tales," *HR,* November 1987, *27*(2):171–188.

49.   Kaj Birket-Smith, *The Eskimos* (London: Methuen, 1959), p. 161.

50.   Franz Boas, *The Central Eskimo* (Lincoln: University of Nebraska Press, 1964), p. 175.

51.   Ibid., pp. 178–179.

52.   Birket-Smith, *The Eskimos.*

53.   Knud Rasmussen, *Across Arctic America* (New York: Putnam's, 1927), p. 385.

54.   Ibid., p. 386.

55.   Ibid., p. 81.

56.   Ibid., p. 86.

57.   Eliade, *Shamanism,* p. 58.

58.   Barry Lopez, *Arctic Dreams* (New York: Charles Scribner's Sons, 1986), brings the reader into this traditional Eskimo sensitivity to the environment.

59.   Clos, "Religions of Illiterate People: Asia," p. 576.

60.   Birket-Smith, *Eskimos,* p. 166.

61.   Collins, *Primitive Religion,* pp. 65–66.

62.   Peter Freuchen, *Book of the Eskimos* (Cleveland: World, 1961).

63.   Boas, *Central Eskimo,* p. 201.

64.   Rasmussen, *Across Arctic America,* p. 261.

65.   See Turnbull, *The Forest People,* p. 252.

66.   John Mbiti, "Traditional Religions in Africa," in *Historical Atlas of the Religions of the World,* ed. I. al Faruqi and D. Sopher (New York: Macmillan, 1974), pp. 61–68; see also Benjamin C. Ray et al., "African Religions," *ER, 1,* 60–96.

67.   David B. Barrett, ed., *World Christian Encyclopedia* (New York: Oxford University Press, 1982), p. 782.

68.   For moving literary presentations, see Hamidou Kane, *Ambiguous Adventure* (New York: Collier Books, 1969), on Islam; and Chinua Achebe, *No Longer at Ease* (New York: Fawcett, 1969), on Christianity.

69.   Evan Zuesse, "Divination and Deity in African Religions," *HR,* 1975, *15*(2):167, note 15.

70.   Henri Frankfort, *Kingship and the Gods* (Chicago: University of Chicago Press, 1978), pp. 33–34. (Originally published 1948.)

71.   Geoffrey Parrinder, *African Traditional Religion,* 3rd ed. (New York: Harper & Row, 1976), p. 17.

72.   Geoffrey Parrinder, "Religions of Illiterate People: Africa," in *Historia Religionum, II,* ed. C. J. Bleeker and G. Widengren (Leiden: E. J. Brill, 1971), p. 556.

73.   John Mbiti, *African Religions and Philosophy* (Garden City, N.Y.: Doubleday, 1969), p. 67.

74.   Parrinder, "Religions of Illiterate People: Africa," p. 561.

75.   W. Richard Comstock, *The Study of Religion and Primitive Religions,* p. 80; see also Luc de Heusch, *Sacrifice in Africa* (Bloomington: Indiana University Press, 1985).

76.   This paragraph is adapted from Denise Lardner Carmody, *Women and World Religions* (Nashville: Abingdon, 1979), p. 34. See Carol P. MacCormack, "Biological Events and Cultural Control," *Signs,* 1971, *3*(1):93–100; also Mbiti, *African Religions and Philosophy,* pp. 165–171.

77.   Turnbull, *The Forest People,* p. 217.

78.   See Ian Barbour, ed., *Finite Resources and the Human Future* (Minneapolis: Augsburg, 1976), especially pp. 55–114.

79. Parrinder, "Religions of Illiterate People: Africa," p. 564.

80. Eliade, *From Primitives to Zen,* p. 269.

81. Ibid., p. 268.

82. Parrinder, "Religions of Illiterate People: Africa," p. 567.

83. Zuesse, "Divination and Deity," pp. 158–182.

84. Ibid., p. 167, note 15.

85. See Parrinder, *African Traditional Religion,* p. 124.

86. This is dramatically portrayed in the anthropological novel by Elenore Smith Bowen, *Return to Laughter* (Garden City, N.Y.: Doubleday, 1964).

87. Geoffrey Barraclough, ed., *The Times Atlas of World History* (Maplewood, N.J.: Hammond, 1979), p. 236.

88. Patrick White, *A Fringe of Leaves* (New York: Viking, 1977). Also, see White's earlier novel *Voss* (New York: Viking, 1957), especially pp. 237 ff; see also Ronald M. Berndt et al., "Australian Religions," *ER, 1,* 529–570.

89. See Mircea Eliade, *Australian Religions* (Ithaca, N.Y.: Cornell University Press, 1973), p. 194.

90. T. G. H. Strehlow, "Religions of Illiterate People: Australia," in *Historia Religionum, II,* ed. C. J. Bleeker and G. Widengren (Leiden: E. J. Brill, 1971), pp. 609–628.

91. Emile Durkheim, *The Elementary Forms of the Religious Life* (New York: Free Press, 1965).

92. Eliade, *Australian Religions,* p. 68.

93. Eliade, *From Primitives to Zen,* pp. 140–141.

94. Ibid., p. 162.

95. Rita M. Gross, "Menstruation and Childbirth as Ritual and Religious Experience in the Religion of the Australian Aborigines," *JAAR,* 1977, *45*(4):1147–1181.

96. Eliade, *Australian Religions,* p. 88.

97. Ibid., p. 92.

98. Ibid., p. 122.

99. Eliade, *From Primitives to Zen,* p. 424.

100. See William Richardson, *Heidegger: Through Phenomenology to Thought* (The Hague: Martinus Nijhoff, 1967).

101. Walker Percy, *The Thanatos Syndrome* (New York: Farrar, Straus & Giroux, 1987).

102. Bernard Lonergan, *Method in Theology* (New York: Herder and Herder, 1972), pp. 101–103.

103. Erik Erikson, *Toys and Reasons* (New York: Norton, 1977), pp. 67–118.

104. Carol P. Christ, "Why Women Need the Goddess: Phenomenological, Psychological, and Political Reflections," in *Woman-spirit Rising,* ed. Carol P. Christ and Judith Plaskow (New York: Harper & Row, 1979), pp. 273–287.

105. E. F. Schumacher, *Small Is Beautiful* (New York: Harper Torchbooks, 1973).

106. Sam Gill, *Beyond the Primitive: The Religions of Non-literate Peoples* (Englewood Cliffs, N.J.: Prentice-Hall, 1982), p. 111.

107. See Michael Harner, *The Way of the Shaman: A Guide to Power and Healing* (New York: Harper & Row, 1980).

Chapter 3:
Hinduism

1. Troy Wilson Organ, *Hinduism* (Woodbury, N.Y.: Barron's, 1974), p. 40; see also Thomas Hopkins, *The Hindu Tradition* (Encino, Calif.: Dickenson, 1971), pp. 3–10; A. L. Basham, *The Wonder That Was India* (New York: Grove Press, 1959), pp. 10–30.

2. On the earliest history and religion of the Indian Aryans, see Mircea Eliade, *A History of Religious Ideas,* vol. 1, *From the Stone Age to the Eleusinian Mysteries* (Chicago: University of Chicago Press, 1978), pp. 186–199.

3. Organ, *Hinduism,* p. 51.

4. See Edward C. Dimock, Jr., et al., *The Literature of India: An Introduction* (Chicago: University of Chicago Press, 1978), pp. 1–2. Also Satsvarupta dasa Gosvami, *Readings in Vedic Literature* (New York: Bhaktivedanta Book Trust, 1977), pp. 3–4. For an overview of Vedic literature, see James A. Santucci, *An Outline of Vedic Literature* (Missoula, Mont.: Scholars Press), 1976.

5. On the polarity of the *asuras* and *devas* in Vedic religion, see F. B. J. Kuiper, "The Basic Concept of Vedic Religion," *HR,* 1975, *15*(2):111.

6. Stella Kramrisch, "The Indian Great Goddess," *HR,* 1975, *14*(4):235–265. As an introduction to the complexity of the Hindu order of the gods, see J. Bruce Long, "Daksa: Divine Embodiment of Creative Skill," *HR,* 1977, *17*(1):29–60.

7. See Organ, *Hinduism,* p. 66; and Brian K. Smith, "Gods and Men in Vedic Ritualism," *HR,* May 1985, *24*(4):291–307.

8. Hopkins, *Hindu Religious Tradition,* pp. 19–35; see also Joseph Henniger, "Sacrifice," *ER, 12,* 544–557. On the horse sacrifice, see Wendy Doniger O'Flaherty, "Horses," *ER, 6,* 464, and *Women, Androgynes, and Other Mythical Beasts* (Chicago: University of Chicago Press, 1980), pp. 149–166; Francis X. Clooney, S. J., "Jaimini's Contribution to the Theory of Sacrifice as the Experience of Transcendence," *HR,* February 1986, *25*(3):199–212.

9. Morton Klass, "Varna and Jati," *ER, 15,* 188.

10. Robert Ernest Hume, *The Thirteen Principal Upanishads* (New York: Oxford University Press, 1971), pp. 5–13.

11. Wendy Doniger O'Flaherty, *Karma and Rebirth in the Classical Indian Tradition* (Berkeley: University of California Press, 1980); William K. Mahoney, "Karman: Hindu and Jain Concepts," *ER, 8,* 261–266.

12. Hume, *The Thirteen Principal Upanishads,* pp. 362–365.

13. For a comparison of the Vedic and Upanishadic mystiques, see S. N. Dasgupta, *Hindu Mysticism* (New York: Frederick Ungar, 1959), pp. 3–57.

14. Mircea Eliade, *A History of Religious Ideas,* vol. 2 (Chicago: University of Chicago Press, 1982), pp. 84–88.

15. Heinrich Zimmer, *Philosophies of India* (Princeton, N.J.: Princeton University Press, 1969), pp. 227–234.

16. For a brief summary of Jainism, see Carlo Della Casa, "Jainism," in *Historia Religionum, II,* ed. C. J. Bleeker and G. Widengren (Leiden: E. J. Brill, 1971), pp. 346–371; see also A. L. Basham, "Jainism," in *The Concise Encyclopedia of Living Faiths,* ed. R. C. Zaehner (Boston: Beacon Press, 1967), pp. 261–266, and Colette Caillat, "Jainism," *ER, 7,* 507–514.

17. See Dasgupta, *Hindu Mysticism,* pp. 113–168; see also Norvin Hein, "A Revolution in Krsnaism: The Cult of Gopala," *HR,* May 1985, *25*(4):296–317.

18. Organ, *Hinduism,* p. 150; see also David R. Kinsley, *The Sword and the Flute* (Berkeley: University of California Press, 1975), pp. 1–78.

19. See John Stratton Hawley, "Thief of Butter, Thief of Love," *HR,* 1979, *18*(3):203–220.

20. See Kinsley, *Sword and the Flute;* see also Basham, *Wonder That Was India,* pp. 304–306; John Stratton Hawley, "Krsna," *ER, 8,* 354–387; and Friedhelm E. Hardy, "Krsnaism," ibid., 387–392.

21. Franklin Edgerton, *The Bhagavad Gita* (New York: Harper Torchbooks, 1964), p. 105; see also R. C. Zaehner, *The Bhagavad-Gita* (New York: Oxford University Press, 1973), pp. 1–41; Ann Stanford, *The Bhagavad Gita* (New York: Seabury, 1970), pp. vii–xxvii; Juan Mascaró, *The Bhagavad Gita* (Baltimore: Penguin, 1962), pp. 9–36; Gerald James Larson, "The *Bhagavad Gita* as Cross-Cultural Process," *JAAR,* 1975, *43*(4):651–669; John B. Carman, "Bhakti," *ER, 2,* 130–134; and Alf Hiltebeitel, "The Two Krsnas on One Chariot," *HR,* August 1984, *24*(1):1–26.

22. Wendy Doniger O'Flaherty, *Asceticism and Eroticism in the Mythology of Shiva* (New York: Oxford University Press, 1973), pp. 83–110; see also Stella Kramrish, *The Presence of Siva* (Princeton, N.J.: Princeton University Press, 1981), and "Siva," *ER, 13,* 338–341. For specimens of later Dravidian devotional Shaivism, see R. K. Ramanujan, *Speaking of Siva* (Baltimore: Penguin, 1973).

23. Dimock et al., *Literature of India,* p. 2.

24. See Sarvepalli Radhakrishnan and Charles A. Moore, ed., *A Sourcebook in Indian Philosophy* (Princeton, N.J.: Princeton University Press, 1957), pp. 184–189.

25. On the "tripartite Indo-European ideology" (priests-warriors-farmers) that George Dumézil has found at the root of Aryan society, see Eliade, *History of Religious Ideas,* vol. 1, pp. 192–195.

26. See Radhakrishman and Moore, *Sourcebook in India Philosophy,* pp. 193–223.

27. Sudhir Kakar, "The Human Life Cycle: The Traditional Hindu View and the Psychology of Erik H. Erikson," *Philosophy East and West,* 1968, *18:*127–136; see also Basham, *Wonder That Was India,* p. 158.

28. Basham, *Wonder That Was India,* pp. 177–188; see also Katherine K. Young, "Hinduism," in *Women in World Religion,* ed. Arvind Sharma (Albany: State University of New York Press, 1987), pp. 59–103.

29. See Roy C. Amore and Larry D. Shin, eds., *Lustful Maidens and Ascetic Kings* (New York: Oxford University Press, 1981), pp. 74–86.

30. See ibid., pp. 166–168.

31. On the six orthodox schools, see Radhakrishnan and Moore, *Sourcebook in India Philosophy,* pp. 349–572; Zimmer, *Philosophies of India,* pp. 280–332 (Samkyha and Yoga), 605–614.

32. See Zaehner, *Hinduism,* pp. 36–56; see also R. C. Zaehner, *Hindu and Muslim Mysticism* (New York: Schocken, 1969), pp. 41–63.

33. Glenn E. Yocum, "Shrines, Shamanism, and Love Poetry," *JAAR,* 1973, *61*(1):3–17.

34. See Zaehner, *Hindu and Muslim Mysticism,* pp. 64–85.

35. On the Puranic Shiva, see Cornelia Dimmitt and J. A. B. van Buitenen, eds., *Classical Hindu Mythology* (Philadelphia: Temple University Press, 1978), pp. 59–146. On Shiva in the Tamil literature, see Glenn E. Yocum, "Manikkavacar's Image of Shiva," *HR,* 1976, *16*(1):20–41; Fred W. Clothey, "Tamil Religions," *ER, 14,* 261–268; David Shulman, "Terror of Symbols and Symbols of Terror," *HR,* November 1986, *26*(2):101–124; Stuart H. Blackburn, "Death and Deification: Folk Cults in Hinduism," *HR,* February 1985, *24*(3):255–274; Norman Cutler, "The Devotee's Experience of the Sacred Tamil Hymns," *HR,* November 1984, *24*(2):91–112.

36. Organ, *Hinduism,* p. 288.

37. See Zimmer, *Philosophies of India,* pp. 560–602; see also Kees W. Bolle, *The Persistence of Religion* (Leiden: E. J. Brill, 1965); Mircea Eliade, *Yoga: Immortality and Freedom* (Princeton, N.J.: Princeton University Press, 1970), pp. 200–273; and André Padoux, "Tantrism," *ER, 14,* 272–280.

38. Ernest Wood, *Yoga* (Baltimore: Pelican, 1962), pp. 140–147; see also Eliade, *Yoga,* pp. 244–249; and Daniel Gold and Ann Grodzins Gold, "The Fate of the Householder Nath," *HR,* November 1984, *24*(2):113–132.

39. For a brief survey of Sikhism, see Khushwant Singh, "Sikhism," in *Historical Atlas of the Religions of the World,* ed. I. al Faruqi and D. Sopher (New York: Macmillan, 1974), pp. 105–108; see also John Noss, *Man's Religions* (New York: Macmillan, 1974), pp. 226–235; and Khushwant Singh, "Sikhism," *ER, 13,* 315–320.

40. However, see Cyrus R. Pangborn, "The Ramakrishna Math and Mission," in *Hinduism: New Essays in the*

History of Religions, ed. Bardwell L. Smith (Leiden: E. J. Brill, 1976), pp. 98–119.

41. See Organ, *Hinduism,* pp. 319–325; and Charlotte Vaudeville, "Kabir," *ER, 8,* 226–227.

42. Nervin J. Hein, "Caitanya's Ecstasies and the Theology of the Name," in *Hinduism: New Essays in the History of Religions,* ed. Bardwell L. Smith (Leiden: E. J. Brill, 1976), pp. 15–32; Joseph T. O'Connell, "Caitanya's Followers and the Bhagavad-Gita," in *Hinduism,* pp. 33–52.

43. See Edward C. Dimock, Jr., and Denise Levertov, trans., *In Praise of Krishna* (Garden City, N.Y.: Doubleday, 1967).

44. Following are some representative works: Swami Prabhupada, *The Nectar of Devotion* (Los Angeles: Bhaktivedanta Book Trust, 1970); *Krishna: The Supreme Personality of Godhead,* 3 vols. (Los Angeles: Bhaktivedanta Book Trust, 1970). On the Hare Krishna movement, see J. Stillson Judah, *Hare Krishna and the Counterculture* (New York: Wiley, 1974).

45. Radical feminist Mary Daly has exposed the full horror of suttee; see Mary Daly, *Gyn/Ecology* (Boston: Beacon Press, 1979), chap. 3.

46. For brief selections from the leading Indian voices of the past century, see Ainslee T. Embree, *The Hindu Tradition* (New York: Vintage, 1972), pp. 278–348.

47. See Walker G. Neevel, Jr., "The Transformations of Sri Ramakrishna," in *Hinduism: New Essays in the History of Religions,* ed. Bardwell L. Smith (Leiden: E. J. Brill, 1976), pp. 53–97.

48. Mohandas K. Gandhi, *An Autobiography: The Story of My Experiments with Truth* (Boston: Beacon Paperbacks, 1957), p. 349.

49. Erik H. Erikson, *Gandhi's Truth* (New York: Norton, 1969), pp. 376–397.

50. Joan Bondurant, *Conquest of Violence,* rev. ed. (Berkeley: University of California Press, 1965).

51. See Adrian C. Mayer, *Caste and Kinship in Central India: A Village and Its Region* (Berkeley: University of California Press, 1960), pp. 99–102; also Thomas B. Coburn, "Hindu Goddesses," *HR,* May 1988, *27*(4):412–414.

52. Gerald D. Berreman, *Hindus of the Himalayas: Ethnography and Change,* new extended ed. (Berkeley: University of California Press, 1972), p. 89.

53. James M. Freeman, "The Ladies of Lord Krishna: Rituals of Middle-Aged Women in Eastern India," in *Unspoken Worlds: Women's Religious Lives in Non-Western Cultures,* ed. Nancy A. Falk and Rita M. Gross (New York: Harper & Row), 1982, pp. 110–126; and Daniel Gold, "Comprehending Indian Devotional Love," *HR,* May 1987, *26*(4):401–421.

54. See Sudhir Kakar, *Shamans, Mystics and Doctors* (New York: Alfred A. Knopf, 1982), pp. 53–88.

55. V. S. Naipaul, *India: A Wounded Civilization* (New York: Vintage Books, 1978), pp. 42–43.

56. Basham, *Wonder That Was India,* pp. 74–231.

57. Kuiper, "Basic Concept of Vedic Religion"; see also Bruce Lincoln, "The Indo-European Myth of Creation," *HR,* 1975, *15*(2):121–145.

58. Basham, *Wonder That Was India,* p. 153.

59. Zaehner, *Hinduism,* p. 102.

60. Vern L. Bullough, *The Subordinate Sex* (Baltimore: Penguin, 1974), pp. 230–231.

61. See Ellison Banks Findley, "Gargi at the King's Court: Women and Philosophical Innovation in Ancient India," in *Women, Religion and Social Change,* ed. Y. Y. Haddad and E. B. Findley (Albany: State University of New York Press, 1955), pp. 37–58.

62. See Basham, *Wonder That Was India,* pp. 186–188.

63. Noss, *Man's Religions,* p. 188. On the role model that the *Mahabharata* described for women in Draupadi, see Nancy Auer Falk, "Draupadi and the Dharma," in *Beyond Androcentrism,* ed. Rita M. Gross (Missoula, Mont.: Scholars Press, 1977), pp. 89–114. For a sensitive fictional treatment of the modern Indian woman, see Kamala Markandaya, *Nectar in a Sieve* (New York: Signet, 1954).

64. Bullough, *Subordinate Sex,* p. 232.

65. Reference in Organ, *Hinduism,* p. 387.

66. Charles S. J. White, "Mother Guru: Jnanananda of Madras, India," in *Unspoken Worlds: Women's Religious Lives in Non-Western Culture,* ed. Nancy A. Falk and Rita M. Gross (New York: Harper & Row, 1980), p. 23.

67. Ibid., p. 27.

68. See Organ, *Hinduism,* p. 29.

69. A popular version is that by Swami Prabhavanada and Christopher Isherwood, *How to Know God* (New York: Mentor, 1969). The commentary is from the viewpoint of Vedanta, whereas Patanjali's own philosophy was Samkhya. See also Georg Feuerstein, "Patanjali," *ER, 11,* 206–207.

70. Basham, *Wonder That Was India,* p. 160.

71. See David Kinsley, "The Portrait of the Goddess in the Devi-mahatmya," *JAAR,* 1978, *46*(4):489–506.

72. A good reminder that most Hindus have not directly known or followed the high literary tradition is found in Philip H. Ashby, *Modern Trends in Hinduism* (New York: Columbia University Press, 1974), pp. 7–24; see also Brian K. Smith, "Exorcising the Transcendent: Strategies for Defining Hinduism and Religion," *HR,* August 1987, *27*(1):32–55.

73. Wendy Doniger O'Flaherty, *The Origins of Evil in Hindu Mythology* (Berkeley: University of California Press Paperback, 1980), p. 5.

74. Ibid., p. 375.

75. Kinsley, *The Sword and the Flute* (note 16), pp. 111–112.

76. V. S. Naipaul, *India: A Wounded Civilization* (New York: Vintage, 1978).

Chapter 4:
Buddhism

1. Richard H. Robinson and Willard L. Johnson, *The Buddhist Religion* (Encino, Calif.: Dickenson, 1977), p. 13; see also Trevor Ling, *The Buddha* (London: Temple Smith, 1973), pp. 37–83; Mircea Eliade, *A History of Religious Ideas,* vol. 2 (Chicago: University of Chicago Press, 1982), pp. 72–86.

2. Edward Conze, *Buddhist Scriptures* (Baltimore: Penguin, 1959), p. 34.

3. Conze, *Buddhist Scriptures,* pp. 48–49; see also Lowell W. Bloss, "The Taming of Mara," *HR,* 1978, *18*(2): 156–176.

4. Robinson and Johnson, *Buddhist Tradition,* p. 28.

5. Ibid., p. 31; see also Edward J. Thomas, *The History of Buddhist Thought* (New York: Barnes & Noble, 1951), pp. 58–70; Henry Clarke Warren, *Buddhism in Translations* (New York: Atheneum, 1973), pp. 202–208.

6. See William Theodore de Bary, ed., *The Buddhist Tradition* (New York: Vintage, 1972), pp. 15–20; see also Edward Conze, *Buddhism: Its Essence and Development* (New York: Harper Torchbooks, 1959), pp. 43–48; I. B. Horner, "Buddhism: The Theravada," in *The Concise Encyclopedia of Living Faiths,* ed. R. C. Zaehner (Boston: Beacon Press, 1967), pp. 283–293; Taitetsu Unno, "Eightfold Path," *ER, 5,* 69–71.

7. See Winston K. King, *In the Hope of Nibbana: Theravada Buddhist Ethics* (La Salle, Ill.: Open Court, 1964).

8. Texts on wisdom, morality, and meditation are available in Stephen Beyer, *The Buddhist Experience* (Encino, Calif.: Dickenson, 1974); see also Conze, *Buddhist Scriptures.*

9. Edward Conze, *Buddhist Meditation* (New York: Harper Torchbooks, 1969); see also Nyanaponika Thera, *The Heart of Buddhist Meditation* (London: Rider, 1969); Winston L. King, "Meditation: Buddhist Meditation," *ER, 9,* 331–336.

10. John Bowker discusses this rather creatively; see Bowker, *The Religious Imagination and the Sense of God* (Oxford: Clarendon Press, 1978), p. 244; see also Willis Stoesz, "The Buddha as Teacher," *JAAR,* 1978, *46*(2):139–158.

11. We have adapted Henry Clarke Warren's presentation of the Fire Sermon. See his *Buddhism in Translations* (note 5), pp. 351–353.

12. See I. B. Horner, "The Teaching of the Elders," in *Buddhist Texts through the Ages,* ed. Edward Conze (New York: Harper Torchbooks, 1954), pp. 17–50. Also Warren, *Buddhism in Translations,* p. 392; Charles S. Prebish, ed. *Buddhism: A Modern Perspective* (University Park: Pennsylvania State University Press, 1975), pp. 16–26, 49–53;

13. On the laity, see Conze, *Buddhism: Its Essence and Development,* pp. 70–88.

14. See Conze, *Buddhist Scriptures,* pp. 182–183.

15. See Robinson and Johnson, *Buddhist Religion;* Lowell W. Bloss, "The Buddha and the Naga," *HR,* 1973, *13*(1):36–53.

16. See Prebish, *Buddhism: A Modern Perspective,* pp. 29–45; see also Edward Conze, *Buddhist Thought in India* (Ann Arbor, Mich.: Ann Arbor Paperbacks, 1967), p. 121; Janice J. Nattier and Charles S. Prebish, "Mahasamghika Origins: The Beginnings of Buddhist Sectarianism," *HR,* 1977, *16*(3):237–272.

17. Robinson and Johnson, *Buddhist Religion,* p. 77; see also John S. Strong, "Gandhakuti: The Perfumed Chamber of the Buddha," *HR,* 1977, *16*(4):390–406.

18. Robinson and Johnson, *Buddhist Religion,* p. 81.

19. Mircea Eliade, *Yoga: Immortality and Freedom* (Princeton, N.J.: Princeton University Press, 1969), pp. 162–199; see also S. N. Dasgupta, *Hindu Mysticism* (New York: Frederick Ungar, 1959), pp. 85–109.

20. Conze, *Buddhist Meditation,* pp. 100–103.

21. Winston L. King, *Theravada Meditation: The Buddhist Transformation of Yoga* (University Park: Pennsylvania State University Press, 1980), pp. 126–127.

22. For general overviews of Mahayana, see Edward Conze, "Buddhism: The Mahayana," in *The Concise Encyclopedia of Living Faiths,* ed. R. C. Zaehner (Boston: Beacon Press, 1967), pp. 296–320; *Buddhist Texts,* pp. 119–217; Erik Zürcher et al., "Buddhism," *ER, 2,* 414–435; Nakamura Hajime, "Buddhism, Schools of: Mahayana Buddhism," ibid., 457–472.

23. Edward Conze, *Buddhist Wisdom Books* (New York: Harper Torchbooks, 1972), p. 77. See also Donald S. Lopez, Jr., "Inscribing the Bodhisvatta's Speech," *HR,* May 1990, *29*(4):351–372.

24. See Joanna Rodgers Macy, "Perfection of Wisdom: Mother of All Buddhas," in *Beyond Androcentrism,* ed. Rita M. Gross (Missoula, Mont.: Scholars Press, 1977), pp. 315–333.

25. Conze, *Buddhist Wisdom Books,* pp. 101–102.

26. Our exposition depends on Edward Conze's translation and study in *Buddhist Wisdom Books* (note 23).

27. See Conze, *Buddhist Thought in India,* pp. 238–244; see also Prebish, *Buddhism: A Modern Perspective,* pp. 76–96; T. R. V. Murti, *The Central Philosophy of Buddhism* (London: Allen & Unwin, 1955).

28. See Conze, *Buddhist Thought in India,* pp. 250–260; Prebish, *Buddhism: A Modern Perspective,* pp. 97–101; Thomas, *History of Buddhist Thought,* pp. 230–248.

29. Juan Mascaró, trans., *The Dhammapada* (Baltimore: Penguin, 1973), p. 1.

30.   D. T. Suzuki, trans., *The Lankavatara Sutra* (London: George Routledge, 1932).

31.   Conze, *Buddhist Thought in India,* pp. 270–274; Robinson and Johnson, *Buddhist Tradition,* pp. 116–127; Thomas, *History of Buddhist Thought,* pp. 245–248; David Snellgrove, "The Tantras," in Edward Conze, ed., *Buddhist Texts through the Ages* (New York: Harper Torchbooks, 1954), pp. 221–273; Conze, *Buddhism: Its Essence and Development,* pp. 174–199; Alex Wayman, "Buddhism, Schools of: Esoteric Buddhism," *ER, 2,* 472–482.

32.   Hellmut Hoffmann, *The Religions of Tibet* (London: Allen & Unwin, 1961); Herbert V. Guenther, *Treasures of the Tibetan Middle Way* (Berkeley: Shambhala, 1976).

33.   Beyer, *Buddhist Experience,* pp. 258–261; Eliade, *Yoga,* pp. 249–254.

34.   Robinson and Johnson, *Buddhist Religion,* p. 120.

35.   Herbert Guenther, trans., *The Life and Teachings of Naropa* (New York: Oxford University Press, 1971), p. 43; see also W. Y. Evans-Wentz, ed., *Tibet's Great Yoga Milarepa* (New York: Oxford University Press, 1969), p. 93.

36.   See Beyer, *Buddhist Experience,* pp. 174–184, 225–229, 258–261.

37.   Stephan Beyer, "Buddhism in Tibet," in *Buddhism: A Modern Perspective,* ed. Charles Prebish (University Park: Pennsylvania State University Press, 1975), pp. 239–247; Herbert Guenther, "Buddhism: Buddhism in Tibet," *ER, 2,* 406–414.

38.   Hoffmann, *Religions of Tibet.*

39.   Evans-Wentz, *Milarepa.*

40.   On modern times, see David L. Snellgrove, "Tibetan Buddhism Today," in *Buddhism in the Modern World,* ed. Heinrich Dumoulin (New York: Macmillan, 1976), pp. 277–293.

41.   See *Tibetan Book of the Dead,* trans. Francesca Freemantle and Chogyam Trungpa (Boulder: Shambhala, 1975).

42.   Alexandra David-Neel, *Magic and Mystery in Tibet* (New York: Dover, 1971), pp. 5–9.

43.   There are major qualifications to this statement, of course. On Hinduism in Southeast Asia, see Robinson and Johnson, *Buddhist Tradition,* pp. 129–136; on Hinduism in Indonesia, see Clifford Geertz, *Islam Observed* (Chicago: University of Chicago Press, 1968), pp. 29–43.

44.   Melford Spiro, *Buddhism and Society* (New York: Harper & Row, 1970), pp. 209–214.

45.   Charles S. Prebish, *American Buddhism* (North Scituate, Mass.: Duxbury Press, 1979), p. 164; Robert S. Ellwood, "Buddhism: Buddhism in the West," *ER, 2,* 436–439.

46.   See Lama Govinda, *The Psychological Attitude of Early Buddhist Philosophy* (New York: Samuel Weiser, 1969), pp. 77–142.

47.   For instance, Spiro found that the goal of Burmese Buddhists was not nirvana but a better rebirth; see Spiro, *Buddhism and Society.*

48.   On the Buddhist shaping of Chinese folk religion, see Daniel L. Overmyer, "Folk-Buddhist Religion: Creation

and Eschatology in Medieval China," *HR,* 1972, *12*(1):42–70. On Thai Buddhist cosmology, see Frank Reynolds and Mani B. Reynolds, trans., *Three Worlds According to King Ruang* (Berkeley: University of California Press, 1982).

49.   Denise Lardner Carmody, *Women and World Religions,* 2d ed. (Englewood Cliffs, N.J.: Prentice-Hall, 1989), pp. 67–92; I. B. Horner, *Women Under Primitive Buddhism* (New York: Dutton, 1930).

50.   See Nancy Falk, "An Image of Woman in Old Buddhist Literature. The Daughters of Mara," in *Women and Religion,* rev. ed., ed. J. Plaskow and J. A. Romero (Missoula, Mont.: Scholars Press, 1974), pp. 105–112.

51.   Frank Reynolds, "The Two Wheels of Dhamma," in *The Two Wheels of Dhamma,* ed. Bardwell L. Smith (Chambersburg, Pa.: American Academy of Religion, 1972), pp. 6–30; Bardwell L. Smith, "The Ideal Social Order as Portrayed in the Chronicles of Ceylon," in *Two Wheels of Dhamma,* ed. Smith, pp. 31–57.

52.   King, *Hope of Nibbana,* pp. 176–210.

53.   Eric Voegelin, *Anamnesis: Zur Theorie der Geschichte und Politik* (Munich: R. Piper, 1966), pp. 179–222. This portion is not available in Gerhart Niemeyer's translation of *Anamnesis* (Notre Dame, Ind.: University of Notre Dame Press, 1978). However, it first appeared under the title "The Mongol Orders of Submission to European Powers," in *Byzantion,* vol. XV (1940/41), pp. 378–413.

54.   See Jane Bunnag, *Buddhist Monk, Buddhist Layman* (Cambridge: Cambridge University Press, 1973); see also Spiro, *Buddhism and Society,* pp. 396–421. On the more spiritual ties among members of the community, see Richard Gombrich, " 'Merit Transference' in Sinhalese Buddhism," *HR,* 1971, *11*(2):203–219.

55.   King, *In the Hope of Nibbana,* pp. 277–284.

56.   G. P. Malalasekera, "Theravada Buddhism," in *Historical Atlas of the Religions of the World,* ed. I. al Faruqi and D. Sopher (New York: Macmillan, 1974), p. 172.

57.   John B. Cobb, Jr., "Buddhist Emptiness and the Christian God," *JAAR,* 1977, *45*(1):11–25.

58.   Yoshito S. Hakeda, trans., *The Awakening of Faith* (New York: Columbia University Press, 1967).

59.   Philip Kapleau, *The Three Pillars of Zen* (Boston: Beacon Press, 1967), p. 207.

60.   E. F. Schumacher, *Small Is Beautiful* (New York: Harper Colophon, 1973), pp. 50–58.

61.   D. T. Suzuki, *Zen Buddhism* (New York: Anchor Books, 1956), pp. 157–226. On the Daoist influence, see Chang Chung-yuan, *Creativity and Taoism* (New York: Harper Colophon, 1970).

62.   The famous Zen ox-herding pictures display the progress toward this freedom. See Kapleau, *Three Pillars of Zen,* pp. 301–313.

63.   See Nagarjuna and Sakya Pandit, *Elegant Sayings,* trans. Tarthang Tulku (Emeryville, Calif.: Dharma Publishing, 1977), pp. 38–39.

64.   Chogyam Trungpa, "Foreword," in *Buddhism: A Modern Perspective,* ed. Charles S. Prebish (University Park:

Pennsylvania State University Press, 1975), p. ix; see also Malcolm David Eckel, "Gratitude to an Empty Savior," *HR,* August 1985, *25*(1):57–75.

65. John Bowker has discussed this matter in the illuminating context of information theory; see Bowker, *Religious Imagination,* pp. 244–307.

66. *Saddharmapundarika,* V:1, 5, 6; in *Buddhist Texts through the Ages,* ed. Edward Conze (note 12), p. 139.

67. See note 66.

68. William Johnston, *The Mirror Mind* (New York: Harper & Row, 1981), pp. 40–41; see also Judith A. Berling, "Bringing the Buddha Down to Earth," *HR,* August 1987, *27*(1):56–88.

Chapter 5:
Chinese Religion

1. Karl Jaspers, *The Origin and Goal of History* (New Haven, Conn.: Yale University Press, 1953), p. 2.

2. Arthur Waley, trans., *Monkey* (New York: Grove Press, 1958).

3. Laurence G. Thompson, *The Chinese Religion: An Introduction,* 3rd ed. (Belmont, Calif.: Wadsworth, 1979), pp. 3–15; Joseph Needham, *Science and Civilisation in China,* vol. 2 (Cambridge: University Press, 1969), pp. 216–345; Schuyler Cammann, "Some Early Chinese Symbols of Duality," *HR,* February 1985, *24*(3):215–254.

4. David N. Keightley, "The Religious Commitment: Shang Theology and the Genesis of Chinese Political Culture," *HR,* 1978, *17*(3–4):213.

5. Hans Steininger, "The Religions of China," in *Historia Religionum, II,* ed. C. J. Bleeker and G. Widengren (Leiden: E. J. Brill, 1971), pp. 479–482; Daniel L. Overmyer, "Chinese Religion: An Overview," *ER, 3,* 257–289.

6. *Chuang Tzu,* sec. 6; see Burton Watson, trans., *Chuang Tzu: Basic Writings* (New York: Columbia University Press, 1964), pp. 76, 81.

7. Thompson, *Chinese Religion: An Introduction,* 3rd ed. (Belmont, Calif.: Wadsworth, 1979), pp. 22–24; Needham, *Science and Civilisation,* pp. 354–363.

8. Arthur Waley, *The Nine Songs: A Study of Shamanism in Ancient China* (London: Allen & Unwin, 1955).

9. Eliade, however, stresses the Chinese shaman's magical flight. See Mircea Eliade, *Shamanism* (Princeton, N.J.: Princeton University Press, 1972), pp. 448–457.

10. On the ritualistic side of early Chinese shamanism, see Jordan Paper, "The Meaning of the 'T'ao-T'ieh,'" *HR,* 1978, *18*(1):18–41.

11. Anna Seidel, "Buying One's Way to Heaven," *HR,* 1978, *17*(3–4):419–431; see also Stephen F. Teiser, "Ghosts and Ancestors in Medieval Chinese Religion," *HR,* August 1986, *26*(1):47–67; and Catherine Bell, "Religion and Chinese Culture: Toward an Assessment of 'Popular Religion,'" *HR,* August 1989, *29*(1):35–57.

12. Donald W. Treadgold, *The West in Russia and China,* vol. 2 (Cambridge: University Press, 1973), pp. 20–26.

13. Quoted in Thompson, *Chinese Religion,* 3rd ed., pp. 32–33; see also Whalen Lai, "Symbolism of Evil in China," *HR,* May 1984, *23*(4):316–343.

14. Mircea Eliade, *A History of Religious Ideas,* vol. 2 (Chicago: University of Chicago Press, 1982), pp. 3–6.

15. Arthur Waley, trans., *The Analects of Confucius* (New York: Vintage, 1938), pp. 27–29.

16. A. C. Graham, "Confucianism," in *The Concise Encyclopedia of Living Faiths,* ed. R. C. Zaehner (Boston: Beacon Press, 1967), p. 367; Wing-Tsit Chan, "Confucian Thought: Foundations of the Tradition," *ER, 4,* 15–24; Laurence G. Thompson, "The State Cult," ibid., 36–38.

17. Laurence G. Thompson, ed., *The Chinese Way in Religion* (Encino, Calif.: Dickinson, 1973), pp. 139–153.

18. Wing-Tsit Chan, *A Source Book in Chinese Philosophy* (Princeton, N.J.: Princeton University Press, 1963), pp. 84–94.

19. Ezra Pound, *Confucius* (New York: New Directions, 1969), p. 219.

20. W.A.C.H. Dobson, trans., *Mencius* (Toronto: University of Toronto Press, 1963), p. 131.

21. Lee H. Yearley, "Mencius on Human Nature," *JAAR,* 1975, *43:*185–198.

22. See Eric Voegelin, *Order and History,* vol. 4 (Baton Rouge: Louisiana State University Press, 1974), pp. 272–299.

23. On Xunzi, see Chan, *Chinese Philosophy,* pp. 115–135; Sebastian de Grazia, *Masters of Chinese Political Thought* (New York: Viking, 1973), pp. 151–181. On Mozi, see Chan, *Chinese Philosophy,* pp. 211–217; de Grazia, *Chinese Political Thought,* pp. 216–246.

24. Arthur Waley, *Three Ways of Thought in Ancient China* (Garden City, N.Y.: Doubleday, 1956), p. 205.

25. On this period, see Werner Eichhorn, *Chinese Civilization* (New York: Praeger, 1969), pp. 43–85; H. G. Creel, *The Birth of China* (New York: Reynal and Hitchcock, 1937), pp. 219–380.

26. Graham, "Confucianism," p. 370; Wing-Tsit Chan, "Confucian Thought: Neo-Confucianism," *ER, 4,* 24–36.

27. See Chan, *Chinese Philosophy,* pp. 588–653.

28. This appears in Rodney L. Taylor, "The Centered Self: Religious Autobiography in the Neo-Confucian Tradition," *HR,* 1978, *17*(3–4):266–283.

29. Thaddeus Chieh Hang T'ui, "*Jen* Experience and *Jen* Philosophy," *JAAR,* 1974, *42:*53–65.

30. Adapted from Thompson, *Chinese Way,* pp. 144–153.

31. Adapted from Thompson, *Chinese Religion,* 3rd ed., pp. 3–15.

32. H. G. Creel, *What Is Taoism?* (Chicago: University of Chicago Press, 1970), pp. 37–47; Farzeen Baldrian, "Taoism: An Overview," *ER, 14,* 288–306.

33.   Thomas Merton, *The Way of Chuang Tzu* (New York: New Directions, 1968).

34.   Arthur Waley, trans., *The Way and Its Power* (New York: Grove Press, 1958).

35.   Waley stresses the mystical; Wing-Tsit Chan's *The Way of Lao Tzu* (Indianapolis, Ind.: Bobbs-Merrill, 1963) stresses the pragmatic.

36.   Denise Lardner Carmody, "Taoist Reflections on Feminism," *Religion in Life,* 1977, *44*(2):234–244.

37.   Holmes Welch, *Taoism: The Parting of the Way* (Boston: Beacon Press, 1966), pp. 35–49.

38.   For a sketch of a utopia that is Daoist in spirit if not in origin, see Ernest Callenbach, *Ecotopia* (New York: Bantam, 1977).

39.   *Tao Te Ching,* chap. 5, in *The Way and Its Power* (New York: Grove Press, 1955), p. 147; Chan, *Lao Tzu,* p. 108, note 2, says: "Straw dogs were used for sacrifices in ancient China. After they had been used, they were thrown away and there was no more sentimental attachment to them."

40.   Current scholarly opinion, however, associates religious Daoism with preaxial religion. See *Encyclopedia Britannica* 15th ed., s.v. "Taoism," "Taoism, History of"; N. Sivin, "On the Word 'Taoist' as a Source of Perplexity," *HR,* 1978, *17*(3–4):303–330.

41.   Werner Eichhorn, "Taoism," in *The Concise Encyclopedia of Living Faiths,* ed. R. C. Zaehner (Boston: Beacon Press, 1967), pp. 389–391; Welch, *Taoism,* pp. 151–158.

42.   Welch, *Taoism,* pp. 130–135; K'uan Yu, *Taoist Yoga* (New York: Samuel Weiser, 1973).

43.   Kristofer Schipper, "The Taoist Body," *HR,* 1978, *17*(3–4):355–386.

44.   Edward H. Schafer, "The Jade Woman of Greatest Mystery," *HR,* 1978, *17*(3–4):393–394.

45.   Chang Chung-yuan, *Creativity and Taoism* (New York: Harper Colophon, 1970), pp. 169–238; Albert C. Moore, *Iconography of Religions* (Philadelphia: Fortress, 1977), pp. 170–180; Raymond Dawson, *The Chinese Experience* (New York: Scribner's, 1978), pp. 199–284.

46.   C. Wei-hsun Fu, "Confucianism and Taoism," in *Historical Atlas of the Religions of the World,* ed. I. al Faruqi and D. Sopher (New York: Macmillan, 1974), p. 121.

47.   For overviews, see R. H. Robinson, "Buddhism: In China and Japan," in *The Concise Encyclopedia of Living Faiths,* ed. R. C. Zaehner (Boston: Beacon Press, 1967), pp. 321–344; C. Wei-hsun Fu, "Mahayana Buddhism (China)," in *Historical Atlas of the Religions of the World,* ed. I. al Faruqi and D. Sopher (New York: Macmillan, 1974), pp. 185–194. Space forbids consideration of the history of Buddhism in the many other Asian lands that it influenced. For treatments on this subject, see Charles S. Prebish, ed., *Buddhism: A Modern Perspective* (University Park: Pennsylvania State University Press, 1975). On contemporary issues, see Heinrich Dumoulin, ed., *Buddhism in the Modern World* (New York: Macmillan, 1976); Erik Zürcher, "Buddhism: Buddhism in China," *ER, 2,* 414–421.

48.   On Buddhist beginnings in China, see Arthur F. Wright, *Buddhism in Chinese History* (Stanford, Calif.: Stanford University Press, 1959), pp. 21–41. Also Kenneth K. S. Ch'en, "The Role of Buddhist Monasteries in T'ang Society," *HR,* 1976, *35*(3):209–230.

49.   See Heinrich Dumoulin, *A History of Zen Buddhism* (Boston: Beacon Press, 1969), pp. 52–136; see also Bernard Faure, "Bodhidharma as Textual and Religious Paradigm," *HR,* February 1986, *25*(3):187–198.

50.   Richard H. Robinson and Willard L. Johnson, *The Buddhist Religion* (Encino, Calif.: Dickenson, 1977), p. 161. For a full discussion of this sutra, see Philip B. Yampolsky, *The Platform Sutra of the Sixth Patriarch* (New York: Columbia University Press, 1967); see also Wing-Tsit Chan, *The Platform Sutra* (New York: St. John's University Press, 1963). Interesting background is Alex Wayman, "The Mirror as a Pan-Buddhist Metaphor-Simile," *HR,* 1974, *13*(4):251–269.

51.   Dumoulin, *History of Zen Buddhism,* p. 88; Yampolsky, *Platform Sutra,* pp. 23–121.

52.   Beatrice Lane Suzuki, *Mahayana Buddhism* (New York: Macmillan, 1969), pp. 63–65; T. O. Ling, *A Dictionary of Buddhism* (New York: Scribner's 1972), pp. 15–16.

53.   Wright, *Buddhism in Chinese History,* p. 70.

54.   See ibid., p. 72.

55.   James J. Y. Liu, *Essentials of Chinese Literary Art* (North Scituate, Mass.: Duxbury Press, 1979), p. 17.

56.   C. K. Yang, *Religion in Chinese Society* (Berkeley: University of California Press, 1970), pp. 265–272; Alvin P. Cohen, "Chinese Religion: Popular Religion," *ER, 3,* 289–296.

57.   Steininger, "Religions of China," p. 486.

58.   See Thompson, *The Chinese Way,* pp. 231–241; Donald E. MacInnes, *Religious Policy and Practice in Communist China* (New York: Macmillan, 1972). See also Yang, *Religion in Chinese Society,* pp. 341–404.

59.   Stuart Shram, *Mao Tse-tung* (Baltimore: Penguin, 1967), p. 23.

60.   Elisabeth Croll, ed., *The Woman's Movement in China* (London: Anglo-Chinese Educational Institute, 1974).

61.   Robert Jay Lifton, *Revolutionary Immortality: Mao Tse-tung and the Chinese Cultural Revolution* (New York: Vintage, 1968).

62.   Mao Tse-tung, *Poems* (Peking: Foreign Language Press, 1976).

63.   *World Christian Encyclopedia,* ed. David B. Barrett (New York: Oxford University Press, 1982), p. 234.

64.   Ibid., p. 231. Figures have been rounded.

65.   N. J. Giradot, "The Problem of Creation Mythology in the Study of Chinese Religion," *HR,* 1976, *15*(4):289–318; see also his "Myth and Meaning in the *Tao Te Ching:* chaps. 25 and 42," *HR,* 1977, *16*(4):294–328.

66.   Alvin P. Cohen, "Concerning the Rain Deities in Ancient China," *HR,* 1978, *17*(3–4):244–265.

67.   See Helmut Wilhelm, *Change: Eight Lectures on the I-Ching* (New York: Pantheon, 1960).

68. This section is adapted from Liu, *Essentials of Chinese Literary Art,* pp. 4–24.

69. Chiang Yee, *The Chinese Eye: An Interpretation of Chinese Painting* (Bloomington: Indiana University Press, 1964), p. 152. We are indebted to Chiang throughout this section. See also Bernard Faure, "Space and Place in Chinese Religious Traditions," *HR,* May 1987, *26*(4):337–356.

70. Richard Mather, "Buddhism Becomes Chinese," in *The Chinese Way,* ed. Laurence G. Thompson (Encino, Calif.: Dickenson, 1973), pp. 77–86.

71. Dumoulin, *History of Zen Buddhism,* pp. 52–136.

72. Philip Kapleau, *The Three Pillars of Zen* (Boston: Beacon Press, 1967), p. 205.

73. Steininger, "Religions of China," pp. 482–487; Creel, *Birth of China,* pp. 204–216.

74. See Arthur F. Wright, ed., *Confucianism and Chinese Civilization* (New York: Atheneum, 1964).

75. This is a major theme in Peter Weber-Schafer, *Oikumene und Imperium* (Munich: P. List, 1968).

76. Vern L. Bullough, *The Subordinate Sex* (Baltimore: Penguin, 1974), p. 249; Teresa Kelliher, "Confucianism," and Barbara Reed, "Taoism," in *Women in World Religions,* ed. Arvind Sharma (Albany: State University of New York Press, 1987), pp. 135–159 and 161–181.

77. Mary Daly, *Gyn/Ecology* (Boston: Beacon Press, 1979), chap. 4. The reference to Dworkin is to her *Woman Hating* (New York: Dutton, 1974), p. 103.

78. Margery Wolf, "Chinese Women: Old Skills in a New Context," in *Woman, Culture, and Society,* ed. M. Z. Rosaldo and L. Lamphere (Stanford, Calif.: Stanford University Press, 1974), pp. 157–172.

79. Denise Lardner Carmody, *Women and World Religions* (Nashville: Abingdon, 1979), pp. 66–72.

80. Ellen Marie Chen, "Tao as the Great Mother and the Influence of Motherly Love in the Shaping of Chinese Philosophy," *HR,* 1974, *14*(1):51–63.

81. Maxine Hong Kingston, *The Woman Warrior: Memories of a Girlhood among Ghosts* (New York: Alfred A. Knopf, 1977).

82. See Nancy Schuster, "Striking a Balance: Women and Images of Women in Early Chinese Buddhism," in *Women, Religion and Social Change,* ed. Y. Y. Haddad and E. B. Findley (Albany: State University of New York Press, 1985), pp. 87–112.

83. Yang, *Religion in Chinese Society,* p. 294.

84. Max Weber, *The Religion of China* (New York: Free Press, 1968), pp. 173–225.

85. Donald J. Munro, *The Concept of Man in Early China* (Stanford, Calif.: Stanford University Press, 1969).

86. A. C. Graham, "Chuang Tzu's Essay on Seeing Things as Equal," *HR,* 1969, *9*:137.

87. Chang, *Creativity and Taoism,* pp. 123–168.

88. In her article "Is There a Doctrine of Physical Immortality in the Tao Te Ching?" (*HR,* 1973, *12*(3):231–249), Ellen Marie Chen argues that Laozi did not propose immor-

tality. She also argues against the Daoist character of *The Secret of the Golden Flower* because it is Confucian in emphasizing the yang principle (p. 246, note 22). For the psychodynamics of *The Golden Flower,* see C. G. Jung, "Commentary," in Richard Wilhelm, trans., *The Golden Flower* (New York: Harcourt, Brace & World, 1962), pp. 81–137.

89. On the original peasant mentality, see Marcel Granet, *The Religion of the Chinese People* (New York: Harper & Row, 1975), pp. 37–56.

90. David C. Yu, "Chinese Folk Religion," *HR,* 1973, *12*:378–387. On the complexity of so small an item as a Daoist talismanic chart, see Michael Saso, "What Is the Ho-t'u?" *HR,* 1978, *17*(3–4):399–416.

91. See Kuang-ming Wu, *Chuang-Tzu: World Philosopher at Play* (New York: Crossroad/Scholars Press, 1982).

Chapter 6:
Japanese Religion

1. Johannes Maringer, "Clay Figurines of the Jomon Period," *HR,* 1974, *14*:128–139.

2. Carmen Blacker, "The Religions of Japan," in *Historia Religionum, II,* ed. C. J. Bleeker and G. Widengren (Leiden: E. J. Brill, 1971), p. 518.

3. H. Byron Earhart, *Japanese Religion: Unity and Diversity,* 2nd ed. (Encino, Calif.: Dickenson, 1974), pp. 11–16.

4. Ichiro Hori, *Folk Religion in Japan* (Chicago: University of Chicago Press, 1968), pp. 181–251. See also Carmen Blacker, *The Catalpa Bow* (London: Allen & Unwin, 1975); and Joseph M. Kitagawa, "Japanese Religion: An Overview," *ER, 7,* 520–538; Alan L. Miller, "Japanese Religion: Popular Religion," ibid., 538–545; Matsumae Takeski, "Japanese Religion: Mythic Themes," ibid., 545–552.

5. G. Bownas, "Shinto," in *The Concise Encyclopedia of Living Faiths,* ed. R. C. Zaehner (Boston: Beacon Press, 1967), p. 349.

6. Ryusaku Tsunoda et al., *Sources of Japanese Tradition,* vol. 1 (New York: Columbia University Press, 1964), pp. 25–26.

7. Bownas, "Shinto," p. 357. For other folk themes, see Alan L. Miller, "Of Weavers and Birds," *HR,* February 1987, *26*(3):309–327; Alan L. Miller, "*Ame No Miso-Ori Me* (The Heavenly Weaving Maiden)," *HR,* August 1984, *24*(1):27–48; and Robert S. Ellwood, "A Cargo Cult in Seventh-Century Japan," *HR,* February 1984, *23*(3):222–239.

8. Ibid.

9. For an introduction to Hua-yan metaphysics, see Francis H. Cook, *Hua-yen Buddhism* (University Park: Pennsylvania State University Press, 1977).

10. Richard J. Robinson and Willard J. Johnson, *The Buddhist Religion* (Encino, Calif.: Dickenson, 1977), p. 175.

11. Francis H. Cook, "Heian, Kamakura, and Tokugawa Periods in Japan," in *Buddhism: A Modern Perspec-*

tive, ed. Charles S. Prebish (University Park: Pennsylvania State University Press, 1975); Tamaru Noriyoshi, "Buddhism: Buddhism in Japan," *ER, 2,* 426–435.

12.   The section adapts materials from Tsunoda et al., *Sources of Japanese Tradition,* vol. 1. pp. 184–260.

13.   Francis H. Cook, "Japanese Innovations In Buddhism," in *Buddhism: A Modern Perspective,* pp. 229–233.

14.   Earhart, *Japanese Religion,* pp. x–xi.

15.   Ibid., p. 73.

16.   See Tsunoda et al., *Sources of Japanese Tradition,* pp. 261–276.

17.   Shusaku Endo, *Silence* (Rutland, Vt.: Tuttle, 1969).

18.   Robert N. Bellah, *Tokugawa Religion* (Boston: Beacon Press, 1970), pp. 90–98.

19.   See Ishida Ichiro, "Kokugaku," *ER, 8,* 360–362; Hirai Naofusa, "Shinto," *ER, 13,* 280–294; Allan G. Grapard, "Japan's Ignored Cultural Revolution," *HR,* February 1984, *23*(3):240–265; whole issue *HR*, February 1980; *27*(3), on Shinto.

20.   See Blacker, *Catalpa Bow,* pp. 130–132.

21.   Earhart, *Japanese Religion,* p. 112.

22.   Ibid., pp. 114–117.

23.   John B. Noss, *Man's Religions,* 5th ed. (New York: Macmillan, 1974), p. 324.

24.   Denise Lardner Carmody, *Women and World Religions* (Nashville: Abingdon, 1979), p. 84.

25.   Edwin O. Reischauer, *Japan Past and Present,* 3rd ed. rev. (Tokyo: Tuttle, 1964), pp. 108–141.

26.   H. Byron Earhart, ed., *Religion in the Japanese Experience: Sources and Interpretations* (Encino, Calif.: Dickenson, 1974), pp. 201–210; see also Tsunoda et al., *Sources of Japanese Tradition,* vol. 2 (New York: Columbia University Press, 1964), pp. 131–210.

27.   Earhart, ed., *Religion in the Japanese Experience,* p. 204.

28.   Joseph Kitagawa, "The Japanese *Kokutai* (National Community): History and Myth," *HR,* 1974, *13*:209–226.

29.   Y. T. Hosoi, "The Sacred Tree in Japanese Prehistory," *HR,* 1976, *16*:95–119.

30.   Manabu Waida, "Symbolisms of the Moon and the Waters of Immortality," *HR,* 1977, *16*:407–423; Manabu Watanabe, "Religious Symbolism in Saigyo's Verse," *HR,* May 1987, *26*(4):382–400.

31.   See Blacker, *Catalpa Bow,* and Hori, *Folk Religion in Japan,* for the shamanistic exceptions to this statement.

32.   See Lynn White, Jr., "The Historical Roots of Our Ecological Crisis," in *Ecology and Religion in History,* ed. David and Eileen Spring (New York: Harper Torchbooks, 1974), pp. 15–31. The other articles in this volume suggest the sort of qualifications one would expect in discussing Jap-

anese ecology. See especially Yi-Fu Tuan, "Discrepancies between Environmental Attitude and Behaviour," pp. 91–113.

33.   This section adapts materials from Robert S. Ellwood, Jr., *An Invitation to Japanese Civilization* (Belmont, Calif.: Wadsworth, 1980), pp. 95–125; see also "Tea Ceremony," in *The New Encyclopaedia Britannica,* vol. II (Chicago: Encyclopaedia Britannica, 1987), pp. 596–597; Theodore M. Ludwig, "The Way of Tea: A Religio-Aesthetic Mode of Life," *HR,* August 1974, *14*(1):28–50; and Richard B. Pilgrim, "Intervals (*Ma*) in Space in Time," *HR,* February 1986, *25*(3):255–277.

34.   On contemporary professional and business life in Japan, see Ichiro Kawasaki, *Japan Unmasked* (Rutland, Vt.: Tuttle, 1969); Nobutaka Ike, *Japan: The New Superstate* (Stanford, Calif.: Stanford Alumni Association, 1973); for further sociological insight, see Chie Nakane, *Japanese Society* (Berkeley: University of California Press, 1972); and Liza Dalby, *Geisha* (Berkeley: University of California Press, 1983).

35.   Earhart, ed., *Religion in the Japanese Experience,* pp. 145–159.

36.   Alfred North Whitehead, *Religion in the Making* (New York: Meridian, 1960), p. 16.

37.   Yukio Mishima has brought this lovely Zen temple into recent Japanese religious consciousness. See his *The Temple of the Golden Pavilion* (Rutland, Vt.: Tuttle, 1959).

38.   "The Seventeen-Article Constitution of Prince Shotoku," *Sources of Japanese Tradtion,* vol. 1, p. 48.

39.   Patrick White, *The Vivisector* (New York: Viking, 1970).

40.   Chang Chung-yun, *Creativity and Taoism* (New York: Harper Colophon, 1970).

41.   Bownas, "Shinto."

42.   Blacker, "Religions of Japan"; see also Denise Lardner Carmody and John Tully Carmody, *How to Live Well: Ethics in the World Religions* (Belmont, Calif.: Wadsworth, 1988), pp. 160–181.

43.   Bellah, *Tokugawa Religion,* pp. 107–132, 178–197; Winston Davis, "Pilgrimage and World Renewal: A Study of Religion and Social Values in Tokugawa Japan," *HR,* November 1983, *23*(2):97–116, and February 1984, *23*(3):197–221.

44.   Mircea Eliade, *From Primitives to Zen* (New York: Harper & Row, 1967), pp. 452–454.

45.   Considering Shinran as a *bodhisattva* would force us to adjust this judgment. See Robert N. Bellah, "The Contemporary Meaning of Kamakura Buddhism," *JAAR,* 1974, *42*:7–9.

46.   See Shunryu Suzuki, *Zen Mind, Beginner's Mind* (New York: John Weatherhill, 1970), pp. 92–95, 102–104.

47.   Earhart, *Religion in the Japanese Experience,* p. 25.

48.   This section adapts materials from Earhart, ed., *Religion in the Japanese Experience,* pp. 19–26.

Chapter 7:
Religions of Ancient Near Eastern Civilizations

1. See James B. Pritchard, ed., *Ancient Near Eastern Texts*, 3rd ed. (Princeton, N.J.: Princeton University Press, 1969), pp. 37–41; Thorkild Jacobsen, "Mesopotamian Religions: An Overview," *ER, 9,* 447–466.

2. Ibid., pp. 60–61; Tikva Frymer-Kensky, "Enuma Elish," *ER, 5,* 124–126.

3. Jacobsen, ibid., pp. 72–100.

4. See William L. Moran, "Gilgamesh," *ER, 5,* 557–560; Tzvi Abusch, "Ishtar's Proposal and Gilgamesh's Refusal," *HR,* November 1986, *26*(2):143–187.

5. Henri Frankfort, *Kingship and the Gods* (Chicago: University of Chicago Press, 1978), pp. 15–214.

6. See Eric Voegelin, *Order and History, I, Israel and Revelation* (Baton Rouge: Louisiana State University Press, 1956), pp. 88–95; John A. Wilson, *The Culture of Ancient Egypt* (Chicago: University of Chicago Press, 1956), pp. 58–60; Leonard H. Lesko, "Egyptian Religion: An Overview," *ER, 5,* 37–54.

7. Voegelin, *Order and History, I,* p. 99.

8. C. J. Bleeker, "The Religion of Ancient Egypt," in *Historia Religionum, I,* ed. C. J. Bleeker and G. Widengren (Leiden: E. J. Brill, 1969), pp. 47–49.

9. Voegelin, *Order and History, I,* p. 108; for an overview of opinions about Akhenaton, see Virginia Lee Davis, "Akhenaton," *ER, 1,* 169–170.

10. James B. Pritchard, ed., *Ancient Near Eastern Texts,* 3rd ed. (Princeton, N.J.: Princeton University Press, 1969), p. 370.

11. Voegelin, *Order and History, I,* p. 86.

12. Hans J. Klimkeit, "Spatial Orientation in Mythical Thinking as Exemplified in Ancient Egypt: Considerations toward a Geography of Religions," *HR,* 1975, *14*(4):266–281.

13. Frankfort, *Kingship and the Gods,* pp. 148–212.

14. C. J. Bleeker, *Egyptian Festivals* (Leiden: E. J. Brill, 1967), pp. 91–123.

15. C. J. Bleeker, *The Rainbow: A Collection of Studies in the Science of Religion* (Leiden: E. J. Brill, 1975), pp. 167–173.

16. Pierre Montet, *Everyday Life in Egypt* (Westport, Conn.: Greenwood Press, 1974), p. 51.

17. Vern L. Bullough, *The Subordinate Sex* (Baltimore: Penguin, 1974), pp. 32–33; for an overview of women's lot in Egypt and other ancient Near Eastern cultures, see Gerda Lerner, *The Creation of Patriarchy* (New York: Oxford University Press, 1986).

18. Bullough, ibid., p. 39.

19. John A. Wilson, *The Culture of Ancient Egypt* (Chicago: University of Chicago Press, 1956), p. 78.

20. James B. Pritchard, ed., *Ancient Near Eastern Texts* (Princeton, N.J.: Princeton University Press, 1969), p. 34.

21. Ibid., p. 35.

22. Jacques Duchesne-Guillemin, *The Hymns of Zarathustra,* trans. M. Henning (Boston: Beacon Press, 1963), p. 1.

23. R. Ghirshman, *Iran* (Baltimore: Penguin, 1954), p. 27; Bruce Lincoln, "Indo-European Religions: An Overview," *ER, 7,* 198–204; Gherardo Gnoli, "Iranian Religions," ibid., 277–280.

24. Arnold Toynbee, *Mankind and Mother Earth* (New York: Oxford University Press, 1976), pp. 91–116.

25. See Richard Frye, *The Heritage of Persia* (New York: World, 1963), pp. 19–20; Jarich G. Oosten, *The Way of the Gods: The Social Code in Indo-European Mythology* (London: Routledge and Kegan Paul, 1985).

26. R. C. Zaehner, *The Dawn and Twilight of Zoroastrianism* (New York: Putnam's, 1961), pp. 60–61.

27. Duchesne-Guillemin, *The Hymns of Zarathustra,* p. 135.

28. Ibid., p. 137.

29. Isma'il R. al Faruqi, "Zoroastrianism," in *Historical Atlas of the Religions of the World,* ed. I. al Faruqi and D. Sopher (New York: Macmillan, 1974), pp. 133–134.

30. Zaehner, *Dawn and Twilight,* p. 99.

31. Frye, *Heritage of Persia,* p. 190; William R. Darrow, "Zoroaster Amalgamated," *HR,* November 1987, *27*(2):109–132.

32. Ghirshman, *Iran,* p. 269.

33. On Manicheanism, see J. P. Asmussen, "Manicheanism," in *Historia Religionum, I,* ed. C. J. Bleeker and G. Widengren (Leiden: E. J. Brill, 1969), pp. 580–610.

34. See Gherardo Gnoli, "Zorastrianism," *ER, 15,* 589–590.

35. Jacques Duchesne-Guillemin, "The Religion of Ancient Iran," in *Historia Religionum, I,* ed. C. J. Bleeker and G. Widengren (Leiden: E. J. Brill, 1969), pp. 366–367.

36. Emily E. Culpepper, "Zoroastrian Menstruation Taboos," in *Women and Religion,* rev. ed., ed. J. Plaskow and J. A. Romero (Missoula, Mont.: Scholars Press, 1974), pp. 199–210.

37. Mary Boyce, "Zoroastrianism," in *Historia Religionum, II,* ed. C. J. Bleeker and G. Widengren (Leiden: E. J. Brill, 1971), pp. 228–229.

38. Eric Voegelin, *Anamnesis* (Notre Dame, Ind.: University of Notre Dame Press, 1978), p. 92.

39. Arnold Toynbee, *Mankind and Mother Earth,* (New York: Oxford University Press, 1976), pp. 77–78.

40. Phillipe Borgeaud, "The Open Entrance to the Closed Palace of the King: The Greek Labyrinth in Context," *HR,* 1974, *14*(1):1–27; Raymond Christinger, "The Hidden Significance of the 'Cretan' Labyrinth," *HR,* 1975, *15*(2):183–191.

41. Mircea Eliade, *A History of Religious Ideas,* vol. 1, *From the Stone Age to the Eleusinian Mysteries* (Chicago: University of Chicago Press, 1978), p. 136; K. Kerenyi, "Voraussentzungen in der Einweihung in Eleusis," in *Initiation,* ed. C. J. Bleeker (Leiden: E. J. Brill, 1965), pp. 59–64; M. Mehauden, "Le secret central de l'initiation aux mystères d'Eléusis," ibid., pp. 65–70; Olivier Pelon, "Aegean Religions," *ER, 1,* 32–39.

42. B. C. Dietrich, *The Origins of Greek Religion* (New York: de Gruyter, 1974), pp. 191–289; see also Louis Gernet, *The Anthropology of Ancient Greece* (Baltimore: Johns Hopkins University Press, 1981); and Jean-Pierre Vernant, *The Origins of Greek Thought* (Ithaca, N.Y.: Cornell University Press, 1982).

43. Eliade, *History of Religious Ideas,* vol. 1, pp. 247–250.

44. W. K. C. Guthrie, *The Greeks and Their Gods* (Boston: Beacon Press, 1955), pp. 73–87; Claude Calame, "Facing Otherness: The Tragic Mask in Ancient Greece," *HR,* November 1986, *26*(2):125–142; Jean-Pierre Vernant, "Greek Religion," *ER, 6,* 99–118.

45. E. R. Dodds, *The Greeks and the Irrational* (Berkeley: University of California Press, 1966), pp. 76–82.

46. Ibid., pp. 270–282.

47. Eliade, *History of Religious Ideas,* vol. 1, p. 360.

48. H. J. Rose, *A Handbook of Greek Mythology* (New York: Dutton, 1959), pp. 91–94.

49. Edith Hamilton, *Mythology* (New York: New American Library, 1942), pp. 103–105.

50. Guthrie, *Greeks and Their Gods,* p. 318.

51. Ibid., pp. 217–253.

52. See Eric Voegelin, *Order and History, II: The World of the Polis* (Baton Rouge: Louisiana State University Press, 1957), pp. 203–331.

53. Ibid., pp. 332–373; Eric Voegelin, *Order and History, IV: The Ecumenic Age* (Baton Rouge: Louisiana State University Press, 1974), pp. 178–183.

54. John Carmody, "Plato's Religious Horizon," *Philosophy Today,* 1971, *15*(1):52–68.

55. Voegelin, *Order and History, IV,* pp. 187–192; Werner Jaeger, *Aristotle* (New York: Oxford University Press, 1962), pp. 366–406.

56. Bernard Lonergan, *Verbum* (Notre Dame, Ind.: University of Notre Dame Press, 1967).

57. Murray, *Greek Religion,* pp. 119–165; Dodds, *Greeks and the Irrational,* pp. 236–269; Walter Burkert, *Ancient Mystery Cults* (Cambridge, Mass.: Harvard University Press, 1987).

58. M. J. Vermaseren, "Hellenistic Religions," in *Historia Religionum, I,* ed. C. J. Bleeker and G. Widengren (Leiden: E. J. Brill, 1969), p. 495; J. Gwyn Griffiths, "Hellenistic Religions," *ER, 6,* 252–266.

59. Sharon Kelly Heyob, *The Cult of Isis among Women in the Graeco-Roman World* (Leiden: E. J. Brill, 1975), pp. 111–127.

60. See Vermaseren, "Hellenistic Religions," pp. 522–533.

61. Ibid., pp. 523–528.

62. See Mircea Eliade, *From Primitives to Zen* (New York: Harper & Row, 1967), p. 55.

63. See Eliade, *History of Religious Ideas,* vol. 1, p. 256.

64. See Bullough, *Subordinate Sex,* p. 59.

65. Eliade, *From Primitives to Zen,* p. 540.

Chapter 8:
Judaism

1. R. J. Zwi Werblowsky, "Judaism," in *Historia Religionum, II,* ed. C. J. Bleeker and G. Widengren (Leiden: E. J. Brill, 1971), p. 1; Eugene B. Borowitz, "Judaism: An Overview," *ER, 8,* 127–148.

2. Herbert May, ed., *Oxford Bible Atlas,* 2nd ed. (New York: Oxford University Press, 1974), p. 57; G. Widengren, "Israelite-Jewish Religion," in *Historia Religionum, I,* ed. C. J. Bleeker and G. Widengren (Leiden: E. J. Brill, 1969), p. 226.

3. Isadore Epstein, *Judaism* (London: Penguin, 1959), pp. 12–14; Eric Voegelin, *Order and History, I: Israel and Revelation* (Baton Rouge: Louisiana State University Press, 1956), pp. 188–195.

4. I. al Faruqi and D. Sopher, eds., *Historical Atlas of the Religions of the World* (New York: Macmillan, 1974), p. 286.

5. See E. E. Urbach, "Torah," *ER, 14,* 556–565; "Torah," *Encyclopedia Judaica* (*EJ*), vol. 15 (Jerusalem: Keter, 1972), pp. 1235–1246; Barry W. Holtz, ed., *Back to the Sources* (New York: Summit, 1984); Jonathan Rosenbaum, "Judaism: Torah and Tradition," in *The Holy Book in Comparative Perspective,* ed. Frederick M. Denny and Rodney L. Taylor (Columbia: University of South Carolina Press, 1985), pp. 10–35; Richard Elliott Friedman, *Who Wrote the Bible?* (Englewood Cliffs, N.J.: Prentice-Hall, 1987).

6. William Foxwell Albright, "The Biblical Period," in *The Jews: Their History,* ed. Louis Finkelstein (New York: Schocken, 1970), pp. 15–19.

7. See Samuel Sandmel, *The Enjoyment of Scripture* (New York: Oxford University Press, 1972), pp. 164–175.

8. For example, Roland Murphy, "Introduction to Wisdom Literature," *The Jerome Biblical Commentary,* vol. 1, ed. R. Brown, J. Fitzmyer, and R. Murphy (Englewood Cliffs, N.J.: Prentice-Hall, 1968), p. 487.

9. John J. Collins, "The Jewish Apocalypse," in *Apocalypse: The Morphology of a Genre,* ed. John J. Collins (Missoula, Mont.: Scholars Press, 1979), pp. 21–59.

10. Eric Voegelin, *Order and History, IV: The Ecumenic Age* (Baton Rouge: Louisiana State University Press, 1974), pp. 117–133, 153–165.

11. Victor Tcherikover, *Hellenistic Civilization and the Jews* (New York: Atheneum, 1974), pp. 152–234.

12. Joseph Fitzmyer, "A History of Israel," in *The Jerome Biblical Commentary,* vol. 2, ed. R. Brown, J. Fitzmyer, and R. Murphy (Englewood Cliffs, N.J.: Prentice-Hall, 1968), p. 692; Judah Goldin, "The Period of the Talmud," in *The Jews: Their History,* ed. Louis Finkelstein (New York: Schocken, 1970), pp. 121–129.

13. *Encyclopedia Judaica,* s.v. "Talmud, Babylonia."

14. See Jacob Neusner, "Form and Meaning in the Mishnah," *JAAR,* 1977, *45*(1):27–54; "History and Structure: The Case of the Mishnah," *JAAR,* 1977, *45*(2):161–192; "Stable Symbols in a Shifting Society," *HR,* November 1985, *25*(2):163–175.

15. R. Travers Herford, *Pirke Aboth: The Ethics of the Talmud* (New York: Schocken, 1962).

16. Renée Bloch, "Midrash," in *Approaches to Ancient Judaism,* ed. William Scott Green (Missoula, Mont.: Scholars Press, 1978), pp. 19–50; Nahum N. Glatzer, ed., *Hammer on the Rock* (New York: Schocken, 1962).

17. Epstein, *Judaism,* pp. 121–194. On the Talmud's view of prophecy (which its law was somewhat trying to replace), see Nahum G. Glatzer, "A Study of the Talmudic-Midrashic Interpretation of Prophecy," in his *Essays in Jewish Thought* (University: University of Alabama Press, 1978), pp. 16–35.

18. See Jacob Neusner, ed., *The Life of Torah: Readings in the Jewish Religious Experience* (Encino, Calif.: Dickenson, 1974), pp. 17–24.

19. Epstein, *Judaism,* p. 140.

20. See Robert Goldenberg, *The Sabbath Law of Rabbi Meir* (Missoula, Mont.: Scholars Press, 1978), pp. 159–264.

21. For a contemporary view of the Sabbath, see Richard Siegel et al., *The Jewish Catalogue* (Philadelphia: Jewish Publication Society of America, n.d.), pp. 103–116.

22. For an overview of the medieval period, see Jacob B. Agus, *The Meaning of Jewish History,* vol. 2 (New York: Abelard-Schuman, 1963), pp. 232–297; Martin A. Cohen, "Judaism: Judaism in Southern Europe," *ER, 8,* 172–180; Ivan G. Marcur, "Judaism: Judaism in Northern and Eastern Europe to 1500," ibid., 180–186.

23. Epstein, *Judaism,* p. 180.

24. On this whole question, see S. D. Goitein, *Jews and Arabs* (New York: Schocken, 1955).

25. Epstein, *Judaism,* p. 191.

26. See Julius Gutmann, *Philosophies of Judaism* (New York: Holt, Rinehart and Winston, 1964).

27. Moses Maimonides, *The Guide for the Perplexed,* 2nd ed., trans. M. Friedlander (New York: Dover, 1956), p. 11; see also Ralph Lerner, "Maimonides' *Treatise on Resurrection,*" *HR,* November 1983, *23*(2):140–155.

28. R. J. Zwi Werblowsky, "Judaism, or the Religion of Israel," in *The Concise Encyclopedia of Living Faiths,* ed. R. C. Zaehner (Boston: Beacon Press, 1967), pp. 45–48; Arthur Green, "Religion and Mysticism: The Case of Judaism," in *Take Judaism, for Example,* ed. Jacob Neusner (Chicago: University of Chicago Press, 1983), pp. 67–91.

29. Gershom G. Scholem, *Major Trends in Jewish Mysticism* (New York: Schocken, 1961).

30. See J. Doresse, "Gnosticism," in *Historia Religionum, I,* ed. C. J. Bleeker and G. Widengren (Leiden: E. J. Brill, 1969), pp. 536–537.

31. Werblowsky, "Judaism," p. 24.

32. See Gershom G. Scholem, ed., *Zohar: The Book of Splendor* (New York: Schocken, 1963), pp. 12–21.

33. Agus, *Jewish History,* pp. 300–485; Cecil Roth, *A History of the Jews* (New York: Schocken, 1961), pp. 235–424.

34. Roth, *History of the Jews,* pp. 180–294.

35. Leon Poliakov, *The History of Anti-Semitism* (New York: Schocken, 1974).

36. See Elie Wiesel, *Souls on Fire* (New York: Vintage, 1973).

37. Mark Zborowski and Elizabeth Herzog, *Life Is with People* (New York: Schocken, 1962); Steven J. Zipperstein, "Judaism: Judaism in Northern and Eastern Europe since 1500," *ER, 8,* 186–195.

38. Meyer Levin, *Classic Hasidic Tales* (New York: Penguin Books, 1975), p. 125. We have adapted Levin's version of the story, found on pp. 125–131.

39. Martin Buber, *Hasidism and Modern Man* (New York: Harper Torchbooks, 1966).

40. Abraham J. Heschel, *Man's Quest for God* (New York: Scribner's, 1954), *God in Search of Man* (New York: Farrar, Straus & Giroux, 1955).

41. Agus, *The Meaning of Jewish History,* p. 152.

42. Jacob Neusner, *The Way of Torah,* 2nd ed. (Encino, Calif.: Dickenson, 1974), pp. 68–71.

43. Arthur Green, "The *Zaddiq* as *Axis Mundi* in Later Judaism," *JAAR,* 1977, *45*(3):327–347.

44. Martin Buber, *Tales of the Hasidim,* 2 vols. (New York: Schocken, 1947–48).

45. Elie Wiesel, *The Gates of the Forest* (New York: Avon, 1966), pp. 6–10.

46. On this conflict in the United States, see Sydney Ahlstrom, *A Religious History of the American People* (New Haven, Conn.: Yale University Press, 1972), pp. 969–984; also Neusner, *Life of Torah,* pp. 156–203.

47. Agus, *The Meaning of Jewish History,* p. 154.

48. Eva Fleischner, "A Select Annotated Bibliography on the Holocaust," *Horizons,* 1977, *4*(1):61–83; *Encyclopedia Judaica,* vol. 8 (Jerusalem: Keter, 1972), pp. 828–918.

49. See, for example, Rosemary Ruether, *Faith and Fratricide* (New York: Seabury, 1974).

50. See, for example, John L. McKenzie, *Dictionary of the Bible* (Milwaukee: Bruce, 1965); Paul J. Achtemeier, ed. *Harper's Bible Dictionary* (San Francisco: Harper & Row, 1985). *The Encyclopedia Judaica,* vol. 12 (Jerusalem: Keter, 1972), does have a three and one-half column article, but only twelve lines deal with the biblical period.

51. Werblowsky, "Judaism, or the Religion of Israel."

52. Geoffrey Wigoder et al., *Jewish Values* (Jerusalem: Keter, 1974).

53. Voegelin, *Order and History: IV,* chaps. 1, 3, 7.

54. Salo Wittmayer Baron, *A Social and Religious History of the Jews,* vol. 1, *Ancient Times,* 2nd ed. (New York: Columbia University Press, 1952), pp. 4–16.

55. Sherry B. Ortner, "Is Female to Male as Nature Is to Culture?" in *Woman, Culture and Society,* ed. M. Z. Rosaldo and L. Lamphere (Stanford, Calif.: Stanford University Press, 1974), pp. 67–88.

56. Phyllis Bird, "Images of Women in the Old Testament," in *Religion and Sexism,* ed. Rosemary Radford Ruether (New York: Simon & Schuster, 1974), pp. 41–88.

57. Judith Hauptmann, "Images of Women in the Talmud," in *Religion and Sexism,* ed. Rosemary Radford Ruether (New York: Simon & Schuster, 1974), pp. 184–212. On Mishnaic menstrual taboos, see Jacob Neusner, *A History of the Mishnaic Law of Purities* (Leiden: E. J. Brill, 1977), p. 22.

58. I. Epstein, "The Jewish Woman in the Responsa: 900 C.E.–1500 C.E.," *Response,* Summer 1973, no. 16, pp. 23–31.

59. For an overview of women in Judaism, see Denise Lardner Carmody, *Women and World Religions* (Nashville: Abingdon, 1979), pp. 92–112. For current issues, see Carol P. Christ and Judith Plaskow, eds., *Woman-spirit Rising* (New York: Harper & Row, 1979); Elizabeth Koltun, ed., *The Jewish Woman: New Perspectives* (New York: Schocken, 1976).

60. See his contributions to *The Life of Torah: Readings in the Jewish Religious Experiences,* ed. Jacob Neusner (Encino, Calif.: Dickenson, 1974), p. 104; see also Elliot R. Wolfson, "Circumcision, Vision of God, and Textual Interpretation," *HR,* November 1987, *27*(2):189–215.

61. Judith Plaskow, "Bringing a Daughter into the Covenant," in *Woman-spirit Rising,* ed. Carol P. Christ and Judith Plaskow (San Francisco: Harper & Row, 1980), p. 181.

62. See *The Jewish Catalogue,* ed. Richard Siegel et al. (Philadelphia: Jewish Publication Society of America, 1973), p. 158.

63. On this point, Robert L. Cohn reminded us of Hillel's saying, "Sever not thyself from the congregation" (*Pirke Avot,* 2:5). (Private communication.)

64. Richard L. Rubenstein, *After Auschwitz* (Indianapolis, Ind.: Bobbs-Merrill, 1966).

65. Emil Fackenheim, *God's Presence in History* (New York: New York University Press, 1970).

66. Hannah Arendt, *Eichmann in Jerusalem* (New York: Viking, 1965).

67. See Elie Wiesel, *The Oath* (New York: Random House, 1973).

68. See, for example, Joel Blocker, ed., *Israeli Stories* (New York: Schocken, 1965).

69. Michael Polanyi and Harry Prosch, *Meaning* (Chicago: University of Chicago Press, 1975). That does not mean, however, that the Talmud did not meditate deeply on Jewish divinity. See A. Cohen, *Everyman's Talmud* (New York: Schocken, 1975), pp. 1–26. For a contemporary view, see Leo Baeck, *The Essence of Judaism* (New York: Schocken, 1961), pp. 83–150.

70. Cynthia Ozick, "Ruth," in *Congregation*, ed. David Rosenberg (New York: Harcourt Brace Jovanovich, 1987), p. 373.

71. See Neusner, ed., *Life of Torah,* pp. 17–24.

Chapter 9:
Christianity

1. For a brief study of Christianity that includes fine maps of its spread, see Gerald Sloyan, "Christianity," in *Historical Atlas of the Religions of the World,* ed. I. al Faruqi and D. Sopher (New York: Macmillan, 1974), pp. 201–236; see also Jaroslov Pelikan, "Christianity: An Overview," *ER, 3,* 348–362; and Williston Walker et al., *A History of the Christian Church,* 4th ed. (New York: Charles Scribner's Sons, 1985).

2. One of the most thorough recent treatments of the critical and theological issues concerning Jesus is Edward Schillebeeckx, *Jesus* (New York: Seabury, 1979).

3. See Raymond E. Brown, *The Birth of the Messiah* (New York: Doubleday, 1977).

4. Geza Vermes, *Jesus the Jew* (London: Fontana, 1976), pp. 18–82.

5. Joachim Jeremias, *New Testament Theology: The Proclamation of Jesus* (New York: Charles Scribner's Sons, 1971), pp. 29–36.

6. Karl Rahner and Herbert Vorgrimler, *Theological Dictionary* (New York: Herder and Herder, 1965), pp. 236–241.

7. A succinct discussion of New Testament ethics is J. L. Houden, *Ethics and the New Testament* (New York: Oxford University Press, 1977); see also Wayne A. Meeks, *The Moral World of the First Christians* (Philadelphia: Westminster, 1986).

8. Jeremias, *New Testament Theology,* pp. 250–257; see also Paula Fredriksen, *From Jesus To Christ* (New Haven, CT: Yale University Press, 1988).

9. See Eric Voegelin, "The Gospel and Culture," in *Jesus and Man's Hope,* vol. 2, ed. D. Miller and D. Hadidian (Pittsburgh: Pittsburgh Theological Seminary, 1971), pp. 59–101.

10. Joseph A. Fitzmyer, "Pauline Theology," in *The Jerome Biblical Commentary,* vol. 2, ed. R. Brown, J. Fitzmyer, and R. Murphy (Englewood Cliffs, N.J.: Prentice-Hall, 1968), pp. 810–827.

11. Pheme Perkins, *Hearing the Parables of Jesus* (Ramsey, N.J.: Paulist Press, 1981), p. 94. Our treatment adapts pp. 94–98.

12. Recent and readable is Stephen Neill, *Jesus through Many Eyes* (Philadelphia: Fortress, 1976). For a literary stress, see Leonard L. Thompson, *Introducing Biblical Literature* (Englewood Cliffs, N.J.: Prentice-Hall 1978), pp.

213–307. For an overview of Jesus that includes a comparison with other great world religious figures, see Denise Lardner Carmody and John Tully Carmody, *Jesus: An Introduction* (Belmont, Calif.: Wadsworth, 1987); see also Jaroslav Pelikan, *Jesus through the Centuries* (New Haven, Conn.: Yale University Press, 1985).

13. Antonio Javierre, "Apostle," in *Sacramentum Mundi,* vol. 1, ed. Karl Rahner et al. (New York: Herder and Herder, 1968), p. 77.

14. Raymond E. Brown et al., eds. *Peter in the New Testament* (Minneapolis, Minn.: Augsburg, 1973).

15. See Maxwell Staniforth, trans., *Early Christian Writings* (Baltimore: Penguin, 1968).

16. J. Doresse, "Gnosticism," in *Historia Religionum, I,* ed. C. J. Bleeker and G. Widengren (Leiden: E. J. Brill, 1969), pp. 536–537.

17. Succinct information on personages such as these is available in F. L. Cross, ed., *The Oxford Dictionary of the Christian Church* (New York: Oxford University Press, 1966).

18. See Jaroslav Pelikan, *The Christian Tradition, 1: The Emergence of the Catholic Tradition* (Chicago: University of Chicago Press, 1971).

19. J. G. Davies, "Christianity: The Early Church," in *The Concise Encyclopedia of Living Faiths,* ed. R. C. Zaehner (Boston: Beacon Press, 1967), pp. 60–69; W. H. C. Frend, *The Rise of Christianity* (Philadelphia: Fortress, 1984).

20. On patristic terminology, see G. L. Prestige, *God in Patristic Thought* (London: Society for the Promotion of Christian Knowledge, 1959).

21. Bernard Lonergan, *The Way to Nicaea* (Philadelphia: Westminster, 1976); Charles Kannengiesser, S.J., "The Athanasian Decade 1974–1984: A Bibliographical Report," *Theological Studies,* September 1985, *46*(3):524–541; Francis M. Young, *From Nicaea to Chalcedon* (Philadelphia: Fortress, 1983); Robert C. Gregg and Dennis E. Groh, *Early Arianism: A View of Salvation* (Philadelphia: Fortress, 1983).

22. William A. Clebsch, *Christianity in European History* (New York: Oxford University Press, 1979), pp. 29–84; Stephen Reynolds, *The Christian Religious Tradition* (Encino, Calif.: Dickenson, 1977), pp. 35–77.

23. Thomas Merton, *The Wisdom of the Desert* (New York: New Directions, 1960).

24. Nicholas Zernov, "Christianity: The Eastern Schism and the Eastern Orthodox Church," in *The Concise Encyclopedia of Living Faiths,* ed. R. C. Zaehner (Boston: Beacon Press, 1967), p. 86; Stanley Samuel Harakac, "Christianity: Christianity in Eastern Europe," *ER, 3,* 372–378.

25. Donald W. Treadgold, *The West in Russia and China,* vol. 1 (Cambridge: Cambridge University Press, 1973), pp. 1–23.

26. On classical Eastern theology, see Jaroslav Pelikan, *The Christian Tradition, 2: The Spirit of Eastern Christendom* (Chicago: University of Chicago Press, 1974); see

also G. P. Fedotov, *The Russian Religious Mind* (Cambridge, Mass.: Harvard University Press, 1966).

27. See Timothy Ware, *The Orthodox Church* (Baltimore: Penguin, 1964).

28. Bernhard Schultze, "Eastern Churches," in *Sacramentum Mundi,* vol. 2, ed. Karl Rahner et al. (New York: Herder and Herder, 1968), pp. 120–130.

29. Sergius Bolshakoff and M. Basil Pennington, *In Search of True Wisdom: Visits to Eastern Spiritual Fathers* (Garden City, N.Y.: Doubleday, 1979).

30. C. W. Monnich, "Christianity," in *Historia Religionum, II,* ed. C. J. Bleeker and G. Widengren (Leiden: E. J. Brill, 1971), p. 65.

31. Jaroslav Pelikan, *The Christian Tradition, 3: The Growth of Medieval Theology* (Chicago: University of Chicago Press, 1978), pp. 268–307.

32. Anthony Kenney, ed., *Aquinas* (New York: Doubleday, 1969); see also H. Francis Davis, "St. Thomas and Medieval Theology," in *The Concise Encyclopedia of Living Faiths,* ed. R. C. Zaehner (Boston: Beacon Press, 1967), pp. 108–112.

33. Lawrence Cunningham and John Reich, *Culture and Values: A Survey of the Western Humanities,* vol. 2 (New York: Holt, Rinehart and Winston, 1982), p. 99. Our treatment adapts pp. 99–103.

34. On the history of the notion of reform, see Gerhart B. Ladner, *The Idea of Reform* (Cambridge, Mass.: Harvard University Press, 1959).

35. Erik H. Erikson, *Young Man Luther* (New York: Norton, 1962).

36. *The New Columbia Encyclopedia,* s.v. "plague."

37. See Pennethorne Hughes, *Witchcraft* (Baltimore: Penguin, 1965).

38. John Kent, "Christianity: Protestantism," in *The Concise Encyclopedia of Living Faiths,* ed. R. C. Zaehner (Boston: Beacon Press, 1967), pp. 117–149; Martin E. Marty, "Protestantism," *ER, 12,* 23–38.

39. Owen Chadwick, *The Reformation* (Baltimore: Penguin, 1964), p. 41.

40. See Lewis Spitz, ed., *The Protestant Reformation* (Englewood Cliffs, N.J.: Prentice-Hall, 1966).

41. C. W. Monnich, "Christianity," p. 72.

42. See William A. Clebsch, *American Religious Thought* (Chicago: University of Chicago Press, 1973), pp. 11–56; Edward S. Gaustad, ed., *A Documentary History of Religion in America,* vol. 1 (Grand Rapids, Mich.: Erdmans, 1982).

43. James Brodrick, *The Origin of the Jesuits* (London: Longmans, 1940); *The Progress of the Jesuits* (London: Longmans, 1946).

44. Sidney E. Mead, *The Lively Experiment* (New York: Harper & Row, 1976); *The Nation with the Soul of a Church* (New York: Harper & Row, 1975); see also Sydney E. Ahlstrom, *A Religious History of the American People* (New Haven, Conn.: Yale University Press, 1972), pp. 121–229.

45. Harvey D. Egan, *The Spiritual Exercises and the Ignatian Mystical Horizon* (St. Louis: Institute of Jesuit Sources, 1976); Gaston Fessard, *La dialectique des exercices spirituels de Saint Ignace de Loyola* (Paris: Aubier, 1956); Antonio T. De Nicolas, *Powers of Imagining: Ignatius de Loyola* (Albany: State University of New York Press, 1986).

46. Robert McAfee Brown, *The Spirit of Protestantism* (New York: Oxford University Press, 1965); Jaroslav Pelikan, *The Christian Tradition,* vol. 4 (Chicago: University of Chicago Press, 1984).

47. Max Weber, *The Protestant Ethic and the Spirit of Capitalism* (New York: Charles Scribner's Sons, 1958).

48. Heribert Raab, "Enlightenment," in *Sacramentum Mundi,* vol. 2, ed. Karl Rahner et al. (New York: Herder and Herder, 1968), p. 230; see also Crane Brinton, "Enlightenment," in *The Encyclopedia of Philosophy,* vol. 2, ed. Paul Edwards (New York: Macmillan, 1967), pp. 519–525; Allen W. Wood, "Enlightenment, The," *ER, 5,* 109–113; George Alfred James, "Atheism," *ER, 1,* 479–490.

49. See the articles by Sidney E. Mead, Sydney E. Ahlstrom, Vincent Harding, and Robert Bellah in *Soundings,* 1978, *61*(3):303–371.

50. Eric Voegelin, *From Enlightenment to Revolution* (Durham, N.C.: Duke University Press, 1975).

51. The breakthrough work was Gustavo Gutierrez, *A Theology of Liberation* (Maryknoll, N.Y.: Orbis, 1973). Especially provocative is Jose Miranda, *Marx and the Bible* (Maryknoll, N.Y.: Orbis, 1974). A fine survey that brings liberation thought to the United States is Robert McAfee Brown, *Theology in a New Key* (Philadelphia: Westminster, 1978).

52. See Sergio Torres and John Eagleson, eds., *Theology in the Americas* (Maryknoll, N.Y.: Orbis, 1976).

53. Martin E. Marty, *Righteous Empire* (New York: Dial Press, 1970).

54. Robert Bellah, *The Broken Covenant* (New York: Seabury, 1975).

55. Emilie Griffin, *Turning: The Experience of Conversion* (Garden City, N.Y.: Doubleday, 1980). We especially draw on pp. 31–49; see also Walter E. Conn, *Christian Conversion* (New York: Paulist Press, 1986).

56. Jorg Splett et al., "Nature," in *Sacramentum Mundi,* vol. 4, ed. Karl Rahner et al. (New York: Herder and Herder, 1969), pp. 171–181.

57. Pieter Smulders et al., "Creation," in *Sacramentum Mundi,* vol. 2, ed. Karl Rahner et al. (New York: Herder and Herder, 1968), pp. 23–37; Conrad Hyers, *The Meaning of Creation* (Atlanta: John Knox, 1984).

58. See Harold K. Schilling, *The New Consciousness in Science and Religion* (Philadelphia: United Church Press, 1973).

59. Alfred North Whitehead, *Process and Reality* (New York: Harper Torchbooks, 1960).

60. See Staniforth, *Early Christian Writings,* pp. 171–185.

61. See Bernard Cooke, *Ministry to Word and Sacrament* (Philadelphia: Fortress, 1976); Monika K. Hellwig, "Christian Sacraments," *ER, 12,* 504–511.

62. Edward Schillebeeckx, *Christ: The Sacrament of Encounter with God* (New York: Sheed & Ward, 1963).

63. Mary Daly, *Gyn/Ecology* (Boston: Beacon Press, 1979), chap. 6.

64. Denise Lardner Carmody, *Women and World Religions* (Nashville: Abingdon, 1979), pp. 113–136; Carol P. Christ and Judith Plaskow, eds., *Woman-spirit Rising* (New York: Harper & Row, 1979); Elizabeth Clark and Herbert Richardon, eds., *Women and Religion* (New York: Harper & Row, 1977); Rosemary Radford Ruether, ed., *Religion and Sexism* (New York: Simon & Schuster, 1974); Mary Daly, *The Church and the Second Sex* (New York: Harper Colophon, 1975); Elisabeth Schüssler Fiorenza, *In Memory of Her* (New York: Crossroad, 1983); George H. Tavard, *Women in Christian Tradition* (Notre Dame, Ind.: University of Notre Dame Press, 1973); Rosemary Radford Ruether and Rosemary Skinner Keller, eds. *Women & Religion in America,* 3 vols. (San Francisco: Harper & Row, 1983).

65. Steven Runciman, *The Orthodox Churches and the Secular State* (Auckland: Auckland University Press, 1971).

66. Karl Rahner, *The Shape of the Church to Come* (New York: Seabury, 1974).

67. See Vladimir Lossky, *The Mystical Theology of the Eastern Church* (Crestwood, N.Y.: St. Vladimir's Seminary Press, 1976); Alexander Schmemann, ed., *Ultimate Questions* (Crestwood, N.Y.: St. Vladimir's Seminary Press, 1977); Marina Warner, *Alone of All Her Sex* (New York: Alfred A. Knopf, 1976).

68. John L. McKenzie, S. J., *The Power and the Wisdom* (Milwaukee, Wis.: Bruce, 1965), pp. 252–255.

69. *The Book of Common Prayer* (New York: Seabury, 1977), p. 308. Our description of the sacramental rituals depends on the *Book of Common Prayer;* see also Charles L. Rice, "Preaching," *ER, 11,* 494–501.

70. A profound interpretation is Karl Rahner's "Thomas Aquinas on the Incomprehensibility of God," *Journal of Religion,* 1978, *58,* supp., 107–125; see also Paul Ricoeur, " 'Response' to Karl Rahner's Lecture on the Incomprehensibility of God," ibid., 126–131; for early Christian background, see Robert M. Grant, *Gods and the One God* (Philadelphia: Westminster, 1986).

71. On the Christian life as a reflection of Jesus' death and resurrection, see Alan Paton, *Ah, But Your Land Is Beautiful* (New York: Charles Scribner's Sons, 1982).

Chapter 10: Islam

1. There are good maps on the spread of Islam in Geoffrey Barraclough, ed., *The Times Atlas of World History* (Maplewood, N.J.: Hammond, 1979), pp. 104–105, 134–135, 138–139; see also I. al Faruqi and D. Sopher, eds., *Historical*

Atlas of the Religions of the World (New York: Macmillan, 1974), pp. 237–281.

2. Annemarie Schimmel, "Islam," in *Historia Religionum, II,* ed. C. J. Bleeker and G. Widengren (Leiden: E. J. Brill, 1971), p. 127; Fazlur Rahman, "Islam: An Overview," *ER, 7,* 303–322; Isma'il R. al Faruqi and Lois Lamya' al Faruqi, *The Cultural Atlas of Islam* (New York: Macmillan, 1986).

3. W. Montgomery Watt, *Muhammad: Prophet and Statesman* (New York: Oxford University Galaxy Books, 1974), pp. 45–55; W. Montgomery Watt, "Muhammad," *ER 10,* 137–146.

4. We have used the translation by A. J. Arberry, *The Koran Interpreted* (New York: Macmillan, 1973).

5. Watt, *Muhammad,* p. 7.

6. On the pre-Islamic background, see Ignaz Goldziher, *Muslim Studies,* vol. 1 (Chicago: Aldine, 1967), pp. 11–44; Marshall G. S. Hodgson, *The Venture of Islam,* vol. 1 (Chicago: University of Chicago Press, 1974), pp. 103–145; M. M. Bravmann, *The Spiritual Background of Early Islam* (Leiden: E. J. Brill, 1972).

7. Schimmel, "Islam," p. 129.

8. Isma'il al Faruqi, "Islam," in *Historical Atlas of the Religions of the World,* ed. I. al Faruqi and D. Sopher (New York: Macmillan, 1974), p. 241.

9. Charles J. Adams, "The Islamic Religious Tradition," in *Judaism, Christianity and Islam,* ed. J. O'Dea, T. O'Dea, and C. Adams (New York: Harper & Row, 1972), p. 166.

10. H. A. R. Gibb, *Mohammedanism,* 2nd ed. (New York: Oxford University Press, 1962), p. 30.

11. See Watt, *Muhammad,* pp. 229–231.

12. H. A. R. Gibb, "Islam," in *The Concise Encyclopedia of Living Faiths,* ed. R. C. Zaehner (Boston: Beacon Press, 1967), p. 179.

13. N. J. Dawood, trans., *The Koran* (Baltimore: Penguin, 1968), p. 10.

14. Kenneth Cragg, *The House of Islam,* 2nd ed. (Encino, Calif.: Dickenson, 1975), pp. 30–34; Arberry, *Koran Interpreted,* p. 28; Charles J. Adams, "Qur'an: The Text and Its History," *ER, 12,* 156–176; Mahmoud M. Ayoub, "Qur'an: Its Role in Muslim Piety," ibid., 176–179.

15. Arthur Jeffrey, ed., *Islam: Muhammad and His Religion* (New York: Bobbs-Merrill, 1975); Isma'il al Faruqi, "Islam," in *The Great Asian Religions,* ed. W. T. Chan et al. (New York: Macmillan, 1969), pp. 307–395.

16. On the development of the *Hadith,* see Ignaz Goldziher, *Muslim Studies,* vol. 2 (Chicago: Aldine, 1975), pp. 17–251; L. T. Librande, "Hadith," *ER, 6,* 143–151.

17. Cragg, *House of Islam,* pp. 5–18.

18. See Martin Lings, *A Sufi Saint of the Twentieth Century,* 2nd ed. (Berkeley: University of California Press, 1973), pp. 121–130; R. C. Zaehner, *Hindu and Muslim Mysticism* (New York: Schocken, 1969), pp. 86–109; Annemarie Schimmel, *The Mystical Dimension of Islam* (Chapel Hill: University of North Carolina Press, 1978); Seyyed Hossein Nasr, ed., *Islamic Spirituality: Foundations* (New York: Crossroad, 1987).

19. W. Montgomery Watt, *The Faith and Practice of al-Ghazali* (London: Allen & Unwin, 1953), pp. 90–130.

20. See Cheikh Hamidou Kane, *Ambiguous Adventure* (New York: Collier, 1969).

21. Cragg, *House of Islam,* pp. 73–108; Frederick Mathewson Denny, "The Meaning of *Ummah* in the Qur'an," *HR,* 1975, *15:*34–70.

22. Dawood, trans., *The Koran,* p. 32. Our treatment of this sura draws on pp. 32–37.

23. See Geoffrey Parrinder, *Jesus in the Qur'an* (New York: Oxford University Press, 1977).

24. al Faruqi, "Islam," in *Historical Atlas,* p. 248.

25. Bernard Lewis, *The Arabs in History,* rev. ed. (New York: Harper Torchbooks, 1966), p. 55; see also Edmund Bosworth, "Armies of the Prophet," in *Islam and the Arab World,* ed. Bernard Lewis (New York: Knopf, 1976), pp. 201–224; V. J. Parry, "Warfare," in *The Cambridge History of Islam,* vol. 2, ed. P. M. Holt et al. (Cambridge: University Press, 1970), pp. 824–850.

26. Lewis, *Arabs in History,* p. 56.

27. See Hodgson, *The Venture of Islam,* pp. 187–217.

28. See W. Montgomery Watt, *The Formative Period of Islamic Thought* (Edinburgh: University Press, 1973), pp. 253–278.

29. Stephen F. Mason, *A History of the Sciences,* rev. ed. (New York: Collier, 1962), p. 95; see also A. I. Sabra, "The Scientific Enterprise," in *Islam and the Arab World,* ed. Bernard Lewis (New York: Alfred A. Knopf, 1976), pp. 181–200; G. Anawati, "Science, in *The Cambridge History of Islam,* vol. 2, ed. P. M. Holt et al. (Cambridge: University Press, 1970), pp. 741–779.

30. Albert C. Moore, *Iconography of the Religions: An Introduction* (Philadelphia: Fortress, 1977), pp. 213–226; see also Richard Ettinghausen, "The Man-Made Setting," in *Islam and the Arab World,* ed. Bernard Lewis (New York: Alfred A. Knopf, 1976), pp. 57–88; G. Fehervari, "Art and Architecture," in *The Cambridge History of Islam,* vol. 2, ed. P. M. Holt et al. (Cambridge: University Press, 1970), pp. 702–740; al Faruqi, *The Cultural Atlas of Islam,* pp. 336–440.

31. Schuyler V. R. Cammann, "Religious Symbolism in Persian Art," *HR,* 1976, *15:*193–205.

32. Oleg Grabar, "Architecture," in *The Legacy of Islam,* 2nd ed., ed. Joseph Schacht and C. E. Bosworth (New York: Oxford University Press, 1979), p. 263.

33. A. J. Arberry, *Aspects of Islamic Civilization* (Ann Arbor: University of Michigan Press, 1967); see also Charles Pellah, "Jewellers with Words," in *Islam and the Arab World,* ed. Bernard Lewis (New York: Alfred A. Knopf, 1976), pp. 141–160; Irfan Shahid et al., "Literature," in *The Cambridge History of Islam,* vol. 2, ed. P. M. Holt et al. (Cambridge: University Press, 1970), pp. 657–701.

34. Oleg Grabar, "Cities and Citizens," in *Islam and the Arab World,* ed. Bernard Lewis (New York: Alfred A. Knopf, 1976), pp. 89–116.

35. Arberry, *Aspects of Islamic Civilization,* p. 257.

36. Ibid.

37. Ibid., p. 111.

38. See J. Schacht, "Laws and Justice," in *The Cambridge History of Islam,* vol. 2, ed. P. M. Holt et al. (Cambridge: University Press, 1970), pp. 539–568; Ann Elizabeth Mayer, "Islamic Law: Shari'ah," *ER, 7,* 431–446; M. Hashim Kamali, "Islamic Law: Personal Law," ibid., pp. 446–453.

39. Fazlur Rahman, *Islam* (Garden City, N.Y.: Doubleday, 1968), p. xxii.

40. al Faruqi, "Islam," in *Historical Atlas,* p. 267.

41. Martin Lings, *What Is Sufism?* (Berkeley: University of California Press, 1977), pp. 45–46; A. J. Arberry, *Sufism* (New York: Harper Torchbooks, 1970), p. 35; Peter J. Awn, "Sufism," *ER, 14,* 104–122.

42. Watt, *Al-Ghazali,* p. 57.

43. Ibid., p. 60.

44. Idries Shah, *The Way of the Sufi* (New York: Dutton, 1970).

45. Ibid., p. 162.

46. Ibid., p. 169.

47. Arberry, *Sufism,* p. 119.

48. Richard M. Eaton, "Sufi Folk Literature and the Expansion of Indian Islam," *HR,* 1974, *14:*117–127.

49. Lings, *Sufi Saint;* see also Clifford Geertz, *Islam Observed* (Chicago: University of Chicago Press, 1971).

50. See Roger Le Tourneau et al., "Africa and the Muslim West," in *The Cambridge History of Islam,* vol. 2, ed. P. M. Holt et al. (Cambridge: University Press, 1970), pp. 209–405; Benjamin Ray, *African Religions* (Englewood Cliffs, N.J.: Prentice-Hall, 1976), pp. 174–191; Nehemiah Levtzion, "Islam: Islam in Sub-Sahara Africa," *ER, 7,* 344–357.

51. Lewis, *Arabs in History,* p. 144.

52. See Norman Itzkowitz, "The Ottoman Empire," in *Islam and the Arab World,* ed. Bernard Lewis (New York: Alfred A. Knopf, 1976), pp. 273–300.

53. Roger M. Savory, "Land of the Lion and the Sun," in *Islam and the Arab World,* ed. Bernard Lewis (New York: Alfred A. Knopf, 1976), pp. 245–272.

54. S. A. A. Rizi, "Muslim India," in *Islam and the Arab World,* ed. Bernard Lewis (New York: Alfred A. Knopf, 1976), pp. 301–320; see also I. H. Qureshi et al., "The Indian Sub-Continent," in *The Cambridge History of Islam,* vol. 2, ed. P. M. Holt et al. (Cambridge: University Press, 1970), pp. 1–120; Peter Hardy, "Islam: Islam in South Asia," *ER, 7,* 390–404.

55. Lewis, *Arabs in History,* pp. 158–159.

56. See Rahman, *Islam,* pp. 237–260.

57. Gibb, "Islam," p. 207.

58. See Wilfred Cantwell Smith, *The Meaning and End of Religion* (New York: Mentor, 1964), p. 79.

59. Anne Sinai and Allen Pollack, *The Syrian Arab Republic* (New York: American Academic Association for Peace in the Middle East, 1976); *The Hashemite Kingdom of Jordan and the West Bank* (New York: American Academic Association for Peace in the Middle East, 1977).

60. Islamic (Student) Association of Cairo University, "Lessons from Iran," in *Islam in Transition,* ed. John J. Donohue and John L. Esposito (New York: Oxford University Press, 1982), p. 246.

61. Ayatullah Ruhullah Khumayni *(sic),* "Islamic Government," *Islam in Transition,* ed. John J. Donohue and John L. Esposito (New York: Oxford University Press, 1982), p. 318 (both quotations).

62. al Faruqi, "Islam," in *Great Asian Religions,* p. 308.

63. Ibid., p. 310.

64. Ibid.

65. Schimmel, "Islam," p. 186.

66. al Faruqi, "Islam," in *Great Asian Religions,* p. 359.

67. Ibid., p. 366.

68. Ibid., p. 374.

69. See Schimmel, "Islam," pp. 160–166.

70. Ibid., p. 163.

71. For an overview, see Denise Lardner Carmody, *Women and World Religions* (Nashville: Abingdon, 1979), pp. 137–155; Jane I. Smith, "Islam," in *Women in World Religions,* ed. Arvind Sharma (Albany: State University of New York Press, 1987), pp. 235–250. On recent attitudes, see Elizabeth Warnock Fernea and Basima Qattan Bezirgan, *Middle Eastern Muslim Woman Speak* (Austin: University of Texas Press, 1977).

72. Joseph Graziani, "The Status of Women in The Contemporary Muslim Arab Family," *Middle East Review,* 1976–77, *9:*48.

73. *Ms.,* March 1977, p. 112.

74. Kari Ka'us Iskander, *A Mirror for Princes* (London: Cresset, 1951), p. 125.

75. George Allgrove, *Love in the East* (London: Gibbs and Phillips, 1962), p. 128.

76. Mary Daly, *Gyn/Ecology* (Boston: Beacon Press, 1979), chap. 5.

77. Jane I. Smith and Yvonne Haddad, "Women in the Afterlife: The Islamic View as Seen from the Qur'an and Tradition," *JAAR,* 1975, *43:*39–50.

78. See Goldziher, *Muslim Studies,* vol. 2, pp. 366–368.

79. On scholarship and saintliness, the Sufis somewhat sponsored women, though their overall view of women was ambivalent; see Schimmel, *Mystical Dimensions of Islam,* pp. 426–435.

80. Watt, *Formative Period of Islamic Thought.*

81. See J. E. Esslemont, *Bahaa'u'llah and the New Era: An Introduction to the Baha'i Faith* (Wilmette, Ill.: Baha'i Books, 1970); Alessandro Bausani, "Baha'is," *ER, 2,* 40–42.

82. This section adapts Patrick J. Ryan's *Imale: Yoruba Participation in the Muslim Tradition* (Missoula, Mont.: Scholars Press, 1978), pp. 249–270; see also John Pemberton III, "Yoruba Religion," *ER, 15,* pp. 535–538.

83. Cragg, *House of Islam,* p. 60.

84. al Faruqi, "Islam," in *Great Asian Religions,* p. 347.

85. Schimmel, "Islam," p. 179.

86. This section draws on Clifford Geertz, *Islam Observed* (Chicago: University of Chicago Press, 1971), pp. 25–35; see also James L. Peacock, "The Creativity of Tradition in Indonesian Religion," *HR,* May 1986, *25*(4):341–351.

87. For a sensitive study of the meaning of *Islam,* more suitable for the end of our survey than the beginning, see Jane I. Smith, *An Historical and Semantic Study of the Term Islam as Seen in a Sequence of Quran Commentaries* (Missoula, Mont.: Scholars Press, 1975).

88. Schimmel, "Islam," p. 142.

89. On the Mutazila, see Watt, *Formative Period of Islamic Thought,* pp. 209–250.

90. See S. Pines, "Philosophy," in *The Cambridge History of Islam,* vol. 2, ed. P. M. Holt et al. (Cambridge: University Press, 1970), pp. 780–823.

91. Earle Waugh, "En Islam Iranien," *HR,* 1975, *14*:322–323.

92. See Gustave Thaiss, "Religious Symbolism and Social Change: The Drama of Husain," in *Scholars, Saints, and Sufis,* ed. Nikki R. Kiddie (Berkeley: University of California Press, 1972), pp. 349–366.

93. Fatima Mernissi, "Women, Saints, and Sanctuaries," *Signs,* 1977, *3*(1):101–112.

94. Schimmel, "Islam," p. 168.

Chapter 11:
Alternatives to Religion—Secularism and Humanism

1. See Bryan Wilson, "Secularization," *ER, 13,* 159–165; Phillip Hammond, ed., *The Sacred in a Secular Age* (Berkeley: University of California Press, 1985); Mary Douglas and Steven Tipton, eds., *Religion and America; Spirituality in a Secular Age* (Boston: Beacon Press, 1983).

2. See Kees Bolle, "Myth: An Overview," and Paul Ricoeur, "Myth and History," *ER, 10,* 261–273, 273–282.

3. See Shaye J. D. Cohen, *From the Maccabees to the Mishnah* (Philadelphia: Westminster, 1987).

4. See Joseph Needham, *Science and Civilization in China* (Cambridge: University Press, 1969).

5. See Stanley Jaki, *The Road of Science and the Ways to God* (Chicago: University of Chicago Press, 1978).

6. See Robin W. Lovin and Frank E. Reynolds, ed., *Cosmogony and Ethical Order* (Chicago: University of Chicago Press, 1985).

7. See Stephen Toulmin, *Human Understanding* (Princeton, N.J.: Princeton University Press, 1972), and Thomas S. Kuhn, *The Structure of Scientific Revolutions,* 2nd ed. (Chicago: University of Chicago Press, 1970).

8. See James Gordon Clapp, "Locke, John," *The Encyclopedia of Philosophy,* vol. 4, ed. Paul Edwards (New York: Macmillan, 1967), pp. 487–503.

9. See Robert Heilbroner, *Marxism: For and Against* (New York: Norton, 1980); Eric Voegelin, *Science, Politics and Gnosticism* (Chicago: Henry Regnery, 1968), and *From Enlightenment to Revolution* (Durham, N.C.: Duke University Press, 1975); Karl Löwith, *From Hegel to Nietzsche* (Garden City, N.Y.: Doubleday Anchor, 1967); Charles C. West, "Marxism," *ER, 9,* 240–249.

10. See Rosemary Haughton, *The Transformation of Man* (Springfield, Ill.: Templegate, 1967), pp. 153–280.

Conclusion:
Summary Reflections

1. C. G. Jung, *Memories, Dreams, Reflections* (New York: Vintage, 1963), p. 235.

2. In our view, Mircea Eliade shows that persuasively; see his *Shamanism* (Princeton, N.J.: Princeton University Press/Bollingen, 1972); *Yoga* (Princeton, N.J.: Princeton University Press/Bollingen, 1970).

3. See Wilfred Cantwell Smith, *The Meaning and End of Religion* (New York: Mentor, 1964); on the rise of the term *religio* with Cicero, see Eric Voegelin, *Order and History,* vol. 4 (Baton Rouge: Louisiana State University Press, 1974), pp. 43–48; Winston L. King, "Religion," *ER, 12,* 282–293.

4. See Joachim Wach, *The Comparative Study of Religions* (New York: Columbia University Press, 1961).

5. Three recent works that illumine religious traditioning are Huston Smith, *Forgotten Truth: The Primordial Tradition* (New York: Harper & Row, 1976); E. F. Schumacher, *A Guide for the Perplexed* (New York: Harper & Row, 1977); Peter Slater, *The Dynamics of Religion* (New York: Harper & Row, 1978).

6. This is a theme in John Bowker, *The Sense of God* (Oxford: Clarendon Press, 1973).

7. See Voegelin, *Order and History,* vol. 4, pp. 330–335.

8. See Marcel Griaule, *Conversations with Ogotemmeli* (New York: Oxford University Press, 1965).

9. Huston Smith, "Frithjof Schuon's *The Transcendent Unity of Religion:* Pro," and Richard C. Bush, "Frithjof Schuon's *The Transcendent Unity of Religion:* Con," *JAAR,* 1976, *44*:715–719, 721–724.

10. See Stanley Jaki, *The Road of Science and the Ways to God* (Chicago: University of Chicago Press, 1978).

11. On religious interpretations of American destiny,

see Conrad Cherry, ed., *God's New Israel* (Englewood Cliffs, N.J.: Prentice-Hall, 1971).

12.   William A. Clebsch, *American Religious Thought* (Chicago: University of Chicago Press, 1973).

13.   Sidney Mead, *The Lively Experiment* (New York: Harper & Row, 1976); R. Laurence Moore, *Religious Outsiders and the Making of Americans* (New York: Oxford University Press, 1986); *The Bible in America,* ed. Nathan O. Hatch and Mark A. Noll (New York: Oxford University Press, 1982).

14.   On American pluralism, see *Soundings,* 1978, *61*(3), entire issue.

ANNOTATED BIBLIOGRAPHY

Introduction:
On the Study of World Religions

Bonnefoy, Yves, Comp., *Mythologies,* 2 vols. (Chicago: University of Chicago Press, 1991). A comprehensive survey of the mythologies of the world's leading cultures.

Carmody, Denise Lardner. *Women and World Religions,* 2nd ed. Englewood Cliffs, N.J.: Prentice-Hall, 1988. A survey of female images and roles in the major religious traditions that describes what being religious as a female has meant in the past and means today.

Carmody, Denise Lardner, and Carmody, John Tully. *Religion: The Great Questions.* San Francisco: Harper & Row, 1983. A comparative study of the major traditions in terms of their positions on the central existential questions of evil, the good life, and so on.

Eliade, Mircea. *The Sacred and the Profane.* New York: Harcourt, Brace & World, 1959. A concise statement of Eliade's view that human beings try to find meaning by making sacred the primary realities of their lives.

Hall, T. William, general editor. *Introduction to the Study of Religion.* San Francisco: Harper & Row, 1978. A team of scholars from Syracuse University tackles the major conceptual topics.

Hick, John H. *Philosophy of Religion,* 3rd ed. Englewood Cliffs, N.J.: Prentice-Hall, 1983. A good survey of the main problems and concepts involved in the study of religion.

Lovin, Robin W., and Reynolds, Frank E., ed. *Cosmogony and Ethical Order.* Chicago: University of Chicago Press, 1985. Studies dealing with how numerous religious traditions have tried to root their ethical systems in the order given at the birth of the physical world.

Smart, Ninian, and Hecht, Richard D., eds. *Sacred Texts of the World: A Universal Anthology.* New York: Crossroad, 1982. A good collection of primary sources on all the traditions that we treat.

Stewart, David, ed. *Exploring the Philosophy of Religion.* Englewood Cliffs, N.J.: Prentice-Hall, 1988. A reader of selections from primary sources in the history of Western thought about religious experience, God, faith, religious language, evil, and death.

Whaling, Frank, ed. *The World's Religious Traditions.* New York: Crossroad, 1986. Essays in honor of Winfred Cantwell Smith, a pioneer in elucidating the function of religious traditions, which examine both what "tradition" has tended to mean in the major world religions and how scholars now tend to approach the study of religious traditions.

Wilson, John F. *Religion: A Preface.* Englewood Cliffs, N.J.: Prentice-Hall, 1982. A short overview of the problems and traditions that one must consider in studying world religion—weak on the East but good on modernity.

Chapter 1:
The Ancient Religious Mind

Auel, Jean M. *The Clan of the Cave Bear.* New York: Bantam, 1981. A persuasive novel about Neanderthal life that focuses on women's roles.

Campbell, Joseph. *The Masks of God: Primitive Mythology.* New York: Viking, 1970. A readable interpretation of prehistoric culture from a Jungian point of view.

Carmody, Denise Lardner. *The Oldest God: Archaic Religion Yesterday and Today.* Nashville: Abingdon, 1981. A study of the ancient religious mentality from prehistoric times to the present.

Gimbutas, Marija. *The Goddesses and Gods of Old Europe: 6500–3500 B.C.* Berkeley: University of California Press, 1982. Reports and guarded speculation about the findings of archeological excavations of prehistoric sites in Eastern Europe. Primary focus is on the varieties of goddesses and fertility figures found.

Jensen, Adolf E. *Myth and Cult among Primitive Peoples.* Chicago: University of Chicago Press, 1963. A rather speculative account of the interaction of stories and ritual actions in terms of the primary mysteries of the lives of hunters-gatherers.

Kurtén, Björn. *Dance of the Tiger.* New York: Berkeley Books, 1981. A good novel focused on the interaction of Neanderthals and Sapientes, by a leading European paleontologist.

Maringer, Johannes. *The Gods of Prehistoric Man.* New York: Knopf, 1960. A dated but lucid reconstruction of religion from early Paleolithic to late prehistoric times.

Marshack, Alexander. *The Roots of Civilization.* New York: McGraw-Hill, 1972. Studies in the cultural significance of archeological remains suggesting early human beings' efforts to calculate the seasons of nature and correlate them with the habits of the game they hunted.

Roe, Derek. *Prehistory.* Berkeley: University of California Press, 1972. A basic survey of the period from the Old Stone Age to the Iron Age.

Tanner, Nancy Makepeace. *On Becoming Human.* New York: Cambridge University Press, 1981. An anthropological study of the evolution from apes to human beings.

Chapter 2:
Religions of Nonliterate Peoples

Coles, Robert. *Children of Crisis.* Vol. 4: *Eskimos, Chicanos, Indians.* Boston: Little, Brown, 1977. Case studies of Eskimo, Chicano, and American Indian children that beautifully describe their current share of their rich traditions.

Eliade, Mircea. *Australian Religions.* Ithaca, N.Y.: Cornell University Press, 1973. A somewhat demanding application of Eliade's theories to the data available on Australian aborigines.

Gill, Sam D. *Beyond the Primitive: The Religions of Non-literate Peoples.* Englewood Cliffs, N.J.: Prentice-Hall, 1982. A good theoretical orientation to the study of nonliterate peoples, informed by recent cultural anthropology and laced with many examples.

Harner, Michael. *The Way of the Shaman.* San Francisco: Harper & Row, 1980. A clear presentation of the nonordinary reality used by shamans, with many tips on how to adapt shamanic techniques to current Western life.

Hultkrantz, Ake. *The Religions of the American Indians.* Berkeley: University of California Press, 1979. A topical study of the main ideas, institutions, and ritual concerns of both the tribes of North and South America and the high cultures of the Incas, Mayas, and Aztecs.

Rasmussen, Knud. *Across Arctic America.* New York: Putnam's, 1927. A firsthand account of Eskimo customs by an explorer sensitive to the richness of Eskimo religion.

Turnbull, Colin M. *The Forest People.* New York: Simon & Schuster, 1962. A study of the pygmies of the Congo by an anthropologist who came to know and love them well enough to be adopted into their tribe.

Turnbull, Colin M. *The Human Cycle.* New York: Simon & Schuster, 1983. Studies illuminating the key moments of the human life cycle from the author's anthropological experience among several African tribes.

Underhill, Ruth M. *Red Man's Religion.* Chicago: University of Chicago Press, 1965. A readable introduction, rich in details, to the principal beliefs and practices of American Indians north of Mexico.

Zahan, Dominique. *The Religion, Spirituality and Thought of Traditional Africa.* Chicago: University of Chicago Press, 1979. An interesting attempt to sketch the general belief system and ritualistic world views of Africans not greatly influenced by Islam or Christianity.

Chapter 3:
Hinduism

Basham, A. L. *The Wonder That Was India.* New York: Grove Press, 1959. A readable and comprehensive study of Indian life before the coming of the Muslims.

Eck, Diana L. *Banaras, City of Light.* New York: Alfred A. Knopf, 1982. A study of a holy city that is a microcosm of Hinduism.

Eliade, Mircea. *Yoga: Immortality and Freedom.* Princeton, N.J.: Princeton University Press, 1970. A classical study of the presuppositions and main features of the various yogic quests to defeat space and time.

Erikson, Erik H. *Gandhi's Truth.* New York: Norton, 1969. A psychoanalytic study of the modern founder of militant nonviolence.

Hawley, John Stratton, ed. *The Divine Consort.* Berkeley: University of California Press, 1982. A colorful study of the major divine wives in Hindu mythology.

Hopkins, Thomas J. *The Hindu Religious Tradition.* Encino, Calif.: Dickenson, 1971. A brief and solid survey of the major religious developments.

Kinsley, David R. *Hinduism.* Englewood Cliffs, N.J.: Prentice-Hall, 1982. A brief introduction that offers a cultural perspective on Hindu history and thought.

McLeod, W. H. *The Sikhs.* New York: Columbia University Press, 1989. A historical study of Sikh traditions and culture.

Markandaya, Kamala. *Nectar in a Sieve.* New York: Signet, n.d. (originally 1954). A simple novel of Indian women caught in the crumbling of traditional culture.

O'Flaherty, Wendy Doniger. *Siva: The Erotic Ascetic.* New York: Oxford University Press, 1973. A study of a major Hindu god that illustrates the many different weights and symbolic associations a Hindu deity can carry.

O'Flaherty, Wendy Doniger. *Women, Androgynes and Other Mythical Beasts.* Chicago: University of Chicago Press, 1980. Studies in Hindu symbolism associated with fertility, vitality, and sacredness.

Stanford, Anne, trans. *The Bhagavad Gita.* New York: Seabury, 1970. A fairly readable verse translation of India's most influential book.

Younger, Paul, and Younger, Susanna. *Hinduism.* Niles, Ill.: Argus, 1978. A very brief, well-illustrated sketch of Hindu traditions, ideas, and practices.

Chapter 4:
Buddhism

Conze, Edward, et al., eds. *Buddhist Texts through the Ages.* New York: Harper Torchbooks, 1964. A good selection of representative primary sources, dealing with most of the major Buddhist sects.

Conze, Edward. *Buddhist Thought in India.* Ann Arbor: University of Michigan Press, 1967. A fairly demanding study of the origin of Buddhist philosophy in Indian dialectics.

King, Winston. *In the Hope of Nibbana: Theravada Buddhist Ethics.* La Salle, Ill.: Open Court, 1964. A solid survey of the framework and content of Theravada ethics, both individual and social.

Nyanaponika, Thera. *The Heart of Buddhist Meditation.* London: Rider, 1969. A thorough study of the Buddha's way of mindfulness that reflects Theravada traditions.

Rahula, Walpola. *What the Buddha Taught,* rev. ed. New York: Grove Press, 1974. A fine exposition, focusing especially on the Four Noble Truths, with selected important texts.

Robinson, Richard H., and Johnson, Willard L. *The Buddhist Religion.* Encino, Calif.: Dickenson, 1977. A comprehensive survey of Buddhist religion throughout the world.

Suzuki, Shunryu. *Zen Mind, Beginner's Mind.* New York: Weatherhill, 1970. A lovely and penetrating vision of Zen by a contemporary master.

Swearer, Donald K. *Buddhism.* Niles, Ill.: Argus, 1977. A good brief sketch of the teachings, history, and practice of Buddhism. Well illustrated.

Tucci, Giuseppi. *The Religions of Tibet.* Berkeley: University of California Press, 1980. A well-regarded investigation of both pre-Buddhist and Buddhist religious thought and practices in Tibet.

Welch, Holmes. *The Practice of Chinese Buddhism, 1900–1950.* Cambridge, Mass.: Harvard University Press, 1967. A valuable window onto the state of Chinese Buddhism (especially monastic life) prior to the antireligious crackdown of the Maoists.

Zwolf, W., ed. *Buddhism: Art and Faith.* New York: Macmillan, 1986. A lavishly illustrated study based on collections in the British Museum.

Chan, Wing-Tsit, ed. *A Sourcebook in Chinese Philosophy.* Princeton, N.J.: Princeton University Press, 1963. The standard one-volume anthology of translated texts, covering the full historical range of pre-Communist Chinese culture.

Eber, Irene, ed. *Confucianism: The Dynamics of Tradition.* New York: Macmillan, 1987. A collection of essays showing how Confucianism responded to various historical challenges.

Giradot, Norman J. *Myth and Meaning in Early Taoism.* Berkeley: University of California Press, 1983. A good analysis of Daoist beginnings.

Jordan, David K., and Overmyer, Daniel L. *The Flying Phoenix: Aspects of Chinese Sectarianism in Taiwan.* Princeton, N.J.: Princeton University Press, 1986. A systematic study of modern Chinese popular sects that brings out the shamanic and folk-religious motifs.

Lagerwey, John. *Taoist Ritualism in Chinese Society and History.* New York: Macmillan, 1987. A study of the roots and intricacies of Daoist ritual.

Maspero, Henri. *Taoism and Chinese Religion.* Amherst: University of Massachusetts Press, 1981. A collection of essays by a pioneering Western scholar that show the Daoist concern for cultivating immortality.

Pound, Ezra. *Confucius.* New York: New Directions, 1951. An idiosyncratic but stimulating translation of major Confucian texts.

Roberts, Moss, ed. *Chinese Fairy Tales & Fantasies.* New York: Pantheon, 1979. A good collection of folktales that often show how Confucian, Daoist, or Buddhist ideas shaped the popular Chinese imagination.

Thompson, Laurence G. *The Chinese Way in Religion.* Encino, Calif.: Dickenson, 1973. A good collection of original sources that represent the span of Chinese religion.

Thompson, Laurence G. *The Chinese Religion: An Introduction,* 3rd ed. Belmont, Calif.: Wadsworth, 1979. An overview of the major components of Chinese religious culture.

Waley, Arthur, trans. *The Way and Its Power.* New York: Grove Press, 1958. A readable version of China's most beguiling classic.

Wright, Arthur F. *Buddhism in Chinese History.* Stanford, Calif.: Stanford University Press, 1959. A straightforward survey of Buddhism's fortunes in the major historical periods.

Chapter 5:
Chinese Religion

Bush, Richard C. *Religion in China.* Niles, Ill.: Argus, 1977. A brief presentation of Chinese religion as a "stream" with several contributing "currents." Well illustrated.

Chapter 6:
Japanese Religion

Anesaki, Masaharu. *History of Japanese Religion,* 2nd ed. Rutland, Vt.: Tuttle, 1963. A standard overview providing a good general introduction.

Bellah, Robert N. *Tokugawa Religion*. Boston: Beacon Press, 1970. A somewhat demanding sociological analysis of Japanese religious culture on the verge of modernity.

Earhart, H. Byron. *Japanese Religion: Unity and Diversity*, 2nd ed. Encino, Calif.: Dickenson, 1974. An exposition of Japanese religious development from prehistoric times to the present.

Earhart, H. Byron. *Religion in the Japanese Experience*. Encino, Calif.: Dickenson, 1974. A good collection of texts that represent the many aspects of Japanese religion.

Ellwood, Robert S., and Pilgrim, Richard. *Japanese Religion: A Cultural Perspective*. Englewood Cliffs, N.J.: Prentice-Hall, 1985. A useful introduction focusing on social and cultural issues.

Franck, Frederick, ed. *The Buddha Eye*. New York: Crossroad, 1982. An anthology of writings by members of the recent Kyoto school, one of the most influential modern circles of Buddhist philosophy.

Hoover, Thomas. *The Zen Experience*. New York: New American Library, 1980. Studies in the thought of major Chinese and Japanese masters.

Hori, Ichiro. *Folk Religion in Japan*. Chicago: University of Chicago Press, 1968. A somewhat specialized study whose richness of detail, especially on shamanism, makes it of interest to the nonspecialist.

Kapleau, Philip, ed. *The Three Pillars of Zen*. Boston: Beacon Press, 1967. A clear view of the practice of Zen in modern Japan.

Nakamura, Hajime. *Ways of Thinking of Eastern People*. Honolulu: University of Hawaii Press, 1964. An interesting study of the cultural assumptions and mind-set that provides a basis for comparing Japanese religion with those of India, China, and Tibet.

Smith, Robert J. *Ancestor Worship in Contemporary Japan*. Stanford, Calif.: Stanford University Press, 1974. A study of postwar Japanese veneration of ancestors and attitudes toward the dead.

Tsunoda, Ryusaku, et al., eds. *Sources of Japanese Tradition*, two volumes. New York: Columbia University Press, 1964. A good anthology of important texts throughout Japanese religious history.

Chapter 7:
Religions of Ancient
Near Eastern Civilizations

Burkert, Walter. *Structure and History in Greek Mythology and Ritual*. Berkeley: University of California Press, 1979. An historical investigation that finds a continuous tradition evolving from Paleolithic to Hellenistic times.

Eliade, Mircea. *A History of Religious Ideas*, I–III. Chicago: University of Chicago Press, 1978, 1982, 1985. These volumes have chapters on Greece, Iran, and Egypt that place these countries in the overall history of religious ideas.

Foy, Whittfield, ed. *Man's Religious Quest: A Reader*. New York: St. Martin's, 1977. This volume includes interesting texts from Greece and Iran.

Frankfort, Henri, et al. *Before Philosophy*. Baltimore: Penguin, 1949. A classic popular presentation of the mythical thought of Egypt and Mesopotamia.

Frye, Richard. *The Heritage of Persia*. New York: World, 1963. An informative if rather fact-laden history of ancient Iran.

Guthrie, W.K.C. *The Greeks and Their Gods*. Boston: Beacon Press, 1955. A thorough commentary on the religion of classical Greece.

Jacobsen, Thorkild. *The Treasures of Darkness: A History of Mesopotamian Religion*. New Haven, Conn.: Yale University Press, 1976. A solid overview by one of the leading scholars and interpreters of Mesopotamian mythology.

Pritchard, James B., ed. *Ancient Near Eastern Texts Relating to the Old Testament*, 3rd ed. Princeton, N.J.: Princeton University Press, 1969. The standard source for key Mesopotamian and Egyptian texts, arranged according to genres for easy comparison.

Renault, Mary. *The Last of the Wine*. New York: Pocket Books, 1964. One of her several historical novels that absorbingly reconstruct the classical Greek world—in this case, that of Socrates and Plato.

Ringgren, Helmer. *Religions of the Ancient Near East*. Philadelphia: Westminster, 1973. A good introduction to Mesopotamian religions.

Wilson, John A. *The Culture of Ancient Egypt*. Chicago: University of Chicago Press, 1956. A general history, not too difficult and good on the principal ideas.

Chapter 8:
Judaism

Carmody, John, Carmody, Denise Lardner, and Cohn, Robert L. *Exploring the Hebrew Bible* (Englewood Cliffs, N.J.: Prentice Hall, 1988). A basic text that analyzes all the books and suggests their lasting significance.

Cohen, A. *Everyman's Talmud*. New York: Schocken, 1975. A topical presentation of rabbinic Judaism's main teachings, rich in quotations and details.

Cohen, Arthur A. *The Tremendum*. New York: Crossroad, 1981. A theological reflection on the significance of the Holocaust.

Encyclopedia Judaica. 16 vols. Jerusalem: Keter, 1971. The standard comprehensive reference work, with articles on all aspects of Jewish history, faith, and practice.

Heilman, Samuel C. *Synagogue Life*. Chicago: University of Chicago Press, 1976. A sociological study of the interactions among Jews at synagogue gatherings.

Neusner, Jacob. *The Life of Torah.* Encino, Calif.: Dickenson, 1974. A selection of readings that illustrate basic aspects of Jewish faith, both traditional and modern.

Neusner, Jacob. *The Way of Torah,* 2nd ed. Encino, Calif.: Dickenson, 1974. A readable introduction to Judaism that delineates its classical structure, the Torah, and the modern situation.

Roth, Cecil. *History of the Jews.* New York: Schocken, 1961. A lucid presentation of Jewish experience from biblical times to World War II.

Rubenstein, Richard L. *After Auschwitz.* Indianapolis: Bobbs-Merrill, 1966. One of the first and most radical interpretations of the implications of the Nazi Holocaust of six million Jews for Jewish faith.

Scholem, Gershom. *Major Trends in Jewish Mysticism.* New York: Schocken, 1961. A classical brief treatment of the evolution of Jewish mysticism stressing Cabalistic and Hasidic developments.

Zborowski, Mark, and Herzog, Elizabeth. *Life Is with People.* New York: Schocken, 1962. An absorbing portrait of *shtetl* life before World War II, based on interviews and personal reminiscences.

Chapter 9: Christianity

Brown, Robert McAfee. *The Spirit of Protestantism.* New York: Oxford University Press, 1965. A lucid analysis of the major emphases in Protestant theology and faith.

Carmody, Denise Lardner, and Carmody, John Tully. *Christianity: An Introduction,* 2nd ed. Belmont, Calif.: Wadsworth, 1988. A basic text that offers an analysis of the Christian world view, a succinct history, and sketches of current schools of Christian religious thought.

Carmody, Denise Lardner, and Carmody, John Tully, *Jesus: An Introduction.* Belmont, Calif.: Wadsworth, 1987. New Testament, historical, recent theological, and comparative studies of Jesus that situate him in both Church history and the full spectrum of the founders of the world religions.

Carmody, John, Carmody, Denise Lardner, and Robbins, Gregory A. *Exploring the New Testament.* Englewood Cliffs, N.J.: Prentice-Hall, 1986. A comprehensive introduction to the New Testament stressing the ideas on which later Christian faith built.

Clebsch, William A. *Christianity in European History.* New York: Oxford University Press, 1979. A somewhat demanding but stimulating view, set in terms of religious studies rather than Church history.

Farmer, David Hugh. *The Oxford Dictionary of Saints,* 2nd ed. New York: Oxford University Press, 1987. A handy reference to many of the great personalities who shaped Christian faith and piety.

Fredriksen, Paula, *From Jesus to Christ* (New Haven, CT: Yale University Press, 1988). A thorough study of the origins of the New Testament's images of Jesus.

Frend, W. H. C. *The Rise of Christianity.* Philadelphia: Fortress, 1984. A massive but readable narrative of the first six hundred years of Christian history when most of the formative ideas and institutions took shape.

Jones, Cheslyn, Wainwright, Geoffrey, and Yarnold, Edward, eds. *The Study of Spirituality.* New York: Oxford University Press, 1986. An excellent handbook guiding readers through the historical development of the major Christian schools of devotion.

Pelikan, Jaroslav. *Jesus through the Centuries.* New Haven, Conn.: Yale University Press, 1985. A good survey of how Christian views of Jesus developed through interaction with succeeding historical cultures.

Schmemann, Alexander. *The Historical Road of Eastern Orthodoxy.* Crestwood, N.Y.: St. Vladimir's Seminary Press, 1977. A view of the development of Orthodoxy from New Testament times, originally written for Russian Christians.

Walker, Williston, et al. *A History of the Christian Church,* 4th ed. New York: Charles Scribner's Sons, 1985. A standard text that has the advantage of offering all the major chronological periods roughly equal space.

Chapter 10: Islam

Al Faruqi, Isma'il. *Islam.* Niles, Ill.: Argus, 1979. A simple introduction that offers an overview of Islamic thought and practice. Well illustrated.

Al Faruqi, Isma'il R., and Al Faruqi, Lois L. *The Cultural Atlas of Islam.* New York: Macmillan, 1986. A large, comprehensive work stressing institutional and cultural themes more than history or theology.

Arberry, A. J. *Aspects of Islamic Civilization.* Ann Arbor: University of Michigan Press, 1971. Selections that illumine major themes of Muslim culture, including science, law, poetry, and mysticism.

Bosworth, C. E., and Schacht, Joseph, eds. *The Legacy of Islam,* 2nd ed. New York: Oxford University Press, 1974. Studies of such major cultural areas as Islamic art and architecture by leading scholars of the previous generation.

Cragg, Kenneth. *The House of Islam,* 2nd ed. Encino, Calif.: Dickenson, 1975. An analysis of major topics in Islam, such as its view of God, the role of Muhammad, liturgy, and Sufism.

Donohue, John J., and Esposito, John L., eds. *Islam in Transition.* New York: Oxford University Press, 1982. Texts from Islamic commentators on recent social changes.

Geertz, Clifford. *Islam Observed.* Chicago: University of Chicago Press, 1968. A brief, somewhat difficult, but rewarding analysis of religious development in Morocco and Indonesia by a leading cultural anthropologist.

Lings, Martin. *A Sufi Saint of the Twentieth Century,* 2nd ed. Berkeley: University of California Press, 1973. A somewhat cumbersome analysis of the impact and teaching of a leading North African sheik.

Rahman, Fazlur. *Islam,* 2nd ed. Chicago: University of Chicago Press, 1979. A solid, fact-filled history of Islam from Muhammad to the present.

Rahman, Fazlur. *Major Themes of the Qur'an.* Chicago: University of Chicago Press, 1980. Systematic presentations of the view of the Qur'an on such themes as God, human nature, and revelation.

Chapter 11:
Alternatives to Religion—
Secularism and Humanism

Buckley, Michael J. *At the Origins of Modern Atheism.* New Haven, Conn.: Yale University Press, 1987. A demanding study of the origins of modern atheism in the shift of Christian apologetics from general appeals to what the life of faith generated to philosophical inferences from the orderliness of nature to the existence of an omniscient God.

Douglas, Mary, and Tipton, Steven, eds. *Religion and America: Spirituality in a Secular Age.* Boston: Beacon Press, 1983. Essays by social scientists and humanists focusing on the resurgence of conservative religious feeling that astounded secularistic observers of American culture during the early 1980s.

Hammond, Phillip, ed. *The Sacred in a Secular Age.* Berkeley: University of California Press, 1985. Studies covering some of the same ground as the book edited by Douglas and Tipton but with more interest in civil religion as the background for the recent contest between secularity and sacrality.

Heilbroner, Robert. *Marxism: For and Against.* New York: Norton, 1980. Analyses by a liberal economist impressed by Marxist insights into the relations between labor and product value but unimpressed by what Marxist economic systems to date have produced.

Jaki, Stanley. *The Road of Science and the Ways to God.* Chicago: University of Chicago Press, 1978. Jaki's Gifford Lectures on the origins of modern science from Christian foundations and the implicitly theistic postulates of even recent scientific geniuses.

Kuhn, Thomas S. *The Structure of Scientific Revolutions,* 2nd ed. Chicago: University of Chicago Press, 1970. Kuhn's thesis that science proceeds by observing normative paradigms until something revolutionary creates a new paradigm (which then becomes normative) aroused great controversy among historians and philosophers of science. As well, historians of other disciplines, theology among them, soon adapted the notion of paradigms and normal science to study the evolution of their own fields.

Löwith, Karl. *From Hegel to Nietzsche.* Garden City, N.Y.: Doubleday Anchor, 1967. A well-regarded, staple study of the evolution of European philosophy in the nineteenth century, when many of the postulates of secularist humanists became fixed.

Toulmin, Stephen. *Human Understanding.* Princeton, N.J.: Princeton University Press, 1972. A study of human cognition greatly indebted to the philosophy of science and ordinary language analysis that deals sufficiently with the historical rise of the institutions that guide formal thought to illustrate the secularization of the modern West.

Voegelin, Eric. *From Enlightenment to Revolution.* Durham, N.C.: Duke University Press, 1975. A portion of Voegelin's discarded history of political ideas that focuses on Marx and other modern political thinkers who were revolting against intellectual and social constraints associated with Christian theism.

Voegelin, Eric. *Science, Politics and Gnosticism.* Chicago: Henry Regnery, 1968. A readable version of Voegelin's thesis that much modern political philosophy amounts to a gnostic effort to direct human development by privileged but nontranscendent revelations about human nature and the laws of history.

Conclusion:
Summary Reflections

Ahlstrom, Sydney. *A Religious History of the American People.* New Haven, Conn.: Yale University Press, 1972. A massive, authoritative treatment of American religion from precolonial times to the end of the 1960s.

Daedalus, Volume 111, Number 1 (Winter 1982). A collection of essays by leading scholars who try to interpret the current significance of religion, both in the United States and on the world scene.

Daedalus, Volume 117, Number 2 (Spring 1988). A discussion among educators about the current function of religion and religious studies in American higher education.

Johnston, William. *The Inner Eye of Love.* New York: Harper & Row, 1978. Shows the contemplative foundations of religion, with special reference to Christianity and Buddhism.

Moore, R. Lawrence. *Religious Outsiders and the Making of Americans.* New York: Oxford University Press, 1986. Chapters on the history of the process by which many groups, either sectarian or marginal to the cultural mainstream, were Americanized.

Neville, Robert C. *Soldier, Sage, Saint.* New York: Fordham University Press, 1978. Typological studies of some of the dominant religious personalities.

Voegelin, Eric. *Order and History,* Vol. 5, *In Search of Order.* Baton Rouge: Louisiana State University Press, 1987. A brief, demanding, but brilliant conclusion to Voegelin's epic study of how human beings have pursued the structures of history and consciousness.

APPENDIX A

ONE HUNDRED KEY DATES IN WORLD RELIGIOUS HISTORY

4.6 billion years ago	Formation of the earth
500,000 years ago	Homo erectus using fire
100,000 years ago	Homo sapiens: ritual burial
50,000 years ago	Homo sapiens in Australia
30,000 years ago	Prehistoric painting and sculpture; Mongoloid peoples cross Bering Strait
8,000–6,000 B.C.E	Agriculture, domestication of animals, rise of towns
4500	Early Jomon period of hunting and gathering in Japan
4000	Casting of bronze
3500	Invention of wheel; Megalith cultures in Britain and Iberia
3100	Unification of Egypt; Invention of writing in Sumer
3000	Farming in central Africa
2750	Growth of civilization in Indus Valley
1600	Shang Bronze Culture in China
1570–1165	New Kingdom in Egypt
1500	Vedas, Rise of Iranian-speaking peoples
1200	Exodus of Hebrews from Egypt
1000	Colonization of Arctic
900	Nubian kingdom of Kush
800–400	Upanishads
750	Homer and Hesiod written down
750–550	Hebrew Prophets
ca. 628–551	Zoroaster
599–527	Mahavira, founder of Jainism
586	Fall of southern kingdom (Judah)
551–479	Confucius
536–476	Buddha
525	Persian conquest of Egypt

525–406	Aeschylus, Sophocles, Euripides
500–200	*Mahabhrata, Ramayana, Bhagavad Gita*
427–347	Plato
350	*Tao Te Ching*
331	Alexander conquers Palestine
273–236	Asoka
200	Rise of religious Taoism
80	Buddhist decline in India
50	Formation of Buddhist canon
5 C.E.	Building of Japanese National Shrine at Ise
30	Death of Jesus of Nazareth
50–95	New Testament writings
70	Romans destroy Jerusalem
80–110	Canonization of Hebrew Bible
220–552	Buddhist missions to China and Japan
304–589	Huns fragment China
325	First Ecumenical Council at Nicaea
400	Fall of Indian Gupta dynasty
451	Council of Chalcedon
500	Compilation of Babylonian Talmud
570–632	Muhammad
637	Islamic invasion of Persia
645	Taika reform—Japan takes Chinese model
650	Canonization of Qur'an
700	Golden Age of Chinese poetry
712–720	Shinto Chronicles
749	First Buddhist monastery in Tibet
750–1258	Abbasid caliphate
762	Foundation of Baghdad
787	Second Council of Nicaea
788–820	Shankara
800–900	Rise of Hindu orthodoxy
845	Persecution of Chinese Buddhists
966	Foundation of Cairo

1054	Mutual anathemas of Rome and Constantinople
1058–1111	Al-Ghazali
1130–1200	Chu Hsi, leading Neo-Confucian
ca. 1135	Maimonides
1175	First Muslim empire in India
1175–1253	Introduction of Pure Land, Zen, and Nichiren schools in Japan
1225–1274	Thomas Aquinas
1453	Ottoman Turks capture Constantinople
1469–1539	Nanak, founder of Sikhism
1473–1543	Nicolaus Copernicus
1492	Expulsion of Jews from Spain
1517	Luther's ninety-five theses
1526–1707	Islamic Mogul Dynasty in India
1549	Francis Xavier in Japan
1565	Roman Catholic colony at St. Augustine
1585	Matteo Ricci in China
1619	Beginning of black slavery in colonial America
1620	Mayflower Compact
1654	Jewish settlement at New Amsterdam
1734	First Great Awakening in New England
1801	Beginnings of revivalism in western United States
1809–1882	Charles Darwin
1818–1883	Karl Marx
1856–1939	Sigmund Freud
1868–1871	Meiji persecution of Buddhism
1869–1948	Mahatma Gandhi
1879–1955	Albert Einstein
1880–1913	Partition of Africa by Western powers
1893	World Parliament of Religions in Chicago
1893–1977	Mao Tse-tung
1894–1905	Japanese victorious in wars with China and Russia
1910	Beginning of Protestant ecumenical movement
1933–1945	Nazi persecution of Jews
1945	Japanese surrender; Disestablishment of Shinto
1947	Partition of Pakistan from India
1948	Creation of state of Israel
1954–1956	Sixth Buddhist Council, Rangoon
1962–1965	Second Vatican Council
1964	Civil Rights Act in United States

APPENDIX B

APPROXIMATE MEMBERSHIP DATA ON MAJOR AMERICAN RELIGIOUS GROUPS (1991)*

Roman Catholics	53,000,000
Baptists	28,250,000
Southern Baptists	14,700,000
Methodists	13,400,000
United Methodist Church	9,200,000
Lutherans	8,500,000
Evangelical Lutheran Church in America	5,350,000
Lutheran Church—Missouri Synod	2,700,000
Pentecostals	8,000,000
Church of God in Christ	3,715,000
Assemblies of God	2,150,000
Reformed	5,750,000
Presbyterian Church (USA)	3,010,000
United Church of Christ	1,700,000
Orthodox	4,750,000
Greek Orthodox	2,000,000
Latter-Day Saints (Mormons)	4,100,000
Church of Jesus Christ of Latter-Day Saints	3,875,000
Christian Churches and Churches of Christ	3,800,000
Episcopalians	2,525,000
Holiness Churches	1,410,000
Jehovah's Witnesses	760,000
Church of Christ, Scientist	700,000
Adventist Churches	700,000
Salvation Army	435,000
Roman Rite Churches	350,000
Mennonites	250,000
Brethren	220,000
Unitarian	175,000
Friends (Quakers)	125,000
Miscellaneous Christians	1,300,000
Jews	6,000,000
Muslims	2,000,000
Buddhists	100,000
Other Non-Christians	500,000

*Source: *The Universal Almanac 1992*

Total Religiously Affiliated	150,000,000
	(Approximately 63% of U.S. Population)
Christian % of Religiously Affiliated	140,000,000
	(Approximately 94%)

INDEX OF NAMES AND PLACES*

Boldface numbers indicate pages on which glossary definitions appear.

INDEX OF SUBJECTS*

Boldface numbers indicate pages on which glossary definitions appear.